WHO LIVED WHERE

A Biographical Guide to Homes and Museums

WHO LIVED WHERE

A Biographical Guide to Homes and Museums

JOHN EASTMAN

BONANZA BOOKS
NEW YORK

This 1987 edition is published by Bonanza Books,
distributed by Crown Publishers, Inc., 225 Park Avenue South,
New York, New York 10003, by arrangement with
Facts on File, Inc.

Printed and Bound in the United States of America

LIBRARY OF CONGRESS CATALOGING-IN-PUBLICATION DATA

Eastman, John.
Who lived where.

Includes indexes.
1. Dwellings—United States—Directories.
2. Historic buildings—United States—Directories.
3. Historical museums—United States—Directories.
4. United States—Directories. I. Title.
E159.E23 1987   973′025   87-6542
ISBN 0-517-64045-7

h g f e d c b a

CONTENTS

"You rows of houses! you window-pierc'd facades! you roofs!
You porches and entrances! you copings and iron guards!
You windows whose transparent shells might expose so much!
You doors and ascending steps! you arches!
You gray stones of interminable pavements! you trodden crossings!
From all that has touch'd you I believe you have imparted to yourselves, and now would impart the same secretly to me,
From the living and the dead you have peopled your impassive surfaces, and the spirits thereof would be evident and amicable with me."

Walt Whitman, *Song of the Open Road*

ACKNOWLEDGMENTS

American writer Gene Fowler once remarked that a book is never really finished, only abandoned. A book of this dimension and scope, however, does not approach even the abandonment stage without engaging the hearts and hands of numerous willing, able and profoundly generous persons. Few writers can have enjoyed such abundant support as I from friends, helpers and associates.

Foremost aide and participant in every phase of this project was my beloved companion Susan Woolley Stoddard. Her constant interest, lively mind, practical abilities and cheerful involvement in the adventure, pressure and drudgery of the task—all at some considerable sacrifice to herself—have taught me much about the meaning of sharing. To Sue I dedicate this book.

I thank James and Sue Eastman, Peter L. Ginsberg, Robert B. Hutchins and Prof. John M. Murphy for valuable support and many favors extended throughout the course of this project. Mike Kennedy's suggestions and editorial eye were right on the mark and much appreciated. Eleanora Schoenebaum and Jo Metsch guided the final production phases.

This book is in large part a tribute to the work of other writers, specifically the noble biographers, who create what is often the most fascinating reading on any shelf. Their literary genre is full of love if not money. One who devotes large chunks of one's own life to recording the life of another is an awesome creature, both in motivation and accomplishment.

A biographical researcher depends heavily upon the competence of people who don't often receive much praise. These include mail clerks and carriers, telephone operators, secretaries and the subordinate office personnel whom everybody knows are more vital to the function of any organization than its managers. Hundreds of you, all over the country, helped make this book. Thank you for your patience and efficiency.

The magnanimous cooperation extended to this writer from every corner of our country has renewed my appreciation for our native intelligence resources, especially in those areas remote from the large population centers. Without the town and county clerks, postmasters, small-town librarians, chamber of commerce personnel and local historical societies and genealogists, this book would not have been possible. The sharpest quality and greatest vitality of American historical research, I have learned, usually reside far from our most publicized resource centers.

I am indebted to the following persons and organizations who took time to hunt and clarify often obscure bits of information for me and to share their knowledge:

ALABAMA: Tyra H. Berry, Oneonta; Eulalia Barrow Bobo, Lafayette; Sherry Bowers, Georgiana; Edward O. Buckbee, Alabama Space and Rocket Center, Huntsville; Robert R. Cason, State of Alabama Dept. of Archives and History, Montgomery; Lucille and Charles S. Hayes, Butler County Historical Society, Greenville; City of Lafayette; Robin A. Lang, Mobile Historic Development Commission; John T. Lissimore, Tuskegee Institute NHS; Jeanie McNees, Helen Keller Property Board, Tuscumbia; Taft Skipper, Entertainment Enterprises, Inc., Greenville; Leon P. Spencer, Talladega College; Daniel T. Williams, Frissell Library, Tuskegee Institute; Norma K. Willis, Ashland.

ARIZONA: The Arizona Biltmore, Phoenix; Lori Davisson, Arizona Heritage Center, Tucson; Joanne Hamilton-Selway, City of Scottsdale; The Haven, Inc., Tucson; Thelma Holveck, Scottsdale Historical Society; Adrienne Lehrer, Tucson; Janet Michaelieu, Central Arizona Museum, Phoenix; Carol Patrick,

Sharlot Hall Historical Society, Prescott; Alma Ready, Pimeria Alta Historical Society, Nogales; Kathy Reed, Parker Area Chamber of Commerce.

CALIFORNIA: David K. Aaker, Palmdale Chamber of Commerce; Roger Abberger, Los Angeles; Val Almendarez, Academy of Motion Picture Arts and Sciences, Beverly Hills; Sylvia Arden, San Diego Historical Society; Harriet L. Axelrod, Pacific Palisades Historical Society; Elizabeth Benjamin, Berkeley Public Library; Robert Benveniste, Los Angeles; Lenore M. Blume, Palos Verdes Library District; R. Bluth, Toluca Lake Chamber of Commerce; Mary E. Bobco, Hawthorne Public Library; Sherman B. Boivin, Santa Rosa; Marabee K. Boone, Pacific Grove Chamber of Commerce; Brookline Homes, Inc., Los Angeles; Mary C. Brooks, Monterey Peninsula Chamber of Commerce; Mary Ann Byrne, Altadena Library District; Anne Caiger, University of California Library, Los Angeles; Alison Stilwell Cameron, Carmel; Lea Comparette, Historical Society of Long Beach; Alan Curl, Riverside Memorial Museum; Danny Dark, Cheviot Hills; Mary DiGrande, Atherton; Walt Disney Archives, Burbank; Margaret Duran, Sierra Madre Public Library; Charles Duarte, International Church of the Foursquare Gospel, Los Angeles; Ray Freed, Los Angeles; Getty Oil Company, Los Angeles; Ted Gibson, Encino; Grass Valley Area Chamber of Commerce; Pam Gregory, Colton Chamber of Commerce; Audrey Hales, Glendale Historical Society; Mary Hanel, Beale Memorial Library, Bakersfield; David W. Haney, Angeles National Forest, Pasadena; Harrison Memorial Library, Carmel; A. Hassett, Chatsworth Branch Library; Mrs. John Heddon, Rancho Santa Fe; Hees Properties, Los Angeles; P. Hong, Oakland; Laura Archera Huxley, Los Angeles; Joseph J. Johnson, Monterey Public Library; Kahngja Kahng, Los Angeles; Russ Kingman, World of Jack London Museum and Bookstore, Glen Ellen; Madonna Korth, Palm Springs Chamber of Commerce; A. Kuyoomjian, Los Angeles; Lake Elsinore Valley Chamber of Commerce; Tammy Lazer, Beverly Hills Visitors Bureau; Ruthann Lehrer, Los Angeles Conservancy; Jack London State Historic Park, Glen Ellen; Linda J. Long, Stanford University Archives; Jerry McBride, Arnold Schoenberg Institute, Los Angeles; Malibu Chamber of Commerce; Georgia Carmichael Maxwell, Los Angeles; Zachary Means, Los Angeles; Lorraine Melton, Ann Scheid, City of Pasadena; Millard M. Mier, Los Angeles; Ann B. Miller, San Simeon Area, State of California Dept. of Parks and Recreation; Nancy Miller, Robinson Jeffers Tor House Foundation, Inc., Carmel; R. A. Miller, Santa Barbara Historical Society; Valentine Miller, Big Sur; Newport Harbor Area Chamber of Commerce, Newport Beach; J. L. Papich, Highland Park Chamber of Commerce; Chuck Park, Duarte Chamber of Commerce; Pebble Beach Corporation; Eric Peterson, Los Angeles; Jerry Peterson, Wrightwood Chamber of Commerce; Placer County Museum, Auburn; Mrs. Ragnar Quale, Los Angeles; Jean A. Quinn, Beverly Hills; Nancy C. Reid, Will Rogers State Historic Park, Pacific Palisades; Nancy Robinson, Palm Springs Public Library; Barbara A. Rush, Encino; San Fernando Valley Historical Society, Mission Hills; Santa Barbara Public Library; Eric A. Saul, Presidio Army Museum, San Francisco; Sue F. Schechter, Pasadena Historical Society; Glen A. Settle, Rosamond; Myron Shane, Beverly Hills; Gwen Silva, Tarzana Chamber of Commerce; Dolores E. Soffer, Beverly Hills;

Jacqueline Spillane, Los Gatos Memorial Library; William W. Sturm, Oakland Public Library; Marie Condon Thornton, Bancroft Library, University of California, Berkeley; Union Bank, Beverly Hills; Valley Guild, Salinas; W. Powell White, National Park Service, San Francisco; Ruth Wilson, Palo Alto Historical Association; Bill Wurtz, History Center, Los Angeles; N. Zohn, Long Beach.

COLORADO: Mary B. Cassidy, Leadville Chamber of Commerce; Catherine Engel, Colorado Historical Society, Denver; Eleanor M. Gehres, Lynn Taylor, Denver Public Library; Marie Jurgendyer, Fort Morgan Heritage Foundation; Darlene Schomberg, Victor/Lowell Thomas Museum; Noreen Stringfellow, Pueblo Library District.

CONNECTICUT: Dorothy Y. Armistead, Henry Whitfield State Historical Museum, Guilford; Jane Atkinson, Library Board, Weston; Miriam Bachner, Ferguson Library, Stamford; Bethel Public Library; Christopher P. Bickford, Connecticut Historical Society, Hartford; Roberta K. R. Bradford, Stowe-Day Foundation, Hartford; Margaret S. Cheney, Mark Twain Memorial, Hartford; Betsy Cooley, Oliver Wolcott Library, Litchfield; Carolyn C. Cooper, Eli Whitney Museum, Whitneyville; Helen M. Cooper, Town of Southbury; Danbury Scott Fanton Museum & Historical Society; Anita T. Daubenspeck, Ridgefield Library and Historical Association; Mary C. Durbrow, New Canaan Historical Society; Town of Enfield; Fairfield Public Library; Michael R. Gannett, Cornwall Historical Society; Office of the Town Clerk, Greenwich; William S. Hass, Westport Public Library; Sylvia Hawkins, Mark Twain Library Association, Redding; Elliott W. Hoffman, Noah Webster Foundation, West Hartford; Mary B. Holzer, Howard Whittemore Memorial Library, Naugatuck; Lauren Kaminsky, Historical Society of the Town of Greenwich; Merle Kummer, Hartford Architecture Conservancy; Judie Lamm, Heritage Properties, Inc., Ridgefield; Kathleen McKula, *Hartford Courant*; Middlesex County Historical Society, Middletown; Carl Mlinar, Town of Easton; New London Public Library; Marion Nicholson, Greenwich Library; Pauline R. Ohmen, New Milford; Judith Paine, State Historic Preservation Office, Hartford; Daniel J. Palmer, New Britain Public Library; Robert Pelton, Barnum Museum, Bridgeport; Town Clerk's Office, Redding; Judith A. Schiff, Yale University Library, New Haven; Trudy J. Schobinger, Antiquarian & Landmarks Society, Inc., Hartford; Paul S. Timpanelli, Trumbull; Janet Camp Troxell, New Haven; Anne H. Willard, New Haven Colony Historical Society; Elmer H. Worthington, Roxbury Historical Society.

DELAWARE: Dr. Barbara E. Benson, Historical Society of Delaware, Wilmington; Larry L. Manuel, Wilmington Library.

DISTRICT OF COLUMBIA: David C. Acheson; Helen C. Adams, American Chemical Society; Edwin C. Bearss, U.S. Dept. of the Interior; Joseph M. Blanton, Jr., National Geographic Society; C. Dudley Brown; Brigitta Carlson, Museum of African Art; Darrell D. Carter, U.S. International Communication Agency; Elizabeth L. Chittick, National Woman's Party; Rudolf A. Clemen, Jr., American Red Cross; Eugene Frank, M.D.; Gail Galloway, Barrett McGurn, Betsy Trumble, Supreme Court of the United States; Julia Heflin;

Dora Kelenson, American Federation of Labor and Congress of Industrial Organizations; Constance L. Kibler, George Washington University; Raymond J. Kramer, Securities and Exchange Commission; Alison M. MacTavish, American Institute of Architects Foundation; Marc Mayer, National Air and Space Museum; Bernard R. Meyer, White House Historical Association; Elizabeth J. Miller, Columbia Historical Society; Wayne D. Rasmussen, U.S. Dept. of Agriculture; Charles M. Schneider; Smithsonian Institution; Nora K. Stinson, Naval Historical Foundation; Otton A. Suarez; Mary Ternes, Washingtoniana Reference Library; Meredeth Turshen; U.S. Chamber of Commerce; Mrs. Malcolm Vosburgh; Charles Whitby, Jr.

FLORIDA: Margot Ammidown, Metropolitan Dade County, Miami; Kathleen Barber, Committee of One Hundred, Fort Myers; JoAnn Crawford, Leesburg Public Library; James H. Davis, Clearwater Public Library; Bernice Dickson, Hemingway Home and Museum, Key West; Rodney E. Dillon, Jr., Fort Lauderdale Historical Society; Historical Association of Southern Florida, Miami; Historical Society of Palm Beach County, Palm Beach; Janice S. Mahaffey, Putnam County Archives and History Commission, Palatka; Office of Public Information, City of Miami Beach; Steve Tool, Jacksonville Historic Landmarks Commission; Sharon Wells, Historic Key West Preservation Board; Lois Whitehead, St. Petersburg Historical Society; E. F. Yarnell, Eastern Air Lines, Inc., Miami.

GEORGIA: Augusta-Richmond County Public Library, Augusta; Gerald Becham, Georgia College, Milledgeville; Gayle Christian, William Russell Pullen Library, Georgia State University, Atlanta; Wessie Connell, Roddenbery Memorial Library, Cairo; Ruth Corry, Dept. of Archives and History, Atlanta; Melvin G. Crandell, Jekyll Island Authority; Margaret B. Evans, Thomasville Landmarks, Inc.; Franklin M. Garrett, Atlanta Historical Society; Laurraine Goreau, Carrollton; City of Harlem; Roger Harris, Historic Columbus Foundation; John A. Hayes III, Historic Savannah Foundation; Vivian S. Howard, U.S. Army Infantry School, Fort Benning; S. C. Kaufmann, Sea Island; Elizabeth A. McGahee, Joel Chandler Harris Memorial Association, Atlanta; Karen E. Osvald, Georgia Historical Society, Savannah; A. G. Proctor Company, Inc., Brunswick; City of Richmond Hill; Thomas C. Rosier, Woodrow Wilson House, Augusta; Royston Public Library; Steven W. Schaefer, Uncle Remus Regional Library, Madison; Kenneth H. Thomas, Jr., Georgia Dept. of Natural Resources, Atlanta.

HAWAII: Constance Hagiwara, Hawaii State Library, Honolulu; Kahului Library; Maui Chamber of Commerce, Kahului.

IDAHO: Idaho State Historical Society, Boise; Nancy E. Morris, City of Hayden Lake.

ILLINOIS: Catherine Barker, Gail Downey, Oak Park Tour Center; Hazel Bigelow, William Jennings Bryan Birthplace, Salem; Russell C. Birk, Illinois State Historical Society, Springfield; Margaret Burroughs, Du Sable Museum of African American History, Chicago; Chicago Historical Society Library; Eva Jane Dunn, Galesburg Public Library; Fair-

field Public Library; Adeline Ferry, A. C. Daugherty Memorial Township Library, Dupo; Tom Forte, Glencoe Public Library; Jane Fountaine, Logan Square Neighborhood Association, Chicago; Isabelle Gibson, Chicago Daily Defender; Chris Gilson, Lincoln Public Library; Maxine M. Hamel, Troy Grove; Gail Hancock, Village of Panama; Mrs. Charles Harmon, Mendota; Marie Hoscheid, Moline Public Library; Illinois Institute of Technology, Chicago; Jacksonville Public Library; Walter and Renee Johnson, Chicago; Larry L. Keely, Ravenswood; Patricia Kelly, Evanston Historical Society; Eileen Kloberdanz, Cook Memorial Public Library District, Libertyville; Mary Neff, Waukegan Historical Society; Steven Olderr, Riverside Public Library; Camille J. Radmacher, Warren County Library, Monmouth; Regenstein Library, University of Chicago; Somonauk Public Library; Les Stegh, Deere & Company, Moline; Sallie Streeter, Chicago; Doris Glade Vogel, Holcomb; Marie S. White, Dirksen Center, Pekin; Diane Wilhelm, Illinois State Historical Library, Springfield; Nancy Wilson, Elmhurst Historical Commission; Jimmie Wooten, Maywood Public Library; Iris M. Zimmer, Carlinville Public Library.

INDIANA: Allen County-Fort Wayne Historical Society; Emma F. Andy, Morrisson-Reeves Library, Richmond; Bloomington Daily Herald-Telephone; Stephen T. Day, Jeffersonville Township Public Library, Jeffersonville; Eugene V. Debs Foundation, Terre Haute; Keith Dowden, Purdue University Libraries, West Lafayette; Fairmount Public Library; Frederick P. Fellers, Indianapolis-Marion County Public Library; Judith C. Ferrell, Elkhart Public Library; Max H. Fisch, Indiana University-Purdue University Library, Indianapolis; Paula Garner, North Manchester Public Library; M. Grigsby, Allen County Public Library, Fort Wayne; Willard Heiss, City of Indianapolis; Philip Holliday, Kosciusko County Historical Society, North Webster Indiana University, Bloomington; Ann Lonie, University Libraries, University of Notre Dame, Notre Dame; Gladys McCammon, Elwood; Mooresville Public Library; Joyce E. Oehler, Brazil; Matt Osborne, Evansville; Gladys Otto, Lilly Library, Wabash College, Crawfordsville; Anne Campbell Pearson, Evansville Public Library; Joe Pike, Rush County Historical Society, Rushville; Carolyn Rawles, Clinton Public Library; Timothy J. Sehr, Indiana University Archives, Bloomington; Robert Taylor, Monroe County Public Library, Bloomington; Samuel M. Upton, Cass County Historical Society, Logansport; Linda Walton, Indiana State Library, Indianapolis; Wayne County Museum, Richmond; Winona Lake Christian Assembly.

IOWA: Anamosa Chamber of Commerce; Dora Biederman, Mitchell County Historical Society, Osage; J. C. Briley, Nevada Community Historical Society; Cedar Falls Public Library; Cedar Rapids Public Library; Genevieve M. Curry, Glenwood Public Library; Des Moines Public Library; Linda Dyer, Iowa City Public Library; Marvyl J. Frink, New Hampton Public Library; Grinnell College Archives; H. W. Kennedy, Buffalo Bill Museum, Le Claire; City of Keokuk; Patricia M. McBride, Free Public Library, Council Bluffs; Eleanor Mathews, Iowa State University Library, Ames; Cathy Moore, Ames Public Library; Musser Public Library, Muscatine; Ottumwa Public Library; Earl M. Rogers, University Libraries, University of Iowa, Iowa City; Robert M. Seger, Clinton Public Library; Sioux City Public Library; James H. Som-

mers, Des Moines; Delpha Trindle, Winterset Chamber of
Commerce; Mrs. Melvin Underbakke, Laura Ingalls Wilder
Park and Museum, Inc., Burr Oak; Eugene J. Wagner, Sta-
cyville; Lowell R. Wilbur, Iowa State Dept. of History and
Archives, Des Moines.

KANSAS: Lawrence J. Baker, Buffalo Bill State Park Com-
mittee, Leavenworth; J. Thomas Brown, Watkins Commu-
nity Museum, Lawrence; Karyl L. Buffington, Coffeyville
Public Library; Barbara Richards Buskirk, Hays Public Library; Butler County Historical Society, El Dorado; Virginia
Callahan, Leavenworth Public Library; Charles Clough,
Coffeyville Historical Society; D. Cheryl Collins, Jean C.
Dallas, Riley County Historical Museum, Manhattan; Em-
poria Public Library; Fort Leavenworth Public Affairs Office;
Ethel J. Hunt, Paola; Larry Jochims, Kansas State Historical
Society, Topeka; Kansas Heritage Center, Dodge City; Law-
rence Public Library; Leavenworth County Historical Soci-
ety, Leavenworth; Alice W. Pearson, Little House on the
Prairie, Inc., Independence; John E. Wickman, Dwight D.
Eisenhower Library, Abilene.

KENTUCKY: Linda Anderson, Kentucky Historical Society,
Frankfort; Dr. Robert E. Daggy, Thomas Merton Studies
Center, Bellarmine College, Louisville; Ellen Dickerson,
Louisville Free Public Library; Forest Retreat Farms, Inc.,
Carlisle; Marjorie B. Heilman, City of La Grange; Nicky
Hughes, Kentucky Military History Museum, Frankfort;
Margaret G. Kendall, Mason County Museum, Maysville;
Theodore R. Klein, Crestwood; Claudette Malone, Louis-
ville; Lorraine Seay, Henry Clay Memorial Foundation, Lex-
ington; Steven M. Seven, Abraham Lincoln Birthplace NHS,
Hodgenville; James J. Shannon, Madison County Historical
Society, Richmond; Mary Jo Young, Elizabethtown.

LOUISIANA: Denia Angevine, Shreve Memorial Library,
Shreveport; Dr. Patsy K. Barber, Lecompte Cultural, Recre-
ation & Tourism Commission; Mary Bishop, Royal Sonesta
Hotel, New Orleans; Donna N. Boé, Louisiana State Uni-
versity Library, Baton Rouge; Jim Bowie Museum, Opelou-
sas; Vaughan Glasgow, Louisiana State Museum, New
Orleans; Kathy McCormick, 19th Judicial District Court,
Baton Rouge; New Orleans Historic District Landmarks
Commission.

MAINE: Boothbay Region Historical Society, Boothbay Har-
bor; Bette Copeland, Pejepscot Historical Society; Arthur J.
Gerrier, Ellen G. Torrey, Maine Historical Society, Portland;
Louise D. Hall, Portland Public Library; Nellie A. Hart,
Camden Public Library; Stanley Russell Howe, Bethel Historical Society; Gladys O'Neil, Bar Harbor Historical Society; Brenda Pelletier, Paula Volent, Bowdoin College Museum of Art, Brunswick; Earle G. Shettleworth, Jr., Maine
Historic Preservation Commission, Augusta; Shirley Thayer,
Maine State Library, Augusta; Toby Updyke, Greater Port-
land Landmarks, Inc.

MARYLAND: Historical Society of Cecil County, Elkton;
Ellen Coxe, Maryland Historical Trust, Annapolis; Diana
Digges, Baltimore Commission for Historical and Architec-
tural Preservation; Jean Fulton, Chevy Chase Library; Ruby

Graham, Public Library of Annapolis and Anne Arundel
County; Mary W. Griepenkerl, Bryn Mawr School, Balti-
more; Regina Guay, Silver Spring Library; John McGrain,
Baltimore County Landmarks Preservation Commission,
Towson; University of Maryland Libraries, College Park; Earl
A. Miller, Town of University Park; V. L. Morris, Berlin;
Jenny Murphy, Dorchester County Public Library, Cam-
bridge; Dr. Morgan H. Pritchett, Enoch Pratt Free Library,
Baltimore; Orlando Ridout V, Annapolis; Alex Rose, Edgar
Allan Poe Society, Baltimore; Babe Ruth Birthplace Foun-
dation, Inc., Baltimore; Mary M. Starin, Talbot County Free
Library, Easton; Jane C. Sween, Montgomery County His-
torical Society, Rockville; Joan H. Wise, Historical Society of
Kent County, Chestertown.

MASSACHUSETTS: Lisa J. Arm, Brenda Howitson, Malden
Public Library; Alexander Armour, McLean Hospital, Belmont; Gertrude C. Bardwell, Whately Historical Society; Jane
Beeke, Brockton Public Library System; Vivian Belko, Wellfleet Historical Society; the late Nathaniel Benchley, Nan-
tucket; Richard B. Betts, Belmont; Nancy L. Bigelow, Ritter
Memorial Library, Lunenburg; Marian Boring, Wellesley Free
Library; Isaline L. Bouteiller, Southern Berkshire Chamber
of Commerce, Great Barrington; Brewster Ladies' Library
Association; Public Library of Brookline; Cambridge Histor-
ical Commission; Susan Cobb, Jonathan Bourne Public Li-
brary, Bourne; Dedham Historical Society; Christina M.
DiNapoli, Woburn Public Library; George Dow, Marshfield;
Dukes County Historical Society, Edgartown; Gloria L.
Edinburg, Free Public Library, Oxford; Bryn E. Evans, Krista
I. McLeod, Paul Revere House, Boston; Fall River Public
Library; Phyllis A. Farnsworth, Lancaster Historical Com-
mission; Fiske Public Library, Wrentham; Gina Flannery,
Newton Free Library; Nancy S. Franke, Medfield; Goddard
Library, Clark University, Worcester; Allan B. Goodrich,
William Johnson, John F. Kennedy Library, Boston; Stanley
Greenberg, Forbes Library, Northampton; Joseph D. Ham-
ilburg, Plymouth Rubber Company, Inc., Canton; Hamilton
Public Library; Harvard Public Library; Elsie Haskell, Dart-
mouth Public Libraries, South Dartmouth; Margaret Hinck-
ley, Winthrop Public Library; Bette Hunt, Marblehead His-
torical Society; Mrs. James H. Hunter, Williamstown; The
Jones Library, Amherst; Edmund Kenealy, Canton Public
Library; Margarett M. Kennard, Lenox Library Association;
Virginia A. Knowlton, Conway; Doris Lavigne, East Brook-
field Public Library; Mary Leen, The Bostonian Society, Bos-
ton; Susan Frisch Lehrer, National Trust for Historic Preser-
vation, Stockbridge; Lincoln Public Library; Faith Magoun,
Lynn Historical Society, Inc.; Donna Mailloux, Lowell City
Library; Marlborough Public Library; Mason Library, Great
Barrington; Helen J. Maynard, Groton Public Library; Bar-
bara A. Meade, Truro Historical Society; Elaine M. Melisi,
Whitman Historical Commission; Janet T. Meunier, City of
New Bedford; Jean L. Miller, Haston Free Public Library,
North Brookfield; Jeanne M. Mills, Pilgrim Society, Ply-
mouth; Nantucket Historical Association; Peter E. Nelson,
Natick; Newburyport Public Library; George O'Hare, New
England Telephone Co., Boston; James K. Owens, Medford;
A. W. Phinney, First Church of Christ, Scientist, Boston;
Pauline D. Pierce, Stockbridge Historical Association; Sally
Pierce, Library of the Boston Athenaeum; Raymond J. Purdy,

Massachusetts Charitable Mechanic Association, Boston; Ellie Reichlin, Society for the Preservation of New England Antiquities, Boston; Elizabeth Roland, Sawyer Free Library, Gloucester; Iola C. Scheufele, Natick Historical Society, South Natick; Robert Severey, Boston; Susan Shafer, Longfellow NHS, Cambridge; Patricia Shaheen, Adams NHS, Quincy; Janet H. Smith, Goodnow Library, Sudbury; Somerville Public Library; Town of South Dartmouth; Springfield City Library; Jacqueline C. Tidman, Westborough Public Library; Richard B. Trask, Danvers Archival Center; Tufts Library, Weymouth; G. B. Warden, Cambridge Historical Society; Elizabeth Webber, Beverly Historical Society; Weymouth Historical Society, South Weymouth; Eunice M. Whitman, Franklin Library; Ruth E. Wilbur, Northampton Historical Society; Joyce Woodman, Concord Free Public Library; Woods Memorial Library, Barre; Worcester Historical Museum; F. Young, Brockton.

MICHIGAN: Margaret Bentley, Owosso Public Library; Don Bolthouse, Beth Hartman, Melissa Lynch, Paul Wolbrinks, Spring Lake High School; James E. Conway, Detroit Historical Museum; Cranbrook Academy of Art/Museum, Bloomfield Hills; Flora Hazard, Kalamazoo; Ingham County Library, Mason; Lansing Public Library; Robert G. Lucking, Spring Lake; Peggy Lugthart, Public Libraries of Saginaw; John McCabe, Sault Ste. Marie; Don McMahon, City of Kalamazoo; University of Michigan Library, Ann Arbor; Tim Mulavey, Ann Arbor; Sandra and Robert O'Daniel, Westland; Orion Township Clerk, Lake Orion; Petoskey Public Library; Warner Pflug, Reuther Library, Wayne State University, Detroit; Rev. Guyron J. Philbert, Kalamazoo; Cynthia Read, Edison Institute Archives, Dearborn; Greater Rochester Chamber of Commerce; Peter Schmitt, Western Michigan University Archives, Kalamazoo; Karen J. Stoll, Monroe County Library System, Monroe; Traverse City Public Library; Leslie J. Vollmert, Michigan Dept. of State; Jennifer Williams, Museum of Arts and History, Port Huron; Kathryn Woolley, Kalamazoo; Your Heritage House, Inc., Detroit.

MINNESOTA: Pamela A. Brunfelt, Otter Tail County Historical Society, Fergus Falls; Patricia Harpole, Minnesota Historical Society, St. Paul; Mary Miller, Dept. of Libraries, Duluth; Minneapolis History Collection, Minneapolis Public Library.

MISSISSIPPI: Newton W. Carr, Jr., Beauvoir, Biloxi; Massena F. Jones, Casey Jones Museum, Vaughan; Harry A. Martin, Community Development Foundation, Tupelo; Ronald W. Miller, Historic Natchez Foundation; Mississippi Dept. of Archives and History, Jackson; Annabel Stephens, Smith Library, New Albany; Williams Library, University of Mississippi, Oxford.

MISSOURI: S. S. Adams, Jr., Clayton; Joan Banks, Joplin Public Library; Belton Chamber of Commerce; Bridgeton City & Village Tax Office; T. Carneal, Northwest Missouri State University, Maryville; Judge Larry J. Casey, Potosi; George H. Curtis, Benedict K. Zobrist, Harry S Truman Library, Independence; Ruth Davis, Town & Country Library, Lamar; Nancy Ehrlich, Jackson County Archives, Independence; R. R. Forry, Arrow Rock State Historic Site; City of Grant City; Ann King, St. Charles City-County Library; Kirkwood Public Library; Irene Lichty, Laura Ingalls Wilder Home and Museum, Mansfield; Milton F. Perry, James Farm, Kearney; Sherry Piland, Kansas City Landmarks Commission; *Potosi Independent-Journal*; Sedalia Public Library; Joseph Smith, Kansas City; A. Louise Staman, State Historical Society of Missouri, Columbia; T. C. Stanley, Marceline; Norbury L. Wayman, St. Louis; Linda Wilson, Mid-Continent Public Library, Grandview; Jack Wood, Town & Country Regional Library, Neosho; Reba Earp Young, Lamar.

MONTANA: Dennis Fredrickson, Lewis and Clark Library, Helena; Meg O'Leary, Montana Historical Society Library, Helena; L. Weirather, Parmly Billings Library, Billings.

NEBRASKA: Ann Billesbach, Willa Cather Historical Center, Red Cloud; John E. Carter, Joni Gilkerson, Nebraska State Historical Society, Lincoln; Charles R. Goodale, Pawnee City; Walter Haverkamp, Pawnee City; F. T. Jelinek, Omaha; Loell Jorgensen, Dodge County Historical Society, Fremont; North Platte Public Library; Omaha Public Library; Raymond W. Pettinger, Burchard.

NEVADA: Gary Arent, Elko County Library, Elko; Marie H. Davis, Elko Chamber of Commerce; Phil Earl, Nevada Historical Society; Reno.

NEW HAMPSHIRE: Joanne Adamowicz, Kelley Library, Salem; Historic Society of Amherst; William Copeley, New Hampshire Historical Society, Concord; Mrs. Walter A. Forbes, Wentworth Library, Center Sandwich; Franklin Public Library; Nancy C. Merrill, Exeter Public Library; William H. Teschek, Lane Memorial Library, Hampton; Jean Ulitz, Cook Memorial Library, Tamworth.

NEW JERSEY: Clark Beck, Rutgers University Library, New Brunswick; Burlington County Historical Society, Burlington; Dr. Samuel Engle Burr, Jr., Aaron Burr Association, Hightstown; Leah S. Burt, Edison NHS, West Orange; John E. Callery, Bordentown; Camden County Historical Society, Camden; Joint Free Public Library of the Chathams, Chatham; Wendy Chu, David Sarnoff Research Center, Princeton; M. Cushing, West Orange Public Library; Jane Eigenrauch, Red Bank Public Library; Einstein Free Public Library, Pompton Lakes; Free Public Library, Elizabeth; City of Englewood; Eleanor Firstenberger, Bernardsville Public Library; Frenchtown Free Public Library; Hammonton Community Library; Adell Hern, Englewood; Free Public Library, Hoboken; Helen Kupferle, Paterson Public Library; Lakewood Public Library; Dr. Richard W. Lenk, Bergen County Historical Society, River Edge; Long Branch Public Library; Janice Moriarty, Bordentown Library; Morris County Historical Society, Morristown; Virginia T. Mosley, Borough of Tenafly; Perth Amboy Public Library; Gregory J. Plunges, Monmouth County Historical Association, Freehold; Historical Society of Princeton; Natalie Richman, Kathleen Stavec, New Jersey Historical Society, Newark; Susan Robinovitz, Somerset County Library, Bridgewater; Borough of Sea Girt; Summit Historical Society; Walt Whitman Association, Camden; Jeanne T. Will, Joint Free Public Library, Morristown; David

J. and Nancy R. Woolley, Lebanon; W. Randall Woolley, Lebanon.

NEW MEXICO: Judy Blome, Roswell Public Library; Hedy Dunn, Los Alamos Historical Museum; Marcia Muth Miller, Museum of New Mexico, Santa Fe; Forest Supervisor, Santa Fe National Forest, Santa Fe.

NEW YORK: Bruce Adams, Schenectady County Public Library, Schenectady; American Symphony Orchestra, New York City; Alan H. Anderson, New City; Aurora Town Public Library, East Aurora; Sally Ball, East Hampton; Bedford Free Library; Christopher E. Belson, East Hampton Historical Society; Dr. Helen M. Breitbeck, Oswego County Historical Society, Oswego; Elizabeth C. Britcher, White Plains Public Library; Bronxville Public Library; Charlene F. Bryan, Sherburne; Bulova, Inc., Flushing; Louis R. Burgunder, Town of Woodbury, Central Valley; Robert J. Cammann, New Rochelle Chamber of Commerce; Donald A. Cardwell, Amityville; Chautauqua County Historical Society, Westfield; Mrs. C. A. Church, Schenectady County Historical Society, Schenectady; Marion Cleaver, Andrew S. Dolkart, Landmarks Preservation Commission, New York City; Eleanore R. Clise, Geneva Historical Society and Museum; Lucille Corda, Town of Pound Ridge; Samuel B. Cottas, Brooklyn; Doris Crofut, Tuxedo Park; Croton Free Library, Croton-on-Hudson; Croton-on-Hudson Village Historian; Theresa A. Cuda, Utica Public Library; Marion Culp, Roosevelt Public Library; Frank and Flora Di Costanzo, Brooklyn; Lola Dudley, Sally Poundstone, Mamaroneck Free Library; Prof. Carolyn Eisele, New York City; William R. Emerson, Raymond Teichman, Franklin D. Roosevelt Library, Hyde Park; Mary S. Fargo, Town of Smyrna; Helene S. Farrell, Schoharie County Historical Society, Schoharie; Elizabeth A. Finck, Palisades; Fishkill Historical Society; Caroline Moul Fitz, Amityville Public Library; Kevin J. Gallagher, Adriance Memorial Library, Poughkeepsie; Helen Ver Nooy Gearn, Newburgh; M. Joan Gibson, Chapman Historical Museum, Glens Falls; Village of Goshen; Janet Graham, Hudson River Heritage, Rhinebeck; Great Neck Library; Irma Mae Griffin, Roxbury; Marjorie Mazia Guthrie, New York City; Martha B. Halperin, Wave Hill, Bronx; Mrs. W. C. Handy, Sr., Yonkers; Neil D. Hanson, Archivist, County of Albany; Laurie Harbour, Gloversville *Leader-Herald*; Peter H. Hare, State University of New York at Buffalo; Kitty Carlisle Hart, New York City; William Randolph Hearst, Jr., New York City; Robert Hefner, East Hampton; Clyde E. Helfter, Buffalo and Erie County Historical Society, Buffalo; Marianne W. Hickman, Oneida Ltd., Oneida; Margaret K. Hills, Hudson Area Association Library; Helen A. Hoag, Greenwich Historical Association; Shirley Houck, Delaware County Historical Association, Delhi; Mrs. William C. Houck, Town of Sullivan, Chittenango; Cynthia Howk, Landmark Society of Western New York, Rochester; Russell G. Hubbard, Madison County Historical Society, Oneida; George Hymowitz, Brooklyn; Jermain Memorial Library, Sag Harbor; John Haydn Jones, Westport; Clifford Kachline, National Baseball Hall of Fame and Museum, Cooperstown; R. Kay, New York City; Elizabeth Burroughs Kelley, West Park; Dorothy T. King, East Hampton Free Library; Lois Kuster, Queens Borough Public Library, Maspeth; Betty D. Landon, Schuyler County Historical Society, Montour Falls; Rufus B. Langhans, Town of Huntington; Elisabeth S. Lapham, Wading River Historical Society; Larchmont Public Library; William Lay, Jr., Tioga County Historical Society, Owego; the late Lotte Lenya, New City; Victor T. Liss, Town of Smithtown; Elaine London, White Plains Public Schools; Katie McCummings, Bronx; K. H. MacFarland, Albany Institute of History & Arts; Virginia McGuire, Hastings Historical Society, Hastings-On-Hudson; Mary MacKenzie, Lake Placid-North Elba Historical Society, Lake Placid; Alice Mahardy, Richfield Springs Public Library; Bea Marcks, Quogue; Bernadette T. Mignone, Brewster Public Library; Thomas H. Miner, The Catskill Center, Arkville; Gae Mitchell, Historical Society of Quaker Hill and Vicinity, Pawling; Edward J. Monarski, Syracuse; Mount Kisco Public Library; Mt. Vernon Library; Vijay Nair, Adirondack Museum Library, Blue Mountain Lake; Lawrence Naukam, Rochester Public Library; Colin T. Naylor, Jr., Peekskill; Ruth Neuendorffer, Historical Society of the Tarrytowns, Inc., Tarrytown; New York Public Library; The Nyack Library; Corinne Nyquist, Sojourner Truth Library, State University of New York, College at New Paltz; Malcolm B. Ochs, White Plains; Yoshi Okamoto, Forest Hills; Alex Oland, New York City; Mona Hirsch Oppenheim, Kings Point; Paul R. Palmer, Low Memorial Library, Columbia University, New York City; Ella L. Perry, Homer; Perry Public Library; M. L. Peterson, Waterville Historical Society; Ruth Piwonka, Columbia County Historical Society, Kinderhook; Port Jervis Free Library; B. Powers, Town of New Castle, Chappaqua; Henry Priebe, Buffalo Landmark and Preservation Board; Agnes M. Pryzgoda, City of Peekskill; Wilfred J. Rauber, Town of North Dansville, Dansville; Lilly Reisert, National Park Service, New York City; Roberta Y. Reminio, Ossining Historical Society; Town of Rhinebeck; Town of Riga, Churchville; Lottie Robbins, Dept. of Public Information, United Nations, New York City; Rochester Historical Society; Bonnie L. Ross, Flower Memorial Library, Watertown; Rye Free Reading Room; Rye Historical Society; St. Lawrence County Historical Association, Canton; Saranac Lake Area Chamber of Commerce; Saratoga County Museum, Ballston Spa; Robert J. Scarry, Moravia; Loretta L. Schmidt, Sagamore Hill NHS, Oyster Bay; Ruth Semtner, Waterloo; Seneca Falls Historical Society; Seymour Library, Auburn; Jeanne Sharp, Newburgh Free Library; Gordon C. Sherman, Westport; Madeline H. Sherwood, New York City; Florence Sinsheimer, Scarsdale Public Library; Anita Smith, Montgomery County Dept. of History and Archives, Fonda; Beatrice Sweeney, City of Saratoga Springs; David Szanton, Bronx; Catherine Townsend, Watervliet Public Library; Garry P. Tunmore, Mineola Memorial Library; Ulster County Historical Society, Kingston; Janice and Mark Van Ness, Saranac Lake; Bets Vondrasek, Walt Whitman Birthplace Association, Huntington Station; F. Wagner, Huntington Historical Society; Margaret V. S. Wallace, Rock Tavern; Westchester County Medical Society, Purchase; Westport Chamber of Commerce; Dorothy Wicker-Re, Bronson Alcott Society, Monroe; Carol Williams, Ontario County Historical Society, Canandaigua; Anne Willis, Stamford; Richard A. Winsche, Nassau County Historical Museum, East Meadow; Carol Woodger, Port Chester Public Library; Jean M. Woodruff, Staten Island Historical Society, Richmondtown; Mrs. Jerry E. Wright, Corning; Richard

N. Wright, Onondaga Historical Association, Syracuse; Yonkers Dept. of Development.

NORTH CAROLINA: Asheville-Buncombe Library System, Asheville; Moir C. Bunker, White Plains; Clark Cox, Rockingham; Kate Bunker Cross, Mt. Airy; Benjamin H. Davis, Carl Sandburg Home NHS, Flat Rock; Anne Elkins, Braswell Memorial Library, Rocky Mount; Wendy L. Foxworth, Pinehurst Hotel and Country Club; Cynthia A. Hall, Cumberland County Public Library System, Fayetteville; Tom Hanchett, Charlotte Mecklenburg Historic Properties Commission, Charlotte; Martha H. Holloman, Halifax County Library, Halifax; Jackson Library, University of North Carolina, Greensboro; Mildred B. McIntosh, Givens Memorial Library, Pinehurst; Pat Ann Matthews, Fayetteville Area Chamber of Commerce; William C. Reeves, Weaverville; Carole Treadway, Friends Historical Collection, Guilford College, Greensboro.

NORTH DAKOTA: Minnewaukan City Library.

OHIO: J. Richard Abell, Public Library of Cincinnati and Hamilton County; Boyd Addlesperger, Mansfield-Richland County Public Library; Sheppard Black, Alden Library, Ohio University, Athens; Patricia R. Bristley, Sandusky County Historical Society, Fremont; Lenore Egan Brown, *Columbus Monthly*; Richard Centing, Ohio State University Libraries, Columbus; Howard Chapman, Strongsville; Cincinnati Symphony Orchestra; Jon Cobes, Ohio State University, Mansfield; Public Library of Columbus & Franklin County; Josephine Rickey Copp, Lucasville; Dorothy S. Cowan, Ashtabula County District Library, Ashtabula; Rosemary Crabtree, Lucasville; Dover Public Library; Shirley K. Duskey, Camden; Ann B. Fauver, Elyria Public Library; Frances Forman, Cincinnati Historical Society; Allison L. Gould, Oberlin College Library, Oberlin; Thomas B. Greenslade, Kenyon College, Gambier; Helen Helton, Akron-Summit County Public Library; Village of Hopedale; Jefferson County Historical Association, Steubenville; Herbert S. Karch, Old Tannery Farm, Hudson; Flora McPherson, Kirtland Temple Historic Center; Dorothea Marshall, Newcomerstown; Vicki J. Martin, Village of Andover; Brenda Merrill, Andover; Rebecca Metz, Marion Public Library; Laura J. Moorman, Mount Vernon Public Library; Village of North Bend; Daniel L. Rhodebeck, Bellville; Ralph H. Romig, Uhrichsville; Joanne M. Sawyer, Teachout-Price Memorial Library, Hiram College; Toni Seiler, Garst Museum, Greenville; R. David Snider, Regional Resource Associates, Inc., Somerset; Stokes Learning Resources Center, Wilberforce University; Thomas L. Vince, Hudson Library and Historical Society; Warren Public Library; David Williams, Warren; Public Library of Youngstown and Mahoning County.

OKLAHOMA: City of Okemah; Bernadette Pruitt, Tulsa; V. Hubert Smith, McAlester; Tulsa City-County Library System.

OREGON: Virginia Guest Ferriday, Portland; Lew Merz, Hood River County Historical Society, Hood River; Dorothy Jean Zornman, Library Association of Portland.

PENNSYLVANIA: Cynthia J. Ahmann, Charles Mann, Pattee Library, Pennsylvania State University, University Park; Kathryn Ann Auerbach, Beverly H. Wilson, Bucks County Conservancy, Doylestown; Edmund N. Bacon, Philadelphia; Samuel J. Bernard, Carlisle; Edna H. Bowser, Cameron County Historical Society, Emporium; Ellen R. Boyer, Pottsville Free Public Library; Jerry Bruce, Lancaster County Library, Lancaster; Rachel Carson Homestead Association, Springdale; Citizens Library, Washington; Conococheague District Library, Chambersburg; Helen Davis, Zane Grey House, Lackawaxen; DuBois Public Library; William A. Felker, Free Library of Philadelphia; George J. Fluhr, Shohola; Richard E. Forgay, Borough of Lansford; Jane Gill, Bethlehem Public Library; Charles H. Glatfelter, Adams County Historical Society, Gettysburg; Barbara Pearson Godfrey, Swarthmore; Sidney B. Gornish, Philadelphia; Nada Gray, Lewisburg; Alberta Y. Haught, Altoona Area Public Library; Nancy D. Horn, Malvern Public Library; Robert D. Ilisevich, Crawford County Historical Society, Meadville; Independence NHP, Philadelphia; David W. Kraeuter, Memorial Library, Washington and Jefferson College, Washington; Joanne Kreamer, Lewisburg; Sara Leishman, Cambria County Historical Society, Ebensburg; Lititz Public Library; Don F. Mills, Holicong; Amy V. Morrison, Swarthmore College Library; New Castle Public Library; Ann Niessen, Bucks County Commissioners, Doylestown; Rosemary B. Philips, Chester County Historical Society, West Chester; Pike County Chamber of Commerce, Milford; Mary Pispeky, Lansford; Pittsburgh Symphony Orchestra; Ruth S. Reid, Historical Society of Western Pennsylvania, Pittsburgh; Mary C. Riley, Cox Free Library, Doylestown; Priscilla Schmidt, Holicong; Sewickley Public Library; John A. Shade, Jr., Pearl S. Buck Foundation, Inc., Perkasie; Shenandoah Area Free Public Library; Skillman Library, Lafayette College, Easton; Betty Smith, Susquehanna County Historical Society, Montrose; Eliza Smith, Pittsburgh History & Landmarks Foundation; Springdale Free Public Library; Mrs. Edmund J. Thomas, Factoryville; Tinicum Township, Erwinna; Margaret Toussaint, Historical Society of Schuylkill County, Pottsville; Richard Tyler, Philadelphia Historical Commission; Upper Darby Township & Sellers Memorial Free Public Library, Upper Darby; U.S. Army Military History Institute, Carlisle Barracks; Jean G. Wilk, Cresson Borough.

RHODE ISLAND: Blackstone Valley Chamber of Commerce, Pawtucket; Gladys E. Bolhouse, Newport Historical Society; Marie F. Harper, Maureen Taylor, Rhode Island Historical Society, Providence; Karen M. Light, Westerly Public Library; James H. Van Alen, Newport.

SOUTH CAROLINA: Camden District Heritage Foundation, Camden; Historic Columbia Foundation; Mary Davis, Georgetown County Chamber of Commerce, Georgetown; Vincent F. Downing, Abbeville County Library, Abbeville; Kingstree Chamber of Commerce; Janet Lamb, South Carolina Dept. of Archives and History, Columbia; McCormick County Historical Commission, McCormick; Barbara H. Mixon, Yemassee; David Moltke-Hansen, South Carolina Historical Society, Charleston; Susan L. Moyer, Aiken County Public Library, Aiken; Sue Mushock, Belle W. Baruch Forest Science Institute, Georgetown.

SOUTH DAKOTA: Alyce Bates, Huron Public Library; Dayton W. Canaday, South Dakota Dept. of Education and Cultural Affairs, Pierre; Pauline Rankin, Adams Memorial Hall Museum, Deadwood; Anne Seaman, Mitchell Library, Aberdeen; Wilma Torkelson, City of Doland.

TENNESSEE: Don W. Belcher, Nashville Area Chamber of Commerce; Joe Brady, Memphis Public Library; Margaret Butler, Giles County Historical Society, Pulaski; Mrs. William Coke, Ladies' Hermitage Association, Hermitage; Lydia D. Corbitt, Denver; Fisk University Library, Nashville; Joni Johnson, Graceland, Memphis; Knoxville-Knox County Public Library; Jack Loistan, Nashville; Beryl Lusby, Knoxville Heritage, Inc.; Town of Madisonville; Maryville College Library; Sara M. Secor, Landmarks Chattanooga; Clara W. Swann, Chatanooga-Hamilton County Bicentennial Library; David A. Wright, Bryan College, Dayton.

TEXAS: Paul R. Arreola, Hunt; Austin Public Library; Lincoln Borglum, La Feria; Jane Chapin, Galveston Historical Foundation, Inc.; Jane Clause, Lubbock City-County Library; Dorothy Glasser, Houston Public Library; Jean Herold, General Libraries, University of Texas at Austin; Tina Lawson, Lyndon Baines Johnson Library, Austin; Basilia Martinez, Fredericksburg Chamber of Commerce; Judge Choice Moore, Windom; J. Myler, San Antonio Public Library; Herb Peterson, Butt-Holdsworth Memorial Library, Kerrville; Daniel D. Snider, Lovett Memorial Library, Pampa; E. C. Starnes, U.S. Army Air Defense Center and Fort Bliss, El Paso; Michael E. Sudderth, M.D., Dallas; Tyrrell Historical Library, Beaumont; Michael E. Wilson, Rosenberg Library, Galveston.

UTAH: Keith W. Perkins, Brigham Young University, Provo; William W. Slaughter, Church of Jesus Christ of Latter-day Saints, Salt Lake City; Fran Zedney, Weber County Library, Ogden.

VERMONT: Marilyn Blackwell, Vermont Historical Society, Montpelier; Brooks Memorial Library, Brattleboro; Edmund A. Brown, Peacham Historical Association; Griffith Memorial Library, Danby; Laura Heller, Putney; Charles D. Maurer, Rutland Free Library; Charles L. Parker, East Poultney; Tyler Resch, Bennington College; Carol L. Richards, West Haven; Jennie Shurtleff, Woodstock Historical Society; David L. Thomas, Canfield Library, Arlington.

VIRGINIA: Jack Bales, Horatio Alger Society, Fredericksburg; Rebecca Bonduino, Winchester-Frederick County Historical Society, Winchester; Dr. Katharine L. Brown, Woodrow Wilson Birthplace Foundation, Staunton; Mrs.

William Bushman, Staunton; Leonie M. DeRoche, Alexandria Library; Peter W. Farrell, Alderman Library, University of Virginia, Charlottesville; John K. Gott, Arlington; Hopewell Area-Prince George Chamber of Commerce, Hopewell; Jeanette G. Hurt, Wytheville-Wythe-Bland Chamber of Commerce, Wytheville; Thomas Jefferson Memorial Foundation, Monticello, Charlottesville; Barbara M. Jenner, Staunton Public Library; Jeanne Klitgaard, Loudoun Museum Information Center, Leesburg; Loudoun County Chamber of Commerce, Leesburg; Christine Meadows, Mount Vernon Ladies' Association; Dennis A. Porter, Verona; Anna W. Rups, Styles Public Library, Falls Church; Patricia L. Taylor, Virginia State Library, Richmond; Virginia State Travel Service, Richmond; Mrs. Williams C. Wickham, Jr., Ashland; Elizabeth B. Wingo, Norfolk Historical Society.

WASHINGTON: Lane Anderson, Seattle Public Library; Tillie H. Coble, Bow; Marge Cowan, Forks; Eunice W. Darvill, Skagit County Historical Museum, LaConner; Jeanne Engerman, Washington State Historical Society, Tacoma; Town of Forks; Frances Henneke, Forks Memorial Library; Robert W. Mull, Yakima Valley Museum & Historical Association, Yakima; Debra Peterson, Historical Society of Seattle & King County; Barbara Street, Clallam County Museum, Port Angeles; Ken Twiss, Bing Crosby Historical Society, Tacoma; Ada Ruth Whitmore, Bickleton; Yakima Valley Regional Library, Yakima.

WEST VIRGINIA: Kanawha County Public Library, Charleston; LaVonne R. Leary, Ohio County Public Library, Wheeling.

WISCONSIN: Robert A. Bjerke, University of Wisconsin Center-Manitowoc County, Manitowoc; Chuck Giodana, Green Bay Packer Hall of Fame, Green Bay; Beck Helland, Outagamie County Historical Society, Appleton; Jean C. Houston, Couderay; George R. Johnson, Milwaukee County Historical Society; Errol Kindschy, West Salem Historical Society; Allan Kovan, La Crosse Public Library; Madison Public Library; Town of Manitowish Waters; Dorothy W. Osborne, Racine County Historical Society, Racine; Prof. Thomas C. Reeves, University of Wisconsin-Parkside, Kenosha; Greater Richland Center Area Chamber of Commerce; Shawano City-County Library; Rosemary Young Singh, Manitowoc Public Library; Thomas Tomczak, Milwaukee Public Library; Vaughn Public Library, Ashland; Les Woldt, Town of Grand Chute, Appleton.

WYOMING: Dorothy M. Doyle, Carbon County Public Library, Rawlins; Altamae Markham, Park County Library, Cody.

INTRODUCTION

"Where are you coming from?" That question became a ritual for pop-psychologists during the 1960s and 1970s, a key to what they considered communication. Understanding where a person was emotionally "coming from" provided a "handle" for knowing that person and helping the interaction.

The more literal places we come from are at least equally important. Our life places cannot explain everything about us, but they may account for much. Our personal points of origin, whether emotional or physical, often reveal much about how we structure our existence now. Do we mainly try to preserve, reconstruct or renovate the places we are "coming from"? Or do we raze them for better structures—or for the moral equivalent of parking lots?

Such questions become vital tools when we view the lives of the most influential persons of our history and try to understand where they were "coming from." Does fame arise mainly from timing and circumstance, or from individuals who inspire and originate the conditions that bring themselves to prominence? There are plausible examples for each argument. Certainly many of the persons listed in this book would never have achieved fame without an exact coincidence of the right milieus plus their own talents. Others would probably have reached eminence in any age and almost any circumstances. In detailing the importance of specific places in specific lives, therefore, the connections range from extremely

obvious to invisible. Mark Twain carried Missouri with him throughout his life, though his actual period there occupied only his boyhood years. Another Missourian, Gen. John J. Pershing, could as well have originated in Iowa or Florida for all the discernible effects of Missouri on his public career. Even when such effects are hard to trace, however, they probably do exist. Any life studied in sufficient depth is likely to yield numerous strands of more or less significant connections between person and place. It is part of the biographer's job, of course, to trace these elements and assign them proper weight. While this book does not undertake that job, it assumes that such connections do exist and that their significance is often enormous.

Numerous homes of eminent persons in American history exist today. Seeking them out for ourselves, however, is a quest on many levels; for what, really, are we seeking?

The achievement of fame in American culture generally means that the achiever becomes divided into two entities; the "real person" and the public persona. This persona—over which the "real person," even if living, often holds little control—assumes a "life" of its own in the public mind. It consists in part of a surface which acts as a mirror. In it, people see subconscious aspects of themselves that they can openly view nowhere else. Thus the famed person attracts powerful emotions of both positive and negative character. "Transference," "projection," "hero worship" and "scapegoatism" are other terms for this process. The illusion has no use to us, however, unless we view the persona as the "real person," so that it may function as a vicarious fulfillment or outlet for us. Only in this way can epochal heroes, heroines and scoundrels originate and exist.

One doesn't need to agree with Thomas Carlyle's "great man" theory of history in order to recognize that the power of notable persons in our history and culture springs from the personae into which we shape them; and that such personae form our models of appearance or behavior and give us psychological and social values. By means of such personae we submit to leadership or rebellion, strive for excellence, learn our ways of thinking, acting, loving, hating, being. We probably never quit imitating and emulating these self-creations; as their subconscious creators, we "discover" in them much about ourselves. This holds true even for a person long dead; the illusion of the "real person" survives in history because of his or her persona, a much less fragile creature than flesh. Abraham Lincoln—the part of him that we created and continue to create— goes marching on, as do hundreds of others in our history.

One result is invariably certain: Lincoln, George Washington, Susan B. Anthony, Kit Carson, Martin Luther King, Jr.—none of these people will ever look quite the same to you after you see where they were literally "coming from." You may enter their homes thinking you know them well and leave estranged—or, more often, vice versa. In any case, you will probably leave with a greater knowledge of yourself. Such persons still have this ability because we have invested that power in them.

Today the age of heroes is regularly declared defunct. Wart-by-wart inspections from the press media, we are told, permit little chance for hero awe to blossom, for personae to grow and assume life and meaning in our psyches. Yet one has only to look at the astronauts, at Billy Graham, at the late John Wayne, to know that hero personae still thrive. Those parts of themselves that the assassins of Dr. King, John Lennon and two Kennedys were trying to kill manifest the sometimes terrible power of personae over the individual psyche. The media concentration, if anything, probably increases "persona potential" to vast, often ridiculous levels. If the press magnifies warts, it also enlarges our appetite for

myths and our real needs for them. The fact that we often deserve better personae than the press gives us says as much about our own limited aspirations as about deficiency of the media.

The men and women whom we regard as "great" in our history often undergo phases of "adjustment" to society's needs, cycles of posthumous debunking, rediscovery and revision. The lives of our writers, presidents and military heroes are especially vulnerable to such reassessment. A large percentage of persons in this book were never listed in Who's Who or its older equivalents during their lifetimes; they never "lived," in some sense, until they were dead. Eminent persons become different personae to different times. Some critics admonish us not to judge a historic person's acts or works by present-day criteria. Yet what other criteria are proper for us to use? If we refrain ourselves from negative evaluations based on our present "enlightened" views, we can hardly accept the positive verdicts we may have gained about certain notable persons since their deaths. Melville, Thoreau and many others would today be lost to us on those terms. Not to reassess historic persons from where we ourselves are "coming from"—whether positively or negatively—is to abandon the opportunities that these lives offer us for our ongoing instruction, growth or amusement. Confining our evaluations to the standards of a person's own times and milieu seals a spurious respect that condemns the person to "historical importance," the scholarly equivalent of funeral and burial. That happens often enough in any case; but it should not happen to a Whitman, a Jefferson, a Douglass, a Dickinson. These persons surely speak to us more clearly than to their own times.

When we seek homes or other places associated with "the real person," we are usually searching for reaffirmation, a reinforcement of our own sense of a persona that remains important to us. Far from actually wanting to view aspects of the "real person," most of us seek a closer approach to the useful persona so as to make it more believable. Sometimes this effort fails. A vague sense of disappointment, of somehow failed expectations, is a fairly common experience for visitors who encounter more "real person" in a notable home than they were emotionally prepared for, thus diminishing the persona.

But a greater danger lies with too much reverence, too many questions about our historic great that remain thoughtfully unasked. The persona, as an instructive reflection of ourselves, of our more admirable or more despicable traits, has no value to us as an ethereal creature of Sunday morning sermons and Fourth-of-July speeches. Viewing the homes of notable Americans can help us flee platitude country. It can help us frame the personae we have created so as to increase their meaning to us.

The aims of this book are twofold: to catalog and present data on the American residences of more than 600 persons whose lives had major effects on national society and history; and to enable travelers, students of history and biography and anyone else so inclined to find and view for themselves the homes or sites associated with these famous persons. For the combined aims of creating a reference work and a practical tour guide, several basic items of information are included, where possible, for each home discussed in the text:
—Year of construction
—Year of destruction, if pertinent
—Dates of occupance by the noted inhabitant
—1982 status of home or site, including street address and access information

In some instances, a loss or inaccessibility of records makes the collection of even this minimal amount of data impossible; but these instances are relatively few. When exact years of construction or destruction are unknown, the general period can often be assigned based on the architecture of the dwelling or on the data for subsequent constructions on the site. Dates of occupance are usually well documented by biographers, though imprecise or conflicting information is not uncommon; in these cases, I have generally relied upon the most recent accounts. The status of these dwellings is, of course, ever changing. Only a minority of dwellings once occupied by notables are now owned and maintained by federal, state or municipal governments. Even a home's inclusion in the prestigious National Register of Historic Places, while conferring certain tax benefits to owners, cannot prevent an owner from maiming or destroying the property. Today the care and fate of most historic dwellings remain in the hands of private owners or of organizations formed especially for maintenance and trusteeship. In too many instances, this book will be outdated as it goes to press; a structure present in 1982

will not necessarily survive to 1985. A significant number of privately owned historic dwellings in these pages stood vacant or in various stages of decline—some of them on the verge of demolition or collapse—at the time of writing. Of these, the number that will find saviors or restorers is probably small. For a building "on the verge," one is well advised to check locally before going too far out of one's way to see it.

What qualifies as a home? Generally, for the purposes of this book, a *home* is any currently existing structure, whether house, hotel or apartment dwelling, where the eminent person resided for any extensive length of time. *Extensive* usually means at least a year, though some addresses of shorter durations are included if the place had some outstanding association with the person's life or career. Not listed as homes (with some significant exceptions) are academic lodgings and transient military quarters.

A *site* is the home address minus the eminent person's residence, which was destroyed or moved elsewhere; the site may be currently vacant but is often occupied by another building (or, frequently, a parking lot).

Most famous homes that admit the public are careful *restorations* along original plans and designs, incorporating a large amount of original materials along with some elements necessarily replaced because of destruction or decay; most restorations begin from a basically intact "skeleton," then are "fleshed out" by specialists in historical architecture working from the accumulated data. *Reconstructions* are entirely rebuilt from the ground up, using original plans but little or no original materials. *Preservations*, the least common structures, maintain both original design and materials. National Register status may be granted only to preservations and restorations that remain on their original sites. For convenience in the text, I have used the National Historic Landmark and Site designation in titles of registered buildings and areas, though these words may not always be part of the place's official letterhead. Dwellings that remain in private hands usually show varying degrees of modification by subsequent owners on both interior and exterior aspects. Comparative "then-and-now" drawings or photographs, especially from exactly the same angles, provide a useful, interesting means of contrasting a home's changing appearances through decades or centuries.

The text portion of this book focuses upon (a) homes open to the public, (b) surviving homes that remain privately owned, and (c) museums displaying biographical collections. In a few instances, current private occupants have requested that addresses not be published. I have respected such wishes, noting the essential fact that the house still exists and giving only generalized location data. Anyone with sufficient interest in locating such a place will be able to do so by local inquiry. For the vast majority of homes and sites, visitors must content themselves with exterior views from the street. These homes are subject to the same protection from trespassing as any other private property, regardless of who once lived there. Except during hours specifically advertised as welcoming the public, or during prearranged hours, visitors will be subject to the penalties of trespassing. Most private owners and occupants of historic houses are well aware of their property's significance, and some are not averse to visits arranged well in advance. Many, however, understandably dread the expense of time and energy involved in bringing strangers into their homes and will not admit visitors under any circumstances. In all dealings with private occupants, simple courtesy and a sensitivity to the problems that visits may represent to them should govern.

For houses open to the public and for museums displaying biographical collections, rules vary widely and in all cases are designed to protect the property and aid maintenance. The minimal amount of upkeep necessary for a property that may host several hundred thousand visitors per year is staggering. Most dwellings maintained by the National Park Service and by state governments are models of professional operation. Unless the property is held by federal, state or local government agencies, however, it is private; and visitors have no taxpayer's "rights." Since hours of admission are items of constant change, visitors should check to verify admission times before planning visits. Most of these places, whether publicly or privately operated, are closed on major holidays.

"There is some sense that only a house gives of how someone lives," wrote John Kenneth Galbraith. Aside from the periodically updated National Register of Historic Places, there has never been a national effort to catalog information on the homes of America's noted sons and daughters. The Register is far from biographically comprehensive, since requirements for achieving National Register status exclude the vast majority of extant historical homes; nor is it, for that matter, biographically oriented. Though valuable state, regional and local guidebooks (the foremost being the classic *American Guide* series produced for each state by the Federal Writers Program of the Works Progress Administration) have identified many homes or sites within their borders, these likewise are rarely comprehensive in terms of following noted residents through their progression of homes. Most area travel guides list a few well-known historic homes in catch-all "places of interest" categories. Excellent architectural guides, some quite encyclopedic, exist for almost every state and large city; while paying large, loving attention to details of style, facades, construction and architects, however, they seldom have much to say about who dwelt therein. Various magnificent "coffee-table" opuses and folios of historic homes are fairly common, but these aim for colorful spectacle rather than large scope.

Somewhat more inclusive are specialized guidebooks to certain historical periods or subjects. Excellent among these are *Landmarks of the American Revolution* (1973), by Mark M. Boatner III; the National Park Service series including *Colonials and Patriots* (1964), *Founders and Frontiersmen* (1967), *Explorers and Settlers* (1968), *Soldier and Brave* (1971), and *Here Was the Revolution* (1976); *The American Woman's Gazetteer* (1976), by Lynn Sherr and Jurate Kazickas; Alice Hamilton Cromie's *A Tour Guide to the Civil War* (1975); and a number of fine literary tour guides—*Exploring Literary America* (1979) by Marcella Thum, *No Castles on Main Street* (1979) by Stephanie Kraft, *The Literary Guide to the United States* (1981), edited by Stewart Benedict; and the trilogy *A Literary Tour Guide to the United States* (1978–79), by Emilie C. Harting and Rita Stein. These volumes discuss many notable historic residences within their areas of interest but again focus on only the best-known, most accessible ones. Probably the best general guidebook of houses open to the public—though well-known Americans occupied only a minority of them—is the American Heritage Guide *Historic Houses of America* (1980). Thus a comprehensive guide to the homes of America's past from the primary angle of biography is long overdue.

While the name index to this volume lists

chronological rosters of homes and sites for each person, the wider life context of any dwelling or site must, of course, be sought in a full-length biography. Most visitors to notable homes and sites will probably arrive with some fund of knowledge about the historic resident; the better that one prepares to see, of course, the more will be seen. An actual encounter with these places may be the closest possible approach to historic figures whom we can never meet in the flesh.

While one has no choice of parents or the location of one's early homes, these places often give startling insights, not only into the person's family and economic background but also into sources of psychological advantages or obstacles encountered in adulthood. Adulthood homes, by contrast, generally represent personal choices within the person's range of options; and the locations, styles and features of these homes tell us much about the chooser. Not everyone could choose, of course. Soldiers usually resided in whatever quarters they were assigned; government officials sometimes occupied publicly owned mansions; and poverty, family considerations, health, work or various other sorts of obligations also dictated choices. At some time, however, most noted persons made a relatively free choice of home place that continues to provide vital images and expressions of that person today. A very few notables built their homes with their own hands; many more planned and helped design their own dwellings. Usually the more effort that one put into creating a personal place, the more of that person lingers there today.

The selection of which notable names to include in this book was arbitrary. How does one weigh a person's historical value and importance? What kind of scales does one use? There is no end of opinionated lists and advice on this matter. The best-known names, of course, presented no agonies of decision, but an exceedingly gray area of personal choice governed the rest. My gray-area choices would probably not match another's. In a few cases, a transient lifestyle or lack of identifiable homes dictated omission of a name. Generally I have tried to restrict my choice of prominent individuals to those whose careers bore some national significance. That is why people of such state or regional importance as Stephen F. Austin, John Bidwell, Grenville M. Dodge, Henry M. Flagler and Mariano Vallejo—to name only a few—were omitted. To those who may

wish to protest other name selections or omissions, I herewith save them labor: You are right and have excellent reasons.

While admitting to a preservationist bias, I am not primarily interested in presenting another plea for historical preservation. There is no shortage of people who are vastly willing and able to act as the public conscience. I am more concerned with documenting the choices we have made. While the record eloquently shows that Americans have a much lower regard for biographical artifacts of their past than Europeans for theirs, the main purpose here is to describe, not bemoan or prescribe. This American generation is certainly more sensitive to tangible remnants of the past than previous ones. It is not so easy as it once was to tear down a historic house in defiance of community interest and pave over its basement for more parking lot space.

Information sources included biographies, memoirs, architectural and specialized travel guides, journalistic accounts and numerous personal communications. Though I have visited a fair number of the homes included, it was obviously impossible for one person to view each house or site and still complete a book of this magnitude. Thus I have gratefully relied upon the best qualified extensions I could find: biographical experts on the notable person concerned, local people familiar with their own communities, and in most cases both. In the effort to check and update the accuracy of all information, private correspondence with libraries, historical organizations, local authorities and householders ran into thousands of pieces of mail. Sources that presented conflicting information were cross-checked with others in seeking definitive conclusions regarding the location of a home or site. Much of the information on currently private property has only been published, if at all, in local newspapers, directories or historical records. Yet despite my rigorous care to cover all the accessible bases, the profusion of data and sources makes it unlikely that the book is totally free of error. There are undoubtedly experts I haven't located, historians I haven't consulted, local sources I have missed. From such authorities, wherever they are, I cordially invite any corrections or additions they may offer.

There can be something like coming home in experiencing a place where someone whose life helped shape our own has breathed, worked, suffered, laughed. The narrow staircase of Lincoln's Springfield home is an awesome climb when mounted with the awareness of how many times, on good days and bad, Lincoln himself trudged this diagonal. A component of heart-breaking innocence seems mortared into the immense mansions of Newport, Long Island and Hollywood, ingredients of a wide-eyed child's delight. There are different impressions for us in Custer's peaceful birth site, Whitman's once-cluttered bedroom, Grant's death cottage, Poe's bare rooms, Jack London's futile acreage,

Thoreau's spiritually bottomless Walden Pond. The charred old walls surrounding the brilliant rooms of the White House have endured almost 200 years of heavy national and personal triumphs and griefs. "You rows of houses . . . ." We Americans have raised—yes, and razed—some mighty ones. By experiencing the places where our notables were necessarily more human than famous, we find hinterlands of possibility for the humanity that binds us all. I address this book to those who may share such experiences and think them worthwhile.

WHO
LIVED
WHERE

A Biographical Guide to Homes and Museums

ONE

NEW ENGLAND

Six states, less than one-fourth the size of Texas in total area, form the northeastern region of our country. New England began as a mere shoreline clearing on a continent of huge but vaguely perceived dimensions. Brief European landings had occurred here before the Pilgrims settled in 1620, but not even the most far-sighted of those visionaries could have predicted the outcome of their modest aims. As in all beginnings of historic significance, New England was seen by its creators as a quite sufficient end in itself.

New England was named by English adventurer Capt. John Smith, who thought, as he cruised from Cape Cod to Nova Scotia in 1614, that this part of "Virginia" resembled the southeastern coast of England. The first English colonists wanted precisely a "new England"—but one kinder to their religious aspirations than the old. It was not the fact of orthodoxy that had rankled them there, but rather its majority expression. And the process of dissent and flight did not cease once they arrived in their "new England"; this repeating pattern of resistance became, in fact, the main impetus for colonizing the entire region.

The assumptions underlying this behavior manifested what Maine author Louise Dickinson Rich called "the impossible Yankee dream of perfection." Life's main business was to justify itself, to gain God's grudging approval by a negative approach: foiling "that old deluder Satan." The fact that examples of perfection seemed rather scarce—one's own neighbor invariably fell short—cut no ice against the argument; one simply hadn't tried (and could never try) as hard as one ought. This gut-deep persuasion still finds ample expression in America today. It is the religion of the compulsive doer. In its countless modern guises—the work ethic, equations of cleanliness and godliness, competitive "goals," "getting ahead," all the endlessly creative account-book approaches to life—this religion has shaped our national character for so long that we are, to a very large extent, a nation of New Englanders. The Puritans proselytized better than they knew.

Yet despite the conflicts they cultivated among themselves while striving for perfection, New Englanders were one kind of people. There was never serious disagreement, for example, about how a village should look, how a house should be raised, how schools should be kept or fields tilled. The constant creation of new settlements out of old ones formed a pattern that shaped a regional character. All of these communities, radiating from Boston in protest of various sorts, ultimately looked much alike. And so did the people, for all of their thorny independence. You couldn't predict what a farmer would say, but you could safely guess the direction of his thinking and the way he would say it. You might not know the sectarian bias that ruled his head and heart, but you could correctly judge that one existed—and that there were hosts of others he didn't "hold with." The jealously maintained colonial borders and the love of theological hair-splitting notwithstanding, the fabric was of one weave.

Outside threats, of course, drew settlements together in times of mutual stress. The native Americans ravaged New England in periodic outbursts, sometimes on their own desperate volition, more often as tools of European ambitions. (Today one can hardly imagine these old, quiet towns in Massachusetts, Maine, Connecticut and Rhode Island as frequent scenes of bloody violence.) In time, too, came pressure from the least expected source. The settlements radiating from Boston had always considered, not Boston, but England, their parent; even Boston-born Benjamin Franklin considered England "home" as late as the 1770s.

But mother England, an unduly possessive parent, tried belatedly to rein in these scattershot settlements, treating them not as children but as regular English colonies, existing solely as sources of revenue. Thus Americans have two persuasive forces to thank for uniting their homeland into a nation. Without our natives and creditors, the colonists might never have quit indulging their squabbles long enough to detect where mutual self-interest lay. The dependency upon one's neighbors forced by these foes—despite the generally held New England premise that "good fences make good neighbors"—finally brought compromises that no number of town-meeting or scriptural debates had been able to effect. Ornery independence was far from lost, however; out of its long tradition eventually came our Bill of Rights and other assertive notions concerning what constituted a proper governmental system.

Towns and families split over the issue of national independence. The "good Americans" of those days felt that loyalty to one's country (i.e., England) was a virtue second only to church attendance. But the law-abiding lost, and many descendants of these old patriots populate eastern Canada today. The rebels, meanwhile, audaciously claimed to be England's equal, hotly enumerating the details of ill use. England's crime, we can now see, was not cruelty but vast insensitivity; but a mark of true Puritans, then and now, is that they will sooner tolerate spectacular injustices than slights. Rebellion, and the American nation, thus began in New England. Yet, when it came to the actual bloody work of it,

relatively few colonists defended their independence with much fervor. They were always walking back to the farm when they were most needed, and George Washington's biggest problem all through the Revolution was holding his own army. Had not the British generally treated the entire embarrassing matter so half-heartedly, we might still be "good Americans" in the original sense.

Colonial loyalty had also shown itself in the village layouts and architecture, all strictly patterned after the English model. The typical New England village or town grew from a central open space. This fenced green or common was originally a community cow pasture, since the first residences were actually farmhouses grouped together for protection, with fields extending behind. As the villages grew, streets followed streams or the lay of the land, or widened from paths between houses, as shown by downtown Boston's surviving maze of lanes; later, they were laid out on the grid system devised by Robert Hooke and Sir Christopher Wren for London in 1666—a pattern still used in most American cities today. Bordering the green was always, of course, the parish church and usually the town inn, the secular center of the community. "At first the New England village was crude and raw with mud and stump-studded fields," wrote historian Samuel Eliot Morison. "Given time for flowers to bloom in dooryards and wine-glass elms to rise about the comely houses, it grew into the sort of unconscious beauty that comes of ordered simplicity."

The first roads connecting the settlements were no more than widened Indian trails, raw with stumps and boulders. Improvements came slowly, requiring as they did a degree of cooperation among communities. The first New England road, by which Connecticut was settled, extended from Cambridge to the Connecticut River at Springfield, Mass., via today's U.S. Highway 20 and State Highway 126—still called the "Old Connecticut Path." The colonial King's Highway, later known as the Boston Post Road, began as a mail route in 1673. Poorly marked and perilous, it extended from Washington Street in Boston to Manhattan's city hall, a two-week journey for the first post riders. The route can still be followed on present highways. A later, lower route followed the entire coastal length of today's U.S. Highway 1.

Early colonial houses looked much alike in most

of the settlements. The style followed that found in the medieval English villages from which the first colonists came. By 1700 the typical end-chimney dwelling with one large room on each of two floors had evolved, by additions, to the central-chimney house with two main first-floor rooms; the 1688 birthplace of poet John Greenleaf Whittier in Haverhill, Mass., is a good example. As seen in the Boston house of Paul Revere, a slight projection of the second story over the first—the "hewn overhang"—was common until about 1800. To the "basic box" type was often added a kitchen lean-to, covered by an extension of the main roof. New England is full of these familiar "saltbox" dwellings; one of them is Noah Webster's birthplace in West Hartford, Conn. During the early 1700s the lean-to evolved into a separate wing placed at right angles to the main house, creating an "L"-shaped structure. The central-hall type with chimneys at either end, as in the Old Manse at Concord, Mass., became common after 1750. These six types were the only truly distinctive New England styles, though many examples of the Georgian, Federal, Greek Revival and Victorian styles later appeared. With its characteristic "let fools be" attitude, New England also displays a wealth of eccentric architecture—the Hartford "steamboat house" of Samuel Clemens, Rudyard Kipling's "Naulakha" near Brattleboro, Vt., the avant-garde design of Walter Gropius in Lincoln, Mass. and the palatial "cottages" of Newport, R.I.

New England, said Bernard De Voto, was "the first permanent civilization in America." This region, with a two-century head start on the rest of the country, naturally seemed more polished and "older" to hinterland America. Ralph Waldo Emerson, in fact, believed that America didn't truly begin until one got beyond the Alleghenies; New England was essentially still Europe, populated by "Yankees".* The region quickly worked through some of the same experiences that later stalemated other areas for years on end. Its sour experience with slavery was over by 1784 (not many know that Massachusetts was the first American colony to legalize slavery, in 1641; and

that Vermont was first to abolish it, in 1777); and its emphasis on liberal education and toleration of dissent—in whatever crazy shape it might appear—set a role model that other regions of the country have sometimes resented but never ignored.

Until about 1820, the old Yankee stock remained dominant in New England. Since then, however, the progeny of immigrants from Europe and French Canada have vastly outnumbered those of English descent. Numerous pockets of Yankeedom remain, especially in Vermont and among Boston's brahmin families; but, generally, New England left its rural heritage behind as it transformed into one of the country's main industrial areas. It has also, however, made studious efforts to preserve large chunks of its past. The Society for the Preservation of New England Antiquities, headquartered in Boston, is probably the most efficient house-restoration organization in the country. And in numerous corners of these states—in villages not far off, yet years removed from, the busiest freeways—it is still possible to slow down and step back, to deal with longer thoughts and quieter priorities. Centered here is our longest national experience. Its old people seem wiser, its young more focused. There is, and has always been, an immense vitality seeded throughout the nation by those who called this region home.

CONNECTICUT

The name of the state tempts word-play. Its syllables bear an ancient connection with the land itself; to the native Algonquin tribes, "Quinnehtukqut" meant "beside the long tidal river." Most people say "Conneticut," but painter and notorious word-player Salvador Dali insisted on a *nect* emphasis. Without too much strain, one can find a repeating pattern in the state's history of simultaneous "connect" and "cut."

This "Land of Steady Habits," one nickname for the state, is often regarded these days as a big oblong borough of New York City. Connecticut's south shore is indeed an urban stretch that appears to the traveler along U.S. Highway 1, the old Boston Post Road, as a long seaside extension of metropolis. But Connecticut is not all exurbia. In upper Litchfield and Windham counties, especially, church steeples still rise from scenic pasture country, and long-retired cannons aim

---

*Several theories try to explain how the term "Yankee" originated. Some postulate that the word is an Indian mispronunciation of "English"—"Yengeese"; others that it began as an ethnic put-down by competing Dutch colonists. In either case, most sources agree, the present word probably represents a proud corruption of verbal error.

over the green, meticulous commons. Connecticut has pushed its Yankee antiquity back from the coast, but New England remains not far off the main road.

A "Land of Steady Habits," however, the state has seldom been; few states have hosted so many temporary residents. Connecticut was a foremost source of participants in national expansion. From Connecticut comes the image of the Yankee peddler-fixer-tinkerer, the clever rube who always gets one up on the smart-mouth city slicker, proceeding to show him how it's done. Often enough—and in numerous creative, Connecticut ways—that has exactly happened.

Though the state remained largely rural until 1890, the populace that stayed built Connecticut into one of the most prosperous industrial areas of the nation, with factory growth concentrated in such centers as New London, Naugatuck, Stratford and Bridgeport. There was always more than technology, however; Yale University, dominating the state's long intellectual tradition, still concentrates on its campus some of the most prestigious scholarship in the world.

The first whites were Dutch, who built a fort at Hartford in 1633. They also gave the derisive name "Johnnies" to the English intruders trickling down from Massachusetts. These English were Puritans who had severed themselves from John Winthrop's Boston congregation to establish subcolonies at Windsor, Wethersfield and Hartford. By 1639 the three river towns had consolidated and produced the first written constitution in history, the Fundamental Orders of Connecticut. The colonial charter granted by Charles II in 1662 was an astonishing document, making the colony virtually independent. It also fixed the Connecticut territory from Narragansett Bay clear to the Pacific coast. (Connecticut did not relinquish its claims in Ohio—the Western Reserve of Connecticut, a million acres bigger than Connecticut itself—until 1795.)

Connecticut, fifth of the original 13 states, strongly supported American independence; its royal governor, Jonathan Trumbull, was the only colonial crown official whose views didn't require his replacement during the Revolution. During the early 1800s, when residents began moving out in droves, the once overwhelming English-descended majority disappeared, and Connecticut became almost a way-station for European immigrants headed west. Having itself radiated

from Boston, the state now radiated little Connecticuts to Vermont, New York and beyond, into the Midwest and South.

Connecticut dwellers and their homes have reflected every phase of this mobile history. And the state's restless vigor has both preserved and exported the tradition of action. Noted Americans who lived here included Ethan Allen, P. T. Barnum, Benedict Arnold, Samuel Clemens, J. P. Morgan, Eli Whitney, Noah Webster, the Beechers and Igor Sikorsky, to name only a few. What these and other well-known residents shared was impatience with mere "steady habits," a drive to get on with the job, to tear down and build, connect and sever. Most were peddlers, tinkers or fixers to some degree. And the homes that some of them occupied appear as unique in design as their lives. In many of those that still exist, you will find rare combinations of whimsy and no-nonsense.

ACHESON, DEAN GOODERHAM (1893–1971). In **Middletown,** President Harry S Truman's Secretary of State was born in an earlier parsonage on the site of the present Church of the Holy Trinity (Episcopal) Rectory at 144 Broad St. He told in *Morning and Noon* (1965) how rats invaded the parsonage living quarters when the basement flooded. "My mother after ten years in the old house moved out of it into a rented one, telling the astonished vestry that they had the choice of a new rectory or a new rector." Acheson's birthplace was torn down about 1901.

(See Chapter 3, DISTRICT OF COLUMBIA, MARYLAND.)

ALCOTT, AMOS BRONSON (1799–1888). Northwest of **Wolcott** at Spindle Hill, 1.5 miles off State Highway 69 on Spindle Hill Road, stands the birthplace of the idealistic educator, Transcendentalist philosopher and father of author Louisa May Alcott. The one and one-half-story saltbox house (privately owned) was long believed to be Alcott's later boyhood home; he was born, it was claimed, in a home that stood nearby. According to Dorothy Wicker-Re of the Bronson Alcott Society, however, the extant house is indeed Alcott's actual birthplace and was his home until about 1815.

(See MASSACHUSETTS in this chapter; also Chapter 3, PENNSYLVANIA.)

ALLEN, ETHAN (1738–1789). The Revolutionary soldier's birthplace, a small gambrel-roofed house dating from 1736, stands on Old South Road at High Street in **Litchfield.** This is probably the only house occupied by Allen that survives anywhere. It is privately owned.

(See VERMONT in this chapter.)

ARNOLD, BENEDICT (1741–1801). The celebrated hero-turned-traitor of the American Revolution was born in **Norwich** at Washington Street and Arnold Place, a site repeatedly vandalized through the years. The large colonial house that stood there remained Arnold's home until 1761, when his bankrupt father lost the property. The son bought it back in 1763 and established his older sister there, closely watching her suitors and even shooting at one. After the Revolution, the dwelling stood as a cheap, reputedly "haunted" rooming house, plagued with weird occurrences and a supposed "curse" on its transient residents until its demolition in 1853. The only remnant of this homestead is the Benedict Arnold Well at 299 Washington St. Arnold is hardly a favorite Norwich son to this day. "If only he'd gotten killed before going bad," said a local official during the 1976 U.S. Bicentennial, "we'd have a hero and it would all be so much easier."

In **New Haven,** where Arnold established a pharmacy before the Revolution, he built a magnificent house at 155 Water St. in 1771. He planted 100 fruit trees on his two-acre lot and built stables and a carriage house; his store, for a time, stood just west of the house, which was only half-finished in 1775. Thereafter Arnold spent little time there, returning for the last time in 1778. Connecticut authorities seized the property after his 1780 defection, and lexicographer Noah Webster later acquired it (see the entry on Webster later in this section). Historian Benson Lossing described it in 1848 as "a handsome frame building, embowered in shrubbery." It was demolished in the early 1900s to clear space for a lumber yard.

Exhibit: The **New Haven** Colony Historical Society, 114 Whitney Ave., displays relics from Arnold's pharmacy; a "badly punctuated" store sign, an account book, a medicine chest and a mortar and pestle. There are also remnants from his elegant home, including a fireplace and ornate windows. (Open Tuesday–Friday 10:00–5:00,

Saturday–Sunday 2:00–5:00; 203-562-4183; free.)

(See Chapter 2, MANHATTAN; also Chapter 3, NEW YORK, PENNSYLVANIA.)

BARNUM, PHINEAS TAYLOR (1810–1891). The showman who built a fortune on his roguish notion that Americans like to be humbugged was born at 55 Greenwood Ave. in **Bethel.** The small saltbox dwelling, built about 1790, burned in the 1830s and was rebuilt as a white clapboard house by Barnum's mother in 1835. The house has been extensively remodeled through the years; converted into a private, two-family dwelling in 1954, it was last up for sale in 1980.

Bridgeport is the city most identified with Barnum. Only the last of his four homes, "Court Marina," a massive Victorian brownstone, stands. Located on the block bounded by Waldemere Park and Linden and Park avenues opposite Seaside Park, it is owned by Bridgeport University and is not accessible to visitors. Barnum built this house in 1890 a few feet west of his previous mansion, "Waldemere," an ornate gingerbread castle that he finally razed. A section of Waldemere was floated by barge to **Stratford** in 1889, where it now stands as a private residence at 1 Pauline St. But it was "Iranistan," his first Bridgeport mansion—an exotic palace of domes, spires, minarets and balconies—that drew the most attention. "Everything glittered," wrote Constance Rourke; "the edifice might have been washed with gold or silver." Deer roamed the 17-acre park around it, and many famous visitors came here to gape if not admire (Barnum always preferred gapes anyway). Built between 1846 and 1848, the Byzantine castle burned down in 1857; it stood at the present site of St. John's Episcopal Church, Park and Fairfield avenues.

Exhibit: The best place to sample the showman's hype and to view many of his personal effects is the Barnum Museum, operated by the City of **Bridgeport** at 820 Main St. (Open Tuesday–Saturday 12:00–5:00, Sunday 2:00–5:00; 203-576-7320; free.)

(See Chapter 2, MANHATTAN.)

BEARD, CHARLES AUSTIN (1874–1948).
BEARD, MARY RITTER (1876–1958).
Political scientists and historians, the couple wrote *The Rise of American Civilization* (1927–1939)

as well as other notable studies at their longtime home at 100 Prospect Hill Road in **New Milford.** Beard described it as a "dour, sprawling house, atop a Connecticut valley slope." It dates from about 1850 and is privately owned.

(See Chapter 2, MANHATTAN.)

BEECHER, HENRY WARD (1813–1887). The abolitionist-preacher's birthplace still exists, though not on its original site, near **Litchfield.** On Norfolk Road off State Highway 63, the gray frame structure stands on the campus of Forman School but does not admit visitors. The original homestead site from which the house was moved after the family left in 1826 is marked at Prospect and North streets (State Highway 63) in Litchfield. Also born here was Henry's noted sister, author Harriet Beecher Stowe (see the entry on Stowe later in this section).

(See Chapter 2, BROOKLYN; also Chapter 3, NEW YORK; also Chapter 4, INDIANA, OHIO.)

BEECHER, LYMAN (1775–1863). The "great gun of New England Calvinism" and sire of several notable children (see the entries for Henry Ward Beecher and Harriet Beecher Stowe in this section) was born in **New Haven** on land owned by his grandfather since 1764 at 261 George St. (at the corner of Chapel Street), where his ancestors were blacksmiths. The frame house was demolished in the 1940s.

In 1810 Beecher came to **Litchfield,** where he pastored the First Congregational Church (the site is marked on the village green), conducting "continuous revivals" at the church and a huge household at the Beecher homestead (see the entry on Henry Ward Beecher in this section).

(See MASSACHUSETTS in this chapter; also Chapter 3, NEW YORK; also Chapter 4, OHIO.)

BENÉT, STEPHEN VINCENT (1898–1943). In **Stonington,** the author-poet's summer residence from 1940 through 1942 was the Amos Palmer House, previously the boyhood home of painter James Abbott McNeill Whistler (see the entry on Whistler later in this section).

(See Chapter 2, MANHATTAN; also Chapter 3, NEW YORK, PENNSYLVANIA; also Chapter 5, GEORGIA; also Chapter 6, CALIFORNIA.)

BORGLUM, GUTZON (1867–1941). The sculptor bought and remodeled his home "Borland" on Wire Mill Road, **Stamford,** in 1910. This home has since burned down, but Borglum's studio— a huge structure of rocks dredged from the nearby riverbed and built around him in 1923 as he worked on his "Wars of America" monument— still stands privately owned.

(See Chapter 2, MANHATTAN; also Chapter 4, SOUTH DAKOTA; also Chapter 6, CALIFORNIA, IDAHO, TEXAS.)

BROWN, JOHN (1800–1859). The marked birth site of the abolitionist guerrilla fighter is located on John Brown Road about one mile south of Pother Road near **Goshen.** The house burned down at an unknown date.

(See Chapter 3, MARYLAND, NEW YORK, PENNSYLVANIA, WEST VIRGINIA; also Chapter 4, IOWA, KANSAS, OHIO.)

BURR, AARON (1756–1836). The eventual vice president and slayer of Alexander Hamilton was a law student at **Litchfield** under the informal guidance of his brother-in-law, Tapping Reeve. Reeve House and Law School National Historic Landmark, which dates from 1773, is located on South Street; a restored white cottage containing period furnishings and memorabilia of its noted graduates, it is operated by the Litchfield Historical Society. Burr lived and studied here just before he enlisted as a Revolutionary soldier. (Open mid-May to mid-October, Tuesday–Saturday 11:00– 5:00; 203-567-5862; admission.)

(See Chapter 2, MANHATTAN, STATEN ISLAND; also Chapter 3, NEW JERSEY, NEW YORK, PENNSYLVANIA.)

CALDER, ALEXANDER (1898–1976). Near **Roxbury** on Old Painter Hill Road stands the remodeled 1723 farmhouse purchased on 18 acres by the sculptor. This served as his longtime permanent home. Calder built the adjacent workshop-studio, a structure 25 × 45 feet, in 1938, and also erected many other outbuildings. The unnumbered property is privately owned.

(See Chapter 2, MANHATTAN; also Chapter 3, NEW YORK, PENNSYLVANIA.)

CAMP, WALTER CHAUNCEY (1859–1925). In **New Haven,** the longtime home of the Yale coach who transformed the game of football into a modern American sport, stood at 34 Hillhouse

MARK TWAIN HOUSE. The author built this turkey-red Victorian mansion overlaid with embellishments of his own design in 1874 in **Hartford.** It remained his home for 17 years. The building stands at 351 Farmington Ave. in the Nook Farm colony.
(Courtesy Mark Twain Memorial, Hartford, Conn.)

Ave. This 19th-century dwelling, built for Benjamin Silliman, Jr., was razed in the 1930s.

CLEMENS, SAMUEL LANGHORNE (MARK TWAIN) (1835–1910). Mark Twain House National Historic Landmark at 351 Farmington Ave. in **Hartford** was the author-humorist's home from 1874 through 1891 in Nook Farm, the city's literary colony. He commissioned its red-brick Victorian design with 19 rooms, 18 fireplaces, a billiard-room, study and riverboat porch. "Walt Disney might not have dared the house that Mark built in Hartford," wrote literary historian John Deedy in 1978; "A tour guide recently described the house as one-third riverboat, one-third cathedral, one-third cuckoo clock." The carved woodwork, gaudy wallpaper, and massive furniture reflect the owner's idea of comfort and style. He wrote most of his best-known works there, including *The Adventures of Huckleberry Finn* (1884). Financial losses compelled Clemens to abandon the house in 1891, but it was 1903 before he could sell it for even a fraction of what it cost him. After he left, the house successively became a private school, warehouse, apartment building and branch library. The Mark Twain Memorial, which operates it today, has meticulously restored the rooms with their original furnishings, adding a basement museum that exhibits artwork from his books and the typesetting machine investment that financially ruined him. (Guided tours through the house leave from Nook Farm Visitors' Center at Farmington Avenue and Forest Street. Open June 1–August 31, daily 10:00–4:30; September 1–May 31, Tuesday–Saturday 9:30–4:00, Sunday 1:00–4:00; 203-247-0998; admission.)

At **Redding,** Clemens built an elaborate Italianate mansion on 200 acres in 1908 that he called "Stormfield," where he died two years later. Stormfield, which burned down in 1925, stood on Redding Road (State Highway 53) about a mile west of Mark Twain Memorial Library.

Exhibit: The Mark Twain Memorial Library on Redding Road in **Redding** displays part of Clemens's library and some personal items. (Open Monday–Friday 10:00–5:00, Wednesday 10:00–8:30, Saturday 10:00–1:00; 203-938-2240; free.)

(See Chapter 2, BRONX, MANHATTAN; also Chapter 3, NEW YORK; also Chapter 4, IOWA, MISSOURI; also Chapter 6, CALIFORNIA, NEVADA.)

MARK TWAIN'S HOUSE

BUILT 1874   EDWARD TUCKERMAN POTTER, ARCHITECT

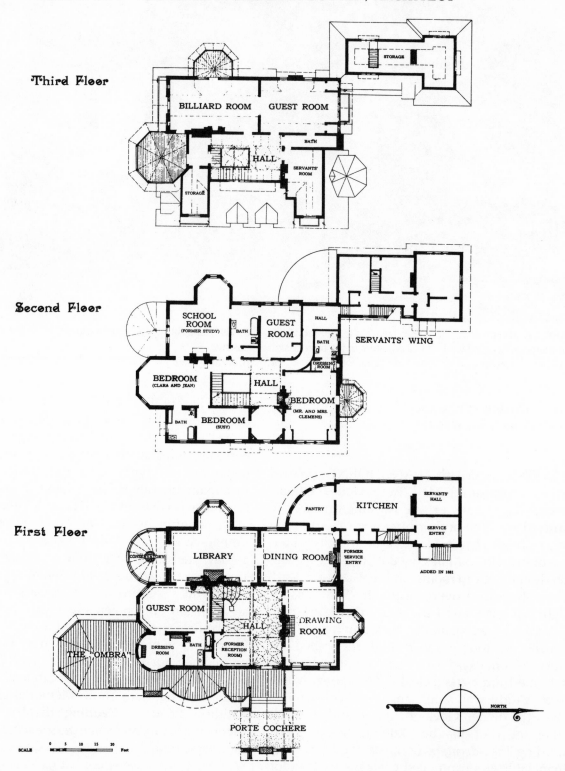

Third Floor

Second Floor

First Floor

FLOOR PLAN OF THE MARK TWAIN HOUSE. The center of this house was, for Clemens, his third-floor billiard room where he played by the hour and also roughed out his best-known books on a small desk. Not shown in this diagram is the basement, now a museum containing the huge Paige typesetter that bankrupted the author.
(Courtesy Mark Twain Memorial, Hartford, Conn.)

COMSTOCK, ANTHONY (1844–1915). Born in **New Canaan,** the aggressively pious reformer with an eagle eye for self-defined "vice" lived in a "plain square cottage" farmhouse on 160 acres until the Civil War. This long-gone house stood east of Oenoke Ridge, north of the present Country Club Road and just south of New Canaan Reservoir. Local residents, perhaps understandably, don't seem anxious to plant a marker on the site.

(See Chapter 2, BROOKLYN; also Chapter 3, NEW JERSEY.)

DORSEY, THOMAS FRANCIS "TOMMY" (1905–1956). The popular bandleader's last home (1953–56) is located at 25 Flagler Drive in **Greenwich.** Built in 1941, the dwelling remains privately owned.

(See Chapter 3, NEW JERSEY, PENNSYLVANIA.)

DOUGLAS, WILLIAM ORVILLE (1898–1980). Douglas taught law at Yale before his entry into public life and his appointment, in 1939, as Supreme Court Justice—a bench he occupied until 1975. In **New Haven,** his home from 1928 to 1933 was 320 Willow St.; and, from 1933 to 1936, he occupied 286 Livingston St. across from East Rock Park. Both dwellings remain privately owned.

(See Chapter 3, DISTRICT OF COLUMBIA; also Chapter 4, MINNESOTA; also Chapter 6, WASHINGTON.)

EDWARDS, JONATHAN (1703–1758). The marked birth site of the New England religious leader and theologian, and his home until he entered Yale at age 13, is located south of the Old Cemetery in **South Windsor,** on the east side of Main Street. The plain, two-story, shingled house with second floor projecting over the first was built by Edwards' grandfather in 1694 and demolished in 1812.

(See MASSACHUSETTS in this chapter.)

FERBER, EDNA (1887–1968). "Treasure Hill," the author's two-story fieldstone house on 140 acres, stands at 190 Maple Road (privately owned) in **Easton.** Now only 15 acres, the property was originally known as the "Oxen Lot," where cattle were turned loose in the fields after harvest. It is situated atop a high hill, from which Long Island can be seen. The novelist considered the 15-room

dwelling her "middle-aged fling . . . in its way, like a late marriage. It represented commitment and security." Still, according to one biographer, "Ferber was house-proud and servant-proud. Her houses were always showplaces, kept just so by the people who worked for her." She resided there from 1938 to 1949, writing fondly of the place in her autobiography *A Peculiar Treasure* (1939).

(See Chapter 2, MANHATTAN; also Chapter 4, IOWA, MICHIGAN, WISCONSIN.)

GIBBS, JOSIAH WILLARD (1839–1903). Founder of the science of physical chemistry, Gibbs was a lifelong resident of **New Haven,** occupying just two houses, neither of which remain. His birthplace stood at 86 Crown St.; and the cream-colored frame house where the bachelor scientist later lived with his sisters stood at 125 High St. (at the corner of Elm Street), the present location of the Berkeley College Master's House.

GOODYEAR, CHARLES (1800–1860). The inventor of vulcanized rubber was born in **New Haven** at a site on Oyster Point (later City Point), present vicinity of the south end of Howard Avenue.

His boyhood home in **Naugatuck** stood for almost 150 years behind modern commercial buildings at North Main and Bridge streets. According to local sources, "this entire area was demolished by the flood of 1955 so that there is no longer any historical site."

(See MASSACHUSETTS in this chapter; also Chapter 3, PENNSYLVANIA; also Chapter 4, OHIO.)

HALE, NATHAN (1755–1776). The young schoolmaster and patriot hanged as a spy by the British, Hale was born on the site of Nathan Hale Homestead National Historic Landmark, on South Street off State Highway 31 at **Coventry.** Part of the birthplace structure was probably incorporated into the presently standing home, a 10-room "L"-shaped mansion built by Hale's father in 1776, but Hale himself never saw the home as it is. Restored and operated by the Connecticut Antiquarian and Landmarks Society, the house displays many Hale family furnishings and possessions. (Open May 15–October 15, daily 1:00–5:00; 203-247-8996; admission.)

Exhibits: In **East Haddam,** the Nathan Hale

Schoolhouse is located behind St. Stephen's Episcopal Church on Norwich Road overlooking the Connecticut River. This red, one-room school was the scene of Hale's first teaching assignment (1773–74) after his graduation from Yale. It originally stood at the junction of State Highway 82 and State Highway 149 but was moved in 1799 and used as a dwelling for 100 years. Operated by the Sons of the American Revolution, the structure displays colonial schoolroom items. (Open summer weekends 1:00–5:00; admission.)

Another Nathan Hale Schoolhouse is located on Captain's Walk in **New London** where Hale taught in 1774 and 1775 just before he joined the Connecticut Militia. This 1774 building, moved from its original site on Mill Street, contains period items and is operated by the City of New London. (Open May 31–October 1, Tuesday–Saturday 2:00–4:30; free.)

Hale's diary may be seen in **Hartford** at the Connecticut Historical Society, 1 Elizabeth St. (Open Monday–Saturday 1:00–5:00; 203-236-5621; free.)

IVES, CHARLES EDWARD (1874–1954). The privately owned birthplace of this composer, a one and one-half-story clapboard house built about 1780, stands at 7 Mountainville Ave. in **Danbury.** Moved three times, it stood originally on Main Street, where a marker identifies the spot. Ives's boyhood home from 1879 to 1889 remains privately owned at 16 Stevens St.

West Redding was the composer's longtime summer residence. The shingled house and barn that he built in 1912 at 240 Umpawaug Road (privately owned) is not visible from the road, though some of the apple trees he planted along the driveway may be seen. Ives resented disturbances of any sort there; when airplanes flew over, he would shake his fist at the sky and shout "Get off my property!"

Exhibit: The Danbury Scott-Fanton Museum and Historical Society at 43 Main St. in **Danbury** displays furnishings from Ives's birthplace and memorabilia of the composer. (Open Wednesday–Sunday 2:00–5:00; 203-743-5200; donation.)

(See Chapter 2, MANHATTAN.)

KELLER, HELEN ADAMS (1880–1968). Near **Easton,** "Arcan Ridge" at 163 Redding Road was the last home of the blind and deaf author-humanitarian. This two-story, 12-room, colonial house, on four and one-half acres where "she knew each tree by touch," is a 1947 replica of her first house there, which she occupied from 1938 and which fire destroyed in 1946. She named the house after the Scottish ancestral home of "Teacher" (Anne Sullivan Macy), who devoted her life to Keller as companion and aide. The residence, located at the end of a birch-lined drive, is privately owned.

(See MASSACHUSETTS in this chapter; also Chapter 2, QUEENS: also Chapter 5, ALABAMA.)

KRUTCH, JOSEPH WOOD (1893–1970). At 33 Limekiln Road in **Redding,** the home of the author, literary critic, and naturalist from 1932 to 1952 remains privately owned. The house dates from sometime before 1867.

(See Chapter 2, MANHATTAN; also Chapter 6, ARIZONA.)

LINDBERGH, CHARLES AUGUSTUS (1902–1974). The famed aviator made his last home at **Darien** on Scotts Cove overlooking Long Island Sound. Lindbergh bought the large Tudor mansion here in 1946 and sold it in the 1960s when his children were grown; then, nearby, he built "Tellina," a white, three-bedroom cottage for his wife Anne Morrow Lindbergh and himself. Both houses, privately owned, stand on Tokeneke Trail off Old Farm Road from State Highway 136.

(See Chapter 3, DISTRICT OF COLUMBIA, NEW JERSEY, NEW YORK; also Chapter 4, MICHIGAN, MINNESOTA: also Chapter 6, HAWAII.)

LUCE, HENRY ROBINSON (1898–1967). In **Greenwich,** "The House," built in 1905, was the publisher's 21-room, Georgian red-brick dwelling. The 60-acre estate at 1275 King St. contained guest cottages, a tennis court, and a swimming pool. Luce and his wife, playwright-diplomat Clare Boothe Luce, lived there from 1938 through 1946, then sold the property when construction of a nearby airport ruined the peace and quiet. Since 1967, the mansion has been home office of the AVCO Corporation, which has enlarged both wings.

Their next estate, "Sugar Hill" at **Ridgefield,** where they lived from 1946 through 1963, was larger yet—a 28-room, Georgian mansion on 70 acres. It was, according to Luce biographer W. A.

Swanberg, the "home of a couple too busy to put down roots . . . of a man still conscious of the value of a dollar and opposed to vulgar display." Luce decorated his study there in the red, white and black color combination of *Life,* one of his most popular magazines. The privately owned estate on Limestone Road dates from the early 1940s.

(See Chapter 2, MANHATTAN; also Chapter 5, SOUTH CAROLINA; also Chapter 6, ARIZONA.)

MONROE, MARILYN (1926–1962). During her marriage to playwright Arthur Miller, the film star frequently resided at Miller's 300-acre farm near **Roxbury.** The 1783 dwelling, their first married home (1957–60), stands unnumbered on Tophet Road and remains privately owned. The woman remembered locally as "Marilyn Miller" was briefly active in local politics.

(See Chapter 2, MANHATTAN; also Chapter 6, CALIFORNIA.)

MORGAN, JOHN PIERPONT (1837–1913). The financier was born in **Hartford** at 153 Asylum Ave., a three-story mansion owned by his grandfather on a site occupied today by downtown office buildings. The family moved to another ancestral mansion since destroyed, a rambling stone-and-wood house on a 100-acre estate at 108 Farmington Ave. (1840–51). The dates of both houses' disappearance are unknown.

(See Chapter 2, MANHATTAN; also Chapter 5, GEORGIA.)

MORSE, SAMUEL FINLEY BREESE (1791–1872). Versatile artist and scientist, Morse lived in his parents' home at **New Haven** from 1821 through 1826. The cottage dwelling, built before 1812 at 320 Temple St., sat so low that every rainstorm flooded the cellar. While living there, Morse made a portable shanty that could be attached to the house or moved into the yard. This was his "painting room," where he labored over his canvases and worked on a marble-carving invention. The frame house, remodeled and greatly enlarged in 1860, was later the home of Yale president Noah Porter and is now owned by Yale University.

(See MASSACHUSETTS in this chapter; also Chapter 2, MANHATTAN; also Chapter 3, NEW YORK.)

OLMSTED, FREDERICK LAW (1822–1903). "Civilizer" of nature in his landscape architecture of parks throughout the nation, Olmsted was born in **Hartford** at an unknown site. His boyhood home stood on a site near the corner of Ann and Asylum streets.

In 1847, Olmsted's father bought his son a small farm near **Guilford.** This 1763 frame farmhouse, where young Olmsted lived for a year, stands at 160 Uncas Point Road (private); it is locally known as the "Reverend Edmund Ward House" after its builder.

(See MAINE, MASSACHUSETTS in this chapter; also Chapter 2, STATEN ISLAND.)

O'NEILL, EUGENE GLADSTONE (1888–1953). Monte Cristo Cottage National Historic Landmark at 325 Pequot Ave. in **New London** was the playwright's boyhood home, the traumatic shadows of which never left him. Victorian parlor and dining room have been meticulously restored with family and period furnishings to the scenes he remembered and described in *Ah, Wilderness* (1933) and *Long Day's Journey into Night* (1941).

Return visits there always plunged him into depression. "Anyone who knows O'Neill and his plays," wrote Emilie C. Harting, "will feel the sense of despair hanging over the house." Built about 1884, the structure was originally a schoolhouse and store joined together and was later enlarged. Restoration was scheduled for completion in 1982. Until regular admission hours are established, visits must be arranged by appointment with the operating authority, the O'Neill Theater Center (203-443-5378). The upstairs museum will display many of O'Neill's letters as well as numerous items relating to stage history.

"Brook Farm" in **Ridgefield,** a large, white clapboard house on 31 acres of lawns, pastures and woodland, was O'Neill's home from 1922 through 1925. Here he worked on his play *Desire Under the Elms* (1924), but "the house was too big and too grand for him," wrote biographers Arthur and Barbara Gelb, "and it oppressed him." The 1909 mansion stands at 845 North Salem Road. O'Neill sold the house in 1928; it was again up for sale in 1981, "listed exclusively" on 16 acres for $595,000.

(See MASSACHUSETTS in this chapter; also Chapter 2, MANHATTAN; also Chapter 5, GEORGIA; also Chapter 6, CALIFORNIA.)

REMINGTON, FREDERIC (1861–1909). The painter and sculptor of Western and ranch scenes, Remington built and occupied his last home on 10 acres only months before he died. The 1909 Remington House National Historic Landmark stands at 154 Barry Ave. in **Ridgefield,** a two-story, fieldstone dwelling of colonial revival style. It is privately owned.

(See Chapter 3, NEW YORK; also Chapter 6, WYOMING.)

ROBESON, PAUL BUSTILL (1898–1976). "The Beeches" at 1221 Enfield St. in **Enfield** had been unoccupied for eight years and was badly run-down when Robeson, the powerful singer, actor and civil rights fighter, bought it in 1940. Before the purchase, Robeson's wife checked the neighborhood thoroughly for racial prejudice that would lead to conflicts—and found Enfield a thoroughly civilized community. Robeson repaired and restored the 19th-century mansion and occupied it as a country house until he sold it in 1953. It remains privately owned. After a period of harassment from a U.S. government that feared his enormous influence among black citizens, Robeson lived in England from 1959 to 1963.

(See Chapter 2, MANHATTAN; also Chapter 3, NEW JERSEY.)

ROBINSON, JACK ROOSEVELT "JACKIE" (1919–1972). Just before his 1956 retirement from the Brooklyn Dodgers, baseball's first black major-league player built his home at 103 Cascade Road in **Stamford.** This large, private acreage, Robinson's last home, included his own lake.

(See Chapter 2, BROOKLYN; also Chapter 3, NEW YORK; also Chapter 5, GEORGIA.)

RODGERS, RICHARD (1902–1979). The composer owned three Fairfield County homes in succession. All of them remain privately owned. "The house was more functional than attractive," he wrote about the 15-room colonial dwelling on six and one-half acres that he bought in 1941—but Rodgers and his wife liked the massive oak tree in the yard. Their home until 1949, this house stands at 4334 Black Rock Turnpike in **Fairfield.**

"Rockmeadow" on Hulls Farm Road near **Southport** was his gray-shingled, three-story, colonial home on 40 acres (1949–65)—"the world's largest croquet ground," he called it.

In 1965, Richard and Dorothy Rodgers built a new home on 10 farmland acres at 4800 Congress St., again at **Fairfield.** This was *The House in My Head* (1967), Dorothy Rodgers' account of its planning and building. "Far from palatial," wrote Rodgers, "the house had a feeling of spaciousness and warmth that made it seem a part of the surrounding landscape." This was his last home.

(See Chapter 2, MANHATTAN.)

SHERMAN, ROGER (1721–1793). The only signer of all four American "founding documents," including the Declaration of Independence and Constitution, Sherman settled at **New Milford** in 1748, where he became a community leader. His residence until 1760 stood on the green on the present site of the Town Hall.

New Haven later became Sherman's permanent home (1760–93). The site of his frame house, demolished in the late 1800s, is marked at 1032 Chapel St.

(See MASSACHUSETTS in this chapter.)

SIKORSKY, IGOR IVAN (1889–1972). Aeronautical engineer and helicopter designer, Sikorsky lived in Connecticut from about 1930. His home at **Trumbull** (1935–50) stood on Long Hill until 1962, when it was moved to 27 Alden Ave. The privately owned house dates from 1935.

In **Easton,** Sikorsky's last home (from 1950), which he described as "a typical farmer's house," stands at 422 Morehouse Road, a privately owned former dairy farm on a scenic hilltop. The house, dating from 1850, has been twice remodeled, the last time by Sikorsky, who added dining and living rooms in 1952.

(See Chapter 2, MANHATTAN.)

STEFFENS, LINCOLN (1866–1936). At **Riverside,** the investigative journalist bought "Little Point," a two and one-half-story, frame farmhouse, in 1906 and resided there until 1911. This house, built about 1855, stands much modified and privately owned on Club Road. Steffens sold it in 1920 to the prominent lawyer and businessman, Owen D. Young.

(See Chapter 2, MANHATTAN; also Chapter 6, CALIFORNIA.)

STEICHEN, EDWARD JEAN (1879–1973). **West Redding** was the famed photographer's permanent residence after 1940. His home at 60 Topstone

Road (private), built in 1940, is a low, rambling bungalow. Steichen acquired 412 acres in this area in 1928, selling more than half to the town of Redding in 1971 for building lots. The nearby Steichen Memorial Wildlife preserve, maintained by the Conn. Audubon Society, conserves 54 acres of Steichen's property as he knew and loved it. (Contact Conn. Audubon Society, 2325 Burr St., **Fairfield,** for information; 203-259-6305.)

(See Chapter 2, MANHATTAN.)

STOKOWSKI, LEOPOLD ANTHONY (1882–1977). During his tenure as conductor of the New York Philharmonic Orchestra, from 1947 to 1950, the English-born musician lived with his wife Gloria Vanderbilt at "Faraway," their mansion at 77 John St. in **Greenwich.** The house remains privately owned.

(See Chapter 2, MANHATTAN; also Chapter 3, PENNSYLVANIA; also Chapter 4, OHIO.)

STOWE, HARRIET BEECHER (1811–1896). The abolitionist author of *Uncle Tom's Cabin* (1852) was born in **Litchfield** (see the entry on Henry Ward Beecher earlier in this section). She described Beecher family life there in her 1878 novel, *Poganuc People.*

Two of the author's later dwellings stand in the Nook Farm literary colony of **Hartford.** Her 12-room "cottage" and last home at 73 Forest Ave. is an 1871 Victorian frame and brick house, now restored with her furnishings and possessions. She lived there from 1873 through 1896 while at the height of her fame, did her last writing, painted, and declined to childlike senility. The house is operated and maintained by the Stowe-Day Foundation; guided tours leave from the Nook Farm Visitors' Center at Farmington Avenue and Forest Street. (Open June 1–August 31, Tuesday–Saturday 9:30–4:00, Sunday 1:00–4:00; 203-522-9258; admission.)

(See MAINE, MASSACHUSETTS in this chapter; also Chapter 4, OHIO.)

HARRIET BEECHER STOWE HOUSE. The author's last home, an 1871 Victorian house, stands at 73 Forest Ave. in Nook Farm in **Hartford.** Like the nearby home of Samuel L. Clemens, Stowe House drew hundreds of visitors eager to meet the woman whom Abraham Lincoln wryly accused of starting the Civil War.
(Courtesy Stowe-Day Foundation.)

SULLIVAN, EDWARD VINCENT "ED" (1902–1974). The first and only house ever owned by this frozen-faced television impresario was "Kettletown Farm" on 185 acres near **Southbury.** Sullivan obtained the property in 1954 "for the consideration of One Dollar and other valuable consideration." Writer Jim Bishop described the 1935 house and working farm as "old spinning wheel." But Sullivan was too much the urbanite to deal for very long with cows; he sold the farm in 1958. It stands privately owned at 367 North Georges Hill Road.

(See Chapter 2, MANHATTAN; also Chapter 3, NEW YORK.)

TAFT, WILLIAM HOWARD (1857–1930). Between his tenures as 27th U.S. president and U.S. Chief Justice, Taft taught law at Yale and resided at four different houses in **New Haven,** none of which stand. He resided longest (1913–18) at his first home here, "Hillcrest," which stood at 367 Prospect St. This was an 1875 Victorian house with a circular porch and painted gables, razed in 1972.

(See Chapter 3, DISTRICT OF COLUMBIA; also Chapter 4, OHIO.)

THURBER, JAMES GROVER (1894–1961). The humorist and cartoonist bought his "Great Good Place," a 14-room, white colonial house amid acres of trees near **Cornwall,** in 1945. In that house he wrote numerous stories, plays and novels, even as total blindness beset him in later years. The privately owned dwelling stands on Great Hollow Road opposite its junction with Essex Hill Road.

(See Chapter 2, MANHATTAN; also Chapter 4, OHIO; also Chapter 5, VIRGINIA.)

TRUMBULL, JOHN (1756–1843). The painter of patriotic scenes and battles of the American Revolution, Trumbull was a native of **Lebanon.** Trumbull House National Historic Landmark, his birthplace near the common, is a 1740 frame dwelling built by his grandfather. Originally it stood at Town Street and Colchester Road but was moved west in 1830 and now fronts State Highway 87. The house, which contains period furnishings, is owned and operated by the Daughters of the American Revolution. (Open May 1–November 30, Tuesday–Saturday 1:00–6:00; admission.)

In **New Haven,** the painter lived with his niece and nephew from 1837 through 1841 in the

Benjamin Silliman House, built before 1807 on Hillhouse Avenue; they added a wing for his studio and library. What remained of this house after many alterations was moved west in 1871 to 87 Trumbull St., where it now stands privately owned.

(See Chapter 2, MANHATTAN.)

TWAIN, MARK. See SAMUEL LANGHORNE CLEMENS.

TWEED, WILLIAM MARCY (1823–1878). Though few of them realized it at the time, New York City taxpayers, bilked of millions by the powerful Tammany politician, built Tweed's country mansion in **Greenwich.** It was a rambling house with replicas of famous statuary on broad lawns and huge, highly publicized stables. "It is better to be one of Mr. Tweed's horses than a poor taxpayer of this city," editorialized the *New York Times.* The mansion didn't last long; built about 1865, it was razed in 1884. Cooperative apartments now occupy the site on East Putnam Avenue.

(See Chapter 2, MANHATTAN.)

WEBSTER, NOAH (1758–1843). Webster Birthplace National Historic Landmark, a frame, saltbox dwelling built about 1676, stands at 227 South Main St. in **West Hartford.** The lexicographer, born in the room above the parlor, lived here until 1774 and often returned to visit his parents thereafter. This five-room dwelling, originally white and once the farmhouse of a 120-acre plot, has been restored on its original site with period furnishings by the Noah Webster House Foundation, which exhibits Webster manuscripts and editions of his spellers and dictionaries. (Open Tuesday and Sunday 1:00–4:00, Thursday 10:00–4:00, and by appointment; 203-521-5362; admission.)

Webster roomed from 1781 through 1782 in the attic of the John Cotton Smith Mansion in **Sharon;** here, it is said, he began compiling his famed "blue-backed speller." The 1760 stone house, located on the east side of State Highway 41 south of the village center, is privately owned.

In **Hartford,** Webster lived from 1789 to 1793 in the elegant Wadsworth House that stood on the present site of Wadsworth Atheneum at 600 Main St.; here he practiced law and experimented with soils and seeds in a small garden.

Webster lived in **New Haven** for two lengthy periods. He bought the former residence of Benedict Arnold (see the entry on Arnold earlier in this section) at 155 Water St. in 1798 and cultivated large gardens on the property until 1812. The site of his last home (1823–43) at Temple and Grove streets is now occupied by Silliman College of Yale University. Henry Ford moved this house to his Michigan Greenfield Village exhibit in 1936.

Exhibit: Webster's writing desk is displayed at the **New Haven** Colony Historical Society at 114 Whitney Ave. (Open Tuesday–Friday 10:00–5:00, Saturday–Sunday 2:00–5:00; 203-562-4183; free.)

(See MASSACHUSETTS in this chapter; also Chapter 4, MICHIGAN.)

WHISTLER, JAMES ABBOTT McNEILL (1834–1903). At Main and Wall Streets in **Stonington,** the 1787 Amos Palmer House (privately owned) was the painter's boyhood home from 1837 through 1843. Earlier, during the war of 1812, this house was heavily damaged by British bombardment; author-poet Stephen Vincent Benét (see the entry on Benét earlier in this section) was a later resident.

(See MASSACHUSETTS in this chapter.)

WHITNEY, ELI (1765–1825). Whitney's 1793 invention of the cotton gin did not gain him financial security, so he turned his energies elsewhere. Several years later near Hamden, he virtually created the technology of using interchangeable parts for manufacturing, extending the small "home factory" capacity into the modern system of industrial mass production at a musket factory. Whitney Armory National Historical Landmark, once a complex of 20 buildings, now includes three restored original structures at 913–40 Whitney Ave. (at the corner of Armory Street) at **Whitneyville.** When Whitney acquired his "Mill Rock" property in 1798, he noted "three things called houses on the farm. . . . I moved into the best of these," a dwelling that stood nearest the old mill. Since 1972, Yale University has conducted extensive archaeological excavations on the site. The recently initiated Eli Whitney Museum on the property will display findings of this research plus exhibits of antique arms and shop replicas (call 203-488-2157 or write Eli Whitney Museum, Whitneyville, Conn., 06511 for hours and admission).

In **New Haven,** Whitney died at the Bowditch House, 275 Orange St. (privately owned), his rented dwelling from 1822. Bowditch House, built about 1810, has been only slightly altered since his occupancy.

(See MASSACHUSETTS in this chapter; also Chapter 5, GEORGIA.)

WILDER, THORNTON NIVEN (1897–1975). In 1930, the author-playwright designed and built his brown-shingled permanent home at 50 Deepwood Drive off Whitney Avenue in **Hamden.** This was, he said, "the house *The Bridge* built" (referring to royalties from his first popular book *The Bridge of San Luis Rey,* 1927). The house is privately owned.

(See NEW HAMPSHIRE in this chapter; also Chapter 4, WISCONSIN.)

MAINE

Maine is where the morning sun, its vast lightfront racing 17.5 miles per minute across the Atlantic, first touches the nation. Mount Katahdin receives the first streak of light, and from this continental gable the new day pours across America. Maine is mainland, as straightforward a name as grateful sailors ever gave to shore. A synonymous expression, "down east," began as a nautical term used by Maine coastal sailors; sailing downwind was sailing east.

This northeasternmost state occupies almost half of New England's land area. Its economy is, and always has been, based on harvest from forest and sea. More than 80 percent of the landscape is living wood; the paper beneath these words may well be a lace of Maine forest fiber. Maine is also Aroostook potatoes and delicious flora known by the local term "pie timber," mostly blueberries. Typical manufactured products consist of well-made gear for plain body needs: footwear and textiles.

"The Sea there is the strangest fishpond I ever saw," reported Capt. John Smith in 1614. Seaward Maine is about 3,500 miles of ocean shoreline and islands. One harvest of these coasts included the cobblestones that paved early American avenues; a few old streets in Boston and Philadelphia are actually transplanted beaches from Maine. Tons of lobsters and fish enter the American diet from Maine nets and boats—and boats themselves, from dinghies to modern ships, emerge from a durable Maine craft and industry.

The first English settlement was at Popham in 1607. Massachusetts acquired Maine as a province 70 years later and held it for almost 150 years. The French, meanwhile, claimed eastern Maine as part of Acadia and set the stage for Maine's long harvest of blood. For fully 85 years during the 18th-century French and Indian wars, not a cabin in the province stood safe from the fiery trails of killing, and a whole generation of Maine settlers never knew complete rest from sudden, nightmarish terror.

Though a part of Massachusetts, Maine lay separated from the lower state by a wedge of New Hampshire. And Maine had separated in spirit long before the War of 1812, when its resentment focused on Massachusetts' indifference to the upper province's welfare. The 1820 Missouri Compromise enabled entry of the province as a free state, the 23rd of the Union.

"To Mainiacs," wrote Maine author Louise Dickinson Rich, "Maine is not merely a place. It is a spiritual home and shelter as perfectly fitting and comfortable and natural as its shell is to a snail; which, like snails, they carry with them wherever they may go." Certainly Sarah Orne Jewett and Edwin Arlington Robinson never left Maine in any vital sense. James G. Blaine, on the other hand, burst Maine horizons sufficiently to attract the label "continental liar"—but he, after all, was a presidential candidate. Likewise Dorothea Dix and Henry Wadsworth Longfellow were hardly "snails"; yet they too carried the marks of their Maine childhoods into old age.

The state has provided "spiritual home and shelter" for numerous writers and artists. Maine-born Edna Millay built lyrical poetry on the rocks of "Ragged Arse"; Harriet Stowe envisioned Uncle Tom from a Brunswick church pew; and Winslow Homer portrayed the incessant roll of the sea on canvases that peer like salt-stained window frames on the gusty coast of Prout's Neck. The list of noted summer people includes those who "discovered" scenic Mount Desert Island, which became the first national park east of the Mississippi. In 1900, Bar Harbor on the island rivaled Newport, R.I., as the elite place for fashionable "rusticators" of the nation's economic stratosphere. America's two most noted Pole seekers, Robert E. Peary and Richard E. Byrd, nourished their rigorous souls in Maine dwellings.

Even the historic homes that remain in private hands offer exterior views that may reward an observer with significant biographical insights. Maine's climate dictates adventuresome angles of thought and vision; its historic homes are centers of individuality embraced by rigor and the dawn's earliest light.

BLAINE, JAMES GILLESPIE (1830–1893). The Republican political leader's first residence in **Augusta** was the Stanwood Homestead, a large duplex dating from 1805 and located at 22–24 Green Street (privately owned). Blaine and his family occupied the seven rooms on the east side from 1851 to 1862, the period in which he began his political career. The house was owned and occupied by Blaine's in-laws from 1826. Number 24 is now a dental office; the other half remains residential. Blaine House National Historic Landmark, Blaine's Augusta residence from 1862 to 1893, has been the State Executive Mansion since 1919. In this 1830 mansion located at Capitol and State streets, Blaine received the good news of his 1876 presidential nomination and the bad news of its failure. The State of Maine displays period furnishings, an art collection, and Blaine's restored study. (Open Monday–Friday 2:00–4:00; 207-289-2121; free.)
(See Chapter 3, DISTRICT OF COLUMBIA.)

BYRD, RICHARD EVELYN (1888–1957). From 1937 to his death, Byrd's summer retreat was "Wickyup" (privately owned), located eight miles northeast of **East Sullivan** off State Highway 183 at the south end of Tunk Lake. This two and one-half-story log dwelling, now a National Historic Landmark, was built as a lodge in 1929 for the Eagle Mountain Lake Club. Here Byrd planned his Antarctic expeditions of 1937, 1946 and 1955, and wrote his classic account *Alone* (1938).

(See MASSSACHUSETTS in this chapter; also Chapter 3, DISTRICT OF COLUMBIA; also Chapter 5, VIRGINIA.)

CARSON, RACHEL LOUISE (1907–1964). Income from her book *The Sea Around Us* (1951) enabled the author-naturalist to buy land and build a one-story summer cottage overlooking Sheepscot Bay at **West Southport**. The 1953 acquisition was a lifelong dream, a place to spend hours wading the tidal pools and studying marine organisms. She enlarged the cottage in 1957 and spent her last summer there in 1963. The privately owned residence stands on Dogfish Head Road.

(See Chapter 3, MARYLAND, PENNSYL-VANIA.)

CHAMPLAIN, SAMUEL DE (1567?–1635). The only residence that this French explorer and colonist really held in the United States was on St. Croix Island on the St. Croix River (1604–05). "Winter in this country lasts six months," he noted; of 79 colonists there during that extremely harsh winter, 35 died of scurvy. This was the second European settlement on the Atlantic coast north of Florida, and it led to the founding of New France in 1608. St. Croix Island National Monument is located on the Canadian border north of **South Robbinston** alongside the river on U.S. Highway 1. There are no remnants of the settlement, and the island is not presently open to the public.

DIX, DOROTHEA LYNDE (1802–1887). A stone archway leads to Dix Memorial Park on U.S. Highway 1A south of **Hampden,** birth site of the single-minded founder of 32 hospitals for the mentally ill. The small, unpainted farmhouse that stood here was her unhappy home until age 12.

(See MASSACHUSETTS in this chapter; also Chapter 3, NEW JERSEY.)

HAMILTON, EDITH (1867–1963). From 1923, the educator and classical historian who brought Athens and Rome alive to countless readers made her summer home near **Manset,** Mount Desert Island. She moved her two-story, white frame house from a spot on State Highway 102 to a site she chose on her 10 acres about a quarter of a mile off the road at Sea Wall Point. The dwelling remains privately owned.

(See Chapter 2, MANHATTAN; also Chapter 3, DISTRICT OF COLUMBIA, MARYLAND; also Chapter 4, INDIANA.)

HAWTHORNE, NATHANIEL (1804–1864). Near **Raymond,** a home that the author occupied briefly as a boy (1818–19) stands on Hawthorne and Raymond Cape roads off State Highway 302, a large, two and one-half story, white barn-like structure with black trim. Hawthorne's uncle built the house from 1812 through 1814 for the boy and his widowed mother in a wilderness clearing. It was there, Hawthorne claimed, that he "first got my cursed habit of solitude." Today neither exterior nor interior resemble the house that Hawthorne knew as a weathered, unpainted, clapboard dwelling. Inside, an entire upper floor was removed in 1877. The building became a tavern, then a church, after his residence. Now restored as a community center and operated by a board of trustees, it hosts receptions and meetings. There is a small display of Hawthorne-related books and pictures. (Open July 1–August 31, Sunday 2:00–5:00, and by appointment at Town Office; 207-655-4742; free.)

(See MASSACHUSETTS in this chapter.)

HOMER, WINSLOW (1836–1910). From 1883, the seascape painter made his permanent home at Prout's Neck near **Scarborough.** "The Sun will not rise or set without my notice and thanks," he said of this spot. Homer Studio National Historic Landmark, a one and one-half-story clapboard house, stands on Winslow Homer Road. Originally built as a stable in 1870, the building was converted and enlarged by Homer on what was then an isolated shoreline. The private studio-home has long since been crowded by other dwellings, but the sunlight, wind and waves that Homer matchlessly captured on his canvases are still here.

Exhibit: Bowdoin College Museum of Art, Walker Art Building at the **Brunswick** campus, displays Homer memorabilia along with a large collection of his paintings. (Open Tuesday–Friday 10:00–4:00, Saturday 10:00–5:00, Sunday 2:00–5:00; 207-725-8731; free.)

(See MASSACHUSETTS in this chapter; also Chapter 2, MANHATTAN.)

JEWETT, SARAH ORNE (1849–1909.) As Louise Dickinson Rich states, "A person planning a first visit to Maine could do worse than read Sarah Orne Jewett in preparation." Though she seldom left **South Berwick,** the novelist who wrote about Maine villages and their people transcended purely local interest because, she believed, "you must know the whole world before you can know the village." Her birthplace is the 1774 Haggens House, now the public library, on Portland Street. From girlhood until death, her home was the Jewett Memorial at 101 Portland St., a two and one-half-story frame house built about 1780. Its central hallway is said to be one of the best preserved, most beautiful interiors in New England. The author's small, upstairs bedroom-study remains exactly as she left it, with personal possessions, furniture and manuscripts. Jewett Memorial with its original family furnishings is maintained by the Society for the Preservation of New England Antiquities. (Open May 1–October 31, Tuesday–Sunday 10:00–5:00; admission.)

LONGFELLOW, HENRY WADSWORTH (1807–1882). The poet's boyhood home, Wadsworth-Longfellow National Historic Landmark, stands dwarfed in downtown **Portland** at 487 Congress St. Built by his grandfather in 1785 with additions made in 1815, the brick dwelling stood solitary amid fields when Longfellow lived here; only a dirt road separated house from shore. Inside, the Maine Historical Society displays original family furnishings as the poet knew them—his cradle, desks, chairs and corn-husk bed. Longfellow often nostalgically returned here to sleep in his boyhood room, the last time in 1881. (Open June 1–September 15, Monday–Friday 9:30–4:30; 207-772-1807; admission.)

In **Brunswick,** Longfellow taught languages at Bowdoin College for six years. His first married home was the 1820 Fales House at 226 Maine St. (privately owned), a one-story boardinghouse when he lived here; its ground floor was raised over an added story in the late 1860s. The couple later resided at the Emmons House, 25 Federal St. (privately owned). Longfellow thought this house "one of the pleasantest in town" but was aghast at the wallpaper: "*Stripes* of the most odious colors . . . and in the front entry *green parrots dancing on the slack wire.*" This house has been extensively altered (including, presumably, the wallpaper). While Longfellow was a student he lived in a house that still hosts Bowdoin students, Stowe House National Historic Landmark, then the cold, bare parsonage of one Rev. Titcomb. The desk Longfellow used is exhibited in his upstairs room (see the entry on Harriet Beecher Stowe later in this section).

Exhibit: The Longfellow Room in Bowdoin College Library, Main and College streets in **Brunswick,** displays a collection of the poet's books and manuscripts. (Open daily during college semesters; 207-725-8731; free.)

(See MASSACHUSETTS in this chapter.)

LOWELL, ROBERT TRAILL SPENCE, JR. (1917–1977). The poet's summer home from 1957 until 1968 was a colonial, white frame house fronting the common at **Castine.** The property, including

a barn overlooking Oakum Bay that Lowell used for his studio, was a gift from his cousin Harriet Winslow and remains in private hands.

(See MASSACHUSETTS in this chapter; also Chapter 2, MANHATTAN; also Chapter 4, OHIO.)

MILLAY, EDNA ST. VINCENT (1892–1950). At **Rockland,** the birthplace of the lyric poet stands at 200 Broadway (privately owned). A marker once attached here was removed at the owner's request.

Camden was her girlhood home from 1903 until 1913; but according to Nellie A. Hart of the Camden Public Library, "the family had no real roots or homestead, and it is not appropriate to call any particular place her girlhood home because the family moved around a great deal." The back section of a house at 42 Chestnut St.—a "shedlike attachment" since removed—was one brief residence. Mrs. Hart believes that the poet wrote "Renascence" (1912) at a later address, 80 Washington St. (privately owned).

Ragged Island (once known as "Ragged Arse") in **Casco Bay** was the solitary, rocky retreat of the poet and her husband, Eugen Boissevain, until 1949. After they bought the island with its abandoned stone house in 1933, they usually came in April and late summer to swim in the sea and spend weeks in the semi-primitive isolation that "Vincent" found so revitalizing. There is no public access to the privately owned island.

Exhibit: In **Camden,** the Millay Room at the Whitehall Inn contains photographs, some of her books and manuscripts, and miscellaneous items. This is the room in which she first recited her poem "Renascence" in the summer of 1912 to an awed gathering of guests. The inn is located at 52 High St. (Open late May–mid-October; 207-263-3391.)

(See Chapter 2, MANHATTAN; also Chapter 3, NEW YORK.)

OLMSTED, FREDERICK LAW (1822–1903). In declining health, the noted landscape architect built a vacation retreat in 1897 on Deer Isle, Penobscot Bay, his summer residence from 1893 until 1898. Olmsted Summer Home (privately owned) is located on State Highway 15 southwest of **Sunset** on the island. Built into a hillside, the two and one-half-story, frame and shingle house with its wraparound porch rises over a high stone basement.

"SAWUNGUN," ROBERT E. PEARY'S HOME. Located in Casco Bay, Peary's 17-acre preserve, **Eagle Island**, where he retreated during most summers from 1880 on, is now a museum open to the public. He built the sprawling house mostly from rocks and wood collected on the island. *(Courtesy Peary-MacMillan Arctic Museum, Bowdoin College, Brunswick, Maine.)*

(See CONNECTICUT, MASSACHUSETTS in this chapter; also Chapter 2, STATEN ISLAND.)

PEARY, ROBERT EDWIN (1856–1920). The earliest surviving residence of the polar explorer is his student residence at 12 Page St. in **Brunswick.** Peary roomed there with his mother from 1873 to 1877 while attending Bowdoin College. The house, built about 1850 and currently undergoing restoration, still holds private apartments.

From 1877 to 1879, Peary resided with his mother in **Fryeburg,** where he practiced surveying and taxidermy. The 1860 house survives with extensive alterations at 9 Elm St.

On 17-acre **Eagle Island** in 1904, Peary designed and built his shingle-and-stone summer residence, mostly from island materials. Peary bought the Casco Bay island called "Sawungun" in 1880 and renamed it for the whaling ship *Eagle* that first carried him to the Arctic. Operated by the Maine Department of Conservation, his home displays relics of his 1909 North Pole expedition, which he planned here. Casco Bay Lines (207-773-2440) provides a ferry to the island from 24 Custom House Wharf in Portland. (Open June 10–Labor Day, 10:00–6:00; admission.)

Exhibit: In **Brunswick,** the Peary-MacMillan Arctic Museum in Hubbard Hall of Bowdoin College, Main and College streets, displays memorabilia and personal items of the explorer. (Open Tuesday–Friday 10:00–4:00, Saturday 10:00–5:00, Sunday 2:00–5:00; 207-725-8731; free.)

(See Chapter 3, DISTRICT OF COLUMBIA, PENNSYLVANIA.)

PULITZER, JOSEPH (1847–1911). From 1893, the New York newspaper publisher spent summers in **Bar Harbor.** He built the ornate, four-story granite mansion he called "Chatwold" in 1895. This building, like all of Pulitzer's later homes, was carefully soundproofed, as intrusive noise of any sort vastly upset him; his employees called it "the Tower of Silence." The mansion lasted until 1944. A modern private residence now occupies the unnumbered site on Seeley Road.

(See Chapter 2, MANHATTAN; also Chapter 4, MISSOURI.)

ROBINSON, EDWIN ARLINGTON (1869–1935). **Head Tide,** the tiny Sheepscot River village in Lincoln County, was the poet's birthplace. The privately owned house is the second dwelling beyond the village store on State Highway 218.

Fifteen miles northwest in **Gardiner,** Robinson House National Historic Landmark on Lincoln Avenue was the poet's home from 1870 through 1896. There, biographer Hermann Hagedorn lushly wrote, Robinson "came to conscious life under a pumpkin-sweet apple-tree, making mudpies in a two-acre kingdom." This two and one-half-story, 19th-century clapboard dwelling is privately owned. Gardiner was the "Tilbury Town" of Robinson's poetry.

Exhibit: Miller Library of Colby College, two miles west of **Waterville,** displays manuscripts in its Robinson Room. (Open Monday–Friday 8:30–4:30; 207-873-1131; free.)

(See NEW HAMPSHIRE in this chapter; also Chapter 2, BROOKLYN, MANHATTAN.)

ROCKEFELLER, NELSON ALDRICH (1908–1979). Few Rockefeller family homes were modest dwellings. **Seal Harbor** on Mount Desert Island was the summer boyhood residence of the New York governor and U.S. vice-president. His father, John D. Rockefeller, Jr., bought the 104-room granite mansion called "The Eyrie" in 1910. Located on a wooded hilltop off State Highway 3, it was torn down in 1964. In 1929, Rockefeller helped architect Wallace K. Harrison design his own 21-room summer residence on scenic Crowninshield Point. A cantilevered balcony over the surf and a lighthouse tower highlight the modern glass, stone and wood dwelling. Rockefeller seldom came here after 1955 and finally sold it in 1978. It remains very privately owned.

(See Chapter 2, MANHATTAN; also Chapter 3, DISTRICT OF COLUMBIA, NEW YORK.)

ROOSEVELT, FRANKLIN DELANO (1882–1945). ROOSEVELT, ELEANOR (1884–1962).

Near **Lubec,** Roosevelt-Campobello Island International Park, jointly operated by the U.S. and Canadian governments, is the location of Roosevelt Cottage National Historic Landmark. Before he became 32nd U.S. president, Roosevelt and his family summered in this elegant 34-room "cottage." Built in 1897, it was given to the couple as a wedding present by Roosevelt's mother. It was there that Roosevelt was stricken with polio in August 1921; the place is the setting for Dore Schary's play *Sunrise at Campobello* (1959). After 1921, Roosevelt made only three brief visits there, the last in 1929. The park, dedicated in 1964, is a 2,600-acre preserve of wooded grounds and nature trails. Most of the house furnishings are original, and both the reception center and home itself display numerous family possessions. His telescope, a birchbark canoe he used from 1900 to 1910 and the improvised stretcher used to carry him off the island after his polio attack are among the items exhibited. Roosevelt himself summered in the area from boyhood; the site of an earlier cottage built by his father in 1883 is marked by its foundation ruins just north of the present house. Visitors to Campobello are free to wander house and grounds and to converse with stationed guides. Access to Campobello Island is by Roosevelt Memorial Bridge (State Highway 189) from Lubec. (Open daily, 9:00–5:00; 506-752-2922; free.)

(See Chapter 2, MANHATTAN; also Chapter 3, DISTRICT OF COLUMBIA, MARYLAND, NEW YORK; also Chapter 4, MICHIGAN; also Chapter 5, GEORGIA.)

STOWE, HARRIET BEECHER (1811–1896). Stowe House National Historic Landmark at 63 Federal St. in **Brunswick** is now a privately owned restaurant ("Harriet's Place") where dinner may be ordered beside the hearth in the Stowe dining room. The 1804 building has been vastly altered from the plain, drafty structure where the author lived from 1850 to 1852. There she wrote *Uncle Tom's Cabin* (1852) in a rush of creative energy and abolitionist fervor after she "saw as in a vision" the death scene of Uncle Tom. Her study has been restored with original items. Adjacent to the house, a modern motel and dining room form parts of the commercial inn establishment, but the Stowe House exterior is well preserved. Guest rooms in the house itself have long been occupied by Bowdoin College students, among whom was Henry Wadsworth Longfellow (see the entry on Longfellow earlier in this section). (Open daily, 6:30–10:00, 12:00–2:00, 6:00–9:00; 207-725-5543; foyer exhibits free.)

Exhibit: The 1846 First Parish Congregational Church, where on Communion Sunday, March 2, 1851, the author suddenly conceived of the character Uncle Tom, is located two blocks from the Stowe **Brunswick** house at Harpswell, Maine and Bath Streets. Pew 23 was the Stowe family seat. (Open daily by side or rear doors or by inquiry at Pilgrim House Parish Center across from the church at the corner of Cleveland Street; free.)

(See CONNECTICUT, MASSACHUSETTS in this chapter; also Chapter 4, OHIO.)

MASSACHUSETTS

Once huge, Massachusetts embraced all of Maine until 1820. Now for smaller geographically, it remains the most populous New England state. Though primarily an industrial state, its main product for America has always been leadership. There is not a corner of the country, not a household, that has not been shaped in some way by someone who wrote, talked, built or breathed in Massachusetts. As the birthplace of some of our most cherished values and assumptions, it has also frequently originated the ideas that most challenge them. Its preachers, intellectuals and politicians created, to a large extent, the ideals we have most liked about ourselves and our land. So massive is this legacy that, even today, public words from Massachusetts bear weight by simple virtue of having originated there. It is the place we "look to" from historical habit for correction and affirmation, for some key criteria of national self-definition.

Massachusetts was christened as such by Capt. John Smith, who cruised its coastline in 1614. The Algonquin word means "at the great hill," referring to what is now Blue Hills Reservation at Milton. Far from the log houses so dear to Thanksgiving mythology, the first colonial settle-

ments at Plymouth and Boston were conical sod-and-branch huts, soon replaced by clapboard, grass-thatched cabins. The style was medieval European, unlike anything seen in America today except at the museum village of Plimoth Plantation.

In 1620 the Pilgrims, a radical Puritan sect, had intended to settle on the Hudson River in New York. Weather and navigational confusion sent the *Mayflower* far north instead. Ten years later, Boston was founded by Gov. John Winthrop and about 900 Puritans. Settlers fanned out from Boston for essentially the same escapist reasons they had come there—to flee a dominant religious authority. Small scriptural or doctrinal disagreements were enough to send whole congregations packing over the countryside; the land was large, if hostile, and compromise wasn't yet necessary. Boston, the strict parent, cast off its numerous black-sheep progeny—sometimes unwillingly or regretfully, often righteously and spitefully—to all of New England. Since those children rarely questioned the notion of theological rigidity itself, their new, dissenting communities often became tilted versions of parental Boston, with only slightly different emphases on what would best hold off "that old deluder Satan." Thus did Puritanism fragment and denominate itself across America.

This gene of dissent was the most consistent force in Massachusetts history. Born as a colony from religious rebellion, the state was born again in political revolt. The American Revolution began at Lexington; rowdy Massachusetts protesters were our first nationalists; and Massachusetts rebels and reformers have made useful nuisances of themselves ever since. Such persons included blowhard agitator Sam Adams, stubborn Alexander Bell and Robert Goddard, awakeners Jonathan Edwards and Ralph Waldo Emerson; three profoundly radical Williams—Garrison, James, Du Bois; and, of course, the inimitable Henry Thoreau. Anyone who told natives Margaret Fuller, Susan Anthony and Clara Barton that they couldn't and shouldn't found it wasted breath. Further immigration has also strengthened the state: Jack Kerouac of French-Canadian stock became one of the state's most controversial writers; Brockton gave Massachusetts Italians a hero in heavyweight boxer Rocky Marciano; and John F. Kennedy, one of four U.S. presidents from Massachusetts, was proud of his Irish ancestry.

Today Boston lies thick with landmarks and ground sites—many more than have ever gotten into the numerous guidebooks, which seldom get beyond the usual tourist attractions. Owing to Boston's prominence in American letters, several literary guidebooks have attempted a slightly closer focus; but even the best of these have not approached a definitive coverage. Boston has always deserved more and better from its historians. There are two excellent books, however, that describe the city changes in landforms and building patterns. These are *Boston: A Topographical History* (1968), by Walter Muir Whitehill; and *Lost Boston* (1980), by Jane Holtz Kay. *Victorian Boston Today: Ten Walking Tours* (1975), edited by Pauline C. Harrell and Margaret S. Smith, focuses exuberantly on one period of the city's past. For Massachusetts, there could be a fat guidebook of sites for each of several time periods and a dozen different areas of American biography. *Historic Buildings of Massachusetts* (1976), in the Scribner Historic Buildings Series, catalogs all of the state's officially "historic" structures (which include only a few of the homes listed in these pages).

Pick your own Massachusetts. In few other states is the choice of historical landscapes so wide. Other states have had rebels, creators and doers, but Massachusetts has somehow produced more of them per acre. From its Puritan beginnings, this center of New England has taught us our basic lessons of democracy; how to create and bond tradition; and how, suddenly and quite loudly, to break it.

ADAMS, CHARLES FRANCIS (1807–1886). In **Boston,** 57 Mount Vernon St. (privately owned), was the permanent four-story home of the political leader and diplomat from 1842. It was built from 1817 to 1819; Daniel Webster (see the entry on Webster later in this section) was an earlier resident.

A son of President John Quincy Adams (see the entry on Adams later in this section), Charles Francis Adams added the stone library to the Adams family mansion at **Quincy,** and many of his personal possessions are displayed there (see the entry on John Adams later in this section).

(See Chapter 3, DISTRICT OF COLUMBIA.)

ADAMS, HENRY BROOKS (1838–1918). The noted author-historian, son of Charles Francis Adams and grandson of President John Quincy

Adams (see the entries on these men in this section), grew to adulthood in the **Boston** parental home at 57 Mount Vernon St. His first married home (1874–77) was the "small but quite pretty" four-story house standing at 91 Marlborough St. Attached to 273 Clarendon St. in 1890, with a new entrance built onto that street, the 1869 building served for years as the Episcopal City Mission. It was converted to a private rest home in 1973, and the spacious Adams chambers were partitioned into 42 bedrooms.

In **Beverly,** Adams' rustic summer residence "Pitch Pine Hill," which he built on 20 acres in 1876, is privately owned. Adams and his wife designed and supervised all details of "our log-hut in the woods"—at that time about a half-mile from the village—where he did much writing; but after his wife's suicide in 1885, he stayed away until 1917. The house, located at Juniper and Hemlock streets, has been greatly altered and enlarged by subsequent owners.

Adams also spent summers and other lengthy periods at the Adams family mansion in **Quincy,** where some of his memorabilia is exhibited (see the entry on John Adams below).

(See Chapter 3, DISTRICT OF COLUMBIA.)

ADAMS, JOHN (1735–1826).
ADAMS, ABIGAIL SMITH (1744–1818).
The birthplace of Abigail Adams has been much modified, restored and shifted several hundred feet from its original site in **East Weymouth.** There John Adams courted her, and her father married the couple in the parlor in 1764. Dating from 1685 in its oldest portion, the house at North and Norton streets is operated by the Abigail Adams Historical Society and contains no original items, though period furnishings are authentic. (Open July 4–Labor Day, Tuesday–Sunday 1:00–5:00; admission.)

Her husband, the second U.S. president, was born in **Quincy** at John Adams Birthplace National Historic Landmark. This saltbox cottage, operated by the Quincy Historical Society, dates from 1681 and contains period furnishings. Adams lived there until 1764. The Adamses made their permanent home in Quincy at the 1716 saltbox John Quincy Adams Birthplace National Historic Site, also maintained by the Quincy Historical Society. In this 20-year home (1764–84), Abigail Adams wrote much of her remarkable corre-

THE ADAMS MANSION. "Peacefield," a much smaller house when John Adams acquired it in 1788, was enlarged by subsequent family occupants, including John Quincy Adams, Charles Francis Adams and Henry Adams. This Frankenstein painting is a 19th-century view of the house at **Quincy**.
(Courtesy Adams National Historic Site)

spondence. Several original items remain in the house, including her bed, dressing table, and a brown silk dress. (Both houses open mid-June–September 30, daily 9:00–5:00; 617-773-1144; admission.) Returning from England in 1788, Abigail and John Adams bought and occupied a Quincy house located about two and one-half miles from their first home, the Adams Mansion National Historic Site, built in 1731 and christened "Peacefield" by John Adams. The couple spent most of the next decade elsewhere but returned to "Peacefield" permanently in 1801. Abigail Adams died in the west bedroom eight years before her husband. A government brochure suggests that the house at 135 Adams St., enlarged by subsequent Adamses, "may be compared to an archeologist's dig laid bare to reconstruct the domestic life of one of the few dynastic families

America has produced." Adams descendants donated the estate to the U.S. government in 1846. Containing numerous family furnishings and possessions, it is operated by the National Park Service. (Open mid-April–mid-November, daily 9:00–5:00; 617-773-1177; admission.)

(See Chapter 2, MANHATTAN; also Chapter 3, DISTRICT OF COLUMBIA, PENNSYLVANIA.)

ADAMS, JOHN QUINCY (1767–1848). In **Quincy,** the sixth U.S. president, son of the second, was born in John Quincy Adams Birthplace National Historic Site, his home until 1784. Adams Mansion National Historic Landmark became his permanent Quincy residence in about 1801 and displays many of his own furnishings and personal items (see the entry on John Adams above).

(See Chapter 3, DISTRICT OF COLUMBIA.)

ADAMS, SAMUEL (1722–1803). In **Boston,** the Revolutionary patriot's lifelong home, neither of his two dwellings remain. Adams' father, a brewer, bought a lot with a 258-foot frontage on Purchase Street, 62 feet north of Summer Street, in 1712 and built his house and brewery on this spot the following year. His son, no business-man, let the buildings run down and finally had to sell off portions of the property to stay solvent. British troops occupying Boston in 1775 took special pains to leave Adams' house a shambles. His last home (1776–1803) was a large frame house located at Winter Street and Winter Place; the confiscated residence of Tory Robert Hallowell was awarded to Adams in recognition of his services. This house stood until about 1820. The site is marked.

The only extant dwelling that sheltered Adams for any duration (almost a month while he attended sessions of the provincial congress in Concord) is Hancock-Clarke House National Historic Landmark at **Lexington,** where he hid from the British in 1775 with John Hancock. Paul Revere made his famous dash to this place on April 18 in order to warn Adams and Hancock of the redcoat approach (see the entries on Hancock and Revere later in this section).

AGASSIZ, LOUIS (1807–1873). The Swiss-born Harvard zoologist made his permanent home in **Cambridge,** but neither of his two houses remain. The two-story dwelling he built in 1854 at 36 Quincy St. was his last; according to Harvard president Charles W. Eliot, it had "only one bathroom and the tub was not infrequently occupied by turtles." This house burned down in 1917.

ALCOTT, AMOS BRONSON (1799–1888).
ALCOTT, LOUISA MAY (1832–1888).

Rented rooms and brief stays marked the itinerant lives of the philosopher-educator and his daughter the author until the 1840s. Several later, more settled dwellings of this close-knit family exist in Massachusetts, however, and three are open to visitors.

On Prospect Hill Road near the village of **Harvard,** Fruitlands Museums National Historic Landmark was the scene of Bronson Alcott's disastrous utopian experiment in 1843 and 1844, "New Eden." Restoration of the 1740 ochre-red farmhouse began in 1914, and the building now stands as part of a museum complex that exhibits numerous items and documents relating to the Alcotts and other Transcendentalists. Louisa May

WAYSIDE, HOME OF THE ALCOTTS. Bronson Alcott drew this sketch showing the wings he added to the 1775 **Concord** house known to the family as "Hillside." They lived here for three years. This dwelling, now open to visitors, also became author Nathaniel Hawthorne's last home. *(Courtesy Concord Free Public Library.)*

Alcott's *Transcendental Wild Oats* (1873) gave a fictionalized account of the harrowing idealism practiced here. (Open Memorial Day–September 30, Tuesday–Sunday 1:00–5:00; 617-456-3924; admission.)

Three Alcott houses remain in **Concord.** Wayside House National Historic Landmark, originally a four-room cottage built in 1775 and now operated on Lexington Road by the National Park Service, was known as "Hillside" to the Alcotts, who lived there from 1845 to 1848. Bronson Alcott added wings and piazzas, and later additions further enlarged the dwelling. Most of its exhibits, however, concern a later resident, author Nathaniel Hawthorne (see the entry on Hawthorne later in this section). *The Wayside: Home of Authors* (1940), by subsequent resident Margaret M. Lothrop, details its sometimes perilous existence. (Open April 1–October 31, Thursday–Monday 10:00–5:30; admission.) At Orchard House National Historic Landmark, Bronson Alcott reconstructed and combined what was originally two houses, dating from 1650 and 1730, into the single mansion as it still appears at 399 Lexington Road. Some 60 percent of the present furnishings belonged to the Alcotts, who lived there from 1858 to 1877. Exhibits in Bronson Alcott's study reflect the ambitious scope of his intellect, and the kitchen displays many of his inventions. Also preserved there are most of Louisa Alcott's personal possessions and furnishings; she wrote *Little Women* (1868–69) in her upstairs bedroom, and the surrounding orchard inspired her name "Apple Slump" for the house. Hillside Chapel, formerly Alcott's School of Philosophy where he and other Transcendentalists lectured, closed in 1888 but was restored and reopened for summer lectures in 1976. Both chapel and home are operated by the Louisa May Alcott Memorial Association. (Open April 15–November 15, Monday–Saturday 10:00–4:30, Sunday 1:00–4:00; 617-369-4118; admission.) The privately owned Thoreau-Alcott House was the family's last Concord home (1877–85). Louisa Alcott bought it for her parents; there her mother Abigail died and Bronson Alcott suffered a crippling stroke. Henry David Thoreau (see the entry on Thoreau later in this section) was a previous occupant.

Alcott residences in **Boston** were numerous, though seldom long-occupied, and a few still exist. From 1864, the Bellevue Hotel-Apartments at 21 Beacon St. was Louisa's most frequent haven when she needed solitude for writing. Widower Bronson Alcott died in Louisa's Boston residence at 10 Louisburg Square, where she had cared for him from 1885. Both of these structures remain in private hands.

(See CONNECTICUT in this chapter above; also Chapter 3, PENNSYLVANIA.)

ALDEN, JOHN (1599?–1687). In **Duxbury,** the Alden House at 105 Alden St. was the last home (1627–87) of the Pilgrim colonist and his wife Priscilla. This frame house, built in 1653 by their son Jonathan Alden, apparently extended the original John and Priscilla Alden homestead, which stood as the rear portion of the present structure. Nine consecutive generations of Aldens lived there until the early 1900s, when the house was acquired and opened as a museum displaying period furnishings by the Alden Kindred of America. (Open last Saturday in June–Labor Day, Tuesday–Sunday 10:00–5:00; 617-934-2788; admission.)

(See the entry on Miles Standish later in this section.)

Exhibits: (See the entry on William Bradford later in this section.)

ALGER, HORATIO, JR (1832–1899). Most of Alger's New England homes were parsonages, since both his father and he were ministers. The author's 19th-century birthplace in **Revere,** his home until 1844, was a brown, seven-room, two-story house with white shutters. It still stands at 88 Beach St.

In **Marlborough,** he lived from 1844 to 1848 at 9 Broad St., in a home built about 1840.

Alger pastored the Unitarian church at **Brewster** on Cape Cod in 1864 and 1865, but his alleged homosexual seduction of two parishioners' sons outraged the community. He never bothered to deny it but fled to New York, where he turned out some 120 enormously popular books for boys. The Brewster parsonage where he lived was built about the time he arrived there; demolished in 1972, it was replaced by a new parsonage at 1944 Old King's Highway.

The 1820 Parsonage National Historic Landmark at 16 Pleasant St. in **Natick** was the family home from 1852 until 1860. Alger often returned there during summers to write in his second-floor room—a chamber he tried to recreate wherever he lived. The house, a large clapboard dwelling, has been somewhat altered. From 1860, Alger often returned to his sister's Natick home at 29 Florence St.; in 1898 he did so to die. All of Alger's Massachusetts homes remain in private hands.

Exhibit: The Natick Historical Society at 58 Eliot St. in **South Natick** displays Alger books and memorabilia. (Open Wednesday 2:00–4:30, Saturday except July–August 10:00–12:30; 617-653-6730; free.)

(See Chapter 2, MANHATTAN.)

ANTHONY, SUSAN BROWNELL (1820–1906). In **Adams,** the birthplace of the famed feminist and reformer is a three-story frame house built by her father in about 1815, her home until age six. It stands at East Road and East Street and is not presently open to visitors.

(See Chapter 3, NEW YORK.)

BANCROFT, GEORGE (1800–1891). The historian-diplomat began as a teacher who helped establish the preparatory Round Hill School in **Northampton.** Bancroft taught and lived in a building dating from 1807 which consisted of three connected houses. Part of this structure, completely renovated in 1975, remains as a classroom building called Rogers Hall, owned by the private Clarke School for the Deaf at 49 Round Hill Road.

(See RHODE ISLAND in this chapter; also Chapter 3, DISTRICT OF COLUMBIA.)

BARTON, CLARA (1821–1912). The birthplace of the American Red Cross founder in **North Oxford** was also the scene of her first nursing activity; she cared for a chronically sick elder brother at the home built in 1805. On Clara Barton Road, the grounds host a conference center and a camp for diabetic girls. Period furnishings plus Barton family and Red Cross memorabilia are displayed by the Unitarian-Universalist Women's Federation. (Open April 1–November 30, Tuesday–Sunday 1:00–5:00; December 1–March 31, by appointment; 617-987-2132; admission.)

Her summer home in **Oxford,** a 19th-century house at 28 Charlton St., has been restored and is privately owned.

(See Chapter 3, DISTRICT OF COLUMBIA, MARYLAND, NEW JERSEY, NEW YORK.)

BEECHER, LYMAN (1775–1863). The Presbyterian preacher and sire of several eminent Beechers had two homes in **Boston,** neither of which remain. At 18 Sheafe St. on Copps Hill (1826–32), the dynamic cleric kept a sandpile that he furiously shoveled from one side of the cellar to the other when his adrenalin level mounted; he also used a gymnastic apparatus in the back yard. Tenement erection here has moved considerably more sand since the 19th-century parsonage fell.

(See CONNECTICUT in this chapter; also Chapter 3, NEW YORK; also Chapter 4, OHIO.)

BELL, ALEXANDER GRAHAM (1847–1922). The inventor-educator lived in **Salem** from 1873 until 1876 while perfecting the apparatus he would patent as the telephone, using the attic at 292 Essex St. as his workshop and also tutoring the deaf grandson of his landlady. The frame house was demolished in 1898 to clear space for the present YMCA building, which bears a marker.

Bell's main work on the telephone was accomplished in **Boston.** At 109 Court St. (the present location of the John F. Kennedy Federal Office Building) is the marked site of Charles Williams' machine shop. There on June 3, 1875, in a third-floor attic room, Bell first sent speech sounds electrically. All materials from this room were carefully noted and preserved when the building was demolished in the late 1920s. Bell's experiments met final success at 5 Exeter Place off Chauncy Street, where he occupied two rooms above a restaurant. This is the site of his immortal words (plus, no doubt, some others left modestly unrecorded) of March 10, 1876: "Come here, Watson, I want you." Bell made this, the very first emergency phone call, to aide Thomas A. Watson when he spilled battery acid on his trousers. The site of the building, demolished about 1900, is currently a business establishment.

Exhibit: The New England Telephone Company recreated Bell's Court Street workshop room in 1959, using materials from the original room. This exhibit, which also displays items of early telephone history, is located in the company's headquarters building at 185 Franklin St. in **Boston.** (Open Monday–Friday 9:00–5:00; 617-743-9800; free.)

(See Chapter 3, DISTRICT OF COLUMBIA.)

BERRYMAN, JOHN (1914–1972). In **Boston,** the poet's lodging from 1941 to 1943 was an apartment at 49 Grove St. (privately owned). Berryman taught at Harvard University during this period.

(See Chapter 3, NEW JERSEY; also Chapter 4, MINNESOTA.)

BOOTH, EDWIN THOMAS (1833–1893). The **Boston** home of the actor, at 29A Chestnut St., (1883–87) "has a princely, brooding air," wrote one observer, "suggestive of *Hamlet,* Booth's most famous role." The 1799 private dwelling also has several of the original purple windowpanes once fashionable on Beacon Hill. After Booth's daughter left, the widower found the house too large and sold it.

(See RHODE ISLAND in this chapter; also Chapter 2, MANHATTAN; also Chapter 3, MARYLAND.)

BORDEN, LIZZIE ANDREW (1860–1927). The three-story gray house where the ax murders of Borden's parents took place in 1892—murders of which she was accused but acquitted—stands at 234 Second St. in **Fall River,** its ground floor now occupied by a local business. After the sensational trial, she moved into "Maplecroft," an 1889 house at 306 French St., where she reclusively dwelled with her sister for the rest of her life. Both homes are privately owned.

Exhibit: The **Fall River** Historical Society at 451 Rock St. preserves some grisly memorabilia of the murders and trial in its Lizzie Borden Room. (Open March 1–December 31, Tuesday–Friday 9:00–4:30, Saturday–Sunday 2:00–4:00; 617-679-1071; free.)

BRADFORD, WILLIAM (1590–1657). The home of the 30-year governor of Plymouth Colony stood on the north corner of Main Street and Town Square in **Plymouth.** Bradford governed there from 1621 to his death except for five years.

Exhibits: Mayflower II, a replica which duplicated the Atlantic crossing in 1957, lies at Frazier State Pier on Water Street in **Plymouth.** (Open July 1–August 31, 9:00–6:30; 617-746-1622; admission.) The Pilgrim Society at 75 Court St., the oldest historical museum in the United States (1820), contains many Pilgrim portraits and possessions including Bradford's chair and Bible.

(Open daily 9:30–4:30; 617-746-1620; admission.) Plimoth Plantation, two miles south on Warren Avenue, recreates the village layout including Bradford's house as it appeared in 1627. (Open April 1–November 30, daily 9:00–5:00; December 1–March 31, classroom programs by appointment; 617-746-1622; admission.)

In **Boston,** the 1795 Massachusetts State House on Beacon and Park streets contains a basement Archives Museum that displays Bradford's historic manuscript *Of Plimoth Plantation,* lost for more than a century after his death and finally discovered in London. Also encased here is the 1620 Mayflower Compact. (Open Monday–Friday 9:00–5:00; 617-727-2816; free.)

BRADSTREET, ANNE DUDLEY (1612?–1672). America's first published poet, a Puritan colonist, settled briefly in **Boston** (1629–31) at the first Bay Colony sites (see the entry on John Winthrop later in this section).

Her **Cambridge** home site from 1631 to 1635 is marked at 2 Boylston St. at the corner of Massachusetts Avenue.

North Andover was her last home (1645–72); fire destroyed the Bradstreet dwelling here in 1666, and she wrote "Verses Upon the Burning of Our House," perhaps to purge herself of the terrifying event. Though a new house was soon built, probably in the same spot, nobody knows exactly where that was—the best guess of local historians places it somewhere across the street from the 1715 Parson Barnard House at 179 Osgood St. near Academy Road.

BRANDEIS, LOUIS DEMBITZ (1856–1941). **Boston** was the famed jurist's residence before President Woodrow Wilson appointed him to the Supreme Court in 1916. Both of his homes remain—at 114 Mount Vernon St. and 6 Otis Place—and are privately owned. "The furnishings were so plain as to be almost drab," wrote one biographer about his Boston homes.

While occupying his summer house at 194 Village Ave. (privately owned) in **Dedham,** Brandeis endured anti-Semitic exclusion from the "Dedham crowd" of country clubbers and fellow professionals, a recurring ordeal of his brilliant career.

Brandeis House National Historic Landmark at **Chatham** on Cape Cod is a one and one-half-story frame house, built in the early 19th century and enclosing a brick patio. Brandeis lived there during summers from 1922 through 1941. It stands privately owned on Neck Lane off Cedar Street.

(See Chapter 3, DISTRICT OF COLUMBIA; also Chapter 5, KENTUCKY.)

BRYANT, WILLIAM CULLEN (1794–1878). Near **Cummington** stands the white-clapboard Bryant Homestead National Historic Landmark, where the poet-journalist grew up and began writing (1799–1816). There he produced his best-known poem "Thanatopsis" at age 16 in his upstairs bedroom. The oldest portion of this house, located at the intersection of State Highway 112 and State Highway 9, was built by Bryant's grandfather in 1783. The homestead was sold in 1835, but 30 years later Bryant bought it back, raised the original house above a new first floor and did extensive remodeling. He used it for a summer place from 1865 until his death, and his descendants occupied it until 1965. Today the rooms look the same as when Bryant lived here, with numerous family furnishings and personal possessions arranged as if the poet had just stepped out. Of more than 1,000 trees he planted on the grounds, many still grow. The Homestead is operated by the Trustees of Reservations. (Open late June–August 31, Friday–Sunday 1:00–5:00; September 1–mid-October, Saturday–Sunday 1:00–5:00; 413-634-2244; admission.)

Another early home (1821–22) stands privately owned in **Great Barrington,** a 1739 dwelling at 362 Main St. Bryant lived there during his brief law career.

(See Chapter 2, MANHATTAN; also Chapter 3, NEW YORK.)

BULFINCH, CHARLES (1763–1844). It is ironic that not one home of New England's noted architect, who left his stylistic signature on so many churches, houses and public buildings throughout **Boston** and the eastern United States, now exists.* He was born at a marked site on the north side of Boston's Bowdoin Square; lands of the Bulfinch Homestead, his birthplace built by

his grandfather in 1737 and razed about 1850, extended south to Ashburton Place. In this three-story, white clapboard house that stood where the New England Telephone and Telegraph Building now rises, he grew to adulthood (1763–94), and he returned there to spend his last years (1837–44). Bulfinch built his own home (1794–96) at 8 Bulfinch Place, a large brick house painted white; it stood with extensive alterations until 1962, when it fell to an urban renewal project (of which he would probably have approved), and the entire small street was destroyed to make space for the Leverett Saltonstall State Office Building. "At last we find ourselves established in a comfortable house, with a moderate income," wrote Hannah Bulfinch in 1800, referring to the Clap-Bulfinch House at the southeast corner of Bulfinch and Howard streets, the family home from 1799 to 1815. Following the architect's return from Washington, D.C., in 1833, the family resided until 1837 at 3 Bumstead Place, a street demolished in 1868. So Bulfinch's memorials appear only where he always wanted them—in the skyline.

BURBANK, LUTHER (1849–1926). The horticultural wizard's ancestral dwelling, his home until 1870, was built about 1800 on Harvard Road near **Lancaster.** It was a large brick house with a two-story wooden ell in which he was born. In 1938, Henry Ford removed this portion of the home to his Michigan Greenfield Village in Dearborn. The remainder of the house was razed by the U.S. government when Fort Devens acquired the land for training purposes. Since army rifle ranges now enclose the area, the site marker is not generally accessible to the public.

In **Lunenburg,** Burbank acquired 17 acres and developed the white rose (Burbank) potato, his first notable success in plant breeding. Actually a remodeled barn, the white frame, privately owned 1835 Jones House at 42 Main St. has undergone no significant alterations since Burbank's residence from 1872 through 1875.

(See Chapter 4, MICHIGAN; also Chapter 6, CALIFORNIA.)

BURGESS, THORNTON WALDO (1874–1965). Children's author and naturalist, Burgess was born in **Sandwich** on Cape Cod at 6 School St. (privately owned).

From 1928 he spent summers at **Hampden,** and

---

*Rarely do sources conflict to the extent that Bulfinch biographers and site researchers disagree on when the man lived where. No two published or field accounts seem to agree. One of the more recent published accounts is *Bulfinch's Boston: 1787–1817,* by Harold and James Kirker (1964), a source that gives the most congruent and convincing data and on which the present entry mainly relies.

after 1957 this became his permanent home. The Western Mass. Audubon Society maintains his 259-acre property at 789 Main St. as the Laughing Brook Education Center & Wildlife Sanctuary, with five miles of nature trails and a touch-trail for the blind. The house, which he bought because it reminded him of his Sandwich birth-place, is filled with Burgess's own colonial furnishings and possessions. His books and animal collections occupy the barn, and his hill-top writing studio now functions as the center classroom. (Open Tuesday–Sunday 10:00–5:00; 413-566-3571; admission.)

Burgess's "city home" from 1906 to 1957 stands at 61 Washington Road (privately owned) in **Springfield.**

Exhibits: The Thornton W. Burgess Museum at 4 Water St. in **Sandwich,** operated by the Thornton Burgess Society, is a 1756 house that belonged to his aunt and now contains memorabilia of the writer. (Open May 1–December 31, Monday–Saturday 10:00–4:00, Sunday 1:00–4:00; 617-888-4668; free.) Sandwich environs provided the setting for the friendly world of his *Old Mother West Wind* series and some 15,000 newspaper stories about its animal residents. The marked "Old Briar Patch" of these stories can be seen on Chipman Road off State Highway 6A.

BYRD, RICHARD EVELYN (1888–1957). The famed Antarctic explorer's 1867 home at 9 Brimmer St. in **Boston** remains in private hands. He lived there from 1934 until 1957.

(See MAINE in this chapter; also Chapter 3, DISTRICT OF COLUMBIA; also Chapter 5, VIRGINIA.)

CARNEGIE, ANDREW (1835–1919). "Shadow-brook," the industrialist-philanthropist's summer home from 1916 to 1919 in **Lenox** was built by Anson Phelps Stokes in 1893. Sold to the Roman Catholic Jesuit order in 1922, this mansion where Carnegie died burned down with some loss of life in 1956. The Jesuits replaced it with a rectangular utility building of the same name (wags christened it the "Jesus Hilton") just west of the marked site on West Street.

(See Chapter 2, MANHATTAN; also Chapter 3, PENNSYLVANIA.)

CLEVELAND, GROVER (1837–1908). At **Bourne** on Cape Cod, the 22nd and 24th U.S. president

bought a two-story, six-gabled clapboard "cottage" in 1891 that he christened "Gray Gables," a rambling, 1880s structure first known as "Tudor Haven." Bluefish and sea bass attracted Cleveland, a compulsive angler, to this shoreline spot, where he owned about 40 acres. Here he recuperated in 1893 from the secret operation that removed his cancerous left jaw. This summer White House and vacation retreat until 1904 remained in Cleveland's family until 1921, then became Gray Gables Inn, a summer hotel. Fire, locally reported "of suspicious origin," destroyed the old house in 1973. The one and one-half-acre private site, currently vacant on President's Road at Monument Point, is prime real estate because of its seaside residential location.

(See NEW HAMPSHIRE in this chapter; also Chapter 3, DISTRICT OF COLUMBIA, MARY-LAND, NEW JERSEY, NEW YORK.)

COHAN, GEORGE MICHAEL (1878–1942). As a boy, the prominent actor-producer-playwright spent summers at his grandparents' home in **North Brookfield,** a privately owned house of uncertain vintage at 34 Bell St.

(See RHODE ISLAND in this chapter; also Chapter 2, MANHATTAN; also Chapter 3, NEW JERSEY, NEW YORK.)

COOLIDGE, CALVIN (1872–1933). Though a Vermont native, the 30th U.S. president spent most of his pre-presidential years in **Northampton,** where he practiced law and occupied various public offices. No spendthrift, he first rented only half of the 19th-century duplex house at 21 Massasoit St., then later occupied all of it (1906–23, 1929–30). After his retirement, Coolidge and his wife searched for a place with a front porch less visible to tourists and bought "The Beeches," a 12-room house on Hampton Terrace, built in 1914. Its nine fenced and forested acres provided him ample privacy from 1930 to 1933, and he died there. Both homes are privately owned.

Exhibit: The Forbes Library at 20 West St. in **Northampton** displays a Coolidge Memorial Room containing his papers and memorabilia. (Open Monday–Saturday 9:00–8:30; Sunday 2:00–6:00; 413-584-8399; free.)

(See VERMONT in this chapter; also Chapter 3, DISTRICT OF COLUMBIA; also Chapter 4, SOUTH DAKOTA.)

CALVIN COOLIDGE AND FRIENDS IN RETIREMENT. The 30th U.S. president relaxes on the porch of his home at 21 Massasoit St., **Northampton,** in 1930. He soon fled front porch visibility for more seclusion at another Northampton home, "The Beeches." Note the sign at right posted for ice delivery.
(Courtesy Forbes Library, Northampton)

COPLEY, JOHN SINGLETON (1738–1815). The portrait artist, a **Boston** native, was born and raised on Long Wharf, the 1710 pier that jutted into Boston harbor from the colonial waterfront. The wharf is still there, though most of its length has been dry land for over a century; what is now 148 State St. was once its foot. Copley's widowed mother kept a tobacco shop on the wharf, and he lived here until age 10. Long Wharf is undergoing renovation by the Boston Redevelopment Authority. Copley's subsequent boyhood addresses in Boston shifted frequently. In 1769, he began to acquire land on Beacon Hill, a piece

that included the present Louisburg Square. His property by 1773 occupied a 20-acre estate he called "Mount Pleasant" between Beacon and Mount Vernon streets, including three houses fronting Beacon. Copley lived in the two-story middle house until 1774, then rented out the estate until he sold it in the 1790s. The posh Somerset Club at 42–43 Beacon now occupies his home site.

CORNELL, KATHARINE (1893–1974). In 1937 near **Vineyard Haven** on Martha's Vineyard, the actress built "Chip Chop," which she whimsically named because of its location at the apex between the East Chop and West Chop headlands. This sprawling house with a complex of guest cottages and outbuildings included a workroom for her marquetry and weaving and became her permanent summer home. While staying there with guests during the hurricane of 1938, she opened the windows to the winds and found herself washed by two-foot waves in her living room. The privately owned house has no street number.

(See Chapter 2, MANHATTAN; also Chapter 3, NEW YORK.)

CUMMINGS, EDWARD ESTLIN (1894–1962). The satiric poet whose unorthodox punctuation and lower-case letters became badges of his work was born in **Cambridge** at 104 Irving St. and lived there until 1918. This three-story mansion with 13 fireplaces, built by his father in 1893, was recently given to Harvard University and remains a private residence.

Also private is the family's 19th-century summer home (1901–03) at 135 Nahant St. in **Lynn.**

(See NEW HAMPSHIRE in this chapter; also Chapter 2, MANHATTAN; also Chapter 3, NEW JERSEY.)

DeMILLE, CECIL BLOUNT (1881–1959). The birthplace of Hollywood's creator of lavish film spectaculars survives east of the post office on Main Street in **Ashfield.** DeMille's parents summered here, occupying the second floor of what was known as the Bronson house. It remains privately owned.

(See Chapter 3, NEW JERSEY; also Chapter 6, CALIFORNIA.)

DICKINSON, EMILY ELIZABETH (1830–1886). **Amherst** was birthplace and lifelong home of this brilliant recluse, one of America's greatest poets. At Dickinson Home National Historic Landmark she was born, grew up, wrote in the southeast upstairs room from which she rarely emerged as years passed and died. The 16-room brick house, built by her grandfather in 1813, "is as intimidating in its twentieth-century literary eminence," wrote John Deedy, "as it was in its nineteenth-century stateliness." Behind tall hemlock shrubbery, the house now serves as a faculty residence for Amherst College. The poet's room has been restored with a few personal relics and period

recreations, but "just as one approached Emily by prearrangement, so does one visit the Dickinson homestead by appointment." Visits must be prearranged in writing with the Office of the Secretary, Amherst College, Amherst, MA, 01002. (Open for tours by appointment May 1–October 1, Tuesday–Friday 1:00–4:30; October 2–April 30, Tuesday 1:00–4:30; admission.)

Exhibits: Jones Library at 43 Amity St. in **Amherst** displays some Dickinson notes and letters. (Open Monday–Friday 9:00–5:30, Tuesday–Thursday 9:00–9:30, Saturday 10:00–5:30; 413-256-0426; free.)

In **Cambridge,** Harvard University's Houghton Library exhibits most of the original furniture removed from her Amherst bedroom—her writing desk, chair, bureau, jewelry, piano and family items. The Library is located on the southeast side of Harvard Square. (Open Monday–Friday 9:30–4:45; 617-495-2440; free.)

DIX, DOROTHEA LYNDE (1802–1887). In 1814, the girl whose later humanitarian activities would help lift the stigma of disgrace from mental illness came to Orange Court in **Boston** to live with an aunt; this remained her home for more than 20 years. The 18th-century Dix Mansion stood at what is now 499 Washington St., the present location of the 1908 Blake Building.

(See MAINE in this chapter; also Chapter 3, NEW JERSEY.)

DOS PASSOS, JOHN RODERIGO (1896–1970). The author's longtime home (1929–47) at 571 Commercial St. in **Provincetown** is privately owned.

(See Chapter 2, BROOKLYN, MANHATTAN; also Chapter 6, VIRGINIA.)

DOUGLASS, FREDERICK (1818–1895). An escaped slave from Maryland, Frederick Bailey arrived at **New Bedford** in 1838, and was taken in by Nathan Johnson, an operator of the Underground Railroad. Johnson's home, where Bailey lived for about three years, is a two and one-half-story shingled structure (originally two buildings) dating from the late 18th century. There, after taking on the new name suggested by Johnson, Douglass began his career as an abolitionist orator. The Johnson house, located at 21 Seventh St., now contains private apartments.

At **Lynn,** Douglass resided at 20 Newhall St. (1841–45), a house later moved to an undeter-

MARY BAKER EDDY'S HOME. Last residence (1908–10), of the Christian Science leader, a 25-room stone mansion in **Newton,** contains a museum displaying some of her personal possessions. *(Courtesy Christian Science Publishing Society. Used by permission.)*

mined address on Sagamore Street. The altered dwelling probably still exists there, but nobody in Lynn has been able to identify the exact structure.

(See Chapter 3, DISTRICT OF COLUMBIA, MARYLAND, NEW YORK.)

DU BOIS, WILLIAM EDWARD BURGHARDT (1868–1963). At the five-acre Du Bois Memorial Park on State Highway 23 in **Great Barrington,** Du Bois Boyhood Homesite National Historic Landmark contains the foundation and chimney remnants of the educator-reformer's home from

1868 to 1873, his grandparents' simple frame farmhouse. This was "the first home that I remember," he wrote. "On this wide and lovely plain, beneath the benediction of gray-blue mountains and the low music of rivers, lived for a hundred years the black Burghardt clan." Of several subsequent boyhood addresses in the town, according to local sources, his dwellings on South Main and Railroad streets "may still stand, but we have no way of knowing which ones they would be."

(See Chapter 2, BROOKLYN, MANHATTAN; also Chapter 3, MARYLAND, PENNSYLVANIA; also Chapter 5, GEORGIA.)

dences, of which several exist in Massachusetts. Most contain period furnishings.

At **Swampscott** began the course of events in 1865 and 1866 that led to the founding of the Christian Science movement. Mrs. Patterson, as she was then known, slipped on the ice near the corner of Market and Oxford streets, injured her back and reported that she recovered in three days after intensive scripture reading at home. Eddy Historic House, the 19th-century dwelling where she thus "discovered" Christian Science, stands at 23 Paradise Road. (Open May 15–October 31, Monday–Saturday 10:00–5:00, Sunday 2:00–5:00; November 1–May 14, Tuesday–Saturday 10:00–3:00, Sunday 2:00–5:00; admission.)

Stoughton was her home from 1868 to 1870 as Mrs. Glover, and the 19th-century Eddy Historic House at 133 Central St., a white farm dwelling, belonged to the Alanson Wentworth family, her host. There she completed the first teaching manuscript of *Science of Man.* (Open May 1–October 31, Tuesday–Sunday 1:00–4:00; 617-344-3904; admission.)

At **Amesbury,** the red-clapboard Eddy Historic House at 227 Main St. dates from the early 18th century. This was the Sarah Bagley home, where Mary Baker Glover lived from 1868 to 1870 as a guest for two periods and wrote the first complete draft of *Science of Man* in her second-floor room. The house contains original furnishings. (Open May 1–October 31, Tuesday–Sunday 1:00–4:00; admission.)

She owned the 19th-century Eddy Residence at 12 Broad St. in **Lynn** but lived in an attic room while renting out the rest of it for mortgage money. This was her home from 1875 to 1882, and here she completed much of *Science and Health* (1875). There she also married Asa G. Eddy in 1877. This house, operated by Boston's First Church of Christ, Scientist, and containing many original furnishings, was considered the earliest headquarters of the movement. (Open May 1–October 31, Wednesday–Saturday 11:30–4:00, Sunday 2:00–5:00; November 1–April 30, by appointment; free.)

In **Boston,** from the 15-room brownstone house at 385 Commonwealth Ave. (privately owned) she emerged as a national religious figure in 1888 and 1889. This house, dating from 1885, is now the official residence of the First Reader of Boston's "Mother Church."

The leader's last home (1908–10) stands at 400

EARHART, AMELIA MARY (1898–1937?). Flying was originally an avocation for the aviator-feminist. At **West Medford,** she lived with her mother and sister in 1924 and 1925 at 76 Brooks St., a shingled, two and one-half-story house that dates from 1887. A historical marker is planned but has not yet been placed outside the privately owned dwelling.

(See Chapter 3, NEW YORK; also Chapter 4, IOWA, KANSAS, MINNESOTA, MISSOURI.)

EDDY, MARY BAKER (1821–1910). The Longyear Foundation, a Christian Science organization, operates most of the religious leader's later resi-

"THE DOWNS," T. S. ELIOT'S BOYHOOD HOME. The poet's sister, Charlotte Eliot, drew this watercolor view of the family's summer house at **Gloucester** in 1897. Two years old then, the house remains privately owned.
(Courtesy Sawyer Free Library, Gloucester.)

Beacon St. in **Newton,** where she began publishing the *Christian Science Monitor.* She described her 25-room stone house on 12 acres as "a big barn of a place." A second-floor exhibit displays memorabilia. (Open May 1–October 31, Wednesday–Saturday 11:30–4:00, Sunday 2:00–5:00; November 1–April 30, by appointment; 617-262-2300; free.)

Exhibit: The Mary Baker Eddy Museum at 120 Seaver St. in **Brookline** (suburban Boston) contains the main documents and artifacts relating to her life and accomplishments. The pen she used in writing *Science and Health* is prominently displayed. (Open April 1–October 31, Tuesday – Saturday 10:00–5:00, Sunday 1:00–5:00; November 1–January 31, March 1–31, Tuesday–Saturday 10:00–4:00, Sunday 1:00–4:00; 617-277-8943; admission.)

(See NEW HAMPSHIRE in this chapter.)

EDWARDS, JONATHAN (1703–1758). The Calvinist preacher and theologian came to **Northampton** in 1727, where he pastored the Congregational Church from 1727 to 1750 and preached the sermons that led to New England's "Great Awakening." The site of his frame homestead, razed in 1830, is 127 King St.—now occupied on Edwards Square by St. Valentine's Polish National Church, which has refused placement of a Northampton Historical Society marker.

At **Stockbridge,** Edwards pastored to the Indians from 1750 to 1757, and a sundial marks the site of his 1737 dwelling, "Edwards Hall," on the grounds of Austen Riggs Psychiatric Center on South and Pine streets. A makeshift fort was hastily erected around the house in 1754 when Indians threatened to attack the town.

Exhibits: Forbes Library at 20 West St. in **Northampton** displays some of Edward's manuscript letters and sermons. (Open Monday–Saturday 9:00–8:30, Sunday 2:00–6:00; 413-584-8399; free.)

The 1739 Mission House National Historic Landmark at Main and Sergeant streets in **Stockbridge** displays the preacher's writing desk. Mission House is maintained by the Trustees of Reservations. (Open May 24–October 13, Tuesday–Saturday 10:00–5:00, Sunday 11:00–4:00; 617-698-2066; admission.)

(See CONNECTICUT in this chapter.)

ELIOT, THOMAS STEARNS (1888–1965). Before the major American poet moved to England in 1914, he spent boyhood summers at the family vacation home overlooking Eastern Point in **Gloucester.** "The Downs," built by Eliot's father on two acres in 1895, is a large, hip-roofed, shingled house that stands unnumbered and privately owned on Edgemoor Road.

In **Cambridge,** from 1910 to 1912, Eliot resided at 16 Ash St. (privately owned) while attending Harvard. This house dates from 1855.

(See Chapter 3, NEW JERSEY; also Chapter 4, MISSOURI.)

EMERSON, RALPH WALDO (1803–1882). New England's notable essayist and intellectual guru was born in **Boston** at his parents' parsonage home on Summer Street near the Chauncy Street corner. His father died there in 1811; the yellow, gambrel-roofed structure that stood on an acre of orchard and garden land remained Emerson's home until 1814, when the family made the first of many moves to various boardinghouses. The site of the house, which stood until the mid-1800s, is marked on the present Jordan Marsh Co. department store.

Though often absent on travels and lecture tours, Emerson made **Concord** his permanent home. There in Old Manse National Historic Landmark on Monument Street near Old North Bridge, he spent many boyhood and adult years until 1835. Emerson's grandfather built this gray clapboard, gambrel-roofed house about 1770. There the New England Transcendentalist movement actually began with Emerson's *Nature* (1836), which he wrote in the upstairs study. House and furnishings dating from the later occupancy of Nathaniel Hawthorne (see the entry on Hawthorne later in this section) have been maintained since 1939 by the Trustees of Reservations. (Open April 15–May 31, Saturday 10:00–4:30; June 1–October 31, Monday–Saturday 10:00–4:30, Sunday 1:00–4:30; 617-698-2066; admission.) Emerson House National Historic Landmark, his last, longtime home in Concord, dates from 1828. Both inside and outside, the white frame, Victorian dwelling remains essentially as he knew it (except for replicas in the study). Family

possessions and furnishings include a closet of Emerson's clothes. Henry David Thoreau also lived there as caretaker in 1847 and 1848 (see the entry on Thoreau later in this section). Though severely damaged by fire in 1872, this house at Lexington Road and Cambridge Turnpike was completely restored through the generosity of the sage's countless friends and is now operated by the Emerson Memorial Association. (Open April 15–October 31, Thursday–Saturday 10:00–4:30, Sunday 2:00–4:00; 617-369-2236; admission.)

Exhibit: Antiquarian House, the museum operated by **Concord** Antiquarian Society at 200 Lexington Road, contains Emerson's study, removed to a fireproof room here from the Emerson House in 1931. (Open Monday–Saturday 10:00–4:30, Sunday 2:00–4:30; 617-369-9609; admission.)

FIELD, MARSHALL (1834–1906). **Conway** was the birthplace of the Chicago merchandiser and philanthropist. The cellar hole of the small farmhouse where he lived until age 17 still exists on Field's Hill, which is now private farmland overlooking the Connecticut River valley. "Field in his later life," wrote a local historian, "was accustomed to say that one might travel far over the world and see nothing finer" than the view from this hill.

The two-story, white frame birthplace itself remains intact and substantially unaltered on Haydenville Road near **Whately,** where it was moved by the present owner's great-grandfather about 1850. The exact date of the private dwelling remains unknown.

(See Chapter 4, ILLINOIS; also Chapter 5, GEORGIA.)

FRANKFURTER, FELIX (1882–1965). The Supreme Court justice lived in **Cambridge** from 1919 to 1939 during his law professorship at Harvard. His 1907 house at 192 Brattle St. is privately owned. The Cambridge Historical Society reports that the house is "a likely candidate for a marker."

(See Chapter 3, DISTRICT OF COLUMBIA.)

FRANKLIN, BENJAMIN (1706–1790). Controversy still exists over the correct location of Franklin's birth site in **Boston.** General biographical consensus places it at 17 Milk St., where the two-story wooden cabin stood with its side to the street until 1810 and where a Franklin bust now

MARSHALL FIELD BIRTHPLACE. This small farmhouse where the merchant grew up originally stood on Field's Hill near Conway. Presently located on Haydenville Road at **Whately,** it remains unaltered (except perhaps for the rear addition) in this 1970 view. The 1830 posted over the door is intended to date, not address, the house; according to a local historical source, however, the dwelling is probably much older. *(Courtesy Whately Historical Society)*

peers from the old *Boston Post* building front. But Franklin himself reportedly stated that he was born at the "Blue Ball," his father's long-gone tallow shop and dwelling at the southeast corner of Union and Hanover streets. Whether or not he was born at the latter site, it was definitely his boyhood home until 1718. The property included four wooden tenements, later joined by a common front, and the projecting globe identifying the

shop was a well-known colonial landmark. Franklin last visited his parents here in 1753; the building stood until 1858. Apprenticed as a printer to his domineering elder brother, James, he boarded in his brother's shop at 17 Court St. from 1718 to 1723, a site marked at Court Street and Franklin Avenue (actually a part of Brattle Street that Franklin knew as Dassett Alley.) There he learned his lifelong manual trade and began

CHESTERWOOD, HOME OF DANIEL CHESTER FRENCH. The sculptor built his 17-room stucco mansion near **Stockbridge** in 1900. This house replaced an old frame farmhouse on the property that French occupied from 1896.
(Courtesy Paul W. Ivory/ Chesterwood, a property of the National Trust for Historic Preservation; open to the public.)

THE CHESTERWOOD STUDIO OF DANIEL CHESTER FRENCH. This exterior view of the studio that French built in 1897 shows the skylight roof of his warehouse-like working area.
(Courtesy Paul W. Ivory/ Chesterwood, a property of the National Trust for Historic Preservation; open to the public.)

writing pieces on local issues for his brother's *New England Courant,* America's fourth newspaper. But a quarrel with James caused him to flee, ultimately to Philadelphia. The building housed Boston printing firms for 80 years before its destruction.

Exhibits: The blue sphere that adorned Franklin's home may still be seen at the Bostonian Society museum in the Old State House at 206 Washington St. (Open Monday–Friday 10:00–4:00, Saturday 9:30–5:00, Sunday 11:00–5:00; 617-242-5610; admission.) The hand press used by the Franklin brothers is on display at the Boston Museum of Science in Science Park. Science Park is located on State Highway 28, Charles River Dam. (Open Monday–Thursday 9:00–4:00, Friday 9:00–10:00, Saturday 9:00–5:00, Sunday 10:00–5:00; 617-723-2500; admission.)

(See Chapter 3, PENNSYLVANIA.)

FRENCH, DANIEL CHESTER (1850–1931). Noted for his massive bronze statues of historic Americans, the sculptor grew up in **Concord** at 342 Sudbury Road, a privately owned 1787 dwelling. French's father bought the white-trimmed farmhouse with center chimney in 1858, and French lived there at lengthy intervals for 30 years.

French's longtime summer home and studio was Chesterwood National Historic Landmark, two miles west of State Highway 183 near **Stockbridge.** He bought the property in 1896, then in 1900 replaced the 1802 farmhouse with a two and one-half-story, frame and stucco mansion of 17 rooms. The lofty studio building dates from 1897 and contains plaster casts, tools and French's models for his Lincoln Memorial and Concord Minuteman statues. A railroad flatcar on tracks enabled him to move his studio creations outside for daylight viewing. Nature trails and sculptures extend throughout the spacious gardens and woods of one of America's most scenic estates. It is operated by the National Trust for Historic Preservation. (Open May 1–October 31 daily, 10:00–5:00; 413-298-3579; admission.)

(See NEW HAMPSHIRE in this chapter; also Chapter 2, MANHATTAN.)

FROST, ROBERT LEE (1874–1963). Though several of the New England poet's homes are open to visitors, all of his extant Massachusetts dwellings remain in private hands.

Lawrence was Frost's first home in the state. His widowed mother brought her children there in 1885, and they resided briefly at his grandparents' home at 370 Haverhill St. Torn down in 1902, the house was located "approximately where the altar of St. Anne's Roman Catholic Church stands today," according to a Lawrence reporter.

Frost's home in **Amherst,** a dwelling designed by architect Stanford White, stands at 43 Sunset Ave. He lived there from 1932 to 1938.

His 1850 house in **Boston** (1938–41) is located at 88 Mount Vernon St.

In 1941, Frost settled in **Cambridge** at 35 Brewster St., a three-story, Victorian double house built in 1884 that remained the poet's home base for the rest of his life.

(See NEW HAMPSHIRE, VERMONT in this chapter; also Chapter 4, MICHIGAN; also Chapter 5, FLORIDA; also Chapter 6, CALIFORNIA.)

FULLER, MARGARET (1810–1850). In **Cambridge,** the brilliant critic, educator and reformer who became Boston's leading intellectual and feminist was born in the 1807 white clapboard Fuller House National Historic Landmark at 71 Cherry St. There the precocious girl received a liberal education from her scholarly father before she went to school in 1826. The dwelling has been a private settlement house since 1902. Brattle House at 42 Brattle St., now the Cambridge Center for Adult Education, was her 1832 residence. Neither house is open to the public.

The Wharton House on Farmers Row in **Groton,** an 1815 house that remains privately owned, was her home from 1832 to 1838.

West Roxbury in suburban Boston was the site of Brook Farm, the utopian commune founded by George Ripley, where Margaret Fuller lived at intervals in 1841 and 1842. Now Brook Farm Site National Historic Landmark at 670 Baker St., the surviving gabled community house is called Margaret Fuller Cottage—though, according to biographers, it is probably the only building of the complex in which she never stayed. An interesting account of this social experiment is *Autobiography of Brook Farm* (1958), edited by Henry W. Sams.

(See Chapter 2, MANHATTAN.)

GARRISON, WILLIAM LLOYD (1805–1879). The prominent abolitionist-reformer was born in **Newburyport** in the small, much-modified frame house at 5 School St. (privately owned). It dates from about 1800.

Garrison House National Historic Landmark at 125 Highland St., privately owned in **Roxbury,** suburban Boston, is a rambling 19th-century frame house, Garrison's home from 1864 to 1879.

GERRY, ELBRIDGE (1744–1814). In **Marblehead,** privately owned, stands the home of President James Madison's vice president, whose name survives in the term "gerrymander," the political shenanigan of drawing district boundaries for partisan advantage. The clapboard house at 44 Washington St., built about 1744, was raised to three stories from two in 1820. There is no solid evidence, despite the claim on the marker there, that this was Gerry's birthplace, though he lived there from 1744 to 1786.

Gerry's permanent home after 1786 was Elmwood National Historic Landmark in

Cambridge (see the entry on James Russell Lowell later in this section). There he operated 96 acres as a working plantation but refused to plow the front yard where Revolutionary soldiers had been buried. Gerry was sworn in as vice president at Elmwood in 1813.

(See Chapter 3, DISTRICT OF COLUMBIA.)

GODDARD, ROBERT HUTCHINGS (1882–1945). The rocketry pioneer was born in the family ancestral homestead, a frame house on Maple Hill in **Worcester.** Dating from about 1851, the house has been modernized and enlarged and is still a private residence at 1 Tallawanda Drive. After spending his boyhood in Roxbury, this became Goddard's inherited permanent home, to which he returned for lengthy intervals until 1934. At 5 Bishop Ave., the large frame house built by his father in 1914 was Goddard's frequent residence from 1914 to 1924. It too is privately owned.

In **Roxbury** (suburban Boston), Goddard's boyhood home was a spacious Victorian frame house, still standing at 63 Forest St. (privately owned); this is currently a high-crime area of the city.

Exhibit: Goddard Site National Historic Landmark at **Auburn** marks the spot of the first liquid-propelled rocket launched by Goddard on March 16, 1926. The marker is located on the ninth fairway of Pakachoag Golf Course on Pakachoag Road.

(See Chapter 6, NEW MEXICO.)

GOODYEAR, CHARLES (1800–1860). **Woburn** was the 1839 site of the inventor's epochal, accidental discovery of the vulcanized rubber process. His 280 Montvale Ave. home (1838–40) stood until 1972.

(See CONNECTICUT in this chapter; also Chapter 3, PENNSYLVANIA; also Chapter 4, OHIO.)

GREEN, HENRIETTA ROBINSON "HETTY" (1834–1916). The eccentric financier who became the richest woman in America was born Henrietta Howland Robinson at 43 Seventh St. (at the corner of Walnut Street) in **New Bedford.** The 1831 house is privately owned. Her girlhood home (1835–63) was the 1830 box-like stone mansion at 1061 Pleasant St., owned by her aunt and presently a Roman Catholic convent.

Howland House, her grandfather's 1721 gambrel-roofed frame dwelling, stood on a 300-acre tract in **South Dartmouth** until the Newport Restoration Foundation moved it to Newport, R.I., in 1969. This was Hetty Green's girlhood summer home. Later family dwellings now stand on the site at 205 Smith Neck Road.

(See RHODE ISLAND, VERMONT in this chapter; also Chapter 2, MANHATTAN; also Chapter 3, NEW JERSEY).

GROPIUS, WALTER ADOLF (1883–1969). The permanent home of the innovative Harvard architect stands unnumbered in **Lincoln** on Baker Bridge Road. With the help of student Marcel Breuer, Gropius designed his home in 1938 shortly after he arrived from his native Germany. "Like many houses architects design for themselves," wrote one observer, "the house was meant to be a public statement about architecture as well as a private home." Features of the small dwelling include a sun deck, window wall, outdoor spiral staircase and other ideas that have since become familiar marks of modern architecture. Though the house is still private and hardly an "antiquity," the architect's widow has donated it to the eventual care of the Society for the Preservation of New England Antiquities.

HANCOCK, JOHN (1737–1793). In **Lexington,** the Boston merchant-patriot lived at Hancock-Clarke House National Historic Landmark, 36 Hancock St., in 1744 and 1745. He was also residing there with Samuel Adams in 1775 when both were rousted out by Paul Revere (see the entries on Adams and Revere in this section) on a lathered horse from Boston. This is the only Hancock residence that remains. Built of hand-hewn oak by his grandfather in 1698, with a 1734 front addition, the house stood until 1896 across the street from its present location. The Lexington Historical Society displays period furnishings inside. (Open mid-April–October 31, Monday–Saturday 10:00–5:00, Sunday 1:00–5:00; 617-861-0928; admission.)

Hancock's two and one-half-story stone mansion in **Boston,** built by his uncle in 1737, stood at 25 Beacon St. until sold by the family and demolished in 1863—a serious loss that did much to inspire creation of the national historical preservation movement. The marked site, located at the west end of the Massachusetts State House yard, was Hancock's home from 1745 to 1793. At 10 Marshall St. (privately owned), the 1760 Hancock House, oldest brick building in Boston, belonged to John Hancock from 1764 until 1785, when he sold it to his brother, Ebenezer. But if John Hancock ever spent much time here, wrote William G. Schofield, "it was probably just to collect the rent or because he was too tired to make it up to Beacon Hill to his own bed." One Bostonian recently observed that the ground floor has been a shoe store since 1796.

Exhibit: In **Quincy,** the 1706 Quincy Homestead, birthplace and home of Hancock's wife Dorothy at 34 Butler Road, displays Hancock's coach in the carriage shed. The house, containing original furnishings, is operated by the Society of Colonial Dames. (Open mid-April–October 31, Tuesday–Sunday 10:00–5:00; 617-472-5117; admission.)

HAWTHORNE, NATHANIEL (1804–1864). **Salem** was the author's native town and the place where he produced his best creative work. Despite the fact that he disliked Salem and Salem disliked him, the town has done a remarkable job of preserving most of the Hawthorne buildings and sites. The original site of his birthplace, built by his grandfather in 1772 from a 1750 kitchen, was 27 Union St.; the house was restored and moved in 1958, along with two other old Salem houses, to the garden behind the 1668 "House of the Seven Gables" at 54 Turner St., where Hawthorne frequently visited. The entire complex is operated by the House of the Seven Gables Settlement Association. Hawthorne's birthplace contains period furnishings. (Open mid-June–Labor Day, daily 9:30–6:30; fall, Saturday–Sunday 10:00–4:30; 617-744-0991; admission.) Hawthorne's home from 1808 to 1828 stands at 10½–12 Herbert Street, private and much modified. It was a morbid, unhappy place—"Castle Dismal," he called it—where his widowed mother retreated into her room and Hawthorne also isolated himself in his small, two-room apartment for long intervals. There he did his first writing; and there, he said, "fame was won" when he wrote the first volume of *Twice-Told Tales* (1837). His home at 16 Dearborn St. (1828–32), also private, originally stood across that street. After living in Concord for several years, Hawthorne returned to work in Salem at the Custom House as port surveyor. At 14 Mall St. (privately owned), he wrote *The Scarlet Letter* (1850), probably his best-known work. This was his last Salem home (1847–49).

Hawthorne's first married home was Old Manse National Historic Landmark in **Concord,** where he spent the years from 1842 to 1846, probably the happiest of his life (see the entry on Ralph Waldo Emerson earlier in this section). He worked in the small upstairs study, and the stand-up desk on which he wrote *Mosses from an Old Manse* (1846) is preserved here; on the window, the diamond-etched signatures of the couple can still be seen. The clerical gloom and solitude of the house exactly suited Hawthorne's reclusive spirit, but the couple could not afford to remain here and moved back to Salem. They returned to Concord in 1852, however, and bought what is now Wayside House National Historic Landmark (see the entry on Amos Bronson Alcott and Louisa May Alcott earlier in this section), his last home. In 1860, he built the mansion's tower study and enlarged the two wings. The house contains many Hawthorne furnishings and memorabilia.

In **Lenox,** the Hawthornes lived in 1850 and 1851 at "Red Cottage"—"an ugly little house," he called it—located on the present grounds of the Berkshire Music Festival, West Hawthorne Street. Hawthorne Cottage, a replica built on the old foundations, contains practice rooms for musicians. The author's stay was one of his most productive periods—he wrote *The House of the Seven Gables* (1851) and *Tanglewood Tales* (1853) there—though he found much fault with the area. He roamed freely over the 200-acre estate, which he christened "Tanglewood." Hawthorne Cottage does not host visitors, though the grounds are open daily (free).

Hawthorne was one of the utopian group who tried communal living at Brook Farm in **West Roxbury,** but he rapidly soured on the experiment and stayed only briefly in 1841 (see the entry on Margaret Fuller earlier in this section). He used the Brook Farm setting for his 1852 novel *The Blithedale Romance* (see the entry on Horace Mann later in this section).

Exhibits: In **Salem,** the 1819 Custom House—part of Salem Maritime National Historic Site—is where Hawthorne worked as port surveyor from 1846 to 1849 and made notes for *The Scarlet Letter;* the book's introduction describes this building on Derby Street, opposite Derby Wharf, and its surroundings, now operated by the National Park Service. His stand-up desk, stool and pens are in the room he used as an office. (Open daily 8:30–5:00; 617-744-4323; free.) Also in Salem, Essex Institute at 132 Essex St. contains a pane of glass, from his room in the Herbert Street house, on which he scratched his name. (Open June 1–October 15, Monday–Saturday 9:00–4:30, Sunday 1:00–5:00; October 16–May 31, 1:00–5:00; 617-744-3390; admission.)

(See MAINE in this chapter.)

HOLMES, OLIVER WENDELL (1809–1894). The prominent Boston literary figure and physician was born in **Cambridge** on the present site of Harvard's Littauer Center just east of the Cambridge Common. Known as the "gambrel-roofed house" to generations of Cambridge residents, the yellow and white frame dwelling, built about 1700, fronted south very close to the street. Holmes lived there until 1830. "We Americans live in tents," he mourned as he watched it being demolished in 1884.

In **Boston,** his last home (1871–94) stood at 293 Beacon St. until 1951. This red-brick dwelling, where his rear study overlooked the Charles River, dated from about 1870. The adjoining 296 Beacon St., now a private apartment building, was a part of the original house.

At "Canoe Meadows" (also called "Holmesdale"), the author's summer retreat in **Pittsfield,** he spent seven summers (1849–56) and wrote such poems as "The Deacon's Masterpiece" and "The Ploughman." The privately owned house, built in 1847 on a huge tract owned by his great-grandfather, has been extensively altered and modernized at 497 Holmes Road. Holmes owned 300 acres there, including a farm and woodlot.

In his later years, Holmes purchased the two-story, brown-frame house, at 868 Hale St., that he called "Beverly Farms"—now Holmes National Historic Landmark—for a summer place (1890–94) in **Beverly.** He first knew the area as "Screeching Beach," but dated his letters from there as "Beverly-by-the-Depot," mocking the pretensions of neighboring summer colonists at "Manchester-by-the-Sea." The house is privately owned.

Exhibits: The 1711 Old Corner Bookstore, operated by the *Boston Globe* at School and Washington streets in **Boston,** contains a desk that belonged to Holmes. (Open Monday–Friday, 8:30–6:00, Saturday 8:30–2:00; free).

In **Pittsfield,** the original "one-hoss shay" of

Holmes's poem is displayed at the Berkshire Museum, 39 South St., (Open July 1–August 31, Monday 10:00–5:00; September 1–June 30, Tuesday–Saturday 10:00–5:00, Sunday 1:00–5:00; 413-443-7171; free.)

HOLMES, OLIVER WENDELL, JR. (1841–1935). Known as "the Great Dissenter" during his lengthy tenure as Supreme Court justice, Holmes shared the **Boston** homes of his parents until he moved to Washington, D.C. The summer house "Beverly Farms" also became his own longtime vacation retreat (see the entry on Oliver Wendell Holmes above).

(See Chapter 3, DISTRICT OF COLUMBIA.)

HOMER, WINSLOW (1836–1910). In **Boston,** according to biographer Gordon Hendricks, if you stand "at the top of the auto ramp debouching on New Sudbury Street from the John F. Kennedy Federal Building," you will be "at or near the spot where Homer was born." The house at 25 Friend St. (1 Dock Square) was demolished in the 1860s for the Washington Street cut. A marker identifies the site.

The painter's only extant Massachusetts residence—and his home base during years of travel—stands at 39 Centre Ave. (privately owned) in **Belmont.** This small, 19th-century house, which the Homer family rented from 1858 into the 1870s originally stood across the street. Homer's studio was in the second-floor rear.

(See MAINE in this chapter; also Chapter 2, MANHATTAN.)

HOPPER, EDWARD (1882–1967). At **South Truro** on Cape Cod, the "painter of loneliness" built his longtime summer home and studio, a shingled dwelling, in 1930. It stands without significant alterations on a nameless, one-lane dirt road off Fisher Road and remains in private hands.

(See Chapter 2, MANHATTAN; also Chapter 3, NEW YORK.)

HUTCHINSON, ANNE (1591–1643). The Old Corner Bookstore at School and Washington Streets in **Boston** (see the entry on Oliver Wendell Holmes earlier in this section) stands on the site of Hutchinson's home from 1634 to 1638, to which, wrote Samuel Eliot Morison, she "attracted people by her wit and personality in order to discuss sermons." As a result of those discussions, she was banished as a religious heretic by Gov. John Winthrop (see the entry on Winthrop later in this section).

(See RHODE ISLAND in this chapter; also Chapter 2, BRONX.)

INNESS, GEORGE (1825–1894). The painter's home in **Medfield,** where he lived from 1859 to 1864—his "most important years," according to his son—stands at 406 Main St., a two and one-half-story clapboard dwelling that dates from about 1810. It was a double tenement when Inness lived there. The back barn that also stands was his studio; there he completed one of his best-known paintings, "Peace and Plenty." In 1981, local interest in preserving this unrenovated property looked dim despite attempts of owner-artist Nancy S. Franke to enlist support.

(See Chapter 3, NEW JERSEY.)

JAMES, HENRY (1843–1916). **Cambridge** was the novelist's most frequent residence before 1875, when he made his permanent home in Europe, and during his occasional visits to the U.S. thereafter. The family home, dating from about 1850 at 20 Quincy St., stood until 1894 and is the present site of the Harvard Faculty Club.

James also resided at various times in **Boston.** At 102 Mount Vernon St. ("the only respectable street in America," he claimed), he worked in 1882 on the dramatization of his novel *Daisy Miller* (1879) in "bare and ugly, but comfortable" rooms. This house is still occupied by private apartments—as is 131 Mount Vernon St., where he lived with his father and sister in 1882 and 1883.

(See RHODE ISLAND in this chapter; also Chapter 2, MANHATTAN.)

JAMES, WILLIAM (1842–1910). Psychologist and philosopher, William James shared the early Quincy Street home of his parents in **Cambridge** (see the entry on Henry James above). His permanent home, which he designed and built in 1889, was 95 Irving St., where his novelist brother also stopped at lengthy intervals. The square, three-story, cedar-shingled house is now a private residence owned by Harvard University.

(See NEW HAMPSHIRE, RHODE ISLAND in this chapter; also Chapter 2, MANHATTAN.)

JOHNSON, JAMES WELDON (1871–1938). Black author, diplomat and civil rights activist, John-son purchased his **Great Barrington** summer home, "Five Acres," in 1925. Originally a barn of uncertain date and a portion of an old mill complex that Johnson renovated, the dwelling is now a private home with an unchanged exterior on Seekonk Road.

(See Chapter 2, MANHATTAN; also Chapter 5, FLORIDA, TENNESSEE.)

KELLER, HELEN ADAMS (1880–1968). In **Watertown,** the author and humanitarian learned Braille at the 1832 Perkins School for the Blind, where she lived with her teacher, Anne Sullivan from 1889 to 1893. The Museum on the History of Blindness at Perkins School, 175 North Beacon St., contains material on both women plus some of Helen Keller's letters. (Open Monday–Friday 8:30–12:00, 1:00–5:00; 617-924-3434; free.)

Helen Keller's 19th-century home in **Wrentham** (1903–17) stands privately owned at 349 East St.

(See CONNECTICUT in this chapter; also Chapter 2, QUEENS; also Chapter 5, ALABAMA.)

KENNEDY, JOHN FITZGERALD (1917–1963). KENNEDY, ROBERT FRANCIS (1925–1968).

Kennedy National Historic Site in **Brookline** (suburban Boston) is the birthplace of the 35th U.S. president. The modest frame house, built about 1908, contains family furnishings. An arsonist's firebomb that destroyed the kitchen in 1975 enabled government historians to restore the interior, with the help of the president's mother Rose Kennedy, to the way it appeared from 1917 to 1921. Visitors may hear Mrs. Kennedy's recorded voice detailing various aspects of the house and the family years there. The dwelling passed through six owners before the family bought it back in 1966 and deeded it to the federal government. It is operated by the National Park Service. (Open daily 10:00–4:30; 617-566-7937; admission.) Robert Kennedy was born at a later family home (1921–26) at 131 Naples Road, privately owned.

Hyannis Port on Cape Cod has been the permanent Kennedy family home since 1928. Kennedy Compound National Historic Landmark consists of three large frame houses on a 4.7-acre lot. The parents' "Big House," the oldest, dates from 1904. John F. Kennedy's own two-story, white shingled summer home stands to

JOHN F. KENNEDY'S HOME IN THE KENNEDY COMPOUND. In May 1963 the president walks to his white-shingled summer White House in **Hyannis Port** with aides as he prepares to welcome Canadian Prime Minister Lester Pearson. The Kennedy family has occupied the three-house lot since 1928. The Kennedy compound is not open to the public.
(Courtesy John F. Kennedy Library.)

the rear; and the 12-room residence of Robert Kennedy is on the right. Kennedy Compound was home base for the 1960 Democratic presidential campaign and also served as the 1961 summer White House. The entire complex is still owned by the family, and visitors are not admitted.

Exhibit: The John F. Kennedy Library, located adjacent to the University of Massachusetts on Morrissey Boulevard in **Dorchester** (suburban Boston), contains numerous displays of Kennedy memorabilia, including a recreation of the White House Oval Office with his rocking chair and a replica of his desk. Dedicated in 1979, the nine-story concrete and glass structure was designed by architect I. M. Pei and is operated by the General Services Administration. (Open daily 9:00–5:00; 617-929-4535; admission.)

(SEE RHODE ISLAND in this chapter; also Chapter 2, BRONX; also Chapter 3, DISTRICT OF COLUMBIA, NEW YORK; also Chapter 4, MICHIGAN; also Chapter 5, FLORIDA, VIRGINIA; also Chapter 6, CALIFORNIA, TEXAS.)

KEROUAC, JACK (1922–1969). Chronicler of the "beat generation" in his novels, the author was born Jean Louis Lebris Kerouac in **Lowell** in the second-floor apartment at 9 Lupine Road (1922–24), a shingled home. Later boyhood homes (see Name Index and Gazetteer) are all plain, privately owned dwellings built around the turn of the century. Kerouac returned to Lowell often, if briefly, throughout his frenetic life; his last Lowell residence at 271 Sanders Ave., where he lived with his wife and mother in 1967 and 1968, is a modern suburban ranch home.

(See Chapter 2, MANHATTAN, QUEENS; also Chapter 3, NEW YORK; also Chapter 5, FLORIDA; also Chapter 6, CALIFORNIA.)

KOUSSEVITSKY, SERGE (1874–1951). The conductor of the Boston Symphony Orchestra from 1924 to 1949 rented several suburban Boston homes during his American musical career. Koussevitsky liked the Jamaica Pond area because in winter the snowscape reminded him of his native Russia. Until 1932 he lived on Pond Avenue and at 60 Rockwood St.—plain, unpretentious dwellings in **Jamaica Plain.** He rented a more modern dwelling at 265 Goddard Ave. from 1942 to 1945. All of these houses are privately owned.

In **Brookline,** from 1945 to his death, he occupied the only American home he ever owned at 191 Buckminster Rd. (privately owned), built about 1909.

LEWIS, SINCLAIR (1885–1951). "Thorvale Farm," four and one-half miles south of **Williamstown** on Oblong Road, was the author's last home (1946–49) in the United States. The estate, with its numerous outbuildings and superb view of Mount Greylock, now houses the Novitiate of the Carmelite Fathers Chapel. Typically, Lewis bought 750 acres and made a huge project of enlarging and improving the house before growing restless and moving on. Lewis had a genius, wrote biographer Mark Schorer, "for choosing to live in houses that were quite beyond the possibility of being shaken down into homes."

(See VERMONT in this chapter; also Chapter 2, MANHATTAN; also Chapter 3, NEW YORK; also Chapter 4, MINNESOTA.)

LODGE, HENRY CABOT (1850–1924). Historian and U.S. Senator for 31 years, Lodge led Republican opposition to American entry into the League of Nations. His only extant home is the privately owned Lodge House National Historic Landmark at 5 Cliff St. in **Nahant,** an elaborate brick and stucco mansion built about 1868. This property, the site of a hotel where Lodge vacationed from boyhood and which was destroyed by fire in 1861, was long owned by his family before the construction of the present dwelling.

The site of Lodge's **Boston** home from 1859 to 1900 is the present location of his statue on the Massachusetts State House grounds, formerly 31 Beacon St.

(See Chapter 3, DISTRICT OF COLUMBIA.)

LONGFELLOW, HENRY WADSWORTH (1807–1882). At 105 Brattle St. in **Cambridge,** Longfellow National Historic Landmark, a fine Georgian frame mansion built in 1759 by Tory Major John Vassall, contains the poet's personal effects, Victorian furnishings, library and family rooms just as he left them. The study where he wrote his best-known works is meticulously preserved, with his table, stand-up desk and a chair carved from the "spreading chestnut tree." In that room and the library occurred a tragic accident in 1861 when his wife's dress caught fire and fatally burned her. Longfellow, shattered for months, grew his patriarchal beard to hide his own facial scars from the incident. He first lived there as a boarder on the second floor from 1837 to 1843; when he married Fanny Appleton in 1843, his father-in-law bought the house and gave it to the couple as a wedding present and permanent home. Years earlier, in 1775 and 1776, George Washington had used the house as his headquarters during the siege of Boston. Vassall's original estate consisted of several hundred acres, now reduced to gardens behind the house, which is operated by the National Park Service. The carriage house also contains Longfellow exhibits. (Open daily 10:00–4:30; 617-876-4491; admission.)

(See MAINE in this chapter.)

LOWELL, JAMES RUSSELL (1819–1891). In **Cambridge,** Elmwood National Historic Landmark at Elmwood Avenue and Mount Auburn Street was the author-poet's birthplace and lifelong home. This three-story house, built on a huge country estate in 1767, was the earlier home of Elbridge Gerry (see the entry on Gerry earlier in this section) and also served as a hospital after the Battle of Bunker Hill in 1775. Now a Harvard faculty residence, it does not admit visitors.

LOWELL, ROBERT TRAILL SPENCE, JR. (1917–1977). The poet's boyhood home from 1924 to 1927 stands at 91 Revere St. (privately owned) in **Boston.** In his essay "91 Revere Street" in *Life Studies* (1959), Lowell recorded his unhappiness in this "squalid, impractical" brick house that dates from about 1850. His mother, he wrote, complained that "we are barely perched on the outer rim of the hub of decency." From 1927, the parental home until Lowell's mother sold it in 1950 was 170 Marlborough St., a four-story townhouse built in 1874. Lowell bought another four-story house, also dating from 1874, at 239 Marlborough St., which he and his wife occu-

WASHINGTON'S HEAD QUARTERS, AT CAMBRIDGE, MASS., THE RESIDENCE OF PROFESSOR LONGFELLOW.

HENRY WADSWORTH LONGFELLOW HOUSE. This sketch of the 1759 mansion at 105 Brattle Street in **Cambridge,** the poet's idyllic home for 45 years, shows the property as it looked when he lived there. George Washington waited out the British siege of Boston in 1775–76 in this same house.

Rooms containing Longfellow's furnishings appear just as they did when his patriarchal presence made the home a literary mecca.
(Courtesy Longfellow National Historic Site.)

pied from 1954 to 1959. "The idea was to test his heritage," said a friend. "It was their first attempt to be Boston Lowells." And their last. Both houses are privately owned.

(See MAINE in this chapter; also Chapter 2, MANHATTAN; also Chapter 4, OHIO.)

MACK, CONNIE (1862–1956). The baseball player and longtime manager of the Philadelphia Athletics was born Cornelius McGillicuddy in **East Brookfield;** his 19th-century birthplace stands marked at Maple and Main streets and is privately owned.

(See Chapter 3, PENNSYLVANIA.)

MANN, HORACE (1796–1859). Educator,

reformer and congressman, Mann was born in **Franklin** at a marked site on East Central Street. This was "Mann's Plain," location of the homestead established by his great-grandfather in 1720. In 1838, Mann sold the property, but the house was not finally razed until about 1940.

In **Dedham,** where Mann practiced law, his rented home from 1830 to 1832 was 19 Franklin Square (at the corner of Church Street). That home, where his first wife died, was demolished in about 1925; the building has been replaced by a private home. The structure that contained his law office, however, remains at 74 Church St.

"I do not live anywhere, I board," he said for years thereafter. In 1846, he finally settled in **West Newton,** where he built a small home in a two-acre wooded grove. The house had "but one luxury," he wrote, "a room for a friend, and a plate at the table." In 1851, Nathaniel Hawthorne (see the entry on Hawthorne earlier in this section) wrote *The Blithedale Romance* (1852) in the house while staying as the Manns' house guest. Mann lived here until 1853. Torn down sometime after 1900, the house stood on the west side of Chestnut Street (at the corner of Highland Street).

(See Chapter 4, OHIO.)

MARCIANO, ROCKY (1924–1969). The heavyweight boxer who retired undefeated in 1956 was born Rocco Francis Marchegiano in **Brockton** at 80 Brook St. The small house was built before 1898 and belonged to Marciano's grandfather. The family lived in four unheated rooms upstairs until 1939. A 1915, two-story shingled house at 168 Dover St. was the family home from 1939 to 1953. By 1953, Marciano could afford to build a house for his wife and himself at 31 Harlan Drive, and this was his last home. All three dwellings are privately owned.

(See Chapter 5, FLORIDA.)

MARQUAND, JOHN PHILLIPS (1893–1960). The Marquand family homestead was "Curzon's Mill," a seven-acre tract near **Newburyport** consisting of the 18th-century "Yellow House," a frame dwelling originally built as a hunting lodge; the later "Red Brick House"; and an 1846 gristmill. The author's great-grandfather bought the property in 1820, and the "Yellow House" became Marquand's boyhood home from 1907 to 1911. He returned at intervals throughout his life, wrote *The Late George Apley* (1937) here, and used the setting in *Wickford Point* (1939). The property, located on Curzon Mill Road, is privately owned. From 1938, Marquand made his permanent home on Kent's Island at the edge of a salt marsh near Newburyport, adding two immense wings to the small farmhouse over several years; and there he died. Owned by the commonwealth of Massachusetts, the house in 1981 was slated for destruction despite vocal opposition.

In **Boston,** the author whose novels gently satirized a certain type of Bostonian resided longest at 43 West Cedar St. (1927–38). Built in the 1880s, the house is now a private, two-family dwelling.

(See Chapter 2, MANHATTAN; also Chapter 3, DELAWARE, NEW YORK; also Chapter 5, FLORIDA, NORTH CAROLINA.)

MATHER, COTTON (1663–1728). None of the Puritan clergyman's homes have survived the numerous fires of early **Boston.** The highly influential spiritual arbiter of the colonial city and son of Rev. Increase Mather was born in a square, double house that stood near the present Pemberton Square, where he lived with his parents to age seven. The family's next home (1670–76) occupied 19 North Square, the present site of Paul Revere House National Historic Landmark (see the entry on Revere later in this section); the Mather house there was destroyed by fire in wooden Boston's conflagration of 1676. Mather's last home (1685–1728) stood at the southwest corner of Hanover and Prince streets, where he kept a 3,000-volume library, one of the largest in the colonies. On a 1724 visit there, the lad Benjamin Franklin (see the entry on Franklin earlier in this section) cracked his head on a low beam. Never one to miss a chance for admonition, Mather told the smarting Franklin: "You are young and have the world before you. Stoop as you go through it and you will miss many hard thumps."

MELVILLE, HERMAN (1819–1891). Arrowhead National Historic Landmark, the author's home from 1850 to 1863, stands on 14 of the original 160 farmland acres that he bought near **Pittsfield** and found full of Indian arrowheads. The 1780 white frame house at 780 Holmes Road has been extensively altered since his residence, but the Berkshire County Historical Society has undertaken an ambitious renovation program that will eventually restore the entire dwelling to its 1860 appearance. Melville whimsically suggested that "this house would appear to have been built simply for the accommodation of my chimney," which dominated the structure. He wrote *Moby Dick* (1851), *Pierre* (1852), and *The Piazza Tales* (1856) in his upstairs study there. Numerous personal items and furnishings are displayed in the family dining room. (Open May 1–October 31, Monday, Wednesday–Saturday 10:00–5:00, Sunday 1:00–5:00; November 1–April 30, Tuesday–Sunday 2:00–5:00; 413-442-1793; admission.)

Exhibit: The Melville Memorial Room in The Berkshire Athenaeum, 1 Wendell Ave. in **Pittsfield,** displays the largest collection of the author's memorabilia. (Open June 16–September 14, Monday, Thursday 10:00–9:00, Tuesday, Wednesday, Friday 10:00–5:00, Saturday 10:00–1:00;

September 15–June 15, Monday–Thursday 10:00–9:00, Friday–Saturday 10:00–5:00; 413-442-1559; free.)

(See Chapter 2, MANHATTAN; also Chapter 3, NEW YORK.)

MORSE, SAMUEL FINLEY BREESE (1791–1872). In the Charlestown section of **Boston,** the painter-scientist-inventor was born at a once-marked site presently occupied by a store at 199–205 Main St. Morse's birthplace, his home until 1817, was the first house to be rebuilt on fire-leveled Town Hill after British soldiers departed in 1776. It stood until 1928.

(See CONNECTICUT in this chapter; also Chapter 2, MANHATTAN; also Chapter 3, NEW YORK.)

MOTT, LUCRETIA COFFIN (1793–1880). The girlhood home of the pioneering feminist and abolitionist until 1804, a privately owned house dating from 1790, stands at 15 Fair St. in **Nantucket.** Her birthplace stood next door to this house until 1820.

(See Chapter 3, PENNSYLVANIA.)

NABOKOV, VLADIMIR VLADIMIROVICH (1899–1977). In **Cambridge,** the novelist lived from 1942 to 1948 in a rented apartment at 8 Craigie Circle (privately owned) while teaching Russian at Wellesley College. He used scenes from this 1917 structure in his book *Bend Sinister* (1947).

(See Chapter 3, NEW YORK.)

OLMSTED, FREDERICK LAW (1822–1903). Olmsted House National Historic Site at 99 Warren St. in **Brookline,** a two-story clapboard house built in 1810, was the noted landscape architect's home from 1883 to 1898. He enlarged the dwelling to accommodate a northeast ground-floor office, putting his bedroom directly overhead. Recently opened to visitors, the house is operated by the National Park Service. (Call for hours and admission; 617-566-1689).

Olmsted's last years of extreme senility (1898–1903) were spent in Hope Cottage on the grounds of McLean Asylum, now McLean Hospital, at 115 Mill St. in **Belmont.** The two-story brick house, dating from 1896—not a small or inelegant residence—was used until 1978 to house VIP patients. According to hospital archivist Alexander Armour, it now serves "as a sort of halfway house for resident patients." Ironically, Olmsted himself had designed the hospital grounds some 20 years before his admission as a patient.

(See CONNECTICUT, MAINE in this chapter; also Chapter 2, STATEN ISLAND.)

O'NEILL, EUGENE GLADSTONE (1888–1953). The playwright lived on both the east and the west coasts during his peripatetic career, but the first and last homes that he owned were both in Massachusetts. At **Provincetown** on Cape Cod, his summer beach cottage, "Peaked Hill Bar," weathered high tides and storms from 1919 until 1930, when it finally washed into the sea. Before 1920, he also stayed briefly in an apartment at 577 Commercial St. (privately owned), since remodeled and renovated for studios and offices.

The last home he owned was a six-room, Victorian cottage perched on a cliff near **Marblehead;** built about 1900, the house clung by cables to the rocks. Carlotta Monterey O'Neill, his third wife, renovated the cottage, and the volatile couple lived there in almost unbroken solitude from 1948 to 1951. Both ended with nervous breakdowns and separated briefly thereafter. The privately owned house stands on Point O'Rocks Lane at Marblehead Neck.

O'Neill's residence from 1951, and where he died, was Suite 401 of the Shelton Hotel, 91 Bay State Road in **Boston.** Palsied and debilitated after years of physical decline, some of his last words were furious: "I knew it, I knew it! Born in a hotel room—goddamn it—and dying in a hotel room!" That building, which dates from 1923, is now Boston University's Shelton Hall.

(See CONNECTICUT in this chapter; also Chapter 2, MANHATTAN; also Chapter 5, GEORGIA; also Chapter 6, CALIFORNIA.)

PATTON, GEORGE SMITH, JR. (1885–1945). The flamboyant World War II general made his permanent home at "Green Meadows," a 1786 mansion that stands on a broad acreage at 650 Asbury St. in **South Hamilton.** Patton's farm, where he retired between assignments and during annual leaves to ride, hunt and rest, is privately owned.

(See Chapter 3, DISTRICT OF COLUMBIA; also Chapter 5, KENTUCKY, VIRGINIA; also Chapter 6, CALIFORNIA.)

PEIRCE, CHARLES SANDERS (1839–1914). A gray frame house at 11 Mason St. in **Cambridge** was the mathematician-philosopher's birthplace and childhood home. Now considerably altered from its 1835 design, it houses Weston Theological School.

(See Chapter 3, MARYLAND, PENNSYLVANIA.)

PHILLIPS, WENDELL (1811–1884). The birthplace of the abolitionist orator stands at the corner of Beacon and Walnut streets in **Boston.** This was the first brick house built (1805) on Beacon Street and Phillips' home until 1827. It is privately owned. His home from 1841 to 1882 stood at 26 Essex St. near Harrison Avenue. This narrow, brick, three-story house was "not fashionably located," but Phillips deplored the necessity of moving when the house was condemned in 1882 for the extension of Harrison Avenue.

Exhibit: The front door of Phillips' longtime home on Essex Street is displayed by the Bostonian Society in the Old State House, 206 Washington St. (Open Monday–Friday 10:00–4:00, Saturday 9:30–5:00, Sunday 11:00–5:00; 617-242-5610; admission.)

PLATH, SYLVIA (1932–1963). The poet whose tragically short life ended by suicide in England was a Massachusetts native. Her parents' small house at 92 Johnson Ave. in **Winthrop** (1936–42) is being considered for designation as a historical site.

Following the death of Plath's father, her mother purchased a white frame, two-story, 1940 house at 26 Elmwood Road in **Wellesley,** where the poet lived during her high school and college years (1942–55); this was her last home in America. Both houses are privately owned.

POE, EDGAR ALLAN (1809–1849). **Boston** was the birthplace of this major American writer and stylist. The exact site, though once disputed among Poe scholars, is undoubtedly 62 Carver St., an 1801 house that stood until sometime after 1924. The son of an impoverished, itinerant acting couple, the infant lived there for only a year before his deserted mother took him to Richmond, Va. Carver Street now ends at Number 20.

(See Chapter 2, BRONX, MANHATTAN; also Chapter 3, MARYLAND, PENNSYLVANIA; also Chapter 5, VIRGINIA.)

POST, EMILY PRICE (1873–1960). Her *Etiquette* (1922) became the frequently updated arbiter of social manners, though Emily Post said she never intended to become an authority on the subject. At **Edgartown** on Martha's Vineyard, she bought and renovated an early 19th-century house topped with a "widow's walk" in 1926 and made it her permanent summer home. *The Personality of a House* (1948) details her love affair with the place, which stands unnumbered and privately owned on Fuller Street.

(See Chapter 2, MANHATTAN; also Chapter 3, MARYLAND, NEW YORK.)

REVERE, PAUL (1735–1818). The silversmith patriot and horseback-riding hero of the poem by Henry Wadsworth Longfellow (see the entry on Longfellow earlier in this section) was a lifelong resident of **Boston,** where he was born at the site of Prince and Garden streets, near the southwest corner. From Revere's boyhood until 1768, the family lived "near the head of Doctor Clark's Wharf on Fish Street"; this house would have stood on the present North Street between Lewis and Fleet streets. Revere House National Historic Landmark at 19 North Square, built about 1677 and purchased by Revere in 1770, is the only surviving structure from Boston's first half-century, a rare example of the urban dwellings of that period. The two-story frame house, built on the embers of the boyhood home of Cotton Mather (see the entry on Mather earlier in this section) was one of Boston's older buildings even when Revere occupied it, from 1770 to 1880 and from 1789 to 1799. Some observers have suggested that very little of the structure is entirely original. But until 1908, when it was carefully restored, the dwelling underwent "minimal structural alteration," according to Bryn E. Evans, director of the Paul Revere Memorial Association, which maintains the property. Yet "it is erroneous to suggest that we present the house 'as it was,' " Evans writes; "we present it as it *is:* The Revere House is being preserved as restored." Among the period items displayed are five pieces of Revere's furniture and a set of gunners' calipers he used. (Open April 15–October 31, daily 10:00–6:00; November 1–April 14, 10:00–4:00; 617-523-1676; admission.) After Revere sold this dwelling in 1800, he bought a house near the corner of Charter and Unity streets, a three-story, yellow-painted brick dwelling with a 64-foot frontage.

OLD NORTH SQUARE.

OLD NORTH SQUARE. This earliest engraving of the Paul Revere House at 19 North Square in **Boston,** by A. Harrals, dates from about 1870. The Revere House, on the left, is the oldest standing house in Boston, but the home's present appearance resembles this woodcut view only in general outline. Thoroughgoing restoration in 1908 removed the attic floor seen here. This was Revere's residence during most of the Revolution, the house from which he set out on his famous "midnight ride." *(Courtesy Boston Athenaeum.)*

Revere, who proudly wore his Revolutionary War uniform into old age, died there. The house later became a haven for "Penitent Females" and was demolished in 1843.

During summers after 1801, Revere lived at "Canton Dale," a plain, two-story frame house at 91 Neponset St. (privately owned) in **Canton.** Nearby, the brick building in which he established the nation's first copper rolling mill stands on the property of the Plymouth Rubber Co. at 104 Revere St. and is currently used as a rubber mixing area. The structure displays a historical marker.

RIIS, JACOB AUGUST (1849–1914). On his wife's suggestion—"that she raise the crops, I do the Rip Van Winkle act"—the Danish-born urban reformer bought "Crown Hill," a century-old house on 200 acres near **Barre,** in 1911. They restored the house, and Riis died here soon after.

Located off Hubbardston Road, it was razed during the 1930s for the Quabbin Reservoir watershed.

(See Chapter 2, QUEENS.)

ROCKWELL, NORMAN (1894–1978). The popular painter-illustrator came to **Stockbridge** in 1953, occupying the yellow frame house on West Main Street next to Stockbridge Cemetery until 1957. Viewing the tombstones from his breakfast room was, he thought, "a good way to start the day." His last home, also in Stockbridge, is a large, 18th-century, white frame house on South Street. He converted the old carriage house in the rear to a studio and also built a living room addition and a glassed-in porch. Rockwell died there, just of "being 84 years old," said his wife. Both houses are privately owned.

Exhibit: The Old Corner House, opened in 1969 at Main and Elm streets in **Stockbridge,** displays many of his original paintings. (Open daily 10:00–5:00; 413-298-3822; admission.)

(See VERMONT in this chapter; also Chapter 2, MANHATTAN; also Chapter 3, NEW YORK, PENNSYLVANIA.)

ROYCE, JOSIAH (1855–1916). A resident of **Cambridge** from 1882, Harvard's pragmatic philosopher lived in three homes, all of which remain in private hands. These include 14 Sumner Road (1882–85), built in 1853; 20 Lowell St. (1885–89), dating from about 1870; and his last, at 103 Irving St., a new dwelling (1889) on the freshly subdivided estate of Harvard president Charles Eliot Norton.

(See Chapter 6, CALIFORNIA.)

RUTH, GEORGE HERMAN "BABE" (1895–1948). At 558 Dutton Road (at the corner of Hudson Road) near **Sudbury** stands "Home Plate," the handsome frame farmhouse on 80 acres purchased in 1922 by baseball's home run king. The 1880 house was erected on the site of a 1700 dwelling destroyed by fire. Ruth lived there until 1926, when he and his first wife separated. The house is now the private property of the Sudbury Foundation.

(See Chapter 2, MANHATTAN; also Chapter 3, MARYLAND, NEW YORK.)

SANTAYANA, GEORGE (1863–1952). In **Boston,** the author-philosopher's 1869 boyhood home

(1872–81) stood at 302 Beacon St. until 1933. Santayana wrote about this house in *Persons and Places* (1944), describing it as a pretentious "white elephant" with its expansive plate glass, brick facade and narrow width. A five-unit apartment dwelling now occupies the site.

His **Cambridge** residence from 1910 to 1912 is still a private apartment house, built about 1903, at 474 Broadway.

SCHOENBERG, ARNOLD (1874–1951). The Austrian composer came to America in 1933 as a refugee from Nazism. He taught and conducted in Boston for a year and during this time resided at Pelham Hall Apartments in suburban **Brookline.** The 1925 building where he occupied Apartment 720 still stands at 1284 Beacon St. and remains a private apartment residence.

(See Chapter 6, CALIFORNIA.)

SHERIDAN, PHILIP HENRY (1831–1888). The Civil War Union general and later U.S. Army commander built his two-story frame vacation house by the sea in 1888 and died there the same year. The house still stands in **Nonquitt,** privately owned by Carlina Sheridan McElroy; check locally for directions.

(See Chapter 4, OHIO; also Chapter 5, VIRGINIA.)

SHERMAN, ROGER (1721–1793). **Newton** was the Revolutionary patriot's birthplace and home until age two. The dwelling stood at a marked site on Waverly Avenue near Cotton Street.

(See CONNECTICUT in this chapter.)

SPELLMAN, FRANCIS JOSEPH (1889–1967). **Whitman** was the Roman Catholic cardinal's birthplace. Spellman was born in the family apartment over his father's grocery store on South Street. A jewelry store now occupies the former grocery. Spellman's boyhood home from 1895 to 1911 stands at 96 Beulah St. (privately owned), a large 19th-century frame house with few exterior alterations. Though he often returned to Whitman in later years, he revisited this house only once, during the 1960s.

At **Newton Centre,** Spellman resided in Sacred Heart Parish Rectory at 1321 Centre St. from 1933 to 1939.

Exhibit: The Johnston Funeral Home at 760 Washington St., **Whitman,** now occupies the house built by the cardinal for his mother. A room has been set aside there for display of Spellman memorabilia (inquire locally for admission information).

(See Chapter 2, MANHATTAN.)

STANDISH, MILES (1584?–1656). The military leader of Plymouth Colony, Standish resided in **Plymouth** at a site fronting the north side of Leyden Street at the foot of Burial Hill (1620–31), just east of the lot owned by John Alden (see the entry on Alden earlier in this section). In modern Plymouth, this would be near the northwest corner of the town square at the end of Leyden Street.

In **South Duxbury,** Standish's later home (1631–56) stood on a marked site off Columbus Street at Standish Shore overlooking Plymouth Bay.

Exhibits: See the entry on William Bradford earlier in this section.

STILWELL, JOSEPH WARREN (1883–1946). Called "Warren" by his family, the World War II general who led American ground forces in Asia lived in **Great Barrington** as a boy. His father built the frame house at 111 West Ave. in 1892, and the family lived there until 1896. The dwelling remains privately owned.

(See Chapter 6, CALIFORNIA.)

STOWE, HARRIET BEECHER (1811–1896). The novelist and reformer had two residences in **Andover** from 1852. The first was Samaritan House at 6 School St., where she wrote *A Key to Uncle Tom's Cabin* (1853) and awaited completion of remodeling at 80 Bartlett St., her home until 1864. The latter house, originally a shop used for making coffins and wheelbarrows, was built about 1828; royalties from her book *Uncle Tom's Cabin* (1852) paid for its extensive renovation. This stone house, which she called "The Cabin," fronted on Chapel Street during her residence and became the Phillips Inn after she left. In 1929, it was moved back from the street to its present site behind Andover Inn. Both Andover residences are privately owned.

(See CONNECTICUT, MAINE in this chapter; also Chapter 4, OHIO.)

STUART, GILBERT CHARLES (1755–1828). The painter lived in Boston from 1805 to 1828 at several addresses on Washington, Common and Devon-

shire streets, but none of the precise spots are known. In what is today suburban **Jamaica Plain,** he occupied a 1790 house that stood until the late 1800s near the corner of Glen Road and Washington Street, Franklin Park.

His last home in **Boston,** the three-story brick house where he died, stood at 59 Essex St.; a commercial building now occupies the site.

(See RHODE ISLAND in this chapter; also Chapter 3, DISTRICT OF COLUMBIA, PENNSYLVANIA.)

THOREAU, HENRY DAVID (1817–1862). **Concord** was the naturalist-philosopher's home for almost his entire life, and he occupied at least seven houses there at various times. His privately owned birthplace, the girlhood home of his mother, stands on Virginia Road about a half mile from Old Bedford Road. A marker identifies the original site of the frame house, which was moved 100 rods eastward to its present location in 1878. Thoreau, born in the eastern upstairs room, lived there for only his first eight months. The family moved frequently until 1827, then settled at 63 Main St. (privately owned) until 1835. His aunt's house, where the family next lived, had been purchased by his grandfather in 1799; it now forms the eastern end of the Colonial Inn near Concord Square. Parkman House, the family home from 1837 to 1844, stood on the rear half of the lot where the Concord Free Public Library is now located. There Thoreau began keeping a journal in an attic room and he and his elder brother John started a public school in 1838. Thoreau was caretaker of the Emerson House for two periods in the 1840s, occupying the small bedroom at the top of the stairs (see the entry on Ralph Waldo Emerson earlier in this section). The "Texas House," built by Thoreau and his father in 1844, stood next to the present Thoreau Lyceum on Belknap Street. Thoreau dug and stoned the cellar and planted shrubbery around the house; fire and a hurricane destroyed this house in the 1930s. The privately owned Thoreau-Alcott House, still standing at 255 Main St., was Thoreau's last home (1850–62). Known as the "Yellow House," this clapboard dwelling dates from about 1820; Thoreau planted many of the large trees in the yard and helped build the rear extension that housed the family pencil business. His study was the room to the right of the front entrance, and an attic room held his journals and collections of arrowheads, rocks and pressed flowers. He died in the first-floor parlor after a long physical decline. Later residents here were Amos Bronson Alcott and Louisa May Alcott (see the entry on the Alcotts earlier in this section).

Walden (1854), Thoreau's best-known book, described his experiences at Walden Pond, just south of Concord. Thoreau built his cabin on the north shore of the 64-acre pond in 1845 and lived there for two years, two months and two days. The 10-x-15-foot cabin, which he built for $28.12½ on land owned by Emerson, was erected over a six-foot-square cellar hole, which Thoreau dug (and which, a century later, was found to contain hundreds of bent, discarded nails). Thoreau wrote *A Week on the Concord and Merrimack Rivers* (1849) and most of *Walden* here. The exact site of the long-gone cabin, scavenged for roof and timbers by local farmers, was unknown until 1945, when foundation pieces were discovered in the roots of a fallen white pine. Today Walden Pond National Historic Landmark at 915 Walden St. (U.S. Highway 26) is a 200-acre preserve operated by the Mass. Department of Natural Resources. A half-mile rugged path leads from the parking lot to the marked cabin site at the far end of the pond; picnic grounds and a swimming beach are closer to the road. (Open daily during daylight hours; free.)

Exhibits: A room in the **Concord** Antiquarian Society Museum at 200 Lexington Road re-creates the interior of Thoreau's Walden cabin, containing his hand-hewn furniture, writing desk, snowshoes, surveying equipment and flute. Some of his survey maps are also displayed. (Open Monday–Saturday 10:00–4:30, Sunday 2:00–4:30; 617-369-9609; admission.) The Thoreau Lyceum at 156 Belknap St., operated by the Thoreau Foundation, displays his town desk, original surveying maps, Indian artifacts, pencils made at the family shop and pieces of the original Walden cabin. A fine replica of the cabin itself, exact in every detail, stands behind the Lyceum. (Open Monday–Saturday 10:00–5:00, Sunday 2:00–5:00; 617-369-5912; admission.) Concord Free Public Library, 129 Main St., has many Thoreau editions as well as manuscripts and books from his own library. (Open Monday–Friday 9:00–9:00, Saturday 9:00–6:00; 617-369-2309; free).

Another Thoreau exhibit at Fruitlands Museums in **Harvard** includes a desk, driftwood bookcases and a collection of rocks and Indian relics (see

the entries on the Alcotts earlier in this section).

A Thoreau Gazetteer (1970) by Robert F. Stowell is an excellent guide to Thoreau territory in Concord and elsewhere.

TILLICH, PAUL JOHANNES (1886–1965). The theologian rented an apartment at 16 Chauncy St. in **Cambridge** during his teaching years at Harvard (1955–62). The 1929 building, the scene of numerous informal student seminars conducted by Tillich, remains a private apartment dwelling.

(See Chapter 3, NEW YORK; also Chapter 4, ILLINOIS.)

TRUTH, SOJOURNER (1797?–1883). The slave-born abolitionist orator bought a house and 60-square-rod lot in Florence, a suburb of **Northampton,** in 1850. This house, where she lived for seven years during her association with an abolitionist group, is probably the present 45 Park St. (privately owned).

(See Chapter 3, NEW YORK; also Chapter 4, MICHIGAN.)

WASHINGTON, BOOKER TALIAFERRO (1856–1915). The black educator's 11-room summer home in 1902 and 1903 stood at Main and Columbian streets in **South Weymouth** until 1977, when it fell to make room for the present Medical Office Building. Built in the 1870's, the two-story frame house had been vacant and vandalized since 1973, and local sentiment went against restoring the structure. "All the codes would be against you," said its last owner, a builder-developer.

(See Chapter 3, NEW YORK, WEST VIRGINIA; also Chapter 5, ALABAMA, VIRGINIA.)

WEBSTER, DANIEL (1782–1852). Orator, long-time Massachusetts senator and twice secretary of state, Webster lived in **Boston** from 1816 to 1832. From 1816 to 1819 he rented the four-story house at 57 Mount Vernon St., the later home of Charles Francis Adams (see the entry on Adams earlier in this section). In 1824, Webster bought an imposing brick mansion at the corner of High and Summer streets, where he entertained the Marquis de Lafayette in 1824 and lived until 1832. This house, demolished about 1860, is the present site of Daniel Webster Park.

In **Marshfield,** Webster bought a 160-acre farm in 1832 and from this nucleus built a 1,400-acre estate that became his permanent home and the "rural showplace of New England." He enlarged a two-story, 1774 farmhouse on the property and named the estate "Green Harbor." Today the only building remaining from this estate is Webster Law Office and Library National Historic Landmark, a 19th-century, one-room frame cabin. This was moved to the grounds of the 1699 Winslow House at Webster and Careswell streets from another part of the estate in 1966. Inside are Webster's office furniture and numerous photos and documents relating to his public career. The property is operated by the trustees of Historic Winslow House. (Open July 1–Labor Day, Wednesday–Monday 10:00–5:00; 617-834-7329; admission.)

(See NEW HAMPSHIRE in this chapter; also Chapter 3, DISTRICT OF COLUMBIA.)

WEBSTER, NOAH (1758–1843). A founder of Amherst College, the lexicographer bought a large double house in **Amherst,** where he lived from 1812 to 1822. On his 10 acres here, he planted an orchard and gardens and worked on his *American Dictionary* (1828). The site of this home, which stood until 1838 at 46 Main St., is now occupied by the Lincoln commercial block.

(See CONNECTICUT in this chapter; also Chapter 4, MICHIGAN.)

WESTINGHOUSE, GEORGE (1846–1914). "Erskine Park," named for his wife's family, was the inventor's large estate at **Lenox,** including a castle-like mansion he bought on 100 acres—eventually increased to 600—in 1887. Lagoons, spacious lawns, white carriage drives and elaborate gardens surrounded the home, which was razed in 1919. The present house on this Stockbridge Road (U.S. Highway 7) site became Foxhollow School for Girls and now serves as an inn and restaurant for The Center at Foxhollow, a private resort complex.

(See Chapter 3, DISTRICT OF COLUMBIA, NEW YORK, PENNSYLVANIA.)

WHARTON, EDITH (1862–1937). The Mount National Historic Landmark, the author's 29-room mansion on Laurel Lake, stands on U.S. Highway 7 just south of **Lenox.** Wharton designed and built this house on 113 acres in 1901, modeling it after Sir Christopher Wren's Belton House in Lincolnshire, England. Here she wrote *The House of Mirth* (1905) and gathered material for

Ethan Frome (1911), entertaining many literary guests in the elaborate gardens. "The story of Edith Wharton's life at the Mount," wrote Stephanie Kraft, "is the story of a woman's determined effort to create herself—to bring herself to birth as an artist and a self-nurturing person." Following her divorce in 1912, she sold the house and settled permanently in Paris. The Mount served as a dormitory for the Foxhollow School for Girls from 1941 to 1976. Today the elaborate mansion with its lawns and wooded areas is part of The Center resort complex at Foxhollow and is leased as a facility for theatrical study.

(See RHODE ISLAND in this chapter; also Chapter 2, MANHATTAN.)

WHISTLER, JAMES ABBOTT McNEILL (1834–1903). At 243 Worthen St. in **Lowell** stands the 1823 Whistler House and Parker Art Gallery, the expatriate painter's clapboard birthplace and home until 1837. A permanent display of his etchings now shares space there with changing contemporary exhibits. The property is maintained by the Lowell Art Association. (Open Tuesday–Sunday 1:00–4:00; 617–452–7641; admission.)

(See CONNECTICUT in this chapter.)

WHITNEY, ELI (1765–1825). The inventor's farmhouse birthplace and home until 1789 stood in **Westboro** at 36 Eli Whitney St. In his father's workshop, where Whitney repaired violins and manufactured nails and hatpins, the youngster developed his extraordinary mechanical skills. The dwelling stood until about 1850; a private home occupies the site today.

(See CONNECTICUT in this chapter; also Chapter 5, GEORGIA.)

WHITTIER, JOHN GREENLEAF (1807–1892). At 305 Whittier Road in **Haverhill** stands the Whittier Birthplace, a 1688 New England farmhouse operated by the Whittier Homestead trustees. "To pause here," wrote literary historian John Deedy, "is to step not only into New England's past, but almost into the very lines of Whittier's immortal poem *Snow-Bound*." Built by the poet's great-great-grandfather on 148 acres (now reduced to 75 acres), the homestead raised five generations of the family. Original furnishings, utensils and clothing appear exactly as they did when the abolitionist poet lived there. This was his home until 1836, when he sold the property. (Open Tuesday–Saturday 9:00–5:00, Sunday 1:00–5:00; admission.)

The poet made his permanent home in **Amesbury** from 1836 to 1892. At 86 Friend St., Whittier Home National Historic Landmark is the 10-room frame house where he wrote *Snow-Bound* (1866) and many other poems. This house, when he moved in, was a new four-room cottage; he added the second floor and two-story ell. His "garden room" study remains exactly as he left it, and his original furniture, possessions, family memorabilia and manuscripts are amply displayed. The house is operated by the Whittier Home Association. (Open March 1–December 31, Tuesday–Saturday 10:00–4:00; January 1–February 28, by appointment; 617-388-1337; admission.)

(See NEW HAMPSHIRE in this chapter.)

WIENER, NORBERT (1894–1964). The mathematician author of *Cybernetics* (1948) occupied two homes in **Cambridge,** both standing and privately owned. He lived in the 1854 house at 20 Avon St. from 1901 to 1903; and at 2 Hubbard Park, from 1910 to 1926.

"Old Mill Farm," his boyhood home from 1904 to 1909, also stands on Old Mill Road near **Harvard,** an unnumbered private dwelling.

Belmont was Wiener's last home. He bought his 1921 house at 53 Cedar Road in 1940 and occupied it for the rest of his life. "I remember him walking from his home to Belmont Center," reports Town Engineer Richard B. Betts, "holding a cigarette or cigar up to but in front of his mouth; he always seemed to be rushing to catch up to it." The house is privately owned.

(See NEW HAMPSHIRE in this chapter.)

WILSON, EDMUND (1895–1972). At **Wellfleet** on Cape Cod, the literary critic spent summers from 1940 to 1972 in a section called Stony Hill, on the west side of U.S. Highway 6 north of the village. Known as the Betsy Freeman Home and built about 1830, the dwelling is privately owned.

(See Chapter 2, MANHATTAN; also Chapter 3, NEW JERSEY, NEW YORK.)

WINTHROP, JOHN (1588–1649). The Puritan governor's first home in America was a frame house erected at the lower end of Harvard Mall in Charlestown (**Boston**) in 1630. Weeks later, when the colony moved across the Charles River

to "Shawmut," Winthrop had this house disassembled and reconstructed at the present site of the Boston Stock Exchange, 53 State St. This was also the later site of the famed Bunch of Grapes Tavern at the head of Long Wharf—a "breeding ground for bastards and legislators," according to John Adams (see the entry on Adams earlier in this section). Winthrop sold this house to pay off debts and built another, in 1644, at the present location of the 1729 Old South Meeting House, 310 Washington St. The thatch roofs and daubed-wood chimneys of these first Boston dwellings accounted for the "Great Fires" that plagued the city from its beginning and that probably consumed both Winthrop houses before the century ended. *Winthrop's Boston* (1965) by Darrett B. Rutman gives a good picture of the colonial town.

Though his main residence was always Boston, Winthrop raised livestock on his 600-acre "Ten Hills Farm" along the Mystic River at **Somerville.** "It is a strange fact in Somerville history," wrote a local journalist in 1926, "that although this is the last land to be developed in Somerville, it was one of the first to be settled." Winthrop's estate, which extended north along today's Broadway and across to Medford Center, was granted in perpetuity to him and his heirs by the Massachusetts Bay Company. There he fended off wolves from his swine and calves and, at least once, got lost on his own property. Winthrop's stone farmhouse stood until about 1740 on the present marked site of Grimmons School, Governor Winthrop Road and Shore Drive. The ten hillocks of his land were excavated for brick clay and leveled during the mid-1800s.

NEW HAMPSHIRE

Like several of the original English claims in America, New Hampshire began as a huge chunk of private property, granted to Capt. John Mason in 1629 by a king who parceled out New England from rather inaccurate maps. Mason, an absentee landlord from Hampshire, probably didn't spend three minutes deciding on a territorial name that has lasted more than 300 years. His grant encompassed all the country lying between the Merrimack and Piscataqua Rivers, borders that shifted considerably as years passed and Mason's heirs dickered, sued and sold. The "New Hampshire Grants" at one point even included Vermont.

Early settlement consisted of the "four towns"—Portsmouth, Dover, Exeter and Hampton; and most of the settlers came from Massachusetts. These towns remained independent until 1641, when they placed themselves under the protection of Massachusetts. In 1741 New Hampshire became a royal province in its own right and, 14 years later, was the first to declare independence, six months before the united Declaration at Philadelphia. During the Revolution it was the only rebel province not invaded by the British; and as one of the original 13 states, it cast the ninth and deciding ballot for the U.S. Constitution in 1788.

Shaped roughly like a right triangle, New Hampshire is bisected by the granitic White Mountains, which provide some of New England's most scenic country. The state has several major manufacturing centers, but 87 percent is forestland. Its 18 miles of seacoast center on Portsmouth, still a thriving port city. Mountain wilderness, lakes and hiking trails make recreation one of the state's dominant "industries."

New Hampshire has bred several national political figures and provided creative refuge for numerous 20th-century artists and writers. Franklin Pierce, a sharp soldier but as dismal a president as the 19th century ever produced, was a Hillsboro native and lived in Concord for most of his life. But there was also the eloquent, much more influential Daniel Webster, who was born at Franklin and launched his career in the state; and native Horace Greeley, child prodigy of Amherst and virtuoso public gadfly. Those who sought New Hampshire's scenic isolation and found an admirable creative environment included sculptor Augustus Saint-Gaudens and painter Maxfield Parrish, who made their permanent homes and studios near Plainfield. Since 1907 the art colony fashioned from the estate of composer Edward MacDowell at Peterborough has provided conducive space for numerous other composers and writers. Poet Robert Frost began his literary career in New Hampshire and lived in the state for many years—the two "best states," he opined, were New Hampshire and Vermont. Other noted writers and scholars became regular summer residents. Willa Cather often set up a tent at Jaffrey; and William James, e e cummings and Norbert Wiener occupied long-time vacation homes that still stand. President Woodrow Wilson courted in New Hampshire, and ex-President Grover Cleveland and poet John Greenleaf Whittier spent their last summers there.

Today New Hampshire attracts many visitors to the colonial restoration project of Strawbery Banke at Portsmouth, begun in 1960. This remarkable 10-acre museum village of 35 structures dating from the 17th to 19th centuries re-creates the seaport town familiar to John Paul Jones and the royal governors. Places like this function as "time slots" for travelers interested in dimensions of time as well as place in their sight-seeing. Such opportunities exist all over New England, but Strawbery Banke provides one of the best.

CATHER, WILLA SIBERT (1873–1947). From 1917 to 1938, the novelist spent summers in **Jaffrey** at the privately owned Shattuck Inn on Dublin Road. Her two small rooms on the third floor of this rambling, 19th-century hotel looked out on Mount Monadnock. Here she worked on *My Antonia* (1918), *One of Ours* (1922) and several other novels. Across the road from the inn, she often pitched a tent in the woods for an outdoor studio she called "High Mowing."

(See Chapter 2, MANHATTAN; also Chapter 3, PENNSYLVANIA; also Chapter 4, NEBRASKA; also Chapter 5, VIRGINIA.)

CLEVELAND, GROVER (1837–1908). After serving terms as 22nd and 24th U.S. president, Cleveland bought an 1830 farmhouse near **Tamworth** that he used as a summer retreat from 1906 to 1908. The Cleveland House, a low, rambling, frame dwelling that he enlarged to 20 rooms, stands on Cleveland Hill Road (privately owned). One Tamworth historian recorded that Cleveland "regularly played fiery cribbage" during his summers there. The house still remains in the Cleveland family.

(See MASSACHUSETTS in this chapter; also Chapter 3, DISTRICT OF COLUMBIA, MARYLAND, NEW JERSEY, NEW YORK.)

CUMMINGS, EDWARD ESTLIN (1894–1962). The "Lost Generation" poet who created a literary style of lower-case lines and nonpunctuation made his permanent summer home near **Silver Lake.** Joy Farm National Historic Landmark, dating from 1799, stands on Salter Hill Road. The farm, purchased and improved by his father, was a "boy's paradise," Cummings recalled, and he inherited the property in 1929. It is privately owned.

(See MASSACHUSETTS in this chapter; also Chapter 2, MANHATTAN.)

EDDY, MARY BAKER (1821–1910). Founder of Christian Science, Mary Baker Eddy was born near **Bow** in a two and one-half-story, gray frame farmhouse, which stood on what is now Mary Baker Eddy Road (State Highway 3A) off Interstate Highway 93. The hilltop house, its site marked, was surrounded by fields now grown to woods.

According to one biographer, the five years that she and husband Daniel Patterson spent in **North Groton** "were the most miserable of her entire life, fraught with illness, depression, and financial setbacks." The 18th-century gray cottage from which they were finally evicted in 1860 rises from the edge of a tumbling stream just off the town's main street. It is now operated as an Eddy Historic House by the Longyear Foundation. (Open June 1–October 31, Tuesday–Sunday by appointment; contact Custodian, Rumney Historic House, 603-786-9943; admission.)

At **Rumney,** some of the furnishings that the impoverished couple auctioned off from 1860 to 1862 have been restored—as were Eddy's spirits there. This is where Mary Baker Patterson began writing her thoughts and meditations. This Eddy Historic House, an 18th-century frame cottage on Stinson Lake Road, is also operated by the Longyear Foundation. (Open June 1–October 31, Tuesday–Saturday 10:00–5:00, Sunday 2:00–5:00; 603-786-9943; admission.)

In **Concord,** her home from 1889 to 1908, a 15-room Georgian frame mansion on 100 acres called "Pleasant View" was her last residence in the state. There she organized Boston's Mother Church and began publishing the *Christian Science Monitor.* "Welcome to Pleasant View, but not to varying views," she greeted devoted followers at 243 Pleasant St. A new residence (privately owned) was built on the site in 1926 and has since operated as a home for elderly Christian Scientists.

(See MASSACHUSETTS in this chapter.)

FRENCH, DANIEL CHESTER (1850–1931). **Exeter** was the noted sculptor's early home. His birthplace, a rented farmhouse built about 1834 and slightly altered thereafter, is presently a furniture store at 34 Court St. In 1850, his father built a square, white clapboard home at 43 Pine St. This boyhood dwelling, altered and moved in 1965 to 5 Nelson Drive, is a private residence.

(See MASSACHUSETTS in this chapter; also Chapter 2, MANHATTAN.)

FROST, ROBERT LEE (1874–1963). The poet's first home in the state was at **Salem,** where the impoverished family roomed at the Loren Bailey Homestead, 8 Sullivan Court (privately owned); the 19th-century house has been sided and somewhat altered.

Derry was where Frost found his poetic voice. "Biographers now realize," wrote literary historian Emilie C. Harting, "how much Frost's years here from 1901–1909 laid the foundation for the great body of poetry he wrote." Frost Farm National Historic Landmark, a simple frame farmhouse dating from about 1900, stands on State Highway 28 south of the bypass junction. The interior, restored to its original condition with the aid of Frost's daughter, contains only a few original items, among them *The Scottish Chiefs,* the first book he owned. There, while he practiced unconventional farming, Frost wrote "The Death of the Hired Man" and many of the poems in *A Boy's Will* (1912). The property is operated by the New Hampshire Division of Parks. (Open Memorial Day–mid-June, Saturday–Sunday 1:00–5:00; mid-June–Labor Day, Wednesday–Sunday 9:00–5:00; admission.)

On Ridge Road near **Franconia,** the poet and his family resided during summers and at other intervals from 1915 to 1920. This eight-room, white, one and one-half-story farmhouse on 50 acres, now Frost Place National Historic Landmark on eight acres, dates from 1830 to 1840 and currently functions as an arts center and summer residence for a young poet chosen by the *Atlantic.** Frost's own writing desk and replicas of other furnishings are displayed where he produced the poems "The Road Not Taken" and "Stopping by Woods on a Snowy Evening," among others. The tiny town of Franconia, in what would have been

*Commenting in 1977 on such a use for historic landmarks, a writer suggested in *Time* that the Frost "living memorial opens unlimited vistas to monument-minded Americans. What about installing a young novelist in William Faulkner's house in Oxford, Mississippi? A young architect in Frank Lloyd Wright's house in Oak Park, Illinois? A young semanticist in Casey Stengel's house in Glendale, California?"

a splendid act for a community five times its size, purchased the property in 1976 as a Bicentennial project and now maintains it. (Open Tuesday–Saturday 10:00–12:00, 1:00–4:00; admission; Friday evening theatrical and concert programs July–August, 8:00 PM in barn; admission.)

(See MASSACHUSETTS, VERMONT in this chapter; also Chapter 4, MICHIGAN; also Chapter 5, FLORIDA; also Chapter 6, CALIFORNIA.)

GREELEY, HORACE (1811–1872). The editor, reformer and 1872 presidential candidate was born five miles north of **Amherst** in what was then a new one-story cottage. It now stands unnumbered but marked on Horace Greeley Road. On this 40-acre hardscrabble farm, the odd-looking boy with the massive head, wax-pale complexion and prodigious intelligence learned to read at his mother's knee—viewing the book upside down, goes the tale, while she read for herself.

(See VERMONT in this chapter; also Chapter 2, MANHATTAN; also Chapter 3, NEW YORK.)

JAMES, WILLIAM (1842–1910). Pragmatic psychologist-philosopher and member of the noted literary family, James purchased and remodeled a rambling, two-story bungalow on 90 acres at **Chocorua** in 1887 for his summer home. His brother, novelist Henry James, described the forested area as "quite Fenimore Cooper but without the danger of being scalped." William James spent many summers in his cedar-shingled home and died there on a late August day. The privately owned farmhouse, dating from about 1842, has been enlarged and stands off State Highway 16, invisible from the highway near Chocorua Lake.

(See MASSACHUSETTS, RHODE ISLAND in this chapter; also Chapter 2, MANHATTAN.)

JONES, JOHN PAUL (1747–1792). The Revolutionary sea fighter lived at what is now Jones House National Historic Landmark at 43 Middle St. in **Portsmouth** for only one month—October 4 to November 7, 1782—but so rare are Jones landmarks that the house has achieved distinction for even this brief residence. Here Jones boarded while he supervised outfitting of the 74-gun ship *America*. A grateful Congress, having appointed him to this command, then reneged and gave France the ship; Jones never commanded an American vessel again. The 1758 frame house,

operated by the Portsmouth Historical Society, contains period furnishings and regional art—but nothing associated with Jones. (Open June 1–October 15, Monday–Saturday 10:00–5:00; 603-436-8420; admission.)

(See Chapter 5, VIRGINIA.)

MacDOWELL, EDWARD ALEXANDER (1861–1908). MacDowell Colony National Historic Landmark, located north of **Peterborough** on MacDowell Road from U.S. Highway 202, occupies the composer's 60-acre farm, the white farmhouse "Hillcrest," and the log studio he built in 1896 as a working retreat. His widow opened the acreage to other musicians and also to working writers and painters for secluded studio space; and many a noted creator's stay there has enriched American letters, music and visual arts. Today the Colony consists of 42 cabin studios and outbuildings on 500 wood and farmland acreas, administered by the trustees of MacDowell Colony. Colony Hall, the main building, welcomes visitors. (Open Monday–Saturday 2:00–5:00; free.)

(See Chapter 2, MANHATTAN.)

PARRISH, MAXFIELD FREDERICK (1870–1966). South of **Plainfield,** the painter-illustrator made his permanent home on State Highway 12A. The long, white Parrish house and studio known as "The Oaks," which he bought and expanded in 1898, was renovated after his death. It now welcomes tourists as a restaurant/antique shop called "Wells Wood."

PIERCE, FRANKLIN (1804–1869). The 14th US president, a lifelong New Hampshire resident except for his military service and White House tenure, lived from 1804 to 1834 at Pierce Homestead National Historic Landmark in **Hillsboro.** This two-story frame house, built by Pierce's father in 1804, stands on State Highway 31 just north of the State Highway 9 junction. The scenic wallpaper is original, and the New Hampshire Division of Parks displays period furnishings. (Open Memorial Day–mid-June, Saturday–Sunday 9:00–6:00; mid-June–Labor Day, Wednesday–Sunday 9:00–6:00; 603-478-3165; admission.)

Two Pierce homes remain in **Concord.** The 1838 Pierce Manse at 14 Penacook St., the only one he owned in the city, was the family home from 1842 to 1846, during his early law practice, and contains original furnishings and memorabilia.

It is operated by The Pierce Brigade. (Open June 1–Labor Day, Monday–Saturday 10:00–4:00; 603-224-9620; admission.) The Pierce House at 48 South Main St., a Victorian mansion built for the ex-president from 1854 to 1857, was his retirement home from 1857 to 1869. It contains period items and the original bedroom furnished as it was when he died here. The private owners may show the house by appointment (603-225-9268).

Exhibit: The New Hampshire Historical Society at 30 Park St. in **Concord** displays some relics of Pierce's earlier military career. (Open Monday-Tuesday, Thursday–Friday 9:00–4:30, Wednesday 9:00–8:00; 603-225-3381; free.)

(See Chapter 3, DISTRICT OF COLUMBIA.)

ROBINSON, EDWIN ARLINGTON (1869–1935). The poet lived and worked at the MacDowell Colony in **Peterborough** for lengthy intervals from 1911. "There is everything here that I do not deserve," he said (as an accomplished self-putdown artist). His first residence here was "Mannex," the men's dormitory, but he soon had his own studio, a stone cabin back in the woods, where he produced most of the poetry of his later career (see the entry on Edward Alexander MacDowell earlier in this section).

(See MAINE in this chapter; also Chapter 2, BROOKLYN, MANHATTAN.)

SAINT-GAUDENS, AUGUSTUS (1848–1907). Saint-Gaudens National Historic Site, operated by the National Park Service, became the sculptor's summer home and studio in 1885, when he purchased the two-story brick mansion dating from about 1800, remodeled it and named it "Aspet" after his father's birthplace in France. In 1900, it became his permanent home, which still contains his original furnishings and possessions. "Little Studio" and "New Studio" buildings on the property display numerous busts, portraits and models of his immense statuary. The grounds, which host summer concerts, are located off State Highway 12A between Cornish and **Plainfield.** (Open late May–October 31, daily 8:30–5:00, grounds until dark; 603-675-2055; admission.)

(See Chapter 2, MANHATTAN.)

WEBSTER, DANIEL (1782–1852). Near **Franklin,** the political leader's reconstructed birthplace—a small frame house operated by the New Hamp-

shire Division of Parks—stands off State Highway 127 south of town. The original house dated from about 1780; demolished sometime during the 19th century, it was rebuilt on its original foundation in the early 1900s. It contains period furnishings and exhibits relating to Webster and his public career. (Open Memorial Day–mid-June, Saturday–Sunday 9:00–6:00; mid-June–Labor Day, Wednesday–Sunday 9:00–6:00; admission.) Webster's boyhood home was "Elms Farm," located about two miles south of Franklin off U.S. Highway 3. The two and one-half-story, white frame house, which Webster's father operated as a tavern on 110 acres, remained in the family for decades. Webster considered it his native homestead, and often returned in later years. He sold it to a brother in 1807 but acquired it again about 1830, converting it to a 1,000-acre livestock farm. The house became the New Hampshire Orphans' Home in 1871 and is now a privately owned dwelling.

Webster Cottage, the 1780, one and one-half-story dwelling where Webster boarded as a Dartmouth College student, stands on North Main Street in **Hanover.** Restored by the Hanover Historical Society, it contains period items plus a few Webster pieces, including a black leather barrel chair from his Franklin home. Webster's alcove quarters occupied the attic. The original site of the house, until 1955, was another spot on Main Street. (Open June 1–mid-October, Tuesday, Thursday, Saturday–Sunday 3:00–5:00; mid-October–May 31, Saturday 2:00–4:00; free.)

Webster achieved initial fame as a lawyer in **Portsmouth,** where only the last of his three homes remain. This four-room 1785 dwelling, Webster's rented residence from 1813 to 1816, stood originally at 58 High St. Restored with funds donated by schoolchildren of the state, it was moved in 1961 to Portsmouth's colonial restoration project of Strawbery Banke, Hancock and Marcy streets, where it functions as a research library. (Strawbery Banke open mid-April–mid-November, daily 9:30–5:00; winter hours by appointment; 603-436-8010; admission.)

(See MASSACHUSETTS in this chapter; also Chapter 3, DISTRICT OF COLUMBIA.)

WHITTIER, JOHN GREENLEAF (1807–1892). The prominent New England poet and abolitionist summered in the state for many years. He spent his last summer and died at "Elmfield," an early

18th-century house that stands on Lafayette Road (privately owned and unnumbered) near **Hampton Falls.** Check locally for directions.

(See MASSACHUSETTS in this chapter.)

WIENER, NORBERT (1894–1964). Dating from the early 1800s, the longtime summer home of the mathematician and cybernetic scientist stands on Bear Camp Pond Road (unnumbered) near **South Tamworth.** It is privately owned.

(See MASSACHUSETTS in this chapter.)

WILDER, THORNTON NIVEN (1897–1975). MacDowell Colony at **Peterborough** was the author–playwright's frequent working retreat from 1924 (see the entry on Edward Alexander MacDowell earlier in this section). Peterborough became "Grover's Corners" for the setting of Wilder's play *Our Town* (1938).

(See CONNECTICUT in this chapter; also Chapter 4, WISCONSIN.)

WILSON, WOODROW (1856–1924). As 28th U.S. president, Wilson vacationed for three summers at "Harlakenden," an 1898 stone mansion owned by U.S. novelist Winston Churchill, at **Cornish.** Wilson spent hours driving through the quiet countryside; there he courted Edith Bolling Galt, who became his second wife. The house, which burned down in 1923, stood at a marked site on the west side of State Highway 12A just south of the Cornish-Plainfield town line.

(See Chapter 3, DISTRICT OF COLUMBIA, NEW JERSEY; also Chapter 5, GEORGIA, SOUTH CAROLINA, VIRGINIA.)

RHODE ISLAND

Its official name is "the State of Rhode Island and Providence Plantations." The "Island" itself is Aquidneck, largest of the islands comprising Newport. Aquidneck's shape supposedly reminded Italian explorer Giovanni da Verrazano, who visited Narragansett Bay in 1524, of the Greek Isle of Rhodes (the Greek island, about three times larger, is roughly similar in shape); and the colonial settlements revived the designation in 1644. This smallest state is 48 miles long and 37 miles wide with a 250-mile coastline.

In Rhode Island, 16 years after the Pilgrims landed at Plymouth, Mass., the principles of American religious freedom became actualized.

Pastor-founder Roger Williams was one of those Boston black sheep whose "dangerous opinions" couldn't be tolerated there. That was exactly the type of stricture that Williams himself couldn't tolerate; and he established his Providence colony in 1636 as a democratic society with separation of church and state, defending the right of all to worship in ways that even he didn't agree with— a profoundly radical notion for any pastor then and more than a few today. The first four settlements—Providence, Portsmouth, Newport, and Warwick—united under the 1644 colonial charter. From 1652 to the end of the Revolution, the colony was involved in nine Indian conflicts, of which King Philip's War was decisive in clearing the territory of its natives. Newport grew quickly and, before the Revolution, rivaled New York City, Boston and Philadelphia as a leading colonial city. It never recovered its status, however, after British forces occupied the city from 1776 to 1779 and blockaded the port for two more years, disrupting commerce and causing mass exodus. The colony had declared itself independent in 1776 and became the last of the original 13 states to ratify the Constitution. Rhode Island did not replace its colonial charter with a state constitution, however, until 1842, as a result of Dorr's Rebellion, which forced extension of suffrage beyond an extrenched propertied minority. Until 1900 the state had two capitals, finally settling on Providence.

Rhode Island is primarily a manufacturing state. The first American factory, Samuel Slater's cotton mill, began operating at Pawtucket in 1790, and textiles remain a major industry. Sea commerce has also thrived from the beginning.

Rhode Island natives included the Perry brothers, famed in U.S. Navy annals, whose several homes in the state still exist; painter Gilbert Stuart, best-known portrait artist of Revolutionary figures; and George M. Cohan, the "Yankee Doodle Dandy" of show business.

After the Civil War Newport beaches were "discovered" by novelty-seeking New York high society, following the lead of Boston intellectuals. Mass migrations, begun by Caroline Schermerhorn Astor, established the city as a "golden summer" playground for the stylish rich, who competed in building the most grandiose mansions and palaces they could afford. Several of these masonry showpieces, invariably called "cottages," still exist; and the Newport Restoration Society continues its remarkable job of preserving and revitalizing for the public these reminders of a decadent but somehow innocent era when, if you had it, you flaunted it. Richard O'Connor's *The Golden Summers: An Antic History of Newport* (1974) gives an entertaining account of this opulent period and place. Many well-known, less wealth-obsessed persons also followed the fashionable trek to Newport. These included the literary James family, historian George Bancroft, writer Edith Wharton—and, in more recent times, President John F. Kennedy. *Rhode Island: An Historical Guide* (1976), by Sheila Steinberg and Cathleen McGuigan, is a useful handbook of sites.

It is intriguing that, among the noted people who lived in Rhode Island, relatively few made it a lifelong residence. Two exceptions were H. P. Lovecraft, the reclusive author of horror tales; and, from 1636, founder Roger Williams himself. Reclusiveness is not easily achieved in this state, the nation's second most densely populated. And such was the triumph of Pastor Williams for all of us that there has been much less necessity to shelter heretics anywhere in America since.

ASTOR, CAROLINE SCHERMERHORN (1831–1908). *"The* Mrs. Astor," as she liked to be known, was *the* arbiter of New York and Newport society for 40 years—with little help from her mostly absent husband, William Backhouse Astor, Jr., grandson of John Jacob Astor. She began the "golden summer" trek to **Newport,** which her presence established as the fashionable locale for the very rich. Her palatial "cottage" was the 1855 "Beechwood" on Bellevue Avenue, a street still lined with remnants of the era's incredibly conspicuous consumption. In her final years, she lived there as a senile recluse, encased in jewels and hosting imaginary grand receptions. Many of her 1890 furnishings are displayed in this mansion, operated by Beechwood Museum, Inc. (Open daily 1:00–7:00; 401-846-3774; admission.)

(See Chapter 2, MANHATTAN; also Chapter 3, NEW YORK.)

BANCROFT, GEORGE (1800–1891). "Roseclyfe," the historian's summer "cottage" and rose garden on Bellevue Avenue in **Newport,** was destroyed about 1900. The present "Rosecliff," the 1902 Oelrichs mansion open to the public, was built just east of the Bancroft site.

(See MASSACHUSETTS in this chapter; also Chapter 3, DISTRICT OF COLUMBIA.)

BELMONT, ALVA ERTSKIN SMITH VANDERBILT (1853–1933). Two lavish summer residences of the prominent feminist remain in **Newport.** Marble House, built from 1889 to 1892 on Bellevue Avenue by Belmont's first husband, William K. Vanderbilt, for $2 million, was styled after the palaces of Versailles by architect Richard Morris Hunt. Belmont lived there at frequent intervals from 1892 until the 1920s. Suffragists met there in 1909 to enlist support of other wealthy donors for the cause. This mansion, operated by the Preservation Society of Newport, contains all of the original sumptuous furnishings. Restoration is planned for a teahouse she built on the property in 1913. (Open April 1–June 30, mid-September–mid-November, daily 10:00–5:00; July 1–mid-September, Tuesday 10:00–8:00; mid-November–March 31, Saturday–Sunday 10:00–4:00; 401-847-1000; admission.) The 1894 Belcourt Castle, also on Bellevue Avenue, was built for $3 million by the feminist's second husband, Oliver H. P. Belmont, whom she married in 1896. This 60-room mansion, also designed by Hunt, resembles the French palace of Louis XIII. Costumed guides display the huge art and antique collection of the current owners, who operate the mansion. (Open April 1–May 31, daily 10:00–5:00; June 1–August 31, daily 10:00–6:00; September 1–October 31, 10:00–5:00; 401-846-0669; admission.)

(See Chapter 2, MANHATTAN; also Chapter 3, NEW YORK.)

BERKELEY, GEORGE (1685–1753). The Irish bishop and philosopher built "Whitehall," his frame, hip-roofed house, in 1729 at **Middletown.** Located on Berkeley Avenue, this was the seat of his 96-acre estate; he gave the farm to Yale University in 1733 after his return to England. Today the restored house is operated as a Berkeley memorial by the Society of Colonial Dames and contains English period furnishings. (Open July 1–Labor Day, 10:00–5:00; 401-846-3116; admission.)

BOOTH, EDWIN THOMAS (1833–1893). "Boothden," which the actor built as a vacation retreat in 1883, stands in **Middletown** on Indian

Avenue, 2.5 miles south off Green End Avenue. The two and one-half-story, privately owned mansion is a rambling, gabled structure, once part of a large estate that Booth ran as a farm until 1887. Here he raised his own produce, which he arranged to have shipped to him wherever he performed.

(See MASSACHUSETTS in this chapter; also Chapter 2, MANHATTAN; also Chapter 3, MARYLAND.)

BROWN, MARGARET TOBIN "MOLLY" (1867–1932). "Typical Brown luck," said the society matron after her courageous rescue of passengers during the 1912 *Titanic* disaster; "I'm unsinkable." In 1960 her life and legend inspired *The Unsinkable Molly Brown,* a popular stage hit. After the *Titanic* episode in her otherwise remarkable career, she rented a "cottage" in **Newport** at 44 Bellevue Ave. (at the corner of Redwood Street), which she named "Mon Etui." Here, amid exotic decorations, she frequently welcomed guests to "An Evening with Molly Brown," during which she cheerfully amplified her own legend and gave readings from favorite authors. The site of what must have been one of Newport's more interesting acts is now a parking lot.

(See Chapter 4, MISSOURI; also Chapter 6, COLORADO.)

COHAN, GEORGE MICHAEL (1878–1942). The actor-playwright-producer said he spent "mighty little time in **Providence**" after his birth at 536 Wickenden St. a three-story frame house that had been marked by a plaque before its destruction. The entire block is now occupied by the Fox Point Neighborhood Center. Interstate Highway 195 skirts downtown Providence as George M. Cohan Boulevard.

(See MASSACHUSETTS in this chapter; also Chapter 2, MANHATTAN; also Chapter 3, NEW JERSEY, NEW YORK.)

GREEN, HENRIETTA ROBINSON "HETTY" (1835–1916). The girlhood summer home of the eccentric, miserly financier was moved to **Newport** in 1969 from South Dartmouth, Mass. It stands now at 6 Bridge St., a 1721 clapboard, gambrel-roofed, five-room structure owned by the Newport Restoration Foundation and privately

occupied. This was the Henry Howland House, owned by Green's grandfather. Its removal to Newport involved meticulous board-by-board demolition and reconstruction.

(See MASSACHUSETTS, VERMONT in this chapter; also Chapter 2, MANHATTAN; also Chapter 3, NEW JERSEY.)

HUTCHINSON, ANNE (1591–1643). Expelled from Boston as a religious heretic in 1638, Hutchinson led a small group of settlers to **Portsmouth,** where she lived until 1642. The marked site of this early settlement, first in the nation to be founded by a woman, is Founders' Brook off Boyd's Lane.

(See MASSACHUSETTS in this chapter; also Chapter 2, BRONX.)

JAMES, HENRY (1843–1916).

JAMES, WILLIAM (1842–1910).

As youths, the James brothers—Henry a major novelist, William a pioneering psychologist—spent several intervals at rented dwellings in **Newport** with their parents during the 1860s. Their residences at 13 Kay St. and 465 Spring St. (at the corner of Lee Avenue)—the latter built in the 1840s and presently a funeral home—remain privately owned.

(See MASSACHUSETTS, NEW HAMPSHIRE in this chapter; also Chapter 2, MANHATTAN.)

KENNEDY, JOHN FITZGERALD (1917–1963). The eventual 35th U.S. president and Jacqueline Bouvier were married on September 12, 1953, at the 50-acre Hammersmith Farm on Ocean Drive in **Newport.** Owned by the bride's family, this 1887 shingle-style "cottage" frequently hosted the Kennedys from 1953 to 1963 as a vacation retreat and summer White House. It is operated by Camelot Gardens, Inc., and displays original furnishings. (Open March, November, Saturday–Sunday 10:00–5:00; April–May, September–October, daily 10:00–5:00; Memorial Day–Labor Day, daily 10:00–8:00; 401-847-0420; admission.)

(See MASSACHUSETTS in this chapter; also Chapter 2, BRONX; also Chapter 3, DISTRICT OF COLUMBIA, MARYLAND, NEW YORK; also Chapter 4, MICHIGAN; also Chapter 5, FLORIDA, VIRGINIA; also Chapter 6, TEXAS.)

LOVECRAFT, HOWARD PHILLIPS (1890–1937). The gaunt, reclusive author of horror stories in the Poe tradition was born in **Providence** at 454 Angell St., and lived until 1904 in the 15-room frame house owned by his grandfather. Sold and converted to physicians' offices, it finally fell in 1961 to clear space for an apartment development. Lovecraft's other Providence homes remain privately owned. These include 598 Angell St., where he lived with his mother from 1904 to 1924 in a ground-floor apartment and began publishing his tales; 10 Barnes St. (1926–33); and his final upper-floor apartment (1933–37), a building now standing at 65 Prospect St. The site of the latter when Lovecraft lived there was 66 College St., the present location of Brown University's List Fine Arts Building.

(See Chapter 2, BROOKLYN.)

MOORE, CLEMENT CLARKE (1779–1863). The scholar's summer home from 1850 to 1863 was his daughter's large frame house, still standing at 26 Greenough Place (at the corner of Catherine Street) in **Newport.** This house, dating from about 1850, contains private apartments. Until recent years, groups gathered here with candles on Christmas Eve to hear a reading of Moore's famous ballad "A Visit from St. Nicholas."

(See Chapter 2, MANHATTAN.)

PERELMAN, SIDNEY JOSEPH (1904–1979). "What I really am, you see, is a crank," the humorist insisted; and his unique style of sophisticated absurdity, one critic wrote, is "one of American letters' most reliable alternate energy sources." Perelman's boyhood home stands at 8 Bernon St. (privately owned) in **Providence.**

(See Chapter 2, MANHATTAN; also Chapter 3, PENNSYLVANIA.)

PERRY, MATTHEW CALBRAITH (1794–1858).

PERRY, OLIVER HAZARD (1785–1819).
Naval heroes of the nation's first century, the brothers were Rhode Island natives. Oliver's probable birthplace (privately owned) was the family homestead south of **Wakefield** at 184 Post Road (U.S. Highway 1). While some biographers dispute the birthplace claim, there is little doubt that he spent many of his early years in this 1702 dwelling built by his grandfather.

A later home of Oliver Perry and the birthplace of Matthew ("Old Bruin") stands privately owned at 31 Walnut St. in **Newport.** This small, gambrel-roofed dwelling, built about 1750, was Matthew's home until about 1810, though he also lived at intervals at the Wakefield family homestead. The ground floor was replaced after his residence here, and the house has been restored to the 18th-century period. Also in Newport, a house owned briefly by Oliver Perry in 1818 stands at 29 Touro St. This two and one-half-story frame dwelling, restored to its 1760 appearance, is privately owned.

(See Chapter 2, BROOKLYN, MANHATTAN; also Chapter 3, PENNSYLVANIA.)

STUART, GILBERT CHARLES (1755–1828). Near **Saunderstown,** Stuart Birthplace National Historic Landmark is the two-story frame house built by the painter's father in 1751; the family snuff mill has been restored on the first floor. Stuart lived here until 1761. The Gilbert Stuart Association displays period furnishings in the house, which stands on Gilbert Stuart Road about one mile east of U.S. Highway 1. (Open Saturday–Thursday 11:00–5:00; 401-294-3001; admission.)

(See MASSACHUSETTS in this chapter; also Chapter 3, DISTRICT OF COLUMBIA, PENNSYLVANIA.)

WHARTON, EDITH (1862–1937). The author's home in **Newport** was "Land's End" on Ledge Road, a large, 19th-century house perched on one-half acre of a rugged cliff overlooking Rhode Island Sound. This home remains a privately owned summer residence.

(See MASSACHUSETTS in this chapter; also Chapter 2, MANHATTAN.)

WILLIAMS, ROGER (1603?–1683). Religious dissenter and 1636 founder of **Providence,** Williams purchased "Providence Plantations" from the Narragansett Indians and settled at what is now Williams National Memorial, operated by the National Park Service, in "Old Town" Providence. Included in the site is Roger Williams Spring on North Main Street opposite Alamo Lane, declared public property forever in 1721. Williams' house stood across the street from the spring at the corner of Howland Street. (Open daily 9:00–5:00; 401-528-4881; free.)

Just north of **North Kingstown** on the west side of U.S. Highway 1 is the marked site of Williams'

Trading Post, which he established in 1636 and 1637. The spot is located directly south of the 1678 Smith's Castle, where Williams often visited and preached. The precise site of the house he built for himself and occupied from 1644 to 1651 was somewhere nearby but remains unidentified.

VERMONT

Vermont probably has less level ground than any other state. Stamped flat, say the oldtimers, it would cover Texas. The only New England state without a seacoast, Vermont also has fewer people, more cattle and less small talk than any other state of the six. In Vermont you come closest to what rural New England of 1789 looked like, for the industrial revolution, if not quite bypassing the state, touched it lightly. The name Vermont means "green mountain," a corruption of the French "Vert-Mont"; the backbone ridge of the Green Mountains extends the entire 159-mile length of the state. Stone, especially granite and marble, underlies Vermont soil and much of its economy as well. Many of the stone monuments marking homes or sites in this book actually commemorate, beneath their bronze plaques, a Vermont quarry.

The first white intruder into the area was explorer Samuel de Champlain in 1609, and the French controlled Lake Champlain for 150 years. English colonists established a permanent settlement near Brattleboro in 1724. Until 1759, when the French pulled out, the French and Indian wars ravaged this northwestern lake frontier. Meanwhile both New York and New Hampshire provinces claimed Vermont; New York won the decision but not the territory. The guerrilla Green Mountain Boys, led by Ethan Allen, were formed for the purpose of fighting New York "land grabbers" but joined the Revolution as American allies. Vermont, having declared its own independence in 1777, maintained itself as a separate republic for 14 years, coining its own money, operating a postal service and conducting diplomatic relations with the surrounding "foreign" governments. Not until 1789 did New York abandon its claims; Vermont entered the Union as the 14th state in 1791.

The terse, laconic image of Vermonters has probably been carried a bit far. Still, there *was* Calvin Coolidge. . . . More startling than the stereotype, however, is the number of truly radical people who have emerged from these mountains. One was John Humphrey Noyes, whose ideas of group marriage and communal relationships are still far too utopian for wide social consideration, though he made them work for 40 years. Vermonters Joseph Smith and Brigham Young, the Mormon pioneers, also had unorthodox views of how many wives one man's family should contain. In more recent times, philosopher John Dewey revolutionized public education with his progressivism. Other famous residents whose homes still exist included journalist Horace Greeley, poet Robert Frost and painter Norman Rockwell. All one can say about Vermont notables is that they fit no discernible pattern of aims or achievement beyond an exuberant, determined individualism.

Prototype of this Vermonter is, of course, the brawling giant Ethan Allen, whose Revolutionary exploits, mighty profanity and dogged agnosticism have achieved folklore dimensions. Fundamentalist preachers in some parts of the country (probably not Vermont) still shiver their listeners with false tales of how snakes crawl out of his grave—which nobody has been able to locate exactly. His farm site near Burlington is easy to find, however; and the view from the stone towers erected on this property makes it easy to understand why he fought so hard for the right to live and die here.

ALLEN, ETHAN (1738–1789). Revolutionary soldier and loud agnostic, Allen lived in Vermont from about 1775 to the end of his life. One possible residence, the former Ethan Allen Inn on U.S. Highway 7 in **Sunderland,** still exists, but "the building has been so radically modified over the years," according to David L. Thomas of the Russell Vermontiana Collection, "that even if it was the Allen dwelling, its current appearance bears little resemblance to the original."

In **Arlington,** reports Thomas, "his residence was in the vicinity of the present railroad station, but it was long gone before the memory of anyone now living. An 'Ethan Allen well' on the site was presumably filled in around the turn of the century." This is the Studio or Batten Kill Tavern site, where Allen lived with his brother Ira in the 1780s and composed his *Oracles of Reason* (1784).

About 2.5 miles north of **Burlington** on Ethan Allen Parkway (State Highway 127), the old soldier acquired 1,400 acres from his brother Ira and built a two-story farmhouse below the Winooski River falls. As early as 1784, he had written Ira to "git the Bords Sawed"; and here for the last two years of his life, he raised cattle and cultivated 40 acres. No original building exists on the site, part of which is preserved by the Sons of the American Revolution as Ethan Allen Park. Two stone lookout towers, erected in 1905, command an imposing panorama of Allen's scenic acreage from the 12-acre park.

Exhibit: The Vermont Historical Society Museum adjoining the State House on State Street in **Montpelier** contains a few of Allen's personal belongings, including a gun and canteen. (Open Monday–Friday 8:00–4:30; July 1–August 31, Saturday–Sunday 10:00–5:00; free.)

(See CONNECTICUT in this chapter.)

ARTHUR, CHESTER ALAN (1829–1886). The 21st U.S. president was born in a small cottage near **East Fairfield,** though controversy still exists about the precise site. Whether this is the actual birthplace spot, as is officially claimed, or not, it is definitely an early childhood home site, located on a remote hillside road between Fairfield Station and Bordoville (follow the signs for about five miles northeast from State Highway 36 at Fairfield). There on a scenic, 35-acre plot in 1954, the Vermont Division of Historic Sites reconstructed, from an old photograph, the one-story, clapboard dwelling on its original foundation. It contains period furnishings. The itinerant family left here during Arthur's infancy for numerous brief stays elsewhere in Vermont and New York. (Open June 1–mid-October, Tuesday–Sunday 9:00–5:00; 802-828-3226; free.)

(See Chapter 2, MANHATTAN; also Chapter 3, DISTRICT OF COLUMBIA, NEW YORK.)

BUCK, PEARL SYDENSTRICKER (1892–1973). Prolific novelist and humanitarian, Buck "discovered" Vermont in the 1950s and occupied two summer homes, both considerably off the beaten track. Her first stands near **Danby** on Boro Hill; at "Danby House," a 19th-century dwelling, she and her four children lived without modern conveniences as a teaching-learning experience.

She designed and built "Mountain Haunt," a Chinese-style dwelling located off State Highway 30 near **Winhall** and overlooking Stratton Mountain, a short time later.

Both houses are privately owned.

(See Chapter 3, PENNSYLVANIA, WEST VIRGINIA.)

COOLIDGE, CALVIN (1872–1933). The 30th U.S. president was born at **Plymouth Notch.** Coolidge Homestead National Historic Landmark off State Highway 100A includes his birthplace and boyhood home, both of which contain original interiors, family furnishings and possessions. Coolidge lived there until about 1890 but often returned during his public years. There in the homestead parlor at 2:47 AM, August 3, 1923, he was sworn in as president by his father, a notary public, following the sudden death of President Warren G. Harding. The unpretentious, one and one-half-story, white frame house, bought by Coolidge's parents in 1876, was built about 1850. In 1956, his son gave the property to the state. Next door to the Coolidge Homestead is the 1820 Wilder House, birthplace of Coolidge's mother, now a hospitality center and restaurant. Both places are operated by the Vermont Division of Historic Sites. (Both open May 15–October 15, daily 9:00–5:00; 802-828-3226; admission.)

(See MASSACHUSETTS in this chapter; also Chapter 3, DISTRICT OF COLUMBIA; also Chapter 4, SOUTH DAKOTA.)

DEWEY, GEORGE (1837–1917). Admiral Dewey's stars have obviously faded. Acclaimed as the 1898 hero of one of America's less laudable wars, he was a Vermont native and resided in his birthplace at 120 State St. in **Montpelier** until 1851. During the course of another star-tarnishing war in 1969, the house was replaced by a state office building. The one and one-half-story, steep-roofed dwelling originally stood almost directly opposite the State Capitol.

(See Chapter 3, DISTRICT OF COLUMBIA, PENNSYLVANIA.)

DEWEY, JOHN (1859–1952). The educator-philosopher was born at **Burlington** in a house still standing at 186 South Willard St. (privately owned), his home until 1863. Another boyhood home (1876–79), also privately owned, is located at 178 South Prospect St.

(See Chapter 2, MANHATTAN; also Chapter 3, NEW YORK; also Chapter 4, ILLINOIS.)

DOUGLAS, STEPHEN ARNOLD (1813–1861). Lincoln's Democratic opponent in the 1860 presidential election, the "Little Giant" of national politics, was born in **Brandon.** His one and one-half-story, white frame birthplace, dating from the early 1800s and somewhat modified, stands at 2 Grove St., now operated by the Daughters of the American Revolution. Period furnishings include Douglas' cradle, which he had not yet outgrown when the family left. According to local tradition, his father died here suddenly while holding the infant in his lap; the son fell into the fireplace but was quickly rescued by a neighbor. As a presidential candidate accompanied by large campaign crowds, Douglas revisited his birthplace in 1860. (Open by appointment, 802-247-5535; free.)

(See Chapter 3, DISTRICT OF COLUMBIA, NEW YORK; also Chapter 4, ILLINOIS.)

FROST, ROBERT LEE (1874–1963). The poet's first Vermont home (1920–28) was **South Shaftsbury,** where he summered in a 1769 half-stone farmhouse with a steep gable roof. Nearby is the "Gully House," now Frost Farm National Historic Landmark, a one and one-half-story frame dwelling that he purchased on 153 acres and occupied during summers from 1929 until his wife's death in 1938. Both homes, located on Buck Hill Road off U.S. Highway 7, are privately owned.

Near **Ripton,** another Frost Farm National Historic Landmark is occasionally open to the public. This is the Homer Noble Farm, located two miles east of State Highway 125 on an unpaved road adjacent to the Frost Wayside area. Built in the late 1800s, the one and one-half-story frame farmhouse became his final summer home (1940–62). He enlarged the house, converting the cabin outbuilding into his studio and living quarters, a dwelling that remains as he left it in 1962. His simple furnishings there include his Morris chair and lap desk. Frost produced four books of poetry there, including *A Witness Tree* (1942). The farm is owned and maintained by Middlebury College. (Open by appointment or tour arrangement with Middlebury College, Middlebury, VT, 05753; 802-388-2117.)

Exhibit: The Robert Frost Nature Trail is a .75-mile stretch of State Highway 125 between the Frost Wayside, east of **Ripton,** to the Bread Loaf campus of Middlebury College, where the poet often gave outdoor lectures. Seven of his poems are mounted on plaques along this scenic route that he often traveled.

(See MASSACHUSETTS, NEW HAMPSHIRE in this chapter; also Chapter 4, MICHIGAN; also Chapter 6, FLORIDA; also Chapter 9, CALIFORNIA.)

GREELEY, HORACE (1811–1872). Though born in New Hampshire, Greeley always felt emotionally rooted in Vermont. The eventual editor, reformer and 1872 presidential candidate worked in **West Haven** from 1819 to 1822 as a young apprentice printer. In 1981, according to Carol Richards, West Haven Town Clerk, the house he lived in was "beyond the point of being restored or repaired," with only "one side and a couple main beams" still unfallen.

"I have never known a community so generally moral, intelligent, industrious, and friendly," Greeley wrote about **East Poultney,** where he boarded from 1822 to 1830. His first residence was the 1785 Eagle Tavern, a large clapboard inn (now a private home) that stands on State Highway 140 at a corner of the village green. He later resided at the plain white Greeley House on the east side of the center triangle, where he learned the printing trade. This privately operated house, dating from 1823, displays memorabilia from Greeley's years there. (Open July 1–August 31, daily 10:00–4:00; admission.)

(See NEW HAMPSHIRE in this chapter; also Chapter 2, MANHATTAN; also Chapter 3, NEW YORK.)

GREEN, HENRIETTA ROBINSON "HETTY" (1834–1916). With her "Midas touch," the "Witch of Wall Street" was also one of the great misers of history. Her home from 1879 to 1882 and intervals thereafter in **Bellows Falls,** the Tucker House, stood at School and Westminster streets—now the site of a bank, she'd be glad to know. The house was demolished after heavy damage in a 1938 hurricane.

(See MASSACHUSETTS, RHODE ISLAND in this chapter; also Chapter 2, MANHATTAN; also Chapter 3, NEW JERSEY.)

KIPLING, RUDYARD (1865–1936). North of **Brattleboro,** the English author whose work powerfully influenced a generation of writers built "Naulakha," his stone and shingle bungalow—shaped "like a boat on the flank of a distant wave"—in 1892. Here in his southeast study, he wrote *The Jungle Book* (1894) and *Captains Coura-*

geous (1897). He named the house in memory of his wife's brother, with whom he had collaborated on a novel titled *The Naulakha*. Kipling and his family lived here until a property disagreement with his American in-laws caused his abrupt return to England in 1896. The house, located at 19 Terrace St. off Kipling and Black Mountain roads, is privately owned. Kipling's first home in Brattleboro, which he occupied during Naulakha's construction (1892–93) was Bliss Cottage (privately owned), now located on Kipling Road several hundred yards east of its original site near the Experiment for International Living campus. His first daughter was born there during a December blizzard. The house has been extensively altered.

LEWIS, SINCLAIR (1885–1951). The novelist's home "Twin Farms," about two miles south of **Barnard** on the road to South Pomfret, is now the Sonnenberg Ski Area (privately owned). Lewis and his wife, journalist Dorothy Thompson, lived in this large, white frame house (1928–38) during most of their marriage. The 1896 farmhouse, along with another on 300 acres, was the first home that Lewis owned; Dorothy Thompson remained here for many years after their 1942 divorce.

(See MASSACHUSETTS in this chapter; also Chapter 2, MANHATTAN; also Chapter 3, NEW YORK; also Chapter 4, MINNESOTA.)

MOSES, ANNA MARY ROBERTSON "GRANDMA" (1860–1961).

Exhibit: Bennington Museum on West Main Street in **Bennington** displays the one-room schoolhouse the painter attended at Eagle Bridge, N.Y. Moved to Bennington, the school now exhibits family memorabilia, clothing and her art equipment. The museum also contains more than 80 of her primitivist works. (Open March 1–November 30, daily 9:00–5:00; 802-442-2180; admission.)

(See Chapter 3, NEW YORK; also Chapter 5, VIRGINIA.)

HORACE GREELEY HOUSE. This 1823 house facing the village green in **East Poultney** is now a Greeley Museum displaying relics of the journalist's printing apprenticeship, 1822–30. The sketch was drawn by Walter McRoberts of East Poultney.
(Courtesy Helen Cahill, Greeley House Museum.)

The Horace Greeley House, 1823   Helen Cahill

NOYES, JOHN HUMPHREY (1811–1886). This charismatic Vermont preacher founded the largest, most successful group-marriage experiment in history and also popularized male continence—"coitus reservatus"—as a birth control technique; "many considered it to be as great a concept as the telegraph," according to one account. In **Putney,** where Noyes organized his first "Bible Communism" group, his boyhood home, built about 1800, stands on Kimball Hill Road. The house he built about 1840 at Christian Square also survives as an apartment building. Both dwellings remain privately owned and unmarked.

(See Chapter 3, NEW YORK.)

ROCKWELL, NORMAN (1894–1978). The popular illustrator's first home and studio (1939–43) stood two miles west of **Arlington** on State Highway 313. A disastrous fire here destroyed his renovated barn studio along with 30 original paintings and a treasury of priceless antique costumes, almost wiping out his career. The white house with blue shutters remains privately owned.

Near **West Arlington,** however, he later purchased a 1792 colonial, two-story house on State Highway 313, built a studio and tennis court in back, and lived here from 1943 to 1953. This home is now "Grandmother's House"; according to country inn authority Jane Anderson, it is "the most personal inn we know of in New England."

Exhibit: The Norman Rockwell Museum, which claims the world's largest collection of his art, is located on U.S. Highway 4 east of **Rutland.** (Open mid-June–mid-October, daily 9:30–5:00; 215-368-1177; admission.)

(See MASSACHUSETTS in this chapter; also Chapter 2, MANHATTAN; also Chapter 3, NEW YORK, PENNSYLVANIA.)

ROETHKE, THEODORE (1908–1963). From 1943 to 1946, the poet taught at Bennington College and during this period resided at "Shingle Cottage" on the campus at **North Bennington.** This two-story saltbox dwelling dates from at least 1777; from its door, it is said, one "Eleazar Edgerton went forth to fight in the Battle of Bennington." The house seems to have become the college's official poet's residence. Robert Frost (see the entry on Frost earlier in this section) occupied it during the summer of 1927; and W. H. Auden stayed here for one term in 1946. It remains privately occupied on Harlan Road.

(See Chapter 3, PENNSYLVANIA; also Chapter 4, MICHIGAN; also Chapter 6, WASHINGTON.)

SMITH, JOSEPH (1805–1844). Off State Highway 14 north of **Sharon** stands the 38½-foot granite shaft—a foot for each year of his life—marking the birth site of the Mormon leader. The family lived here for only a few months. Smith Birthplace Memorial, operated by the Church of Jesus Christ of Latter-Day Saints, also contains a Mormon library and museum. (Open May 1–November 30, daily 8:00–6:00; free.)

(See Chapter 3, NEW YORK, PENNSYLVANIA; also Chapter 4, ILLINOIS, MISSOURI, OHIO; also Chapter 6, UTAH.)

STEVENS, THADDEUS (1792–1868). Fierce leader of the post-Civil War Radical Republicans, Stevens lived most of his life in Pennsylvania but was a Vermont native. Several miles south of **Peacham,** his boyhood home (1807–15) stands on Town Highway 4, a farm since about 1800. The privately owned house has been considerably altered. Excluded from many activities because of a clubfoot, the youth apparently suffered rejection traumas here that made him prefer the image of a crusty loner throughout his life.

(See Chapter 3, DISTRICT OF COLUMBIA, PENNSYLVANIA.)

YOUNG, BRIGHAM (1801–1877). A 14-foot granite monument marks the Mormon leader's birth site off State Highway 100 east of **Whitingham,** his home until 1803.

(See Chapter 3, NEW YORK; also Chapter 4, ILLINOIS; also Chapter 6, UTAH.)

TWO

NEW YORK CITY

(See Chapter 3 for upstate New York)

Because so many notable figures in every realm of activity and occupation lived at some time in New York City, this chapter interrupts the regional format of *Who Lived Where* to focus on that metropolis, the nation's largest. Some observers maintain that New York City—plus parts of Connecticut, New Jersey and upstate Westchester County—indeed forms an indigenous urban region; and there is much to support that point of view. This chapter, however, deals strictly with the five boroughs of the city.

The borough system, established with the annexations of 1898, created the entity of Greater New York. Each borough has its own municipal government represented in the New York City mayor's office. Each borough is also a separate county containing administrative units that often overlap in function with borough offices. During its first 250 years, the city consisted solely of Manhattan, which was also the first borough settled, by Dutch whites in 1626. Permanent settlements then followed in Brooklyn, the Bronx, Queens and—by 1661—Staten Island (Richmond). Queens is the largest in total square mileage, followed by Brooklyn, Staten Island and the Bronx, with Manhattan ranking a low fifth; an astonishing amount of the city's total land area lies in parks and playgrounds—almost one-fifth. Brooklyn ranks first in population number, followed by Queens, Manhattan, the Bronx and Staten Island.

New York has been the nation's most populous city since 1820, when it surged ahead of Philadelphia. Today, its population of barely 8 million ranks ninth among world cities. Averaged out, some 26,000 people occupy each square mile. New York is the financial, business, and entertainment capital of the United States; but as headquarters of the United Nations and as one of the world's great seaports, it is also a hugely diverse international center.

It is easier to count the noted Americans who have never lodged here than those who have. For artists and writers, the city's magnet was the proximity of exhibits, publishers and each other, plus the adrenal atmosphere of creativity. For politicians, it was the lure of contest and power. For ex-presidents and retired military men, New York granted the most convincing illusion of continuing power and busy affairs. Business tycoons came to New York because, in the words of bank-robber Willie Sutton, "that's where the money was." For show people, Broadway was simply the greatest show on Earth. Attracting them all was simple quantity; New York held more of most things, and probably at least one of anything, to be found anywhere. Most of all, there were more people and possibilities. It is still true. The excitement of New York for many is that despite its old age (by American standards), it remains the front line and cutting edge of our society, the place to be for what is happening. It is still, in that sense, our frontier. Americans have always been a frontier people, we're told, and New York City provides that ongoing "rush" of experience, challenge and discovery that seems so important to our national bloodstream. What looks to an outsider like a general state of hypertension in New Yorkers is, one finds, merely their common pace; speed is treasured there like nowhere else in the world. Often a newcomer is first startled, then amused, then appalled; but, in the end, one is usually caught up in this lifestyle that makes sense, of course, only in its own unique milieu.

The New York City Landmarks Preservation Commission, established in 1965, has been active in researching, designating, and preserving historic buildings all over the city. This agency is an excellent model for any city interested in doing well for its past. Unfortunately, much of the collection and ongoing research gathered by the Commission's trained, enthusiastic staff remains unpublished owing to budgetary limits. The Commission has concentrated its investigations and inventory work in 39 identified historic districts throughout all boroughs, 23 of them in Manhattan. *A Guide to New York City Landmarks* (1978), a booklet published by the Commission, briefly describes these districts and other designated buildings. Other fine treatments, with mainly architectural emphasis, include *History Preserved: A Guide to New York City Landmarks and Historic Districts* (1974), by Harmon H. Goldstone and Martha Dalrymple; and *New York: A Guide to the Metropolis* (1975), by Gerard R. Wolfe. Nathan Silver's *Lost New York* (1971) is a marvelous photographic record of a New York City gone but—thanks to books like these—far from forgotten.

Sources for identifying New York City sites and homes are plentiful; but where there are many observers, there are also many versions. While the following account of the homes occupied by notable New York residents is probably the most ambitious ever attempted, readers already familiar with the city's landmarks may note a few glaring omissions. For example, Manhattan guidebooks through the years have referred to the site of Mme. Katharine Branchard's rooming house at 61 Washington Square as the so-called "House of Genius," where writers including Willa Cather, Stephen Crane, John Dos Passos, Theodore Dreiser, O. Henry, Eugene O'Neill, John Reed and Lincoln Steffens supposedly roomed. But Susan Edmiston and Linda D. Cirino dispelled that myth in their excellent *Literary New York* (1976); they found no evidence that any of these authors ever resided there. Another apparently phoney association is that of the house at 130 MacDougal St. with philosopher Bronson Alcott and his daughter, the author Louisa May Alcott; it is reported by even some of the most reputable city guides that she wrote *Little Women* (1868–69) here. Yet no Alcott biography mentions this house; and the Bronson Alcott Society has no information on the address and cannot verify either of the Alcott's presence there. The inescapable conclusion is that probably neither Alcott ever stayed there, much less wrote anything on the spot— yet numerous guidebooks continue to identify the place as an Alcott residence. The Branchard and Alcott examples illustrate fairly common cases of oblivious repetition, errors apparently copied from one guidebook to the next with a touching degree of trust but scant respect for fact or reader. Thus at least some of the "glaring" omissions herein are vastly deliberate, with not-too-optimistic hopes of "glaring them out" of the street-guide literature.

As for New York City guidebooks of various sorts, there is no dearth. Many are excellent, particularly those focusing on architecture, museums, restaurants and what to do with the kiddies. Yet New York City, like most of America's major urban centers, has never received its just due in any comprehensive inventory of its historical sites. The Landmarks Commission has certainly made an auspicious beginning, but one has only to look at some of the detailed, street-by-street historical guides for London to note how far New York City lags in this regard. As one of the world's great cities, New York owes a better record to itself, to its posterity and to all of us.

THE BRONX

Ranaque and Tackamuck only wanted "two guns, two kettles, two coats, two adzes, two shirts, one barrel of cider and six bits of money." That was the 1641 market value of the 500 acres between the Harlem and Bronx rivers that Jonas Bronck, a Dane, bought and settled north of today's Port Morris area.

Suspended like a loose purse draping from the Westchester County line into the East River and

Long Island Sound, the Bronx is the city's northernmost borough, the only one situated on mainland New York State. New England colonists followed Bronck and formed numerous settlements. Caught between hostile natives and the claims of Dutch Manhattan, these villages endured grievous hardship and many disappeared. After England took over the New York colony, class-conscious gentry built large estates, and the area acquired the genteel look of English country domains and the Southern plantation system. The Bronx was all part of Westchester County until 1874, when New York City annexed the western townships; acquisition of the eastern portions followed in 1895. Today the borough occupies 42.5 square miles.

Like Queens, the Bronx was an early refuge for Manhattan dwellers seeking wooded countryside and pure air. Foothills of the Berkshires and Green Mountains begin here, accounting for the borough's lumpy topography. The look of rural Bronx is well preserved in the borough's extensive park system, especially in Pelham Bay and Van Cortlandt parks. Irish and German immigration tripled urban population here in the decade from 1850 to 1860, and population again tripled from 1910 to 1940. In 1939 it was reported that 92 percent of existing Bronx houses arose after 1900; that figure is certainly higher now. The borough remains primarily residential.

Why is it *the* Bronx, and not *the* Brooklyn, *the* Manhattan, *the* Queens? According to George R. Stewart's *American Place Names* (1970), "People came to speak of going to the Broncks" (estate) for country excursions, and *the* simply survived the phonetic transfer of household name into borough name—a plausible guess, at least.

Noted New Yorkers who sought stylish Riverdale dwellings included the Kennedy family, Mark Twain, Fiorello La Guardia and Arturo Toscanini. Leon Trotsky roomed in the Bronx just before the Russian revolution plunged him into a historic vanguard; and plumber George Meany arose to labor leadership in the borough. The haunted Edgar Allan Poe spent most of his last days here, and his little Fordham house remains one of the borough's oldest.

Today too much of the Bronx is ravaged by the worst kind of urban decay—blocks upon blocks of derelict buildings and desolate lots are symbols of boarded-up hopes. The degradation of these once-pastoral acres and their current inhabitants exacts a continuing price on New York's beleaguered social and economic stability. It seems tragic that, were Trotsky alive in the Bronx today, he would not need to travel many blocks to find his audience.

BARTÓK, BÉLA (1881–1945). At 3242 Cambridge Ave. in **Riverdale,** the Hungarian composer resided for three years following his 1940 flight from Europe. "We have five fine rooms and a sun-parlour (where we have put the two pianos)," he wrote in a letter, "and for all this the monthly rent is $70." The building still contains private apartments.

(See MANHATTAN, QUEENS in this chapter; also Chapter 3, NEW YORK.)

CLEMENS, SAMUEL LANGHORNE "MARK TWAIN" (1835–1910). Before his wife's death there in 1903, the author spent what were probably the last happy years of his life at Wave Hill House in **Riverdale.** This fieldstone mansion at 675 West 252nd St. (at the corner of Sycamore Avenue), built from 1820 to 1830, occupies a 28-acre estate on the Hudson. To Clemens, when he moved there in 1901 at the height of his literary success, Wave Hill's most attractive feature was the dining room—by his account, it was "60 feet long, 30 feet wide and had two great fireplaces in it." Theodore Roosevelt lived there earlier, and Arturo Toscanini was a later dweller there (see the entries on Roosevelt and Toscanini later in this section). Today the mansion is owned by the Wave Hill Foundation and, known as Wave Hill Environmental Center, features art exhibits. (Open daily 9:30–4:30; 212-549-2055; admission.)

(See MANHATTAN in this chapter; also Chapter 1, CONNECTICUT; also Chapter 3, NEW YORK; also Chapter 4, IOWA, MISSOURI; also Chapter 6, CALIFORNIA, NEVADA.)

GEHRIG, HENRY LOUIS "LOU" (1903–1941). The nation kept a long death watch for the "Iron Horse" of baseball after a paralytic illness forced him to quit the New York Yankees team in 1939. He died in his last home at 5204 Delafield Ave. in **Fieldston,** a privately owned dwelling that dates from 1925.

(See MANHATTAN in this chapter; also Chapter 3, NEW YORK.)

HUTCHINSON, ANNE (1591–1643). In what is now **Eastchester,** the widowed Puritan colonist who had been banished from Boston for daring to challenge America's first moral majority settled in 1642 with her six children. The next year, she and five of her family were slain there by local Siwanoy Indians, providing the Boston elders with a lip-smacking celebration of "divine justice." After years of locating the Hutchinson cabin site in Pelham Bay Park, historians now believe that she lived on the west shore of the Hutchinson River near today's Boston Road bridge (U.S. Highway 1).

(See Chapter 1, MASSACHUSETTS, RHODE ISLAND.)

KENNEDY, JOHN FITZGERALD (1917–1963).
KENNEDY, ROBERT FRANCIS (1925–1968).
As boys, the 35th U.S. president and his brother, a later presidential aspirant, resided from 1926 to 1929 in what was then the parental home at 5040 Independence Ave., **Riverdale.** This mansion remains privately owned.

(See Chapter 1, MASSACHUSETTS, RHODE ISLAND; also Chapter 3, DISTRICT OF CO-LUMBIA, NEW YORK; also Chapter 4, MICHIGAN; also Chapter 5, FLORIDA, VIRGINIA; also Chapter 6, CALIFORNIA, TEXAS.)

LA GUARDIA, FIORELLO HENRY (1882–1947). In 1921, the blustery little congressman who would become one of New York City's most beloved mayors bought the two-story, white stucco house at 1852 University Ave. in **Riverdale.** La Guardia, hoping that the move from Manhattan would benefit the health of his ailing first wife (she died that same year), added a sun porch and resided there until the early 1930s. The house is still a private residence. La Guardia's last home, from his retirement as mayor in 1945 until his death, stands at 5020 Goodridge Ave. (privately owned), also in Riverdale.

(See MANHATTAN in this chapter.)

MEANY, GEORGE (1894–1980). The boyhood home from 1899 to 1919 of the plumber who became the longtime chief of the American Federation of Labor stood until the 1970s at 695 East 135th St., a three-story brick house close to the northern piers of Triborough Bridge (Interstate Highway 278) in **Port Morris.**

Meany's home from 1923 until 1948 was a row house at 1626 Mayflower Ave. (privately owned), now located within the grounds of the Bronx Psychiatric Center, **Westchester Heights.**

(See Chapter 3, MARYLAND.)

OSWALD, LEE HARVEY (1939–1963). "When Lee became a truant from school, I feel that he also became a truant from life," wrote his brother Robert. The alleged assassin of President Kennedy (see the entry on John Fitzgerald Kennedy earlier in this section) lived with his mother in an apartment north of **Crotona Park** at 825 East 179th St. from 1952 to 1954, spending daytime hours alone there until school authorities took disciplinary action.

Earlier (1952) the pair resided in a smaller basement apartment at 1455 Sheridan Ave., **Morrisania.** "Lee hated it," reported his brother.

Both addresses remain private.

(See Chapter 5, LOUISIANA; also Chapter 6, TEXAS.)

POE, EDGAR ALLAN (1809–1849). Poe Cottage, a one and one-half-story frame farmhouse in Poe Park at 2640 Grand Concourse and East Kingsbridge Road, **Fordham,** was the author's last residence of any lengthy duration. Though well-known when he arrived there in 1846 with his ailing child-wife Virginia and mother-in-law Maria Clemm, he was, as usual, direly impoverished, and Mrs. Clemm begged their meals on the street. "Eddie rarely left his beautiful home," she recalled. "I attended to his literary business; for he, poor fellow, knew nothing about money transactions." There Poe wrote his poems "Annabel Lee" and "The Bells," among others; and there in 1847, to his wild grief, Virginia Poe finally succumbed to tuberculosis. Her bed is still there, along with Poe's rocking chair. Poe left the small house in 1848 for a rootless year of mental and physical decline before his sordid death in Baltimore. The house, dating from about 1812 and now surrounded by urban traffic, stood solitary in peaceful meadowland in Poe's day. In 1913, the city moved it from its original location on Kingsbridge Road about 400 feet to its present site. After a long history of neglect and vandalism, the house is presently well-maintained by the New York City Department of Parks. (Open Tuesday–Saturday 10:00–1:00, 2:00–5:00, Sunday 1:00–5:00; 212-881-8900; admission.)

(See MANHATTAN in this chapter; also Chapter 1, MASSACHUSETTS; also Chapter 3, MARYLAND, PENNSYLVANIA; also Chapter 5, VIRGINIA.)

ROOSEVELT, THEODORE (1858–1919). In **Riverdale,** a summer boyhood home of the 26th U.S. president was Wave Hill House (see the entry on Samuel Langhorne Clemens earlier in this section). Here, in 1870 and 1871, the frail, near-sighted child roamed in nearby fields and woods and developed his lifelong interest in nature and the outdoors. The Roosevelt children, who took French and German lessons from private tutors during this period, used the small room left of the main entrance for their ongoing studies.

(See MANHATTAN in this chapter; also Chapter 3, DISTRICT OF COLUMBIA, NEW YORK; also Chapter 4, NORTH DAKOTA; also Chapter 6, NEW MEXICO.)

SETON, ELIZABETH ANN BAYLEY (1774–1821). The ancestral homestead from 1763 of America's first native saint was "Cragdon," located in **Edenwald** at what is now Seton Falls Park, Seton Avenue and 233rd Street. At this site, the home of her grandparents, she spent summers as a child. Seton Manor surmounted the hill near the falls. The city acquired the site in 1903 for a hospital it never built, and established the park in 1930.

(See MANHATTAN in this chapter; also Chapter 3, MARYLAND, NEW YORK.)

TOSCANINI, ARTURO (1867–1957). At age 70, when he became conductor of the NBC Symphony Orchestra, Toscanini moved into "Villa Pauline," a five-acre estate overlooking the Hudson River at the crest of Independence Avenue in **Riverdale.** The house was described by one biographer as "a cross between a Swiss mountain chalet and a late Victorian mansion." The volatile maestro, a podium terrorist whose stomping tantrums and piercing expletives in several languages could wither platoons of prim orchestral egos, was charmingly sweet outside the pit. He often entertained lavishly at his mansion; not infrequently his guests included astonished, still-quivering players whom, during a day's work, he had all but stoned. The final result of such tyranny was, of course, the rare perfection of music preserved on Toscanini records. Toscanini

lived at Villa Pauline from 1939 to 1942, then bought and returned to the mansion a few years later and died there. During the mid-1940s, he lived briefly at "Wave Hill House" (see the entry on Samuel Langhorne Clemens earlier in this section).

(See Chapter 3, NEW JERSEY.)

TROTSKY, LEON (1879–1940). The Russian revolutionist lived briefly in a three-room apartment at 1522 Vyse Ave., **Claremont,** in 1917, just before the upheaval in his homeland that brought the Bolshevik party to power. Trotsky was lecturing and publishing a small newspaper in Manhattan at this time (see the entry on Wystan Hugh Auden in the section on Manhattan). He and his children were fascinated by the modest enough "modern conveniences" they found in the apartment, for which he paid $18 per month. The building still contains private apartments.

TWAIN, MARK. See SAMUEL LANGHORNE CLEMENS.

BROOKLYN

The most populous borough and second largest in area, encompassing 72.8 square miles, Brooklyn caps the western end of Long Island. The East River separates it from Manhattan, and Queens borders on the east. Brooklyn long resisted formal merger with New York City—though when it did join, for purposes of sheer practicality, in 1898, the merger had been all but official for years. More than the Bronx, Queens or Staten Island, Brooklyn jealously maintains a sense of civic individuality. Whereas other borough residents may, without visible trauma, identify New York City as their home, a true Brooklynite always comes from Brooklyn first, New York City second if at all.

Flatlands, or New Amersfoort, was the first tiny village established by Dutch settlers in 1624. The Dutch towns of Flatbush, Brooklyn, Bushwick, New Utrecht and the English settlement of Gravesend followed. Breukelen (later Brooklyn), named after a village in Utrecht, Holland (meaning "broken land"), arose in the present vicinity of Hoyt and Fulton streets in 1637. When the bloody Battle of Long Island raged at Gowanus during the American Revolution, the town numbered some 3,000; almost 12,000 Continental soldiers died on British prison ships in Wallabout Bay. Brooklyn gradually annexed surrounding communities, became a city in 1834, and was the third largest in America by 1855. The borough reached its present boundaries in 1896, and two years later became part of New York City. Today a sizable percentage of American foreign commerce passes over Brooklyn's 202-mile waterfront. Though one of the extensive industrial and business centers of the nation, the borough remains primarily residential.

The celebrated "Brooklyn accent"—that curious dialect which transforms "th" to "d" and transposes the sounds "er" and "oi"—is apparently fast disappearing. A project of the Long Island Historical Society is to record and "presoive dose Noo Yawk verces," certainly a worthwhile historical and conservation effort.

Noted Brooklyn residents have included American preachers as diverse in message and motivation as Henry Ward Beecher, Anthony Comstock, and W. E. B. Du Bois. Winston Churchill's mother was a good Brooklyn girl and author Henry Miller a sad Brooklyn boy. The borough gave America George Gershwin and Al Capone four months apart. Walt Whitman and Woody Guthrie were lyrical Brooklyn brothers. Synonymous with Brooklyn for most Americans until their 1958 shift to Los Angeles, the Dodgers brought Jackie Robinson and Branch Rickey to town. Many homes of Brooklyn notables have survived in private hands.

In Brooklyn stands the oldest dwelling in both New York City and State. This is the 1652 Pieter Wyckoff House, currently awaiting restoration at Clarendon Road and Ralph Avenue in Flatlands. Especially noteworthy areas for viewing buildings of Brooklyn's past are Brooklyn Heights and the borough's 10 other designated historic districts.

AUDEN, WYSTAN HUGH (1907–1973). The English-born poet made New York City his permanent home in 1945. Earlier in **Brooklyn Heights,** however, Auden rented rooms for a year during 1939 and 1940 at 1 Montague Terrace (privately owned), where he kept regular writing hours. A later nearby residence (1940–41) stood at 7 Middagh St., where he paid $25 per month for the third floor, collected rents for the landlord, and shared household tasks with Carson McCullers (see the entry on McCullers later in this section), Gypsy Rose Lee and frequent well-

known guests. "It was just a nice old house," wrote resident Paul Bowles, "with a comfortable atmosphere and rather uncomfortable furnishings . . . Auden sat at the head of the table and conducted the conversations." This house, located on the north side of the street, fell to wreckers in 1945 when the entire block became a widened access to the Brooklyn-Queens Expressway (U.S. Highway 278).

(See MANHATTAN in this chapter.)

BEECHER, HENRY WARD (1813–1887). In 1847, the controversial spellbinding preacher assumed the pulpit of the new Plymouth Church of the Pilgrims in **Brooklyn Heights,** where he remained for the rest of his life. Two of his area homes (both privately owned) still stand: the 1847 house of brick and brownstone at 22 Willow St., where he lived in 1848; and 176 Columbia Heights, his home from 1851 to 1855. The latter house, a three-story frame dwelling dating from 1846, has a modern brick veneer but still utilizes the original cast-iron railings in front. Beecher died at his last home, which stood at 124 Hicks St. (at the corner of Clark Street), where he resided from the 1860s. Preacher Beecher also practiced a bit of lechery with a comely parishioner, it was alleged, while living there; and the sensational Tilton Affair, in which he was acquitted of adultery by a hung jury, rocked the country. Plymouth Church, now a National Historical Landmark and still holding regular services, is located at 75 Hicks St.

(See Chapter 1, CONNECTICUT; also Chapter 3, NEW YORK; also Chapter 4, INDIANA, OHIO.)

BOW, CLARA GORDON (1905–1965). The silent-film actress became known as "the It Girl" for some supposedly vague, provocative quality she exuded that her publicists were careful not to define; it was, of course, plain slinky sex, 1920s style. A Brooklyn native, Bow was born in an apartment over a storefront Baptist church on Bergen Street.

The three-story house where she spent most of her nubile adolescence and from which she departed to begin her Hollywood career stands at 857 73rd St., **Bay Ridge.** She lost her mother to a traumatic mental illness there, an episode that left lifelong emotional scars on the actress herself. The Bows occupied the second story of this 19th-century private dwelling.

(See Chapter 6, CALIFORNIA, NEVADA.)

CAPONE, ALPHONSE "AL" (1899–1947). Some sources give the Chicago gangster's birthplace as Naples, Italy, but biographer John Kobler states that Capone was born on Navy Street in Brooklyn, the area just east of **Manhattan Bridge** (Interstate Highway 78). Unless sentiment overcomes the Mafia, there will never be a monument there to celebrate the parental Capones' sordid gift to their adopted country. Nor will a plaque improve 38 Garfield Place (privately owned), his boyhood home from 1907 to 1915, a two-story cold-water tenement further south. Scarface Al's most attractive monument is probably his tombstone in a Chicago cemetery.

(See Chapter 4, ILLINOIS, WISCONSIN; also Chapter 5, FLORIDA; also Chapter 6, CALIFORNIA.)

CHURCHILL, JENNIE JEROME (1854–1921). Addressing the U.S. Congress in 1941, British Prime Minister Winston Churchill remarked, "If my father had been American and my mother British, instead of the other way 'round, I might have got here on my own." Churchill's mother, who married Lord Randolph Churchill, was the stunningly beautiful daughter of sportsman-financier Leonard Jerome. Her **Cobble Hill** birthplace and home to age four stands at 197 Amity St. (privately owned), a house built in 1849 but much altered except for the front ironwork. "Children were heard and seen and hugged" at Amity Street, wrote biographer Anita Leslie of Jennie Jerome's pleasant childhood. The marker at 426 Henry St. claiming that house as her birthplace is in error, though her parents lived there just before her birth.

(See MANHATTAN in this chapter.)

COMSTOCK, ANTHONY (1844–1915). Crusading suppressor of vice, with supersensitive antennae for any art or literature that remotely suggested the presence of genitals (and he could detect such "vice" where no one else could), Comstock is the patron saint of censors; he spent a voyeuristic, purse-lipped lifetime joyously rooting out and arresting victims of his morality. His longtime **Williamsburg** home from 1871 at 354 Grand Ave. is now a private, two-apartment dwelling.

(See Chapter 1, CONNECTICUT; also Chapter 3, NEW JERSEY.)

CRANE, HART (1899–1932). *The Bridge* (1930), Crane's epic poem to the symbolic majesty of Brooklyn Bridge, was composed over several years at various New York City addresses, but he finished it while residing in **Brooklyn Heights.** Intermittently from 1924 to 1929, he occupied a room on the fourth floor of 110 Columbia Heights (privately owned) with a superb view of the bridge and the Manhattan skyline. A previous resident of this building was Washington Roebling, designer of the bridge; and a concurrent roomer with Crane was author John Dos Passos (see the entry on Dos Passos below). Crane briefly occupied a room at 77 Willow St. (privately owned) in 1928. In 1929, he finished his opus at 130 Columbia Heights, since replaced by the 1968 world headquarters building of the Watchtower Bible and Tract Society (Jehovah's Witnesses).

(See MANHATTAN in this chapter; also Chapter 4, OHIO.)

DOS PASSOS, JOHN RODERIGO (1896–1970). In 1924 the author briefly occupied a **Brooklyn Heights** room at 106–110 Columbia Heights (see the entry on Hart Crane above), where he worked on *Manhattan Transfer* (1925).

(See MANHATTAN in this chapter; also Chapter 1, MASSACHUSETTS; also Chapter 5, VIRGINIA.)

DREISER, THEODORE (1871–1945). The author lived in the private apartment building at 1799 Bedford Ave., **Bedford Stuyvesant,** with his longtime companion and later wife Helen Richardson during almost all of 1925. This was where he completed *An American Tragedy* (1925), his best-known novel.

(See MANHATTAN in this chapter; also Chapter 3, NEW YORK; also Chapter 4, ILLINOIS, INDIANA; also Chapter 6, CALIFORNIA.)

DU BOIS, WILLIAM EDWARD BURGHARDT (1868–1963). At 31 Grace Court in **Brooklyn Heights,** the educator-reformer who joined the Communist Party in 1961 lived for a decade; this was his last U.S. home before his 1962 emigration to Ghana. "We couldn't have rented here," said Du Bois, "we had to buy. When we first came, the FBI swarmed around the neighborhood asking questions." The stucco-covered house, which Du Bois bought from playwright Arthur Miller, is where Miller wrote *Death of a Salesman* (1949). It is privately owned.

An earlier Brooklyn home at 650 Greene Ave. (privately owned) was his residence before 1920, the period of his active leadership in the NAACP.

(See MANHATTAN in this chapter; also Chapter 1, MASSACHUSETTS; also Chapter 3, MARYLAND, PENNSYLVANIA; also Chapter 5, GEORGIA.)

GERSHWIN, GEORGE (1898–1937). Born Jacob Gershvin in the two-story brick house at 242 Snediker Ave., **East New York,** the composer lived there only for his first eight months. The dwelling, originally frame, was remodeled to its present appearance in 1914. On Gershwin's 65th anniversary in 1963, a marker was dedicated and placed on the privately owned house.

(See MANHATTAN in this chapter; also Chapter 6, CALIFORNIA.)

GUTHRIE, WOODROW WILSON "WOODY" (1912–1967). The nation's foremost balladeer and composer of folk songs lived in Brooklyn before and during the cruel progression of the hereditary Huntington's Disease that finally rendered him helpless. In 1943 he lived briefly at 3755 Cypress Ave. (privately owned) south of **Williamsburg.**

His home from 1943 to 1950 was 3520 Mermaid Ave. on **Coney Island,** a small, three-room apartment in a building since demolished.

The three-story Beach Haven Apartments at 59 Murdoch Court near the intersection of Shore and Ocean parkways in the **Gravesend** area was his family home for the next two years.

(See MANHATTAN, QUEENS in this chapter; also Chapter 6, OKLAHOMA, TEXAS.)

JEROME, JENNIE. See JENNIE JEROME CHURCHILL.

LOVECRAFT, HOWARD PHILLIPS (1890–1937). Author of macabre tales, Lovecraft was an eccentric, reclusive introvert whose hypochondria, cadaverous appearance and assorted neuroses kept him mostly at home behind drawn shades. Home was mainly Rhode Island, but in 1924 he

mistakenly ventured marriage, and the couple occupied two successive apartments in Brooklyn. Both of the buildings remain: at 259 Parkside Ave. in **Flatbush,** their 1924 home; and further north at 169 Clinton St., where they lived from 1924 until their 1926 separation and Lovecraft's return to Providence.

(See Chapter 1, RHODE ISLAND).

McCULLERS, CARSON SMITH (1917–1967). Shattered by ill health and personal tragedy in her later years, the novelist was young, pretty, and vivacious during her residence at 7 Middaugh St. in **Brooklyn Heights** (see the entry on Wystan Hugh Auden earlier in this section). She resided there longer (1940–41, 1943) than the other occupants of this spontaneous literary colony, and she immortalized some of the neighborhood characters in her short stories and a 1941 *Vogue* article titled "Brooklyn Is My Neighborhood."

(See MANHATTAN in this chapter; also Chapter 3, NEW YORK; also Chapter 5, GEORGIA, NORTH CAROLINA.)

MILLER, HENRY VALENTINE (1891–1980). The author whose *Tropic* books provoked a series of obscenity trials but won him eventual recognition as a major American writer grew up in Brooklyn, which he affectionately described in *This Is Henry, Henry Miller from Brooklyn* by Robert Snyder (1974). In infancy Miller moved with his family to the **Williamsburg** section, where they occupied the three-story brick house at 662 Driggs Ave. (privately owned) until his tenth year. His next home, until 1916, stood at 1063 Decatur St. (his "street of early sorrows"), now occupied by a school.

In 1924, having married a second time and quit his Western Union job to write full-time, Miller occupied an apartment far beyond his means at 91 Remsen St. (privately owned) in **Brooklyn Heights.** There, he wrote, "I refused to clutter the place with furniture . . . and thought I was in Japan all the time, everything so clean, so polished, so decorative, so bare." And so futile. Miller soon lost his creative initiative (temporarily) along with his apartment and marriage.

(See MANHATTAN in this chapter; also Chapter 6, CALIFORNIA).

MOORE, MARIANNE CRAIG (1887–1972). The

poet lived for 35 years and wrote most of her best-known works in the **Fort Greene** area at 260 Cumberland St., the six-story Cumberland apartment building which remains there. She occupied fifth-floor quarters from 1931 to 1966.

(See MANHATTAN in this chapter; also Chapter 3, PENNSYLVANIA; also Chapter 4, MISSOURI).

PAINE, THOMAS (1737–1809). Several Brooklyn sources state that the famed patriot spent a portion of his final years in a boardinghouse at Sands and Fulton streets. However, since nobody can say just when, and since none of Paine's many biographers mention the place at all in detailing his last years, this may be a case of simple error compounded by frequent repetition.

(See MANHATTAN in this chapter; also Chapter 3, NEW JERSEY, NEW YORK, PENNSYLVANIA.

PERRY, MATTHEW CALBRAITH (1794–1858). Perry House National Historic Landmark stands at Hudson Avenue and Evans Street in the **U.S. Naval Shipyard** (Naval Station Annex), a large, two and one-half-story frame dwelling built in 1805 and 1806. Encircled by porches and also known as the Commandant's House or Quarters A, this was "Old Bruin's" residence for the two years he commanded the shipyard (1841–43). It was still used until recently as the official residence of Shipyard commanders and is not open to the public.

(See MANHATTAN in this chapter; also Chapter 1, RHODE ISLAND.)

RICKEY, BRANCH WESLEY (1881–1965). As president of the Brooklyn Dodgers, Rickey made sports history in 1946 when he signed Jackie Robinson (see the entry on Robinson later in this section) to the team, thus beginning the racial integration of major league baseball. Rickey's apartment home from 1943 to 1950 stood at 215 Montague St. in **Brooklyn Heights,** the present site of the 1962 Brooklyn Savings Bank.

(See Chapter 3, MARYLAND, PENNSYLVANIA; also Chapter 4, MISSOURI, OHIO.)

ROBINSON, EDWIN ARLINGTON (1869–1935). The poet occupied a dingy apartment at 810 Washington Ave. (at the corner of Eastern Parkway) near **Prospect Park** with his friend Seth Pope

from 1918 to 1922. This building still contains private apartments.

(See MANHATTAN in this chapter; also Chapter 1, MAINE, NEW HAMPSHIRE.)

ROBINSON, JACK ROOSEVELT "JACKIE" (1919–1972). As the first black major-league baseball player, Robinson joined the Brooklyn Dodgers in 1946 and played in Brooklyn until his retirement a decade later. His home from 1947 to 1949 stands in **Flatbush** at 5224 Tilden St., a two and one-half-story brick duplex built about 1912. It remains privately owned.

(See Chapter 1, CONNECTICUT; also Chapter 3, NEW YORK; also Chapter 5, GEORGIA.)

ROCKEFELLER, JOHN DAVISON (1839–1937).

Exhibit: After the financial titan's death, John D. Rockefeller, Jr., demolished his father's Manhattan mansion but donated several intact rooms to New York museums. The Brooklyn Museum, 188 Eastern Parkway at Washington Avenue, **Prospect Park,** displays Rockefeller's ornate sitting room on the museum's fourth floor. The room is lavish, to say the least, a vista of plush velvet and candelabra—also faced with Moorish tiles, gold-brocaded walls, and fine ebony and oak paneling. Here is the baronial style that oil prices paid for 100 years ago. (Open Wednesday–Saturday 10:00–5:00, Sunday 11:00–5:00; 212-638-5000; admission.)

(See MANHATTAN in this chapter; also Chapter 3, NEW JERSEY, NEW YORK; also Chapter 4, OHIO; also Chapter 5, FLORIDA, GEORGIA.)

WHITMAN, WALT (1819–1892). Whitman's Brooklyn occupies the **Manhattan Bridge** and **Fort Green Park** areas, vicinities in which he lived at numerous addresses over many years. In *Walt Whitman on Long Island* (1971), Bertha H. Funnell records 18 separate Brooklyn residences for Whitman between 1823 and 1859. Not a single one remains. The poet reminisced in *Specimen Days* (1882) that "from 1824 to '28 our family lived in Brooklyn on Front, Cranberry and Johnson streets. In the latter my father built a nice house for a home, and afterwards another in Tillary street. We occupied them, one after the other, but they were mortgaged, and we lost them." The houses that Whitman or his carpenter father built on these streets have been long since replaced by housing projects and bridge approaches. Except for their dwelling on Cranberry Street in **Brooklyn Heights,** all of them stood north of Fulton Street and west of Washington Avenue. Later, as a printer and newspaper editor, Whitman occupied several homes and lodgings in the same general area. In 1849 he built a three-story, square-frame house at 106 Myrtle Ave. and lived there with his family for three years, using the lower floor for his office; this house also disappeared years ago. A few of his more long-standing or significant addresses included 41 Tillary St. (1827–32); 120 Front St. (1833–44); 142 Skillman St. (1854–55), where he began writing poems for *Leaves of Grass;* and 107 Portland Ave. (1859–63), his last Brooklyn home. In 1855, he helped set type for *Leaves of Grass* in a print shop that stood on the southwest corner of Cranberry Street and Cadman Plaza West, a building razed in 1964.

(See MANHATTAN in this chapter; also Chapter 3, DISTRICT OF COLUMBIA, NEW JERSEY, NEW YORK.)

WOLFE, THOMAS CLAYTON (1900–1938). Immense in talent, wordage and physical size, the author of five autobiographical novels occupied several **Brooklyn Heights** apartments during four years of prodigious creativity during the 1930s; of the three remaining, his first (1931) was 40 Verandah Place, a three-story brick house between Clinton and Henry streets; his long, boxcar-like room there was poorly lighted at either end by small, barred windows. He moved to 111 Columbia Heights, a row house, later in 1931 and occupied an entire floor for a year. In 1933, he occupied the 1886 pristine brownstone at 5 Montague Terrace, where he lived on the fourth floor until 1935 and completed *Of Time and the River* (1935). A visitor described his scarred work table there as "dented like a shield after a hard battle." All of these residences, where Wolfe continued to pour out the crateloads of prose that editor Maxwell Perkins carved into separate novels, remain privately owned.

(See MANHATTAN in this chapter; also Chapter 5, NORTH CAROLINA.)

WRIGHT, RICHARD (1908–1960). At 175 Carlton Avenue, a three and one-half-story brick house that stood deserted in 1981, the author began writing his best-known work, *Native Son* (1940). He finished the book at 87 Lefferts Place, a three and one-half-story private brownstone. These were the **Bedford Stuyvesant** homes of his friends Jane and Herbert Newton, with whom he lived in 1938. Wright lived in a three-room apartment at 11 Revere Place (privately owned) in 1941 and 1942. Then, until 1945, he and his wife occupied a large apartment at 89 Lefferts Place, a four-story, brick apartment building where he organized a successful tenants' strike and worked on his autobiographical *Black Boy* (1945).

(See MANHATTAN in this chapter; also Chapter 5, MISSISSIPPI, TENNESSEE.)

MANHATTAN

The 23-square-mile finger of Manhattan extends from the Harlem River 12.5 miles south to Battery Park. New Jersey lies across the Hudson River on the west; on the east, over the East River, are the boroughs of Queens and Brooklyn. The finger is 2.5 miles wide at its broadest.

In contrast to the other large colonial cities of Boston and Philadelphia, where religion was such a dominant force in settlement, Manhattan began as a strictly commercial venture. It was peltry, stinking animal hides, that motivated the Dutch West India Company to build and arm a colony here in 1626, an action based on territorial claims from the explorations of the Dutch-employed English seaman Henry Hudson. Supposedly at today's Inwood Hill Park, a party of Manhattan Indians greeted Hudson in 1609; and he greeted them with rum, thus inspiring a tale that the word "Manhattan" literally means "where we all got drunk," or "place of the first colossal hangover." At any rate, when Hudson descended the river on his return journey, his erstwhile drinking guests attacked his ship, apparently convinced that he had laid some very bad medicine on the land. More sober students of the language believe that the word derives less exotically, meaning "island of the hills," which it was but now isn't. Actually Manhattan was more peninsula than island in these early days, since no continuous waterway bounded the northern end; not until 1895 was the link between Spuyten Duyvil Creek and the Harlem River dredged to provide a navigable channel between the Hudson and East rivers.

The colony's first governor, Peter Minuit, began negotiating for purchase with the Manhattan natives, who apparently used the peninsula only as a hunting ground. On behalf of the Company,

Minuit bought the entire land-finger, estimated at 22,000 acres (it is actually closer to 14,000), paying the equivalent of $24—a transaction completed, it is said, in what is now Bowling Green Park. According to George Stimpson in *A Book About American History* (1956), "Just what tribe received these presents is not known for certain. Some authorities say it was collected by the Canarsees on Long Island. The Indians had no conception of land ownership in the white man's sense and such sales meant little more to them than a few presents. But such transactions quieted the consciences of the Dutch and gave a color of legality to their occupation of Indian lands." The fourth and most notable Dutch governor was Peter Stuyvesant, who ruled New Amsterdam from 1647 until the English takeover—and renaming of the colony as New York—in 1664. Today's Pearl Street marked the original waterfront, along which waves lined rows of sea shells. The first of many landfills created Water Street during the late 1600s. Front Street was laid about 1785, and by 1800 the landfill waterfront extended to South Street, where it remains. All but a small upper portion of Battery Park lies on landfill.

By 1653, the town had grown north as far as Wall Street—by 1771 to Grand Street—and by 1800 to Greenwich Village. In 1776, the city's first "Great Fire" wiped out most of the Dutch colonial aspect, but as late as 1835, Manhattan still retained some of its original structures. In that year a gas pipe exploded at Beaver and Hanover streets, and a day later 17 blocks of the city— some 674 buildings, including the last Dutch colonial structure—lay in a smoking plain of ashes. Manhattan's oldest surviving structures today were new when the city was 140 years old. And today in this Lower Manhattan site, writes Sol Stember, "despite the modern, towering commercial structures that now line these streets, the area still retains something of its old character, perhaps because the streets wind about and so many of them are little more than narrow alleys, reminders of the cobblestone roads they once were."

Lower Manhattan is usually considered as everything south of 14th Street. The Chelsea, Gramercy Park and Madison Square districts lie north. Midtown is usually identified as lying between 34th Street and Central Park South (59th Street); and everything north is Upper Manhat-

tan. From Greenwich Village north, 5th Avenue divides east from west.

From the end of the American Revolution, when New York served as national capital for five years, Manhattan's finger has beckoned the country's foremost doers and creators. Some came to struggle and "make it," then left. Many stayed. Others had built careers elsewhere and arrived in the bloom of their fame. There is no city kinder to fame; in success, one had at hand the only audience that somehow mattered. But as Moss Hart once remarked, New York is not a place in which to be poor or unsuccessful, although one had loads of company. Not only did the world's greatest concentration of opportunity cluster here but so did the stimulation and satisfaction of experiencing an immense variety in people and things. In this thick stew bubbled a sense of creative potential and unlimited possibility that Americans found in short supply elsewhere. The sense of movement and direction here is vertical; one does not "spread out" but "moves up"—or down. Like tree competition in a dense forest, "Manhattan towers" inspire quick reach and height rather than leisurely amplitude. Thus the very architecture of the city reflects a profound ideal of striving. Washington, D.C., is the capital of our country, but Manhattan remains the chief headquarters for what is happening.

Apartment and hotel rooms form most of the domestic walls in Manhattan. It is not astonishing that many of the structures in which some of America's most notable people resided are gone and continue to go. More surprising is the number of such buildings that survive and are cared for. Most of these, by far, remain in private hands. The New York City Landmarks Preservation Commission has a better handle on historic structures today than the city has ever had; and disappearance of Manhattan's tangible past is not so simple and individual a decision as it was before 1965. Yet the pulse of a city where demolition and new construction is constant dictates that one may not always see what a guidebook leads one to expect. The only thing certain and incessant about Manhattan is its ongoing change. Most noted Americans would never have lived here otherwise.

KEY TO MANHATTAN STREET NUMBERS

Correct use of this formula will locate the cross-street of virtually any address in Manhattan.

North-South Avenues

Step A: Cancel the last figure of the house number.
Step B: Divide the remainder by 2.
Step C: Add the key number, or deduct as indicated.
Example: 1165 3rd Ave. **A:** Cancel the last figure—result 116. **B:** Divide by 2—result 58. **C:** Add to (key number for 3rd Ave.)—result 68th St.

*On streets or address numbers preceded by an asterisk, omit Step B from the computation.

Ave. A, B, C, D 3	10th Ave. 13
1st Ave. 3	11th Ave. 15
2nd Ave. 3	Amsterdam 59
3rd Ave. 10	Columbus 59
4th Ave. 8	Lexington 22
5th Ave.:	Madison 27
1–200 13	Park 34
201–400 16	West End 59
401–600 18	*Central Park West 60
601–775 20	*Riverside Dr.:
*776–1286 . . . . Deduct 18	*1–567 73
Avenue of the Americas	*Above 567 78
Deduct 12	Broadway:
7th Ave.:	1–754 are below 8th St.
1–1800 12	754–858 . . . . Deduct 29
Above 1800 20	858–958 . . . . Deduct 25
8th Ave. 9	Above 1000 . . . . . . Deduct 31
9th Ave. 13	

East-West Numbered Streets

Addresses begin at the streets listed below.

East Side		West Side	
1 . . . . 5th Ave.		1 . . . . 5th Ave.	
101 . . . . Park Ave.		101 . . . . 6th Ave.	
201 . . . . 3rd Ave.		201 . . . . 7th Ave.	
301 . . . . 2nd Ave.		301 . . . . 8th Ave.	
401 . . . . 1st Ave.		401 . . . . 9th Ave.	
501 . . . . .York or Ave. A.		501 . . . . 10th Ave.	
601 . . . . Ave. B.		601 . . . . 11th Ave.	

ADAMS, JOHN (1735–1826).
ADAMS, ABIGAIL SMITH (1744–1818).

As the nation's first vice presidential family, the Adamses occupied the Mortier House, also called "Richmond Hill," a mansion that surmounted a 100-foot scenic rise at the present site of Charlton Street between Varick and MacDougal streets in **Greenwich Village.** The manor house built by British Maj. Abraham Mortier in 1767 had served as a headquarters for George Washington in 1776 and earlier for Lord Jeffrey Amherst. Adams bought the country estate, which overlooked a brook and pond, in 1788, and resided there until the national capital moved to Philadelphia in 1790. Abigail Adams conducted numerous official receptions, and the site elegantly hosted most of the nation's forefathers. A later owner was Aaron Burr. Today nothing remains as even a vague reminder of the mansion's pastoral setting; the hill was leveled in 1811, pond and brook are long gone, and John Jacob Astor bought and subdivided the land in 1817 (see the entries on Washington, Burr, and Astor later in this section). The house itself lasted somewhat longer. Moved first to 34–38 Charlton St., then two blocks south, it occupied from 1831 the present site of the Butterick Building, 161 Sixth Ave. (at the corner of Spring Street), as the Richmond Hill Theatre. It was finally razed in 1849.

Exhibit: See *Exhibits*, in the entry on George Washington later in this section.

(See Chapter 1, MASSACHUSETTS; also Chapter 3, DISTRICT OF COLUMBIA, PENNSYLVANIA.)

ALGER, HORATIO, JR. (1832–1899). The prolific author whose books for boys repeated the same basic plot line some 120 times—poor but honest boy overcomes adversity and gets ridiculously rich on pluck and platitudes—achieved massive readership if not riches himself with his immensely popular fantasies of "success." Alger spun off his formula fiction at several Manhattan rooming houses, none of which remain. He probably resided longest (1872–76) at 26 West 34th St. in **Midtown.**

According to biographer Edwin P. Hoyt, Alger "moved around constantly from one room to another, and although he spent a good deal of time at the Newsboys' Lodging House, he never claimed it as his place of residence." Yet he apparently did have a room set aside for him there. This boys' home, founded in 1853 as an adjunct of the Children's Aid Society by Charles Loring Brace, was Alger's longtime emotional if not physical residence in **Lower Manhattan.** He frequented the place, brought gifts, talked with the boys, and found there the ideas and characters for his tales. His homosexuality never became an overt problem, at least, and he was a well-liked if often lonely man of somewhat larger ambition than ability. The Lodging House stood at William and New Chambers streets, present site of the 1972 Police Headquarters Building at 1 Police Plaza.

(See Chapter 1, MASSACHUSETTS.)

ALGONQUIN HOTEL. This French Renaissance structure at 59 West 44th St. in **Midtown** dates from 1902, originally called the Puritan Hotel. Its longtime owner and manager, Frank Case, renamed it and built its reputation as "the writers' and actors' hotel"; and 30 years after his death it continues to host notable literary and show folk. Case's *Tales of a Wayward Inn* (1938) details his love affair with the hotel itself and his adventures in playing father figure to the famed and creative who resided here. "There is something in me that does not respond to the Social Register," he wrote. "Now, an actor, that's different. Or a writer, or a musician, or a painter. I was determined to get the Arts." Residents who occupied rooms here for more than brief or occasional stops included John Barrymore, Douglas Fairbanks and James Thurber. The hotel is probably best known for its celebrated Round Table, where writers including Franklin Pierce Adams, Robert Benchley, Dorothy Parker and Robert E. Sherwood gathered during the 1920s to lunch and try out their acerbic wits on each other. Edna Ferber, also a member, believed that "theirs was a tonic influence on the world of American letters"; while to Parker, "The Round Table was just a lot of people telling jokes and telling each other how good they were." (See the entries on Barrymore, Fairbanks, Thurber, Benchley, Parker, Sherwood and Ferber in this section). One of the best accounts, written by Case's daughter, Margaret Case Harriman, is *The Vicious Circle* (1951). Formerly located in the Rose Room of the dining area, the legendary table now stands in the Oak Room. The Rose Room has been restored to its original 1920s appearance, and the lobby, which retains its oak paneling and winged chairs, is still a favorite literary watering hole. Exuding dignity and a sense of lofty tradition, the Algonquin remains the kind of place where the headwaiter insists that men wear coat and tie but keeps a rack of clothes on hand to loan for the purpose.

ANDERSON, SHERWOOD BERTON (1876–1941). Just before publication of his best-known book *Winesburg, Ohio* (1919), Anderson was living in the **Chelsea** area at 427 West 22nd St., a brownstone painted gray. "It was a good room,"

he wrote. "I was in the back of the house, upstairs, and looked across little city back yards into many other people's rooms . . . There were people making love, dining, quarreling."

In 1922, he rented a floor in **Greenwich Village** at 12 St. Lukes Place, one in the row of three-story, Italianate, red-brick houses built in 1852 and 1853. Anderson made his city home during the 1930s at the house of his friend and patron Mary Emmett at 54 Washington Mews; this house was one of the 1834 brick row of five stables converted to dwellings on the cobbled court behind Washington Square North—but he found it a difficult place for writing. "There is too much ringing of phones . . . Mary is too rich. There are too many rare books and art objects about. I like bare walls."

All three of these residences are privately owned.

(See Chapter 4, OHIO; also Chapter 5, LOUISIANA, VIRGINIA.)

ANDRÉ, JOHN (1751–1780). During the British occupation of Manhattan, the popular adjutant of the British army, later tried and hanged by the Americans as a spy for collusion with Benedict Arnold (see the entry on Arnold later in this section), occupied quarters in 1779 and 1780 at the Beekman House. This 1766 colonial mansion called "Mount Pleasant" stood at 455 East 51st St. (at the corner of First Avenue) in **Midtown.** Here André received his final instructions in September, 1780, to meet Arnold on the Hudson, and thus began the cycle of events that put André on a rope and Arnold on America's permanent hate list. Four years earlier, it was reputedly here that the British brought American patriot Nathan Hale just before they summarily hanged him. Other occupants of the house at various times were British generals Sir Henry Clinton, Sir William Howe and Sir Guy Carleton. Beekman House was later moved a block south (to the northeast corner of First Avenue and East 50th Street), where it stood until 1874.

André resided earlier in 1779 at the Archibald Kennedy House, 1 Broadway in **Lower Manhattan,** and there wrote his coded correspondences to Arnold using the name John Anderson. This brick dwelling served as British and later American army headquarters and was used by both Clinton and George Washington (see the entry on Washington later in this section). It stood at the present site of the 1921 United States Lines-Panama Pacific Lines Building. A large building marker that faces Bowling Green describes this historic area of lower Broadway. Arnold, ironically, quartered next door at 3 Broadway just after André's capture.

Exhibit: The reconstructed parlor, a bedroom and three original mantelpieces from the Beekman House are displayed by the New York Historical Society, 170 Central Park West, **Upper West Side.** (Open Tuesday–Friday 1:00–5:00, Saturday 10:00–5:00, Sunday 1:00–5:00; 212-873-3400; donation.)

(See Chapter 3, NEW YORK, PENNSYLVANIA.)

ANDROS, SIR EDMUND (1637–1714). The third British colonial governor of New York (1674–81), Andros occupied "White Hall," the stone mansion in **Lower Manhattan** built by former Dutch governor Peter Stuyvesant (see the entry on Stuyvesant later in this section), as his official residence.

(See Chapter 5, VIRGINIA.)

ARENDT, HANNAH (1906–1975). The German-born political scientist and historical analyst made her permanent home in the United States after 1940. Her **Upper West Side** apartment dwellings included two semifurnished rooms at 317 West 95th St. (1941–51); 130 Morningside Drive from 1951 to the late 1960s; and her last, 370 Riverside Drive. All of these buildings remain privately occupied.

(See Chapter 4, ILLINOIS.)

ARNOLD, BENEDICT (1741–1801). After Gen. Arnold's 1780 defection to the British, his wife Peggy joined him in **Lower Manhattan** at the Watts House, a narrow, red-brick dwelling that stood across from Bowling Green at 3 Broadway. This was their home until their departure for England in 1781. The house was demolished in 1882 for construction of the ornate Washington Building, itself razed in 1919; today the enormous United States Lines-Panama Pacific Lines Building, dating from 1921, occupies the site.

(See Chapter 1, CONNECTICUT; also Chapter 3, NEW YORK, PENNSYLVANIA.)

ARTHUR, CHESTER ALAN (1829–1886). Before entering national politics, the 21st U.S. president made Manhattan his permanent home. He occu-

pied several hotel residences but resided longest near **Gramercy Park** at what is now Arthur House National Historic Landmark at 123 Lexington Ave., which he purchased in 1867. Arthur took the presidential oath here at 2:00 AM, September 20, 1881, following the death of President Garfield; and here he returned in 1885 after completing Garfield's term. Built in 1855, the present four-story brownstone house with its three bays encloses only a remnant of the original dwelling. The first and second floors are storefronts, and the two upper stories have been converted to apartments. Publisher William Randolph Hearst (see the entry on Hearst later in this section) was a later occupant. The building remains privately owned.

(See Chapter 1, VERMONT; also Chapter 3, DISTRICT OF COLUMBIA, NEW YORK.)

ASTOR, CAROLINE SCHERMERHORN (1831–1908). Socially you were nobody in Manhattan of the late 19th century unless *the* Mrs. Astor, as she titled herself, deigned to receive you—and she received, with few exceptions, only *old* money. The top 400 members of New York society thus accepted were about as dreary and dim-witted a company as most people would want to tolerate for 20 minutes. Stunted as only the very rich can be, however, they found little to do besides contending for Caroline Astor's favor; this became the favorite upper-crust game for 40 years. She, at least, took it all quite seriously. Husband William Backhouse Astor, Jr., a grandson of John Jacob Astor (see the entry on Astor below), was an unwilling floater; all she insisted from him was that he drop that dreadful middle name. "Today as you stand near the rear of the Empire State Building's main lobby," wrote Theodore James, Jr., in *The Empire State Building* (1975), "you will be near the spot where 'The' Mrs. Astor received her guests." Her four-story brownstone at 350 Fifth Ave. in **Midtown** was the glittering site for decades of New York's most glittering social event: Mrs. Astor's annual ball on the third Monday of January. When the Waldorf Hotel arose on adjacent Astor property, the doyenne grew restive: "There is a glorified tavern next door," she complained, and had architect Richard Morris Hunt build her a new mansion in 1894 at the southeast corner of Fifth Avenue and 65th Street, the present site of the Temple Emmanu-El; this was her last city home. The Astoria Hotel, meanwhile, arose in 1895 on the site of her previous mansion. Combined later into the first Waldorf-Astoria, it was demolished for the Empire State Building in 1929.

(See Chapter 1, RHODE ISLAND; also Chapter 3, NEW YORK.)

ASTOR, JOHN JACOB (1763–1848). The German-born merchant-businessman, whose descendants still own some of Manhattan's most expensive real estate, arrived in 1784 and made the city his permanent home. None of his several residences remain; their sites, thanks greatly to his own progeny's business dealings, have experienced multiple constructions and razings so that hardly more than a list of his successive addresses is possible. His first American lodging (1785–90) with a German baker stood at what is now 362 Pearl St. in **Lower Manhattan.** As affluent years passed, Astor moved steadily up Broadway, acquiring property and occupying three fashionable addresses: a house at 149 (1794–1803); then a new, two-story house at 223, which diplomat Rufus King had built; and finally a mansion at 585 Broadway between East Houston and Prince streets, a four-story, richly furnished brownstone where, in senile old age, he gummed a wet-nurse for nourishment. The site of his second Broadway home became the celebrated Astor House hotel in 1836, demolished in 1913 but illustrated on a tablet affixed to the 1915 Transportation Building at 225 Broadway.

Astor's summer house, variously called "Astoria" or "Hell Gate Farm," stood on what is now the south side of East 87th Street between York and East End avenues on the **Upper East Side.** His 13 acres fronted on the East River, occupying much of today's Carl Schurz Park. A grandson sold the property to a convent, and descendant Vincent Astor eventually bought it back for East End real estate development.

Astor's first land purchase, incidentally, was a **Lower Manhattan** plot between the Bowery and Elizabeth Street in 1789, acquired for £47.

(See Chapter 3, NEW JERSEY.)

AUDEN, WYSTAN HUGH (1907–1973). An English-born poet, Auden lived mostly in the United States after 1938. He occupied a succession of Manhattan apartments wherein neatness was disdained in favor of the touseled, unmade-bed look of the poet himself. His earliest Manhattan residence (1938–39) was 237 East 81st St., still a three-apartment dwelling on the **Upper East Side.**

At 7 Cornelia St. in **Greenwich Village,** the poet lived from 1945 to 1953. Visitors here, wrote biographer Charles Osborne, "found it a cosy place, despite its almost unbelievable untidiness, and its permanent smell of cat piss."

In 1953 Auden moved to the old brick tenement at 77 St. Mark's Place on the **Lower East Side,** and this remained his winter home until 1972. In this fantastically cluttered, second-floor, four-room apartment, Auden hosted friends for gourmet meals amid stacks of phonograph records, books and manuscripts. Auden enjoyed this section of the city and liked to point out that Russian revolutionist Leon Trotsky had printed his paper *Novy Mir* in the basement there in 1917. In August, 1976, three years after Auden's death in Austria, the *New York Times* reported that a "cache of seedy mementos" had been removed from this apartment and unconscionably placed on the front sidewalk. Auden's furniture, books, records and papers rapidly disappeared— "everybody grabbed, nothing's left," said a building resident.

All of Auden's Manhattan apartments remain privately occupied.

(See BROOKLYN in this chapter.)

AUDUBON, JOHN JAMES (1785–1851). A painter and naturalist, Audubon scrounged in poverty for years before the success of his *Birds of America* folio (1827–38) enabled him to buy 24 acres along the Hudson River in 1841. At what is now 765 Riverside Drive (at the corner of West 156th Street) in **Washington Heights,** he built "Minnie's Land," a three-story, flat-topped house that he presented as a gift to his long-suffering wife Lucy; the name represented a Scots term of endearment for "mother." He rented the laundry room for telegraph experiments to Samuel Finley Breese Morse (see the entry on Morse later in this section) in 1846. Audubon planted an orchard, caught sturgeon in the Hudson and declined to helpless senility before he died there. Lucy Audubon could not afford to keep the property after his death and finally sold it. The house, however, lasted in decrepit condition until 1930 when, surrounded and dwarfed by public buildings, it was razed— a tragic loss to both city and nation. Today the Washington Heights Museum Group occupies

Audubon's former estate along with nearby Trinity Church Cemetery, where he is buried.

(See Chapter 3, PENNSYLVANIA; also Chapter 5, FLORIDA, KENTUCKY, LOUISIANA.)

BARA, THEDA (1890–1955). At the height of her career (1916–19), the silent-film actress known as "the Vamp" for her sultry come-hitherness occupied 132 East 19th St. near **Gramercy Park,** a 1910 house where actress Mrs. Patrick Campbell and writer Ida M. Tarbell have also lived. It remains privately owned.

Theda Bara lived in the **Upper West Side** apartment building at 500 West End Ave. (at the corner of West 84th Street) in 1920, about the time she quit her fading movie career.

(See Chapter 6, CALIFORNIA.)

BARNUM, PHINEAS TAYLOR (1810–1891). Genial showman and professional hoaxer with his "American Museum" and "Greatest Show on Earth," the circus entrepreneur built his gaudy career in Manhattan. Though usually a hotel dweller in the city, he operated a private boardinghouse at 52 Frankfort St. on the **Lower East Side** from 1835 to about 1840.

He bought a **Midtown** brownstone mansion at 438 Fifth Ave. (at the corner of East 39th Street) in 1868, and this was his Manhattan home for several years. Neither of these structures now exist.

(See Chapter 1, CONNECTICUT.)

BARRYMORE, JOHN (1882–1942). During his early stage career, the "Great Profile" often occupied rooms in the Algonquin Hotel (see the entry on the Algonquin Hotel earlier in this section) for various intervals. The hotel "played a very pungent part in the kaleidoscopic fabric of my early manhood," he purply assessed in 1933.

His numerous rooming houses included the "narrowest house in the city" at 75½ Bedford St. in **Greenwich Village,** residence of Edna St. Vincent Millay (see the entry on Millay later in this section) in the 1920s. A later Village residence, from 1917 to 1920, was the top-floor apartment at 132 West Fourth St. (privately occupied). To the consternation of his landlady, he had tons of topsoil hauled to the roof and planted a jungle variety of flowers and shrubs for his own countryside in the city.

From about 1910 to 1916, Barrymore and his

first wife, Katherine Harris, occupied an apartment at 36 **Gramercy Park** East, where he indulged his taste for antiques, old silver and rare books. This building, privately owned, dates from 1905.

(See Chapter 3, PENNSYLVANIA; also Chapter 6, CALIFORNIA.)

BARTÓK, BÉLA (1881–1945). The last home, from 1944, of the Hungarian composer who fled Nazism in 1940 was a **Midtown** suite at 309 West 57th St., still a private apartment building.

(See BRONX, QUEENS in this chapter; also Chapter 3, NEW YORK.)

BARUCH, BERNARD MANNES (1870–1965). Wall Street financier and frequent presidential advisor, Baruch lived in Manhattan from boyhood. About 1880 his family resided in a **Midtown** top-floor apartment at 144 West 57th St., subsequent **Upper West Side** addresses were 51 West 70th St. and 345 West End Ave. These apartment buildings are probably the same ones still on the sites.

His last suite on the **Upper East Side** at 4 East 66th St. (privately occupied) "was a reflection of Baruch's formalities," wrote one biographer, "which had nothing to do with pomposity" but which had "something of that bare, ordered look that comes in a big house with too many servants with too little to do." Baruch lived here from about 1948.

(See Chapter 3, DISTRICT OF COLUMBIA; also Chapter 5, SOUTH CAROLINA.)

BEARD, CHARLES AUSTIN (1874–1948).
BEARD, MARY RITTER (1876–1958).

The husband-wife team of political scientists and historians lived for a decade (1907–17) at 400 West 118th St. (privately occupied), **Upper Manhattan,** when he taught at Columbia University.

(See Chapter 1, CONNECTICUT.)

BEIDERBECKE, LEON BISMARCK "BIX" (1903–1931). In 1924, when he was playing at the Roseland Ballroom with a group called the Wolverines, the jazz cornetist lived on the **Upper West Side** at 119 West 71st St., still a private apartment building.

His city lodgings from 1928 were usually cheap rooms, frequently changed; he cared only for music and alcohol, paying scarce attention to necessities of health or comfort. Beiderbecke resided in Room 605 of the 44th Street Hotel in 1930 and 1931. Babe Ruth (see the entry on George Herman Ruth later in this section) often visited him here. According to Edward J. Nichols in *Jazzmen* (1967), Ruth "could never get through the rooms of the little apartment, so he would unscrew the doors from the hinges and set them aside." The hotel, dating from about 1920, stands at 120 West 44th St. in **Midtown.** The aforementioned Roseland Ballroom, a famous Manhattan landmark of musical history, reopened in 1956 at Broadway and West 52nd St., a block north of its 1919 site.

(See QUEENS in this chapter; also Chapter 4, IOWA; also Chapter 5, LOUISIANA.)

BELASCO, DAVID (1853–1931). Dubbed "the bishop of Broadway" for his affected clerical garb, the stage producer-playwright built the Stuyvesant Theater—now called the Belasco Theater—in 1906 at 111 West 44th St. in **Midtown,** and maintained a luxurious, six-room private suite in its rococo interior. His rooms overflowed with all sorts of bric-a-brac collected without any apparent aim or system. Belasco's last home, from about 1926, was a suite at the Hotel Gladstone, which stood at 114 East 52nd St. until the 1960s.

BELMONT, ALVA ERTSKIN SMITH VANDERBILT (1853–1933). The "matron saint" of the woman's movement lived in two lavish mansions, neither of which remain. Earlier, as the new wife of railroad magnate William K. Vanderbilt, she occupied her first city home from 1875 to 1881, a small **Midtown** house at 5 East 44th St., appropriately the present site of an organization called Shareholders Services. Here she found herself excluded from the "cream" of Manhattan society, so she determined to crash the elite "400" by building a $3-million mansion in 1881. Architect Richard Morris Hunt designed it in the style of Francis I at 660 Fifth Ave. (at the northeast corner of 52nd Street), thereby beginning an upper-crust vogue for fake chateaus that, in 25 years, would line Fifth Avenue from 52nd to 79th streets. There Alva Vanderbilt launched herself grandly into high society in 1883. The house was razed in 1925. In 1896, she married financier Oliver H. P. Belmont and occupied their opulent mansion at 677 Fifth Ave. until his death in 1908. The town house she next built at 477 Madison Ave. was her last city home, now the site of a commercial building; but she spent most of her last years in Paris.

Exhibit: The 1927 Sherry-Netherland Hotel lobby at 781 5th Ave. (at the corner of East 59th Street) in **Midtown** displays sculptured panels salvaged from Alva Vanderbilt's 5th Avenue mansion.

(See Chapter 1, RHODE ISLAND; also Chapter 3, NEW YORK.)

BENCHLEY, ROBERT CHARLES (1889–1945). Versatile writer, humorist, and actor, Benchley resided in 1919 at the Algonquin Hotel (see the entry on the Algonquin Hotel earlier in this section), where he became a charter member of the famed Round Table group of Manhattan writers and wits. Almost across the street, at 44 West 44th St., stands the Royalton Hotel, where Benchley maintained a two-room suite for 24 years. "Oh, so they think they're Victorian," he growled. "I'll show them something Victorian," and proceeded to overfurnish his rooms with the most grotesque assortment of Victoriana he could find plus a book collection assembled for titles alone (e.g., *Talks on Manure*). "Dig It Up, Dust It Off, and Give It to Benchley" was his motto here. The Royalton in **Midtown** dates from about 1900.

Exhibit: Benchley was also a regular at the "21" Club, which occupied 42 West 49th St. Today his table at "21" is identified by a plaque in the club's present location at 21 West 52nd St.

(See Chapter 3, NEW YORK; also Chapter 6, CALIFORNIA.)

BENÉT, STEPHEN VINCENT (1898–1943). Both of the poet's **Upper East Side** apartment homes are gone, demolished to make way for the huge apartment complex that now covers both sites. At 220 East 69th St., which he said had "more wasted hall-space than the Grand Canyon," he entertained young writers during the 1930s. He moved to 215 East 68th St., his last home, in 1939.

(See Chapter 1, CONNECTICUT; also Chapter 3, NEW YORK, PENNSYLVANIA; also Chapter 5, GEORGIA; also Chapter 6, CALIFORNIA.)

BIERSTADT, ALBERT (1830–1902). **Greenwich Village** was Bierstadt's favorite Manhattan locale during the late 19th century. At intervals, the painter of Western and Hudson River scenes occupied the famed Studio Building for artists at 51–55 West 10th St. (see the entry on Winslow

Homer later in this section). Another of his residences during his frequent city stays was an apartment at the 1854 Brevoort, which stood at the northeast corner of Fifth Avenue and Eighth Street; this building, one of Manhattan's finest hotels, was demolished after World War II. The present massive apartment structure called "The Brevoort" on the site of 11 5th Ave. dates from 1953.

BILLY THE KID. See WILLIAM H. BONNEY.

BLACKWELL, ELIZABETH (1821–1910). The physician who came from England to find herself reforming sexist American medical practice pioneered the entry of women into the profession over fierce opposition from the medical establishment. She lived and practiced in Manhattan for almost 20 years, but none of her homes remain. Her **Lower East Side** address from 1860 to 1869—her last home in America—was 126 2nd Ave., the present site of the Orpheum Theatre.

In 1857, she founded the New York Infirmary, staffed entirely by women, at 64 Bleecker St. on the **Lower West Side.** Now located at Stuyvesant Square East and 15th Street, the women's hospital is, according to *The American Woman's Gazetteer* (1976), "so progressive that male physicians were admitted to the attending staff in the 1960s."

BOGART, HUMPHREY DEFOREST (1899–1957). The actor's childhood home until about 1917 was the four-story limestone mansion at 245 West 103rd St. on the **Upper West Side.** Today this privately owned house is easily recognized by its greenish painted surface.
(See Chapter 6, CALIFORNIA.)

BONNEY, WILLIAM H. "BILLY THE KID" (1859–1881). Surprisingly, the legendary western outlaw was apparently a Manhattan native, born at an unknown address on Rivington Street, **Lower East Side.** According to biographer Carl W. Breihan, subsequent boyhood addresses from 1860 to 1862 may have been 386 East 10th St. and 271 East 12th St.
(See Chapter 6, NEW MEXICO.)

BOOTH, EDWIN THOMAS (1833–1893). In **Gramercy Park,** the famed actor's last home was The Players Club National Historic Landmark at 16 Gramercy Park South. Booth founded this organization for struggling actors and writers in 1888 and hired architect Stanford White (see the entry on White later in this section) to remodel the five-story, Gothic Revival brownstone that dates originally from 1845. Booth's own third-floor rooms in front are well preserved and contain his furnishings, costumes and library, but these are not accessible to the public. The Club has become a travesty of Booth's intentions, with its membership now restricted to men definitely successful and mostly retired.

The marked site of the Edwin Booth Theater, which Booth managed and where he frequently starred from 1869 to 1883, is the southeast corner of 6th Avenue and 23rd Street in **Chelsea.**
Exhibits: The bust of Shakespeare that adorned the Edwin Booth Theater, and for which Booth himself may have posed, is now in New York University Library, 70 Washington Square South in **Greenwich Village** (call 212-598-2450 for hours).
(See Chapter 1, MASSACHUSETTS, RHODE ISLAND; also Chapter 3, MARYLAND.)

BORGLUM, GUTZON (1867–1941). The sculptor's home from about 1902 to 1912 stood in **Midtown** at 166 East 38th St. An old stable behind a row of brownstones there was remodeled for his studio, where he created his famed head of Lincoln, among other pieces. He sold the property in 1924.
(See Chapter 1, CONNECTICUT; also Chapter 4, SOUTH DAKOTA; also Chapter 6, CALIFORNIA, IDAHO, TEXAS.)

BRADY, JAMES BUCHANAN "DIAMOND JIM" (1856–1917). Rotund financier and likable exhibitionist who made sure that his friends lived well, too, Brady was a Manhattan native and seldom ventured long or far from the Broadway where he socialized and indulged his formidable appetite. He was born on the **Lower West Side** above his father's saloon at Cedar and West streets, his home to age 11; the 23-story West Street Building at 90 West St. has occupied this site since 1905.

On the **Upper West Side,** Brady's large brownstone mansion, his permanent home from about 1900, stood at 7 West 86th St. Tiring of the same expensive furnishings day after day, he annually cleared out his whole house and installed new furniture in all the rooms.

(See Chapter 3, NEW JERSEY.)

BRADY, MATTHEW B. (1823?–1896). The famed cameraman's first Manhattan studio (1844 to 1853) was located in a second-story loft at the **Lower Manhattan** corner of Broadway and Fulton Street. There he gained an increasingly successful reputation as a portrait photographer. His second, luxurious studio at 359 Broadway (from 1853 to 1860) over Thompson's Saloon had rosewood furniture, rose carpets and a roof skylight. Many of the most eminent persons of the day (including Abraham Lincoln) came to have their photos taken in his third studio at Broadway and East 10th Street—"Brady and the Cooper Institute made me President," said Lincoln. Brady had no permanent residence during his Manhattan years but roomed in a succession of long-gone houses near his studios.

His last residence (1896) stood at 127 East 10th St., **Lower East Side;** impoverished and forgotten, he went from there to a hospital charity ward, where he died.

(See Chapter 3, DISTRICT OF COLUMBIA.)

BRYANT, WILLIAM CULLEN (1794–1878). Dissatisfied with his life, the lawyer-poet came to Manhattan in 1825 and from 1829 to his death edited the *New York Evening Post,* which stood at Broadway and Fulton Street in **Lower Manhattan.** Bryant occupied several rooming houses in the area during his first years in the city.

In 1867, he purchased the **Greenwich Village** house still standing at 24 West 16th St. (privately owned) and lived there for the rest of his life. "Wherever Bryant lived," wrote the authors of *Literary New York* (1976), "he followed the same regime. He rose at five-thirty and did an hour's exercises, which included . . . jumping back and forth over his bed, aided by a vaulting pole. Then, after a small breakfast, he walked to his office in lower Manhattan." Bryant died at the house. Two later literary residents were editor Margaret Anderson and poet Hart Crane (see the entry on Crane later in this section).

(See Chapter 1, MASSACHUSETTS; also Chapter 3, NEW YORK.)

BURR, AARON (1756–1836). Politician, soldier, vice president, duelist, and adventurer, Burr practiced law in Manhattan from 1783 to 1804 and again from 1812 to 1836. His many residences included 3 Wall St. (1783–84) "next door but one to the City Hall"—i.e., adjoining what is now Federal Hall National Memorial at 28 Wall St. Other **Lower Manhattan** addresses were 10 Maiden Lane (1784–90) and 4 Broadway (1790–94). None of these residences have survived.

Burr lived most of the time from 1794 to 1804 at the Mortier House in **Greenwich Village** (see the entry on John and Abigail Smith Adams earlier in this section). From here in 1804 he departed to duel Alexander Hamilton, an encounter that left Hamilton fatally wounded and Burr forever disgraced (see the entry on Hamilton later in this section). Two Federal houses built for Burr in 1829 remain at 127 and 131 MacDougal Street (privately owned), among the oldest houses in the city with dormer windows and cast-iron newel posts.

Morris-Jumel Mansion National Historic Landmark at Edgecomb Avenue and West 160th Street in **Washington Heights** dates from 1765 and has been renovated three times: in 1810, 1903 and 1945. In 1833, Burr married its wealthy owner, Eliza Jumel, in the parlor, but his philandering habits so enraged her that she chased him out months later (with fire tongs, the story goes). George Washington (see the entry on Washington later in this section) had used this house as his headquarters in autumn 1776; then British and Hessian commanders occupied it until 1783. The city acquired the Georgian colonial mansion in 1903. It is now operated by the N.Y.C. Department of Parks in conjunction with the Daughters of the American Revolution and displays period furnishings. One of the few Burr items exhibited is the desk he used here. (Open Tuesday–Sunday 11:00–4:30; 212-923-8008; admission.)

(See STATEN ISLAND in this chapter; also Chapter 1, CONNECTICUT; also Chapter 3, NEW JERSEY, NEW YORK, PENNSYLVANIA.)

CALDER, ALEXANDER (1898–1976). Born into a noted family of sculptors, Calder spent several years as an art student in various **Greenwich Village** rooms. At 249 West 14th St., now a restaurant, he occupied a second-floor room in 1925 that he found "painted with robins egg blue & crimson paint, & tobacco juice. There were crimson incrustations which . . . peeled off and fell on me. So I whitewashed it."

(See Chapter 1, CONNECTICUT; also Chapter 3, PENNSYLVANIA, NEW YORK.)

CARNEGIE, ANDREW (1835–1919). The steel industrialist and philanthropist occupied two Manhattan homes: from 1887 to 1901 at 5 West 51st St., no longer standing; and from 1901 at 2 East 91st St. (at the corner of Fifth Avenue), his last. Carnegie built this three-story, red-brick, 64-room mansion on the **Upper East Side** for $1.5 million in what was then the edge of the city, transplanting full-grown trees to the grounds. Better known as the Cooper-Hewitt Museum, Carnegie Mansion National Historic Landmark now houses the Smithsonian Institution's National Museum of Design. The huge art collection displays not only paintings but various types of decorative objects. (Open Tuesday 10:00–9:00, Wednesday–Saturday 10:00–5:00, Sunday 12:00–5:00; 212-860-6898; admission.)

CARUSO, ENRICO (1873–1921). Probably the greatest opera tenor who ever lived, the Italian singer resided in Manhattan during his many years of Metropolitan performances. He was a hotel dweller primarily, but having chosen a favorite, he liked to settle in for a long duration. He stayed longest (from 1908 to 1920) at the Hotel Knickerbocker, now the Knickerbocker Building converted to offices at the southeast corner of Broadway and West 42nd Street near **Times Square.** Caruso's last home in America (1920–21) was the 1912 Vanderbilt Hotel, which stood on the southwest corner of Park Avenue and East 34th Street, **Midtown.**

Caruso made many of his recordings from 1904 to 1906 on an upper floor (Room 826) of Carnegie Hall National Historic Landmark at 154 West 57th St. in **Midtown.** The old Metropolitan Opera House, where he made his debut in 1903 and last performed in 1921, stood at Broadway and West 39th Street from 1883 to 1966.

CATHER, WILLA SIBERT (1873–1947). The author whose best-known novels and stories portrayed pioneers of the West was a Manhattan resident for 40 years. Several of her apartment dwellings remain. She first resided in **Greenwich Village.** From 1908 to 1913, her address was 82 Washington Place, the six-story private apartment building erected in 1903; Richard Wright was a later dweller there (see the entry on Wright later in this section). In 1913, Cather moved to 5 Bank St., occupying seven rooms on the second floor of a large brick house. She wrote six novels there, including *My Antonia* (1918) and *Death Comes for the Archbishop* (1927). This house fell in 1927 to make way for construction of the 7th Avenue subway, but a plaque marks the site on the present 1929 apartment building. The 1925 Grosvenor Hotel at 35 Fifth Ave. (at the corner of East 10th Street) was her home from 1927 to 1932, the place in which she wrote *Shadows on the Rock* (1931). A tablet notes her residence in this 15-story building, now the Samuel Rubin International Hall of New York University.

Her last home, from 1932, was the **Upper East Side** apartment building still at 570 Park Ave., where her only windows faced the blank wall of the Colony Club. She died there.

(See Chapter 1, NEW HAMPSHIRE; also Chapter 3, PENNSYLVANIA; also Chapter 4, NEBRASKA; also Chapter 5, VIRGINIA.)

CERF, BENNETT ALFRED (1898–1971). Publisher, editor, columnist and television panelist, Cerf was an **Upper Manhattan** native. A boyhood home from 1911, the Riviera Apartments, remains at 790 Riverside Drive, where Cerf's family occupied a 12th-floor suite. He made the Navarro Hotel at 112 Central Park South his home during the 1940s; and his last city dwelling, from the 1950s, was 132 East 62nd St. (privately owned).

(See Chapter 3, NEW YORK.)

CHELSEA HOTEL. "A proud survivor of the quarter's Golden Age," according to architectural historian Gerard R. Wolfe, Hotel Chelsea National Historic Landmark opened in 1884 as a cooperative apartment house at 222 West 23rd St.—in, of course, the **Chelsea** area. Construction of the 11-story, Victorian Gothic edifice was sponsored by a group of artists who sought studio space; only in 1905 did it become a hotel. Its roster of noted literary residents have included some of the best-known names of the century. When built, the Chelsea was one of Manhattan's tallest buildings, displaying the city's first penthouse and duplex apartments, ornate iron balconies, a dormer roof and tall chimneys. The broad interior staircase that spirals to the roof is now closed, and the altered lobby hosts an art gallery that displays works of former and present Chelsea residents. But the old suites remain, many with fireplaces and rosewood gingerbread on the windows, continuing to host a devoted clientele—such as one noted occupant who recently observed, "It has big, quiet rooms. Some of them need painting, of course."

CHURCHILL, JENNIE JEROME (1854–1921). It was "more of a display place than a home," wrote biographer Ralph G. Martin of Lady Churchill's childhood dwelling. The mother of Sir Winston Churchill resided from 1860 to 1867 at the opulent, six-story, brick mansion built in 1859 by her father, sportsman Leonard Jerome, at the southeast corner of Madison Avenue and 26th Street near **Madison Square.** This was her last American home. The first of Manhattan's "private palaces," the Jerome house later became the Manhattan Club, demolished in the 1960s for construction of the present Merchandise Mart Building at 41 Madison Ave.

(See BROOKLYN in this chapter.)

CLEMENS, SAMUEL LANGHORNE "MARK TWAIN" (1835–1910). When the author-humorist returned in 1900 from a lengthy stay in Europe, he moved into a town house at 14 West 10th St. (privately occupied) in **Greenwich Village.** The house, built in 1854 and 1855, is a four-story red brick structure with stonework, large windows, and a basement entrance; a historical marker is attached. Huge numbers of guests went there to meet him, and "every day was like some great festive occasion," recalled his daughter Clara. "One felt that a large party was going on." The family lived there for a year. Clemens returned to the Village in 1904 and occupied a three-story brick house at 21 Fifth Ave. (at the corner of East 9th Street) until 1908. This was the period when he began wearing the white serge-suits of his later photographs. But he also spent much of his time in bed there, dictating, smoking cigars, completing *Adam's Diary* (1904) and writing *The Mysterious Stranger* (1916). This 1851 Romanesque building, called "one of the most architecturally notable houses in all New York," was torn down about 1950, its site now thoroughly covered by the massive Brevoort Apartment complex (see the entry on Albert Bierstadt earlier in this section). If Mark Twain's white-serge ghost isn't grumbling in the halls there, his spirit is much reformed indeed.

(See BRONX in this chapter; also Chapter 1, CONNECTICUT; also Chapter 3, NEW YORK; also Chapter 4, IOWA, MISSOURI; also Chapter 6, CALIFORNIA, NEVADA.)

CLINTON, DE WITT (1769–1828). As New York's lieutenant governor and 1812 presidential candidate, Clinton resided in the Mortier House, **Greenwich Village,** from 1811 to 1815 (see the entry on John and Abigail Smith Adams earlier in this section).

Sources regarding his subsequent Manhattan dwellings are vague and conflicting. When elected governor in 1817, he may have been residing in the Franklin House at 3 Cherry St., **Lower East Side,** formerly occupied by George Washington (see the entry on Washington later in this section); or at 9 Cherry St. Neither of these houses remain.

(See QUEENS in this chapter; also Chapter 3, NEW YORK.)

CLINTON, GEORGE (1739–1812). Revolutionary soldier, governor, vice president and uncle of De Witt Clinton (see the entry on De Witt Clinton above), George Clinton lived on the **Lower East Side** at 80 Pine St. (at the corner of Pearl Street) from 1784 to 1791. Mayor Abraham de Peyster built the three-story mansion that stood there from the late 17th century.

Clinton next occupied, until 1794, the 1791 Government House, a two-story porticoed mansion erected on the site of Fort George just south of Bowling Green; the house was razed after a fire in 1815. This site is occupied today by the 1907 U.S. Custom House, **Lower Manhattan.**

Clinton's **Yorkville** farm, which he occupied as a summer home from 1794 to 1800, consisted of a large orchard, gardens and a 1747 rambling house of brick and wood. The house stood until 1901, when John Davison Rockefeller (see the entry on Rockefeller later in this section) built Rockefeller Institute for Medical Research on the site, now Rockefeller University National Historic Landmark, 1230 York Ave. (at the corner of East 66th Street).

(See Chapter 3, DISTRICT OF COLUMBIA, NEW YORK.)

COHAN, GEORGE MICHAEL (1878–1942). Information is thin on addresses and durations of Cohan's Manhattan hotel residences. The last apartment of the composer-playwright-actor, where he died, was located in the 993 Fifth Avenue Building, **Upper East Side.** Another favorite city residence of Cohan until converted to an office building in 1921 was the Knickerbocker Hotel (see the entry on Enrico Caruso earlier in this section).

(See Chapter 1, MASSACHUSETTS, RHODE ISLAND; also Chapter 3, NEW JERSEY, NEW YORK.)

COLTRANE, JOHN WILLIAM (1926–1967). The saxophone virtuoso lived in Manhattan from 1957 to 1959 at 203 West 103rd St., **Upper West Side.** He occupied rooms on the second floor of the present six-story private apartment building.

(See Chapter 3, NEW YORK, PENNSYL-VANIA; also Chapter 5, NORTH CAROLINA.)

COOPER, JAMES FENIMORE (1789–1851). Cooper moved to Manhattan from Scarsdale, N.Y., following the success of his novel *The Spy* (1821), to pursue a literary career. His first city home stood at the northeast corner of Broadway and Prince Street, the site of Niblo's Garden Theater from 1829 to 1895. In 1823, the family moved to 3 Beach St., a narrow, three-story brick house with marble steps, where Cooper wrote *The Pilot* (1823). "The number of rats was really alarming," recalled Cooper's daughter of this house. In 1825 and 1826, just before Cooper's departure for an extended stay in Europe, the family lived at 345 Greenwich St., a quiet, dignified neighborhood at the time. All of these **Lower Manhattan** houses are long gone.

On his return, Cooper rented a winter house at 145 Bleecker St. (privately owned), a house in **Greenwich Village** selected by his friend Samuel Finley Breese Morse (see the entry on Morse later in this section). Though Cooper's wife thought the house "too magnificent for our simple French tastes," the family lived there with four Swiss servants at two intervals from 1833 to 1836. This four-story dwelling, probably new at the time, survives in decrepit condition.

In 1834, Cooper also rented the red-brick home at 6 St. Mark's Place (privately owned), now St. Mark's Baths, **Lower East Side.** The building's original two stories, with a scaffolding of fire escapes, has been topped with an addition.

(See Chapter 2, NEW JERSEY, NEW YORK.)

CORNELL, KATHARINE (1893–1974). The stage actress's longtime home with her husband, director Guthrie McClintic, was 23 Beekman Place (privately owned) on the **Upper East Side,** a high-

ceilinged old house they occupied from 1921 to 1952. Her last home, from 1961, was a suite at a nearby undisclosed address on East 51st Street.

(See Chapter 1, MASSACHUSETTS; also Chapter 3, NEW YORK.)

COWARD, SIR NOEL PIERCE (1899–1973). The versatile English composer-playwright-actor maintained various Manhattan lodgings at irregular periods over many years. In 1936, he took over a luxurious **Midtown** penthouse apartment at 450 East 52nd St. from Alexander Woollcott, and this was his city home until 1940. A rented apartment at 1 Beekman Place in 1933 and the 1915 Hotel des Artistes at 1 West 67th St., actually a cooperative apartment house designed by and for artists, were other Coward residences. He spent relatively little time at his last Manhattan suite at 404 East 55th St. All of these addresses remain private.

CRANE, HART (1899–1932). *The Bridge* (1930), Crane's poetic tribute to Brooklyn Bridge as an American metaphor, was composed over several years at various New York addresses. In **Greenwich Village,** he roomed at 54 West 10th St. in 1917, in a five-story, red-brick house with a basement entrance—the original lower portion of this dwelling dates from 1839; and at 25 East 11th St. (1917–18, 1919), a house dating from 1845. Both buildings, which were cheap rooming houses in Crane's day, have been finely restored and remain privately owned. In 1919, Crane roomed on the top floor of 24 West 16th St. (privately owned), where Margaret Anderson edited the *Little Review* and where William Cullen Bryant (see the entry on Bryant earlier in this section) last lived. Crane occupied a room at 45 Grove St. in 1923 and 1924, and also in 1930. He appreciated the good writing table there and the absence of an "inquisitive landlady always looking through the keyhole." The N.Y.C. Landmarks Commission has called this 1830 house "one of the finest and largest Federal residences in Greenwich Village." Once surrounded by spacious grounds, it was remodeled in 1870 and remains a privately owned apartment dwelling. Crane's address in 1924 was 79 Charles St. (then 15 Van Nest Place) in the 1866 row of privately owned, three-story, brick houses. The poet usually moved several times a year and briefly occupied additional rooming houses during the period from 1917 to 1924. The addresses given here are only those residences of some duration that are known to exist.

(See BROOKLYN in this chapter; also Chapter 4, OHIO.)

CRANE, STEPHEN (1871–1900). The author-journalist came to Manhattan in 1892 and occupied a succession of lodgings for the next four years. In the Art Students League Building near **Gramercy Park** at 143 East 23rd St., an ancient, dilapidated structure that has long since disappeared, the bohemian studio he shared with three friends in 1893 became the setting of his story "The Third Violet" (1898); there he also completed *The Red Badge of Courage* (1895) in 1894.

In 1895 and 1896, Crane resided on the top floor of 165 West 23rd St. (privately owned) in the **Chelsea** area and filled it with impressionistic art and Civil War trophies. This old brownstone survives but in sad condition at recent report.

(See Chapter 3, NEW JERSEY.)

CUMMINGS, EDWARD ESTLIN (1894–1962). Though born in Massachusetts, e e cummings, as he styled himself, lived for most of his life in **Greenwich Village.** His permanent home after his return from Europe in 1923 was 4 Patchin Place (privately owned), an 1848 dwelling where he first resided on the top floor. Over the years, he acquired most of this three-story brick house that he occupied during winters for the rest of his life. There, at various times, he hosted poet friends including T. S. Eliot, Ezra Pound and Dylan Thomas (see the entry on Thomas later in this section). According to literary historian Emilie C. Harting, "At one point a city agency tried to evict him because the building did not conform to health codes. The whole affair created such a furor that the mayor had to intervene and make a special exception for him."

(See Chapter 1, MASSACHUSETTS, NEW HAMPSHIRE.)

DEAN, JAMES BYRON (1931–1955). An ambitious "Method actor," Dean began his career on the stage. In 1954, just before he began making the films that brought him a national audience, he occupied a fifth-floor apartment at 19 West 68th St. (privately occupied), **Upper West Side.**

(See Chapter 4, INDIANA; also Chapter 6, CALIFORNIA.)

DEWEY, JOHN (1859–1952). The philosopher resided in **Upper Manhattan** during most of his long career, and his addresses were numerous. From 1913 to 1927, he lived at 2880 Broadway, the present site of Goddard Institute for Space Studies; at 125 East 62nd St. from 1927 to 1938; at 1 West 89th St. from 1939 to 1945; and at 1158 5th Ave., his last from 1945. All of these buildings, except the Goddard site, still house private apartments.

(See Chapter 1, VERMONT; also Chapter 3, NEW YORK; also Chapter 4, ILLINOIS.)

DEWEY, THOMAS EDMUND (1902–1971). Gang-busting attorney, governor and two-time presidential candidate, Dewey had a magnificent baritone voice that gave him early hopes of a singing career and belied his somewhat Chaplinesque appearance—"How do you vote for a man who looks like a bridegroom on a wedding cake?" Alice Roosevelt Longworth once remarked. Dewey maintained an **Upper Manhattan** apartment suite at 1148 5th Ave. during his days as Manhattan district attorney in the 1930s. The building there is known as the 1148 5th Corporation. His retirement city dwelling after 1955 was 141 East 72nd St., still a private apartment building.

(See Chapter 3, NEW YORK; also Chapter 4, MICHIGAN.)

DOS PASSOS, JOHN RODERIGO (1896–1970). The author moved in and out of the city frequently during the 1920s ("Young women I met at cocktail parties liked to tell me I was running away from myself," he wrote). In 1922, he rented a studio in the 1884, five-story, brick apartment building at 14A Washington Mews (behind 3 Washington Square North between 14 and 15 Washington Mews) in **Greenwich Village,** where he worked on *Manhattan Transfer* (1925).

He briefly occupied an **Upper West Side** apartment at 214 Riverside Drive in 1932 while working on his trilogy *U.S.A.* (1930–36).

(See BROOKLYN in this chapter; also Chapter 1, MASSACHUSETTS; also Chapter 5, VIRGINIA.)

DREISER, THEODORE (1871–1945). Dreiser first came to Manhattan in 1895 and resided at various addresses and intervals until 1935. His first lodging was in **Greenwich Village** at the Greenwich Hotel (Mills Hotel in 1895), still at 160 Bleecker

St. (at the corner of Thompson Street), where he paid 25¢ a night for a bed. The residence at which he stayed longest (from 1914 to 1920) was 165 West 10th St., where he completed his controversial novel *The Genius* (1915); the present two-story, brick house on this site dates from 1929. In 1922, he moved into 16 St. Luke's Place, a barely furnished, two-room apartment with polished plank flooring, and worked at a massive desk made from a piano. This private residence remains one of five brick houses in a row built in 1852 and 1853; Sherwood Anderson and James John Walker (see the entries on Anderson and Walker in this section) were his noted neighbors in this row off Leroy Street. In 1923 Dreiser moved to 118 West 11th St. in "Rhinelander Gardens," a row of eight houses built after 1854 and razed in 1955 to clear space for the Greenwich Village School (PS 41). Here he wrote *An American Tragedy* (1925), one of his best-known novels.

Dreiser occupied an apartment from about 1925 to 1931 at 200 West 57th St., presently a **Midtown** office building.

The two-room Suite 1454 at the Ansonia Hotel, 2101–2119 Broadway on the **Upper West Side,** was Dreiser's last Manhattan home, from 1931 to 1935. This elegant, 17-story bastion, built from 1899 to 1904, was once one of Manhattan's most opulent hotels, a favorite hostelry for many noted musicians and singers. Florenz Ziegfeld lived there earlier (see the entry on Ziegfeld later in this section).

(See BROOKLYN in this chapter; also Chapter 3, NEW YORK; also Chapter 4, ILLINOIS, INDIANA; also Chapter 6, CALIFORNIA.)

DU BOIS, WILLIAM EDWARD BURGHARDT (1868–1963). The Paul Laurence Dunbar Apartments, six brick buildings erected from 1926 to 1928, stand at 2594 7th Ave. in **Harlem.** Du Bois, among the first tenants, bought two small apartments and resided there until 1934. At 409 Edgecomb Ave., known as the choicest address in Harlem's exclusive Sugar Hill area, the educator-reformer occupied a small 13th-floor apartment from 1944 to 1951 during his leadership of the NAACP.

(See BROOKLYN in this chapter; also Chapter 1, MASSACHUSETTS; also Chapter 3, MARYLAND, PENNSYLVANIA; also Chapter 5, GEORGIA.)

DULLES, JOHN FOSTER (1888–1959). Before President Eisenhower (see the entry on Eisenhower below) appointed him secretary of state in 1952, Dulles practiced law for many years in Manhattan. His **Upper East Side** home from the 1920s, a town house, stands at 72 East 91st St., now occupied by a doctor's office and private apartments.

(See Chapter 3, DISTRICT OF COLUMBIA, NEW YORK.)

DVOŘÁK, ANTONÍN (1841–1904). The Czech composer resided in a dwelling that stood at 328 East 17th St. near **Gramercy Park** during his teaching tenure with the National Conservatory of Music in 1892 and 1893. The Steinway firm installed a grand piano for him in the building, where he worked on his *New World Symphony* (1893).

(See Chapter 4, IOWA.)

EISENHOWER, DWIGHT DAVID (1890–1969). Between his army retirement in 1948 and election as the 34th U.S. president in 1952, Eisenhower occupied the presidential chair of Columbia University. His four-year residence in **Morningside Heights** was 60 Morningside Drive (at the corner of West 116th Street), the official university president's house designed by McKim, Mead & White in 1912 and previously occupied by Nicholas Murray Butler. "The most compassionate judgment of Eisenhower at Columbia," wrote biographer Peter Lyon, "is that he was not a bad president because he was no president at all." The position was mutually advantageous for letterhead purposes, however, and neither employer nor employee bothered each other much. The mansion remains official and private. Into a former water-tank room on the roof, Eisenhower recalled, "Mamie and I moved furniture utterly ineligible for a place in the gracious rooms below but dear from long association and worn by the years." This room, where he often retired to paint, was "the one place I could be by myself."

(See Chapter 3, DISTRICT OF COLUMBIA, MARYLAND, PENNSYLVANIA; also Chapter 4, KANSAS, MICHIGAN; also Chapter 5, GEORGIA, VIRGINIA; also Chapter 6, COLORADO, TEXAS.)

ELLINGTON, EDWARD KENNEDY "DUKE" (1899–1974). Prolific jazz composer, pianist and bandleader, Ellington spent most of his time on the road playing clubs and concerts all over the globe. His permanent base after 1923, however, was Manhattan, where he occupied several addresses through his long career. During the 1930s, he lived at 381 Edgecomb Ave. in the Sugar Hill district of **Harlem**. For 22 years (1939–61), he resided in Apartment 4A of 935 St. Nicholas Ave., a six-story masonry structure. His last address from 1961 was an apartment suite at 333 Riverside Drive. All of these buildings remain privately owned.

(See Chapter 3, DISTRICT OF COLUMBIA.)

FAIRBANKS, DOUGLAS (1883–1939). The muscular, boisterous actor performed on the stage in Manhattan before films lured him to Hollywood and made him one of the first "stars" in the modern sense. He resided from 1907 to 1915 at the Algonquin Hotel (see the entry on the Algonquin Hotel earlier in this section), **Midtown** where he also performed rope-jumping exercises on the roof.

(See Chapter 6, CALIFORNIA.)

FARRAGUT, DAVID GLASGOW (1801–1870). In 1865, the Union naval hero of the Civil War bought a **Midtown** house at 113 East 36th St., which became his last, most frequent residence. This house remained in the Farragut family for years and is probably the same one now standing unmarked at this address.

(See Chapter 3, NEW YORK; also Chapter 5, MISSISSIPPI, TENNESSEE.)

FERBER, EDNA (1887–1968). In 1923, the popular novelist moved into the ornate apartment house at 50 Central Park West, her home until 1929. She wrote *Show Boat* (1926) there. During the early 1930s, she resided in the Hotel Lombardy, still at 111 East 56th St. Her next residence until 1938 was 791 Park Ave. At the author's last address from 1949, an apartment at 730 Park Ave., she wrote *Giant* (1952) and *Ice Palace* (1958). All of these **Midtown** and **Upper Manhattan** buildings still house private apartments.

Ferber was a prominent member of the Round Table group at the Algonquin Hotel during the 1920s (see the entry on the Algonquin earlier in this section).

(See Chapter 1, CONNECTICUT; also Chapter 4, IOWA, MICHIGAN, WISCONSIN.)

FITZGERALD, F. SCOTT (1896–1940). "New York was a dreamland to Fitzgerald," wrote critic Alfred Kazin. "It represented his imagination of what is forever charming, touched by the glamour of money, romantically tender and gay." Fitzgerald lived mainly in hotels, but in 1919, while working for an advertising agency and struggling to become a writer, he took rooms in "a high, horrible apartment house in the middle of nowhere," where he pinned 122 rejection slips in a frieze around his bedroom. This brick "nowhere" building stands at 200 Claremont Ave. on the **Upper West Side** and still houses private apartments.

In **Midtown**, Scott and Zelda Fitzgerald spent their honeymoon of April 1920, in Room 2109 of the Hotel Biltmore, still standing (but no longer a hotel) at 55 East 43rd St. (at the corner of Madison Avenue), but were thrown out because of their incessantly exuberant antics, such as handstands in the lobby. Later that year they occupied an apartment in a brownstone at 38 West 59th St., the present site of the Park Lane Hotel, 36 Central Park South. The 1907 Plaza Hotel National Historic Landmark, which figures in *The Great Gatsby* (1925), stands at Fifth Avenue and Central Park South near the Pulitzer Fountains where wild child Zelda took her celebrated, impulsive dips. Rarely has "fun city" been taken so literally as by this nonstop couple whose gaiety was always grimly intense.

(See Chapter 3, MARYLAND, NEW YORK; also Chapter 4, MINNESOTA; also Chapter 5, ALABAMA, NORTH CAROLINA; also Chapter 6, CALIFORNIA.)

FOSTER, STEPHEN COLLINS (1826–1864). The songwriter moved to New York in 1860, beginning the end of a long decline plagued by debt, domestic troubles and alcohol. He occupied several **Lower Manhattan** lodging houses, including his first city residence at 97 Greene St. in 1860 and 1861, now occupied by an 1881 office building; 6 Greenwich St., the present site of the 14-story, 1929 Women's House of Detention; and his last room at 15 Bowery (at the corner of Bayard Street), where stood the 1828 New England Hotel, the site of the puzzling accident that caused his death. Apparently he fell against his washbowl, severely gashing his face and neck. He died shortly after in Ward 11 of Bellevue Hospital, First Avenue and East 27th Street. The New England Hotel was demolished in 1891.

(See Chapter 3, NEW JERSEY, PENNSYLVANIA; also Chapter 4, OHIO; also Chapter 5, FLORIDA, KENTUCKY.)

FRENCH, DANIEL CHESTER (1850–1931). The sculptor's longtime home, a four-story brick house dating from 1849 with a two-story studio in the rear, stands privately owned at 125 West 11th St. in **Greenwich Village.** French designed the interior when he bought the property in 1888 and resided there and in New Hampshire at intervals for the rest of his life. In 1931, French's "Chesterwood Studio" at 12 West Eighth St. was integrated with two adjacent dwellings, all dating from 1838, into the building that became the Whitney Museum of American Art. Today it houses the New York Studio School of Drawing, Painting and Sculpture.

(See Chapter 1, MASSACHUSETTS, NEW HAMPSHIRE.)

FULLER, MARGARET (1810–1850). See HORACE GREELEY.

(See Chapter 1, MASSACHUSETTS.)

FULTON, ROBERT (1765–1815). Engineer and steamboat inventor, Fulton made his last home in a mansion at 1 State St. (at the corner of Whitehall Street) in **Lower Manhattan,** site of the earlier home of Peter Stuyvesant (see the entry on Stuyvesant later in this section). The South Ferry Building presently occupies this historic ground. Fulton's first steamboat, the *Clermont,* was launched in 1807 from a pier at Cortlandt Street for its maiden voyage up the Hudson to Albany, thus demonstrating the viability of steam power for navigation.

(See Chapter 3, NEW YORK, PENNSYLVANIA.)

GARLAND, HAMLIN (1860–1940). Apparently the only existing Manhattan residence of Garland, author of Midwestern sketches and novels, is 23 **Gramercy Park** South (privately owned), where he lived in 1897.

He wrote his best-known book, *A Son of the Middle Border* (1917) in an **Upper East Side** "ugly, out-of-date" apartment, his home from 1916 to 1929 at 71 East 92nd St. (at the corner of Park Avenue), no longer standing.

(See Chapter 4, ILLINOIS, IOWA, SOUTH DAKOTA, WISCONSIN; also Chapter 6, CALIFORNIA.)

GEHRIG, HENRY LOUIS "LOU" (1903–1941). The New York Yankees hitter who played 14 consecutive seasons from 1925 without missing a game was born of German parentage and raised on the **Upper East Side.** His birthplace stood at 1994 2nd Ave.

(See BRONX in this chapter; also Chapter 3, NEW YORK.)

GERSHWIN, GEORGE (1898–1937). During his boyhood and musical career beginnings between 1900 and 1917, the composer occupied 25 Manhattan apartment residences, according to one biographer. In 1919, he wrote his first hit song "Swanee" at 520 West 144th St. in **Harlem,** still a private apartment building.

On the **Upper West Side** at 316 West 103rd St., Gershwin occupied the entire fifth floor of the five-story, white granite house from 1925 to 1928; his family lived in the rest of the house, which held three pianos. *Concerto in F* (1925) and *An American in Paris* (1928) were written there. The floors have since been divided into private apartments. From 1928 to 1933, the composer resided in a 17th-floor penthouse apartment at 33 Riverside Drive (at the corner of West 75th Street), a highly social place where he lived in the "feverish atmosphere of a railroad station." Another composer, Sergei Rachmaninoff, also lived here for part of the same period (see the entry on Rachmaninoff later in this section).

Gershwin's next apartment on the **Upper East Side,** where he worked on *Porgy and Bess* (1935), remains at 132 East 72nd St., a 14-room duplex with a gym and an art studio. It was his last Manhattan home, from 1933 to 1936. Today it holds private apartments and doctors' offices.

(See BROOKLYN in this chapter; also Chapter 6, CALIFORNIA.)

GETTY, JEAN PAUL (1892–1976). From 1936 to 1942, the oil billionaire established his home base in a large, rented penthouse suite at 1 Sutton Place South, where he surrounded himself with part of his expensive art collection; it was typical of Getty, however, to make sure he got the correct change at the building news stand. The One Sutton Place Building, **Upper East Side,** remains a private apartment complex.

(See Chapter 4, MINNESOTA; also Chapter 6, CALIFORNIA, OKLAHOMA.)

GOLDMAN, EMMA (1869–1940). The fiery anarchist speaker and writer occupied several Manhattan apartments and rooms, mostly cheap, run-down places, from 1889 to 1917. Few of the addresses are known. From 1903 to 1913, she lived with fellow anarchist Alexander Berkman and published the journal *Mother Earth* on the **Lower East Side** at 210 East 13th St. They called this two-room tenement apartment "the home for lost dogs" because of the number of down-and-out intellectuals and "radicals" they took in. The brown brick structure remains in private hands.

GOMPERS, SAMUEL (1850–1924). Cigar-maker and eventual founder of the American Federation of Labor, Gompers emigrated with his parents from London in 1863. Their first American home stood at Houston and Attorney streets on the **Lower East Side** (1863–64), a section then known as "Little Germany." Gompers moved about once a year for more than 20 years in Lower Manhattan, occupying a succession of squalid, over-crowded tenements.

Finally prosperous enough to move uptown in 1886, he resided in 1888 at an unidentified apartment on East 91st St., **Upper East Side,** his first home with indoor plumbing and a bath. He moved several more times until union activities took him permanently to Washington, D.C., in 1895.

What is now the Hotel Washington-Jefferson (1890) at 318 West 51st St. became Gompers' **Midtown** home during his Manhattan stays thereafter.

(See Chapter 3, DISTRICT OF COLUMBIA.)

GOULD, JAY (1836–1892). The last home from 1882 of the railroad magnate, financier, and prototype of the "robber baron" capitalist stood in **Midtown** at 579 5th Ave. (at the northeast corner of 47th Street); the four-story brownstone was later converted to a furniture store and is presently the site of a bank.

(See Chapter 3, NEW YORK; also Chapter 6, TEXAS.)

GRANT, ULYSSES SIMPSON (1822–1885). After his retirement as the 18th U.S. president, Grant made his final home from 1881 at 3 East 66th St., a handsome, red-brown, four-story brownstone with a mansard roof. The **Upper East Side** house was a gift to the luxury-loving, easily manipulated old soldier from a group of businessmen cronies whose motives may have been less than altruistic; at any rate, Grant went disastrously bankrupt there after following their "sound advice." The house stood until 1930, when a developer razed it for the apartment building presently on the site.

(See Chapter 3, DISTRICT OF COLUMBIA, NEW JERSEY, NEW YORK; also Chapter 4, ILLINOIS, MICHIGAN, MISSOURI, OHIO; also Chapter 5, VIRGINIA; also Chapter 6, WASHINGTON.)

GREELEY, HORACE (1811–1872). The profoundly influential journalist and 1872 presidential candidate lived at several Manhattan addresses from 1831. His first lodging in the city was the second floor of a saloon-boardinghouse, long gone, at 168 West St. where he paid $2.50 per week in 1831 and 1832. The site of Greeley's home in 1842 and 1843 is marked at 63 Barclay St. Both sites are on the **Lower West Side.**

From 1844 to 1850, Greeley resided in the **Upper East Side** Turtle Bay area (now the site of United Nations Park) on the East River. The "old, desolate rookery of a house," nicknamed "Castle Doleful" by friends because of the Greeleys' unpleasant domestic life, stood on eight country acres between East 48th and 49th Streets. Margaret Fuller boarded there from 1844 to 1846 while writing for Greeley's *New York Tribune*. When his adored only son died there in 1850, he moved back down to the city.

The three-story, brick row house he bought and occupied from 1850 to 1853 stands at 35 East 19th St. (privately owned). He kept a goat in the back yard there to remind him of the farm life he loved. This building near **Gramercy Park** now has a commercial facade.

(See Chapter 1, NEW HAMPSHIRE, VERMONT; also Chapter 3, NEW YORK.)

GREEN, HENRIETTA ROBINSON "HETTY" (1835–1916). Born wealthy, the redoubtable "witch of Wall Street," so-called for her skill as a major financial operator and for grimly holding on to her millions, lived with her son during her frequent Manhattan sojourns. She died at his home, no longer standing at 7 West 90th St. on the **Upper West Side.**

(See Chapter 1, MASSACHUSETTS, RHODE ISLAND, VERMONT; also Chapter 3, NEW JERSEY.)

GREY, ZANE (1875–1939). Before he became a bestselling western novelist, Grey was a practicing dentist in Manhattan, from 1896 to 1903. His office occupied the private apartment building at 100 West 74th St. (at the corner of Columbia Avenue), **Upper West Side.** He roomed nearby at an unknown location.

(See Chapter 3, PENNSYLVANIA; also Chapter 4, OHIO; also Chapter 6, ARIZONA, CALIFORNIA.)

GUGGENHEIM, MARGUERITE "PEGGY" (1898–1979). A self-styled "art addict," patron and collector, the silver-spoon granddaughter of Meyer Guggenheim (see the entry on Meyer Guggenheim below) was a Manhattan native who said she lived a "gilt-edged childhood" until about 1914 in her parents' five-story town house. It stood at 5th Avenue and 72nd Street.

The four-story, **Upper East Side** brownstone (called the "Hale House") where she lived with husband Max Ernst from 1942 became the hub of the New York art world before she moved permanently to Venice in 1946. This privately owned house stands at 440 with a terrace overlooking the East River.

GUGGENHEIM, MEYER (1828–1905). On the **Upper West Side** at 36 West 77th St., just opposite the American Museum of Natural History, the mining industrialist and founder of a financial dynasty made his home from 1888 in a large brownstone mansion, where he invariably celebrated Jewish Sabbath eves with gatherings of his large family. The house no longer stands.

(See Chapter 3, PENNSYLVANIA.)

GUTHRIE, WOODROW WILSON "WOODY" (1912–1967). Though the legendary singer-composer created his music from the Western dust bowl and migrant camps of his own experience, he was not the country hick he often liked to pretend; actually he resided longer in New York City than anywhere else in the country. He wrote the song "This Land Is Your Land" in 1940, as a Marxist rejoinder to Irving Berlin's "God Bless America," while bunked in the Hanover House, a "fleabag hotel" that stood near **Times Square** at Sixth Avenue and West 43rd Street. The old storefront building on the southwest corner there may be the same place.

The original "Almanac House," where the Almanac Singers including Guthrie lodged in 1941 and 1942, stands at 130 West 10th St. (privately owned) in **Greenwich Village,** a small dwelling that dates from 1862. Guthrie completed his book *Bound for Glory* (1943) in a small room at 148 West 14th St. in 1942, a private storefront building. "El Rancho del Sol," the place he named for its dusty, dingy appearance, stands at 74 Charles St., a six-story brick apartment building built in 1871. Guthrie roomed there in 1942 and 1943.

(See BROOKLYN, QUEENS in this chapter; also Chapter 6, OKLAHOMA, TEXAS.)

HALSEY, WILLIAM FREDERICK, JR. (1882–1959). After his 1950 retirement, Admiral "Bull" Halsey made his last home in Manhattan, where he served on the boards of several major corporations. Widowed, he lived in a friend's **Midtown** suite at 530 Park Ave., a private apartment building.

(See Chapter 3, NEW JERSEY; also Chapter 5, VIRGINIA.)

HAMILTON, ALEXANDER (1755–1804). Residing in Manhattan from 1783, Hamilton became the new nation's strongest conservative voice and first secretary of the treasury. He occupied many **Lower Manhattan** residences, most of them long since replaced by towering office buildings. While co-authoring *The Federalist* (1788) with John Jay and James Madison (see the entries on Jay and Madison later in this section), Hamilton lived at 58 Wall St., his home from 1783 to 1790.

Only his last home remains. Hamilton Grange National Memorial at 287 Convent Ave., **Washington Heights,** contains numerous family items, period furnishings, and exhibits. Built for Hamilton on a 16-acre tract he purchased in 1800, this two-story, clapboard country house culminated his long desire for a "dream house," and this was the only home he ever owned. It originally stood about 500 feet (two blocks) north on the south side of West 143rd Street. St. Luke's Church acquired it and moved it to the present site in

HAMILTON GRANGE NATIONAL MEMORIAL. In 1802, Alexander Hamilton built his country home on West 143rd Street in **Washington Heights,** but occupied it only for the two years preceding his death. This 1895 engraving by E. D. French shows the front of the house before the house was moved to its present site at 287 Convent Ave. *(Courtesy National Park Service)*

HAMILTON GRANGE TODAY. When moved 500 feet south to 287 Convent Ave. in 1889, the house was turned around and its front and side porches were removed. This "front view" of the house, then, was actually the back of the mansion when Hamilton lived there. Country acres, obviously, no longer surround the home. *(Courtesy National Park Service)*

1889 for use as a temporary chapel. The house, now maintained by the National Park Service, has undergone considerable restoration, but the basic structure, including the siding, beams and mouldings remain original. (Open daily 9:00–4:30; 212-283-5154; free.)

A day after his duel with Aaron Burr (see the entry on Burr earlier in this section), Hamilton died from his wound at the 1750 country home of William Bayard, which survived in **Greenwich Village** as the "Mansion House" tavern until 1886. The site is still occupied by the five-story apartment houses that replaced it at 80½ and 82 Jane St.

Exhibits: See *Exhibits* in the entry on George Washington later in this section.

The Museum of the City of New York at 1220 5th Ave. (at the corner of 103rd Street) displays a collection of Hamilton memorabilia. (Open Tuesday–Saturday 10:00–5:00, Sunday 1:00–5:00; 212-534-1672; free.)

(See Chapter 3, NEW JERSEY, NEW YORK.)

HAMILTON, EDITH (1867–1963). The educator retired in 1924 to 24 **Gramercy Park** South to begin her long career writing classical studies on Greece and Rome. She lived there until 1943. The house, probably remodeled from a 19th-century dwelling, holds private apartments.

(See Chapter 1, MAINE; also Chapter 3, DISTRICT OF COLUMBIA, MARYLAND; also Chapter 4, INDIANA.)

HAMMARSKJÖLD, DAG (1905–1961). As second U.N. Secretary-General (1953–61), the Swedish diplomat occupied an apartment suite at 778 Park Ave. (at the corner of East 73rd Street), **Upper East Side,** still a private residence building.

(See Chapter 3, NEW YORK.)

HAMMERSTEIN, OSCAR, II (1895–1960). The lyricist for some of Broadway's best-known stage musicals was an **Upper Manhattan** native, born at an unidentified apartment address on East 116th Street. His main adulthood residences, however, were located elsewhere, and he lodged only at intervals in Manhattan. Hammerstein's first married home, in 1917, was a small suite in the private apartment house at 509 West 121st St., **Harlem.** At 1067 5th Ave., **Upper East Side,** he occupied an apartment during 1930 and 1931 in the present building.

(See Chapter 3, NEW YORK, PENNSYLVANIA.)

HANDY, WILLIAM CHRISTOPHER (1873–1958). The musician and blues composer operated his own music-publishing company in Manhattan for about 30 years. His home during the 1920s and 1930s, preceding his final move upstate, was the private apartment building at 400 Convent Ave. in **Harlem.**

(See Chapter 3, NEW YORK; also Chapter 5, ALABAMA, TENNESSEE.)

HART, MOSS (1904–1961). Although he died in California, the writer and director of numerous popular stage hits had been a Manhattan resident for virtually all of his life. The remodeled Victorian brownstone he occupied from the 1930s to 1961 stands at 1185 Park Ave. (privately occupied), **Upper Manhattan.**

(See Chapter 3, PENNSYLVANIA; also Chapter 6, CALIFORNIA.)

HARTE, BRET (1836–1902). During the late 1840s, Harte briefly occupied the handsome 1825 Federal house at 487 Hudson St. in **Greenwich Village,** now the Parish Office for nearby St. Luke's in the Fields Church. A St. Luke's Thrift Shop is also located in the house (phone 212-924-9364). The writer whose tales of Western mining camps made him famous in the East returned in 1870 to Manhattan, where his career rapidly skidded. He lived with his sister at 16 5th Ave. for three years; this five-story apartment has since been combined with Number 14, both built in 1848 and 1849 and much modified with a stucco veneer.

(See Chapter 3, NEW JERSEY; also Chapter 6, CALIFORNIA.)

HEARN, LAFCADIO (1850–1904). Just before leaving to make his final home in Japan, the brilliant author-translator resided during 1889 and 1890 at 149 West 10th St., a three-story row house in **Greenwich Village** dating from 1833–34. It is privately owned.

(See Chapter 5, LOUISIANA.)

HEARST, WILLIAM RANDOLPH (1863–1951). Probably the most powerful publisher in American history, Hearst founded and ruled a press empire whose "yellow journalism" created some of the shabbier moments of our media's past.

"The public is even more fond of entertainment than it is of information" was his lifelong journalistic credo. Hearst operated in Manhattan from 1895 to 1926. As a bachelor, the first home he owned in the city was 123 Lexington Ave., now Arthur House National Historic Landmark (see the entry on Chester Alan Arthur earlier in this section), near **Gramercy Park.** Hearst lived there with editor Arthur Brisbane from about 1900 until Hearst's marriage to Millicent Willson in 1903; the couple then resided there until 1907.

"Any Hearst domicile was a place where one stumbled over statuary," wrote biographer W. A. Swanberg. Hearst found a larger home and haven for his ever-burgeoning art collection at the Clarendon Apartments, 137 Riverside Drive, where he took 30 rooms on the top three floors plus a roof garden and eventually a penthouse. This "overstuffed museum" remained his **Upper West Side** home until 1926, when he moved to California; his family continued to occupy the home until 1938. The interior was later remodeled into smaller private apartments, which remain.

Accompanied by actress Marion Davies, Hearst made his occasional city home from 1928 to 1938 at the 11-story Ritz Tower Hotel, dating from 1926, which he owned. It stands in **Midtown** at Park Avenue and East 57th Street.

(See Chapter 3, DISTRICT OF COLUMBIA; also Chapter 6, CALIFORNIA.)

HECHT, BEN (1894–1964). Prolific journalist, playwright, and screenwriter, Hecht occupied a 14th-floor apartment at 39 West 67th St. (privately occupied), **Upper West Side,** during his last years and died there.

(See Chapter 3, NEW YORK; also Chapter 4, ILLINOIS, WISCONSIN.)

HENDRIX, JIMI (1943–1970). Virtuoso rock guitarist and flamboyant leader of "the Jimi Hendrix Experience," the gifted performer who neither wrote nor read music occupied numerous Manhattan lodgings from 1963. "Jimi had several places where he stayed," wrote biographer David Henderson. "Sometimes it was not cool to go to one place, so he had others to go to. All of his pads had lovely young ladies taking care of them for him." His first city residence (1963–64) was Room 406 of the Theresa Hotel (see the entry on the Theresa Hotel later in this section) in **Harlem.** He sometimes kept a room

in Howard Johnson's Motor Lodge at Eighth Avenue and West 51st Street; and by 1968 occupied a 17th-floor "business suite" at the Drake Hotel, 440 Park Ave., **Upper Manhattan.**

In **Greenwich Village** at 55 West Eighth St., Hendrix designed and converted rooms of this 1890s apartment building into his Electric Lady Studio, giving him freedom to record his music the way he wanted. Hendrix probably spent more time there during the late 1960s than in any of his other "pads."

(See Chapter 6, WASHINGTON.)

HENRY, O. See WILLIAM SYDNEY PORTER.

HERBERT, VICTOR (1859–1924). The composer-conductor's **Upper West Side** home from 1904, his last, was 300–321 West 108th St. (at the corner of Broadway), possibly in the present large apartment building on this site.

Exhibit: Herbert's stand-up desk, from which flowed many of his operetta compositions, is displayed at the Songwriters' Hall of Fame, 1 **Times Square.** (Open Monday–Saturday 11:00–3:00; 212-221-1252; free.)

(See Chapter 3, NEW YORK, PENNSYLVANIA.)

HILL, JAMES JEROME (1838–1916). The financier and railroad magnate's last home, from 1906, was 8 East 65th St., **Upper East Side.** This five-story building, refaced and presently used as a private residence of the Pakistan Mission to the United Nations, dates from about 1900.

(See Chapter 4, MINNESOTA; also Chapter 5, GEORGIA.)

HOLIDAY, BILLIE (1915–1959). From 1928 "Lady Day," the blues and club singer, occupied numerous Manhattan apartments, mainly in **Harlem,** at intervals between her road engagements. During her peak years (ca. 1940), she lived at 286 West 142nd St., Apartment 2E (privately occupied).

Her last home, from 1957, was a one and one-half-room apartment at 26 West 87th St. (privately occupied), **Upper West Side.** According to biographer John Chilton, the doorbell (marked with her real name, Eleanora Fagan) "rarely rang." Ravaged from years of hard use and heroin addiction, she died at an aged 44.

HOMER, WINSLOW (1836–1910). The painter's only extant Manhattan dwelling stands near **Gramercy Park** at 128 East 16th St. (privately owned), his residence in 1859 and occasionally thereafter.

During the 1870s in **Greenwich Village,** he lived in the 1857 Studio Building at 51 West 10th St., the residence and studio of numerous 19th-century artists including Albert Bierstadt, Frederick E. Church, Eastman Johnson, John La Farge, and Augustus Saint-Gaudens (see the entries on Bierstadt and Saint-Gaudens in this section). The site of the building demolished in 1954 is now occupied by the 1959 Peter Warren Apartment building. At the southeast corner of Washington Square North and University Place stood the 1837 neo-Gothic New York University building; there in a top-floor studio, Homer lived and painted from 1882 to 1884. The Main Building of New York University, erected in 1894, now stands there.

(See Chapter 1, MAINE, MASSACHUSETTS.)

HOOVER, HERBERT CLARK (1874–1964). The 31st U.S. president retired from office to Suite 31A of the Waldorf Towers (see the entry on the Waldorf Towers later in this section), his permanent home from 1934. This was the longest period that Hoover ever resided in one place.

(See Chapter 3, DISTRICT OF COLUMBIA; also Chapter 4, IOWA; also Chapter 5, VIRGINIA; also Chapter 6, CALIFORNIA, OREGON.)

HOPPER, EDWARD (1882–1967). The painter's longtime home and studio was a house in "The Row," 3 Washington Square North in **Greenwich Village.** This elegant Greek Revival house, one of five remaining here (Numbers 7–13 are only facades), dates from about 1832 and was remodeled as a studio building in 1884. Hopper lived here permanently from 1913. "Growing a little shabby, but not yet mutilated as it is today," wrote John Canaday in 1980, "the square was still a garden spot where uptown met downtown. Life on the square and in the Village came as close to artists' life in Paris as life ever came in America. Yet Hopper, who loved Paris, never accepted this American Bohemia as part of his life or as subject matter for his painting, remaining circumspectly apart from it." Other residents of this house at various times included painters William Glackens and Rockwell Kent, and writer Edmund

Wilson (see the entry on Wilson later in this section).

(See Chapter 1, MASSACHUSETTS; also Chapter 3, NEW YORK.)

HOUDINI, HARRY (1874–1926). The magician's last home, from 1904, is probably the same four-story private brownstone now on the site at 278 West 113th St., **Upper West Side.** Here the showman retired between engagements, worked out new escape acts to baffle his audiences and waged incessant war against charlatan mediums and spiritualists.

(See Chapter 4, MICHIGAN, WISCONSIN.)

HUGHES, CHARLES EVANS (1862–1948). As a practicing lawyer in Manhattan—just before beginning the public career that took him to Albany and Washington, D.C.—the future governor and U.S. chief justice lived on the **Upper West Side.** His home from 1893 to 1905 stood on the marked site at 325 West End Ave. (at the corner of West 75th Street).

(See Chapter 3, DISTRICT OF COLUMBIA, NEW YORK.)

HUGHES, LANGSTON (1902–1967). Author and "original jazz poet," Hughes made his last home from 1948 in his beloved **Harlem** at 20 East 127th St., the three-story, private brownstone where he lived with Mr. and Mrs. Emerson Harper. Hughes worked in a third-floor study here and grew ivy near the front door, "the only green thing on that Harlem block," said a friend. Earlier (from 1942 to 1947) he had resided with the Harpers in a three-room apartment at 634 St. Nicholas Ave., still a private apartment building.

(See Chapter 4, KANSAS, MISSOURI.)

IRVING, WASHINGTON (1783–1859). America's first professional man of letters was born in **Lower Manhattan** at 131 William St. (at the corner of Fulton Street) and grew up at 128 William St. The small, two-story, brick and wood cottage that stood at the latter address, with its lovely garden, was Irving's home from 1783 to 1802. From 1802 until about 1810, he lived at the northwest corner of Ann and William streets; there he wrote his *Knickerbocker's History of New York* (1809). A marker identifies the site.

In 1836, he occupied a **Lower East Side** dwelling in Colonnade Row, nine marble town houses built in 1833 and united by a long, two-story colonnade. The private four that remain (428–434 Lafayette Street) have suffered disfigurement owing to alterations and neglect through the years.

Irving's usual city residence after he settled in 1836 at Irvington, N.Y., was his nephew's home, the four-story, brownstone, John Trent Irving House still standing at 46 East 21st St. (privately owned) near **Gramercy Park.** Irving never lived at 122 East 17th St., despite the marker there that says so; the confusion apparently resulted from another Irving having once dwelled in that 1845 house.

The marker at 11 Commerce St. (privately owned) in **Greenwich Village,** the site of his sister's house, states that Irving wrote "The Legend of Sleepy Hollow" there in 1816. According to the New York Landmarks Preservation Commission, however, the present brick row dates from 1826.

(See Chapter 3, NEW YORK.)

IVES, CHARLES EDWARD (1874–1954). The composer whose symphonic and instrumental works created a distinctive American idiom did another distinctively American thing for most of his life—sold insurance. Most of his several Manhattan dwellings still exist, all privately owned. He occupied a succession of three apartment dwellings with friends in the decade from 1898 to 1908, each of which they labeled "Poverty Flat." Two of the buildings—at 65 Central Park West (1901–07) and 34 Gramercy Park East—remain. The latter address was New York's first cooperative apartment dwelling, dating from 1883.

Ives's first married home (from 1908 to 1911) was 70 West 11th St. in **Greenwich Village,** a five-story brownstone apartment building that dates from 1879. His address in 1911 and 1912 was 118 Waverly Place, an 1842, brick, four-story house; in 1914 and 1915 he occupied another apartment at 29 West 11th St., a six-story house built in 1889.

From 1917 to 1926, Ives lived near **Gramercy Park** at 120 East 22nd St. above what is now a coffee shop; and by the end of this period, he had completed most of his major activity as a composer.

Ives's last home, from 1926, stood on the **Upper East Side** at 164 East 74th St., razed since his death there.

(See Chapter 1, CONNECTICUT.)

JAMES, HENRY (1843–1916).

JAMES, WILLIAM (1842–1910).

Both brothers were born in Manhattan: William, the famed psychologist, at the Astor House Hotel, which stood until 1913 at 225 Broadway, the present site of the 1915 Transportation Building; and Henry, expatriate novelist and critic, at 27 (then called 21) Washington Place east of Greene Street in **Greenwich Village.** The latter dwelling fell when the Main Building of New York University was erected in 1894, much to Henry James's displeasure; he said he felt "amputated of half his history." Today, according to the authors of *Literary New York* (1976), "there is a tablet commemorating James, but he would doubtless consider it ironic that it is in the wrong place—on the NYU Brown Building half a block from his birthplace." The brothers spent most of their childhood years at 57 West 14th St., long gone. Their grandmother's house, where they also spent many boyhood hours, stood at what today would be 18 Washington Square North, the setting for Henry's novel *Washington Square* (1881); this 1836 brick dwelling fell in 1950 to make way for the present 20-story apartment house extending from 2 Fifth Ave. The only surviving Manhattan house where Henry James spent a period of any duration is 21 East 11th St., where he occupied first-floor rooms in 1904 during an American visit. This fine, brick town house, erected in 1848, was the home of his friend Mary C. Jones, noted for her salons and many famous guests. Still privately owned, the house appears just as James knew it from his youth in this neighborhood.

In 1875, Henry James occupied 111 East 25th St. near **Madison Square** for six months while completing *Roderick Hudson* (1875). An armory now stands on the site.

(See Chapter 1, MASSACHUSETTS, NEW HAMPSHIRE, RHODE ISLAND.)

JAY, JOHN (1745–1829). The first U.S. chief justice resided at various **Lower Manhattan** sites during and after his six-year court tenure. While co-authoring *The Federalist* (1788) with Alexander Hamilton and James Madison, Jay lived at 133 Broadway between Cedar and Liberty streets, on the west side. He resided in Government House as New York's governor from 1795 to 1801 (see the entries on George Clinton, Hamilton and Madison, all in this section).

(See Chapter 3, NEW YORK.)

JEFFERSON, THOMAS (1743–1826). As the nation's first secretary of state when New York was the federal capital, the eventual third U.S. president wanted a house on Broadway but settled for a dwelling at 57 Maiden Lane. He resided there for only three months in 1790 but added a rear gallery and expensive cabinetry. This house stood as late as 1929; its **Lower Manhattan** site is marked on the triangular plaza between Maiden Lane and John Street.

Exhibit: See *Exhibits,* in the entry on George Washington in this section.

(See Chapter 3, DISTRICT OF COLUMBIA, PENNSYLVANIA; also Chapter 5, VIRGINIA.)

JOHNSON, JAMES WELDON (1871–1938). Author, poet and civil rights leader, Johnson wrote songs when he came to Manhattan in 1901. He lived in **Midtown** on the second floor of the Marshall Club, which stood at 260 West 53rd St.— called "The Club" in his novel *Autobiography of an Ex-Colored Man* (1912).

In the 1920s, Johnson resided at 2311 Seventh Ave., now a **Harlem** gift shop and doctors' offices. His "well-appointed" last home, from 1925, stands at 187 West 135th St., a five-story brick dwelling built about 1900. It remains privately owned.

(See Chapter 1, MASSACHUSETTS; also Chapter 5, FLORIDA, TENNESSEE.)

JOPLIN, SCOTT (1868–1917). The ragtime composer's first Manhattan residence, from 1911 to 1915, was an old, six-story, brick apartment house at 252 West 47th St., recently standing in **Midtown** but slated for demolition. This was his home when he produced his opera *Tremonisha* (1911).

During his last declining years, Joplin continued to compose and teach, renting **Harlem** rooms at 133 West 138th St. (1915–16), now a two-apartment dwelling.

Joplin died at his final pathetic residence, the 1863 Manhattan State Hospital (now Manhattan Psychiatric Center) on **Ward's Island** in the East River.

(See Chapter 4, MISSOURI.)

KAUFMAN, GEORGE SIMON (1889–1961). Acerbic humorist and playwright who wrote or directed at least one Broadway hit each year from 1921 to 1941, Kaufman resided at least part-time in Manhattan apartment suites during all of those years. He apparently occupied all of his later dwellings by the decade. In 1932, he was living at 158 East 63rd St., still a private residence. From 1932 to 1942, he occupied an apartment in the white town house at 14 East 94th St. His apartment for the next decade (1942–51) was at 410 Park Ave. Kaufman's last home from 1951 was 1035 Park Ave., a penthouse suite. All of these **Upper East Side** structures still house private apartments.

Kaufman was also a Round Table regular at the Algonquin Hotel during the late 1920s (see the entry on the Algonquin Hotel earlier in this section).

(See Chapter 3, PENNSYLVANIA.)

KERN, JEROME DAVID (1885–1945). The composer of almost 50 musical-comedy scores was born in **Midtown** at 411 East 56th St., his home to age five. The present private building here, possibly the same, houses doctors' offices.

In **Upper Manhattan,** his three-story boyhood home until 1895 stood at 128 East 74th St. Here he was introduced to the piano, a meeting that ultimately resulted in such stage classics as *Show Boat* (1927) and *Roberta* (1933; "Smoke Gets in Your Eyes"). Kern's last Manhattan apartment residence stands at 226 West 70th St. (privately occupied), his home from 1914 to 1916, the years when he firmly "made it" on Broadway.

(See Chapter 3, NEW YORK; also Chapter 6, CALIFORNIA.)

KEROUAC, JACK (1922–1969). In **Harlem,** the literary avant-garde "beat movement" was born, according to poet Allen Ginsberg, at Amsterdam Avenue and West 118th Street when Ginsberg, Kerouac and William Burroughs shared an apartment there from 1943 to 1945 with two women, one of whom (Edie Parker) Kerouac later married. Which building on this corner housed their apartment is uncertain.

In 1951, Kerouac wrote *On the Road* (1957), typing nonstop on a 120-foot roll of teletype paper, in a brownstone loft at 149 West 21st St. (privately owned) in the **Chelsea** area.

"Paradise Alley," an inner brick courtyard of

the tenement at 501 East 11th St., **Lower East Side,** was the scene of *The Subterraneans* (1968); Kerouac lived with a woman friend there in 1953.

(See QUEENS in this chapter; also Chapter 1, MASSACHUSETTS; also Chapter 3, NEW YORK; also Chapter 5, FLORIDA; also Chapter 6, CALIFORNIA.)

KIDD, WILLIAM (1645?–1701). The Scottish-born seaman, convicted and hanged in London for piracy, was a stable Manhattan citizen from 1690 to 1695 before he became a privateer for the English, then a pirate in Madagascar. Captain Kidd owned what is now some of the most expensive real estate in the world. According to one biographer, the "scrolled dormers and fluted chimneys of his tall house were landmarks for ships bound in to New York moorage." This house stood in **Lower Manhattan** at what is now 119–21 Pearl St. in Hanover Square. He also owned the land at 56 Wall St., 86–90 Pearl St., 52–56 Water St., and 25–29 Pine St.

Kidd's "Saw Kill" farm, his summer home, stood at East 74th St. on the East River, **Upper East Side.**

KRUTCH, JOSEPH WOOD (1893–1970). Author, critic and naturalist, Krutch resided in **Greenwich Village** for about 40 years, including the period from 1937 to 1952 when he taught dramatic literature at Columbia University. Earlier, during the 1920s, he lived with friend and fellow teacher Mark Van Doren at 43 Barrow St., a three-story brick house dating from 1828, where Krutch roomed in the back apartment heated by a gas radiator. From about 1940 to 1958, Krutch's last Manhattan home was 11 West 11th St., a four-story, brick town house built in 1831, still privately owned.

(See Chapter 1, CONNECTICUT; also Chapter 6, ARIZONA.)

LA GUARDIA, FIORELLO HENRY (1882–1947). New York's most popular mayor, a volatile dumpling of a politician who delightedly offended everybody except the voters, was a longtime Manhattan resident, born at 177 Sullivan St. on the **Lower West Side,** a presently unlisted address.

His home from about 1915 to 1921, during his first terms in Congress, was 39 Charles St. in **Greenwich Village,** one of five town houses in an 1869 row and still privately owned.

From 1929 to 1932, La Guardia occupied an apartment at 23 East 109th St. on the **Upper East Side** (at the corner of Madison Avenue), still a private residence building.

La Guardia was living in a simply furnished apartment on the top floor of the building at 1274 Fifth Ave. in **Harlem** when elected mayor in 1933 and stayed there until 1942, when city officials decided that "hizzoner" deserved a more prestigious dwelling.

He thus became the first city mayor to occupy what has been the official Mayor's Residence ever since—Gracie Mansion National Historic Landmark, East End Avenue at East 88th Street in Carl Schurz Park, **Upper East Side.** La Guardia chose the new official residence as cheaper to maintain than the Schwab chateau on Riverside Drive that was originally proposed. Gracie Mansion, a two-story Federal frame house, dates from 1799 with additions from 1811 and a north wing from 1966. "It now holds the distinction," wrote Gerard R. Wolfe, "of being the only original country seat in Manhattan still occupied as a home." The city has owned it since 1893. In 1923, it was being used as a comfort station in the park but was restored in 1927. There is no public admittance. La Guardia lived there until the end of his three-term mayoral tenure in 1945.

(See BRONX in this chapter.)

LEE, GYPSY ROSE (1914–1970). The woman for whom H. L. Mencken coined the word "ecdysiast" to honor her art as a striptease performer was also a detective novelist. Her last home, from 1940, stands on the **Upper East Side** at 153 East 63rd St., a white stucco Spanish colonial dwelling with 24 rooms, built from 1917 to 1919. It remains privately owned.

(See Chapter 3, NEW YORK; also Chapter 6, CALIFORNIA.)

LEHMAN, HERBERT HENRY (1878–1963). Banker, reform governor and U.S. senator, Lehman became one of the state's most liberal and popular politicians. He was a Manhattan native, born and raised in a "quiet, solid home," a four-story brownstone that stood at 5 East 62nd St., **Upper East Side.** Lehman's permanent city home from about 1930 was a second-floor suite at 820 Park Ave., which still houses private apartments. He died there just before he was to receive the Presidential Medal of Freedom from President Lyndon B. Johnson.

(See Chapter 3, NEW YORK.)

LENNON, JOHN (1940–1980). The English-born musician-composer-peace activist retained his almost mythic if somewhat faded aura as one of the hugely successful Beatles into his last days. Apparently beginning a new creative phase after a long hiatus, he was brutally gunned down by a homicidal young psychopath—the type that, in America, has always found handguns easily available—in front of Lennon's Manhattan home. This, from 1975, was the Gothic fortress-like Dakota Apartments National Historic Landmark, one of Manhattan's most prestigious dwellings at 1 West 72nd St. (at the corner of Central Park West) on the **Upper West Side.** This eight-story, yellow-brick structure dates from 1880–84 and has been the subject of at least two books—Jack Finney's fantasy novel *Time and Again* (1970) and Stephen Birmingham's *Life at the Dakota* (1979). Here Lennon and his family reclusively occupied 25 rooms in five seventh-floor apartments, where he and his wife collected Egyptian artifacts and ran a $235-million financial empire that included large real estate holdings and a prize Holstein herd. Part of the huge Lennon suite was the former home of actor Robert Ryan, whose wife died there. Lennon also maintained an office and studio on the Dakota ground floor. Dakota residents have always valued their privacy, and security has been especially tight there since Lennon's death.

LEWIS, SINCLAIR (1885–1951). As a struggling young writer in 1911, the novelist lived in **Greenwich Village** at 69 Charles St. (10 Van Nest Place at that time) in a private row of four-story brick houses dating from 1866 and 1867. Just after their marriage in 1928, Lewis and his wife, the journalist Dorothy Thompson, occupied the private town house at 37 West 10th St., built in 1838 and 1839.

Each partner had a sitting room for separate entertaining in the apartment-office building still at 21 East 90th St., their **Upper East Side** home in 1931.

Lewis, after their divorce, rented a 29th-floor duplex apartment at the Eldorado Towers, 300 Central Park West, in 1943 and 1944. He called the place "Intolerable Towers" and "a cross between Elizabeth Arden's Beauty Salon and the horse-stables at Ringling Circus Winter Headquarters." A huge map of his native Minnesota dominated the study. The Eldorado, built about 1930, still houses private suites on the **Upper West Side.**

(See Chapter 1, MASSACHUSETTS, VERMONT; also Chapter 3, NEW YORK; also Chapter 4, MINNESOTA.)

LIPPMANN, WALTER (1889–1975). The journalist and political philosopher, a Manhattan native, spent his first and last years on the **Upper East Side.** Boyhood homes stood at 121 East 79th St., a four-story brick dwelling; and, from 1902 to 1917, at 46 East 80th St. From 1929 to 1937, when he moved to Washington, D.C., Lippmann lived at 245 East 61st St., a town house where he entertained many noted guests and installed a soundproof study—his "pool of silence"—on the top floor. Returning from Washington in 1966, he bought a 17-room duplex at 1021 Park Ave., but lived there for only a year. His last apartment dwelling was a suite at the "discreetly fashionable" Lowell Hotel, 28 East 63rd St.

As a staff member of the *New Republic,* a journal he helped found, he lived in **Greenwich Village,** first at 50 Washington Mews, a converted stucco carriage house built before 1854 and extensively remodeled in 1888. This was Lippmann's home from 1923 to 1926. At 39 Fifth Ave., he rented a large apartment in 1926 and 1927 in the 14-story brick building that dates from 1922.

All of Lippmann's extant dwellings remain privately owned.

(See Chapter 3, DISTRICT OF COLUMBIA, NEW YORK.)

LOUIS, JOE (1914–1981). As heavyweight boxing champion from 1937 to 1949, Louis was a modest, self-effacing man—except in the ring, which he ruled longer than anyone else. His Manhattan residences, where he frequently resided from the 1930s to the 1970s, consisted mainly of two **Upper Manhattan** apartment suites. The first, occupied during his prime boxing years, was the Theresa Hotel (see the entry on the Theresa Hotel later in this section); and from the 1960s, he occupied a 24th-floor suite at the Park Sheraton Hotel, 870 7th Ave.

(See Chapter 4, ILLINOIS; also Chapter 6, CALIFORNIA, COLORADO, NEVADA.)

LOWELL, ROBERT TRAILL SPENCE, JR. (1917–1977). "The last gasp of true Nineteenth-Century Capitalistic Gothic" was the poet's assessment of his studio duplex at 15 West 67th St. (privately owned), **Upper West Side.** His poem "The Golden Middle" also describes this residence, Lowell's home for the decade of the 1960s. In 1963, the first issue of the *New York Review of Books* was born here as a group of Manhattan literati gathered around the dining room table.

(See Chapter 1, MAINE, MASSACHUSETTS; also Chapter 4, OHIO.)

LUCE, HENRY ROBINSON (1898–1967). The publisher of mass circulation magazines that reflected his strongly conservative political credo, Luce resided for much of his life in Manhattan and occupied a variety of apartment dwellings. When he founded *Time* with co-editor Briton Hadden in 1923, he was living with his missionary parents at 514 West 122nd St. in **Morningside Heights.**

The large town house at 234 East 49th St. (privately owned) was his **Midtown** home from 1927 to about 1933. Built in 1926 by violinist Efrem Zimbalist and his wife, singer Alma Gluck, the house served as the 17th Precinct Police Station from 1957 to 1960. From 1936, Luce and his wife, Clare Boothe Luce, occupied a luxurious suite in "River House," the posh complex of duplex and triplex apartments built in 1931 at 435 East 52nd St.; and this remained their Manhattan base for almost 25 years. They also occupied various suites for 12 years, from 1938, in the Waldorf Towers, their last on the 41st floor (see the entry on the Waldorf Towers later in this section). Their final Manhattan home, from about 1960, was a smaller but still grand apartment at 950 5th Ave.

All of these residences remain privately occupied.

(See Chapter 1, CONNECTICUT; also Chapter 5, SOUTH CAROLINA; also Chapter 6, ARIZONA.)

MacARTHUR, DOUGLAS (1880–1964). The old soldier of World War II and Korea who said he would "just fade away" did so in characteristic baronial style at the Waldorf Towers, his final home (see the entry on the Waldorf Towers later

in this section). After President Harry S. Truman relieved him from Asian command in 1952, MacArthur occupied the $133-per-day Suite 37A for $450 per month.

(See Chapter 3, MARYLAND, NEW YORK; also Chapter 4, KANSAS; also Chapter 5, ARKANSAS, VIRGINIA; also Chapter 6, NEW MEXICO, TEXAS.)

McCLELLAN, GEORGE BRINTON (1826–1885). After his Civil War military career and presidential candidacy of 1864, McClellan retired briefly in 1865 to a four-story brick mansion, bought for him by well-heeled friends, at 22 West 31st St. in the **Chelsea** area. The house, though primarily rented out, stayed in the McClellan family as late as 1934; a son who lived there served as New York City mayor from 1904 to 1909. Today a cafe occupies this site.

(See Chapter 3, DISTRICT OF COLUMBIA, NEW JERSEY, PENNSYLVANIA.)

McCULLERS, CARSON SMITH (1917–1967). A novelist whose work reflected her Southern origins and whose life was marked by ill health and domestic tragedy, McCullers lived in 1940 with her husband, Reeves McCullers (who committed suicide in 1953), at 321 West 11th St. in **Greenwich Village.** They occupied an apartment on the top floor of this private, five-story building that dates originally from 1838 and 1839; it was much altered in 1873. This was the period when she launched her career with her first novel *The Heart is a Lonely Hunter* (1940).

(See BROOKLYN in this chapter; also Chapter 3, NEW YORK; also Chapter 5, GEORGIA, NORTH CAROLINA.)

MacDOWELL, EDWARD ALEXANDER (1861–1908). None of MacDowell's Manhattan dwellings remain. The birthplace of the pianist-composer and first American musician to gain a serious audience in Europe stood at 220 Clinton St., his **Lower East Side** home until about 1876.

During most of the years he taught at Columbia University (1898 to 1902), MacDowell occupied an apartment in the vicinity of Central Park West and West 96th Street, **Upper West Side.**

(See Chapter 1, NEW HAMPSHIRE.)

MADISON, JAMES (1751–1836). The fourth U.S. president and "father of the Constitution,"

Madison co-authored *The Federalist* (1788) with Alexander Hamilton and John Jay (see the entries on Hamilton and Jay earlier in this section). His **Lower Manhattan** residence before the federal capital moved to Philadelphia in 1790 was the Elsworth boardinghouse at 19 Maiden Lane near the corner of Liberty Place. The house is long gone.

(See Chapter 3, DISTRICT OF COLUMBIA, PENNSYLVANIA; also Chapter 5, VIRGINIA.)

MARQUAND, JOHN PHILLIPS (1893–1960). In 1937 after winning the Pulitzer Prize for *The Late George Apley* (1937), the novelist took a duplex apartment at 1 Beekman Place and lived there until 1940. This immense apartment building known as One Beekman Place, Inc., still houses prestigious private suites. Previous residents were Sir Noel Pierce Coward (see the entry on Coward earlier in this section) and actress Gertrude Lawrence. Before winning his prize money, Marquand occupied an apartment at 161 East 75th St., also privately occupied. Several of his novels are set in the **Upper East Side.**

(See Chapter 1, MASSACHUSETTS; also Chapter 3, DELAWARE, NEW YORK; also Chapter 5, FLORIDA, NORTH CAROLINA.)

MARX, ADOLPH ARTHUR "HARPO" (1893–1964).
MARX, JULIUS HENRY "GROUCHO" (1895–1977).
MARX, LEONARD "CHICO" (1891–1961).
The Marx brothers, whose chaotic style of film and vaudeville comedy made utter shambles of the pompous, serious and sensible, were Manhattan natives. Groucho's birthplace, a brownstone at 239 East 114th St. on the **Upper East Side,** no longer stands; but the boyhood home of all three brothers from 1895 to 1910, is probably the same four-story brownstone still at 179 East 93rd St., and they considered the three-bedroom apartment there as their ancestral home. An art gallery currently occupies the first floor.

From 1924 to 1926, when the brothers made their first hit on the musical stage, Groucho lived in the apartment building still at Riverside Drive and West 161st Street, **Upper West Side.**

(See Chapter 3, NEW YORK; also Chapter 6, CALIFORNIA.)

MASTERS, EDGAR LEE (1869–1950). The Midwestern poet's residence of longest duration was Manhattan, not Illinois; he occupied one of the city's best-known literary lodgings, the Chelsea Hotel, from 1931 to 1944 (see the entry on the Chelsea Hotel earlier in this section). In Room 214 there he produced most of his later poetic and biographical works.

(See Chapter 4, ILLINOIS, MICHIGAN.)

MEAD, MARGARET (1901–1978). The famed anthropologist and author, long associated with the American Museum of Natural History, lived in various Manhattan apartments throughout her long career. During the 1940s and 1950s, she occupied the attractive 1868 brownstone house at 72 Perry St. in **Greenwich Village.** In the 1960s she lived at 193 Waverly Place, a fine Greek Revival house built from 1845 to 1847. Both houses remain privately owned.

(See Chapter 3, NEW JERSEY, PENNSYLVANIA.)

MELVILLE, HERMAN (1819–1891). One of America's great writers, all but ignored during his lifetime, Melville was a **Lower Manhattan** native. He was born at 6 Pearl St., where a marker on an office building near the corner of State Street identifies the site.

In **Greenwich Village,** later boyhood addresses included 33 Bleecker St. (1824–28), presently shops and apartments; and 675 Broadway (1828), the later site of the Broadway Central Hotel, also gone.

After his marriage in 1847, Melville settled at 103 Fourth Ave. on the **Lower East Side,** where he lived until 1850 and wrote *Redburn* (1849) and *White-Jacket* (1850), beginning an apparently futile literary career.

After a long Massachusetts residence, Melville bought his last home in 1863, a yellow-brick row house at 104 East 26th St. near **Gramercy Park.** There he wrote *Billy Budd*, his last masterpiece, unpublished until 1924. During most of his years at this house (1866 to 1885), Melville dutifully supported his family in a dreary job as customs inspector in offices at 207 West St. The house was replaced by the National Guard Armory at 68 Lexington Avenue; none of Melville's Manhattan homes stand.

(See Chapter 1, MASSACHUSETTS; also Chapter 3, NEW YORK.)

MERTON, THOMAS (1915–1968). As a student at Columbia University, the eventual author, poet, and Trappist monk resided in 1939 and 1940 at 35 Perry St. in **Greenwich Village.** Merton especially enjoyed the upstairs balcony in this 1855 house and sat there for hours observing Village activity and reading. The house remains privately owned.

(See Chapter 5, KENTUCKY.)

MILLAY, EDNA ST. VINCENT (1892–1950). The Maine poet arrived at **Greenwich Village** in 1917, intending to become an actress; she settled with her sister Norma in an unheated room—"hardly large enough for a bed and a typewriter and some cups and saucers"—at 139 Waverly Place, where she entered community spirit by living in "gay poverty" for a year. This two-story, 1829 dwelling is wooden frame with brick facing; its front was recently remodeled to provide a basement entrance. The sisters moved with their mother in 1918 to 25 Charlton St., a brick house where they occupied the top floor and held countless literary soirees. The poet's early married home in 1923 and 1924, often identified as the "Millay House," is the three-story, 9.5-foot-wide, pink toy town house at 75½ Bedford Street, a former residence of John Barrymore (see the entry on Barrymore earlier in this section). Built in 1873, it is popularly known as the "narrowest house in the city." All of these dwellings remain in private hands.

(See Chapter 1, MAINE; also Chapter 3, NEW YORK.)

MILLER, HENRY VALENTINE (1891–1980). The controversial author whom critic Karl Shapiro called "Gandhi with a penis" was born in **Yorkville** at 450 East 85th St. (at the corner of York Avenue), his home until 1892. The family apartment in the top floor above a saloon might have occupied the building still on the site.

(See BROOKLYN in this chapter; also Chapter 6, CALIFORNIA.)

MONK, THELONIOUS SPHERE (1920–1982). Jazz pianist, composer and bebop innovator, Monk lived at one **Upper West Side** address for almost his entire life—a two-room apartment at 243 West 63rd St. (privately occupied), his home from 1924.

MONROE, JAMES (1758–1831). The retired fifth U.S. president's last home, from 1830, was the **Lower Manhattan** residence of his son-in-law, Samuel Gouverneur, which stood at the northeast corner of Lafayette and Prince streets. The small, Dutch-roofed dwelling survived as late as 1925. Monroe died there.

(See Chapter 3, DISTRICT OF COLUMBIA; also Chapter 5, VIRGINIA.)

MONROE, MARILYN (1926–1962). The film actress who studio employers and the public built into a sex goddess occupied a small Waldorf Towers suite in 1955 and 1956 (see the entry on the Waldorf Towers later in this section). Later she lived with her husband, playwright Arthur Miller, in Apartment 13E at 444 East 57th St., **Midtown.** This address is the "front entrance" to Sutton Place, one of modern Manhattan's most prestigious bastions of the wealthy. The seven-room suite, decorated in white, was the actress' city home from 1957 until her death.

(See Chapter 1, CONNECTICUT; also Chapter 6, CALIFORNIA.)

MOORE, CLEMENT CLARKE (1779–1863). The prominent scholar whose language studies are largely forgotten, Moore's fame is resurrected each Christmas with his ballad "A Visit from St. Nicholas" (1823). Moore's ancestral home and birthplace in **Chelsea** was Chelsea Mansion, a two-story brick homestead built in 1777 and located between Ninth and 10th avenues north of West 22nd Street. The large estate, which he inherited in 1809, extended along Eighth Avenue and the Hudson River from 19th to 24th streets. Moore subdivided the property for building lots as the city grew northward, and by 1831 streets gridded the former estate. The mansion was demolished in 1854. Moore later built a home, also long gone, at the southwest corner of Ninth Avenue and West 23rd Street.

(See Chapter 1, RHODE ISLAND.)

MOORE, MARIANNE CRAIG (1887–1972). In **Greenwich Village** from 1918 to 1929, the poet and her mother occupied an apartment on the ground floor of 14 St. Luke's Place, a brick row house built in 1852 and 1853. She returned to the Village after 35 years in Brooklyn, and her last home, from 1966, occupied the nine-story brick building at 35 West Ninth St., Apartment 7B. This apartment has been reassembled for public view at the Rosenbach Foundation in Philadelphia. Both

Village buildings remain privately occupied.

(See BROOKLYN in this chapter; also Chapter 3, PENNSYLVANIA; also Chapter 4, MISSOURI.)

MORGAN, JOHN PIERPONT (1837–1913). The powerful financier and noted art collector made Manhattan his permanent home after 1865 and occupied several increasingly opulent residences, none of which remain. His last residence, at 219 Madison Ave. in **Midtown,** was one in a group of three large brownstones he owned at the corner of East 36th Street. All dated from about 1850. In 1882, when Morgan moved in, his mansion became the first private house in the world to be electrically lighted throughout, under the personal supervision of Thomas A. Edison. Morgan used this mansion as a winter residence. In 1900, he projected construction of an adjacent library building to house his art treasures, and this white marble structure designed by McKim, Mead & White was completed in 1906. Morgan's will directed that his home should be demolished for extension of the Morgan Library, which was accomplished in 1928. The extension covering the site of Morgan's home is now the library entrance annex at 29 East 36th St. Standing at nearby 231 Madison Ave. (at the corner of East 37th Street) is the only house of his original group that remains. This was the longtime residence of his son and successor, J. P. Morgan, Jr. It has served as national headquarters of the Lutheran Church in America since 1943.

Exhibit: Pierpont Morgan Library National Historic Landmark, 33 East 36th St., **Midtown,** displays one of the world's great collections of sculpture, paintings, jewelry, and rare books and manuscripts, assembled by the financier and his dynastic heirs. The West Room here was Morgan's study, where he hosted daily guests and held the consultation with bankers that averted a national financial panic in 1907. The room has red silk damask walls. (Open Tuesday–Saturday 10:30–5:00, Sunday 1:00–5:00; 212-685-0008; free.)

(See Chapter 1, CONNECTICUT; also Chapter 5, GEORGIA.)

MORGENTHAU, HENRY, JR. (1891–1967). Agriculturist and secretary of the treasury from 1934 to 1945, the namesake son of a prominent lawyer and diplomat was born in the Beresford Apartments, still at 211 Central Park West (at the corner of West 81st Street), **Upper West Side.** There

is little information available on other Manhattan dwellings he may have occupied until 1913, when he moved upstate.

(See Chapter 3, NEW YORK.)

MORSE, SAMUEL FINLEY BREESE (1791–1872). Morse, a versatile painter as well as inventor, developed the electrical telegraph in Manhattan. As the nation's first professor of fine arts, he taught and occupied rooms from 1835 to the early 1840s in the old main building of New York University in **Greenwich Village.** His five rooms in the northwest tower, where he perfected the telegraph, overlooked Washington Square. Morse also operated a daguerrotype studio on the roof there. The huge Gothic Revival building completed in 1837 also became a later residence of artist Winslow Homer (see the entry on Homer earlier in this section). Torn down in 1894, it was replaced by the present Main Building at the corner of Washington Square North and East.

In 1846, while trying to figure a method of spanning the telegraph line from Baltimore to New York across the Hudson from Fort Lee, N.J., Morse rented a room and conducted experiments at "Minnie's Land," the home of John James Audubon in **Washington Heights** (see the entry on Audubon earlier in this section). Workmen who demolished Audubon's home in 1930 reputedly found scraps of Morse's telegraph wires in the laundry room.

Morse's winter home, and the site of his death, was 5 West 22nd St., demolished about 1900. A furniture shop and other businesses now occupy this **Chelsea** site.

(See Chapter 1, CONNECTICUT, MASSACHUSETTS; also Chapter 3, NEW YORK.)

MURROW, EDWARD ROSCOE (1908–1965). "Listen to Murrow . . . tomorrow" was the announcer's sign-off line for Murrow's daily news commentaries, and millions tuned in to hear Murrow's portentous "This . . . is the news" and his grim "Good night . . . and good luck." Murrow's journalistic skill and integrity set the high standard of excellence that television news broadcasting has generally maintained. The private apartment building at 580 Park Ave. on the **Upper East Side** was his last Manhattan address, to 1961.

Exhibit: At the Museum of Broadcasting, 1 East 53rd St. in **Midtown,** visitors may review programs in private booths from a massive collection of radio and television broadcasting tapes. Murrow's years of network news service, as well as transcriptions of numerous other news and entertainment personalities, are preserved here for public listening or viewing. Special features are

NAST, THOMAS (1840–1902). Nast, whose brilliant editorial cartoons forged Northern support for the Civil War and helped break up the infamous graft ring bossed by William Marcy Tweed (see the entry on Tweed later in this section), lived in **Harlem** from 1864 to 1873, the period of his greatest influence. "Harlem Lane," the first home he had ever owned, stood at an undetermined spot on 125th Street near 5th Avenue. He built a large studio in the rear of his property, and from there issued most of his famous caricatures of the corrupt that spoke louder than words.

(See Chapter 3, NEW JERSEY.)

NIN, ANAÏS (1903–1977). The French-born author, whose major literary work was her intimate *Diary* that spanned some 50 years, began that huge opus in 1914 at 158 West 75th St. (privately owned), where she lived with her mother and brother. They occupied the first floor of this **Upper West Side** dwelling of brick and stone until 1919.

Much later, after living for years in Europe, she took a skylight studio apartment in **Greenwich Village** at 215 West 13th St. This four-story building, combined from two houses built in 1851, was her home from 1940 to the 1960s. During her last years, she kept an apartment in Washington Square Village, the complex behind the Loeb Student Center of New York University between Bleecker and 3rd streets.

(See Chapter 6, CALIFORNIA.)

OCHS, ADOLPH SIMON (1858–1935). By introducing "All the News That's Fit to Print"—in contrast to the popular "yellow journalism" of 1896—the Tennessee publisher built the *New York Times* into a bastion of journalistic integrity and one of the world's leading newspapers. Ochs's longtime **Upper West Side** home stood at 308 West 75th St. He sold the house about 1930, and this address is the present site of Manhattan Day School.

(See Chapter 3, NEW YORK.)

O'HARA, JOHN HENRY (1905–1970). The novelist whose realistic treatment of urban life and death made him one of the most popular writers of his generation lived at several Manhattan addresses while establishing his career. His first **Midtown** lodging (1933–34) was the Pickwick Arms Hotel, still at 230 East 51st St., where he began his first novel, *Appointment in Samarra* (1934). In the brownstone at 103 East 55th St., since demolished, he wrote *Butterfield 8* (1935), which firmly established him as a major writer. shown on a large screen from 1:30 to 3:00. (Open Tuesday–Saturday 12:00–5:00; 212-752-7684; admission.)

(See Chapter 3, DISTRICT OF COLUMBIA, NEW YORK; also Chapter 5, NORTH CAROLINA; also Chapter 6, WASHINGTON.)

NASH, OGDEN (1902–1971). The writer whose eccentric rhymes and deceptively light verse often conveyed sharp poetic insight occupied a **Midtown** suite at the private 333 East 57th Street Building from the 1950s until 1965.

(See Chapter 3, MARYLAND; also Chapter 5, GEORGIA.)

O'Hara occupied a **Chelsea** suite from 1937 to 1939 at the London Terrace Apartments, the current Penthouse Club of London Terrace at 470 West 24th St., built in 1930; when out of town, he often sublet the apartment.

By the early 1940s, O'Hara could afford an apartment on the ground floor of an **Upper East Side** town house at 27 East 79th St. (privately owned). His last city address, from 1945 to 1949, was 55 East 86th St., the 15-story apartment building where he wrote *Rage to Live* (1949).

(See Chapter 3, NEW JERSEY, NEW YORK, PENNSYLVANIA.)

O'NEILL, EUGENE GLADSTONE (1888–1953). The morose playwright who dramatized the darker sides of human aspiration was born in Room 236 of the 1883 Barrett House, the eight-story hotel that stood until 1940 at the northeast corner of Broadway and West 43rd Street in **Times Square;** a marker identifies the site, which O'Neill liked to point out. "There is only empty air now where I came into the world," he mourned.

O'Neill used many scenes and locales from his early Manhattan years in his plays. Thus the vermin-infested, **Lower Manhattan** flophouse over Jimmy the Priest's Saloon at 252 Fulton St., where

O'Neill bunked as a seaman in 1911, lives in *Anna Christie* (1922), though the brick building itself is long gone.

In **Greenwich Village,** he occupied rooms at 38 Washington Square South in a "garbage flat" during 1915; and, in 1916, at 42 Washington Square South (see the entry on John Silas Reed in this section). These places helped set the stage for *Strange Interlude* (1928) and *The Iceman Cometh* (1946). Both structures are gone, the sites now occupied by New York University buildings.

O'Neill and his wife, Carlotta Monterey, occupied an **Upper East Side** six-room penthouse suite at 35 East 84th St. (privately owned) from 1946 to 1948. By this time, a crippling disease had ended his writing; and here the pair endured (and apparently cherished) a torturous, love-hate existence not unlike that portrayed in some of O'Neill's plays.

Exhibit: O'Neill's New York stage career began in 1917 at 133 MacDougal St. in **Greenwich Village,** where he and others established the Provincetown Playhouse in a converted stable and presented many of his plays for a decade. The theater is still in business. (Call 212-777-2571 for current performance schedules.)

(See Chapter 1, CONNECTICUT, MASSACHUSETTS; also Chapter 5, GEORGIA; also Chapter 6, CALIFORNIA.)

OPPENHEIMER, J. ROBERT (1904–1967). The physicist who directed the Los Alamos project during World War II and became known as "father of the atomic bomb" was later declared a security risk by the government that had sponsored that research—a judgment never officially revoked, though he received the Fermi Award in 1963. An **Upper West Side** native, Oppenheimer grew up in the 11th-floor apartment home of his parents at 155 Riverside Drive, probably the same building on the site today, his home from 1912 to about 1922.

(See Chapter 3, NEW JERSEY; also Chapter 6, CALIFORNIA, NEW MEXICO.)

PAINE, THOMAS (1737–1809). After the American Revolution, which his eloquent pen had done nearly as much to win as the mistakes of British troops in the American geography, Paine was largely snubbed—sometimes politely, more often rudely—by his former compatriots. He had remained an outspoken radical, but it was his deistic *The Age of Reason* (1794–96) that sat least well with Americans, who even then liked their heroes prayerful; and to transform this brilliant, alcoholic founding father into a pious man was a job beyond even the best efforts of our often-skilled historical mythologists. Paine spent his last years, from 1804, in Manhattan, ostracized by the public and all but a few friends. The "first modern internationalist" and "America's godfather," as various biographers have called him, was regarded as more dangerous, wrote historian Vernon Parrington, "than a common felon and outlaw." None of his last boardinghouse residences stand. On the **Lower West Side,** he lived at 16 Gold St. in 1804; at 36 Cedar St., where he suffered a stroke, from 1804 to 1806; at 85 Church St. from 1806 to 1807; and at 63 Partition St. (now West Fulton Street) from 1807 to 1808.

He declined in health from 1808 in the two-story house that stood until 1932 on the site of 309 Bleecker St. in **Greenwich Village.** The two combined structures dating from 1933 on this site were recently occupied by a food market. Paine spent his last month in bed at 59 Grove St., a frame farmhouse site now marked and occupied by Marie's Crisis Restaurant. The present building dates from 1839.

(See BROOKLYN in this chapter; also Chapter 3, NEW JERSEY, NEW YORK, PENNSYLVANIA.)

PARKER, CHARLES CHRISTOPHER "CHARLIE" (1920–1955). The jazz saxophonist, a creative musician without peer, occupied numerous apartments, often those of friends and usually briefly, during his generally rootless Manhattan years. His married home during the early 1940s was the private apartment building at 411 Manhattan Ave. in **Harlem.**

"Bird" died in the apartment suite of an admirer at the Hotel Stanhope, still at Fifth Avenue and 81st Street, **Upper Manhattan.**

(See Chapter 4, KANSAS.)

PARKER, DOROTHY ROTHSCHILD (1893–1967). The short-story writer and critic whose hilarious, throw-away wit flashed razors from velvet gloves was a legendary Manhattan creature who occupied cheap boardinghouses and hotel rooms for much of her adult life. According to biographer John Keats, "She said that all she needed was enough space 'to lay a hat—and a few friends.' "

Her **Upper West Side** childhood home stands at 57 West 57th St., now an office building.

Her residence of longest duration, from 1953, was the Volney Hotel, still at 23 East 74th St. on the **Upper East Side,** where she died alone and impoverished.

(See Chapter 3, PENNSYLVANIA; also Chapter 6, CALIFORNIA.)

PEGLER, WESTBROOK (1894–1969). The newspaper columnist whose fanged abuse of almost everybody in national politics won him last employment as a writer for the John Birch Society made his Manhattan lair at the Park Lane Hotel, formerly in the building at 299 Park Ave. in **Midtown.**

(See Chapter 3, NEW YORK; also Chapter 4, MINNESOTA; also Chapter 6, ARIZONA.)

PERELMAN, SIDNEY JOSEPH (1904–1979). Last home of the humorist, whose disgust with American cultural affectations produced some of the most wildly original satire of the 20th century, made his last home from 1972 at the Gramercy Park Hotel, 52 **Gramercy Park** North. Perelman died there.

(See Chapter 1, RHODE ISLAND; also Chapter 3, PENNSYLVANIA.)

PERRY, MATTHEW CALBRAITH (1794–1858). "Old Bruin," the naval officer who led Mexican War squadrons and extorted a trade treaty from the Japanese, made his final home, no longer standing, at 38 West 32nd St. bordering the **Chelsea** area. He died in his brick house there three years after he built it.

(See BROOKLYN in this chapter; also Chapter 1, RHODE ISLAND.)

POE, EDGAR ALLAN (1809–1849). Poe, contrary to popular mythology, was an esteemed, highly successful writer during his lifetime. He was, however, a bad money manager, undisciplined in everything except his literary craft. He lived in Manhattan at three separate times and occupied some 10 brief addresses. Only one of these houses remains, the privately owned, much modified four-story brick house in **Greenwich Village** at 85 West 3rd St. (Amity Place in his day). He resided there in 1845 while editing the *Broadway Journal*, which operated on the southwest corner of Beekman and Nassau streets.

A marker on West 84th Street just west of Broadway identifies the site of the **Upper West Side** farmhouse he occupied during the summers of 1843 and 1844 while working on his poem "The Raven" (1844).

Exhibit: The mantelpiece, on which Poe carved his name, from the farmhouse mentioned is now displayed in Philosophy Hall of Columbia University, Amsterdam Avenue near 116th Street in **Morningside Heights.** (Open daily; guided tours Monday–Friday at 3:00, from Low Memorial Library; 212-280-1754; free.)

(See BRONX in this chapter; also Chapter 1 MASSACHUSETTS; also Chapter 3, MARYLAND, PENNSYLVANIA; also Chapter 5, VIRGINIA.)

POLLOCK, JACKSON (1912–1956). Reacting against realism in art, the founder of the "action painting" school—whose splash-and-drip methods of conveying paint to canvas often startled the uninitiated—resided for the decade from 1935 to 1945 in his brother's apartment at 46 East Eighth St. on the **Lower East Side.** He used a large front room on the top floor of the old five-story building that stood there for his studio, and there began the canvas experimentation that led to the abstract expressionist movement in art.

(See Chapter 3, NEW YORK; also Chapter 6, CALIFORNIA.)

PORTER, COLE ALBERT (1893–1964). The lyricist-composer's **Midtown** home from October to June, from 1936 until his death, was Suite 33A of the Waldorf Towers, where the management charged him only $35 per day for his 14-room suite as a loss leader, in hopes that his presence would attract other lessees (see the entry on the Waldorf Towers later in this section). His library there, designed in 1955, had bookcases of brass tubing and walls of tortoise-shell leather. From Porter's piano there first sounded the songs of such musical hits as *Kiss Me Kate* (1948), *Can-Can* (1953) and *Silk Stockings* (1955).

(See Chapter 4, INDIANA; also Chapter 6, CALIFORNIA.)

PORTER, KATHERINE ANNE (1890–1980). In 1919 and 1920, before she began publishing her short stories, the author occupied a room in one of the oldest surviving houses in **Greenwich Village,** 17 Grove St. Built in 1822, this small frame dwelling remains privately owned.

Years later, in 1953, she briefly resided in a small basement apartment near **Gramercy Park** at 117 East 17th St., where she worked on her only novel *Ship of Fools* (1962). This building also remains in private hands.

(See Chapter 3, DISTRICT OF COLUMBIA, MARYLAND, NEW YORK.)

PORTER, WILLIAM SYDNEY "O. HENRY" (1862–1910). "Bagdad on the Subway" was his term for Manhattan, and his short stories pictured the sentimental glitter and pathos of city lives—shopgirls, Broadway bums, street people. He knew the city, especially the **Chelsea** area, on its most intimate levels as probably no other observer before or since. Porter arrived in 1902 and first lived at the seedy Martz Hotel, which stood at 47 West 24th St., now the General Envelope Co.

In 1903 he moved to 55 Irving Place, where he watched passers-by from a large bay window; this house near **Gramercy Park,** which he occupied until 1907 and where he wrote "The Gift of the Magi" (1906), stands with a remodeled facade incorporating the two adjacent houses into one apartment building. Porter's parlor is now occupied by Sal Anthony's Restaurant.

Back in **Chelsea,** his most frequent home after 1906, and his last, was the seven-story Caledonia Hotel, now a private apartment building at 28 West 26th St.; nine empty whiskey bottles were found under his bed there after his death from cirrhosis. Porter also lived at the Chelsea Hotel in 1907 and 1910 (see the entry on the Chelsea Hotel earlier in this section); his six-room apartment contained only a table, chair and bed.

Exhibit: Pete's Tavern in the five-story brick building at 129 East 18th St. near **Gramercy Park** was Healy's Cafe when Porter hung out there. Never gregarious and often secretive in his slouch hat, he usually came in at midnight, drank alone at the end of the bar, then left without a word. On the walls hang newspaper articles and photos relating to O. Henry and his associations there. Porter described this bar in his story "The Lost Blend."

(See Chapter 5, NORTH CAROLINA; also Chapter 6, TEXAS.)

POST, EMILY PRICE (1873–1960). From age 12 until adulthood, the woman who would write and constantly update society's norms of *Etiquette* (1922) lived at 12 West 10th St. in **Greenwich Village,** a large town house built in 1845 and 1846 and renovated by her father, architect Bruce Price, in 1895. President Wilson, it is said, proposed to his second wife, Edith Bolling Galt, while visiting there on Thanksgiving Day in 1915. The house remains privately owned.

Post built her own **Upper East Side** apartment house at 39 East 79th St. (privately occupied), a portion of which she occupied as her permanent home from about 1925.

(See Chapter 1, MASSACHUSETTS; also Chapter 3, MARYLAND, NEW YORK.)

PULITZER, JOSEPH (1847–1911). The aggressive publisher of the *New York World* for almost 30 years, Pulitzer lived in **Midtown** from 1887 to 1900 at 10 East 55th St., a four-story, 1883 mansion. Fire destroyed it in 1900, killing two of his servants and consuming scores of paintings in his art collection. The St. Regis Hotel Pharmacy occupies this site today.

Pulitzer's **Upper East Side** home, his last, was 9 East 73rd St., a five-story, white stone house designed by Stanford White in 1904 (see the entry on White later in this section). Pulitzer installed cork floors and massive walls to insure total silence while he played his huge church organ—but pronounced the effort a "wretched failure" when muffled sounds still penetrated. His double-walled rear annex was termed "the Vault" by bemused employees. This handsome mansion fell in 1930 when Pulitzer's sons leased the property for construction of the present building on the site.

(See Chapter 1, MAINE; also Chapter 4, MISSOURI.)

RACHMANINOFF, SERGEI (1873–1943). The Russian-born pianist and classical composer lived in the private apartment building at 33 Riverside Drive, **Upper West Side,** from 1921 to 1942. His suite here became a center for other expatriate Russian artists who were living in or passing through Manhattan.

RANDOLPH, ASA PHILIP (1889–1979). "The most dangerous Negro in America," he was called when beginning his stormy career as a union organizer. The first national labor leader among American blacks was also a powerful orator and civil-rights activist whose persistent lobbying and personal confrontations with two presidents hastened desegregation in war industry employment and the armed forces. Randolph's first married home, which he occupied in 1914, is probably the same apartment building now standing at 2453 7th Ave. in **Harlem.** From 1933 until 1968, he resided in a suite on the third floor of the Paul Laurence Dunbar Apartments, 230 West 150th St. (see the entry on William Edward Burghardt Du Bois earlier in this section). Widowed and frail in 1968, Randolph was mugged by toughs in the hallway of his dwelling here, and friends moved him to a safer residence.

He spent his final years and died in a sparsely furnished apartment on the fifth floor at 280 Ninth Ave. (at the corner of West 27th Street) in **Chelsea.**
(See Chapter 5, FLORIDA.)

REED, JOHN SILAS (1887–1920). Ebullient political activist and writer, Reed occupied a "romantically shabby" back room in **Greenwich Village** on the second floor at 42 Washington Square South in 1911 and 1912. These were the years when he began writing for the left-wing *Masses* and allying himself with strikers and the labor movement. "Within a block of my house," he wrote, "was all the adventure in the world. . . . There I first saw that reality transcended all the fine poetic inventions." This house, where writer-reformer Lincoln Steffens occupied two front rooms below at the same time, no longer exists. It is the present site of the New York University Law Library. In 1918, while standing trial for sedition, the "Golden Boy of the Village" lived in a small, dingy apartment at 1 Patchin Place (privately owned), a three-story, 1848 brick house. He wrote his first-hand report of the Russian Revolution, *Ten Days That Shook the World* (1919), in a room just above a restaurant at 147 West Fourth St.; formerly Polly Holliday's, where Village writers and artists socialized during this period, the restaurant is now Bertolotti's. The four-story structure dates from 1849 and 1850. Reed lived with his paramour Mabel Dodge, hostess of the Village's most notable bohemian salon, in her mansion at 23 5th Ave. in 1913 and 1914. This house, whose aged owner, Gen. Daniel E. Sickles, lived on the first floor and where Mabel Dodge entertained almost every notable painter and writer of the time, is long gone. It stood on the present site of the 13-story apartment building at 25 5th Ave., which dates from 1921.

(See Chapter 3, NEW YORK; also Chapter 6, OREGON.)

RICE, GRANTLAND (1880–1954). Longtime sports columnist, commentator and versifier, Rice came to Manhattan in 1910 and lived for a year with cartoonist Rube Goldberg at 616 West 116th St. in **Morningside Heights.**

His home from 1911 to 1930 was an **Upper West Side** suite at 450 Riverside Drive; and he occupied an apartment at 1158 Fifth Ave., his last residence, from 1930.

All three of Rice's Manhattan homes remain in use as private apartment buildings.
(See Chapter 3, NEW YORK; also Chapter 5, TENNESSEE.)

RICKENBACKER, EDWARD VERNON "EDDIE" (1890–1973). From 1937 until the 1970s, the businessman and World War I flying ace made his home in **Upper Manhattan.** His residence during the 1940s and until 1954 was a suite at 130 East End Ave. (privately occupied). Later he occupied three suites in the Stanhope Hotel, 5th Avenue and 81st Street (1954 to 1956); the Regency Hotel at 540 Park Ave. (1950s–60s); and the Dorset Hotel, 30 West 54th St., his last New York City home.

(See Chapter 3, NEW YORK; also Chapter 4, INDIANA, MICHIGAN, OHIO; also Chapter 5, FLORIDA; also Chapter 6, TEXAS.)

ROBESON, PAUL BUSTILL (1898–1976). The prominent singer, athlete, actor and civil rights activist resided from 1939 to 1941 in **Harlem** at Robeson Home National Historic Landmark, the 13-story, private apartment house at 555 Edgecomb Ave., built in 1916. In 1956, during the height of his harassment by the House Un-American Activities Committee, he resided at 16 Jumel Terrace (privately owned), his last Manhattan home. Silenced finally by ill health, he lived there reclusively from 1963 to 1966.

(See Chapter 1, CONNECTICUT; also Chapter 3, NEW JERSEY.)

ROBINSON, EDWIN ARLINGTON (1869–1935). Impoverished for much of his life, the poet occupied a room from 1901 to 1905 on the top floor of the four-story brownstone at 450 West 23rd St. (privately owned), **Chelsea.** He acquired this lodging through the charity of the brownstone's owner, who ran a nearby cafe that Robinson frequented.

From 1905 to 1909, Robinson occupied quarters at the Hotel Judson in **Greenwich Village.** Now Judson Hall, a private dormitory for New York University, the five-story building at 51 Washington Square South dates from 1877. In 1909, Robinson was again lucky in finding a patron. He moved into a one-room studio built for him by Clara P. Davidge behind her 1832 brick home at 121 Washington Place (privately owned) and lived there at intervals for several years. At 28 West Eighth St. (privately owned), a three-story brick house which now has a storefront ground floor, he resided with his friends, sculptor James Earle Fraser and his wife Laura, from 1922 to 1927; he occupied the skylighted room on the top floor and there wrote his most popular work, *Tristram* (1927).

From 1927, Robinson lived in **Midtown** with the Frasers at 328 East 42nd St., and this was his last home. It is now the site of Woodstock Tower in Tudor City Place at the street's eastern terminus.

(See BROOKLYN in this chapter; also Chapter 1, MAINE, NEW HAMPSHIRE.)

ROCKEFELLER, JOHN DAVISON (1839–1937). The razor-lipped industrialist's **Midtown** home was 4 West 54th St. a four-story brownstone built about 1860. Rockefeller, wrote biographer William Manchester, "lived virtually all his life within a triangle bound by 26 Broadway [his office], the [Union] Baptist Church on Fifth Avenue, and the West 54th Street house." Rockefeller bought the house in 1884, and it remained his city home for the rest of his life. It was torn down in 1938; the garden of the Museum of Modern Art, 11 West 53rd St., now occupies the site.

Exhibit: The fifth floor of the Museum of the City of New York, 1220 Fifth Ave. (at the corner of East 103rd Street), **Upper East Side,** displays the preserved bedroom and dressing room from Rockefeller's Manhattan home. These rooms, decorated in fine satinwood and rosewood, were modeled after designs by English architect Charles L. Eastlake. (Open Tuesday–Saturday 10:00–5:00, Sunday 1:00–5:00; 212-534-1672; free.)

(See BROOKLYN in this chapter; also Chapter 3, NEW JERSEY, NEW YORK; also Chapter 4, OHIO; also Chapter 5, FLORIDA, GEORGIA.)

ROCKEFELLER, NELSON ALDRICH (1908–1979). The sunniest, most extroverted member of his solemn clan, this grandson of John Davison Rockefeller (see the entry on John D. Rockefeller above) became a politician, eventually achieving the vice presidency by appointment. His boyhood home stands in **Midtown** at 13 West 54th St., a brownstone town house that he used at intervals throughout his life for a residence and office. There he was stricken with a heart attack and apparently lay dying for at least an hour in most puzzling circumstances before futile emergency help was summoned by the people present. Rockefeller's last city home was a 32-room duplex apartment (he actually occupied only 20 of the rooms) at 812 Fifth Ave. Both of these addresses remain among the private Rockefeller holdings.

(See Chapter 1, MAINE; also Chapter 3, DISTRICT OF COLUMBIA, NEW YORK.)

ROCKWELL, NORMAN (1894–1978). The painter of homey folk scenes best described as "warm-hearted" was born "in the fifth-floor back bedroom of a shabby brownstone front" on the **Upper West Side** at Amsterdam Avenue and West 103rd Street, his home to age two. The Rockwells then occupied a succession of long, narrow "railroad flat" apartments in **Harlem,** none of which have been exactly identified. They probably resided longest (from 1896 to 1900) at St. Nicholas Avenue and West 147th Street.

(See Chapter 1, MASSACHUSETTS, VERMONT; also Chapter 3, NEW YORK, PENNSYLVANIA.)

RODGERS, RICHARD (1902–1979). Composer of numerous popular songs and shows for the musical theater, Rodgers occupied several Manhattan apartments during his long career. His **Morningside Heights** boyhood home until 1911 was 3 West 120th St., a brownstone unlisted in current directories but as late as 1964, when Rodgers visited the house, being used as a drug rehabilitation center.

From 1911 until 1929, Rodgers lived on the fifth floor of 161 West 86th St., **Upper West Side,** still a private apartment-office building; there he collaborated with Lorenz Hart to produce such hits as *Connecticut Yankee* (1927) and *Spring Is Here* (1929).

Rodgers's first married home in 1929 and 1930

was a **Midtown** three-room suite on the 19th floor of the Hotel Lombardy, still at 111 East 56th St.

On the **Upper East Side** from 1931 to 1941, he occupied a suite at 50 East 77th St., part of the 1929 Hotel Carlyle complex, and during this period wrote the music for *Babes in Arms* (1937) and *The Boys From Syracuse* (1938), among others. (The Hotel Carlyle, with an entrance address at 35 East 76th St., later served as Manhattan headquarters for two Democratic Presidents—Harry S. Truman and John F. Kennedy—and was their usual residence when they visited the city.) Rodgers occupied an apartment in the Volney Hotel (see the entry on Dorothy Rothschild Parker earlier in this section) from 1941 to 1945, when he produced *Oklahoma!* (1943) with Oscar Hammerstein II. From 1945 to 1971, he owned and occupied a 15-room duplex apartment at 70 East 71st St., his residence when he composed *South Pacific* (1949) and *The Sound of Music* (1959); this, actually the same building as 730 Park Ave., was his last city dwelling. Edna Ferber was a concurrent resident there (see the entries on Hammerstein and Ferber earlier in this section).

All of Rodgers's extant homes remain privately occupied.

(See Chapter 1, CONNECTICUT.)

ROOSEVELT, ELEANOR (1884–1962).

The dynamic, remarkable wife of the 32nd U.S. president was a Manhattan native, born Anna Eleanor Roosevelt and raised by her grandparents, the Halls; her alcoholic father, whom she worshipped, was a brother of Theodore Roosevelt and died young (see the entry on Theodore Roosevelt below). Her mother, beautiful but invalid, lived just long enough to imprint Eleanor with an "ugly duckling" self-image that took her years to overcome. The brownstone Hall mansion, where she lived from 1893 until her marriage with sixth cousin Franklin, stood at 11 West 37th St., now the site of **Midtown** shops. The couple's first married home was a rented dwelling still at 125 East 36th St. (privately occupied), their residence from 1905 to 1908.

Their permanent city home from 1908 was the double town house standing at 47–49 East 65th St., **Upper East Side.** This was the residence built by autocratic Sara Delano Roosevelt, Franklin's mother, as a home for herself (Number 47) and the couple (Number 49). As a lawyer, state legis-

lator and New York governor, Franklin Roosevelt used Number 49 for his Manhattan residence until 1932. There, in the front bedroom on the fourth floor, he began his long recovery from polio during the 1920s. Following his mother's death in 1941, he sold the house to Hunter College, for which it presently functions as a social and interfaith student center. After President Roosevelt's death, Eleanor continued her political, diplomatic and humanitarian activities at an astonishing pace for almost 20 years. Her later city dwellings included 29 Washington Square West (1945–53), **Greenwich Village,** a place she had chosen earlier for the presidential retirement home; 211 East 62nd St., a five-story brick house on the **Upper East Side** where she leased a four and one-half-room, garden duplex suite on the first two floors in 1953 and lived until 1959; and 55 East 74th St., her last city home and the site of her death. All three residences remain privately owned.

(See Chapter 1, MAINE; also Chapter 3, DISTRICT OF COLUMBIA, MARYLAND, NEW YORK; also Chapter 4, MICHIGAN; also Chapter 5, GEORGIA.)

ROOSEVELT, FRANKLIN DELANO (1882–1945).
ROOSEVELT, THEODORE (1858–1919). Roosevelt Birthplace National Historic Site, operated by the National Park Service, stands at 28 East 20th St. near **Gramercy Park.** This is not the original 1848 house where the sickly, asthmatic child who became the strenuous 26th U.S. president lived until age 15, but an exact, four-story replica built on the original site in 1922. Five rooms have been refurnished with their original contents, and museum rooms display memorabilia and items relating to Roosevelt's numerous interests and activities. (Open Monday–Friday 9:00–4:30; 212-260-1616; admission.)

At 6 West 57th St., the family lived from 1873 until the 1884 illnesses that took the lives of Roosevelt's mother and first wife Alice Lee Roosevelt (on the same day). This **Midtown** brownstone is now occupied by the Festival Theatre.

(See BRONX in this chapter; also Chapter 3, DISTRICT OF COLUMBIA, NEW YORK; also Chapter 4, NORTH DAKOTA; also Chapter 6, NEW MEXICO.)

THE YOUNG ROOSEVELT VIEWS LINCOLN'S FUNERAL.
Six-year-old Theodore Roosevelt stands on the right in the
second-story window of his birthplace at 28 East 20th St. as
soldiers line up to march in Abraham Lincoln's 1865 funeral
procession. Black crepe decorates the house front that only
a few days before had cheered the end of the Civil War with
flags and bunting. The present house on this site near
Gramercy Park is an exact replica of the one in the
photograph.
*(Courtesy Theodore Roosevelt Collection, Harvard College
Library)*

ROOT, ELIHU (1845–1937). The prominent
corporation lawyer who became a reliable cabinet
member and workhorse diplomat for four U.S.
presidents, Root built his Georgian manor at 733
Park Ave. (at the corner of East 71st Street) in
1903. It remains as a private apartment dwelling
and awaits likely designation as an **Upper East
Side** landmark. A 20-room suite at prestigious
998 Fifth Ave. (at the corner of East 81st Street)
was Root's last city home from about 1912. He
occupied the suite as a loss leader for $15,000 per
year. This 11-story, Italian Renaissance-style
building, erected in 1911, became a "watershed"
in Manhattan society's living habits. "When 998
was erected," wrote John Tauranac in *Essential
New York* (1979), "90 percent of Society lived in
private homes; within twenty-five years, 90
percent of Society would be living in apartments,
with much of the change due to the kind of quality this house inspired."

A marker at 20 Irving Place near **Gramercy Park**
identifies the site of Root's early Manhattan resi-

dence (1871–78) while he built his law career.

(See Chapter 3, DISTRICT OF COLUMBIA, NEW YORK.)

ROTHKO, MARK (1903–1970). The Russian-born painter, raised in Oregon, occupied numerous Manhattan lodgings from the 1920s. From 1936 to 1940, he resided at 313 East Sixth St., **Lower East Side,** still a private apartment building.

He lived from 1960 to 1964 at 118 East 95th St. (privately owned), an **Upper East Side** brownstone in which he converted the fourth floor into a studio and storage area. Rothko, whose abstract expressionist canvases became increasingly obsessed with death, resided at 157 East 69th St. from 1964 until his suicide. He modified the illumination in this three-story, brick arena-studio by draping a parachute over the skylight, and this was the locale of his last work. It was later occupied by Marlborough Studios and remains privately owned.

RUNYON, DAMON (1880–1946). The Broadway columnist and recorder of Manhattan night life occupied several city apartments, most of which remain privately occupied. According to biographer Tom Clark, "Between 1913, when Damon rented the Runyons' first Manhattan apartment (at 111th Street and Broadway), and 1928, when he 'officially' moved out of the family home (then at 113th Street and Riverside Drive), there were some half dozen different Runyon households. All were within a single mile-square area on the **Upper West Side,** but in terms of luxury, the early apartments and the later Riverside Drive places were light years apart." Early addresses also included an apartment on the seventh floor at 251 West 95th St., a corner of Broadway that Runyon claimed was a haunt "of the bootleggers and gangsters of the period." Sources other than Clark give 320 West 102nd St. (at the corner of Riverside Drive) as the address that he and his family occupied from 1920 until he separated from them in 1928.

Runyon began writing his tales of Manhattan nightbirds about 1930 in **Midtown** bachelor quarters at 224 West 49th St., at that time the Hotel Forrest, his residence from 1928 to 1932. In 1940, he was residing at 350 West 57th St. Runyon's last city home, from 1945, was a suite at the Hotel Buckingham, still at 101 West 57th St.

(See Chapter 4, KANSAS; also Chapter 5, FLORIDA; also Chapter 6, COLORADO.)

RUSSELL, LILLIAN (1861–1922). "A vision of loveliness and a voice of gold," was how producer Tony Pastor introduced her in 1880 at his 585 Broadway theater. She really wasn't a very good singer, and her acting suggested an actress playing an actress. But she was beautiful, by hefty-peach 1890s standards, she read comedy well, and there was always something flamboyant happening in her private life. So she entertained millions and became a great star, and, later, an outspoken feminist. During the 1880s, Lillian Russell occupied the four-story, stucco house with red shutters at 57 East 54th St., **Midtown.** Bill's Gay Nineties restaurant, a sing-along and vaudeville cafe described by writer James Dale Davidson as "patronized by the geriatrics set and by nostalgia buffs of all ages," appropriately occupies the first floor today.

A favorite residence during the height of her career was the top floor of the Wilbraham Apartments, 284 5th Ave., one of the first residential apartment buildings for the wealthy, erected about 1885 and still housing private suites.

(See Chapter 3, PENNSYLVANIA; also Chapter 4, IOWA.)

RUTH, GEORGE HERMAN "BABE" (1895–1948). The last residence of the "Home Run King" from about 1935 was 110 Riverside Drive on the **Upper West Side,** a large, comfortable apartment where his widow maintained rooms full of his baseball memorabilia until her own death in 1976. The building remains privately occupied.

(See Chapter 1, MASSACHUSETTS; also Chapter 3, MARYLAND, NEW YORK.)

SAINT-GAUDENS, AUGUSTUS (1848–1907). Born in Ireland, the noted sculptor was raised from infancy in a succession of **Lower Manhattan** dwellings from 1848 to 1860. His later addresses included 22 Washington Place in **Greenwich Village** (1880–90); and in **Midtown,** his 148 West 36th St. studio (from 1884), and 51 West 45th St. (1890–97). None of these buildings remain.

(See Chapter 1, NEW HAMPSHIRE.)

SANGER, MARGARET HIGGINS (1883–1966). The pioneer reformer in birth control and family planning lived at 4 Perry St. in **Greenwich Village** in 1914, when she founded the National Birth Control League. This 1849, brick row house remains privately owned. Painter Rockwell Kent lived there in 1911. In 1917, just after her release from prison for "creating a public nuisance"—i.e., establishing the nation's first birth-control clinic—she lived at 236 West 14th St., occupying two rooms on the ground floor of an old brownstone, long gone. From about 1930, she resided at 17 West 16th St., an 1846 town house located on what, in the 17th century, was the farmland of a free black man, Simon Congo. The Margaret Sanger Clinic was located there from 1930 to 1973. The house is now a private residence.

(See Chapter 3, NEW YORK; also Chapter 6, ARIZONA.)

SARNOFF, DAVID (1891–1971). The Russian-born electronic engineer and businessman-founder of the National Broadcasting Company, "General" Sarnoff, as he liked to be called, resided primarily on the **Upper East Side.** During the 1930s, he occupied a suite at 11 East 68th St., presently an office building. He bought his five-story, 28-room town house at 44 East 71st St. in 1937 and resided there—"his orbit [was] confined to Rockefeller Center on the south and 71st Street on the north," according to one biographer—until his death. The house, currently unlisted in directories, has apparently been demolished.

(See Chapter 3, NEW JERSEY, NEW YORK.)

SCOTT, WINFIELD (1786–1866). "Old Fuss and Feathers," a stickler for the fine points of military courtesy, commander of the U.S. Army from 1841 to 1861, and 1852 presidential candidate, was given a new house in the latter year by a group of admirers headed by U.S. Senator Hamilton Fish. The four-story brownstone, built in 1851 and 1852, stands at 24 West 12th St. in **Greenwich Village.** Now designated as Scott House National Historic Landmark, it is privately owned.

(See Chapter 3, NEW JERSEY; also Chapter 5, VIRGINIA.)

SETON, ELIZABETH ANN BAYLEY (1774–1821). The Roman Catholic nun, teacher and (since 1975) saint occupied about seven different Manhattan dwellings from 1785 to 1808 before she took her vows. The only residence that remains, however, is the present St. Elizabeth Seton Shrine, a three-story brick house at 7 State St. near Battery Park

in **Lower Manhattan.** This house, the sole survivor of an elegant 1793 row, was formerly the James Watson House. Today the remodeled interior serves as the church of Our Lady of the Rosary, displaying a large stained-glass window and a statue in memory of the saint who lived there from 1801 to 1804.

(See BRONX in this chapter; also Chapter 3, MARYLAND, NEW YORK.)

SHERMAN, WILLIAM TECUMSEH (1820–1891). "War is hell," said the fierce Union general of the Civil War after he did his huge part to make it so. In retirement, he bought a new, four-story house at 75 West 71st St. (at the corner of Columbus Avenue), **Upper West Side,** and this was his last home from 1888. The present brick building on this site dates from more recent construction.

(See Chapter 3, DISTRICT OF COLUMBIA; also Chapter 4, MISSOURI, OHIO; also Chapter 6, CALIFORNIA, OKLAHOMA.)

SHERWOOD, ROBERT EMMET (1896–1955). Playwright, historian and writer of presidential speeches, Sherwood occupied many Manhattan apartments throughout his career, but biographical records are sparse on specific addresses. His first married home in 1922, however, was 71 West 12th St. in **Greenwich Village,** a building described by the Landmarks Preservation Commission as an "unobtrusive six-story brick apartment house built in 1922," still containing private apartments. The Sherwoods occupied one of the smallest—his mother said it was "very pretty and filled with new furniture and wedding loot."

Sherwood's last home from 1937 was 25 Sutton Place South on the **Upper East Side.**

(See Chapter 3, NEW YORK.)

SIKORSKY, IGOR IVAN (1889–1972). The Russian-born aircraft designer and builder arrived as an immigrant in 1919 and taught mathematics to other immigrants for four years. His first American home, until 1923, was a two-room apartment at 506 West 135th St. in **Harlem,** still a private apartment building.

(See Chapter 1, CONNECTICUT.)

SMITH, ALFRED EMANUEL (1873–1944). With his brown derby and ever-present cigar as trademarks, the four-term governor and 1928 Democratic presidential candidate was a lifelong

Manhattan resident. He was born on the **Lower East Side** above a German grocery store, in a narrow brick tenement at 174 South St., his home until the building was demolished in 1884. This is the present site of Alfred E. Smith Houses, a public residential development consisting of almost 2,000 units, completed in 1953. Smith's birthplace stood in the shadow of Brooklyn Bridge, under construction during his boyhood. "The Bridge and I grew up together," he said. His first married home, in 1900 and 1901, is now the site of St. Joseph's Convent (this would not displease him) at 83 Madison St. Smith House National Historic Landmark, a three-story, brick row house built in the late 1800s, stands at 25 Oliver St. (privately owned); this was his home from 1909 to 1924, though he occupied only half of the house until 1921. Earlier, from 1904 to 1909, he had resided in a third-floor apartment across the street at 28 Oliver, also private.

After his unwilling political retirement in 1929, Smith resided in a penthouse apartment at 51 Fifth Ave. near **Greenwich Village.**

His last home was a **Midtown** suite in the Apartment 820 Building at 820 Fifth Ave.

(See Chapter 3, NEW YORK.)

SPELLMAN, FRANCIS JOSEPH (1889–1967). As the Roman Catholic archbishop of New York and then as a cardinal, Spellman resided from 1939 until his death in the five-story Gothic Archbishop's Mansion at 452 Madison Avenue (northwest corner of 50th Street), **Midtown.** He occupied a private apartment on the second floor of this 1882 house near St. Patrick's Cathedral, the seat of the archdiocese.

(See Chapter 1, MASSACHUSETTS.)

STANTON, ELIZABETH CADY (1815–1902). The prominent feminist and author occupied four Manhattan dwellings at intervals from 1863. Her last, from 1898, was 250 West 94th St., her son's home, which remains privately owned. She said she regretted giving up her own home in Tenafly, N.J., to spend her final years here.

(See Chapter 3, NEW JERSEY, NEW YORK.)

STEFFENS, LINCOLN (1866–1936). See JOHN SILAS REED.

(See Chapter 1, CONNECTICUT; also Chapter 6, CALIFORNIA.)

STEICHEN, EDWARD JEAN (1879–1973). An innovative lens master who helped win recognition for photography as an art form, Steichen opened a studio, his New York City base from 1902, at 291 5th Avenue. This studio became famous as the "291 Gallery," where Steichen and other "photo-secessionists" exhibited their works. His many Manhattan addresses are elusive. Two during the 1930s, both private buildings, include 80 West 40th St., **Midtown;** and 139 East 69th St., **Upper East Side.**

(See Chapter 1, CONNECTICUT.)

STEINBECK, JOHN ERNST (1902–1968). "New York is an ugly city, a dirty city," wrote the novelist, "but there is one thing about it—once you have lived in New York and it has become your home, no place else is good enough." Steinbeck moved permanently to Manhattan in 1943 and, in **Midtown,** occupied two floors of a three-story brick house at 330 East 51st St. (privately owned) until 1951. He created a garden from "a small sootfield" of a yard and raised tomatoes in huge pots.

His last home, from 1951, was an **Upper East Side** brownstone at 206 East 72nd St., recently razed.

(See Chapter 3, NEW YORK; also Chapter 6, CALIFORNIA.)

STEVENSON, ADLAI EWING (1900–1965). As U.S. ambassador to the United Nations from 1961 to his death, the twice-defeated presidential candidate occupied the official embassy suite, Apartment 42A of the Waldorf Towers (see the entry on the Waldorf Towers later in this section). This was Stevenson's last home.

(See Chapter 3, DISTRICT OF COLUMBIA; also Chapter 4, ILLINOIS; also Chapter 6, CALIFORNIA.)

STOKOWSKI, LEOPOLD ANTHONY (1882–1977). The English-born orchestra conductor, a brilliant, controversial musician who spoke in an affected "foreign accent" unlike any heard in the world, lived in a 12-room penthouse suite at 10 Gracie Square (privately occupied), **Upper East Side,** from 1945 to about 1956. Later, during his leadership of the American Symphony Orchestra in the 1960s, until 1972, he occupied a suite at 1067 Fifth Ave., still a private apartment building.

(See Chapter 1, CONNECTICUT; also Chapter 3, PENNSYLVANIA; also Chapter 4, OHIO.)

STRAVINSKY, IGOR FEDOROVICH (1882–1971). The Russian-born composer whose orchestral works revolutionized 20th-century classical music was a permanent Manhattan dweller during his last years. His residence from 1969 was a suite at the Essex House Hotel, 160 Central Park South in **Midtown.**

(See Chapter 6, CALIFORNIA.)

STUYVESANT, PETER (1610–1672). The autocratic, peg-legged governor of the Dutch colony of New Netherland from 1647 to 1664, Stuyvesant ruled from New Amsterdam (now **Lower Manhattan**), the site of his "costly and handsome" mansion called "White Hall," known in his day as "Stuyvesant's Great House." He built his two-story stone house about 1655 at the present intersection of Whitehall and State streets, bought the property from the Dutch West India Company in 1658, and made it his official residence until 1664. Its fine interior with paintings and rare china was said to resemble homes of the Dutch upper middle class. The locale at the time was a tiny peninsula projecting from the east end of the Battery. "White Hall" became the later residence of British governors Thomas Dongan and Sir Edmund Andros; it burned in 1716. Robert Fulton later lived on this site, now occupied by the South Ferry Building (see the entries on Andros and Fulton earlier in this section). Before "White Hall," Stuyvesant's residence was the Governor's House that stood within the walls of Fort Amsterdam. It was demolished in 1790; the U.S. Custom House now stands on the site.

In 1651, Stuyvesant bought a large farm called "Great Bouwery Number 1," which he had been renting. His cropland and pastures occupied much of present Manhattan's **Lower East Side,** extending north from East Fifth to East 17th streets and east from Broadway and Fourth Avenue to the East River, an area including Stuyvesant Square. The Bowery (4th Avenue) was Stuyvesant's route from the city to his farm, and the driveway to his mansion became the present Stuyvesant Street. His manor house stood approximately at the intersection of today's Stuyvesant and East 10th streets and Second Avenue. This was Stuyvesant's last home from 1664. It too burned to the ground in 1774. In 1660 Stuyvesant added a private chapel to the estate at the present site of the 1779 St. Marks-in-the-Bowery Church at Second Avenue and East 10th Street. Restoration proceeds after a 1978 fire badly damaged the church.

SULLIVAN, EDWARD VINCENT "ED" (1902–1974). The powerful television impresario and Broadway gossip columnist, whose hunched, wizened appearance, chirping voice and petty feuds made him a favorite butt for comic impressionists, was a Manhattan hotel dweller for his final 34 years. From 1940 to 1944, he resided at the famed Hotel Astor on **Times Square,** the present site of One Astor Plaza, a 50-story office tower erected in 1969. Sullivan's last city home, from 1944, was Delmonico's Hotel at 502 Park Ave. (at the corner of East 59th Street, **Midtown**), in an 11th-floor suite containing both his apartment and offices. The ulcer-ridden Sullivan was about as knotted up as he looked; he often used a stomach pump on himself there when he couldn't digest meals.

(See Chapter 1, CONNECTICUT; also Chapter 3, NEW YORK.)

TEILHARD DE CHARDIN, PIERRE (1881–1955). From 1951 to 1954, the French Jesuit priest, controversial philosopher and evolutionary anthropologist—a giant of scientific humanism whose work frightened Roman Catholic officials into censoring many of his "dangerously Darwinian" propositions—resided at St. Ignatius Loyola Church Rectory at 980 Park Ave., on the **Upper East Side.** He lived in a room on the fourth floor there until clerical housing became scarce and he was evicted. His last address, from 1954, was a small room at the Fourteen Hotel, which occupied 14 East 60th St. Teilard died suddenly while visiting with friends in an apartment at 39 East 72nd St. (privately occupied).

THERESA HOTEL. Long a favorite Harlem landmark and meeting place, this recently renovated structure—now known as Theresa Towers, Ltd.— stands at 2090 Seventh Ave. (at the corner of West 125th Street) in **Harlem.** Probably every notable black American of the past 40 years has, at one time or another, lodged here. From 1940, when it began admitting blacks, this hotel provided Manhattan's foremost refuge for distinguished citizens who were often turned away from the

City's "prestigious" hotels. Joe Louis maintained a suite for years; Room 406 became the first New York address of Jimi Hendrix (see the entries on Louis and Hendrix earlier in this section); and Muslim leader Malcolm X established his Harlem "rectory" in Suite 128. The hotel is also noted for its distinctive terra cotta facade.

THOMAS, DYLAN (1914–1953). Everybody's favorite Welsh poet of the 1950s, the flamboyant cherub had turned to flab after years of hard drinking and died in Manhattan after an alcoholic binge during his fourth lecture trip to America. His last residence in October and November of 1953 was the Chelsea Hotel, from which he was carried to St. Vincent's Hospital in a coma. In 1952, during a previous trip, Thomas and his wife had occupied a kitchenette apartment at the Chelsea (see the entry on the Chelsea Hotel earlier in this section). John Malcolm Brinnin's *Dylan Thomas in America* (1955) details the last, lush escapades of the poet and his harried "keepers" on the U.S. college circuit.

THOMAS, NORMAN MATTOON (1884–1968). The six-time Socialist candidate for president gave the first political exposure to many "dangerous ideas" that later became embodied in legislation, including the five-day work week, minimum wage and abolition of child labor. As an outspoken enemy of capitalism, yet a devout foe of Communism, he was more "radical" at 80 than most left-wing activists at 20, usually moving 30 years ahead of conventional thinking and politics. Thomas made Manhattan his base from the 1930s. He and his family occupied an apartment at 206 East 18th St. (privately owned) near **Gramercy Park** until the early 1940s. They moved in 1945 to 71 Irving Place, a building owned by his wife—who, oddly enough in that milieu, was a remarkable businesswoman. They occupied the two upper floors over the tea room-restaurant she had operated there since 1932. Shops and private apartments remain there. In 1949, the widowed Thomas moved to a small apartment at 39-A Gramercy Park East (privately occupied), his last city home.

(See Chapter 3, NEW YORK, PENNSYLVANIA.)

THURBER, JAMES GROVER (1894–1961). The *New Yorker* humorist whose stories and deft cartoons transformed banal situations into crystals of quiet hysteria was a frequent Manhattan dweller. His early apartment residences are gone, but his most frequent lodging from 1929 was the Algonquin Hotel. Sick, totally blind and emotionally strung out, Thurber fled to the Algonquin from his Connecticut home in 1961 after a domestic squabble flared into crisis; and the hotel was his last residence (see the entry on the Algonquin Hotel earlier in this section).

Exhibit: A mural sketched by Thurber depicting the war between the sexes is still displayed at Costello's Bar and Grill, 225 East 44th St. in **Midtown.** Costello's, a favorite Thurber hangout, was located at 3rd Avenue and East 44th Street when he drew and drank.

(See Chapter 1, CONNECTICUT; also Chapter 4, OHIO; also Chapter 5, VIRGINIA.)

TIFFANY, LOUIS COMFORT (1848–1933). A painter, craftsman and decorator whose "art nouveau" style became high fashion from 1890 to 1915, Tiffany was a Manhattan native and the son of jeweler Charles Lewis Tiffany. None of his city homes remain. He was born at 57 Warren St. on the **Lower West Side.**

Tiffany's last home was a five-story, 50-room Romanesque structure on the **Upper East Side,** erected by his father at 19 East 72nd St. (at the corner of Madison Avenue). A house built in 1936 presently occupies this site.

(See Chapter 3, NEW YORK; also Chapter 5, FLORIDA.)

TILDEN, SAMUEL JONES (1814–1886). A brilliant lawyer and governor, Tilden won the popular vote but not the electoral vote in the 1876 presidential election. Tilden, who is credited with inventing the phrase "See you later," resided during the 1850s in **Greenwich Village** at 11 5th Ave., a town house later combined with two others to create the 1854 Brevoort Hotel. This landmark structure was replaced in 1953 by the present 14-story apartment building called "The Brevoort" (see the entry on Albert Bierstadt earlier in this section).

Tilden's last city home, from 1864, stands at 15 **Gramercy Park** South. This house was originally two houses dating from 1845; Tilden had them remodeled and combined in 1874 and also installed a tunnel leading to East 19th St. for an escape from unruly crowds. The National Arts

Club bought the mansion for a clubhouse in 1906 and still owns it today. Tilden's old library is now the club's bar. Like the Players Club next door (see the entry on Edwin Thomas Booth earlier in this section), National Arts Club National Historic Landmark no longer serves any important purpose for creative people. Admittance is by invitation only.

(See Chapter 3, NEW YORK.)

TRUMBULL, JOHN (1756–1843). The painter of grandiose American Revolutionary scenes resided in **Lower Manhattan** at lengthy intervals from 1804, but none of his several residence-studios remain. His first city home, from 1804 to 1808, stood at 128 Broadway (at the corner of Pine Street). From 1818 to 1825, when completing his four famous canvases for the U.S. Capitol's rotunda, Trumbull lived and worked in a mansion at 27 Park Place (at the corner of Church Street), currently the site of a commercial building. Trumbull lived longest (1825–37, 1841–43) and died in a large boardinghouse at 256 Broadway, currently the site of shops.

(See Chapter 1, CONNECTICUT.)

TWAIN, MARK. See SAMUEL LANGHORNE CLEMENS.

TWEED, WILLIAM MARCY (1823–1878). The prototypical crooked politician at the center of the "Tweed Ring" that bilked New Yorkers of perhaps $200 million in elaborate graft schemes, Tweed was a Manhattan native. None of his homes remain. His birthplace and home until 1844 lasted until 1862 at 1 Cherry St. on the **Lower East Side** near the site of his father's small chair factory at 24 Cherry St. The yellow-brick birthplace stood ominously next to the first U.S. Executive Mansion (see the entry on George Washington later in this section) and fell to make way for a coalyard. Tweed's first married home, from 1844 to 1846, was that of his in-laws at 193 Madison St. He lived from 1866 to about 1870 in a brownstone at 41 West 36th St., **Midtown.**

His four-story brownstone mansion, which New Yorkers didn't know they bought for him and which he occupied about 1870, stood in **Times Square** at 511 Fifth Ave. (at the corner of East 43rd Street), the site of his arrest in 1871. The Israel Discount Bank now operates legally here.

Tweed's last, more fitting home from 1876 was the Ludlow Street Jail, where he died. The jail occupied the western half of the block now improved by Seward Park High School, 350 Grand St., on the **Lower East Side.** Tammany Hall, when Tweed ran it, stood at Chatham and Frankfort streets.

(See Chapter 1, CONNECTICUT.)

VANDERBILT, CORNELIUS (1794–1877). "Commodore" Vanderbilt, the shipping and railroad magnate and founder of a financial dynasty, built his four-story brick mansion in 1846 at 10 Washington Place in **Greenwich Village.** His estate there included extensive grounds and stables. Today a New York University business administration building appropriately occupies the site where the almost illiterate Vanderbilt redefined the meaning of "wealthy," credulously held seances and died leaving a fortune of $100 million.

Vanderbilt's earlier Manhattan residences during the 1830s stood at unidentified sites on Stone and Madison streets and East Broadway on the **Lower East Side.**

(See STATEN ISLAND in this chapter; also Chapter 3, NEW JERSEY.)

VANDERBILT, WILLIAM HENRY (1821–1885). Father Cornelius Vanderbilt (see the entry on Cornelius Vanderbilt above) didn't think son William had the stomach for making money, but William's financial talents finally went beyond those of the patriarch. William inherited and almost doubled the vast wealth accumulated by his father and became a railroad baron by conducting business under the matter-of-fact philosophy "the public be damned" (an attitude that, concerning railroads, has seemingly come full circle). His piratical methods of acquisition and control eventually brought government regulation to the railroads, but not before he gained a fortune, some of which would successfully disguise him as a great philanthropist. In 1879, Vanderbilt built twin brownstone mansions on Fifth Avenue that occupied the entire block between West 51st and 52nd streets in **Midtown,** his last home. Three generations of the family, in addition to industrialist Henry Clay Frick, occupied this site, and later Vanderbilts also erected mansions on the opposite side of Fifth Avenue. The last of the "twins" at 640 Fifth Ave., where Vanderbilt died, fell in 1947 for construction of a 19-story office building. Paramount Studios bought much of the lavish interior woodwork and fixtures for movie sets.

(See STATEN ISLAND in this chapter; also Chapter 3, NEW JERSEY.)

WALDORF TOWERS. At 100 East 50th St. in **Midtown** stand the 47-story, chrome-capped twin towers of the Waldorf-Astoria Hotel. The towers, reserved for residential suites, date from 1931. Here, among many other noted figures who occupied luxurious apartments for long durations, lived former President Herbert Clark Hoover, publisher Henry Robinson Luce, Gen. Douglas MacArthur, actress Marilyn Monroe, composer Cole Albert Porter, and diplomat Adlai Ewing Stevenson (see the entries on Hoover, Luce, MacArthur, Monroe, Porter and Stevenson earlier in this section).

WALKER, JAMES JOHN "JIMMY" (1881–1946). The lawyer, songwriter, state politician and enormously popular if not obsessively honest mayor of New York City from 1926 to his 1932 resignation cultivated the debonair image of a playboy "night mayor." New Yorkers adored him, their affection undimmed by his retirement under a cloud of official charges and suspected financial impropriety. Walker was born in a flat that stood at 110 Leroy St. in **Greenwich Village,** his home to age five. From 1886 to 1934, he resided at 6 St. Lukes Place, which his father bought in 1891. This three-story, brick row house, built in 1852 and 1853, still bears the traditional "lamps of honor" signifying a mayor's residence on the front newel posts. The house remains privately owned.

Walker's last home, from 1944, was a 10-room apartment he leased on the seventh floor at 120 East End Ave., **Upper East Side,** still a private apartment building.

WASHINGTON, GEORGE (1732–1799). The nation's first president lived in Manhattan at several intervals in his life. As commander of the Revolutionary army during his unsuccessful defense of Manhattan island in 1776, he headquartered at the Mortier House (see the entry on John Adams earlier in this section) and at the Morris-Jumel Mansion (see the entry on Aaron Burr earlier in this section). In the latter house he occupied a three-room suite on the second floor.

The first Executive Mansion of the United States stood on Manhattan's **Lower East Side.** This was the home of importer Walter Franklin, a show-place mansion built in 1770 at 3 Cherry St. in what was then the most fashionable part of the city. George and Martha Washington resided there from his inauguration in April, 1789, to February, 1790. Franklin House was demolished in 1856, and the site was long occupied by warehouse-cellars for fish, wine and rubber heels. The Manhattan pier of Brooklyn Bridge now covers this site where Washington indeed slept on his first night as president. "One can tour the spot," reported James Dale Davidson, "by going to the Brooklyn Bridge and nicely asking the gentleman in charge if you can see the catacombs. The damp, the silence and the peeling walls give the place an atmosphere like that described in the 'Cask of Amontillado.' "

The next presidential dwelling was the Alexander McComb Mansion, its drier site marked by a plaque at 39 Broadway, **Lower Manhattan.** Washington lived there from February to August in 1790, then departed to the new capital city of Philadelphia.

Exhibits: Washington was sworn into office on April 30, 1789, at the present site of Federal Hall National Memorial, Wall and Nassau streets, **Lower Manhattan.** He took the oath on the balcony of the original City Hall, a building sold for scrap in 1812 and replaced in 1842 by the present columned structure, which served as the Subtreasury Building until 1920. Washington stood about where his statue now surveys Manhattan's financial district. Inside the Memorial, exhibits displayed by the National Park Service include the stone of the balcony on which he stood, a brown suit of the style he wore that day, and a pair of his shoe buckles. There the first national Congress also met and the Bill of Rights was shaped and adopted. Earlier, this site figured prominently in the sedition trial of John Peter Zenger (see the entry on Zenger later in this section); it was also the location of the Dutch colonial Stadt Huys from 1699 to 1703. Enter at 15 Pine St. (Open Memorial Day–Labor Day, daily 9:00–4:30; Labor Day–Memorial Day, Monday–Friday 9:00–4:30; 212-344-3830; free.) What has been called "the most notable object in the city's possession" is Washington's writing table, used at Federal Hall and now exhibited in the Governor's Room at City Hall, Broadway and Park Row. Here too are desks used by John Adams, Alexander Hamilton and Thomas Jefferson (see the entries on Adams, Hamilton and Jefferson earlier in this section). (Open Monday–Friday 10:00–4:00; 212-566-5525; free.)

On the **Upper East Side,** the Museum of the City of New York, 1220 Fifth Ave. (at the corner of East 103rd Street), displays Washington memorabilia in a room on the second floor. (Open Tuesday–Saturday 10:00–5:00, Sunday 1:00–5:00; 212-534-1672; free.)

(See Chapter 3, NEW JERSEY, NEW YORK, PENNSYLVANIA; also Chapter 5, VIRGINIA.)

WHARTON, EDITH (1862–1937). Born Edith Newbold Jones in a three-story brownstone at 14 West 23rd St. in the **Chelsea** area, the novelist lived there until 1882. Most sources state that the present building with a cast-iron front at this address replaced the original brownstone in 1882; but architectural historian Gerard R. Wolfe believes that the present structure, now owned by Hammacher Schlemmer Co., is the same building vastly altered. Jones moved with her mother to 28 West 25th St., from which she married banker Edward Wharton in 1885 and where the couple lived until 1889. This neighborhood was the New York she chronicled in *The Age of Innocence* (1920). The latter house is definitely gone, but Trinity Chapel where she married—now the Serbian Orthodox Cathedral of St. Sava—still remains at 15 West 25th St.

In 1891, she bought a small, **Upper East Side** town house at 884 Park Ave., which she tastefully furnished. This, her last Manhattan residence, has been replaced by an apartment building.

In 1882, she and her mother briefly occupied 7 Washington Square North in **Greenwich Village,** one of perhaps only two surviving Wharton residences in the city. It is part of "The Row," a line of elegant Greek Revival town houses built in 1832 and 1833. Today Numbers 7 to 13 retain their original appearance but are nevertheless all one facade, in which the doors are rarely used; major alterations in 1939 converted this row of seven dwellings into one private apartment house, entered from Fifth Avenue.

(See Chapter 1, MASSACHUSETTS, RHODE ISLAND.)

WHITE, STANFORD (1853–1906). The architectural firm of McKim, Mead & White, founded by White in 1879, was probably the most creative and original influence in American buiding design until the later 20th century, usually combining several styles into new, versatile elements. Many White-designed structures remain in New York City—among them, the Washington Arch and the Judson Church and Tower in **Greenwich Village,** The Players National Historic Landmark in **Gramercy Park,** the Cable Building at 611–621 Broadway, and the Prison Ship Martyrs' Monument near Fort Greene in Brooklyn.

White was born in a house that still stands at 110 East 10th St., **Lower East Side,** his home to age five.

White built **Madison Square** Garden at Madison Avenue and East 26th Street in 1890; the second Madison Square Garden on the spot, its central tower was second highest in the city. On the elaborate roof garden there White was shot and killed by Harry K. Thaw, the aggrieved husband of showgirl Evelyn Nesbit, on June 25, 1906. Madison Square Garden was twice rebuilt elsewhere after its 1925 demolition. The site is now occupied by the New York Life Insurance Company Building. Noted roué as well as brilliant architect, White achieved almost as much fame for his busy sexual life as for his buildings. According to Robert Baral in *Turn West on 23rd* (1965), "White had three hideaway spots to take his girls. One, his studio in the tower of Madison Square Garden, was a sort of prelude to his other two places. He apparently analyzed his young lady guests here to see how far he could go." White's two other "bordello apartments" were located near Madison Square at 122 East 22nd St., now Gramercy East Apartments; and the upper floors of 22 West 24th St. The latter building, containing private apartments, is probably the same one now on the site. A secret door led from the street directly to the love nest on the upper floor, reputedly outfitted in plush couches with a red velvet swing for exotic games.

White's conventional home, his last from 1901, stood at the northwest corner of Lexington Avenue and **Gramercy Park** North, the present site of the Gramercy Park Hotel. A feature of this elaborate mansion was a music room containing nine harps on a stage, all for effect since nobody there played them. "He used his Gramercy Park house," wrote Michael M. Mooney, "to charm, buffalo, wheedle, and convince clients of what they surely

always thought their plans should have included."
  (See Chapter 3, NEW YORK.)

WHITMAN, WALT (1819–1892). In 1842, the poet
edited the *New York Aurora* and lodged at Mrs.
Chipman's "quiet, clean" boardinghouse, long
gone from 12 Centre St. in **Lower Manhattan.**
Whitman lunched there each day and walked to
the Battery before returning to the newspaper
office at 111 Nassau St. His essay "New York
Boarding Houses," written during this period, is
contained in *Walt Whitman of the New York Aurora*
(1950), by Joseph Jay Rubin and Charles H. Brown.

  (See BROOKLYN in this chapter; also Chapter
3, DISTRICT OF COLUMBIA, NEW JERSEY,
NEW YORK.)

WILKINS, ROY (1901–1981). Wilkins, a longtime
civil rights activist and executive of the NAACP,
occupied a suite from 1932 to 1952 at 409 Edgecomb Ave. in the Sugar Hill section of **Harlem.**
The building still contains private apartments.

  (See QUEENS in this chapter; also Chapter 4,
MINNESOTA.)

WILLKIE, WENDELL LEWIS (1892–1944).
Corporation lawyer, businessman, and 1940
Republican presidential candidate, Willkie
achieved wider renown for the international
outlook conveyed in his book *One World* (1943),
which laid important groundwork for the later
organization of the United Nations. Because he
"disliked changes of residence," he occupied his
last home steadily from 1929. It was an **Upper
Manhattan** apartment suite at 1010 5th Ave.
(privately occupied) near the Metropolitan
Museum of Art.

  (See Chapter 4, INDIANA, KANSAS, OHIO.)

WILSON, EDMUND (1895–1972). The prolific
author and literary critic called "Bunny" by his
friends was a frequent Manhattan dweller from
1919 to 1955 but seldom stayed long in any of the
numerous apartments he occupied. As the
"discoverer" and lover of Edna St. Vincent Millay
in 1920 and 1921 (see the entry on Millay earlier
in this section), he lived at 136 West 16th St.
(privately owned) near **Greenwich Village.** In the
Village itself, also during the 1920s, he occupied
3 Washington Square North (see the entry on
Edward Hopper earlier in this section).

  One of his longest stays, from 1933 to 1935,

was at the **Midtown** address of 314 East 53rd St.,
presently the site of attorneys' offices.

  At 14 Henderson Place off East 86th Street near
York Avenue in **Yorkville,** the brick house where
he lived in 1944 and 1945 with his second wife,
novelist Mary McCarthy, remains privately
occupied.

  (See Chapter 1, MASSACHUSETTS; also
Chapter 3, NEW JERSEY, NEW YORK.)

WINCHELL, WALTER (1897–1972). "Not many
men in this country have had such a profound
influence on American manners and thought,"
wrote biographer Bob Thomas of the Broadway
columnist and broadcaster whose immense power
over public opinion in the 1930s and 1940s
extended even into national politics. Basically a
showman and publicist with a talent for innu-
endo, show-biz feuds, original slang expressions
and a staccato radio delivery that milked adrenalin from every line, Winchell cultivated a
disheveled, comic-book "reporter" image that he
apparently believed himself—in 30 years, somebody said, he never took off his hat or tightened
his tie, for that was how one looked "on the go."

  A Manhattan dweller for all but his final soured
and obscure years, Winchell lived for most of his
frenetic life in small apartments and hotel rooms.
There is little specific information about his lodgings, though it is known that his birthplace was
a three-room tenement apartment near Madison
Avenue and 117th Street, **Upper East Side.**

  During the heyday of his career, he lived for
years apart from his wife and children in the St.
Moritz Hotel, still at 50 Central Park South in
Midtown.

WODEHOUSE, SIR PELHAM GRENVILLE
(1881–1975). The English writer who created and
chronicled the stylishly zany, upper-class adventures of Jeeves and Bertie Wooster in a stream of
comic novels lived in Manhattan for two main
periods of his life. His early married home (1914–
15) was an apartment at 375 Central Park West,
Upper West Side.

  After World War II, Wodehouse moved permanently to the United States. He occupied **Upper
East Side** suites at the Hotel Adams, 2 East 86th
St., in 1947 and 1948; then at 1000 Park Ave., a
duplex apartment with a rooftop garden and
panoramic view of Central Park, from 1948 to
1952. These buildings remain privately occupied.

(See Chapter 3, NEW YORK; also Chapter 6, CALIFORNIA.)

WOLFE, THOMAS CLAYTON (1900–1938). "The most homesick city in the world," was how the novelist described New York. Yet the city fascinated him, and he spent much time here. Wolfe, a boisterous, stuttering moose of a man, came to Manhattan in 1923 to teach at New York University, where he conducted writing classes in the Brown Building sporadically until 1928. His first lodging was Room 2220 of the Albert Hotel, which stood at University Place and East 11th Street in **Greenwich Village.** In 1927 stage designer Aline Bernstein, who became his mistress and exerted a profound influence on his work, rented him a loft on the top floor of 13 East Eighth St., a filthy, ramshackle place, formerly the elegant home of editor Richard Watson Gilder. Here Wolfe began his novel *Of Time and the River* (1935). The site of this house is now occupied by the massive Brevoort Apartment Building, erected between 1953 and 1965, which fills the block. Wolfe and Bernstein then lived together on the second floor of 263 West 11th St., a four-story, private brick dwelling that dates from 1836. Wolfe completed *Of Time and the River* there in 1927 and 1928; he describes a similar house, transposed to 12th Street, in *You Can't Go Home Again* (1940). In 1928 and 1929, Wolfe lived at 27 West 15th St., at the rear of the second floor. This five-story house, privately owned, has been remodeled since his occupancy.

Wolfe occupied a three-room apartment on the 14th floor of 865 First Ave., **Upper East Side,** from 1935 to 1937, while working and quarreling with editor Maxwell Perkins on carving Wolfe's voluminous pages into presentable novels. The apartment was, he said, "one of the coolest places and one of the most wonderful views of New York." This private apartment building dates from about 1928.

Wolfe's last home of any duration was the Chelsea Hotel, to which he moved in 1937 (see the entry on the Chelsea Hotel earlier in this section). He occupied a corner suite with high ceilings on the eighth floor. Here in 1938, just four months before his death, he assembled the pages that were to become *The Web and the Rock* (1939) and *You Can't Go Home Again* from the packing cases full of manuscript that he piled on the living room floor.

(See BROOKLYN in this chapter; also Chapter 5, NORTH CAROLINA.)

WOODHULL, VICTORIA CLAFLIN (1838–1927). An outspoken feminist, successful businesswoman, and the first woman presidential nominee (in 1872), Woodhull moved to Manhattan with 24 relatives and servants in 1868. She lived at 15 East 38th St. (at the corner of Madison Avenue), a four-story **Midtown** mansion from which they were all evicted in 1871. A liquor store now stands at the site.

The Woodhull-Claflin clan was likewise evicted for spreading "immoral doctrines" at 118 East 23rd Street near **Madison Square** in 1872. They briefly occupied numerous other brownstone addresses through the 1870s until Victoria's final departure for England in 1877. Apparently none of the Manhattan houses identified with her have survived.

The site of the 1870 stockbrokerage firm that Woodhull ran with her sister Tennessee Claflin is 44 Broad St. in **Lower Manhattan.** *Who's Who* gave her euphemistic recognition just before she died as "a banker in New York."

(See Chapter 4, OHIO.)

WRIGHT, RICHARD (1908–1960). The novelist whose books documented America's racial tragedy in powerful, brutally frank prose lived in Manhattan in 1937 and again from 1945 to 1947, after which he fled America for the kinder racial climate of Paris and never returned. His first Manhattan lodging was in **Chelsea** with white friends at 235 West 26th St., still a private apartment building.

In 1945, he resided in a large, four-room apartment on the third floor of 82 Washington Place in **Greenwich Village,** a previous residence of Willa Sibert Cather (see the entry on Cather earlier in this section). The following year, Wright bought an 1847 brownstone at 13 Charles St., his final American home. This site has been occupied by the 18-story Village Towers Apartment, 15 Charles St., since 1961.

(See BROOKLYN in this chapter; also Chapter 5, MISSISSIPPI, TENNESSEE.)

ZENGER, JOHN PETER (1697–1746). Manhattan became the stage for one of the world's most significant jury trials in 1735, when the German-born newspaper editor was arrested for printing antigovernment opinions. His acquittal established the principle of freedom of the press, later given constitutional status. Zenger resided in **Lower Manhattan** for most of his life from age 13, but none of his addresses are definitely known except for that of William Bradford's printing shop, marked at 81 Pearl St. Zenger apprenticed there from 1711 to 1719. His later homes included lodgings on Smith Street (now William Street) near Maiden Lane (1726 to 1734); and on Broad Street (from 1734). For almost a year before his famous trial, however, he was imprisoned in City Hall, where the trial also occurred. Trial exhibits are displayed on the site at Federal Hall National Memorial.

Exhibit: See the entry on George Washington earlier in this section.

ZIEGFELD, FLORENZ (1869–1932). The theatrical producer was a frequent Manhattan hotel resident over a period of almost a quarter-century during the annual staging of the *Ziegfeld Follies,* a revue intended, he said, to "glorify the American girl." From the revue's chorus lines, which Ziegfeld personally selected, came the American ideal of slimness in women. During the 1890s, he usually resided at the Netherland Hotel, the present **Midtown** site of the 1927 Sherry-Netherland at 781 Fifth Ave. (at the corner of East 59th Street).

His permanent suite after 1900, however, was a 13-room apartment in the Ansonia Hotel (see the entry on Theodore Dreiser earlier in this section). There he lived with his first wife, French starlet Anna Held, and continued to occupy the suite long after his second marriage, to actress Billie Burke in 1914. His quarters were later divided into three smaller apartments.

(See Chapter 3, NEW YORK; also Chapter 4, ILLINOIS; also Chapter 6, CALIFORNIA.)

QUEENS

By far the largest borough (109.6 square miles), Queens extends New York City to its easternmost border on Long Island. Brooklyn and the East River bound the west, and Nassau County continues east.

Whites arrived here about 1635. Dutch settlers acquired title from the Rockaway Indians in 1639 and founded Mespat (Maspeth) in 1642. Numerous other settlements, both Dutch and English,

rapidly arose, and the new British government organized Queens County (named for Catherine of Braganza, the consort of England's monarch Charles II) in 1683. The majority of these villages favored the British side during the American Revolution. Until the early 20th century, Queens remained prime farmland. Heavy industrialization began along the East River and Newtown Creek in the 1870s, and the entire western portion of Long Island consolidated with New York City in 1898.

Numerous dwellings of the 17th and 18th centuries survive in Queens. Since De Witt Clinton established his summer residence there in 1796, the borough's fashionable residential communities have attracted many notable New Yorkers seeking homes away from Manhattan hyperactivity.

An impressive number of musicians made their homes in Queens. Among these were Louis Armstrong, Béla Bartók, John Coltrane, Glenn Miller and Fats Waller. Several social reformers and public activists, including Helen Keller, Malcolm X, Jacob Riis and Roy Wilkins, lived there for lengthy periods; and one of America's most influential extroverts, Dale Carnegie—who taught us not only how to influence people but how to "win" friends—lived in Forest Hills.

Visitors to the historic houses listed in Queens must currently be satisfied with exterior views, since almost all of them remain privately owned and occupied.

ARMSTRONG, LOUIS DANIEL (1900–1971). The gravel-voiced singer and trumpeter's last permanent home was the two-story brick house with marble trim at 34–56 107th St. in **Corona,** where he lived from 1942. Now Armstrong House National Historic Landmark, the home dating from about 1900 is still private, though Armstrong's widow has announced her intention of leaving it to the city as a memorial to the jazz giant.

(See Chapter 5, LOUISIANA.)

BARTÓK, BÉLA (1881–1945). In **Forest Hills,** the refugee composer occupied an apartment at 110–31 73rd Road (privately occupied) just after he arrived from Europe in 1940.

(See BRONX, MANHATTAN in this chapter; also Chapter 3, NEW YORK.)

BEIDERBECKE, LEON BISMARCK "BIX" (1903–1931). The influential jazz cornetist retired in July of 1931 to a ground-floor room containing only a bed, bureau and piano at 43–30 46th St. in **Sunnyside.** Beset by a faded career and violent delirium tremens, he died there on August 7. The apartment building, which dates from about 1930, remains privately occupied.

(See MANHATTAN in this chapter; also Chapter 4, IOWA; also Chapter 5, LOUISIANA.)

CARNEGIE, DALE (1888–1955). Modern salespersons, speakers and evangelists owe much to Carnegie's upbeat *How to Win Friends and Influence People* (1936), the father of all "how to," self-therapy books. Carnegie was probably the first to make a lucrative career as a professional optimist. His longtime home in **Forest Hills,** built about 1930, stands at 27 Wendover Road and remains a private residence.

(See Chapter 4, MISSOURI.)

CLINTON, DE WITT (1769–1828). A prominent mayor of the city and New York governor, and the 1812 presidential candidate, Clinton occupied a summer farm (his wife's ancestral homestead) in what is now **Maspeth** from 1796. This became his frequent residence and retreat until his death. Built in the early 1700s, the frame house with a gambrel roof stood as late as 1928, "a pathetic wreck about ready to fall down," reported H. D. Eberlein. There, it is said, Clinton planned the scheme for the Erie Canal, opened in 1825. Lois Kuster of the Queens Borough Public Library describes the site as "at the foot of 56th Terrace on the right and before the railroad tracks." A trucking firm now occupies the leveled ground.

(See MANHATTAN in this chapter; also Chapter 3, NEW YORK.)

COLTRANE, JOHN WILLIAM (1926–1967). In **St. Albans,** the saxophonist and jazz innovator resided from 1959 to 1963 in the two-story brick house at 116–60 Mexico St., still privately occupied.

(See MANHATTAN in this chapter; also Chapter 3, NEW YORK, PENNSYLVANIA; also Chapter 5, NORTH CAROLINA.)

GUTHRIE, WOODROW WILSON "WOODY" (1912–1967). The wandering ballad singer, prolific songwriter and author spent intervals from 1952 with his family at his last home, located in **Howard Beach,** while suffering the final ravages of the genetic Huntington's Disease that truncated his life and career. His residence at 15913 85th St. remains privately owned.

Guthrie died at Creedmoor State Hospital, Winchester Boulevard and Hillside Avenue in **Queens Village,** where he received constant care from 1966.

(See BROOKLYN, MANHATTAN in this chapter; also Chapter 6, OKLAHOMA, TEXAS.)

KELLER, HELEN ADAMS (1880–1968). The humanitarian-author whose work, both because of and despite her own enormous handicaps, enlightened a generation of attitudes toward the blind and deaf lived in **Forest Hills** for 21 years, from 1917. Her home at 7111 112th St., bordering Flushing Meadow Park, is a brick mansion of odd peaks and angles that she called her "Castle on the Marsh." It remains privately owned.

(See Chapter 1, CONNECTICUT, MASSACHUSETTS; also Chapter 5, ALABAMA.)

KEROUAC, JACK (1922–1969). The two-story frame house where the author lived with his mother at intervals from 1952 to 1963 and wrote *The Subterraneans* (1958) and *Doctor Sax* (1959) stands at 94–21 134th St. (privately owned) in **Richmond Hill.**

(See MANHATTAN in this chapter; also Chapter 1, MASSACHUSETTS; also Chapter 3, NEW YORK; also Chapter 5, FLORIDA; also Chapter 6, CALIFORNIA.)

MALCOLM X (1925–1965). According to biographer Peter Goldman, "The 'X,' said Malcolm, announced what you had been and what you had become: 'Ex-smoker. Ex-drinker. Ex-Christian. Ex-slave.' " The Black Muslim leader, powerful orator and religious reformer made his last home, from 1954, in **East Elmhurst.** The seven-room brick bungalow at 23–11 97th St., owned when he lived there by the Nation of Islam, became the scene of violence on February 13, 1965; a fire-bomb damaged the house badly after Malcolm had broken publicly from the Nation and fought eviction. He and his family were unhurt, but Malcolm had long considered himself a marked man, and he was fatally shot at Audubon Auditorium in Harlem one week later.

(See Chapter 4, MICHIGAN, NEBRASKA.)

MILLER, GLENN (1904–1944). The popular bandleader achieved his early reputation as a talented arranger in the 1930s. In **Astoria,** he lived at 30–60 29th St. (privately occupied) in 1929 and 1930.

A later Queens home, until 1939, was 37–60 88th St. in **Jackson Heights.**

(See Chapter 3, NEW JERSEY; also Chapter 4, IOWA, MISSOURI, NEBRASKA; also Chapter 6, COLORADO.)

RIIS, JACOB AUGUST (1849–1914). In 1887, the Danish-born urban reformer and photographer built a two-story Victorian house and rear study in **Richmond Hill,** his home until 1911. Though the property was declared a National Historic Landmark in 1971, the designation was not enough to save it. The house and study at 84–41 120th St. fell to wreckers two years later. Shortly before the house was razed, hundreds of his glass negatives showing city slums and tenement districts were discovered in the attic, providing a valuable historical record of 19th-century New York City.

(See Chapter 1, MASSACHUSETTS.)

WALLER, THOMAS WRIGHT "FATS" (1904–1943). Composer, jazz pianist and bandleader—also the first prominent jazz organist—Waller lived at 173–19 Sayres Ave. (privately occupied) in **St. Albans** from 1939. Shortly after moving there, he was welcomed to the neighborhood by a burning cross in his lawn; but Waller and his family outlasted their inferiors there, and this was his last home.

WILKINS, ROY (1901–1981). The civil-rights fighter and longtime leader of the NAACP made his last home, from 1952, at 147–15 Village Road (privately occupied) in **Jamaica.**

(See MANHATTAN in this chapter; also Chapter 4, MINNESOTA.)

STATEN ISLAND

Officially known as the Borough of Richmond, Staten Island is New York City's southernmost extension. Encompassing 55.8 square miles, 13.9 miles long and 7.3 miles broad at its widest, it is the third largest borough in size, but is smallest in population. The inland hills of Staten Island are the highest on the Atlantic coast from Maine to Florida. Only a channel separates this pear-shaped chunk of land from New Jersey; Manhattan is a five-mile ferry ride across Upper New York Bay. Staten Island's only direct contact with its sibling boroughs is the Verrazano Narrows Bridge, the world's longest suspension span, which extends to Brooklyn. Geographic logic should thus place Staten Island with New Jersey rather than New York, but political boundaries march to different drummers—in this case, British ones.

Henry Hudson supposedly named it Staaten Eylandt (State Island) in 1609, honoring his expedition sponsor, the ruling States-General of the Netherlands. Dutch colonial attempts, repeatedly wiped out by native Americans, did not finally succeed there until 1670. Each time the colonists were driven off and wanted to return, the Dutch-wise Indians made them rebuy the island, five times in all. The first permanent white settlement was probably Oude Dorp (Old Town) near the present site of Fort Wadsworth Military Reservation on the easternmost point. Somewhat whimsically, British colonial successors made the island a province of New York rather than New Jersey, a decision never seriously challenged since. Stock raising and shipbuilding became important occupations under the British, who named the province after the Duke of Richmond, the son of Charles II; and Staten Island remained predominantly a rural area of farming and fishing communities until the 1830s. Subsequent growth as a fashionable resort center and as a residential community for workers in expanded New Jersey factories effectively urbanized the island, though sizable rural acreage still remains. Today industrial development crowds along the northern shore, while the rest of the borough remains primarily residential.

The only native Staten Islander listed in these pages is Cornelius Vanderbilt, whose early homes are long gone. The last residence of Aaron Burr has likewise disappeared. Frederick Law Olmsted's farmhouse survives, however; and Italian nationalist Giuseppe Garibaldi's home is open to visitors. The list of Staten Island homes is short because, though many notable persons visited or vacationed there, few stayed for any duration. For most people with enough business or pleasure in New York City to warrant a residence in the area, Staten Island was an impractical choice.

BURR, AARON (1756–1836). The long, colorful life of the ambitious vice president, political intriguer and slayer of Alexander Hamilton ended in a **Port Richmond** hotel. Winant's Inn, built about 1787 and subsequently named St. James Hotel and Port Richmond Hotel, served Burr frequently during his travels, and there he spent his last weeks. The old inn stood at 2040 Richmond Terrace; a bronze plaque that once marked the site has disappeared.

(See MANHATTAN in this chapter; also Chapter 1, CONNECTICUT; also Chapter 3, NEW JERSEY, NEW YORK, PENNSYLVANIA.)

GARIBALDI, GIUSEPPE (1807–1882). The Italian patriot whose military leadership helped achieve his dream of a united Italy, Garibaldi spent two years in American exile before his "Thousand Redshirts" conquered Naples and Sicily. Garibaldi and Meucci Memorial Museum, the one and one-half-story, clapboard dwelling where he lived with inventor Antonio Meucci as a candlemaker from 1851 to 1853, stands at 420 Tompkins Ave. in **Rosebank.** Dating from 1845 and originally located across the street, the little house is operated as a museum by the Sons of Italy in America and displays several Garibaldi artifacts. (Open Tuesday–Friday 10:00–5:00, Saturday–Sunday 1:00–5:00; 212-442-1608; admission.)

OLMSTED, FREDERICK LAW (1822–1903). At **Eltingville,** Olmsted first practiced landscape architecture on his 130-acre "Tosomock Farm," an estate formerly called "Woods of Arden" and "Oakland Farm." There from 1848 to 1854, he raised 40 bushels of wheat to the acre, imported saplings, and cultivated orchards. This holding, later divided into "seaside estates," occupied the present area of Woods of Arden Road. Olmsted's old farmhouse, considerably altered and neglected, still stands nearby at 4515 Hylan Blvd. (privately owned).

(See Chapter 1, CONNECTICUT, MASSACHUSETTS, MAINE.)

VANDERBILT, CORNELIUS (1794–1877). Founder of a financial dynasty, Vanderbilt was born at **Port Richmond** in a small farmhouse overlooking Kill van Kull. He grew up at nearby **Stapleton,** in a small, two-story frame house that stood on Bay Road, his home from 1795 to 1813.

(See MANHATTAN in this chapter; also Chapter 3, NEW JERSEY.)

VANDERBILT, WILLIAM HENRY (1821–1885). An unscrupulous railroad magnate, the well-taught son of Cornelius Vanderbilt (see the entry on Cornelius Vanderbilt above) farmed 70 acres that his father gave him at **New Dorp.** It was his first enterprise, a kind of test in the senior's skeptical eyes, and he succeeded, especially after he added a large adjacent acreage. Vanderbilt's farmhouse, which he enlarged to a country villa in 1855, stood north of New Dorp Lane between the Old Moravian Church and the bay. He occupied this site from 1840 to 1864.

(See MANHATTAN in this chapter; also Chapter 3, NEW JERSEY.)

THREE

MIDDLE ATLANTIC REGION

The Middle Atlantic States are usually designated as those five lying between New England and Virginia that have Atlantic Ocean ports. They are Delaware, Maryland, New Jersey, New York and Pennsylvania. Some classifications list only Delaware, Maryland and Pennsylvania—New Jersey and New York being the "Gateway States." West Virginia, having no Atlantic port, is anomalous yet more congruent with this region than with the South. For the purposes of this book, it is most convenient to include West Virginia and the District of Columbia, in addition to the basic five states, as part of the Middle Atlantic complex. New York City was covered in the previous chapter.

Unlike New England, this region has little historic, cultural or economic unity. Bounded on the north by the St. Lawrence River and Lake Erie, by Virginia to the south, by New England and the Atlantic on the east and by Ohio and the Ohio River on the west, the region includes five of the original 13 states. Maryland was the only one of those five originally colonized by the English; the rest began with small Swedish or Dutch settlements which, before 1700, were all subdued and claimed by the English.

Two of these colonies—those of the Catholic Lord Baltimore in Maryland and of the Quaker William Penn in Pennsylvania—were founded by religious minorities for the express purpose of seeking spiritual freedom from oppression in the home country. As a region, however, the Middle Atlantic was never particularly obsessed with religion, again much unlike New England. European settlement in this area did not proceed from common doctrinal assumptions about the world and humanity's place in it. While occasional episodes of religious fanaticism did occur, there was nothing like the witchcraft hysteria nurtured by God's elect in the northern region. Maryland's Catholics welcomed Protestant settlers; and to Penn's Quakers, the ideal of peace and brotherhood, even with Indians, far outweighed any matter of doctrinal nit-picking. The large influx of German pietistic sects into Pennsylvania during the 1700s maintained this tradition. Unlike so many of the restless crowds that pressed national frontiers constantly westward, these people came to settle, and they stayed put. Their numerous progeny still prosper on the ancestral homesteads of the Pennsylvania Dutch country.

Having claimed ownership of the Middle Atlantic territory, British royalty proceeded to carve it up. Huge colonial land grants were awarded in gratitude for services or settlement of royal debts. These proprietors, while loyal to the Crown, had absolute power within their domains to make and enforce their own laws, regulate industry and trade and determine who could settle. Owing to imprecise or arbitrary property lines, the colonial borders often fell into dispute; some of the first warfare in America involved white men shooting at each other over land that belonged to Indians.

Except in the early days of Penn's colony, the natives of this region were used and abused for colonial ends. Actual conflict between settlers and Indians never reached the bloody pitch experienced in New England, but New York and Pennsylvania colonies were far from secure during the pre-Revolutionary frontier wars. French influence was strong west of the Hudson beginning in 1609, when Champlain laid eyes on the lake that bears his name. The Iroquois Confederacy, that fierce, remarkable band of five nations centered in New York, allied itself early on with the French cause; and the French and British used their tribal allies as buffers, contesting the area for five decades until the final British conquest in 1763. This region and period forms the melodramatic background of James Fenimore Cooper's novels.

If Boston was the soul of the Revolution, Philadelphia became its body. It was all very well for New Englanders to riot, dump tea in harbors and provoke fights with bewildered redcoats; but to do systematic battle required somewhat finer talents and the cooler emotional climate provided by the largest colonial city. Pennsylvania, the central colony, expressed itself extremely cool, in fact, to the idea of independence, mainly owing to Quaker sentiment. But once the decision to revolt was made, the very locale of that decision inspired confidence that the matter had been thoroughly weighed—Samuel Adams was a Yankee hothead, but men like Benjamin Franklin and Thomas Jefferson were anything but.

The Middle Atlantic region took the brunt of Revolutionary fighting. Key battles were fought in New York, New Jersey and Pennsylvania. At Saratoga, thanks to Benedict Arnold, the eventual traitor, the tide of losses presided over by Gen. George Washington definitely turned; the American losers, whose main achievements had been simply to endure in winter camps, suddenly sensed victory as a distinct possibility. The concluding battles were fought in the South, but the drive to success was fashioned in the Middle Atlantic region.

In 1790 Philadelphia became the nation's capital for 10 years. Here emerged the second founding document, the Constitution, amid even greater vocal fireworks than the earlier Declaration had provoked. None of the united colonies bore any excess trust toward one another; the document's final passage was as much a brave endorsement of the high character of Franklin and Washington as the result of any burning confidence in the plan. Nevertheless, miraculously, the United States was born. The delivery room, Independence Hall, stands today in Independence National Historical Park, much more reverent and polished a place these days than the chamber familiar to that crowd of sweating politicians.

Two of the politicians in that 18th-century equivalent of a smoke-filled room—Alexander Hamilton and Jefferson—worked out the compromise that led to locating the nation's capitol in a Potomac swamp. Congress decided to build a city from the damp ground up and move there by 1800. President Washington, who chose its site, personally finagled with the farming property owners to acquire land for streets and public buildings, and the city began to rise. Amid half-finished stone buildings, mudhole avenues, a shacktown of boards, rubble, manure and marsh miasma, the Congress, Supreme Court and President John Adams moved into Washington, D.C., at the century mark. Complaints about the fetid site continued for the next 75 years, and Congress more than once verged on choosing another. When legislators finally perceived, however, that the city was perceived abroad as the symbol of the nation, the more astute among them felt that improving the existing image would be worthwhile. Over the years and not without furious opposition, the city was remarkably rebuilt; and Washington, with its parks, gardens and monuments, ranks today as one of the most beautiful capitals in the world.

Transportation became a vital component in this region that contains some of the largest cities on the continent. Baltimore launched the first American common-carrier railway service in 1827 when the Baltimore & Ohio Railroad began laying tracks to the Ohio River at Wheeling, W. Va., a roadbed completed in 1852. Most of the first highways of this region may still be traveled, including the former King's Highways from New York to Philadelphia and Philadelphia to Virginia, and the Braddock (U.S. Highway 40) and Forbes (U.S. Highway 30) Roads cut through Pennsylvania by British armies from 1755 to 1758. The road across New Jersey, along which the native Lenni-Lenape tramped east to obtain fish and oysters on New York Bay, existed before colonial times; the first recorded use of the route was by Peter Stuyvesant's 1651 invasion force into Delaware. State Highway 27 and U.S. Highway 206 follow the path today, and U.S. Highway 13 tracks it to Philadelphia.

The types of homes constructed by residents of this region varied enormously. Log cabins, introduced to America in Pennsylvania and Delaware by the earliest Swedish colonists, were quickly adapted for frontier use all over the region. Pioneers took the style west, and the "log cabin birthplace" became a patriotic symbol for aspiring presidential contenders—especially as such domiciles sagged into increasingly relict reminders of "good old days." Examples of such cabins may be seen today in the two Millard Fillmore birthplace restorations in New York. New York Dutch colonial architecture, using stone and brick, exists in the Sojourner Truth birthplace in Hurley and the Hasbrouck House (Washington's Headquarters) in Newburgh. The Pennsylvania colonial farmhouse, prevalent in Bucks County and west, is a mixture of English and German styles.

Philadelphia was the focal point of Middle Atlantic architecture. The Georgian or Colonial style exemplified the neoclassic designs that flourished in England and became common in America from 1720 to 1820. Philadelphia's brick row houses, of which many survive, represent the typical type; Mount Pleasant mansion, the home in Fairmount Park bought by status-seeker Benedict Arnold, is probably the most notably refined showpiece of the style. Annapolis also preserves some of the best Georgian examples in the nation. During the Federal period (1790–1830), a distinctively American style developed, combining Roman classicism with simple, restrained proportions and facades. Fine examples include the Caldwell-Monroe and Stephen Decatur houses in Washington, D.C. The Greek Revival style for houses became enormously popular throughout the region and nation after 1820. George Eastman's birthplace at Mumford, N.Y., and Nicholas Biddle's imposing home in Andalusia, Pa., offer notable views of this architectural phase.

The Middle Atlantic Region is so various in landscape, culture and history that general statements attempting to package the area with neat edges are unwise if not impossible. Many of America's best-known makers and doers found this variety most conducive to their own expectations of life and home.

DELAWARE

"Delaware has three counties at low tide," noted one observer. Surface of the second-smallest state is indeed one-sixth water; with an average height above sea level of only 60 feet, it is also the lowest state. Its population, less than Rhode Island's, ranks third lowest in number among all states but sixth highest in density.

Henry Hudson claimed Delaware Bay for the Dutch in 1609, but English Capt. Samuel Argall spotted it the next year and named its western cape for his superior Thomas West, Lord De La Warr, the provincial governor of Virginia. That gentleman probably never set foot there, but in time the entire territory became known to the English as Delaware. Native Americans promptly wiped out the Dutch colonists who had settled near Lewes in 1631. In 1638, Swedes planted a colony at Wilmington, and the Dutch settled anew in 1651 at New Castle. For years Dutch and Swedes contested whether the area would be New Sweden or an outpost of New Netherlands. The English resolved the quarrel by seizing the entire territory in 1664 and making it part of the colonial Pennsylvania grant, and it remained under the Penn proprietorship until 1776. By being first to ratify the Constitution in 1787, Delaware became the first state. Its position during the Civil War was ambigious; technically a slave state, it refused to secede, and Delaware residents served both sides in the state's own microcosm of the national split.

Today Delaware is a manufacturing state, specializing in the massive chemical industry that grew from the Du Pont munitions works, which kept many of the world's guns going for a century. That well-preserved complex near Wilmington has been Delaware's economic center for almost as long as the state has existed. Miles of Atlantic beach have also made the state a major resort center.

Though relatively few figures of national importance have lived here, Delaware's record of preserving the noted homes that do exist has been excellent.

DICKINSON, JOHN (1732–1808). The shrine of the "Penman of the Revolution" whose eloquent patriotic writings laid the rationale for American independence, Dickinson Mansion National Historic Landmark stands on Kitts Hummock Road about one-half mile off U.S. Highway 113, six miles south of **Dover.** His father built the original two and one-half-story brick plantation house on a 1,300-acre tract in 1740. Dickinson himself left about 1750 but often returned at intervals throughout his life. After a fire destroyed all but the original brick walls in 1804, Dickinson rebuilt the house as a tenant residence. Restoration in 1952, however, re-created its original interior appearance. Most items displayed are period pieces, but a few Dickinson possessions remain— dishes, his desk, cradle, clock and some small personal items. The home is maintained by the Delaware Department of State. (Open Tuesday–Saturday 10:00–4:30, Sunday 1:30–4:30; 302-736-4266; admission.)

(See MARYLAND, PENNSYLVANIA in this chapter.)

DU PONT DE NEMOURS, ÉLEUTHÈRE IRÉNÉE (1771–1834). At **Greenville,** the French immigrant chemist built the gunpowder mill that founded the Du Pont industrial dynasty. Eleutherian Mills National Historic Landmark, his 1803 home, with 1805 and 1853 additions, is a buff-colored, three-story, stucco mansion that remained occupied by the Du Pont family until 1958. It is located within the 185-acre Hagley Museum complex at the site of the original Du Pont enterprise off State Highway 141. This was the founder's only home in America, and also served as the factory office until 1837—built close to the mills, it is said, so that labor and management would share the risk of explosions. After an 1890 blast, however, family occupants reconsidered and relocated until 1921, when operations ceased there. The mansion, operated by Eleutherian Mills-Hagley Foundation, contains furnishings of early American, Federal and Empire styles from five family generations. (Open Tuesday–Saturday 9:30–4:30, Sunday 1:00–5:00; 302-658-2400; admission.)

Exhibits: The Hagley Museum on Barley Mill Road off State Highway 141 includes numerous outdoor and indoor displays of the early powder-making process and company history as well as several of the original shop buildings. (Open same hours as Eleutherian Mills; admission.)

MARQUAND, JOHN PHILLIPS (1893–1960). The novelist's birthplace, a three-story Victorian dwelling that was probably new in 1893, stands at 1301 Pennsylvania Ave. (privately owned) in **Wilmington.** Local historical sources know little about the house beyond the fact that Marquand's parents resided there until 1894.

(See NEW YORK in this chapter; also Chapter 1, MASSACHUSETTS; also Chapter 2, MANHATTAN; also Chapter 6, FLORIDA, NORTH CAROLINA.)

SINCLAIR, UPTON BEALL (1878–1968). In 1911, the prolific author, early consumer activist and political reformer built a two-story cottage in the single-tax utopian community of **Arden,** six miles north of Wilmington on Grubb's Road. He lived there three years and also rented Scott Nearing's cabin next door as a study. The house stands at Woodland Lane and Theater Path (privately owned).

(See MARYLAND, NEW JERSEY in this chapter; also Chapter 6, CALIFORNIA.)

DISTRICT OF COLUMBIA

The District of Columbia, now coterminous with the city of Washington, has been a political anomaly since its 1790 creation as the nation's capital. It exists outside any state constituency. Because this notch of territory belongs to "all" the people, it often, in seeming effect, belongs to none. Unlike most other world capitals, Washington is perceived not solely as a place but as a personified force and source. Washington, we often hear, is "what's wrong with the country," a criticism not referring to cherry blossoms. Recent presidents have even taken remarkable pains to seem "anti-Washington." "The President may find temporary shelter in the roomy house on Pennsylvania Avenue," wrote Roger Rosenblatt, "but when he looks toward green Lafayette Square and creamy St. John's Church, he will not see his home town." To paraphrase Calvin Coolidge (though he wouldn't like the paraphrase), "The business of Washington is government." The district and the city, with all of their complex American symbology, were built and maintained for the sole purpose of seating the federal government and have done so since 1800. As eighth largest metropolitan area in the nation, the District is the constituency of every senator and member of Congress; but because this constituency has no elective voice in their home districts, its own needs and problems usually come low on the national priority scale.

Several communities predated Washington in what became the District of Columbia. The site, long occupied by Algonquin villages, was inspected by Capt. John Smith in 1608, and a few Irish and Scots farmers settled there. Georgetown, established in 1751, and what is now Alexandria, Va., settled in 1731, were distinct communities within the original 100-square-mile district. Alexandria, comprising almost one-third of that area, was returned to Virginia on the petition of its residents in 1846.

The controversy of where to locate a permanent national capital threatened to wreck the Union only three years after passage of the Constitution. Francis Hopkinson satirically suggested putting the capital on wheels. When agreement was finally reached, George Washington himself chose the Potomac site for its central waterway location and for its boondock isolation from the politics and overly influential money of the established eastern cities.

It was not the ideal site in other ways. Malarial Potomac swamps and steamy summer heat made it one of the most uncomfortable capitals in the world. Before the days of air conditioning, presidents usually fled the stifling White House for higher ground; and Congress, of course, has always deserted the city in summer. Not until after the Civil War did extremely vocal minorities stop trying to move the capital elsewhere.

"With the French passion for formalizing the landscape," wrote Mary Mitchell, architect Pierre L'Enfant "envisioned a mall reclaimed from the swamps and stretching to the river." From the geographic center of the Capitol, he divided the city into quadrants, correctly assuming that city and district would ultimately be coextensive. Each lettered (east-west) and numbered (north-south) street was duplicated in each quadrant (NW, SW, NE, SE), and this quadrant designation remains a vital part of any Washington address. (Most of the nation's public business is conducted in the northwest quadrant—the others are primarily residential.) Upon his basic gridiron pattern,

L'Enfant superimposed long, radiating avenues named for the states "to connect the separate and most distant objects with the principal." The finished pattern, however, departed in many details from L'Enfant's original scheme.

In many ways the most beautiful and imposing city on the continent, Washington was also the most backward. While magnificent structures arose like temples to house the federal machinery, paving, curbs, sewers, decent water and sanitation—all of the practical urban necessities taken for granted in most American cities—lagged far behind. One could easily step from marble grandeur into knee-deep mud—or worse—on the very best avenues. The city had the raw, rutted look of a busy construction site; shacks surrounded parthenons. Fine carpets soaked with tobacco juice in White House offices symbolized the entire grand-and-gross aspect of the federal city.

That began to change when national legislators themselves migrated from city boardinghouses and "congressional messes" into private dwellings and began bringing in their own families. More than any single person, Alexander R. "Boss" Shepherd converted Washington from a provincial town of dust, mud and shacks into a modern city. His board of public works in the 1870s "knocked the town down and built it up again" in three whirlwind years. In 1902, the McMillan Commission, adapting L'Enfant's design, planned a modern park system, and the results of this project form the city as seen today. The trend of modern city planning is to restore as much of L'Enfant's original scheme as possible; the long-neglected Mall has gradually been restored as he envisioned it, and today Pennsylvania Avenue National Historic Site protects the city's first, main and most historic avenue.

Noted residents have crowded Washington from the beginning, but most have lived there only because their jobs required it. Exceptions included two important city natives, composer Duke Ellington and FBI director J. Edgar Hoover. Boardinghouses and hotels lodged most public officials until far into the 20th century, and buying or building a Washington home may still denote more than modest faith in one's political alliances.

Historical buildings in Washington usually experience one of two extremes: Either they are given lavish restoration and care as public monuments; or, in civic haste to improve and beautify, they are torn down. Though distinct exceptions exist, Washington holds less interest than most American cities in maintaining historic private homes apart from any public purpose. The old Willard Hotel survives but only after a long fight; present plans to convert it into a useful office building go against the Washington grain of all-out embalming or summary bulldozing. For all of the eminent people who have lived in the District during almost 200 years of history, relatively few eminent homes that predate 1920 have survived.

Probably the best guide to the "life histories" of specific Washington structures (and of city streets and neighborhoods as well) is *Capital Losses* by James M. Goode (1979). Aside from a few specialized efforts like Goode's, few publications provide convenient sources of historical information on Washington buildings and streets. There is presently no up-to-date, comprehensive "Washington guidebook" for anyone who wants much beyond the latest restaurant and hotel rates. This is indeed a capital loss.

ACHESON, DEAN GOODERHAM (1893–1971). The secretary of state under President Truman (see the entry on Harry S. Truman later in this section), Acheson bought his 19th-century home at 2805 P St. NW (privately owned) in 1922, subsequently enlarged it and remained there for the rest of his life. He hosted the Trumans for their final Washington dinner there just before their retirement to Missouri in 1953.

(See MARYLAND in this chapter; also Chapter 1, CONNECTICUT.)

ADAMS, CHARLES FRANCIS (1807–1886). The son of President John Quincy Adams lived in the White House during the last two years (1827–29) of his father's term (see the entry on John Qunicy Adams later in this section). Later, as an influential diplomat and Republican leader, he occupied the Caldwell-Monroe House (see the entry on James Monroe later in this section), which contains no Adams memorabilia.

(See Chapter 1, MASSACHUSETTS.)

ADAMS, HENRY BROOKS (1838–1918). The historian and grandson of President John Quincy Adams (see the entry on John Quincy Adams later in this section) achieved monumental status in Washington for his astute, brittle comments on national politics. None of his three homes, all

located close together on H Street NW, remain. His wife, Marion "Clover" Adams, committed suicide in 1885 in their home at 1607 H St., razed in 1922. The 1927 Hay-Adams Hotel stands on the site of his last house at 1603 H St. (1885–1918), a three-story brick mansion designed by architect Henry Hobson Richardson to resemble a medieval fortress. Adams did much writing and remained a widower until his death there.

(See Chapter 1, MASSACHUSETTS.)

ADAMS, JOHN (1735–1826).
ADAMS, ABIGAIL SMITH (1744–1818).

As first occupants of the still-unfinished White House (1800–01), the Adamses suffered extreme inconvenience, detailed in Abigail's letters to friends. "The country around is romantic but a wilderness at present," she reported. The new Executive Mansion was, in fact, a solitary eminence surrounded by shacks and a sea of mud. Today it is hard to reconcile the polished gloss of the East Room with the picture of Abigail Adams hanging her washing there, as lack of usable space forced her to do. Later generations would occasionally worry about other types of "dirty linen" in the White House, despite John Adams's prayer "to bestow the best of Blessings on this House. . . . May none but honest and wise men ever rule under this roof." (See the entry on the White House later in this section for tour information.)

(See PENNSYLVANIA in this chapter; also Chapter 1, MASSACHUSETTS; also Chapter 2, MANHATTAN.)

ADAMS, JOHN QUINCY (1767–1848). As secretary of state for President Monroe, Adams lived at 1333 F St. NW from 1817 to 1825. This three-story brick mansion, "only second in importance to the President's," wrote Esther Singleton, was the earlier home of James Madison (see the entries on James Monroe and James Madison later in this section). Adams returned there in 1834 and made it his last city home. In 1883 an observer noted that the building was "still a boarding house sandwiched between a grocery store and a millinery shop, while a physician uses its parlors for his office." Probably soon after, it was "sandwiched out" entirely.

As the sixth U.S. president, Adams occupied the White House from 1825 to 1829. His days there consisted of a precisely ordered routine, beginning with a dawn swim in the Potomac during summer and ending with billiard games at night. The high social point of his tenure was hosting Gen. Lafayette at the White House in 1825. (See the entry on the White House later in this section for tour information.)

Adams' Washington home from 1829 to 1834 was "Meridian Hill," an 1816 mansion on 110 acres successively owned by naval officers David Porter and John Rodgers. It straddled 16th Street NW at the present location of Meridian Hill Park and burned down, spectacularly, in 1863.

(See Chapter 1, MASSACHUSETTS.)

ARTHUR, CHESTER ALAN (1829–1886). The 21st U.S. president occupied the White House from 1881 to 1885. Before he moved in, he insisted on moving loads of things out—24 wagons of furniture and household articles—and on renovating the mansion, never thoroughly done since its 1816 reconstruction after British soldiers burned it. "I will not live in a house looking this way," he said, but his discomfort with his predecessor, James Abram Garfield (see the entry on Garfield later in this section), probably motivated this clean sweep as much as Arthur's own sense of style and elegance. He chose famed craftsman-decorator Louis Tiffany to restyle the rooms, and Tiffany's "art nouveau" provided the drape-heavy Victorian setting that lasted until the next renovation in 1902. Since Arthur's wife had died in 1880, hostess duties were performed by his sister, Mary Arthur McElroy. (See the entry on the White House later in this section for tour information.)

(See NEW YORK in this chapter; also Chapter 1, VERMONT; also Chapter 2, MANHATTAN.)

BANCROFT, GEORGE (1800–1891). The last home, from 1874, of the historian and diplomat was 1623 H St. NW, a three-story brick house with a plaster front, demolished for commercial expansion in 1922. Here the "Father of American History" completed his 10-volume *History of the United States* in 1874 and wrote several later works.

(See Chapter 1, MASSACHUSETTS, RHODE ISLAND.)

BARTON, CLARA (1821–1912). The founder of the American Red Cross occupied several Washington lodgings from 1860 to 1897. Her residence from 1886 to 1892 was a house she purchased in 1878 at 947 T St. NW (privately owned); she rented

it out before and after her own occupancy but kept it for the rest of her life. This row house, its front now painted green, has been only slightly altered. All of her other Washington residences are long gone.

Exhibit: The 1917 Memorial Building of the American National Red Cross headquarters at 17th and D Streets NW contains a basement museum with several Barton items. (Open Monday–Friday 9:00–4:00; 202-666-0111; free.)

(See MARYLAND, NEW JERSEY, NEW YORK in this chapter; also Chapter 1, MASSACHUSETTS.)

BARUCH, BERNARD MANNES (1870–1965). Wall Street financier, advisor to eight U.S. presidents and famed park-bench sage, Baruch spent much time in Washington, where he usually occupied a nondescript suite at the 1925 Carlton-Sheraton Hotel, 16th and K Streets NW. He found little solitude there; the apartment sometimes became so crowded with callers that he fled, and what began as an escape resulted in his habitual use of a bench at Lafayette Square for an informal "office."

Exhibit: Saunterers may freely sit on the bench where Baruch held forth on public issues and even had his mail delivered. To find it, walk 11 paces northwest of Andrew Jackson's equestrian statue in Lafayette Square—and sit. An adjacent memorial plaque will confirm your pacing. Does the "Bench of Inspiration" live up to its name? "Yes," said a park attendant recently, "sometimes I do see people get up from it as though they'd suddenly thought of something."

(See Chapter 2, MANHATTAN;   also Chapter 5, SOUTH CAROLINA.)

BELL, ALEXANDER GRAHAM (1847–1922). The inventor's first Washington home (1882–89) was the 1879 Bell-Morton House, a three-story mansion of gables and turrets located at 1500 Rhode Island Ave. NW, Scott Circle. Later tenants included Vice President Levi P. Morton and Secretary of State Elihu Root (see the entry on Root later in this section); the building now serves as headquarters of the National Paint and Coatings Association. In 1891, Bell built a three-story house of brick and stone at 1355 Connecticut Ave. NW, which he occupied for the rest of his life. After standing vacant for eight years following his death, it was sold and demolished in 1930. In

1881 he established his parents at the Alexander Melville Bell House at 3434 Volta Place NW (privately owned), where he set up a laboratory in the old rear stable and perfected a primitive recording device called a disk-graphophone. This house, built about 1845 around an 18th-century farmhouse, diminished in size as portions were removed and added to an adjacent house on the south; what is left faces 35th Street. The carriage house-laboratory also became a separate property. Walter Lippman was a later occupant (see the entry on Lippman later in this section).

(See Chapter 1, MASSACHUSETTS.)

BLAINE, JAMES GILLESPIE (1830–1893). In 1881, the political leader and "Plumed Knight" of the Republican party built his rambling, red-brick Victorian mansion at 2000 Massachusetts Ave. NW (at the corner of 20th Street), but lived there only until 1883. "The home had recommended itself to larger purses than Mr. Blaine's," commented a tactful observer. Blaine rented it out, and a later owner was inventor George Westinghouse. Today, surrounded by urban blight, it houses government offices. None of Blaine's other Washington homes remain. His last was 17 Madison Place on Lafayette Square; Blaine remodeled and occupied this former mansion of William Henry Seward (see the entries on Westinghouse and Seward later in this section) from 1889 and died there.

(See Chapter 1, MAINE.)

BOOTH, JOHN WILKES (1838–1865). The assassin of President Lincoln (see the entry on Abraham Lincoln later in this section) often stayed at the National Hotel, his favorite Washington residence. Booth checked in and out 10 times during the month preceding his crime of April 14, 1865, and was occupying Room 228 on that day (see the entry on Henry Clay later in this section).

The neatly painted antebellum house at 604 H St. NW (privately owned) was Mary Surratt's boardinghouse. There Booth and his fellow conspirators plotted the deed in the early spring of 1865. Today the building is a grocery store in the heart of Washington's Chinatown district.

Exhibits: The Lincoln Museum in the basement of Ford's Theatre at 511 10th St. NW contains Booth's derringer pistol, knife, compass and diary, among other items. (Open daily 9:00–5:00; 202-426-6924; free.) The 1863 theater itself, recon-structed and functional since 1968, may also be visited. (Open daily 9:00–5:00; on days when performances are scheduled, 9:00–1:00.) Another exhibit on the assassination may be seen at the Armed Forces Medical Museum in the Armed Forces Institute of Pathology, 6825 16th St. NW. (Open daily 12:00–6:00; 202-576-2341; free.)

(See MARYLAND, PENNSYLVANIA in this chapter.)

BORAH, WILLIAM EDGAR (1865–1940). The famed Idaho Republican, a highly respected political maverick, lived at only two addresses in Washington for most of his 34-year senatorial career. He occupied Apartment 21 at what is now Windsor Lodge National Historic Landmark, 2139 Wyoming Ave. NW, from 1913 to 1929. This four-story, brick apartment building dates from about 1912. Later Borah occupied a larger apartment at 2101 Connecticut Ave.

(See Chapter 4, ILLINOIS; also Chapter 6, IDAHO.)

BRADY, MATTHEW B. (1823?–1896). Noted as "Mr. Lincoln's camera man," the Civil War photographer opened the Brady National Photographic Gallery, his second Washington studio, at 627 Pennsylvania Ave. NW in 1858. That four-story brick building, built in 1855 and occupied by Gilman's Drug Store until 1967, probably hosted more national figures on its upper floors than any place in the city except the White House. Many of the notable faces peering from the past in Brady's photos were posing, braced by metal headrests, in that building. Brady himself lived there in 1880 and 1881. His home for most of his Washington years, however, was the National Hotel (see the entry on Henry Clay later in this section). When his fortunes declined after the war, he moved to his nephew's red-brick residence at 494 Maryland Ave. SW. That house remained standing until recent years.

(See Chapter 2, MANHATTAN.)

BRANDEIS, LOUIS DEMBITZ (1856–1941). The prominent liberal Supreme Court justice came to Washington in 1916 and lived until 1926 at Stoneleigh Court Apartments, on the southeast corner of Connecticut Avenue and L Street NW. This 1902 building was razed in 1965; the Blake Office Building presently occupies the site. His last home (1926–41) was 2205 California St. NW, Apartment 505. Dating from 1903, the building was renovated for condominiums in 1978.

(See Chapter 1, MASSACHUSETTS; also Chapter 5, KENTUCKY.)

BRYAN, WILLIAM JENNINGS (1860–1925). Three times nominated and defeated for the presidency, the "Great Commoner" spent much of his long, often stormy public career in Washington. His home during the early 1900s at 2101 R St. NW stands with a slightly altered facade; the privately owned building has been converted to three town-house apartments. As secretary of state for President Wilson (see the entry on Woodrow Wilson later in this section), Bryan resided at "Calumet Place," the John A. Logan mansion, which stood until 1925 at Clifton and 13th Streets NW, until his 1915 resignation.

(See Chapter 4, ILLINOIS, NEBRASKA; also Chapter 5, FLORIDA, TENNESSEE.)

BUCHANAN, JAMES (1791–1868). From 1857 to 1861 the White House was bachelor's hall for Buchanan, the 15th U.S. president. His hostess, niece Harriet Lane Johnson, whom he had raised, presided over social Washington at superbly styled dinners and receptions. During these harried years preceding the Civil War, social life sparkled in the Executive Mansion, reaching heights of elegance that imitated the pattern of European courts, where Buchanan had served as a diplomat. A tall, striking figure with a constant myopic head tilt, Buchanan was brilliant in society if flustered in power; and he gratefully stepped aside for Abraham Lincoln. (See the entry on Lincoln later in this section; see also the entry on the White House for tour information.)

Because of Washington's dank, malarial swamps, Buchanan considered the White House an unfit residence during warm weather, and he was the first president to use Anderson Cottage at the U.S. Soldier's Home—now U.S. Soldiers' and Airmen's Home National Historic Landmark—for a summer retreat. The stuccoed, neo-Gothic Anderson Cottage, dating from 1843, served as the first structure of this haven for retired military men founded by Gen. Winfield Scott in 1851. Closed to the public, it stands inside the grounds at Rock Creek Church Road and Upshur Street NW.

(See PENNSYLVANIA in this chapter.)

BYRD, RICHARD EVELYN (1888–1957).

Exhibits: Two museums display items used by the naval officer and explorer in his various polar expeditions. Explorers Hall of the National Geographic Society, 17th and M streets NW, contains his Bumstead sun compass among other equipment—even the stuffed body of his lead sled dog. (Open Monday–Friday 9:00–6:00; Saturday 9:00–5:00, Sunday 12:00–5:00; 202-857-7588; free.) The U.S. Navy Memorial Museum (Building 76 at Washington Navy Yard, 8th and M streets SE) also exhibits some of his expedition equipment. (Open Monday–Friday 9:00–4:00, Saturday–Sunday 10:00–5:00; 202-433-2651; free.)

(See Chapter 1, MAINE, MASSACHUSETTS; also Chapter 5, VIRGINIA.)

BYRNES, JAMES FRANCIS (1879–1972). Senator, Supreme Court justice, secretary of state and governor of South Carolina, Byrnes was one of Washington's most influential public figures from 1930 to 1947. His residence for those 17 years was the 1929 Shoreham Hotel at 2500 Calvert St. NW.

(See Chapter 5, SOUTH CAROLINA.)

CALHOUN, JOHN CALDWELL (1782–1850). In 1823, the powerful pro-slavery senator from South Carolina moved into Dumbarton Oaks at 1703 32nd St. NW, an 1801 Georgian mansion loaned to him by his brother. He occupied it as vice president until 1826, when he left because of maintenance expense and sold it for his brother in 1829. Extensively altered and enlarged since his day, it is now an art museum and center of medieval studies owned and operated by Harvard University. Fifteen acres of formal gardens surround the mansion. (Open Tuesday–Sunday 2:00–4:45; closed July 1–Labor Day; 202-338-8278; free.)

The U.S. Supreme Court Building now occupies the site of Calhoun's last Washington residence—Hills' Boardinghouse (First and A streets NE). Erected in 1815 as a temporary hall for Congress while the burned Capitol was being restored, the imposing brick structure stood until 1867 as a lodging house, then as the Old Capitol Prison for Confederate spies. President Monroe was inaugurated outside the building in 1817 (see the entry on James Monroe later in this section), and Calhoun died there. Also known as the Old Brick Capitol, the building was razed in 1932.

(See Chapter 5, SOUTH CAROLINA.)

CLAY, HENRY (1777–1852). Known as "the Great Compromiser" for his efforts to mediate between the North and the South, the Kentucky political leader and presidential candidate lived in Washington at various boardinghouses and hotels during his public career. During his tenure as secretary of state for President John Quincy Adams, he boarded on Lafayette Square at 17 Madison Place NW, the later home of William Henry Seward (see the entries on Adams and Seward in this section); then moved to the present Decatur House National Historic Landmark, at 748 Jackson Place NW (see the entry on Stephen Decatur later in this section).

One of his favorite residences was the National Hotel, where he died in Room 116. This 1816 structure, which with 300 rooms became one of the largest hotels in the nation, operated until 1931, then became the National Guard Armory. The building stood at the northeast corner of Pennsylvania Avenue and 6th Street NW until demolished in 1942.

(See Chapter 5, KENTUCKY, VIRGINIA.)

CLEVELAND, GROVER (1837–1908). Cleveland occupied the White House during two separate periods as the 22nd (1885–89) and 24th (1893–97) U.S. president. One staffer noted the bad cockroach problem that existed during his first term. The most notable social event of that term was his marriage in the Blue Room on June 2, 1886, to Frances Folsom, his 21-year-old ward. One of their five children was born in the Executive Mansion. (See the entry on the White House later in this section for tour information.)

Following their marriage, the couple's frequent refuge from the White House from 1886 to 1888 was an 1868 suburban farm called "Oak View" that Cleveland purchased; the press dubbed it "Red Top" because of its roof color. Located at 3536 Newark St. NW, its 27 wooded acres gave them some privacy from the rudely aggressive press of that era. Cleveland later sold the estate, and the house was razed in 1927. The present residence on the site retains the stone wall, driveway posts, and steps and walks from the original property. This area is now known as Cleveland Park.

(See MARYLAND, NEW JERSEY, NEW YORK in this chapter; also Chapter 1, MASSACHUSETTS, NEW HAMPSHIRE.)

CLINTON, GEORGE (1739–1812). As vice president from 1804 to 1812, Clinton resided in Washington hotels and boardinghouses. His last residence (1811–12), and where he died, was O'Neale's Hotel, long gone from the northwest corner of 21st and I streets NW.

(See NEW YORK in this chapter; also Chapter 2, MANHATTAN.)

COOLIDGE, CALVIN (1872–1933). "He don't say much," was a frequent description of the astringent, moody little man with the quacking voice who became the 30th U.S. president. He actually prided himself on doing little and saying less. As vice president under President Harding, Coolidge maintained a suite at the Willard Hotel because "a hotel apartment is plenty good enough for them," ranted Mrs. Harding (see the entries on Warren Gamaliel Harding and the Willard Hotel later in this section). There on August 21, 1923, Coolidge repeated the oath of office first administered to him by his father three weeks earlier in Vermont.

Coolidge occupied the White House from 1923 to 1929, except for several months in 1927. He concerned himself greatly with the mansion's expense accounts, checking into menus and the small affairs of staffing and running the household. Whatever social success the Coolidges enjoyed was due almost entirely to Grace Goodhue Coolidge, as sparkling and pleasant a personality as her husband was dour. Tragedy struck the White House in 1924 when their youngest son Calvin died of blood poisoning from a toe blister received while playing lawn tennis on the south grounds. This event, Coolidge believed from his puritan point of view, was the "price exacted for occupying the White House."

When the White House underwent renovation in 1927, the executive residence moved to the home of Eleanor Patterson at 15 Dupont Circle NW. In this four-story, 30-room brick dwelling, the Coolidges entertained Col. Charles Augustus Lindbergh on his return from Paris after his solo flight across the Atlantic (see the entry on Lindbergh later in this section). The 1903 house, designed by architect Stanford White, has hosted the Washington Club, a private women's organization, since 1951.

(See Chapter 1, MASSACHUSETTS, VERMONT; also Chapter 4, SOUTH DAKOTA.)

DAVIS, JEFFERSON FINIS (1808–1889). Before becoming president of the Confederate States, Davis served many years in Washington as congressman, cabinet member and senator. None of his homes survive. His last Washington residence (1857–60), the scene of many brilliant entertainments hosted by his attractive wife, Varina Howell Davis, stood at 1736 I St. NW.

(See Chapter 5, ALABAMA, GEORGIA, KENTUCKY, LOUISIANA, MISSISSIPPI, TENNESSEE, VIRGINIA.)

DECATUR, STEPHEN (1779–1820). The naval hero of the War of 1812 who first toasted "our country, right or wrong," Decatur built his home at 748 Jackson Place NW on Lafayette Square in 1818 and 1819. But he missed enemy guns, so he dueled with a naval colleague and died there—in the front room left of the entrance—from excruciatingly painful wounds but with "honor" intact. Decatur House National Historic Landmark is owned by of the National Trust for Historic Preservation, which maintains the three-story, red-brick Federal mansion. Designed by architect Benjamin Latrobe, the house was restored to its original inner dimensions in 1944 and contains notable woodwork, period furnishings and Decatur memorabilia. Later residents there included Henry Clay and Martin Van Buren (see the entries on Clay and Van Buren in this section). (Open Monday–Friday 10:00–2:00, Saturday–Sunday 12:00–4:00; 202-673-4030; admission.)

(See MARYLAND, PENNSYLVANIA in this chapter.)

DEWEY, GEORGE (1837–1917). The Spanish-American War made Admiral Dewey a hero in an age of national imperialism, and a public subscription was raised to buy him a Washington house. "Although 'simplicity' was part of his legend," wrote Dixon Wecter, "it was found that he would accept a house only in the most fashionable district." He married a widow and deeded the house to her, which didn't sit well either. This home, his last from 1908, stood at 1601 K St. NW until sometime after 1940. An office building now occupies the site.

(See Chapter 1, VERMONT.)

DILLINGER, JOHN HERBERT (1903–1934?).
Exhibit: The FBI Museum in the Hoover FBI Building, Pennsylvania Avenue between 9th and 10th streets NW, displays several items removed from the corpse of the man ambushed outside Chicago's Biograph Theater in 1934. Evidence seems shaky at best, however, that the G-men, anxious to get the outlaw who had run circles around them, got the right man. Documents missing for years revealed later that the corpse's fingerprints and eye color didn't match Dillinger's, and there were other discrepancies. The Bureau maintains official silence—perhaps the better part of valor—on the matter. (E Street entrance open Monday–Friday 9:00–4:00; 202-324-3000; free.)

(See Chapter 4, ILLINOIS, INDIANA, WISCONSIN.)

DIRKSEN, EVERETT McKINLEY (1896–1969). The longtime national legislator was mainly noted for his mellifluous baritone oratory on "applehood and mother pie" topics. Illinois sent him to Washington for two lengthy periods. As congressman for the decade from 1938 to 1948, he resided at the Mayflower Hotel, 1127 Connecticut Ave. NW; Huey Pierce Long was an earlier occupant there (see the entry on Long later in this section).

From 1950 to 1959, as a U.S. senator, Dirksen occupied an eighth-floor suite in the Berkshire Apartment building, 4201 Massachusetts Ave. NW.

(See Chapter 4, ILLINOIS; also Chapter 5, VIRGINIA.)

DOUGLAS, STEPHEN ARNOLD (1813–1861). The "Little Giant" of American Democratic politics, who fought hard to gain the White House but lost to Abraham Lincoln, lived in Washington hotel suites until 1857, then bought "Mount Julep"—so-called from its renown during his residence as "a resort for those who are fond of good eating and drinking." This four-story, brick dwelling at 201 I St. NW was the corner house of three attached homes known as "Douglas Row" (or "Minnesota Row"), later occupied by Ulysses Simpson Grant and William Tecumseh Sherman (see the entries on Lincoln, Grant and Sherman later in this section). Douglas lived there until 1861. The row was demolished over the period from 1934 to 1965.

(See NEW YORK in this chapter; also Chapter 1, VERMONT; also Chapter 4, ILLINOIS.)

DOUGLAS, WILLIAM ORVILLE (1898–1980). Controversial Supreme Court justice for 36 years, prominent outdoorsman, author and libertarian, Douglas's first Washington address (1936–38) was 3135 Ellicott St. NW (privately owned), built about 1920. He lived from 1949 to 1951 in the large private apartment house at 2029 Connecticut Ave. NW, dating from the early 1900s. His last home was 4852 Hutchins Place NW (privately owned).

(See Chapter 1, CONNECTICUT; also Chapter 4, MINNESOTA; also Chapter 6, WASHINGTON.)

DOUGLASS, FREDERICK (1818–1895). Both of the abolitionist leader's homes in Washington remain and are open to the public. The restored Victorian Douglass Townhouse at 316 A St. NE dates from about 1870 and was his home from 1871 to 1877. Today it houses the Museum of African Art, which owns and operates the building. Inside, the Douglass Memorial Room displays period furnishings and memorabilia, including his re-created study. (Open Monday–Friday 10:00–5:00, Saturday–Sunday 12:00–5:00; 202-287-3490; donation.)

Douglass' last home stands at 1411 W St. SE. This is "Cedar Hill," now Douglass Home National Historic Landmark, dating from about 1855. Douglass took special delight in living there, not only because of its scenic view but because the property's original owner had specified that no Negro or Irishman should ever acquire title. The two-story, 20-room brick home that he bought on 15 acres overlooking the Anacostia River is now operated by the National Park Service and has been restored and decorated as it looked when Douglass died there. Visitors may see the desk given to him by Harriet Beecher Stowe, his library, canes and many other personal possessions. Here Douglass wrote his classic autobiography *The Life and Times of Frederick Douglass* (1881). (Open April 1–August 31, daily 9:00–5:00; September 1–March 31, Monday–Friday 9:00–4:00, Saturday–Sunday 10:00–5:00; 202-889-1736; free.)

(See MARYLAND in this chapter; also Chapter 1, MASSACHUSETTS.)

DULLES, JOHN FOSTER (1888–1959). The secretary of state remembered for his "brinkmanship" Cold War policies was born at the home of his grandfather, diplomat John Watson Foster, at 1405 I St. NW, the present site of a government building. His last home (1953–59) was 2740 32nd St. NW (privately owned).

(See NEW YORK in this chapter; also Chapter 2, MANHATTAN.)

EISENHOWER, DWIGHT DAVID (1890–1969). Popular World War II commander and 34th U.S. president, "Ike" occupied the White House from 1953 to 1961. "Strangely," wrote First Lady Mamie Eisenhower in 1961, "my husband and I have lived in this home longer than in any other." "Mamie pink" became the dominating color of furnishings and carpets. The White House was virtually a new building when they moved in, its interior having been rebuilt from the ground up during the previous administration of Harry S. Truman (see the entry on Truman later in this section). Eisenhower's unofficial life was mostly devoted to grinning and golf, a game he passionately practiced on the south grounds of the Executive Mansion as well as on countless greens elsewhere. Yet for all his outdoor activity, he suffered several major illnesses in office and spent long, bedridden intervals during both his terms. Most Washington observers believed that he left few permanent marks of his stay aside from golf-shoe indentations on the floor of the Oval Office in the west wing. But historians are beginning to give him higher marks, especially for his astute foresight and warnings regarding the nuclear arms race. (See the entry on the White House later in this section for tour information.)

(See MARYLAND, PENNSYLVANIA in this chapter; also Chapter 2, MANHATTAN; also Chapter 4, KANSAS, MICHIGAN; also Chapter 5, GEORGIA, VIRGINIA; also Chapter 6, COLORADO, TEXAS.)

ELLINGTON, EDWARD KENNEDY "DUKE" (1899–1974). A Washington native, the composer-bandleader enjoyed an early musical success, enabling him to move his parents to his home at 1212 T St. NW in 1916. The house, which dates from about 1885, remains privately owned. Its current owner reports that he is considering application for National Register status.

(See Chapter 2, MANHATTAN.)

FILLMORE, MILLARD (1800–1874). The forgettable 13th U.S. president, a man of great rectitude if not surpassing intellect, occupied the White House from 1850 to 1853—"this temple of inconvenience," he called it—following the death of President Taylor (see the entry on Zachary Taylor later in this section). A handsome but unpopular president, Fillmore was often called a "wife-made man" because of his reliance on schoolteacher Abigail Powers Fillmore for rounding out his poor, late-adolescent education. She, in fact, installed the first White House library on the second floor in what is today the Yellow Oval Room. In this room, the heart of the Fillmore White House, the family received informal visitors and spent an hour together late each night before retiring. (See the entry on the White House later in this section for tour information.)

(See NEW YORK, WEST VIRGINIA in this chapter.)

FRANKFURTER, FELIX (1882–1965). Noted for his legal scholarship, brilliant mind and tireless talk, the Supreme Court justice had several homes in Washington. As a minor bureaucrat rooming with other ambitious young men, he occupied his first from 1912 to 1914, a high, red-brick row house at 1727 19th St. NW—dubbed the "House of Truth" for all of the late-night debates that settled Everything. Walter Lippmann was a later occupant there (see the entry on Lippmann later in this section). The house, built about 1890, remains privately owned.

Much later when Frankfurter became an associate justice, he lived at 1511 30th St. NW, an 1840 home that remains a private residence. His rented home from 1947 to 1962 was 3018 Dumbarton Ave. NW, also private.

(See Chapter 1, MASSACHUSETTS.)

GARFIELD, JAMES ABRAM (1831–1881). The 20th U.S. president and second assassination victim in that office built a three-story brick home at the northeast corner of 13th and I streets NW in 1869, enlarged it in 1878 and resided there until he entered the White House for an occupancy that lasted only six months in 1881. His home, sold by his wife in 1895, was demolished in 1964.

Garfield was interested in the history of the Executive Mansion and intended to refurnish it based on his research at the Library of Congress, but Charles Guiteau's bullet ended that. He lingered on, mostly in the White House, for 80 days of clumsy medical attempts to save his life; his back wound, though serious, would hardly

be considered life-threatening today. (See the entry on the White House later in this section for tour information.)

(See NEW JERSEY in this chapter; also Chapter 4, OHIO.)

GOMPERS, SAMUEL (1850–1924). The founder of the American Federation of Labor, which he headed for all but one year between 1886 and 1924, owned only one home; it stands at 3501 Ordway St. NW, a 1917 dwelling that gratified his "intense desire to have a home with four separate walls that were not attached to anyone else's walls." His previous, rented home (1902–19) stands at 2122 First St. NW. Both houses are privately owned though identified by markers.

(See Chapter 2, MANHATTAN.)

GRANT, ULYSSES SIMPSON (1822–1885). The Civil War commander of the Union armies and the 18th U.S. president lived from 1867 to 1869 at 205 I St. NW. The four-story double house stood next door to a house in "Douglas Row" earlier occupied by Stephen Arnold Douglas. Grant, unable to afford this dwelling himself, accepted the purchase price from a group of New York financiers who raised the amount for him. When he entered the White House, he sold this home to his army compatriot William Tecumseh Sherman (see the entries on Douglas and Sherman in this section).

Grant occupied the White House from 1869 to 1877. Like the public who elected the war hero, Grant considered the presidency more a reward than a responsibility. For the mansion itself, however, he undertook a major renovation in 1873 that replaced rotting timbers and cracked, sagging ceilings. He also replaced its Georgian interior simplicity with fashionable ornamentation that later received the name "steamboat gothic." In the plush East Room he witnessed the wedding of his daughter Nellie in 1874. Julia Dent Grant's writing table and a Grant sofa were returned to the White House public rooms in 1961 and 1962. In contrast to the experience of most first ladies there, Mrs. Grant wrote that "life at the White House was like a bright and beautiful dream and we were immeasurably happy"—but she was, in many ways, an extraordinary woman. (See the entry on the White House later in this section for tour information.)

(See NEW JERSEY, NEW YORK in this chapter; also Chapter 2, MANHATTAN; also Chapter 4, ILLINOIS, MICHIGAN MISSOURI, OHIO; also Chapter 5, VIRGINIA; also Chapter 6, WASHINGTON.)

HAMILTON, EDITH (1867–1963). The educator and classical scholar bought her last home in 1943. Privately owned, the house at 2448 Massachusetts Ave. NW backs against Rock Creek Park.

(See MARYLAND in this chapter; also Chapter 1, MAINE; also Chapter 2, MANHATTAN; also Chapter 4, INDIANA.)

HANNA, MARCUS ALONZO "MARK" (1837–1904). The businessman, Republican senator, and political mentor of President McKinley occupied the 1828 brick Tayloe-Cameron House at 23 Madison Place NW, Lafayette Square, during McKinley's administration from 1897 to 1901 (see the entry on William McKinley later in this section). So influential was Hanna as an advisor that this dwelling was dubbed "the Little White House." It is privately owned.

(See Chapter 4, OHIO; also Chapter 5, GEORGIA.)

HARDING, WARREN GAMALIEL (1865–1923). Probably the most jovially inept chief executive that Americans have somehow found and elected, the handsome 29th U.S. president and his dowdy, snappish wife ("The Duchess") made the oddest of White House odd couples during their residence from 1921 to 1923. Though Harding supported Prohibition, bootleg liquor flowed freely (The Duchess mixing) at the crony poker parties that became the main social activity for their tenure. Harding's extramarital affair with Nan Britton took place amid the umbrellas and galoshes of White House closets. Also on the sly was the Teapot Dome scandal, the consequences of which Harding died just in time to avoid. The only remnant of this bemusing period is located on the White House lawn outside the East Wing, where a magnolia tree planted by Harding still grows. (See the entry on the White House later in this section for tour information.)

The Hardings occupied 2314 Wyoming Ave. NW during his senatorial career from 1915 to 1921; the house dates from about 1914 and is privately owned.

(See Chapter 4, OHIO; also Chapter 6, CALIFORNIA.)

HARRISON, BENJAMIN (1833–1901). As the 23rd U.S. president, grandson of the ninth, Harrison lived in the White House from 1889 to 1893, his term sandwiched between the two of Grover Cleveland (see the entry on Cleveland earlier in this section). Electricity was installed in the building during his tenure, and lights were often left burning because of the Harrisons' timidity with the switches. An accomplished painter of china, Caroline Scott Harrison began the White House china collection, to which many presidents have added and which is still used at state functions. Some five layers of old flooring, stacked like geological strata, were removed during these years from the mansion's ground floor, and rooms were redesigned—though the result was far from the "new White House" that the First Lady envisioned. The capable Mrs. Harrison died in the White House in 1892, and her funeral was held in the East Room. (See the entry on the White House later in this section for tour information.)

(See Chapter 4, INDIANA, OHIO.)

HARRISON, WILLIAM HENRY (1773–1841). The 68-year-old Indian fighter who became the ninth U.S. president had held the office for only a month in 1841 when exhaustion and pneumonia from the "log-cabin campaign" caught up with him, ending the shortest presidential tenure in the nation's history. Harrison, actually a Virginia aristocrat who knew little of log cabins, was the first president of only two to die within the walls of the White House itself and the first to lie in state in the East Room. (See the entry on the White House later in this section for tour information.)

(See Chapter 4, INDIANA, OHIO; also Chapter 5, VIRGINIA.)

HAYES, RUTHERFORD BIRCHARD (1822–1893). Hayes, as 19th U.S. president, was probably the most puritanical chief executive to occupy the White House. The first couple brought an unrelenting righteousness into the mansion with daily family worship, Sunday singing of hymns and complete abstention from alcohol. Lucy Webb Hayes, tagged "Lemonade Lucy," gently but firmly refused to serve alcoholic beverages; water, buttermilk and fruit punch flowed like wine, joked thirsty guests, countless numbers of whom departed the premises healthier, if seldom more edified than they arrived. The couple celebrated their silver wedding anniversary in the White House. Hayes was the second of three Presidents not popularly elected, the first being John Quincy Adams (see the entry on Adams earlier in this section), the third, Gerald R. Ford. Samuel J. Tilden had more votes in 1876, but a stacked electoral commission gave Hayes the presidency. After his gratuitous term, the couple retired with unflagging rectitude to years of additional good works in their native Ohio. (See the entry on the White House later in this section for tour information.)

(See Chapter 4, OHIO.)

HEARST, WILLIAM RANDOLPH (1863–1951). As a two-term New York City congressman ambitious for a much larger political career than voters saw fit to grant him, the powerful publisher leased the former dwelling of Elihu Root (see the entry on Root later in this section) at 722 Jackson Place NW across from the White House. "He would not have far to move if his hopes were realized," as one biographer wrote. This was Hearst's city home from 1903 to 1907.

(See Chapter 2, MANHATTAN; also Chapter 6, CALIFORNIA.)

HENRY, JOSEPH (1797–1878). As first secretary of the Smithsonian Institution, the physicist famed for his pioneering research in electromagnetism lived in the first Smithsonian building, sometimes called the "Castle on the Mall." The red-sandstone structure with Norman towers, designed and built by architect James Renwick from 1847 to 1855, housed the entire Smithsonian complex for 30 years. Henry occupied rooms in the east wing from 1847 to his death. Today the building, much remodeled and enlarged, is still a Washington landmark and serves as the Institution's administrative headquarters and visitors' information center. It is located at 1000 Jefferson Drive SW. (Open daily 10:00–5:30; 202-357-1300; free.)

(See NEW JERSEY in this chapter.)

HOLMES, OLIVER WENDELL, JR. (1841–1935). The first Washington home of the Supreme Court justice stands at 716 Jackson Place on Lafayette Square. Built in the late 1860s, this three-story brick house more recently contained offices of former President Lyndon Baines Johnson and Vice President Nelson Aldrich Rockefeller (see the

entries on Johnson and Rockefeller later in this section). In 1969 it was designated as the official Washington residence for former presidents. Holmes's later permanent home (1904–35) stands at 1720 I St. NW, a four-story, privately owned brick house.

(See Chapter 1, MASSACHUSETTS.)

HOOVER, HERBERT CLARK (1874–1964). As a bright, popular cabinet member for two presidents, the affluent mining engineer who would become the 31st U.S. president lived and entertained lavishly at 2300 S St. NW (1921–29), a three-story brick house that is now occupied by the Chancery of Burma.

Those were his best Washington days. In the White House, which he occupied from 1929 to 1933, Hoover became a glum, workaholic President in a bad time, a man whose political philosophy prevented any real address to the social and economic plight of the Great Depression. He used the Lincoln Bedroom as a study but was probably unable to enjoy his historic environs; his cruel, unproductive hours might have soon killed him if voters had granted him another term. As it was, he lived to a mellow 90. Lou Henry Hoover, the gracious, accomplished First Lady, did much to locate and restore White House treasures, and social functions under her guidance achieved unprecedented brilliance. (See the entry on the White House later in this section for tour information.)

(See Chapter 2, MANHATTAN; also Chapter 4, IOWA; also Chapter 5, VIRGINIA; also Chapter 6, CALIFORNIA, OREGON.)

HOOVER, JOHN EDGAR (1895–1972). The 48-year director of the FBI—an untouchable public icon in his time but whose questionable uses of his immense power heavily damaged his posthumous reputation—occupied only two homes throughout his life. He was born at 413 Seward Square SE, a two and one-half-story, stone house where he lived with his mother until her death in 1938. This house no longer stands.

In 1939 he bought a recently built house at 4936 30th Place in Forest Hills, a two-story dwelling of red brick. Hoover planted rose gardens and filled his home with antique jade pieces and bronzes. After he died there, his closest friend and FBI associate, Clyde Tolson, occupied the property until his own death. It remains privately owned.

HOPKINS, HARRY LLOYD (1890–1946). Prominent social worker and close advisor to President Franklin Delano Roosevelt, Hopkins was a transient dweller who never settled in one place for long. His lengthiest Washington residence was the White House, where Roosevelt installed him from 1940 to 1943 in the second-floor Lincoln Bedroom. (See the entry on Roosevelt later in this section; see also the entry on the White House later in this section for tour information.)

A later residence (1943–45) stands at 3340 N St. NW, a private house dating from about 1830.

(See Chapter 4, IOWA.)

HUGHES, CHARLES EVANS (1862–1948). Hughes served twice on the Supreme Court during his long public career. As associate justice from 1911 to 1916, he built a house in 1910 at 2100 16th St. NW (privately owned), which he sold when he became the Republican presidential candidate in 1916. This is the Bulgarian Embassy today. His rented home from 1921 to 1925, during his tenure as secretary of state, was 1529 18th St. NW (privately owned). Hughes House National Historic Landmark at 2223 R St. NW, Sheraton Circle, was the last home (1930–47) of the chief justice, a four-story structure built in 1907 and presently the Burmese Embassy.

(See NEW YORK in this chapter; also Chapter 2, MANHATTAN.)

HULL, CORDELL (1871–1955). From 1941 until his death, the longtime congressman, secretary of state, and "father of the United Nations" resided in a seven-room suite at the 1916 Wardman Park Hotel—now the Sheraton Park—located at 2660 Woodley Road NW.

(See Chapter 5, TENNESSEE.)

HUMPHREY, HUBERT HORATIO (1911–1978). The last home, from 1966, of the ebullient liberal senator and vice president was a 20th-century condominium at 550 N St. SW, still privately owned.

(See MARYLAND in this chapter; also Chapter 4, MINNESOTA, SOUTH DAKOTA.)

JACKSON, ANDREW (1767–1845). The seventh U.S. president, a thin-skinned old soldier whose duels outnumbered most men's fistfights, often took political criticism as personal insult and liked to threaten opponents with shooting or hanging. He occupied the White House from 1829 to 1837. The largest mob scene the building has ever experienced occurred on his inauguration day, when thousands of citizens inundated the stately East Room in a swinish grab for refreshments, leaving draperies in rags, windows broken, china smashed, puddles of punch on the floor and mud on the furniture. The executive skill of "the people's president" consisted mostly of intimidation and verbal abuse; he went through cabinet secretaries like figs for breakfast. Yet, in a crude, frontier country, Jackson's bluster made him the most enormously popular president before Franklin Delano Roosevelt. He refurnished and enlarged the ravaged mansion elegantly, adding the North Portico and making palatial showplaces of the public rooms. With only fireplaces for heat, however, those rooms remained drafty for the old warrior: "Hell itself couldn't warm that corner," he snarled. Today those same public rooms display several of Jackson's expensive acquisitions for the White House, and the magnolia trees he planted in memory of his wife Rachel still flower brilliantly near the Rose Garden. (See the entry on the White House later in this section for tour information.)

(See Chapter 5, NORTH CAROLINA, SOUTH CAROLINA, TENNESSEE.)

JARRELL, RANDALL (1914–1965). As consultant in poetry for the Library of Congress from 1956 to 1958, the brilliant poet-critic and teacher resided at 3916 Jenifer St. NW (privately owned).

(See Chapter 4, OHIO; also Chapter 5, NORTH CAROLINA; also Chapter 6, CALIFORNIA, TEXAS.)

JEFFERSON, THOMAS (1743–1826). America's third President, probably the brainiest, most innovative and accomplished man ever to occupy the White House (1801–09), was a longtime widower whose egalitarian behavior rankled status-conscious Washington. He canceled all orders of ranking, precedence and seating, even shaking hands instead of receiving bows from his guests. When Jefferson moved in, the mansion was still unfinished; he made the first sketches for the south portico himself and drew up plans for the long terraces and colonnades that are still retained in the west-wing pavilion. Jefferson described the mansion as "big enough for two emperors, one pope, and the grand lama in the bargain." Whispering in the White House was unnecessary, he assured his guests, because "we are alone and our walls have no ears." The first infant born in the White House was a Jefferson grandson. All that remains of Jefferson's tenure today is his 1804 bronze inkstand in the Red Room—and, of course, the venerable outer walls and porticos of his exterior design. (See the entry on the White House later in this section for tour information.)

Jefferson's residence in 1800 and 1801 as vice president—and for 15 days after his first inauguration as president—was Mrs. Conrad's 1796 boarding house at the northwest corner of C Street and New Jersey Avenue SE. There he occupied a parlor and bedroom and sat at the foot of a table for 30. This building later became the Varnum Hotel, razed in 1929 for the present Longworth House Office Building.

(See PENNSYLVANIA in this chapter; also Chapter 2, MANHATTAN; also Chapter 5, VIRGINIA.)

JOHNSON, ANDREW (1808–1875). The 17th U.S. president, who had the thankless task of following Abraham Lincoln to the White House (see the entry on Lincoln later in this section), occupied the mansion from 1865 to 1869. Despite his drunken inauguration speech as vice president, Johnson was probably one of the most principled and courageous men, not excepting Lincoln himself, who has ever graced the White House. Basically a Southern Democrat, he directly confronted the vindictive rage of Northern Republican radicals against the South while steadily maintaining Lincoln's liberal reconstruction aims. As a result, he became the most maligned, futile and persecuted president of our history, escaping conviction of an unjust impeachment bill by only one vote. Johnson's Cabinet Room on the second floor is now the restored, Victorian-furnished Treaty Room containing many original pieces. It was used for cabinet meetings by every succeeding president until 1902. (See the entry on the White House later in this section for tour information.)

(See Chapter 5, NORTH CAROLINA, SOUTH CAROLINA, TENNESSEE.)

JOHNSON, LYNDON BAINES (1908–1973). The 36th U.S. president, a man of domineering personality and consummate political skills, might have entered history as one of our greatest executives; his decision to maintain a war without popular support, however, ended his career in an abyss. A longtime senator and Washington resident before he entered the White House, Johnson dwelled longest (1943–61) at 4921 30th Place NW in the Forest Hills area, a three-story brick house (privately owned). As vice president, he bought "The Elms" at 4040 52nd St. NW from Washington hostess Perle Mesta and lived there from 1961 to 1963. Johnson installed piped music in each room plus a heated swimming pool. This hilltop French chateau, set far back from the street and secluded by tall shrubbery, now belongs to the Republic of Algeria and serves as its embassy.

Johnson occupied the White House from 1963 to 1969 and provided for its constant care by establishing a full-time curator to supervise all future renovation. Claudia Taylor "Lady Bird" Johnson became the most publicly active first lady since Eleanor Roosevelt (see the entry on Roosevelt later in this section). *A White House Diary* (1970), her memoir, details six of the mansion's long years. (See the entry on the White House later in this section for tour information.)

(See MARYLAND in this chapter; also Chapter 4, MICHIGAN; also Chapter 6, TEXAS.)

KEFAUVER, ESTES (1903–1963). The popular senator, foe of organized crime and 1956 vice presidential candidate bought his two-story, white brick home at 4848 Upton St. NW (privately owned) in 1948. His last Washington residence, from 1958, also remains privately owned at 4929 Hillbrook Lane NW.

(See Chapter 5, TENNESSEE.)

KENNEDY, JOHN FITZGERALD (1917–1963). As congressman and senator from Massachusetts for 14 years, Kennedy rented and occupied four Georgetown houses, all privately owned. The two-story, white brick dwelling at 3271 P St. NW was his first married home (1953–54) in Washington; and the couple's last residence (1956–61) before moving into the White House was 3307 N St. NW, a red brick, 18th-century townhouse.

The Kennedys occupied the White House from 1961 to 1963. This period, cut tragically short by the assassination of the 35th president, achieved a retrospective aura of "Camelot," when a youthful vigor and grace permeated the mansion. Small children romped the halls again, and America had never seen such a glamorous first lady as Jacquelyn Bouvier Kennedy. She took upon herself the authentic refurnishing of the White House public rooms with antiques, paintings and historical items, leaving a permanent heritage there for all Americans. "Everything in the White House must have a reason for being there," she said. "It would be sacrilege merely to 'redecorate' it—a word I hate. It must be restored—and that has nothing to do with decoration." (See the entry on the White House later in this section for tour information.)

(See MARYLAND, NEW YORK in this chapter; also Chapter 1, MASSACHUSETTS, RHODE ISLAND; also Chapter 2, BRONX; also Chapter 4, MICHIGAN; also Chapter 5, FLORIDA, VIRGINIA; also Chapter 6, TEXAS.)

KENNEDY, ROBERT FRANCIS (1925–1968). The brother of President Kennedy, and his advisor and attorney general—also a Democratic political leader and contender for the 1968 presidential nomination—Robert Kennedy lived at 3214 S St. NW (1951–57) during his early public career as counsel for various Senate committees. The house remains privately owned.

(See NEW YORK in this chapter; also Chapter 1, MASSACHUSETTS; also Chapter 2, BRONX; also Chapter 5, FLORIDA, VIRGINIA; also Chapter 6, CALIFORNIA.)

KEY, FRANCIS SCOTT (1779–1843). The prominent lawyer, chiefly remembered for writing "The Star-Spangled Banner" as he observed the 1814 British bombardment of Fort McHenry in Baltimore, bought "The Maples" at 630 South Carolina Ave. SE in 1815 but lived there only briefly. This brick, two-story, 1796 dwelling is now the privately owned Friendship House, with its entrance at 619 D St. SE.

The last remnant of Key's longtime earlier home at 3518 M St. NW, a two and one-half-story brick dwelling built about 1802, stood 100 feet west of Key Bridge over the Potomac River until 1948. Key lived there from 1808 to 1828, the period when he saw the flag under fire and wrote the anthem. Parts of the house were removed to storage according to plans and promises to rebuild

it; but house, plans and promises are still in storage.

(See MARYLAND in this chapter.)

LA FOLLETTE, ROBERT MARION (1855–1925). The longtime senator and Progressive Party candidate for president in 1924, La Follette rented several addresses during his Washington career. He lived from 1909 to 1913 at 1864 Wyoming Ave. NW, a four-story home built about 1900 and presently occupied by private apartments. La Follette's last home (1923–25), and where he died, is located at 2112 Wyoming Ave. NW, now the Senegalese Chancery.

(See Chapter 4, WISCONSIN.)

L'ENFANT, PIERRE CHARLES (1754–1825). Engaged in 1791 by President Washington to plan the federal city of Washington, D.C., the Paris-born architect did exactly that, and the basic layout he drew is seen today in the city's malls and rayed avenues. Unfortunately L'Enfant was a devilish man to work with, and his unbending perversity led to his dismissal in 1792; what remains of his scheme is a triumph over insistent self-defeat. His lodging site remains unknown, but long tradition holds that he headquartered himself in one of Washington's oldest buildings—the 1765 Old Stone House National Historic Landmark at 3051 M St. NW—while surveying and drawing plans for the city. This will probably never be verified, and some authorities discredit the story altogether. The house predates L'Enfant's streets, at any rate; restored in 1959 by the National Park Service, it displays period furnishings and craft demonstrations. (Open daily 9:00–5:00; 202-426-6851; free.)

LEWIS, MERIWETHER (1774–1809). Virginia soldier and co-leader of the Lewis and Clark Expedition, Lewis served as private secretary to President Jefferson from 1801 to 1803 and helped the president plan the expedition. He occupied White House quarters during this period and left from there to recruit and train his exploring party for the two-year journey to and from the Pacific coast. (See the entry on the White House later in this section for tour information.)

(See Chapter 4, MISSOURI, NORTH DAKOTA; also Chapter 5, TENNESSEE, VIRGINIA; also Chapter 6, OREGON, WASHINGTON.)

LINCOLN, ABRAHAM (1809–1865).
LINCOLN, MARY TODD (1818–1882).

Lincoln's first residence in the city during his one term in Congress (1847–49) was Mrs. Sprigg's boardinghouse, which stood in the block of five houses known as Carroll Row, now occupied by the main building of the Library of Congress, First Street and Independence Avenue SE.

As the 16th president, Lincoln and his family occupied the White House from 1861 to 1865. His office and cabinet room, where he signed the Emancipation Proclamation, is now the Lincoln Bedroom on the second floor, reserved for overnight White House guests and containing furnishings and items used during his administration. Mary Lincoln, a witty, intelligent but also extremely high-strung woman whose unpredictably emotional behavior made her the object of much unkind gossip, was a compulsive buyer of new White House furnishings and clothing for herself. On one occasion, when the President was asked to approve an overextended purchase, he angrily refused. "I'll pay it out of my own pocket first," he raged. "It would stink in the nostrils of the American people to have it said that the President had approved a bill overrunning an appropriation of $20,000 for *flub dubs* for this damned old house, when the soldiers cannot have blankets." The Lincolns lost their 11-year-old son Willie there in 1862, a grief that deranged Mrs. Lincoln for a time and that neither of the couple completely surmounted. (See the entry on the White House later in this section for tour information.)

Lincoln often used Anderson Cottage at the U.S. Soldiers' Home as a summer retreat; he prepared the final draft of the Emancipation Proclamation there in 1862 (see the entry on James Buchanan earlier in this chapter).

Exhibits: Lincoln's death site, the Petersen House, stands directly across the street from Ford's Theater at 516 10th St. NW. Built by tailor William Petersen in 1849, this three-story, brick rooming house, purchased by the government in 1896, remains substantially as it looked in 1865. The tiny bedroom where the president lingered throughout the night after being shot—and where Secretary of War Edwin M. Stanton uttered the words, "Now he belongs to the ages" when Lincoln died at 7:22 AM on April 15—has been restored with period furnishings (original contents of the room are displayed by the Chicago Histor-

ical Society; see Chapter 4). Mary Todd Lincoln kept a nightlong vigil in the front parlor, and Vice President Andrew Johnson numbered among the stunned officials who stopped that night to sit with her. Memorabilia of Lincoln's last hours there are displayed by the National Park Service. (Open daily, 9:00–5:00; free.)

Also see *Exhibits,* in the entry on John Wilkes Booth in this section.

(See PENNSYLVANIA in this chapter; also Chapter 4, ILLINOIS, INDIANA, MICHIGAN, OHIO; also Chapter 5, KENTUCKY, TENNESSEE.)

LINDBERGH, CHARLES AUGUSTUS (1902–1974).

Exhibit: The aviator's Ryan monoplane, *The Spirit of St. Louis,* in which he made the first solo flight across the Atlantic in 1927, is enshrined and displayed in the Air and Space Building of the Smithsonian Institution, Independence Avenue and 9th Street SW. (Open 10:00–5:30 daily; 202-357-1300; free.)

(See NEW JERSEY, NEW YORK in this chapter; also Chapter 1, CONNECTICUT; also Chapter 4, MICHIGAN, MINNESOTA, MISSOURI; also Chapter 6, HAWAII.)

LIPPMANN, WALTER (1889–1975). The first married home (1917) of the highly influential journalist and political observer was the privately owned brick house at 1727 19th St. NW, the former bachelor quarters of Felix Frankfurter. In 1938, he bought the house in which Alexander Graham Bell had formerly installed his parents at 3434 Volta Place NW, Lippmann's home until 1946 (see the entries on Frankfurter and Bell earlier in this chapter).

His home from 1946 to 1967 was 3525 Woodley Road NW (privately owned)—"only a little smaller than Grand Central Station," as one observer described it, ample space for the dinner parties that sometimes welcomed hundreds of Lippmann's carefully selected guests. This house was the former deanery of Washington Cathedral.

(See NEW YORK in this chapter; also Chapter 2, MANHATTAN.)

LODGE, HENRY CABOT (1850–1924). As the chief opponent of U.S. entry into the League of Nations, the Republican senator and historian from Massachusetts became one of the most powerful men in Washington. His longtime home stood at 1765 Massachusetts Ave. NW, a double house combined into one. Lodge had a special door cut from the garden so that President Theodore Roosevelt could enter unobserved from the back yard to consult with Lodge (see the entry on Roosevelt later in this section). The site of this house is now occupied by the Brookings Institution.

(See Chapter 1, MASSACHUSETTS.)

LONG, HUEY PIERCE (1893–1935). The senatorial career of "the Kingfish," the political demagogue and virtual dictator of Louisiana whose presidential aspirations were cut short by assassination, lasted only three years. He resided from 1932 to 1934 in the luxury Mayflower Hotel, located at 1127 Connecticut Ave. NW since 1925.

(See Chapter 5, LOUISIANA.)

McCARTHY, JOSEPH RAYMOND (1908–1957). "McCarthyism," a synonym for witch-hunting, was this Wisconsin senator's lasting, destructive contribution to the political lexicon. In Washington, he bunked casually with friends or associates during much of his 11-year tenure. He resided in Apartment 12 at 3335 C St. SE in 1950 when he began making his sensational, phony "disclosures" of Communists in government. His last home from 1953 remains privately owned at 20 3rd St. NE, a duplex the McCarthys shared with his mother-in-law.

(See Chapter 4, WISCONSIN.)

McCLELLAN, GEORGE BRINTON (1826–1885). The vain commander of the Army of the Potomac (though a hesitant fighter) and 1864 presidential candidate, McClellan occupied a house in 1861 and 1862 that stood at the northwest corner of H and 15th streets NW. Such was the general's high opinion of himself that when President Lincoln came to consult, McClellan would keep him waiting in the parlor or go to bed without seeing him (see the entry on Lincoln earlier in this section).

(See NEW JERSEY, PENNSYLVANIA in this chapter; also Chapter 2, MANHATTAN.)

McKINLEY, WILLIAM (1843–1901). As a Republican congressman, the eventual 25th U.S. presi-

dent resided at the Ebbitt House hotel, which stood until 1926 at the southeast corner of F and 14th streets NW, the present site of the National Press Club. He also maintained an office there but rarely entertained because of his wife's epilepsy.

The political protege of Ohio promoter Mark Hanna, McKinley occupied the White House from 1897 to 1901. He was a gentle—some said saintly—bear of a man, well-meaning if not overly bright. As a leader, he meekly permitted the "yellow journalism" of William Randolph Hearst to result in the Spanish-American War and several other imperialistic ventures—which did, however, make him an enormously popular president (see the entries on Hanna and Hearst earlier in this section). During his White House residence, according to Smithsonian historian Margaret B. Klapthor, "the house itself was in extremely bad condition. When large public receptions were held, the staff had to bolster up the floors on the first floor with beams and bricks in the cellar." (See the entry on the White House later in this section for tour information.)

(See NEW YORK in this chapter; also Chapter 4, OHIO.)

MADISON, JAMES (1751–1836).
MADISON, DOLLEY PAYNE TODD (1768–1849).
As secretary of state for President Jefferson, Madison resided at 1333 F St. NW from 1801 to 1809. The three-story brick house, long gone, was one of official Washington's brightest gathering places; and the city has probably never seen a more brilliant, extroverted hostess than Dolley Madison, who also served frequently as the White House hostess for the widowed Jefferson. The F Street house, with its coach and stable outbuildings, was later owned by John Quincy Adams and stood just east of a house occupied by James Buchanan (see the entries on Jefferson, Adams and Buchanan earlier in this section).

The fourth U.S. president and his jolly wife, who towered above his 5'4" birdlike frame (she called him "my darling little husband"), occupied the White House from 1809 to 1814. The War of 1812 was unfortunately the main business of this administration. Though president until 1817, Madison left the mansion in August of 1814 to assume personal command of a military unit in Maryland—the only president who has ever exercised rank as commander-in-chief on an actual battlefield. The British broke through and burned the White House plus many other public buildings. Just before they arrived, however, Dolley Madison insisted on removing the 1800 Gilbert Stuart portrait of George Washington—the only item saved from the "first" (pre-1814) White House; today this painting hangs permanently in the East Room. The mansion was not reconstructed in time for further Madison residence. (See the entry on Stuart later in this section; see also the entry on the White House later in this section for tour information.)

Octagon House National Historic Landmark at 1799 New York Ave. NW was the nation's Executive Mansion in 1814 and 1815. There in the tower treaty room just over the entrance, Madison signed the Treaty of Ghent ending the War of 1812; and the round, inlaid table on which he did so, plus other original and period furnishings, may be seen there. Now owned and maintained by the American Institute of Architects, the 1798–1800 Federal house is actually hexagonal in shape. (Open Tuesday–Friday 10:00–4:00, Saturday–Sunday 1:00–4:00; 202-638-3105; donation.)

The Madisons next moved to the corner house of the "Seven Buildings" (at the northwest corner of Pennsylvania Avenue and 19th Street NW), where the President finished out his term (1815–17). This dwelling at 1901 Pennsylvania Ave., part of a row built about 1796 and demolished in 1959, housed the first State Department in the city under John Marshall, a later chief justice, as well as other notable residents (see the entry on Marshall later in this section).

After Madison's death, Dolley Madison remained socially prominent, and her last home (1836–49) became the elite center of Lafayette Square. She rescued her husband's papers from a fire there in 1848. This house at Madison Place and H Street NW, built from 1818 to 1820 and bought by Madison in 1828 for his retirement home, has been extensively altered over the years and is now occupied by the Federal Judiciary Center.

Exhibit: Tradition insists that Dolley Madison, during her 1814 flight from the burning White House, stopped briefly at Dumbarton House, 2715 Q St. NW, where a second-floor display shows some of her clothing; people always noticed what Dolley wore, and visitors there still can. The restored 1799 mansion, moved in 1915 from its

original site on a spot where the street was later extended, is national headquarters of the Society of Colonial Dames and contains fine colonial furnishings and interiors. (Open September 1– June 30, Monday–Saturday 9:00–12:00; 202-337-2288; donation.)

(See PENNSYLVANIA in this chapter; also Chapter 2, MANHATTAN; also Chapter 5, NORTH CAROLINA, VIRGINIA.)

MARSHALL, GEORGE CATLETT (1880–1959). As a staff assistant to Gen. John Joseph Pershing following World War I (see the entry on Pershing later in this section), the soldier who would become army chief of staff himself in World War II resided in a leased apartment suite at the Envoy Towers, 2400 16th St. NW, from 1919 to 1921. Rose Page Wilson details an account of Marshall when he lived there in *General Marshall Remembered* (1968). Private apartments still occupy this building.

(See PENNSYLVANIA in this chapter; also Chapter 5, GEORGIA, NORTH CAROLINA, VIRGINIA; also Chapter 6, WASHINGTON.)

MARSHALL, JOHN (1775–1835). The nation's most notable chief justice lived for years during Court sessions at Mrs. Peyton's exclusive boardinghouse, a brick dwelling that stood at the northwest corner of Pennsylvania Avenue and John Marshall Place NW—the present area of a new court facility complex. One of Marshall's rooming houses that still stands is the Ringgold-Carroll House at 1801 F St. NW (privately owned), a four-story brick house built in 1825.

(See Chapter 5, VIRGINIA.)

MELLON, ANDREW WILLIAM (1855–1937). The building now used as headquarters of the National Trust for Historic Preservation at 1785 Massachusetts Ave. NW was originally the luxury McCormick Apartments. Mellon occupied a fifth-floor suite there as secretary of the treasury (1921–23) and intermittently from 1933 to 1937.

(See PENNSYLVANIA in this chapter.)

MONROE, JAMES (1758–1831). Caldwell-Monroe House National Historic Landmark at 2017 I St. NW was Monroe's home during his tenure as secretary of state under President Madison and during his own first six months as president (1811–17). This house, built from 1802 to 1806 and a later residence of Charles Francis Adams (see the entries on Madison and Adams earlier in this section), is now owned and operated by the Arts Club of Washington. It displays fine period furnishings and interiors. (Open daily 10:00–4:00; 202-331-7282; free.)

As the fifth U.S. president (1817–25), Monroe was the first occupant of the rebuilt "second White House," and he immediately began purchasing large quantities of exquisite items and furnishings from France for the mansion. As Bess Furman wrote in *White House Profile* (1951), "any claim which the White House ever would have to antiques would be in these works of art which arrived in America in the autumn of 1817. Statesmen all down the years would come to know them like old friends." Some of these objects are still present, including a gilt pier table, a mahogany center table, bronze mantelpieces and clocks. Restoration of the Monroe-period appearance, undertaken by Jacqueline Kennedy in the early 1960s, included all of the public parlors; and this restoration is essentially what visitors see today. The Monroes reinstituted the formality and protocol earlier practiced by John Adams and dismissed by Thomas Jefferson (see the entries on Adams and Jefferson earlier in this section), giving the mansion a regal atmosphere it has seldom experienced since. (See the entry on the White House later in this section for tour information.)

(See Chapter 2, MANHATTAN; also Chapter 5, VIRGINIA.)

MURROW, EDWARD ROSCOE (1908–1965). The famed radio and television newsman headed the U.S. Information Agency from 1961 to 1964 and lived during that time at 5171 Manning Place NW (privately owned).

(See NEW YORK in this chapter; also Chapter 2, MANHATTAN; also Chapter 5, NORTH CAROLINA; also Chapter 6, WASHINGTON.)

NATIONAL MUSEUM OF AMERICAN HISTORY, Smithsonian Institution, Constitution Avenue and 13th Street NW.

Exhibits: This is the central national repository for biographical memorabilia. Its list of holdings, far too long to itemize, includes displays on almost every major figure of American history as well as material on many lesser greats. Personal clothing is a frequent part of Smithsonian biographi-

cal exhibits, and one can gain a very realistic idea of the person's size and physical presence through these displays of uniforms, formal attire or more conventional apparel. The highlight of dress exhibits is probably the First Ladies' Hall, showing original inaugural gowns on wax models for each president's wife from Martha Washington on. Other common items displayed here include personal chairs and desks, awards of various sorts, weapons, saddles, watches—countless belongings, in short. Like homes, these help tell us who these people were; and help us retrieve what may be "just names" to the here-and-now experience of identities that were attached, like ours today, to plain and personal things. This national treasury is a good place to begin a search for the people of our past whom we would most want to meet or question. For some of them, it is the closest we can come. (Open daily 10:00–5:30; 202-357-1300; free.)

NIMITZ, CHESTER WILLIAM (1885–1966). Pacific naval commander of World War II, Adm. Nimitz resided at three Washington addresses before and after the war. From 1936 to 1938, he lived at 5515 39th St. NW. An apartment dwelling at 2222 Q St. NW was his residence from 1939 to 1942, when he assumed command of the Pacific Fleet. The admiral's postwar address (1945–47) as chief of naval operations was the "Admiral's House," his official quarters and later the U.S. vice presidential mansion (see the entry on Nelson Aldrich Rockefeller later in this section).

(See Chapter 6, CALIFORNIA, TEXAS.)

PATTON, GEORGE SMITH, JR. (1885–1945). The flamboyant World War II general, one of the few in our history who never proclaimed a love for peace, lived at "Woodley" during the early 1920s (see the entry on Martin Van Buren later in this section). He occupied 3117 Woodland Drive NW from 1928 to 1931 during army staff duties in Washington. This house, of uncertain date, is privately owned.

(See Chapter 1, MASSACHUSETTS; also Chapter 5, KENTUCKY, VIRGINIA; also Chapter 6, CALIFORNIA.)

PEARSON, DREW (1897–1969). Scourge of Washington political cloakrooms, the engaging muckraker lived at 2820 Dumbarton Ave. NW (privately owned), his 18th-century, three-story mansion where he kept his notorious files under tight lock and key. Sitting beside a teletype and several telephones there, he wrote his daily column "Washington Merry-Go-Round," which earned him countless enemies in high places. No saint himself, he was nevertheless on the mark often enough to become the most hated, feared and powerful journalist in the capital. Pearson also raised one of the best gardens in Washington there.

(See MARYLAND, PENNSYLVANIA in this chapter; also Chapter 4, ILLINOIS.)

PEARY, ROBERT EDWIN (1856–1920). The admiral who devoted his life to planting the nation's flag on a barren ice plain at the North Pole—and claimed to have done so, not without challenge from even recent skeptics—often resided in Washington after his 1909 exploit. The home razed from 1831 Wyoming Ave. NW was his last; there he died a national hero.

Exhibit: Explorers Hall of the National Geographic Society, 17th and M streets NW, displays the sledge Peary rode to the North Pole and the tattered flag that he carried. (Open Monday–Friday 9:00–6:00, Saturday 9:00–5:00, Sunday 12:00–5:00; 202-857-7588; free.)

(See PENNSYLVANIA in this chapter; also Chapter 1, MAINE.)

PERSHING, JOHN JOSEPH (1860–1948). Walter Reed Center, the U.S. Army hospital at 6825 16th St. NW, was the World War I AEF commander's final home. He had fought what was supposed to be "the war to end wars." But during his last eight years, the semi-invalid all but forgotten by a once-idolatrous nation watched the world erupt again. He "faded away" in his two-room penthouse apartment on the third floor.

(See Chapter 4, MISSOURI; also Chapter 6, CALIFORNIA, NEW MEXICO.)

PIERCE, FRANKLIN (1804–1869). The 14th U.S. president, who occupied the White House from 1853 to 1857, was not then the dashing hero he had been when he led troops in the Mexican War. He was probably the most handsome president we've ever had but also one of the weakest, both politically and personally. Alcoholism beset him; the loss of his 12-year-old son in a railroad accident just before his inauguration and the incapacitating grief of the already morose Jane

Appleton Pierce kept the mansion a somber, depressing place throughout his term. Beyond these factors, he was one of our several presidents who were plainly not intellectually cut for the job. One useful thing he did was install the first furnace in the White House. (See the entry on the White House later in this section for tour information.)

(See Chapter 1, NEW HAMPSHIRE.)

POLK, JAMES KNOX (1795–1849). As the 11th U.S. president, Polk lived in the White House from 1845 to 1849. A meticulous, parsonlike little man who resented every moment away from his desk, he saw his main tasks during his self-allotted single term as territorial expansion and tariff reduction. The Polks were strict Calvinists who banned dancing and drinking in the mansion. Gaiety was regarded as an "unprofitable" expense of time, and the precise rigidity of White House social events reflected this peculiarly recurrent American attitude. Polk was probably the first of our several "workaholic" presidents—dedicated, driven men who equated office hours with degree of accomplishment. History indicates that this equation has seldom balanced in the White House, however, and that the country has rarely benefitted from such leadership. Polk always cleared his desk; he died of exhaustion at 53, only three months after his term ended. (See the entry on the White House later in this section for tour information.)

(See Chapter 5, NORTH CAROLINA, TENNESSEE.)

PORTER, KATHERINE ANNE (1890–1980). From 1960 to about 1975, the author dwelled in her own Georgetown home at 3601 49th St. NW (privately owned), which she furnished with antiques and occupied longer than any of her many other residences. She finished her only novel, *Ship of Fools* (1962), there.

(See MARYLAND, NEW YORK in this chapter; also Chapter 2, MANHATTAN.)

POUND, EZRA LOOMIS (1885–1972). The brilliant poet, translator and critic, a vastly influential force of 20th-century literature, posed a problem for the U.S. government after World War II. As a resident of fascist Italy, he had made virulent propaganda broadcasts and was indicted for treason after the war. Instead of convicting him for that, however, U.S. courts declared him "mentally unfit" and jailed him for 12 years at St. Elizabeth's Hospital. Staff personnel there frankly considered him a Soviet-style political prisoner. Despite his long confinement in the hospital's noisy Chestnut Ward, Pound continued to write, received occasional visitors who braved gauntlets of hospital "security," and perversely remained in good spirits. Following his release in 1958, he lingered hardly at all before heading back to Italy, declaring that "all America is an insane asylum." The Pound literary shrine of St. Elizabeth's is located at 2700 Martin Luther King Jr. Ave. SE. Only patients and patients' visitors are admitted.

(See PENNSYLVANIA in this chapter; also Chapter 6, IDAHO.)

RAYBURN, SAMUEL TALIAFERRO (1882–1961). "Mister Sam," influential Texas congressman and Speaker for 17 years, made his Washington bachelor home at the Anchorage Apartments, 19th and Q streets NW, from 1929 to 1961. He began with a two-room apartment, but in time the owner tore out some partitions to give Rayburn a larger place—which still, by his own preference, lacked a kitchen.

(See Chapter 5, TENNESSEE; also Chapter 6, TEXAS.)

ROCKEFELLER, NELSON ALDRICH. (1908–1979). "I never wanted to be *vice* president of anything!" he ruefully exclaimed. As the appointed U.S. vice president from 1974 to 1977, however, Rockefeller moved back into his 25-acre estate at 2500 Foxhall Road NW (privately owned), which he had purchased in 1941 and occupied from then until 1956. He expanded the 1885 mansion to include a swimming pool, tennis court and pond. When he sold the property to a real estate developer in 1978, neighbors protested plans to subdivide it until a compromise assured preservation of the land's forested character.

The 33-room "Admiral's House," a white, 1893 Victorian mansion at Massachusetts Avenue and 34th Street NW, became the officially designated vice presidential residence in 1975. Though Rockefeller held several opening receptions, he never actually lived there, preferring his own more comfortable estate. Admiral Chester William Nimitz was an earlier resident (see the entry on Nimitz earlier in this section).

(See NEW YORK in this chapter; also Chapter 1, MAINE; also Chapter 2, MANHATTAN.)

ROOSEVELT, FRANKLIN DELANO (1882–1945). ROOSEVELT, ELEANOR (1884–1962). The house presently occupied as the Mali Embassy at 2131 R St. NW was the Roosevelt residence from 1917 to 1920, during part of his tenure as assistant secretary of the navy.

Returning to Washington as the 32nd U.S. president, Roosevelt occupied the White House longer than any president before or since (1933–45). He used the Blue Room as his first office in the mansion while the present west-wing Oval Office was being modified and enlarged. The gregarious Roosevelts brought *joie de vivre* to a high art inside the sagging old house, and their overwhelming self-confidence radiated from the White House to every corner of a deeply depressed nation. Eleanor Roosevelt, a dynamo of supercharged energy, managed this complicated household with aplomb and seemed to be everywhere else besides. To her, the upstairs living quarters had an aged "atmosphere of solemn responsibility—you couldn't live up there and not feel it." The present design of the East Room is essentially President Roosevelt's. During World War II, the mansion was strictly off-limits to the public for the only time in its history. (See entry on the White House later in this section for tour information.)

(See MARYLAND, NEW YORK in this chapter; also Chapter 1, MAINE; also Chapter 2, MANHATTAN; also Chapter 4, MICHIGAN; also Chapter 5, GEORGIA.)

ROOSEVELT, THEODORE (1858–1919). The 26th U.S. president, with a large family as irrepressible as himself, occupied the White House from 1901 to 1909—though they spent four months of 1902 in the temporary White House at 736 Jackson Place NW, a previous home of James Gillespie Blaine (see the entry on Blaine earlier in this section), while the mansion underwent major renovation and the west-wing office extension was built. The remodeling, while badly needed, was too hasty and careless, however; only in 1948, when the old interior was demolished and rebuilt from the ground up, did architects discover how much hazardous weight had been added and poorly secured to the old walls. New floors had simply been laid over old ones, and tons of new plaster were held to ceilings by nails; why the edifice never collapsed during the next half-century is one more marvel of its history. In 1902, however, its appearance, at least, was greatly improved. It was Roosevelt who officially designated the mansion as the White House, previously only a colloquial term. "I don't think any family has ever enjoyed the White House more than we have," he wrote to his son Kermit. In the East Room, his daughter Alice married Nicholas Longworth in 1906, and "Princess Alice" continued to reign socially in Washington for 70 years. (See the entry on the White House later in this section for tour information.)

The home where Roosevelt lived from 1889 to 1895, when he was employed as a U.S. Civil Service commissioner, stands at 1215 19th St. NW. The privately occupied building, dating from about 1880, now contains law offices.

(See NEW YORK in this chapter; also Chapter 2, BRONX, MANHATTAN; also Chapter 4, NORTH DAKOTA; also Chapter 6, NEW MEXICO.)

ROOT, ELIHU (1845–1937). Prominent cabinet member, senator and diplomat, Root was one of the sharpest legal minds and esteemed public workhorses that Washington has ever seen. As secretary of war for President McKinley, he resided from 1903 to 1905 in the 1820 Ewell House, long gone from 722 Jackson Place NW, a later residence of William Randolph Hearst. Back in Washington as secretary of state for President Theodore Roosevelt, he lived from 1907 to 1909 at the Bell-Morton House, the former home of Alexander Graham Bell (see the entries on William McKinley, Hearst, Roosevelt and Bell earlier in this section). His address from 1909 to 1915 was 1155 16th St. NW, the present site of the 1959 American Chemical Society building.

(See NEW YORK in this chapter; also Chapter 2, MANHATTAN.)

SEWARD, WILLIAM HENRY (1801–1872). The pragmatic, cigar-smoking politician made secretary of state by President Lincoln rented the brick, three and one-half-story home built by Commodore John Rodgers (1831) at 17 Madison Place NW in 1861 and lived there for eight years. This 30-room house, which had served as a congressional boardinghouse (known as the "Old Club

House") for many years before Seward occupied it, faced Lafayette Square from a pleasant grove of trees. Rodgers had acquired the lot in 1827 from Henry Clay by trading him a jackass. Here Seward was viciously attacked in his bed by knife-wielding conspirator Lewis Payne on the same night in 1865 that John Wilkes Booth shot Lincoln. Seward recovered but aged quickly and bore facial scars for the rest of his life. The house was later the residence of James Gillespie Blaine (see the entries on Abraham Lincoln, Clay, Booth and Blaine earlier in this section). Torn down in 1894, it was replaced by the Belasco Theater, which stood there until the 1960s. The U.S. Court of Claims Building now occupies the site.

(See NEW YORK in this chapter.)

SHERMAN, WILLIAM TECUMSEH (1820–1891). After the Civil War, the fierce, popular Union general became commander of the army and bought the former home of Ulysses Simpson Grant (see the entry on Grant earlier in this section) at 205 I St. NW in Douglas Row. Sherman lived unhappily there from 1869 to 1874; house expenses were beyond his means, and "my family rarely had any rest from entertaining people, most of them utter strangers." In 1872, he partitioned off the house, rented out half and was relieved to sell the entire dwelling two years later.

(See Chapter 2, MANHATTAN; also Chapter 4, MISSOURI, OHIO; also Chapter 6, CALIFORNIA, OKLAHOMA.)

SMITHSONIAN INSTITUTION. See NATIONAL MUSEUM OF AMERICAN HISTORY.

SOUSA, JOHN PHILIP (1854–1932). Composer of military music and conductor of the U.S. Marine and Navy bands, the "March King" was born in the 19th-century house standing at 636 G St. SE. The brick and frame house where he grew up (1859–76) and which he always considered home also stands, at 527 Seventh St. SE. Both dwellings are privately owned.

(See NEW YORK in this chapter; also Chapter 2, MANHATTAN.)

STANTON, EDWIN McMASTERS (1814–1869). Brusque and abrasive but a notably effective secretary of war for President Lincoln, Stanton lived at 1323 K St. NW, his last home, during the

Civil War. The house has long since disappeared. (See Chapter 4, OHIO.)

STEVENS, THADDEUS (1792–1868). The club-footed congressman, a fierce abolitionist, master of invective and harsh foe of President Andrew Johnson, rented a small, run-down brick house at 279 Independence Ave. SE (then B Street), where he lived from 1859 to 1868 with his mistress, Lydia Smith. The Library of Congress occupies this site today.

(See PENNSYLVANIA in this chapter; also Chapter 1, VERMONT.)

STEVENSON, ADLAI EWING (1900–1965). From 1941 to 1943, as legal assistant to the secretary of the navy, the future Illinois governor, presidential candidate and diplomat rented a furnished house at 1904 R St. NW. This 1919 building now contains private apartments and doctors' offices.

Stevenson had no later Washington residence of his own; but during frequent stays in the city until his death, he occupied quarters in the home of his friends, Dr. and Mrs. Paul B. Magnuson, at 3121 O St. NW (privately owned).

(See Chapter 2, MANHATTAN; also Chapter 4, ILLINOIS; also Chapter 6, CALIFORNIA.)

STUART, GILBERT CHARLES (1755–1828). The noted portrait painter lived hand-to-mouth from 1803 to 1805 in Washington at a studio (actually only a small room) hastily built for him at Sixth and C streets NW, the present vicinity of a new court facility. Stuart, who painted only faces from life and copied or improvised bodies and backgrounds, completed many portraits of Washington notables there.

(See PENNSYLVANIA in this chapter; also Chapter 1, MASSACHUSETTS, RHODE ISLAND.)

TAFT, ROBERT ALPHONSO (1889–1953). "Mr. Republican," the influential Ohio senator and son of President Taft (see the entry on William Howard Taft below), lived in the White House with his parents at intervals from 1909 to 1913, but never fulfilled his own presidential aspirations. He rented the 15-room brick house at 1688 31st St. NW from 1941 to 1945, then bought and occupied it for the rest of his life. Built in the 1880s, Taft's home remains privately owned.

(See Chapter 4, OHIO.)

TAFT, WILLIAM HOWARD (1857–1930). The 27th and heaviest U.S. president (300–322 pounds) occupied the White House from 1909 to 1913. In contrast to the previous administration of Theodore Roosevelt, Taft's was dull and he admitted it. First Lady Helen Herron Taft, who suffered a stroke soon after she moved in but recovered, is responsible for the presence of Washington's famous Japanese cherry trees; because of her enthusiasm for them, Tokyo sent 3,000 saplings, from which the colorful blossoms have become an early spring feature of the city. (See the entry on the White House later in this section for tour information.)

When Taft returned to Washington as chief justice, he bought 2215 Wyoming Ave. NW, his last home (1922–30). This brick house with white pillars, nine bedrooms, several fireplaces and an elevator installed by Taft is one of the few former presidential homes in the city identified by a historical marker. It is privately owned.

(See Chapter 1, CONNECTICUT also Chapter 4, OHIO.)

TAYLOR, ZACHARY (1784–1850). "Old Rough and Ready," our 12th president, a seamed old Indian fighter and Mexican War commander, occupied the White House in 1849 and 1850. He was the second of two presidents to die in the mansion itself. With little political experience and scant education, he gave indications of a solid, temperate intelligence; he might have been a notable president had he lived. "Old Whitey," his war horse, munched grass in peaceful retirement on the White House lawn while invalid Margaret Taylor resented the denial of retirement years for her husband and stoutly refused the active role of first lady. Their daughter Betty Bliss cheerfully assumed the role of hostess, and the popular general himself strolled on the lawns, mixing easily with people of every station. Taylor died in the family quarters after a brief illness, fulfilling his wife's dire predictions. (See the entry on the White House later in this section for tour information.)

(See Chapter 5, ARKANSAS, KENTUCKY, LOUISIANA, VIRGINIA.)

TRUMAN, HARRY S. (1884–1972). As senator and vice president, Truman lived in a two-bedroom apartment at 4701 Connecticut Ave. NW

(1941–45). The building's lobby displays a historical marker.

The peppery 33rd U.S. president was the last to occupy the "second White House" (1945–48) and the first to reside in the new mansion (1952–53) with its completely rebuilt and faithfully restored interior. By the time the Trumans temporarily vacated in 1948, the place had become hazardous indeed. Chandeliers tinkled ominously; sudden, eery knockings and vibrations startled guests; and inspection revealed that "the second floor was staying up there purely from habit." Truman, a voracious student of history, probably knew more than any previous tenant about the mansion's past occupants—and had firm opinions about all of them. (See the entry on the White House later in this section for tour information.)

Blair-Lee House National Historic Landmark across the street at 1651–53 Pennsylvania Ave. NW became the temporary White House from 1948 to 1952, and there Bess Truman re-created the state rooms on a small scale. While President Truman napped in his second-floor bedroom there on November 1, 1950, two Puerto Rican nationalists attempted an assassination, trying to shoot their way into the house. Until 1982, when it was closed to await renovation, the four-story Blair House, built from 1824 to 1827 as the residence of political leader Francis Preston Blair, served as the official president's guest house for visiting dignitaries and heads of state. Lee House, built later, was joined to its neighbor in 1948. Neither are open to the public.

(See Chapter 4, MICHIGAN, MISSOURI; also Chapter 5, FLORIDA.)

TYLER, JOHN (1790–1862). The 10th U.S. president lived in the White House from 1841 to 1845, the first vice president to succeed to the highest office through death, that of President William Henry Harrison (see the entry on Harrison earlier in this section). Tyler, a somewhat ferret-faced political pro, confronted an immediate challenge to his position from congressional opponents who claimed he was only "Acting President"—but he quickly established the pattern of assuming full executive powers that has ruled vice presidential succession ever since. Partly because he stubbornly insisted on *being* president, Tyler was abandoned by his party and was probably the most unpopular president of the 19th century.

Letitia Tyler, a long-time reclusive invalid, was the first wife of any president to die in the White House (1842). Two years later, Tyler at 54 married 24-year-old Julia Gardiner, and the social pace of the mansion picked up brilliantly. A polite, southern gentleman to the last, Tyler retired not much the worse for wear, fathered seven more children, and became an outspoken secessionist before he died. (See the entry on the White House later in this section for tour information.)

(See WEST VIRGINIA in this chapter; also Chapter 5, VIRGINIA.)

VAN BUREN, MARTIN (1782–1862). The eighth U.S. president occupied the White House from 1837 to 1841. "Little Van" had been a widower for 19 years when he assumed office, and his hostess in the mansion was his beautiful daughter-in-law Angelica Van Buren. A protege of his predecessor Andrew Jackson, whose popularity won him the election, Van Buren rapidly lost control, and the master political intriguer soon found himself intrigued against. He maintained superb aplomb, however, while his support crumbled and a slanderous campaign cost him reelection. Though he returned to the fray as a strong presidential contender in 1844 and 1848 and never lost interest in politics, he long outlived his day of power and public service. (See the entry on the White House later in this section for tour information.)

Van Buren was the first of four presidents to use "Woodley," the Georgian manor house at 3000 Cathedral Ave. NW, as a summer White House. General George Smith Patton, Jr., was also a later resident (see the entry on Patton earlier in this section), as was Secretary of War Henry L. Stimson. Built in 1836, the mansion now hosts the private Maret School.

(See NEW YORK, WEST VIRGINIA in this chapter.)

WALLACE, HENRY AGARD (1888–1965). Liberal idealist, prominent New Dealer and second vice president of Franklin Delano Roosevelt, Wallace occupied a suite during all of his Washington years (1933–48) at the Wardman Park Hotel, now the Sheraton Washington at 2660 Woodley Road NW.

(See NEW YORK in this chapter; also Chapter 4, IOWA.)

WARREN, EARL (1891–1974). One of the most notable and controversial chief justices in the nation's history, Warren made his permanent Washington home from 1953 in the seven-room Apartment I-140 at the Sheraton Washington Apartment Annex (see the entry on Cordell Hull earlier in this section).

(See Chapter 6, CALIFORNIA.)

WEBSTER, DANIEL (1782–1852). "Black Dan," so nicknamed because of his swarthy complexion, owned two Washington homes. In 1841 the noted orator and political leader bought the 1828 house later owned by art collector William W. Corcoran at 1611 H St. NW (at the corner of Connecticut Avenue) on Lafayette Square. Webster lived there for the duration of his tenure as secretary of state until 1843, negotiated the Webster-Ashburton Treaty there and finally sold the house in 1847. Demolished in 1922, it is the present site of the U.S. Chamber of Commerce building. Webster's desk is displayed in the Chamber library room. (Open Monday–Friday 8:30–5:00; 202-659-6000; free.)

In 1845 Webster bought "Vine Cottage," located on the north side of D Street NW between Fifth and Sixth streets, a house he described as "about as big as two pigeon boxes." The house was Webster's last in Washington and is long gone.

(See Chapter 1, MASSACHUSETTS, NEW HAMPSHIRE.)

WESTINGHOUSE, GEORGE (1846–1914). Inventor of air brakes and electrical power systems, Westinghouse rented the old Blaine Mansion at 2000 Massachusetts Ave. NW in 1898. He bought it in 1901, installed a passenger elevator and made it his last home (see the entry on James Gillespie Blaine earlier in this section).

(See NEW YORK, PENNSYLVANIA in this chapter; also Chapter 1, MASSACHUSETTS.)

WHITE HOUSE. There have actually been three separate White Houses within the familiar Aquia sandstone walls at 1600 Pennsylvania Ave. NW. The first interior, designed by architect James Hoban in 1792 at a site chosen by Pierre L'Enfant, was barely finished when torched in 1814 by British soldiers in revenge for the gratuitous American firing of Niagara-on-the-Lake, Ontario. Today the East Room where Abigail Adams hung her wet wash is not, in fact, the same room she knew, though its location and dimensions remain the same. The same applies for the "second White House" interior, rebuilt on the Hoban plan from the ashes of 1814 and finished in 1817. Except for a few superimposed floors and upper-story additions, this same interior served the nation's presidents until 1948, when it threatened to collapse around Harry S. Truman. The third interior, completed in 1952 from the ground up and duplicating the previous Hoban layout, is the White House that visitors see today. It is supposed to last for a century without major renovation; certainly its steel beams are more structurally solid than its timber predecessors. The first-floor public rooms are, except for modern construction materials, the same ones known by James Monroe, and he would recognize them—though succeeding presidents who decked every inch with ornate Victorian decor and heavy plush fabrics might not.

For the 35 presidential families of this book who have lived there, these rooms have held a full range of human experience. The mansion has seen marriage, birth and death; celebration, riot and wailing grief. Too often it has sheltered profound ache and unhappiness. At times, mediocrity and mean spirit have ruled, and outright corruption is not unknown to its experience. But the old house has occasionally known greatness too.

An excellent history of the mansion is *The White House: An Historic Guide* (1979), compiled by the White House Historical Association.

To visit the White House, go to the East Gate on East Executive Avenue. Tours start there, proceed through the East Wing, and include the first-floor public rooms of the mansion. It is best to check with the office of your congressional representative before you go; he or she may be able to arrange a somewhat more extended tour for you. If the flag is flying, your Chief Tenant is in residence. (Open summer, Tuesday–Saturday 10:00–12:30; winter, Tuesday–Friday 10:00–12:00; tickets available during summer at 8 for day of tour; 202-456-1414; free.)

WHITMAN, WALT (1819–1892). America's major poet, an eternal optimist for democracy and the country, saw plenty to discourage a less hardy sort in Civil War Washington, where he visited wounded soldiers and worked as a government clerk. Whitman occupied a succession of shabby,

WHITE HOUSE IN RUINS, 1814. A burned-out shell is all that remained of the Executive Mansion after the British raid on Washington during the War of 1812. The exterior walls were repaired and preserved, however, and remain standing today. This engraving by Strickland views the desolate scene from the north. Note the 1807 pavilion-terrace designed by Thomas Jefferson on the left. This reconstructed colonnade now connects to the western Executive Wing, which contains the President's Oval Office.
(Courtesy Library of Congress)

WHITE HOUSE NORTH FACADE IN 1820. This drawing by artist George Catlin shows the Mansion shortly after its restoration during the presidency of James Monroe. The north portico was not added until 1829.
(Courtesy Library of Congress)

unheated rooms from 1863 to 1873, among them two houses on M Street NW near 12th Street. In his attic room at 535 15th St. NW, he suffered a crippling stroke in 1873. These houses are long gone. One that was still standing recently is 1407 L St. NW, a narrow brick house remodeled in the 1920s and converted to a small office building. Whitman rented a second-floor bedroom there in 1863.

(See NEW JERSEY, NEW YORK in this chapter; also Chapter 2, BROOKLYN, MANHATTAN.)

WILLARD HOTEL. Poet Carl Sandburg wrote that "Willard's Hotel could more justly be called the center of Washington and the nation than either the Capitol or the White House." An earlier reporter, Nathaniel Hawthorne, called it "the meeting-place of the true representatives of this country. . . . Never, in any other spot, was there such a miscellany of people." Two Willards have occupied the same site at 14th and F streets NW. The 1847 hotel hosted Andrew Jackson and Abraham Lincoln (just before his first inauguration), among numerous other public figures. The present 1901, 13-story building was likewise a Washington social center, though it finally closed its doors as a hotel in 1968. Presidents Taft, Wilson, Harding and Coolidge were among those who stayed there at various times. Until 1981 its status remained in limbo; advocates firmly opposed the landmark's destruction, and a court decision finally ruled that renovation and conversion into an office building could proceed. *Willard's of Washington*, a 1954 account by Garnett L. Eskew, gives an interesting history of this notable corner.

WILSON, WOODROW (1856–1924). The 28th U.S. president, a professional scholar turned politician, served in the White House from 1913 to 1921. Wilson entered the presidency as a vigorous intellectual at the peak of his powers— and left it a broken, stroke-paralyzed old man. His first wife, Ellen Axson Wilson, died in the White House in 1914, and his grief made the mansion a somber place until his 1915 marriage to widow Edith Bolling Galt. World War I and its aftermath of controversies involving the Versailles Treaty and League of Nations aged and exhausted him, and his popularity declined. Inside the White House in 1919, he suffered the stroke that paralyzed his left side; and from then until the end of his term, Edith Wilson was virtually "acting president" while Wilson's helpless condition was kept secret.

He never fully recovered, lingering as an invalid until his death at Wilson House National Historic Landmark, 2340 S St. NW. "I am showing President Harding how an ex-President should behave," he was able to joke. This 1915, 23-room mansion, owned and maintained by the National Trust for Historic Preservation, contains original furnishings and Wilson memorabilia, carefully assembled and saved by his widow until her own death in 1961. (Open Monday–Friday 10:00–2:00, Saturday–Sunday 12:00–4:00; 202-673-4034; admission.)

(See NEW JERSEY in this chapter; also Chapter 1, NEW HAMPSHIRE; also Chapter 5, GEORGIA, SOUTH CAROLINA, VIRGINIA.)

WRIGHT, ORVILLE (1871–1948).
WRIGHT, WILBUR (1867–1912).
Exhibit: The wooden biplane "Flyer," built and flown by the Wright brothers at Kill Devil Hill, N.C., in 1903—the machine that introduced the air age—is displayed in the Air and Space Building of the Smithsonian Institution (see the entry on Charles Augustus Lindbergh earlier in this section).

(See PENNSYLVANIA in this chapter; also Chapter 4, INDIANA, MICHIGAN, OHIO.)

MARYLAND

Capt. John Smith, that English sea dog who saw more of America than many living Americans have seen, found agricultural Algonquin tribes in Maryland when he explored Chesapeake Bay in 1608. The territory's first white owner was George Calvert, the first Lord Baltimore, who was granted a royal charter by Charles I to establish a colony north of Virginia. Calvert wanted to name it Crescentia, "Land of Plenty." He knew, however, that Charles liked to christen his gifts, so Calvert deferred in the matter. Religious scruples also weighed in the decision: Calvert was a Catholic in Protestant England; Queen Mary was also Catholic. So Protestant Charles named the territory in honor of his queen.

Calvert's ambition was to found a colony in which Catholics would have equal rights with Protestants, but he also wanted Protestant colonists. Thus, from the beginning, he promised freedom from a "moral majority," and the promise was carried out by the historic Maryland Toleration Act of 1649. Calvert himself never set foot in his colony. His younger son Leonard Calvert brought two shiploads of colonists in 1634 and built his capital, St. Marys City; it remained the capital until 1694, when Annapolis, founded by Virginia Puritans in 1649, assumed the role. Annapolis has been the capital ever since.

Royal charters sometimes overlapped, and when they did the inevitable result was colonial conflict far from the king's map table. The later grant of Pennsylvania to William Penn intruded onto Calvert's grant, and border disputes continued until the Mason-Dixon surveys from 1763 to 1767. Employed to settle the dispute, English astronomer-mathematicians Charles Mason and Jeremiah Dixon ran a 230-mile line, eventually extending to the Ohio River, that established the Maryland-Pennsylvania-Delaware borders. This line also became the highly emotional symbol of division between freedom and slavery in America. (In 1974 the National Geodetic Survey resurveyed the Maryland-Delaware line and restored many of the 81 Mason-Dixon markers that had been lost.) One result of the original survey was Maryland's curious "wasp waist"; the state is about two miles wide at Cumberland.

Maryland became the seventh of the original 13 states when it ratified the Constitution in 1788. This state was a main arena of the War of 1812; observing the British bombardment of Fort McHenry at Baltimore, Francis Scott Key emotionally penned "The Star-Spangled Banner," its patriotic sentiments undimmed by a fiendishly difficult (English) melody. As a slave state, Maryland would have seceded at the outbreak of the Civil War had not Union troops immediately occupied it, and its Confederate sympathies remained strong throughout the conflict. The bloodiest single day's engagement of that war occured at Antietam in 1862.

Today Maryland's economy, once based solely on tobacco, relies mainly on manufacturing and commerce. Chesapeake Bay, from three to 30 miles wide, is the state's primary recreational and fishing resource. Vestiges of old rural Maryland are best seen today in the Eastern Shore section of the state, where abolitionist Frederick Douglass grew up. Maryland takes southern pride in its colonial dwellings, of which several thousand survive throughout the state—Annapolis alone has about 100—and has done much to preserve and maintain them. The state's largest city, Baltimore, achieved early prominence from 1729 as a port. Its reputation for what Baltimore historian John C. French called "a quickness of temper that easily flared into violence, and a marked fondness for civic pomp and ceremony" faded with time and growth. Today's Baltimore is a cosmopolitan center that still retains numerous old row houses among its historic structures. Poe and Fitzgerald wrote in dwellings still standing, and the houses of natives Babe Ruth and H. L. Mencken are open to visitors. Maryland suburban cities adjoin Washington, D.C., and many national officials including Vice President Hubert Humphrey and labor leader George Meany found homes in such surrounding communities as Bethesda, Silver Spring and Chevy Chase.

Other Maryland natives and residents included

Clara Barton, Harriet Tubman and Rachel Carson. The presence of these and many other notables has given the "Old Line State" a diverse legacy of freedom, dissent and excellence, qualities often spiced by an underlying rambunctious streak that doesn't seem to diminish Maryland's traditional tone of style and elegance.

ACHESON, DEAN GOODERHAM (1893–1971). Secretary of state for President Truman, Acheson retired to his 1792 farmhouse "Harewood" near **Sandy Spring** in 1953. Acheson bought the farm in 1925 as a weekend and summer retreat. There he wrote several volumes of memoirs including the Pulitzer Prize-winning *Present at the Creation* (1969), and there he died. The two and one-half-story frame house stands privately owned at 17600 Meeting House Road.

(See DISTRICT OF COLUMBIA in this chapter; also Chapter 1, CONNECTICUT.)

BARTON, CLARA (1821–1912). Barton National Historic Site at 5801 Oxford Road in **Glen Echo** was the home built by the founder of the American Red Cross in 1891. Fondly modeled on the

CLARA BARTON HOME INTERIOR. Visitors in **Glen Echo,** may view these rooms as she personally designed and arranged them. The dynamic Red Cross founder died in this parlor-bedroom in 1912. *(Courtesy American Red Cross)*

CLARA BARTON HOME. This unique dwelling on Oxford Road in **Glen Echo,** built by the American Red Cross founder in 1891 and now a National Historic Site, became her perma- nent dwelling in 1897. Barton stands second from left in this 1904 photo.
(Courtesy American Red Cross)

style of a Mississippi riverboat, her home displays galleries, gothic interiors and gardens after her own design; she salvaged lumber for the house from field hospitals at the 1889 Johnstown, Pa., flood site. Visitors may view her original furnishings plus numerous gifts and awards she received from all over the world. The house is operated by the National Park Service. (Open Saturday 10:00–5:00, Sunday 1:00–5:00, Thursday–Friday by appointment; 301-492-6245; donation.)

(See DISTRICT OF COLUMBIA, NEW JERSEY, NEW YORK in this chapter; also Chapter 1, MASSACHUSETTS.)

BOOTH, EDWIN THOMAS (1833–1893).
BOOTH, JOHN WILKES (1838–1865)

The actor brothers, Edwin a noted tragedian and John Wilkes a strutting psychopath and the assassin of President Lincoln, were born in a log house near the present "Tudor Hall," three miles northeast of **Bel Air** on Tudor Lane off State Highway 22. Tudor Hall, an Elizabethan-style, eight-room brick dwelling built in 1853 by their father, actor Junius Brutus Booth, stands about 50 yards from the birthplace site. This remained the family homestead, to which both brothers returned at intervals into adulthood. Much modified over the years, it is privately owned.*

In **Baltimore,** the brothers had several child-hood homes. A spacious backyard at what is now 152 North Exeter St. provided space for a make-shift stage, where they gave impromptu perfor-mances for neighborhood children. The original dwelling, their home from 1846 to 1852, is long gone.

(See DISTRICT OF COLUMBIA, PENNSYL-VANIA in this chapter; also Chapter 1, MASSA-CHUSETTS, RHODE ISLAND; also Chapter 2, MANHATTAN.)

BROWN, JOHN (1800–1859). Near **Samples Manor,** John Brown Headquarters National Historic Landmark (privately owned) stands on Chestnut Grove Road off Harpers Ferry Road. This brick and stone, two and one-half-story farmhouse was the final staging area for Brown's 1859 attack on Harpers Ferry; from there, Brown and his terrorist band rode out for the last time to instigate slave rebellion and proclaim a "free state" of antislavery guerrilla fighters.

(See NEW YORK, PENNSYLVANIA, WEST VIRGINIA in this chapter; also Chapter 1, CON-NECTICUT; also Chapter 4, IOWA, KANSAS, OHIO.)

CALVERT, LEONARD (1606–1647). Brother of Lord Baltimore, whose colonists he brought in the *Ark* and the *Dove* in 1634, Calvert founded Maryland and **St. Marys City.** There he built his capital and governed the colony until his death. Only the foundations of the colony's many build-ings—including more than 60 brick structures—survive in today's St. Marys City. Marked site of the original "pallizado" or fort where the colo-nists lived is located at Church Point about a half mile from State Highway 5 on State Highway 584.

CARSON, RACHEL LOUISE (1907–1964). In **Silver Spring,** the biologist author of *Silent Spring* (1962) built a house "that gives me everything I need" on an acre lot at 11701 Berwick Road, her last home from 1957. According to a local reporter,

*In 1980, newspaper stories reported that the house's current owners "say strange voices, crashing mirrors and other strange events have marked their 12 years in the house and they believe they are from the spirits of the Booth family. 'But they're friendly spirits,' insisted one resident. 'They play little tricks on us.'"

"Rachel Carson left half of her lot in its natural wooded habitat for small animals, and the present owners have left it this way." Her previous home (1949–57), a 1941 dwelling, stands at 204 Wil-liamsburg Drive. Both houses remain privately owned.

(See PENNSYLVANIA in this chapter; also Chapter 1, MAINE.)

CLEVELAND, GROVER (1837–1908). When the 22nd and 24th U.S. president married Frances Folsom in 1886, the couple honeymooned in a "cottage" still standing near **Deer Park.** A marker identifies the frame, two and one-half-story house (privately owned) as "Grover Cleveland Cottage," located on Deer Park Hotel Road off State High-way 135.

(See DISTRICT OF COLUMBIA, NEW JERSEY, NEW YORK in this chapter; also Chapter 1, MASSACHUSETTS.)

DECATUR, STEPHEN (1779–1820). Naval offi-cer, foe of pirates and hero of the War of 1812, Decatur was born in the town of **Berlin.** The site of the log cabin, vacated by the family soon after his birth, is located about 200 yards from the present Stephen Decatur Park on Tripoli Street bordering U.S. Highway 113.

(See DISTRICT OF COLUMBIA, PENNSYL-VANIA in this chapter.)

DICKINSON, JOHN (1732–1808). Called "Penman of the Revolution" for his colonial protest documents, Dickinson was born at an estate called "Crosiadore" southwest of **Trappe.** This tract remained in the Dickinson family for almost 300 years from 1669. The marked site of the house, destroyed in 1976, is located on Grubin Neck Road west off U.S. Highway 50.

(See DELAWARE, PENNSYLVANIA in this chapter.)

DOUGLASS, FREDERICK (1818–1895). Born a slave named Frederick Bailey at Anthony Farm about two miles south of **Queen Anne,** the boy who became the eloquent abolitionist orator and writer lived on this site (also called "Holme Hill Farm") beside Tuckahoe Creek until 1824. It is located a few hundred yards east of Kingston Landing Road off State Highway 303 just south of the Tappers Corners junction; Douglass himself pointed out the place on a return visit there in 1878.

His next home was a wooden kitchen extension that stood at the rear of the 1785 brick "Captain's House," which survives on what was the Lloyd Plantation, located northwest of **Longwoods** on the bay coastline. It is privately owned and difficult of access by a complex of country lanes. Neither of these spots had historical markers at last report. A Douglass marker seven miles away on State Highway 328 has no associations with any place where he lived. Dickson J. Preston's *Young Frederick Douglass: The Maryland Years* (1980) is an admirable guide to the territory.

(See DISTRICT OF COLUMBIA, NEW YORK in this chapter; also Chapter 1, MASSACHUSETTS.)

DU BOIS, WILLIAM EDWARD BURGHARDT (1868–1963). In **Baltimore,** the educator, author and reformer built the house at 2302 Montebello Terrace during the 1940s for his wife and daughter but spent only brief intervals there himself. When at the home, now privately owned, he enjoyed gardening in the spacious grounds.

(See PENNSYLVANIA in this chapter; also Chapter 1, MASSACHUSETTS; also Chapter 2, BROOKLYN, MANHATTAN; also Chapter 5, GEORGIA.)

EISENHOWER, DWIGHT DAVID (1890–1969). The 34th U.S. president was the second president to frequent the mountain retreat of **Camp David,** which he renamed after his grandson. There Eisenhower conferred with British Prime Minister Harold Macmillan and with Soviet Premier Nikita Khruschev in 1959 (see the entry on Franklin Delano Roosevelt later in this section).

(See DISTRICT OF COLUMBIA, PENNSYLVANIA in this chapter; also Chapter 2, MANHATTAN; also Chapter 4, KANSAS, MICHIGAN; also Chapter 5, GEORGIA, VIRGINIA; also Chapter 6, COLORADO, TEXAS.)

FITZGERALD, F. SCOTT (1896–1940). At **Towson** the novelist and his wife Zelda lived in 1932 and 1933 at the 1885 Bayard Turnbull estate "La Paix," where he wrote most of *Tender Is the Night* (1934). This 18-room, rambling Victorian house, wrote Zelda, was "surrounded by apologetic trees and warning meadows and creaking insects." When a fire broke out during his stay, Fitzgerald handed

out drinks to the firemen. The house was razed in 1961, and St. Joseph Hospital at 7620 York Road now stands near the site on LaPaix Lane.

In **Baltimore,** the city of his great-uncle Francis Scott Key (see the entry on Key later in this section), Fitzgerald lived from 1933 to 1935 in a row house at 1307 Park Ave. (privately owned); and in 1935 at Apartment 7K of the Cambridge Arms Apartments, still standing at 3337 North Charles St. "I belong here," he wrote, "where everything is civilized and gay and rotted and polite."

(See NEW YORK in this chapter; also Chapter 2, MANHATTAN; also Chapter 4, MINNESOTA; also Chapter 5, ALABAMA, NORTH CAROLINA; also Chapter 6, CALIFORNIA.)

HAMILTON, EDITH (1867–1963). Educator and interpreter of ancient history in her books on Greece, Rome and Israel, Hamilton lived in **Baltimore** from 1896 to 1922 as the headmistress of Bryn Mawr School. Her home from 1908 to 1917 stands privately owned at 1312 Park Ave., erected about 1880. The school itself was located at Cathedral and Preston streets during her lengthy tenure.

(See DISTRICT OF COLUMBIA in this chapter; also Chapter 1, MAINE; also Chapter 2, MANHATTAN; also Chapter 4, INDIANA.)

HUMPHREY, HUBERT HORATIO (1911–1978). When first elected to the Senate in 1948, the eventual vice president and 1968 presidential candidate bought a recent tract house at 3216 Coquelin Terrace (privately owned) in **Chevy Chase,** a Washington suburb. This remained his home until 1966.

(See DISTRICT OF COLUMBIA in this chapter; also Chapter 4, MINNESOTA, SOUTH DAKOTA.)

JOHNSON, LYNDON BAINES (1908–1973). The 36th U.S. president used the executive retreat at **Camp David** for palaver with cronies and occasional meetings of state (see the entry on Franklin Delano Roosevelt later in this section).

(See DISTRICT OF COLUMBIA in this chapter; also Chapter 4, MICHIGAN; also Chapter 6, TEXAS.)

JOHNSON, WALTER PERRY (1887–1946). Longtime pitcher with the Washington Senators and one of the first players chosen for membership in the National Baseball Hall of Fame, Johnson purchased a farm near **Germantown** (Montgomery County) in the early 1900s. He resided there, when he wasn't traveling with the team, for the rest of his life. Johnson's home on Germantown Road (State Highway 118), according to a county historian, "was a nondescript farmhouse of uncertain age. The property is slated for development, which probably means it will disappear shortly."

(See NEW YORK in this chapter; also Chapter 4, KANSAS.)

KENNEDY, JOHN FITZGERALD (1917–1963). As the 35th U.S. president, Kennedy came to appreciate the space and solitude of **Camp David** only during the last year of so of his truncated administration. The family horses were kept there; though Kennedy himself did not ride, his wife and daughter Caroline enjoyed the wooded trails (see the entry on Franklin Delano Roosevelt later in this section).

(See DISTRICT OF COLUMBIA, NEW YORK in this chapter; also Chapter 1, MASSACHUSETTS, RHODE ISLAND; also Chapter 2, BRONX; also Chapter 4, MICHIGAN; also Chapter 5, FLORIDA, VIRGINIA; also Chapter 6, TEXAS.)

KEY, FRANCIS SCOTT (1779–1843). The prominent lawyer, chiefly remembered for writing "The Star-Spangled Banner" (1814) to an old English tavern tune, was a Maryland native. His birthplace "Terra Rubra" stood about one mile from **Keysville** on Keysville-Bruceville Road. The original tract, named for the color of its soil, was farmed by Key's grandfather, who built the homestead in 1770. A storm demolished it in 1850; the present brick dwelling on the site is privately owned.

Exhibits: The Roger Brooke Taney Home and Key Museum at 123 South Bentz St. in **Frederick** displays memorabilia of Key and of Chief Justice Taney, Key's brother-in-law. It is operated by the Francis Scott Key Foundation. (Open summer, Tuesday–Sunday 9:00–4:00, or by appointment; admission.)

In **Baltimore,** the Maryland Historical Society at 201 West Monument St. exhibits Key's original manuscript of the national anthem. (Open Tues-

day–Saturday 11:00–4:00, Sunday 1:00–5:00 except July and August; 301-685-3750; admission.)

(See DISTRICT OF COLUMBIA in this chapter.)

MacARTHUR, DOUGLAS (1880–1964). "Rainbow Hill," the 1917 mansion owned by his first wife, Louise Brooks MacArthur, stands near **Owings Mills** on the east side of Park Heights Avenue, a half mile north of Green Spring Valley Road. MacArthur lived there from 1925 to 1928—most of the time alone (the couple separated during this period)—while serving in an army general staff position. The private Baptist Home of Maryland, Inc., presently occupies the house.

(See NEW YORK in this chapter; also Chapter 2, MANHATTAN; also Chapter 4, KANSAS; also Chapter 5, ARKANSAS, VIRGINIA; also Chapter 6, NEW MEXICO, TEXAS.)

MEANY, GEORGE (1894–1980). In **Bethesda,** a Washington suburb, the labor leader's home from 1949 to 1980 stands at 8819 Burdette Road (privately owned), built probably during the 1940s. One of Meany's favorite relaxations, it is said, was mowing his lawn there.

(See Chapter 2, BRONX.)

MENCKEN, HENRY LOUIS (1880–1956). The "Sage of **Baltimore**"—acerbic journalist, language scholar and social commentator—was a lifelong resident of that city. His birthplace, long gone, stood at 380 West Lexington St. But from 1883, Mencken lived for all but the five years of his marriage at 1524 Hollins St., a narrow, brick three-story town house now used as a University of Maryland dormitory. His own matchless account of growing up there is *Happy Days: 1880–1892* (1940). The house "is as much a part of me as my two hands," he wrote. He began his writing career in a room on the third floor; he moved his study in 1936 to a second-floor room with a window overlooking the Convent of the Good Shepherd. "The Holy Ghost stands beside me, guiding me to the truth," he assured friends. In 1920, he walled in his back yard, laying the bricks himself; visitors may still see this wall and his insertions of Beethoven's death mask and a bronze memorial to his dog "Tessie." As a widower, Mencken kept a bachelor house with his brother August for the last 20 years of his life and died there, silenced in his last decade by a stroke but audaciously good-humored to the last. The house, willed by August Mencken to the University of Maryland, now holds graduate students; but visitors are admitted to the yard and first floor, which contains the original family furniture, one afternoon each week. (Call or write University of Maryland School of Social Work, 525 West Redwood, Baltimore, MD, 21201; 301-528-7794; free.) Mencken's married home (1930–36) is a private apartment dwelling at 704 Cathedral St.

Exhibit: The Mencken Room at the Enoch Pratt Free Library, 400 Cathedral St. in **Baltimore,** displays a collection of memorabilia, correspondence and manuscripts. (Open at irregular intervals; check with the library; 301-396-5430.)

NASH, OGDEN (1902–1971). The poet whose outrageous rhymes often conveyed depth of feeling in deceptively light verse had two homes in **Baltimore,** both of which remain in private hands. His first, at 4300 Rugby Road, dates from 1927. Nash's last home (1965–71) is a modern townhouse at 30 Olmstead Green.

(See Chapter 2, MANHATTAN; also Chapter 5, GEORGIA.)

OAKLEY, ANNIE (1860–1926). "Miss Annie Oakley, the peerless Lady Wing-Shot," a star performer with Buffalo Bill's Wild West Show for 17 years, retired briefly in 1914 and 1915 to **Cambridge.** She lived at 28 Bellevue Ave., a private, four-bedroom house overlooking Hambrook Bay. Such a scene, one observer suggested, was too placid to hold the energetic Annie for long.

(See NEW JERSEY in this chapter; also Chapter 4, OHIO; also Chapter 5, FLORIDA, NORTH CAROLINA.)

PEALE, CHARLES WILLSON (1741–1827). Famed painter of Revolutionary portraits, Peale was born near **Centreville** in the schoolmaster's house, a 40-x-18-foot structure where his father taught until 1742 and which stood until 1804. According to Historic Sites Surveyor Orlando Ridout, "the precise location has never been determined, but it is in the vicinity of the intersection of State 18 and Tilghman Neck Road. This site today consists of plowed fields, a wooded streambed, and several modern houses." The marker at State Highway 18 and Wright's Neck

Road is about a quarter of a mile east.

Peale's home in **Annapolis,** a small brick house on North Street, was still standing in 1900, but local sources profess ignorance of the exact site. Pearle lived there from 1769 to 1775, working in a small studio he added to the house.

(See PENNSYLVANIA in this chapter.)

PEARSON, DREW (1897–1969). Near **Potomac,** the scandalmongering columnist owned a 450-acre working farm. The stone mansion, which he built in 1937, surmounts a bluff overlooking the Potomac River. He went there for the relaxation of physical work and earned up to $150,000 annually from the sale of his dairy herd's manure. The bags read "Pearson's Best Manure—Better Than The Column—All Cow, No Bull" and became collectors' items. He named bulls and boars after political figures (his hog pen was "the State Department"). Pearson wanted to be buried there under the epitaph "Here Lies an S.O.B.," an unfulfilled wish. The estate at 13130 River Road is privately owned and, at last report, was "being developed."

(See DISTRICT OF COLUMBIA, PENNSYLVANIA in this chapter; also Chapter 4, ILLINOIS.)

PEIRCE, CHARLES SANDERS (1839–1914). Mathematician and pragmatic philosopher, Peirce taught at Johns Hopkins University in **Baltimore** from 1879 to 1884. He lived at least part of that time in a rented house still standing at what is now 1020 North Calvert St. (privately owned).

(See PENNSYLVANIA in this chapter; also Chapter 1, MASSACHUSETTS.)

POE, EDGAR ALLAN (1809–1849). "The striking thing about Poe's homes," wrote Stephanie Kraft, "is that they are so empty, not of period furnishings but of actual memorabilia of him and his family." Yet for a writer who spent most of his years as a drug addict in the direst sort of poverty, a surprising number of his dwellings remain. Poe House National Historic Landmark at 203 North Amity St. in **Baltimore**—a tiny brick dwelling where he lived from 1832 to 1835 with his aunt, grandmother, brother and two cousins (including Virginia Clemm, whom he later married)—dates from 1830. The interior of roughly plastered walls and painted woodwork probably looks much less dismal after its 1978 renovation than when the family crowded together in the back kitchen there.* Poe's room was the garret. The Baltimore City Commission on Historic and Architectural Preservation maintains the house, which contains a few portraits and furnishings like those the family may have used (plus a surprising piano like the one Poe "would have wanted" for Virginia); but the only aspect he would probably recognize today is the cramped,

---

*"With thousands of visitors coming to see Poe's home annually," said the curator of Poe House in 1978, "it's imperative the facility be kept in top-notch condition as a showplace for Baltimore." Poe, a supreme ironist, must have had a sly grin in his grave over his home's present "showplace" status.

HOME OF EDGAR ALLAN POE. The author resided in this small brick house in **Baltimore** with five relatives for about three years, seeking privacy for writing in the attic. Aside from the sense of tightly confined space, however, visitors will find few direct associations with Poe among the period items exhibited. *(Courtesy Edgar Allan Poe Society, Baltimore)*

oppressive space. (Open Wednesday–Saturday 1:00–4:00; 301-396-4866; admission.) Fourteen years after leaving the house, Poe was picked up from the gutter in Lombard Street and carried to what is now Church Home Hospital, 100 North Broadway, where a marker identifies the spot of his long-sought release from life.

(See PENNSYLVANIA in this chapter; also Chapter 1, MASSACHUSETTS; also Chapter 2, BRONX, MANHATTAN; also Chapter 5, VIRGINIA.)

PORTER, KATHERINE ANNE (1890–1980). At **College Park,** the author's home from 1975 to 1979 was the Westchester Park Apartments, a condominium at 6100 Westchester Park Drive (privately owned).

Her last residence was the 1968 Carriage Hill Nursing Home at 9101 2nd Ave. (at the corner of Hanover Street) in **Silver Spring,** where she died.

Exhibit: The Katherine Anne Porter Room at the University of Maryland's McKeldin Library in **College Park** contains a replica of her library plus papers and memorabilia. (Open by appointment; 301-454-2853; free.)

(See DISTRICT OF COLUMBIA, NEW YORK in this chapter; also Chapter 2, MANHATTAN.)

POST, EMILY PRICE (1873–1960). The author who became the nation's foremost arbiter of social *Etiquette* (1922) through numerous updated editions of her book was born in **Baltimore** at 14 East Chase St. (privately owned), her home until age 12. Description of the home is lacking, but since her father was the well-known architect Bruce Price, the home was probably quite new in the 1870s.

(See NEW YORK in this chapter; also Chapter 1, MASSACHUSETTS; also Chapter 2, MANHATTAN.)

RICKEY, BRANCH WESLEY (1881–1965). The baseball executive who inaugurated the farm system for training young players and led the major leagues in desegregating the sport, Rickey maintained a large stock farm near **Chestertown** from 1943 to 1951. The private farmhouse, located at Mill Creek in what is now the housing development of Chesapeake Landing about six miles from town, stands hidden on a lane.

(See PENNSYLVANIA in this chapter; also

Chapter 2, BROOKLYN; also Chapter 4, MISSOURI, OHIO.)

ROOSEVELT, FRANKLIN DELANO (1882–1945). In the center of Catoctin Mountain National Park near **Thurmont,** 75 miles from Washington, the 32nd U.S. president's wartime retreat was "Hi-Catoctin," a 143-acre compound built in 1939 by the Civilian Conservation Corps and Works Progress Administration. Roosevelt renamed it "Shangri-La" after novelist James Hilton's fictional mountain paradise; and President Eisenhower again renamed it "**Camp David**" after his grandson in 1953 (see the entry on Dwight David Eisenhower earlier in this section). The retreat during Roosevelt's time, with rough pine cabins and generally austere conditions, looked like a boot camp, which was how he preferred it. Since then, the compound has been developed into a luxurious, comfortably rustic resort maintained by the U.S. Marines for presidents, seven of whom have lived there since 1945 for varying intervals. Aspen Lodge is the executive domicile, and surrounding lodges also named for trees are for the president's staff and guests. British Prime Minister Winston Churchill visited Roosevelt five times there during World War II; and numerous foreign statesmen of subsequent years have also enjoyed the later installations of heated swimming pool, sauna, golf course and other amenities. Though still designated a presidential retreat, it is essentially a military post, complete with an underground fortress; marines guard the double row of barbed-wire-topped fences, and plain taxpayers are unwelcome. You can, however, glimpse the perimeter fencing on Park Central Road north of the Park Visitor's Center on State Highway 77.

(See DISTRICT OF COLUMBIA, NEW YORK in this chapter; also Chapter 1, MAINE; also Chapter 2, MANHATTAN; also Chapter 4, MICHIGAN; also Chapter 5, GEORGIA.)

RUTH, GEORGE HERMAN "BABE" (1895–1948). Doomed for demolition in 1967, the small row house at 216 Emory St. in **Baltimore** where baseball's "Sultan of Swat" was born has been saved and restored by the Babe Ruth Birthplace Foundation—which also maintains the three adjacent, combined houses in "a kind of Danish modern museum style," according to one biographer. Ruth memorabilia and photos plus period furnishings

are displayed. (Open Wednesday–Sunday 10:30–4:00; 301-727-1539; admission.) Between 1895 and 1906, the impoverished family lived at nine different city addresses. From 1903 to 1914, however, the boy's most frequent residence—and where he developed his prodigious baseball skills—was St. Mary's Industrial School for Boys. Contrary to fond, nostalgic legends about the school fostered by Ruth himself, this was actually a reform institution run by strict lay brothers to confine 800 tough city kids—among whom "Nigger Lips Ruth," as he was known, entered as one of the youngest. The 1866 "school," which stood at the southeast corner of Wilkens and Caton avenues until it was razed during the 1950s, is the present site of Cardinal Gibbons High School for Boys.

(See NEW YORK in this chapter; also Chapter 1, MASSACHUSETTS; also Chapter 2, MANHATTAN.)

SETON, ELIZABETH ANN BAYLEY (1774–1821). Mother Seton, Roman Catholic educator and founder of the first American order of nuns, was also "the first American girl who 'made good' according to God's exact standards," observed Jesuit writer Leonard Feeney, an accomplishment signaled to believers by her 1975 canonization as the first saint born in the United States. In **Baltimore,** she lived in 1808 and 1809 at 600 North Paca St., a small "new-built" brick house that she called her "mansion." The dwelling, operated by trustees of Mother Seton's House, displays period furnishings and Seton memorabilia. (Open Saturday–Sunday 1:00–4:00 and by appointment; 301-523-3443; free.)

At **Emmitsburg,** Mount St. Mary's College and Seminary three miles south on U. S. Highway 15 contains the Seton Shrine Center, where she lived from 1809 to 1821 and established the Sisters of Charity of St. Joseph community. Their first residence, the small "Stone House," was an uncomfortable lodging they held for a year until the nearby "St. Joseph's House" was ready. Mother Seton resided there for the rest of her life. Visitors may receive information there for a self-guided tour of sites on the grounds and a museum of items associated with the saint. (Open daily, daylight hours; free.)

(See NEW YORK in this chapter; also Chapter 2, BRONX, MANHATTAN.)

SINCLAIR, UPTON BEALL (1878–1968). Prolific author and utopian reformer, Sinclair was born in **Baltimore**—in a boardinghouse on Biddle Street, he said. Other sources state the address as 417 North Charles St., an 1812 house demolished in 1969. His childhood was unusual for its constant shifting between the vermin-infested rooms rented by his impoverished parents and the contrasting mansions of rich relatives. "No Aladdin of fairy lore," he wrote, "ever stepped back and forth between the hovel and the palace as frequently as I." His Grandfather Harden's home, where he spent much time during his boyhood, is a mansion still standing at 2010 Maryland Ave. (privately owned).

(See DELAWARE, NEW JERSEY in this chapter; also Chapter 6, CALIFORNIA.)

STEIN, GERTRUDE (1874–1946). Before she established her permanent residence in Paris as the center of the American expatriate movement, the avant-garde author and art patron studied medicine in **Baltimore.** Her residence from 1897 to 1900 was 215 East Biddle St. (privately owned), where she lived with her brother Leo. She left for Europe one month short of taking her medical degree. An earlier brief residence was 2408 Linden Ave. in 1892. City officials plan to identify this late-19th-century private dwelling by historical marker as the Gertrude Stein House.

(See PENNSYLVANIA in this chapter.)

TUBMAN, HARRIET (1820–1913). The "Moses of her people," an escaped slave herself, risked her life and precarious health by personally conducting hundreds of slaves north on the Underground Railroad during the 1850s. She was born of slave parents near **Bucktown** on the plantation of Edward Brodas, where she spent almost a third of her life. The one-room windowless cabin—and, indeed, all of the plantation buildings—are long gone; but the site on Greenbriar Swamp Road is still private farmland.

(See NEW YORK in this chapter.)

NEW JERSEY

Linguistically, at least, Rome never fell. The word "Jersey," for example, is a direct descendant of "Caesar." Wrapped around Norman and Saxon tongues, the largest of the English Channel Islands that Roman troops had named "Caesa-rea" became "Chesrea," "Jesrie," and finally "Jersey." Sir George Carteret, who defended the Isle during England's Parliamentary wars, received the colonial grant of what is today eastern New Jersey in 1664 and named it for his life's great scene.

New Jersey itself is very nearly an island. Besides its Atlantic coast, two large rivers, the Delaware and Hudson, border it with water on all sides except for its 48-mile boundary with New York. The path of the Lenni-Lenape, New Jersey's Algonquin natives, ran across the territory and long predated colonial settlement; the route closely approximated today's State Highway 27 and U.S. Highway 206.

New Jersey's first colonists were Swedes who settled the Delaware valley and Dutch who settled the eastern portion from Manhattan. The state's oldest permanent settlement is Bergen, founded by the Dutch in 1618. New Amsterdam seized the colony in 1655 and was, in turn, displaced by the English in 1664. From 1676, when split into east and west portions, the colony was known as "the Jerseys," and the name is still sometimes pluralized. East Jersey, dominated by New England Puritanism, was economically oriented toward New York City; while West Jersey, influenced by English Quakers, looked to Philadelphia. Though the colony had reunited as one province by 1702, reminders of this split still exist in economic and cultural differences between the Jerseys. More than 100 Revolutionary battles and skirmishes occurred on the territory owing to its important midway position between the two largest colonial cities. Hosting Congress twice, in Princeton and Trenton, New Jersey became the third of the original 13 states in 1787. Our bicameral system of representation—specifically, the creation of the U.S. Senate—resulted from the insistence of constitutional delegates from New Jersey.

Today this state is one of the most highly industrialized in the nation. Manufacturing concentrates in the urbanized complexes that extend from New York City on the east and Philadelphia on the west. New Jersey has the densest population per square mile of any U.S. state—974.2 persons—though it ranks ninth in total numbers. Between its two main urban centers, large portions of New Jersey are still rural with "pine barrens," Appalachian forests and tidal wetlands. It is a state of astonishing contrasts.

In New Jersey resided some of the most eminent people in our history: two U.S. presidents, Grover Cleveland and Woodrow Wilson; inventor Thomas A. Edison; America's foremost poet, Walt Whitman; world-shaker Albert Einstein; maligned activist and music-maker Paul Robeson; and writers James Fenimore Cooper and John O'Hara. Their homes plus those of numerous colonial and Revolutionary figures still exist, though not all can be entered by the public. In quiet Princeton, the state's main educational center, stand homes of the eminent scholars who resided there—most of these remain in private hands also. The larger urban centers, by contrast, offer relatively few intact homes of early notables.

A useful if aging guide for visitors is Sibyl Groff's *New Jersey's Historic Houses: A Guide to Homes Open to the Public* (1971).

ASTOR, JOHN JACOB (1763–1848). Fur entrepreneur and founder of a financial dynasty that still owns much of New York City's most valuable real estate, Astor built his summer mansion "Astor Villa" at **Hoboken** in 1828 but used it only occasionally thereafter. A four-story brick tenement replaced it at 132–134 Washington St. in 1889.

(See Chapter 2, MANHATTAN.)

BARTON, CLARA (1821–1912).
Exhibit: The eventual founder of the American Red Cross boarded at an unknown site in **Bordentown** when she volunteered to organize a free public school there (one of the nation's first). It was so successful that town officials installed a male principal, and Barton resigned within a year. The school, a one-room brick cottage with period schoolroom items, still stands at 142 Crosswicks St. and is operated by the Bordentown Historical Society. (Open by appointment; 609-298-1740; admission.)

(See DISTRICT OF COLUMBIA, MARYLAND, NEW YORK in this chapter; also Chapter 1, MASSACHUSETTS.)

BERRYMAN, JOHN (1914–1972). While teaching English at Princeton University in **Princeton,** the poet lived in Apartment M-1 at 120 Prospect Ave., (1944–54), a large, brick structure that dates from about 1910 and is currently a university housing facility. Here Berryman wrote much of his *Homage to Mistress Bradstreet* (1956).

(See Chapter 1, MASSACHUSETTS; also Chapter 4, MINNESOTA.)

BRADY, JAMES BUCHANAN "DIAMOND JIM" (1856–1917). Vast in wealth, generosity, appetites and bulk, the financier and *bon vivant* of Broadway bought Ellesdale Manor Farm near **South Branch** in 1901. "I ain't gonna get anything elaborate, just a place for weekends and the like," he stated—then promptly spent thousands of dollars renovating and enlarging the estate, where he entertained cronies and show people on a lavish scale. He raised livestock, squab and acres of produce, shipping barrels of foodstuffs on ice to rich and not-so-rich friends alike. "Hell, we got so goddamn much food down there that I hadda do somethin' with it," he explained. "It's a case of feedin' it to the pigs, or sendin' it to my friends—and the pigs get too much to eat as it is." Brady's Raritan River farm purchased in 1906, remains privately owned.

In **Atlantic City,** a favorite playground, his years of incessant eating finally did him in, and he died with no regrets at the Shelburne Hotel after a six-month residence. Typically he had renovated his enormous, $1,000-per-week apartment there with a glass veranda facing the ocean. This hotel still stands on the ocean front at Boardwalk and South Michigan Avenue.

(See Chapter 2, MANHATTAN.)

BURR, AARON (1756–1836). Burr, the vice president under President Jefferson and a brilliant, enigmatic figure of American history, was born in **Newark**. The two-story, brownstone parsonage at Broad and William streets was his home for only a few months before the family moved to Princeton, where Burr's father became the second president of Princeton College. A commercial building now occupies his birth site.

At **Princeton,** the family lived for two years at President's House National Historic Landmark, the yellow-brick, two and one-half-story residence of Princeton's presidents from 1756–1879; the Burrs were its first occupants. Many famous guests were entertained there, including George Washington (see the entry on Washington later in this section), John Adams, Henry Clay and Andrew Jackson. The house stands on the Princeton University campus just west of Nassau Hall National Historic Landmark, in which Burr attended classes and graduated in 1772.

(See NEW YORK, PENNSYLVANIA in this chapter; also Chapter 1, CONNECTICUT; also Chapter 2, MANHATTAN, STATEN ISLAND.)

CLEVELAND, GROVER (1837–1908). The 22nd and 24th U.S. president was born in a Presbyterian parsonage at **Caldwell,** the only New Jersey native to occupy the White House. Cleveland Birthplace State Historic Site, a two and one-half-story frame house built in 1832, has been restored at 207 Bloomfield Ave. There the New Jersey Dept. of Environmental Protection displays many of his belongings including his infant cradle, the cane rocking chair he used in the White House, his huge Victorian bed, and the desk he used as the mayor of Buffalo, N.Y. (Open Wednesday–Friday 9:00–12:00, 1:00–6:00, Saturday 9:00–12:00, 1:00–5:00, Sunday 1:00–6:00; 201-226-1810; free.)

At **Princeton,** the ex-President's last home, and where he died, was Westland National Historic Landmark at 58 Bayard Lane (privately owned). This stucco mansion dates from 1854.

(See DISTRICT OF COLUMBIA, MARYLAND, NEW YORK in this chapter; also Chapter 1, MASSACHUSETTS, NEW HAMPSHIRE.)

COHAN, GEORGE MICHAEL (1878–1942). Versatile performer, playwright and composer, Cohan resided at frequent intervals in **Atlantic City,** where he occupied suites from 1909 at the venerable Shelburne Hotel (see the entry on James Buchanan "Diamond Jim" Brady earlier in this section). "Throughout the years," wrote biographer Ward Morehouse, "Cohan's ideal workshop was a hotel room. It was always his notion that whatever inspired moments he ever had were those when he was in his slippers and robe in the suite of a big hotel." Cohan wrote his autobiography, *Twenty Years on Broadway,* during a stay at the Shelburne in 1924.

(See NEW YORK in this chapter; also Chapter 1, MASSACHUSETTS, RHODE ISLAND; also Chapter 2, MANHATTAN.)

COMSTOCK, ANTHONY (1844–1915). "Comstockery," a term coined by George Bernard Shaw for America's chronic puritanical spasms, originated from the surname of the most powerful prude in our history. As an official "vice suppressor," Comstock built "Breeze Crest," his last home (1897–1915), in **Summit.** Privately owned, the turreted Victorian mansion stands at

35 Beekman Road—"as solid and upright as the Victorian virtues he tried to champion," in the words of a local historian.

(See Chapter 1, CONNECTICUT; also Chapter 2, BROOKLYN.)

COOPER, JAMES FENIMORE (1789–1851). In **Burlington,** the Cooper House at 457 High St. was the author's birthplace. Built about 1780, the red-brick colonial home displays period furnishings and a bed warmer that belonged to the family. Also exhibited are some of Cooper's first editions and part of his manuscript of *The Spy* (1821). The house is operated by the Burlington County Historical Society. (Open Wednesday 1:00–4:00, Sunday 2:00–4:00; 609-386-4773; free.)

(See NEW YORK in this chapter; also Chapter 2, MANHATTAN.)

CRANE, STEPHEN (1871–1900). The author's birthplace in **Newark** stood at 14 Mulberry Place until 1941, an elegant, three-story brick parsonage that was his home to age three. A small playground, with a memorial marker and low brick wall that displayed 34 ceramic plaques depicting scenes from Crane stories and poems, replaced the dwelling. This site, vandalized and neglected along with Crane's memory since then (while European cities continue to note his anniversaries), remains a littered receptacle for "the dreary kind of refuse that only a city without poets could produce," wrote a Newark reporter. Even the bronze marker has been removed to the Newark Public Library to prevent its thievery.

(See Chapter 2, MANHATTAN.)

DeMILLE, CECIL BLOUNT (1881–1959). "Pamlico," the three-story white frame house built by the eventual film producer's father in 1891, stood on 76 hilltop acres overlooking Pompton Lake. DeMille's father died there in 1893, and his mother organized a school at Pamlico to support the family. A prominent student was socialite Evelyn Nesbit, removed there by her lover, architect Stanford White, to escape the amorous attentions of actor John Barrymore. Barrymore pursued, and when Nesbit refused to see him, left passionate love notes strewn about the grounds. DeMille and his elder brother William (also a film director) lived there until 1896. The estate adjoined "Sunnybank," the boyhood home of the popular writer of dog stories, Albert Payson

Terhune. Today only the gatehouse to Pamlico survives, marked by a tablet at 266 Terhune Drive in **Wayne.** The estate itself has been subdivided and holds many recently built houses.

(See Chapter 1, MASSACHUSETTS; also Chapter 6, CALIFORNIA.)

DIX, DOROTHEA LYNDE (1802–1887). **Trenton** was the mental-health reformer's last home. In 1848, the New Jersey Lunatic Asylum opened at a site she selected along the Delaware River. She considered this institution her "first-born child" among the mental hospitals she established, and she occupied an apartment there from 1881 to 1887. The site is now occupied by Trenton State Hospital on Sullivan Way.

(See Chapter 1, MAINE, MASSACHUSETTS.)

DORSEY, THOMAS FRANCIS "TOMMY" (1905–1956). In **Bernardsville,** trombonist-bandleader Tommy Dorsey's home from 1935 to 1941 was a 1909 house that he remodeled in 1937. It stands privately owned at 200 Old Army Road.

(See PENNSYLVANIA in this chapter; also Chapter 1, CONNECTICUT.)

DOUBLEDAY, ABNER (1819–1893). The Civil War general who supposedly fired the first defensive shot for the Union at Fort Sumter in 1861—and who also, some claim, invented baseball—made **Mendham** his permanent home from about 1874. He built his home on Hilltop Road opposite the present Hilltop School, a dwelling razed about 1940. In Mendham, wrote a local historian, " 'The General' never walked; he marched, hands behind him, slowly and in perfect form . . . with his little black-clad wife always a pace or so behind him. He took his constitutional daily and occasionally gave voice to a cough of shattering magnitude." Local folk grew accustomed to "old Major Twodays, just a-coughin'."

(See NEW YORK in this chapter.)

EDISON, THOMAS ALVA (1847–1931). At **Menlo Park,** Edison developed his most notable inventions, including the phonograph (1877) and the incandescent bulb (1879). His original complex of six buildings where he lived and worked from 1876 to 1886, was moved intact to Henry Ford's Greenfield Village in Dearborn, Mich., in 1929. Today Edison State Park and Museum, operated by the New Jersey Department of Environmental

Protection, marks the site on Christie Street three blocks north of State Highway 27. There the 131-foot Edison Memorial Tower incorporates several of his devices and inventions, including a 13-foot eternal light bulb, which Edison himself switched on in 1929. (Open Tuesday–Saturday 10:00–12:00, 1:00–5:00, Sunday 1:00–5:00; 201-549-3299; admission.)

Edison National Historic Site at West Main Street and Lakeside Avenue in **West Orange** became the inventor's permanent home and laboratory complex in 1886. Original models of his inventions, showings of his first movies in his "Black Maria" studio, his machine shop, library and science laboratory are displayed. His home "Glenmont," a 23-room Victorian house built about 1880 and where he died at age 84, exhibits original furnishings and memorabilia, including his "thought bench," a massive desk overlooking the 13½-acre estate. The taped voices of Edison's daughter and son evoke scenes of their childhood home. Glenmont stands in Llewellyn Park, Glen Avenue off Main Street, about half a mile from the museum compound. The National Park Service conducts hourly guided tours through the home and laboratory, beginning at the Main Street location. (Open daily 9:30–5:00; 201-736-5050; admission.)

(See Chapter 4, MICHIGAN, OHIO; also Chapter 5, FLORIDA, KENTUCKY.)

EINSTEIN, ALBERT (1879–1955). The most influential physicist since Sir Isaac Newton, Einstein made his permanent home in **Princeton** from 1933, after he fled Nazi Germany. His first home was 2 Library Place, a house dating from 1848 but much altered before his residence. It is now a private apartment dwelling owned by Princeton Theological Seminary. His last home (1935–55) was 112 Mercer Road, a modest, two-story house built about 1835 and moved to its present site in 1876. It is privately owned.

(See Chapter 6, CALIFORNIA.)

ELIOT, THOMAS STEARNS (1888–1965). The poet born in St. Louis who became a naturalized Englishman, T. S. Eliot came to lecture and write at the Institute for Advanced Study in **Princeton** in 1948 and 1949, residing in the white frame house at 14 Alexander St. (privately owned). He wrote his drama *The Cocktail Party* (1949) during his Princeton stay.

THOMAS A. EDISON AND "GLENMONT." The inventor made this rambling Victorian mansion in **West Orange** his permanent home in 1886. Edison's rustic chair in this 1917 photo may have been a gift from his naturalist friend John Burroughs. *(Courtesy Edison National Historic Site)*

(See Chapter 1, MASSACHUSETTS; also Chapter 4, MISSOURI.)

FERMI, ENRICO (1901–1954). The Italian-born physicist who became the "father of the atomic age" by creating the first sustained nuclear chain reaction taught at Columbia University in New York City from 1939 to 1942. During this period he resided in a home he purchased at 382 Summit Ave. in **Leonia.** The house remains privately owned.

(See Chapter 4, ILLINOIS; also Chapter 6, NEW MEXICO.)

FOSTER, STEPHEN COLLINS (1826–1864). The only dwelling of the popular songwriter from Pittsburgh that still stands anywhere is the three-story brick house at 601 Bloomfield St. in **Hoboken.** Foster, down on his luck as usual and separated from his wife, occupied rooms there in 1854; while living there, he composed one of his best-known songs, "Jeanie With the Light Brown Hair," supposedly written with his wife Jane in mind. The building, which was probably quite new in 1854, now houses basement stores and private apartments above.

(See PENNSYLVANIA in this chapter; also Chapter 2, MANHATTAN; also Chapter 4, OHIO; also Chapter 5, FLORIDA, KENTUCKY.)

GARFIELD, JAMES ABRAM (1831–1881). On September 6, 1881, two months after being shot in the back by assassin Charles Guiteau, the 20th U.S. president was taken at his own request to **Long Branch,** the fashionable coastal resort where he had settled his family away from Washington's heat earlier in the summer. To avoid moving him by jolting carriage, a railroad spur was laid in one night to the door of Franklyn Cottage on the grounds of the Elberon Hotel, where Garfield lingered for two more weeks, then died, as much a victim of bungling doctors as of the madman's bullet. The site of the hotel is on Ocean Avenue opposite Lincoln Avenue; at 6 Garfield Terrace, the granite monument marking the cottage site resulted from the 1962 fund-raising efforts of 12-year-old local resident Bruce Frankel.

(See DISTRICT OF COLUMBIA; also Chapter 4, OHIO.)

GRANT, ULYSSES SIMPSON (1822–1885). After the old soldier and 18th U.S. president first visited **Long Branch** in 1869, the resort community on the Atlantic coast became a status summer place for the very rich and influential. Grant wasn't rich, but plenty of his cronies were; and several of them with sudden faith in the future of Long Branch bought him an 1866, two and one-half-story Tudor "cottage" at 991 Ocean Ave., which soon became known as "the summer capital." Grant, naive in all but war, apparently thought they did it because they liked him. There, wrote Thomas Fleming, he liked to sit on his porch "in a white plug hat and linen duster, smoking a cigar and swapping yarns." Grant returned there almost every summer for 15 years; and there he began writing his classic *Personal Memoirs* to rescue his family from the financial ruin he suffered when his summer pals defrauded him. The house was demolished in 1963.

(See DISTRICT OF COLUMBIA, NEW YORK in this chapter; also Chapter 2, MANHATTAN; also Chapter 4, ILLINOIS, MICHIGAN, MISSOURI, OHIO; also Chapter 5, VIRGINIA; also Chapter 6, WASHINGTON.)

GREEN, HENRIETTA ROBINSON "HETTY" (1835–1916). Probably the richest woman in America as well as a legendary miser and eccentric, Green lived at lengthy intervals in **Hoboken.** The five-story, yellow-brick apartment house at 1203 Washington St., where she resided in different flats and under various names from 1895, is still a private apartment dwelling.

(See Chapter 1, MASSACHUSETTS, RHODE ISLAND, VERMONT; also Chapter 2, MANHATTAN.)

HALSEY, WILLIAM FREDERICK, JR. (1882–1959). The World War II Pacific naval commander was born and raised in **Elizabeth** at 134 West Jersey St., a house built about 1864. It has been converted into a restaurant called Polly's Elizabeth Inn.

(See Chapter 2, MANHATTAN; also Chapter 5, VIRGINIA.)

HAMILTON, ALEXANDER (1755–1804). Revolutionary soldier, controversial founding father and first secretary of the treasury, Hamilton is believed to have boarded in 1773 at Boxwood Hall National Historic Landmark, 1073 East Jersey St. in **Elizabeth,** while attending school in the town. This two-story, shingle house, built about 1755, was the home of Revolutionary statesman Elias Boudinot. Period furnishings are displayed by the New Jersey Department of Environmental Protection. (Open Wednesday–Friday 9:00–12:00, 1:00–6:00, Saturday 10:00–12:00, 1:00–6:00, Sunday 1:00–6:00; 201-352-3559; admission.)

(See NEW YORK in this chapter; also Chapter 2, MANHATTAN.)

HARTE, BRET (1836–1902). In **Morristown,** the tale spinner of Western mining camps lived in 1874 and 1875 at "The Willows," the Joseph W. Revere House on Mendham Avenue. Designed in 1854 by a grandson of Paul Revere, the two and one-half-story, clapboard house is privately owned.

(See Chapter 2, MANHATTAN; also Chapter 6, CALIFORNIA.)

HENRY, JOSEPH (1797–1878). At **Princeton,** the physicist pioneered research in electromagnetism. The 1837 Henry House, a two and one-half-story brick dwelling that he may have designed himself, originally stood between West College and Stanhope Hall on the Princeton campus. Since 1870 it has been thrice shifted on the campus but since 1946 has stood northeast of Nassau Hall. Henry resided in this house from 1837 to 1848. It is now the private official residence of the Dean of Faculty.

(See DISTRICT OF COLUMBIA in this chapter.)

INNESS, GEORGE (1825–1894). Childhood home of the painter in the 1830s and 1840s stood at High Street and Central Avenue in **Newark.**

At **Perth Amboy,** Inness resided at "Eagleswood," a 19th-century house at 313 Convery Blvd. He completed almost 150 canvases there, a period in which he began branching out from landscape painting. Now used to store junked auto parts and surrounded by wrecked cars, the house has been much altered, but the distinctive mansard roof and thick stone walls remain. The owner, who unsuccessfully fought designation of the building as a state historic site, considers interested visitors "a pain in the neck."

(See Chapter 1, MASSACHUSETTS.)

KINSEY, ALFRED CHARLES (1894–1956). The biologist whose pioneering research into human sexuality unaccountably met most resistance from the scientific community was born in **Hoboken** at 611 Bloomfield St., a brick, three-story house built about 1883. The family soon moved to 621 Bloomfield St., where Kinsey grew to adulthood. Both dwellings are privately owned.

(See Chapter 4, INDIANA.)

LINDBERGH, CHARLES AUGUSTUS (1902–1974). Near **Hopewell,** the house that riveted the nation's attention during the sensational 1932 kidnap-murder of the aviator's two-year-old son stands on Lindbergh Road off Stoutsville-Wertsville Road. Now known as "Highfields," the two-story, ten-room fieldstone house that Lindbergh built in 1930 on 350 wooded acres is a private state center for juvenile offenders. The Lindberghs first viewed this site from the air and selected it for its isolation. They seldom lived there after the kidnapping and, in 1941, donated the house and grounds to the state.

The home of Anne Morrow Lindbergh's parents, "Next Day Hill" in **Englewood,** was also the frequent home of the aviator and his wife during long intervals before and after the tragedy. Ambassador Dwight Morrow built this Georgian mansion at 435 Lydecker St. in 1928. The structure now houses the Elisabeth Morrow School, named for Lindbergh's mother-in-law.

(See NEW YORK in this chapter; also Chapter 1, CONNECTICUT; also Chapter 3, DISTRICT OF COLUMBIA; also Chapter 4, MICHIGAN, MINNESOTA, MISSOURI; also Chapter 6, HAWAII.)

McCLELLAN, GEORGE BRINTON (1826–1885). The Union commander of the Potomac built his home "Maywood" in 1870 at **West Orange.** It stood until 1938 in the St. Cloud section of the city between Ridgeway Road and Prospect Avenue.

(See DISTRICT OF COLUMBIA, PENNSYLVANIA in this chapter; also Chapter 2, MANHATTAN.)

MANN, THOMAS (1875–1955). At **Princeton,** the German novelist lived from 1938 to 1941 at 65 Stockton St. (at the corner of Library Place) while lecturing and writing at Princeton University. The building now houses the Aquinas Institute of Princeton.

(See Chapter 6, CALIFORNIA.)

MEAD, MARGARET (1901–1978). "However far away we moved and however often," wrote the famed anthropologist in *Blackberry Winter* (1972), "we always came home again to Hammonton." Her frequent home from 1902 to 1911 and the source of some of her happiest childhood memories, the 19th-century house stands at 338 Fairview Ave. (privately owned) in **Hammonton,** a five-acre estate when she and her parents lived there.

(See PENNSYLVANIA in this chapter; also Chapter 2, MANHATTAN.)

MILLER, GLENN (1904–1944). The popular bandleader's last home (from 1939) was the Cotswold Apartments, 1 Byrne Lane off Serpentine and Inness roads in **Tenafly.** Miller had moved to New Jersey from New York City on the advice of his agent for state income tax purposes. He and his family occupied rooms on the first floor of the building, which had previously been remodeled from the 45-room French castle mansion of a large estate. It still contains privately occupied apartments.

(See Chapter 2, QUEENS; also Chapter 4, IOWA, MISSOURI, NEBRASKA; also Chapter 6, COLORADO.)

NAST, THOMAS (1840–1902). "Villa Fontana," the brilliant editorial cartoonist's home from 1873, stands at MacCulloch Avenue and Miller Road in **Morristown.** The two and one-half-story frame house dates from 1860 and 1861 and is privately owned. Nast's pictorial legacy includes the Democratic donkey, the Republican elephant and the modern version of Santa Claus.

(See Chapter 2, MANHATTAN.)

NEUMANN, JOHN VON (1902–1957). At **Princeton,** where the Hungarian-born mathematics prodigy taught, he bought the dwelling at 26 Westcott Road in 1939 as his permanent residence. Built about 1925, it is privately owned.

OAKLEY, ANNIE (1860–1926). In 1892, the sharpshooter who amazed audiences for almost 50 years with her incredible skill built a spacious frame house in **Nutley,** where she and husband Frank Butler lived until 1913. Because both were so accustomed to living out of trunks, they designed the house without closets. This home at 300 Grant Ave. has since been replaced by two private dwellings at 303 and 306 Grant.

Exhibit: The **Nutley** Historical Society Museum at 65 Church St. displays several of Annie Oakley's guns and letters.

(See MARYLAND in this chapter; also Chapter 4, OHIO; also Chapter 5, FLORIDA, NORTH CAROLINA.)

O'HARA, JOHN HENRY (1905–1970). Prolific novelist and story writer, O'Hara made his permanent home in **Princeton.** In 1957, he built "Linebrook" in French provincial style on three acres at Pretty Brook and Province Line roads. There in his study wing, he wrote his later works including *From the Terrace* (1958) and *Ourselves to Know* (1960). The white-brick house with ten rooms is privately owned. O'Hara's fascinating study in this house has been re-created at Pennsylvania State University.

(See NEW YORK, PENNSYLVANIA in this chapter; also Chapter 2, MANHATTAN.)

OPPENHEIMER, J. ROBERT (1904–1967). The nuclear physicist who became a victim of the anti-Communist hysteria of the 1950s—the only declared "security risk" who was later given the prestigious Fermi Award (1963)—Oppenheimer directed the Institute for Advanced Study from 1947 to 1966. His **Princeton** home, "Olden Manor," dates in its oldest portion (the west wing) from 1697; the middle and east portions are 18th- and 19th-century additions. The frame mansion, still the official private residence of the Institute's director, stands on Olden Lane.

(See Chapter 2, MANHATTAN; also Chapter 6, CALIFORNIA, NEW MEXICO.)

PAINE, THOMAS (1737–1809). In 1783, the patriot and revolutionist bought five acres in **Bordentown,** and his home still stands at 2 West Church St., today a private dwelling and dental office. Paine lived there at intervals between his travels until 1787, when he went to live for years in France. At Bordentown, he worked on his model for an iron bridge and other technical designs but never resided there after 1803.

(See NEW YORK, PENNSYLVANIA in this chapter; also Chapter 2, BROOKLYN, MANHATTAN.)

ROBESON, PAUL BUSTILL (1898–1976). Civil rights activist and one of the nation's greatest singing and acting performers—widely acclaimed in almost every country but his own—Robeson was born in **Princeton** at 110 Witherspoon St. (at the corner of Green Street). The 19th-century house, now sided with aluminum, was the scene of a 1904 accident in which Robeson's mother was fatally burned. It is privately owned.

(See Chapter 1, CONNECTICUT; also Chapter 2, MANHATTAN.)

ROCKEFELLER, JOHN DAVISON (1839–1937). The multimillionaire was an avid golfer and bought the 1895 Ocean County Hunt Club in **Lakewood** for his private summer preserve in the late 1890s. "Golf House" burned in 1917, and its razing was completed after Rockefeller's death. The site is currently Rockefeller Park in Lakewood.

(See NEW YORK in this chapter; also Chapter 2, BROOKLYN, MANHATTAN; also Chapter 4, OHIO; also Chapter 5, FLORIDA, GEORGIA.)

SARNOFF, DAVID (1891–1971). The communications engineer, television pioneer and founder of the National Broadcasting Company frequently occupied an office and living quarters from about 1951—though he never stayed overnight—at the David Sarnoff Library in **Princeton.** The library is part of the David Sarnoff Research Center, operated by the Radio Corporation of America, and illuminates Sarnoff's private, public and military careers, mainly through items of personal correspondence with world leaders and display cases of citations, gifts and awards. This place was "the closest Sarnoff came to having a country estate," wrote one biographer. Sarnoff Library is located at 201 Washington Road. (Open Monday–Friday 10:00–3:00; 609-734-2000; free.)

(See NEW YORK in this chapter; also Chapter 2, MANHATTAN.)

SCOTT, WINFIELD (1786–1866). Though often absent on various military assignments, "Old Fuss and Feathers," the dominant U.S. military leader of his time and an 1852 presidential candidate, made his home in **Elizabeth** for more than 30 years. "Hampton Place," an 18th-century Federal mansion at 1105 East Jersey St., was razed in 1928 for a gas station. A replica of this house was built in the late 1960s at 507 Westminster Ave. (privately owned).

(See Chapter 2, MANHATTAN; also Chapter 5, VIRGINIA.)

SINCLAIR, UPTON BEALL (1878–1968). Trying to establish himself as a writer and committed utopian, Sinclair bought a 60-acre farm three miles northwest of **Princeton** in 1904 at Province Line and Drakes Corner roads. He set up in a tar paper shack he had previously used for a studio and practiced a naive, idealistic celibacy with his unenthusiastic first wife, Meta Fuller Sinclair—a two-year experience that led to their divorce. The 19th-century farmhouse, the scene of so much domestic agony, was also the locale of great success—for there Sinclair wrote his best-known novel *The Jungle* (1906). The house remains privately owned.

(See DELAWARE, MARYLAND in this chapter; also Chapter 6, CALIFORNIA.)

STANTON, ELIZABETH CADY (1815–1902). The prominent feminist writer lived in **Tenafly,** where her home from 1868 to 1887 stands at 135 Highwood Ave. The two and one-half-story, clapboard dwelling that she built and later sold is privately owned.

(See NEW YORK in this chapter; also Chapter 2, MANHATTAN.)

TOSCANINI, ARTURO (1867–1957).

Exhibit: The volatile orchestra conductor, one of the world's greatest, left his largest heritage in the form of many excellent recordings. He also left a baton, letters and a Verdi musical score inscribed with his handwritten notes. These personal items may be seen at the David Sarnoff

Library in **Princeton** (see the entry on David Sarnoff earlier in this section).

(See Chapter 2, BRONX.)

VANDERBILT, CORNELIUS (1794–1877).
VANDERBILT, WILLIAM HENRY (1821–1885).

The elder Vanderbilt, founder of the financial dynasty, began his climb to wealth by operating a ferry boat from New York City to **New Brunswick.** In 1818, he acquired the 1801 "Bellona Hall," a three-story clapboard inn on the waterfront at New Brunswick, to serve the passengers he carried. Named after his steamboat, the inn was efficiently managed by Vanderbilt's wife, Sophia, and was the Vanderbilt home until 1829. Son William, the eventual railroad magnate, was born there. This building, located on Burnet Street, was demolished along with the entire street in 1951 to make way for construction of State Highway 18.

(See Chapter 2, MANHATTAN, STATEN ISLAND.)

WASHINGTON, GEORGE (1732–1799). New Jersey has three residences in which the Revolutionary commander settled for intervals of several months with his wife Martha during the course of the war.

At **Somerville,** they occupied the two-story, white frame Wallace House in 1778 and 1779. It's not generally noted that Washington's main activities there were partying with Revolutionary brass and planning the Sullivan Expedition that ravaged New York Iroquois settlements in 1779. Dating from 1778 and operated by the New Jersey Department of Environmental Protection, the house is located at 38 Washington Place. Exhibited there are Revolutionary War relics, period furnishings and Washington's metal campaign chest. (Open Wednesday–Friday 9:00–12:00, 1:00–6:00, Saturday 10:00–12:00, 1:00–6:00, Sunday 1:00–6:00; 201-725-1015; admission.)

At **Morristown** National Historical Park, the Washingtons occupied Ford Mansion National Historic Landmark during the bitter winter of 1779–80, a period that made the previous year's encampment at Valley Forge seem like a picnic. The large Georgian mansion at 230 Morris Ave. dates from 1774; inside, short legends on doorways describe the use of each room. About 80 percent of the furnishings are original to the house. Behind is a historical museum contain-

WALT WHITMAN'S LAST HOME. This photograph shows 330 Mickle St. in **Camden** as it looked shortly after the poet's death there. Chatting in the doorway is Mary O. Davis, the widow who served him for many years as housekeeper and nurse. The adjacent houses also remain standing. *(Courtesy Walt Whitman House, Camden.)*

ing, it is claimed, the best collection of Washington's personal items in the country, along with numerous Revolutionary weapons, clothing, furnishings and Morristown relics. Both buildings are operated by the National Park Service. (Open daily 9:00–5:00; 201-539-2016; admission.)

When the war ended in 1783, Washington did much official entertaining at "Rockingham," the two-story frame house where he wrote and delivered his Farewell Address to the armies. This twenty-room mansion, dating from the 1730s, became his residence for three months just before he retired to Mount Vernon. Located east of **Rocky Hill** on County Highway 518 just west of the State Highway 27 junction, the house stands about three-quarters of a mile from its first location on the Millstone River; quarrying operations have destroyed the original hill site. Period furnishings exhibited by the New Jersey Department of Environmental Protection include some original items used by Washington. (Open Wednesday–Friday 9:00–12:00, 1:00–6:00, Saturday 10:00–12:00, 1:00–6:00, Sunday 1:00–6:00; 609-921-8835; admission.)

(See NEW YORK, PENNSYLVANIA in this chapter; also Chapter 2, MANHATTAN; also Chapter 5, VIRGINIA.)

WHITMAN, WALT (1819–1892). **Camden** was the poet's last home from 1873, when he suffered a stroke that partially incapacitated him. In 1884, he bought the only house he ever owned; he revised his *Leaves of Grass* and welcomed many noted guests there. Whitman House National

Historic Landmark at 330 Mickle St., a small, two-story frame dwelling that dates from 1848, remains just as it was when Whitman lived and died there. During those years, Whitman had no steady income, but he was such an intriguing literary curiosity that friends donated occasional "purses" to meet his expenses. The only furnishings he owned were a rocking chair, bed, oil stove, brass lamp and some wooden crates. His downstairs parlor-study displays a rich trove of personal items: the huge rocking chair where he sat while reading or conversing, numerous mementoes, letters and photographs—even a lock of his flowing gray hair. Upstairs is the bedroom from which he rarely emerged after a second stroke in 1888, though he continued to work. Visitors can compare the present appearance of these rooms with displayed photos taken when the poet lived there; the only real difference today is that they lack the imposing disarray of papers heaped around him—"a sort of result and storage collection of my own past life," he remarked, a pile from which he could instantly retrieve anything he wanted. The New Jersey Department of Environmental Protection maintains the home. (Open Tuesday–Saturday 10:00–12:00, 1:00–5:00, Sunday 2:00–5:00; 609-964-5383; admission.) Another Whitman residence—rarely noticed but where the poet spent 11 of his 19 Camden years—also stands, at 431 Stevens St. (privately owned). This 1873 dwelling, a three-story brick house built by his brother George, was the poet's lodginghouse before he moved to Mickle Street. It was converted to apartments sometime before 1950.

(See DISTRICT OF COLUMBIA, NEW YORK in this chapter; also Chapter 2, BROOKLYN, MANHATTAN.)

WILSON, EDMUND (1895–1972). In **Red Bank,** the birthplace of the famed literary critic stands at 100 McLaren St., a large, 19th-century frame house recently renovated into private apartments. Wilson's father, a chronically depressed man and one-time state official, owned the dwelling that his only child described in *Piece of My Mind* (1958) as "ugliness and gloom." This was Wilson's home until age 11.

(See NEW YORK in this chapter; also Chapter 1, MASSACHUSETTS; also Chapter 2, MANHATTAN.)

WILSON, WOODROW (1856–1924). Long before considering politics as a career, the eventual 28th U.S. president taught political science at **Princeton** and served the university as president from 1902 to 1910. All of his four homes remain in private hands. Dr. Wilson owned 72 Library Place and lived there until 1896. This two-story frame house was built in 1836 and restored 100 years later. His next home, which he built in 1896, stands at 82 Library Place. As president of the university, he occupied "Prospect," the 1849 official residence on the campus southeast of Nassau Hall. Wilson's last Princeton residence, where he lived as New Jersey's governor from 1910 to 1913—and from which he entered the White House—was 25 Cleveland Lane, built about 1905.

"Shadow Lawn," Wilson's 52-room summer White House at **West Long Branch,** stood on the site of the present Woodrow Wilson Hall, on the Shadow Lawn campus of Monmouth College, until destroyed by fire in 1927. This was his campaign headquarters in 1916; on election night, he retired there thinking he had lost to Charles Evans Hughes but awoke to celebrate victory instead.

(See DISTRICT OF COLUMBIA in this chapter; also Chapter 1, NEW HAMPSHIRE; also Chapter 5, GEORGIA, SOUTH CAROLINA, VIRGINIA.)

NEW YORK

(See Chapter 2 for New York City boroughs.)

Most of us who live outside the state think of New York solely as a city that lies hyperactive and noisy somewhere around New Jersey. New York State, however, is not easily overshadowed in its historical or national importance.

New York was the site of a native organization unique in world history, the Iroquois Confederation. The five nations comprising the original Confederation were peoples of different languages and customs who combined a high degree of tribal independence with a mutual security and support system. This remarkably sophisticated structure, America's own "United Nations," operated far in advance of any peacekeeping system devised by the so-called civilized nations of Europe. The New York Iroquois demonstrated to the jealously separate colonies that unification was workable. Benjamin Franklin, for one, was so impressed with the system that he suggested its use as a model for colonial unification 20 years before the Revolution. (Unfortunately, the Iroquois concept is still far too advanced for modern international politics.) From colonial times forth, however, governmental and administrative skills have always been New York strong points; and many of the state's public officials have gained national prominence for their ability to enlarge focus beyond immediate parochial demands.

Henry Hudson, an Englishman sailing under Dutch colors, approached the vicinity of modern Albany in 1609, searching for the fabled northwest passage to the East Indies. Coincidentally, it was during the same year that Frenchman Samuel de Champlain was exploring the lake to the west that would bear his name. Thus the chief world powers began squaring off for 150 years of European wars, fought most fiercely and destructively between their American colonies. For the natives, cynically used as tools and weapons of war, these conflicts spelled incessant, total defeat.

In eastern New York, the Dutch controlled the Hudson area or New Netherlands until 1664, surrendering it finally to the English 10 years later; Fort Orange, settled by the Dutch in 1624, became Albany. The new proprietor, to whom Charles II had granted the entire colony, was the Duke of York (later James II), and the colony-state has been New York ever since.

Much more violence occurred in western New York. Each of the French and Indian wars coursed across this territory, though the scale of fighting was less intense and barbaric than in New England. France and its Iroquois allies remained in sporadic control of the Champlain and Niagara country until 1760, when Montreal fell to the British.

Almost one-third of all Revolutionary War action occurred on New York soil. "New Yorkers have shown an exceptional interest in preserving their Colonial and Revolutionary history," wrote a recent observer, "perhaps partly because of their not being diverted by the Civil War interest that predominates in the South." The state entered the Union as 11th of the original 13 in 1788. Much of its rapid commercial growth resulted from construction of the Buffalo-to-Albany Erie Canal, opened in 1825. Today New York is the nation's foremost industrial state; manufacturing concentrates in Long Island, the Hudson and Mohawk valleys, and the central and southern parts of the state.

Smaller communities produced such natives as George Westinghouse, George Eastman, Elizabeth Cady Stanton, Margaret Sanger and Sojourner Truth. Westchester County, just north of Manhattan, has hosted many prominent names in the arts and business—Theodore Dreiser, Ethel Barrymore and the Rockefellers, to name only a few; and Long Island was long noted for the palatial retreats of Manhattan's upper crust, writers and show people. Residents Washington Irving and James Fenimore Cooper created the first distinctively American literature in New York. Samuel L. Clemens did much of his best work upstate, and Walt Whitman was a native Long Islander. In art, the Hudson River School, founded by Thomas Cole in Catskill, gave Americans extraordinary views of the country's scenic wonders; painter Frederic Remington opened the West, as much as any pioneer, to our perceptions; and Edward Hopper from Nyack revealed fresh, sobering views of our cities. New York's master politicians have included the Clintons, Martin Van Buren, Samuel Tilden, Charles Evans Hughes, Elihu Root, the Roosevelts and Nelson Rockefeller. Susan B. Anthony, Frederick Douglass, Jackson Pollock and John Coltrane, all longtime residents, made social and creative waves that have not yet subsided.

Taking a cue from George Washington, who labeled the state America's "seat of Empire," New York named itself the "Empire State" when it surpassed all other states in population and wealth during the 1820s. Though its population fell second to California's in 1964, the nickname is not likely to change. Its experience and current contributions make the state a vastly more diversified "seat of Empire" than Washington could have imagined.

ANDRÉ, JOHN (1751–1780). At **Tappan,** the British spy spent the last week of his life imprisoned in the stone Mabie Tavern, now a public restaurant called " '76 House" on Main Street. This building, constructed as a Dutch-style farmhouse before 1750, has been a tavern for most of its existence, carefully restored when on the verge of collapse in 1897. Inside, look for the narrow room, visible through a half-door from the dining area, where André anxiously hoped for reprieve and finally reconciled himself to death. His trial occurred in the old Dutch church that stood until 1836 on the present site of Tappan Reformed Church on King's Highway.

Exhibit: In **Tarrytown,** the "Captors' Room" at the Historical Society of the Tarrytowns, 1 Grove St., contains items associated with André and his capture. (Open Tuesday–Saturday 2:00–4:00; 914-631-8374; free.)

(See PENNSYLVANIA in this chapter; also Chapter 2, MANHATTAN.)

ANTHONY, SUSAN BROWNELL (1820–1906). From her Massachusetts birthplace, the family of the eventual suffragist-reformer moved to **Battenville,** where her father built a two-story brick house with 15 rooms and four fireplaces, known as the "finest house in that part of the country." This house still stands as a private residence on State Highway 29, excellently maintained by its owner. Anthony lived there from 1833 to 1839.

In 1866, her widowed mother purchased the 1850 red-brick house at 17 Madison St. in **Rochester,** a residence that became the feminist's home base for the rest of her long, active life. Now an ivy-covered National Historic Landmark operated by the Susan B. Anthony Memorial, the home is full of her furnishings and possessions plus memorabilia of the suffrage movement. (Open Monday–Saturday 11:00–4:00, and by appointment; 716-381-6202; admission.)

(See Chapter 1, MASSACHUSETTS.)

ARNOLD, BENEDICT (1741–1801). At the marked site of Arnold's 1780 defection to the British stood the Col. Beverly Robinson House, just south of **Garrison** on State Highway 9D. Arnold and his wife occupied this house during his short tenure as commandant of West Point, which he meant to betray and which is located just across the Hudson River from Garrison. Having learned that spy John André had been captured with papers that detailed the plot, Arnold jumped on his horse and galloped from the house down a path (marked Arnold's Lane, about 50 feet north of the house) to the river, where he commandeered a rowboat and crew and boarded a British vessel. George Washington, who arrived there moments later, was confronted by a mock-hysterical Peggy Arnold, who later joined her husband in Manhattan (see the entries on André and Washington in this section). The white frame colonial farmhouse,

destroyed by fire in 1892, stood on the grassy plot just north of the present farmhouse. Its original well remains.

(See PENNSYLVANIA in this chapter; also Chapter 1, CONNECTICUT; also Chapter 2, MANHATTAN.)

ARTHUR, CHESTER ALAN (1829–1886). One of the 21st U.S. president's boyhood homes (1835–37) still stands at 7 Elm St. (privately owned) in the village of **Perry.**

The family later occupied a parsonage in **Greenwich.** Dating from the early 19th century and formerly located adjacent to Bottskill Baptist Church on Church Street, where Arthur's father pastored, the house with asbestos shingles now stands on Woodlawn Avenue (privately owned). A historical marker is planned.

(See DISTRICT OF COLUMBIA in this chapter; also Chapter 1, VERMONT; also Chapter 2, MANHATTAN.)

ASTOR, CAROLINE SCHERMERHORN (1831–1908). The country estate of New York City's foremost social arbiter, "the" Mrs. Astor, was "Ferncliff" on River Road near **Rhinebeck.** This estate, built by her husband, William B. Astor, Jr., about 1870 and where he bred racehorses, extended 1.5 miles along, and two miles back from, the Hudson shore. Later acquired by the Roman Catholic Archdiocese of New York, the property has been subdivided. The huge mansion was demolished in 1941. A sports casino, designed by architect Stanford White and converted to a private dwelling, survives from the original complex (see the entry on White later in this section). The largest modern building on the property is the Roman Catholic Ferncliff Nursing Home.

(See Chapter 1, RHODE ISLAND; also Chapter 2, MANHATTAN.)

BARRYMORE, ETHEL (1879–1959). The actress's longtime **Mamaroneck** home, a house built about 1840 at the tip of Taylor's Lane, overlooked Long Island Sound. She had the three-story, barn-red dwelling painted white with green shutters, planted an orchard on her nine acres and entertained many well-known stage people from 1914 to 1945. This house survived until the early 1960s. Today the area is occupied by Barrymore Estates (privately owned), a posh, fenced-in suburban development. Only the remodeled caretaker's cottage from the original estate remains as part of the current development.

(See PENNSYLVANIA in this chapter; also Chapter 6, CALIFORNIA.)

BARTÓK, BÉLA (1881–1945). The Hungarian composer, a refugee of World War II, retired to **Saranac Lake** with its Manhattan street names for three summers. In 1943 and 1944, he resided at 32 Park Ave., a former "cure house" for tubercular patients built about 1920 and presently an apartment dwelling; in 1945 he lived at 89 Riverside Drive. Both houses are privately owned.

(See Chapter 2, BRONX, MANHATTAN, QUEENS.)

BARTON, CLARA (1821–1912). In **Dansville,** the founder of the American Red Cross resided from 1877 to 1886 in a two-story frame house on Health Street at the head of Perine Street—a dwelling sometimes called "Red Cross Cottage" because the first local chapter of the organization was established there in 1881. This house was razed in the late 1960s, and the important site, at last report, remained unmarked.

(See DISTRICT OF COLUMBIA, MARYLAND, NEW JERSEY in this chapter; also Chapter 1, MASSACHUSETTS.)

BAUM, LYMAN FRANK (1856–1919). The village of **Chittenango** was the author's birthplace. Local historian Clara Houck has traced the site to "the edge of the village near the barrel factory" owned by Baum's father. This would be on Falls Boulevard (State Highway 13) at the south edge of town near a creek, but the exact location remains unknown. Mrs. Houck believes that the house may have burned down in 1864 after the Baum family left, though one of Baum's sons stated in 1956 that the birthplace had been razed. A historical marker is planned for the approximate spot.

During the 1880s, Baum's family occupied several homes in the **Syracuse** area, three of which stand, privately owned and probably much altered. These include 107 Shonnard St., 112 Slocum Ave., and 268–270 Holland St. "Rose Lawn," the family's large country estate at suburban Mattydale, was razed in the late 1800s.

Exhibit: In 1981 **Chittenango** completed laying a yellow-brick sidewalk in its business district. It won't lead to Baum's Land of Oz, but the familiar "yellow-brick road" has become a popular attraction of the town.

(See Chapter 4, ILLINOIS, SOUTH DAKOTA.)

BEECHER, HENRY WARD (1813–1887). The popular Brooklyn preacher's frequent summer retreat from 1861 to 1878 was **Peekskill** on the Hudson River, where he built "Boscobel," a rambling, neo-Gothic house of wood and stone on 36 acres in 1874.* It stands unmarked on East Main Street, occupied until recently by St. Peter's School for Boys. Beecher planted trees there that he received from all over the world.

(See Chapter 1, CONNECTICUT; also Chapter 2, BROOKLYN; also Chapter 4, INDIANA, OHIO.)

BEECHER, LYMAN (1775–1863). The parents of Henry Ward Beecher and Harriet Beecher Stowe, among other notable children, lived from 1800 to 1810 in the house still standing at 84 Main St. (at the corner of Huntting Lane) in **East Hampton,** Long Island, where the senior Beecher pastored the Presbyterian Church for that decade (see the entries on Henry Ward Beecher and Harriet Beecher Stowe in this section). "In the spring of 1800," Beecher wrote, "I bought a house and five acres of ground for $800. I laid new pitch-pine floors, had a new fireplace made, and finished the back rooms and chambers, also a small bedroom below." The two and one-half-story house has since undergone extensive alterations to the roof and north side. Educator Catherine Esther Beecher and clergyman son Edward Beecher were born there. The old homestead, dating from 1740 and privately owned, is excellently maintained by its current owner, realtor Sally Ball, who has "tried to keep the facade pretty much as it was in his time."

(See Chapter 1, CONNECTICUT, MASSACHUSETTS; also Chapter 4, OHIO.)

BELMONT, ALVA ERTSKIN SMITH VANDERBILT (1853–1933). The prominent feminist and high-society competitor of Caroline Schermerhorn Astor built her large medieval "Castle" at **Sands Point,** Long Island, in 1920 (see the entry on Astor earlier in this section). Her five-acre

---

*This structure should not be confused with "Boscobel," the restored mansion open to the public a few miles north at Garrison; the Garrison home has no Beecher associations.

LYMAN BEECHER HOME. This privately owned residence at 84 Main St. in **East Hampton,** Long Island, dates in its original portions from 1740. Beecher's wife Roxanna, mother of Henry Ward Beecher and Harriet Beecher Stowe, drew this sketch of the home sometime during their residence from 1800 to 1810.
(Courtesy Sally Ball, Realtor)

estate, located near Sands Point Lighthouse, extended back from the shoreline on Long Island Sound to what is now Lighthouse Road off State Highway 101 at the western end of Sands Point. She died a year after the mammoth building was completed. Publisher William Randolph Hearst then acquired it for storing his collection of art works and statuary. Originally valued at $500,000, the mansion found no buyers at $19,000 a few years later, and it was demolished in 1938. All that remains in the present residential area is the main iron gate and gatehouse on Lighthouse Road.

(See Chapter 1, RHODE ISLAND; also Chapter 2, MANHATTAN.)

BENCHLEY, ROBERT CHARLES (1889–1945). From 1920, the humorist, actor and author made his permanent family home at **Yonkers** but resided there himself only occasionally. The privately owned dwelling stands at 2 Lynwood Road.

(See Chapter 2, MANHATTAN; also Chapter 6, CALIFORNIA.)

BENÉT, STEPHEN VINCENT (1898–1943). Benét's father, an unusually brilliant and cultivated career soldier, occupied posts at several military installations during the author-poet's boyhood; and the precocious son, constantly exposed during boyhood to drill and parade, remained attracted to the military life throughout his life. Only weak eyes prevented him from emulating his father's vocation. The family lived at the 1813 **Watervliet** Arsenal for two separate periods. From 1900 to 1904, they inhabited Quarters 2, a two-story brick dwelling built in 1889; and from 1919 to 1921, when Col. J. Walker Benét commanded the post, the family lived in the 1842

Quarters 1, the Commanding Officer's House. Neither dwelling at the federal complex on South Broadway is accessible to civilians except during infrequent public tours or military holidays.

(See PENNSYLVANIA in this chapter; also Chapter 1, CONNECTICUT; also Chapter 2, MANHATTAN; also Chapter 5, GEORGIA; also Chapter 6, CALIFORNIA.)

BLOOMER, AMELIA JENKS (1818–1894). The feminist editor, speaker and dress-reform advocate was born in **Homer,** her home until 1824. According to Town Historian Ella L. Perry, her birthplace may have stood "at or near what is now 43 North Main St." on a small plot owned by her father. The site, however, has not been sufficiently authenticated to be marked.

Her first and only extant home in **Seneca Falls,** where she resided from 1840 to 1853 and began publishing her temperance paper, the *Lily,* is the two-story, white clapboard dwelling at 53 East Bayard St. This property has been acquired by the Elizabeth Cady Stanton Foundation for the new Women's Rights National Historical Park, which will exhibit the house as soon as restoration is completed (see the entry on Stanton later in this section).

Exhibit: **Seneca Falls** Historical Society at 55 Cayuga St. displays a collection of Bloomer's handwritten speeches in its Woman's Rights Room. (Open May 1–October 31, Monday–Tuesday, Thursday–Friday 1:00–4:00; 315-568-8412; admission.)

(See Chapter 4, IOWA.)

BROWN, JOHN (1800–1859). The abolitionist's son-in-law built a clapboard farmhouse for him on 214 acres south of **Lake Placid** in 1855, and Brown lived there intermittently until his 1859 execution. That is also where "John Brown's body" lies. Restored in 1958 and operated by New York State Parks and Recreation, John Brown Farm State Historic Site contains original furnishings and possessions of this violent man to whom ends always justified means; the farm is located on John Brown Road, half a mile south of State Highway 73. (Open early May–late December, Wednesday–Sunday 9:00–5:00; 518-523-3900; free.)

(See MARYLAND, PENNSYLVANIA, WEST VIRGINIA in this chapter; also Chapter 1, CONNECTICUT; also Chapter 4, IOWA, KANSAS, OHIO.)

BRUCE, LENNY (1926–1966). Born Leonard Alfred Schneider, the "black humorist" and satirist lived with his parents from 1937 to 1943 at 710 Hughes St. (at the corner of Newbridge Road), privately owned, in **Lawrence,** Long Island.

(See Chapter 6, CALIFORNIA.)

BRYANT, WILLIAM CULLEN (1794–1878). At **Roslyn,** Long Island, stands "Cedarmere," Bryant's summer home overlooking Long Island Sound. This gray stucco house, privately owned on Bryant Avenue off Northern Boulevard, dates from 1787; Bryant purchased his "little place in a most healthy neighborhood" in 1843, renovated the house, and lived there at intervals for the rest of his life. Landscapist Frederick Law Olmsted designed the gardens. Walt Whitman, who visited there, described Bryant's 40 acres as "a beautiful place," but "rather cliffy" (see the entry on Whitman later in this section).

Exhibit: Bryant Library on Paper Mill Road in **Roslyn** displays the poet's books. (Open Monday–Friday 9:00–12:00, 3:00–6:00; 516-621-2240; free.)

(See Chapter 1, MASSACHUSETTS; also Chapter 2, MANHATTAN.)

BUNTLINE, NED. See EDWARD ZANE CARROLL JUDSON.

BURR, AARON (1756–1836). The first married home of the enigmatic political figure who became vice president, killed Alexander Hamilton in a duel, and conspired to set up an independent western nation was in **Albany,** where he began practicing law in 1782 and 1783 (see the entry on Hamilton later in this section). "Our House is roomy but inconvenient," wrote Theodosia Prevost Burr of their two-story frame dwelling at 110 Washington Ave., a site presently occupied by the Fort Orange Club.

(See NEW JERSEY, PENNSYLVANIA in this chapter; also Chapter 1, CONNECTICUT; also Chapter 2, MANHATTAN, STATEN ISLAND.)

CALDER, ALEXANDER (1898–1976). The rumpled sculptor, creator of mobiles and stabiles, lived in 1911 and 1912 at **Croton-on-Hudson,** where his family occupied the "Old Gate House," on the 1907 Stevenson Estate at 1184 Old Post Road. Calder's father, the noted sculptor Alexander Stirling Calder, installed a skylight in the garage he used for his studio. The medieval-style stone and brick buildings are privately owned.

(See PENNSYLVANIA in this chapter; also Chapter 1, CONNECTICUT; also Chapter 2, MANHATTAN.)

CERF, BENNETT ALFRED (1898–1971). Publisher, columnist and television panelist, Cerf made his last and permanent home at **Mount Kisco.** "The Columns," a mansion dating from about 1930, stands privately owned on Orchard Road.

(See Chapter 2, MANHATTAN.)

CLEMENS, SAMUEL LANGHORNE "MARK TWAIN" (1835–1910). In **Elmira,** the author-humorist courted and married Olivia Langdon in 1870. Langdon Homestead, the site of the ceremony, stood at Church and Main streets, where Clemens also corrected proofs for his first book, *Innocents Abroad* (1869). "Quarry Farm," the Langdon country place nearby, was also the author's summer home from 1874 to 1903. There he wrote most of *The Adventures of Tom Sawyer* (1876) and completed numerous other books; his isolated study stood in the orchard. The large, pre-1849 family house is a frame stucco dwelling located on Crane Road near the intersection of State Highways 7 and 17 and is privately owned.

The couple's first married home was in **Buffalo,** where Clemens edited the *Buffalo Express* from 1869 to 1871. They lived at 472 Delaware Ave., a new house presented as a wedding gift from the bride's father. The house was razed in 1963, and the Cloister restaurant now occupies the former stable on the site.

Exhibit: Clemens's octagonal writing study, removed from the Langdon orchard at "Quarry Farm" in 1952, now stands on the Elmira College campus, Park Place, **Elmira.** This workroom, an 1872 gift from his sister-in-law, has the riverboat pilothouse shape with windows all around that Clemens found nostalgically salubrious in several of his dwellings. Study furnishings include his typewriter, round desk and various favorite chairs. Mark Twain Study is maintained by Elmira College. (Open daily 9:00–5:00; 607-734-3912; free.)

(See Chapter 1, CONNECTICUT; also Chapter 2, BRONX, MANHATTAN; also Chapter 4, IOWA, MISSOURI; also Chapter 6, CALIFORNIA, NEVADA.)

CLEVELAND, GROVER (1837–1908). **Fayetteville** was the boyhood home of the 22nd and 24th U.S. president. The 1841 house where he lived from 1841 to 1850 stands unaltered at 109 Academy St. (privately owned).

Cleveland served as governor of New York from 1883 to 1885 and during this period resided at **Albany** in the red-brick State Executive Mansion (see the entry on Samuel Jones Tilden later in this section).

(See DISTRICT OF COLUMBIA, MARYLAND, NEW JERSEY in this chapter; also Chapter 1, MASSACHUSETTS, NEW HAMPSHIRE.)

CLINTON, DE WITT (1769–1828). The prominent New York governor and political leader, a nephew of George Clinton, was born probably at the Clinton ancestral homestead, built about 1730 at the village of **Little Britain,** Clinton's home until about 1785 (see the entry on George Clinton below). According to area historians, a small section of the original one and one-half-story cottage may be enclosed in the present 1856 stone house on the property, which has repeatedly changed hands and remains privately owned. A large boulder marker identifies the homestead site on Bull Road.

Some authorities have insisted that Clinton was born in **New Windsor,** where the 1760 frame house long identified as his birthplace and home until 1773 stands "on the west side of [River] Road near the foot of New Windsor hill." It is privately owned.

(See Chapter 2, MANHATTAN, QUEENS.)

CLINTON, GEORGE (1739–1812). Revolutionary soldier and vice president, Clinton was born at the ancestral homestead in **Little Britain** (see the entry on De Witt Clinton above) and lived there at intervals until 1770.

In 1770, he bought a 350-acre farm at **New Windsor** on a hillside above the Hudson River, his home until 1777. British soldiers seeking Clinton raided this place during the Revolution. A small section of the house exists in the present dwelling marked on Maple Street.

Clinton's first home in **Poughkeepsie** (1777–84) was the large 1740 Crannell House, which stood until about 1880 at 448 Main St. A marker is located inside the Mid-Town Pharmacy that presently occupies this site. His last home (1806–12), a small, brick house that he built, stood until destroyed by fire in 1874 on Sheafe Road. Though a marker is present, the property is owned by a quarrying firm and is not open to the public. The 1786 Clinton House, a two-story fieldstone structure at 549 Main St., may have been used as Governor Clinton's headquarters from 1777 to 1782 when the town served as state capital, though his occupancy has never been authenticated. Operated by New York State Parks and Recreation, the house displays Dutch and English colonial furnishings. (Open Wednesday–Saturday 9:00–5:00; 914-471-1630; free).

(See DISTRICT OF COLUMBIA in this chapter; also Chapter 2, MANHATTAN.)

COBB, TYRUS RAYMOND "TY" (1886–1961). See NATIONAL BASEBALL HALL OF FAME AND MUSEUM.

(See Chapter 5, GEORGIA; also Chapter 6, CALIFORNIA.)

COHAN, GEORGE MICHAEL (1878–1942). At **Highland Mills,** the playwright, composer of patriotic songs and Broadway producer-actor bought "Sunnycroft," a farm near Cromwell Lake, in 1909. He installed his parents and spent much time there during the off-season months of his busy career. The farm remains privately owned on Bakertown Road.

From 1914 to 1927, Cohan owned the mansion at 100 Kings Point Road in the Elm Point section of **Kings Point,** Long Island. There he wrote his popular patriotic song "Over There" (1917). Both the house and former servants' quarters across the road are private residences.

(See NEW JERSEY in this chapter; also Chapter 1, MASSACHUSETTS, RHODE ISLAND; also Chapter 2, MANHATTAN.)

COLE, THOMAS (1801–1848). Founder of the Hudson River School in American painting, Cole made his permanent home in **Catskill** from 1820 to 1848. Cole House National Historic Landmark, his Federal-style brick home and studio dating from 1812, stands at 218 Spring St. (privately owned) near the west end of Rip Van Winkle Bridge, State Highway 23. His property originally extended to the Hudson River shore. In 1979 Cole's great-granddaughter sold the home and studio to the Catskill Center for Conservation and Development, which may open the buildings to visitors in the near future.

COLTRANE, JOHN WILLIAM (1926–1967). In the Dix Hills section of **Huntington,** Long Island, the master saxophonist bought his 10-room, split-level ranch house in 1966, his last home. This privately owned dwelling stands on Candlewood Path in a recent subdivision.

(See PENNSYLVANIA in this chapter; also Chapter 2, MANHATTAN, QUEENS; also Chapter 5, NORTH CAROLINA.)

COOPER, JAMES FENIMORE (1789–1851). At **Cooperstown,** the author's father built "The Manor," a two-story frame house facing Main Street and Otsego Lake, and this was the boy's home from 1790 to 1798. William Cooper then built the much larger "Otsego Hall" on Main Street opposite Fair Street, occupied by the family from 1798. Otsego Hall became the author's permanent home in 1833 and he died there, a fierce old squire worried about his real estate and little else. Cooper described this home in *The Pioneers* (1823); fire destroyed it in 1853.

In **Mamaroneck,** Cooper lived for lengthy periods from 1811 to 1814 with his in-laws at the 18th-century DeLancey House (privately owned), located at 404 West Post Road, at the foot of Fenimore Road. There in the west parlor, Cooper and Susan DeLancey married in 1811; the house at that time stood atop Heathcote Hill overlooking Long Island Sound. Removed to its present location in 1900, it became a saloon and at last report was a combination restaurant-service station with pper apartments. The house, once a Mamaroneck showplace, is currently in sore decline.

To get away from those in-laws, Cooper built an 1817 house in **Scarsdale.** The marked site of his long-gone "Angevine Farm," where he lived from 1818 to 1822 as a gentleman farmer and fledgling novelist, is located on Mamaroneck Road just past Scarsdale High School. Cooper began his literary career there with his novel *The Spy* (1821).

Exhibits: Historical markers around Otsego Lake near **Cooperstown** point out various locales of scenes from Cooper's novels. Also at Cooperstown, on the site of a cottage he owned, stands Fenimore House, a 1932 brick mansion operated as a museum by the New York State Historical Society, one mile north on State Highway 80. A room there displays Cooper papers and memorabilia. (Open May 1–October 31, daily 9:00–5:00; winter schedule, call 607-547-2533; admission.)

(See NEW JERSEY in this chapter; also Chapter 2, MANHATTAN.)

CORNELL, KATHARINE (1898–1974). The girlhood home of the actress was 484 Delaware Ave. in **Buffalo,** an 1894 dwelling since converted into private apartments.

"Peter Rock," a mansion with 16 rooms and three levels that she built of shingle and stone on seven acres at Sneden's Landing near **Palisades,** was her home with husband Guthrie McClintic from 1951 to 1961. Anchored in rock high above the Hudson River and blending into the rugged landscape, this elegant, sprawling mansion was the mutual creation of architect Eric Gugler and the actress, who wanted something "simple on the outside but the last word in comfort and elegance on the inside"—including a 45-x-31-foot drawing room, formerly a barn removed from Long Island. The estate, located on Woods Road, was recently sold to the Isley Brothers, a popular rock-and-roll group.

(See Chapter 1, MASSACHUSETTS; also Chapter 2, MANHATTAN.)

DEWEY, JOHN (1859–1952). On Greenlawn Road near **Huntington,** Long Island, stood the summer home of the philosopher-educator, who lived there from 1910 to 1923. According to the Huntington Historical Society, the 18th-century house was "torched" by an arsonist in 1977 when plans were developed to use it as a hotel for handicapped adults. Dewey, were he alive, might have had some choice ironic words about "handicaps" in this situation.

(See Chapter 1, VERMONT; also Chapter 2, MANHATTAN; also Chapter 4, ILLINOIS.)

DEWEY, THOMAS EDMUND (1902–1971). A gangbusting attorney and twice the Republican presidential candidate, Dewey made his permanent home from 1938 near **Pawling** on Reservoir Road. According to local sources, the mansion and grounds that Dewey called "Dapplemere" have been poorly maintained with "no feeling for history" since his death; the property is currently a private multifamily dwelling.

As New York's governor, Dewey resided in the State Executive Mansion in **Albany** from 1942 to 1955 (see the entry on Samuel Jones Tilden later in this section).

(See Chapter 2, MANHATTAN; also Chapter 4, MICHIGAN.)

DOUBLEDAY, ABNER (1819–1893). He probably didn't originate the game of baseball, as once was widely claimed; but Doubleday, a professional soldier, did contribute to the sport's development. He was born at **Ballston Spa** in a house built about 1800, still standing at 24 Washington St. (privately owned).

Exhibit: The National Baseball Hall of Fame and Museum (see entry later in this section) in **Cooperstown** displays a few Doubleday items—most notably his home-made baseball.

(See NEW JERSEY in this chapter.)

DOUGLAS, STEPHEN ARNOLD (1813–1861). The Douglas family moved from Vermont to **Clifton Springs** in 1830; and from there in 1832 the future political leader—called 'the Little Giant" for his stubby physique and furious energy—left to achieve a vast reputation in Illinois. His home, built about 1830, stands on Steven Street Extension and is privately owned.

(See DISTRICT OF COLUMBIA in this chapter; also Chapter 1, VERMONT; also Chapter 4, ILLINOIS.)

DOUGLASS, FREDERICK (1818–1895). In **Rochester,** the abolitionist orator founded his newspaper, the *North Star,* in 1847. His home stood at 297 Alexander St., a station on the Underground Railroad. Douglass strongly suspected arson when this house burned down in 1872, and he moved to Washington, D.C.

(See DISTRICT OF COLUMBIA in this chapter; also Chapter 1, MASSACHUSETTS.)

DREISER, THEODORE (1871–1945). In 1929, the novelist built his country home "Iroki" (a Japanese word for "beauty"), a 37-acre tract on Croton Lake Road near **Mount Kisco.** Designed and constructed of local fieldstone with the help of numerous friends, the house started out as a garage, then became a writing studio and finally a two-story dwelling, as Dreiser constantly revised his plans and intentions. Thus some of the portions normally built first in a house (e.g., the basement) were afterthoughts. Dreiser lived there until 1938 but succeeded in selling it only shortly after his last visit in 1944. "He had done no great writing there," wrote biographer W. A. Swanberg. *"That* had all been done when he was poor." The private residence that stands today consists of the original stone exterior and fireplaces. A cabin he built and used as a studio also remains on the property. Vandals have recently destroyed the "Iroki" name plate on the entrance gate.

(See Chapter 2, BROOKLYN, MANHATTAN; also Chapter 4, ILLINOIS, INDIANA; also Chapter 6, CALIFORNIA.)

DULLES, JOHN FOSTER (1888–1959). "I will always look on **Watertown** as my real home," said the lawyer and secretary of state under President Eisenhower of the town where he grew up. The Presbyterian parsonage occupied by his family from 1886 to 1897 stands at 162 Clinton St., a private residence built in 1828 and considerably modified since then. The marker there commemorates the house, not specifically for Dulles, but as one of Watertown's oldest houses. His later boyhood home (1897–1904) stood until 1959 at 124 Mullin St., the present corner site of Watertown Savings Bank at 111 Clinton St.

The family summer home was "Underbluff," built in 1890 at **Henderson Harbor** by Dulles' grandfather and still privately occupied.

Always a lover of water and an expert boatman, Dulles purchased **Main Duck Island** (privately owned), an isolated, windswept spot in eastern Lake Ontario, in 1941. The rustic log cabin he built there became his frequent vacation home until his death.

(See DISTRICT OF COLUMBIA in this chapter; also Chapter 2, MANHATTAN.)

EARHART, AMELIA MARY (1898–1937?). The aviator's home in **Harrison** stands on Amelia Earhart Lane. She occupied the dwelling, her last home, between lecture tours and flights for six years with her husband, publisher George P. Putnam. A 1934 fire during their absence partially destroyed this house, portions of which they rebuilt. It is privately owned.

(See Chapter 1, MASSACHUSETTS; also Chapter 4, IOWA, KANSAS, MINNESOTA, MISSOURI.)

EASTMAN, GEORGE (1854–1932). In **Waterville,** the inventor's birth site and home until 1860 is presently a parking lot at 189' Stafford Ave. (formerly 29 Stafford Ave.).

The house itself stands in Genessee Country Village at **Mumford,** recently moved there from Eastman's Rochester property where it was first taken from Waterville. The 1847 house is one of more than 50 historic buildings from upstate New York, restored at Mumford to create an early American village. The complex is operated by the Genessee Country Museum. (Open mid-May–mid-October, daily 10:00–5:00; 716-538-2887; admission.)

Rochester, where Eastman built his film and camera industry, became his permanent home. Eastman House National Historic Landmark, a mansion with 49 rooms at 900 East Ave., was designed for the inventor from photographs he took of similar houses. He bequeathed this 1905, two-story, concrete home (with 1919 additions) to the University of Rochester. A photography museum since 1949, the house exhibits Eastman's original furnishings along with antique cameras, many photographs and push-button displays on optics and color. It is operated by the International Museum of Photography. (Open Tuesday–Sunday 10:00–4:30; 716-271-3361; admission.)

FARRAGUT, DAVID GLASGOW (1801–1870). The Civil War sailor for whom the rank of admiral was created made his home in **Hastings-on-Hudson** from 1861 to 1866. His own stays in the town were infrequent owing to his naval service, but his family waited out the war for him there. They lived briefly at 60 Main St. but stayed longest at 128 Washington Ave., a two and one-half-story, frame duplex now sided. That house dates from about 1850, and both homes are privately owned.

(See Chapter 2, MANHATTAN; also Chapter 5, MISSISSIPPI, TENNESSEE.)

FILLMORE, MILLARD (1800–1874). "Where would America be today had there been no Millard Fillmore?" This is the topic of the annual essay contest sponsored by the Millard Fillmore Society, a tongue-in-cheek national organization founded in 1963 "to perpetuate the memory of the 13th president, holding his actions as exemplary examples of inconsistency."

Fillmore was born in a log cabin in **Summer Hill,** the marked site of which is a picnic area located on Fillmore Road. The cabin, torn down in 1852, has been re-created at Fillmore Glen State Park four miles west, a 21-x-16-foot replica containing period furnishings from 1800–1830. The park, not itself a site where he lived, is located one mile south of **Moravia** on State Highway 38 and is operated by New York State Parks and Recreation. (Open May 15–October 16, daily 8:00–10:00; admission.)

Only the well of Fillmore's boyhood home (1802–19) remains at **New Hope.** The site of the house, demolished in 1937, is marked on Carver Road, where a picnic area is planned for 1983.

Fillmore House National Historic Landmark at 24 Shearer Ave. in **East Aurora,** one and one-half-story clapboard dwelling, was the home Fillmore built in 1826 after he finished law school; he and his wife lived there until 1830. The original site of the house is also marked at 681 Main St. Now a museum operated by the Aurora Historical Society, the house has been restored and contains period furnishings. (Open June 1–October 31, Wednesday, Saturday–Sunday 2:30–4:30; 716-652-3280; free.) The earlier family homestead (1820–26), privately owned, stands at Olean and Lapham roads.

Fillmore's retirement home was in **Buffalo.** His last residence (1858–74), known to be "a home of industry and temperance," stood at West Genesee and Delaware avenues (52 Niagara Square) until 1929.

Exhibits: Fillmore certainly has his "fans," as evidenced by the number of memorials devoted to him. At **Auburn,** the grounds of the Cayuga Museum of History and Art, 203 Genessee Street, display the Millard Fillmore Memorial, another log cabin replica of his birthplace. (Open Tuesday–Friday 1:00–5:00; Saturday 9:00–5:00, Sunday 2:00–5:00; 315-253-8051; free.)

(See DISTRICT OF COLUMBIA, WEST VIRGINIA in this chapter.)

FITZGERALD, F. SCOTT (1896–1940). The novelist spent a decade of his boyhood, except for two years in Syracuse, in **Buffalo.** From 1903 to 1905, the family resided at 29 Irving Place, a small dwelling now included within the Allentown Preservation District. The last Fitzgerald home in Buffalo, from 1905 to 1908, stands at 71 Highland Ave. Both of these 19th-century frame houses remain privately owned.

Two of Fitzgerald's three **Syracuse** residences also stand, both privately owned. The Kasson Apartment building at 622 James St., built in 1899, has been recently renovated. Fitzgerald lived there

in 1902 and 1903. The family apartment dwelling in 1903 at 735 East Willow St. (at the corner of Catherine Street) dates from 1898.

In 1922, Fitzgerald rented a large colonial mansion at **Great Neck,** Long Island, and there began work on *The Great Gatsby* (1925). With his wife Zelda and countless weekend guests, his social life was typically hectic and alcoholic; neighbors often found him asleep early mornings on the lawn. He did find time to write, however, and worked in a room over the garage until 1924. Dating from the early 1900s, house and garage stand at 6 Gateway Drive (privately owned).

(See MARYLAND in this chapter; also Chapter 2, MANHATTAN; also Chapter 4, MINNESOTA; also Chapter 5, ALABAMA, NORTH CAROLINA; also Chapter 6, CALIFORNIA.)

FRÉMONT, JOHN CHARLES (1813–1890). Soldier, explorer and first Republican presidential candidate (1856), Frémont bought his luxurious 1848 mansion "Pokahoe," a gray stone house at **North Tarrytown,** in the early 1860s. Financial disaster involving his railroad investments in 1873 forced him to give up the 100-acre estate. Also known as the Webb-Frémont House, it has been altered to a one-story private residence at 7 Pokahoe Drive.

(See Chapter 6, ARIZONA, CALIFORNIA.)

FULTON, ROBERT (1765–1815). The summer home from 1808 to 1815 of the engineer and steamship inventor-promoter was "Teviotdale," his father-in-law's 1774 palatial mansion in **Linlithgo,** a village near Hudson. Now restored and identified by a historical marker, the address of the two and one-half-story stucco house is withheld by the current private owners; but "those of an inquiring mind," suggests the local historical society, "will probably manage to discover it."

(See PENNSYLVANIA in this chapter; also Chapter 2, MANHATTAN.)

GEHRIG, HENRY LOUIS "LOU" (1903–1941). The "Iron Horse" of baseball who played for the New York Yankees from 1925 to 1939, Gehrig occupied two houses in **New Rochelle,** both of which stand privately owned. He lived at 9 Meadow Lane from 1928 to 1932, and at 5 Circuit

THE DYING ULYSSES S. GRANT AT HIS ADIRONDACK COTTAGE. Four days before his death in 1885, this photo was taken of the cancer-stricken old soldier who came to the cottage at Mount McGregor near **Wilton** in a race with time to complete his *Personal Memoirs*. He had finished the autobiography that would rescue his survivors from financial ruin just hours before this last picture was made. (*Courtesy Library of Congress*)

Road, his first residence after marriage, from 1932 to 1937.

Exhibit: See NATIONAL BASEBALL HALL OF FAME AND MUSEUM later in this section.

(See Chapter 2, BRONX, MANHATTAN.)

GOULD, JAY (1836–1892). A white saltbox house on a 150-acre farm near **Roxbury** was the financier's birthplace and home until 1852. It is a private residence, owned and restored by the Chem-Tex Corp. on West Settlement Road, fire number 758.

Lyndhurst National Historic Landmark at 635 South Broadway in **Tarrytown,** an 1838 Gothic marble castle that Gould rented in 1878 and purchased in 1880, became his permanent summer home. He enlarged and renovated the mansion, adding a 400-foot greenhouse where he spent most of his leisure time. Opulent, gilded-age furnishings include Gould's art collection and lavish knickknacks and toys of the absurdly rich. There are 15 buildings on the 67 parklike acres maintained by the National Trust for Historic Preservation. If one wants to see what a typical "robber baron" lived like, this is the place to visit. (Open May 1–October 31, Tuesday–Sunday 10:00–5:00; November 1–April 30, Tuesday–Sunday 10:00–4:00; 914-631-0313; admission.)

(See Chapter 2, MANHATTAN; also Chapter 6, TEXAS.)

GRANT, ULYSSES SIMPSON (1822–1885). Impoverished in retirement because of bad business investments, the former 18th U.S. president came to the frame Drexel Cottage at Mount

McGregor three weeks before he died of throat cancer. Unable to speak, he worked feverishly to complete his *Personal Memoirs* (1885) in order to leave his family an income, and he finished the book just four days before his death. The 19th-century cottage, containing original furnishings and some of Grant's clothing, is operated by New York State Parks and Recreation and is located northwest of **Wilton** off State Highway 50. (Open Wednesday–Sunday 9:00–5:00; 518-584-2000; admission.)

(See DISTRICT OF COLUMBIA, NEW JERSEY in this chapter; also Chapter 2, MANHATTAN; also Chapter 4, ILLINOIS, MICHIGAN, MISSOURI, OHIO; also Chapter 5, VIRGINIA; also Chapter 6, WASHINGTON.)

GREELEY, HORACE (1811–1872). The hugely influential newspaperman, presidential aspirant, abolitionist and well-meaning if often wrong-headed public gadfly made his summer home in **Chappaqua** for the last 18 years of his life. Friends called it "Greeley's Bog," a 78-acre rocky hillside with a morass at the foot. Greeley drained the bog along with his pocketbook and attempted farming there without much success except for turnips. His last book, nevertheless, was *What I Know About Farming* (1871)—"kussed little," was Josh Billings's review. Greeley built three dwellings there. "The House in the Woods" was his favorite retreat, a two-story frame dwelling located in a glen southeast of the present Church of Saint Mary the Virgin off South Greeley Avenue. The house burned down in 1875; portions of the present Senter Street are remnants of the entrance road to Greeley's farm. To house his family, Greeley bought "the House on the Main Road" in 1864. This two and one-half-story frame dwelling that dates from about 1820 was the family country home until Greeley's death. Located in a gatehouse position to the Greeley farm, it fell into disrepair but was restored by new owners in 1940 and still stands at 100 King St., now a gift shop. Greeley built a larger "Hillside House" in 1871, but never lived there; it stood on the hill above Senter Street until 1890, when it too burned. "Rehoboth," Greeley's concrete barn that he designed and built in 1865, "will be abidingly useful long after I shall have been utterly forgotten," he believed. Greeley's daughter converted it to a residence in 1892, and it remained in the family until 1954. A new owner restored it to its original simpler lines as one of the first concrete buildings in America, and it remains a privately owned dwelling at 33 Aldridge Road.

Exhibit: The **Chappaqua** Historical Society in New Castle Town Hall, 200 South Greeley Ave., displays what is probably the best collection of Greeley items anywhere. Included are his infant crib, spectacles, desk from the *New York Tribune*, a printing stand he used in Vermont and many odd pieces of memorabilia. (Open September 1–July 31, Wednesday 1:00–4:00; other times by appointment; 914-238-4771; free.)

(See Chapter 1, NEW HAMPSHIRE, VERMONT; also Chapter 2, MANHATTAN.)

HAMILTON, ALEXANDER (1755–1804). The young Revolutionary soldier, later Federalist leader and first secretary of the treasury resided at Schuyler Mansion National Historic Landmark in **Albany,** the home of his in-laws, while studying law from 1780 to 1783. He married Elizabeth Schuyler there in 1780 (see the entry on Philip John Schuyler later in this section).

(See NEW JERSEY, PENNSYLVANIA in this chapter; also Chapter 2, MANHATTAN.)

HAMMARSKJÖLD, DAG (1905–1961). Swedish economist and second U.N. secretary-general, Hammarskjöld used the Brewster House on Foggintown Road in **Brewster** as a frequent weekend retreat from 1954 to 1961. The two-story, early 19th-century house on 76 acres, including a secluded lake, was leased to the United Nations for Hammarskjöld's use; there he hiked, fished and canoed, "seldom seen in other than short lederhosen, in winter as well as summer," reported a local historian. The dwelling, no longer a U.N. residence, is privately owned.

(See Chapter 2, MANHATTAN.)

HAMMERSTEIN, OSCAR, II (1895–1960). At **Great Neck,** Long Island, the famed lyricist built his Tudor-style mansion of 22 rooms in 1926 on a lot shaped like a slice of pie. This house at 40 Shore Drive, his home until 1940 and still privately owned, was featured in the 1971 film *The Anderson Tapes*.

(See PENNSYLVANIA in this chapter; also Chapter 2, MANHATTAN.)

HANDY, WILLIAM CHRISTOPHER (1873–1958). **Tuckahoe** in suburban Yonkers was the blues musician-composer's last home. His house at 19 Chester Drive (now called W. C. Handy Place) in Colonial Heights remains privately owned.

(See Chapter 2, MANHATTAN; also Chapter 5, ALABAMA, TENNESSEE.)

HECHT, BEN (1894–1964). An 18th-century mansion on Perry Lane, **Upper Nyack,** became the journalist-playwright's permanent home, which he renovated in 1929. His writing studio was a stone tower that overlooks the Hudson. The property is well-maintained and privately owned.

(See Chapter 2, MANHATTAN; also Chapter 4, ILLINOIS, WISCONSIN.)

HERBERT, VICTOR (1859–1924). The composer-conductor spent summers from the late 1890s at **Lake Placid.** He built "Camp Joyland" in 1903 on the lakeshore, made this his permanent summer home and composed many of his operettas there. The privately owned house at 69 Victor Herbert Drive stands hidden from the road.

(See PENNSYLVANIA in this chapter; also Chapter 2, MANHATTAN.)

HOPPER, EDWARD (1882–1967). In **Nyack,** the painter of lonely urban scenes was born and raised in the 1861 house at 82 North Broadway, where restoration continues under direction of the Hopper Landmark Preservation Association. The first floor is now a gallery featuring the work of local artists and offering Hopper books and prints for sale. (Open Friday 12:00–4:00, Saturday–Sunday 1:00–5:00; free.)

Hopper also frequented the art colony of Yaddo (see the entry on Yaddo later in this section).

(See Chapter 1, MASSACHUSETTS; also Chapter 2, MANHATTAN.)

HUGHES, CHARLES EVANS (1862–1948). Governor, presidential candidate, secretary of state and U.S. chief justice, Hughes was one of the foremost national figures of his time. His birthplace in **Glens Falls** stands at 20 Center St., a shingled, clapboard dwelling built about 1850 and moved from 135 Maple St. shortly after the family left in 1863. The privately owned house has been nominated for National Register status.

In **Albany** as New York's governor, Hughes occupied the State Executive Mansion from 1906

to 1910 (see the entry on Samuel Jones Tilden later in this section).

(See DISTRICT OF COLUMBIA in this chapter; also Chapter 2, MANHATTAN.)

IRVING, WASHINGTON (1783–1859). Irving's spirit is well maintained along the scenic banks of the Hudson, the setting for his best literary work. Sunnyside National Historic Landmark on West Sunnyside Lane at **Irvington** was a 17th-century farmhouse with four rooms when the author bought it in 1835. He added rooms, a Moorish tower, stepped gables and roof weather vanes, transforming the house into a jumbled, exotic looking, but still basically simple "fairyland manor." "No restoration in the nation," wrote Carl Carmer, "makes visitors feel more at home—perhaps because it continues to exist in the company of more august castles and mansions that grace the countryside." Irving, the nation's first professional man of letters, called the house his "Roost" and "an elegant little snuggery." There he lived the good life, entertained numerous famous guests and did all of his later writing. John D. Rockefeller, Jr., bought and restored the house in 1945, and today it looks exactly as it did when English novelist William Makepeace Thackeray visited Irving there in 1855. Irving's study is arranged as he left it with his desk, library and couch; and other original furnishings and possessions are displayed throughout the profusion of nooks and corners that he never stopped remodeling and elaborating. Guides in period costume conduct tours through the house and immaculate grounds, maintained by Sleepy Hollow Restorations. A reception center exhibits Irving manuscripts, letters, photos and paintings. (Open daily 10:00–5:00; 914-631-8200; admission.)

(See Chapter 2, MANHATTAN.)

JAY, JOHN (1745–1829). Prominent Federalist and first U.S. chief justice, Jay retired in 1801 to his farm near **Katonah,** where he remained for the rest of his life. Jay Homestead, located on Jay Street (State Highway 22 south of town), has been preserved essentially as Jay knew it. The two-story clapboard house, which dates from about 1800, and the outbuildings stand on land bought from the Indians by Jay's grandfather; and Jay's descendants occupied the property until 1958, when it was restored. Many of his furnishings are displayed, and a wing added in 1925 contains a portrait collection. The property is operated by New York State Parks and Recreation. (Open Wednesday–Sunday 9:00–5:00; 914-232-5651; free.)

The two-story Van Wyck-Jay House on State Highway 52 at **East Fishkill** was Jay's refugee home from 1776 to 1781 during the Revolution. Built about 1740, the frame house had only one floor when he rented there but was remodeled and enlarged about 1870. It is privately owned.

(See Chapter 2, MANHATTAN.)

JOHNSON, WALTER PERRY (1887–1946).
Exhibit: See National Baseball Hall of Fame and Museum later in this section.

(See MARYLAND in this chapter; also Chapter 4, KANSAS.)

JUDSON, EDWARD ZANE CARROLL "NED BUNTLINE" (1823–1886). Boisterous adventurer, incessant opportunist and author of some 400 "dime novels" under his Buntline pseudonym, Judson was also a master publicist and mob agitator. Through his novels featuring an easygoing frontiersman named William F. Cody, he virtually created "Buffalo Bill," hero to a generation. Judson moved around, sometimes voluntarily, often chased, seldom lingering in one place longer than it took to stir up a fuss. An exception to this rule was his birthplace and final dwelling in **Stamford.** His home in infancy may have occupied the present Westholen Hotel site; according to Village Historian Anne Willis, however, "there is a little old house behind the hotel which could possibly be the one he was born in." Judson designed and built his final Stamford home, "Eagle's Nest," in 1871 on his father-in-law's farm. There in his elaborate gun room, library and conservatory, he nourished and amplified his own legend to numerous curious and credible visitors. "To interview Ned Buntline at Eagle's Nest became one of the things cub reporters were assigned to do," wrote biographer Jay Monaghan in *The Great Rascal* (1951). The well-kept house stands on South Delaware Street. Though it remains privately owned, reports Anne Willis, "there has been some talk of turning the house into a Ned Buntline museum."

Judson also built another "Eagle's Nest," this one a hunting lodge on the northwestern shore of Eagle Lake high in the Adirondacks, where he lived at intervals from 1856 to 1861, built another

cabin and a two-story farmhouse and buried his third wife, who died there in childbirth. The nearest community is **Blue Mountain Lake;** inquire at the Adirondack Museum there for directions to the unnumbered site.

KAISER, HENRY JOHN (1882–1967). The marked birthplace of the versatile industrialist stands in the village of **Sprout Brook** southwest of Canajoharie. Built about 1875, the Italianate frame dwelling remains in excellent shape and is privately occupied. Kaiser lived there until age 13, when he struck out on his own in Horatio Alger fashion.

To such men, the first job of their lives often assumes a vast nostalgic aura, and Kaiser liked to recall his youthful days in **Utica** as a drygoods helper. He lived during this period at 2 Jewett Place, now the local chapter residence of the American Red Cross.

(See Chapter 6, CALIFORNIA, HAWAII.)

KENNEDY, JOHN FITZGERALD (1917–1963).
KENNEDY, ROBERT FRANCIS (1925–1968).

The 35th U.S. president and his brother, who became attorney general and a prominent political leader, grew up from 1929 to 1942 in the family home at 294 Pondfield Road in **Bronxville.** From there the elder brother enlisted in the Navy, becoming a war hero in 1943 when his PT-109 crew was rescued after a Japanese destroyer rammed the boat. The palatial, brick Georgian home on six acres was torn down in 1951, and the property has been subdivided.

(See DISTRICT OF COLUMBIA in this chapter; also Chapter 1, MASSACHUSETTS, RHODE ISLAND; also Chapter 2, BRONX; also Chapter 4, MICHIGAN; also Chapter 5, FLORIDA, VIRGINIA; also Chapter 6, CALIFORNIA, TEXAS.)

KERN, JEROME DAVID (1885–1945). In **Bronxville,** the composer of some of the most popular and enduring Broadway show music ever written rented a two-story stucco dwelling at Sagamore and Avon roads (privately owned) as a refuge from Manhattan from 1916 to 1918. He liked the town so much that, in 1918, he bought property at Dellwood Road and Gentian Lane and built a three-story, colonial mansion and barn. Kern seldom left there until 1936, when he sold the property and moved to California. Fronting

Dellwood Road in the Cedar Knolls area, this house also remains privately owned.

(See Chapter 2, MANHATTAN; also Chapter 6, CALIFORNIA.)

KEROUAC, JACK (1922–1969). At **Northport,** Long Island, the "beat-generation" author resided with his mother in 1963 and 1964 at 7 Judy Ann Court, the most elaborate house, with its fireplace and two bathrooms, that the pair had ever occupied in years of moving about. It remains privately owned.

(See Chapter 1, MASSACHUSETTS; also Chapter 2, MANHATTAN, QUEENS; also Chapter 5, FLORIDA; also Chapter 6, CALIFORNIA.)

LARDNER, RINGGOLD WILMER "RING" (1885–1933). Sports journalist and master of perverse humor and American vernacular in his short stories, Lardner occupied two Long Island homes in later life. His first, a three-story house on two acres at **Kings Point,** stands on East Shore Road. Lardner, who lived there from 1921 to 1928, called this place "The Mange." It is privately owned.

At **East Hampton** in 1927, he built a shingled house of 13 rooms which he named "Still Pond" because he planned "no more moving"; and this was, true to plan, his last home. The house stands privately owned and unnumbered on Apaquogue Road, next to the house owned by Grantland Rice (see the entry on Rice later in this section), who built there at the same time. Dune erosion after a 1931 hurricane necessitated the removal of both houses back from their original shoreline site.

(See Chapter 4, ILLINOIS, MICHIGAN.)

LEE, GYPSY ROSE (1914–1970). The country estate of the noted strip-tease artist and novelist was "Witchwood," located at **Highland Mills** on State Highway 208 near Ridge Road. She acquired the place in the 1930s, but until 1942 the village acknowledged her presence only in the tax bills she received. When she donated a performance for a local fund-raising effort, however, she suddenly became persona grata. Witchwood Manor Farm remains privately owned.

(See Chapter 2, MANHATTAN; also Chapter 6, CALIFORNIA.)

LEE, ROBERT EDWARD (1807–1870). Commander of the Confederate armies, the brilliant career soldier headed the U.S. Military Academy at **West Point** for three years (1852–55) before the Civil War. During this time he occupied the Superintendent's Quarters at Jefferson and Washington roads, a brick and iron-grill structure dating from about 1820. Douglas MacArthur was a later resident (see the entry on MacArthur later in this section). West Point tours begin from the Visitor Information Center at Thayer Gate. (Open April 15–November 15, Monday–Saturday 9:00–5:00, Sunday and holidays 11:00–5:00; 914-938-4658; free.)

(See Chapter 5, VIRGINIA.)

LEHMAN, HERBERT HENRY (1878–1963). As a New York reform governor, Lehman occupied the State Executive Mansion at **Albany** from 1932 to 1942 (see the entry on Samuel Jones Tilden later in this section).

"Meadowfarm," the summer home he built and occupied from 1911 to 1942 at **Purchase,** stands at 84 Purchase St. Lehman and his wife bred boxer showdogs there until 1938. The building, its interior converted to offices, currently houses the Westchester County Medical Society.

(See Chapter 2, MANHATTAN.)

LEWIS, SINCLAIR (1885–1951). The novelist and his wife, journalist Dorothy Thompson, lived from 1933 to 1937 at 17 Wood Lane in **Bronxville,** where he wrote *It Can't Happen Here* (1935) and several plays. This was the couple's last married home; it burned down about the time of their divorce in 1942.

(See Chapter 1, MASSACHUSETTS, VERMONT; also Chapter 2, MANHATTAN; also Chapter 4, MINNESOTA.)

LINDBERGH, CHARLES AUGUSTUS (1902–1974). In 1927, two months after his historic flight from New York to Paris, the aviator resided at "Falaise," the 1924 Norman-style mansion of Harry F. Guggenheim at **Sands Point,** Long Island. There in his suite, Lindbergh wrote *We* (1927), his first account of the flight. The 26-room house, operated by the Nassau County Department of Recreation and Parks, displays antique furnishings, and the 80-acre estate is undergoing development as Sands Point Park and Preserve. (Open May 15–November 15, Sunday–Wednesday; call 516-883-1612 for admission information.)

Exhibit: The first plane owned by Lindbergh, a

Curtiss "Jenny" discovered rotting in an Iowa barn in 1976, has been restored and is displayed by Nassau County Historical Museum in **East Meadow,** Long Island. Lindbergh barnstormed in such machines through the Midwest and South in 1923. The museum is located in Eisenhower Park, Old Country Road and Hempstead Turnpike. (Open daily 9:00–5:00; 516-364-1050; free.)

(See DISTRICT OF COLUMBIA, NEW JERSEY in this chapter; also Chapter 1, CONNECTICUT; also Chapter 4, MICHIGAN, MINNESOTA, MISSOURI; also Chapter 6, HAWAII.)

LIPPMANN, WALTER (1889–1975). On Sound Road near **Wading River,** Long Island, stands the two and one-half-story summer home of the famed journalist from 1920 to 1937. The south end of the house dates from about 1750, with the main structure added in 1858. Lippmann's study there was the apartment over the garage. According to the state inventory form for this structure, "it is recorded that the first commercial radio message was sent from the front steps, with Theodore Roosevelt in attendance." That would have been before Lippmann's occupancy, since Roosevelt died in 1919. The property remains privately owned.

(See DISTRICT OF COLUMBIA in this chapter; also Chapter 2, MANHATTAN.)

MacARTHUR, DOUGLAS (1880–1964). As Superintendent of the U.S. Military Academy at **West Point** between the two World Wars, MacArthur occupied the Superintendent's Quarters from 1919 to 1922. He lived with his mother there until his 1922 marriage. (See the entry on Robert Edward Lee earlier in this section.)

(See MARYLAND in this chapter; also Chapter 2, MANHATTAN; also Chapter 4, KANSAS; also Chapter 5, ARKANSAS, VIRGINIA; also Chapter 6, NEW MEXICO, TEXAS.)

McCORMICK, CYRUS HALL (1809–1884). Inventor and industrialist, McCormick built his summer home "Clayton Lodge" in 1882, a large, oddly shaped mansion encircled by a veranda on Sunset Hill in **Richfield Springs.** It was razed in 1958, though much of the woodwork and antique furnishings were saved and sold. The carriage house and caretakers' dwelling remain on the privately owned property.

(See Chapter 4, ILLINOIS; also Chapter 5, VIRGINIA.)

McCULLERS, CARSON SMITH (1917–1967). The novelist made her last home in **Nyack** at 131 South Broadway, a large Victorian house in which she occupied the first floor. She bought the house from her mother in 1951, and both resided in it thereafter. It is currently a private apartment building.

McCullers was also a frequent summer resident of Yaddo (see the entry on Yaddo later in this section).

(See Chapter 2, BROOKLYN, MANHATTAN; also Chapter 5, GEORGIA, NORTH CAROLINA.)

McKINLEY, WILLIAM (1843–1901). In **Buffalo,** where the 25th U.S. president was shot by assassin Leon Czolgosz, he lingered for the last eight days of his life at the Milburn House, which stood until the 1950s at 1168 Delaware Ave.—now a parking lot for Canisius High School. The third president in our history to die from gunshot wounds, McKinley would probably have survived if antibiotic drugs had been available in 1901.

Exhibits: McKinley was shot as he shook hands in a reception line at the **Buffalo** Temple of Music on Fordham Drive between Elmwood Avenue and Lincoln Parkway. A monument marks the site. At Theodore Roosevelt Inaugural National Historic Site, 641 Delaware Ave., the National Park Service displays several items and a slide program relating to the assassination. (Open Monday–Saturday 10:00–5:00, Saturday–Sunday 12:00–6:00; 716-884-0095; admission.)

(See DISTRICT OF COLUMBIA in this chapter; also Chapter 4, OHIO.)

MARQUAND, JOHN PHILLIPS (1893–1960). A social chronicler and gentle satirist in his fiction, Marquand spent much of his boyhood at **Rye,** where his grandparents' mansion at 355 Boston Post Road now functions as the Aurora Health Institute, a private nursing home "where retired dwell in dignity."

(See DELAWARE in this chapter; also Chapter 1, MASSACHUSETTS; also Chapter 2, MANHATTAN; also Chapter 5, FLORIDA, NORTH CAROLINA.)

MARX, JULIUS HENRY "GROUCHO" (1895–1977). At **Great Neck,** Long Island, the leering, cigar-flicking comedian and member of the Marx Brothers vaudeville and film team lived at 21 Lincoln Road (privately owned), a 10-room, stucco dwelling on an acre lot during the 1920s. "There was a sewer on the corner," he recalled. "Rats from the sewer used to come into our basement. During Prohibition, Frenchy [his father] made some wine in the basement. The bottles exploded and killed the rats."

(See Chapter 2, MANHATTAN; also Chapter 6, CALIFORNIA.)

MATHEWSON, CHRISTOPHER "CHRISTY" (1880–1925). "Big Six," the legendary New York Giants pitcher, spent his last years undergoing unsuccessful therapy for tuberculosis at **Saranac Lake.** His home from 1922 stands privately owned at 21 Old Military Road.

Exhibit: See the entry on National Baseball Hall of Fame and Museum later in this chapter.

(See PENNSYLVANIA in this chapter.)

MELVILLE, HERMAN (1819–1891). In the Lansingburgh section of **Troy,** Melville wrote his first two novels (*Typee*, 1846; *Omoo*, 1847) in a portion of the house standing at First Avenue and 114th Street (privately owned), where he lived with his family in 1838 and 1839 and from 1844 to 1847. There is some interest among Melville admirers in restoring the house as a museum, since it is one of only two existing Melville houses.

(See Chapter 1, MASSACHUSETTS; also Chapter 2, MANHATTAN.)

MILLAY, EDNA ST. VINCENT (1892–1950). Steepletop National Historic Landmark, the 700-acre farm and two-story, white frame house named for the wild steeplebush that decorates the meadows, stands on East Hill Road off State Highway 22 northeast of **Austerlitz.** The poet lived there from 1925 to 1950, writing in her upstairs study under a sign that said "Silence," while househusband Eugen Boissevain gladly attended to daily chores. Vincent Sheean described their life here in *The Indigo Bunting* (1951). Millay's cabin-studio stands in the woods beyond the house, which dates from about 1870. The Millay Colony for the Arts owns the estate and manages it as a creative haven for writers, artists and composers, as specified in her will. The colony eventually plans to make the estate accessible to the public on a limited basis, with a museum to display memorabilia of the poet. In the meantime, visits must be arranged with Millay Colony for the Arts, Austerlitz, NY, 12017 (518-392-3103).

(See Chapter 1, MAINE; also Chapter 2, MANHATTAN.)

MORGENTHAU, HENRY, JR. (1891–1967). Near **Hopewell Junction,** the secretary of the treasury who financed New Deal programs under President Franklin Delano Roosevelt (see the entry on Roosevelt later in this section) bought several hundred acres in 1913 and became a prosperous farmer, raising apples and dairy cattle. He retired there in 1946, continuing to manage the farm until his death. The 1885 farmhouse built by brewer Adolf Hupfel stands on East Hook Road and is privately owned.

(See Chapter 2, MANHATTAN.)

MORSE, SAMUEL FINLEY BREESE (1791–1872). Locust Grove National Historic Landmark at 370 South Road in **Poughkeepsie** is a clapboard, two and one-half-story house built about 1830. The versatile painter-inventor enlarged it after he purchased the property in 1847, and this was his last home. It is now operated as the Yount-Morse Historic Site museum by private trustees and contains period furnishings, costumes and dolls. (Open May 15–October 31, Wednesday–Sunday; call 914-454-4500 for hours; admission.)

(See Chapter 1, CONNECTICUT, MASSA-CHUSETTS; also Chapter 2, MANHATTAN.)

MOSES, ANNA MARY ROBERTSON "GRANDMA" (1860–1961). The "American primitive" painter lived in rural New York for all but 18 years of her long life. Her farm home from 1905 to 1951 near **Eagle Bridge** stands on Grandma Moses Road; across the road from this old homestead is her ranch-style last home (1951–61), built for her by her sons. Both dwellings are privately owned.

(See Chapter 1, VERMONT; also Chapter 5, VIRGINIA.)

MURROW, EDWARD ROSCOE (1908–1965). Famed radio and television newsman, Murrow occupied two homes near **Pawling** from 1946 to 1965. His first was a 1940 cedar log house on Berry Lane at the crest of a high hill overlooking the distant Hudson River. In 1954 Murrow acquired his 280-acre "Glen Arden" estate at

Quaker Hill, a colonial mansion dating from the early 1800s. George Washington stopped there briefly in 1778, and that same year the house was the scene of the court martial of Gen. Philip John Schuyler (see the entries on Washington and Schuyler later in this section). Murrow operated this as a working farm with a dairy herd of 60 head. His ashes were scattered on the estate in 1965. Both homes are privately owned.

(See DISTRICT OF COLUMBIA in this chapter; also Chapter 2, MANHATTAN; also Chapter 5, NORTH CAROLINA; also Chapter 6, WASHINGTON.)

NABOKOV, VLADIMIR VLADIMIROVICH (1899–1977). In **Ithaca,** where the novelist taught at Cornell University from 1948 to 1959, he lived in several apartments; but his "best Cornell house," where he occasionally took in lodgers and lived for some 18 months, stands at 880 Highland Road (privately owned).

(See Chapter 1, MASSACHUSETTS.)

NATIONAL BASEBALL HALL OF FAME AND MUSEUM. On Main Street in **Cooperstown,** this institution built to celebrate the national institution displays relics and memorabilia of the game's most notable players. These include Tyrus Raymond "Ty" Cobb, Henry Louis "Lou" Gehrig, Walter Perry Johnson, Christopher "Christy" Mathewson, Jack Roosevelt "Jackie" Robinson, George Herman 'Babe" Ruth, and Cy Young (see the entries on Gehrig and Mathewson earlier in this section). Films, photos and recordings recapture their golden moments. (Open May 1–October 31, daily 9:00–9:00; November 1–April 30, daily 9:00–5:00; 607-547-9988; admission.)

NOYES, JOHN HUMPHREY (1811–1886). In **Kenwood,** the utopian reformer established his commune of expelled Vermonters in 1848, a social experiment that functioned with notable success for 32 years. Out of this unorthodox society of "perfectionists" developed Oneida Ltd., modern manufacturers of tableware and silver goods. Many descendants of the Oneida colony still work in the vastly expanded corporation, which has retained some cooperative features. The large brick "Mansion House," dating from 1860, stands on the site of the original wooden communal building, which it replaced, and today houses company employees. This structure, still in excellent shape,

was the nucleus of the longest lasting group-marriage commune in American history. Pierrepont Noyes wrote an account of growing up there in *My Father's House* (1937).

(See Chapter 1, VERMONT.)

OCHS, ADOLPH SIMON (1858–1935). The publisher of the *New York Times* bought "Hillandale," a 60-acre estate in **White Plains,** in 1929, and it became his last permanent home in 1931. The Ochs family held it until 1949. Built from 1914 to 1916, the homestead mansion is now owned and occupied by White Plains Board of Education at 5 Homeside Lane on eight of the original acres.

(See Chapter 2, MANHATTAN.)

O'HARA, JOHN HENRY (1905–1970). From 1937, the novelist made his summer home in **Quogue,** Long Island, where his house dating from the 1920s stands privately owned and unnumbered on Dune Road.

(See NEW JERSEY, PENNSYLVANIA in this chapter; also Chapter 2, MANHATTAN.)

PAINE, THOMAS (1737–1809). He was a good man, if not a very likeable one, to have on your side. Americans owe him a lot, but only New Yorkers countered the general pattern of abuse and neglect that dogged him in death as well as life. "In spite of Theodore Roosevelt's 'dirty-little-atheist' remark," wrote Stewart H. Holbrook, "**New Rochelle** has been described as being pretty much in the Paine business." Paine Cottage National Historic Landmark is the two-story, shingled house where the Revolutionary writer, called "the first modern internationalist," lived intermittently from 1803 to 1806. The state awarded Paine a confiscated Tory estate in 1784 for his services, but he took up residence and expanded the small 1793 dwelling only after a lengthy stay in France. Impoverished during his last years, Paine owned practically no furnishings and lived mostly on "tea, milk, fruit pies, plain dumplings and a piece of meat" through neighborhood charity; he also sold off portions of the 100-acre estate to pay expenses. A debtor shot at him there on Christmas of 1804 from outside, and visitors may still see the thumb-size bullet hole just below a window sill. The house, containing period furnishings, is operated by the Huguenot and Thomas Paine Historical Associa-

"MANSION HOUSE," COMMUNAL DWELLING OF THE ONEIDA COLONY. The sprawling 1860 building that housed the most successful group-marriage commune in U.S. history was established in **Kenwood** by utopian John Humphrey Noyes. Still used by Oneida Ltd. for housing and offices, the complex is not open to the public. (*Courtesy Oneida Ltd.*)

tion. (Open Wednesday–Sunday 2:00–5:00; free.)

Exhibit: Paine Memorial Building at 983 North Ave. in **New Rochelle** displays many personal effects and memorabilia of this complex historical figure. (Open Wednesday–Sunday 2:00–5:00; 914-632-5376; free.)

(See NEW JERSEY, PENNSYLVANIA in this chapter; also Chapter 2, BROOKLYN, MANHATTAN.)

PEGLER, WESTBROOK (1894–1969). The once-respected and powerful newspaper columnist whose self-styled "opinions of the average man" became slashing, sometimes libelous attacks on public figures, Pegler spent his bitter last years writing for the only audience that would finally tolerate him, the John Birch Society. From 1926 to 1929, before his spleen ruptured into national syndication, he rented a house at the ironic address of 10 Harmony Drive in **Larchmont.** This structure, still privately occupied, dates from about 1920.

From 1929 to 1941, Pegler's home was a Bavarian-type stone house with nine rooms that he built on 25 hilly acres at **Pound Ridge.** The property, including his stone writing studio and a small lake, is located on Eastwoods Road, unnumbered and still private.

(See Chapter 2, MANHATTAN; also Chapter 4, MINNESOTA; also Chapter 6, ARIZONA.)

POLLOCK, JACKSON (1912–1956). The painter's two and one-half-story frame home, a 19th-century farmhouse where he lived from 1945 to 1956 with his barn studio behind, stands with a scenic view of Gardiners Bay near the village of **Springs,** Long Island, on Fireplace Road. There Pollock virtually founded the movement of abstract expressionism with his celebrated "action painting" of huge canvases on the floor or on rollers—a frenzied process of splashing, dripping, "attacking" the canvas with paint. The property, which Pollock bought on money loaned by patron Peggy Guggenheim, remains privately owned.

(See Chapter 2, MANHATTAN; also Chapter 6, CALIFORNIA.)

PORTER, KATHERINE ANNE (1890–1980). Near **Ballston Spa,** the writer of short stories and novelist bought "South Hill," a small colonial house dating from the 18th century, in 1941 and lived there for a year. The house, one of the first in the area, was built by relatives of Benedict Arnold; but there is no evidence supporting the local tradition that Arnold himself occupied it (see the entry on Arnold earlier in this section). It remains privately owned on Cramer Road.

(See DISTRICT OF COLUMBIA, MARYLAND in this chapter; also Chapter 2, MANHATTAN.)

POST, EMILY PRICE (1873–1960). The author of ten editions of *Etiquette* from 1922 spent her summers as a child at **Tuxedo Park,** built as an exclusive Orange County resort in 1884 and still maintained as such. Her girlhood home on West Lake Road no longer exists; but "Rocklawn Cottage," the 1897 home designed and built by her father, the noted architect Bruce Price, stands privately owned on Pepperidge Road. Post occupied it during summers until the 1920s. There is no admission to Tuxedo Park without a local friend.

(See MARYLAND in this chapter; also Chapter 1, MASSACHUSETTS; also Chapter 2, MANHATTAN.)

REED, JOHN SILAS (1887–1920). "My sanctuary" and "Mount Airy Soviet," the leftist journalist called his cottage retreat at **Croton-on-Hudson,** probably his last American residence. He lived there at intervals from 1915 to 1920. In the latter year he headed the Communist Labor Party and became an expatriate victim of the 1919 and 1920 "Red Scare." The 19th-century dwelling with the one-room studio where Reed lodged next to what is known as the Abraham Victor house stands unnumbered and privately owned on Mount Airy Road. Reed's wife sold the house after his death from typhus in Moscow.

(See Chapter 2, MANHATTAN; also Chapter 6, OREGON.)

REMINGTON, FREDERIC (1861–1909). The painter-sculptor's birthplace, built from 1825 to 1830, stands at 55 Court St. in **Canton,** his home to age 11. Privately owned, the frame house has been enlarged at the rear and side but otherwise remains essentially as built.

Forty miles west of Canton, the five-acre **Ingleneuk Island** in Chippewa Bay of the St. Lawrence River was Remington's summer home and studio from 1898 to 1908. The house he enlarged there burned down about 1970, but the fireplace and tennis court remain. His boathouse and studio have been renovated as private summer cottages.

Remington's boyhood home in **Ogdensburg** stood at 218 Hamilton St.

Exhibit: Remington Art Memorial Museum, operated by the city of **Ogdensburg** at 303 Washington St., contains the most complete single collection of his art. Also displayed there are his library and personal items. (Open June 1–September 30, Monday–Saturday 10:00–5:00, Sunday 1:00–5:00; October 1–May 31, Monday–Saturday 10:00–5:00; 315-393-2425; admission.)

(See Chapter 1, CONNECTICUT; also Chapter 6, WYOMING.)

RICE, GRANTLAND (1880–1954). In 1927 and 1928, the sportswriter and versifier built a large two-story, frame summer home on a four-acre tract he had purchased with his friend Ring Lardner in **East Hampton,** Long Island (see the entry on Lardner earlier in this section). This house, along with Lardner's, was damaged in a 1931 hurricane and moved back 200 feet behind the dunes to its present location on West End Avenue. Rice resided at long intervals there for the rest of his life. The house remains privately owned.

(See Chapter 2, MANHATTAN; also Chapter 5, TENNESSEE.)

RICKENBACKER, EDWARD VERNON "EDDIE" (1890–1973). The aviator-businessman, a popular World War I hero and flying ace, resided from 1931 to 1937 in **Bronxville** at 8 Prescott Ave. in the Lawrence Park residential section. This stone house, still privately occupied, dates from 1845. It was originally the manor house of the farm from which Lawrence Park was subdivided, then served as an inn for prospective home buyers.

(See Chapter 2, MANHATTAN; also Chapter 4, INDIANA, MICHIGAN, OHIO; also Chapter 5, FLORIDA; also Chapter 6, TEXAS.)

ROBINSON, JACK ROOSEVELT "JACKIE" (1919–1972).

Exhibit: See National Baseball Hall of Fame and Museum earlier in this section.

(See Chapter 1, CONNECTICUT; also Chapter 2, BROOKLYN; also Chapter 5, GEORGIA.)

ROCKEFELLER, JOHN DAVISON (1839–1937). The birth site of the oil magnate is in Tioga County, a rise of ground called Michigan Hill three miles northeast of a village called **Richford,** believe it or not. Built about 1835 by the financier's father, the modest, one-story dwelling on 160 acres was the site of nostalgic annual pilgrimages by Rockefeller for many years until 1928, when a buyer dismantled the house and big plans to display it elsewhere fizzled.* The unmarked site today is virtually inaccessible except by off-road vehicle.

A historical marker does identify the site of his boyhood home from 1843 to 1850 on Rockefeller Road near **Moravia.** Fire destroyed this home in 1924. It was the site of Rockefeller's first business venture—raising turkeys.

East of **Owego,** a later boyhood home (1850–53) stands on State Highway 17C between Day Hollow Road and Tioga Gardens. The one and one-half-story farmhouse is a privately owned residence.

At Pocantico Hills near **North Tarrytown,** Rockefeller purchased his 3,500-acre estate in 1893. Pocantico Hills, 10 times the size of Monaco, five

---

*As author Dixon Wecter has remarked, Americans do not consider billionaires as heroes in the same league with founding fathers, great presidents, sports figures or noted writers. Thus the landmarks of the very rich draw relatively minor preservation interest. The strange fate of Rockefeller's birthplace is a case in point. In 1928 Mrs. Sarah S. Deneen of the Coney Island Chamber of Commerce purchased the small farmhouse, intending to display it on Coney Island for public edification as a solid "inspiration to future generations." Then, according to William Lay, Jr., Curator of the Tioga County Historical Society, "her plans miscarried. She first planned to move the house intact. When that proved impractical, she had it dismantled and loaded on a truck for transportation to Coney. Various complications arose, financial and otherwise, and it never arrived there. For a long while it was stored in Binghamton. Its present whereabouts are unclear. One story has it stored in Berkshire; another has it still in Binghamton."

times larger than Central Park in Manhattan, is the "spiritual center of the family's existence," wrote biographers Peter Collier and David Horowitz, "as much involved with being a Rockefeller as Blenheim was with being a Churchill." Or, as a Broadway wit once proclaimed, the estate "is an example of what God could have done if He'd only had the money." Rockefeller built his four-story, neo-Georgian mansion "Kykuit" (Dutch for "the lookout") in 1905; he laid out 70 miles of roads, a huge golf course, gymnasium and stables. The six square miles of Rockefeller's estate encompass some of the most scenic country in Westchester County. Located on State Highway 117 between the Hudson and Saw Mill Rivers, it is fenced with high stone walls and barbed wire—but some of the acreage is now open for hiking and horse riding (see the entry on Nelson Aldrich Rockefeller below).

Exhibit: The Historical Society of the Tarrytowns, 1 Grove St. in **Tarrytown,** displays Rockefeller memorabilia including a mahogany desk, boyhood account book and papers. (Open Tuesday–Saturday 2:00–4:00; 914-631-8374; free.)

(See NEW JERSEY in this chapter; also Chapter 2, BROOKLYN, MANHATTAN; also Chapter 4, OHIO; also Chapter 5, FLORIDA, GEORGIA.)

ROCKEFELLER, NELSON ALDRICH (1908–1979). A New York governor, U.S. vice president and grandson of John Davison Rockefeller, Nelson Rockefeller announced in 1970 that the family intended to preserve its Pocantico Hills estate near **North Tarrytown** for ultimate public use as a recreation area and would not allow commercial subdivision (see the entry on John D. Rockefeller above). Now consisting of about 4,200 acres with 60 buildings, the estate remains the private center of the Rockefeller family. It was Rockefeller's summer home and frequent retreat throughout his life.

As governor, Rockefeller occupied the State Executive Mansion in **Albany** from 1958 to 1973 (see the entry on Samuel Jones Tilden later in this section).

(See DISTRICT OF COLUMBIA in this chapter; also Chapter 1, MAINE; also Chapter 2, MANHATTAN.)

ROCKWELL, NORMAN (1894–1978). During his early career, the popular illustrator of down-home

Americana occupied several houses and studios in **New Rochelle.** The home he occupied longest (1927–39) was built about 1926 and stands at 24 Lord Kitchener Road. Both house and studio, connected by a "Florida room," are privately owned.

Rockwell's boyhood home (1903–12) in **Mamaroneck** is at 415 Prospect Ave., built about 1900 and privately owned.

(See PENNSYLVANIA in this chapter; also Chapter 1, MASSACHUSETTS, VERMONT; also Chapter 2, MANHATTAN.)

ROGERS, WILL (1879–1935). The grinning rope artist and monologuist was still nationally unknown when he began performing on the Ziegfeld Follies stage in 1915. He and his family rented a house in **Amityville** for about a year; and during this period his career began the rise that would make him the most beloved humorist and general gadabout in national history. The house at 425 Clocks Blvd., dating from about 1890, remains essentially unaltered and privately owned.

(See Chapter 6, CALIFORNIA, OKLAHOMA.)

ROOSEVELT, FRANKLIN DELANO (1882–1945). ROOSEVELT, ELEANOR (1884–1962).

Roosevelt Home National Historic Site at **Hyde Park** was the 32nd U.S. president's lifelong permanent residence. His father bought the original 1826 frame house in 1867 and massively enlarged it by 1916 to the present stone and stucco mansion with 50 rooms on 187 acres (only a remnant of the 1,365 acres President Roosevelt owned there at his death). "Big House," as family members called it, is Roosevelt's birthplace, served as his summer White House and frequent retreat from 1933 to 1945, and is preserved exactly as it appeared during his lifetime by the National Park Service, with original furnishings and family heirlooms. Eleanor Roosevelt describes the rooms via tape recording for visitors. A 1982 fire seriously damaged several third-floor rooms and the roof. (Open daily 9:00–5:00; 914-229-9115; admission.)

Two miles east of the ancestral mansion stands Val-Kill National Historic Site, the fieldstone cottage of Eleanor Roosevelt on a 173-acre wooded tract. She built this house in 1926 as a refuge from the "Big House," where her autocratic

BIRTHPLACE AND LIFELONG HOME OF FRANKLIN D. ROOSEVELT. The Roosevelt family grouped on the lawn in this October, 1917, snapshot shows the later president on his pony "Bobby" at right; Eleanor Roosevelt stands third from left. Four of their children plus Roosevelt's maternal grandfather and a family friend complete the informal gathering at the **Hyde Park** estate. A frontal view shows the mansion at the same season exactly 60 years later. (*Courtesy Franklin D. Roosevelt Library*)

1917

SAGAMORE HILL, HOME OF THEODORE ROOSEVELT.
The 26th U.S. president helped design his permanent home
from 1885, this rambling Victorian mansion on Cove Neck
Road at **Oyster Bay**, Long Island.
(*Courtesy National Park Service*)

THE TROPHY ROOM AT SAGAMORE HILL. Crowded with
objects from a lifetime of hunting and exploring expeditions,
this room probably best reflects the macho president's spectacular interests and lifestyle.
(*Courtesy National Park Service*)

mother-in-law, Sara Delano Roosevelt, reigned. At Val-Kill, alone and with selected friends, Eleanor Roosevelt forged the dynamic, positive personality admired by the world from a painfully shy woman obsessed with failure. She also made this her home base during her last, widowed years of nonstop activity. Val-Kill, undergoing restoration by the National Park Service since its 1978 public acquisition, will probably be ready for visitors by the time of Eleanor Roosevelt's centenary in 1984.

In **Albany** during his tenure as New York's governor (1929–33), Roosevelt resided in the State Executive Mansion, where, huddled by radio and phones, he received word of his 1932 presidential nomination (see the entry on Samuel Jones Tilden later in this section).

Exhibit: The Roosevelt Library and Museum, adjacent to the **Hyde Park** estate, displays personal memorabilia of the couple. Roosevelt built this structure as a library-office in 1939, and it now houses his ship models, White House desk and chair, the President's Room from which he broadcast, the Eleanor Roosevelt Gallery and the Gift Room, among numerous exhibits. (Open

daily 9:00–5:00; 914-229-8114; admission.)

(See DISTRICT OF COLUMBIA, MARYLAND in this chapter; also Chapter 1, MAINE; also Chapter 2, MANHATTAN; also Chapter 4, MICHIGAN; also Chapter 5, GEORGIA.)

ROOSEVELT, THEODORE (1858–1919). Near **Oyster Bay,** Long Island, Sagamore Hill National Historic Site was the permanent home of the 26th U.S. president. He helped design the three-story, 23-room, informal Victorian mansion on 83 acres in 1884 and 1885 and resided there for the rest of his life. During his tenure as president from 1901 to 1909, it served as the summer White House. Today it remains as he left it. Visitors there can see family furnishings, Roosevelt's hunting trophies and gun collection, clothing, art treasures and a large assortment of mementoes that reflect the variety of this president's interests and activities. "At Sagamore Hill," he wrote, "we love a great many things—birds and trees, and books . . . and horses and rifles, and children and hard work and the joy of life." Sagamore Hill, located on Cove Neck Road, is operated by the National Park Service. (Open Memorial Day–Labor Day, daily 9:30–6:00; Labor Day–November 30, March 1–Memorial Day, 9:30–5:00; December 1–February 28, 9:30–4:30; 516-922-4447; admission.)

As New York's governor from 1899 to 1901, Roosevelt occupied the State Executive Mansion in **Albany** (see the entry on Samuel Jones Tilden later in this section).

Exhibits: Old Orchard Museum near Sagamore Hill at **Oyster Bay,** formerly the home of Gen. Theodore Roosevelt, Jr., displays numerous items relating to the president's family life and public career. (The hours are the same as for Sagamore Hill.)

At **Buffalo,** Roosevelt Inaugural National Historic Site at 641 Delaware Ave. is the house where Roosevelt took the oath of office on September 14, 1901, following the death of President McKinley (see the entry on McKinley earlier in this section). The brick house dates from 1838 and has been restored with period furnishings by the National Park Service. Roosevelt became president in the library room. (Open Monday–Saturday 10:00–5:00, Sunday 12:00–6:00; 716-884-0095; admission.)

(See DISTRICT OF COLUMBIA in this chapter; also Chapter 2, BRONX, MANHATTAN; also

Chapter 4, NORTH DAKOTA; also Chapter 6, NEW MEXICO.)

ROOT, ELIHU (1845–1937). Prominent secretary of state, senator and diplomat, Root was a native of **Clinton.** His two-story clapboard home, Root House National Historic Landmark at 101 College Hill Road dates from 1817. Root made this his summer home in the early 1900s and later retired there permanently. He took great interest in the trees and shrubs on his property, knew each by its Latin name, and spent hours in gardening and walking the grounds. In 1906 he purchased adjacent land and a small house to the west of his home, which remains privately owned. The 1845 Buttrick Hall on Hamilton College campus was his grandparents' home and his birthplace.

(See DISTRICT OF COLUMBIA in this chapter; also Chapter 2, MANHATTAN.)

RUTH, GEORGE HERMAN "BABE" (1895–1948).
Exhibit: See National Baseball Hall of Fame and Museum earlier in this section.

(See MARYLAND in this chapter; also Chapter 1, MASSACHUSETTS; also Chapter 2, MANHATTAN.)

SANGER, MARGARET HIGGINS (1883–1966). Until age 20, the pioneer birth-control reformer lived in **Corning** at several rented addresses, few of which are firmly identified—"houses not only on the wrong side of the tracks, but often right next to them," as one biographer wrote. One privately owned house occupied by her family during the 1890s stands at 238 West Second St.

At **Hastings-on-Hudson,** she lived from 1908 to 1911 at 155 Edgar's Lane (privately owned). Her first husband designed this three-story tile house, and a fire burned out the first floor the same night they moved in.

"Willowlake" on Van Wyck Lake Road at **Fishkill** was her large fieldstone house in later life. Her second husband built it in 1922, and it remained their home until his death in 1943. They named the house for the trees planted around the adjacent pond. There she wrote *Happiness in Marriage* (1926), among other books; but though she was often a happy, sexually liberated woman, the contentment she herself experienced in marriage amounted to little enough. She sold this property in 1947, and it remains privately owned.

(See Chapter 2, MANHATTAN; also Chapter 6, ARIZONA.)

SARNOFF, DAVID (1891–1971). The communications engineer and businessman who pioneered in both radio and television broadcasting industries occupied a modest part-time home in **Mount Vernon** from 1921 to 1926, the period when he first assumed direction of the Radio Corporation of America. This house, still private, stands at 180 Pennsylvania Ave.

(See NEW JERSEY in this chapter; also Chapter 2, MANHATTAN.)

SCHUYLER, PHILIP JOHN (1733–1804). The ancestral mansion and frequent boyhood home of the wealthy country squire and Revolutionary general was "The Flats" in **Watervliet,** a 1666 house that stood on First Street until fire destroyed it in 1962; the site is marked.

In **Albany,** Schuyler's birthplace, built in 1667, was a double brick dwelling that stood on the southeast corner of State and Pearl streets, now a commercial block. Also in Albany, Schuyler Mansion National Historic Landmark at 27 Clinton St., the two and one-half-story, red brick dwelling built for him by slaves and off-duty British soldiers in 1761 and 1762, retains its original appearance—only the vestibule is a post-1800 addition. "By any criteria," wrote Revolutionary War historian Mark M. Boatner, "The Schuyler Mansion is among the most noteworthy historic houses in America." Schuyler named his home "The Pastures"; there his daughter Elizabeth married Alexander Hamilton, who lived there for a time; Benjamin Franklin visited in 1776; and the house became the unofficial headquarters of northern political and military activity during the Revolution. Former president Millard Fillmore married his second wife in the parlor there in 1858 (see the entries on Hamilton and Fillmore earlier in this section). Completely restored in 1950, the house contains many original furnishings and period antiques and is maintained by New York State Parks and Recreation. (Open Wednesday–Sunday 9:00–5:00; 518-474-3953; free.)

At **Schuylerville,** Schuyler House National Historic Landmark centered the general's 900-acre summer estate, which he operated as a farming and milling complex. British troops retreating from Saratoga burned the second house on the site in 1777, and Schuyler rebuilt it in three weeks as the two-story, white frame house seen today. Restored with period furnishings, it occupies a 25-acre detached portion of Saratoga National Historic Park. It is operated by the National Park Service and Old Saratoga Historical Association. (Open June 15–Labor Day, daily 10:00–5:00; Labor Day–October 15, Saturday–Sunday 10:00–5:00; 518-695-3664; admission.)

SETON, ELIZABETH ANN BAYLEY (1774–1821). The frequent girlhood home of the Roman Catholic nun and saint until she turned 14 was the home of her uncle, William Pell Bayley, in **New Rochelle.** Originally built in 1720, the rambling, clapboard house stood on Bayley's 250-acre shoreline farm overlooking Long Island Sound. According to a recent owner, this dwelling at 145 Shore Road was rebuilt in 1850 and again at an unrecorded later date. Local authority Robert J. Cammann states that "the home is situated directly on the border line (which runs through the master bedroom) of New Rochelle and Pelham, and taxes are paid to both communities." Identified by marker, the house remains privately owned.

(See MARYLAND in this chapter; also Chapter 2, BRONX, MANHATTAN.)

SEWARD, WILLIAM HENRY (1801–1872). President Lincoln's secretary of state lived in **Westfield** while practicing law from 1836 to 1841. The Old McClurg Mansion, his home for his first two years in the town, stands at the junction of U.S. Highway 20 and State Highway 17. The Chautauqua County Historical Society displays period furnishings in the 1820 house. (Open mid-April–June 30, September 1–mid-October, Tuesday–Saturday 10:00–12:00, 1:00–4:00; July 1–August 31, hours as above plus Sunday 2:00–5:00; 716-326-2977; admission.) His later house in Westfield was moved to South Portage Road in 1967.

Seward House National Historic Landmark at 33 South St. in **Auburn** was his permanent homestead from 1824. Built in 1816 by Seward's father-in-law, the brick, two and one-half-story house contains original furnishings plus items and letters pertaining to Seward's career and his 1867 Alaska purchase. It is operated by the Foundation Historical Association. (Open March 1–December 31, Monday–Saturday 1:00–5:00; 315-252-1283; admission.)

(See DISTRICT OF COLUMBIA in this chapter.)

SHERWOOD, ROBERT EMMET (1896–1955). Two of the playwright's boyhood homes survive under private ownership in **Westport.** "Beach Hill," where he lived with his parents from 1899 to 1906, is a gray stone house with Tudor gables at 115 South Main St. Dating in its earliest stone-cottage portion from 1830, the structure's later additions include an 1890 north wing designed by architect Stanford White (see the entry on White later in this section) and a 1915 south wing. "Skene Wood," the 40-room mansion designed by White and Sherwood's remarkable mother, was the family's home and 300-acre estate from 1906 to 1917. It has no numbered address.

(See Chapter 2, MANHATTAN.)

SMITH, ALFRED EMANUEL (1873–1944). The popular New York governor and 1928 presidential candidate resided in the State Executive Mansion at **Albany** in 1919 and 1920 and from 1923 to 1928 (see the entry on Samuel Jones Tilden later in this section). Smith, an animal lover, converted the mansion's back yard to a private zoo that he enjoyed showing off to guests.

(See Chapter 2, MANHATTAN.)

SMITH, JOSEPH (1805–1844). At **Palmyra,** the boyhood home (1822–25) of the founder of the Mormon Church stands on Stafford Road. He helped his father and brothers build the clapboard farmhouse in 1822 and 1823. There in his southeast bedroom, say the Mormons, Smith had the 1823 vision that led to his discovery of buried golden plates at Hill Cumorah; these he later deciphered and published as *The Book of Mormon* (1830). The house, containing original floorboards and period furnishings, is operated by the Church of Jesus Christ of Latter-day Saints. (Open daily 8:00–6:00; 315-597-4383; free.)

The Peter Whitmer Farm site on Aukst Road west of State Highway 96 near **Waterloo** is the spot where Smith organized the Mormon church in 1830 and from which he led his band of followers to Ohio in 1831. The present farmhouse dates from 1852, with period furnishings maintained by the church as a Mormon museum. (Open daily 8:00–6:00; 315-539-2552; free.)

Exhibit: Hill Cumorah, four miles south of **Palmyra** on State Highway 21, is the sacred spot in Mormon theology where, according to Smith, he recovered the golden plates buried in the fifth century by the angel Moroni. A 40-foot statue of

Moroni crowns the hill, and a visitor center is operated by the Church of Jesus Christ of Latter-day Saints. (Open daily 8:00–6:00; 315-597-5851; free.)

(See PENNSYLVANIA in this chapter; also Chapter 1, VERMONT; also Chapter 4, ILLINOIS, MISSOURI, OHIO; also Chapter 6, UTAH.)

SOUSA, JOHN PHILIP (1854–1932). Wildbank National Historic Landmark at 14 Hicks Lane in **Sands Point,** Long Island, was the 1907 mansion on three acres owned by the "March King" composer-conductor. Sousa added a wing to this, his last home (1914–32), which remained in the Sousa family until 1965. It is still privately owned.

(See DISTRICT OF COLUMBIA in this chapter.)

STANTON, ELIZABETH CADY (1815–1902). In **Seneca Falls,** Stanton House National Historic Landmark at 32 Washington St. is the two-story, 19th century dwelling the pioneer feminist's father gave her in 1847. The place was decrepit and run-down. "You believe in woman's capacity to do and dare," he told her. "Now go ahead and put your place in order." She did and managed a household of husband and three children besides. It remained her home until 1862. There she met collaborator Susan Brownell Anthony in 1851 and helped organize the suffrage movement that would absorb them for the rest of their lives. The house has been acquired by the Stanton Foundation, which is developing this property along with the home of Amelia Jenks Bloomer into Women's Rights National Historic Park for eventual public visitation (see the entries on Anthony and Bloomer earlier in this section).

Her birth site and home until 1842 is in **Johnstown,** present site of the State Bank of Albany at Main and Market streets.

Exhibits: **Seneca Falls** Historical Society at 55 Cayuga St. displays some Stanton furnishings and memorabilia including a piano and rocking chair in its Woman's Rights Room. (Open May 1–October 31, Monday–Tuesday, Thursday–Friday, 1:00–4:00; 315-568-8412; admission.)

Johnstown Historical Society at 17 North Williams St. in **Johnstown** contains more personal artifacts. (Open Tuesday–Saturday 1:30–5:00; 518-762-7076; admission.)

(See NEW JERSEY in this chapter; also Chapter 2, MANHATTAN.)

STEINBECK, JOHN ERNST (1902–1968). **Sag Harbor** was the novelist's frequent summer home from 1955, when he bought a small house in an oak grove outside the village. It remains privately owned on Bluff Point.

(See CHAPTER 2, MANHATTAN; also Chapter 6, CALIFORNIA.)

STEUBEN, FRIEDRICH VON (1730–1794). The Prussian soldier, stern chief drillmaster of the raw farmboys who fought the American Revolution, was awarded 16,000 acres in the Mohawk Valley in 1786 by a grateful New York. Near **Remsen,** a 1930s replica of his 1794 cabin on this land grant stands three miles west of town on Starr Hill Road. The Steuben Memorial, operated by New York State Parks and Recreation, contains some original furnishings and personal belongings, including his uniform. "German-Americans," noted military historian Mark M. Boatner recently, "are showing increasing interest in the Steuben Memorial as an ethnic shrine." (Open May 30–Labor Day, Wednesday–Sunday 9:00–5:00; 315-768-7224; free.)

(See PENNSYLVANIA in this chapter.)

STEVENSON, ROBERT LOUIS (1850–1894). At **Saranac Lake** during the winter of 1887–88, the Scottish author submitted himself to a physician's care for the chronic tuberculosis that was slowly killing him. He settled into a new, two-story cottage-farmhouse at 11 Stevenson Lane, enchanted by the rustic setting and natural beauty of the area, which he called an "American Switzerland." There he wrote most of his novel *The Master of Ballantrae* (1888), pacing on the veranda while working out plot details, as well as several essays. Stevenson Memorial Cottage, operated by the Stevenson Society of America, houses the largest U.S. collection of Stevenson material, including his desk, clothing, letters, photos and many other items. Leaving a trail of cigarette burns wherever he went, his marks on the mantelpiece are still evident. (Open July 1–September 15, Tuesday–Sunday 9:30–12:00, 1:00–4:30; 518-891-4480; admission.)

(See Chapter 6, CALIFORNIA, HAWAII.)

SULLIVAN, EDWARD VINCENT "ED" (1902–1974). The newspaper columnist and longtime television impresario whose wooden style inspired countless comic imitations grew up in **Port Ches-**

ter from 1907 to 1920. The parental home stands at 119 Pearl St., a 1900 private dwelling with a store attached.

(See Chapter 1, CONNECTICUT; also Chapter 2, MANHATTAN.)

THOMAS, LOWELL JACKSON (1892–1981). He did almost everything in his long life, knew everybody, went everywhere, worked hard, made no real enemies and lived extremely well. In **Pawling,** the news broadcaster, author and world traveler built what amounted to a baronial estate including a 90-acre lake, ski chalet and lift and several mansions. He also contributed land and buildings to the community and sold homes to his friends, attracting such public luminaries as Thomas Edmund Dewey and Edward Roscoe Murrow to the area (see the entries on Dewey and Murrow earlier in this section). Thomas successively occupied three locations on Quaker Hill. He bought "Cloverbrook Farm" in 1926, a 32-room, white frame, colonial mansion with two barns and 80 acres, to which he added 350 woodland acres. Thomas later sold this property, which is now privately occupied as a horse farm and riding school. He next acquired "Hammersley Hill," an estate built by Manhattan entrepreneur Fred F. French during the 1920s. This 50-room, red brick mansion became the focus of the 3,000-acre Thomas "empire," surrounded by his 140-acre golf course, the aforementioned lake and a 1,000-foot slope, a softball field, stable, viewing tower and the 13-room broadcasting studio he built in 1931, the source of his nightly newscasts until his 1976 retirement. It was, in the words of local historian Gae Mitchell, "an establishment, in the true sense." Thomas lived there until 1979. The complex remains privately owned. Nearby, Thomas built his last home, a smaller Georgian colonial mansion called "Main-top," in the late 1970s and died there.

Exhibit: See Edward Roscoe Murrow, *Exhibit,* Chapter 2, MANHATTAN.

(See Chapter 4, OHIO; also Chapter 6, COLORADO.)

THOMAS, NORMAN MATTOON (1884–1968). Six-time Socialist presidential candidate, Thomas never indulged any hopes of winning but saw many of his proposals eventually adopted by the major political parties and become law; thus as a "conscience candidate" and often unpopular

anticapitalist, he was highly influential. His longtime home (1929–68) stands at 106 Goose Hill Road near **Huntington,** Long Island. Thomas built this 14-room farmhouse on five acres after his wife's U-shaped design. It remains privately owned.

(See PENNSYLVANIA in this chapter; also Chapter 2, MANHATTAN.)

TIFFANY, LOUIS COMFORT (1848–1933). "Laurelton Hall," Tiffany's 580-acre estate two miles east of **Oyster Bay,** Long Island, included the 80-room castle described as a "Moorish pile," which "sprawled for 275 feet across the top of a hill, and three stories down the side" and was built by the artist-designer in 1904. Until 1942, it housed the Tiffany Foundation, then lingered as a white elephant until a fire razed it in 1953.

"Tiffany Park" in **Irvington** was the family's 65-acre country estate acquired by Tiffany's father, jeweler Charles Lewis Tiffany, in the 1860s. The main house was demolished in the early 1900s, but two elegant stone houses that were also part of the property remain in private hands, located just south of Sunnyside National Historic Landmark, the home of Washington Irving, west of U.S. Highway 9 (see the entry on Irving earlier in this section).

(See Chapter 2, MANHATTAN; also Chapter 5, FLORIDA.)

TILDEN, SAMUEL JONES (1814–1886). Sometimes called the 19th U.S. president, since he actually won the popular vote for that office in 1876 (though a slanted electoral commission gave the election to Rutherford B. Hayes), Tilden achieved renown as an able political reformer. As governor of New York, he was the first to occupy the **Albany** State Executive Mansion (1875–76), which he first rented; the state, on his recommendation, bought it. Located at 138 Eagle St., this two and one-half-story, brick structure dates from about 1860, was remodeled in 1887 and has served as the official residence of each governor since Tilden—several of whom likewise achieved or aspired to the presidency.

In **Yonkers,** "Graystone" was Tilden's country home from 1879. There he raised cattle and operated the estate as a working farm. He also died there. His 1868 stone mansion at 919 Broadway was extensively remodeled by noted lawyer Samuel Untermyer, who purchased the estate in

1899, extensively landscaped the 113-acre grounds, and maintained the property until his death in 1940. Since 1946, the property has belonged to the city of Yonkers, which undertook complete restoration during the 1970s. Untermyer Park at Warburton Avenue and North Broadway now displays Untermyer's renovated formal gardens and layout scheme.

Tilden's birth site is marked in **New Lebanon.** The large frame house, his home until about 1835, burned down in 1914.

(See Chapter 2, MANHATTAN.)

TILLICH, PAUL JOHANNES (1886–1965). The prominent philosopher-theologian made his permanent home in America after fleeing Nazi Germany in 1933. His summer home in **East Hampton,** Long Island, dating from about 1915, stands at 84 Woods Lane (privately owned). The small, two-story frame house, badly run-down when Tillich bought it in 1943, was slowly renovated. His American homes, wrote one biographer, "were all simple and modern, producing a certain barren or monastic effect and never pretentious." Tillich wrote most of his major work *Systematic Theology* (1951–63) there.

(See Chapter 1, MASSACHUSETTS; also Chapter 4, ILLINOIS.)

TRUTH, SOJOURNER (1797?–1883). A two and one-half-story stone dwelling built before 1752, the Hardenbergh House stands much modernized and privately owned on School House Lane in **Hurley.** The emancipated slave and electrifying orator was born there and lived in the cellar until separated from her parents at a young age.

In **Bloomington,** the home to which she fled and where owner Isaac Van Wagener befriended her stands marked on Main Street. Built from 1726 to 1730, the central portion is the original house. The property is still privately occupied by a Van Wagener descendant.

(See Chapter 1, MASSACHUSETTS; also Chapter 4, MICHIGAN.)

TUBMAN, HARRIET (1820?–1913). The abolitionist and skilled conductor of the Underground Railroad, a former slave herself, moved to **Auburn** in the late 1850s. Tubman House National Historic Landmark at 180 South St., a two and one-half-story white clapboard house built before 1850 and her last home, stands on

the 26-acre property sold to her in 1857 by Gov. William Henry Seward (see the entry on Seward earlier in this section). The large collection of Tubman memorabilia includes her furnishings, huge Bible and other personal items. She deeded house and land in 1908 to the AME Zion Church as a home for indigent blacks, and the church now operates it as a shrine to "the Moses of her people." (Open Monday–Friday 11:00–5:00, Saturday–Sunday by appointment; 315-253-2621; admission.)

(See MARYLAND in this chapter.)

TWAIN, MARK. See SAMUEL LANGHORNE CLEMENS earlier in this section.

VAN BUREN, MARTIN (1782–1862). In 1839, the eighth U.S. president, called the "most Machiavellian of politicians," bought "Lindenwald," a brick, two and one-half-story, 1797 mansion, in his native **Kinderhook.** He wanted to make a Venetian villa of it, so he hired architect Richard Upjohn to design the wing and four-story tower in 1850; the front portico is a 1958 addition. This was Van Buren's retirement home, now Van Buren National Historic Site, located east of town on State Highway 9H. Operated by the National Park Service, it displays period furnishings. (Open May 1-September 30, daily 9:00-5:00; 518-758-9689; free.)

Exhibit: Also in **Kinderhook,** the House of History museum at 16 Broad St. displays some Van Buren memorabilia. (Open May 30–September 15, Tuesday–Saturday 10:30–4:30, Sunday 1:30–4:30; 518-758-9265; admission.)

(See DISTRICT OF COLUMBIA, WEST VIRGINIA in this chapter.)

WALLACE, HENRY AGARD (1888–1965). Near **South Salem,** the former vice president and political maverick bought his 115-acre "Farvue Farm" in 1945, and this became his last home after his 1948 retirement from public life. There he raised exotic plants and experimented with hybrid corn, continuing his lifelong interest and occupation as an agriculturist. The 19th-century house situated on a high knoll had earlier belonged to Wallace's sister. Stone gates mark the privately owned property a short distance off State Highway 124 in upper Westchester County.

(See DISTRICT OF COLUMBIA in this chapter; also Chapter 4, IOWA.)

WASHINGTON, BOOKER TALIAFERRO (1856–1915). The educator's Long Island summer home after 1905 stands on Cousins Lane in **Fort Salonga** on the north shore. There is little precise data available about this 19th-century dwelling except that it has undergone alterations since Washington's occupancy.

(See WEST VIRGINIA in this chapter; also Chapter 1, MASSACHUSETTS; also Chapter 5, ALABAMA, VIRGINIA.)

WASHINGTON, GEORGE (1732–1799). Whatever the merits of any individual claim that "Washington slept here," the fact is that he occupied guest bedrooms (never less than comfortable) all over the state during his constant movements as commander-in-chief of the Continental army—and many of these houses still stand as proud memorials of famous trousers hung on an antique chair, a quick shave in the looking glass and a night's repose. At a few places, however, the fortunes of war enabled him to settle in and establish a domestic routine. The most prominent of these in New York is Washington's Headquarters National Historic Landmark at 84 Liberty St. in **Newburgh**—also known as Hasbrouck House. This fieldstone farmhouse, built from 1725 to 1750, served as the center of the Continental troops' final winter encampment at New Windsor (1782–83). Washington lived there for 17 months, longer than anywhere else during the Revolution; his wife Martha was also present for much of this period. It was there that he flatly rejected the proposal that he become king; there he also squelched the incipient mutiny called the Newburgh Conspiracy and created the Order of the Purple Heart, the first American military award (only three were presented until the revival of the order in 1932). This house also represents the first historic preservation effort of any state, when New York acquired it in 1850 and restored it to its 1782 appearance. Operated by New York State Parks and Recreation, it now displays period furnishings; a museum next door contains historical exhibits, and the seven-acre park in which the buildings stand has also preserved some appearance of the original setting. (Open Wednesday–Sunday 9:00–5:00; 914-562-1195; free.)

(See NEW JERSEY, PENNSYLVANIA in this chapter; also Chapter 2, MANHATTAN; also Chapter 5, VIRGINIA.)

WEILL, KURT (1900–1950). Near **New City,** the German-born composer and his wife, Lotte Lenya, bought and remodeled an 1878 farmhouse of wood and stone on 14 acres at 116 South Mountain Road. "Brook House," where they lived from 1941 to 1950, and which Lotte Lenya used as a summer home until her death in 1981, remains privately owned.

WESTINGHOUSE, GEORGE (1846–1914). Just east of State Highway 7 near the Schoharie River in the village of **Central Bridge** stands the inventor's birthplace and childhood home, a small, white frame house with a large bronze marker in front. The privately owned dwelling was up for sale in 1981.

In **Schenectady,** Westinghouse bought and occupied a double brick house from 1865 to 1868 at what is now 1416 State St. opposite the present YMCA in Liberty Park. The house stood until about 1925, when it was cleared for bridge construction.

(See DISTRICT OF COLUMBIA, PENNSYLVANIA in this chapter; also Chapter 1, MASSACHUSETTS.)

WHITE, STANFORD (1853–1906). "Box Hill" northwest of **St. James,** Long Island, was the architect's permanent summer estate from 1884. Built in 1872, the two and one-half-story house of pebbles and stucco stands privately owned on Moriches Road, Head of the Harbor, St. James. White's later home on the estate, which dates from 1892 and which he enlarged several times, stands nearby on Harbor Road, also private.

(See Chapter 2, MANHATTAN.)

WHITMAN, WALT (1819–1892). Near **Huntington Station,** Long Island, the poet's birthplace and boyhood home stands at 246 Walt Whitman Road. There is still some controversy about whether Whitman was born in this house or in one of the nearby ancestral dwellings; but documentation provided by Bertha H. Funnell in her *Walt Whitman on Long Island* (1970) sufficiently authenticates the birthplace claim for this dwelling. The two-story, shingle farmhouse built by his father about 1810 sits on an acre island amid heavy traffic and urban development very different from the peaceful surroundings of fields and woods Whitman knew. He would, however, recognize the first floor of his sparsely furnished

WALT WHITMAN BIRTHPLACE. Built by his father, this shingled homestead near **Huntington Station** was the poet's home until 1823. It was a house made to last. The wooden pegs holding its hand-hewn beams display an excellent example of native American craftsmanship. *(Courtesy Walt Whitman Birthplace Association)*

home, with colonial kitchen, parlor and "borning room," though most of the furnishings are not original. Upstairs are exhibit rooms with a library, Whitman manuscripts, letters, schoolmaster's desk and other memorabilia. The house is maintained by New York State Parks and Recreation. (Open Monday–Friday 9:00–4:00; Saturday–Sunday 10:00–5:00; 516-427-5240; free.) "Fish-shape Paumanok," Whitman's name for the clean, wild Long Island of his youth, was a place to which he often returned for restoration of body and soul during his drifting years as schoolteacher, journalist, printer, carpenter and clerk. His ancestors had farmed in the Huntington area since the early 1700s, and the original family homestead, which he revisited at age 63 and nostalgically described in *Specimen Days* (1882), stood at South and Old Coast Roads. A number of other Whitman family homes that he remembered from childhood remain standing near the intersection of West Hills and Chichester roads, including the Whitman-Place houses owned by his great-grandfather.

At 313 Main St. in **Huntington** is the building (privately owned) in which Whitman edited and published the *Long Islander* in 1838 and 1839, sleeping upstairs over the shop and entertaining villagers with poems and stories in the evenings.

(See DISTRICT OF COLUMBIA, NEW JERSEY in this chapter; also Chapter 2, BROOKLYN, MANHATTAN.)

WILLARD, FRANCES ELIZABETH (1839–1898). The noted feminist and temperance leader's birthplace stood until the 1890s on a marked site at 24 South Main St. in **Churchville.** A hardware store and apartments now occupy the spot, her home to age 2.

(See Chapter 4, ILLINOIS, WISCONSIN.)

WILSON, EDMUND (1895–1972). South of **Port Leyden** on Talcottville Road stands the famed literary critic's two and one-half-story limestone dwelling. The house, built from 1789 to 1803 and bought by Wilson's father, became his lifelong country retreat and the subject of his book *Upstate* (1971). It remains privately owned.

(See NEW JERSEY in this chapter; also Chapter 1, MASSACHUSETTS; also Chapter 2, MANHATTAN.)

WODEHOUSE, SIR PELHAM GRENVILLE (1881–1975). The English humorist occupied a house in **Great Neck,** Long Island, for three years before World War II. Privately owned, this dwelling stands at 121 Arrandale Ave.

At **Remsenburg,** Long Island, P. G. Wodehouse bought "Blandings Castle," his last home, in 1952 and lived permanently on the 10-acre estate from 1959. His 10-room home, renovated by his wife, remains privately owned on Basket Neck Lane.

(See Chapter 2, MANHATTAN; also Chapter 6, CALIFORNIA.)

YADDO. In **Saratoga Springs,** the longtime haven for artists and writers is a complex of studio buildings that stands off Union Avenue. The 400-acre estate, willed for such a purpose in 1926, took its name from the mispronunciation of "shadow" by children of the original owner, stockbroker Spencer Trask. Elizabeth Ames, who died at 99 in 1977, ran the colony with "softly imperious" finesse for more than 40 years. Working guests there have included painter Edward Hopper and writers Carson Smith McCullers, Flannery O'Connor, Sylvia Plath, Katherine Anne Porter and Theodore Roethke (see the entries on Hopper, McCullers and Porter earlier in this section). Rose gardens and a part of the wooded grounds are open to the public. (Open daily 8:00–6:00; free.)

YOUNG, BRIGHAM (1801–1877). One spot the Mormon Church has somehow missed in paying its ordinarily vast attention to the sites of its founders is the boyhood home site of Brigham Young. From 1803 to 1813, he resided with his parents in a rented farmhouse on Cole Road near **Smyrna.** Beyond Young's own statements and those of a few local people who claim to have seen the old house foundations, almost nothing is known of this important spot.

In **Mendon,** the Mormon leader underwent conversion and baptism into the church while residing from 1829 to 1832 in a house long gone from the southeast corner of Boughton Hill and Pittsford-Ionia Roads. This was also the site of his sawmill and a small workshop where he made chairs.

Exhibit: Valentown Museum at Valentown Square in **Fishers** exhibits items excavated from Young's furniture shop. (Open April 1–November 30 daily, 1:00–5:00; 716-924-2645; admission.)

(See Chapter 1, VERMONT; also Chapter 4, ILLINOIS; also Chapter 6, UTAH.)

ZIEGFELD, FLORENZ (1869–1932). The home of the theatrical producer was "Burkeley Crest," an 1868 marble mansion of 19 rooms at 360 Broadway, **Hastings-on-Hudson.** Ziegfeld's wife, actress Billie Burke, acquired the 22-acre property in 1910 before her marriage, and the couple resided there from 1916 to 1931. Extensive gardens, tennis courts, a swimming pool, menagerie and a playhouse that was an exact scale model of Mount Vernon were features of the lavish estate. The house was razed before 1936, and its white stucco replacement is currently owned and leased out by the local board of education.

(See Chapter 2, MANHATTAN; also Chapter 4, ILLINOIS; also Chapter 6, CALIFORNIA.)

PENNSYLVANIA

A company of Swedes and Finns established the first Pennsylvanian colony on Tinicum Island in 1643. This New Sweden became a part of New Netherlands in 1655 when New Amsterdam's Peter Stuyvesant took over the colony; the English took possession in 1664. Only then were circumstances right for the utopian "holy experiment" by English Quaker William Penn, who acquired the enormous grant in 1681 as payment for a family debt against Charles II.

Penn's experiment consisted of building a colony where good people could live together in peace and religious freedom. "Sylvania"— ("Woodland") (Latin *sylva,* forest)—he thought, expressed the pastoral quality of his ideal as well as the actuality of the landscape—but Charles II wanted to honor Penn's admiral father, so "Pennsylvania" it has been ever since. No ascetic, Penn liked the good life, as you will see if you visit Pennsbury Manor near Tullytown. He was also a scrupulously honest man, perhaps the purest example of Plato's "philosopher-king" who has ever lived. Unlike the Puritan brethren in other colonies, he combined love of life and permissiveness in all matters of belief with high personal character, avoiding self-righteousness. He promised his colonists that "you shall be governed by laws of your own making," and kept the promise. So fair and impartial were his ethics that he even treated native tribespeople like human beings—an astonishing approach among English colonists (with the result that this colony experienced no Indian conflicts until long after Penn's death). Penn planned his capital of Philadelphia ("brotherly love") with meticulous care, supervising street layout on a pattern that remains basically unchanged after 300 years. By 1685 the city numbered about 1,500 souls, mostly Quaker.

Later settlers representing almost every European religious faith also found welcome in the colony. The most numerous of these were members of several German sects, including Mennonites, Amish, Dunkards and Moravians— the "Pennsylvania Dutch" who peopled the Lancaster area; today their many descendants give this region one of the nation's most distinctive subcultures. To these Americans we owe the holiday traditions of the Christmas tree, Santa Claus and the Easter Bunny. Their energy and agricultural skill also made Pennsylvania one of the wealthiest colonies in America.

A third ethnic group was the Scotch-Irish, who gravitated to southwestern Pennsylvania, an area that became the first colonial extension across the Alleghenies. Unlike the peaceful Quakers and domestic Germans, these people were scrappers and pioneer types, too restless for cities and farms.

New France had claimed portions of the western colony and the Ohio Valley in 1749 but finally relinquished Fort Duquesne (presently Pittsburgh) to the British in 1758 after holding out fiercely for almost a decade. Until the Revolution, the Penn family retained ownership of the colony, but William Penn's descendants fell far short of the founder's intelligence and idealism. The Pennsylvania Assembly paid the family £130,000 for giving up their proprietary rights during the Revolution.

Philadelphia, the midpoint between the American colonies and by far the largest American city in 1776, hosted the several meetings and Continental Congresses that led to final signing of the Declaration of Independence in Independence Hall. British troops soon occupied the city and held it for almost nine months. After the Revolution, the Convention of 1787 framed the Constitution, using Penn's "frame of government" as an important source, and Pennsylvania became the second of the original 13 states. Philadelphia became the nation's second capital (1790–1800). Today Independence National Historical Park preserves and maintains several key homes and sites of this period as their residents knew them.

In Pennsylvania came the 1863 turning point of the Civil War at the three-day Battle of Gettysburg; four months later, President Lincoln delivered a brief address on the field that set forth the national purpose—"a new birth of freedom"—in 266 concise words, one of the great speeches in all history. Pennsylvania factories produced the Conestoga wagon and Kentucky rifle that pushed the national frontiers incessantly west. The state, an industrial giant by 1890, today produces about one-fourth of the nation's steel plus vast coal tonnages from its Appalachian fields.

Pennsylvania's noted residents have included some of the nation's weightiest minds and muscles. Daniel Boone and John Audubon grew up there. In Philadelphia, Washington, Adams and Jefferson changed from Revolutionary warriors into national administrators, a different kettle entirely. Gilbert Stuart and Charles Willson Peale documented the founders' faces in their Philadelphia portrait studios. Businessmen Carnegie, Mellon and Guggenheim reigned like lords, controlling the lives and destinies of thousands of factory laborers. Show people—the Barrymores, W. C. Fields, Tom Mix—made their first entrances in Pennsylvania. Louisa Alcott, Stephen Foster, Gertrude Stein and John O'Hara were Pennsylvania natives; and Edgar Allan Poe,

Pearl Buck, Zane Grey, George Kaufman and Willa Cather wrote prolifically during their Pennsylvania years.

The Pennsylvanian for the ages was, of course, the sage, dumpy figure of Dr. Benjamin Franklin, who, in his genius, skepticism and rectitude made all sorts of risk-taking seem conventional. After Penn, the idealistic "philosopher-king," it was the sedately rebellious Franklin who not only glorified creative individualism but also established the American tradition of community service. He carried the Pennsylvania "holy experiment" to secular success, demonstrating Penn's ambitions of brotherly love in shop practice.

ADAMS, JOHN (1735–1826).
ADAMS, ABIGAIL SMITH (1744–1818).

As a delegate to the first Continental Congress in 1774, John Adams boarded in **Philadelphia** at the "Slate Roof House," which stood at the southeast corner of Second and Sansom streets (see the entry on William Penn later in this section). "Bush Hill," a mansion built by lawyer Andrew Hamilton in 1740, became the rural residence of the nation's first vice president when the national capital transferred to Philadelphia in 1790. Abigail Adams was hostess there for about three years. "We are only two miles from town," she wrote in 1791, "yet have I been more of a prisoner this winter than I ever was in my life," an isolation resulting from the treacherous road she described as a "bed of mortar without a bottom." Nothing remains of the spacious country estate at what is now the northeast corner of 18th and Buttonwood streets. It declined to a tavern, then a "resort of some reputation" until a fire left only the outside walls in 1808. These housed a textile factory finally razed in 1875. As second U.S. president, Adams occupied the Robert Morris Mansion, also called the Masters House, at 526–30 Market St. from 1797 until 1800, when he moved to the new Executive Mansion in Washington, D.C. (see the entry on George Washington later in this section).

(See DISTRICT OF COLUMBIA in this chapter; also Chapter 1, MASSACHUSETTS; also Chapter 2, MANHATTAN.)

ALCOTT, AMOS BRONSON (1799–1888).
ALCOTT, LOUISA MAY (1832–1888).

In 1832 the itinerant teacher-philosopher and

his family were rooming at "Rookery Cottage," Pine Place, in **Philadelphia**'s Germantown; and there, in a house long gone from 5425 Germantown Ave. (at the corner of Church Street), his daughter Louisa was born. The family soon headed for Boston, commencing a long series of moves that ended only when they settled in Concord, Mass.

(See Chapter 1, CONNECTICUT, MASSACHUSETTS.)

ANDRÉ, JOHN (1751–1780). In **Lancaster**, the British officer who would later be executed as a spy was paroled as a war prisoner at the Cope house, which stood at Lane and Grant streets. During his four-month residence there (1775–76), André charmed his hosts and gave youngster John Cope lessons in drawing and painting. After André's exchange, he became a major and adjutant of the British army.

During the British occupation of **Philadelphia** (1777–78), André was quartered in the new home of Benjamin Franklin (see the entry on Franklin later in this section) on Orianna Street. He took from the house a Benjamin Wilson portrait of Franklin which was returned from England in 1906 and now hangs in the White House, Washington, D.C.

(See NEW YORK in this chapter; also Chapter 2, MANHATTAN.)

ARNOLD, BENEDICT (1741–1801). The so-called "Slate Roof House," earlier occupied by William Penn and John Adams, became Arnold's first residence as the American military commander of **Philadelphia** from 1778 to 1779 (see the entries on Penn and Adams in this section). The lavish parties he threw there while courting Peggy Shippen put him in great debt, which contributed to his defection in 1780. Always a high-living status seeker, Arnold kept an elaborate coach-in-four and servants in livery to befit his post.

Arnold and his fiancee married at 212 South Fourth St. in the Shippen home on April 8, 1779—a site now occupied by the 1836 Philadelphia Contributionship for the Insuring of Houses from Loss by Fire—the nation's oldest (and certainly longest titled) fire insurance company. The couple then moved to the leased Morris Mansion, also gone from 526–30 Market St. (see the entry on George Washington later in this section), where

they lived for a year. There began Arnold's treasonous correspondence with British Maj. John André. The only house owned by Arnold that still exists is the 1762 Mount Pleasant National Historic Landmark in Fairmount Park, Mount Pleasant Drive. No evidence exists that he actually resided there, however. Arnold bought the stuccoed brick mansion, which Adams called "the most elegant seat in Pennsylvania," as a gift for his bride in 1779 but installed his sister and three sons from his first marriage instead. The 100-acre Schuylkill estate was confiscated when Arnold defected in 1780; he secretly repurchased it later, then sold it. The City of Philadelphia acquired it in 1868, and today it remains one of the most beautiful colonial houses in America. Now furnished in elaborate period style, it is operated by the Philadelphia Museum of Art. (Open daily 10:00–5:00; 215-763-8100; admission.)

(See NEW YORK in this chapter; also Chapter 1, CONNECTICUT; also Chapter 2, MANHATTAN.)

AUDUBON, JOHN JAMES (1785–1851). "Mill Grove," the 1762 stone farmhouse and 300-acre estate purchased in 1789 by Audubon's father, is located near the junction of Pawling and Audubon roads, one mile east of **Audubon**. There the youth developed his first interest in wildlife and nature study, rambling all over the estate, collecting specimens and drawing his first bird sketches. Visitors can ramble there too, over six miles of hilly hiking trails along Perkiomen Creek. Now an Audubon Wildlife Sanctuary on 130 acres of the original estate, it is operated by the Commissioners of Montgomery County. The ivy-covered house where Audubon lived from 1804 to 1806 contains numerous Audubon prints, stuffed birds, modern murals, family furniture pieces from his New York City home and other exhibits. The attic has been restored to a studio and taxidermy room that duplicates the naturalist's workshop there. (Open Tuesday–Sunday 9:00–5:00; 215-666-5593; free.)

Bakewell Estate (also known as "Fatland Ford" and "Vaux Hall"), located half a mile west of "Mill Grove" on Pawling Road, was the home of Lucy Bakewell Audubon, whom the naturalist married there on April 5, 1808. The couple lived there briefly before moving to Kentucky. The original mansion, dating from 1776, was one place where

George Washington authentically slept, in September 1777 (see the entry on Washington later in this section). It burned to the ground about 1830, and the present stuccoed mansion with 20 rooms and Greek Revival columns dates from 1843. A well-known site of the Underground Railroad during the Civil War, it is privately owned.

(See Chapter 2, MANHATTAN; also Chapter 5, FLORIDA, KENTUCKY, LOUISIANA.)

BARRYMORE, ETHEL (1879–1959).
BARRYMORE, JOHN (1882–1942).
BARRYMORE, LIONEL (1878–1954).

All three siblings in this theater family were born in **Philadelphia,** but none of their childhood homes remain. John Barrymore's birth site at 2008 West Columbia Ave. is now a vacant lot. Their grandmother's house at 140 North 12th St., between Race and Cherry streets, was their home until about 1885. The present two-story brick structure there dates from 1895. Ethel Barrymore recorded her childhood recollections of the former dwelling on this site in her *Memories* (1955).

(See NEW YORK in this chapter; also Chapter 2, MANHATTAN; also Chapter 6, CALIFORNIA.)

BENÉT, STEPHEN VINCENT (1898–1943). The poet and story writer was born near Bethlehem at 827 North Bishopthorpe St. (at the corner of Ostrum Street) in **Fountain Hill.** Marked but privately owned, the house has been subdivided into apartments. Benét's family lived there only briefly after his birth.

(See NEW YORK in this chapter; also Chapter 1, CONNECTICUT; also Chapter 2, MANHATTAN; also Chapter 5, GEORGIA; also Chapter 6, CALIFORNIA.)

BIDDLE, NICHOLAS (1786–1844). The imposing **Philadelphia** mansion of the banker, diplomat and progenitor of socially prominent Biddles, an 1821 double dwelling now known as the Whitten Evans House, stands at 715 Spruce St. (privately owned). Biddle lived there during the financial crisis and damage to his own career caused by President Jackson's withdrawal of government funds from the Second Bank of the United States, which Biddle headed. The site of Biddle's early law office is 181 Chestnut St.

Along the Delaware River near the town of

Andalusia, just north of the Philadelphia city limits, stands Biddle's country house, Andalusia National Historic Landmark on State Road. Built by his father-in-law in 1794, the two-story house of brick and stucco reflects Biddle's love for Greek Revival architecture; he added the huge Doric columns and the southern extension in 1834. Biddle spent years improving and landscaping the estate, planting hedges, orchards and shrubs, and conducting horticultural experiments. Also standing is the little two-story gaming house he built in 1830 as his safe "den of iniquity" for billiards and cards. After 1839, Biddle retired permanently to Andalusia. Still occupied by his descendants, the house hosts visitors only by appointment, which can be made at 6401 Germantown Ave., Philadelphia, PA, 19144.

BOONE, DANIEL (1734–1820). The frontiersman's log-cabin birthplace no longer exists on the Boone Homestead, located one mile north of **Baumstown** on Boone Road. On its old foundation, however, stands the two-story stone house built by his father before 1750, when the family moved to North Carolina. Now restored as a museum along with outbuildings and operated by the Pennsylvania Historical and Museum Commission, the farmhouse contains period furnishings and exhibits. The 600 surrounding acres where the boy roamed and hunted until age 16 now form a state wildlife sanctuary. (Open May 1–October 31, Tuesday–Saturday 10:00–4:30; Sunday 12:00–4:30; November 1–April 30, Tuesday–Saturday 9:00–5:00, Sunday 12:00–5:00; 215-582-4900; admission.)

(See WEST VIRGINIA in this chapter; also Chapter 4, MISSOURI; also Chapter 5, KENTUCKY, NORTH CAROLINA.)

BOOTH, JOHN WILKES (1838–1865).
Exhibit: In **Franklin,** the Venango County Museum at 415 12th St. contains an exhibit of Booth memorabilia. (Open April 1–November 30, Tuesday–Sunday 1:00–5:00; free.)

(See DISTRICT OF COLUMBIA, MARYLAND in this chapter.)

BRADLEY, OMAR NELSON (1893–1981).
Exhibit: At the U.S. Army Military History Institute in Carlisle Barracks, located north of **Carlisle** on U.S. Highway 11, the Omar N. Brad-

ley Museum displays memorabilia of the World War II general. (Open Monday 8:00–12:00, Wednesday, Friday 1:00–4:00; 717-245-4114; free.)

(See Chapter 4, MISSOURI; also Chapter 5, GEORGIA, VIRGINIA; also Chapter 6, CALIFORNIA, TEXAS.)

BROWN, CHARLES BROCKDEN (1771–1810). The author's birth site at 117 South Second St. is now occupied by Society Hill Towers apartment building in **Philadelphia.** Brown's last home (1805–10) stood at 124 South 11th St. on the west side between Chestnut and Walnut streets. An observer described it as a "low, dirty, two-story brick house, standing a little in from the street, with never a tree or a shrub near it." Painter Thomas Sully movingly wrote of his final November view of Brown there: "Passing a window one day, I was caught by the sight of a man, with remarkable physiognomy, writing at a table in a dark room. The sun shone directly upon his head. I shall never forget it. The dead leaves were falling then. It was Charles Brockden Brown." Commercial buildings now cover the site.

BROWN, JOHN (1800–1859). At **New Richmond,** the future abolitionist avenger operated a leather tannery from 1825 to 1835, employing up to 15 men. This period was the longest sustained residence of Brown's migratory life. It may also have been the most peaceful period of his existence. Brown cleared and tilled 100 acres there and built a log-cabin home, a two-story tannery building and a large barn. He buried his first wife and an infant son at "the highest spot on the farm." Only this family cemetery and the stone foundation walls of the tannery remain after a 1907 fire destroyed its upper portions. The John Brown Amphitheater Association of Meadville acquired trusteeship of the site in 1975 and intends to restore the tannery. Brown's homestead stood on the east side of Local Road 20118, just south of the village off State Highway 77; the tannery walls stand opposite on the west side of the road. The site is freely accessible to the public.

While collecting arms at **Chambersburg** in 1859 for his abortive raid at Harper's Ferry, W. Va., Brown posed as Dr. Isaac Smith and lived at 225 East King St., which he made his base of operations. The two and one-half-story, 19th-century house, made originally of logs covered with clapboard, was restored by the commonwealth of Pennsylvania in 1980 as Brown knew it and will probably admit visitors in the near future.

(See MARYLAND, NEW YORK, WEST VIRGINIA in this chapter; also Chapter 1, CONNECTICUT; also Chapter 4, IOWA, KANSAS, OHIO.)

BUCHANAN, JAMES (1791–1868). The 15th U.S. president, the only one from Pennsylvania, was born at **Cove Gap,** located between Mercersburg and McConnellsburg on State Highway 16. A stone pyramid marking the log cabin site stands in the 18-acre Buchanan's Birthplace State Historic Park in Buchanan State Forest Monument; this is also a good place to fish and picnic. The place was called "Stony Batter" in Buchanan's day. Now a "wild and gloomy gorge," the site was a main channel through the mountains for westward-bound pioneers during Buchanan's infancy. The log cabin birthplace itself, his home to age three, is now displayed on the campus of Mercersburg Academy in **Mercersburg** and contains period furnishings (open by appointment). And what is now the James Buchanan Hotel at 17 North Main St. was built by his father, Buchanan's boyhood home from 1796 to 1807.

At **Lancaster,** Wheatland National Historic Landmark at 1120 Marietta Ave. became Buchanan's permanent home from 1848 until his death. Built for a local banker in 1828, this two and one-half-story brick mansion has 17 rooms restored as they appeared when Buchanan lived there and displays his furnishings and personal possessions. The ex-president returned there to write in 1861 and sat out the Civil War he had been unable to prevent; and there he died. The house is operated by the James Buchanan Foundation for the Preservation of Wheatland. (Open April 1–November 30, 10:00–4:30; 717-392-8721; admission.)

(See DISTRICT OF COLUMBIA in this chapter.)

BUCK, PEARL SYDENSTRICKER (1892–1973). At 520 Dublin Road, one mile west of **Dublin,** Green Hills Farm National Historic Landmark was the author's home from 1934 to her death. She and her husband renovated and enlarged the 1835 stone farmhouse on 60 acres; today visitors may see her collection of Oriental art and antiques, writing desk, 1938 Nobel Prize for Literature and many personal possessions. The cottage she used

PEARL BUCK AT "GREEN HILLS FARM." Taken during her later years, this pensive view of the author also shows the living room of the 19th-century Bucks County farmhouse near **Dublin** that she and her husband renovated, her last permanent home.
(*Courtesy Pearl S. Buck Foundation, Inc.*)

for her study stands apart from the main house. A barn on the property contains offices of the charitable Pearl S. Buck Foundation, Inc., which operates the estate and is "dedicated to the education and general welfare of the displaced children of the world." (Open for tours Monday–Friday 10:30–2:00; 215-242-6779; admission.)

In **Philadelphia,** a city she loved, her occasional home and working quarters for the last years of her life were 2019 Delancey Place (privately owned) in a row of 1850 Federal townhouses.

(See WEST VIRGINIA in this chapter; also Chapter 1, VERMONT.)

BUNKER, CHANG and ENG (1811–1874).
Exhibit: The Mütter Museum, located in the College of Physicians at 19 South 22nd St. in **Philadelphia,** comes as close to displaying the actual fused bodies of the original Siamese twins as anyone could want. Exhibits in this medical museum are not for everyone, but included in the panoply of various human fragments is a body cast taken of the twins immediately after their death. Their shared liver is entombed in a jar there, and a wooden chair they used is also displayed. (Open Monday–Friday 9:00–4:30; 215-561-6050; free.)

(See Chapter 5, NORTH CAROLINA.)

BURR, AARON (1756–1836). As orphaned infants, the future vice president and his sister were brought to **Philadelphia** from New Jersey by Dr. William Shippen and raised from 1758 to 1760 in the physician's home at 240 South Fourth St. (at the southwest corner of Locust Street). The brick Shippen-Wistar House, built about 1750, is now a part of the 19th-century Cadwalader House; this combined building has contained the offices of the Mutual Assurance Company since 1912.

(See NEW JERSEY, NEW YORK in this chapter; also Chapter 1, CONNECTICUT; also Chapter 2, MANHATTAN, STATEN ISLAND.)

CALDER, ALEXANDER (1898–1976). The sculptor's birthplace in **Philadelphia,** destroyed sometime after 1917, was a double stone farmhouse at 1903 North Park Ave., the present site of a Temple University science building.

(See NEW YORK in this chapter; also Chapter

1, CONNECTICUT; also Chapter 2, MANHATTAN.)

CARNEGIE, ANDREW (1835–1919). Along with the millions this Scots-born industrialist made and gave in philanthropic donations came his "gospel of wealth" to justify the pursuit. None of Carnegie's early homes in **Pittsburgh,** where he began his financial rise, survives. The Pittsburgh History & Landmarks Foundation has no information regarding his residences on Rebecca Street (1848–52) or in Homewood (1860–67).

Carnegie's summer mansion from 1879 to 1886 at **Cresson,** "Braemar Cottage," stands in a dilapidated condition on the grounds of old Mountain House resort, which stood from 1800 to 1916 at the present intersection of U.S. Highway 22 and State Highway 53. By 1881 this was Carnegie's only Pennsylvania home; according to one account, "he courted his wife there, went on bird walks, read, and talked and talked." Carnegie's house has been converted to private apartments.

(See Chapter 1, MASSACHUSETTS; also Chapter 2, MANHATTAN.)

CARSON, RACHEL LOUISE (1907–1964). The naturalist author of *The Sea Around Us* (1951) and *Silent Spring* (1962) was born at **Springdale** on the 65-acre farm purchased by her father in 1900. This 1870 house, a two-story clapboard structure at 613 Marion Ave., was her home until age 22. In 1975 the Rachel Carson Homestead Association was organized to maintain and restore this property and to display memorabilia of the writer. The residence, currently used for ecology lectures and meeting rooms, has no regular admission hours as yet. Visits may, however, be arranged by appointment. (Write Rachel Carson Homestead Association, 613 Marion Ave., Springdale, PA, 15144.)

(See MARYLAND in this chapter; also Chapter 1, MAINE.)

CASSATT, MARY (1844–1926). "I do not admit that a woman can paint like that," said artist Edgar Degas of Mary Cassatt's impressionist work, a statement that revealed more about him than her. She was born on Reedsdale Street in **Pittsburgh,** but local historical sources know nothing of the present site.

CATHER, WILLA SIBERT (1873–1947). In **Pittsburgh,** the author wrote her novels *O Pioneers!* (1913) and *The Song of the Lark* (1915). She lived in the McClung home at 1180 Murray Hill Ave. (on the northwest corner of Fair Oaks) while teaching English in Pittsburgh high schools (1896–1906) and later as a full-time writer (1912–13), working in an attic study there. The two and one-half-story house, built about 1880, remains privately owned.

(See Chapter 1, NEW HAMPSHIRE; also Chapter 2, MANHATTAN; also Chapter 4, NEBRASKA; also Chapter 5, VIRGINIA.)

COLTRANE, JOHN WILLIAM (1926–1967). The jazz saxophonist lived in **Philadelphia** from 1951 to 1956 at 1511 North 33rd St., a three-story brick dwelling with a frame porch, still privately owned.

(See NEW YORK in this chapter; also Chapter 2, MANHATTAN, QUEENS; also Chapter 5, NORTH CAROLINA.)

DECATUR, STEPHEN (1779–1820). The naval hero's boyhood home in **Philadelphia** (1780s–96) stood at 611 South Front St., a three-story brick mansion demolished about 1870 at the present site of a warehouse. "Mount Airy," the family summer home from 1779 into the 1780s, a two-story dwelling on 120 acres, survived in the 10000 block of Decatur Road until 1969, when it was finally razed for expansion of the North Philadelphia Airport.

Exhibit: When the 18th-century Decatur dwelling on Decatur Road fell for airport expansion, 18 architectural specimens from the house were donated to the National Park Service. These included hinges, metal locks, batten doors and casement window sashes with blown crown-glass panes. The items may been seen at the old Second Bank of the United States, 420 Chestnut St., part of Independence National Historical Park in **Philadelphia.** (Open daily 9:00–5:00; 215-597-7132; free.)

(See DISTRICT OF COLUMBIA, MARYLAND in this chapter.)

DEWEY, GEORGE (1837–1917).
Exhibit: USS Olympia National Historic Landmark, permanently docked at Pier 40, Delaware Avenue and Spruce Street in **Philadelphia,** was the flagship used by the admiral in Manila Bay during the Spanish-American War (1898). The steel-hulled warship, built from 1890 to 1893, also brought the body of the Unknown Soldier back from Europe in 1922. Restored with its heavy artillery intact, the ship displays many relics of its crew, including Dewey's cabin and the bridge where he uttered those surprisingly well-preserved if hardly clarion words, "You may fire when you are ready, Gridley." (Open daily 9:00–9:00; 215-922-1898; admission.)

(See DISTRICT OF COLUMBIA in this chapter; also Chapter 1, VERMONT.)

DICKINSON, JOHN (1732–1808). "Fair Hill," a 1717 mansion called "the most beautiful seat in Pennsylvania," was the patriot's **Philadelphia** home for seven years. British raiders burned it to the ground in 1777. His extensive gardens on the 600-acre estate he inherited from his father-in-law, Isaac Norris, were a showplace of colonial Pennsylvania. The house, which stood in the approximate area of Fairhill Cemetery, Germantown Avenue and Cambria Street, was similar in design to the present Woodford National Historic Landmark, the 1735 house at 33rd and Dauphin streets in Fairmount Park. Woodford, restored in 1929 and operated by the Estate of Naomi Wood, displays 18th-century furnishings of the type familiar to Dickinson. (Open Tuesday–Sunday 9:30–5:00; 215-229-6115; admission.)

(See DELAWARE, MARYLAND in this chapter.)

DOOLITTLE, HILDA "H.D" (1886–1961). None of the imagist poet's early dwellings survive, and from 1912 she resided permanently in Europe. Her birthplace and home until 1895 stood until 1963 at 10 East Church St., now the City Center Plaza, in **Bethlehem.**

In **Upper Darby,** where her father taught astronomy at the University of Pennsylvania, the family occupied a house on the grounds of Flower Observatory, St. Lawrence Road. H.D. lived there from 1895 to 1910.

DORSEY, THOMAS FRANCIS "TOMMY" (1905–1956). The bandleader was born in **Shenandoah** at 17–19 North Chestnut St. (privately owned), where he lived until age two.

His boyhood home from 1907, to which he and his clarinetist brother Jimmy Dorsey often returned for home-cooked meals during years of constant travel and road engagements, stands privately owned at 227 East Abbott St. in **Lans-**

ford. Dorsey's father carved his initials in fresh concrete over the old coal-bin window there in 1938; they're still visible from the walk. The brick house dates from 1907.

(See NEW JERSEY in this chapter; also Chapter 1, CONNECTICUT.)

DU BOIS, WILLIAM EDWARD BURGHARDT (1868–1963). "Murder sat on our doorsteps, police were our government, and philanthropy dropped in with periodic advice," wrote the black educator-reformer of his one-room lodging over a cafeteria at Seventh and Lombard streets in **Philadelphia.** He and his bride of three months resided there in 1896 and 1897 while Du Bois taught at the University of Pennsylvania and wrote *The Philadelphia Negro* (1899), an early sociological study. The building is long gone.

(See MARYLAND in this chapter; also Chapter 1, MASSACHUSETTS; also Chapter 2, BROOKLYN, MANHATTAN; also Chapter 5, GEORGIA.)

EAKINS, THOMAS COWPERTHWAIT (1844–1916). Eakins House National Historic Landmark at 1729 Mount Vernon Place in **Philadelphia** was the notable painter's family home from age 13. The studio where he did most of his later work was on the top floor of that four-story dwelling built in 1854. Eakins, a lifelong Philadelphia resident, was born in an 1831 private house at 539 North 10th St. (then 4 Carrollton Square), recently demolished, and lived there until 1852. His boyhood home in 1853 and 1854 is apparently the only other Eakins residence surviving, a three-story brick structure at 1201 Green St. (at the northwest corner of 12th Street).

EISENHOWER, DWIGHT DAVID (1890–1969). The 34th U.S. president made his permanent retirement home near **Gettysburg.** Eisenhower National Historic Site, located at the southwestern edge of Gettysburg National Military Park off Wheatfield Road, was the only home Eisenhower ever owned in his peripatetic military career. He bought the pre-1921 brick farmhouse on 189 acres before he entered the White House, completely redesigned and rebuilt it using many of the original materials and first occupied it in 1955. Following his two presidential terms, he bred Black Angus show cattle there and increased his holdings to almost 500 acres. One of his deepest wishes, he said, was to leave some piece of land better than he found it. His widow Mamie Doud Eisenhower resided there until her own death in 1979. (Open April 1–November 23, daily 8:00–5:00; November 24–March 31, daily 8:30–4:30; 717-334-1124; admission.)

(See DISTRICT OF COLUMBIA, MARYLAND in this chapter; also Chapter 2, MANHATTAN; also Chapter 4, KANSAS, MICHIGAN; also Chapter 5, GEORGIA, VIRGINIA; also Chapter 6, COLORADO, TEXAS.)

FIELDS, W. C. (1880–1946). Born William Claude Dukenfield, the surly comedian with a proboscis resembling a ravaged beet made a lifelong patter of disliking his native **Philadelphia**—though he generously allowed he'd rather be back there than dead. Tracking down the Fields birthplace was not an easy task for Philadelphia historian Milton Kenin, who devoted years to the project and finally discovered it to be 6320 Woodland Ave. The house was torn down in 1924.

(See Chapter 6, CALIFORNIA.)

FOSTER, STEPHEN COLLINS (1826–1864). Born on **Pittsburgh**'s north side, the popular composer of sad romantic songs lived in the same area, usually with relatives, for most of his life. Henry Ford was convinced he had Foster's birthplace when he moved a house to his Michigan Greenfield Village in 1935, but careful research by historians outside the Ford domain established in 1953 that Ford's prize had never been occupied by any Foster. The actual birthplace, a white cottage built by Foster's father in 1815 and occupied by the family to about 1830, stood at 3600 Penn Ave. (at the corner of Denny Street) until razed in 1865. Foundations of the Foster house remain but were concealed by construction of the brick McKee Mansion in about 1870. The interior of this house is presently being remodeled for an art gallery, concert hall and offices of the Pittsburgh Wind Symphony, to be named Stephen Foster Museum. (To make music on the site where Foster entered the world represents an innovative approach to historical site commemoration, one that calls for emulation.) Foster's various homes until 1857 were his brother's and parents' several residences, most of which stood in the East Commons area—now Allegheny Center Shopping Mall.

Exhibits: Foster memorabilia and manuscripts

THE EISENHOWERS AT HOME. Near **Gettysburg**, the old brick farmhouse completely rebuilt by the 34th U.S. president became the couple's permanent retirement dwelling in 1961. The President and Mamie Doud Eisenhower stroll in the garden of their recently completed home during September of 1956, shortly before the Suez crisis erupted. Today visitors may also stroll there.

(*Courtesy Abbie Rowe, National Park Service, and Dwight D. Eisenhower Library*)

are displayed at Foster Memorial Hall on the University of **Pittsburgh** campus, Forbes Avenue and Bigelow Boulevard. (Open Monday–Friday 9:00–4:45; 412-624-4100; free.)

In **Athens,** Tioga Point Museum at 724 South Main St. also shows a Foster exhibit. (Open Monday 7:00–9:00 PM; Wednesday, Saturday 2:00–5:00; 717-882-7225; donation.)

(See NEW JERSEY in this chapter; also Chapter 2, MANHATTAN; also Chapter 4, OHIO; also Chapter 5, FLORIDA, KENTUCKY.)

FRANKLIN, BENJAMIN (1706–1790) **Philadelphia** claimed Franklin permanently from his arrival there as a penniless boy in 1723. Throughout his long life, though often absent on colonial business or during lengthy European residences, he considered the city his only home. In view of his vast importance to the city–as well as his national and international reputation—it is remarkable that not one of the seven Philadelphia dwellings where he resided for sustained periods has survived. Indeed, Franklin is our only major founding father with no extant home anywhere in his own country—though England and France proudly mark his lodgings in those countries. The best account of Franklin's early years in Philadelphia is contained in his classic *Autobiography* (1868). His first home in the city stood at 139 Market St., where he opened his first printing shop, began publishing *Poor Richard's Almanack* and lived for 11 years. In 1739 he moved shop and residence up to 131 Market, the site of Franklin's "New Printing Office" for 26 years, though he lived there for only nine. At these two Market Street sites, Franklin gained most of his self-education, laid the foundation for his public career and grew to comfortable prosperity. If any single American locale can be labeled "birthplace of the work ethic," these sites near the old Jersey Market district may best qualify.

During the time that Franklin conducted his electrical experiments, he lived at 325 Market St. He designed his final dwelling, "Franklin Court," in 1763 but did not return from England to occupy it until 1775. This was a three-story brick mansion 34 feet square, now outlined by steel beams on a section of Orianna Street, part of Independence National Historical Park. An "arch'd Passage" between what are now restored street-front houses on Market Street led to his door in the center of the block. In 1785, he added a 16.5-foot extension to the east, writing his sister that he could hardly "justify building a library at an age that will soon oblige me to quit it; but we are apt to forget that we are grown old, and building is an amusement." Most of the early notables of the republic came to pay homage to the aged Franklin there; and he completed his *Autobiography* in the house. After 1787 he rarely ventured beyond his garden; surrounded by lawns, shrubbery and grandchildren, he took opium for his pain and sat beneath a large mulberry tree while his declining strength, he reported, "weans me from the world." After his death there, the home underwent steady deterioration as an embassy, school, boardinghouse and coffee house until Franklin's grandchildren razed it in 1812. Lack of precise information has prevented full reconstruction by the National Park Service, but 1975 archaeological excavations exposed the foundations, and the dig remains open to view. Franklin's courtyard is laid out with mulberry and plane trees as he knew it.

Exhibits: The underground Franklin Court Museum, operated by the National Park Service at 318 Market St. near the reconstructed alley, displays audiovisual material on Franklin's versatile roles as statesman, author and scientist, plus Franklin portraits and some original furniture from his home. (Open daily 9:00–5:00; 215-597-7132; free.) The Benjamin Franklin Memorial, located at 20th Street and Franklin Parkway at Franklin Institute of Science, also displays personal belongings and scientific apparatus. (Open Monday–Saturday 10:00–5:00, Sunday 12:00–5:00; 215-448-1000; admission.)

(See MASSACHUSETTS in this chapter.)

FULTON, ROBERT (1765–1815). At U.S. Highway 222 and Swift Road near **Goshen** stands Fulton Birthplace National Historic Landmark—not the steamboat inventor's actual birthplace, which burned down in 1822, but the two and one-half-story, stone house rebuilt from the ruins of the original house. Now a Fulton memorial, the house contains period furnishings and memorabilia. The site, where he lived until age six, occupied his father's 400-acre farm. It is operated by the Pennsylvania Historical and Museum Commission. (Open May 1–September 30, Wednesday–Saturday 9:00–5:00, Sunday 12:00–5:00; October 1–April 30, Wednesday–Saturday 10:00–4:30, Sunday 12:00–4:30; 717-548-2679; admission.)

(See NEW YORK in this chapter; also Chapter 2, MANHATTAN.)

GOODYEAR, CHARLES (1800–1860). The inventor lived from 1826 to 1834 in **Philadelphia,** where he occupied a dwelling with his father and ran a hardware business in what is now the 200 block of Church Street. The pair introduced an improved steel pitchfork there but suffered commercial disaster. Goodyear recovered financially only when he discovered the rubber vulcanization process in 1839.

(See Chapter 1, CONNECTICUT, MASSACHUSETTS; also Chapter 4, OHIO.)

GREY, ZANE (1875–1939). The author of 54 novels that set the stereotype of the "western" began his hugely successful career at **Lackawaxen.** Giving up dentistry in 1904, he bought a cottage on five acres at the confluence of the Lackawaxen and Delaware rivers, where he could cast a fishing line 30 feet into either river—and often did. There, with his wife's editing help, he taught himself to write fiction. After writing *The Heritage of the Desert* (1910) and *Riders of the Purple Sage* (1912), his future was secure and he moved in 1918 to the locale of his stories, the West. Grey's cottage, much enlarged and extended, later became the Zane Grey Inn, now containing the Zane Grey Museum. Possessions and memorabilia of the writer include family furniture, ranch clothing, his dental drill, desk, book jackets and photographs. The museum, privately operated, is located on Roebling Road between the two rivers. (Open April 15–September 15, Tuesday–Sunday 10:00–4:00; 717-685-7522; admission.)

(See Chapter 2, MANHATTAN; also Chapter 4, OHIO; also Chapter 6, ARIZONA, CALIFORNIA.)

GUGGENHEIM, MEYER (1828–1905). Mining entrepreneur and founder of a financial dynasty, the Swiss-born Guggenheim started small and gained his fortune in **Philadelphia.** He moved about every five years from 1854 to 1873, the size of his houses and their neighborhoods reflecting his rise to wealth. Guggenheim resided longest at 1420 North 16th St. (1873–88), Philadelphia's "street of affluence," before moving to New York City. This home site is currently a vacant lot.

(See Chapter 2, MANHATTAN.)

HAMILTON, ALEXANDER (1755–1804). While residing at the southeast corner of Walnut and Third streets in 1791, wrote **Philadelphia** historian John Francis Marion, the first secretary of the treasury "had a liaison with a Mrs. Mary Reynolds, only to be blackmailed later by her husband James." Hamilton had to write a confessional book about the affair in order to rescue his career from disgrace. Hamilton's later Philadelphia residence, from 1794, was somewhere on Market Street. Several Hamilton biographers casually mention that he resided at Robert Morris's mansion "The Hills" in Fairmount Park (the present site of Lemon Hill Mansion), but Richard Tyler of the Philadelphia Historical Commission finds no evidence that Hamilton ever lived there.

(See NEW JERSEY, NEW YORK in this chapter; also Chapter 2, MANHATTAN.)

HAMMERSTEIN, OSCAR, II (1895–1960). Noted lyricist in the musical theater with Richard Rodgers and other composers, Hammerstein moved in 1940 to Bucks County, where he bought his 40-acre "Highland Farm" at 70 East Road near **Doylestown.** The privately owned farmhouse probably dates from 1848. There on the side porch, it is said, Hammerstein wrote the song "Oh, What a Beautiful Mornin'." Since his death there, the acreage has been subdivided and the U.S. Highway 202 Bypass now cuts through Hammer-

stein's former tennis court and landscaped garden area. There has been some interest expressed in placing the well-preserved house on the National Register.

(See NEW YORK in this chapter; also Chapter 2, MANHATTAN.)

HART, MOSS (1904–1961). The Bucks County home of the playwright-director, located on Aquetong Road north of U.S. Highway 202 near **Aquetong,** is somewhat run down today. Dating from about 1750, the mansion has undergone considerable alteration and enlargement, much of it during Hart's residence. It is said that he entered a rivalry with neighbor-collaborator George Simon Kaufman over who could more lavishly landscape his estate, and that both spent immense sums importing exotic plants and trees (see the entry on Kaufman later in this section). Hart bought this property, typically, on impulse and reportedly sank 17 wells before he found water. He and his wife, the singer Kitty Carlisle, occupied their country house during the 1940s.

(See Chapter 2, MANHATTAN; also Chapter 6, CALIFORNIA.)

HERBERT, VICTOR (1859–1924). Herbert's home was located at what is now 503–519 Aiken Avenue in **Pittsburgh** during his tenure as conductor of the Pittsburgh Symphony Orchestra from 1898 to 1904. A prominent feature of the house was his billiard room—the game was the only one he enjoyed. Arlington Apartments and the First Methodist Church now occupy this site.

(See NEW YORK in this chapter; also Chapter 2, MANHATTAN.)

JEFFERS, ROBINSON (1887–1962). The poet was born John Robinson Jeffers in **Pittsburgh** at 723 Ridge Ave., no longer standing.

Jeffers's father built a three-story brick dwelling in **Sewickley** at 44 Thorn St. in 1888, the family residence until 1893. A two-story addition has closed in the former porch area of this privately owned house.

(See Chapter 6, CALIFORNIA, WASHINGTON.)

JEFFERSON, THOMAS (1743–1826). Graff House National Historic Landmark at 7th and Market streets in **Philadelphia** is the 1975 reconstruction of the 1775 narrow brick house, razed in 1883, where Jefferson wrote the Declaration of Independence. Jefferson occupied two tiny upstairs rooms there in 1776, and the recreated bedroom and parlor display his lap desk and pen. Downstairs is a small exhibit on the founding document itself. The house, part of Independence National Historical Park, is operated by the National Park Service. (Open daily 9:00–5:00; 215-597-7132; free.) As the first secretary of state, Jefferson's later lodging in the city (1790–93) was the Thomas Leiper House, which stood on the south side of Market Street, the fourth house west of 8th Street. The site is a vacant lot today.

(See DISTRICT OF COLUMBIA in this chapter; also Chapter 2, MANHATTAN; also Chapter 5, VIRGINIA.)

KAUFMAN, GEORGE SIMON (1889–1961). The playwright-director's birthplace in **Pittsburgh** no longer stands at 6230 Station St., the current site of a housing project.

From 1900 to 1903, Kaufman lived at what is now 458 Croton Ave. (privately owned) with his parents in **New Castle.** Now a double family dwelling, this house was listed as vacant in 1981.

Kaufman bought his 57-acre Bucks County estate "Barley Sheaf Farm" in 1936. The Pennsylvania Dutch fieldstone house dates in its original part from 1740. There he wrote some of his best-known plays, entertained many famous guests and resided at long intervals. He referred to the place as "Cherchez La Farm." Kaufman's first wife, Beatrice, died there in 1945, and he sold the property in 1953. Located on U.S. Highway 202 at **Holicong** near Buckingham, the mansion now hosts visitors as a bed-and-breakfast tourist inn.

(See Chapter 2, MANHATTAN.)

LAFAYETTE, MARIE-JOSEPH, MARQUIS DE (1757–1834). The French aristocrat who became one of Washington's most reliable and effective generals during the Revolution joined the American army at **Valley Forge** in 1777 (see the entry on George Washington later in this section). He resided during that winter at a square stone house on Wilson Road southwest of the Park. Lafayette's quarters occupied the lower floor in what is now the east wing of a later frame addition. The aspect of this house on Valley Creek, renovated in 1948, was bleak when the young officer quartered there, "a small barrack scarcely more

cheerful than dungeons," he wrote. It is privately owned.

Exhibit: The **Valley Forge** Historical Society on State Highway 23 displays several of Lafayette's personal effects, including his camp stove and a check for $120,000 from Congress as partial payment for his services. (Open Monday–Saturday 9:00–4:30, Sunday 1:00–5:00; 215-783-0535; admission.)

LINCOLN, ABRAHAM (1809–1865).
Exhibits: Wills House at Lincoln Square in **Gettysburg** is the 1849 dwelling where the 16th U.S. president completed writing his Gettysburg Address and slept on November 18, 1863, the night before he spoke on the battlefield. Original furniture is arranged in the Lincoln bedroom just as it was that night, and other rooms display further memorabilia of his stay. Lincoln Room Museum is privately owned by LeRoy E. Smith. (Open spring and fall, daily 9:00–5:00; summer, daily 9:00–9:00; 717-334-8188; admission.)

A fine collection of Lincoln material is displayed in **Philadelphia** at the War Library and Museum of the Military Order of the Loyal Legion of the United States, 1805 Pine St. Exhibits include campaign materials, life masks, a lock of his hair and a large collection of Civil War mementos. (Open Monday–Friday by appointment 10:00–4:00; 215-735-8196; admission.) Also in Philadelphia, the Historical Society of Pennsylvania at 1300 Locust St. exhibits Lincoln's wardrobe, a heavy sofa, his complete law library and life masks. (Open Monday 1:00–9:00, Tuesday–Friday 9:00–5:00; 215-732-6200; free.)

(See DISTRICT OF COLUMBIA in this chapter; also Chapter 4, ILLINOIS, INDIANA, MICHIGAN; also Chapter 5, KENTUCKY, TENNESSEE.)

McCLELLAN, GEORGE BRINTON (1826–1885). The Civil War Union general was born in **Philadelphia** at 700 Walnut St., a "home of culture" and the present site of the Philadelphia Savings Fund Society. McClellan left there to attend West Point in 1842.

(See DISTRICT OF COLUMBIA, NEW JERSEY in this chapter; also Chapter 2, MANHATTAN.)

McGUFFEY, WILLIAM HOLMES (1800–1873). The birth site of the educator who authored the schoolbooks known as "McGuffey's Readers" stood near **Washington,** but the site has not been definitely determined. Henry Ford moved what his researchers believed was the cabin birthplace from the Blayney farm in West Finley Township to his Michigan Greenfield Village in 1934.

(See Chapter 4, MICHIGAN, OHIO; also Chapter 5, VIRGINIA.)

MACK, CONNIE (1862–1956). "Mr. Baseball," longtime mentor and manager of the Philadelphia Athletics, lived for most of his career at 620 West Phil-Ellena St. His last residence was a suite at the School Lane House apartments, 5450 Wissahickon Ave. Both private addresses are located in Germantown, **Philadelphia.**

(See Chapter 1, MASSACHUSETTS.)

MADISON, JAMES (1751–1836).
MADISON, DOLLEY PAYNE TODD (1768–1849).

As a congressman in the national capital at **Philadelphia,** the man who would be the fourth U.S. president resided from 1780 to 1793 during his city stays at Mrs. House's boardinghouse, long gone from Market and 5th streets. His vivacious future wife, a brilliant hostess, occupied several girlhood houses in the city; the first (ca. 1785) stood at 410 South Third St. Her later married home stands as Todd House National Historic Landmark at Walnut and Fourth streets, a 1777 brick dwelling, the home of John and Dolley Todd from 1790 until the death of John Todd and their infant son, both of yellow fever, in 1792. She was still living there when she met, through Aaron Burr, the congressman she called "the great little Madison" (see the entry on Burr earlier in this section). The house looks just as it did then, thanks to her own inventory of contents; and furnishings include many original items. A later occupant was Revolutionary Gen. Stephen Moylan. Now part of Independence National Historical Park, it is maintained by the National Park Service. (Open daily 9:00–5:00; 215-597-7132; free.) After their 1794 marriage, the Madisons moved to 429 Spruce St., a surviving three-story brick house they rented from 1795 to 1797, now privately owned.

(See DISTRICT OF COLUMBIA in this chapter; also Chapter 2, MANHATTAN; also Chapter 5, NORTH CAROLINA, VIRGINIA.)

MARSHALL, GEORGE CATLETT (1880–1959).

One of the few professional soldiers of U.S. history who became a notable statesman, Gen. Marshall was born in **Uniontown** at 130 West Main St., his home until age 17, when he enrolled at the Virginia Military Institute. The actual site of the two-story brick house rented by the family beside Coal Lick Run has been long covered; Uniontown "buried my childhood under twenty feet of fill," lamented the general in later years. Today, reports one biographer, "asphalt and grime pave the Marshalls' back yard," recently a filling station site.

(See DISTRICT OF COLUMBIA in this chapter; also Chapter 5, GEORGIA, NORTH CAROLINA, VIRGINIA; also Chapter 6, WASHINGTON.)

MATHEWSON, CHRISTOPHER "CHRISTY" (1880–1925). Known as "Big Six" (after a famous fire engine), the legendary pitcher for the New York Giants was born in **Factoryville,** his home until 1898. His family dwelling, still occupied and privately owned, stands unidentified on Mathewson Terrace just off U.S. Highway 6 in the delightful mountain town.

(See NEW YORK in this chapter.)

MEAD, MARGARET (1901–1978). The famed anthropologist's girlhood home was her parents' 107-acre farm just north of **Holicong** on Holicong Road. The large, 1845 farmhouse stands at the end of a long lane. Basically unaltered and in good condition, what is now the 15-acre property had been up for sale for more than a year in 1981. Mead lived there from 1911 to 1925.

(See NEW JERSEY in this chapter; also Chapter 2, MANHATTAN.)

MELLON, ANDREW WILLIAM (1855–1937). Financier, art collector and secretary of the treasury from 1921 to 1933, Mellon bought his 1897 Tudor brick mansion in **Pittsburgh** in 1917. He renovated and enlarged the two and one-half-story house, adding tennis courts, bowling alleys and a swimming pool. The house remained in the Mellon family until 1940, when it was given to Chatham College. It now functions as Mellon Center, the Chatham student center, located on Woodland Road. The estate's nearby Carriage House houses the Chatham post office and bookstore. An earlier Mellon residence, built in 1909 and razed about 1939, stood at 5052 Forbes

Ave. The site of his mansion birthplace and home until 1900 (irreverently tagged "the Mellon patch" by local wags) is now a cul-de-sac called Rippey Place, formerly 401 North Negley Ave.

(See DISTRICT OF COLUMBIA in this chapter.)

MIX, THOMAS EDWIN "TOM" (1880–1940). "Just a big devil, too busy playing with guns to learn much." That's how his mother described the future star of Hollywood "oaters" as a boy. He was born and lived until age four in a rural house built about 1860 at **Mix Run** on Bennett's Branch of the Susquehanna River. An official of Cameron County Historical Society reports that the dwelling was never maintained and, in the year of Tom's death, "literally fell down" and that "only the river stone foundation is still on the site." It is located on Bennett's Branch Road. A highway marker stands on State Highway 555 directly across the river from the birthplace.

The family home in nearby **Driftwood** (1884–88) is long gone, its exact site on Front Street unknown.

(See Chapter 6, CALIFORNIA, OKLAHOMA.)

MOORE, MARIANNE CRAIG (1887–1972). In **Carlisle** the poet's childhood home remains privately owned at 343 North Hanover St. The two-story stone-fronted house, Moore's residence from 1894 to 1916, dates from at least the 1880s.

Exhibit: The Rosenbach Foundation Museum at 2010 Delancey Place in **Philadelphia** displays the recreated apartment that the poet last occupied in Greenwich Village, New York City. Contents she donated to the exhibit include furnishings, letters and manuscripts. (Open September 1–July 31, Tuesday–Sunday 11:00–4:00; 215-732-1600; admission.)

(See Chapter 2, BROOKLYN, MANHATTAN; also Chapter 4, MISSOURI.)

MOTT, LUCRETIA COFFIN (1793–1880). The last home from 1857 of the Quaker abolitionist and feminist was "Roadside," a rambling frame house sheltered by a large oak grove at Old York and Township Line roads just south of **Jenkintown.**

An earlier brick home in **Philadelphia** may still stand, according to the Philadelphia Historical Commission, at either 226 or 228 North 9th St., where Lucretia Mott lived during the 1840s. Because of changes in the address system, "it is

impossible to locate this house exactly" in relation to the former address of 136—but "it is probably one of the two mentioned."

Exhibit: Germantown Historical Society at the Clarkson-Watson Museum, 5275 Germantown Ave. in **Philadelphia,** displays the plain Quaker garment and shawl Mott wore while preaching, as well as her rocking chair and a few other personal items. (Open Tuesday, Thursday, Saturday 1:00–5:00; 215-844-0514; admission.)

(See Chapter 1, MASSACHUSETTS.)

O'HARA, JOHN HENRY (1905–1970). In **Pottsville,** the novelist's birthplace stands at 125 Mahantongo St., where the family occupied the rear of the house until 1913. O'Hara's father, a surgeon, used the front part for his office. The house, dating probably from the 1880s, now contains a beauty shop and private apartments. The next family residence, O'Hara's home from 1913 to 1928, also survives at 606 Mahantongo St., a three-story house built about 1875; O'Hara's room was on the top floor. This dwelling has also been converted to private apartments.

Exhibit: John O'Hara's Study, recreated with original contents from his home in Princeton, N.J., is displayed by appointment at Pattee Library of Pennsylvania State University Park at **State College.** (Open Monday–Friday 8:00–5:00; 814-865-7056; free.)

(See NEW JERSEY, NEW YORK in this chapter; also Chapter 2, MANHATTAN.)

PAINE, THOMAS (1737–1809). Controversial journalist and revolutionist, Paine resided in **York** when the Continental Congress refuged there in 1777 and 1778 (York was, in fact, the first U.S. capital city). The Cookes House at 438–40 Cordorus St., the earliest (1761) stone house in the city, was Paine's probable residence. It is privately owned.

(See NEW JERSEY, NEW YORK in this chapter; also Chapter 2, BROOKLYN, MANHATTAN.)

PARKER, DOROTHY ROTHSCHILD (1893–1967). Overlooking the Delaware River, "Fox Hollow Farm," located on Mt. Airy Road east of Cafferty Road near **Tinicum,** was the author's 112-acre country estate with husband Alan Campbell from 1934 to 1945. The fieldstone farmhouse with a slate roof, built in 1883, remains privately occupied. Parker gutted and remodeled the interior of this, the only house she ever owned, hosted literary friends, and generally enjoyed what was probably the most peaceful period of her troubled life. She sold the property in 1947.

(See Chapter 2, MANHATTAN; also Chapter 6, CALIFORNIA.)

PEALE, CHARLES WILLSON (1741–1827). The painter occupied several **Philadelphia** residences, two of which survive. In the 1785 Philosophical Hall, now the headquarters of the American Philosophical Society at 104 South Fifth St., Peale opened his first museum in 1794, displaying paintings and natural history exhibits; he also resided with his family in the building until 1810. Now part of Independence National Historical Park, Philosophical Hall is not open to visitors. Belfield National Historic Landmark at 2100 Clarkson Ave. is the 1750 stone farmhouse that the painter bought as a retirement home on 100 acres in 1810. He first called it "Farm Persevere," planted acres of exotic trees and shrubbery, raised livestock and resided there until 1821. The house is privately owned. Peale's last home (1821–27) was the residence of his son, painter Rubens Peale, which stood at the present site of 617 Walnut St.

(See MARYLAND in this chapter.)

PEARSON, DREW (1897–1969). The boyhood home of the muckracking newspaper columnist was Benjamin West Birthplace National Historic Landmark on the **Swarthmore** College campus (see the entry on West later in this section). Pearson lived there from 1903 to 1913. From 1913 until 1919, the family occupied a new house at 516 Walnut Lane, still privately occupied.

(See DISTRICT OF COLUMBIA, MARYLAND in this chapter; also Chapter 4, ILLINOIS.)

PEARY, ROBERT EDWIN (1856–1920). At State Highway 176 and U.S. Highway 22 in **Cresson,** the Admiral Peary Monument commemorates the polar explorer's birthplace, which stood a few hundred feet west of the junction. The two-story frame farmhouse, long gone when Peary associates dedicated his statue there in 1937, was the infant's home until his father's death in 1859. A picnic area surrounds the statue. (Open Tuesday–Saturday 10:00–4:30, Sunday 12:00–4:30; grounds 9:00–8:00; 814-886-2293; free.)

(See DISTRICT OF COLUMBIA in this chapter; also Chapter 1, MAINE.)

PEIRCE, CHARLES SANDERS (1839–1914). "The house is not in the least Queen Anne or any other style," wrote the pragmatist philosopher-mathematician about the rambling wooden mansion he bought in 1888 near **Milford;** "It is our original style." He named the house "Arisbe" after an ancient Greek city mentioned in Homer's *Iliad,* greatly enlarged it and resided in virtual isolation there for the rest of his life, occasionally hiding in the attic from creditors. The farmhouse, dating from the 1880s, was acquired by the National Park Service in 1972 as an attraction for the Delaware Water Gap National Recreation Area and for eventual restoration as a Peirce museum and study center. While Congressional action has been pending on the project for a decade, the N.P.S. maintains a caretaker for the property, located two and one-half-miles northeast of Milford on U.S. Highway 6.

(See MARYLAND in this chapter; also Chapter 1, MASSACHUSETTS.)

PENN, WILLIAM (1644–1718). From Charles II in 1681, the Quaker preacher acquired charter to the tract named Pennsylvania in his father's honor and proceeded to colonize it as a "holy experiment." He resided there himself, however, for only two brief intervals.

In 1683 and 1684, the small clapboard house he built in **Philadelphia** stood on Letitia Court between Market and Chestnut streets. (This is not, however, the same house moved to Fairmount Park in 1883 from Letitia Street and long identified as Penn's. That house, which now stands on Lansdowne Drive near West Grand Avenue, dates from about 1715). During his second Philadelphia stay (1694–1701), Penn occupied the "Slate Roof House," built about 1687. "The building is of imported brick," wrote Benson Lossing in 1859, except for an addition between the wings "now occupied as a clothing store by an Israelite . . . doubtless the broom of improvement will soon sweep it away, as a cumberer of valuable ground." Indeed, it was demolished in 1868; and its site at the southeast corner of Second and Sansom streets is occupied by the Commercial Exchange Building.

Pennsbury Manor, built from 1683 to 1700 on the Delaware River, was Penn's 8,400-acre country seat, where he lived and entertained like the stylish, extravagant aristocrat he was. He employed a vast work force of servants, gardeners and slaves to maintain his orchards, vineyards, outbuildings and half-brick, half-timbered mansion. The house fell to ruins after Penn's involuntary departure to settle his financial affairs in England but in 1939 was meticulously recreated on its original 40-x-60-foot foundation. The entire plot now occupies 40 acres of the once-massive holding. Inside Pennsbury Manor are authentic pegged-oak floors, tinted panes, original fireplace tile and a few pieces of Penn's own furniture—a carved chair, Jacobean chest and highboy. The collection of 17th-century period furnishings there is the largest in Pennsylvania. Follow the signs off U.S. Highway 13 from **Tullytown**—Pennsbury is a short distance northeast along the river, which was Penn's own route here. Pennsbury Manor National Historic Landmark is operated by the Pennsylvania Historical and Museum Commission. (Open May 1–September 30, Tuesday–Saturday 9:00–5:00, Sunday 12:00–5:00; October 1–April 30, Tuesday–Saturday 10:00–4:30, Sunday 12:00–4:30; 215-946-0400; admission.)

Exhibit: A collection of Penn's furniture may be seen at the Historical Society of Pennsylvania, 1300 Locust St. in **Philadelphia.** (Open Monday 1:00–9:00, Tuesday–Friday 9:00–5:00; 215-732-6200; free.)

PERELMAN, SIDNEY JOSEPH (1904–1979). The prolific humorist whose outrage at American cultural pretensions (especially Hollywood) fueled a lifetime of wildly funny prose, Perelman and author Nathanael West, his brother-in-law, bought an 83-acre farm they called "The Rising Gorge" near **Erwinna** in 1932. The early 19th-century farmhouse, a Dutch stone mansion with a barn and converted milkhouse that he used for a studio, stands privately owned on Geiger Hill Road. Perelman tried unsuccessfully to raise turkeys there. He found the blessings of country life not unmixed, and his outspoken lack of faith in pastoral virtues offended some of the local people. Perelman was the first among New York City literati to move to Bucks County, soon followed by Moss Hart, George Simon Kaufman and others (see the entries on Hart and Kaufman earlier in this section). After his wife died in 1970, Perelman sold the farm and moved to England.

(See Chapter 1, RHODE ISLAND; also Chapter 2, MANHATTAN.)

PERRY, OLIVER HAZARD (1785–1819).
Exhibit: The naval hero of the 1813 Battle of Lake Erie ("He met the enemy and they was his," as one sailor told the deed) prepared for the engagement at **Erie.** The little wooden vessel *USS Niagara*, to which Perry moved during the 1813 battle when his flagship was gunned down, is docked at the State Street lake-front. Twice sunk through neglect and refloated—the last time in 1963—the ship has been virtually reconstructed; a long section of keel is about the only original part of it. With full rigging and cannon, however, its appearance is exactly that of the commander's vessel. (Open Monday–Saturday 10:00–4:30; Sunday 12:00–4:30; 814-871-4596; admission.) The shipyard site where the *Niagara* was built is located at 6th and Cascade streets.

(See Chapter 1, RHODE ISLAND.)

POE, EDGAR ALLAN (1809–1849). Poe House National Historic Site at 530–32 North Seventh St. in **Philadelphia** was the author's home from 1842 to 1844. This small dwelling, known to Poe as "Spring Garden Cottage," is the birthplace of the modern detective story. There Poe crafted "The Gold-Bug," "The Murders in the Rue Morgue," "The Tell-Tale Heart," and several other of his best-known tales; and also wrote the first draft of "The Raven." Poe allowed no mirrors in the house he shared with his mother-in-law, Mrs. Clemm, and his dying wife. He marked on the walls wherever he stayed, however, and visitors may see the cryptic words "Death to the" carved in the parlor. He also did most of his writing in this 12-foot-square room and an upstairs bedroom, now restored but much less bare than when he occupied it. Mrs. Clemm sold most of the sparse furnishings to pay Virginia Poe's medical bills and gave the rest to the landlord for rent. When Poe left the city, it is said that he carried nothing but his books under one arm and his two cats under the other. Poe House, built about 1800, was restored in 1927 and is now operated by the National Park Service, which also displays a Poe exhibit in the adjoining building. (Open daily 9:00–5:00; 215-597-8780; free.)

(See MARYLAND in this chapter; also Chapter 1, MASSACHUSETTS; also Chapter 2,

BRONX, MANHATTAN; also Chapter 5, VIRGINIA.)

POUND, EZRA LOOMIS (1885–1972). The poet occupied several residences in or near Philadelphia during his early years. At age four, he came to **West Philadelphia** with his parents and lived in the three-story, brick row house at 208 South 43rd St. for a year.

At **Jenkintown,** they lived for the next two years at 417 Walnut St., a three-story house with a mansard roof.

Wyncote, however, was his 15-year boyhood home (1892–1907), where he occupied the tower bedroom at 166 Fernbrook Ave., a house with white shingles. Upon his release as a 12-year political prisoner in 1958, Pound briefly revisited there, inspecting the house and grounds thoroughly, commenting that the place had been "dolled up a bit." *Ezra Pound's Pennsylvania* (1976) by Noel Stock details the poet's years in these homes, all of which remain privately owned.

(See DISTRICT OF COLUMBIA in this chapter; also Chapter 6, IDAHO.)

PRIESTLEY, JOSEPH (1733–1804). English chemist and discoverer of oxygen, Priestley settled in America in 1794 and built a two and one-half-story frame house in **Northumberland.** Priestley House National Historic Landmark at 346 Ninth St. contains a small museum of personal items and his laboratory, operated by the Pennsylvania Historical and Museum Commission. (Open May 1–September 30, Wednesday–Saturday 9:00–5:00, Sunday 12:00–5:00; October 1–April 30, Wednesday–Saturday 10:00–4:30, Sunday 12:00–4:30; 717-473-9474; admission.)

RICKEY, BRANCH WESLEY (1881–1965). In 1950 the innovative baseball executive became general manager of the Pittsburgh Pirates and bought a 100-acre estate at **Fox Chapel,** his last home. The property included a large colonial house, a tenant dwelling and riding stables. Still privately owned, this property is located at 333 Old Mill Road.

(See MARYLAND in this chapter; also Chapter 2, BROOKLYN; also Chapter 4, MISSOURI, OHIO.)

ROCKWELL, NORMAN (1894–1978).
Exhibit: The privately operated Rockwell

Museum at 601 Walnut St. in **Philadelphia** displays a replica of the painter's Stockbridge, Mass., studio as well as paintings and an audiovisual program. (Open daily 10:00–4:00; 215-922-4345; admission.)

(See NEW YORK in this chapter; also Chapter 1, MASSACHUSETTS, VERMONT; also Chapter 2, MANHATTAN.)

ROETHKE, THEODORE (1908–1963). Before Roethke began publishing his poetry, he taught English at Lafayette College in **Easton** from 1932 to 1935. He resided in a ground-floor room at 100 Easton Hall on the campus. This building, still used, dates from 1926.

The poet published his first volume *Open House* (1941) while teaching at Pennsylvania State University in **State College** from 1936 to 1943. He occupied two residences: from 1936 to 1938, a room on the top floor of the 1913 University Club, still at 331 West College Ave.; and a suite at the 1932 Glennland Apartments, 205 East Beaver Ave., from 1938 to 1943. Both buildings remain privately functional. In the words of one biographer, Roethke "made a sty of all his habitations" and lost possessions for months at a time under the clutter. Such self-created chaos seemed to provide a necessary seedbed for the perfection of his craft.

(See Chapter 1, VERMONT; also Chapter 4, MICHIGAN; also Chapter 6, WASHINGTON.)

ROSS, BETSY (1752–1836). Born Elizabeth Griscom, the **Philadelphia** upholsterer supposedly made the first national flag in either 1776 or 1777 after consulting with George Washington (see the entry on Washington later in this section). There is considerable dispute about whether she ever resided—let alone stitched—in the Betsy Ross House at 239 Arch St. The Philadelphia Historical Commission states that no good evidence exists for either claim. Her more probable home site (ca. 1776) was 233 Arch St.; and a later site was probably 241 Arch. All were nevertheless in the immediate vicinity of the standing house, which is an interesting example of colonial city dwellings and certainly worth a visit. Built before 1720 and restored in 1937, the two and one-half-story brick house contains period furnishings. The City of Philadelphia owns and maintains it. (Open May 1–October 31, daily 9:00–6:00; November 1–April 30, daily 9:00–5:00; 215-627-5343; free.)

RUSSELL, BERTRAND (1872–1970). "Little Datchet Farm," a country acreage with a century-old stone farmhouse, barn, orchard and woodland, was the English philosopher's rented dwelling from 1941 to 1943, while he taught at the Barnes Foundation in Philadelphia. Russell auctioned his household goods there in 1944 shortly before his return to England. Now called the Minfeldler property, the house and land remain privately owned on Street Road in West Pikeland Township near **Malvern.**

(See Chapter 6, CALIFORNIA.)

RUSSELL, LILLIAN (1861–1922). The last home of the singer-actress stood in the Point Breeze section of **Pittsburgh** at the southwest corner of Penn and Linden avenues.

(See Chapter 2, MANHATTAN; also Chapter 4, IOWA.)

SIAMESE TWINS. See CHANG and ENG BUNKER.

SMITH, BESSIE (1898?–1937). The "world's greatest blues singer" made her permanent home in **Philadelphia** after 1923. With husband Jack Gee, she rented an apartment at 1236 Webster St., still a private apartment building that dates from about 1905, as a place to stay between road engagements. In 1926, she moved into her last home at 7003 South 12th St., also private.

(See Chapter 5, TENNESSEE.)

SMITH, JOSEPH (1805–1844). Near **Oakland,** the Mormon founder occupied the farmhouse of Isaac Hale in 1825 and there claimed to have translated the golden tablets revealed to him by an angel at Palmyra, N.Y. This work became the *Book of Mormon,* which Smith completed there in 1830. Known locally as the "Old Joe Smith House," the two and one-half-story dwelling burned down in 1919, but the Mormon monument identifies the approximate site along State Highway 171 between Oakland and Great Bend.

(See NEW YORK in this chapter; also Chapter 1, VERMONT; also Chapter 4, ILLINOIS, MISSOURI, OHIO; also Chapter 6, UTAH.)

STEIN, GERTRUDE (1874–1946). A rose by any other name would have deprived her of one of her best-known, typically obscure lines. The expatriate author's birthplace was recently restored and a marker dedicated at 850 Beech Ave. in **Pittsburgh.** The brick house, her home only during infancy, remains privately owned.

(See MARYLAND in this chapter.)

STEUBEN, FRIEDRICH VON (1730–1794). Baron von Steuben, the stern Prussian drill-master of the Revolution, began his task of turning 10,000 raw Continental troops into soldiers at the fierce winter camp of **Valley Forge** in 1778. Despite his weak English, he rapidly acquired a useful store of English profanity and became quite popular with his men. During his four months there, he occupied what is now Steuben Headquarters National Historic Landmark on State Highway 23 just outside Valley Forge National Historical Park (see the entry on George Washington later in this section). The two and one-half-story stone house, built as a tavern, was restored in 1965. It had also served as a camp hospital, and there is a display of the surgical instruments used there.

(See NEW YORK in this chapter.)

STEVENS, THADDEUS (1792–1868). Strong abolitionist and master of invective as a fire-breathing Radical Republican congressman, Stevens made his first Pennsylvania home in **Gettysburg,** where he bought an 1815 house at 51 Chambersburg St. He lived there from about 1818 to 1843, selling the house in 1848. Used for years as a business building and apartment house, it still stands, privately owned and much altered.

In **Lancaster,** where he moved in 1843, Stevens bought a brick double house that became his permanent home at 45 South Queen St., a site now marked by a bronze plaque.

(See DISTRICT OF COLUMBIA in this chapter; also Chapter 1, VERMONT.)

STOKOWSKI, LEOPOLD ANTHONY (1882–1977) In 1912 the English-born conductor came to **Philadelphia** where he directed the Philadelphia Orchestra for the next 26 years. Along with his brilliant, unorthodox musical interpretations, Stokowski was a keenly skilled publicist, well aware of his value as an *enfant terrible* for building an audience. If that audience coughed too much, he stopped the music to scold Philadelphians in his ingeniously "foreign" accent. Stowkowski lived at 2117 Locust St., a dwelling built about

1860 and still a private residence, until 1923. During his occupancy with his wife, the pianist Olga Samaroff, his later home at 1716 Rittenhouse St. became one of Philadelphia's high-status social centers.

(See Chapter 1, CONNECTICUT; also Chapter 2, MANHATTAN; also Chapter 4, OHIO.)

STUART, GILBERT CHARLES (1755–1828). That picture of George Washington on the dollar bill originated in a stone studio at the rear of 5140 Germantown Ave. in **Philadelphia,** where the famed portrait painter of Revolutionary figures resided from 1796 to 1799 (see the entry on Washington later in this section). The studio was partially destroyed by fire in 1854 and razed in 1900.

(See DISTRICT OF COLUMBIA in this chapter; also Chapter 1, MASSACHUSETTS, RHODE ISLAND.)

SUTTER, JOHN AUGUSTUS (1803–1880). In 1871, the German-born pioneer of California on whose lands began the 1849 Gold Rush moved to **Lititz,** having lost his once vast holdings. He attempted to interest the federal government in verifying his western claims and helping him recover his property but had little success and died a near-pauper. In 1871, however, he had enough money to build his two-story brick house in Lititz, the first home there with indoor plumbing and said to be the finest house in town. Sutter's last home was faithfully restored in 1980 by Farmers First Bank, which maintained much of the original woodwork and now occupies the building at 9 East Main St.

(See Chapter 6, CALIFORNIA.)

THOMAS, NORMAN MATTOON (1884–1968). The Presbyterian parsonage in **Lewisburg** was the Socialist political leader's family home from 1900 to 1915. This brick Victorian house at 14 Market St., next to the 1856 church pastored by his father, dates from about 1869 and is still a private parsonage.

(See NEW YORK in this chapter; also Chapter 2, MANHATTAN.)

THORPE, JAMES FRANCIS "JIM" (1888–1953). *Exhibit:* From 1907 to 1912, the Sac and Fox Olympic star from Oklahoma attended Carlisle Indian School at **Carlisle,** beginning his remark-

ably versatile athletic career. The 1777 Hessian Guard House at Carlisle Barracks, the site of the school, which existed from 1879 to 1918, displays material pertinent to the school and its most famous student. Carlisle Barracks, operated by the U.S. Army, is located just north of town on U.S. Highway 11. (Museum open May 15–October 15, Saturday–Sunday 1:00–4:30; 717-245-3131; free.)

(See Chapter 4, OHIO; also Chapter 6, OKLAHOMA.)

WASHINGTON, GEORGE (1732–1799). The Revolutionary commander's winter camp at **Valley Forge** (1777–78) marked one of the low points of the war, not because the weather blew exceptionally cold but because graft and war profiteering on the "home front" deprived the callow new army of minimal supplies. About 3,000 men died there in consequence. Yet it proved a bottoming-out period, for "it was here," wrote military historian Mark M. Boatner, "that the losers of earlier campaigns were transformed into the winners of Monmouth and Yorktown." There is no evidence that Washington's kneeling to pray in the snow had anything to do with this; this was a tale concocted almost 30 years later by Parson Weems for parsonly purposes (Washington apparently never even knelt in church). Indeed, he lived rather comfortably with his wife Martha in the 1758 stone farmhouse known as Washington Headquarters National Historic Landmark in Valley Forge National Historic Park. About 90 percent of this structure is completely original, including woodwork, fireplaces and floors. Along with period furnishings, the only Washington possession in the house with period furnishings, however, is an iron candlestand. Valley Forge National Historic Park is administered by the National Park Service. The reception center entrance is located at the junction of State Highways 23 and 363. (Open June 15–Labor Day, daily 8:30–6:00; Labor Day–June 14, daily 8:30–5:00; 215-783-7700; free.)

As the first U.S. president, Washington occupied the three-story Morris Mansion in **Philadelphia** for all but the first year of his two terms; he thought it "the best single House in the city." Sir William Howe and Sir Henry Clinton, British commanders of the city, lived there in 1777 and 1778, as did Benedict Arnold and John Adams later (see the entries on Arnold and Adams earlier in this section). This dwelling, which dated from 1772, decayed to a cheap rooming house and was demolished in 1832. The site at 526–30 Market St. is on Independence Mall. As his summer haven in 1793 and 1794, Washington occupied Deshler-Morris House National Historic Landmark at 5442 Germantown Ave. This 1772 stone house, operated by the National Park Service, has fine interior woodwork and some original furnishings plus excellent period pieces and a life mask of Washington. It is definitely a Philadelphia showpiece. (Open Tuesday–Sunday 1:00–4:00; 215-596-1748; admission.)

Exhibits: Washington items are displayed at **Valley Forge** National Historical Park in the Museum of the Valley Forge Historical Society, located adjacent to the Washington Memorial Chapel on State Highway 23, including the field tent, flag and expensive silver cups he used there. (Open Monday–Saturday 9:00–4:30, Sunday 1:00–5:00; 215-783-0535; admission.)

Some of the furniture Washington used in the Morris Mansion is displayed at the Historical Society of Pennsylvania, 1300 Locust St. in **Philadelphia.** (Open Monday 1:00–9:00, Tuesday–Friday 9:00–5:00; 215-732-6200; free.)

(See NEW JERSEY, NEW YORK in this chapter; also Chapter 2, MANHATTAN; also Chapter 5, VIRGINIA.)

WAYNE, ANTHONY (1745–1796). Often called "Mad Anthony" for his dashing aggressiveness and storming tactics, the Revolutionary general and Indian fighter was born at Waynesborough National Historic Landmark on Waynesborough Road off State Highway 252 east of **Paoli.** Wayne lived at this ancestral homestead (still privately owned by Wayne descendants) and worked as a tanner until the Revolution. The restored, well-maintained fieldstone mansion dates in its oldest, left-wing portion from 1724 and was built by Wayne's grandfather. Its main section was added in 1735 and the right wing in 1792. British troops raided the house looking for Wayne and stuck their bayonets into the boxwood hedge, hoping to flush him out. The hedge, almost 300 years old, is still visible behind the left wing.

Exhibit: In **Erie,** the Wayne Blockhouse at 560 East Third St. is a replica of the Fort Presque Isle structure in which Wayne died. The blockhouse was built over the general's original grave and is maintained on the grounds of the Pennsylvania

Home for Soldiers and Sailors. (Open Memorial Day–Labor Day, daily 9:00–11:30, 1:00–4:30, 5:30–9:00; otherwise by appointment; 814-871-4531; free.) Erie Historical Museum at 356 West Sixth St. displays a macabre object associated with Wayne: the cauldron his son used to boil the general's bones apart from his flesh for transportation back to the family graveyard at Radnor. The flesh residue was redeposited back in the first grave. (Open Tuesday–Sunday 1:00–5:00; 814-453-5811; free.)

WEST, BENJAMIN (1738–1820). On Swarthmore College campus at **Swarthmore** stands the 1724 house where the painter was born and lived until age five, in the southeast corner of the first floor. West Birthplace National Historic Landmark, a two and one-half-story dwelling of cut stone stands on its original site, extensively altered after an 1874 fire. It is owned by the college and does not admit visitors. A later resident was Drew Pearson (see the entry on Pearson earlier in this chapter).

WESTINGHOUSE, GEORGE (1846–1914). The inventor's home "Solitude," a brick villa he bought in 1871, became his permanent home in **Pittsburgh.** Always tinkering and experimenting, Westinghouse conducted natural gas tests there; he wired his home for electricity but kept the wiring exposed from the woodwork in order to rig up changes and new systems. He also built a tunnel from a corner of his lawn to the nearby depot for quick boarding of his private railroad car. The estate had a stable and large gardens. Torn down in 1919, the house stood in what is now Westinghouse Park at North Murtland and McPherson streets.

(See DISTRICT OF COLUMBIA, NEW YORK in this chapter; also Chapter 1, MASSACHUSETTS.)

WRIGHT, ORVILLE (1871–1948).
WRIGHT, WILBUR (1867–1912).
Exhibit: The Franklin Institute of Science at 20th Street and Franklin Parkway in **Philadelphia** displays most of the extant artifacts of the aviation pioneer brothers in its Hall of Aviation. Included there are their personal sketches and notes, original test equipment, a replica of their Dayton, Ohio, bicycle shop and the last craft they

flew—a Model B biplane. (Open Monday–Saturday 10:00–5:00, Sunday 12:00–5:00; 215-448-1000; admission.)

(See DISTRICT OF COLUMBIA in this chapter; also Chapter 4, INDIANA, MICHIGAN, OHIO; also Chapter 5, NORTH CAROLINA.)

WEST VIRGINIA

"West (By God) Virginia" does not constitute profanity. So ruled Judge Ernest A. See in 1949 when a state resident was charged with corrupting morals by using the old phrase, originally intended to highlight the state's distinction from its parent Virginia.

Profanity aside, West Virginia is a state of notable irregularities. Its chopped topography and uneven boundaries formed by Appalachian ridges and the Ohio and Potomac rivers are obvious; but the state also entered the Union in an irregular, probably illegal manner. Isolated by geography and antislavery sentiment, West Virginia's 40 counties (now 55) had chafed under Richmond dominance for almost a century. Since Virginia slaves counted in figuring legislative representation, the almost slaveless western region carried little political clout. Virginia's secession in 1861 led Union loyalists at Wheeling to meet and declare the secession void. Confederate defeats contributed to the separatist movement; and although the Federal Constitution prohibits the formation of new states from existing states, Congress approved West Virginia's statehood as "a war measure" in 1863. West Virginia became the last state east of the Mississippi to enter the Union, 35th in rank.

Pioneered largely from the North, West Virginia has always held more in common with Pennsylvania and Ohio interests than with its eastern transmountain neighbor. Rough country and fierce Shawnee natives deterred white settlement until 1726, when one Morgan Morgan made a permanent home near what is now Charles Town. The last battle of the Revolution occurred at Wheeling in 1782.

Strata of bituminous coal underlie 80 percent of this rugged terrain, but the coal industry's decline after World War II and West Virginia's narrow economic base have given the state a depressive familiarity with hard times; and the term "Appalachia" became synonymous with hard-core poverty. The state is now beginning to benefit from more enlightened management of its still-vast resources, one of which is the imposing scenery that attracts increasing tourism.

West Virginia hills have nourished some rugged people. Natives included Gen. Stonewall Jackson, who untypically allied himself with the Confederate cause, novelist Pearl Buck and labor leader Walter Reuther. Daniel Boone and Booker T. Washington were notable residents, and so was John Brown, briefly and violently. The state has been a favorite vacation retreat for several U.S. presidents. Though sites are often well-marked, relatively few homes of well-known West Virginians, even among the more recent, survive. A partial reason for such absence is that many of these residents only became well-known long after their presence there—and by that time, interest in preserving their dwellings was too late. Of West Virginians listed in this section, not one stayed long enough to die there (except, of course, the outsider John Brown by rope), plainly indicating that opportunity lay elsewhere. The state has historically been so concerned with hardscrabble survival that its attention to the tangible reminders of its past, like historic dwellings, has generally been short-spanned. Despite these overriding worried-man themes of coal mine and living wage, however, the healthy defiance and tough, fibrous character of "West (By God) Virginia" is well demonstrated in the eminent lives shaped there.

BOONE, DANIEL (1734–1820). In **Charleston,** the two-room cabin where Boone lived from 1788 to 1795 stood at the marked site of Fort Lee, at 1202 East Kanawha Blvd. He served during this period as a member of the Virginia Assembly and as a lieutenant colonel of militia.

At **Point Pleasant,** Boone ran a trading post in 1790 and 1791; this site is also marked at City Park on U.S. Highway 35.

Exhibit: The West Virginia Department of Culture & History, located in the State Capitol on East Kanawha Blvd. in **Charleston,** displays a rifle and beaver trap used by Boone. (Open Monday–Friday 9:00–9:00; Saturday–Sunday 1:00–9:00; 304-348-0232; free.)

(See PENNSYLVANIA in this chapter; also Chapter 4, MISSOURI; also Chapter 5, KENTUCKY, NORTH CAROLINA.)

BROWN, JOHN (1800–1859).

Exhibits: **Harpers Ferry,** the culminating point of Brown's violent abolitionist career, preserves the scene of his 1859 attempt to take the town by force and mount a slave rebellion. Harpers Ferry National Historical Park, operated by the National Park Service, is one of the few landmarks set aside by the government to commemorate an insurrection. Notable features that relate specifically to Brown include the Visitor Center on Shenandoah Street (open daily 8:00–5:00; 304-535-6371; free); John Brown's Fort, the 1848 brick firehouse where Brown and his men held out for two days, at Old Arsenal Square (moved in 1893 from alongside the B&O railroad depot, where a monument marks the original site, and placed in the Square in 1968); and the John Brown Museum in the 1838 Wager Building, with exhibits on Brown's life.

In **Charles Town,** the Jefferson County Museum at East Washington and North Samuel streets contains Brown memorabilia (open April 1–October 31, Tuesday–Saturday 10:00–4:00; free); and the site of the Old Jail, where Brown was held for over a month preceding his execution, is marked at South George and Washington streets.

(See MARYLAND, NEW YORK, PENNSYLVANIA in this chapter; also Chapter 1, CONNECTICUT; also Chapter 4, IOWA, KANSAS, OHIO.)

BUCK, PEARL SYDENSTRICKER (1892–1973). Buck Birthplace National Historic Landmark, a brick Victorian house with vertical wood siding built by the author's great-grandfather about 1847, stands on U.S. Highway 219 northeast of **Hillsboro.** Restored to its 1892 appearance, her "goodly, twelve-room house" amid 16 farm acres contains family furnishings and possessions. It is operated by the Pearl S. Buck Birthplace Foundation, an organization she created for the education of displaced children. The 1939 Nobel Prize winner spent her first three months there before being taken to China by her missionary parents; she returned at age nine and left for the last time at 17. She wrote of this place that "I would like it to belong to everyone. . . . From that home there has come so much life that it ought never to die or fall into ruin." (Open Monday–Saturday 9:00–5:00; Sunday 1:00–5:00; 304-653-4430; admission.)

(See PENNSYLVANIA in this chapter; also Chapter 1, VERMONT.)

FILLMORE, MILLARD (1800–1874). The 13th U.S. president was the last of three to use Presidents' Cottage at **White Sulphur Springs** (1850–52) as a summer White House (see the entry on Martin Van Buren later in this section.)

(See DISTRICT OF COLUMBIA, NEW YORK in this chapter.)

JACKSON, THOMAS JONATHAN "STONEWALL" (1824–1863). The Confederate general's birth site and home until age two is marked at 328 West Main St. in **Clarksburg,** where the three-room brick house was built by his father in 1818.

Further south at **Jacksons Mill,** two miles west of U.S. Highway 19, a state 4-H camp now occupies the 532-acre site of Jackson's boyhood home (1830–42). The Jackson Homestead there was his grandfather's farm, where an 1837 grist mill, farm equipment and pioneer relics typify sights familiar to Jackson.

(See Chapter 5, VIRGINIA.)

REUTHER, WALTER PHILIP (1907–1970). The prominent labor leader was born in Wheeling. Most of his boyhood years were spent in the six-room frame house built by his father at 3640 South Wetzel St. in **South Wheeling,** Reuther's home until 1927. An unusual feature installed by the elder Reuther was the family outhouse attached to the back porch. Neither house nor outhouse remain on the property, which was cleared in the early 1970s for construction of Interstate Highway 470.

(See Chapter 4, MICHIGAN.)

TYLER, JOHN (1790–1862). The 10th U.S. president honeymooned in 1844 with his second wife at **White Sulphur Springs,** his summer White House from 1841 (see the entry on Martin Van Buren later in this section.)

(See DISTRICT OF COLUMBIA in this chapter; also Chapter 5, VIRGINIA.)

VAN BUREN, MARTIN (1782–1862). Though a total of 14 U.S. presidents have visited the house, the eighth president was the first of three chief executives to use Presidents' Cottage at **White Sulphur Springs** for a frequent summer White

House (1837–40). The 1816 house with its double gallery is now a museum of period furnishings operated by the Greenbriar Hotel, U.S. Highway 60 on the west edge of town. Presidents' Cottage stands on the hotel grounds. (Open April 1–November 30, Monday–Saturday 10:00–12:00, 1:00–4:30; December 1–March 31, by appointment; 304-536-1110; admission.)

(See DISTRICT OF COLUMBIA, NEW YORK in this chapter.)

WASHINGTON, BOOKER TALIAFERRO (1856–1915). The site of the boyhood home from 1865 to 1872 of the educator-reformer born a slave is marked on U.S. Highway 60 near **Malden.** While living in a small cabin there from age nine, though technically emancipated, he worked slavish hours in a nearby salt furnace and coal mine.

(See NEW YORK in this chapter; also Chapter 1, MASSACHUSETTS; also Chapter 5, ALABAMA, VIRGINIA.)

FOUR

GREAT LAKES AND GREAT PLAINS

The 12 states that make up the country's midsection also form its economic backbone. In this region the nation centers its heavy industry and agriculture, the wheels and wheat that energize the entire structure, drive its growth and power, and control its security and prosperity. Usual labels divide it into such subregions as Mideast, Midwest, North Central States, Northern and Central Plains, and so on; but the boundaries for such classifications differ among various authors and, unlike New England borders, have no absolute definition. This chapter combines the six key industrial states that front on one or more Great Lakes—Illinois, Indiana, Michigan, Minnesota, Ohio and Wisconsin—with the six "breadbasket states" that lie further west: Iowa, Kansas, Missouri, Nebraska and the Dakotas. Today this western portion feeds not only America but much of the world, including the Soviet Union. (As Joel Garreau points out in *The Nine Nations of North America* [1981], "the Breadbasket has become the ratifier of social change on the continent—an idea is really nothing more than a regional idiosyncrasy until it 'plays in Peoria.' ") While agriculture is of major importance in all 12 states, and all likewise contain industrial complexes, the difference in primary economic activity generally corresponds with this division into lake states and plains states.

There are other differences, of course. The continental glaciation that capped much of North America with ice about 10,000 years ago formed most of this region's topography. Pioneers found hardwood forest stretching virtually unbroken to the Mississippi River. Beyond lay the relatively treeless expanses of tallgrass prairie—and further still, the shortgrass prairie—though long fingers and islands of both forest and grassland created broad transitional zones between them. Thus in the east, settlement was generally a matter of clearing timber; and in the west, of "busting" a thick, gluey sod entirely unlike the lighter forest soils.

The first human natives we know anything about constructed the great Moundbuilding cultures that flourished at the time of Christ, peoples who left earthworks of graves, temples, and effigies all over North America. Some of the most numerous and best preserved of these remain in southern Ohio and the Mississippi Valley. Early archaeologists refused to connect this evidence of highly developed cultures with the "primitive" natives they observed on the scene, seeking explanation in various pseudoscientific theories about European "lost tribes" or transplanted peoples. The modern scientific consensus, however, is that the Moundbuilders indeed produced the tribes encountered by whites.

Jacques Marquette and Louis Jolliet, that French team of God bringer and fur taker who typified in themselves the entire French colonial effort in America, were the first whites to view much of this region. As for those "primitive" forest and plains peoples, each new investigation adds to the mounting impression that most native American tribal societies contained elements, at least, of profound cultural sophistication. Historically they produced some of the most notable leaders, diplomats and warriors in American history. Men like Pontiac, Tecumseh, Charles Langlade, Little Turtle, Crazy Horse and Sitting Bull usually had no "homes" in the sense of a settled residence but nevertheless lived "at home" in the region to an extent that no modern American can ever fully experience. It was to preserve their rights to live "at home," of course, that they fought the intruding European culture with its peculiar notions of land ownership and competitive economies. The shift in the region's human consciousness became quickly reflected in the appearance of the land itself. Trees fell, towns grew, soil turned; and the immigrant attitude of exploitation, from furs to minerals to crops, transformed the country's mental slant of millennia into a philosophy of "use." Instead of "being at home," the fundamental consciousness of the outsider aimed toward (and still is) "making a home."

Almost the entire American midcontinent occupies two enormous land acquisitions. The Ordinance of 1787 named the region west of Pennsylvania extending to the Mississippi and south from the Great Lakes to the Ohio River—a chunk ceded by Great Britain at the end of the American Revolution—as the Northwest Territory. This included the present states of Ohio, Michigan, Indiana, Wisconsin, Illinois and part of Minnesota. Congress split the Northwest Territory vertically in 1800, and the western portion became an enormous Indiana Territory, subsequently divided into Michigan, Illinois and Wisconsin Territories. The eastern Northwest Territory became the state of Ohio in 1803.

That same year, President Jefferson increased U.S. area by almost 100 percent with a stroke of his pen and a payment to Napoleon's France of about four cents per acre for some 7 billion acres known as Louisiana Territory. Its boundaries were vaguely defined, and the original title was complicated and clouded; as historian George Stimpson wrote, "In a sense, Napoleon had no right to sell it and Jefferson had no right to buy it." Prior Spanish claims were involved, but the political timing was just right for a fast deal. Soon after, Meriwether Lewis and William Clark tra-

versed this immensity to the Pacific. The seven states of this chapter that lie west of the Mississippi—Kansas, Missouri, Nebraska, Iowa, Minnesota and the Dakotas—were, in due course, carved from Louisiana Territory.

Our nation was settled on the raw principle that might makes right; to teach or believe otherwise today is willful ignorance or vulgar deception. Nowhere did this settlement philosophy become more evident than in the territorial conflicts with the native Americans in this midsection area. In the end, it was cunning and duplicity that won the Lakes and Plains. Subjugation of native resistance, the Homestead Act of 1862 and rapid extension of railroads brought floods of settlers to and through the region. The last third of the 19th century saw immigration swell and peak; from Europe the tides of German and Scandinavian influx were especially heavy.

Main access routes were the Great Lakes and river highways of the Ohio, St. Joseph, Wabash, Illinois, Mississippi, Missouri and others. In 1811 work began on construction of the great National Road, now U.S. Highway 40, from Cumberland, Md., across Ohio and Indiana to Vandalia, Ill. Farther west, from Old Franklin, Mo., began the Santa Fe Trail, and the Oregon Trail snaked westward from Independence.* St. Louis, of course, became the great gateway for this westward fanning. All 12 states underwent similar sequences of political arrival into the Union. Large territories divided and subdivided into smaller territories; when any subdivision reached a population of 60,000, it could apply for statehood. In Kansas and Missouri, especially, proslavery and abolitionist factions exploded beyond the passionate oratory of Eastern chambers and blazed into fierce border warfare. Missouri, however, was the region's only state to secede for a brief period.

From this vast, fertile region have emerged some of the nation's most dynamic, creative people. Though many of them went east or west to fulfill their ambitions, some stayed, many returned, and relatively few forsook, in any absolute sense, their long roots in lake or prairie country. From this ground germinated · the American prairie traditions of art, literature and architecture; the archetypes of Paul Bunyan, the "Western," and "God's country" in the popular

---

*The Santa Fe Trail Museum near Larned, Kan., and the Oregon Trail Museum at Scottsbluff, Neb., offer excellent displays on these pioneer routes.

arts; the reformist political traditions of Minnesota and Wisconsin; the existence of a brawling Chicago in the national psyche. Sod houses of the prairie (with notable examples displayed at Sod Town Prairie Pioneer Museum in Colby, Kan.) gave way to solid frame constructions often based on New England models. But Frank Lloyd Wright's belief that a building's form should extend and complement its natural environment revolutionized thinking about shelter. His low-swept houses with long overhangs and horizontal lines, best seen at Oak Park, Ill., were immensely sophisticated refinements on the prairie sod house theme.

Recurrent names in the roster of notables include Marquette, Lewis and Clark, Hamlin Garland, Laura Ingalls Wilder, Ulysses S. Grant, and Thomas Edison. Epitomizing the heartland's significance was the individual whom many regard as America's greatest man: Abraham Lincoln.

Among the several excellent guidebooks to regional homes and museums are Rita Stein's *A Literary Tour Guide to the United States: West and Midwest* (1979); John Drury's dated but still informative *Historic Midwest Houses* (1977 reprint); and *The Great Lakes Guidebook* series (1978–) by George Cantor. A fine, detailed travel guide for modern Oregon Trail pilgrims is Gregory M. Franzwa's *The Oregon Trail Revisited* (1972).

ILLINOIS

Is it pronounced *noy* or *noise*? Pedagogues like to pretend that a mongrelized English French *illinoy* is correct, but if one insists on a "right" way, the early French settlers pronounced their home *eel-ee-nwah*. Acerbic old John Quincy Adams had his own "ill-annoyed" version: In the 1847 Congress in which both he and Abraham Lincoln sat, Adams reputedly said that "if one were to judge from the character of the representatives in this Congress from that state, I should decide unhesitatingly that the proper pronunciation is *All-Noise*." Whatever pronunciation one prefers, the word has come far; *Illinois* today is an anglicized version of a Frenchified revision of the native Algonquian term for "man"—long variations, one might say, on a sexist theme.

From late 17th century settlement, Illinois was ruled—on paper, at least—by seven separate governments before achieving statehood. New France laid first claim to the territory through the effective priest-merchant team of Jacques Marquette and Louis Jolliet, the first white visitors, in 1673. Sieur de La Salle, with dreams of creating a massive fur empire, followed in 1680 and established the first outposts near today's East Peoria and Utica. French pioneers founded the oldest permanent community in the Mississippi valley, Cahokia, in 1699. Kaskaskia, settled in 1703 and washed into the Mississippi in 1910, served as a territorial capital and as the state's first capital. Canadian Illinois remained mostly French populated even after France ceded the territory to Great Britain in 1763. The British centered military control at Fort de Chartres until the American Revolution, when George Rogers Clark—on behalf of Virginia only—took fort and colony without a shot. Until 1784 Illinois officially existed as the western county of a long-stretched Virginia. It became part of the newly created Northwest Territory in 1787. Illinois Territory, carved from Indiana Territory in 1809, also included Wisconsin. Finally in 1818, Illinois entered the Union as the 21st state. The settlement of southern Illinois proceeded mainly from the southeastern states; and after Black Hawk's futile attempt to hold traditional Sac lands in 1832, white settlers poured into the central and northern parts of the state.

Great waters border Illinois on three sides: Lake Michigan and the Mississippi, Ohio and Wabash Rivers. The Great Plains reach their easternmost extension in Illinois, a level terrain and flat horizon fingered only by the towers of grain elevators that enable one to sight towns from miles away on the ruler-straight roads. Agriculture transformed the grassland into a breadbasket terrain, vital to the economy but a caricature of the original landscape; and relict plots of the tallgrass prairie are as scarce there as the descendants of Marquette's hosts. The deep, glutinous soil of Illinois, still almost gelatinous in early spring, now produces more soybeans than any other state, and Illinois is second in corn and hog production. It is first in the production of coal, and the Illinois Waterway system connecting the St. Lawrence Seaway with the Mississippi has become a vital national shipping lane.

Illinois history, far from analogous to its table-flat rectangles of road and field, is gouged with craters of shadow and violence. Black Hawk's valiant fight for hopeless rights—"that disgraceful affair," as one historian called it—was blood spilled from desperation. The slavery controversy split the state into vicious south-north factions, but Illinois gathered itself and overwhelmingly supported the Union during the Civil War. Chicago, dating as a city only from 1837, has ranked second largest in the nation since 1890 and today holds about 27 percent of the Illinois population. The Chicago Portage channeled a main passage between the Great Lakes and Mississippi valley for Indian, explorer and trader; as a main station on the interior waterways from the beginning, it grew into the key industrial port of mid-America. Chicago's plentiful traumas included the disastrous fire of 1871 that probably did not begin when Kate O'Leary's cow kicked over a lantern at 558 West De Koven St. The swinish Al Capone rule of the Prohibition years made Chicago law the bitter laughingstock of a generation, an image hard to live down. And nobody who viewed the televised spectacle of Mayor Daley's space-helmeted cops attacking unarmed protestors during the 1968 Democratic National Convention can forget it. "Hog butcher for the world," Carl Sandburg waxed, but Chicago's once-vast stockyards have shrunk as the industry decentralized. Yet, because or in spite of its rowdy lack of subtlety, the city has powerful charms and still no lack of the tense, dynamic atmosphere celebrated by Sandburg.

And despite or because of its turmoil, Illinois has produced some of the nation's most notable public figures, though many were not natives of the state. Foremost, of course, was Abraham Lincoln, who resided for most of his adult life in Springfield, the capital since 1837. Adlai Stevenson also came to national prominence there. Perhaps Stephen A. Douglas and natives William Jennings Bryan and Everett M. Dirksen, each a more impressive orator than either Lincoln or Stevenson, spoke less durable words; but all except Douglas are represented by standing homes and museums in the state. Illinois writers, most notably Sandburg and Ernest Hemingway, made a large impact on the national literature. Reformers Frances E. Willard and Jane Addams built powerful international bases of temperance and social work in the Chicago area. Two of the most important farmers in U.S. history lived and worked in Illinois. Neither John Deere nor Cyrus McCormick were natives but in Illinois perfected the plow and reaper technology that would not only transform the Great Plains but revise the entire American pattern of settlement and agriculture. Architects Frank Lloyd Wright and Mies Van Der Rohe created new concepts of how people should occupy their landscape and urban environments. Beneath a Chicago stadium in 1942, Enrico Fermi anxiously ignited the atomic age— while not far away in Greater Salem Baptist Church, gospel singer Mahalia Jackson made a considerably more "joyful noise." The prestigious University of Chicago attracted a succession of noted scholars and teachers—Hannah Arendt, John Dewey and Paul Tillich, among others. Illinois, in short, has raised food for the national body, mind and soul in fairly equal proportions. It has also taught hard lessons by example. It has been, on the whole, one of America's most efficient providers.

Though dated, John Drury's *Old Illinois Houses* (1977 reprint) remains one of the best sources of historic-home information for this intriguing state. Several excellent books on Chicago's neighborhoods and architecture are also available for city specialists.

ADDAMS, JANE (1860–1935). The birthplace of the humanitarian and 1931 Nobel Peace Prize recipient is a two-story house on Mill Street, **Cedarville,** where she lived until 1881. Her father built this brick and white frame homestead in 1854. It remains privately owned.

For 45 years, from 1889 to 1935, Addams lived at Hull House National Historic Landmark, 800 South Halsted St. (at the corner of Polk Street) on Chicago Circle, **Chicago.** "I gradually became convinced that it would be a good thing to rent a house in a part of the city where many primitive and actual needs are found," she wrote. She converted this 1856 brick mansion to a settlement house in 1889 and made it an influential hub and training center for social workers. Temporary residents of Hull House have included Canadian Prime Minister William L. Mackenzie King, Russian revolutionary Prince Peter Kropotkin, Czech leader Thomas G. Masaryk and social worker Julia Lathrop. Addams's own rooms there have been restored and display possessions, awards and memorabilia. Hull House is operated by the University of Illinois Chicago Circle campus. (Open summer, Monday–Friday 10:00– 4:00, Sunday 12:00–4:00; 312-996-2793; free.)

Exhibit: The Jane Addams Room at the

Stephenson County Historical Society, 1440 South Carroll Ave. in **Freeport,** houses articles from her Cedarville birthplace, assorted pictures and letters and her infant cradle. (Open Friday–Sunday 1:30–5:00; 815-232-8419; donation.)

ARENDT, HANNAH (1906–1975). German-born political scientist and penetrating analyst of social revolution and violence, Arendt taught at the University of **Chicago** from 1963 to 1967. Her residences included the 1921 Quadrangle Club, still a university residence at 1155 East 57th St., and 1126 East 59th St. Both remain privately occupied.

(See Chapter 2, MANHATTAN.)

BAUM, LYMAN FRANK (1856–1919). The author whose *Oz* books achieved most of their popularity after his death lived in **Chicago** from 1891 to 1910, the period when he wrote his best-known fantasy, *The Wonderful Wizard of Oz* (1900). Baum's home, a 19th-century, three-story stone dwelling, stands unmarked at 5423 South Michigan Ave., the south half of a double house (privately owned).

(See SOUTH DAKOTA in this chapter; also Chapter 3, NEW YORK.)

BENNY, JACK (1894–1974). Born Benjamin Kubelsky in a Chicago hospital, the comedian always claimed **Waukegan** as his birthplace because his mother carried him there for nine months. There is, however, considerable confusion about the location of his Waukegan boyhood homes. When Benny last visited his hometown in 1974, he told a news conference that "we lived in a house at 518 Clayton St." Waukegan mayor Robert Sabonjian corrected him, indicating the address was 418; "I was here before you were," Benny quipped. According to biographer Irving A. Fein, Benny's first home was a small apartment over a butcher shop on Glendon Street. Later, when he dropped out of high school, the family was living at 224 South Genesee St., where he listed himself in the city directory as "Jack Kubelsky, Violinist." This building still remains, its ground floor now a grocery store and the upper apartment privately occupied. As for Clayton Street, the Waukegan Historical Society finds no evidence that Jack Benny ever resided there.

(See Chapter 6, CALIFORNIA.)

BIRTHPLACE OF "THE GREAT COMMONER." The father of William Jennings Bryan built this frame house in 1852. Visitors to the **Salem** dwelling may view numerous items displaying various aspects of the statesman's life and career. (*Courtesy William Jennings Bryan Birthplace, City of Salem*)

BORAH, WILLIAM EDGAR (1865–1940). The birthplace of the longtime senator from Idaho, one of the most respected and influential legislators in American history, stood about six miles northeast of **Fairfield** in Jasper Township. The low, frame farmhouse, Borah's home until 1883, recently "fell down," reported a Fairfield source in 1981.

(See Chapter 3, DISTRICT OF COLUMBIA; also Chapter 6, IDAHO.)

BRYAN, WILLIAM JENNINGS (1860–1925). The political leader was born in **Salem,** where the 1852 Bryan House built by his father stands at 408 South Broadway. Bryan lived there until 1866; the two-story clapboard home, operated by the City of Salem Historical Commission, contains many personal and family effects. These include his Spanish-American War uniform, his spectacles, first editions of his books and souvenirs of the 1896 Democratic Convention where his rousing "Cross of Gold" speech swept him into presidential candidacy. (Open daily 10:00–5:00; 618-548-1236; admission.) Bryan's later boyhood home—a three-story, brick house built in 1862—stood until 1955 on Bryan Lane in northwest Salem.

In **Jacksonville,** Bryan occupied two residences, neither of which exist. A marker identifies the site of his last dwelling there at 1225 West College Ave., where Bryan lived while practicing law from 1884 to 1887.

(See NEBRASKA in this chapter; also Chapter 3, DISTRICT OF COLUMBIA; also Chapter 5, FLORIDA, TENNESSEE.)

BURROUGHS, EDGAR RICE (1875–1950). The creator of "Tarzan" and author of numerous science-fiction novels was born in **Chicago** at 646 Washington Blvd., a three-story brick house where he lived until 1891. The house presently on the site may well be the same private building with a remodeled front.

In **Oak Park,** suburban Chicago, Burroughs resided from 1917 to 1919 at 414 Augusta Blvd. (at the corner of Linden Avenue), the first home he owned. This three-story stucco dwelling—the "house that Tarzan bought"—remains privately owned.

(See Chapter 6, CALIFORNIA.)

CAPONE, ALPHONSE "AL" (1899–1947). The bloody gang warlord of the 1920s lived in the Chicago suburb of **Cicero** for many of those years. His main hangout from 1923 to 1929 was the infamous Hawthorne Inn at 4833 West 22nd St.; this place, renamed Towne Inn, stayed in Chicago syndicate hands until 1970, when it burned down. It was the site of Capone's brutal murdering of three cronies with a baseball bat in 1929.

The two-story, 15-room brick home where he installed his numerous family and, from 1922 to 1933, sometimes even resided himself, stands at 7244 South Prairie Ave. in **Chicago.** The upstairs parlor there had mirrors from floor to ceiling, and a steel gate led from the rear alley to a reinforced concrete basement. Built about 1920, the house is now a private, two-family apartment dwelling.

(See WISCONSIN in this chapter; also Chapter 2, BROOKLYN; also Chapter 5, FLORIDA; also Chapter 6, CALIFORNIA.)

CARNAP, RUDOLF (1891–1970). Philosopher and leading developer of the doctrine of logical positivism, the German-born Carnap taught at the University of **Chicago** from 1936 to 1952. Three of his four residences in the university area remain, all private: 5438 South University Ave.

(1937 to 1941), 5724 South Kenwood Ave. (1941 to 1944), and 5642 South Drexel Ave. (1944 to 1952).

(See Chapter 6, CALIFORNIA.)

DALEY, RICHARD JOSEPH (1902–1976). Daley, the powerful mayor of **Chicago** from 1955 until his death, became a nationally controversial figure during the 1968 Democratic National Convention. His use of thuggish Chicago police against unarmed street demonstrators at that time did little to dispel Chicago's old reputation for tolerating—if not occasionally preferring—violence. Daley occupied only two houses, both on the same street, during his entire life. He was born at 3502 South Lowe Ave. in Chicago's Bridgeport area, a "two-flat" residence that he occupied until 1939. Daley built his seven-room brick bungalow at 3536 South Lowe in 1939, residing there for the rest of his life. Both houses remain privately occupied.

DARROW, CLARENCE SEWARD (1857–1938). The prominent labor lawyer, defense attorney and civil libertarian, whose rumpled appearance and mastery of oral argument in a career of dramatic trials made him a highly visible public figure, resided in **Chicago** from 1887. In 1892 he built the house still standing at 4219 Vincennes Ave.—though his first wife, whom he later divorced, complained that he only came home to sleep. Darrow left this wife and house in 1897. None of his subsequent dwellings remain. His last home, from 1907, was the nine rooms of the top floor at 1537 East 60th St., a six-story apartment building overlooking Jackson Park and the University of Chicago. He died there in his big brass bed. The site is a parking lot today.

(See OHIO in this chapter; also Chapter 5, TENNESSEE.)

DEERE, JOHN (1805–1886). Deere's development of the heavy steel plow in 1837 opened the Great Plains to successful farming. The Vermont blacksmith came to Illinois in that year and established his shop and home at what is now John Deere Historic Site just off State Highway 2 in **Grand Detour,** where he lived and worked until 1847. Buildings include remnants of his original shop, his reconstructed blacksmith forge and his 1836, two-story clapboard house (Deere House National Historic Landmark) containing period furnishings. The complex is operated by trustees of John Deere Historic Site. (Open March 1–November 30, daily 9:00–5:00; December 1–February 28, by appointment; 815-652-4551; free.)

In **Moline** as a prosperous manufacturer of farm implements, Deere occupied several homes from 1847 to his death. His only surviving and clearly identified home is the early 19th-century structure now known as the Red Cliff Apartments, overlooking Moline and the Mississippi River at 11th Avenue and 12th Street. This stucco dwelling, bought, rebuilt and enlarged by Deere in 1880, has been recently renovated and continues to house private apartments. Deere built an air-conditioning shaft from a low point on the bluff to his hallway and anchored the house with long iron bolts running from upper rafters to the foundation.

Exhibit: Past and present implements manufactured by the Deere factory can be seen at Deere & Company Administrative Center, seven miles south of **Moline** on John Deere Road. (Open Monday–Friday 9:00–4:00, tours 10:30, 1:30; 309-752-4881; free.)

DEWEY, JOHN (1859–1952). The philosopher and educational innovator taught at the University of **Chicago** from 1895 to 1904. His first residence, the Del Prado Hotel, stood on the present site of the University International House, 1414 East 59th St. Dewey occupied five more apartment addresses during his Chicago stay (see Name Index and Gazetteer); these buildings, located in deteriorated neighborhoods in the vicinity of the university, have fallen as a result of slum clearance projects.

(See Chapter 1, VERMONT; also Chapter 2, MANHATTAN; also Chapter 3, NEW YORK.)

DILLINGER, JOHN HERBERT (1903–1934?).
Exhibit: The fugitive who eluded massed law-enforcement agencies for two years was finally gunned down by FBI agents in **Chicago.** At least that's the official version; a long-missing autopsy record recently brought to light raises some legitimate doubt that the person buried as Dillinger was actually he. Whoever may have been the victim of J. Edgar Hoover's urgency to close the file, he was shot on July 22, 1934, as he emerged from the Biograph Theater, 2433 North Lincoln Ave. He fell in an alley toward the rear of the building. Nothing much has changed in this neighborhood since 1934. The Biograph remains functional as an art theater; in 1981 it was hosting a Truffaut festival. The only reminder of Dillinger was grafitti—his name scrawled in red crayon on the aforesaid alley wall.

(See INDIANA, WISCONSIN in this chapter; also Chapter 3, DISTRICT OF COLUMBIA.)

DIRKSEN, EVERETT McKINLEY (1896–1969). According to his wife's account, "the Wizard of Ooze," longtime senator noted for his mellow, emphysematous-bass voice and old-fashioned oratory, habitually gargled with cold cream to oil those pipes. Dirksen was born in **Pekin** and made his lifelong home there. His farmhouse birthplace, dating from about 1880, stands at 802 Catharine St. His boyhood home at 1201 Hamilton St., like his birthplace, has been much modified from its original appearance. Dirksen's permanent home from 1927, an 1865, two-story clapboard dwelling that belonged to his mother-in-law, is identified by a marker at 335 Buena Vista. All of these houses remain privately owned.

Exhibit: The Dirksen Center—"devoted to the study of Congress and congressional leadership in the United States"—is a nonprofit research organization located at 301 South 4th St. in **Pekin.** Memorabilia of the senator are displayed in its "Honorable Mr. Marigold" collection. (Open Monday–Saturday 9:00–5:00; 309-347-7113; free.)

(See Chapter 3, DISTRICT OF COLUMBIA; also Chapter 5, VIRGINIA.)

DOUGLAS, STEPHEN ARNOLD (1813–1861). The "Little Giant" of national politics—congressman, senator, debate opponent of Abraham Lincoln (see the entry on Lincoln later in this section) and 1860 presidential candidate—lived in Illinois from 1833. None of his Illinois lodgings survive, though the sites of all seven of his debates with Lincoln are marked by tablets in the communities where they were held. Douglas is buried in **Chicago** on a portion of his estate "Oakenwald," a 53-acre lakeshore tract he purchased in 1849. His small, one-story, clapboard house stood near what is now East 35th Street and Martin Luther King Jr. Drive until the early 1900s.

Exhibit: Personal memorabilia plus a life mask of Douglas are displayed in the Illinois Room of the **Chicago** Historical Society, North Clark Street and North Avenue. (Open Monday–Saturday

9:30–4:30, Sunday 12:00–5:00; 312-642-4844; admission.)

(See Chapter 1, VERMONT; also Chapter 3, DISTRICT OF COLUMBIA, NEW YORK.)

DREISER, THEODORE (1871–1945). In 1884 the eventual author moved to **Chicago** with his family. Biographer Ellen Mores wrote that Dreiser "would never forget how the big city looked to the child that first time," a view that became "the basis for all his subsequent imaginative encounters with Chicago experience." The large, fatherless family occupied a third-floor apartment at West Madison and Throop streets—the tenth dwelling and fifth town of Dreiser's boyhood years. He made this area in the vicinity of 1300 West Madison St. the first home of his heroine *Sister Carrie* (1900). The building is long gone. Dreiser's first stay lasted only a few months. Later, as a less than proficient Chicago newspaper reporter, he briefly occupied rooms at several unidentified addresses.

(See INDIANA in this chapter; also Chapter 2, BROOKLYN, MANHATTAN; also Chapter 3, NEW YORK; also Chapter 6, CALIFORNIA.)

EARP, WYATT (1848–1929). Frontier gambler, part-time lawman and brawling gunfighter, Earp was born Wyatt Berry Stapp Earp (named after his father's commanding officer in the Mexican War) in **Monmouth.** His birthplace, a small, two-story frame house stands at 406 South Third St., thrice-moved from its original location at 213 South Third. Earp lived there with his parents and brothers until 1850. One owner of this still-private dwelling, it is said, found the names of Earp and his brother written on a closet wall.

(See IOWA, KANSAS in this chapter; also Chapter 6, ARIZONA, CALIFORNIA.)

FERMI, ENRICO (1901–1954). From 1942 the Italian-born physicist resided at intervals in **Chicago,** where he headed the secret Manhattan Project that produced the first nuclear chain reaction, leading to quick development of the atomic bomb. His last home, from 1946, stands privately owned at 5327 South University Ave., a three-story house built about 1900.

Exhibit: On South Ellis Avenue between East 56th and 57th streets stands the Henry Moore sculpture that marks First Self-Sustaining Nuclear Reaction National Historic Landmark, the site of Fermi's laboratory. The spot where Fermi built his atomic pile, which almost exploded prematurely, was a squash court beneath the west stadium of Stagg Field. Fermi made the successful test of the atomic pile on December 2, 1942.

(See Chapter 3, NEW JERSEY; also Chapter 6, NEW MEXICO.)

FIELD, MARSHALL (1834–1906). Prominent **Chicago** sales innovator, merchant, philanthropist and founder of a business dynasty, Field organized the Marshall Field and Company department store in 1881, a merchandising firm still thriving. He came to Chicago in 1856 and occupied a long-gone house at 306 South Michigan Ave. Architect Richard Morris Hunt designed Field's last home in 1876 at 1905 South Prairie Ave. The interior of this three-story, red brick palace was remodeled in 1937 as the New Bauhaus, ironically sheltering one of the most advanced schools of modern American architecture until 1939. This mansion, the city's first with electric lights, was razed after World War II.

(See Chapter 1, MASSACHUSETTS; also Chapter 5, GEORGIA.)

GARLAND, HAMLIN (1860–1940). Near **Oregon** the author was one of the literary group attracted to "Eagle's Nest," the art colony established on the 15-acre estate of the lawyer and businessman Wallace Heckman on Rock River. Heckman built his two-story stone home, which he called "Ganymede," in 1893, and Garland spent frequent summers there from 1898 through the 1920s; he wrote *A Daughter of the Middle Border* (1921) in the guest room of the house. Sculptor Lorado Taft was also a frequent resident. The site and its buildings, acquired by the State of Illinois in 1943, are included in the 207-acre Lowden State Park, located 2 miles north of Oregon via State Highway 64. (Open daily.)

Garland's last **Chicago** residence, from 1907 to 1915, stands at 6427 South Greenwood Ave., a three-story brick dwelling that is still a private residence. He wrote several obscure novels there before winning recognition with his memoir *A Son of the Middle Border* (1917).

(See IOWA, SOUTH DAKOTA, WISCONSIN in this chapter; also Chapter 2, MANHATTAN; also Chapter 6, CALIFORNIA.)

GRANT, ULYSSES SIMPSON (1822–1885). The Union army commander during the Civil War and later 18th U.S. president occupied two homes in **Galena** at separate intervals. Following six years of unsuccessful farming in Missouri, he moved to Galena in 1860, clerked in his father's leather-goods store and rented the two-story brick house at 121 High St. (privately owned). The amiable, hard-drinking retired captain left this house as an aimless loser in 1861 to resume a military career that would bring him national renown. His family remained in this dwelling throughout most of the war. Grant's return to Galena at the war's end in 1865 was a vastly different occasion from his unceremonious departure. Galena citizens purchased the two-story, brick Italianate house at 511 Bouthillier St. and gave it to him. Grant and his family lived there until 1867, when he moved to Washington, D.C.—and again for a period after his presidency (1879–81). Today Grant Home National Historic Landmark displays family furnishings and possessions plus elegant silver and china used in the White House during his two terms. The restored 1859 house is operated by the Illinois Department of Conservation. (Open daily 9:00–5:00; 815-777-0248; free.)

Exhibits: Jesse Grant's leather store, where the eventual president clerked in 1860 and 1861, stood at 120 South Main St., a site identified by a marker in **Galena.** A reconstruction of the Grant Leather Store stands at 211 South Main St.

In **Chicago,** the table on which Grant and Gen. Robert E. Lee signed the document of Confederate surrender at Appomattox is displayed at the Chicago Historical Society, North Clark Street and North Avenue. (Open Monday–Saturday 9:30–4:30, Sunday 12:00–5:00; 312-642-4844; admission.)

(See MICHIGAN, MISSOURI, OHIO in this chapter; also Chapter 2, MANHATTAN; also Chapter 3, DISTRICT OF COLUMBIA, NEW JERSEY, NEW YORK; also Chapter 5, VIRGINIA; also Chapter 6, WASHINGTON.)

HECHT, BEN (1894–1964). The 1920s for literary **Chicago** has been called the "Age of Hecht." Newspaperman, author, playwright and screenwriter, Hecht underwent his Chicago journalistic apprenticeship from 1910, a period richly detailed in his *1001 Nights in Chicago* (1922) and in his autobiography, *Child of the Century* (1954). The residence where he roomed until 1924 stands privately occupied at 5210 South Kenwood Ave., a lovely old Victorian frame mansion.

(See WISCONSIN in this chapter; also Chapter 2, MANHATTAN; also Chapter 3, NEW YORK.)

HEMINGWAY, ERNEST MILLER (1899–1961). Probably the foremost American novelist of the 20th century, Hemingway was an Illinois native. Though his early life in **Oak Park,** suburban Chicago, was outwardly conventional and materially advantaged, it was also, in many ways, a middle-class catalog of horrors. His birthplace and home until 1905 stands at 339 North Oak Park Ave. This two-story, Victorian mansion built by Hemingway's maternal grandfather dates from 1890. Hemingway was born in the second floor south bedroom. From 1906 to 1917, he lived with his parents at 600 North Kenilworth Ave. His father, a physician, shot himself there in 1928—an action Hemingway would compulsively emulate. Both houses remain privately owned.

Just before his first marriage in 1921, Hemingway occupied an apartment at 1239 North Dearborn St. in **Chicago,** a three and one-half-story brick structure then known as The Belleville and still privately occupied.

Exhibit: The Historical Society of **Oak Park** and River Forest at Home Avenue and Pleasant Street (Farson-Mills House) displays Hemingway memorabilia. (Tours Sunday 1:00–3:00; 312-848-6755; free.)

(See MICHIGAN in this chapter; also Chapter 5, FLORIDA; also Chapter 6, IDAHO.)

HICKOK, JAMES BUTLER "WILD BILL" (1837–1876). A state monument marking the site of the frontier gunslinger's birthplace stands in a grove of evergreens on Main Street (East Fourth Road) one block south of U.S. Highway 52 in **Troy Grove.** According to Mrs. Charles Harmon, a Hickok descendant, this frame house stood until 1929, "when it was torn down to make way for the state park in memory of the birthplace of James B. Hickok." Hickok grew up on a long-gone farm, his home until 1856, at an unidentified spot north of Troy Grove. "A cellar hole was visible until recent times," says Mrs. Harmon. This cellar built by Hickok's father was apparently used as a station on the Underground Railroad.

(See SOUTH DAKOTA in this chapter.)

JACKSON, MAHALIA (1912–1972). The "world's greatest gospel singer" made her home in **Chicago** from 1927, but only her last two residences remain. In 1956, she integrated the neighborhood at 8358 South Indiana Ave. by moving into the brick, ranch-style house, the first home she had owned. Her first months there gave her frightening welcome with a chorus of obscene phone calls and a smashed picture window. She endured, however, and a better class of people soon moved into the area. In 1969, she occupied a 26th-floor condominium called Cornell Village at 5201 South Cornell Ave. overlooking Lake Michigan, and that was her last home.

(See Chapter 5, LOUISIANA.)

JOHNSON, JACK ARTHUR (1878–1946). The greatest boxer of his time—and perhaps of any time—spent a lifetime infuriating whites with his clear superiority over the best of white opponents and his attractiveness to white women. He also endured numerous injustices from lesser men because of his race—was even driven out of the country at one point—and spent a year in prison for violation of the notorious Mann Act. He held the heavyweight championship title from 1908 to 1915; Jess Willard finally took it from him after a 26-round bout in Cuba. In 1910, when Johnson beat "the great white hope" Jim Jeffries, his home was 3344 South Wabash Ave. in **Chicago,** a large brick mansion since razed, where he lived with his mother and sisters. It stood on what is now Illinois Institute of Technology grounds. Johnson's Cafe de Champion, whose liquor license was revoked by the state in 1912, stood at 42 West 31st St. Johnson occupied a second-floor apartment there in 1911 and 1912.

(See Chapter 6, TEXAS.)

LARDNER, RINGGOLD WILMER "RING" (1885–1933). The sportswriter and popular author of vernacular stories lived in **Riverside,** suburban Chicago, from 1914 to 1917 while writing his "Wake of the News" column for the *Chicago Tribune.* His home at 150 Herrick Road, new in 1913, remains privately occupied. Lardner sold it in 1919.

A three-story row house that he occupied in **Chicago** from 1912 to 1914 stands at 6002 South Prairie Ave. (at the corner of East 60th Street), also private.

(See MICHIGAN in this chapter; also Chapter 3, NEW YORK.)

LA SALLE, ROBERT CAVELIER, SIEUR DE (1643–1687). The French explorer who claimed and named the domain of Louisiana for Louis XIV spent considerable time in Illinois, both before and after his epochal 1682 journey from Canada to the mouth of the Mississippi. The staging area for the expedition was Fort Crevecoeur on the Illinois River, a small redoubt he erected in 1680. The location of this site has long been disputed; what seems fairly certain is that Fort Crevecoeur State Park, two miles south of **East Peoria** on State Highway 29, does not mark the true site but was selected by the Daughters of the American Revolution and the Illinois State Historical Society as the closest landform matching La Salle's description. According to Russell C. Birk, Historical Markers Supervisor, this site "was the only one that met the essential requirements and to which there was access, and therefore would have to suffice unless and until further indisputable evidence should prove otherwise." The likeliest site, however, is that identified by civil engineer Arthur Lagron in 1913, an unmarked spot graded for the extensive Peoria and Pekin Union Railroad yards about half a mile north of the official fort site.*

In 1683 after the successful river expedition, La Salle built Fort St. Louis atop Starved Rock, the 125-foot-high sandstone outcrop on the Illinois River at what is now Starved Rock State Park. He intended it as the first of a chain of forts that would command the main passage south from Canada and hold the territory for France; it soon became the center of a large Indian settlement, and La Salle himself only stayed for about five months. Until about 1690, when decline of the fur trade caused its abandonment, it remained the seat of government for the Illinois territory. The fort burned about 1720. The cliff received its name only later, when according to Indian legend a band of Illinois natives starved to death there when besieged by Ottawa-Potawatomi warriors in 1769. Today the park is maintained by the Illinois Department of Conservation and encompasses 2,520 acres of hiking trails, picnic areas, campgrounds and an interpretive center. There is, of course, no remnant of La Salle's fort on Starved Rock, though 1949 excavations established outlines of the fort and recovered some

---

*These railroad yards are off-limits, as the writer discovered in the summer of 1980 when two squads of grim security people interrupted his efforts on behalf of posterity to pinpoint the fort site from this dismal complex of rails and cinders.

French artifacts. The park is located several miles southeast of **Utica** on State Highway 71, five miles east of La Salle. (Open daily 8:00–10:00; 815-667-4726; free.)

(See MICHIGAN in this chapter; also Chapter 6, TEXAS.)

LEWIS, JOHN LLEWELLYN (1880–1969). The powerful, fierce-browed president of the United Mine Workers for 40 years arose to union leadership in the coal town of **Panama,** where he lived from 1908 to 1917. His home, privately owned and sided since he occupied it, stands just north of the post office on Main Street, the only house on the block.

The first home that Lewis owned stands at 1132 West Lawrence Ave. in **Springfield.** He bought this three-story, Victorian frame dwelling in 1917, when it was the largest house on the street, and lived there until 1933. Last up for sale in 1980, it remains privately occupied. Lewis also owned two other neighborhood houses in which he established his parents and sisters.

(See IOWA in this chapter; also Chapter 5, FLORIDA, VIRGINIA.)

LINCOLN, ABRAHAM (1809–1865).
LINCOLN, MARY TODD (1818–1882).

Illinois is, of course, Lincoln country, and it is impossible to travel far in the state without encountering reminders of his presence—for Lincoln journeyed widely during his days as circuit lawyer, congressman and political speaker. Places where he addressed crowds, courthouses in which he argued cases, even houses where he bunked for a night or a week are abundantly marked and revered throughout the state. He actually resided in or near only three communities, however, from the year he entered Illinois with his parents (1830) until he left Springfield (1861) to become the 16th U.S. President.

His first Illinois home, near **Decatur,** is now Lincoln Trail Homestead State Park, located 10 miles southwest of the city off U.S. Highway 36; follow directional markers from the highway. The family farmed 15 acres and lived there for a year (1830–31), marooned that winter in their crude log cabin by six feet of snow. That is the main locale of Lincoln's reputation as rail-splitter; he cut hundreds there for neighboring farmers. The original cabin was removed from the site in 1865 for exhibition elsewhere and eventually disappeared. The park is operated by the Illinois Department of Conservation. (Open daily; 217–963-2729; free.)

In 1831 Lincoln left his parents and drifted to New Salem, a Sangamon River town laid out two years before. Lincoln spent six years there; during this period, he clerked for merchant Denton Offutt, volunteered brief service in the Black Hawk War, kept a store with William Berry, served as postmaster and surveyor, won election to the state legislature and was licensed to practice law. He lived in the loft of Rutledge Tavern, owned by the father of Ann Rutledge—a nebulous person whom romantic mythologizers have transformed into the great love of Lincoln's life. After Lincoln left, New Salem soon faded, trade moved elsewhere and by 1839 the village lay almost deserted. But history has been remarkably kind to this settlement that lasted only a decade and was overgrown weeds by the time Lincoln became President. Publisher William Randolph Hearst bought the village site in 1906 and conveyed it to the Old Salem Chautauqua Association—which, in 1919, gave it to the State of Illinois. With the aid of the Civilian Conservation Corps, village reconstruction began during the 1930s and continued for a decade. Today 12 timber houses plus the Rutledge Tavern, shops and a school stand meticulously rebuilt on their original sites. The only original structure there is the Onstot Cooper Shop, restored on its foundation in 1922. Authentic furnishings, both period and original, and yard gardens, hedges and native tree plantings recreate the village as Lincoln knew it. A walk through New Salem, one of the nation's most notable museum villages, is a jaunt into a decade of America's pioneer past. Lincoln's New Salem State Park, operated by the Illinois Department of Conservation, lies two miles south of **Petersburg** off State Highway 97. Interpretive programs, exhibits and audiovisual aids are available to visitors. (Open daily 9:00–5:00; 217-632-3846; free.)

Lincoln left New Salem for **Springfield** as an ambitious politician in 1837. His first residence was shared quarters above the store of Joshua Speed, which stood at 101–103 South Fifth St. (at the corner of Washington Street), the later site of the Lincoln-Herndon Law Office. Lincoln resided with Speed from 1837 to 1841. The first married home of the Lincolns, in 1842 and 1843, was Globe

JOHN L. LEWIS HOME. The first home owned by the union leader, at 1132 West Lawrence Ave. in **Springfield**, this dwelling also saw his rise to eminence as the president of the United Mine Workers. Lewis resided there from 1917 to 1933. The photo shows the house as it looked in 1980, still privately owned.
(Author's photo)

ABRAHAM LINCOLN'S HOME. This house in **Springfield**, one of America's most popular landmarks, was a one and one-half story dwelling when Lincoln bought it in 1844. Twelve years later, the Lincolns enlarged it to its present dimensions, then left it permanently when he became president in 1861. It was the only home they ever owned, the center of national attention in 1860, and the scene of domestic tragedy as well as political success. This engraving probably dates from the period of Lincoln's presidency.
(Courtesy Library of Congress)

Tavern, a hotel boardinghouse that stood at 315 East Adams St. Their first son, Robert Todd Lincoln, was born there in 1843. The Lincolns then moved to a rented three-room cottage at 214 South Fourth St., also long gone. The next year (1844), they bought the only home they ever owned at Eighth and Jackson streets, now Lincoln Home National Historic Site. Built in 1839 for Rev. Charles Dresser, who had married the couple, the house was a one and one-half-story, five-room cottage framed in oak when the Lincolns moved in. They paid Dresser $1,200 cash for the home and $300 for the 50 × 152-foot lot. Lincoln installed the front fence and brick wall in 1850. In 1856 Mary Lincoln used an endowment from her deceased father to enlarge the house to the two full stories seen today, for $100 more than the original cash price—$1,300. Of the three Lincoln sons born there, one ("Eddie") died in the house in 1850. The Lincolns occupied this home, except for part of his congressional term in 1847 and 1848, until 1861, when they left Springfield for the White House. Lincoln received his formal notification of the presidential nomination in the north parlor on May 19, 1860. Most of the Lincolns' household furnishings, which they auctioned in 1861, were moved to Chicago and destroyed in the Great Fire of 1871. A succession of residents occupied the Lincoln home until son Robert Todd Lincoln deeded the property to the state in 1889. Full restoration of the house, begun in 1950, used old prints and documented descriptions of the rooms to recreate the dwelling as the Lincolns knew it, and it was opened to the public in 1955. Many of the original, widely scattered surviving contents have returned from collectors and museums; by 1980, about 60 percent of the interior furnishings were original Lincoln possessions (for security reasons, attendants are reluctant to identify precisely which items these are). The Quaker-brown exterior and the yard are also faithfully restored. What with his rampaging youngsters and numerous guests and delegations, Lincoln's home received hard enough use when he lived there. Today, with some 700,000 visitors per year, it endures even harder wear. Visitors are astonished to note that the Springfield politician, though not wealthy, had obviously come far from splitting rails when he lived there. He was prosperous, and his home would rank as very upper middle-class by today's standards. National Park Service personnel handle the crowds with typical professionalism and perform a remarkable job of maintenance and interpretation. The entire neighborhood is a pedestrian court, closed to vehicle traffic. (Open daily 8:00–5:00; 217-789-2357; free.)

A shattered Mary Todd Lincoln returned to Springfield after her husband's death. Her intermittent home from 1865 and last permanent residence was the house of her sister, Mrs. Ninian Edwards, which stood on the present site of the Centennial Building at Second and Edwards streets. The Lincolns were married there in 1842, and there Mary Lincoln died. That 1836 house has been replicated at 406 South Eighth St. as the Lincoln Marriage Home and Museum, containing dioramas. (Open April 1–October 31, daily 9:00–5:00; admission.)

Mary Lincoln also resided in **Chicago** after the assassination. In 1866 she impulsively bought a stone row house at 375 West Washington St., lived there for a year with her son Tad, then rented it out and finally sold it in 1874. This house has long since disappeared.*

One of Mary Lincoln's saddest residences was a sanitarium in **Batavia,** where anguished son Robert committed her briefly in 1875. Bellevue Place Rest Home, an 1853 limestone building with wings added about 1890, stands at 333 South Jefferson St. Now called Batavia Institute, it has served as a home for adolescent girls since 1966.

Exhibits: Illinois displays a wealth of Lincolniana, some of it vastly worth seeing, much of it just as well bypassed. Dozens of remote county courthouses have an obligatory Lincoln Room containing a few items of faded trivia to identify the community with greatness. Outstanding, of course, are many of the various displays in Lincoln's hometown of **Springfield.** Local buildings and sites associated with him include his various law offices: the Lincoln-Stuart office (1837–41) in the remodeled building at 109 North Fifth St. (privately occupied); the Logan-Lincoln office (1841–44), 203 South Sixth St. (at the corner of Adams Street, open daily 9:00–5:00; 217-523-1010; admission); and the Lincoln-Herndon office site (1843–61), 101–103 South Fifth St. (at the corner

---

*An old man raised in Chicago once told the author's father of a childhood incident he recalled from his childhood. He and a group of boys had accidentally spattered mud on some clothes hanging in a Washington Street yard. A woman burst from the house and showered them with a torrent of profanity. "That woman," he said, "was Mary Todd Lincoln."

of Washington Street). The Lincoln Depot Museum at 10th and Monroe streets, where Lincoln made an emotional farewell to Springfield, has been restored to its 1861 appearance (open April 1–November 1, Monday–Saturday 9:00–5:00, Sunday 12:00–5:00; 217-785-3856; admission.) Probably the wisest first stop in Springfield is the National Park Service visitor center at 426 South Seventh St., where maps and information regarding all of the Springfield Lincoln sites and buildings may be obtained (open daily 8:00–5:00; 217-525-4241; free.)

Next to Lincoln's home, by far the nation's most significant Lincoln display is housed in the Chicago Historical Society, North Clark Street and North Avenue in **Chicago.** Replicas include those of his Kentucky birthplace cabin, of the Springfield home parlor and of the Peterson Bedroom, which contains the bed on which he died in Washington, D.C. The exhibit also features the table on which he signed the Emancipation Proclamation and a White House piano bought by Mary Lincoln, plus personal items such as his watch, spectacles and clothing. (Open Monday–Saturday 9:30–4:30, Sunday 12:00–5:00; 312-642-4844; admission.)

(See INDIANA, MICHIGAN, OHIO in this chapter; also Chapter 3, DISTRICT OF COLUMBIA, PENNSYLVANIA; also Chapter 5, KENTUCKY, TENNESSEE.)

LINDSAY, VACHEL (1879–1931). The **Springfield** birthplace of the "vagabond poet" remained his lifelong home base. He was born at 603 South Fifth St., a two-story, white frame house dating from about 1830. Displayed there along with period furnishings are many of his letters, manuscripts and drawings, plus his tiny upstairs study and bedroom. Lindsay, whose popular chanting recitals of his poetry took him all over the country, became increasingly eccentric and emotionally unstable, and finally took his own life there. The Vachel Lindsay Association owns and maintains the house. (Open June 1–August 31, Tuesday–Saturday 10:00–3:00, Sunday 12:00–4:00; September 1–May 31, by appointment; 217-528-9254; admission.)

(See Chapter 6, WASHINGTON.)

LOUIS, JOE (1914–1981). Professional boxer, idol of his generation and a man of great natural class and dignity, Louis made his home in **Chicago** during most of the 12 years he reigned as heavyweight champion. From about 1934, when he won his first professional fight, until the 1950s, he resided in a suite of eight rooms at 4320 South Michigan Ave., still a private apartment building.

(See Chapter 2, MANHATTAN; also Chapter 6, CALIFORNIA, COLORADO, NEVADA.)

McCORMICK, CYRUS HALL (1809–1884). "The reaper is to the North what Slavery is to the South," claimed Edwin M. Stanton. McCormick's reaper and Deere's plow did more to settle the West than any number of Custers and Buffalo Bills. The inventor of the mechanical reaper, which revolutionized harvest methods and also spelled the eventual end of small farms, built the device in 1831. After 1848 he manufactured the implements in **Chicago,** where his firm prospered, and he became one of the city's wealthiest industrialists. He resided until 1879 in a succession of homes, none of which stand. In that year, he completed building a huge brownstone mansion at 675 North Rush St., where he entertained lavishly in a 200-seat private theater and, according to Chicago historian Stephen Longstreet, "suffered from carbuncles and enjoyed major lawsuits" on numerous patent infringements. Three generations of McCormicks dwelled there until the mansion finally stood vacant and was demolished in 1955.

(See Chapter 3, NEW YORK; also Chapter 5, VIRGINIA.)

MARQUETTE, JACQUES (1637–1675). French Jesuit missionary and 1673 explorer of the Mississippi with Louis Jolliet, Marquette resided during the winter of 1674–75 in a crude log shelter at the present site of **Chicago.** Hemorrhaging from what was probably recurrent tuberculosis, "he told his two companions," wrote historian Francis Parkman, "that this journey would be his last. In the condition in which he was, it was impossible to go farther. The two men built a log hut by the river . . . while Marquette, feeble as he was, began the spiritual exercises of Saint Ignatius, and confessed his two companions twice a week. . . . Pierre and Jacques killed buffalo and deer and shot wild turkeys close to their hut." The priest and his two companions thus became the first white Illinois residents. Marquette survived that winter but died in Michigan the following spring. His marked cabin site is located at the northern edge of the Damen Avenue bridge across the Chicago River.

(See MICHIGAN, WISCONSIN in this chapter.)

MASTERS, EDGAR LEE (1869–1950). The poet's boyhood home from 1870 to 1880 is the Masters Memorial Museum at Eighth and Jackson streets in **Petersburg.** "Altogether I was not happy in this house," he wrote in 1936, though he later spoke of Petersburg as his "heart's home." This house stood at 528 Monroe St. on Braham Hill when Masters lived there. His grandfather bought the small frame dwelling that dates from about 1850 and gave it to the improvident family. Visitors may see the cherrywood desk Masters used during his long residence at the Chelsea Hotel in New York City, furniture from his grandparents' home and photos of local people who became prototypes for his *Spoon River Anthology* (1915). The house is operated by the Edgar Lee Masters Museum Board. (Open May 15–September 15, Tuesday–Sunday 1:00–5:00; free.)

Lewistown, also in Spoon River country, was the family's next stop; Masters's boyhood home from 1883 to 1891 stands at the southeast corner of Main and C streets, a private building now used for offices.

Masters lived for almost 30 years in **Chicago,** where he practiced law and wrote his best-known book. He occupied seven addresses from 1895, only three of which remain. The elegant three-story mansion at 4200 South Drexel Blvd., where Masters married and where he resided with his in-laws from 1898 to 1900, was in sad condition by 1981—vacant, vandalized and probably soon to be demolished. He lived at 4219 South Ellis St., a three-story brick residence, from 1903 to 1905. From 1909 to 1923, he lived in the lovely, well-maintained Georgian brick house at 4853 South Kenwood Ave., where he wrote much of *Spoon River Anthology.* The last two houses remain privately occupied.

(See MICHIGAN in this chapter; also Chapter 2, MANHATTAN.)

MIES VAN DER ROHE, LUDWIG (1886–1969). German-born architect, head of the famed Bauhaus school at Dessau, Mies came to America as one of the vast number of creative intellectuals driven from the Nazi state. He worked and taught in **Chicago** from 1938, producing some of the nation's most notable glass-and-steel architec-

ture. Inside his large apartment in the 200 East Pearson Street Building, he surrounded himself with off-white walls and Paul Klee paintings. Mies said he "did his thinking" there, guided by his philosophy, since popular, that "less is more." This building remains occupied by private apartments.

PEARSON, DREW (1897–1969). The muckraking columnist and powerful though unpredictable confidant of the mighty in government and politics was born in **Evanston.** Between the year of his birth and 1901, when the family left Evanston, the Pearsons occupied five different homes, all of which stand privately owned. Pearson was born at 1104 Foster St. The four remaining addresses are on Garnett (formerly Ayars) Street: 1100, 1117, 1103, and 1121.

(See Chapter 3, DISTRICT OF COLUMBIA, MARYLAND, PENNSYLVANIA.)

SANDBURG, CARL (1878–1967). Poet, folklorist and biographer of Abraham Lincoln, Sandburg cultivated in himself the "scholarly hick" qualities he admired in his heroes Lincoln (see the entry on Lincoln earlier in this section) and Walt Whitman. The literary intellectual was vastly talkative about his Illinois roots. His **Galesburg** birthplace, an 1875 frame cottage, stands at 331 East Third St., his home until 1881. Unplastered and sided with rough lumber, the three-room dwelling was heated by the kitchen stove; newspapers pasted over the walls served for insulation. Efforts of Galesburg schoolchildren and the Sandburg Birthplace Association resulted in the 1948 restoration of this house. An 1889 owner had clapboarded the exterior and added a rear room, which is now the Lincoln Room containing Sandburg memorabilia. "The little room which heard his first cry," wrote Adda George, "now echoes to his great tones" by means of his song and narrative recordings in the bedroom where he was born on a cornhusk mattress. Visitors may see family utensils, furniture, photographs and the typewriter on which Sandburg wrote parts of *Rootabaga Stories* (1922) and *The Prairie Years* (1926). Sandburg's ashes lie beneath "Remembrance Rock," the boulder monument behind his birthplace, which is operated by the Illinois State Historical Library. (Open Tuesday–Saturday 9:00–12:00, 1:00–5:00, Sunday 1:00–5:00; 309-342-2361; free.) In 1881 the family moved for a year to 641

East South St. a private dwelling now sided. In 1882 Sandburg's father bought what is now 808–810 East Berrien St., a stucco, two-family house, the ten rooms of which he divided into four apartments. The family rented out three of these and lived in the fourth until 1899. Across the street at 809 East Berrien stands the "Turn of the Century House," their home from 1899 to 1905. All of these later boyhood dwellings remain privately owned and unmarked. Sandburg details his Galesburg upbringing in *Always the Young Strangers* (1953).

In **Chicago,** Sandburg and his wife Lilian Steichen lived from 1911 to 1914 at 4646 North Hermitage Ave., Ravenswood. They occupied a second-floor apartment in this two-story, 1875 frame house, which remains private. There Sandburg wrote his famed poem "Chicago" (1914).

Maywood, a suburb of Chicago, was their residence from 1914 to 1919, when Sandburg edited feature copy for the *Chicago Daily News*. Their two-story home at 616 South Eighth Ave. (privately owned) dates from about 1895 and remains substantially unaltered.

The site of the 1860 dwelling they called "Happiness House" at 331 South York St. in **Elmhurst,** another suburb of Chicago, was cleared for a Baptist Church parking lot in the late 1960s. Sandburg lived there from 1919 to 1928.

(See MICHIGAN, WISCONSIN in this chapter; also Chapter 5, NORTH CAROLINA.)

SMITH, JOSEPH (1805–1844). History teaches that religious differences can often be counted upon to provoke the ultimate in hateful behavior, as the Mormon experience in western Illinois again demonstrated. In 1839, the visionary founder of this church led his followers to **Nauvoo,** where they settled and established their headquarters. Mormon converts swelled the town population to 18,000, making it one of the largest cities in Illinois by 1845. The oldest dwelling in Nauvoo is the Joseph Smith Homestead, an 1803 log structure that Smith occupied until 1843; it contains original and period furnishings, as does Smith's 1843 Mansion House. The latter dwelling, a two-story, oblong structure of white pine displays Smith's desk plus numerous documentary exhibits. There he was arrested for the last time following a church schism and general community uprising. "Every year," wrote Harry

M. Beardsley, "scores of earnest young men visit Nauvoo to spend a night in meditation in Joseph Smith's room in the Mansion House before setting out on their missionary journeys. . . . A few miles away at Carthage, other equally earnest young men arrive every year from Utah to spend a night in solemn contemplation in the cell tower at Carthage jail in which Joseph Smith was murdered, so that they may set forth on their missions imbued with the spirit of the Prophet." (Earnestness is not yet sufficient to qualify women for such missions among the Mormons.) Both Nauvoo dwellings are a part of Joseph Smith Historic Center at Maine and Water streets, operated by the Reorganized Church of Jesus Christ of Latter-Day Saints. (Open Memorial Day–Labor Day 8:00–8:00, Labor Day–Memorial Day 8:30–5:00; 217-453-2246; free.) *Nauvoo: Kingdom on the Mississippi* (1965), by Robert Bruce Flanders, gives an interesting history.

In **Carthage,** Smith and his brother Hyrum were shot and killed by an anti-Mormon mob at the Old Carthage Jail, where they had been imprisoned for instigating destruction of an opposition printing press. This building, also maintained by the aforesaid church, stands at 307 Walnut St. and offers a film and tour. (Open May 1–September 30, 9:00–sunset; October 1–April 30, 9:00–5:00; 217-357-2989; free.)

Exhibit: **Nauvoo** Historic District National Historic Landmark includes more than a dozen buildings associated with this troubled period that brought violence upon the town and death to Smith himself. Nauvoo Restoration, Inc. Visitor Center offers historical displays, a film and self-guiding maps to the old Mormon community. (Open June 1–October 31, daily 8:00–9:00; November 1–May 31, daily 9:00–6:00; 217-453-2237; free.)

(See MISSOURI, OHIO in this chapter; also Chapter 1, VERMONT; also Chapter 3, NEW YORK, PENNSYLVANIA; also Chapter 6, UTAH.)

STEVENSON, ADLAI EWING (1900–1965). The ancestral home (though not the birthplace) of the popular governor, presidential candidate and diplomat was **Bloomington.** His boyhood home from 1906 to 1916 stands privately owned at 1316 East Washington St. The original clapboard exterior of this two-story, 10-room Victorian house was faced with stucco in 1912. The 1867 brick mansion of Stevenson's grandfather, Adlai E.

Stevenson I, a U.S. vice president, stands at 901 North McLean St., also private. The grandson spent much time there as a youngster.

As a practicing lawyer, Stevenson occupied several **Chicago** apartment dwellings from 1927 to 1936. These included brownstone buildings at 70 East Elm St., 1434 Astor St., and 1246 North State St. All remain privately occupied.

In 1936 Stevenson bought 70 country acres on the Des Plaines River near **Libertyville,** a portion of the Hawthorne Farm estate once owned by utilities magnate Samuel Insull. Ellen Borden Stevenson designed the low, white wooden house, which the couple built in 1938 after fire destroyed their first dwelling on the property. "It is very much home," Stevenson once rhapsodized to reporters, "because I built it out of field and forest. I love it because I worked over every inch of it." And yet he resided at his farm for something less than a decade in total duration though he often went there to rest and stay for brief intervals until his death. The 14-room house, briefly occupied by his biographer John Bartlow Martin after Stevenson's death, "was quite modest at the time we lived there," said Martin. "The chairs were a bit threadbare and the tables wobbled—Stevenson never spent any money or fixed anything." Owned since 1974 by the Lake County Forest Preserve District, the house has since hosted a succession of carefully screened occupants. Of Stevenson's original property, 41 acres still surround the private dwelling, identified by a marker on St. Mary's Road.

As a reform governor, Stevenson occupied the Governor's Mansion in **Springfield** from 1949 to 1953. This 28-room, white brick Victorian house stands on the square bounded by Jackson, Edwards, Fourth, and Fifth streets. All Illinois governors since the mansion's 1855 construction have resided there. Abraham and Mary Todd Lincoln guested frequently until Lincoln's 1860 election as president (see the entry on the Lincolns earlier in this section). The mansion remains owned and operated by the State of Illinois. (Open Tuesday, Thursday 9:30–11:00, 2:00–3:30; 217-782-6450; free.)

Exhibit: The Stevenson Memorial Room in Stevenson Hall of Illinois State University, **Normal-Bloomington,** displays manuscripts, letters and other personal and political memorabilia. Stevenson Hall is located on School Street within the campus. (Open spring and fall semesters, Monday–Friday 10:00–5:00; summer, Tuesday, Thursday, Sunday 1:00–5:00; 309-829-6331; free.)

(See Chapter 2, MANHATTAN; also Chapter 3, DISTRICT OF COLUMBIA; also Chapter 6, CALIFORNIA.)

SUNDAY, WILLIAM ASHLEY "BILLY" (1862–1935). The professional baseball player who turned his athleticism to the pulpit made his summer home until 1913 on the farm he purchased from his in-laws in 1899 near **Sleepy Hollow,** a suburb of Chicago. The private property is identified by a state historical marker along State Highway 72.

(See INDIANA, IOWA in this chapter; also Chapter 6, OREGON.)

TILLICH, PAUL JOHANNES (1886–1965). The final residence of the German-born philosopher-theologian was a large suite he maintained in **Chicago** from 1962 at the Windermere Hotel, still at 1642 East 56th St. Tillich taught at the nearby University of Chicago during his last years.

(See Chapter 1, MASSACHUSETTS; also Chapter 3, NEW YORK.)

WILLARD, FRANCES ELIZABETH (1839–1898). In **Evanston,** the educator and temperance reformer lived with her family from 1858 to 1865 at "Swampscott," long gone from the southeast corner of Judson Avenue and Church Street. Her last home, from 1865, was Rest Cottage National Historic Landmark, now national headquarters of the Women's Christian Temperance Union, which owns and maintains the Victorian house built by her father. After his death, she occupied the north wing, and her mother lived in the south extension. Willard memorabilia include her furnishings, family Bible, the bicycle she learned to ride six years before her death and a unique bell cast from 1,000 opium and tobacco pipes (she apparently never said they couldn't be used for *something*). Rest Cottage stands at 1730 Chicago Ave. (Open Monday–Friday 9:00–12:00, 1:00–4:30; Saturday–Sunday by appointment; 312-864-1397; donation.)

(See WISCONSIN in this chapter; also Chapter 3, NEW YORK.)

WRIGHT, FRANK LLOYD (1867–1959). Probably the most influential architect of his time, Wright resided and built his practice in **Oak Park,** a suburb of Chicago. Wright House and Studio at 951 Chicago Ave. (at the corner of Forest Avenue) is the house he began building in 1889 and constantly remodeled and enlarged until 1911 as his family grew and his architectural style evolved. Wright used his own home as an experimental model for developing his Prairie School of building design. "The Wright home and studio," wrote Paul Goldberger in 1978, "is a laboratory—not a masterwork but a place in which a visitor can see ideas tried out without concern as to how they would fit into a coherent whole." Wright himself lived there until 1909, the year selected as the home's restoration date for public viewing. Playwright Charles MacArthur was a later occupant. The property is owned by the National Trust for Historic Preservation and operated by the Wright Home and Studio Foundation. (Open September 1–June 30, Tuesday, Thursday 1:00–2:30, Saturday–Sunday 1:00–4:00; July 1–August 31, Friday 1:00–2:30, Saturday 11:00–4:00; 312-848-1976; admission.)

Exhibits: The Frank Lloyd Wright Prairie School of Architecture National Historic District in **Oak Park** preserves 120 buildings in this style, 25 of them designed by Wright. Oak Park Visitor Center at 158 North Forest Ave. provides maps and tour information. (Open March 1–November 30, daily 10:00–5:00; 312-848-1978; free.) Wright memorabilia is displayed at the Historical Society of Oak Park and River Forest, Pleasant Street and Home Avenue. (Tours Sunday 1:00–3:00; 312-848-6755; free.)

(See WISCONSIN in this chapter; also Chapter 6, ARIZONA.)

YOUNG, BRIGHAM (1801–1877). A founder with Joseph Smith (see the entry on Smith earlier in this section) of the Mormon settlement at **Nauvoo** in 1839, the church's eventual prophet and leader of the Utah branch preached in England for a year, then returned to Nauvoo in 1841. His two-story home, built of handmake brick, has one-story wings—Young's office occupied the east wing. From there the persecuted "Saints" began their two-year trek to Utah in 1846. Young's house stands recently restored at Kimball and Main streets as part of Nauvoo Historic District National Historic Landmark.

(See Chapter 1, VERMONT; also Chapter 3, NEW YORK; also Chapter 6, UTAH.)

ZIEGFELD, FLORENZ (1869–1932). The theatrical producer whose vaudeville stagings and popular *Follies* made the chorus line of nubile femininity a standard show item, Ziegfeld was a **Chicago** native. His home from 1882, a narrow, beautifully shaped house to which he returned at intervals until his last years, stood until the 1970s at 1448 West Adams St., now a playground.

(See Chapter 2, MANHATTAN; also Chapter 3, NEW YORK; also Chapter 6, CALIFORNIA.)

INDIANA

Indiana was officially declared Indian domain, the American territory beyond the 1800 borders of the United States. The nation considered itself generous in allotting this land to the natives driven westward as well as to those who had always lived there. America has had many Indianas in that sense, but none stayed that way very long as new, white Americans phalanxed westward.

Prehistoric Moundbuilders left earthen evidence of their villages in about one-third of Indiana's counties. In 1680 the French explorer La Salle found the Miami tribe of Algonquians inhabiting what is now the South Bend area. Later the French established three early posts, the only permanent one being Vincennes in 1732. In 1763 paper possession of the territory went to Great Britain, which ceded it to the United States 20 years later. Indiana soon became part of the Northwest Territory, then formed the nucleus of the Indiana Territory created in 1800. For a brief period, Gen. William Henry Harrison ruled the half of the nation then existing under the rubric of Indiana Territory, and immediately commenced his dishonorable dealings with the native residents. Operating on instructions from the national capital, this master of carefully legitimized deceit and the *fait accompli* method of "purchase" took huge acreages of land on ludicrous terms for the purpose of white settlement. The Battle of Tippecanoe, a Harrison-manipulated action, gave a final stamp of legitimacy to the territorial acquisition. When Michigan and Illinois were created as separate territories, Indiana emerged with its present borders and entered the Union as the 19th state in 1816.

Prairie-spotted and undulant in the north, hilly in the south, Indiana's original landscape was mainly hardwood forest. Settlers who flooded in after Harrison's efficient acquisitions cleared the timber; and agriculture, primarily grain and live-stock, remains the central activity of a state which remains largely rural. The major industrial area is the northwestern Calumet section, where Hammond and Gary form a contiguous extension of Chicago's metropolitan spread. Over southern Lake Michigan, Gary's large steel industry has cast a severe pall of air pollution, which residents seem inclined to live with.

"Isn't it wonderful how many bright people come from Indiana!" someone once gushed to Indiana humorist George Ade. He replied, "Yes, and the brighter they are, the faster they come." With a few notable exceptions, Ade's facetious observation seems correct—few great Americans born in Indiana stayed there for much of their lives. Indiana has traditionally offered sparse comforts to the untypical and exceptional among us. This is still demonstrated in the state's curious treatment of its genuine historical greats—on the one hand, devoting large resources to polishing faded progeny like Paul Dresser, James Whitcomb Riley and Gene Stratton Porter—and on the other, almost studiously ignoring people like author Theodore Dreiser and scientist Alfred Kinsey, whose lives and work brought Indiana vast national significance. Indiana's own notions of what constitutes greatness among its children often bewilder visitors who come looking for Dreiser and get Dresser. The state has always cut itself shorter than it deserves in this regard.

One brilliant exception to the flight of the eminent was Eugene Debs, when he wasn't in federal prison for preaching socialism. Kinsey, though not a native, spent most of his life in Bloomington and made it, of all places, the sex education center of America. And Knute Rockne, pudgy shepherd of 105 Notre Dame football wins, exhorted as passionately in the locker room as did Billy Sunday (another adopted son) in the pulpit. In politics, Indiana has produced three presidents (both Harrisons plus Lincoln, who spent his boyhood there) and the strong contender Wendell Willkie. Carole Lombard and James Dean, screen artists, were Indiana natives—as was John Dillinger, perhaps as artistic in his own lawless way. Inventor Wilbur Wright and songwriters Hoagy Carmichael and Cole Porter also added renown to their birthplace state. Most Indiana homes of these persons plus many noted others still exist, but only a few are publicly designated or open to visitors.

BEECHER, HENRY WARD (1813–1887). The first pastorate of the eloquent preacher's career was in **Lawrenceburg,** where he and his wife occupied two bare rooms over a livery stable from 1837 to 1839. This building, razed about 1950, stood at 22 East High St.

In **Indianapolis,** both of Beecher's homes from 1839 to 1847 are gone. His last, which he helped build in 1847 at 327 East Ohio St., stood until about 1930. "I worked on it with my own hands and painted it myself," he recalled years later, "mostly after evening meetings were over . . . my wife holding the lantern for me while I painted." The site of his nostalgia is now a downtown parking lot.

(See OHIO in this chapter; also Chapter 1, CONNECTICUT; also Chapter 2, BROOKLYN.)

BIERCE, AMBROSE GWINNETT (1842–1914?). "Bitter Bierce," as he was called by his fellow journalists, grew up on his parents' 80-acre farm about three miles southwest of **Warsaw.** The presently vacant site at the southwest corner of roads 200S and 200W was the later writer's home from 1846 to about 1857.

Bierce later lived at 518 West Franklin St. in **Elkhart,** 1859–61. This was the parental home from which he enlisted in the Union army at 19. The unmarked, two-story frame house, privately owned, has been extensively altered since his residence.

(See Chapter 6, CALIFORNIA.)

CARMICHAEL, HOAGLAND HOWARD "HOAGY" (1899–1981). A **Bloomington** native, the composer was born in a house on South Grant Street, apparently no longer standing. A later boyhood home remains unmarked on South Fess Avenue just off East Third Street.

"By 1916," wrote Carmichael, "our house was the thin dark side of a double-fronted place" in **Indianapolis,** his home until 1919. This house stands privately owned at 27 North Warman Ave.

Exhibit: "A randy temple smelling of socks, wet slickers, vanilla flavoring, face powder and unread books" was how Carmichael described the university student hangout known as the Book Nook, later the Gables Restaurant, at 114 South Indiana Ave. in **Bloomington.** Pecking on an old upright piano there from 1921 to 1926, Carmichael composed some of his earliest songs, including "As Time Goes By" and "Barrelhouse

Stomp," and also began working on ideas for "Stardust." Bloomington Restorations, Inc., placed a marker honoring Carmichael on the building in 1979. The old Book Nook is now a pizza parlor. (See Chapter 6, CALIFORNIA.)

CLARK, GEORGE ROGERS (1752–1818). The frontiersman, soldier and explorer founded the settlement of **Clarksville** in 1784 across the Ohio River from Louisville, Ky. There he built a two-story cabin in 1803, operated a grist mill and declined into alcoholism until paralysis and a leg amputation in 1809 forced his removal to a Kentucky relative's care. The site of Clark's long-gone cabin—where he lived with his younger brother William in 1803 prior to William's joint command of the Lewis and Clark expedition—is marked on Harrison Avenue. The State of Indiana, which owns the plot on what was Clark's Point, vaguely foresees a cabin replica on the site.

Exhibit: In **Vincennes,** George Rogers Clark National Historic Park at 401 South Second St. commemorates the soldier's achievement in capturing the British Fort Sackville in 1779, thus opening the Northwest for U.S. expansion. The 24-acre plaza operated by the National Park Service occupies part of the fort site. Films and recorded commentary trace Clark's campaign there. (Open daily 8:30–5:00; 812-882-1776; free.)

(See Chapter 5, KENTUCKY, VIRGINIA.)

CLARK, WILLIAM (1770–1838). See GEORGE ROGERS CLARK.

(See MISSOURI, NORTH DAKOTA in this chapter; also Chapter 5, KENTUCKY, VIRGINIA; also Chapter 6, OREGON, WASHINGTON.)

DEAN, JAMES BYRON (1931–1955). A small boulder identifies the **Marion** birth site of the popular film actor and cult hero. The house with seven gables stood at the southwest corner of South McClure and East Fourth streets—now a parking lot. It was Dean's home until 1936.

Near **Jonesboro,** the farm of his uncle Marcus Winslow became the youngster's home in 1940 after his mother died. Dean grew up there, left in 1949, but returned at intervals until an auto crash ended his life in California. The farm, privately owned, is located at 7184 South 150th Road East.

(See Chapter 2, MANHATTAN; also Chapter 6, CALIFORNIA.)

DEBS, EUGENE VICTOR (1855–1926). "While there is a lower class," he said, "I am in it; while there is a criminal element, I am of it; while there is a soul in prison, I am not free." The founder of industrial unionism and five-time Socialist presidential candidate, Debs was a lifelong resident of **Terre Haute.** A stone monument marks his birth site in front of the Indiana State University Gymnasium at 457 North Fourth St. The 1885 Debs Home National Historic Landmark at 451 North Eighth St. is a large, two and one-half-story frame house standing amid the buildings of downtown Terre Haute. "Kate and Eugene didn't really need a large house," wrote biographer Ray Ginger of the childless couple, "but they built one anyway," using money from their savings and Kate Metzel Debs's inheritance. Debs himself designed the house, an odd melange of peaks and angles with a fireplace of blue tile in almost every room. This was Debs's last home from 1890. His study and library, and the guest chamber where James Whitcomb Riley often stayed (see the entry on Riley later in this section), are especially notable restorations. Original furnishings and memorabilia are maintained by the Eugene V. Debs Foundation. (Open Saturday–Thursday 2:00–5:00, or by appointment; 812-232-2163; free.)

DILLINGER, JOHN HERBERT (1903–1934?). The outlaw (who pronounced his surname with a hard *g*) lived on the 60-acre Dillinger family farm near **Mooresville** from 1920 to 1924 and there began the criminal career that he turned into a national, deadly game of cops and robbers. The Dillinger home, to which he occasionally returned between prison terms and as a fugitive, remains privately occupied at 535 State Highway 267. Sightseers are not appreciated.

Exhibit: In **Nashville,** the John Dillinger Historical Museum displays numerous items associated with the outlaw's career, including the wooden gun he used in one of his jail escapes and a death mask. Joseph Pinkston's collection also exhibits some Dillinger bank robbery plans and features the recreated Chicago funeral parlor—complete with wax corpse and music—where he supposedly lay in death. In the words of one observer, this museum "is as much a shrine as it is a study of Dillinger's extraordinary criminal personality." The museum is located at Franklin and Van Buren streets. (Open March 1–November 30, daily

10:00–6:00; December 1–February 28, call 317-342-3120; admission [free to police].)

(See ILLINOIS, WISCONSIN in this chapter; also Chapter 3, DISTRICT OF COLUMBIA.)

DREISER, THEODORE (1871–1945). **Terre Haute,** Dreiser's birthplace, still wishes he would go away, preferring to honor obscure songwriter Paul Dresser rather than his vastly better known and more accomplished younger brother. Paul Dreiser, who changed his name to Dresser, wrote "On the Banks of the Wabash," but Theodore made waves of a more significant sort with his prose and realistic fiction. According to biographer W. A. Swanberg, "Whatever small interest Terre Haute and Indiana had in TD dwindled after publication of *A Hoosier Holiday,* which spoke critically of the state, and still more of his later involvement in radical causes." The family was dirt-poor and moved five times during Dreiser's first seven years. Dreiser claimed that his birthplace stood on South Ninth and Chestnut streets, but he was notoriously inaccurate about such details. More likely, according to Swanberg, the long-gone residence stood on South Ninth near Oak Street. The carefully restored and maintained Paul Dresser Birthplace at First and Farrington streets was never a Theodore Dreiser residence, having been occupied by his parents during a more affluent period 12 years before his birth.

Dreiser also lived in **Evansville** and **Warsaw** during his boyhood, but neither home exists.

(See ILLINOIS in this chapter; also Chapter 2, BROOKLYN, MANHATTAN; also Chapter 3, NEW YORK; also Chapter 6, CALIFORNIA.)

HAMILTON, EDITH (1867–1963). The educator and scholarly popularizer of classical and Biblical history grew up in **Fort Wayne.** The "Old House," a three-story brick mansion built in 1840 by her grandfather, stood on the same property as her parents' frame "White House." Both are long gone from the present site of the Central Catholic High School at 130 East Lewis St. (at the corner of Clinton Street). Hamilton's sister Alice, who became a prominent public-health physician, told of their childhood there in her book *Exploring the Dangerous Trades* (1943).

"Veraestau," an 1810 house of frame and brick, stands one mile south of **Aurora** on State Highway 56. The Hamilton sisters occupied this family country residence at intervals during their childhood. Still privately owned, the original house was enlarged in 1913 and 1937.

(See Chapter 1, MAINE; also Chapter 2, MANHATTAN; also Chapter 3, DISTRICT OF COLUMBIA, MARYLAND.)

HARRISON, BENJAMIN (1833–1901). The 23rd U.S. president and grandson of the ninth made his home base in **Indianapolis** from 1854. Harrison occupied three dwellings, none of which survive, until 1874, when he built Harrison Home National Historic Landmark, his permanent residence at 1230 North Delaware St. This 16-room brick mansion contains original family possessions including furniture, clothing of First Lady Caroline Scott Harrison and Harrison's recreated law office. Among the rooms that remain exactly furnished are the back parlor where Harrison received official notification of his presidential nomination on July 4, 1888, and the bedroom in which he died. At this house in 1888 he conducted his "front-porch campaign" for the presidency (though the large porch seen today dates from the 1890s). Harrison Home is owned and operated by the Arthur Jordan Foundation. (Open Monday–Saturday 10:00–4:00, Sunday 12:30–4:00; 317-631-1898; admission.)

(See OHIO in this chapter; also Chapter 3, DISTRICT OF COLUMBIA.)

HARRISON, WILLIAM HENRY (1773–1841). Before becoming the ninth U.S. president in 1841, the grandfather of President Benjamin Harrison (see the entry on Benjamin Harrison above) was the first governor of the immense Indiana Territory and resided at the territorial capital in **Vincennes.** Grouseland National Historic Landmark, the house he built in 1804 and occupied until 1812, was known as the "White House of the West." Harrison had the residence on his 300-acre estate designed after the Virginia plantation houses familiar to him from his youth. The walnut grove that once surrounded the mansion— and where the Shawnee statesman Tecumseh uttered a desperate, futile defiance to the governor in 1811 that ended with the Battle of Tippecanoe—has disappeared. The Daughters of the American Revolution display Harrison furnishings and possessions. (Open January 1–March 1, daily 11:00–4:00; March 1–December 31, daily 9:00–5:00; 812-882-2096; admission.)

Exhibit: Indiana Territory State Memorial, the small frame house originally adjoining Grouseland, served as the territorial capital from 1800 to 1813. It stands relocated since 1949 at Harrison Historical Park on **Vincennes** University campus, First and Harrison streets. The desk that Harrison used in administering territorial affairs is displayed along with other original and period furnishings. The home is owned and operated by Vincennes University. (Open March 1–November 1, daily 9:00–5:00; November 2–February 28, Saturday–Sunday 9:00–5:00 or by appointment; 821-885-4364; admission.)

(See OHIO in this chapter; also Chapter 3, DISTRICT OF COLUMBIA; also Chapter 5, VIRGINIA.)

HOFFA, JAMES RIDDLE (1913–1975). The labor leader whose mobster pals apparently did worse to him than his numerous enemies (his body was never discovered after an appointment with those pals), Hoffa was born in **Brazil,** his home until 1922. The site of the A-frame Hoffa house at 103 North Vandalia St. is currently occupied by a mobile home.

(See MICHIGAN in this chapter.)

KINSEY, ALFRED CHARLES (1894–1956). Zoologist and first scientific researcher into human sexual behavior, Dr. Kinsey founded the Institute for Sex Research at Indiana University in 1942. His purely descriptive work aroused notable resistance among embarrassed scientific colleagues, who astonishingly viewed the whole subject unfit for study and better left alone. Kinsey taught, researched and resided in **Bloomington** from 1920 until his death. His first home there, in 1921, was 620 South Fess St. From 1921 to 1927, he lived at 615 South Park St. (at the corner of University Street). Kinsey built his last home in 1926 at 1320 East First St. In accordance with his maxim "Straight is the line of duty but curved the line of beauty," he designed this brick house in an L-shape to encircle a persimmon tree on his two and one-half-acre property. All three residences remain privately occupied.

(See Chapter 3, NEW JERSEY.)

LINCOLN, ABRAHAM (1809–1865). Indiana claims one of the main childhood home sites of the 16th U.S. president near **Lincoln City.** Lincoln Boyhood Home National Memorial, the reconstructed farm near Little Pigeon Creek operated by the National Park Service, stands on State Highway 162 just south of town. This was the Lincoln family home from 1816 to 1830, the site of his mother's death in 1818 and of his early self-education encouraged by his stepmother Sally Bush Lincoln. The authentically furnished log cabin and farm buildings, an exhibit shelter and visitor center detail this crucial period of Lincoln's life and interpret the surroundings of his formative years there. (Open late April–late October, daily 9:00–6:00; rest of year, daily 8:00–5:00; 812-937-4757; free.)

Exhibit: The Louis A. Warren Lincoln Library and Museum at 1300 South Clinton St. in **Fort Wayne** contains a remarkable collection of Lincoln photos, portraits, literature and miscellaneous personal items. It is operated by the Lincoln National Life Foundation. (Open May 15–November 30, Monday–Friday 8:30–4:30, Saturday 10:00–4:30; December 1–May 14, Monday–Thursday 8:00–4:30, Friday 8:00–12:30; 219-424-5421; free.)

(See ILLINOIS, MICHIGAN, OHIO in this chapter; also Chapter 3, DISTRICT OF COLUMBIA, PENNSYLVANIA; also Chapter 5, KENTUCKY, TENNESSEE.)

LOMBARD, CAROLE (1908–1942). The film actress and comedienne was born Jane Alice Peters at 704 Rockhill St. (privately owned) in **Fort Wayne.** This large house, owned by her parents until 1914, served as rescue headquarters and makeshift hospital during the catastrophic 1913 flooding of the St. Marys River.

(See Chapter 6, CALIFORNIA.)

PORTER, COLE ALBERT (1893–1964). The birthplace and childhood home of the lyricist and composer stands at 102 East Third St. (at the corner of Huntington Street) in **Peru.** Identified by a marker, this huge frame mansion of his wealthy family remains privately owned. Porter lived there until age 13, when he went away to school, but he returned for visits throughout his life.

Exhibit: Miami County Historical Museum, located in the county courthouse at U.S. Highways 24 and 31-Business in **Peru,** displays Porter mementos. (Open Monday–Friday 9:00–12:00, 1:00–4:00; 317-472-3075; free.)

COLE PORTER BIRTHPLACE. At 102 East 3rd St. in **Peru**, the songwriter lived until adolescence in the large Porter family mansion, still privately occupied in this 1980 view. *(Author's photo)*

(See Chapter 2, MANHATTAN; also Chapter 6, CALIFORNIA.)

RICKENBACKER, EDWARD VERNON "EDDIE" (1890–1973).

Exhibit: The Indianapolis Motor Speedway Hall of Fame Museum, located five miles northwest of **Indianapolis** at 4790 West 16th St., displays trophies, souvenirs and photos of Rickenbacker's early pre-aviation career as a daredevil speed driver. (Open daily, 9:00–5:00; 317-241-2501; admission.)

(See MICHIGAN, OHIO in this chapter; also Chapter 2, MANHATTAN; also Chapter 3, NEW YORK; also Chapter 5, FLORIDA; also Chapter 6, TEXAS.)

RILEY, JAMES WHITCOMB (1849–1916). Riley was the literary forerunner and counterpart of painter Norman Rockwell. His dialect verse and palaverous sentiments about rural Indiana have won lavish efforts to preserve his homes; judging by these efforts alone, he ranks only with long-faded novelist Gene Stratton Porter in Hoosier affection. The hard-drinking bachelor versifier who glorified barefoot boys "with cheek of tan" and dropped his *g*'s only in writing was born in **Greenfield**—"Griggsby's Station" in his verse—at 250 West Main St. This house is "a bit ramshackle now," wrote reporter Shirley Barnes in 1979, "with drooping shutters and sagging porch." Originally a two-room log cabin, round which Riley's father built the 10-room, white frame

house in 1850, the dwelling's original portion in which Riley was born is now its kitchen. His family lost the house after the Civil War, but Riley bought it back in 1894 and spent nostalgic summers there. Numerous family furnishings are displayed by the Riley Old Home Society. (Open May 1–November 1, Monday–Saturday 10:00–5:00, Sunday 1:00–5:00; 317-462-5462; admission.)

Riley Home National Historic Landmark at 528 Lockerbie St. in **Indianapolis** was his last home from 1893 (though he had guested there frequently before that). He never owned the house but continued to reside as a paying guest. This two-story, brick Victorian dwelling, built in 1872, is a genuine preservation, not a restoration—little has been moved or even touched since Riley died in the upstairs bedroom, where he shut himself away for hours to write and imbibe. The entire two blocks of Lockerbie Square are undergoing restoration as a historical district that, with cobblestone streets and old lamp posts, recreates the neighborhood as Riley knew it. Riley Home is operated by the James Whitcomb Riley Association. (Open Tuesday–Saturday 10:00–4:00, Sunday 12:00–4:00; 317-631-5885; admission.)

Exhibit: In **Greenfield,** the setting for much of Riley's nostalgic verse is preserved in Riley Park, U.S. Highway 40 near State Highway 9, locale of the original "Old Swimmin' Hole." (Open daily.)

ROCKNE, KNUTE KENNETH (1888–1931). The Norwegian-born Notre Dame football coach famed for his locker-room oratory, ingenious use of the forward pass and stunning record of wins, lived in **South Bend** from 1914. Probably his first home there was 1715 College St. From about 1918, when he became head football coach, until 1930, Rockne resided in a small house at 1006 St. Vincent St. His last home, from 1930, was 1417 East Wayne St., an English Tudor house where he became an avid gardener and where he lay in state after the plane crash that claimed his life. This home remained in the Rockne family until 1952. All of these houses remain privately owned.

SUNDAY, WILLIAM ASHLEY "BILLY" (1862–1935). Evangelist and temperance crusader noted for his pulpit athletics and crowd-pleasing stunts, the fundamentalist Sunday made his permanent home after 1911 in **Winona Lake.** The two-story cottage built with nine rooms in that year was occupied after 1935 by his widow, "Ma" Sunday, until her own death and was deeded by her to the Winona Lake Christian Assembly and Bible Conference. Located at 1111 Sunday Lane on the Conference grounds, Sunday's home contains original furnishings, gifts and memorabilia. (Open mid-June–mid-August, daily 1:00–5:00; admission.)

(See ILLINOIS, IOWA in this chapter; also Chapter 6, OREGON.)

WILLKIE, WENDELL LEWIS (1892–1944). The lawyer and corporation executive who became the 1940 Republican presidential candidate and far-sighted world statesman was born at **Elwood** in a house that stood at 1900 South A St. (at the corner of 19th Street), a three-story frame dwelling built by his father in 1891 and the boy's home until age two. His two later boyhood residences survive: at 2302 North A St. (at the corner of 23rd Street, 1894 to 1900); and 1836 North A St. (at the corner of 19th Street, 1900 to 1917). Willkie's father built the latter three-story frame house in 1900. Both houses remain privately owned.

(See KANSAS, OHIO in this chapter; also Chapter 2, MANHATTAN.)

WRIGHT, ORVILLE (1871–1948).
WRIGHT, WILBUR (1867–1912).
The eldest of the aviation pioneer brothers was born near **Millville** at what is now Wilbur Wright State Memorial, a five-acre park with a replica of the farmhouse occupied by the family until 1868.

The original 1867 frame farmhouse, which burned in 1884, was rebuilt on this solitary country site in 1973 by the Indiana Department of Natural Resources, which displays period furnishings. A mounted U.S. Air Force surplus fighter plane rather overwhelms the picnic area, lending the false impression that the Wrights' achievements were predominantly military-oriented; actually they skillfully managed the military establishment for their own ends quite as much as the military derived benefit from their tinkering genius. The Memorial is located on County Road 750 East, northeast of Millville. (Open March 1–October 31, daily 9:00–12:00, 1:00–5:00; November 1–February 28, Tuesday–Saturday 9:00–12:00, 1:00–5:00; 317-332-2513; admission.)

From 1881 to 1884 the family resided at three rented addresses in **Richmond,** all 19th-century frame houses that remain privately owned: 211 North 14th St., vacant in 1981, where the brothers made and flew "the best kites in Richmond"; 309 North 12th St.; and 38 South 13th St., the family residence when Wilbur Wright attended high school. Apartments now occupy the latter two dwellings.

Exhibit: Henry County Historical Museum at 614 South 14th St. in **New Castle** displays a collection of Wright memorabilia. (Open Monday–Saturday 1:00–4:30; 317-529-4028; donation.)

(See MICHIGAN, OHIO in this chapter; also Chapter 3, DISTRICT OF COLUMBIA, PENNSYLVANIA; also Chapter 5, NORTH CAROLINA.)

IOWA

According to American historian George Stimpson, "There is more controversy over the origin, meaning and correct pronunciation of *Iowa* than over any other State name." Only one other, Ohio, combines three vowels in a four-letter word. The name evolved from a condescending Sioux label for a small prairie tribe. French and Spanish phonetics confused the sound, and English spelling followed the French pronunciation, *Ioway.* Lewis and Clark spelled it four different ways in their journals. The Sioux root word apparently meant either "sleepy or drowsy one" or "putter to sleep." Despite this anaesthetic etymology, Iowans have never been a sleepy folk.

Pioneers found Iowa topsoil almost two feet deep, a thickness now depleted to an average depth of eight inches. Today barely a tenth of one percent remains of the original tall grass prairie that once covered the state, but these portions are carefully preserved. Until John Deere's heavy plow came on the scene in 1837, most farming was confined to the wooded river valleys; but about 94 percent of Iowa's present surface is farmland, a higher proportion than for any other state. "If you're talking corn and beans, you're talking Iowa," say those citizens best qualified to know. From the development of hybrid corn during the 1920s, early promoted by native Iowan and eventual vice president Henry A. Wallace, Iowa's most profitable energies have been devoted to raising corn, rotated with nitrogen-restorative soybeans. Today the state leads the nation in the production not only of corn, but of corn-eating hogs. Accordingly, agribusiness and food processing are Iowa's primary industries.

The earliest known Iowans were the Moundbuilders, who left hundreds of earthworks in the northeastern part of the state. Near Marquette, Effigy Mounds National Monument preserves these people's land record, dating from about 600 BC. In Iowa, as in so many Mississippi valley states, the first pale faces were those of Marquette and Jolliet; on the basis of their brief riverbank view in 1673, France claimed the territory as part of Louisiana, ignoring an earlier Spanish claim based on the explorations of Columbus, who never sailed quite this far. The first waves of white settlers came into this section of Louisiana Territory beginning about 1830 and established the towns of Dubuque and Davenport. Attached to Michigan Territory in 1834, Iowa became part of Wisconsin Territory in 1836; by 1838 Iowa Territory had been established to include Minnesota and parts of the Dakotas. Iowa became the 29th U.S. state in 1846. Most members of the numerous plains tribes had unwillingly vacated by 1851, and German immigrants soon established the communal Amana Colonies near Iowa City.

Today visitors discover that Iowa isn't as flat as they pictured; its subtle tilts and swells, and sometimes outright hills, produce a landscape hardly as level as parts of Kansas, Nebraska or the Dakotas. Despite the massive rural acreage, most Iowans are urban residents. The largest city is the capital, Des Moines, also a major insurance center. Now a joint stock corporation, the Amana Society produces kitchen equipment and a variety of food and household items. The University of Iowa's Writer's Workshop has made Iowa City one of the nation's best-known cultural centers.

Diverse Iowa natives included the first U.S. president born west of the Mississippi, Herbert Hoover; regionalist painter Grant Wood; New Dealers Henry Wallace and Harry Hopkins; musicians Bix Beiderbecke and Glenn Miller; and entertainers Buffalo Bill, John Wayne, Lillian Russell—and, of course, Billy Sunday. Others who lived in the state for extensive periods included Mark Twain, Amelia Earhart and Wyatt Earp. One of the state's most unlikely residents was the Czech composer Antonin Dvořák, who found inspiration in Spillville for some of his best-known music. The homes of most nationally well-known Iowans still exist, though many remain privately owned. Iowa's low priority on tourism probably accounts for its moderate interest in maintaining historic homes for the public. Except where individual family farmsteads are concerned, Iowans are not greatly concerned with heritage; obviously where so much depends on the immediate conditions of weather and crops, "who lived where" ranks far below "who lives how" in general topics of concern. The land itself and naturally conservative living patterns, however, have been conducive to preservation regardless of official policy. Unlike some states, Iowa has no subtle, unstated program of destruction for its own compulsively "progressive" sake.

BEIDERBECKE, LEON BISMARCK "BIX" (1903–1931). The legendary jazz cornetist's birthplace and permanent family home stands privately owned at 1934 Grand Ave. in **Davenport.** From there the "young man with a horn" went to perform in road bands, and there he often returned to vacation or recuperate—the last time only shortly before alcoholism finished him at age 28. Proud of the recordings he made with Paul Whiteman's band, he sent a copy of each home for his parents—only to discover one day that all of them lay neatly stacked and unopened in a closet.

Exhibit: A Bix Beiderbecke Memorial Jazz Festival is held each July in **Davenport,** featuring concerts, art fairs and drama. For information, write to Bix Beiderbecke Memorial Society, 2225 West 17th St., Davenport, IA, 52804.

(See Chapter 2, MANHATTAN, QUEENS; also Chapter 5, LOUISIANA.)

BLOOMER, AMELIA JENKS (1818–1894). The last home from 1855 of the feminist and dress-reform advocate whose new cut of trousers came to be labeled "bloomers" (she had ceased wearing them by 1860) was 123 Fourth St. in **Council Bluffs.** The house, which sat amid aster beds and an apple orchard, was razed about 1950. Its site is now occupied by a real estate agency.

(See Chapter 3, NEW YORK.)

BROWN, JOHN (1800–1859). At **Tabor,** Brown used the Todd House on Park Street as a secret headquarters for his Kansas border raids in 1856. He stored arms in the cellar that was also a stop on the Underground Railroad. This house, built by Rev. John Todd of native lumber in 1853, has been restored with period furnishings by the Tabor Historical Society. (Open in summer by appointment.)

(See KANSAS, OHIO in this chapter; also Chapter 1, CONNECTICUT; also Chapter 3, MARYLAND, NEW YORK, PENNSYLVANIA, WEST VIRGINIA.)

BUFFALO BILL. See WILLIAM FREDERICK CODY.

CLEMENS, SAMUEL LANGHORNE "MARK TWAIN" (1835–1910). In **Keokuk,** the author-humorist worked as a printer for his brother Orion from 1854 to 1856 and boarded at the 1850 Ivins House, Second and Main streets. While residing there, he wrote his first articles for the *Saturday Post* under the name Thomas Jefferson Snodgrass and listed himself in the first city directory as "antiquarian." Ironically, a home for senior citizens now occupies the site of this building, later known as the Hawkeye Hotel, which stood for about a century after Clemens's stay.

Exhibit: The **Keokuk** Public Library at 210 North Fifth St. displays a small collection of Mark Twain memorabilia. (319-524-1483.)

(See MISSOURI in this chapter; also Chapter 1, CONNECTICUT; also Chapter 2, BRONX, MANHATTAN; also Chapter 3, NEW YORK; also Chapter 6, CALIFORNIA, NEVADA.)

CODY, WILLIAM FREDERICK "BUFFALO BILL" (1846–1917). **LeClaire** was the scout and showman's birthplace, but the actual frame house he occupied until 1851 was moved to Cody, Wyo.,

in 1934. The site of the 1840 homestead is marked at 1034 North Cody Road.

His boyhood residence, Cody Homestead, stands three miles southwest of **McCausland** off U.S. Highway 61 (follow the signs). Cody's father built this house in 1851, and the youngster lived there until 1853, when the family moved to Kansas. The homestead, with a later frame addition, is operated by the Society of Colonial Dames and contains period furnishings. (Open May 1–October 31, daily 9:00–6:00; 319-225-2981; donation.)

Exhibit: The Buffalo Bill Museum at 206 North River Road in **LeClaire** contains Cody memorabilia and artifacts. (Open May 15–October 15 daily, 9:00–5:00; November 1–April 30, Saturday–Sunday 10:00–5:00; 319-289-5580; admission.) (See KANSAS, NEBRASKA in this chapter; also Chapter 6, COLORADO, WYOMING.)

DE FOREST, LEE (1873–1961). In **Council Bluffs,** the parsonage birthplace of the electronics scientist whose 1906 audion tube created billion-dollar industries and millions of jobs—but who was himself declared a bankrupt failure in 1936—stood at a heretofore undetermined location on Fourth Street near Fifth Avenue. Various local sources have given the address of his home to age three as 543 and 523.

(See NEBRASKA in this chapter; also Chapter 5, ALABAMA; also Chapter 6, CALIFORNIA.)

DVOŘÁK, ANTONIN (1841–1904). In 1893 the Czech composer brought his family to the Bohemian settlement of **Spillville** for the summer and there composed his *American Quartet* (1893). The two-story, eight-room house where he resided dates from 1865. Built of sandstone blocks with a brick front, it now houses the Bily Clock Exhibit, an unusual collection of hand-carved time pieces. This museum, operated by the town of Spillville on State Highway 325 in the town center, contains no memorabilia of the composer. (Open May 1–October 31, 8:00–5:30; March, November, Saturday–Sunday 10:00–4:00; April daily 10:00–4:00; other times by appointment; 319-562-3569; admission.)

(See Chapter 2, MANHATTAN.)

EARHART, AMELIA MARY (1898–1937?). The aviator spent five years of her girlhood in **Des Moines.** Of the four homes occupied by her family during this period, the two standing remain privately owned; she lived at 1443 8th St. in 1908 and 1909, and at 1530 8th St., a four-family apartment house, in 1910.

(See KANSAS, MINNESOTA in this chapter; also Chapter 1, MASSACHUSETTS; also Chapter 3, NEW YORK.)

EARP, WYATT (1848–1929). Frontier gunslinger and gambler whose exploits hardly resembled what Hollywood and television made of them, Earp spent his boyhood years in **Pella**. The two-story brick home at 507 Franklin St., where he lived with his family from 1850 to 1864, dates from 1849 and is part of Pella Historical Village, operated by the Pella Historical Society. Period furnishings and a Dutch pioneer museum occupy the house. (Open Monday–Friday 9:00–11:30, 1:00–4:30; 515-628-4311; admission.)

(See ILLINOIS, KANSAS in this chapter; also Chapter 6, ARIZONA, CALIFORNIA.)

FERBER, EDNA (1887–1968). **Ottumwa** was the novelist's childhood home from 1890 to 1897. She loathed the town for its religious bigotry; "I don't think there was a day when I wasn't called a sheeny," she remembered. When she revisited Ottumwa in 1933, however, she was inclined to forgive and forget. The two-story dwelling at 410 North Wapello Ave. dates from about 1887 and has been converted to private apartments. The exterior remains basically unaltered.

(See MICHIGAN, WISCONSIN in this chapter; also Chapter 1, CONNECTICUT; also Chapter 2, MANHATTAN.)

GARLAND, HAMLIN (1860–1940). One of the author's boyhood homes stands identified by a county historical marker in Burr Oak Township near **Osage**. Extensive remodeling and additions have altered the small frame prairie cottage he occupied with his parents from 1869 to 1876. Because of these structural changes, the National Register of Historic Places has rejected formal listing of the privately owned house. Its current address is given only as Postal Route 3.

(See ILLINOIS, SOUTH DAKOTA, WISCONSIN in this chapter; also Chapter 2, MANHATTAN; also Chapter 6, CALIFORNIA.)

HOOVER, HERBERT CLARK (1874–1964). The humanitarian and 31st U.S. president, and the first president born west of the Mississippi, Hoover was born in **West Branch** at what is now Herbert Hoover National Historic Site, operated by the National Park Service. He lived there until 1884, then moved as an orphan to Oregon. The restored, two-room frame cottage, built about 1870, displays some of the original Hoover furnishings. There is also a replica of his father's blacksmith shop and a Quaker meetinghouse where his mother, Hulda Minthorn Hoover, often spoke. The Hoover complex is located at Parkside Drive and Main Street. (Open daily, 8:00–5:00; 319-643-2541; free.)

Exhibit: Hoover Presidential Library and Museum at 234 South Downey St. in **West Branch** has been the central repository since 1966 for Hoover papers and items relating to his administration. Personal memorabilia and films are also displayed. As might be expected, staffers are partial to the president whom they believe "got a bum rap" from history.* The library-museum is operated by the National Archives and Records Service. (Open Memorial Day–Labor Day, Monday–Saturday 9:00–6:00, Sunday 10:00–6:00; Labor Day–Memorial Day, Monday–Saturday 9:00–5:00, Sunday 12:00–5:00; 319-643-5301; admission.)

(See Chapter 2, MANHATTAN; also Chapter 3, DISTRICT OF COLUMBIA; also Chapter 5, VIRGINIA; also Chapter 6, CALIFORNIA, OREGON.)

HOPKINS, HARRY LLOYD (1890–1946). The social worker who became one of the New Deal's most prominent figures, a cabinet member and close advisor to President Franklin D. Roosevelt, was born in **Sioux City** at 512 10th St., his home until age one. The two-story clapboard house, dating from the 1880s, has been sided and converted to private apartments.

At **Grinnell**, Hopkin's boyhood home from about 1901 to 1909 stands privately owned at 1033 Elm St. This frame house dates from about 1880.

(See Chapter 3, DISTRICT OF COLUMBIA.)

---

*In 1981, Professor John Whiteclay Chambers, a Columbia University historian, expressed concern over the tendency of tax-funded presidential museums (seven at present count) to distort the historical record. "I'm struck by the fact that in the Hoover Library it's as if the Great Depression never occurred," he stated. "In the [Lyndon Baines] Johnson Library, the Vietnam War is relegated to a couple of display cases on an upper floor."

LEWIS, JOHN LLEWELLYN (1880–1969). Leonine in manner as well as looks, the miner who became one of the nation's most powerful labor leaders was born in Iowa's coal country. Neither his **Cleveland** "company home" birthplace nor boyhood homes in **Beacon, Lucas** and **Des Moines** are traceable. From infancy to age 17, wrote biographers Melvyn Dubofsky and Warren Van Tine in 1977, "his life seems almost a closed book" as far as identifying specific residences. Lewis himself, reticent about his early years, offered scant information to the friendliest of his inquirers.

(See ILLINOIS in this chapter; also Chapter 5, FLORIDA, VIRGINIA.)

MILLER, GLENN (1904–1944). In **Clarinda,** the popular bandleader was born at 601 16th St. (privately owned), his parental home until 1909.

Exhibit: The Glenn Miller music festival is held each May in **Clarinda.** A museum displaying memorabilia is also planned. (Call 712-542-2166 for information.)

(See MISSOURI, NEBRASKA in this chapter; also Chapter 2, QUEENS; also Chapter 3, NEW JERSEY; also Chapter 6, COLORADO.)

RUSSELL, LILLIAN (1861–1922). This singer-actress, the gay-nineties ideal of blooming beauty but also an early feminist, was born Helen Louise Leonard in **Clinton.** Her birthplace was actually a shack located on a north-south alley in the block bounded by First and Second streets and Third and Fourth avenues. Later the family moved to a larger house at 408 Seventh Ave., her home until age two. Both residences are long gone, and their sites remain unmarked.

(See Chapter 2, MANHATTAN; also Chapter 3, PENNSYLVANIA.)

SUNDAY, WILLIAM ASHLEY "BILLY" (1862–1935). An ex-baseball player, Sunday became one of the first "pulpit jocks." One observer estimated that Sunday "walked, pranced, ran, slid, staggered and jumped" one and one-half miles during a single sermon; for news photographers, he liked to pose for buffoon "action shots." Sunday (his real name) revived the camp meeting as a distinctively American entertainment, and his strenuous body language and colorful fulminations against saloons and bootleggers captivated thousands. Sources disagree on the site of the two-room log cabin near **Ames** in which

he was born. The 1938 Iowa *American Guide* stated that the cabin was then being used as a smokehouse on a farm three and one-half miles east on U.S. Highway 30; but earlier local accounts placed the site three miles south and one mile west of Ames off U.S. Highway 69. Present Ames sources have been unable to verify either location as the precise site. In 1868 the youngster whose father died as a soldier in the Civil War went to live with his grandparents at the Martin Cory farm, his home until 1874. The Cory farm included the present area south of 16th Street, east of South Duff Avenue, and north of the State Forest Nursery; the farmhouse stood at the present location of an auto dealership at the intersection of U.S. Highways 30 (Bypass) and 69.

From 1874 the youngster resided for two years with his older brother at two Soldiers' Orphans Homes: in **Glenwood,** at the 1866 building that is now the Glenwood State Hospital School at 711 South Vine St.; and, until 1876, in **Davenport** at what is now the Annie Wittenmyer Home, 2800 Eastern Ave., the 1867 site of deserted army barracks. Both places are still state-operated institutions.

In **Nevada,** the John Scott home, a two-story frame house dating from about 1860, stands privately owned at 711 10th St. Scott, former lieutenant governor of Iowa, hired Sunday to take care of his Shetland ponies while the orphaned youngster completed high school, and Sunday lived in the Scott home from about 1877 to 1881.

(See ILLINOIS, INDIANA in this chapter; also Chapter 6, OREGON.)

TWAIN, MARK. See SAMUEL LANGHORNE CLEMENS.

WALLACE, HENRY AGARD (1888–1965). Four miles southeast of Greenfield off State Highway 25 near **Orient** stands the ancestral homestead and birthplace, "Catalpa," of the prominent agriculturist, vice president and 1948 Progressive presidential candidate. The small, two-story, clapboard farmhouse, built in the 1870s, was his home until age four. It remains privately owned.

His last Iowa home is the private residence at 3821 John Lynde Road in **Des Moines,** the two-story house built by his father in 1912 and Wallace's summer residence until the late 1940s. He performed numerous home gardening experiments on this property.

(See Chapter 3, DISTRICT OF COLUMBIA, NEW YORK.)

WAYNE, JOHN (1907–1979). Rugged actor in macho film roles who achieved the status of real-life hero and patriotic symbol for many Americans, Wayne was born Marion Michael Morrison—"a very severe name to inflict on a boy," he stated—in **Winterset,** where his father operated a pharmacy. His cottage birthplace at 224 South Second St. has been recently acquired by the City of Winterset, which displays Wayne memorabilia in the house. In 1981 the parlor and kitchen had been restored to their 1907 appearance, and other rooms will be exhibited as restoration proceeds. Wayne resided in this rented dwelling, which dates from about 1880, until 1910, when the family left for California. (Open April 1–October 31, daily 9:00–3:30; November 1–March 31, Monday, Wednesday, Friday 9:00–3:30; 515-462-1185; donation.)

(See Chapter 6, CALIFORNIA.)

WILDER, LAURA INGALLS (1867–1957). One of the several childhood homes of the children's author stands restored in **Burr Oak** as the Laura Ingalls Wilder Park and Museum. The building now posted as the "Little Hotel in the Village" was the two-story Masters Hotel, located on the covered wagon route that is now U.S. Highway 52, a hostel managed by her parents from 1876 to 1878. "For Laura," wrote biographer Donald Zochert, "Burr Oak was a crossroads of the spirit. . . . where gently and imperceptibly she crossed the line between childhood and adolescence." The saltbox structure is privately operated by trustees and contains period furnishings. Picnic facilities are available in the park. (Open May 1–September 30, Monday–Friday 10:00–5:00, Sunday 12:00–5:00; other times by appointment; 319-735-5436; admission.)

(See KANSAS, MINNESOTA, MISSOURI, SOUTH DAKOTA, WISCONSIN in this chapter.)

WOOD, GRANT (1892–1942). An Iowa native and resident for most of his life, the "Painter of the Soil" was an important launcher of the regionalist movement in American art.

Wood's home for most of his life was **Cedar Rapids,** where he occupied four dwellings that remain. From 1903 to 1914 his family home was 318 14th St. NE. He lived at 1532 B Ave. NE from 1914 to 1916; and from 1918 to 1925 at 3178 Grove Court, a stucco house he built. Probably Wood's best-known residence—the place where he painted his most important works, including the lugubrious classic "American Gothic" (1930)—was the coach house behind the John B. Turner and Son Mortuary at 800 Second Ave. SE. Wood designed his own studio-lodging there, dubbing the address "5 Turner Alley." It remained his home for the decade from 1925 to 1935. He completely remodeled it after a 1932 fire damaged the interior. All of Wood's Cedar Rapids houses remain privately owned.

In **Iowa City,** Wood's last home from 1935 was the two-story, 1858 brick mansion—whose builder, said Wood, "didn't stint on the brick"—at 1142 East Court St. He restored this house with 12 rooms and high ceilings to its original form. Wood "was frequently to be seen in overalls," wrote John Drury, "working around the grounds of his mid-Victorian residence, tending rose or lilac bushes, planting pine trees, or making flagstone walks." Identified by marker, this house remains privately owned.

KANSAS

Named after the Kansa Indians, a Sioux tribe inhabiting the Kansas River valley when French traders and explorers penetrated there in the 18th century, Kansas was spoken "Kansaw" until at least 1820. Early whites from Mexico had seen Kansas as members of Coronado's 1541 expedition, which sought the fabled seven cities of Cibola, indicating this region as *Quivira* on its maps. Juan de Padilla, a Spanish priest left by Coronado, was murdered near Lyons by the natives, thus becoming America's first Christian martyr. After the area of Kansas became U.S. territory in 1803, it served as a kind of dumping ground for eastern native tribes displaced by the General Removal Act of 1830. Forest peoples of ancient lineage strained to fit their place-centered cultures to unfamiliar plains, ruler-straight horizons and a tremendous bowl of sky. But as white officials and soldiers well knew, Indians removed from their native grounds always became, in some vital spiritual sense, dead Indians.

White settlement proceeded mainly from Missouri, Ohio, Kentucky and the Middle Atlantic states. Both the Santa Fe and Oregon trails passed through Kansas prairie, but not until

Kansas itself became an immigrant destination did severe trouble begin. Kansas Territory, organized under the 1854 Kansas-Nebraska Act, soon rent itself into a hotbed of fanatic violence, "bleeding Kansas," over the slavery issue. Its civil insurrections and guerrilla warfare between pro- and antislavery settlers gave the nation an anguished preview of the Civil War. Vengeful abolitionist John Brown found the territory ripe for exercising his homicidal psychosis, and he righteously quoted Scripture while slaughtering innocents. In line with majority "Jayhawker" opinion, Kansas entered the Union as a free state in 1861 and contributed proportionately more soldiers to the Union army than any other state. Kansas continued as a guerrilla battleground during the war; in 1863 William Quantrill and his Confederate band virtually wiped out Lawrence in one of the most brutal, gratuitous atrocities of any American war.

After the war railroad construction made Abilene and Dodge City two of the most important "cow town" terminals for longhorn cattle drives from Texas. Drifters like Wyatt Earp found sporadic niches as "peace officers" in such places, and from these dusty Kansas towns grew the national mythology of the "western," so large a part of our popular culture. Forts Leavenworth and Riley, which became important staging areas for subduing native resistance to "manifest destiny," remain as functional military installations. On private land south of Osborne is located the historic geodetic center of the United States, base point of all surveys and mapping of North America.

Kansas borders repeat on a large scale the rectangular patterns of its checkerboard farm landscape. Kansas is the nation's leading grain producer, and never far from where one stands in Kansas are "Kansas towers," the concrete grain elevators that rise like monoliths from the plains. Kansas concentrates its manufacturing on food processing and aircraft building. Topeka has been its capital since statehood, but Kansas City, founded by transplanted Wyandot Indians in 1859 and famed for its stockyards and meat-packing, is the largest city. It is contiguous with its counterpart, Kansas City, Mo.; the Missouri River marks the official dividing line between states.

Kansas natives have included some of the nation's most active and accomplished people: two "birds," aviator Amelia Earhart and musician Charlie Parker; baseball pitcher Walter Johnson; and writers Damon Runyon and William Allen White. Carry Nation, Buffalo Bill Cody and Dwight D. Eisenhower numbered among non-native residents who lived there for extensive periods. Visitors may see many notable Kansan homes and enter two, those of President Eisenhower and the hatchet-swinging Nation. Only White, editor of the small but highly influential *Emporia Gazette*, made his lifelong home in Kansas—and by so doing made the state a national center in more ways than one.

BROWN, JOHN (1800–1859). In **Osawatomie,** John Brown Memorial Park at 10th and West Main streets, operated by the Kansas State Historical Society, contains the 1854 log cabin owned by his brother-in-law and used by Brown in 1855 and 1856 during the border warfare which included the Potawatomie Massacre, in which he and seven others murdered five suspected proslavery settlers. The cabin, containing period furnishings plus a cherrywood table used by Brown, was dismantled and moved there from its original site on Osawatomie Road in 1910. A stone pergola has sheltered it since 1928. (Open Tuesday–Saturday 10:00–5:00, Sunday 1:00–5:00; 913-755-4384; free.)

Exhibit: The Kansas State Historical Society Museum in the Memorial Building at 10th and Jackson streets in **Topeka** contains Brown memorabilia from his violent stay in Kansas. (Open Monday–Saturday 8:00–5:00, Sunday 1:00–5:00; 913-296-3251; free.)

(See IOWA, OHIO in this chapter; also Chapter 1, CONNECTICUT; also Chapter 3, MARYLAND, NEW YORK, PENNSYLVANIA, WEST VIRGINIA.)

BUFFALO BILL. See WILLIAM FREDERICK CODY.

CARVER, GEORGE WASHINGTON (1864?– 1943). Two miles south of **Beeler,** the black agricultural genius occupied a homestead for two years (1886–88) after being refused admittance to white colleges. The site is marked on State Highway 96.

(See MISSOURI in this chapter; also Chapter 5, ALABAMA.)

CODY, WILLIAM FREDERICK "BUFFALO BILL"

(1846–1917). The army scout, buffalo slayer, showman and all-around frontier hero as created by writer Ned Buntline came to **Leavenworth** with his parents in 1853. His father took a homestead and built a log cabin in Salt Creek Valley, Cody's home until 1861. From there, the youngster joined his first wagon train west and began his frontier career. A private dwelling stands on what is apparently part of the Cody house stone foundation at the base of Cody Hill, north of town on U.S. Highway 73. The site remains unmarked.

Cody achieved his "Buffalo Bill" moniker in 1867 and 1868 at Fort Hays, where he was hired to supply 12 buffalo per day to 1,200 railroad tracklayers. He earned his name by killing, it is said, 4,280 buffalo in 18 months. Occupying 7,000 acres, Fort Hays was abandoned in 1889. The site contains restored fort buildings at Fort Hays Frontier Historical Park on U.S. Highway 183A south of **Hays**. Exhibits on military and pioneer history are displayed by the State of Kansas. (Open May 30–September 1, Tuesday–Saturday 9:00–9:00, Sunday–Monday 1:00–5:00; September 2–May 29, Tuesday–Saturday 10:00–5:00, Sunday–Monday 1:00–5:00; 913-625-6812; free.)

(See IOWA, NEBRASKA in this chapter; also Chapter 6, COLORADO, WYOMING.)

CUSTER, GEORGE ARMSTRONG (1839–1876). At Fort Riley Military Reservation, nine miles southwest of **Manhattan** on State Highway 18, Custer's residence is privately occupied, a limestone house built in 1855. Fort Riley was headquarters of the Indian-fighting Seventh Cavalry, which Custer flamboyantly commanded until impetuously leading himself and his regiment to death at Little Bighorn. He and his wife resided at these quarters in 1866 and 1867.

(See MICHIGAN, NORTH DAKOTA, OHIO, SOUTH DAKOTA in this chapter; also Chapter 5, KENTUCKY; also Chapter 6, MONTANA.)

EARHART, AMELIA MARY (1898–1937?). The aviator's birthplace and frequent residence until 1908 stands privately owned at 223 North Terrace (at the corner of Sante Fe Street) in **Atchison**. She was born in the southwest bedroom of this two-story, frame dwelling, her grandparents' home. Dolls were not for this child—she preferred football, shooting and raising insects and tadpoles. Her "unladylike" behavior in preferring to jump fences rather than stay on sidewalks like a "good

little girl" gave her grandmother fits. Unlike most women of her generation, however, Earhart never did acquiesce to sidewalks; though she eventually married, wifehood and domesticity for her ranked second to piloting across mountains and oceans.

In **Kansas City,** the simultaneous family home and summer residence until 1908 is located at 1021 Ann Ave., a building now consisting of five private apartments. Her maternal grandfather gave this house to the family; despite (or perhaps because of) such largesse, her father became an alcoholic burden on the family.

Exhibit: **Atchison** County Museum at 409 Atchison St. displays a collection of Earhart memorabilia including clothing and some of her craft work. (Open spring and fall, Saturday–Sunday 2:00–5:00, or by appointment; 913-367-3046; free.)

(See IOWA, MINNESOTA in this chapter ; also Chapter 1, MASSACHUSETTS; also Chapter 3, NEW YORK.)

EARP, WYATT (1848–1929). A gambler and part-time lawman who liked to brawl and kept generally unpleasant company despite the "good guy" reputation later concocted by Hollywood, Earp hung out in **Wichita** during 1875 and 1876. In **Dodge City,** where he served two terms as assistant marshal from 1876 to 1879, his probable residence was the two-story, 38-room Dodge House hotel. This long building stood until about 1920 at the corner of Front Street and Central Avenue, today a parking lot.

Exhibit: Both Wichita and Dodge City have recreated portions of their old cow towns into highly commercialized, Hollywood-set streets and buildings. As tourist attractions, these sights offer reasonable facsimiles of film and television versions of history. Suffice to say that more gunfire was staged for tourists there in 1979 than was heard in all of Kansas 100 years earlier. Hombres like Earp, of course, wouldn't think much of Dodge City's imitation Boot Hill cemetery, which is actually the remains of a Rotarian Club hoax staged in 1930—the real Boot Hill lies under City Hall. For visitors who can imagine lots of grime, manure, tobacco juice and ripe body odors in these impossibly clean and varnished atmospheres, a visit may offer something more than carnival hype—for the physical reconstruction work itself is highly accurate.

Historic **Wichita** Cow Town, operated by trustees, is a 37-building complex reproducing the 1870s, located at 1871 Sim Park Drive. Included there is a jail used by Earp when he was marshal. (Open March 1–November 1 daily, 10:00–5:00; November 2–February 28, Monday–Friday 10:00–5:00; 316-264-0671; admission.)

Historic Front Street in **Dodge City,** also privately operated, is a two-block reconstruction beginning at 500 West Wyatt Earp Blvd. "Marshal Dillon," if not old con-man Earp himself, would certainly recognize the place. (Open May 30–August 22, daily 8:00–10:00; August 23–May 29, daily 9:00–5:00; 316-227-8188; admission.)

(See ILLINOIS, IOWA in this chapter; also Chapter 6, CALIFORNIA.)

EISENHOWER, DWIGHT DAVID (1890–1969). The World War II general and 34th U.S. president grew up in **Abilene,** his home from 1891 to 1911. The two-story frame house occupied by the family from 1898 stands as part of Eisenhower Center, a 15-acre plot at 201 Southeast Fourth St.—known as "Devil's Addition" during Abilene's cow-town days, the place where all of the town's prostitutes were sequestered. Today the Eisenhower complex includes the Presidential Library, Museum and "Place of Meditation," the chapel containing his tomb. His boyhood home, dating from 1870, contains the original furnishings from those early years. Eisenhower returned to visit his mother at intervals until her death there in 1946. Eisenhower Center, visited by about 150,000 persons annually, is operated by the National Archives and Records Service. (Open daily 9:00–4:45; 913-263-4751; free.) The family's first home in Abilene, from 1891 to 1898, was a small rented house at an unmarked site on Southeast Second Street.

Exhibit: The Eisenhower Museum within the Center of **Abilene** is the main repository for items and memorabilia associated with the military and political careers of "Ike," as he liked to be called. Included there are his command staff car, some of his paintings, golf clubs, gifts, awards and numerous other displays. (Hours and phone same as above; admission.)

(See MICHIGAN in this chapter; also Chapter 2, MANHATTAN; also Chapter 3, DISTRICT OF COLUMBIA, MARYLAND, PENNSYLVANIA; also Chapter 5, GEORGIA, VIRGINIA; also Chapter 6, COLORADO, TEXAS.)

HUGHES, LANGSTON (1902–1967). The widely traveled black poet who wrote the classic "The Negro Speaks of Rivers" (1921) spent part of his boyhood in **Lawrence.** He resided from about 1914 to 1916 at the James Reed house, a frame dwelling which stood until 1969 at 731 New York St.

(See MISSOURI in this chapter; also Chapter 2, MANHATTAN.)

JOHNSON, WALTER PERRY (1887–1946). "Big Train," hard-throwing pitcher of the Washington Senators for 21 years, built a house on his farm near **Coffeyville** in 1920, raised Holstein cattle and chickens and spent autumns and winters there until 1930, when his wife died and he sold the place. The two-story frame house remains privately owned at 1701 East Eighth St.

Exhibit: The **Coffeyville** Historical Museum, also known as the Dalton Museum, is operated by trustees at 113 East Eighth St. and displays memorabilia and items related to the Kansas farm boy who showed 'em how to pitch. (Open daily, 8:00–4:00; admission.)

(See Chapter 3, MARYLAND, NEW YORK.)

MacARTHUR, DOUGLAS (1880–1964). From 1908 to 1911 the career army officer noted for his strutting ambition and leadership of Pacific forces in World War II and the Korean War was a lieutenant stationed at **Fort Leavenworth.** His 1834 residence at 12–14 Sumner Place is the oldest building on the fort and possibly the oldest extant dwelling in Kansas. Andrew J. Reeder had lived in this house of log and stone as the first territorial governor in 1854, and it remains privately occupied. According to Fort Leavenworth's Public Affairs Officer, "The story is that it is called the 'Rookery' because it once served as a bachelor officers' quarters and the men who lived there were 'wild birds.' " Fort Leavenworth is open to public visitation year-round.

(See Chapter 2, MANHATTAN; also Chapter 3, MARYLAND, NEW YORK; also Chapter 5, ARKANSAS, VIRGINIA; also Chapter 6, NEW MEXICO, TEXAS.)

NATION, CARRY AMELIA MOORE (1846–1911). Hatchet-wielding temperance activist who reasoned that saloons selling liquor illegally were outside legal protection, Nation invaded and smashed the strongholds of demon rum across the country, leaving a trail of broken glass, cringing bartenders, souvenir hatchets and bemused observers. She began her crusade in Kansas, making shambles of barrooms in Kiowa, Topeka and Wichita. Nor did **Medicine Lodge,** her home from 1889 to 1902, escape her righteous wrath—she dried up that seven-tavern town in 1899—in fact, began her crusade there with a stout umbrella after undergoing a "baptism of the Holy Ghost" during a severe electrical storm. She used the basement of her house for prayers, meditation and reading. The Carry Nation Home, operated by the Women's Christian Temperance Union, stands at 211 West Fowler Ave. (at the corner of Oak Street), a one-story brick dwelling built in 1884. Now a temperance museum, it displays furniture and memorabilia—including, of course, the inevitable hatchet. (Open daily 9:00–6:00; 316-886-5234; admission.)

Exhibit: The Kansas State Historical Society at Memorial Building, 10th and Jackson streets in **Topeka,** displays relics of Carry Nation's "hatchetations," including miscellaneous saloon wreckage, glass shards, hatchets and war clubs. (Open Monday–Saturday 8:00–5:00, Sunday 1:00–5:00; 913-296-3251; free.)

(See MISSOURI in this chapter; also Chapter 5, ARKANSAS, KENTUCKY; also Chapter 6, TEXAS.)

PARKER, CHARLES CHRISTOPHER "CHARLIE" (1920–1955). "Bird," the saxophone jazz master, was a **Kansas City** native born at 852 Freeman St. No marker identifies the site of the long-gone house.

(See Chapter 2, MANHATTAN.)

QUANTRILL, WILLIAM CLARKE (1837–1865). The so-called "bloodiest man in American history"—at least until My Lai and Cambodia—scavenged the troubled border area of Kansas as a guerrilla raider with no particular allegiance to either side—at least until 1862, when he formally joined the Confederates. He took a land claim in 1857 at what is now the northeast edge of **Rantoul.**

While teaching school in 1857 and 1858 in a log classroom on the present site of Stockwell School, located north of Osawatomie in the southeastern corner of Stanton Township, he boarded at a home that stood on the west side of the Marais des Cygnes bridge just west of **Stanton.** Acording to a 1973 report, "In the unfinished second-story room, Quantrill carved his

name on one of the rafters. The name could be seen until the house was rebuilt recently."

The man who later led the massacre and destruction of **Lawrence** boarded there at intervals from 1858 to 1861, using the name Charlie Hart, in the Durfee House hotel. This 27-room frame structure stood until the 1880s on the southwest corner of Pinckney and New Hampshire streets. During the infamous guerrilla raid of August 21, 1863, he used the hotel as headquarters and prisoner area. The unmarked site is now a city parking lot.

Exhibit: "Miami County, Heart of Bleeding Kansas" is the theme of the 36-mile Quantrill's Trail of 1863, a series of road markers extending from the Franklin County line to the Missouri border. The beginning point is one mile east of State Highway 33, via county road, and one and one-half miles south of Interstate Highway 35, **Wellsville** exit. The trail and campsites are sponsored by the Miami County Historical Society, Paola, Kan.

(See OHIO in this chapter.)

RUNYON, DAMON (1880–1946). Journalist and fictional chronicler of New York City night life, Runyon was native of a **Manhattan** far removed from the haunts of his *Guys and Dolls* (1931). The birthplace of Alfred Damon Runyan—he later dropped his first name and changed the spelling of his surname—stands at 400 Osage St. (at the corner of Fourth Street), a two-story, white frame house built about 1870, his home to age two. A kitchen, bathroom and porches have been added to the five rooms of the original dwelling. Runyon's birth date on the outside marker—as in most of his synoptic biographies—is wrongly listed as 1884. The house remains privately owned.

(See Chapter 2, MANHATTAN; also Chapter 5, FLORIDA; also Chapter 6, COLORADO.)

WHITE, WILLIAM ALLEN (1868–1944). "The Sage of **Emporia,**" one of the nation's most influential and respected newspapermen, was a lifelong Kansan. None of his earliest dwellings remain, but "Red Rocks," White's mansion of Colorado sandstone at 927 Exchange St., is now the privately owned White House National Historic Landmark. White redesigned this house when he acquired it in 1899 and occupied it until his death. He described the house as "covered with towers and turrets and fibroid tumors and minarets, and all useless ornaments that an architect in 1885 could think of." After a damaging fire in 1920, architect Frank Lloyd Wright remodeled the ground floor.

Exhibit: The *Emporia Gazette*, White's newspaper, displays mementos of the editor-publisher in its building at 517 Merchant St. in **Emporia.** (Open Monday–Friday 8:00–5:00, Saturday 8:00–12:00; 316-342-4800; free.)

(See Chapter 6, COLORADO.)

WILDER, LAURA INGALLS (1867–1957). There really was a "Little House on the Prairie," and Laura Ingalls lived there in 1869 and 1870. The family arrived in a covered wagon, settled mistakenly on Osage tribal lands and moved on when it looked like they would be dispossessed (they could have stayed, for the land was opened to white settlement six months later). Wilder wrote about living there in her second *Little House* book in 1935. A 1977 cabin reconstruction, operated by private trustees, stands on the site 13 miles southwest of **Independence** (follow the signs on U.S. Highway 75). (Open May 15–September 15, Monday–Saturday 10:00–5:00, Sunday 1:00–5:00; donation.)

(See IOWA, MINNESOTA, MISSOURI, SOUTH DAKOTA, WISCONSIN in this chapter.)

WILLKIE, WENDELL LEWIS (1892–1944). The 1940 presidential candidate and world statesman taught high school for five semesters from 1913 to 1915 in **Coffeyville,** where he roomed at 611 Elm St. This house was razed in 1961 from a lot currently owned by the local Episcopal Church.

Exhibit: A display relating to Willkie's stay in **Coffeyville** may be seen at the Coffeyville Historical Museum, 113 East Eighth St. (Open daily 8:00–4:00; admission.)

(See INDIANA, OHIO in this chapter; also Chapter 2, MANHATTAN.)

MICHIGAN

First used by French explorers for the Great Lake on the western side, the name apparently meant either "big water" or "large clearing" in the native Algonquian tongue. The state consists of two jutting peninsulas bordered by four Great Lakes; loosely translated, the Latin state motto advises "If you seek a nice peninsula, look no further." Lower and upper peninsulas are divided by the Straits of Mackinac (pronounced "Mackinaw"), which also separate lakes Huron and Michigan. Those bordering waters, providing more than 3,000 miles of coastline, are lakes only in name and freshwater—anywhere outside North America, such basins would show on the maps as seas.

The upper peninsula ("U.P.," in local parlance) was the scene of the earliest French missionary activity as well as the first area of settlement. Father Jacques Marquette of that front-line order, the Jesuits, established the first outpost at Sault Ste. Marie in 1668. The military garrison of Detroit, founded in 1701, and the 1715 Fort Michilimackinac at today's Mackinaw City were the only white settlements for the next century. Except for Ottawa Chief Pontiac's year-long siege of Detroit in 1763 and 1764 and a 1763 massacre at Fort Michilimackinac, Michigan escaped most of the Indian conflicts that ravaged bordering states. British troops, who had replaced French caretakers in 1763, held the wilderness bastions of Mackinac and Detroit until 1796, long after the American Revolution had forced their general evacuation from the country.

The great westward movement of the early 19th century passed Michigan by, partly because of bad publicity from surveyors. Sandy soil, swamps and heavy forests were distinct second choices for farmland—but this was incomplete information, as settlers began to discover in the 1830s. Michigan offered fertile land, particularly in the south, where black muck lay in glacial lake beds and large "oak openings" interspersed with hardwood forest. The discovery of copper ore brought a tide of European immigrants to the U.P. in the 1840s; and the pine forests that stretched virtually unbroken from Saginaw north brought a generation of loggers. As part of that immense holding, formerly Virginia's, included in the Northwest Territory, Michigan achieved its own territorial status in 1805. Statehood followed in 1837, when Congress gave the small but controversial "Toledo Strip" along the southern border to Ohio and awarded Michigan the entire U.P., then a part of Wisconsin Territory, in compensation. Lansing became permanent capital a decade later.

Michigan today is classified as a leading manufacturing state; but in contrast to the earlier period, its modern industrial centers mainly occupy the southern third. Detroit, hub of the nation's auto industry, is also a powerful headquarters of organized labor. Nationally the state ranks second in both copper and iron mining; fruit, dairy cattle and cereals also number among its major industries. More than 11,000 inland lakes plus the Great Lakes and northern wilderness areas focus a large part of the economy on year-round recreation and tourism. The U.P. is linked to the mitten-shaped lower state only by the five-mile Mackinac Bridge, whereas it shares a border of over one hundred miles with northern Wisconsin—a fact that periodically gives rise to the suggestion that the U.P should revert to Wisconsin. More vocal is an occasional petition for a separate, modestly named state of Superior.

As much as anyone, auto industrialist Henry Ford, who permanently resided in the Detroit area, created the modern age of transportation; yet, philosophically, Ford was anything but an "apostle of change." Despite his clanging assembly lines, the very center of planned obsolescence, Ford wanted to preserve—selectively, of course. He brought homes of his own American heroes—Edison, especially, but also those of William H. McGuffey, Noah Webster and others—into his museum, Greenfield Village in Dearborn. This large complex, probably the nation's foremost collection of 19th-century Americana, represents Ford's own bootstrap view of history. He cherished the familiar McGuffey maxims of honesty, hard work and an implied "pie in the sky" for smiling through today; and he erected what he called "my Smithsonian institute" to demonstrate these values. Ford never really comprehended that his own accomplishments in providing cheap auto transportation that radically transformed American lifestyles had done much to sever the nation forever from the simple sufficiency of his own values.

Ford was one of Michigan's few notable natives who made lifelong careers in the state. Other natives included Edna Ferber, Theodore Roethke, Thomas E. Dewey and Charles A. Lindbergh; but all arrived at eminence elsewhere. Noted people who lived in Michigan for extensive periods included Gen. George A. Custer, Sojourner Truth, Carl Sandburg, Malcolm X, Walter Reuther, Thomas Edison and Ernest Hemingway. Of those homes listed that remain extant, however, none stand open to the public except at Greenfield Village. Compared to other regional states, Michigan has expended little economic or scholarly effort to interpret the homes of its noted

progeny and make them accessible. Some of the earliest sites associated with French explorers Marquette and La Salle might well offer valuable archaeological data, but tentative searches in this direction ended more than a decade ago at St. Ignace. This state, with its enormous scholarly resources, owes itself more attention to its rich past.

BURBANK, LUTHER (1849–1926). The horticultural genius never lived in Michigan, but his Massachusetts birthplace—at least the original parts of it—stands in Greenfield Village at **Dearborn.** The two-story, frame, L-shaped dwelling on South Dearborn Road and Burbank Street, Burbank's home until 1870, became two wings of a brick dwelling after Burbank left. When this house was demolished, Henry Ford salvaged the wings and rejoined them in 1937. Behind the house stands Burbank's small garden office, moved there in 1929 from his experimental gardens in Santa Rosa, Calif. His oak rolltop desk may be seen inside. (See the entries on Ford and the Edison Institute later in this section).

(See Chapter 1, MASSACHUSETTS; also Chapter 6, CALIFORNIA.)

CUSTER, GEORGE ARMSTRONG (1839–1876). Flamboyant, blond-tressed soldier and Indian-killer whose military prowess was finally outmatched by Crazy Horse, Custer made his permanent home at **Monroe** from age 13 to his death. His family home, dating from about 1840, stood until 1911 at the northwest corner of Monroe and Second streets. Now sided with aluminum at 703 Cass St. (at the corner of West Seventh Street), it remains privately owned. The Monroe Street site, to which Custer and his wife returned at intervals between military assignments, is now the locale of the Monroe County Historical Museum (see below), formerly the city post office.

Exhibit: **Monroe** County Historical Museum at 126 South Monroe St. displays Custer exhibits. (Open May 1–October 31, Tuesday–Sunday 10:00–5:00; November 1–April 30, Tuesday–Sunday 1:00–5:00; 313-243-7137; free.) The main archive of Custeriana is the Lawrence A. Frost Collection, available by research appointment at the Monroe County Library, 3700 South Custer Road. (Open Monday–Friday 9:00–4:00; 313-241-5277; free.)

(See KANSAS, NORTH DAKOTA, OHIO, SOUTH DAKOTA in this chapter; also Chapter

5, KENTUCKY; also Chapter 6, MONTANA.)

DEWEY, THOMAS EDMUND (1902–1971). Loser in the presidential races of 1944 and 1948, the lawyer and New York governor was a native of **Owosso.** His birthplace, an apartment over his grandfather's grocery store, stands at 323 West Main St., presently a furniture and appliance center. The upper rooms of this structure, built before 1890 by Dewey's grandfather, remain privately occupied. In 1915 after various moves, the family bought the Victorian house at 421 West Oliver St., and Dewey lived there until 1919. This dwelling, identified by marker, is also privately owned.

(See Chapter 2, MANHATTAN; also Chapter 3, NEW YORK.)

EDISON INSTITUTE. Henry Ford built the 260-acre complex best known as the Henry Ford Museum and Greenfield Village in **Dearborn,** a suburb of Detroit. Though he had once opined history as "bunk," few persons did more to collect and preserve tangible Americana—the objects, crafts, tools, machines and buildings of our national past—than this quirky industrialist whose own auto manufacturing career created a revolution in American living patterns. What Ford meant by history as "bunk," it developed, was "book history" as learned in school by date and rote. He wanted to show a past that one could lay hands on, see, experience. "Our country has depended more on harrows than on guns or speeches," he elaborated. "I thought that a history which excluded harrows and all the rest of daily life is bunk and I think so yet." He launched his massive collecting program in 1920. The museum and village were dedicated as The Edison Institute, in honor of his admired friend Thomas Edison in 1929; and until 1944 the additions of historic buildings to the complex came rapidly. Homes gathered in Greenfield Village include those of the following: Luther Burbank, Thomas Alva Edison, Henry Ford, Robert Lee Frost, William Holmes McGuffey, Noah Webster and the Wright brothers (see the entries on each of these people in this section). Ford insisted on precise historical accuracy in all house restoration projects. A fascinating account of how his workmen dismantled, transported and reconstructed some of the nation's most historic homes is Geoffrey C. Upward's *A Home for Our Heritage*

(1979). The Edison Institute continues to grow, though at a slower pace. One of the most recent additions is "The President's Car," displaying five vehicles used by nine U.S. presidents (see the entries on Dwight David Eisenhower, Lyndon Baines Johnson, John Fitzgerald Kennedy, Franklin Delano Roosevelt and Harry S. Truman later in this section). Located at 20900 Oakwood Blvd., Edison Institute requires a minimum of two days to be viewed with any degree of thoroughness. (Open June 15–Labor Day, daily 9:00–6:00; Labor Day–June 14, Monday–Friday 9:00–5:00, Saturday–Sunday 9:00–6:00; 313-271-1620; admission.)

EDISON, THOMAS ALVA (1847–1931). The inventor's boyhood home, a large, two-story frame house built in 1840, stood in **Port Huron** overlooking Fort Gratiot and Lake Huron. The Edison family lived there from 1854 to 1863. After the house burned in 1867, railroad tracks covered the site for many years. Intensive excavations by the Port Huron Archaeological Project in 1979 and 1980 pinpointed the exact site of the dwelling on the southwest corner of Thomas and Erie streets, an unmarked vacant lot. Portions of old walls, floors and many small artifacts were recovered. Edison began experimenting with chemistry and electricity there and printed his own newspaper, which he distributed on the trains that ran between Port Huron and Detroit.

The Edison Homestead on South Dearborn Road in Greenfield Village, **Dearborn,** is his grandparents' 1816 clapboard farmhouse that stood in Vienna, Ontario. Edison's parents were married in this house in 1828, and the boy spent many summers there. (See the entry on the Edison Institute above.)

Exhibit: In 1928 Henry Ford (see the entry on Ford later in this section) decided to restore Edison's six-building "invention factory" and move it from Menlo Park, N.J., where Edison worked from 1876 to 1886 and had developed the incandescent bulb, among many other devices. Reconstruction at Edison Institute, **Dearborn,** was meticulous, using many of the original materials from the Menlo Park site, even to the directional orientation and placement of buildings. Edison himself was present at the 1929 dedication and pronounced the complex faithful in every detail—except, he said, for the missing clutter and dirt. His furnishings, laboratory equipment, even soil and stumps from the site, were exactly resituated at Middlesex Avenue and Christie Street. Edison's winter laboratory building from Fort Myers, Fla., which he used from 1886 to 1926, was also re-erected at Monmouth and Christie streets in 1928 and hosted the Institute's first dedication ceremony. The restored Building 11 from the inventor's West Orange, N.J., complex was added to the Menlo Park compound in 1941 and stands at the corner of Middlesex Avenue and Washington Boulevard.

(See OHIO in this chapter; also Chapter 3, NEW JERSEY; also Chapter 5, FLORIDA, KENTUCKY.)

EISENHOWER, DWIGHT DAVID (1890–1969). See the entry on Harry S. Truman.

(See KANSAS in this chapter; also Chapter 2, MANHATTAN; also Chapter 3, DISTRICT OF COLUMBIA, MARYLAND, PENNSYLVANIA; also Chapter 5, GEORGIA, VIRGINIA; also Chapter 6, COLORADO, TEXAS.)

FERBER, EDNA (1887–1968). The novelist's birthplace, a house built by her merchant father and her home for a year, was moved sometime after 1910 from 817 South Park St. in **Kalamazoo.** According to City Archivist Don McMahon, the modified house may stand at another location, so far unidentified, on the same street. A more recent apartment building occupies the unmarked original site.

(See IOWA, WISCONSIN in this chapter; also Chapter 1, CONNECTICUT; also Chapter 2, MANHATTAN.)

FORD, HENRY (1863–1947). Machinist, assembly line innovator and powerful industrialist, Ford revolutionized American transportation and culture with his mass-produced Model T automobile. A paradoxical man of vast mechanical skill and business sense—but with odd, profound lapses of deeply opinionated ignorance and prejudice—he fought any changes in manufacturing and employment practices that were not of his own bold innovation. Ford was born on his parents' 40-acre farm, now a marked site on Greenfield and Ford roads in **Dearborn.** In 1944, he moved the two-story clapboard farmhouse, his birthplace and home until 1879, to Greenfield Village, where it stands at Main Street and Michigan Avenue. Inside this 11-room house, which dates from 1860, are his infant crib, the foot-pedal organ he liked to poke at and other simple

furnishings of the family. Ford even had the yard soil of his homestead sifted so that artisans could recreate the dishes used by his family from samples of broken fragments. Also in Dearborn, Ford's 1,369-acre estate and permanent home from 1916, now Fair Lane National Historic Landmark, stands at 4901 Evergreen Road. The two-story, 56-room limestone mansion he built with outbuildings and extensive landscaping has been owned by the University of Michigan since 1956 and operates as a conference center for the Dearborn campus. Ford died there by candlelight in a wood-heated room—duplicating the conditions of his birth—during a power outage on the estate. (Open Sunday; call 313-593-5590 for admission information.)

From 1891 to 1915 Ford occupied some 11 addresses in **Detroit** (See Name Index and Gazetteer). Most of his residences are long gone, but his brick mansion at what is now 140 Edison Ave. (at the corner of Second Avenue) remains standing and privately owned. Ford resided there from 1907 to 1915, just before he moved back to Dearborn. He built his first auto in a workshop behind his house at 58 Bagley Ave., where he lived from 1893 to 1897. The house had disappeared by 1930.

Exhibit: The Henry Ford Museum in **Dearborn** contains seven rooms devoted to the industrialist, depicting his life and accomplishments through letters, photos, gifts and artifacts. Included are Ford's 1896 Quadricycle, his first auto, which he last drove around the streets of Greenfield Village in 1946; and the 15-millionth Model T, made in 1927. In 1933, Ford reconstructed the 1896 workshop that stood behind his 58 Bagley Ave. home in Detroit. The brick shed in which he built the Quadricycle was reproduced with characteristic fidelity to detail and contents at Main Street and Bagley Avenue in Greenfield Village. (See the entry on the Edison Institute earlier in this section.)

(See Chapter 5, FLORIDA, GEORGIA.)

FROST, ROBERT LEE (1874–1963). The New England poet taught at the University of Michigan in **Ann Arbor** for two durations. The large Victorian house he occupied in 1921 and 1922 at 1523 Washtenaw Ave. is gone. So is the small, white frame dwelling at 1223 Pontiac Road, where he lived from 1924 to 1926, presently the site of a 1940 private dwelling.

HENRY FORD AT FAIR LANE, 1917. The auto industrialist and his wife (at right) had just moved into their new **Dearborn** mansion when they hosted these two unidentified visitors in the garden. Thirty years later, Ford died there. Fair Lane is now used as a university conference center.
(Courtesy Henry Ford Museum, The Edison Institute)

The latter house, however, a six-room, Greek Revival structure built in 1830, was moved to Edison Institute in **Dearborn** (see the entry on the Edison Institute earlier in this section), where it is known as Ann Arbor House. Located on South Dearborn Road, it is furnished with 19th-century items.

(See Chapter 1, MASSACHUSETTS, NEW HAMPSHIRE, VERMONT; also Chapter 5, FLORIDA; also Chapter 6, CALIFORNIA.)

GRANT, ULYSSES SIMPSON (1822–1885). The young lieutenant who would command the Union army during the Civil War and become the 18th U.S. president was stationed at **Detroit** on return from duty in the Mexican War. He and his wife occupied a two-story clapboard house at 1369 East Fort St. in 1849 and 1850. This dwelling, which dates from about 1840, was donated to the state and moved to the Michigan State Fairgrounds in 1936. A marker identifies the restored structure in the center of the fairgrounds at State Fair and Woodward avenues. It is open only during the annual Michigan State Fair week in August, when visitors may enter and view period furnishings. (Call 313-833-1805 for scheduling information.)

(See ILLINOIS, MISSOURI, OHIO in this chapter; also Chapter 2, MANHATTAN; also Chapter 3, DISTRICT OF COLUMBIA, NEW JERSEY, NEW YORK; also Chapter 5, VIRGINIA; also Chapter 6, WASHINGTON.)

HEMINGWAY, ERNEST MILLER (1899–1961). Some Hemingway students maintain that the author's best works were his early "Nick Adams" stories set in northern Michigan, where he spent all of his summers as a boy and young man. Now known as Windemere National Historic Landmark, the one-story, frame cottage built by Hemingway's father in 1900 stands privately owned on the north shore of **Walloon Lake,** Lake Grove Road near Petoskey. Hemingway returned there to recover from wounds received as an ambulance driver in World War I, writing all fall and half the winter of 1919–20.

In **Petoskey,** the setting for his first novel, *The Torrents of Spring* (1926), he briefly occupied a room at 602 State St. (privately owned) in 1919. After 1920 Hemingway returned to this area only once—quietly and briefly in 1947. Hunting and fishing were his main occupations in what has since become one of the state's major resort areas.

(See ILLINOIS in this chapter; also Chapter 5, FLORIDA; also Chapter 6, IDAHO.)

HOFFA, JAMES RIDDLE (1913–1975). The teamster union leader's **Detroit** home, a two-story brick bungalow at 16154 Robson St. that he occupied from the 1950s, remains privately owned.

Hoffa's summer home also stands privately owned at 1614 Ray Court in the Avalon Beach subdivision on Big Square Lake, **Lake Orion.** He added the kitchen wing to the two and one-half-story house built in 1950 and placed stone statuary on his seven landscaped acres. On July 30, 1975, Hoffa left this house for an appointment with mobster pals, who apparently made him an "offer he couldn't refuse." Last seen alive at the Machus Red Fox Restaurant in Bloomfield Township, Hoffa never returned.

(See INDIANA in this chapter.)

HOUDINI, HARRY (1874–1926).
Exhibit: The American Museum of Magic at 107 East Michigan Ave. in **Marshall** displays Robert Lund's collection of the showman's escape equipment and other apparatus used in his performances. Lund says he knows Houdini's secrets of releasing himself from chains, padlocks, underwater coffins and the like—but "will not expose how he did it. Magic loses its charm and mystery once you know how it's done. It's really just very simple." (Open March 1–October 31, Tuesday–Sunday 1:00–5:00; other times by appointment; 616-781-7666; admission.)

(See WISCONSIN in this chapter; also Chapter 2, MANHATTAN.)

JOHNSON, LYNDON BAINES (1908–1973). See the entry on John Fitzgerald Kennedy below.

(See Chapter 3, DISTRICT OF COLUMBIA, MARYLAND; also Chapter 6, TEXAS.)

KENNEDY, JOHN FITZGERALD (1917–1963).
Exhibit: The 1961 Lincoln Continental convertible in which the 35th U.S. president was slain while riding in a Dallas, Tex., motorcade is displayed in "The President's Car" exhibit at Edison Institute, **Dearborn.** Four subsequent presidents, including Kennedy's successor, Lyndon B. Johnson, also used the car until it was retired from White House service in 1977. Following Kennedy's assassination, this car was rebuilt with a permanent roof and armor plating that increased its weight by almost a ton. Another auto earlier used by Kennedy is also displayed there (see the entries on the Edison Institute and Harry S. Truman in this section).

(See Chapter 1, MASSACHUSETTS, RHODE ISLAND; also Chapter 2, BRONX; also Chapter 3, DISTRICT OF COLUMBIA, MARYLAND, NEW YORK; also Chapter 5, FLORIDA, VIRGINIA; also Chapter 6, TEXAS.)

LARDNER, RINGGOLD WILMER "RING" (1885–1933). The author's birthplace overlooks the St. Joseph River in **Niles** at 519 Bond St., his home until 1905. This 14-room, one and one-half-story dwelling, built of frame and stucco about 1850 by the town banker and mayor, was occupied by the wealthy Lardner family from 1875 to 1940. It remains privately owned.

(See ILLINOIS in this chapter; also Chapter 3, NEW YORK.)

LA SALLE, ROBERT CAVELIER, SIEUR DE (1643–1687). French explorer of the Mississippi River and claimer of the vast Louisiana Territory for Louis XIV, La Salle established a preparatory base at the mouth of the St. Joseph River on Lake Michigan in 1679. He built a crude log stockade and cabins on a forested bluff overlooking the river channel and named it Fort Miami, after the French name of the river. La Salle was there for eight brief periods through 1682; from this spot in 1680, he departed on his epochal overland journey to Canada for supplies when his ship, the fabled *Griffon,* failed to arrive at the fort. The site of Fort Miami, which might well yield interesting archaeological data, is marked at Lake Boulevard and Ship Street in **St. Joseph.**

(See ILLINOIS in this chapter; also Chapter 6, TEXAS.)

LINCOLN, ABRAHAM (1809–1865).
Exhibit: In Edison Institute, **Dearborn,** stands the 1840 Logan County Courthouse where the future 16th U.S. president practiced law early in his career. Henry Ford found this building being used in 1929 as a private residence in Postville, Ill. He bought it and had it shipped to Dearborn before suddenly interested townspeople could stop him (see the entries on the Edison Institute and Ford earlier in this section). The main item of interest in the restored building is the encased, dilapidated chair in which Lincoln was sitting when shot by John Wilkes Booth at Ford's Theater in Washington, D.C. "Lincoln Courthouse" stands on Middlesex Avenue across from Greenfield Village Green.

(See ILLINOIS, INDIANA, OHIO in this chapter; also Chapter 3, DISTRICT OF COLUMBIA, PENNSYLVANIA; also Chapter 5, KENTUCKY, TENNESSEE.)

LINDBERGH, CHARLES AUGUSTUS (1902–1974). Aviator, isolationist spokesman, conservationist and national hero, Lindbergh was born in **Detroit.** The three-story brownstone built by his grandfather in 1895 stood at 1120 West Forest Ave. until 1973, when—after years of neglect, vandalism and 1972 fire damage—it was demolished. Lindbergh lived there only briefly as an infant, though he returned at intervals during boyhood visits to his grandparents. The loss of this house, its sturdy walls still capable of reconstruction after the fire, marked a severe failure of preservationist interest and effort.

Exhibit: The Henry Ford Museum, **Dearborn,** displays an extensive collection of Lindbergh memorabilia, including his 1919 Excelsior motorcycle, a Franklin Airman Sedan that he drove, a replica of his plane "The Spirit of St. Louis" (used in the 1957 film of that title), a travel trailer, photos, letters and autographed books. (See the entry on the Edison Institute earlier in this section.)

(See MINNESOTA, MISSOURI in this chapter; also Chapter 1, CONNECTICUT; also Chapter 3, DISTRICT OF COLUMBIA, NEW JERSEY, NEW YORK; also Chapter 6, HAWAII.)

McGUFFEY, WILLIAM HOLMES (1800–1873). The log-cabin birthplace of the educator and author whose *Reader* series became standard American school texts for almost a century stands in Edison Institute, **Dearborn,** moved there from Washington, Pa., in 1934. There was some controversy over the exact location of the McGuffey homestead in Pennsylvania, but Henry Ford bought what his researchers believed to be the authentic two-story cabin of McGuffey's grandfather, the child's home until age two. Small as it is, this structure was supposedly the largest home in the area where McGuffey was born. McGuffey descendants donated family items including the home-made furniture seen there (see the entries on Ford and the Edison Institute earlier in this section).

Exhibit: To Henry Ford, McGuffey's homespun adages represented the ideal in elementary education; and the philosophy and intention of Ford's **Dearborn** museum project was based largely on McGuffey precepts. One of the largest world collections of McGuffey *Eclectic Readers,* assembled by Ford, is displayed in the Henry Ford Museum. (See the entry on the Edison Institute earlier in this section).

(See OHIO in this chapter; also Chapter 3, PENNSYLVANIA; also Chapter 5, VIRGINIA.)

MALCOLM X (1925–1965). A marker at 4705 South Logan St. identifies the site of the **Lansing** house where Malcolm Little lived with his parents during the 1930s. Local records do not support the Black Muslim leader's statement that white men set fire to the house and destroyed it, though there was a fire. A private apartment building now occupies this site.

(See NEBRASKA in this chapter; also Chapter 2, QUEENS.)

MARQUETTE, JACQUES (1637–1675). The site of the Mission of Sainte Marie de Sault, which the French Jesuit missionary and explorer established in 1668, is located in Brady Park at the foot of Bingham Avenue in **Sault Ste. Marie.** Marquette stayed there for only one winter en route to a mission assignment further west. There he first met Louis Jolliet, with whom he would explore much of the Mississippi River in 1673.

In 1671 Marquette founded the St. Ignace Mission, and from there in 1673 departed on his epochal journey with Jolliet, never to return alive. The officially designated St. Ignace Mission National Historic Landmark is a small waterfront area on the Straits of Mackinac called Marquette Park, located in downtown **St. Ignace** at Marquette and State streets. Abandoned by the French in 1705, the site underwent archaeological investigations in 1877 and 1971, but these failed to establish its authenticity, and controversy remains. One respected researcher, Catherine L. Stebbins, believes that Great Lakes water levels were six feet higher in 1670, ruling out Marquette Park, and that the mission site lies near Castle Rock, a cliff formation located four miles north on Castle Rock Road.

(See ILLINOIS, WISCONSIN in this chapter.)

MASTERS, EDGAR LEE (1869–1950). The lawyer and poet best known for his *Spoon River Anthology* (1915) bought a 12-acre farm near **Spring Lake** in 1917 and made many improvements on the property, but occupied it only that summer. It remained in his family, however, until 1926. Although the original house burned in 1946, the present, privately owned property, a rebuilt house at 18067 Fruitport Road, retains Masters' fireplace chimneys, his ice house and a concrete sea wall he built on the edge of Spring Lake. His book *Toward the Gulf* (1918) includes many poems written there that relate to this area.

(See ILLINOIS in this chapter; also Chapter 2, MANHATTAN.)

REUTHER, WALTER PHILIP (1907–1970). Prominent union organizer and leader of the United Auto Workers from 1946 to his death, Reuther lived in **Detroit** from 1927 to 1952. From 1941 until 1948 he owned and occupied 20101 Appoline St., a six-room bungalow of brick and frame that hosted numerous organizational meetings and strategy sessions in its cellar workshop. There, on April 20, 1948, Reuther was seriously wounded when a hidden gunman fired through the kitchen window. The house remains privately owned—as does his three-story brick dwelling (1948–52) at 2292 Longfellow St., where he installed watchdogs and bullet-proof windows.

In **Rochester,** Reuther designed and built his summer home on Paint Creek in 1949, exercising his shattered right arm as he did most of the construction himself. As a result, he said, he "got a good house and a good hand—all for the same price." Reuther made this four-acre tract his permanent home in 1952. Having altered the course of a trout stream to surround the house, he quipped that he was "the only union leader who lives behind a moat." The property remains privately owned on Ellamae Street.

(See Chapter 3, WEST VIRGINIA.)

RICKENBACKER, EDWARD VERNON "EDDIE" (1890–1973). Rickenbacker, World War I air ace and businessman, lived in **Detroit** from 1922 to 1932 and there organized the Rickenbacker Motor Company. After it folded in 1926, he worked for the Cadillac division of General Motors. He occupied several apartment buildings, most of which survive. These include Indian Village Manor at 8120 East Jefferson Ave. (1923 to 1925); and the Whittier Towers, 415 Burns Drive (at the corner of Jefferson Avenue, 1927–28).

(See INDIANA, OHIO in this chapter; also Chapter 2, MANHATTAN; also Chapter 3, NEW YORK; also Chapter 5, FLORIDA; also Chapter 6, TEXAS.)

ROETHKE, THEODORE (1908–1963). The poet and teacher, a **Saginaw** native, was born in an uncle's home at 1624 Gratiot Ave. Both this house and Roethke's boyhood home, a white frame dwelling built in 1910 by his father at 1805 Gratiot, remain privately owned. The latter house stands on what was formerly his family's greenhouse acreage, the basis of the plant imagery that suffused much of Roethke's poetry. He lived there until 1925 and returned at intervals thereafter. A private real estate development, Roethke Court, now occupies this land. It is said that when Roethke died, no book of his was available in Saginaw.

(See Chapter 1, VERMONT; also Chapter 3, PENNSYLVANIA; also Chapter 6, WASHINGTON.)

ROOSEVELT, FRANKLIN DELANO (1882–1945).
Exhibit: "The President's Car" exhibit at Edison Institute, **Dearborn,** displays the 1939 Lincoln "Sunshine Special" sedan used by the 32nd U.S. president—and, until 1950, by his successor, Harry S. Truman (see the entries on the Edison Institute and Truman in this section). This was the first car ever custom-built as a presidential parade vehicle. During World War II (1942), it was armor-plated and equipped with other security features.

(See Chapter 1, MAINE; also Chapter 2, MANHATTAN; also Chapter 3, DISTRICT OF COLUMBIA, MARYLAND, NEW YORK; also Chapter 5, GEORGIA.)

SAARINEN, EERO (1910–1961).
SAARINEN, ELIEL (1873–1950).
The Finnish-born father and son, architects who worked together, lived in **Bloomfield Hills,** where the elder Saarinen headed Cranbrook Academy of Art, in 1925. He designed and completed "Saarinen House," his permanent home on Academy Way, in 1929—now the main building of Cranbrook Academy. His son lived there until he bought his own Victorian home at 1045 Vaughan Road, which dates from 1901; and this was Eero Saarinen's last home from the 1930s. It remains privately owned.

SANDBURG, CARL (1878–1967). "Chikaming Goat Farm," the poet-folklorist's Lake Michigan estate, stands on Birchwood Court in **Harbert.** Sandburg built this two and one-half-story, large frame house with enclosed porches and more than 75 windows in 1928, and this was his permanent home until 1945. While his wife raised goats, he wrote *The People, Yes* (1936) and finished his epochal Lincoln biography. "The Sandburgs never seemed to worry about appearances," wrote one biographer. Yet, realizing that a certain farm-boy scruffiness added to his Whitmanesque appeal, Sandburg did cultivate a mild disorder of person and surroundings. The Harbert property remains privately owned.

(See ILLINOIS, WISCONSIN in this chapter; also Chapter 5, NORTH CAROLINA.)

SITTING BULL (1831–1890).
Exhibit: Artwork and clothing of the Dakota Sioux chief, who outfought the U.S. Army but was finally beaten by tribal famine and treachery, is displayed in the Fort St. Joseph Museum, operated by the Niles Historical Commission at 508 East Main St. in **Niles.** (Open Tuesday—Saturday 10:00–4:00, Sunday 1:00–4:00; 616-683-4702; free.)

(See SOUTH DAKOTA in this chapter; also Chapter 6, MONTANA.)

TRUMAN, HARRY S. (1884–1972).
Exhibit: The 33rd U.S. president's official White House vehicle, which he used from 1950 to the end of his term in 1953, is displayed in "The

President's Car" exhibit at Edison Institute, **Dearborn.** This 1950 Lincoln Cosmopolitan convertible lacked the security features of the earlier auto that Truman (and Franklin Delano Roosevelt) had used; Truman, Dwight D. Eisenhower and John Fitzgerald Kennedy, all of whom used this same car for presidential motorcades, were more concerned with public visibility than protection (see the entries on the Edison Institute, Roosevelt and Kennedy earlier in this section). It was Eisenhower who conceived of the transparent "bubble top" dome for this convertible, enabling him to be seen in bad weather.

(See MISSOURI in this chapter; also Chapter 3, DISTRICT OF COLUMBIA; also Chapter 5, FLORIDA.)

TRUTH, SOJOURNER (1797?–1883). Abolitionist, feminist and magnetic orator, the uneducated ex-slave electrified audiences wherever she spoke. Her last home from about 1867 stood in **Battle Creek** at 38 College St., a barn she bought and remodeled. Until about 1880, however, she was rarely there, using her home only as a base from which to travel and lecture widely. She died there.

(See Chapter 1, MASSACHUSETTS; also Chapter 3, NEW YORK.)

WEBSTER, NOAH (1758–1843). In 1936 Henry Ford bought the dictionary author's two-story, white frame mansion from Yale University, which had planned to demolish it. Ford had it dismantled into numbered pieces at New Haven, shipped to Edison Institute, **Dearborn,** and meticulously reconstructed on South Dearborn Road. This was Webster's last home from 1823, the place where he finished his *American Dictionary* (1828). The rooms and furnishings are preserved as he knew them; Webster's upstairs study is especially noteworthy with its fireplace, globes, table and books. The building, which dates from 1822 and 1823, functioned as a live-in home economics laboratory for high school girls at Greenfield Village through the 1940s and was opened to the public in 1962 (see the entries on Ford and the Edison Institute earlier in this section).

(See Chapter 1, CONNECTICUT, MASSACHUSETTS.)

WRIGHT, ORVILLE (1871–1948).

WRIGHT, WILBUR (1867–1912).

The two-story frame house where the aviation pioneer brothers lived for almost 40 years was removed from Dayton, Ohio, to Edison Institute, **Dearborn,** in 1937. This dwelling, built in 1870, was Orville Wright's birthplace, and Wilbur Wright died there. After their father bought the seven-room house in 1871, the family lived there until 1878, and again from 1885 to 1914. Today it stands on Michigan Avenue next to the two-story Wright Cycle Co., the brothers' bicycle workshop also transported and reconstructed brick-by-brick from its original Dayton site. In this shop the Wrights built their first plane in 1903. The two buildings were dedicated at the institute (see the entry on the Edison Institute earlier in this section) with great fanfare in 1938, with Orville Wright in attendance.

(See INDIANA, OHIO in this chapter; also Chapter 3, DISTRICT OF COLUMBIA, PENNSYLVANIA; also Chapter 5, NORTH CAROLINA.)

MINNESOTA

If all of Minnesota's surface water were land and all the land water, there would still be an ample Minnesota. This glacier-pitted topography holds some 15,000 lakes, ranging from the huge twin Red Lakes of the north to the many thousands of lakes 10 acres and less that become progressively shallower toward the south. North of Minnesota lie Ontario and Manitoba. From Lake Superior the state's eastern edge drops along the St. Croix and Mississippi rivers bordering Wisconsin; the source of the Mississippi is Lake Itasca near Bemidji. Below Alaska, the northernmost town of the United States is Angle Inlet, Minn.

From the first recorded visit of Frenchmen in 1660 until it became the 32nd state, Minnesota existed under 12 different flags, both national and territorial. Most of this ownership was mere paper shuffling. Few whites except occasional fur traders had the remotest notion of what the territory looked like until 1805, when Lt. Zebulon Pike made an inspection and declared formal U.S. possession. In 1819 Fort Snelling, the early nucleus of St. Paul, became the nation's northwesternmost military outpost, keeping an eye on the Sioux and Chippewa natives who held fast until treatied out of their homeland in the 1850s. Settlers soon arrived in such numbers that Minnesota separated from Wisconsin Territory in 1848 and qualified for statehood a decade later. After the Civil War, in which Minnesota was first to declare for the Union side, Scandinavian and German immigration peaked. These newcomers transplanted their old-country livelihoods of farming and dairying to the new land and established ethnic communities that still thrive.

Lumbering, still a major industry, was dominant until about 1910—Bemidji is known as Paul Bunyan's "birthplace"—then agriculture centered the state's economy until World War II. Commerce and service industries have since taken the lead, and food processing—milling, packing, canning—is now Minnesota's major activity. Livestock farming and dairying remain important, however; the state grows more sweet corn, oats, wild rice and turkeys than any other. The nation's richest source of iron ore is Minnesota's three mining ranges north of Duluth. With more inland fresh water than any other state and a dense northern forest region, Minnesota has built recreation and tourism into a major source of income.

Urban Minnesota consists almost exclusively of Duluth and the Twin Cities. Partially separated by the Mississippi River, contiguous Minneapolis and St. Paul display interesting differences in style and values: St. Paul, heavily Roman Catholic and blue collar, is the state capital, an extroverted government town; while Minneapolis, more self-contained, conservative and commercially focused, impresses visitors as the big-city twin. Or, according to Garrison Keillor of National Public Radio's "Prairie Home Companion," "The difference between St. Paul and Minneapolis is the difference between pumpernickel and Wonder Bread."

It is easy to affix a certain "northern voyageur" quality to Minnesota's relatively few notable progeny. Native writers F. Scott Fitzgerald and Sinclair Lewis fled the state but kept returning. Businessman J. Paul Getty did not return, but railroad baron James J. Hill came south from Canada and settled permanently. Jurist-outdoorsman William O. Douglas and Hubert Humphrey blended their Minnesota iron qualities with warm capacities for pure palaver. Homes exist for all of these residents except Douglas; but only those of Hill and Lewis host visitors.

BERRYMAN, JOHN (1914–1972). The poet's last home from 1964, the only house he ever owned,

stands privately owned at 33 Arthur Ave. SE in **Minneapolis.**

(See Chapter 3, NEW JERSEY.)

DOUGLAS, WILLIAM ORVILLE (1898–1980). The 36-year Supreme Court Justice, also a prominent conservationist and author, was born in the 1889 Presbyterian manse at Maine, his home until 1901. There the infant suffered an attack of polio, from which he eventually made complete recovery. He remembered "sawdust pitched high around the foundation of our house for winter insulation." This house, razed in 1948, stood on the site of a manse that has replaced it next to the Maine Presbyterian Church in the present community of **Underwood.**

(See Chapter 1, CONNECTICUT; also Chapter 3, DISTRICT OF COLUMBIA; also Chapter 6, WASHINGTON.)

EARHART, AMELIA MARY (1898–1937?). In **St. Paul,** a childhood home of the aviator who disappeared on a Pacific flight stands at 825 Fairmount Ave. Her parents rented the house from 1913 to 1915, and from there she began high school. The dwelling remains privately owned.

(See IOWA, KANSAS in this chapter; also Chapter 1, MASSACHUSETTS; also Chapter 3, NEW YORK.)

FITZGERALD, F. SCOTT (1896–1940). A native of **St. Paul,** the novelist of the "jazz age" was named after Francis Scott Key, a collateral ancestor. His birthplace stands at 481 Laurel Ave., a three-story, balconied brick building that is now a condominium. Fitzgerald lived there until age two. Back in the city after a decade elsewhere, the family occupied a succession of houses on Laurel, Holly and Summit avenues (see Name Index and Gazetteer). In 1918 they settled at what is now Fitzgerald National Historic Landmark, 599 Summit Ave. (Summit Terrace), an 1889 brownstone row house where he lived with his family until 1920 and returned for occasional visits thereafter. Fitzgerald called the 19th-century Summit Avenue row "a museum of American failures." There in his front bedroom on the third floor he wrote his first novel, *This Side of Paradise* (1920). In 1921 and 1922, he and his wife Zelda occupied 626 Goodrich Ave., a two-story frame house where he completed *The Beautiful and the*

Damned (1922). All of Fitzgerald's St. Paul homes remain privately owned and occupied.

(See Chapter 2, MANHATTAN; also Chapter 3, MARYLAND, NEW YORK; also Chapter 5, ALABAMA, NORTH CAROLINA; also Chapter 6, CALIFORNIA.)

GETTY, JEAN PAUL (1892–1976). One of the world's richest men when he died, the oil magnate was born in **Minneapolis** at what is now the Hampshire Arms Hotel, 900–912 Fourth Ave. South (at the corner of Ninth Street South), an apartment hotel dating from 1891. This was Getty's home until 1906.

(See Chapter 2, MANHATTAN; also Chapter 6, CALIFORNIA, OKLAHOMA.)

HILL, JAMES JEROME (1838–1916). The railroad builder and financier was born in Ontario but made **St. Paul** his home from 1856. His last residence, from 1891, is the 1887 Hill House National Historic Landmark, which he built at 240 Summit Ave., a three and one-half-story, red sandstone chateau. The mansion, now owned by the Minnesota Historical Society, is currently undergoing restoration and will exhibit original furnishings in at least some of the rooms. (Call 612-296-7129 for information.)

"From 1883 until his death," wrote biographer Albro Martin, "Hill's real home would be North Oaks Farm," an estate that eventually included more than 5,000 acres of "typical Minnesota landscape" on the south shore of Pleasant Lake about 10 miles north of St. Paul. The "Empire Builder" resided there from spring through fall, raised large herds of beef and dairy cattle and constantly expanded his holdings. Hill's descendants retained possession until 1950, when a grandson subdivided the property for development of a "model residential community." Today the Village of **North Oaks,** incorporated in 1956, remains an exclusive, very expensive tract of private homes, golf courses and amenities for the wealthy. North Oaks lies gated at the end of Rice Street (State Highway 49) on State Highway 96.

(See Chapter 2, MANHATTAN; also Chapter 5, GEORGIA.)

HUMPHREY, HUBERT HORATIO (1911–1978). Senator, vice president and 1968 presidential candidate, the ebullient liberal became noted for what he called the "politics of joy" throughout his long public career. During his **Minneapolis** years as student, teacher and mayor, he occupied several dwellings, all of which remain privately occupied. In 1939 when he graduated from the University of Minnesota, Humphrey resided at 1112 Southeast Fourth St. He lived at 707 University Ave. SE while teaching political science at the University in 1940 and 1941; and as mayor from 1945 to 1949, Humphrey lived at 890 19th Ave. SE. This was his last city residence.

His last Minnesota home, from 1956, was "Triple H Ranch" at **Waverly,** a lakefront house he built and later slyly named as counterpart to the Texas "LBJ Ranch" of President Lyndon B. Johnson. Humphrey's widow sold their home in 1979 to the Louis Whitbeck Fraser School, which now maintains it as an educational retreat center for the mentally retarded.

(See SOUTH DAKOTA in this chapter; also Chapter 3, DISTRICT OF COLUMBIA, MARYLAND.)

LEWIS, SINCLAIR (1885–1951). The "Gopher Prairie" of Lewis's best-known novel *Main Street* (1920) was **Sauk Centre,** his birthplace and childhood home. "In a sense," wrote literary historian Rita Stein, "Sauk Centre has lived up to the satire in the book by turning negative criticism into positive thinking, honoring its most famous citizen, who made Sauk Centre itself famous for the wrong reasons." Born Harry Sinclair Lewis in a house razed from what is now 811 Sinclair Lewis Ave., the author lived in the parental home at 812 (across the street) from 1889 to 1903, returning at intervals thereafter. This two-story frame house, dating from about 1882, is now Lewis Boyhood Home National Historic Landmark operated by the Sinclair Lewis Foundation. Original family furnishings include heavy Victorian pieces typical of 19th-century, smalltown America. According to Lewis, his father, a physician, never forgave him for writing *Main Street*. (Open Memorial Day–Labor Day, Monday–Saturday 10:00–6:00, Sunday 1:00–6:00; Labor Day–Memorial Day, by appointment; admission.)

Though Lewis never again lived in Sauk Centre for any duration, he resided elsewhere in Minnesota at various times throughout his career; indeed, he seemed unable to stay away for long. He spent the winter of 1917–18 in a large rented room at 516 Summit Ave. in **St. Paul.** In **Minneapolis,** he resided at 1500 Mount Curve Ave., a

1929 Tudor mansion, in 1942. Both of these dwellings remain privately owned.

In 1944 and 1945, Lewis occupied 2601 East Second St. in **Duluth,** where he worked on his novel *Cass Timberlane* (1945). This 30-room brick mansion, dating from 1912, is now occupied by the Dominican Holy Rosary Convent.*

Exhibit: **Sauk Centre** read Lewis, swallowed hard, took a deep breath and proudly named U.S. Highway 71 through town as "The Original Main Street"; by so successfully commercializing his name there, the town richly fulfills its "Gopher Prairie" image. The main exhibit outside his boyhood home is the Sinclair Lewis Interpretive Center (as if he needed much interpretation), maintained by the Sinclair Lewis Foundation at the junction of Interstate Highway 94 and U.S. Highway 71 on the edge of town. Visitors there may see a slide show on Lewis's life plus a collection of his manuscripts, letters and memorabilia. (Open Memorial Day–Labor Day, daily 10:00–6:00; Labor Day–Memorial Day, Monday–Saturday 9:00–4:00; 612-352-6892; free.

(See Chapter 1, MASSACHUSETTS, VERMONT; also Chapter 2, MANHATTAN; also Chapter 3, NEW YORK.)

LINDBERGH, CHARLES AUGUSTUS (1902–1974). Lindbergh State Memorial Park near **Little Falls** contains the aviation hero's boyhood home, now operated by the Minnesota Historical Society. The large frame house, which his father, a congressman, built in 1907 to replace the original dwelling destroyed by a 1905 fire, stands two miles southwest on County Road 52. Inside the restored farm home where Lindbergh resided until 1920 are family memorabilia, original furnishings and audiovisual programs. A slide show features a description of Lindbergh's solo Atlantic flight of 1927 in his own voice. The park encompasses 110 acres of the 1898 original property. Lindbergh last visited the homestead in 1969. His book *Boyhood on the Upper Mississippi* (1972) details his life there. (Open May 1–October 31, Monday–Saturday 10:00–5:00, Sunday 1:00–5:00; 612-632-9050; free.)

(See MICHIGAN, MISSOURI in this chapter; also Chapter 1, CONNECTICUT; also Chapter 3, DISTRICT OF COLUMBIA, NEW JERSEY, NEW YORK; also Chapter 6, HAWAII.)

*A contemplative religious order also followed a Lewis occupancy in Massachusetts (see Chapter 1).

PEGLER, WESTBROOK (1894–1969). The libelous newspaper columnist lived in **Minneapolis** until 1904. His first home, a three-story brick apartment house built about 1885, stands at 2838 Eighth Ave. South, still privately occupied.

(See Chapter 2, MANHATTAN; also Chapter 3, NEW YORK; also Chapter 6, ARIZONA.)

VEBLEN, THORSTEIN BUNDE (1857–1929). The boyhood home of the reclusive economic genius and social critic who originated the phrase "conspicuous consumption" stands decaying near **Nerstrand.** Last occupied about 10 years ago, the property has recently become the focus of a nationwide fundraising campaign instigated by economist John Kenneth Galbraith to acquire and restore the Greek Revival house and eventually establish a scholarly retreat on the site. Veblen's father, a prominent farmer and craftsman, built this house of handhewn timbers in 1865 and 1866 on his 290 acres, 10 of which are being acquired. This was Veblen's home until 1874. The house stands on an unnumbered road half a mile north and about a mile east of the village. National Historic Landmark status seems certain, but in 1981 the property remained unmarked. For updated information on this important historical treasure, contact the Veblen Preservation Project, Inc., Box 372, Northfield, MN, 55057.

(See MISSOURI, WISCONSIN in this chapter.)

WILDER, LAURA INGALLS (1867–1957). In 1870 the pioneering Ingalls family settled on Plum Creek near **Walnut Grove,** an area where Wilder lived until 1880 and which she described in her book *On the Banks of Plum Creek* (1937). Only a ground depression remains of the family dugout home, identified by a marker one and one-half miles north of town off U.S. Highway 14.

(See IOWA, KANSAS, MISSOURI, SOUTH DAKOTA, WISCONSIN in this chapter.)

WILKINS, ROY (1901–1981). The boyhood home of the civil rights leader and longtime NAACP executive stands at 906 Galtier St. in **St. Paul.** Wilkins lived with an uncle and aunt, who enlarged the original frame cottage to two stories soon after his arrival. He resided there from 1905 to 1923, the year of his graduation from the University of Minnesota. The house remains privately owned.

(See Chapter 2, MANHATTAN, QUEENS.)

MISSOURI

"I'm from Missouri, you'll have to show me" is ascribed not to Thomas of the Twelve but to Doubting Willard. Congressman Willard D. Vandiver, who represented a state district from 1897 to 1905, reputedly said it during an exchange with an Iowa congressman.

To non-Missourians, the "show me" requirement has, at times, seemed a lot to ask, more mulelike than sensible. Missouri's best-known residents, however, have always preferred the reverse act, that of showing, over spectatoring. From Meriwether Lewis and William Clark, who showed us the half of our country that President Jefferson bought on bargain—and Mark Twain, who revealed how harmless and sane it was to laugh at ourselves—to Harry S. Truman, who demonstrated how to stand heat in the political kitchen, Missouri notables have always demanded much more "watch me" than "show me." The literal meaning of the tribal name "Emissourita" remains unknown.

The Frenchmen Jacques Marquette and Louis Jolliet were the first whites to view Missouri during their 1673 passage down the Mississippi. Based on Sieur de La Salle's completion of that exploration in 1682, France claimed Missouri as part of its Louisiana and established St. Genevieve as the Missouri area's first permanent settlement in 1735. By the time St. Louis sprouted in 1763, the area had passed to Great Britain except for the Missouri River valley, where Spanish pioneers built St. Charles and New Madrid. The American flag arose over St. Louis in 1804, but Spanish land titles and residual Indian conflicts delayed the main surge of settlement until 1815. When Louisiana proper became a state in 1812, a large chunk of Upper Louisiana Territory became Missouri Territory, only part of which would form the State of Missouri in 1821. The upper Missouri fur trade, channeled through St. Louis, brought a profitable wildcat commerce to the region. By the 1850s, Missouri was less a final destination than the new starting point and supply center for the overland route to Oregon and the California gold fields. The St. Louis status as "Gateway to the West" has been symbolized by Eero Saarinen's Jefferson National Expansion Memorial, the 630-foot soaring steel arch that is visible for miles distant from the Mississippi shore. At St. Joseph began the pony express route west, and from Arrow Rock and Old Franklin commenced the Santa Fe Trail.

Application for statehood caused the first real clash between North and South. The temporary solution, which only deferred the problem, was the Missouri Compromise of 1820: Let Missouri enter as a slave state, conceded the North, but prohibit slavery in the rest of Upper Louisiana. As a state without a plantation-slave economy, Missouri's economic interests were clearly aligned with the North, yet opinion was strongly pro-Southern. The state sought desperately for compromise, but federal interference in a tense situation apparently tilted the issue, and Missouri reluctantly seceded late in 1861. The Confederate state government never achieved actual control, however; collapse of civil order made the state a perpetual war zone as roaming guerrilla bands and local insurrections ravaged farms and settlements, neutral ones first. "To southern Missouri," wrote Duncan Aikman, "the struggle was not so much a volcanic national emergency as an open season for neighborhood malice." A new state government managed a return to the Union by 1864, but Missouri endured a long legacy of border hatred and radical internal politics plus a severely damaged economy.

The rugged Ozark range, one of the mid-continent's most scenic areas, divides the state's northwestern prairies from the lowlands of the Mississippi, the river that forms Missouri's eastern boundary. The Missouri River, which bisects the state from west to east, forms the northeast boundary. A broad economic diversity centers on manufacturing, with auto production ranking second nationally. Agriculture consists mainly of livestock industries. Missouri's main urban areas of St. Louis and Kansas City, both major industrial centers, bracket the state on the east and west. Centrally located Jefferson City has been the state capital from the beginning.

Missouri retains many homes of its illustrious residents. Pioneer Daniel Boone spent his last years there as did frontier scout Jim Bridger. Some of the nation's most unique women—Calamity Jane Burke, Molly Brown and Carry Nation, among others—plus two U.S. presidents, Ulysses S. Grant and Harry S. Truman—were either natives or lived in Missouri for extensive periods. Missouri writers included T. S. Eliot, Marianne Moore, Laura Ingalls Wilder and, of course, Mark

Twain, who made his Hannibal boyhood a metaphor of national growth and place. The only bank in history that memorializes the crook who robbed it—Jesse James, the son of a Missouri preacher and our native Robin Hood surrogate—stands in Liberty. Scientist George Washington Carver, born a slave, became humanity's creditor; when all is said, he was perhaps Missouri's greatest man. Each in his or her own way were essential frontier spirits, and Missouri exhibits a proud, familial knowledge of its progeny in its energetic care for their dwelling places. As elsewhere, sites outnumber structures; but on the comparative scale, the state ranks high in the awareness of its history. After all the banter, Missouri plainly means "show *them*."

BOONE, DANIEL (1734–1820). Cheated out of his Kentucky landholdings, the frontiersman accepted a Missouri River grant of 845 acres from Spanish colonial authorities in 1799. Above this Darst Bottom property, Boone built a log cabin and rude fort as protection from Indians. He resided there as civil administrator for the Femme Osage District of the Spanish colony until Missouri territory became part of the United States. Boone then lost his position and, again, most of his land. The marked site of the Boone Farm, which he occupied until 1804, is still a privately owned farm located south of **Matson** on State Highway 94. His double log house stood until 1854 just south of the present 1848 farmhouse; the stone fort stood in the front yard. "The spring was the inducement which led Boone to build his cabin there," wrote William S. Bryan in 1909. "Those old pioneers valued a spring more than they did the land surrounding it, for it was sure to be a meeting place for deer and other game. Boone could sit in the door of his cabin, which stood fifty feet or more eastwardly from the spring, and lay in a winter's supply of meat for his family without the trouble of hunting." A stone shed—built, it is said, with rocks from Boone's fort there—now shelters this spring.

Six miles northwest of **Defiance** on local Highway 7 (County Road F) off State Highway 94 stands Boone Home National Historic Landmark, the frontiersman's last residence, built from 1803 to 1810 by himself and his youngest son, Nathan. This building is actually a small, L-shaped fortress of native blue limestone with two stories and gunports. Boone himself handcarved most

of the interior woodwork. From 1810 he occupied the two small rooms to the right of the main entrance. His wife died seven years before his own death there. Boone's home, operated by the Shelband Corporation, displays many family furnishings and memorabilia. (Open March 15–December 14, daily 8:30–dusk; December 15–March 14, Saturday–Sunday 9:30–dusk; 314-987-2221; admission.)

Exhibit: Bates County Museum of Pioneer History at 106 East Fort St. in **Butler** displays a collection of Boone memorabilia in a log cabin adjacent to the museum. (Open daily 1:30–5:00; 816-679-4777; admission.)

(See Chapter 3, PENNSYLVANIA, WEST VIRGINIA; also Chapter 5, KENTUCKY, NORTH CAROLINA.)

BRADLEY, OMAR NELSON (1893–1981). The birthplace of the World War II general, probably the most intelligent field commander in American history and first chairman of the Joint Chiefs of Staff, was a farm located two and one-half miles west of **Higbee** in a house that has since burned. His marked boyhood home, a frame house of four rooms on one story built about 1900, survives at the east end of Grand Street (County Route B).

A brief home during Bradley's infancy, a two-story frame dwelling, stands at Railroad and Cross streets in **Clark.**

Both houses remain privately owned.

(See Chapter 3, PENNSYLVANIA; also Chapter 5, GEORGIA, VIRGINIA; also Chapter 6, CALIFORNIA, TEXAS.)

BRIDGER, JAMES "JIM" (1804–1881). Mountain man, trapper and scout, Bridger spent most of his life in the far West. His permanent home, however, was in south **Kansas City,** where he owned a 375-acre farm plus timber between Wornall and State Line roads just east of the Leawood subdivision. He retired temporarily there from 1853 to 1857 and permanently after 1868. There he died, wrapped in a blind old man's memories of a West that nobody now alive has seen. Bridger's two-story farmhouse, located approximately across from Notre Dame de Sion High School at 10631 Wornall Road, fell in 1908, though foundation ruins remained as late as 1941.

(See Chapter 6, WYOMING.)

BROWN, MARGARET TOBIN "MOLLY" (1867–1932). The life of the irrepressible woman who survived the 1912 *Titanic* disaster and became known as "the Unsinkable Molly Brown" was the subject of a 1960 musical comedy and later film. She was born in the small frame house at Denkler Alley and Butler Street (U.S. Highway 36) in **Hannibal,** her home until 1884. Fired with enthusiasm about the Western mining camps (partially inspired by Samuel Langhorne Clemens [see the entry on Clemens later in this section] at the Park Hotel, where she waited tables), she left for Colorado and a lifestyle that entered American folklore. Her pre-Civil War birthplace contains period furnishings. (Open May 30–Labor Day, daily 10:00–6:00; Labor Day–May 29, by appointment; 314-221-8979; admission.)

(See Chapter 1, RHODE ISLAND; also Chapter 6, COLORADO.)

BURKE, MARTHA JANE CANARY "CALAMITY JANE" (1848?–1903). Hard-drinking and hard-riding, this legendary frontier figure was born in a log cabin probably near Ollen Owen Corner on U.S. Highway 136 west of **Princeton,** the site identified by marker. If not her birthplace, it was apparently her childhood home until 1865.

(See SOUTH DAKOTA in this chapter; also Chapter 6, MONTANA, WYOMING.)

CALAMITY JANE. See MARTHA JANE CANARY BURKE.

CARNEGIE, DALE (1888–1955). His *How to Win Friends and Influence People* (1936) became the extrovert's bible. The patron saint of self-helpers, public speakers and people who yearn to be liked, Carnegie was born on a farm west of **Ravenwood,** a one-story frame cabin torn down in 1977 after a long vacancy. The site is located on a gravel road four miles north of State Highway 46.

A 1910 house owned by his parents in **Belton** stands privately owned and unmarked on the south side of Carnagey Street (Carnegie changed the spelling of his surname to make it easier for people to remember by associating it with his businessman hero, Andrew Carnegie).

Exhibit: The City Hall Museum, operated by the Belton Historical Society at 512 Main St. in **Belton,** plays broadcast tapes of Carnegie's popular "Five Minute Biographies" in its Carnegie display. (Open Monday–Friday; 816-331-6565; donation.)

(See Chapter 2, QUEENS.)

CARSON, CHRISTOPHER HOUSTON "KIT" (1809–1868). Boone's Lick State Historic Site marks the vicinity of the frontier scout's boyhood home. Established in 1805 by two sons of Daniel Boone (see the entry on Boone earlier in this section), the community of Boone's Lick grew around the salt springs from which arose one of central Missouri's earliest industries, the processing and shipping of salt. Carson lived there from 1811 to 1824, though the exact site of his parental home has been lost. The Missouri Department of Natural Resources maintains this 17-acre preserve located on Howard County Road MM off State Highway 87, 19 miles northwest of **Boonville.** (Open daily 8:00–5:00; 816-837-3392; free.) Opposite Boonville on the Missouri River stood Old Franklin, a town that existed from 1816 to about 1828 near what is now State Highway 87 about one mile west of U.S. Highway 40. There Carson's mother apprenticed him to a saddle maker in 1824, and he remained until 1826 when he ran away to join a wagon train headed for Santa Fe. Franklin was the original eastern head of the Santa Fe Trail that channeled westward expansion for 50 years. The shifting river had cut away the entire town site by 1829, but a later shift has since rebuilt the bottomland site to its approximately original level.

(See Chapter 5, KENTUCKY; also Chapter 6, COLORADO, NEW MEXICO.)

CARVER, GEORGE WASHINGTON (1864?–1943). The famed agricultural chemist was born a slave at what is now Carver National Monument, two and one-half miles southwest of **Diamond** on County Road V. His birthplace cabin, about 14 feet square, is outlined by logs on the site. The infant Carver and his mother were kidnapped from there by guerrilla bushwhackers, and only the boy was retrieved by his owner, Moses Carver—for a $300-racehorse. The youth lived there until the mid-1870s in the barely larger Carver cabin, which stood next to the birthplace cabin. A visitor center contains Carver exhibits, and a nature trail extends to various points of the Moses Carver farm, now maintained by the National Park Service. (Open daily 8:30–5:00; 417-325-4151; free.)

MARK TWAIN VISITS HIS BOYHOOD HOME. "It all seems so small to me," said Samuel L. Clemens on the ceremonious occasion of his visit to **Hannibal** in June of 1902. "A boy's home is a big place to him. I suppose if I should come back ten years from now it would be the size of a bird house." At right in the photo is a remnant of the fence described in *The Adventures of Tom Sawyer*, obviously needing a good whitewash.
(Courtesy Mark Twain Memorial, Hartford, Conn.)

(See KANSAS in this chapter; also Chapter 5, ALABAMA.)

CLARK, WILLIAM (1770–1838). See MERIWETHER LEWIS and WILLIAM CLARK.

CLEMENS, SAMUEL LANGHORNE "MARK TWAIN" (1835–1910). **Florida** was the humorist's birthplace, more exactly a small, two-room frame cabin now enclosed in Mark Twain Birthplace Memorial Shrine National Historic Landmark, Mark Twain State Park on State Highway 107. "Someone in Missouri," he wrote, "has sent me a picture of the house I was born in. Heretofore I have always stated that it was a palace but I shall be more guarded now." The museum there displays some of his possessions, first editions, the original manuscript of *The Adventures of Tom Sawyer* (1876) and a riverboat pilothouse. The Clemens family lived there only briefly, also occupying several other long-gone Florida houses, before moving to Hannibal in 1839. The original site of the Clemens birthplace cabin is about a quarter of a mile north of the Shrine on State Highway 107, where a pedestal and tablet mark the spot. The Shrine is operated by the Missouri State Park Board. (Open June 1–August 31, Monday–Saturday 10:00–4:00, Sunday 12:00–6:00; September 1–May 31, Monday–Saturday 10:00–4:00, Sunday 12:00–5:00; 314-565-3449; admission.)

Hannibal, of course, is the place most associated with Clemens. Some visitors may find the Mississippi River town of Tom Sawyer and Huckleberry Finn a bit oversaturated in commercial Huckleberriana. According to River traveler Jonathan Raban in *Old Glory: An American Voyage* (1981), Hannibal "adopted Twain's angry masterpiece and civilized it into a nice, profit-making chunk of sentimental kitsch." But Clemens himself, a frustrated businessman, might well glow at his name's present merchandising value. Mark Twain Boyhood Home National Historic Landmark, where he spent most of the years from 1839 to 1853, stands at 206 Hill St. It was cheaply built by Clemens's father in 1844 as a one-story dwelling; Samuel's brother Orion added the second floor about 1850. This frame house now stands as it looked when Clemens lived there and contains period furnishings. It is operated by the Mark Twain Home Board. (Open June 1–September 1, daily 8:00–6:00; fall and spring, daily 8:00–5:00; winter, daily 10:00–5:00; 314-221-9010; donation.)

The Pilaster House, on the southwest corner of Hill and Main streets, became the Clemens home in 1846 and 1847, when financial reverses forced them to vacate the Hill Street house (though they moved back there in 1847). They lived above the Grant Drug Store that occupied the ground floor. The two and one-half-story frame house, also operated by the Mark Twain Home Board, is one of the better-built 19th-century houses in Hannibal, though it was prefabricated in Pittsburgh and came to Hannibal by steamboat. Clemens's father died there in 1847. (Same admission schedule as Mark Twain Boyhood Home.)

Exhibit: The 1937 Mark Twain Museum adjacent to his Boyhood Home displays many personal articles and original Clemens manuscripts (same admission schedule as Mark Twain Boyhood Home). Visitors interested in the many sites associated with Clemens in **Hannibal** may pick up a brochure and map from the local chamber of commerce at 623 Broadway (PO Box 230, Hannibal, MO, 63401).

(See IOWA in this chapter; also Chapter 1, CONNECTICUT; also Chapter 2, BRONX, MANHATTAN; also Chapter 3, NEW YORK; also Chapter 6, CALIFORNIA, NEVADA.)

DISNEY, WALT (1901–1966). The commercial artist and film tycoon whose humanized cartoon animals became some of America's best-known celebrities spent part of his boyhood on a 45-acre farm near **Marceline**. From 1906 to 1909 the youngster lived with his family in a one-story farmhouse at the corner of State Highway 5 and West Broadway. "My first impression of it," recalled Disney, "was that it had a beautiful front yard with lots of weeping willow trees." He sold some of his first sketches to neighbors while living there. Disney returned to his boyhood home for visits in 1933, 1956 and 1960. Much altered and enlarged, the house remained privately owned.

The **Kansas City** home of the Disney family from 1914 to 1921 is the 1905 dwelling at 3028 Bellefontaine Ave. (privately owned). Disney himself resided in this house, now Disney Home National Historic Landmark, from 1914 to 1917 and from 1919 to 1921. Behind, the garage built by his father in 1917 became Disney's first studio, where he experimented with film animation and created his first "Laugh-O-Gram" cartoons.

(See Chapter 6, CALIFORNIA.)

ELIOT, THOMAS STEARNS (1888–1965). Staunch traditionalist in everything but his poetry, which revolutionized modern literature, Eliot was a **St. Louis** native. His family home at 2635 Locust St., where he lived until about 1910, is long gone.

(See Chapter 1, MASSACHUSETTS; also Chapter 3, NEW JERSEY.)

GRANT, ULYSSES SIMPSON (1822–1885). His military career seemingly at a dead end, the later Union army commander and 18th U.S. president resigned his captain's commission in 1854 and went to **St. Louis**. His farm "Hardscrabble," where he halfheartedly scraped the soil from 1854 to 1860, is located at 10501 Gravois Road (at the corner of Grant Road), a 281-acre tract now operated by Anheuser-Busch, Inc., as a zoo, game preserve and Clydesdale horse stables. Grant's restored, two-story log cabin, dating from 1856, contains period items. Moved and rebuilt three times since Grant constructed it, the cabin originally stood in the northwest corner of St. Paul's Churchyard Cemetery on Rock Hill Road near Laclede Station Road. Brewer Adolphus Busch moved it to the present location on Grant's farm in 1907. (Open April 15–May 31, September 1–October 15, Thursday–Sunday; June 1–August 31, Tuesday–Sunday; reservations required one month ahead; write Grant's Farm Tours, St. Louis, Mo, 63123; 314-843-1700; free.)

(See ILLINOIS, MICHIGAN, OHIO in this chapter; also Chapter 2, MANHATTAN; also Chapter 3, DISTRICT OF COLUMBIA, NEW JERSEY, NEW YORK; also Chapter 5, VIRGINIA; also Chapter 6, WASHINGTON.)

HARLOW, JEAN (1911–1937). The birthplace and childhood home of the film actress born Harlean Carpenter stands privately owned and unmarked at 3344 Olive St. in **Kansas City,** her home until 1927. This house dates from about 1906.

(See Chapter 6, CALIFORNIA.)

HUGHES, LANGSTON (1902–1967). "In some countries he is the only known American writer," remarked Professor Max Baird of the black author-poet born in **Joplin,** "and some African nations identify America from Hughes' works. Joplin comes late in honoring him. But as a man who always understood humanity and its weaknesses, he would have understood." According to Baird, also a Joplin native, Hughes was born at 1602 Missouri Ave., still a privately owned dwelling; but other authorities believe that his birthplace stood at 1046 Joplin Ave., now a commercial block. He probably lived in either of these houses less than a year but maintained a lifelong interest in his native city.

(See KANSAS in this chapter; also Chapter 2, MANHATTAN.)

JAMES, JESSE WOODSON (1847–1882). The birthplace and lifelong "old home place" of the legendary outlaw and folk hero was the James Homestead, located about three miles northeast of **Kearney** (follow the signs to Jesse James Farm Drive). The sagging log cabin, built in 1822, was a strict religious home where Rev. Robert James, father of Jesse and Frank, farmed the surrounding acres. There the family was attacked by a squad of Union militia in 1863, and from there Jesse James rode off to become a Confederate guerrilla. After the war, he turned his energies to banks and trains, often returning to visit his mother there under the alias "Mister Howard"; sometimes he even brought Robert Ford, the "friend" who "laid Jesse James in his grave," which was in the front yard until relatives moved his bones in 1902. Frank James built the adjoining two-story frame house in 1893 and died there

in 1915. Both structures, operated by Clay County Department of Parks, display family mementos, furnishings, weapons and photos. (Open daily 9:30–5:30; 816-635-6065; admission.)

Ford, "that dirty little coward who shot Mister Howard," did so on April 3, 1882, at 1318 Lafayette St. in **St. Joseph,** where Jesse had hidden out with his wife and children. They occupied the one and one-half-story, 1879 cottage at what is now 12th and Penn streets. Interior items include Jesse's shaving mug, rocking chair and the hole in the wall supposedly made by the bullet that laid him low. It is operated by the Pony Express Historical Association. (Open April 1–May 31, September 1–November 30, Saturday–Sunday 1:00–5:00; June 1–August 31, Monday–Saturday 10:00–5:00, Sunday 1:00–5:00; closed December–January; 816-232-8206; admission.)

Exhibit: The Jesse James Bank Museum at 104 East Franklin St. in **Liberty** is the 1858 building that housed a bank robbed by the James gang on February 13, 1866. Pictures and documents relating to the gang are displayed by private owner Jack B. Wymore. (Open May 1–August 31, Monday–Saturday 10:30–4:30, Sunday 1:00–4:30; September 1–April 30, Monday–Wednesday, Friday–Saturday 10:30–4:30; 816-781-4458; admission.)

(See Chapter 5, TENNESSEE.)

JOPLIN, SCOTT (1868–1917). In **St. Louis,** the ragtime pianist and composer occupied the row house at what is now 2658A Delmar Ave. (privately owned) from 1901 to 1903. Funds were being raised in 1982 for its restoration as a city landmark.

The marked site of the Maple Leaf Club, the 1899 "birthplace" of ragtime, is on Main Street west of Lamine Avenue in **Sedalia.** Joplin's rooms at 135 West Henry St. (1897–1901) are long gone.

(See Chapter 2, MANHATTAN.)

LEWIS, MERIWETHER (1774–1809).
CLARK, WILLIAM (1770–1838).
The Lewis and Clark Expedition, assigned by President Jefferson to explore the newly acquired Louisiana Territory, assembled and organized during its first winter encampment (1803–04) at a Mississippi River site in Illinois. Because of subsequent natural changes in the river channel, however, this spot now occupies the opposite bank, in Missouri. The site of Camp Wood, where

Clark sternly drilled 43 men into physical shape for the two-year expedition, formerly at the junction of Wood River and the Mississippi, remains inaccessible by road; its approximate location is east of U.S. Highway 67, two and one-half miles north of the Missouri River mouth. **West Alton** is the closest town.

Exhibit: A collection of material from the Lewis and Clark Expedition may be viewed at the Jefferson Memorial in **St. Louis** (see the entry on Charles Augustus Lindbergh below).

(See INDIANA, NORTH DAKOTA in this chapter; also Chapter 3, DISTRICT OF COLUMBIA; also Chapter 5, KENTUCKY, TENNESSEE, VIRGINIA; also Chapter 6, OREGON, WASHINGTON.)

LINDBERGH, CHARLES AUGUSTUS (1902–1974).
Exhibit: Probably the most idolized hero in U.S. history, the aviator who not only guided the "Spirit of St. Louis" across the Atlantic but unwillingly personified the nation's image of itself for years afterward had been funded for that 1927 solo flight by **St. Louis** businessmen—hence the name of his plane. The Lindbergh exhibit at the Jefferson Memorial, operated by the Missouri Historical Society, 5700 Lindell Blvd., Forest Park, holds the huge collection of medals, awards and citations he received from nations, organizations and apparently almost anyone who could get close enough to beribbon him. He deposited all of this loot—with profound relief, no doubt—in the showcases of St. Louis. (Open daily, 9:30–4:45; 314-361-1424; free.)

(See MICHIGAN, MINNESOTA in this chapter; also Chapter 1, CONNECTICUT; also Chapter 3, DISTRICT OF COLUMBIA, NEW YORK; also Chapter 6, HAWAII.)

MILLER GLENN (1904–1944). The boyhood home from about 1915 to 1918 of the popular bandleader who disappeared on a wartime flight over the English Channel stands at 304 South High St. in **Grant City.** A local bandleader gave Miller his first trombone lessons when the boy lived there. The house remains privately owned.

(See IOWA, NEBRASKA in this chapter; also Chapter 2, QUEENS; also Chapter 3, NEW JERSEY; also Chapter 6, COLORADO.)

MOORE, MARIANNE CRAIG (1887–1972). The poet's residence until age seven was the home of her grandparents, a two-story Presbyterian parsonage long gone from 325 North Taylor St. in **Kirkwood.** The site is now occupied by the Kirkwood YMCA.

(See Chapter 2, BROOKLYN, MANHATTAN; also Chapter 4, PENNSYLVANIA.)

NATION, CARRY AMELIA MOORE (1846–1911). The temperance activist whose "hatchetation" raids on saloons won her much notoriety had a personal score to settle with booze—it had ruined her first marriage and killed her husband, Dr. Charles Gloyd. During that brief, difficult period, the couple lived in a three-room house she built in **Holden,** her home from 1867 to 1872. The privately owned dwelling stands in the town center across from the Holden Community Building.

(See KANSAS in this chapter; also Chapter 5, ARKANSAS, KENTUCKY; also Chapter 6, TEXAS.)

PERSHING, JOHN JOSEPH (1860–1948). American General of the Armies, a rank created for George Washington but never again held until 1919, the commander of the World War I American Expeditionary Force was a Missouri native. Pershing State Park, two miles west of **Laclede** on U.S. Highway 36, marks the site of his farm birthplace. Just where the house stood on this 2,000-acre tract remains a matter of some dispute. The state historical marker in Laclede's City Park maintains that he was born "in a section house (no longer standing) on old Hannibal-St. Joseph Railroad one-half mile west of Laclede." In 1866, the family moved to what is now Pershing Boyhood Home National Historic Landmark, a two-story, 11-room frame house dating from about 1857 at State and Worlow streets; and this remained Pershing's home until his 1882 entry into West Point. His own room in the house occupied the northwest corner of the second floor. Period furnishings, exhibits and Pershing memorabilia are displayed by the Missouri State Park Board. (Open June 1–August 31, Monday–Saturday 10:00–4:00, Sunday 12:00–6:00; September 1–May 31, Monday–Saturday 10:00–4:00, Sunday 12:00–5:00; 816-963-2525; admission.)

(See Chapter 3, DISTRICT OF COLUMBIA; also Chapter 6, CALIFORNIA, NEW MEXICO.)

PULITZER, JOSEPH (1847–1911). Founder of the *St. Louis Post-Dispatch* in 1880, the Hungarian-born publisher began his journalistic career in **St. Louis.** His home at 2920 Washington Ave. from 1879 to 1882, then the "best residential section" of the city, is long gone, as is his dwelling at 2648 Locust St. (1882–83). The first office of the *Post-Dispatch* stood at 321 Pine St.

(See Chapter 1, MAINE; also Chapter 2, MANHATTAN.)

RICKEY, BRANCH WESLEY (1881–1965). As president and manager of the St. Louis Cardinals, the baseball executive lived at 5405 Bartmer Ave. (privately owned) in **St. Louis.** He bought the three-story brick house in 1917 and resided there for a decade.

In 1927 Rickey purchased his farm estate "Country Life Acres" in **Bridgeton,** a suburb of St. Louis. His 33 acres included a lake, orchard, tennis court and several outbuildings, and he raised livestock and poultry on the farm. He sold the property in 1943, after a fire damaged the house in that year. A new owner rebuilt the house on its original plan, and it remains privately owned on seven acres at 25 Country Life Acres, a residential subdivision.

(See OHIO in this chapter; also Chapter 2, BROOKLYN; also Chapter 3, MARYLAND, PENNSYLVANIA.)

SHERMAN, WILLIAM TECUMSEH (1820–1891). None of the Union army general's several **St. Louis** residences exist. At 912 North Garrison Ave., he occupied a new brick, two-story house given to him in appreciation of his Civil War service. Sherman resided there at three separate intervals: from 1865 to 1869, 1874 to 1876, and 1883 to 1886. By one account, "he wrangled endlessly with the St. Louis authorities over taxes. A neighbor protested that General Sherman was wasting water sprinkling the street in front of his house." When he received his water bill, he "refused to pay it, and the newspapers resounded with his roars." This house was razed sometime after 1965.

(See OHIO in this chapter; also Chapter 2, MANHATTAN; also Chapter 3, DISTRICT OF COLUMBIA; also Chapter 6, CALIFORNIA, OKLAHOMA.)

SMITH, JOSEPH (1805–1844).

Exhibit: The founder of the Mormon Church stayed briefly in western Missouri after having led his followers there from Kirtland, Ohio. In **Liberty,** ironically, he spent four months (1838–39) in jail for antagonizing other settlers. The 1833 Historic Liberty Jail, reconstructed in cutaway form by the Church of Jesus Christ of Latter-day Saints, stands at 210 North Main St. There Smith is said to have experienced the revelations that led him to move his group to Illinois. (Open June 1–September 15, daily 8:00–9:00; September 16–May 31, daily 8:00–6:00; 816-781-3188; free.)

(See ILLINOIS, OHIO in this chapter; also Chapter 1, VERMONT; also Chapter 3, NEW YORK, PENNSYLVANIA; also Chapter 6, UTAH.)

STENGEL, CHARLES DILLON "CASEY" (1891–1975). The nickname of the colorful player, manager and "Old Perfessor" of baseball originated from his "KC" birthplace, which stands privately owned at 1229 Agnes St. in **Kansas City,** his home until about 1910. This house dates from about 1890.

(See Chapter 6, CALIFORNIA.)

TRUMAN, HARRY S. (1884–1972). The birthplace of the 33rd U.S. president stands at 1009 Truman Ave. (at the corner of 11th Street) in **Lamar,** a two-story, six-room frame house built about 1881 and Truman's infant home for almost a year. Truman Birthplace National Historic Landmark, operated by the Missouri State Park Board, displays period furnishings. (Open May 1–September 30, Monday–Saturday 10:00–4:00, Sunday 12:00–6:00; October 1–April 30, Monday–Saturday 10:00–4:00, Sunday 12:00–5:00; 417-682-2279; free.)

About five miles southeast of **Belton** on a hilltop stands the two-story, white frame house occupied by the Trumans from 1885 to 1887. Truman's father farmed a tract of 71 acres there. The original house, built in 1848, was rebuilt around a southeast room of the first dwelling before the Trumans occupied it. Union troops in the Civil War burned a slave cabin, smokehouse and barn but left the house untouched. Privately

THE 37TH PRESIDENT VISITS THE 33RD. Harry S. Truman never understood how the American people could have elected Richard M. Nixon, whom he held in profound personal contempt long before the feeling grew generally popular. Nevertheless he respected the presidential office, and when the Nixons came to the **Independence** home of the ailing ex-president on March 21, 1969, the Trumans dutifully accompanied their guests to the Truman Library, where Nixon presented a piano. The birthplace of Bess Wallace Truman at 219 North Delaware St., shown here, became the couple's permanent residence for more than half a century.   (*Ollie Atkins, White House Photograph, Courtesy Harry S. Truman Library*)

occupied on the C. K. Frank farm, the dwelling is identified by a small lawn marker.

Harry Truman said he "plowed, sowed, reaped, milked cows, fed hogs, doctored horses, baled hay and did everything there was to do on a 600-acre farm." "He could plow the straightest row of corn in the country," boasted Martha Truman of her son. But he recalled that "if a crooked row or blank space showed up in the corn field or the wheat, I'd hear about it for a year." The **Grand-**

view farm bought by his maternal grandfather in 1842 was Truman's home twice—from 1887 to 1890, and from 1906 to 1917, both times with his parents. From there he left to become a combat officer in World War I and never returned except to visit. The original colonial farmhouse burned down in 1893. "Harry planned almost monthly to rebuild the big place," recalled a friend, "but he never found the time or money to do so." The two-story, white frame house in which the family lived from 1906 remains privately occupied. it stands on a 13-acre portion of the original property directly behind Truman Corners Shopping Center at 12300 South 71st Highway. In 1981 a recently organized Truman Home Foundation in Grandview purchased the house and lot, planning restoration and a public park by Truman's centennial birthday in 1984. In the center of the aforesaid shopping mall, a historical marker identifies the commercial tract as a portion of the Truman farm.

In **Kansas City,** the family occupied 2108 Park Ave. from 1902 to 1905. This house, built in 1899, remains privately owned.

Three of Truman's 19th century **Independence** homes stand, all privately occupied as of 1981. From 1890 to 1896, he lived with his parents in the two-story dwelling at 619 South Crysler St. His father sometimes kept as many as 500 goats in the back lot there and also drilled the first natural gas well in Missouri on the property. From 1896 to 1902 the family occupied 909 West Waldo St., a two-story frame house. Truman's longtime residence from 1919, the year of his marriage to Elizabeth "Bess" Wallace, was the two-story Victorian frame mansion at 219 North Delaware St., now Truman House National Historic Landmark. This is Mrs. Truman's birthplace, the Wallace ancestral homestead built by her businessman grandfather in 1865. From 1935 to 1953—Truman's public years as senator, vice president, and president—the family occupied the rambling house intermittently, but the couple retired there permanently in 1953. The ex-president became a virtual recluse during his later years as age and infirmities advanced, and he no longer emerged for his customary morning "constitutionals" that had for years delighted reporters and his neighbors on Delaware Street. The house, a part of Truman Historic District National Historic Landmark, will eventually become U.S. government property and accessible to public visitation according to the Trumans' wishes.

Exhibits: The Harry S. Truman Library and Museum, located on U.S. Highway 24 at Delaware Street in **Independence,** is the main repository for Truman papers, memorabilia and displays relating to his life and public service. Highlights of the exhibit include the 1941 Chrysler coupe he drove as a senator, the piano he played in the White House, audiovisual programs and important documents and displays on virtually every

significant event of his presidential years. Tours through an exact replica of the Oval Office as it looked when he occupied it are guided by Truman's own tape-recorded voice. Visitors may also view (from the exterior) the library office suite he occupied from 1957 to 1966. Truman Library and Museum is operated by the National Archives and Records Service. (Open Memorial Day–Labor Day, daily 9:00–7:00; Labor Day–Memorial Day, daily 9:00–5:00; 816-833-1400; admission.) Truman's Office and Courtroom, which he occupied as the presiding judge of Jackson County Court from 1926 to 1934, has been restored in the 1836 Independence Square Courthouse at Main and Lexington streets. Maintained by Jackson County Parks and Recreation Department, it contains office memorabilia of Truman's early political career. (Open Tuesday–Saturday 9:00–5:00; 816-881-4467; admission.)

(See Chapter 3, DISTRICT OF COLUMBIA; also Chapter 5, FLORIDA.)

TWAIN, MARK. See SAMUEL LANGHORNE CLEMENS.

VEBLEN, THORSTEIN BUNDE (1857–1929). Few people in his lonely life knew what to make of him; his cryptic humor, ponderous intellect, amoral behavior and generally unconventional presence and opinions evoked mixtures of outrage, admiration, and puzzlement. The brilliant eccentric economist and social scientist preferred to leave no residential tracks whatever and stated in his will that he wanted no memorials or markers. **Columbia,** where he taught at the University of Missouri from 1911 to 1918, has obliged his wish, partly because he often lodged with associates at uncertain addresses. One residence that survives is 106 Lathrop St. (privately owned). Veblen guested there with a fellow professor, occupied the basement and, at least part of the time, a tent on the front lawn, where he made his own crude furniture from boxes covered with burlap.

(See MINNESOTA, WISCONSIN in this chapter.)

WILDER, LAURA INGALLS (1867–1957). "Rocky Ridge Farm," one and a quarter miles east of **Mansfield** on U.S. Business Route 60, was the author's permanent home from 1895. Almanzo Wilder, her husband, built the original two-room cabin that is now the kitchen and added frame portions until 1912. Not until the 1920s, however, did Laura Wilder begin writing the memoirs of her pioneer childhood that resulted in the popular *Little House* series. Her daughter, Rose Wilder Lane, grew up there and became a noted writer long before her mother. The Wilders expanded their farm from 40 to 200 acres. Displayed in the farmhouse where Laura Wilder wrote all of her nine books and in the next-door museum are the original furnishings, craftwork, school-tablet manuscripts and Ingalls family heirlooms. She died there at age 90. House and museum are operated by the Wilder Home Association. (Open May 1–October 15, Monday–Saturday 9:00–4:00; 417-924-3626; admission.)

(See IOWA, KANSAS, MINNESOTA, SOUTH DAKOTA, WISCONSIN in this chapter.)

NEBRASKA

The center of the Great Plains, Nebraska—an Otoe name meaning "flat water" of the Platte River—also marks the transition zone between the native shortgrass and tallgrass prairie; or, in agricultural terms, between cattle and corn country. The amount of annual rainfall, declining almost six inches from eastern to western borders, makes the difference. The state's topography resembles a ramp gently ascending from its Missouri River boundary toward the Rocky Mountain foothills. Hills and buttes chop the western panhandle wedge. Thin strips of forest occupied only about three percent of presettled Nebraska, mainly along streams and rivers. Sizable woodlands exist today—but only because people took trouble to plant them; Arbor Day (April 22) was established in 1885 principally to increase the number of trees in Nebraska. The chief crop in one of America's leading breadbasket states is corn, which occupies about one-third of Nebraska's cultivated acreage; wheat and oats follow in major importance, while stock ranching prevails in the drier west. Nebraska's dominant urban industry is food processing.

Nebraska's native tribes included the Omaha, Pawnee, Cheyenne, Arapaho and Sioux. Though he probably never arrived there himself, Coronado claimed this territory for Spain in 1541. The few French fur traders who penetrated this far emerged with such unfavorable reports about the "Great American Desert" that little actual exploration began until 1804, when Lewis and Clark noted the billowing Nebraska grassland as they ascended the Missouri River. For white Americans during the next half-century, this sea of grass was mainly an area to be "gotten by" as quickly as possible, a long, dusty bridge for passage elsewhere. Between 1840 and 1866 almost 400,000 persons crossed Nebraska in covered wagons. Pioneers, goldseekers, missionaries and Mormons swelled in number along the Platte valley and Oregon Trail, hardly lingering on a sod that seemed too thick and dry for promise, always in motion westward. For the same motive of passage, to bridge Nebraska by a transcontinental railroad, territorial status was sought and obtained in 1854, with Colorado and the Dakotas included in Nebraska Territory until 1861. Though the oldest permanent community, Bellevue, dates from 1820, settlement in Nebraska itself remained sparse until the 1862 Homestead Act brought thousands of land-hungry Easterners and Europeans. Homestead National Monument near Beatrice preserves an original quarter-section of the 126 million acres claimed under this act. Groundbreaking for that first transcontinental railroad, the Union Pacific, occurred at Omaha in 1863, and settlements sprouted along the tracks' westward advance. Beleaguered native Nebraskans fought fierce, well-organized battles against this course of events, but with the 1877 death of Crazy Horse, resistance collapsed; and almost all of this exclusive "Indian country," so designated by Congress in 1834, had been "ceded" to the new Americans only four decades later. Nebraska became the 37th U.S. state in 1867, and its open-prairie capital was named Lincoln in honor of the slain president. The single-chamber, nonpartisan legislature of this state, operating only in odd-numbered years since 1937, is unique in a nation that ranks two-party systems and bicameral congresses second only to the King James Bible.

Also unique are those noted individuals who, from Nebraska's deep soil and wide-sky plains, have broadened the national horizons. Native Nebraskans included film comedian Harold Lloyd and Black Muslim religious leader Malcolm X, but neither stayed into adulthood. The foremost Nebraskan, though not by birth, was probably novelist Willa Cather; her matchless prairie descriptions completed, for the national consciousness, what Lewis and Clark had begun. Cather left Nebraska, at least physically, when she was still young; but Buffalo Bill Cody, William

Jennings Bryan and Sen. George Norris settled there more or less permanently. Preserved homes of eminent Nebraskans number proportionally among the highest of any state. Perhaps because relatively few national historic figures have lived there, homes of those residents who brought renown to the state are particularly treasured.

BRYAN, WILLIAM JENNINGS (1860–1925). The first residence in **Lincoln** of the "Great Commoner" was 1425 D Street, a two-story, white frame house he built in 1888. There Bryan began the Democratic political career that would make him a major public figure and presidential contender for the next quarter-century—despite the fact that he never won another election after his 1892 return to Congress. The privately owned house has been considerably altered. Bryan built Fairview National Historic Landmark at 4900 Summer St. in 1902. "A home of brick and stone had been in my mind from youth," he said, and he broke ground for it on his 17th wedding anni-

versary, eventually accumulating more than 300 acres there. The rural "fair view" that attracted him has been long built over, but Fairview, a conglomerate of shapes and styles that remained his home until 1921, has been well preserved. Only the first floor, which contains many Bryan family furnishings, gifts and memorabilia, admits visitors. The house is operated by the Nebraska State Historical Society, the Junior League of Lincoln and Bryan Memorial Hospital, which now owns the grounds. (Open summer 8:00–5:00; winter Saturday–Sunday 1:00–5:00; 402-471-3270; admission.)

(See ILLINOIS in this chapter; also Chapter 3, DISTRICT OF COLUMBIA; also Chapter 5, FLORIDA, TENNESSEE.)

BUFFALO BILL. See WILLIAM FREDERICK CODY.

CATHER, WILLA SIBERT (1873–1947). At **Red Cloud,** Cather Childhood Home National Historic

WILLA CATHER'S CHILDHOOD HOME. The Willa Cather Historical Center is unable to date this picture or identify the persons posing; but presumably it shows Charles Cather and his family sometime during the period 1884–90, when they resided in the 1878 dwelling now open to the public at Third

and Cedar Streets in **Red Cloud**, Nebraska. Willa Cather is probably the child leaning against the porch at left, just below her father. The house—even the picket fence—remains unchanged today.
(*Courtesy Nebraska State Historical Society.*)

Landmark, a home and environment that frequently appeared in her stories and novels, sheltered the author's adolescence from 1884 to 1890. Located at Third and Cedar streets, this 1878 white frame dwelling held "everything a little on the slant," she wrote. Her own attic bedroom, with a slanting ceiling, still displays the now-faded wallpaper she placed; and childhood possessions and Cather family furnishings remain as she remembered and described them. The house is operated by the Nebraska State Historical Society. (Open April 1–November 15, Monday–Saturday 8:00–5:00, Sunday 1:00–5:00; November 16–March 31, Monday–Friday 8:00–5:00; admission.) Cather's first home in this area (1883–84) after her family moved west from Virginia was her grandfather's homestead, located northwest of Red Cloud on Bladen Road off State Highway 4. The small, frame Dane Church now occupies the site.

Exhibits: "There is perhaps no small town in America that has been described more often in fiction," wrote James Woodress, and the entire town of **Red Cloud** has, in a sense, become a Willa Cather exhibit. The Willa Cather Historical Center has identified the landmarks familiar to her readers with signs all over town and maintains a branch museum of the Nebraska State Historical Society at 338 North Webster St. (U.S. Highway 281). There one may view a slide show about Willa Cather and Red Cloud, see her manuscripts, letters and mementoes, and obtain guidebooks and maps to the local Cather sites. (Open April 1–November 15, Monday–Saturday 8:00–5:00, Sunday 1:00–5:00; November 16–March 31, Monday–Friday 8:00–5:00; 402-746-3285; free.) Tour maps can also be obtained at Red Cloud Chamber of Commerce, Webster Street; and at Webster County Historical Museum, 721 West Fourth Ave. (open April 1–October 31 daily, 8:00–5:00; closed November 1–May 31; 402-746-2444; admission). To see the land as it looked when she lived there, drive to the 610-acre Willa Cather Memorial Prairie, operated by the Nature Conservancy five miles south of town on U.S. Highway 281. This plot of virgin grassland typifies the Nebraska that Willa Cather loved and never, in spirit, left. Returning on periodic trips until her last visit in 1931, she wrote that "the very smell of the soil tore me to pieces."

(See Chapter 1, NEW HAMPSHIRE; also Chapter 2, MANHATTAN; also Chapter 3,

PENNSYLVANIA; also Chapter 5, VIRGINIA.)

CODY, WILLIAM FREDERICK "BUFFALO BILL" (1846–1917). At **North Platte,** Cody occupied two successive homes that he called "Welcome Wigwams" from 1877 to 1908, both gone. The present Scouts Rest Ranch State Park became the showman's permanent winter quarters from 1886. This frame Victorian mansion—not a typical ranch dwelling at all but "rather like an old-fashioned Ohio farm home," wrote John Drury—contains original furnishings plus many Cody possessions and memorabilia, including his personally designed wallpaper. Cody built his complex of house and outbuildings on the 4,000-acre ranch that represented the huge commercial success of his Wild West Show, which originated there and toured nationally for more than 30 years. Cody's Ranch, located one mile north on Buffalo Bill Avenue, is operated by the Nebraska State Game and Parks Commission. (Open May 14–September 5, daily 9:00–8:00; September 6–May 14, Monday–Friday 8:00–5:00; 308-532-4795; free.)

(See IOWA, KANSAS in this chapter; also Chapter 6, COLORADO, WYOMING.)

DE FOREST, LEE (1873–1961).
Exhibit: De Forest's 1906 development of the audion tube led to the rapid growth of the electronics industry. Some of his early radio and communications gear plus personal memorabilia from his Iowa birthplace are displayed in the Western Heritage Museum, 801 South 10th St. in **Omaha.** (Open Tuesday–Friday 10:00–5:00, Saturday–Sunday 1:00–5:00; 402-444-5071; admission.)

(See IOWA in this chapter; also Chapter 5, ALABAMA; also Chapter 6, CALIFORNIA.)

LLOYD, HAROLD CLAYTON (1894–1971). The bespectacled silent-film comedian was born in a one-story cottage still standing in **Burchard** at 24 Pawnee St., his home for only a year. He returned throughout his childhood to visit his grandmother, who continued to reside there. Built about 1880 and slightly modified, the house stood vacant in 1981.

Lloyd's boyhood home also stands privately occupied at 1008 Eighth St. in **Pawnee City.** The present long-time owner recalls that "when Harold was here to look over the house several years ago, he said he sat many a Sunday afternoon by the window, for his father wouldn't let him go out and play on Sundays."

(See Chapter 6, CALIFORNIA.)

MALCOLM X (1925–1965). **Omaha** historical sources believe that the infant home of the Black Muslim leader, born Malcolm Little, stood at 3448 Pinkney St., a currently vacant site. His Baptist preacher father moved the family to Michigan soon after Malcolm's birth.

(See MICHIGAN in this chapter; also Chapter 2, QUEENS.)

MILLER, GLENN (1904–1944). The popular bandleader lived with his parents in **North Platte** from 1912 to 1916. Their home has been rebuilt at 720 West A St. (privately owned), where his mother worried that his horn playing would disturb the neighbors.

(See IOWA, MISSOURI in this chapter; also Chapter 2, QUEENS; also Chapter 3, NEW JERSEY; also Chapter 6, COLORADO.)

NORRIS, GEORGE WILLIAM (1861–1944). Nebraska's longtime senator, the "Gentle Knight of Progressive Ideals" is chiefly remembered as the father of public control over power resources, resulting in the landmark creation of the Tennessee Valley Authority. In **McCook,** Norris Home National Historic Landmark stands at 706 Norris Ave., operated as a memorial by the Nebraska State Historical Society. Norris built this two-story, stucco dwelling in 1886 as his permanent home, spent summers there during his public career, and retired there in 1943 to write his autobiography *Fighting Liberal* (1945). The house contains family furnishings and heirlooms plus many letters, photos and memorabilia of this farsighted public servant. (Open April 1–May 31, September 1–October 31, Saturday–Sunday 1:00–5:00; June 1–August 31, Monday–Saturday 8:00–5:00, Sunday 1:00–5:00; 308-345-5293; free.)

(See OHIO in this chapter.)

REED, WALTER LAWRENCE (1851–1902). As a U.S. Army physician, Reed served at Fort Robinson from 1884 to 1887. The fort, established in 1874 to protect the Red Cloud Indian Agency, served as a base for a number of campaigns against the Sioux and remained an active military installation through World War II. Sioux war chief Crazy Horse was killed in the guardhouse

there in 1877. Nebraska State Historical Society maintains several structures dating from Dr. Reed's time. A visitor center and museum on the 22,672-acre property displays Indian, pioneer and military exhibits. Fort Robinson State Park National Historic Landmark is located three and one-half miles west of **Crawford** on U.S. Highway 20. (Park open Memorial Day–Labor Day; 308-665-2660; free; Fort Robinson Museum open April 1–November 15, Monday–Saturday 8:00–5:00, Sunday 9:00–5:00; November 16–March 31, by appointment; 308-665-2852; free.)

(See Chapter 5, ALABAMA, VIRGINIA.)

NORTH DAKOTA

Not New York City, not Chicago, but Blanchard, N.D., boasts the nation's tallest structure—the 2,063-foot transmission tower of KTHI-TV. Exactly the midpoint of continental North America, North Dakota borders Canadian Manitoba and Saskatchewan on the north. Three broad steps of prairie ascend westward, culminating in hilly plateaus and a jagged finger of Badlands. To casual observers, however, most of North Dakota's landscape seems mainly horizon.

The first white face there was probably that of French trader-explorer Pierre de la Vérendrye, who sought a water route to the Pacific in 1738 and left a lead plate claiming French possession near Menoken. The 1803 Louisiana Purchase, massive as it was, included only the southwestern portion of present North Dakota. Lewis and Clark spent the winter of 1804–05 near Stanton and raised the first U.S. flag, also making their luckiest discovery there: the Shoshone guide Sacagawea. Pembina, begun as a fur trading post in 1797, became the first permanent settlement in 1812; and the British-claimed portion of what is now North Dakota passed to American ownership by the Canadian boundary agreement of 1818. Successively placed under eight U.S. territorial flags, the final Dakota Territory split into North and South in 1889, when both Dakotas became states. Violent native resistance and a rigorous climate discouraged much settlement until post-Civil War railroad extension brought a large influx of homesteaders, almost one-third of them from Norway.

North Dakota's population is 44 percent urban, but Fargo, the largest city, numbers only 57,000. Today this state grows the nation's second largest wheat crop and is also a major livestock producer. Oil from the Williston Basin has become an important national resource along with lignite coal, and commercial power companies hold mineral leases on vast tracts of the state. Among the state's interesting museums that focus on native and pioneer culture, wildlife and agriculture, the Geographical Center Museum at Rugby marks the hub of North America.

North Dakota's roster of nationally famed residents is small. Gen. Custer spent his final days at Fort Abraham Lincoln. Probably the most noted dweller was the pre-presidential Theodore Roosevelt, who came to this spacious land seeking emotional recovery from personal tragedy. Visitors may roam portions of his two large ranches.

CLARK, WILLIAM (1770–1838). See MERIWETHER LEWIS and WILLIAM CLARK.

CUSTER, GEORGE ARMSTRONG (1839–1876). From Fort Abraham Lincoln, Custer and his Seventh Cavalry rode to their last battle at the Little Bighorn in Montana. The fort, abandoned in 1891, has been reconstructed on its 1872 site, but only the cornerstone remains of the house where Custer and his wife resided from 1873; the original flagpole and a historical marker identify the spot. Elizabeth Bacon Custer's *Boots and Saddles* (1885) details their final years together there. The 750-acre Fort Abraham Lincoln State Park, operated by North Dakota Park Service, is located on State Highway 1806, three miles south of **Mandan.** (Open May 1–31, September 1–30, daily 9:00–5:00; June 1–August 31, daily 9:00–9:00; October 1–April 30, Monday–Friday 9:00–5:00; 701-633-3049; free.)

(See KANSAS, MICHIGAN, OHIO, SOUTH DAKOTA in this chapter; also Chapter 5, KENTUCKY; also Chapter 6, MONTANA.)

LEWIS, MERIWETHER (1774–1809).

CLARK, WILLIAM (1770–1838).
During the bitter winter of 1804–05, the expedition assigned by President Jefferson to explore the newly acquired Louisiana Territory camped from November 2 to April 3 on the Missouri River shore about eight miles east of today's **Stanton** at Fort Clark. Fort Mandan State Historic Site, a 35-acre state park located off State Highway 200A on County Road 17, marks the approximate spot where the 40-odd men built two rows of log huts and a stockade. They celebrated a boisterous Christmas with "musick" and brandy, though ailments and unpredictable natives harassed them. It was there that the Shoshone woman Sacagawea joined the expedition as guide and interpreter and gave birth to a boy in February of 1805. The actual site of Fort Mandan, lost by 1833, lies about one and three-quarters miles south and slightly east of the state historical marker. Repeated flooding and alluvial changes in almost 200 years of shifting Missouri shorelines have long obliterated any trace of the actual fort.

Exhibits: A full-size replica of Fort Mandan, operated by the state, stands three miles west of **Washburn** on County Road 17. (Open daily; free.)

The Lewis and Clark Trail Museum on U.S. Highway 85 in **Alexander** exhibits a diorama of Fort Mandan plus pioneer items. (Open Memorial Day–Labor Day, Monday–Saturday 9:00–6:00, Sunday 1:00–6:00; 701-828-3595; admission.)

(See INDIANA, MISSOURI in this chapter; also Chapter 3, DISTRICT OF COLUMBIA; also Chapter 5, KENTUCKY, TENNESSEE, VIRGINIA; also Chapter 6, OREGON, WASHINGTON.)

ROOSEVELT, THEODORE (1858–1919). Following the simultaneous deaths of his mother and first wife in 1884, the eventual 26th U.S. president returned to the Maltese Cross Ranch in which he had bought partnership the previous year and stayed until 1886. Roosevelt renamed it "Chimney Butte Ranch"; it stood along the Little Missouri River about seven miles south of **Medora.** He also established his own "Elkhorn Ranch" about 35 miles north of Medora. After 1886 Roosevelt's ranch visits were brief and he sold all of this Badlands property in 1898. The restored Maltese Cross Ranch Cabin National Historic Landmark stands relocated at the Medora Visitor Center of Theodore Roosevelt National Memorial Park, a 70,436-acre preserve that contains, in its South Unit, acreage from the Roosevelt ranches. Audiovisual programs and memorabilia of Roosevelt's stay are presented by the National Park Service. A 38-mile scenic road loops through the South Unit, while the North Unit is accessible via U.S. Highway 85 south of Watford City. (Open June 1–Labor Day, daily 8:00–8:00; Labor Day–May 31, daily 8:00–4:30; 701-623-4467; free.) Elkhorn Ranch site occupies land outside the park limits; follow signs north from Medora, but check on unpaved road conditions first.

(See Chapter 2, BRONX, MANHATTAN; also Chapter 3, DISTRICT OF COLUMBIA, NEW YORK; also Chapter 6, NEW MEXICO.)

OHIO

Perhaps not more than a half-dozen of our 50 states have been absolutely pivotal to national direction and development. A major reason for Ohio's pivotal importance lies in the number of prominent Ohioans who profoundly influenced how we work, perceive and live today. Ohio's history, from its ancient Moundbuilding culture and the French and Indian conflicts that raged over its soil to its Civil War trauma and mighty industrial growth, has also mirrored and condensed the entire American past in both positive and negative images. The name of the state apparently derives from an Iroquois word meaning the "great river" of its southern boundary.

Ohio's earliest known dwellers, the Mound-builders, left abundant marks of their presence on mid-America's most durable tablet, the land. The natives encountered by the first whites, however, were relative newcomers themselves— detached bands of Miamis, Shawnees, Wyandots and Delawares, perhaps 15,000 total. Pierre Céloron de Bienville, an explorer strangely neglected by historians, claimed this region for France in 1749, but the area rapidly fell to the dispute of European powers as English colonial traders intruded. The resistance of the French and their Indian allies was bloody but not victorious. After their final withdrawal, Ohio officially became part of the British Province of Quebec in 1774. The American Revolution, as experienced by Ohio, blazed into savage frontier warfare between the British-supplied natives and American frontiersmen. British defeat vindicated the Ohio land claims of Virginia; along with Connecticut's large Western Reserve in northeastern Ohio, these claims were ceded to the new national government, which created the Northwest Territory with Ohio as its main seat in 1787. Organized settlement proceeded rapidly, mainly from New England, and Marietta became first town and capital of the new territory. After the 1794 Battle of Fallen Timbers crushed the last native resistance, the influx of settlers became a flood via the Ohio River and, later, the National Road. Indiana Territory split off in 1800, and Ohio entered the Union as the 17th state three years later. By 1840 Ohio was the third most populous state, a position it maintained until 1890 (today it ranks sixth). No important Civil War battles occurred on Ohio soil, but the state was strongly pro-Union, and Confederate forces invaded to their northernmost point at Salineville in 1863.

Ohio's landscape, a relic of the ice age, gently rolls and swells except in the unglaciated southeast, a region of outright hills. Pioneers found dense hardwood forest covering most of this surface, and for more than a generation the first task of any Ohio settler lay with axe and saw. Today, as one of America's foremost industrial states, Ohio manufactures a huge diversity of the products that characterize the machine age. Steel, rubber and transportation equipment rank highest. In commerce, Ohio River cargo traffic exceeds that of the Panama Canal, and nine Lake Erie ports rank among the nation's busiest. Ohio's likewise diversified agriculture produces almost 6 percent of the nation's corn; and the world's entire supply of Liederkranz cheese comes from Van Wert. Columbus, the capital since 1816, ranks second in size after Cleveland; Cincinnati is third largest.

More than for most states, Ohio's rich past is woven into the biographical fabric of its noted residents. Influential Ohio writers included Sherwood Anderson, Zane Grey, Hart Crane, Harriet Beecher Stowe and James Thurber. Inventors Thomas Edison and the Wright Brothers were Ohio men; teachers Horace Mann and William H. McGuffey patterned much of the nation's educational system there; and natives Annie Oakley and Clark Gable became star entertainers of their times. Ohio has produced eight U.S. presidents (including William Henry Harrison, not a native)—more than any state except Virginia—though deciding which of them was "greatest" may not be a very rewarding task. John D. Rockefeller originated his endless fortune in Cleveland, and in Hudson and Akron John Brown cultivated his blood-lust over the slavery issue. Prominent Ohio soldiers included the nation's largest chunk of Union top brass: Ulysses S. Grant, Philip H. Sheridan, William T. Sherman and George A. Custer. As advanced in historical preservation as in almost every other enterprise, Ohio welcomes visitation to homes, sites and museums associated with most of these residents plus many others.

ANDERSON, SHERWOOD BERTON (1876–1941). The author's birthplace, a small one-story cottage, remains privately owned at 142 South Lafayette St. in **Camden,** his infant home to 1877.

In **Clyde,** the model for Anderson's *Winesburg, Ohio* (1919), the author's boyhood home from 1884 until 1896 stands at 120 Spring Ave., a private dwelling that has been considerably altered.

Elyria, where Anderson managed his own small paint factory and suffered the nervous breakdown that would turn him to writing, contains two of his residences, both privately owned. He lived at the Gray Apartment building at West and Second streets in 1907 and 1908; and, from 1908 to 1913, at 229 Seventh St., a house dating from about 1900.

Exhibit: The Clyde Public Library at 222 West Buckeye St. in **Clyde** contains Anderson memorabilia and photos in a small basement museum. (Open Wednesday 5:30–8:30 and on request; 419-547-7174; free.)

(See Chapter 2, MANHATTAN; also Chapter 5, LOUISIANA, VIRGINIA.)

BEECHER, HENRY WARD (1813–1887).
BEECHER, LYMAN (1775–1863).

Lyman Beecher, the fiery Calvinist preacher, arrived in **Cincinnati** with his family in 1832 to assume the presidency of Lane Theological Seminary. They occupied what is now Stowe House Community Center, the two-story, L-shaped brick house built for him at 2950 Gilbert Ave. (at the corner of U.S. Highway 22 and State Highway 3) in the Walnut Hills section, at that time a virgin hardwood forest. The energetic senior Beecher lived there until 1850; his study on the ground floor, to which a separate entrance opened from outside, was usually littered ankle-high in papers. His clergyman son Henry resided there until 1837 while attending the seminary; and daughter Harriet Beecher Stowe also lived there (see the entry on Stowe later in this section). Later known as the Edgement Inn and now containing exhibits of Ohio Black history, the house operated by the State of Ohio displays one room of Beecher family items. (Open June 1–September 20, Wednesday–Sunday 10:00–5:00; 513-221-0004; free.)

(See INDIANA in this chapter; also CONNECTICUT, MASSACHUSETTS; also Chapter 2, BROOKLYN; also Chapter 3, NEW YORK.)

BROWN, JOHN (1800–1859). In **Hudson,** the violently righteous abolitionist grew up, worked in his father's tannery and married his first wife. Several local houses where he resided no longer stand, but the frame house he built with his own hands in 1823 and 1824 remains on 66 acres purchased by Brown's father, the site of John Brown's earlier house and tannery (1818–24). Brown returned there periodically after he moved to Pennsylvania in 1825, and the house remained in the Brown family until 1869. It stands at 1842 Hines Hill Road (privately occupied). A later addition has left the original portion intact.

While raising sheep and selling wool in **Akron,** Brown lived from 1842 to 1846 in the frame house that stands remodeled at 514 Diagonal Road. Now the John Brown Home Museum, this 1835 house was built by Brown's employer and given by him to Brown. Though considerably altered, the house contains the original six-inch oak flooring in the dining room plus period furnishings. It is operated by the Summit County Historical Society. (Open Tuesday–Sunday 1:00–5:00; 216-535-1120; admission.)

Exhibit: The Ohio Historical Center at 17th Avenue off Interstate Highway 71 in **Columbus** displays Brown memorabilia and relics. (Open Monday–Saturday 9:00–5:00, Sunday 1:00–5:00; 614-466-1500; free.)

(See IOWA, KANSAS in this chapter; also Chapter 1, CONNECTICUT; also Chapter 3, MARYLAND, NEW YORK, PENNSYLVANIA, WEST VIRGINIA.)

CRANE, HART (1899–1932). His personal life was a shambles of neurotic conflicts and compulsions, but his poetic vision resembled Whitman's in its mystical affirmation of American symbol and meaning. Crane's **Garrettsville** birthplace, a large, frame Victorian mansion, stands privately owned and unmarked near the center of town at 10688 Freedom St., his infant home until 1903.

From 1903 to 1908 Crane lived with his parents in **Warren** at what is now 340–350 High St. A brick front has been added to this building, which now contains offices.

Crane spent most of an unhappy boyhood marked by extreme family dissension in **Cleve-**

land from 1908 and at adulthood intervals to 1925. He began writing poetry in his north tower room at 1709 East 115th St., a large Victorian house that remains privately owned. The family home from 1920 stood at 11431 Euclid Ave., razed in 1963.

After Crane's businessman father moved to **Chagrin Falls** in 1929, the poet frequently came for lengthy visits and stayed at "Canary Cottage," the senior Crane's restaurant-dwelling located at 87 West St. off U.S. Highway 422, still a commercial building. The father and son occupied the upper floor there.

(See Chapter 2, BROOKLYN, MANHATTAN.)

CUSTER, GEORGE ARMSTRONG (1839–1876). Flamboyance is not a historically unusual characteristic in American generals, but in reckless bravado this long-haired soldier and Indian exterminator had few peers. A monument, bronze statue and exhibit pavilion mark the one-acre Custer homestead site, his birthplace, at Custer Memorial State Park, State Highway 646 near **New Rumley.** The youngster called "Autie" by his family lived there until age 13 and for occasional intervals thereafter. Today a picnic area pacifies this seedbed of so much strut, gratuitous violence and inglorious martyrdom.

(See KANSAS, MICHIGAN, NORTH DAKOTA; SOUTH DAKOTA in this chapter; also Chapter 5, KENTUCKY; also Chapter 6, MONTANA.)

DARROW, CLARENCE SEWARD (1857–1938). The famed trial lawyer's boyhood home from 1864 to 1878 stands at **Kinsman,** a two-story, octagonal, white frame house built in 1850. Darrow Octagon House stands just north of the town public square at the intersection of State Highways 5 and 7. It is privately owned.

Darrow practiced law in **Ashtabula** from 1884 to 1887 and lived at what is now 4744 Park Ave. To his agnostic ghost's chagrin, no doubt, that residence became a Jehovah's Witness chapel in 1948; later converted to a warehouse, it fell in 1956, and a bank parking lot now occupies the site. As a local librarian recently expressed in an oft-heard civic lament, Darrow "didn't make much impression on the city until recent years when everyone is doing research on outstanding citizens!"

(See ILLINOIS in this chapter; also Chapter 5, TENNESSEE.)

EDISON, THOMAS ALVA (1847–1931). Edison Birthplace National Historic Landmark, the 1842 brick cottage where the inventor lived with his parents until 1854, stands at 9 Edison Drive in **Milan.** As a boy, he was known to his family and playmates as "Al." "Little Al's curiosity and the scrapes it got him into soon were the talk of the town," wrote John Drury. "Seeing a hen sitting on eggs in the barn behind the house, he decided to sit on some eggs too, eager to know if he could hatch out little chicks. And in that same barn Al tried to solve the mystery of fire. The barn was destroyed, and the spanking Al's father gave him was staged in the public square, as a lesson to other boys." The light bulbs we take for granted, of course, witness to Edison's stubborn, lifelong failure to learn conventional lessons. Edison bought back his birthplace in 1906 and retained ownership for the rest of his life. Today the Edison Birthplace Association exhibits family and period furnishings, invention models and personal memorabilia of the great tinkerer. (Open January 2–May 31, Tuesday–Sunday 1:00–5:00; June 1–November 30, Tuesday–Saturday 9:00–5:00, Sunday 1:00–5:00; 419-499-2135; admission.)

(See MICHIGAN in this chapter; also Chapter 3, NEW JERSEY; also Chapter 5, FLORIDA, KENTUCKY.)

FOSTER, STEPHEN COLLINS (1826–1864). From 1846 to 1850 the popular songwriter worked as a bookkeeper for his brother in **Cincinnati** and lived at Mrs. Griffin's boardinghouse. The site of this long-gone dwelling is marked by a tablet at the Guilford Public School, 421 East Fourth St. This was where Foster wrote "O Susannah" (1848), among others of his earliest songs.

(See Chapter 2, MANHATTAN; also Chapter 3, NEW JERSEY, PENNSYLVANIA; also Chapter 5, FLORIDA, KENTUCKY.)

GABLE, CLARK (1901–1960). The film actor known as the "King of Hollywood" was born in the two-story, white frame house at 138 Charleston St. in **Cadiz,** his home until his mother died there in 1902. The family occupied an apartment in this two-family dwelling, which remains privately owned.

Gable's father built a six-room house on four acres at **Hopedale** in 1905. This two-story frame dwelling, also private, stands marked on Mill Street across from the Methodist Church near

LAWNFIELD, HOME OF JAMES A. GARFIELD. In **Mentor**, the 20th U.S. president lavished time and attention on his farm, shown here in an engraving that dates from about 1880.

The house remains much the same today except for a wing constructed in 1886 to hold a memorial library. (*Courtesy Library of Congress*)

the village center. Gable lived there until 1917.

In **Akron,** Gable roomed at 1163 Getz St. (privately owned) in 1917 and 1918 while holding factory jobs in the city.

(See Chapter 6, CALIFORNIA.)

GARFIELD, JAMES ABRAM (1831–1881). The 20th U.S. president, third from Ohio and second to die by assassin's bullet, was born near the present community of **Moreland Hills,** where a marker identifies Abram Garfield Farm Site Park at the southwest corner of S.O.M. Center and Jackson roads. After his father died from the effects of fighting a forest fire that threatened their cabin, Garfield supported his widowed mother by working the farm. A new frame house replaced the cabin in 1843, and his mother sold the property a decade later. This wooded acreage, which contains no remnant of the farmstead, was Garfield's home until about 1850.

Access to the park, which remains undeveloped with a woodland trail, is via an entrance beside the Moreland Hills Town Hall. (See below for information on the birthplace replica.)

In **Hiram,** where Garfield lived during his early congressional career, he bought the two-story frame house at 6825 Hinsdale St. in 1863. Garfield and his wife enlarged the original 1852 dwelling—their first owned home—and resided there until they sold the property in 1872. It remains privately occupied.

At 8095 Mentor Ave. in **Mentor** stands Garfield Home National Historic Landmark ("Lawnfield"), a rambling Victorian mansion dating in its oldest part from 1831, with 1876 and 1886 additions. Garfield acquired this dwelling in 1876 while serving as an Ohio congressman and spent long hours remodeling the house and working his adjacent fields. From there he conducted his 1880 presidential race, the first "front-porch" political campaign in national history. The small building used as a campaign office and equipped with telegraph wires stands at a corner of the house. Also on the property is a replica of Garfield's Moreland Hills birthplace, a structure that earned him credentials as one of our few genuine "log-cabin" presidents; it contains period furnishings. The 26-room house itself displays Garfield family furnishings and possessions including the hat he was wearing when shot, the Bible on which he took the presidential oath, his inaugural address manuscript, a set of White House china used by the Garfields, part of his library and numerous other items. Lawnfield is operated by Lake County Historical Society. (Open April 15–November 15, Tuesday–Saturday 9:00–5:00, Sunday 1:00–5:00; 216-255-8722; admission.)

(See Chapter 3, DISTRICT OF COLUMBIA, NEW JERSEY.)

GOODYEAR, CHARLES (1800–1860).

Exhibit: In **Akron,** the Goodyear World of Rubber displays memorabilia of the New England inventor whose 1839 accidental discovery of vulcanized rubber keyed the development of the tire industry, among others. Exhibits include Goodyear's desk and cane, both made of hard rubber, plus letters and a replica of his workshop. This museum is operated by the Goodyear Tire & Rubber Co. at 1144 East Market St. (Open Monday–Friday 8:30–4:30; 216-794-2044; free.)

(See Chapter 1, CONNECTICUT, MASSACHUSETTS; also Chapter 3, PENNSYLVANIA.)

GRANT, ULYSSES SIMPSON (1822–1885). The Civil War general and 18th U.S. president was the first of eight Ohio natives sent to the White House. Grant Birthplace State Memorial, a small frame house dating from 1817, stands on State Highway 232 at **Point Pleasant,** an Ohio River town where the infant lived with his parents for only a year. Period furnishings and memorabilia are displayed by the Ohio Historical Society. (Open April 1–October 31, Wednesday–Saturday 9:30–5:00, Sunday 1:00–5:00; 614-466-1500; admission.)

From 1823 to 1839 Grant lived in the two and one-half-story brick house built by his father at 219 East Grant Ave. in **Georgetown.** Grant Boyhood Home, restored to its former appearance, is privately maintained by Mr. and Mrs.

John A. Ruthven. (Open by appointment; 513-378-3760).

Exhibit: In **Georgetown,** the Ohio Historical Society displays Grant memorabilia in the 1809 Grant Schoolhouse, the youngster's first classroom, on South Water Street. (Open April 1–November 1, Tuesday–Sunday 9:30–5:00; admission.)

(See ILLINOIS, MICHIGAN, MISSOURI in this chapter; also Chapter 2, MANHATTAN; also Chapter 3, DISTRICT OF COLUMBIA, NEW JERSEY, NEW YORK; also Chapter 5, VIRGINIA; also Chapter 6, WASHINGTON.)

GREY, ZANE (1875–1939). The birthplace of the author, who started out as a dentist but turned to writing Westerns and produced 54 adult novels plus numerous boys' books, stands privately owned at 705 Convers Ave. in **Zanesville,** a town named for a Grey ancestor. Pearl Zane Grey (he later dropped his first name) lived in this seven-room frame house until 1890 and wrote his first story in a rocky cave "hideout" at the rear. His dentist father, convinced that teeth offered life's highest destiny for the boy, discovered him there one day and tore his first manuscript to shreds, thus guaranteeing his perseverance as a writer. Grey revisited his birthplace and the cave of his destiny in 1921.

Exhibit: The National Road-Zane Grey Museum, operated by the Ohio Historical Society at 8850 East Pike on U.S. Highway 40 at **Norwich,** displays Grey manuscripts, first editions, sports equipment, a replica of his Altadena, Calif., study and other exhibits of his life as baseball player, dentist, outdoorsman and writer. (Open Monday–Saturday 9:30–5:00, Sunday 11:00–5:00; 614-872-3143; admission.)

(See Chapter 2, MANHATTAN; also Chapter 3, PENNSYLVANIA; also Chapter 6, ARIZONA, CALIFORNIA.)

HANNA, MARCUS ALONZO "MARK" (1837–1904). The businessman, senator, and powerful political manager and advisor of President McKinley (see the entry on William McKinley later in this section), was born at **Lisbon** in a privately owned house at Park Avenue and Market Street, his home until 1852.

In **Cleveland,** Hanna's first married home (1864–90s) stands at 2905 Franklin Ave., now the Cuyahoga County Archives building. McKinley was a frequent visitor at Hanna's last permanent home, a large mansion that stood on Lake Avenue.

(See Chapter 3, DISTRICT OF COLUMBIA; also Chapter 5, GEORGIA.)

HARDING, WARREN GAMALIEL (1865–1923). The 29th U.S. president—our first absolutely "foul ball" in the White House and therefore of more than ordinary interest—was a man of low intelligence and ability, chosen by Republican kingmakers apparently for his jovial eagerness to please and his dark good looks. Still, he was smart enough to learn that he wasn't smart enough for the job. Sudden death rescued him from the consequences of the Teapot Dome scandal. He was born in a saltbox cottage at a marked site, now a field, on State Highway 97 just east of its junction with County Road 20 near **Blooming Grove.** Almost half a mile further east stands a two-story, white frame house on the north side of the highway, Harding's earliest extant home (to 1873). It remains privately owned. Tiny Blooming Grove, according to the Harding Memorial Association, was "the glamor spot of young Warren's early life."

Harding spent most of his boyhood, from 1873 to 1880, in **Caledonia.** The family home was the white frame house identified by a marker on the northwest corner of South and Main streets, still privately owned.

Harding made his permanent home in **Marion** as a newspaper publisher, state legislator, and U.S. senator until elected president. The parental dwelling where he lived from 1882 to 1891—and where his funeral was conducted—stood at 500 East Center St., a site now occupied by a commercial building. In 1891 Harding married Mrs. Florence Kling De Wolfe, nicknamed "the Duchess," in the home they had planned and built in 1890 at 380 Mount Vernon Ave., their permanent residence until the couple left Marion for the last time in 1921. This large, green-frame Victorian mansion, now Harding House National Historic Landmark, has been restored to its 1900 appearance and contains original furnishings and household items—their pajamas are even laid out on their twin beds. In the back yard stands the small cottage that served as the press office during Harding's 1920 front-porch campaign. It now houses a museum of political memorabilia including his inaugural lectern and infant cradle (but nothing remotely resembling a teapot). The

Harding Memorial Association efficiently maintains this property with understandable reticence about its two unhappy former occupants and the national trauma it inevitably represents. (Open April 1–October 31, Wednesday–Saturday 9:30–5:00, Sunday 1:00–5:00; 614-387-9630; admission.)

(See Chapter 3, DISTRICT OF COLUMBIA; also Chapter 6, CALIFORNIA.)

HARRISON, BENJAMIN (1833–1901). "I want it understood that I am the grandson of nobody," he overstated while attempting to carve his own political niche. The 23rd U.S. president, grandson of William Henry Harrison (see the entry on William Henry Harrison below), was born on the Harrison family homestead at **North Bend,** his home until age two. In 1833 the grandfather built a two-story brick house for his son's family on 600 acres near his own Ohio river home, and this became Benjamin Harrison's home until 1853. "Point Farm," as he called it, stood in the present area of Harrison State Memorial, a 14-acre state park which contains the tomb of the elder Harrison and overlooks the Ohio River just off U.S. Highway 50 on Loop Avenue.

(See INDIANA in this chapter; also Chapter 3, DISTRICT OF COLUMBIA.)

HARRISON, WILLIAM HENRY (1773–1841). The first Ohio frontier home in 1795 and 1796 of the soldier who would become territorial governor and ninth U.S. president occupied the southeast bastion of Fort Washington, constructed in 1789 and the largest military post of the Northwest Territory. The site is marked on Fort Washington Way near Third Street in **Cincinnati.**

In 1796, mainly by inheritance from his father-in-law, Harrison acquired a baronial acreage along the Ohio River west of Cincinnati at **North Bend.** Over the years he expanded his original 160 acres to 2,200, with a 600-acre detached piece to the west that he gave his son, a portion that became the boyhood home of grandson Benjamin Harrison (see the entry on Benjamin Harrison above). In 1796 the elder Harrison built a five-room, two-story log cabin at what is now the southwest corner of Symmes and Washington avenues; he later incorporated this cabin into his 13-room dwelling of log and frame—the "Big House" on the same site. This rambling structure, "wholly without architectural graces," according to one biographer, became the emblem of Harrison's "log-cabin" campaign for the presidency. Harrison retired there in 1829 and stayed until he entered the White House in 1841. The house burned down in 1858.

(See INDIANA in this chapter; also Chapter 3, DISTRICT OF COLUMBIA; also Chapter 5, VIRGINIA.)

HAYES, RUTHERFORD BIRCHARD (1822–1893). The 19th U.S. president, elected not by the people but by a slanted electoral commission, was born in **Delaware;** a marker identifies the site of the two-story house of frame and brick where he lived until 1836 at the northeast corner of East William and Winter streets.

Most ex-presidents become more conservative with age and the lapse of power, but Hayes considerably enlarged his horizons after his White House tenure. Active in several reform causes following his 1881 retirement to **Fremont,** he became increasingly sympathetic to Socialist ideas. Spiegel Grove National Historic Landmark at 1337 Hayes Ave. is Hayes's 25-acre wooded estate and Victorian mansion, now operated by the Ohio Historical Society. A Hayes uncle had purchased the estate in 1846 and built the original two-and one-half-story brick house as a summer retreat for his nephew. When Hayes inherited the property in 1874, he made extensive additions—and again in 1880 and 1889. After 1889 only two rooms—the parlor and his uncle's room above—remained of the original house. Original furnishings and family possessions are displayed in the 20-bedroom house that is rimmed with a broad veranda where the ex-president often sat with family and guests. Hayes planted numerous trees on his estate and christened the old oaks with names of his noted visitors; most of these name-plated trees survive. The six iron entrance gates surrounding the estate stood on the White House grounds during Hayes's presidential term. Hayes died at Spiegel Grove. (Open Sunday–Tuesday 2:00–5:00, Wednesday–Saturday 9:00–5:00; admission.) Hayes memorabilia, including his library, carriage and numerous other items, are also displayed in the adjacent Hayes Library and Museum. (Open Monday–Saturday 9:00–5:00, Sunday 1:30–5:00; 419-332-2081; admission.)

(See Chapter 3, DISTRICT OF COLUMBIA.)

JARRELL, RANDALL (1914–1965). The poet and critic taught English at Kenyon College in **Gambier** from 1937 to 1939 and resided during this period in the home of his mentor John Crowe Ransom (see the entry on Ransom later in this section).

(See Chapter 5, NORTH CAROLINA; also Chapter 6, CALIFORNIA, TEXAS.)

LINCOLN, ABRAHAM (1809–1865).
Exhibit: The desk used in the White House by the 16th U.S. president and several successors is displayed at the Hayes Library and Museum in **Fremont** (see the entry on Rutherford Birchard Hayes earlier in this section).

(See ILLINOIS, INDIANA, MICHIGAN in this chapter; also Chapter 3, DISTRICT OF COLUMBIA, PENNSYLVANIA; also Chapter 5, KENTUCKY, TENNESSEE.)

LOWELL, ROBERT TRAILL SPENCE, JR. (1917–1977). Noted poet and descendant of the famed New England Lowells, Robert Lowell studied at Kenyon College in **Gambier** from 1937 to 1940. During this period, he shared quarters with Randall Jarrell in the home of John Crowe Ransom (see the entries on Jarrell and Ransom earlier in this section).

(See Chapter 1, MAINE, MASSACHUSETTS; also Chapter 2, MANHATTAN.)

McGUFFEY, WILLIAM HOLMES (1800–1873). "McGuffey's *Readers,*" wrote one observer, "were in their time almost as influential as the Bible in making the little Johnnies and Annies of a crude, expanding frontier region conscious of right and wrong, of good and bad." The locale of the educator's first Ohio residence is marked as McGuffey Boyhood Home Site National Historic Landmark on McGuffey Road, east of State Highway 616 north of **Coitsville Center** near Youngstown. McGuffey grew up there from 1802 until he left the 165-acre family farm about 1815 to begin his teaching career. The homestead itself is long gone.

In **Oxford,** McGuffey House National Historic Landmark is the two-story brick house built by the Miami University professor and Presbyterian minister in 1833, his home until 1836. There McGuffey conceived the idea of his *Eclectic Readers* and wrote the first four of the eventual six volumes; he also taught in his home the first children's classes that used the readers. The six-room house at 401 East Spring St. (at the corner of Oak

Street), now owned and operated by Miami University, has undergone important alterations, both inside and out, and there has been no effort to retrieve a 19th-century appearance. It was originally attached to an earlier frame dwelling on the site. Today the house contains many McGuffey furnishings, including his personally designed octagon desk with swivel top, items from his last home in Virginia, and a large collection of McGuffey *Readers* and *Spellers*. (Open Tuesday, Sunday 2:00–4:30; other times by appointment; closed during August; 513-529-4917; free.)

McGuffey endured the unhappiest period of his life during his presidency of Ohio University in **Athens** from 1839 to 1843. Townspeople resented taxes levied to support the struggling campus and subjected McGuffey himself to violent personal abuse. His two-story frame house stood on East Union Street facing the campus near the northeast corner of Court Street. Ohio University archivists cannot estimate how long it stood. The eastern portion of the Beckley Building now occupies this site.

(See MICHIGAN in this chapter; also Chapter 3, PENNSYLVANIA; also Chapter 5, VIRGINIA.)

McKINLEY, WILLIAM (1843–1901). The nation's 25th president, exceedingly popular for his pious sincerity if not for his striking abilities, was also the third assassination victim of that office. None of his dwellings (except the White House) remain. His two-story birthplace, part of which served as a village grocery store, is long gone from the Main Street center of **Niles,** where he lived until 1852.

In **Canton,** McKinley's white frame house—an 1871 wedding gift from his father-in-law—stood at the southwest corner of North Market Avenue and Eighth Street. McKinley sold the dwelling after his 1877 election to Congress but rented it as the base for his 1896 presidential campaign, which he conducted on the front porch. In 1899 he bought it back and last returned just before his assassination in Buffalo, N.Y. The McKinleys, a devoted couple, experienced early happiness and much sorrow on this site where both of their infant girls died and where Ida Saxton McKinley became a lifelong invalid from the 1870s. "More than a dwelling place," wrote biographer Margaret Leech, "this was the shrine of their early joys and sorrows." In decrepit condition by 1934, the

house was razed for the later Mercy Hospital on the site.

As Ohio governor (1891–96), McKinley occupied a suite in the Neil House Hotel in **Columbus.** This structure on South High Street near the State Capitol lasted until 1981, when it was razed.

Exhibits: The National McKinley Birthplace Memorial at 40 North Main St. in **Niles** occupies the site of the small white schoolhouse first attended by McKinley. Operated by the McKinley Memorial Association, the museum displays career relics and biographical exhibits. (Open Monday–Friday 10:00–8:00, Saturday 9:30–5:30; 216-652-1704; free.)

In **Canton,** Stark County Historical Center at 749 Hazlett Ave., Monument Park, contains the McKinley Museum with personal memorabilia and displays. (Open Tuesday–Friday 10:00–5:00, Saturday 12:00–5:00, Sunday 1:30–5:00; 216-455-7043; admission.)

(See Chapter 3, DISTRICT OF COLUMBIA, NEW YORK.)

MANN, HORACE (1796–1859). From 1853 the innovative educator lived in **Yellow Springs** as president of Antioch College. The site of his home is now occupied by the Horace Mann Library on the campus.

(See Chapter 1, MASSACHUSETTS.)

NORRIS, GEORGE WILLIAM (1861–1944). Birthplace of the "Fighting Liberal" who represented Nebraska for 30 years in the U.S. Senate stands privately owned at 2148 County Road 270, just east of **Clyde.** This two-story, frame farmhouse built by Norris's father in 1841 has been carefully maintained by the present owners. Norris left the family homestead about 1880.

(See NEBRASKA in this chapter.)

OAKLEY, ANNIE (1860–1926). Phoebe Anne Oakley Mozee, vaudeville sharpshooter without peer, was born in a weatherbeaten log cabin northeast of the village of **Willowdell,** her home to age nine. The site of the cabin, which burned down about 1900, was precisely located by a research team in 1980, and a marker identifies the spot on Spencer Road, about one mile south of State Highway 705.

The site of her girlhood home from 1872 to 1876 is also marked on U.S. Highway 127 south of **North Star.** There, while still a child, she developed amazing skill in hunting game, marketed the meat and paid off the farm mortgage for her widowed mother. The house on this property lasted until the 1950s.

She returned to her native area in 1926 and roomed at the home of friends in **Greenville,** dying there in the privately owned house at 225 East Third St., a frame structure dating from about 1895.

Exhibit: The Garst Museum, operated by Darke County Historical Society at 205 North Broadway in **Greenville,** displays the largest collection of Oakley memorabilia—her guns, costumes, trophies, traveling trunk and gifts—in its Annie Oakley Room. (Open Tuesday–Sunday 1:00–5:00; closed January; 513-548-5250; free.)

(See Chapter 3, MARYLAND, NEW JERSEY; also Chapter 5, FLORIDA, NORTH CAROLINA.)

QUANTRILL, WILLIAM CLARKE (1837–1865). The schoolmaster who turned gambler, then thief, Quantrill found the Kansas border warfare opportune for waging violence on both sides until he joined the Confederates as a guerrilla captain and led the notorious 1863 massacre at Lawrence, Kan. Quantrill, one of the most unsavory characters in national history, was born at **Dover,** his home until about 1857. His birthplace, then a one-story frame house, still exists, though neither the town nor the house occupants like to broadcast the fact. It stands much modified as a physician's office near Factory and Fourth streets. Quantrill's mother sold the house in 1885.

(See KANSAS in this chapter.)

RANSOM, JOHN CROWE (1888–1974). Important in literature for the distinctive students he trained as well as for his own poetry and criticism, Ransom taught at Kenyon College in **Gambier** from 1937 and occupied three residences there. His first was the 1833 Walton House, the two-story frame building at 103 College Drive on the campus, now used as the Kenyon financial center. There Ransom rented out a second-floor room to his students Randall Jarrell and Robert Traill Spence Lowell, Jr., who later became distinguished poets (see the entries on Jarrell and Lowell earlier in this section). An expert gardener, Ransom raised flowers as well as poets there. His next home, occupied during the 1940s and 1950s, also stands on the campus, at 304 Gaskin St. It now houses extracurricular craft activities for Kenyon students. In 1958 Ransom built the first and only home he ever owned, also his last home, at 220 North Ackland St.; it remains privately occupied.

(See Chapter 5, TENNESSEE.)

RICKENBACKER, EDWARD VERNON "EDDIE" (1890–1973). The World War I flying ace and business executive was a native of **Columbus.** His boyhood home at 1334 East Livingston Ave. stands in a deteriorating neighborhood, though initial steps have been taken to give the house National Register status. Rickenbacker's father, a Swiss immigrant, built the one and one-half-story, L-shaped dwelling about 1894, and this remained the son's permanent home until his 1922 marriage. Rickenbacker himself helped add the north ell and a cellar in about 1900; after his father's death there in 1904, he paid off the mortgage. This house remained in the Rickenbacker family until 1960, when the present shingle siding was added over the construction of frame and brick. Just north of the house stands the shed in which Rickenbacker tinkered and made mechanical experiments. The property remains privately owned.

Exhibit: The U.S. Air Force Museum, located at Old Wright Field on Springfield Pike northeast of **Dayton,** shows Rickenbacker medals, albums, diaries and other memorabilia. (Open Monday–Friday 9:00–5:00, Saturday–Sunday 10:00–6:00; 513-255-3284; free.)

(See INDIANA, MICHIGAN in this chapter; also Chapter 2, MANHATTAN; also Chapter 3, NEW YORK; also Chapter 5, FLORIDA; also Chapter 6, TEXAS.)

RICKEY, BRANCH WESLEY (1881–1965). The boyhood home of the lawyer who, in 1946, brought professional baseball into the 20th century by signing black player Jackie Robinson to the Brooklyn Dodgers stands in a rural area near **Lucasville.** This privately owned farmhouse, dating from the 1880s and Rickey's home from about 1892 to 1899, is located at Duck Run and is still occupied by Rickey family members.

(See MISSOURI in this chapter; also Chapter 2, BROOKLYN; also Chapter 3, MARYLAND, PENNSYLVANIA.)

ROCKEFELLER, JOHN DAVISON (1839–1937). The parsonlike oil magnate and philanthropist founded the Rockefeller family fortune while living in **Cleveland,** his home from 1853 to 1918. In 1858 the already prosperous youth built a large brick home for his parents at 33 Cheshire St., which also became Rockefeller's first married home. In 1865 he and his bride rented a nearby house at 29 Cheshire St., their home for three years. Cheshire Street, formerly a part of Cleveland's most beautiful and prestigious neighborhood, is now East 19th Street. Both houses fell when Carnegie Street was laid out; the original Rockefeller lot occupies what is now the southwest corner of Carnegie and East 19th. The first house owned by Rockefeller himself was a new two-story brick dwelling he bought in 1868 at 997 Euclid Ave. (at the corner of East 40th Street), a house much less pretentious than some that stood near it. Broad lawns, trees and a two-story carriage house in the rear completed the estate. There his second child, Alice, died in 1870—an event, it is said, that impelled her parents to establish the Rockefeller Institute for Medical Research. John D. Rockefeller, Jr., was born there in 1874. After 1878 though the house stayed in the family, the Rockefellers resided there only briefly during spring and fall seasons—and not at all after 1918. John D. Rockefeller, Jr., had this home demolished, along with his parents' New York City dwelling, a year after his father's death. It was replaced by a parking lot and filling station "for a Standard Oil competitor." According to Grace Goulder in *John D. Rockefeller: The Cleveland Years* recognize Euclid Avenue today. . . . The land is now taken over by the incredibly ugly concrete masses that house Cleveland State University."

Rockefeller's summer residence from 1878 was "Forest Hill," his 79-acre estate overlooking Lake Erie in **East Cleveland.** There he completed building an immense, 1875 wooden structure of turrets and towers, intending to run it as a hotel. When his enterprise with "paying guests" aborted, he adopted it for his permanent summer "Homestead." Over the years he extended his acreage to 700, installed a half-mile race track, stock barns, stables, a golf course, 18 miles of roadway and two lakes. "Puritanical was the word which best described the Rockefeller household," wrote biographer Allan Nevins, "a Puritanism not of New England but of the Baptist West." Forest Hill, wrote Nevins, "struck most visitors as a rather ugly house." Rockefeller rarely came there after 1913; the four-story "Homestead" burned to the ground one night in 1917. John D. Rockefeller, Jr., subdivided the huge property in the 1920s, and Forest Hill Boulevard was cut through the grounds. The son set aside the 266 acres in the heart of the original estate at 13400 Euclid Avenue for today's public Forest Hills Park.

(See Chapter 2, BROOKLYN, MANHATTAN; also Chapter 3, NEW JERSEY, NEW YORK; also Chapter 5, FLORIDA, GEORGIA.)

SHERIDAN, PHILIP HENRY (1831–1888). Probably born on the Atlantic Ocean during his parents' emigration from Ireland, the Civil War general and Indian fighter grew from infancy in **Somerset,** his home until 1848. The privately owned house at 114 West Sheridan Ave., originally a three-room frame cottage built about 1825, now has a rear addition. A former marker has apparently been stolen and not replaced. Sheridan returned there at intervals throughout his career.

(See Chapter 1, MASSACHUSETTS; also Chapter 5, VIRGINIA.)

SHERMAN, WILLIAM TECUMSEH (1820–1891). This Union general in the Civil War was a **Lancaster** native, the elder brother of noted senator John Sherman. Both were born at what is now Sherman House National Historic Landmark, the small house of frame and brick at 137 East Main St., and lived there until orphaned in 1829. Dating from 1811 in its oldest portion, the dwelling exhibits period furnishings plus war relics from Gen. Sherman's own collection. The house, operated by the Ohio Historical Society, was saved from demolition in the 1940s by the quick action of local citizens. (Open May 1–October 31, Wednesday–Saturday 9:30–5:00, Sunday 1:00–5:00; 614-653-5634; admission.) Sherman's boyhood home from 1829 until he entered West Point in 1836 was the Thomas Ewing House at 163 East Main St. (privately owned). Ewing, an Ohio politician appointed the nation's first secretary of the interior in 1849, became Sherman's unofficial guardian and father-in-law.

(See MISSOURI in this chapter; also Chapter 2, MANHATTAN; also Chapter 3, DISTRICT OF COLUMBIA; also Chapter 6, CALIFORNIA, OKLAHOMA.)

SMITH, JOSEPH (1805–1844). Having led his Mormon followers to Kirtland in 1831, Smith himself withdrew to **Hiram** with his family and occupied the 1830 farmhouse of convert John Johnson until 1832. Smith was severely beaten there by local toughs who resented Mormon settlement in the area. The clapboard Johnson House, now operated by the Church of Jesus Christ of Latter-Day Saints, stands at 6203 Pioneer Trail. Exhibits relate to Smith's period of residence there. (Open May 1–October 31, daily 9:00–9:00; November 1–April 30, daily 1:00–5:00; free.)

Smith's **Kirtland** lodging in 1831 was the Whitney Store, still a privately owned structure at the intersection of Chillicothe and Kirtland-Chardon roads. His son Joseph Smith III was born there.

Exhibit: Kirtland Temple Historic Center at 9020 Chillicothe Road in **Kirtland** commemorates the Mormon founders in the 1833 structure they erected and that served as church headquarters until 1838. It is operated by the Reorganized Church of Jesus Christ of Latter-Day Saints. (Open daily 9:00–12:00, 1:00–5:00; 216-256-3318; free.)

(See ILLINOIS, MISSOURI in this chapter; also Chapter 1, VERMONT; also Chapter 3, NEW YORK, PENNSYLVANIA; also Chapter 6, UTAH.)

STANTON, EDWIN McMASTERS (1814–1869). The birthplace of the controversial secretary of war under President Lincoln (see the entry on Abraham Lincoln earlier in this section) stood at 524 Market Place in **Steubenville** until 1977. Site of the two-story brick house where he lived until 1831 is now a parking lot for the Ohio Valley Tower.

(See Chapter 3, DISTRICT OF COLUMBIA.)

STOKOWSKI, LEOPOLD ANTHONY (1882–1977). The prominent conductor first gained national attention when he headed the **Cincinnati** Symphony Orchestra from 1909 to 1912. His home survives at 270 McGregor Ave. and remains privately owned.

(See Chapter 1, CONNECTICUT; also Chapter 2, MANHATTAN; also Chapter 3, PENNSYLVANIA.)

STOWE, HARRIET BEECHER (1811–1896). Though she lived in the parental Lyman Beecher home in **Cincinnati** for only two years (1832–34), the house at 2950 Gilbert Ave. has been named Stowe House Community Center in the author's honor. There she became exposed to the ugly reality of slavery just across the border and came into contact with fugitives escaping into the North—experiences that later ripened into one of the mightiest weapons ever produced by a pen, her book *Uncle Tom's Cabin* (1852). This house was probably also the scene of Harriet Beecher's 1836 wedding to Professor Calvin Stowe, the ceremony performed by her father (see the entry on Henry Ward Beecher and Lyman Beecher earlier in this section). Harriet and Calvin Stowe lived for 11 years (1839–51) in a frame house near that of her parents, enduring many privations on Professor Stowe's meager teaching salary from Lane Theological Seminary. In this long-gone dwelling, a site now occupied by Assumption Roman Catholic Church and Parish House at 2622 Gilbert Ave., Harriet Stowe published her first book *The Mayflower* (1843), a collection of stories and sketches.

(See Chapter 1, CONNECTICUT, MAINE, MASSACHUSETTS.)

TAFT, ROBERT ALPHONSO (1889–1953). The prominent senator and presidential aspirant, this son of President Taft (see the entry on William Howard Taft below) was a **Cincinnati** native and made the city his lifelong permanent home. He resided in 1913 and 1914 with his uncle, Charles P. Taft, at what is now Taft Museum National Historic Landmark at 316 Pike St. This 1820 mansion, operated as an art museum by the Cincinnati Institute of Fine Arts, is one of the finest examples of classical revival architecture in the Midwest. Before Charles Taft's ownership, Congressman Nicholas Longworth resided there. (Open Monday–Saturday 10:00–5:00, Sunday 2:00–5:00; 513-241-0343; free.) In 1917 the Tafts bought their 46-acre Indian Hill estate overlooking the Little Miami River. They renovated and enlarged the 19th-century, eight-room farmhouse to a 16-room, white frame colonial house that became their permanent Ohio home, "Sky Farm," in 1924. Taft raised crops and livestock there but never succeeded in making the farm a paying operation. The large two-story mansion remains privately owned at 4300 Drake Road.

(See Chapter 3, DISTRICT OF COLUMBIA.)

TAFT, WILLIAM HOWARD (1857–1930). The rotund 27th U.S. president and later chief justice was born in the first-floor bedroom at Taft National

Historic Site, 2038 Auburn Ave. in **Cincinnati.** The two-story brick house purchased by his father dates from about 1850. Taft began his law career and involvement in local politics while living there, his home until age 25. The National Park Service displays family furnishings, Taft memorabilia and exhibits on a career as well-rounded as the president's waistline. (Open Memorial Day–Labor Day, daily 8:00–4:30; Labor Day–Memorial Day, Monday–Friday 8:00–4:30; 513-684-3262; free.)

(See Chapter 1, CONNECTICUT; also Chapter 3, DISTRICT OF COLUMBIA.)

THOMAS, LOWELL JACKSON (1892–1981). World traveler, author and lecturer, but best-known as a news broadcaster for almost half a century from radio's infancy, Thomas was born in the tiny village of **Woodington** north of Greenville but lived there only briefly as a child. Built about 1875, the privately owned house stands on State Highway 49 within the village, at both ends of which are signs bidding farewell with Thomas's tag line: "So long until tomorrow!"

Exhibit: The Garst Museum at 205 North Broadway in **Greenville** displays a Lowell Thomas Room containing objects and gifts from his travels plus photos and other memorabilia. Thomas himself narrated the tapes that explain the exhibits. The museum is operated by Darke County Historical Society. (Open Tuesday—Sunday 1:00–5:00; closed January; 513-548-5250; free.)

(See Chapter 3, NEW YORK; also Chapter 6, COLORADO.)

THORPE, JAMES FRANCIS "JIM" (1888–1953). *Exhibit:* The Pro Football Hall of Fame, operated by nonprofit trustees at 2121 Harrison Ave. NW next to Fawcett Stadium in **Canton,** displays films, relics and memorabilia of football greats including the amazing halfback who emerged from Carlisle Indian School to become an Olympic champion. (Open Memorial Day–Labor Day, daily 9:00–8:00; Labor Day–Memorial Day, daily 9:00–5:00; 216-456-8207; admission.)

(See Chapter 3, PENNSYLVANIA; also Chapter 6, OKLAHOMA.)

THURBER, JAMES GROVER (1894–1961). Despite the fact that the author-cartoonist never lived in his native **Columbus** after 1922, he recognized that, for better and worse, he had never fully left. His birthplace at 251 Parsons Ave. no longer stands. The family owned and resided in the three-story brick building at 921 South Champion Ave. (privately owned) from 1898 to 1901. There, according to one biographer, Thurber spent "the only truly joyous time of his childhood." From 1913 to 1917 the family resided at 77 Jefferson Ave., a two and one-half-story brick house built about 1873 and still privately owned. Thurber fictionalized the address of this house to 77 Lexington Ave. when he wrote about it in *My Life and Hard Times* (1933). The Thurber family occupied about six other addresses in what is now Columbus's inner city, but these two dwellings are the only ones that remain.

(See Chapter 1, CONNECTICUT; also Chapter 2, MANHATTAN; also Chapter 5, VIRGINIA.)

WILLKIE, WENDELL LEWIS (1892–1944). The lawyer-businessman, who won more votes in 1940 than any previous Republican candidate but still lost the presidency, resided during his early corporate law practice in **Akron.** From 1920 to 1929, when he moved to New York City, he lived at 180 Beck Ave. (privately owned). Willkie, then a Democrat, was told by rubber magnate Harvey S. Firestone that "no Democrat can ever amount to much" and apparently believed him, though Willkie's politics always remained more liberal than the platforms of his adopted party.

(See INDIANA, KANSAS in this chapter; also Chapter 2, MANHATTAN.)

WOODHULL, VICTORIA CLAFLIN (1838–1927). One of the nation's earliest feminist activists was an Ohio native, but none of her numerous residences remain, there or elsewhere. Her birthplace and home for about a decade was a ramshackle dwelling in the village of **Homer,** where her father operated a gristmill. The shack burned to the ground in the late 1840s. Long after the woman labeled "Mrs. Satan" for her outspoken advocacy of equal rights for women and free love moved permanently to England in 1877, she built two cottages on her Cotswold estate, naming them "Homer" and "Ohio."

The large Claflin clan lived on its wits and often one step ahead of the law, stirring up talk and scandal wherever they settled. In **Cincinnati** they took up residence in a three-story, brick building that stood on the north side of West Fifth Street near Mound Street. Neighbors uneasily observed the mother and daughters Victoria and Tennes-

BOYHOOD HOME OF THE WRIGHT BROTHERS. This dwelling of the aviation pioneers, at 7 Hawthorne St. in Dayton, still stands, but not at the site of this 1900 photo. Today visitors may inspect the Wright house and belongings at Green-field Village in **Dearborn**, Mich., where industrialist Henry Ford moved it in 1937.
(*Courtesy National Air & Space Museum, Smithsonian Institution*)

see brewing patent medicine in the back yard there and spoke darkly of witchcraft, especially after the sisters hung out a shingle announcing themselves as clairvoyants. The family lived there from 1864 to 1866, when complaints that they were operating a "house of ill repute" forced them to pack up again. The dense traffic complex of Interstate Highway 71/75 now covers this area of Cincinnati.

(See Chapter 2, MANHATTAN.)

WRIGHT, ORVILLE (1871–1948).

WRIGHT, WILBUR (1867–1912).

The aviation pioneer brothers resided permanently in **Dayton** from 1885. Earlier, however, they had lived there in a frame house that stood at 7 Hawthorne St., bought by their father, a bishop, in 1871. That was Orville Wright's birthplace. The family left in 1878, then returned to the house in 1885. The parents and Wilbur Wright died there, but Orville Wright stayed until 1914; this is the frame dwelling that Henry Ford moved with much pomp to his Dearborn, Mich., Greenfield Village in 1937. In 1914 Orville Wright bought

"Hawthorne Hill," the large, columned mansion at Harmon and Park avenues in Dayton's Oakwood section, and this was his final home. It remains privately owned.

Exhibits: The bachelor brothers prepared for their epochal 1903 flight of a motor-powered aircraft in a succession of **Dayton** bicycle shops and work sheds. The Wright Cycle Co. brick shop they occupied after 1895, and where they actually built the "plane that flew," stood at 22 South Williams St. This structure was also moved to Greenfield Village in 1937. In Carillon Park, 2001 South Patterson Blvd., Wright Hall displays the Wright Flyer III, the 1905 plane described by Orville Wright as the one in which he and his brother "learned to fly"—after, of course, they had already flown at Kitty Hawk, N.C. There too is a replica of their Cycle Co. workshop. Carillon Park is maintained by a Board of Trustees. (Open May 1–October 31, Tuesday–Saturday 10:00–8:30, Sunday 1:00–8:30; 513-293-3412; free.)

(See INDIANA, MICHIGAN in this chapter; also Chapter 3, DISTRICT OF COLUMBIA, PENNSYLVANIA; also Chapter 5, NORTH CAROLINA.)

SOUTH DAKOTA

Dakota, meaning "friends" or "allies," originally labeled the confederation of northwestern Sioux, from which emerged some of America's best fighters and most intelligent statesmen. The U.S. Army, it is clear, could never have subdued these rugged plains peoples by confronting them on remotely equal terms—each time that happened, the Indians won. Finally, however, the latter possessed only spiritual weapons, and a last, desperate fervor of Indian mysticism against bullets ended in the Wounded Knee atrocity of December 29, 1890. This episode in which American soldiers systematically gunned down more than 100 starving men, women and children on their own reservation—like another December day 51 years later—lives in infamy.

The agricultural Arikara inhabited South Dakota when the French explorer Pierre de la Vérendrye became the first white man to wander this far in 1743. Displaced Sioux from Minnesota and Iowa displaced, in turn, the Arikara. Until 1858 when Yankton arose as the first permanent settlement, few whites except fur traders came. Congress carved Dakota Territory from Nebraska Territory in 1861, and both South and North Dakota entered

the Union as states on November 2, 1889. The extension of rail lines in the 1870s, plus free homestead land and the discovery of gold in the Black Hills, brought the first large influx of settlers onto sacred native lands, resulting in the bloody frontier clashes that led to Wounded Knee.

South Dakota's almost rectangular shape is bisected by the Missouri River. Flat and undulating prairie suddenly breaks into a choppy topography of western buttes, Badlands and Black Hills, folded roots of ancient mountains that extend about 60 miles across and 100 miles long. Gutzon Borglum carved one of the world's largest sculptures from Mount Rushmore. Some observers, though finding his four huddled presidential heads not, perhaps, the classiest use of a matchless topography, are gratified that at least the faces aren't smiling; the scene has become as functional for satire as Grant Wood's "American Gothic" painting. The face of the only president who actually spent much time in South Dakota—dour Calvin Coolidge, who liked to pose in Sioux headgear—would have been much more adaptable to granite. Near Custer, Korczak Ziolkowski's huge mountain effigy of Crazy Horse, when finished, will hugely surpass Borglum's—as it should, if the size of the geological visage is to reflect regional historical importance.

Pierre became the state's permanent capital in 1890, though the largest city is Sioux Falls, with 72,500 residents. South Dakota's economy depends mainly on agriculture and tourism. A larger proportion of people earn farm income there, primarily from hay crops and stockraising, than in any other state. Black Hills gold still provides an important mineral resource.

South Dakota's interesting citizens included writers L. Frank Baum, Hamlin Garland and Laura Ingalls Wilder. Sitting Bull's country also held early homes of public chieftain Hubert H. Humphrey. Of notable residences that exist, however, only Wilder's home stands open to visitors.

BAUM, LYMAN FRANK (1856–1919). Baum's books have increased in popularity over the years, especially since the 1939 film version of *The Wonderful Wizard of Oz* (1900). In **Aberdeen,** however, his fantasy fiction still lay ahead, and he operated a variety store and published a weekly newspaper there from 1888 to 1891. His home, built about 1887 and hardly changed, stands at 512 South Kline St. and is privately owned.

(See ILLINOIS in this chapter; also Chapter 3, NEW YORK.)

BORGLUM, GUTZON (1867–1941). The sculptor whose material was mountains lived and worked intermittently from 1929 to 1940 at Borglum Ranch and Studio, seven miles east of **Hermosa** on State Highway 36. This was his headquarters for carving nearby Mount Rushmore National Memorial; exhibited there are models, tools, paintings and original furnishings. (Open May 30–September 30, 7:30–7:30; admission.)

Exhibits: Borglum's best-known exhibit, of course, is his chiseled quartet of presidents staring dourly "head and shoulders" above everybody else in the world. These massive granitic crania, measuring 60 feet from scalp to mandible, cost Borglum 14 years to plan and complete. Perhaps some viewers feel a surge of patriotism on viewing the faces of four U.S. politicians capping a mountain—but for many, the impression is mainly to marvel at the colossal engineering feat; according to one cynical observer, "The magnitude of its accomplishment is outdone only by the banality of its conception." Borglum, let it be said, did much finer and more inspired work than this in his lifetime. Mount Rushmore National Memorial, operated by the National Park Service, is located three miles west of **Keystone** via U.S. Highway 16A and State Highway 244. The Visitor Center displays special programs and exhibits plus a replica of the sculptor's studio. (Open June 1–August 31, daily 7:00–10:00; September 1–May 31, daily 8:00–6:00; 605-574-2523; free.) The Rushmore-Borglum Story on Main Street in Keystone displays Borglum's original models, tools, furniture and audiovisual programs. (Open May 1–June 14, September 1–October 15, daily 8:00–7:00; June 15–August 31, daily 8:00–10:00; 605-666-4449; admission.)

(See Chapter 1, CONNECTICUT; also Chapter 2, MANHATTAN; also Chapter 6, IDAHO, TEXAS.)

BURKE, MARTHA JANE CANARY "CALAMITY JANE" (1848?–1903).

Exhibit: Transient throughout the mining camps and army posts of the West, the legendary frontier woman bested many a man at cards, drink,

guns—and, most of all, tall tales. "She liked men and she liked whiskey," wrote J. Leonard Jennewein, "and where men were, there was whiskey." As a frequent resident of **Deadwood,** she returned there in July of 1903, rode on the ore train to nearby Terry, became violently ill in a saloon and died about a week later at the Calloway Hotel. The entire town of Terry is now extinct. In Deadwood the Adams Memorial Hall Museum displays pictures of Calamity Jane (see the entry on James Butler "Wild Bill" Hickok later in this section).

(See MISSOURI in this chapter; also Chapter 6, MONTANA, WYOMING.)

COOLIDGE, CALVIN (1872–1933). The 30th U.S. president, first to summer west of the Mississippi, came to South Dakota in 1927. In the apt words of Bess Furman, "he responded to the Black Hills atmosphere like a wrinkled prune plopped into a glass of water." The State Game Lodge of stone and pine where he wore cowboy hats on the front porch was his residence and the spot where he tersely chose "not to run for President in 1928"—big news to his wife as well as to the country. State Game Lodge is located on U.S. Highway 16A in the Custer State Park community of **Game Lodge** and is now a privately operated resort claiming "Food fit for Presidents." (Open May 15–October 1; 605-255-4541.)

(See Chapter 1, MASSACHUSETTS, VERMONT; also Chapter 3, DISTRICT OF COLUMBIA.)

CUSTER, GEORGE ARMSTRONG (1839–1876).

Exhibit: In **Custer,** Way Park Museum in Way City Park, Mt. Rushmore Road, displays relics of Custer's Seventh Cavalry. This 1875 building of hewn logs is reputedly the oldest in the Black Hills. (Open June 1–August 31, 8:00–8:00; admission.)

(See KANSAS, MICHIGAN, NORTH DAKOTA, OHIO in this chapter; also Chapter 5, KENTUCKY; also Chapter 6, MONTANA.)

GARLAND, HAMLIN (1860–1940). The Garland Homestead Site, where the author lived from 1881 to 1884, is marked on State Highway 10 northeast of **Aberdeen,** two miles north and half a mile west of Ordway. At age 24, Garland escaped the homestead where he had watched his parents, like so many other pioneer farmers, grind away their lives with relentless toil. He briefly returned, however, in 1887; angered by the drudgery and human waste he observed, he wrote his first short, bitterly realistic story there, "Mrs. Ripley's Trip." He last visited in 1915; the frame house burned down a year later.

Exhibit: Friends of the Middle Border Museum—also known as the Museum of Pioneer Life—is located at 1311 South Duff St. on the Dakota Wesleyan University campus in **Mitchell.** While few items there relate directly to Garland (aside from some manuscripts), the environment he described is brought richly to life in the museum's displays. (Open May 1–31, September 1–30, Monday–Friday 9:00–5:00, Saturday–Sunday 1:00–5:00; June 1–August 31, Monday–Saturday 8:00–9:00, Sunday 10:00–9:00; 605-996-2122; admission.)

(See ILLINOIS, IOWA, WISCONSIN in this chapter; also Chapter 2, MANHATTAN; also Chapter 6, CALIFORNIA.)

HICKOK, JAMES BUTLER "WILD BILL" (1837–1876).

Exhibits: The frontier gambler, part-time lawman and deadeye marksman drew his last hand in **Deadwood,** just before Jack McCall shot him dead in Nuttall and Mann's No. 10 Saloon, which stood at 620 Main St. Hickok's camp site during his brief, final stay in Deadwood is marked with a sculptured bust by Korczak Ziolkowski on Sherman Street. Adams Memorial Hall Museum, operated by a board of trustees at 54 Sherman St. (at the corner of Deadwood Street), displays pictures of Hickok plus pioneer relics of this old mining town. (Open May 15–October 31, daily 9:00–6:00; 605-578-1714; donation.) "The Trial of Jack McCall for the Murder of Wild Bill Hickok" is staged in Old Towne Hall on Lee Street during the summer, with the purchase of advance tickets advised. (Performances June 1–August 29, Monday–Saturday 8:00 PM; 605-578-3583; admission.)

(See ILLINOIS in this chapter.)

HUMPHREY, HUBERT HORATIO (1911–1978). Only a vacant lot and locally made sign currently mark the birth site of the liberal political leader in **Wallace.** A brick building that stood on Main Street near the east end of town was the drug store owned by his father; the family resided above the store until 1915. "A suitable bronze marker"

will be placed on the site, according to recent information.

"I just loved that town," said the irrepressibly emotive vice president in reminiscing about his **Doland** boyhood. His father's pharmacy, now a cafe, stands marked on Dakota Street as the "Original Humphrey Drug Store." The family lived from 1915 to 1927 in one of the town's best houses, a two-story, white frame dwelling at the corner of South First and Iowa streets. When the Depression all but wiped out the store, Humphrey's father sold the house to pay family bills; and the family retreated to a smaller rented dwelling on Iowa Street until 1931, when they moved to Huron.

In **Huron,** where Humphrey learned the pharmacy trade and often kept store for his father, the family resided at three separate addresses: 760 Illinois Ave. SW in 1932 and 1933; 459 Seventh St. SW in 1934 and 1935; and 766 Colorado Ave. SW, 1935 and 1936. Humphrey's first married home in 1936 was 1043 Beach St. SE, where the couple lived for a year before moving to Minnesota. All of these houses remain privately owned.

(See MINNESOTA in this chapter; also Chapter 3, DISTRICT OF COLUMBIA, MARYLAND.)

SITTING BULL (1831–1890). The redoubtable chief of the Hunkpapa Sioux, who led an angry confederacy of tribes against the broken words and traitorous deeds of much more recent and paler Americans, wandered for much of his troubled life in what is now South Dakota. He was born, it is said, a few miles below the present village of **Bullhead**—not far from where he died—on the south bank of the Grand River. The place was known as "Many-Caches" because of the number of food-storage pits long used there by the Hunkpapa band. As a child, he was nicknamed "Slow" and had to earn his adult name—Tatanka Iyotake—on a buffalo hunt.

In 1881 a fugitive Sitting Bull and his dwindled band of 150 followers surrendered to the army, and he was imprisoned until 1883 at Fort Randall. The site of this 1856 fort, abandoned in 1884, is marked by its only remnant building, the Fort Randall Chapel, across from **Pickstown** at one end of Fort Randall Dam on the Missouri River. Observation points and audiovisual displays of the area and its history are presented from the dam powerhouse, operated by the U.S. Army

Corps of Engineers on U.S. Highways 18 and 281. (Open daily, 8:00–4:30; 605-487-7844; free.)

Sitting Bull was paroled to Standing Rock Reservation in 1883. Now confined almost entirely to North Dakota, the reservation then included the eastern half of Corson County below the present state line, and this area near his birth site was the leader's main residence until his arrest and apparently plotted murder. This event occurred near his cabin site on the north bank of the Grand River four miles west of State Highway 63. Follow the signs from U.S. Highway 12 north of **Mobridge.**

(See MICHIGAN in this chapter; also Chapter 6, MONTANA.)

WILDER, LAURA INGALLS (1867–1957). **De Smet** was the final destination of the Ingalls family as chronicled in her popular *Little House* series of six volumes; and De Smet was *The Little Town on the Prairie* (1941). The first family home was the Surveyor's House, the small frame dwelling now restored at 101 Olivet Ave. SW (at the corner of First Street) where they spent the fall and winter of 1879–80. The site of the "claim shanty" where the family settled in 1880 is marked on U.S. Highway 14 east of town. From 1887 to 1928 the Ingalls family resided at the house built by the father on Third Street between Poinsett and First avenues. It displays exhibits on the author. The Wilder Homestead site, where the author lived from her 1885 marriage to Almanzo Wilder until their 1894 departure for Missouri, is also marked on State Highway 25 about one and one-half miles north of town. Fire destroyed this claim shanty, the birthplace of their daughter, the author Rose Wilder Lane. All of these places and more—some 18 Ingalls and Wilder sites in the area—may be seen on tours conducted by the Laura Ingalls Wilder Memorial Society, which operates and maintains the Ingalls and Surveyor's houses. (Tours begin at Surveyor's House, June 1– September 30, daily 9:00–5:00; October 1–May 31, by appointment; 605-854-3383; admission.)

Exhibit: The **De Smet** City Library displays Ingalls family mementos. (Call 605-854-3842 for hours; free.)

(See IOWA, KANSAS, MINNESOTA, MISSOURI, WISCONSIN in this chapter.)

WISCONSIN

Jean Nicolet, voyageur and the emissary of French Governor Champlain, stepped ashore at Red Banks near Green Bay in 1634, so confident he had reached China that he dressed in oriental robes for the occasion. He quickly learned that his hosts were the Winnebago natives of "Miskonsing" (the word's meaning, apparently conjectural even to them, evolved through various spellings into "Wisconsin"), and he retired in profound confusion to Quebec. The Jesuit missionary and explorer Jacques Marquette manned two stations on the shores of the Great Lakes in the 1660s and from Green Bay, with trader Louis Jolliet, began the epochal river voyage of 1673 that heralded colonialism in the region. At Prairie du Chien on June 17, they became the first whites (after de Soto) to view the Mississippi. In their wake, Wisconsin trails, waterways and portages soon routed a main access into the midcontinent. Fur was the main pull in Wisconsin itself until the region passed to nominal U.S. ownership in 1783 (actually, British outposts remained until 1816). While native subjugation progressed and finally terminated in the Black Hawk War of 1832, lead deposits brought the first rush of white settlers to southwestern Wisconsin in 1822. Wisconsin achieved its own territorial status in 1836, splitting off from Michigan Territory, and became the 30th state in 1848. A huge influx of German and Swiss immigration is still reflected in the population of Wisconsin's cities and farms.

By the turn of the century, Wisconsin was the nation's major timber producer but soon emerged as "the great pasture state" and still maintains the leading position in dairying and associated industries. Manufacturing, however, has become the major element of the state's diverse economy, which includes heavy metalworking, machinery, shipbuilding and paper among its dominant technologies. Heavy industry centers in Milwaukee, Racine, Kenosha and Janesville. Beer, cheese, and truck-farmed vegetables are some of Wisconsin's best-known and most visible products, and its lake ports handle an international commerce. Carved by glaciers and pitted with almost 9,000 lakes, Wisconsin's rolling plain breaks off sharply in the southwestern coulee country, a rugged "Driftless Area" bypassed by glaciation. Regional prairie, hardwood and coniferous forest zones are interspersed, and the state's variety of season and landscape makes tourism a major economic resource.

Wisconsin's history is loaded with intriguing facts. The nation's first kindergarten was established at Watertown in 1856. The greatest forest fire disaster in U.S. history occurred at Peshtigo in 1871 on the same night that fire destroyed Chicago. That year also marked the largest recorded nesting ground of the now-extinct passenger pigeon—some 850 square miles of Jackson County, containing an estimated 136 million birds. Milwaukee residents originated the first practical typewriter (1869) and made the first Colby cheese (1885). The home of the ice-cream sundae is marked in Manitowoc; and Flag Day (June 14) began at Stony Hill School near Waubeka in 1885. The Gideons, worldwide Bible distributors, organized at a Boscobel hotel in 1898.

Wisconsin has often provided national leadership in progressive politics and farsighted social reform. The Republican Party, liberal haven of its day, originated at Ripon in 1854, and Robert M. La Follette led the Progressive Party to its zenith in 1924. Milwaukee is one of the few American cities that has repeatedly elected Socialist mayors. Some observers viewed the advent of Senator Joseph McCarthy as an uncharacteristic political nose dive, but the state's diversity in politics, as in most other features, makes occasional anomalies inevitable.

An impressive roster of natives, besides the contrasting politicians La Follette and Joseph McCarthy, included two massively influential iconoclasts, Thorstein Veblen and Frank Lloyd Wright. Native writers included Hamlin Garland, Ben Hecht and Laura Ingalls Wilder. Coach Vince Lombardi achieved near-legendary status, both as a sports figure and a macho ideal, during his Green Bay Packer years. Harry Houdini escaped from Wisconsin to New York, and Milwaukee-born actor Spencer Tracy gave American film some of its finest moments. To spice the generally constructive impression of Wisconsin's progeny, however, one must add criminals Al Capone and John Dillinger to the state's north-woods creatures—and hasten to qualify that neither lasted in God's country for long. Despite Wisconsin's rich legacy of eminent Americans, relatively few of their homes stand open to the public. Where such homes still exist—and many do—visitors must usually settle for exterior views.

CAPONE, ALPHONSE "AL" (1899–1947). The most powerful man in Chicago during the lawless Prohibition era owned a vacation estate near **Couderay,** to which he retired at intervals during the 1920s just like any respectable person. The thug's 400-acre northwoods retreat contained a two-story stone lodge, an eight-car garage and a gun tower where his lackeys guarded the "Boss" from intrusion. It is now a privately operated restaurant-resort called "The Hideout," where visitors may tour the estate plus eat and drink in lavish gangland style. The estate, dating from about 1925, is located six miles north of town on County Highway CC. (Open May 15–September 13, daily 12:00–11:00; September 14–October 11, Friday–Sunday 12:00–11:00; 715-945-2746; admission.)

(See ILLINOIS in this chapter; also Chapter 2, BROOKLYN; also Chapter 5, FLORIDA; also Chapter 6, CALIFORNIA.)

DILLINGER, JOHN HERBERT (1903–1934?). The outlaw whose reputed death on a Chicago street was never satisfactorily verified holed up with cronies in 1934 at Little Bohemia Resort south of **Manitowish Waters** on U.S. Highway 51. FBI agents traced them there and, on April 22, opened a barrage of gunfire that killed one innocent man and wounded two others, somehow managing to let Dillinger and his four friends escape. Little Bohemia on Star Lake is still a privately operated lakefront restaurant and bar. The two-story timber structure dates from 1930. Memorabilia and items that the outlaws left behind are displayed.

(See ILLINOIS, INDIANA in this chapter; also Chapter 3, DISTRICT OF COLUMBIA.)

FERBER, EDNA (1887–1968). At 218 North St. in **Appleton,** the novelist lived from 1897 until 1906, years in which she completed high school and became the local newspaper's first female reporter. After four years in Milwaukee, she returned to this family home in 1910 and wrote her first novel, *Dawn O'Hara* (1911) there. Private apartments now occupy this house.

Edna Ferber's century-old **Milwaukee** boardinghouse residence fell to make way for a parking lot in 1974. An architectural historian had declared that the two-story brick mansion had "no historical value" (reaffirming the fact that historical preservation, like war, is too important to leave exclusively to the "generals"). The house she occupied while working for the *Milwaukee Journal*, from 1906 to 1910, stood at 760 North Cass St.

(See IOWA, MICHIGAN in this chapter; also Chapter 1, CONNECTICUT; also Chapter 2, MANHATTAN.)

GARLAND, HAMLIN (1860–1940). Recorder of the raw hardships of pioneer life in his fiction and memoirs, Garland was born in a log cabin, long-gone, near **West Salem.** Garland Homestead National Historic Landmark at 357 West Garland St. was the 1860 home he bought on four acres for his parents in 1893. He enlarged and remodeled the two-story frame house and, until 1915, spent most of his summers there. Through the years profits from his writing enabled him to make further improvements. After a 1912 fire severely damaged the house, he had it quickly rebuilt but soon moved to the East. Garland detailed much of his life in the house in his Pulitzer Prize-winning *A Daughter of the Middle Border* (1921). The West Salem Historical Society, which operates the restored house, also displays Garland furnishings and memorabilia. (Open May 15–Memorial Day, Labor Day–September 15, daily 1:00–4:00; Memorial Day–Labor Day, daily 10:00–5:00; 608-786-1399; admission.)

(See ILLINOIS, IOWA, SOUTH DAKOTA in this chapter; also Chapter 2, MANHATTAN; also Chapter 6, CALIFORNIA.)

HECHT, BEN (1894–1964). In **Racine,** the house where the author-playwright grew up was demolished in 1961, and the site—supposedly cleared for a motel—is now a parking lot. This residence, Hecht's home from early childhood until 1910, was a two-story, rambling frame house of "capricious contours" at 838 Lake Ave. Actually a boardinghouse in which the Hecht family occupied deluxe rooms, the dwelling was managed by the widow of Dan Castello, a circus contemporary of P. T. Barnum. Mrs. Castello's boardinghouse also hosted all sorts of transient circus performers, who stirred Hecht's imagination and whom he fondly recalled in *Child of the Century* (1954).

(See ILLINOIS in this chapter; also Chapter 2, MANHATTAN; also Chapter 3, NEW YORK.)

HOUDINI, HARRY (1874–1926). The Hungarian-born showman's reputed boyhood home from 1874 to 1883 stands unmarked in **Appleton.** According to a local historical source, "The city of Appleton would dearly love to flatten it and replace it with a department store or two parking spaces," but in 1981 the dwelling still stood on Appleton Street. The historical connection of this house with the boy named Ehrich Weiss is supported only by oral tradition, which has, however, proven accurate in many local instances. It is said that he erected a homemade trapeze behind the house and began cultivating the muscular physique and endurance demanded by his later strenuous performances and escape acts.

(See MICHIGAN in this chapter; also Chapter 2, MANHATTAN.)

LA FOLLETTE, ROBERT MARION (1855–1925). Longtime senator and 1924 Progressive Party candidate for president, La Follette was born in a rural log cabin near Madison. He worked the family farm there until 1873. The site is marked three miles north of **Stoughton** on County Road B.

La Follette lived in **Madison** during his years as a practicing lawyer and congressman. His home at 405 West Wilson St. (1881–1900) now houses private apartments. From 1900 to 1906, La Follette occupied the State Executive Mansion in Madison as Governor. Located at 130 East Gilman St., this two-story sandstone edifice dates from 1854 and served as official Governor's Residence from 1883 to 1950. An earlier resident was concert violinist Ole Bull. The house is now privately owned.

From 1906, La Follette's permanent Wisconsin home was La Follette Home National Historic Landmark, a two-story brick dwelling he purchased at 733 Lakewood Blvd. in **Maple Bluff,** a suburb of Madison. The house, still privately occupied, dates from about 1860.

(See Chapter 3, DISTRICT OF COLUMBIA.)

LOMBARDI, VINCENT THOMAS (1913–1970). "Winning isn't everything. It is the only thing." So, it is popularly believed, said the legendary fire-breathing coach (1959–69) of the Green Bay Packers football team. Lombardi lived at 667 Sunset Circle (privately owned) in **Green Bay.** In *Coach* (1970), Tom Dowling relates that after Lombardi sold this house, the new owner and friends fine-combed the place for Lombardi "holy relics." Dowling doesn't say what, if anything, they found.

Exhibit: The Green Bay Packer Hall of Fame at 1901 South Oneida St. in **Green Bay** shows memorabilia and films of Lombardi and outstanding players. The nonprofit museum is operated by the Green Bay Area Visitor & Convention Bureau, Inc. (Open daily 10:00–5:00; 414-499-4281; admission.)

McCARTHY, JOSEPH RAYMOND (1908–1957). The controversial Republican senator who found Communists in every closet (or said he did) was extremely reticent about his childhood, and his living intimates have maintained a terse blackout toward biographers who might have cleared up some of the "misinformation" which those intimates have deplored but refuse to correct. McCarthy's birthplace and home until 1923 was a 142-acre farm in Grand Chute Township just south of the village of **Center** in Outagamie County. The eight-room, white frame house remains privately owned at 5711 North McCarthy Road.

The young lawyer began his political career in **Shawano** (as a Democrat); in 1939, he switched parties and was elected state circuit judge. During the period from 1936 to 1940, the bachelor attorney resided in the two and one-half-story, stucco dwelling at 404 South Main St. (privately owned), then known as the Edith Green boardinghouse. This house dates from about 1910.

In **Appleton,** McCarthy lived with relatives in a new house he bought in 1942 at 514 South Story St. (privately owned), and this remained his permanent Wisconsin address. The house remained in his family until 1960.

(See Chapter 3, DISTRICT OF COLUMBIA.)

MARQUETTE, JACQUES (1637–1675). In what is now **Ashland,** the French Jesuit missionary, later explorer of the Mississippi River, labored at La Pointe du Saint Esprit, the Chequamegon Bay mission established by Father Claude Allouez in 1665. Marquette spent 18 months (1669–71) there and learned much from the natives about the Illinois country he would penetrate with Louis Jolliet in 1673. The site of this first Christian chapel in Wisconsin stood in the Ottawa Indian village located on Fish Creek west of Ashland. State Highway 112 crosses the creek at the approximate village site.

After the exhausting exploratory journey, Marquette spent the winter of 1673–1674 at St. Francis Xavier Mission in what is now **De Pere.** The mission stood until 1717 on the bank of Fox River; its site is marked at the east end of Allouez Bridge in town.

(See ILLINOIS, MICHIGAN in this chapter.)

MEIR, GOLDA MABOWEHZ (1898–1978). The dynamic Ukrainian-born Israeli Prime Minister spent most of her childhood years in **Milwaukee.** From 1906 to 1912, she and her family occupied a five-room apartment behind the small grocery they operated at 623 West Walnut St. The young daughter worked long hours in the store. "It became the bane of my life," she wrote in her autobiography. "It began as a dairy store and then developed into a grocery; but it never prospered and it almost ruined the years I spent in Milwaukee." She went to Denver in 1912 but returned in 1914 to the family apartment and delicatessen at 750 North 10th St., where she lived while finishing high school. She married Morris Myerson there in 1917. Neither structure survives.

(See Chapter 6, COLORADO.)

SANDBURG, CARL (1878–1967). The poet and folklorist lived in **Milwaukee** from 1908 to 1912 as a Socialist political activist. For part of that period, he occupied the 1895 frame house at 3325 North Cambridge Ave., which remains privately owned.

(See ILLINOIS, MICHIGAN in this chapter; also Chapter 5, NORTH CAROLINA.)

TRACY, SPENCER BONAVENTURE (1900–1967). Two of the film actor's childhood homes remain in **Milwaukee,** both privately owned: at 2970 South Kinnickinnic Ave., and at 2447 South Graham St.

(See Chapter 6, CALIFORNIA.)

VEBLEN, THORSTEIN BUNDE (1857–1929). "He was not a popular teacher but attracted dedicated followers to his extreme social and economic ideas. His books and articles have been described as perhaps 'the most considerable and creative body of social thought that America has produced.'" So reads, in part, the state historical marker in the village park of **Valders** near Veblen's 160-acre farm birthplace, his home until 1865. The site of that farm lies unmarked on County Highway JJ, Section 29 of Cato Township, Manitowoc County.

According to a 1981 communication from Robert A. Bjerke, Veblen researcher of the University of Wisconsin Center in Manitowoc, "The house on that farm today is a modern construction. When it was built, the old house was moved to the village of Valders and divided into three separate houses. However, I don't think this older house can have been the same house that was built in 1855. On the other hand, it is possible that the original house served as part of the big farmhouse that was moved to Valders. I am presently trying to locate information which would indicate what happened to the original house." Thus, for now, the first home of the reclusive mental giant who wrote *The Theory of the Leisure Class* (1899) remains as elusive as he could have wished.

(See MINNESOTA, MISSOURI in this chapter.)

WILDER, LAURA INGALLS (1867–1957). *Little House in the Big Woods* (1932), her first in the series of novels detailing her pioneer childhood, concerns her birthplace near **Pepin,** her home until 1869. The site of the long-gone, one-room cabin is marked on State Highway 183 about seven miles northwest of town.

(See IOWA, KANSAS, MINNESOTA, MISSOURI, SOUTH DAKOTA in this chapter.)

WILDER, THORNTON NIVEN (1897–1975). All of the author-playwright's earliest residences survive and remain privately occupied in **Madison.** His birthplace stands at 14 West Gilman St. From 1898 to 1900 the family lived at 25 Mendota Court. Then, until 1906, when the Wilders moved to a consulate in China, their Madison home was 211 West Gilman St., now split into five apartments. Author Zona Gale lived almost directly across the street there in 1895.

(See Chapter 1, CONNECTICUT, NEW HAMPSHIRE.)

WILLARD, FRANCES ELIZABETH (1839–1898). "Forest Home" at 1816 South River Road in **Janesville** is the frame house built by Willard's father in 1846, the childhood home of the teacher and temperance activist until 1857. This privately owned dwelling stood originally on the marked site at 1720 South River Road. The Willard homestead, which she described as "half prairie, half forest on the banks of the Rock River," was one of the largest stock farms in the state. Against family wishes, her father sold the place in 1862.

Exhibit: In the Frances Willard Schoolhouse at 1401 East Craig Ave. in **Janesville,** she began her 16-year teaching career in 1858. The 1853 building, owned by Rock County Historical Society, is currently undergoing restoration and will display period schoolroom items. (Call 608-756-4509 for information.)

(See ILLINOIS in this chapter; also Chapter 3, NEW YORK.)

WRIGHT, FRANK LLOYD (1867–1959). Whether regarded as a hero or villain of American architecture, there was seldom much middle ground of opinion concerning this builder. Wright's birthplace stands at 300 South Church St. in **Richland Center,** a small, privately owned frame house that was undergoing remodeling in 1982. It was Wright's home until 1869.

From 1911, Wright centered his activities near **Spring Green,** where he chose a site on the Wisconsin River to build a rambling mansion after his own design. There he also established an architectural school to train his student-disciples. Wright's first two houses on the site burned in 1914 and 1924; his rebuilt third, now known as Taliesin East National Historic Landmark, continues to teach "the nature of Style" and Wright's theories of design. The Taliesin Fellowship Buildings, operated by the Frank Lloyd Wright Foundation, are located three miles south of town on State Highway 23. (Open for tours, June 15–Labor Day, Monday–Saturday 10:00–4:00; 608-588-2511; admission.)

(See ILLINOIS in this chapter; also Chapter 6, ARIZONA.)

FIVE

THE SOUTHEAST

Eleven states form the most homogeneous yet rapidly changing region of the United States. These states include Alabama, Arkansas, Florida, Georgia, Kentucky, Louisiana, Mississippi, North Carolina, South Carolina, Tennessee and Virginia. Five of them memorialize English royalty in their names. Except for Arkansas and Louisiana, all lie east of the Mississippi. Maryland, the District of Columbia and Delaware are sometimes included within this region; though they do contain strong southeastern elements, one could also argue that cosmopolitan Atlanta, Birmingham, New Orleans and Miami hardly represent the "typical South."

So what is the "typical South"? Basically, it is a historical concept, that of a region based on a cotton economy and on rebellion from the United States. One can easily find remnants of old "Dixie" in all 11 states; but "Dixie" today is like the nostalgia of old family scrapbooks—helping define who you are, but mostly occupying fond shelf space. Only in New England does one encounter a similar regional affection for the past; but not even there has the rate of socioeconomic change become such a dynamic, wholehearted embrace of the future. Though agriculture is and probably always will be a major economic activity, the Southeast has become a primary industrial region of startling vigor. This region has a higher native-born population—mainly of English-Scotch-Irish and African ancestry—than any other, but more minorities are moving in than out, reversing a

century-long trend; and the innovation and sharp intelligence applied to area and community problems far outshines the efforts of most other national regions. Thus, while the scrapbooks retain an honored place, the "typical South" is far from what it was.

This region borders the Atlantic Ocean on the east, the Gulf of Mexico south, and the Southwestern, Great Lakes and Middle Atlantic regions on the west and north. Several distinct subregions include the eastern seaboard, settled by the English and part of the 13 original colonies; the Florida peninsula with its Spanish history; the Gulf Coast area with its strong French heritage; the Appalachian mountains and hill country populated by Scotch-Irish and Elizabethan English descendants; and the broad interior plains and bayous. It is a region known for its "belts": the agricultural cotton and black belts; the religious Bible belt of Baptist and Methodist fundamentalism; and most recently, the "sun belt," a term used mainly in connection with the startling economic vigor and development of both the Southeast and Southwest.

In contrast to other regions, the Southeastern past may seem more traumatic, even tragic, because it stands less distant from us than the nightmarish history of neighboring regions. It is easy, in viewing the "Southern trauma," to lose sight of the general context and climate of violence in which the nation evolved. Secession was hardly a dreadful idea to the national founders, who assumed that somewhere along the line one or more states would secede; if not exactly a pleasing foresight, it was far from alarming. In 1861 "the act of secession," wrote Edward Porter Alexander, "was passed by each State in full confidence that the legal right peaceably to secede was assured by the Constitution." Creating "united" states, after all, had been a practical design for benefitting individual states, not an excuse to make a new nationality. When unity with others no longer served the self-interests of a state, it was assumed that such a state would quite naturally break off.

The states never became united in the modern sense until the growing morality expressed by abolitionism and the commercial ties of the railroad and telegraph—plus rising world nationalism—forced a far larger emphasis on unity than this nation had ever imagined. The notion of the Union as something sanctified and untouchable began to transform the permissive attitude of the founders; in the North, the very word *secession* took on the weight and meaning of treason. Lincoln defined this new self-image as a creation beyond the sum of its parts when he said that the nation could not exist half-slave and half-free. Not a few of his predecessors had simply asked, "Why not?" But this self-image has seldom, since the Civil War, been questioned, for that war baptized it firmly in the national consciousness. In the rural Southeast, this new notion of patriotism and "national interest" lagged, even long after the war. Thus slavery, the issue that originally divided the nation, was not the only conflict; the war disputed the larger question of a state's right to self-government.

Probably a stronger case can be made for economic determinism in the Southeast than in any other region. Before 1800 slavery was not popular in most of the South. It was, in fact, a rapidly dying anachronism when the invention of the cotton gin transformed the region almost overnight. The new cotton economy gave Southern landowners a massive stake in holding cheap labor.

Of the 11 southeastern states, only the border state of Kentucky did not secede, remaining disputed territory with delegations on each side. The Confederate States of America, organized at Montgomery, Ala., in February of 1861, soon transferred its capital to Richmond, Va., where it remained until the 1865 Confederate surrender.

Internally the Confederate States confronted strife between executive and legislative branches plus insurrection on local levels, finally paralyzing civil government. The final outcome was inevitable. With a population about half as large as the Union's and including 4 million slaves, with an economy based on one-crop agriculture in contrast to the commerce and industry of the North, with an army outnumbered by about three to one, the Confederacy knowingly embraced a lost cause on patriotic principle. Its most optimistic aim was to endure and wear out the adversary. The Confederates suffered about 300,000 casualties in the war, the North almost 400,000. Yet at Bull Run, Cold Harbor, and its advance to Gettysburg, the Confederacy struck a deep fear in the North. The South's best general was bound to a desk during much of the war by an executive fiat; when Jefferson Davis finally allowed him to take the field, Robert E. Lee found himself presiding over the desperate motions of defeat. But the wonder, in looking back, is not that the Confederates misused their resources; but that they could field armies at all and engage much larger, better supplied forces for four bitter years.

At least as bitter as the war itself was the Reconstruction period that followed. The economy of the Southeast lay in ruins, and the policy of vengeance forced by Congress in the aftermath of Lincoln's assassination deprived the region of any effective political voice, rubbed salt in the wounds of conflict and prevented any actual reconstruction of economic and political autonomy. The carpetbag governments under which most of the states reentered the Union were sadistic indulgences of the victors, and the scars of this vicious treatment lasted well into the 20th century. As for American blacks in the South, they could no longer be owned as property; otherwise, their situation remained a national disgrace for almost a century. Under the euphemism "separate but equal," their segregation in every aspect of Southern life—schools, churches, civic buildings, transportation, restaurants, even bathrooms—clearly told them that, as second-class citizens, they had best "keep their place." Terrorism—the Ku Klux Klan, lynch law and much more insidious types of threat—intimidated the "uppity nigger" who presumed to vote or exercise other civil rights. Leaders like Booker T. Washington, attempting to deal with things as they were, preached that blacks must prove their worth to white society. Later black activists W. E. B. Du Bois and Martin Luther King, Jr., recognized that no amount of such "Uncle Tomism" would effect change in vested economic and social interests, and that only direct challenge to the nation's vaunted principles of freedom and equality would do the job. Accordingly King and his followers proceeded to break the law in a carefully orchestrated, systematic display of civil disobedience, forcing confrontations with long-ingrown social patterns and presumptions. Black Americans, in the tradition of our colonial forebears, did not ask for their rights but took them in the teeth of the entrenched system that had illegally deprived them. Yet in doing so, they also displayed a profound faith in the fundamental justice of American courts and public opinion. And they did succeed in revolutionizing Southern society. While nobody could claim that the success was final and the task finished, the major foundation had been laid for the entry of black citizens into their full constitutional birthright. Today, where Southern bigotry exists, it tends to be an open wound, easier dealt with than some of its more insidious forms in the North. People of good will, saddled by generations of a system not of their own making, are revitalizing the region with innovative vigor and lifting the burden of human oppression and guilt that kept it, in the words of an old blues lament, "down so long."

Some of the nation's most notable literature has emerged from the South. A distinctively American musical idiom, jazz, was born in New Orleans and Memphis. In architecture, the Southern colonial style featured end chimneys and high ceilings for cooling. Virginia refined the American Georgian style, typically brick and characterized by rectangular symmetry and wood ornamentation; fine examples of this style may be seen in the homes of William Byrd, Thomas Jefferson and George Washington, among many others. French and Spanish colonial styles, best seen in New Orleans, reveal the strong European heritage of this intriguing blend of cultures. Memphis, Tenn., is the region's largest city.

Channels of settlement included, of course, the great river roads of the Ohio and Mississippi. The Great Road from Philadelphia angled southwest from Maryland between the mountains of Virginia to Bristol, N.C. From there, Daniel Boone's Wilderness Road through the Cumberland Gap into Kentucky brought thousands of pioneers west during its 60 years. The Federal Road through Georgia and the Natchez Trace also became vital national highways.

From its status as backward redneck of the nation, the Southeast has probably come furthest from its past than any other region. The surge of energy resulting from its social reforms has probably played no small part in its present dynamism and prosperity. Each state attracts annual crowds of tourists and vacationers to its winter resort areas. And in the former cotton fields of an antebellum "golden age" that masked much fear, oppression and depression, space technology is now a major concern.

Two handbooks that will interest seekers of Southern biographical heritage include Alice Hamilton Cromie's *A Tour Guide to the Civil War* (1975) and *A Literary Tour Guide to the United States: South and Southwest* (1979), by Rita Stein.

ALABAMA

Alabama's boundaries, straight as a politician's lips, bear little relation to any natural borders, except in the southeast and extreme northwest, where rivers smudge their neatness; and in the state's western toe, carved by the Gulf.

The native Americans who left few reminders beyond their tribal name (Alabama) bridged the time gap between the ancient moundbuilding cultures and the four powerful C's: the Cherokee, Chickasaw, Choctaw and Creek peoples. The first Europeans to traverse and claim this country were Spaniards in 1540. France, however, established the first permanent settlement above Mobile in 1702. Mobile (a name originating from the Mabila tribe that Hernando de Soto found and slaughtered there) remained the capital of France's Louisiana Territory until 1722, when the seat of government transferred to New Orleans. The 1763 Treaty of Paris gave southern Alabama, known as West Florida, to England, which ceded it back to Spain in 1795, and Spain held this portion until the War of 1812. Northern Alabama had become a part of Mississippi Territory in 1798; actually, however, the "four C's" controlled this area until Andrew Jackson's 1814 victory in the Battle of Horseshoe Bend. Settlers quickly poured in. Alabama achieved separate territorial status in 1817 and became the 22nd state just two years later. A plantation economy based almost exclusively on cotton rapidly developed. By 1869

Alabama's population was 45 percent black.

The Confederate States of America, organized in Montgomery following the state's 1861 secession, elected Jefferson Davis as president. Most of the state saw little fighting until 1864, when Union Adm. David G. Farragut ignored the torpedoes to break through Mobile Bay. After Alabama's readmission to the Union in 1868, Reconstruction brought political and economic turmoil until 1876, when effective self-government was finally restored. Racial segregation remained a bulwark of public law, however, until the 1950s. In Montgomery, the state capital since 1846 and the first seat of the Confederacy, began the historic 1955 bus boycott led by Baptist minister Martin Luther King, Jr. Scenes of similar nonviolent protest in Birmingham and Selma became notable landmarks of the national civil rights struggle. Since then, the state has made notable progress in racial harmony. As one black activist states, "Everything isn't rosy here, but we'll never go the way of the subtle segregation you have in the North. Here it's all honest, even the bigotry; it's all out front."

By 1922 depredations of the boll weevil had wiped out the exclusive cotton economy. Cotton still ranks as an important product in the "black belt" of rich prairie soil that crosses the central state, but the boll weevil is memorialized today (by a statue in Enterprise) as the catalyst for bringing Alabama's economy into the 20th century. Agronomist George Washington Carver, in his work at Tuskegee, helped give not only Alabama but the entire South a new range of agricultural options. Today, however, farming ranks below Alabama's leading industries of tourism, mining and manufacturing. Birmingham, the state's largest city and one of the nation's main steel producers, uses iron and coal mined from Appalachian fields; and pine forestry feeds a major pulp and lumber industry. Most products are channeled through the state's major port of Mobile. In Huntsville's Marshall Space Flight Center originated the nation's first space satellite, *Explorer I*, plus the design for the 1969 rocket that carried the first moon explorers.

Alabama's roster of notable historic figures is impressive. The nation's two foremost black leaders, Dr. Washington and Dr. King, came to prominence there. Native Helen Keller revealed through her own life and career that abilities are not confined to the sense organs. Other natives included one of the U.S. Supreme Court's most liberal justices, Hugo L. Black; and popular musicians Nat King Cole, W. C. Handy and Hank Williams. Dr. Wernher von Braun, a captured prize of World War II, did most of his significant postwar work in Huntsville, an unlikely spot for a mind trained under Nazi technology to shoot for the stars. Visitors will find surviving residences of each; and Handy, Keller, King and Washington homes welcome the public in the style of Southern hospitality for which the state is famed.

BLACK, HUGO LAFAYETTE (1886–1971). U.S. Supreme Court Justice for 34 years, the Alabama native grew up in **Ashland,** his home from 1889 to 1907. The privately owned house on Second Avenue South was recently described by a local official as "very old and falling down." A 1972 plan to restore the residence has not yet advanced beyond good intentions.

(See VIRGINIA in this chapter.)

BRAUN, WERNHER VON (1912–1977). The German-born engineer who developed the V-2 rocket ("Revenge Weapon 2") for the Nazis in World War II came to the United States in 1945 and immediately resumed work in missile research. As the director of the Space Flight Center at **Huntsville** from 1950 to 1970, he helped develop launch vehicles for the first U.S. satellites and became an active consultant-researcher for numerous space programs. His home from about 1950 to 1957 was 907 McClung St.; and his home until 1970, built in 1957, stands at 1516 Big Cove Road. Both remain privately owned.

Exhibit: The Alabama Space and Rocket Center at Tranquility Base, west of **Huntsville** on State Highway 20, displays a large library of von Braun memorabilia. (Open June 1–August 31, daily 8:00–6:00; September 1–May 31, daily 9:00–5:00; 205-837-3400; admission.)

(See VIRGINIA in this chapter.)

CARVER, GEORGE WASHINGTON (1864?–1943). At **Tuskegee,** the chemist and educator taught and researched at Tuskegee Institute National Historic Site from 1896 to his death, producing hundreds of useful products from peanuts, sweet potatoes, soybeans, even wood shavings. Because of his work, the South was able to diversify from a strict cotton economy, renew worn-out land and become a major supplier of new agricultural products. The versatile bachelor scientist occupied rooms on the ground floor of Rockefeller Hall, a boys' dormitory then but now a women's residence hall, from its 1903 construction. Carver's quarters there, according to one observer, resembled "a combination of library, picture gallery, museum and hothouse." Tuskegee Institute is located one mile north of town on U.S. Highway 80.

Exhibit: Carver Museum, dedicated by Henry Ford on the **Tuskegee** campus in 1941, houses the scientist's collections and memorabilia plus research exhibits and African art works. Located at 399 Old Montgomery Road, the museum is operated by the National Park Service. (Open daily 9:00–5:00; 205-727-6390; free.)

(See Chapter 4, KANSAS, MISSOURI.)

COLE, NAT KING (1919–1965). Born Nathaniel Adams Coles, this Baptist minister's son who became one of the world's most popular singers was born in **Montgomery,** his home until age 4. His privately owned birthplace stands at 1524 St. John St.

(See Chapter 6, CALIFORNIA.)

DAVIS, JEFFERSON FINIS (1808–1889). In **Montgomery,** the First White House of the Confederacy at 626 Washington St. (at the corner of Union Street) became the Davis family's residence immediately after he was sworn in as provisional Confederate President in 1861. This two-story, white frame house, dating from about 1835, stood on the southwest corner of Bibb and Lee streets when Davis occupied it. He lived there for only three months before his formal inauguration and the removal of the Confederate capital to Virginia; before her death, his widow Varina Howell Davis sketched the rooms and contents as she remembered them, and the present arrangement of period furnishings, Civil War relics and Davis memorabilia is based on her detailed recollections. Among items included there are Davis's sword, possessions from his last home in Biloxi, Miss. and the table on which he wrote *The Rise and Fall of the Confederate Government* (1881). Removed to its present location in 1921, the home is operated by the White House Association. (Open Monday–Friday 8:00–5:00, Saturday–Sunday 8:00–12:00, 1:00–5:00; 205-832-5269; donation.)

Exhibit: The Bible on which Davis took his presidential oath is a treasured relic of the Alabama State Archives, displayed in the World War Memorial Building at Monroe and Jackson streets in **Montgomery.** (Open daily 8:00–5:00; 205-832-6510; free.)

(See GEORGIA, KENTUCKY, LOUISIANA, MISSISSIPPI, TENNESSEE, VIRGINIA in this chapter; also Chapter 3, DISTRICT OF COLUMBIA.)

DE FOREST, LEE (1873–1961). Electronics genius and inventor, De Forest grew up in **Talladega,** where his father, a minister, headed the College for the Colored. From 1882 to 1891 he resided with his parents in a new brick house at 702 West Battle St. that still serves as the private home for the president of Talladega College. De Forest revisited the house in 1918 and slept in his old bedroom.

(See Chapter 4, IOWA, NEBRASKA; also Chapter 6, CALIFORNIA.)

FITZGERALD, F. SCOTT (1896–1940). **Montgomery** was Zelda Sayre Fitzgerald's 1900 birthplace. Her parental home is long gone from South Street, but the large house where she and her novelist husband resided in 1931 remains privately owned at 919 Felder Ave.

(See NORTH CAROLINA in this chapter; also Chapter 2, MANHATTAN; also Chapter 3, MARYLAND, NEW YORK; also Chapter 4, MINNESOTA; also Chapter 6, CALIFORNIA.)

GERONIMO (1829?–1909). The Apache leader and guerrilla chieftain who fiercely resisted white settlement in his Arizona homeland was taken prisoner in 1887 and moved, along with his family and tribal members, completely out of Arizona territory. From 1888 to 1894 he lived in semiconfinement at Mount Vernon Barracks, a 2,000-acre military reservation established in the 1830s. The marked site of Fort Stoddert, where he occupied a small house, lies about two miles east of **Mount Vernon** on County Road 96 off U.S. Highway 43. Dr. Walter Lawrence Reed served there for part of the same period (see the entry on Reed later in this section).

(See Chapter 6, OKLAHOMA.)

HANDY, WILLIAM CHRISTOPHER (1873–1958). The birthplace and boyhood home of the "Father of the Blues" stands at 620 West College St. (at

the corner of Marengo Street) in **Florence.** This three-room log cabin, built by the musician-composer's grandfather about 1870, was moved to this location from its original site on three acres near Cypress Creek. The Florence Historical Board displays Handy's piano, trumpet, period furnishings and personal mementoes. (Open Tuesday–Saturday 9:00–12:00, 1:00–4:00; 205-764-4661; admission.)

(See TENNESSEE in this chapter; also Chapter 2, MANHATTAN; also Chapter 3, NEW YORK.)

KELLER, HELEN ADAMS (1880–1968). The frame cottage birthplace of the gifted but severely handicapped woman, whose life and humanitarian accomplishments surmounted a childhood illness that made her blind, deaf and mute, stands at "Ivy Green," her family home in **Tuscumbia.** This cottage, originally built by her grandfather as a plantation office in the yard adjacent to the one-story, frame ancestral home, also served as living quarters for the child and "Teacher" Anne Sullivan from 1887 to 1896. At the pump still standing between the outdoor kitchen and main house occurred the event dramatized in William Gibson's play *The Miracle Worker* (1959) when the unruly child suddenly seized the connection between water and the word "water"—so this pump marks, in a more significant sense, Keller's true birthplace. Both houses, operated by the Helen Keller Property Board, date from 1820 and display family furnishings plus personal memorabilia of the author-lecturer. Gibson's play is presented on the 10-acre grounds at 300 West North Commons on Friday and Saturday nights from late June through July. For ticket information, write Ivy Green, 300 West North Commons, Tuscumbia, AL, 35674. (Open Monday–Saturday 8:30–4:30, Sunday 1:00–4:30; 205-383-4066; admission.)

"IVY GREEN," HELEN KELLER'S BIRTHPLACE. Helen Keller herself saw little of her 1820 ancestral home in **Tuscumbia,** but she experienced it vividly through the eyes and ears of her "translator" and longtime companion Anne Sullivan Macy. At (top) is the parental home. The former plantation office (middle), in which Helen Keller was born, also became the scene of her earliest education when Helen and "Teacher" resided here. Both structures have been restored to their 1880s appearance.
(Courtesy Helen Keller Property Board)

(See Chapter 1, CONNECTICUT, MASSACHUSETTS; also Chapter 2, QUEENS.)

KING, MARTIN LUTHER, JR. (1929–1968). Foremost civil rights leader, winner of the Nobel Peace Prize and moral force of the midcentury, King pastored the Dexter Avenue Baptist Church in **Montgomery** from 1954 to 1960, the period of his landmark organization of the Montgomery bus boycott and formation of the Southern Christian Leadership Conference. The King home, an unpretentious, seven-room frame dwelling, stands at 309 South Jackson St., still a private parsonage. King's life there was fraught with peril. Burning crosses flared on the lawn, and on January 30, 1956, a bomb thrown on the front porch exploded, but King's family escaped injury. Another bomb planted on the porch a year later did not explode.

Exhibits: Dexter Avenue King Memorial Baptist Church at 454 Dexter Ave. in **Montgomery** was given National Historic Landmark status in 1977. The church, dating from 1878, conducts regular services.

In **Birmingham,** the solitary cell in which Dr. King composed his historic 19-page "Letter from Birmingham Jail" (1963) is located in the city jail building at 501 Sixth Ave. South. Mayor David Vann ordered the small cell preserved as a memorial in 1979 when renovation knocked out partitions and combined cells. As no public viewing policy has been established, however, visits must be prearranged with city authorities.

(See GEORGIA, TENNESSEE in this chapter.)

REED, WALTER LAWRENCE (1851–1902). From 1887 to 1890 the U.S. Army physician whose research would virtually wipe out yellow fever served at **Mount Vernon** Barracks (see the entry on Geronimo earlier in this section).

(See VIRGINIA in this chapter; also Chapter 4, NEBRASKA.)

WASHINGTON, BOOKER TALIAFERRO (1856–1915). The educator-reformer and 1881 founder of Tuskegee Institute built his home "The Oaks" on the Tuskegee campus in 1899. Bricks for his three-story house were made from local clay by Tuskegee students. Located on Old Montgomery Road at Tuskegee Institute National Historic Site, one mile north of **Tuskegee** on U.S. Highway 80, the mansion displays Dr. Washington's restored study with original furnishings plus exhibits of his life and career. It is operated by the National Park Service. (Open Monday–Friday 8:00–12:00, 1:00–4:30; 205-727-6390; free.) The site of the shanty where Washington began building this prestigious learning center is marked by the Founder's Monument on the campus.

Exhibits: Both the Carver Museum and the Art Center on the **Tuskegee** campus display Washington mementoes (see the entry on George Washington Carver earlier in this section).

(See VIRGINIA in this chapter; also Chapter 1, MASSACHUSETTS; also Chapter 3, NEW YORK, WEST VIRGINIA.)

WILLIAMS, (HIRAM) HANK (1923–1953). The hard-traveling country singer who wrote such hits as "Cold, Cold Heart" and "Jambalaya" was born in a log dwelling that was also his parents' country store at **Mount Olive** off State Highway 106 in southwestern Butler County. The site of the house on County Road 7 is now an overgrown field.

The family moved frequently until 1935, occupying various dwellings in and around Georgianna.

In **Greenville,** his mother's boardinghouse, where he learned to play the guitar and wrote his first songs, stands at 707 Walnut St. The one-story dwelling with raised porch now serves as a county storage area. Williams lived there until 1937.

Montgomery became the permanent family residence in 1937. At 114 South Perry St., Williams's mother operated a two-story frame boardinghouse, and this remained the singer's home until after his 1946 marriage to Audrey Sheppard. He formed his backup musical group, the Drifting Cowboys, while living there and began performing professionally. This dwelling fell during construction of the Interstate Highway, and the Montgomery County Health Department now occupies the site at 515 West Jeff Davis Ave. Williams authority Tyra Berry also gives 406 McDonough St. as a Williams address in Montgomery.

Exhibit: The Alabama State Department of Archives and History at 624 Washington Ave., **Montgomery,** displays Williams memorabilia including song drafts and clothing. (Open daily 8:00–5:00; 205-832-6510; free.)

The annual Hank Williams Memorial Festival in **Greenville,** a musical jamboree commemorating the composer, occurs in late May or early June. (Contact Entertainment Enterprises, Inc., PO Box 184, Greenville, AL, 36037; 205-382-6858.)

(See TENNESSEE in this chapter.)

ARKANSAS

The pronunciation has been "Arkansaw" from the beginning, but what the word originally meant to the French explorers who originated it from a native word has been lost. When Arkansas split as a territory from Missouri Territory in 1819, the official spelling was also "Arkansaw"; but by 1836, when Arkansas entered the Union as the 25th state, the final letter had become s. The 1881 legislature, however, declared the *saw* pronunciation official.

Hernando de Soto viewed the area in 1541 but probably never got further west than the vicinity of Camden. For the French team of Marquette and Jolliet in 1673, the mouth of the Arkansas River marked the furthest point of their Mississippi River exploration. The area was included in the immense region that La Salle formally claimed as Louisiana Territory in 1682; and Arkansas Post, the first permanent settlement in the Mississippi Valley, arose in 1686. France ceded the region to Spain in 1763; it reverted back to France briefly in 1800, then became part of U.S. territory with the 1803 Louisiana Purchase. Arkansas Territory also included what is now Oklahoma. The state was ninth to join the Confederacy in 1861. Two years later, the capture of Little Rock, capital from the year of statehood, secured Union control; and the state reentered the Union in 1868.

The Mississippi River forms the entire eastern border facing Tennessee and Mississippi. Southeastern bottomlands of Arkansas became broad cotton plantations; mountain folk from the southern Appalachians migrated to the hollows of the Ozarks and Ouachitas and maintained fiercely independent traditions; and the western border became a frontier and staging area for Texas settlement, Mexican War troops and California wagon trains. U.S. Highway 67, which bisects the state from the northeast to the southwest, is also the approximate dividing line between lowlands and highlands. Though industry is decentralized and diverse, the state remains predominantly agricultural; cotton, rice and soybeans are the main crops, while cattle and turkeys rank as important livestock. Origi-

nally 85 percent wooded, Arkansas still has a large timber industry of yellow pine and leads the nation in the production of red gum, oak and hickory timber. Almost all of the nation's bauxite comes from the Ouachita range. Recreation and tourism bring many visitors; the nation's best-known spa is probably Hot Springs National Park.

Arkansas contributions of nationally historic figures, though not numerous, are significant. Gen. Douglas MacArthur was born there, and Carry Nation ended her colorful career of smashing up saloons there. Jim Bowie and President Taylor dwelled in Arkansas for awhile. The state is associated with some of the nation's most notable frontier weapons; the Bowie knife, it is claimed, originated in Washington, and the side-arms of several notorious gunslingers lie unloaded at last in the Saunders Memorial Museum at Berryville.

BOWIE, JAMES "JIM" (1796–1836).

Exhibit: The restored 1831 Blacksmith Shop at Old Washington State Historic Park is reputedly the place where someone made the first Bowie knife, a stout hunting blade that did a fair amount of damage to human flesh during the Civil War and later. Various historical sources assign Bowie himself, his brother Rezin Bowie or village smith James Black as the inventor-designer. And other communities in Louisiana, Mississippi and Texas also claim the "actual" knife-making site. The Gun Museum in the park displays many Bowie knives. Old Washington was a popular stopping point on the Southwest Trail (Franklin Avenue) to Texas, and there is little question that Bowie spent time there. Operated by the Pioneer Washington Restoration Foundation, the park and reconstructed building complex stands eight miles south of **Washington** on State Highway 4. (Open Monday, Wednesday–Saturday 9:00–4:00, Sunday 1:00–5:00; 501-983-2588; admission.)

(See LOUISIANA in this chapter; also Chapter 6, TEXAS.)

DE SOTO, HERNANDO (1496?–1542). In 1541 and 1542 the Spanish explorer of the southeast built a stockade and spent his last winter on a bluff above the Ouachita River at an Indian village called Utiangue. Historians remain uncertain of the exact spot, but the description left by expedition narratives indicates one of the two present towns, **Camden** or **Calion,** as the site. Only archaeological investigation might confirm one or the other place.

Exhibit: A plaque at **Caddo Gap** on State Highway 8 marks the furthest westward point reached by de Soto as established by the 1939 U.S. De Soto Expedition Commission.

(See FLORIDA, TENNESSEE in this chapter.)

MacARTHUR, DOUGLAS (1880–1964). The birthplace of the stentorian World War II Pacific commander was the towered arsenal of Fort Dodge, an army post established at **Little Rock** in 1836 and functional until 1893. MacArthur's idolized father, also a soldier, was stationed there in 1880; and the family occupied the arsenal building, just previously converted into a two-family officers' dwelling, for 18 months following the child's birth. Today this structure houses the Museum of Science and History, located at the north end of MacArthur Park on East Ninth Street. Visitors, however, will find few reminders of MacArthur's infancy there. (Open Monday–Saturday 9:00–5:00, Sunday 1:00–5:00; 501-376-4321; free.)

(See VIRGINIA in this chapter; also Chapter 2, MANHATTAN; also Chapter 3, MARYLAND, NEW YORK; also Chapter 4, KANSAS; also Chapter 6, NEW MEXICO, TEXAS.)

NATION, CARRY AMELIA MOORE (1846–1911). "My name is Carry A. Nation. That means 'Carry a nation.' " she said. The last home of the hatchet-wielding temperance crusader was "Hatchet Hall," her 14-room frame boardinghouse at 31 Steel St. in **Eureka Springs.** She bought the 1883 house in 1908, opened a school and resided there until a few months before her death. Operated by Hatchet Hall Museum, the structure now houses an art gallery. (Open March 1–November 30, Monday–Saturday 9:00–5:00; admission.)

(See KENTUCKY in this chapter; also Chapter 4, KANSAS, MISSOURI; also Chapter 6, TEXAS.)

TAYLOR, ZACHARY (1784–1850). In 1841 the frontier soldier and later 12th U.S. president took command of unfinished **Fort Smith** and remained until 1844. Taylor described his house as a "plain one-story concern with stone chimneys outside and ample porches in front and rear." All that remains of it today is a single chimney and fire-

place at Garrison Avenue and North 13th Street, converted into a grotto-shrine on the Roman Catholic Convent of Mercy grounds. The ruin may be viewed from Garrison Avenue.

(See KENTUCKY, LOUISIANA, VIRGINIA in this chapter; also Chapter 3, DISTRICT OF COLUMBIA.)

FLORIDA

Geologically, much of the 500-mile peninsula that separates the Atlantic Ocean from the Gulf of Mexico is the youngest area of the continental United States. The Floridian Plateau with its almost square limestone base, of which the surface of Florida forms only the cap, is also one of the stablest areas of the earth's crust. Florida's coastal lowlands, a rim 10 to 125 miles wide, mark a wet transition zone between continent and ocean, a region of cypress and mangrove swamps, sawgrass prairie and some of the most popular winter resorts in the nation. The peninsula's highest point, in Walton County, rises only 345 feet above sea level. Of Florida's more than 30,000 lakes, the largest is Lake Okeechobee, the second biggest freshwater lake inside the contiguous United States. The northern panhandle resembles its Georgia and Alabama border states in its red clay hills and pine forests, while the low spine of the peninsula slopes down to the wide, creeping river known as the Everglades and ends in the 135-mile hook of the Florida Keys. Long barrier beaches enclose the Intracoastal Waterway and buffer Florida's 350-mile Atlantic coast. The state's 8,462-mile tidal coastline, longest of any state's except Alaska, is deeply indented on the western side with large bays enclosed by land. Florida's climate ranges from subtropical at Miami to temperate in the north.

The state's southeasternmost location has deceptive aspects. Its northernmost border is more than 100 miles south of California's southernmost point, while its largest city, Jacksonville, lies almost directly south of Cleveland, Ohio, and some 800 miles west of Maine's coast. And most of the state lies entirely west of continental South America.

Juan Ponce de León, the Spanish governor of Puerto Rico who landed somewhere between St. Augustine Inlet and the St. Johns River in 1513, affixed the Spanish feminine adjective meaning "flowery" to the peninsula. It is hard to believe that he did not concoct his fountain of youth nonsense for Florida's first travel brochure; or that the natives, perhaps snickering, did not feed him tales worthy of a modern chamber of commerce. De Soto continued the Spanish penetration in 1539 and cut a swath of bloody destruction to the Mississippi. French Huguenots, however, established the first colony at what is now Jacksonville in 1564. A year later, Pedro Menendez de Avilés asserted Spain's claim, destroyed this colony and built St. Augustine, the first permanent European settlement in the United States. After Sir Francis Drake burned it in 1586, English settlers began arriving in force. Spain swapped Florida to the British for Havana in 1763; England split its new territory into East and West Florida, and the area remained agressively Tory during the American Revolution. By 1783 Spain was again in possession, but—pestered by revolts inside the colony and by U.S. pressure from without—finally sold Florida to the United States in 1821.

Tallahasee became the capital of Florida Territory in 1823. Until 1841 the native Seminoles fiercely resisted attempts to displace them, and the U.S. army suffered one of the worst defeats in its history near Bushnell when Major F. L. Dade's entire troop was wiped out in 1835. The army simply abandoned the project, and a number of Seminoles fled deep into the Everglades, where some 1,500 of their descendants remain today, officially unconquered and in a formal state of war with the United States. Florida became the 27th state in 1845 and, in 1861, the third state to secede. No major Civil War battles occurred there. The state verged on bankruptcy during Reconstruction, but railroads heralded a Florida land boom during the 1880s. After World War I, speculators ruled a fantastic period of wild promotions and real estate schemes, mostly mountains of promises. The Great Depression came early to Florida when banks began to fail in 1926. Paper fortunes vanished overnight, and killer hurricanes piled damage and death upon economic woe. Florida never really recovered until the 1950s, with the beginning of its second land boom. During the decade from 1950 to 1960, Florida gained more than two million residents, including a huge retirement population. Today the state hosts some 32 million visitors annually, more in summer than in winter.

From a plantation cotton economy in the north, Florida's agriculture has diversified to tobacco, sugarcane and vegetable produce. Today about 35 percent of the state's total crop is citrus fruit, supplying two-thirds of the nation's oranges, grapefruits and tangerines. Florida's main industry, aside from tourism, is food processing, especially of frozen juices. South Florida looks increasingly toward Latin America for its economic future. "Caribbean trade and migration," wrote Joel Garreau in 1981, "have become far more important than flocks of pasty-faced tourists from the North."

Most of Florida's notable residents, like much of its general population, were escapees from cold and snow. These included figures as diverse in aims and accomplishments as Robert Frost, Thomas Edison, the Kennedys, Annie Oakley, Harry S. Truman and John D. Rockefeller. A few, like William Jennings Bryan, Al Capone, Ernest Hemingway and Edward V. Rickenbacker established homes for the year round. James Weldon Johnson and Asa P. Randolph numbered among Florida's relatively few eminent natives. Of these names, only the Edison and Hemingway homes invite visitors inside, though most other eminent dwellings do survive and may be externally viewed.

AUDUBON, JOHN JAMES (1785–1851).
Exhibit: Audubon House, 205 Whitehead St. in **Key West,** features a display of the painter's double elephant folios of *The Birds of America* (1827–38). Audubon used the yard there for painting backgrounds of cordia trees in 1832, but no evidence supports widely published claims that he resided there during his stay. It is more likely that he lived aboard the boat *Marion* docked at Key West. The two-story frame house dates from about 1830 and is operated by the Mitchell Wolfson Family Foundation. (Open daily 9:00–12:00, 1:00–5:00; 305-294-2116; admission.)

(See KENTUCKY, LOUISIANA in this chapter; also Chapter 2, MANHATTAN; also Chapter 3, PENNSYLVANIA.)

BRYAN, WILLIAM JENNINGS (1860–1925). "Villa Serena," the home built by the political warhorse of the Democratic party in 1916 and his permanent dwelling after 1921, stands privately owned at 3115 Brickell Ave. in **Miami.** "The Great Commoner," in common with many investors of his day, had bought into the Florida land boom earlier and finally decided to move there. Bryan's political career had faded by the time he occupied the home with its red tile roof and three sun-porches, and he became increasingly verbal in issues of religious fundamentalism. From there he departed in July of 1925 to prosecute John T. Scopes in the celebrated "Monkey Trial" at Dayton, Tenn., and never returned.

(See TENNESSEE in this chapter; also Chapter 3, DISTRICT OF COLUMBIA; also Chapter 4, ILLINOIS, NEBRASKA.)

CAPONE, ALPHONSE "AL" (1899–1947). At the height of his power in 1928, the Chicago gang warlord bought his winter estate on Palm Island in **Miami Beach,** where he fished, entertained cronies and pretended respectability behind rings of bodyguards and a high wall. He also installed what was reputedly the largest private swimming pool in the nation. Capone used the fact that he was at his Palm Island house as an alibi when under investigation for the Chicago St. Valentine's Day Massacre in 1929. His long absence in Alcatraz (1933–39) left the estate in care of his minions; but from 1939 to his death, Capone faded away and died there as a helpless paretic, his brain withered in disease. The privately owned mansion, dating from 1922, stands with its green tile roof at 93 Palm Ave.

(See Chapter 2, BROOKLYN; also Chapter 4, ILLINOIS, WISCONSIN; also Chapter 6, CALIFORNIA.)

DE SOTO HERNANDO (1496?–1542). Spanish explorer in the Pizarro mold, the gold-thirsty de Soto began his ill-fated 4,000-mile expedition into the North American interior, probably at Tampa Bay, in 1539.* The site of Anhayea, the Indian village where the army of some 600 spent its first winter (1539–40), is an undetermined location probably in the vicinity of **Tallahassee.**

Exhibit: Five miles west of **Bradenton** on 75th Street NW off State Highway 64, De Soto National Memorial commemorates the first major European exploration of southeastern North America. The 25-acre memorial, operated by the National Park Service, includes displays of 16th-

century arms and armor, replicas of buildings, crossbow and cooking demonstrations, a nature trail and a film on de Soto's expedition. (Open daily 8:00–5:30, 813-792-0458; free.)

De Soto's actual landing and staging site was probably Ucita, a deserted Indian village located on Terra Ceia Island near **Terra Ceia** on U.S. Highway 19 north of Bradenton. On a "high fortified hill" above the beach, he occupied the vacated chief's lodging. There are no roads leading to the private site.

(See ARKANSAS, TENNESSEE in this chapter.)

EDISON, THOMAS ALVA (1847–1931). In 1886 the inventor had a large house prefabricated in Maine and shipped to **Fort Myers,** and this became his permanent seasonal home. Edison Winter Home National Historic Landmark, operated by the City of Fort Myers, stands on a 13-acre estate at 2350 McGregor Blvd. The grounds include his large botanical garden, the source of materials for his chemical experiments. Visitors may see Edison's original furnishings in his office-laboratory, his workshops and a museum displaying a large collection of his inventions. Some of Edison's light bulbs have been burning 12 hours a day there since he made them (such extremely efficient bulbs would be obviously too unprofitable to mass-produce). Another laboratory building from the property was moved to Dearborn, Mich., in 1928. (Open Monday–Saturday 9:00–4:00, Sunday 12:30–4:00; 813-334-3614; admission.)

(See KENTUCKY in this chapter; also Chapter 3, NEW JERSEY; also Chapter 4, MICHIGAN, OHIO.)

FORD, HENRY (1863–1947). In 1916 the auto industrialist bought a two-story gabled house for $20,000 next to the winter estate of his friend and hero Thomas Alva Edison (see the entry on Edison above) at 2400 McGregor Blvd. in **Fort Myers.** The house, hidden from view behind a high picket fence, remains privately owned. Ford lost interest in his Florida property after Edison's death and did not return after 1934.

(See GEORGIA in this chapter; also Chapter 4, MICHIGAN.)

FOSTER, STEPHEN COLLINS (1826–1864).
Exhibit: "Way down upon the Swanee River" on U.S. Highway 41 east of Interstate Highway

---

*In 1966, however, Florida historian Rolfe F. Schell published an interesting and plausible argument that de Soto landed further south near Fort Myers.

ERNEST HEMINGWAY HOME. The author wrote several of his best-known novels in this Spanish colonial mansion at **Key West**. He owned it from 1931 until his death, but lived here with his second wife, Pauline Pfeiffer Hemingway, only until 1939. Hemingway planted many of the abundant trees and shrubs on this acre lot.
(Courtesy Bernice Dickson)

75 near **White Springs,** Stephen Foster State Folk Culture Center is a 250-acre wooded preserve (on the Suwannee River) that memorializes the composer. Displayed there by the Florida Department of Natural Resources are dioramas depicting his life and songs, plus manuscripts and other memorabilia. Period exhibits, song recitals, riverboat trips and picnic grounds offer much to do and see even for those not fond of Foster. Foster himself never ventured remotely near this place. (Open daily 9:00–5:00; grounds open 8:00–sunset; 904-397-2192; admission.)

(See KENTUCKY in this chapter; also Chapter 2, MANHATTAN; also Chapter 3, NEW JERSEY, PENNSYLVANIA; also Chapter 4, OHIO.)

FROST, ROBERT LEE (1874–1963). The white-thatched poet affectionately associated with New England spent much of his later life (1941–62) wintering in the warmer climes of **South Miami.** He built his dwelling "Pencil Pines"—actually two prefabricated houses—at 5340 Southwest 80th St., which remains privately owned.

(See Chapter 1, MASSACHUSETTS, NEW HAMPSHIRE, VERMONT; also Chapter 4, MICHIGAN; also Chapter 6, CALIFORNIA.)

HEMINGWAY, ERNEST MILLER (1899–1961). In 1931 the novelist bought the Spanish colonial mansion at 907 Whitehead St. in **Key West,** now known as the Hemingway Home and Museum National Historic Landmark. The two-story house of native stone—quarried by slave labor in 1850–dates from 1851. With ornate iron railings and French windows, the house stands back from the street in a junglelike yard surrounded by a brick wall that Hemingway built to discourage sightseers. In his "pool house" study beside a swimming pool installed by his second wife, Pauline Pfeiffer Hemingway, in 1937, the author wrote *Death in the Afternoon* (1932), *The Green Hills of Africa* (1935), *To Have and Have Not* (1937), and began *For Whom the Bell Tolls* (1940). His small, round writing table and cigar maker's chair are still there. Yet he spent so much time abroad during the 1930s "that he regarded this house not so much as a permanent residence," wrote Rita Stein, "as a place to come home to." Money for purchase of the house was put up by Pauline Hemingway's uncle, and the novelist resented the affluence of her family; this may have helped undermine their marriage, which had all but ended by 1936. After 1939 he rarely visited, and he moved to Cuba with his third wife Martha Gellhorn in 1940. Pauline Hemingway resided there until her death in 1951, and the property remained in the Hemingway family until 1963. Today the house, privately owned by Bernice Dickson, displays original Hemingway furnishings, hunting and travel trophies and other mementoes. A brightly tiled trough in the yard is actually a urinal that Hemingway lifted from the local Sloppy Joe's saloon after one drinking bout. Visitors are sure to see descendants of Hemingway's nearly 50 cats that still live there. (Open daily 9:00–5:00; 305-294-1575; admission.)

Exhibit: Sloppy Joe's, the **Key West** bar where the writer hung out with local fishermen every afternoon, still exists on Duval Street. Photos and newspaper clippings of its best-known patron line the walls. Today, where draft beer formerly cost a nickel per glass and bar gin a dime, wrote reporter Art Sills, "you go up against top prices. It is all furnished in a style best described as Tourist Rustic. The crowd at the bar is chiefly composed of young Navy guys who are still working on their first pack of razor blades." Today, like most bars made famous by writers, it frowns on serving the scraggly; Hemingway, who usually appeared there in dirty shorts, rope belt and ragged t-shirt, would probably not get in. As Sills caustically notes, "Hemingway does not live here anymore."

(See Chapter 3, ILLINOIS, MICHIGAN; also Chapter 6, IDAHO.)

JOHNSON, JAMES WELDON (1871–1938). In 1869 the father of the brilliant author, diplomat and reformer bought an old house at the northwest corner of Lee and Houston streets in **Jacksonville.** Johnson, born there, stayed until 1901, when he moved with his brother, the composer John Rosamond Johnson, to New York City. Both brothers wrote songs, and James Weldon Johnson composed "Lift Every Voice and Sing," often called the Negro national anthem, while living there. The house lasted until sometime after their father's death in 1912. Today a brick building

occupies the marked site of Johnson's first home at 138 Lee St.

(See TENNESSEE in this chapter; also Chapter 1, MASSACHUSETTS; also Chapter 2, MANHATTAN.)

KENNEDY, JOHN FITZGERALD (1917–1963). KENNEDY, ROBERT FRANCIS (1925–1968).
The 35th U.S. president and his brother, who became U.S. attorney general and a later presidential aspirant, often resided at the parental family's winter home and vacation retreat in **Palm Beach.** Father Joseph P. Kennedy acquired the white stucco villa on two acres overlooking the ocean in 1933. The six-bedroom house, designed by architect Addison Mizner and built in 1923 for Rodman Wanamaker, was the scene of John Kennedy's long convalescence during the 1950s from a back operation. On the front lawn he wrote much of his Pulitzer Prize–winning *Profiles in Courage* (1956). The house also became his pre-inaugural headquarters in 1960 and 1961; he visited there only four days before his assassination. Located at 1113 North Ocean Blvd., this property remains off limits to visitors.

(See VIRGINIA in this chapter; also Chapter 1, MASSACHUSETTS, RHODE ISLAND; also Chapter 2, BRONX; also Chapter 3, DISTRICT OF COLUMBIA, NEW YORK; also Chapter 4, MICHIGAN; also Chapter 6, CALIFORNIA, TEXAS.)

KEROUAC, JACK (1922–1969). Author and a primary figure of the "beat generation," Kerouac made his last home with his wife and mother in **St. Petersburg.** Alcoholism and waning popularity ravaged his final years, far declined from the fervor of experience that had produced *On the Road* (1957). The modest house of concrete blocks that he bought and occupied from 1968 stands privately owned at 5169 10th Ave. North

(See Chapter 1, MASSACHUSETTS; also Chapter 2, MANHATTAN, QUEENS; also Chapter 3, NEW YORK; also Chapter 6, CALIFORNIA.)

LEWIS, JOHN LLEWELLYN (1880–1969). The longtime winter home of the former miner and powerful labor leader stands privately owned on Pineland Road at Pine Island near **Fort Myers.** This was Lewis's vacation residence from the 1940s.

(See VIRGINIA in this chapter; also Chapter 4, ILLINOIS, IOWA.)

MARCIANO, ROCKY (1924–1969). The heavyweight boxer who retired undefeated in 1956, Marciano occupied two **Fort Lauderdale** residences, both remaining under private ownership. He lived from 1960 to 1968 in a new house at 2561 Del Lago Drive. From 1968 to his death, his home was 2700 North Atlantic Blvd., built about 1966.

(See Chapter 1, MASSACHUSETTS.)

MARQUAND, JOHN PHILLIPS (1893–1960). The novelist bought a small winter home he called "Nervana" at **Hobe Sound** in 1946—"a terrific-looking house with funny stuffy old grounds but right on the most beautiful beach you ever saw," gushed his wife Adelaide Hooker Marquand. Another observer described the property as "scruffy grounds full of bushes and fallen coconuts." Because of the strongly anti-Semitic cast of this insular community, however, Marquand, though not Jewish himself, decided he could not stay and sold the house in 1952. Its exact location remains a guarded secret of local inhibitants who still incline to wall themselves from the world. "You can't see anything except high shrubs hiding estates," notes one recent Florida guidebook. "Roads, parks and even a post office have been fought off in the pursuit of nontourism."

(See NORTH CAROLINA in this chapter; also Chapter 1, MASSACHUSETTS; also Chapter 2, MANHATTAN; also Chapter 3, DELAWARE, NEW YORK.)

OAKLEY, ANNIE (1860–1926). During the 1920s, the performer who amazed audiences for four decades by her sharpshooting skills wintered in **Leesburg** with her husband and manager, Frank Butler. Lakeview Hotel, which stood until 1957 at Main and Palmetto streets, became their home, and the couple often presented impromptu exhibitions on the front veranda for local residents. The accident-prone Oakley first arrived there in 1922 as a convalescent recovering from a fractured hip and ankle suffered in an auto accident, and the couple returned each year until 1926. When the hotel was razed, reports JoAnn Crawford of the Leesburg Public Library, its bricks were sold for $1 apiece; funds collected helped build the Leesburg General Hospital. "There is a story

that Annie's dog died there and she wanted it buried in the local cemetery," reports Ms. Crawford. "This was not allowed," but a grave marker for the dog stood for many years in a woodland off Center Street now occupied by homes. The site of the old hotel is now a parking lot.

(See NORTH CAROLINA in this chapter; also Chapter 3, MARYLAND, NEW JERSEY; also Chapter 4, OHIO.)

RANDOLPH, ASA PHILIP (1889–1979). The boyhood home of the prominent civil rights leader and union organizer was a two-story frame house in the 600 block of Jesse Street (between Spearing and Palmetto streets) in **Jacksonville.** A brick bungalow replaced it during the 1940s. Randolph lived there for two decades, from 1891 to 1911.

(See Chapter 2, MANHATTAN.)

RICKENBACKER, EDWARD VERNON "EDDIE" (1890–1973). From 1960 the retired president of Eastern Airlines resided at his winter home, 4115 Kiaora St. (privately owned) in the Coconut Grove suburb of **Miami.** He sold this house about 1970, however, and his last residences were Villa 68, then Villa 74 in the Key Biscayne Hotel and Villas at 701 Ocean Drive on Key Biscayne, Miami. The latter villa, a two-story house on the sea wall, overlooks the ocean.

(See Chapter 2, MANHATTAN; also Chapter 3, NEW YORK; also Chapter 4, INDIANA, MICHIGAN, OHIO; also Chapter 6, TEXAS.)

ROCKEFELLER, JOHN DAVISON (1839–1937). "Neighbor John," he liked to be regarded by his millionaire cronies at **Ormond Beach,** where the oil magnate established his winter home in 1917. Each morning before he went golfing, his valet filled Rockefeller's pockets with freshly minted nickels and dimes. On the links, the aged financier dispersed nickels to "encourage the downcast" and dimes to "reward the triumphant" in his games. When he disapprovingly observed several players give up hunting for a lost ball after several hours, he commented: "They must have lots of money." Located at 15 East Granada St., "The Casements" is an unpretentious house with many windows on the Halifax River and remains privately owned. Rockefeller died there, two years short of his goal of living to 100. Ormond Beach has not been so lavishly nickel-and-dimed since.

(See Chapter 2, BROOKLYN, MANHATTAN; also Chapter 3, NEW JERSEY, NEW YORK; also Chapter 4, OHIO.)

RUNYON, DAMON (1880–1946). "Las Melaleuccas," the New York City columnist's winter home from about 1933 to 1940, stands much modified at 271 Hibiscus Island in **Miami.** It was the "one happy home Damon had known," according to biographer Edwin P. Hoyt. Runyon built the house, which remains privately owned, in 1931.

(See Chapter 2, MANHATTAN; also Chapter 4, KANSAS; also Chapter 6, COLORADO.)

TIFFANY, LOUIS COMFORT (1848–1933).
Exhibit: Probably the best collection of the craftsman's works, including windows, lamps, furniture and paintings, may be seen in the Morse Gallery of Art, operated by the Charles Hosmer Morse Foundation at 133 East Welbourne Ave. in **Winter Park.** (Open Tuesday–Saturday 9:30–4:00; Sunday 1:00–4:00; 305-644-3686; admission.)

(See Chapter 2, MANHATTAN; also Chapter 3, NEW YORK.)

TRUMAN, HARRY S. (1884–1972). The 33rd president often came to sun and swim at **Key West** during his term of office. He first occupied the ten-room frame Commandant's Quarters of the U.S. Naval Station in 1946 and returned for ten more working vacations until the end of his presidency in 1953. Called the "Little White House" since Truman's first visit, the building is officially known as "Quarters A and B" and dates from 1890. The president occupied Bedroom 4 on the second floor to the north. A constant feature of his vacations there were the afternoon poker games he enjoyed with his staff and friends on the south porch. Located behind the 1942 Naval Administration Building at Key West Naval Station, the area of the house, almost an acre, is surrounded by a wrought-iron fence at the southwest corner of Front and Caroline streets. The Historic Key West Preservation Board plans to restore and refurnish the house as a Truman museum; currently it remains closed under custody of the General Services Administration.
Exhibit: Until the proposed Little White House Museum at **Key West** becomes fact, some of the dwelling's original furnishings are displayed at the East Martello Gallery and Museum, operated by the Key West Art and Historical Society at 3500 South Roosevelt Blvd. These items include Truman's poker table, chairs and piano. (Open daily 9:30–5:00; 305-296-3913; admission.)

(See Chapter 3, DISTRICT OF COLUMBIA; also Chapter 4, MICHIGAN, MISSOURI.)

GEORGIA

As one of those states whose names are epitaphs to long-dead royalty (in this case the English George II, who named the colony after himself), Georgia preserves many memorials to its colonial past. The main purpose of the colony was to provide a buffer between the English Carolina and Spanish Florida by establishing a place "out-of-sight-and-mind" for English debtors, prisoners, scalawags and religious refugees. Gen. James Oglethorpe founded Savannah, the first permanent settlement, in 1733 and conducted several campaigns against the Spanish colonies further south. Few of the outcast sought this asylum, however; when Georgia became a royal province in 1755, its population numbered only about 2,000 whites and 1,000 black slaves. Almost 200 years earlier, Hernando de Soto's 1541 expedition had given the native Cherokees and Creeks their first ominous look at white faces. Hardly more reassuring to them were the Spanish Franciscan missions established on St. Simons and Jekyll islands in 1566. The signs of Georgia's earliest dwellers in the Okmulgee and Etowah mound groups near Macon and Cartersville reveal de Soto to be a relatively recent passer-by.

Despite its slow growth, the colony prospered, and immigrants from Massachusetts, Virginia and the Carolinas formed a core of radicalism. As one of the 13 original colonies, Georgia voted unanimously for independence. Several important Revolutionary battles occurred there, and British forces held Georgia during much of the war. Becoming the fourth state in 1788, Georgia extended to the Mississippi River but ceded the future states of Alabama and Mississippi to the federal government in 1802.

The slavery issue divided the state, but the up-country proslavery faction won out in 1807 and secured the capital at Milledgeville, where it remained until transferred to Atlanta in 1868. Georgia was the fifth state to secede from the Union, and the state became the most vital economic bastion of the Confederacy. It not only contributed the most food and supplies to the Southern armies but also the wispy Alexander H. Stephens as Confederate vice president. Georgia suffered almost complete physical annihilation during Gen. William T. Sherman's 1864 march from Atlanta to the sea. His objective: "the utter destruction of its roads, houses, and people." "My orders are not designed to meet the humanities of the case," he said. "Those who brought war into our country deserve all the curses and maledictions a people can pour on." Georgia became the last state to reenter the Union in 1870.

Racial segregation denied the state much of its human potential until the 1954 Supreme Court school desegregation decision. One of the nation's greatest leaders, Rev. Martin Luther King, Jr., shaped the civil rights crusade from Atlanta, calling the nation to fulfill its long-delayed promise of full equality to all citizens.

Georgia is the largest state east of the Mississippi River. From the Appalachian ranges in the north, the land drops abruptly to coastal plain. The 100-mile Atlantic coastline includes the Sea Islands, a popular resort area. Georgia's primary industry is textiles, followed by lumber. The state leads the nation in the production of peanuts, pecans and pulpwood, and is second in poultry and egg production. Its agriculture has become widely diverse since the cotton decline of the 1920s and now includes the justly famous Elberta peach. Atlanta, the largest city by far, has become the major commercial and cultural center of the Southeast. Rapid growth, urban renewal and a fresh start from its 1864 ruins has enabled Atlanta to avoid much of the urban blight that afflicts most American cities of its size.

Besides Dr. King, notable Georgia residents who have enriched the nation included two presidents: Woodrow Wilson and, in a highly significant sense, Franklin D. Roosevelt. If not for Warm Springs, where this politician crippled by polio restored his physical and emotional strength, the nation might not have heard more of Roosevelt after 1930. And earlier, if not for a friendly plantation that hosted inventor Eli Whitney near Port Wentworth, the cotton gin's enormous socioeconomic repercussions might not have exploded across the South in quite the same way. Among natives and lifelong residents were authors Joel Chandler Harris, Margaret Mitchell and Flannery O'Connor. Stephen Vincent Benét, Carson McCullers and Ogden Nash spent crucial childhood years in the state. Various World War II military leaders lived at Fort Benning; and Jekyll Island served as a moated retreat for American money barons. The English Wesley brothers preached there early in their pulpit careers; auto magnate Henry Ford created a domain south of Savannah; Eugene O'Neill brooded on an island and wrote his only comic play; and President Eisenhower played tremendous amounts of golf. More recently, the state attracted wide national attention as the home of former governor and president James Earl Carter.

Among the states of the old Confederacy, Georgia has probably advanced furthest of all in applying its physical and intellectual wealth to constructive social policy. This progressive attitude also carries to the treatment of its often turbulent past and to the homes of its noted residents. Many of their dwellings survive and welcome visitors.

BENÉT, STEPHEN VINCENT (1898–1943). Commandant's House National Historic Landmark at 2500 Walton Way, former chief quarters of the **Augusta** military arsenal, was the author-poet's boyhood home when his father commanded the arsenal from 1911 to 1915. Today the campus of Augusta College occupies the old arsenal grounds, and the two-story brick mansion where Benét wrote his first stories serves as the official dwelling of the college president. The house dates from about 1828.

(See Chapter 1, CONNECTICUT; also Chapter 2, MANHATTAN; also Chapter 3, NEW YORK, PENNSYLVANIA; also Chapter 6, CALIFORNIA.)

BRADLEY, OMAR NELSON (1893–1981). Career soldier, World War II general and one of the few to hold the final rank of general of the army, Bradley spent two periods of duty on the staff of **Fort Benning** Infantry School. From 1930 to 1934, as a major, he served as an instructor and resided in officers' quarters at 126 Rainbow Ave. As school commandant in 1941 and 1942, he lived at "Riverside" (Quarters One), 100 Vibbert Ave. This two-story frame dwelling dates from about 1910; it was enlarged from an old meetinghouse that had been moved to this site before the 1918 establishment of the Infantry School. Both residences remain occupied by U.S. Army personnel. Fort Benning stands five miles southeast of

Columbus on U.S. Highway 27.

(See VIRGINIA in this chapter; also Chapter 3, PENNSYLVANIA; also Chapter 4, MISSOURI; also Chapter 6, CALIFORNIA, TEXAS.)

COBB, TYRUS RAYMOND "TY" (1886–1961). Longtime outfielder for the Detroit Tigers and probably baseball's greatest singles hitter, Cobb was a Georgia native and also spent his last years in the state. His boyhood home stood on South Cobb Street in **Royston.**

In 1958 he built his last home on Chenocetah Mountain near **Cornelia.** "I'm going to be hard to find up on my mountain," he said—but he also maintained a town apartment on Grier Street. Precise dates and addresses have been unusually difficult to verify for Cobb; the bad old man of baseball would be delighted that he is still "hard to find."

(See Chapter 3, NEW YORK; also Chapter 6, CALIFORNIA.)

DAVIS, JEFFERSON FINIS (1808–1889).

Exhibit: Jefferson Davis Memorial State Park on State Highway 32 north of **Irwinville** marks the site of Davis's capture by Union soldiers on May 10, 1865. The Confederate President, intending to escape southwest and continue resistance after Lee's surrender at Appomattox, camped there during his flight. When a troop of Michigan cavalry appeared at dawn, he attempted to disguise himself in his wife's clothing but was recognized and arrested. A small museum, operated by the Georgia Department of Natural Resources, displays Confederate relics and a few Davis items. (Open Tuesday–Saturday 9:00–5:00, Sunday 1:00–5:00; 912-831-2335; admission.)

(See ALABAMA, KENTUCKY, LOUISIANA, MISSISSIPPI, TENNESSEE, VIRGINIA in this chapter; also Chapter 3, DISTRICT OF CO-LUMBIA.)

DU BOIS, WILLIAM EDWARD BURGHARDT (1868–1963). The black educator and civil rights leader lived and taught at **Atlanta** University for two lengthy intervals (1897–1910 and 1932–44). Both times he occupied campus quarters—at 50 Chestnut St. SW during the latter period, a site now occupied by a campus dormitory. Atlanta University is located at 223 Chestnut St. SW.

(See Chapter 1, MASSACHUSETTS; also Chapter 2, BROOKLYN, MANHATTAN; also Chapter

3, MARYLAND, PENNSYLVANIA.)

EISENHOWER, DWIGHT DAVID (1890–1969). From 1949 the World War II general and 34th U.S. president, an avid golfer, vacationed at least once each year with big business cronies at the Augusta National Golf Club on Washington Road in **Augusta.** Eisenhower friends erected a three-story country house for "Ike" and his wife near the tenth tee in 1953—a structure that became known as "Mamie's Cabin"—and the presidential couple resided there during their Augusta stays. The club remains one of the most exclusive golfing establishments in the nation, with admittance to the grounds and "Mamie's Cabin" by membership only.

(See VIRGINIA in this chapter; also Chapter 2, MANHATTAN; also Chapter 3, DISTRICT OF COLUMBIA, MARYLAND, PENNSYLVANIA; also Chapter 4, KANSAS, MICHIGAN; also Chapter 6, COLORADO, TEXAS.)

FIELD, MARSHALL (1834–1906). The Chicago businessman was one of the founders of the resort for the very rich at Jekyll Island (see the entry on Jekyll Island later in this section). He resided during winters from 1888 at the Jekyll Island Club House there.

(See Chapter 1, MASSACHUSETTS; also Chapter 4, ILLINOIS.)

FORD, HENRY (1863–1947). The Detroit auto industrialist began acquiring thousands of acres in Bryan and Chatham counties in 1925 and eventually developed a community which survives today as **Richmond Hill.** Eventually his holdings included 17 plantations totaling 69,000 acres. In 1936 he began restoring and rebuilding an old, two-story colonial mansion burned by Sherman's troops during the Civil War, drained hundreds of swampland acres, began a timber industry and resided there during winters until his death. Ford, always a lover of historic materials, used bricks from an early 19th-century Savannah plantation called "The Hermitage" in reconstructing his mansion on the Ogeechee River. His widow held the property until her own death in 1950, and the vast estate was then sold to the International Paper Company to satisfy Ford inheritance taxes on property elsewhere. The building stood vacant for about a decade after Mrs. Ford's death, then became an exclusive restaurant. In 1981, however, it again stood vacant. A marker on State Highway 144 west of Richmond Hill indicates the structure's locale, which is secluded far from the highway.

(See FLORIDA in this chapter; also Chapter 4, MICHIGAN.)

HANNA, MARCUS ALONZO "MARK" (1837–1904). An Ohio businessman and political promoter of President McKinley, Hanna resided during winters from 1895 to 1900 in a rented house at **Thomasville.** McKinley, it is said, decided to run for president while visiting Hanna there. Built about 1883, the house has undergone much enlargement and modification since Hanna's occupancy. It remains privately owned at 830 North Dawson St.

(See Chapter 3, DISTRICT OF COLUMBIA; also Chapter 4, OHIO.)

HARDY, OLIVER NORVELL (1892–1957). The rotund, cherubic half of the film comedy team of Laurel and Hardy was a Georgia native, born on an unmarked site now occupied by a laundromat behind the city hall in **Harlem.** He spent only his first few months there.

None of Hardy's subsequent boyhood homes in Madison and Milledgeville survive.

(See Chapter 6, CALIFORNIA.)

HARRIS, JOEL CHANDLER (1848–1908). Chronicler of dialect slave folktales in *Uncle Remus: His Songs and His Sayings* (1880) and subsequent volumes, Harris never realized that the "Br'er Rabbit" stories he heard on the "Turnwold" plantation where he grew up were actually Housa and Ashanti legends passed by oral tradition from Africa and somewhat changed to fit the slaves' new country. Harris always refused to take credit for making up the stories and was one of the first writers to recognize literary value in the experiences of black Americans. "Turnwold" stood at a marked site eight miles northeast of **Eatonton** on Phoenix Road. Harris worked as an apprentice printer on the estate from 1862 to 1866.

In **Atlanta,** as an editorial writer for the *Atlanta Constitution,* Harris resided from 1876 to 1881 at 201 Whitehall St., where he wrote his first "Uncle Remus" tales; the house is long gone. Still standing, however, is Harris's last home from 1881, now Wren's Nest National Historic Landmark, a gabled Victorian house at 1050 Gordon St. SW.

In 1883 the author enlarged this dwelling built in 1871, leaving the four original rooms intact as he added around them. Harris named his rambling, gray frame house for a wren that had nested in his mailbox. The Joel Chandler Harris Memorial Association displays his original furnishings, personal possessions, first editions and letters. (Open Monday–Saturday 9:30–5:00, Sunday 2:00–5:00; 404-753-8535; admission.)

Exhibit: Uncle Remus Museum in Turner Park, half a mile south of **Eatonton** on U.S. Highway 441, is a log structure built from two slave cabins; Georgia writer Flannery O'Connor described it as "the only air-conditioned slave cabin in the South" (see the entry on O'Connor later in this section). Period furnishings depict the setting of the Uncle Remus stories—carvings and paintings of the animal characters plus some Harris memorabilia and first editions. (Open Monday, Wednesday–Saturday 10:00–12:00, 1:00–5:00, Sunday 2:00–5:00; 404-485-6856; admission.)

HILL, JAMES JEROME (1838–1916). The railroad builder made his winter home from 1888 at Jekyll Island, where he occupied rooms in the Jekyll Island Club House (see the entry on Jekyll Island below).

(See Chapter 2, MANHATTAN; also Chapter 4, MINNESOTA.)

JEKYLL ISLAND. From 1899 to 1942, when President Roosevelt (see the entry on Franklin Delano Roosevelt later in this section) ordered the island evacuated to prevent wartime international kidnappings, the residents of this exclusive "100 Millionaires" resort on one of Georgia's Sea Islands numbered among the nation's richest, most powerful families. Those residents, who generally occupied the island from January to March, were often insular in more ways than one, and stories of their peculiar mores are legion. A clannish, anti-Semitic society based on the assumption that surplus money somehow equaled a surplus of brains or ability, the "Millionaires Village" is one of the nation's more intriguing anthropological sites. "For sixty years," said one veteran tribesman of the clan, "no unwanted foot ever walked Jekyll soil." The project began in 1888, when publicity-fatigued John Pierpont Morgan, James Jerome Hill (see the entries on Morgan and Hill in this section) and about 50 others cast about for a refuge from reporters, salesmen and "people who would make them dress for dinner." Membership eventually grew to 294 of the *crème de la crème*. Most of the best-known residents did not own cottages but resided in the Jekyll Island Club House, the 125-room gingerbread mansion that centered the "club." Cleveland Amory, in his entertaining book *The Last Resorts* (1952), detailed the island's social decline into a competitive status thicket. "Jekyll," he wrote, "was unquestionably the island epitome of this country's Big Business Society. Furthermore, whether Jekyll fell solely because of its high age limit or whether also because it ran the matter of privacy into the ground and in the end, like Old Guard Society, simply bored itself to death . . . its fall was the largest in the history of old-line resorts." The State of Georgia acquired the property in 1947, and today the Jekyll Island State Park Authority welcomes as many feet as care to tread in the footsteps of the absurdly rich. The two-hour tour of Millionaires Village National Historic Landmark on the island's western side begins at 375 Riverview Drive with a slide show; and, at scheduled intervals, there is guided transportation to the Club House and several of the restored cottages. (Open May 30–September 1, Monday–Saturday 9:00–6:00, Sunday 10:00–5:00; September 2–May 29, Monday–Saturday 9:00–4:00, Sunday 12:00–5:00; 912-635-2236; admission.)

KING, MARTIN LUTHER, JR. (1929–1968). The birthplace and boyhood home of the murdered civil rights leader stands at 501 Auburn Ave. in **Atlanta.** Built about 1900, this two-story, 13-room frame house belonged to his grandparents, and the family resided there until 1941. Now restored and containing many of the King family's furnishings, it is owned and operated by the Martin Luther King, Jr., Center for Social Change (see *Exhibit* below). King's rented parsonage as co-pastor of Ebenezer Baptist Church from 1960, his last home, stands at 234 Sunset Ave. NW. This two-story brick house remains privately owned.

Exhibit: The Martin Luther King, Jr., Center for Social Change at 671 Beckwith St. SW in **Atlanta** contains a museum, library and archives relating to Dr. King's work. This building is included in an area of several blocks containing the neighborhood where he grew up, his birthplace, tomb and the Ebenezer Baptist Church. The entire complex now constitutes the King Historic District National Historic Landmark. (Open Tuesday–Saturday 10:30–4:00, Sunday 1:30–4:30; 404-524-1956; admission.)

(See ALABAMA, TENNESSEE in this chapter.)

McCULLERS, CARSON SMITH (1917–1967). The birthplace of the novelist born Lulu Carson Smith no longer stands at Fifth Avenue and 13th Street in **Columbus.** Her childhood home from 1927 to 1934, however, remains privately owned and unmarked at 1519 Starke Ave. The author's mother owned this one-story stucco dwelling until 1945. The house dates from about 1917.

(See NORTH CAROLINA in this chapter; also Chapter 2, BROOKLYN, MANHATTAN; also Chapter 3, NEW YORK.)

MARSHALL, GEORGE CATLETT (1880–1959). From 1927 to 1932 the career soldier, World War II chief of staff and later secretary of state served in a staff position at the U.S. Army Infantry School at **Fort Benning,** located five miles south of Columbus on U.S. Highway 27. Lt. Col. Marshall's address was 118 Eames Ave., an old plantation house built in 1850 and still privately occupied by army personnel.

(See NORTH CAROLINA, VIRGINIA in this chapter; also Chapter 3, DISTRICT OF COLUMBIA, PENNSYLVANIA; also Chapter 6, WASHINGTON.)

MITCHELL, MARGARET MUNNERLEIN (1900–1949). The author's only novel *Gone With the Wind* (1936) became the largest-selling work of fiction in national history. A lifelong **Atlanta** resident, she was born at 296 Cain St., her home to 1903. The two-story frame house stood about 75 feet back from the street. From age 12 to 24, she lived at 1401 Peachtree St. NE, a house built by her father and demolished in 1952; there is a marker on the office building that now occupies this site. Mitchell wrote her novel in apartment dwellings at 979 Crescent Ave. NE, her married home from 1925 to 1932, and at 4 East 17th St. where she lived from 1932 to 1939. Her last home from 1939 was a suite in the Della Manta apartment house, where she lived with her husband John R. Marsh on the second floor at 1268 Piedmont Ave. NE. All three of these dwellings remain privately occupied.

Exhibits: The Margaret Mitchell Room at the **Atlanta** Public Library, 126 Carnegie Way NW, displays personal memorabilia, her reference library, typewriter, handwritten notes and the world's largest collection of *Gone With the Wind* editions. (Open Monday–Friday 9:00–9:00, Saturday 9:00–6:30, Sunday 2:00–6:00; 404-688-4636; free.) The Atlanta Historical Society at McElreath Hall, 3101 Andrews Drive NW, also exhibits a collection of Mitchell items in its James M. Cox Museum. (Open Tuesday–Saturday 10:30–4:30, Sunday 2:00–4:30; 404-261-1837; free.) The Atlanta Museum, operated by J. H. Elliott, Jr., at 537-39 Peachtree St. NE contains film memorabilia of *Gone With the Wind.* (Open Monday–Friday 10:00–5:00; 404-872-8233; admission.)

South of Atlanta at **Jonesboro** stands the authentic setting for *Gone With the Wind.* Buffs disagree on the model for "Tara," Scarlett O'Hara's mansion in the novel; some claim it is the clapboard "Fitzgerald place," owned by Mitchell's great-grandfather, at Tara and Folsom roads five miles west of Jonesboro; others believe it is "Stately Oaks," the 1849 Greek Revival mansion that closely resembles her description of "Tara." The latter house, a two-story frame structure located at Margaret Mitchell Park on Carnegie Drive, was moved in 1972 from its original site on Tara Boulevard and restored with period furnishings. It is operated by Historical Jonesboro, Inc. (Open by appointment; 404-478-8881.) A Gray Line "Gone With the Wind Tour" provides bus transportation from Atlanta to Jonesboro for visitors interested in a commercial tour to the sites described in the novel (contact Gray Line of Atlanta, 309 Walker St. SW, Atlanta, GA, 30313; 404-524-6086).

MORGAN, JOHN PIERPONT (1837–1913). The financier vacationed often at Jekyll Island (see the entry on Jekyll Island earlier in this section), where he built the Sans Souci Apartments in 1899 and occupied an opulent chamber therein. The building stands on Old Plantation Road.

(See Chapter 1, CONNECTICUT; also Chapter 2, MANHATTAN.)

NASH, OGDEN (1902–1971). A boyhood home of the author of deceptively "light" verse—loaded puns and outrageous rhymes—is a **Savannah** landmark identified with another worthy resident, Juliette Gordon Low. The 1849 Low House (also called "Colonial Dames House"), a Victorian dwelling of stuccoed brick, stands at 329 Abercorn St.; there Low founded the first Girl Scout troop in 1912, and she died there in 1927. Nash's parental family rented the house from her for several years before 1912. The Society of Colonial Dames now displays the antiquarian rooms with their carved woodwork and period furnishings. No official recognition of the Nash presence has yet filtered into this stately scene, however; Juliette Low, an impish sort herself, would be disappointed not to share the historical honors of her house with a humorist. Guests there included English novelist William Makepeace Thackeray in 1853 and 1856—he worked on his novel *The Virginians* (1857) there—and Gen. Robert E. Lee in 1870. (Open Monday–Saturday 10:30–5:00; 912-233-6854; admission.)

(See Chapter 2, MANHATTAN; also Chapter 3, MARYLAND.)

O'CONNOR, FLANNERY (1925–1964). Fame, the unpretentious author assured one awed correspondent, is "a comic distinction shared with Roy Rogers's horse and Miss Watermelon of 1955." Her **Savannah** birthplace, a stately old brownstone mansion, stands privately owned at 207 East Charlton St.

Before her father died in 1941 of the lupus erythematosus that would afflict the author herself in 1950, the family moved to the **Milledgeville** home where her mother had grown up. This 1820 white frame mansion with four columns at 305 West Green St. (privately owned), which once served briefly as Georgia's executive mansion, remained the home of the mother and daughter until 1951. O'Connor's last home from 1951 was the 500-acre "Andalusia Farm" inherited by her mother. "You run the farm," Flannery O'Connor told Regina O'Connor, "and I'll do the writing"—an arrangement that succeeded, despite Regina's inexperience and Flannery's degenerative illness, until the daughter's death. There she wrote all of her published fiction, raised geese, swans and peacocks, painted and welcomed visitors. From 1955 she walked only with the aid of crutches. "There is something enormously monotonous and still about the farm," wrote biographer Josephine Hendin. The large, two-story, white frame dwelling, where the author occupied a bedroom-study on the ground floor, was originally a plantation house for the tract which Regina O'Connor eventually turned into a cattle farm. The property remains privately owned five miles north of Milledgeville on U.S. Highway 441. *Flannery O'Connor's Georgia* (1980) by Barbara McKenzie provides an excellent introduction to O'Connor country.

Exhibit: At 231 West Hancock St. on the Georgia College campus in Milledgeville, the Ina Dillard Russell Library displays furnishings from the author's last home. The main repository for her papers and memorabilia is the library's O'Connor Memorial Room. (Call 912-453-4047 for hours; free.)

O'NEILL, EUGENE GLADSTONE (1888–1953). In 1932 the playwright and his wife, Carlotta Monterey, built a 22-room Spanish-style house they christened "Casa Genotta" (combining their first names) at the resort colony of **Sea Island.** Overlooking the ocean at Agramont (19th) Street, O'Neill's study surmounted the house and could be reached only by a narrow spiral stair. There, while attempting to patch his always faltering marriage, he wrote his only comedy *Ah, Wilderness!* (1933), beachcombed, swam and entertained Somerset Maugham, Sherwood Anderson and Bennett Cerf, among others. But peace of mind eluded the morose dramatist there as everywhere else he lived, and he sold the property in 1936. Today it remains privately owned as cottage number 57 on the Sea Island Company list.

(See Chapter 1, CONNECTICUT, MASSACHUSETTS; also Chapter 2, MANHATTAN; also Chapter 6, CALIFORNIA.)

ROBINSON, JACK ROOSEVELT "JACKIE" (1919–1972). The baseball player who courageously pioneered the entry of black players into the major leagues, Robinson was born near **Cairo.** Only a chimney of the house where Robinson spent his first 16 months remains on the marked site about nine miles southwest of Cairo off Pine Hill Road, east of Calvary Highway (State Highway 111).

(See Chapter 1, CONNECTICUT; also Chapter 2, BROOKLYN; also Chapter 3, NEW YORK.)

ROCKEFELLER, JOHN DAVISON (1839–1937). The richest man of his time never became a member of the super-exclusive Jekyll Island "club," but he often guested there during winters from about 1890 and played golf extensively (see the entry on Jekyll Island earlier in this section). He hated to lose golf balls, and at least once spent an entire day looking for one; he never found it but tipped his caddy a dime anyway. Rockefeller resided at the Jekyll Island Club House. The 1892 Rockefeller Cottage ("Indian Mound") on Riverview Drive was owned by his younger brother William.

(See FLORIDA in this chapter; also Chapter 2, BROOKLYN, MANHATTAN; also Chapter 3, NEW JERSEY, NEW YORK; also Chapter 4, OHIO.)

ROOSEVELT, FRANKLIN DELANO (1882–1945). The 32nd U.S. president first came to **Warm Springs** in 1924 in a desperate attempt to recover the use of his legs, paralyzed by polio. According to Betsy Fancher, "Warm Springs was Roosevelt's last and not very promising hope. He had spent three years consulting the country's leading orthopedists and was still a hopeless cripple." The 88-degree waters of an underground spring that fed a pool in the Meriwether Hotel were said to have remarkable therapeutic effects. Roosevelt was lifted in and out of the water each day and thought he began feeling "life in my toes." Soon other polio victims began arriving, and Roosevelt founded the Georgia Warm Springs Foundation with two-thirds of his personal fortune. In 1926 he built his first dwelling there, a simple frame structure later known as "McCarthy Cottage." By 1928 he owned a 1,750-acre farm atop Pine Mountain south of Warm Springs, began raising cattle, corn and peaches, and became the community's main benefactor, funding a schoolhouse and civic improvements. There in 1928 he also made a crucial decision to reenter politics, his first step to the presidency. At Warm Springs he threw away his crutches, learned to walk with a cane and helping arm, learned to drive again and gained the self-confidence that enabled a rather avocational politician to become one of the century's greatest leaders. Roosevelt built his six-room "Little White House," a frame cottage, in 1932—the same year he won the presidency—on a scenic site where he liked to picnic. During the war years, his trips there declined to annual Thanksgiving Day pilgrimages. On March 30, 1945, however, he arrived for the last time, trembling with fatigue after the historic Yalta Conference plus 12 years as chief executive, including four during wartime. Thirteen days later, while posing for a portrait, he collapsed in the cottage and died there a few hours later. The "Little White House," operated by the Franklin D. Roosevelt Memorial Commission, stands half a mile south of town on State Highway 85W. A museum depicts Roosevelt's life and times with exhibits and a film. Furnished as in 1945, the cottage itself displays the president's leather chair, wheelchair, ship models, the bedroom where he died and the unfinished portrait by Elizabeth Shoumatoff. In the garage stands his Ford with special hand controls that he liked to drive around the surrounding countryside. Always a genial host to his Georgia neighbors, Roosevelt would be pleased that there are picnic accommodations on the grounds. (Open daily 9:00–5:00; 404-655-3511; admission.) The memorial property also includes the "McCarthy Cottage," Roosevelt's first.

(See Chapter 1, MAINE; also Chapter 2, MANHATTAN; also Chapter 3, DISTRICT OF COLUMBIA, MARYLAND, NEW YORK; also Chapter 4, MICHIGAN.)

STEPHENS, ALEXANDER HAMILTON (1812–1883). The vice president of the Confederacy, a frail, anemic little man of vast legislative experience and ability, bought his permanent home "Liberty Hall," an unpretentious frame dwelling, in 1845. After the Civil War, he tore down the original 1834 structure except for two rear rooms and built the enlarged two-story frame house that stands today. Now a part of Stephens Memorial State Park, located half a mile north of **Crawfordville** on State Highway 12, his restored home operated by the Georgia Department of Natural Resources displays many original furnishings and Stephens' possessions, including his wheelchair. An adjacent Confederate Museum also exhibits Stephens relics and documents. (Open Tuesday–Saturday 9:00–5:00, Sunday 1:00–5:00; 404-456-2221; admission.)

Stephens was elected governor of Georgia in 1882, and his last residence in **Atlanta** was the Georgia Governor's Mansion—not the present one, but a house known as the John H. James Mansion that stood at Peachtree and Cain streets until 1921, when it was declared unsafe. Stephens died there.

WESLEY, CHARLES (1707–1788).
Exhibit: Fort Frederica National Monument at the east end of **St. Simons Island** marks the site of a British fortification and town laid out by Gen. James Oglethorpe in 1736, an important post in England's colonial struggle against Spain for Georgia and Florida. The English preacher and hymnwriter accompanied his brother John Wesley (see the entry on John Wesley below) to Georgia in 1736 and served as Oglethorpe's secretary at Fort Frederica for almost a year. Among the numerous marked sites on the island is the spot where Charles Wesley conducted religious services the first Sunday after his arrival. Christ Church displays a cross carved from the large oak under which he preached. A visitor center, operated by the National Park Service on Frederica Road, presents exhibits, maps and a film relating to the area. (Open daily, 9:00–5:00; 912-638-3639; free.)

WESLEY, JOHN (1703–1791). The English founder of Methodism (a word without religious significance as first used) who never formally abandoned the Church of England himself, Wesley spent a year in **Savannah** preaching to the English colonists. According to Wesley, the second rise of Methodism occurred "at Savannah in 1736 when twenty or thirty persons met at my house." His tenure there (1736–37) was marked by his halfhearted courtship of Sophia Hopkey and much strife when she finally married someone else. Given to much agonizing self-examination, Wesley resided in a one-story cabin parsonage—the largest dwelling in the tiny settlement—that stood isolated on the present Reynolds Square on Abercorn Street between East Bryan and East Congress streets.

Exhibits: Wesley preached his first sermon in America at the outdoor site of the 1852 U.S. Customs House, Bull and East Bay streets, in **Savannah.** He usually spoke in church, however; Christ Episcopal Church, now facing Johnson Square at Bull and East St. Julian streets, is the third church to occupy the site of his weekly pulpit. The present structure was erected in 1838, over a century after Wesley last preached on the spot. (Christ Church is open Tuesday–Friday 9:00–5:00; 912-232-4131; free.) *Strange Fires: John Wesley in Georgia* (1971), by Willie Snow Ethridge, details the evangelist's brief, troubled months in Savannah.

In **Atlanta,** the John Wesley Room of Candler School of Theology at Emory University, 1380

South Oxford Road NE, possesses what is probably the world's largest collection of Wesleyana, including a pulpit he used and books owned by the Wesley brothers. (Call 404-329-7322 for hours of admission; free.)

(See NORTH CAROLINA in this chapter.)

WHITNEY, ELI (1765–1825). Inventor of the fibre-cleaning device that enabled the Southeast to hinge its entire economy on cotton for generations—and inadvertently gave the fading institution of slavery a new lease on life—Whitney developed the machinery, from which he reaped hardly a cent, in Georgia. As a guest of Revolutionary Gen. Nathanael Greene's widow in 1793 at Greene's "Mulberry Grove" plantation, Whitney designed and built his hand-operated cotton gin. Only the brick foundation of the original plantation house remains at the site of Mulberry Grove, where Greene died in 1786. The ravaging troops of a later general, William T. Sherman, burned the 1735 structure in late 1864 or early 1865, and a storm wrecked the rebuilt mansion in the early 1900s. The site, marked on State Highway 21 north of **Port Wentworth,** remains private and unexcavated.

Exhibit: In **Atlanta,** J. H. Elliott, Jr., displays an original Whitney cotton gin and Whitney's gun collection in the Atlanta Museum, 537-39 Peachtree St. NE. (Open Monday–Friday 10:00–5:00; 404-872-8233; admission.)

(See Chapter 1, CONNECTICUT, MASSACHUSETTS.)

WILSON, WOODROW (1856–1924). From 1857 to 1871, the eventual 28th U.S. president resided in the Presbyterian parsonage located at 419 Seventh St. (at the corner of Telfair Street) in **Augusta.** His father pastored the adjacent old First Presbyterian Church at 642 Telfair St. The three-story, restored brick manse, built in 1822, is now a privately operated National Historic Landmark. (Open Tuesday–Saturday 9:00–5:00; 404-722-4556; admission.)

Exhibit: Wilson practiced law briefly in **Atlanta** (1882–83). His law office stood at the present site of First Federal Savings and Loan Co., 40 Marietta St. NW (at the corner of Forsyth Street). The bank has established a replica of his office in its building. (Open Monday–Friday 9:00–4:00; 404-525-7681; free.)

(See SOUTH CAROLINA, VIRGINIA in this chapter; also Chapter 1, NEW HAMPSHIRE; also Chapter 3, DISTRICT OF COLUMBIA, NEW JERSEY.)

KENTUCKY

One noted Kentucky writer described the shape of the state as that of a camel trying to arise. The Ohio River directs the long meanderings of its northern border, giving the top of Kentucky a bunched, irregular profile and progressively narrowing the state in the west. From the deep gorges and forested mountains of its Appalachian east, Kentucky's furrowed plain slants toward the Mississippi River, which fronts the state's westernmost edge. Its greatest length from east to west is 425 miles; its broadest width is 180 miles.

Moundbuilders along the Ohio were the first known Kentuckians. Their Shawnee and Cherokee descendants warred extensively over Kentucky soil during the 18th century; "dark and bloody land," the Cherokees called it. That fact plus the Appalachian barrier effectively isolated the area from much white intrusion until 1775, when Daniel Boone cut the Wilderness Road through Cumberland Gap, a mountain passage 700 feet deep, to found Boonesboro. The first permanent white settlement west of the Alleghenies was Harrodsburg in 1774. For Kentucky, the American Revolution consisted of unrelenting Indian attacks, fomented by British suppliers, on the few precarious settlements along Boone's trail. Despite Boone's key role in founding Kentucky and his current publicity value to the state, Kentucky treated him shabbily while he was alive, cheating him of his extensive land holdings and rendering him a pauper. When Boone left for Missouri, he vowed never to return; he did return, but only when his coffin was clandestinely removed to Frankfort from a Missouri country cemetery.

Kentucky became a county of Virginia in 1776. In 1783 George Rogers Clark arrived at what is now Kentucky's largest city, Louisville; and by 1784 some 30,000 settlers had entered by the mountain route. Sentiments for political separation rapidly arose, and Kentucky became the 15th state in 1792, with Frankfort as capital. Ohio River commerce gave Kentucky strong interest in national and international affairs from the beginning; it was no accident that Henry Clay, the skilled political mediator between North and

South, was a Kentucky man. Though strongly sympathetic to the Confederate cause, the state never officially seceded, but did send troops—including 41 Union and 38 Confederate generals—to both sides of the conflict. Again, as a border state, Kentucky became a "dark and bloody ground" of the Civil War. Ironically, the presidents of both sides—Abraham Lincoln and Jefferson Davis—were born in Kentucky.

Increasing river and railroad commerce, developing agriculture and labor unrest marked Kentucky's 20th-century growth. "Bloody Harlan," where the violence of "goons and ginks and company finks" could not stamp out the United Mine Workers, remains the bituminous coal capital of the nation. The state also leads the nation in burley tobacco production and is high in corn, soybeans, livestock and dairying. But Kentucky is probably best known for its thoroughbred horses, raised in the 1,200-square-mile bluegrass country around Lexington; and for its production of bourbon whiskey in the north-central area. The state's fourth largest employer is its recreation and tourism industry.

Kentucky's noted sons and daughters have long enriched the nation's experience, and many structures they inhabited survive. Besides the figures already mentioned, Kentucky gave us frontiersman Kit Carson, reformer Carry Nation, film pioneer D. W. Griffith and jurist Louis D. Brandeis. Kentucky ranks high on the list of states that not only take pains to preserve their biographical heritage but also know how to share this accomplishment with visitors.

AUDUBON, JOHN JAMES (1785–1851). Always armed with the best of intentions, the painter-naturalist was constitutionally unable to settle for long into the domestic role of "good provider." "I have a rival in every bird," stated Lucy Bakewell Audubon regarding her obsessed husband. The couple made their first frontier home at **Louisville** (1807–10), where he established a store that stood, it is believed, near the north end of North Third Street. Inside this store in 1810 he met the transient pioneer ornithologist Alexander Wilson, a crucial event that probably set Audubon's future course as a wanderer with a purpose. The Audubons lived at Gwathmey's Indian Queen Hotel (waterfront site unknown) during this period.

In 1813, having failed in Louisville, Audubon

bought a log cabin beside another general store he opened in **Henderson.** This property included "four acres of orchard and meadow for livestock, poultry, caged wild birds, and a variety of pet rodents," wrote biographer Alice Ford. "Three or four slaves made an artificial pond to assure a supply of his favorite turtle soup." No remnant of his cabin and store, located near the corner of Main and Second streets, survives, though plaques mark the site. In 1816 Audubon also built a steam sawmill and gristmill on the property, a structure that lasted in ramshackle condition until fire destroyed it in 1913. A two-acre park marks this site at the foot of Main Street. Fundamentally uninterested in business, Audubon finally abandoned Henderson and all merchant pretenses in 1819 to follow his dream and the birds of America.

Exhibit: In 1813 Audubon purchased two lots, an area now included in the 812 acres of Audubon Memorial State Park, located three and one-half miles north of **Henderson** on U.S. Highway 41. Visitors to this public park and bird sanctuary may roam numerous woods trails and climb Wolf Hill, one of Audubon's favorite haunts. Somewhere on the tract, biographers believe, lies the unmarked grave of Audubon's daughter Lucy, who died in infancy. Also in the park stands the Audubon Memorial Museum, containing a collection of Audubon's prints, mounted specimens, a life mask and family items. The "French Garden" contains two bird baths constructed from grindstones found on the site of Audubon's Henderson mill. Both park and museum are operated by the Kentucky Department of Parks. (Park open daily 7:30–sunset; 502-826-2247; free; museum open April 1–October 31, daily 9:00–5:00; November 1–March 31, Saturday–Sunday 9:00–5:00; 502-564-6957; admission.)

An entertaining account of a couple who recently searched out Audubon's homes and traced his journeys is *On the Road with John James Audubon* (1980), by Mary Durant and Michael Harwood.

(See FLORIDA, LOUISIANA in this chapter; also Chapter 2, MANHATTAN; also Chapter 3, PENNSYLVANIA.)

BOONE, DANIEL (1734–1820). At **Boonesboro** stands a replica of the solitary wilderness fort constructed in 1775 by the frontiersman and 30 axmen that became Kentucky's second white settlement. Isolated and unwelcome in the Cherokee warground along the Kentucky River, Fort Boonesborough's four blockhouses and palisade withstood sustained Indian attacks in 1778, grew to boom-town proportions by 1780, then declined and disappeared. Boone himself moved on after the safety of the fort was assured. No trace of the original fort remains on the site, now operated by the Kentucky Department of Parks as the 108-acre Fort Boonesborough State Park. Cabins with pioneer artifacts, craft demonstrations, a pioneer museum and films depict life at this early Kentucky outpost. The reconstructed fort stands on State Highway 388 about a quarter of a mile southeast of the State Highway 627 junction. (Open April 1–Labor Day, daily 10:00–6:30; Labor Day–October 31, Wednesday–Sunday 10:00–6:30; 606-527-3328; admission.)

In 1795 Boone built a cabin west of what is now **Carlisle,** cleared 10 acres and stayed until 1797. The old cabin stood on its original site until 1944, when it was privately restored by the Asbury family and moved a short distance back from a creek. It now stands marked at their Forest Retreat Farms on U.S. Highway 68 just south of the State Highway 36 junction. Henry Ford offered $10,000 for the cabin before restoration, intending to move it to his Greenfield Village museum in Dearborn, Mich. He was refused. (Open by appointment; 606-289-7136; donation.)

Exhibits: The Kentucky History Museum, operated by the Kentucky Historical Society in the annex of the Old State Capitol at Broadway and St. Clair streets in **Frankfort,** displays "Boon's Best Fren," the flintlock rifle he used and inscribed, plus a powder horn. Boone's rifle became a symbol of the entire post-Revolutionary frontier. (Open Monday–Saturday 9:00–4:00, Sunday 1:00–5:00; 502-564-3016; free.)

The Filson Club at 118 West Breckinridge St. in **Louisville** displays many Kentucky historical items including a tattered buckskin shirt reputedly worn by Boone. (Open October 1–June 30, Monday–Friday 9:00–5:00, Saturday 9:00–12:00; July 1–September 30, Monday–Friday 9:00–5:00; 502-582-3727; free.)

Cumberland Gap National Historical Park preserves the Appalachian pass through which Boone and his band of axmen cleared the Wilderness Road for settlers in 1775. This 20,222-acre park at the juncture of three states had channeled 300,000 pioneers westward by 1800.

About two miles of the original road blazed by Boone (U.S. Highway 58) remains in the park. The visitor center operated by the National Park Service half a mile south of **Middlesboro** on U.S. Highway 25E displays historical and audiovisual exhibits. (Open June 15–Labor Day, daily 8:00–7:00; Labor Day–June 14, daily 8:00–5:00; 606-248-2817; free.)

Summer outdoor dramas relating to Boone's key role in opening Kentucky for settlement include "The Legend of Daniel Boone," presented at Old Fort Harrod State Park on U.S. highways 127 and 68 north of **Harrodsburg** (mid-June–late August, Monday–Saturday 8:30 PM; 606-734-3346; admission); and "Song of the Cumberland Gap" in Pine Mountain State Park Amphitheater, one mile south of **Pineville** on U.S. Highway 25E as marked by signs (June 22–August 29, Monday–Saturday 8:45 PM; 606-337-3800; admission).

(See NORTH CAROLINA in this chapter; also Chapter 3, PENNSYLVANIA, WEST VIRGINIA; also Chapter 4, MISSOURI.)

BRANDEIS, LOUIS DEMBITZ (1856–1941). The exact address of the noted jurist's birth site in **Louisville,** his home until 1875, remains unknown to local historical authorities. The house stood in the 500 block of Armory Place, then known as Center Street, on the present site of an office building or parking lots.

(See Chapter 1, MASSACHUSETTS; also Chapter 3, DISTRICT OF COLUMBIA.)

CARSON, CHRISTOPHER HOUSTON "KIT" (1809–1868). Frontier scout and soldier, Carson was born in a log cabin near **Richmond,** his infant home until 1811. The dwelling stood on Tates Creek Road near Goggins Lane about one mile southwest of town. A marker placed by Carson's grandson formerly identified the knoll where the cabin stood; according to Madison County historical authorities, the present state historical marker "in front of the adjoining hill" is wrongly located.

(See Chapter 4, MISSOURI; also Chapter 6, COLORADO, NEW MEXICO.)

CLARK, GEORGE ROGERS (1752–1818).
CLARK, WILLIAM (1770–1838).
"Conqueror of the Old Northwest," George Rogers Clark established his permanent base of

"ASHLAND," HOME OF HENRY CLAY. The house seen by visitors to **Lexington** is actually a faithful reconstruction of the statesman's permanent home from 1811, completed five years after his death on its original foundation. Clay family furnishings and memorabilia provide notable insights into the personality and public career of this master politician and peace-maker. *(Courtesy Henry Clay Memorial Foundation)*

operations at the present site of **Louisville** in 1778. His first fortified camp, where he settled 13 pioneering families, was above the Ohio River falls on Corn Island, long since washed away. Clark soon built a mainland fort opposite the island near the present river terminus of 12th Street, his headquarters until 1782. In that year, he erected Fort Nelson, a site marked at the northwest corner of West Main and Seventh streets; this stockaded post extending along the river shore to Ninth Street is regarded as the nucleus of Louisville settlement. Clark himself resided until 1803 at the 600-acre "Mulberry Hill" plantation he established for his family in 1785. His mother named the estate for its high, forested site overlooking the settlement. The six-room log house had a stone chimney at either end and glass panes, unusual on the frontier. Clark's brother William, explorer of the Louisiana Territory with Meriwether Lewis, lived at Mulberry Hill until age 19, returned there in 1796 and ran the estate until his venture with Lewis in 1803. All of the original buildings on the property had disappeared by World War I, when the federal government requisitioned the grounds for an army post—named, unaccountably, Camp Zachary Taylor. Three of Clark's grandnephews bought 43 acres of the property in 1921 and deeded the land to the City of Louisville. Today the home site of Louisville's founder is, appropriately, George Rogers Clark Park, located at the south-

eastern edge of the city on Poplar Level Drive—formerly Clark's Lane that ran from his front gate to the main road. Sadly declined by alcoholism and paralysis in 1809, the old warrior returned from the Indiana side of the river to spend his remaining years in his sister's Louisville home. That stands as Locust Grove National Historic Landmark, a two-story brick house built about 1790 by Clark's brother-in-law, Maj. William Croghan, and a fine example of frontier Georgian architecture. Restored and operated on 55 acres at 561 Blankenbaker Lane by the Historic Homes Foundation, the mansion displays period furnishings. Eight outbuildings include a smokehouse, log cabin and slave quarters; a visitor center features an audiovisual program on this notable restoration. (Open Monday—Saturday 10:00–4:30, Sunday 1:30–4:30; 502-897-9845; admission.)

(See VIRGINIA in this chapter; also Chapter 4, INDIANA, MISSOURI, NORTH DAKOTA; also Chapter 6, OREGON, WASHINGTON.)

CLAY, HENRY (1777–1852). "I'd rather be right than be president," said "the Great Pacificator." He tried hard and often to be both but was finally neither. Probably the foremost national legislator of the period preceding the Civil War, Clay represented Kentucky in Congress for almost 40 years. His permanent home from 1811 stood at Ashland National Historic Landmark, 1400 Richmond Road (at the corner of Sycamore Road) in

Lexington, though he never lived in the actual house now on this site. Clay's home, an 1805 structure that became known as the "White House of the West" because of his immense power and prestige, was structurally weak even during his lifetime. In 1857 it was razed and reconstructed on the original foundation, following the original Italianate 20-room design. The Henry Clay Memorial Foundation maintains 20 woodland acres of Clay's 600-acre estate, on which he built one of the nation's first private racetracks; most of his grounds are now occupied by adjacent residential areas. Family furnishings plus numerous Clay possessions and memorabilia recall the troubled times of this peacemaker whose failures may have been nobler than most of his peers' successes. (Open daily, summer 9:30–4:30, winter 10:00–4:00; 606-266-8581; admission.)

(See VIRGINIA in this chapter; also Chapter 3, DISTRICT OF COLUMBIA.)

CUSTER, GEORGE ARMSTRONG (1839–1876). The cavalry officer resided during a temporary disbandment of the Seventh Cavalry, which he ultimately led to its destruction, in **Elizabethtown** from 1871 to 1873. While serving as the military governor of Kentucky, he resided in a small tenant dwelling that stood next door to the 1825 Brown-Pusey Community House, 128 North Main St. (at the corner of Poplar Street). This two-story brick structure, a stagecoach inn in Lt. Col. Custer's day, is now a community center and historical library containing many original furnishings. Custer wrote *My Life on the Plains* (1874) while stationed there. (Open Monday–Saturday 10:00–4:00; 502-765-2515; free.)

(See Chapter 4, KANSAS, MICHIGAN, NORTH DAKOTA, OHIO, SOUTH DAKOTA; also Chapter 6, MONTANA.)

DAVIS, JEFFERSON FINIS (1808–1889). The birth site of the Confederate president is marked by a 351-foot obelisk, similar in design to the Washington Monument, at **Fairview.** Jefferson Davis Monument State Park, east of town on U.S. Highway 68, offers visitors a scenic view from the top of the obelisk plus a 22-acre tract that includes a replica of his two-room, log-cabin birthplace. The site of the original cabin, it is said, was the vestibule of the 1886 Bethel Baptist Church adjacent to the park. "It was quite a good house for those pioneer days," wrote biographer Hudson Strode, "and peculiarly distinguished from comparable homes because it was the first in the district to have glass windows." Davis's father farmed some 600 acres there, raising tobacco and breeding horses. The family moved to Mississippi before Davis reached age two. The Kentucky Department of Parks maintains this site. (Open daily, June 1–August 31, 9:00–5:30; March 1–May 31, September 1–November 30, Tuesday–Sunday 9:00–5:30; December 1–February 28, Saturday–Sunday 9:00–5:30; 502-564-6957; admission.)

A marker at 102 West High St. in **Lexington** identifies the Ficklin House site, where Davis roomed as a Transylvania University student from 1821 to 1824.

(See ALABAMA, GEORGIA, LOUISIANA, MISSISSIPPI, TENNESSEE, VIRGINIA in this chapter; also Chapter 3, DISTRICT OF COLUMBIA.)

EDISON, THOMAS ALVA (1847–1931). A house where the inventor resided in 1866 and 1867, when he worked as telegrapher for Western Union, stands at 729 East Washington St. in **Louisville.** About a year after Edison lived there, he patented his first device, an electrical vote recorder. The restored house, operated by Butchertown, Inc., displays period furnishings, a library, and a museum. (Open Monday–Friday 9:00–4:00, Saturday–Sunday 2:00–4:00; guided tours Saturday–Sunday; 502-587-1447; free.)

(See FLORIDA in this chapter; also Chapter 3, NEW JERSEY; also Chapter 4, MICHIGAN, OHIO.)

FOSTER, STEPHEN COLLINS (1826–1864).
Exhibit: According to hallowed tradition, the minstrel songwriter was inspired to compose "My Old Kentucky Home" when he visited his Rowan cousins at their "Federal Hill" estate near **Bardstown** in 1852. While no documentary evidence exists that Foster ever went there, much less wrote his song on the premises as is often claimed, the Kentucky Department of Parks maintains the 1795 plantation house in My Old Kentucky Home State Park as a Foster memorial. Original furnishings and Foster memorabilia are displayed three-quarters of a mile south of town on U.S. Highway 150. (Open January 7–June 6, Labor Day–December 20, daily 9:00–5:00; June 7–Labor Day,

daily 9:00–7:30; except closed Monday in December, January, February; 502-348-3502; admission.) In summer, "The Stephen Foster Story," a Paul Green musical drama, is presented in the park amphitheater (June 12–September 5, Tuesday–Sunday 8:30 PM; 502-348-5971; admission; write PO Box D, Bardstown, KY, 40004, for reservations).

(See FLORIDA in this chapter; also Chapter 2, MANHATTAN; also Chapter 3, NEW JERSEY, PENNSYLVANIA; also Chapter 4, OHIO.)

GRIFFITH, DAVID LEWELYN WARK (1875–1948). "Overqualified" and shabbily cast aside by the motion picture industry he did much to create, the pioneer director made his last film in 1931 and spent his final bitter years seeking menial directing jobs from movie moguls who owed their success to him. A Southern gentleman of courtly manners and distinctly Confederate sympathies, Griffith resided mainly in hotel rooms throughout his adult life. His farm birthplace, razed either in 1911 or 1918, stood on what is now the Ray Deible farm, State Highway 22 about three miles east of **Crestwood.** According to local authority Theodore Klein, "some of the material from the old house was used in construction of the new one" on the site. "This included most of the old yellow poplar studding and a yellow poplar beam that was 32 feet long."

Sometime after 1885 the family moved to **Louisville,** where his widowed mother operated boardinghouses at several addresses. One that survives is located at 421 West Chestnut St., an 1860 building that now houses a lounge.

From about 1920 to 1939, Griffith returned at occasional intervals to his native area of **La Grange,** where he bought the two-story frame house at 206 North Fourth St. (at the corner of Madison Street). Built about 1905 by a local funeral director, the house was divided into four apartments during the 1940s. The present private owners have excellently restored and remodeled the dwelling. Though not ordinarily open to visitors, the house is occasionally included in holiday tours of local homes. (Contact City of La Grange, 121 West Main St., La Grange, KY, 40031.)

(See Chapter 6, CALIFORNIA.)

LINCOLN, ABRAHAM (1809–1865). The 16th U.S. president, like his Confederate counterpart Jefferson Finis Davis (see the entry on Davis earlier in this section), was born in Kentucky. Neither Davis nor Lincoln remembered anything of their birthplaces, since both were infants when their frontier families moved on. Lincoln Birthplace National Historic Site includes 100 acres of Thomas Lincoln's 300-acre "Sinking Spring Farm," named for the deep limestone spring that still runs on the property. The small log-cabin birthplace, built about 1808, stands on or very near its original site atop a knoll, sheltered and enshrined by a templelike granite edifice since 1911. Before that year, the cabin underwent various treatments and fortunes. "Its history prior to 1860 is a matter of controversy and doubt," admits the National Park Service brochure; its claim to authenticity is based on the fact that in 1860 it was standing in decrepit condition on the former Lincoln farm. Repaired and moved to a farm about two miles north in that year, it served as a one-room school and residence there until 1894. In 1895 a New York businessman bought it and returned it to its original site. It was dismantled in 1897, moved and exhibited at the Nashville (Tenn.) Centennial; and the Buffalo (N.Y.) Exposition displayed it in 1901.

Ten years later (exactly 100 years after the Lincolns left this farm), the cabin was re-erected on its original and present site. Today the National Park Service maintains this historic ground, also displaying the Lincoln family Bible, a film and a diorama of the farm's 1809 appearance. There are also picnic areas and nature trails. Lincoln's Birthplace is located three miles south of **Hodgenville** on U.S. Highway 31E and State Highway 61. (Open June 1–September 1, daily 8:00–6:45; September 2–May 31, 8:00–4:45; 502-358-3874; free.)

In 1811 a defective land title to "Sinking Spring Farm" forced the family's move to a better farm of 230 acres northeast of Hodgenville. "Knob

ABRAHAM LINCOLN BIRTHPLACE SHRINE. In a still-rural area of central Kentucky rises this templelike edifice sheltering the probable cabin in which the nation's greatest President entered the world. His father, Thomas Lincoln, it is believed, hewed and laid these logs on the exact hilltop site where the cabin now sits carefully protected. This old wood has undergone many ordeals since Lincoln's birth. Dismantled, moved and reconstructed several times during its history, the cabin was finally returned to the spot that Thomas Lincoln chose. He would hardly recognize the grand approach to it today, but the surrounding spring and farmland would look familiar.

(*Courtesy Abraham Lincoln Birthplace National Historic Site*)

Creek Farm," Lincoln's home from 1811 to 1816, was the first place he remembered; he and his sister Sarah attended their first two terms of school two miles away. The original log cabin was torn down in 1870. Located just east of **New Hope** on State Highway 52, a 1931 reconstruction of the cabin is privately operated and maintained on the site.* (Open June 1–August 31, daily 9:00–7:00; April 1–May 31, September 1–October 31, daily 9:00–5:00; 502-549-3741; admission.)

(See TENNESSEE in this chapter; also Chapter 3, DISTRICT OF COLUMBIA, PENNSYLVANIA; also Chapter 4, ILLINOIS, INDIANA, MICHIGAN.)

LINCOLN, MARY TODD (1818–1882). The emotionally high-strung Mary Todd married Abraham Lincoln in 1842 (see the entry on Lincoln above). She, like her husband, was born in Kentucky but lived in the state for a much longer period. Her birthplace at 501 West Short St. in **Lexington** is long gone. Her later family home, however, stands at 578 West Main St., a two-story, Georgian brick structure built about 1803. Constructed as an inn, it was purchased by her father in 1832 and remained her home until 1839. As Lincoln's wife, she returned there with her husband for three subsequent visits. The Kentucky Mansions Preservation Foundation displays period furnishings plus Todd and Lincoln family items. (Open April 1–December 31, Tuesday–Saturday 10:00–4:00; 606-233-9999; admission.)

(See Chapter 3, DISTRICT OF COLUMBIA; also Chapter 4, ILLINOIS.)

MERTON, THOMAS (1915–1968). From 1941 the prolific poet-author and religious mystic resided as a Trappist monk—ordained as Father M. Louis in 1949—in the Abbey of Our Lady of Gethsemane at **Trappist.** The world's largest monastery of the Roman Catholic Trappist order, the Abbey is located 12 miles south of Bardstown on U.S. Highway 31E. From 1964 Merton occupied a solitary cabin, "The Hermitage," built especially for him on the woodland grounds where he meditated and did most of his writing. Monks there practice an austere discipline of silence. (Guided tours and scheduled retreats for men only; dona-

tion; contact Abbey of Our Lady of Gethsemane, Trappist, KY, 40073.)

(See Chapter 2, MANHATTAN.)

NATION, CARRY AMELIA MOORE (1846–1911). The birthplace and home until 1853 of the hatchet-wielding temperance activist stands privately owned near **Bryantsville.** The 10-room, one-story house on her father's hog farm, with wooden frame now covering its original hewed logs, is located on Herrington Lake, State Highway 34 off Fisher Ford Road near Pope's Landing.

(See ARKANSAS in this chapter; also Chapter 4, KANSAS, MISSOURI; also Chapter 6, TEXAS.)

PATTON, GEORGE SMITH, JR. (1885–1945).
Exhibit: At **Fort Knox,** the Patton Museum of Cavalry and Armor displays memorabilia of "Old Blood and Guts," the World War II general who, almost alone among America's military pantheon, never professed himself a man of peace. Amid examples of the tanks and armored vehicles that became his specialty, visitors may see his celebrated collection of pistols and the staff car in which he was fatally injured in Germany. The museum, operated by the U.S. Army, is located in Keyes Park, 4554 Edmunson Ave. (Open May 1–September 30, Monday–Friday 9:00–6:00, Saturday–Sunday 10:00–6:00; October 1–April 30, Monday–Friday 9:00–4:30, Saturday–Sunday 10:00–4:30; 502-624-3812; free.)

(See VIRGINIA in this chapter; also Chapter 1, MASSACHUSETTS; also Chapter 3, DISTRICT OF COLUMBIA; also Chapter 6, CALIFORNIA.)

TAYLOR, ZACHARY (1784–1850). Rough-hewn soldier and 12th U.S. president, Taylor served in many frontier outposts during his military career but made his permanent home until 1829 at one location near **Louisville.** Taylor was nine months old when his parents arrived at the present site of Springfield National Historic Landmark, 5608 Apache Road, seven miles east of Louisville off U.S. Highway 42. His father built their first home there, a log cabin that later became the quarters for some of the plantation's 26 slaves; it survives at the rear of the two and one-half-story brick house. Dating from 1790 in its earliest portions and with additions built from 1810 to 1830, this house hosted Taylor's marriage to Margaret Mackall Smith on June 21, 1810. The privately owned house suffered damage during a 1974

---

*In 1981, however, its owner had placed the farm up for sale, so visitors should check locally on current accessibility.

tornado but has been restored. Taylor's nearby tomb in Taylor National Cemetery, 4701 Brownsboro Road, occupies part of the former 700-acre estate, now mainly housing developments.

(See ARKANSAS, LOUISIANA, VIRGINIA in this chapter; also Chapter 3, DISTRICT OF COLUMBIA.)

LOUISIANA

Shaped like a tattered boot, the 18th state channels the nation's mightiest river down at last to the Gulf of Mexico. There the runoff from 31 states and two Canadian provinces joins sea level through five mouths into the Gulf.

Like the Mississippi River, Louisiana itself gathers many streams. Few states are so diverse in history, landscape and culture. De Soto's expedition, bringing the first whites, sailed the entire length of Louisiana in 1543, and de Soto himself left his bones in the Mississippi. Near Venice at the Head of Passes, La Salle ceremoniously planted a cross in 1682, claimed the territory drained by the entire river—a watershed whose immensity he had no way of knowing— and named it for the "Sun King," Louis XIV of France. Louisiana Territory encompassed most of the present midcontinental United States.

The present state's oldest permanent settlement, founded in 1714, is Natchitoches. French-Canadian colonist Sieur de Bienville founded New Orleans in 1718 at the first reasonably dry spot about 100 river miles north of the Gulf. In 1762 France ceded Louisiana Territory to Spain, which supported the American colonies with arms and supplies during the American Revolution. France again briefly controlled the territory from 1800 until Napoleon's epochal 1803 decision to sell it to America for an urgently needed $15 million. American settlers poured into present Louisiana, conflicting at first with the refined Creole culture evolved in New Orleans during the generations of French-Spanish settlement.* Louisiana entered the Union in 1812. During the final phase of the War of 1812, English troops launched a massive invasion of Louisiana, and Andrew Jackson achieved the military renown that would propel him to the White House when he and his ragtail army defeated the British at Chalmette—the celebrated Battle of New Orleans, actually fought two weeks after the peace document was signed in England. New Orleans, the first capital, became the staging area for the Mexican War. The state was the sixth to secede, and Louisiana's Gen. Beauregard ordered the first shot of the Civil War fired at Fort Sumter, S.C., in 1861. Union Adm. David G. Farragut took New Orleans in 1862, but most of the state resisted until almost the very end. The Reconstruction period was chaotic and corrupt; not until 1877 did federal occupation cease and the state resume its own political control. State politics attracted outside attention in 1927 when Gov. Huey P. Long, a colorful demagogue, upset the traditional power structure and became the virtual dictator of the state and a national political figure. From his base at Baton Rouge, the permanent state capital from 1882, Long's autocratic methods brought many modern improvements, but often at the expense of due process and other democratic guarantees; and the lawless political climate culminated in Long's assassination by a fellow Louisianian.

Today Louisiana thrives as one of the most prosperous Southeastern states. Its northern portion differs greatly from the south. German immigrant farmers settled the low hill country above the Red River; alcohol remains prohibited and politics conservative in this area. In contrast, New Orleans, Louisiana's largest city and second largest American seaport, is one of the nation's most cosmopolitan urban areas, dominantly French-Catholic and relatively liberal in politics. The city meticulously preserves its old European heart in the Vieux Carre, the 70-block French Quarter. At what is now Beauregard Square, West African slaves performed tribal dances to crude drums and banjos, creating the ancestral sounds of an entire musical culture known as jazz, later born in the Tenderloin district. New Orleans has never needed excuses to dress up and celebrate.

---

*Outside Louisiana there is much confusion about the terms *Creole* and *Cajun.* Creoles are descendants of the original French and Spanish settlers. Formerly the term was exclusively reserved for whites but later came to include those of mixed Negro and white ancestry who formed the aristocratic colonial class—mainly in New Orleans, though not restricted there. Creoles, proud of their heritage, bear much the same genealogical status in Louisiana as Pilgrim descendants in New England. John James Audubon, Gen. P. G. T. Beauregard and musician Jelly Roll Morton were among the noted Americans who claimed Creole ancestry.

Creole is more of a racial designation than Cajun, which is primarily a cultural identity. A much smaller and more cohesive group, Cajuns descend from French-Canadian expatriates, the Acadians cast out of Nova Scotia by the British in 1755. Today they inhabit the Lafayette area.

Jazz funerals, Creole cuisine, Sugar Bowl games, Mardi Gras and shrimp harvests provide only a few of the occasions for festivity, a vital part of life for this thoroughly mixed populace. The French heritage continues in the Code Napoléon, the legal system framed by the Emperor of this region; and French remained an official language in the state until 1915.

Today Louisiana's chief income derives from industry, mainly the processing of oil and foods. Nationally, the state ranks first in the production of natural gas, and second in oil and petrochemicals. Rice, cotton, sugarcane and strawberries are leading crops. Some of the world's largest salt mines operate there, and an extensive nutria and muskrat fur industry grows.

Louisiana gave the nation a treasure in Louis Armstrong, probably America's foremost jazz artist. Jefferson Davis's troubled life ended there. Sherwood Anderson, William Faulkner and Lafcadio Hearn wrote extensively in New Orleans, and John James Audubon painted some of his best bird portraits in Louisiana. Jean Lafitte, the useful scoundrel, and Jim Bowie, the bold opportunist, created legends in this state where song and story, romance and adventure, are respected components of living. Most historic homes center in New Orleans and Baton Rouge. The number of extant dwellings associated with national figures is not large, and fewer still are open to visitors. What does survive in Louisiana, however, is something often rarer than historic structures—the style and ambiance of a rich past than can still be shared.

ANDERSON, SHERWOOD BERTON (1876–1941). In 1924 and 1925 the author inhabited rooms at 540B St. Peter St. in **New Orleans.** This address is a section of the Upper Pontalba building that, with its Lower Pontalba counterpart on St. Ann Street, flanks Jackson Square. Built in 1849, the brick apartment buildings with their ornamental iron balconies each extend for an entire block and are two of the city's most elegant structures. There in 1924, Anderson met the young writer William Cuthbert Faulkner, who briefly roomed with Anderson (see the entry on Faulkner later in this section). According to one account, the two "used to sit on their adjoining French Quarter balconies, dropping BBs on unsuspecting passers-by in the alley below. A direct hit on a woman carrying laundry was worth one point, a

priest brought two and a tourist three. The loser bought coffee and doughnuts for both at the nearby Morning Call Coffee Stand," which closed in 1974. The Upper Pontalba is owned by the City of New Orleans, but apartments there remain privately occupied. In 1925 Anderson's wife bought an old house at 715 Governor Nicholls St.; she owned the house until 1930, but the couple lived there only briefly. Once known as "Casa Correjolles" for its 1834 builder, this privately owned house shows one of the more interesting wrought-iron railings in the French Quarter. Faulkner and painter William Spratling scored a ten-pointer with their satire of the French Quarter artistic clique of this period, titled *Sherwood Anderson and Other Famous Creoles* (1926); Anderson wasn't overjoyed at this BB shot.

(See VIRGINIA in this chapter; also Chapter 2, MANHATTAN; also Chapter 4, OHIO.)

ARMSTRONG, LOUIS DANIEL (1900–1971). Jazz innovator, trumpeter and possibly the first scat singer, "Satchmo" was born in **New Orleans,** his home until 1917. According to biographers Max Jones and John Chilton, "It was only by bad luck, it seems, that Louis' birthplace was not preserved. The shack . . . was discovered by an enthusiast just before the wreckers leveled the site. He bought the shack for $50 and told the New Orleans Jazz Museum, which arranged to move it. Unfortunately they could not meet the demolition firm's deadline and the building was burned down." This occurred in 1964. The 26-by-24-foot shack stood at 2723 Jane Alley off South Broad Street. Armstrong identified "my corner" as the intersection of Liberty and Perdido streets, the site of his boyhood home in a brick tenement row and of his first professional "gigs" in nearby taverns.

Exhibit: The **New Orleans** Jazz Museum, formerly located in the Royal Sonesta Hotel, was held in the Louisiana State Museum archives in 1982. According to Chief Curator Vaughan Glasgow, however, this notable collection will be installed and displayed in the restored New Orleans Branch U.S. Mint Building, 400 Esplanade Ave., in 1983. Prominent in the collection are Armstrong's first bugle and cornet, Bix Beiderbecke's cornet, plus many other artifacts, photos and recordings from the early days of jazz. (Call 504-568-6968 for information.)

(See Chapter 2, QUEENS.)

AUDUBON, JOHN JAMES (1785–1851). Of French-Creole ancestry, the naturalist and bird artist liked Louisiana but experienced some of his most difficult times there. He resided in **New Orleans** for two hungry periods, sketching portraits and living hand-to-mouth. Audubon rented a room at 706 Barracks St., a low brick house of uncertain vintage, where he lived with an assistant from February 22 to June 20, 1821. Later (1821–22) he and his family approached starvation in the small wooden cottage he rented at 505 Dauphine St. Both of these dwellings remain privately owned.

Audubon State Commemorative Area, three miles east of **St. Francisville** on State Highway 965, contains the restored 1799 "Oakley Plantation House," where Audubon worked on his *Birds of America* series in 1821 while tutoring Eliza Pirrie, the owner's daughter. This modest, two-story frame dwelling, operated by the Louisiana State Park and Recreation Commission, displays period furnishings and Audubon prints. Audubon completed 32 paintings during his residence there from June to October. Nature trails wind through the park's 100 acres. (Park open Monday–Saturday 9:00–7:00, Sunday 1:00–7:00; house open Monday–Saturday 9:00–5:00, Sunday 1:00–5:00; 504-635-4593; admission.)

At "Weyanoke Plantation House" near **Wakefield,** Audubon taught himself to paint with oils and found the subject of one of his best-known paintings, *The Wild Turkey.* He lived there briefly in 1822 and again in 1824 and 1825; his wife, Lucy Bakewell Audubon, joined him there after a long separation and taught school on the plantation, then known as "Beech Woods." "For three years, while JJA bounced from pillar to post in England, it was the closest thing the Audubon family had to a permanent residence," wrote Michael Harwood in 1980. According to Harwood, no trace of this 1802 plantation remains in the forks of a dirt road about four miles west off State Highway 124. Since it was still listed in the revised Louisiana *American Guide* of 1971, however, its disappearance presumably occurred fairly recently.

(See FLORIDA, KENTUCKY in this chapter; also Chapter 2, MANHATTAN; also Chapter 3, PENNSYLVANIA.)

BEAUREGARD, PIERRE GUSTAVE TOUTANT (1818–1893). The birthplace of the Creole Confederate general who modeled himself on Napoléon was destroyed by vandals for firewood about 1910. The large, one-story house, his home until about 1826, centered the prosperous family's sugar cane plantation. The site is marked at **Contreras** on State Highway 46.

In **New Orleans,** where the widowed Beauregard retired to a business career after the Civil War, he first occupied rented rooms with his son at 1113 Chartres St. while looking for a job (1866–67). This 1827 "raised cottage" was the 1837 birthplace of chess master Paul Morphy. After undergoing numerous vicissitudes, the house was purchased in 1944 by novelist Frances Parkinson Keyes, who restored it and used it as her winter residence until her death in 1970. Her novel *Madame Castel's Lodger* (1961) is based on Beauregard's brief stay there. Today the house, operated as a Beauregard-Keyes memorial by the Keyes Foundation, contains period items collected by the author. (Open Monday–Saturday 10:00–4:00; 504-523-7257; admission.) With his son and a widowed sister, Beauregard moved in 1867 to the two-story house at 934 Royal St., which remained his home until 1875. It remains privately owned. His last home from 1881 at 1631 Esplanade St. also remains private; it dates from about 1880.

Exhibit: The Confederate Museum, operated by the Louisiana Historical Association at 929 Camp St. in **New Orleans,** displays Beauregard items including a uniform he wore. (Open Monday–Saturday 10:00–4:00; 504-523-4522; admission.)

BEIDERBECKE, LEON BISMARCK "BIX" (1903–1931).
Exhibit: See *Exhibit* entry for Louis Daniel Armstrong earlier in this section.

(See Chapter 2, MANHATTAN, QUEENS; also Chapter 4, IOWA.)

BOWIE, JAMES "JIM" (1796–1836). The Texas revolutionary leader who died at the Alamo was a Louisiana resident from 1802 to 1828. A Spanish land grant acquired by his father in Section 40 of **Catahoula Parish** was Bowie's home until 1812. The unmarked site is located at Township 9 North, Range 6 East.

A marker on the First National Bank building at 1790 South Union St. in **Opelousas** identifies the site of one of his dwellings, from about 1812 to 1820. While living there, Bowie profitably engaged with Jean Lafitte in smuggling slave cargoes into the country (see the entry on Lafitte later in this section.)

During the 1820s Bowie acquired extensive sugar plantations and timber lands in Avoyelles, Rapides, Terrebonne and Lafourche parishes. None of his dwellings remain, and exact sites are, in most cases, uncertain.

Exhibit: The Jim Bowie Museum, 220 South Academy St. in **Opelousas,** displays documents and relics relating to Bowie, his family and the celebrated knife. (Open Monday–Friday 8:00–4:00; 318-948-6263; admission.)

(See ARKANSAS in this chapter; also Chapter 6, TEXAS.)

DAVIS, JEFFERSON FINIS (1808–1889). The last lodging of the Confederate president stands privately owned at 1134 First St. in **New Orleans.** En route from his Mississippi plantation, Davis was taken ill and brought to this home of Judge Charles E. Fenner. He died in a guest room on the ground floor. The two-story dwelling of brick covered by concrete, now called the Forsyth House, was built by slaves in the early 1850s.

Exhibit: A Louisiana Historical Society collection of Davis clothing and possessions, including his infant crib, may be seen at the Confederate Museum, 929 Camp St. in **New Orleans.** (Open Monday–Saturday 10:00–4:00; 504-523-4522; admission.)

(See ALABAMA, GEORGIA, KENTUCKY, MISSISSIPPI, TENNESSEE, VIRGINIA in this chapter; also Chapter 3, DISTRICT OF COLUMBIA.)

FAULKNER, WILLIAM CUTHBERT (1897–1962). The novelist wrote mostly stories and poetry when he lived in **New Orleans** at intervals for about a year (1924–25), first sharing the apartment of his idol Sherwood Anderson (see the entry on Anderson earlier in this section). He soon moved to another shared apartment, that of painter William Spratling at 624 Orleans (Pirates) Alley between St. Peter Street and St. Louis Cathedral. Later he occupied rooms on the second floor of one of the city's most interesting old structures, the 1811 Le Monnier Mansion at 640 Royal St. (at the corner of St. Peter Street). This four-story brick building with its ornate ironwork was supposedly the city's first "skyscraper" of three stories; the fourth story was added in 1876. All of these lodgings remain privately occupied.

(See MISSISSIPPI, VIRGINIA in this chapter.)

HEARN, LAFCADIO (1850–1904). "Over each essay," wrote Allan Nevins, "the near-sighted word-jeweler toiled like a lapidary over his precious gems." The half-blind but prolific journalist, author, translator and critic, Hearn worked for **New Orleans** newspapers from 1877 to 1887 and wrote his first books there. His first lodging in the city was the Mary Bustillos boardinghouse, a two and one-half-story brick dwelling built about 1845 and still at 813 Baronne St. Only the staircase remains of the original interior, which now contains private law offices. "Baronne Street was to be only the first stop on an erratic, zigzagging course he would pursue through ten years of living in the city," wrote biographer Elizabeth Stevenson. Hearn moved from one bare room to another on St. Louis, Constant and Canal streets. In 1880 he lived at 516 Bourbon St., built in 1827 and still privately occupied. He finally settled at his last city lodging in 1881, Kate Higgins's two-story, brick boardinghouse at what is now 1565 Cleveland St. (privately owned), where he occupied two rooms on the second floor. The site of "The Hard Times," a restaurant he briefly operated in 1878 ("Satisfies hunger for one nickel") is 160 Dryades St.

(See Chapter 2, MANHATTAN.)

JACKSON, MAHALIA (1912–1972). Mountainous in both appearance and talent, the irrepressible gospel singer was a native of **New Orleans,** her home until 1927. Her Water Street birthplace, a levee cottage, is long gone. An aunt's house where she spent years of her childhood, however, remains privately owned at 7467 Esther St. The house, according to biographer Laurraine Goreau, "has been materially rebuilt and upgraded."

(See Chapter 4, ILLINOIS.)

LAFITTE, JEAN (1780?–1825?) Fact will probably never be sorted from legend concerning this Gulf privateer and slave smuggler who preyed on Spanish vessels and aided Gen. Andrew Jackson during the 1815 Battle of New Orleans. From about 1810 to 1817, Lafitte made his headquarters on **Grand Isle** at the head of Barataria Bay. Other sites associated with him include **Lafitte Village,** a rendezvous point for his smugglers; a log fort and embankment he may have built on the present site of the 1850 Barbé House at 2709 Shell Beach

Drive in **Lake Charles;** and the Irish Channel waterfront district of **New Orleans** in the vicinity of St. Thomas Street, a favorite haunt of Lafitte's men during the waterfront's brawling, lawless days. No surviving structure can be definitely linked to Lafitte today. His association with the so-called "Lafitte's Blacksmith Shop" at 941 Bourbon St. in New Orleans, though the shop is an ancient little structure, has never been authenticated, despite the words on the plaque there and valiant local efforts to trace some connection.

Exhibit: The Louisiana State Museum displays Lafitte relics, including a compass, weapons, coins and glassware in the historic 1795 Cabildo on Jackson Square, **New Orleans.** (Open Tuesday–Sunday 9:00–5:00; 504-522-8832; admission.)

(See Chapter 6, TEXAS.)

LONG, HUEY PIERCE (1893–1935). By demagoguery and corrupt politics, "the Kingfish" held a virtual dictatorship in Louisiana from 1930 until his assassination. As governor, senator, founder of a political dynasty and serious presidential aspirant, he was far from the backwoods buffoon type he pretended to be. "Like all true patriots he was born in a log cabin," biographer Carleton Beals wrote satirically. "Writing in his autobiography," wrote T. Harry Williams, Long "said correctly that it was a 'comfortable, well-built' house. In his speeches over the years, however, it appeared as something quite different, something much more humble." Long's sister remarked that "every time I hear of that cabin it gets smaller and smaller." The large, split-log dwelling stood on the present rear lawn of 1107 Maple St. in **Winnfield.** When Long was about a year old, the family moved into a larger saltbox house on the same property, a 320-acre cotton farm. His father moved the house in 1907 and built on its site a large, two-story, frame house, Long's home until about 1918. That house burned down a few years later; the saltbox house stood until 1962, when it was demolished to enlarge the Earl K. Long State Commemorative Area, named after Huey Long's younger brother, also a controversial governor. Picnic facilities are offered there by the Louisiana State Park and Recreation Commission. (Open Monday–Saturday 9:00–5:00, Sunday 1:00–5:00; free.)

Long's home from 1925 to 1930 stands at 305 Forest Ave. in **Shreveport,** a white brick, Span-

ish-style house that he built for $40,000. The wrought-iron balcony above the entrance of this two-story dwelling still shows the monogram "HPL."

Long built the Governor's Mansion at 502 North Blvd., **Baton Rouge,** in 1930 as his own lavish seat of power. This Georgian building of brick and stucco, now known as the "Old Governor's Mansion," is occupied by the Louisiana Arts and Science Center, which displays a variety of historical and art exhibits, including rooms of memorabilia donated by former Louisiana governors. (Open Tuesday–Saturday, 10:00–5:00, Sunday 1:00–5:00; 504-344-9463; free.) From 1932 Long's usual city residence was a suite on the 24th floor of the State Capitol building at Riverside Mall and Boyd Avenue, a monumental (34 stories) marble structure built during his administration in 1931. In a corridor of this building he was shot by Dr. Carl A. Weiss, a young idealist, on September 8, 1935, and died two days later; Weiss was gunned down and overkilled on the spot, which is pointed out by tour guides. The observation deck on the 27th floor gives a spectacular view of the city. (Open daily 8:00–4:15; 504-342-7317; free.)

In **New Orleans** Long occupied a suite in the Roosevelt Hotel from 1930; now called The Fairmont, this 1893 structure still operates at University Place and Baronne Street. He also bought a 1923 Spanish colonial house at 14 Audubon Blvd. (privately owned) in 1932, and this was his last family home, though he seldom stayed there himself. This house was used as a Louisiana State Museum building during the 1940s. Until the 1970s it served as the official Dean's Residence of Louisiana State University Medical School.

(See Chapter 3, DISTRICT OF COLUMBIA.)

OSWALD, LEE HARVEY (1939–1963). Apparent lone assassin of President Kennedy, the loser was born in **New Orleans,** his home until 1944. His mother, Marguerite C. Oswald, operated Oswald's Notion Shop at 1010 Bartholomew St., a house she owned until 1941; she and her children resided behind the shop. They occupied an apartment at 831 Pauline St. from 1941. Oswald himself was shipped to Bethlehem Children's Center, 4430 Bundy Road, in 1943 and resided there for a year. All of these addresses remain private, and their occupants are less than pleased at their notorious association.

(See Chapter 2, BRONX; also Chapter 6, TEXAS.)

TAYLOR, ZACHARY (1784–1850). From 1845 to 1849 the career soldier who became the 12th U.S. president made his home in a one-story "Spanish cottage" of four rooms on the **Baton Rouge** military reservation overlooking the Mississippi River. A marker identifies the site of Taylor's long-gone house on the State Capitol grounds at 752 Lafayette St. There Taylor, who had never voted in a presidential contest and knew nothing of politics, received the astonishing news of his 1848 Whig nomination and final election, and from there departed to his 1849 inauguration and brief presidency. The Pentagon Barracks, part of the former military post Taylor commanded, stand nearby on Riverside Mall at State Capitol Drive. This group of four buildings (originally five) dates from 1824. From 1886 to 1925, they housed Louisiana State University cadets; another soldier, Gen. Claire L. Chennault of World War II "Flying Tiger" fame, resided there as a student. State offices now occupy the old barracks.

(See ARKANSAS, KENTUCKY, VIRGINIA in this chapter; also Chapter 3, DISTRICT OF COLUMBIA.)

MISSISSIPPI

Similar in general outline to its eastern neighbor Alabama (but flipped, with its "toe in the Gulf" portion snugged against the Alabama "toe"), Mississippi took its name from the serpentine river forming its western border. Whether the Algonquin etymology was "maesi" (fish) or "missi" (great)—or whether "fish river" or "great river" specifically labeled this river apart from any large river—is beyond knowing. "Father of Waters," at any rate, is out, the concoction of a sexist poet or Hollywood Indian. The Spanish explorer de Soto viewed the river in 1541, probably near Clarksdale—and what a moment that must have been, even for a soldier whose sensitivity resembled his armor. By 1673, when Marquette and Jolliet came downriver as far as Arkansas, the name Mississippi was firmly established, though each took the explorer's liberty of renaming it. Chickasaws, Choctaws and Natchez tribes were the first Americans found there. In 1682 La Salle conferred with a solemn native aristocracy at the Great Village of Natchez

a few weeks before he claimed the entire region for France. Pierre le Moyne, Sieur d'Iberville, established Mississippi's first pemanent settlement in 1699 at what is now Ocean Springs. France ceded all of its lands east of the river to Great Britain in 1763, and a tide of, Virginia, Georgia and Carolina immigrants swelled west to Mississippi. After two decades of Spanish control in the southwestern portion, Mississippi Territory, created in 1798, added that portion of Spanish West Florida (now the "toe") in 1813. Mississippi became the twentieth state in 1817 and located its capital at Jackson in 1822.

Mississippi's cotton economy, river commerce and slave labor made it one of the South's most prosperous states, one with large stakes in the status quo. The second state to secede, it lost about three-quarters of its young white male population during the Civil War. The decisive Union victory at Vicksburg after a siege of 47 days in 1863 was the turning point of the war; Vicksburg National Military Park preserves this key battlefield of our history. Because Grant accepted the city's surrender on July 4, Vicksburg ignored Independence Day until after World War II and even today gives only token recognition. Few Southern historians dwell on it, but much Unionist sympathy occurred in Mississippi throughout the war. The "Free State of Jones" (Jones County) formed a large pocket of resistance to the Confederacy, but was only one of many such pockets. Mississippi reentered the Union in 1870, but Reconstruction's harsh political period lasted until the Democratic Party's takeover in 1876.

The state became a major focus of the civil rights struggle during 1964 black voter registration drives. Tragic episodes of racial violence entered Mississippi's legacy during the decade of the 1960s, but the state also achieved notable progress in desegregation. From its former national image as a "closed society" of fearful people, Mississippi continues to enlarge its horizons, moving toward fulfillment of a promise that fear, violence and self-defeat were unable to vanquish.

Though agriculture—especially soybeans and cotton—remains extremely important in the Yazoo-Mississippi delta country, industry has become the state's chief source of income. Food processing, chemicals and space technology form the expanding core of the state's economy. Mississippi is also a major timber producer; the southern half of the state is mostly longleaf pine forest. The Gulf coast portion encompasses the world's longest human-made beach—28 miles—a white strand dredged from the Intracoastal Waterway and now a major resort area of the South. The famed 450-mile Natchez Trace from Natchez to Nashville, Tenn., became an important supply route in the nation's westward expansion and military history. Today the scenic Natchez Trace Parkway parallels, crosses and occasionally covers this old route.

Highly aware of its past, Mississippi has done much to preserve the bittersweet record of its history. Plantation homes, though atypical of how most Mississippians lived, are especially notable in the Natchez area. Confederate President Jefferson Davis spent most of his life in the state; and Union Adm. David G. Farragut, ironically, was born about as far south in Mississippi as one can go. Other natives included singer-actor Elvis Presley, almost more of a cultural phalanx than a person, and expatriate novelist Richard Wright. Mississippi's most enduring gift was probably writer William Faulkner, whose creation of fictional Yoknapatawpha County illustrates Sara Orne Jewett's belief that the keenest view of the world comes through a close look at the village. Visitors will find many of these houses extant, open and welcoming.

DAVIS, JEFFERSON FINIS (1808–1889). The earliest home of which the Confederate president had any recollection was "Rosemont Plantation," the one and one-half-story frame house built by his father in 1810 and Davis's home until about 1825. It stands east of **Woodville** on State Highway 24. Privately operated, the house displays period furnishings and a detailed genealogy of the Davis family. (Open March–December, Monday–Friday 9:00–5:00; 601-888-6809; admission.)

Davis's first married home in 1835 was a three-story mansion on the 5,000-acre "Hurricane Plantation," owned by his brother Joseph at the peninsula of Davis Bend—which, since 1867, has been **Davis Island**—in the Mississippi River. Sara Knox Taylor Davis died of malaria in that same year, and Davis stayed a heartbroken recluse working his brother's plantation there until 1838. In that year he designed and built his own adjacent one-story plantation house, "Brierfield,"

which he and "Knox" had long before planned. Until the outbreak of Civil War in 1861, this plantation of about 2,400 acres was Davis's permanent home with his second wife, Varina Howell Davis. Union troops advancing toward Vicksburg burned and ravaged "Hurricane Plantation" in 1862; "Brierfield," though defaced, was spared. In 1866 the Davis brothers sold both plantations to one of their former slaves. The new owner defaulted on payments, however, and complicated legal maneuvers finally resulted in the 1881 restoration of "Brierfield" to the aged ex-president. Though Davis never returned there to live, he visited a few days before his death and had ambitious plans to rebuild the plantation. "Brierfield," plagued by increasingly higher spring floods, was raised 10 feet on brick pillars by Davis's grandson in 1924. Finally, in 1931, it burned to the ground. The Davis family retained the property until 1953. Today only the overgrown ruins of "Brierfield" remain on what is now a private game preserve, accessible mainly by plane to Dale air strip on the island. Davis Island lies about 15 miles south of Vicksburg. In *The Pursuit of a Dream* (1981), Janet Sharp Hermann describes the cooperative living experiment developed there by ex-slave Isaiah T. Montgomery until 1880. *Brierfield: Plantation Home of Jefferson Davis* (1971), by Frank E. Everett, Jr., gives an intriguing history and modern description of the site.

Davis's last home from 1877 was Beauvoir National Historic Landmark, located on West Beach Boulevard (U.S. Highway 90), five and one-half miles west of **Biloxi**. This one and one-half story house, built in 1852, has been restored by the Sons of Confederate Veterans, which has owned the house since Varina Howell Davis sold it to the organization in 1898. From 1903 until 1955, Beauvoir was the Jefferson Davis Memorial Home for Confederate veterans and their wives. Davis furnishings and the 70-acre grounds now authentically re-create the scene where Davis spent his last 12 years. In the separate Library Pavilion, a cottage east of the main dwelling, Davis wrote *The Rise and Fall of the Confederate Government* (1881). (Open daily 8:30–5:00; 601-388-1313; admission.)

Exhibit: "The Briars," located on Briars' Lane off U.S. Highway 65–84 Bypass in **Natchez,** was the ancestral home of Varina Howell, who married Davis there in 1845. The 1814 plantation house stands high on a bluff overlooking the Mississippi River. Period furnishings are displayed by the private owners. The Pilgrimage Garden Club arranges regular tours. (Open daily, 9:00–5:00; 601-446-7441; admission.)

(See ALABAMA, GEORGIA, KENTUCKY, LOUISIANA, TENNESSEE, VIRGINIA in this chapter; also Chapter 3, DISTRICT OF CO-LUMBIA.)

DE SOTO, HERNANDO (1496?–1542).

Exhibit: The Spanish explorer spent the winter of 1540–41 at the present site of **Tupelo**. On May 21, 1541, he sighted the Mississippi River, the first European to do so. The U.S. De Soto Exposition Commission in 1939 established the probable site of this epochal arrival at Sunflower Landing, identified by marker about 15 miles west of **Clarksdale** on the river. This site, as with most significant locations on de Soto's old, cold trail, is contested—in this case, with Memphis, Tenn. Only new discoveries, not of rivers but of documents or artifacts, could settle the matter beyond controversy.

(See ARKANSAS, FLORIDA, TENNESSEE in this chapter.)

FARRAGUT, DAVID GLASGOW. (1801–1870) Ironically, the Union admiral whose 1864 damning of torpedoes and capture of Mobile Bay dealt a death blow to the Confederacy was a native Southerner. His boyhood home from 1809 to about 1821, when he became a midshipman, was the 900-acre Farragut plantation on the Pascagoula River. The site of the long-gone plantation is Farragut's Point on the west side of Farragut Lake, about two miles north of **Gautier**. A marker on U.S. Highway 90 near Gautier indicates the approximate site.

(See TENNESSEE in this chapter; also Chapter 2, MANHATTAN; also Chapter 3, NEW YORK.)

FAULKNER, WILLIAM CUTHBERT (1897–1962). The author whose fictional Yoknapatawpha County traced the saga of Southern social change, Faulkner made his lifelong home in Mississippi. The original spelling of the family name, which he changed, was Falkner. His birthplace and home until 1898, a one-story frame house at 204 Cleveland St. (at the corner of Jefferson Street) in **New Albany** was razed for the present Presbyterian parsonage in 1953.

The family lived in **Oxford** from 1902 and occu-

pied several houses on Second South Street and South Street. In 1929 Faulkner married Estelle Oldham, and the couple occupied a ground-floor apartment at 803 University Ave. (privately owned) for a year. Their last home, from 1930, was Rowan Oak National Historic Landmark located at 719 Garfield St. off Old Taylor Road. Known as the "old Shegog place," the two and one-half-story, white frame house built in 1848 was in decrepit shape when Faulkner bought it, and he restored the house himself. "For the rest of his life," wrote Stephanie Kraft, "Faulkner put his own labor and most of the money from his books into Rowan Oak. During the first summer, he and a few helpers jacked up one section of the house after another and replaced the foundation beams." Then he laid a new roof, installed new plumbing and wiring, and added the study where he produced most of his best-known novels. Faulkner named his home from an ancient Scottish practice of placing rowan tree branches across thresholds to deflect evil spirits and bad luck. Not until 1948, when the author achieved financial security from film scripts, was he able to quit worrying about a possible foreclosure on Rowan Oak. Today the University of Mississippi displays Faulkner's home and 31 acres with most of his furnishings and possessions intact. Of particular interest is the outline he wrote on his study wall for his novel *A Fable* (1954). (Open during university sessions, Monday–Friday 10:00–12:00, 2:00–4:00, Saturday 10:00–12:00; 601-234-3284; free.)

"Greenfield Farm," Faulkner's 320-acre property that he bought in 1938 and hired a brother to operate, is located 17 miles northeast of Oxford off State Highway 30 near **Woodson Ridge** in Holly Springs National Forest. Against all advice, Faulkner specialized in raising mules there—not very successfully—and often hunted on this isolated rural property, still privately owned.

Faulkner's County: Yoknapatawpha (1964) by Martin J. Dain is an interesting photo pilgrimage.

Exhibit: The Mary Buie Museum at 510 University Ave. in **Oxford** contains Faulkner memorabilia. (Open Tuesday–Wednesday, Saturday 10:00–12:00, Tuesday–Sunday 1:30–4:30; closed August; 601-232-7073; free.)

(See LOUISIANA, VIRGINIA in this chapter.)

JONES, JOHN LUTHER "CASEY" (1864–1900).
Exhibit: "He was characterized by the moaning and wailing whippoorwill sound of his whistle,"

wrote Massena F. Jones, the unrelated curator of the Casey Jones Museum at **Vaughan.** The engineer for the Illinois Central Railroad who rode "Old 382," his locomotive, into a stalled freight train near Vaughan and achieved fame from a ballad written about the event, Casey Jones was the only human casualty of the wreck, apparently the result of his own carelessness. The site of the pileup is marked about three-quarters of a mile north of the village. The museum, operated by the Mississippi Department of Natural Resources in the 1900 depot on Main Street, displays items from the accident plus other railroad memorabilia. (Open Wednesday–Saturday 10:00–5:30, Sunday 1:30–5:30; 601-961-5262; admission.)

(See TENNESSEE in this chapter.)

PRESLEY, ELVIS ARON (1935–1977). Dominant figure of rock and roll music and symbol of a generation, the singer was born in **Tupelo** and spent his first 13 years there. His birthplace stands in a section of town called East Heights. The small, frame two-room house, restored and furnished by the East Heights Garden Club, is operated by the City of Tupelo. Presley himself donated a large amount of money for Elvis Presley Park, which now surrounds the dwelling at 305 Elvis Presley Drive. (Open Monday–Friday 10:00–5:00, Sunday 2:00–5:00; 601-842-9765; admission.) Subsequent Presley residences in Tupelo stood on Kelly and Berry streets.

Near **Walls,** Presley bought his "Circle G Ranch," a former cotton and cattle farm of 163 acres, in 1967 and used it for horse riding. The one-story house of frame and brick stands four miles west of U.S. Highway 51 on Horn Lake Road. Presley, who surrounded his acres with a wire fence eight feet high, sold the property in 1969, and it remains privately owned.

(See TENNESSEE in this chapter; also Chapter 6, CALIFORNIA.)

WRIGHT, RICHARD (1908–1960). Regarding the novelist's birthplace and early boyhood home, "the truth of the matter is not certain," according to Ronald W. Miller, Executive Director of the Historic Natchez Foundation in 1982. The unknown site was definitely near Roxie, however, where his parents sharecropped on a farm until 1911.

In that year, his mother brought him to the home of her parents in **Natchez,** where Wright lived until 1914. One biographer identifies this house as 20 Woodlawn Ave., a small, one-story frame dwelling that remains privately owned. Miller, however, states that the home may have been located on North Union Street. The matter awaits some original research for its resolution.

(See TENNESSEE in this chapter; also Chapter 2, BROOKLYN, MANHATTAN.)

NORTH CAROLINA

Bridging Virginia and South Carolina, North Carolina has been labeled the "vale of humility between two mountains of conceit" by at least one state politician. Its motto is *Esse Quam Videri*— "To be, rather than to seem." Actually, most visitors agree, North Carolina seems quite all right. Geographically, the state consists of three steps down to the sea: the Appalachian convergence of the Blue Ridge and Great Smoky mountains, where Mount Mitchell towers as the highest point in the eastern United States; the gradually sloping Piedmont plateau that occupies almost half of the state; and the level coastal plain, pocketed with lakes. Offshore, the linear barrier islands of Cape Hatteras and Cape Lookout strung along the 120-mile Atlantic coast form the Outer Banks.

North Carolina hosted England's first colonial attempt in America. Fort Raleigh National Historic Site on Roanoke Island marks the 1585 site of this shortlived settlement sponsored by Sir Walter Raleigh. The first white child born in the New World, Virginia Dare, cried there in 1587. She apparently didn't live long, for this was also the famed "Lost Colony," which by 1590 had vanished without a trace—except for the cryptic word "CROATOAN" carved on a tree. In 1663 Charles II granted the entire area of the Carolinas—a name deriving from *Carolus*, the Latin form of Charles— to eight lords proprietor. Bath, incorporated in 1705, is North Carolina's oldest town. Though officially united until the American Revolution, the Carolina colony had split into northern and southern portions by 1712. North Carolina became a royal province in 1729 and by 1765 was England's fourth largest American colony, pioneered mainly by Scots and Pennsylvanians. As the first colony to authorize a vote for independence in 1776, North Carolina was the last of the 12 originals to ratify the 1789 Constitution, successfully insisting on a religious freedom clause and thus becoming the 13th state. The American

Revolution faced two fronts of opposition there— the British with their Tory sympathizers and Cherokee natives.

The state reluctantly seceded in 1861, 10th of the 11 to do so. During the Civil War, its troops suffered more casualties than any other southern state. It was reputedly during this period that the term "Tarheel" originated as a putdown or as praise (probably each successively). The feet of North Carolinians were said to be coated with the tar produced by the state, accounting for their fierce persistence in battle; if they retreated, they had forgotten to "tar their heels." The state reentered the Union on July 4, 1868.

Economic prosperity gathered momentum after World War I, and North Carolina became a national pioneer in supporting school and road systems. Today the state, though broadly diverse in industry, remains primarily agricultural. Two-thirds of the nation's bright-leaf tobacco, supported by federal subsidies, grows there, along with corn, soybeans, peanuts, livestock and timber. The dominant industries include textiles (most of the hosiery we wear), tobacco products, furniture and tourism.

North Carolina became a runway for the air age when two Ohio brothers named Wright went there to try their laboriously built wings. Two better-than-average U.S. presidents, James Polk and Andrew Johnson, were natives, and their birth sites are appropriately memorialized. Authors O. Henry and Thomas Wolfe returned at intervals to their native cities, and other prominent literary residents included Randall Jarrell, Carson McCullers and Carl Sandburg. The resort area of Pinehurst attracted such names as Annie Oakley, John P. Marquand and Gen. George C. Marshall, probably the most notable soldier-statesman in our history. North Carolina was also Daniel Boone's early home. Other intriguing residents better known by sobriquets than surnames were Edward Teach (Blackbeard) and Chang and Eng Bunker (the Siamese Twins). Today the dwellings of most notable North Carolinians do survive, thanks to an active care for "Tarheel" history and liberal efforts to preserve and display it.

BLACKBEARD. See EDWARD TEACH.

BOONE, DANIEL (1734–1820). Years before the frontiersman cut the Wilderness Road and led pioneers into Kentucky, he farmed, hunted and explored widely in North Carolina. The first North Carolina home of the family (1751–52), who came from Pennsylvania, was a cave in what is now Daniel Boone Memorial State Park along the Yadkin River, southwest of **Lexington** off State Highway 703. In 1752 his father, Squire Boone, built a 20-foot-square log cabin on his tract of 640 acres there. A replica cabin on 110 acres of this property contains a small museum of pioneer relics. The site, operated by the North Carolina Department of Natural and Economic Resources, is undeveloped; visitors may picnic and hike.

About two miles west of **Mocksville** on U.S. Highway 64 is the site of the family's Bear Creek home where Squire Boone built an 18- × -22-foot cabin, probably in 1754. Daniel Boone farmed there, bought the land from his father in 1759 and sold it about 1763. A later house on this plot, using some of Boone's old logs, became the 1829 birthplace of racist abolitionist author Hinton Rowan Helper. A highway marker indicates the site.

Boone himself married Rebecca Bryan in 1756 and acquired a 640-acre tract on Sugartree Creek, his home base for most of the next decade. Boone farmed and hunted there but often left for months at a time on long exploring journeys while Rebecca Boone raised their first four children and bore a daughter by his brother. This site is located two miles east of **Farmington** on the present Bryant Smith farm (privately owned), Rainbow Road.

From 1766 to 1775, Boone settled his family on the upper Yadkin River at what is now **Boone.** His cabin stood at the present Faculty and Newland streets, its site marked with an 18-foot stone monument.

Exhibit: Daniel Boone Native Gardens, located half a mile off U.S. Highway 421 on Horn in the West Drive, **Boone,** displays frontier relics in Squire Boone Cabin Museum. (Open May 1–June 30, September 1–October 31, Tuesday–Sunday 9:00–5:00; July 1–August 31, Tuesday–Sunday 9:00–7:00; admission.) The historical drama *Horn in the West,* performed in an outdoor amphitheater, is a musical treatment of Boone's life and accomplishments. (Performances mid-June–mid-August, Tuesday–Sunday 8:30 PM; 704-264-2120; admission.)

(See KENTUCKY in this chapter; also Chapter 3, PENNSYLVANIA, WEST VIRGINIA; also Chapter 4, MISSOURI.)

BUNKER, CHANG AND ENG (1811–1874). Their carnival billing as "the Siamese Twins" gave rise to the term describing all such congenitally united siblings. Attached together at the waist, they settled in North Carolina in 1839 and became prosperous farmers who owned 28 slaves by 1860. Despite the unconventional living arrangements their condition required, both brothers raised large families with numerous descendants. Near **Mount Airy,** each brother built a house in 1845; they resided in each dwelling for three-day intervals, and each twin governed the actions of both in his own household. Chang's two-story frame house has been sided and re-roofed on U.S. Highway 601 near Stewarts Creek, just south of town and on the west side of the highway. It remains privately owned.

Eng's house, where the twins died, burned down in 1955. It stood further south nearer **White Plains** on the east side of the same highway. A private brick residence now occupies this marked site, though an original log corn crib remains on the property.

(See Chapter 3, PENNSYLVANIA.)

COLTRANE, JOHN WILLIAM (1926–1967). The birthplace of the jazz saxophonist stood unmarked, dilapidated and vacant in 1981 at 318 Bridges St. in **Hamlet.** Coltrane was born in an upstairs apartment of this building with a brick veneer, his home to about age three.

(See Chapter 2, MANHATTAN, QUEENS; also Chapter 3, NEW YORK, PENNSYLVANIA.)

FITZGERALD, F. SCOTT (1896–1940). The novelist resided frequently from 1936 to 1939 at the Grove Park Inn in **Asheville** in order to stay near his wife Zelda Sayre Fitzgerald, who remained hospitalized for schizophrenia at Highland Hospital until her death in 1948. Grove Park Inn, a large stone structure built in 1913 with recent wing additions, still hosts tourists at 290 Macon Ave.

(See ALABAMA in this chapter; also Chapter 2, MANHATTAN; also Chapter 3, MARYLAND, NEW YORK; also Chapter 4, MINNESOTA; also Chapter 6, CALIFORNIA.)

HENRY, O. See WILLIAM SYDNEY PORTER.

JACKSON, ANDREW (1767–1845). North and South Carolina have long contested over the seventh U.S. president's birth site. While scholarly consensus favors South Carolina's claim, the two sites straddle the state line only a few miles apart, occasionally resulting in a Carolina "border warfare" of highway markers. The signs "have been torn down by stealth, and replaced with tenacity," wrote Dixon Wecter. The general vicinity of both sites, an area known as "the Waxhaws" in frontier times, was familiar country to Jackson the boy.* North Carolina marks the locale of the McCamie Cabin, locally claimed as Jackson's actual birth site, southwest of **Waxhaw** via State Highway 75 or U.S. Highway 521.

There is no historical doubt about Jackson's residence in **Salisbury** (1784–87), where he began studying law and earned his license to practice. His boarding residence was the Hughes Hotel, later the Rowan House hotel, still standing at Church and Fisher streets.

(See SOUTH CAROLINA, TENNESSEE in this chapter; also Chapter 3, DISTRICT OF COLUMBIA.)

JARRELL, RANDALL (1914–1965). Poet, critic and longtime professor of literature at the University of North Carolina, Jarrell resided mainly in **Greensboro** from 1947. He lived at 1200 West Market St. from 1954 to 1956, and at 123 Tate St. from 1958 to 1960. His last home from 1960—a "rustic, improbable house in a small forest of pines and hardwood the bulldozers forgot," as Mary von Schrader Jarrell described it—stands at 5706 South Lake Drive. All of these dwellings remain privately owned.

(See Chapter 3, DISTRICT OF COLUMBIA; also Chapter 4, OHIO; also Chapter 6, CALIFORNIA, TEXAS.)

JOHNSON, ANDREW (1808–1875). The 17th U.S. president, peering down from his portraits as one of America's great scowling, politically battered faces, was a native of **Raleigh.** His 12- × 18-foot birthplace, a tiny frame house built with a gambrel roof about 1795, stood originally at 123 Fayetteville St.; a marker designates the site. Today the house stands along with other 18th-century restorations in the re-created village square at Mordecai Historic Park, 1 Mimosa St. The walls

---

*Other spots claimed at various times for the entrance of "Old Hickory" into this world have included Virginia, West Virginia, Pennsylvania, England, Ireland and the high seas.

and upstairs flooring are original. Restorers found that Johnson's birthplace had been constructed partly of used lumber showing old nail holes. The house was first moved during Johnson's presidency and several times thereafter; at one point, during the early 20th century, railroad hoboes used it for a shelter. Johnson lived there until 1824. Period furnishings are displayed by the Mordecai Square Historical Society. (Open June 1–September 30, Wednesday 10:00–12:00, Sunday 2:00–4:00; October 1–May 31, Tuesday–Thursday 10:00–1:00, Sunday 2:00–4:00; 919-834-4844; admission.)

(See SOUTH CAROLINA, TENNESSEE in this chapter; also Chapter 3, DISTRICT OF COLUMBIA.)

McCULLERS, CARSON SMITH (1917–1967). Carson Smith married Reeves McCullers in 1937, and their first married home was a two-room furnished apartment at 311 East Blvd. in **Charlotte.** Today this one and one-half-story Victorian structure in the Dilworth neighborhood is a posh restaurant. In 1938 the couple lived upstairs at 806 Central Ave., razed during the 1960s. There the author wrote the early chapters of her first novel *The Heart is a Lonely Hunter* (1940).

Sources differ on the couple's **Fayetteville** residence (1938–40) where she completed the novel. One biographer identifies it as an upstairs apartment at "Cool Spring Place," the 1789 former public tavern building at 119 North Cool Spring St.; but city directories and local historical sources give their address as 1104 Clark St., currently unlisted.

(See GEORGIA in this chapter; also Chapter 2, BROOKLYN, MANHATTAN; also Chapter 3, NEW YORK.)

MADISON, DOLLEY PAYNE TODD (1768–1849). The fourth U.S. first lady, Dorothea Payne was born in a house that stood behind the four-ton boulder marker at 5505 West Friendly Ave. in **Guilford College,** her infant home until 1769.

Exhibit: The Dolley Madison Room in the **Greensboro** Historical Museum, 130 Summit Ave., features objects relating to the vivacious woman who set the first real example of "class" in the White House—one that few presidential families have matched since, not by what she did but by her own exuberant sense of style. Visitors may see several of her gowns, manuscripts and personal items. (Open Tuesday–Saturday 10:00–5:00, Sunday 2:00–5:00; 919-373-2043; free.)

(See VIRGINIA in this chapter; also Chapter 3, DISTRICT OF COLUMBIA, PENNSYLVANIA.)

MARQUAND, JOHN PHILLIPS (1893–1960). "A place devoid of intellect and concerned only with bridge and golf, but a place which I find pleasant because on the whole people let me alone and I can write in the morning and play golf in the afternoon." Thus the novelist described his winter home in **Pinehurst,** which he called "the Golf Capital of America." The house he bought in 1959 and occupied for only a few months before his death arose in 1925 as a cooperative effort to build a dwelling that would reflect the ideal average of Pinehurst domestic needs. Six floor plans of representative area houses were combined to produce a structure of aggressively average dimensions, promptly labeled "Ideal House"; a restrictive deed on the property prevented "said premises to be occupied by a Jew or a Negro or any person affected by tuberculosis or consumption." The name was later changed to "Nandina." Still privately owned and apparently free of disease (and, one hopes, discrimination), the house stands at the junction of Palmetto, Cherokee and Midland roads.

(See FLORIDA in this chapter; also Chapter 1, MASSACHUSETTS; also Chapter 2, MANHATTAN; also Chapter 3, DELAWARE, NEW YORK.)

MARSHALL, GEORGE CATLETT (1880–1959). Shortly before his 1945 retirement as U.S. Army Chief of Staff, Gen. Marshall bought "Liscombe Lodge" in **Pinehurst** and resided there during winters until his death. His stays were usually brief and infrequent, however, until his permanent retirement from public service in 1951. Built in 1927, the sprawling house remains privately owned on Linden Road.

(See GEORGIA, VIRGINIA in this chapter; also Chapter 3, DISTRICT OF COLUMBIA, PENNSYLVANIA; also Chapter 6, WASHINGTON.)

MURROW, EDWARD ROSCOE (1908–1965). The news broadcaster and courageous foe of McCarthyism was born Egbert Roscoe Murrow of Quaker parentage in the Pleasant Garden Center Community of Friends. His birthplace was apparently a small house that stood on the 320-

acre Polecat Creek farm of his parents. The house traditionally ascribed as his birthplace near **Pleasant Garden** at the northeast corner of State Highway 62 and Davis Mill Road is probably the home his father enlarged from an 18th-century log cabin shortly after Murrow's birth and the boy's home until 1913. The present small wings on the two-story sided house, which remains privately owned, were more recently added by a Murrow uncle. Nearby on the south side of State Highway 62, east of its Sunrise Drive junction, stands the two-story, frame Josh Murrow farmhouse (also privately owned), built in 1895 by Murrow's grandfather.

(See Chapter 2, MANHATTAN; also Chapter 3, DISTRICT OF COLUMBIA, NEW YORK; also Chapter 6, WASHINGTON.)

OAKLEY, ANNIE (1860–1926). The star of Buffalo Bill's Wild West Show and a deadly accurate sharpshooter during a performing career of almost half a century, Oakley and her husband Frank Butler made their winter home from 1915 to 1920 at the Carolina Hotel in **Pinehurst,** with occasional visits thereafter. The hotel employed them to operate the gun club, give exhibitions and teach sharpshooting. "In the gun room or on the sunny terrace," wrote Walter Havighurst, "they talked about guns, golf, and game birds with John Philip Sousa, John Bassett Moore, Walter Hines Page, John D. Rockefeller. They exchanged Ohio and Indiana memories with Booth Tarkington, and Frank Butler quoted homely verse to author Edgar A. Guest." This massive, 1900 wooden complex in the shape of a triple cross, now the Pinehurst Hotel and Country Club, stands off Ritter Road and continues to harvest much publicity from Oakley and Butler.

(See FLORIDA in this chapter; also Chapter 3, MARYLAND, NEW JERSEY; also Chapter 4, OHIO.)

POLK, JAMES KNOX (1795–1849). The reconstructed log-cabin birthplace of the 11th U.S. president stands half a mile south of **Pineville** at Polk Memorial State Historic Site on U.S. Highway 521. This is the site of his parents' 260-acre farm, acquired in 1776, and Polk's home until 1806. The North Carolina Department of Cultural Resources maintains a visitor center with exhibits and a film on Polk's life and career. There is also a picnic area. (Open Tuesday–Saturday 9:00–5:00,

Sunday 1:00–5:00; 704-889-7145; free.)

(See TENNESSEE in this chapter; also Chapter 3, DISTRICT OF COLUMBIA.)

PORTER, WILLIAM SYDNEY "O. HENRY" (1862–1910). The author's **Greensboro** birthplace, a small, one-story frame house owned by his grandparents, no longer stands. Its marked site at 426 West Market St. is now occupied by the Masonic Temple Museum, which displays Masonic relics. Porter lived on this property until 1882, though he saw his actual birthplace dwelling demolished about 1874.

Exhibit: At 130 Summit Ave., the **Greensboro** Historical Museum displays several exhibits relating to Porter and his early life in the town. Replicas of the schoolhouse he attended until age 15 and of the W. C. Porter Drug Store, his uncle's pharmacy where he worked from ages 17 to 19, are prominent features. Also displayed is an extensive collection of O. Henry manuscripts, pictures and first editions. (Open Tuesday–Saturday 10:00–5:00, Sunday 2:00–5:00; 919-373-2043; free.)

(See Chapter 2, MANHATTAN; also Chapter 6, TEXAS.)

SANDBURG, CARL (1878–1967). The poet, folklorist and biographer made his last home at Sandburg Home National Historic Site in North Carolina. He and his wife, Lilian Steichen Sandburg, purchased the 240-acre farm called "Connemara" near **Flat Rock** in 1945. According to the National Park Service brochure, "Mrs. Sandburg was the one who discovered the western North Carolina mountain area for the family. . . . The farm had everything the family wanted, including ample pasture for the goats and seclusion for writing." There Sandburg wrote *Remembrance Rock* (1948), *Always the Young Strangers* (1953), and his Pulitzer Prizewinning *Complete Poems* (1950); while Lilian Sandburg managed the working farm and also won prizes with her large goat herd. The two and one-half-story frame house was built over a raised basement in 1838 as the summer home of Christopher G. Memminger, Confederate secretary of the treasury. No curtains cover the windows there. According to granddaughter Paula Steichen, "There was no one to peek in, and we all wanted the sun. The trees and vistas framed by the windows took the place of paintings on the walls."

"CONNEMARA FARM," LAST HOME OF CARL SAND-BURG. Sandburg, with his socialist sympathies, had qualms of guilt about owning this 240-acre estate near **Flat Rock**. Ironically for the biographer of Abraham Lincoln, his mansion had been constructed by a man who later became a prominent Confederate official. Sandburg's large family lived there from 1945, and he wrote all of his later works in his cluttered upstairs study. Sandburg died there at age 89. In 1974 the property became the first national park established to commemorate a writer.
(*Courtesy Carl Sandburg Home National Historic Site*)

Sandburg habitually worked at night in his upstairs study, where his eyeshade, cigars and typewriter on an upended crate remain as he left them. "Sandburg also loved to stroll around the property," wrote Rita Stein, "and the visitor is free to retrace Sandburg's steps along paths to the farm buildings or through the woods." Original family furnishings and Sandburg possessions may be viewed on tours conducted from a basement information center. Amid scores of federal sites that preserve areas or homes associated with political and military leaders, this is the only national park thus far created to honor a literary figure. Sandburg died peacefully there after a remarkably full and fulfilled lifetime. "Connemara Farm" stands on Little River Road west off U.S. Highway 25 as marked by signs. (Open daily 9:00–5:00; 704-693-4178; free.)

(See Chapter 4, ILLINOIS, MICHIGAN, WISCONSIN.)

SIAMESE TWINS. See CHANG AND ENG BUNKER.

TEACH, EDWARD "BLACKBEARD" (1680?–1718). Not to be confused with the fictitious Bluebeard, this pirate also had many wives but apparently remained courteous to all of them, if to hardly anyone else. Colonial authorities deeply resented his plundering attacks on coastal shipping and finally went after him. In a clean-shaven age, Teach (or perhaps his name was Thatch—no one is sure) cultivated a fearsome appearance with his leonine black, braided whiskers and the sputtering fuses stuck into his hat. In 1718 shortly before his bloody demise, he occupied a house on Plum Point overlooking Pamlico Bay at **Bath.** There he entertained lavishly and perhaps married his 14th wife. One source says his residence stood on Bay Street. Until recent years, the marked site showed a ground depression, probably left by modern treasure seekers who haven't done very well at recovering his supposed troves of booty.

The pirate's favorite anchorage was **Ocracoke Island** on the Outer Banks, where he intercepted many a ship threading through the chief trade lane of Ocracoke Inlet. "Teach's Hole," where he was separated from his bushy head by Lt. Robert Maynard of the royal sloop *Ranger,* is located at Ocracoke. The old fishing village is accessible by ferry from Hatteras, Cedar Island or Swan Quarter.

WESLEY, JOHN (1703–1791).
Exhibit: At **Lake Junaluska,** the World Methodist Commission on Archives and History of the United Methodist Church displays memorabilia of the English evangelist, including letters and his portable pulpit. The museum is located at 39 Lakeshore Drive. (Open summer, Monday–Saturday 9:00–5:00; rest of year, Monday–Friday 9:00–5:00; 704-456-9433; free.)

(See GEORGIA in this chapter.)

WOLFE, THOMAS CLAYTON (1900–1938). A shambling tower of a man whose explosive ener-gies created some of the most monumental novels of the 20th century, Wolfe did everything in a large, keyed-up, compulsively wordy way. His **Asheville** birthplace at 92 Woodfin St. is long gone; but the rambling boardinghouse opened by his mother in 1906—which she called "My Old Kentucky Home" and which Wolfe thinly fiction-alized as "Dixieland" in *Look Homeward, Angel* (1929)—stands at 48 Spruce St. Now Thomas Wolfe Memorial National Historic Landmark, the two and one-half-story frame house dating from the 1890s looks just as it did when Wolfe's family lived there. The interior brings poignant remind-ers of his meticulous love-hate descriptions of the place. Almost all of the furnishings are orig-inal, including personal items and possessions from Wolfe's birthplace; an entire room also recreates his New York City apartment. Some idea of Wolfe's size is revealed by a clothing exhibit. Literary historian Stephanie Kraft calls this excel-lently preserved and maintained landmark "a specimen *par excellence* of an early twentieth-century boardinghouse." These dining room tables and oak sideboards so indented into Wolfe's own consciousness still serve luncheons to visi-tors—once each year on October 3, his birthday. The house is operated by the North Carolina Department of Cultural Resources. (Open Tues-day–Saturday 9:00–5:00, Sunday 1:00–5:00; 704-253-8304; admission.)

(See Chapter 2, BROOKLYN, MANHATTAN.)

WRIGHT, ORVILLE (1871–1948).

WRIGHT, WILBUR (1867–1912).
Exhibit: Wright Brothers National Memorial designates the site of their aviation experiments from 1900 to 1903 that finally culminated in the first sustained flights by a machine heavier than air. The epochal flight of December 17, 1903, occurred at Kill Devil Hill on the Atlantic sandbar of the Outer Banks. This windy tract of 431 acres, operated by the National Park Service, marks the site "where the world was given wings," the 120-foot span between takeoff and landing. Build-ings include replicas of the Wrights' hangar-workshop and living quarters and a visitor center containing their experimental wind tunnel, tools and replicas of their 1902 glider and the 1903 wooden biplane "Flyer" that prone pilot Orville Wright lifted into history. (The original plane is

on permanent exhibition at the Smithsonian Institution, District of Columbia.) Long known as Kitty Hawk, the park is adjacent to the community of **Kill Devil Hills** on U.S. Highway 158 Bypass. The event is annually commemorated there on December 17. (Open Memorial Day–Labor Day, daily 8:30–6:30; winter, daily 8:30–4:30; spring and fall, daily 9:00–5:00; 919-473-2111; free.)

(See Chapter 3, PENNSYLVANIA; also Chapter 4, INDIANA, MICHIGAN, OHIO.)

SOUTH CAROLINA

The heart-shaped wedge of South Carolina, eighth colony of the original 13 to become a state in 1788, was first settled in 1670 at Charles Towne (now Charleston), a community named like the colony after Charles II who had granted the territory to proprietary lords. Earlier, the first European settlement in North America, though shortlived, occurred at Paris Island, when Jean Ribault led a group of French Huguenots there in 1562. The southern Carolina colony, separated from its northern neighbor in 1712, rallied strongly in support of the independence movement. America's first decisive victory of the Revolution occurred at Fort Moultrie in 1776, and the battles of Kings Mountain and Cowpens proved significant turning points in the war. But political tension over states' rights and the slavery issue stirred a hotly defensive temper in the state almost from the beginning; and John C. Calhoun became the leading Southern spokesperson for the nullification method of dealing with unpopular federal laws. South Carolina led 11 states in secession on December 20, 1860, and the Civil War began when Confederates fired from Fort Johnson on Fort Sumter at Charleston. The city remained in Confederate hands until almost the last month of the war. Though readmitted to the Union in 1868, the state's continued refusal to extend suffrage to its black population led to 12 years of military rule and carpetbag government; and the economic disruption of those years lasted well into the 20th century.

South Carolina's previously agrarian economy, based chiefly on cotton and rice, has shifted since World War II to a primarily industrial base, with emphasis on textile manufacturing and tourism. Tobacco has overtaken cotton as the main cash crop. Columbia, the largest city, has been state capital since 1790.

Geographically, South Carolina continues the coastal state pattern of mountain, piedmont and plain (called Up Country, Midlands, and Low Country in South Carolina). In the northwest, the Blue Ridge range marks the highest point, and extensive salt marshes and islands buffer the transition from land to sea. The main central watershed is the Santee River system, modified by several huge artificial lakes created for power and recreation purposes. Charleston, major seaport and the second largest city, retains portions of its colonial heritage in houses, historic walking trails and spectacular gardens.

South Carolina has produced several political figures of national prominence. Besides the redoubtable Calhoun, three presidents—Andrew Jackson, Andrew Johnson and Woodrow Wilson—had early homes in the state. James F. Byrnes and Bernard M. Baruch were natives and longtime residents; and editor Henry R. Luce, a major political influence, occupied a massive estate near Charleston. The state's unlikeliest dweller, perhaps, was English author W. Somerset Maugham, who produced most of his later novels there. While most of these homes survive, relatively few stand open to the public; and several are so sequestered on private grounds that even exterior views may be difficult. Various localities do offer entrance to many older homes worth seeing, especially in the Charleston area. Few of these, however, have associations with South Carolina's best-known residents.

BARUCH, BERNARD MANNES (1870–1965). In **Camden,** the birth site of the Wall Street financier, longtime presidential advisor and "park-bench statesman" is marked on Broad Street, at the present location of the First Baptist Church educational building. The two-story frame dwelling in which Baruch lived until 1880 was demolished during the 1950s.

"Hobcaw Barony," Baruch's longtime winter hunting preserve, encompassed his plantation of 17,500 acres at the southern end of Waccamaw Neck, a peninsula between the Atlantic Ocean and the Waccamaw River. This vast coastal forest and marshland property remains isolated and relatively undisturbed. On this site in 1526, some 600 Spanish colonists attempted to establish Spain's first settlement in North America but gave it up after a year. George I granted 12,000 acres to Lord Carteret in 1718, and Carteret named his barony "Hobcaw." As many as 13 rice plantations once worked the area. Baruch acquired the original barony lands in 1905 and added 5,000 acres in 1907. His first mansion, a Victorian frame structure called "Friendfield House," overlooked Winyah Bay at the end of Hobcaw Road. Fire destroyed this house during Christmas of 1929. Baruch immediately built his two-story Georgian "Hobcaw House" of brick, steel and concrete on the same site and entertained numerous public figures, including British prime minister Winston Churchill, during 30 years of VIP hobnobbing. A weary president, Franklin D. Roosevelt, rested there for a month in 1944. Belle Baruch acquired the estate from her father in 1958 and made provision to leave the property in trust for outdoor educational and research purposes. Today Hobcaw Barony, owned by the Belle W. Baruch Foundation, provides field laboratory environments for Clemson University's Baruch Forest Science Institute and the Baruch Institute of Marine Biology and Coastal Research of the University of South Carolina. A portion of the Baruch mansion, now used for offices and conference rooms, has been maintained with its original interior; according to an official policy statement, however, "groups permitted upon the property must relate to the areas of research" specified in the 1964 will of Belle W. Baruch, and "the property is not open to the general public." Hobcaw Barony is located about five miles north of **Georgetown** off U.S. Highway 17. (Contact Belle W. Baruch Foundation, PO Box 578, Georgetown, SC, 29440 for information.)

(See Chapter 2, MANHATTAN; also Chapter 3, DISTRICT OF COLUMBIA.)

BYRNES, JAMES FRANCIS (1879–1972). "Jimmy" Byrnes enjoyed a long, controversial political career as congressman, senator, Supreme Court justice, New Deal official, secretary of state and South Carolina governor. His early homes in Charleston and Aiken no longer stand.

Byrnes occupied the Governor's Mansion at Richland and Lincoln streets in **Columbia** during his tenure as the state's chief executive from 1951 to 1955. This two-story, white stucco building dates from 1855, originally an officers' barracks. It remains the official residence of South Carolina's governors. In 1955 Byrnes bought and renovated

a house at 12 Heathwood Circle, and this was his last home. It is presently owned by the McKissic Museum of the University of South Carolina.

(See Chapter 3, DISTRICT OF COLUMBIA.)

CALHOUN, JOHN CALDWELL (1782–1850). One of the most powerful senators and cabinet members of the period preceding the Civil War, Calhoun was also twice vice president. His defense of sectional interests, however, defeated his presidential hopes; when he died, he was the strongest states' rights leader in Congress. His birthplace, the first two-story house in the Long Canes settlement on Calhoun Creek near **Abbeville,** lasted almost a century before fire destroyed it. Calhoun lived there until about 1800. The site is marked on Mt. Carmel Road (State Highway 823) about nine miles southwest of Abbeville. The approximate site of his law office is also marked on Court House Square in town.

Calhoun's permanent home from 1825 was Fort Hill National Historic Landmark, the 14-room, white frame mansion that stands on the Clemson University campus at **Clemson.** Calhoun enlarged the original 1802 dwelling on his 1,100-acre plantation, which his son-in-law eventually deeded to the state for the establishment of the university. Visitors may see many of Calhoun's original furnishings and possessions, including a sideboard made from timbers of "Old Ironsides" (*U.S.S. Constitution*), a gift from Henry Clay; and a chair and sofa once owned by George Washington. Floride Colhoun Calhoun, his gifted wife, designed much of the furniture there. Among the outbuildings is Calhoun's private office. Fort Hill is operated by United Daughters of the Confederacy and Clemson University. (Open Tuesday—Saturday 10:00–12:00, 1:00–5:30, Sunday 2:00–6:00; 803-656-2475; free.)

Floride Calhoun's widowed home from 1854 to her death in 1866 stands privately owned at 430 South Mechanic St. in **Pendleton.**

(See Chapter 3, DISTRICT OF COLUMBIA.)

JACKSON, ANDREW (1767–1845). The generally accepted birth site of the short-fused soldier and seventh U.S. president—"if for no other reason than that Jackson himself believed it was his birthplace," wrote biographer Robert V. Remini—is located near the North Carolina state line on U.S. Highway 521 about eight miles north of **Lancaster.** Andrew Jackson State Park, operated by the South Carolina Department of Parks, Recreation and Tourism, occupies 360 acres that include nature trails, a log schoolhouse and a museum of Waxhaw frontier relics. A five-room reconstructed log house on the site is similar to Jackson's first home on the farm of James Crawford, his uncle. Jackson resided there until about 1781. (Park open daily during daylight hours; museum open daily, 10:00–5:00; 803-285-3344; free.)

Exhibit: Fort Jackson Museum, Building 4442 at the U.S. Army post of **Fort Jackson** near Columbia, displays several possessions of "Old Hickory" plus military relics of the colonial frontier period. (Open Tuesday–Sunday 1:00–4:00; 803-751-7419; free.)

(See NORTH CAROLINA, TENNESSEE in this chapter; also Chapter 3, DISTRICT OF COLUMBIA.)

JOHNSON, ANDREW (1808–1875). At **Laurens,** the tailor's apprentice who conquered illiteracy and became the 17th U.S. president lived and worked with his elder brother in a cabin tailor shop that stood on a marked site north of the town square. While there (1824–25) Johnson also designed coverlets for young quiltmakers—probably our only president skilled in that particular craft.

(See NORTH CAROLINA, TENNESSEE in this chapter; also Chapter 3, DISTRICT OF COLUMBIA.)

LUCE, HENRY ROBINSON (1898–1967). A humorless man whose heavy brows often bristled in patriotic consternation, the powerful, conservative editor-publisher of Time Inc. bought Mepkin Plantation for $150,000 in 1936, and it became the center of his family life until 1949. This estate of 7,200 acres on the Cooper River above Charleston was the historic residence of Revolutionary merchant-diplomat Henry Laurens. The original plantation house, long gone, stood on the site of the Luce mansion at the end of a one-mile drive from River Road south of **Moncks Corner.** Numerous outbuildings, guest houses and ancient trees survive on this magnificent estate. The Luce family turned this property over to the Roman Catholic contemplative Trappist order, which operates a tree plantation there. The Abbey of Our Lady of Mepkin has opened a portion of

the grounds to public visitation. (Call 803-723-0245 for information.)

(See Chapter 1, CONNECTICUT; also Chapter 2, MANHATTAN; also Chapter 6, ARIZONA.)

MARION, FRANCIS (1732?–1795). The Revolutionary guerrilla leader, known as "the Swamp Fox" for his sudden strike-and-fade tactics, was a lifelong South Carolina resident, though biographers find him almost as elusive as the British did. None of his several homes exist, and historians have not even been able to pinpoint the sites for most. His birthplace and home until age six, called "Goatfield" or "Belle Isle Plantation," may have stood in the present vicinity of his tomb, about one mile off State Highway 45 west of **Pineville** as indicated by signs. Apparently Marion lived there with a brother during the 1750s and 1760s; according to Mark M. Boatner III, "the house survived until modern times." Today the property surrounding Marion's tomb is private and fenced off.

A possible boyhood home site of the little Huguenot soldier, also called "Belle Isle," is now Belle Isle Gardens on Winyah Bay, about five miles south of **Georgetown** off U.S. Highway 17. This landscaped preserve of 5,000 acres, privately operated, is also the site of a Confederate battery captured by the Union navy in 1865. The colorful grounds occupy a former rice plantation. Marion, if he lived there at all, left about 1750.

He bought his own plantation "Pond Bluff" on the Santee River in 1756, found it in ruins after the war, and rebuilt it in 1786. This was Marion's last home, where he married Mary Videau and died a few years later. From hearsay, Benson J. Lossing drew a sketch of the two-story frame house and said it had been demolished several years before his 1849 visit. Boatner, on the other hand, wrote in *Landmarks of the American Revolution* (1973) that the house burned in 1816 and that the "present structure built in that year" on the site contains some of Marion's original furniture. To cap the confusion, Sol Stember's *Bicentennial Guide to the American Revolution* (1974) stated that Marion's plantation site is "now under the water of Lake Marion." To clear the confusion: Marion's mansion burned to the ground in 1816; a one and one-half-story home built on the site in 1820 was removed before the 1939 Santee River impoundment; and Marion's original acreage, located four miles southeast of **Eutaw Springs,** now lies beneath Lake Marion.

MAUGHAM, W. SOMERSET (1874–1965). In 1941 his American publisher Nelson Doubleday built the English novelist a white frame house on Doubleday's "Bonny Hall" plantation near **Yemassee** on the Combahee River. Though Maugham traveled often, he made this his home base with companion Alan Searle until 1946. Besides the house, he used a cottage as a writing studio and there wrote *The Razor's Edge* (1944), *Then and Now* (1946) and *Catalina* (1948). Both structures are now occupied by a private owner about nine miles east of Yemassee and two miles west of U.S. Highway 17.

WILSON, WOODROW (1856–1924). A boyhood home (1872–75) of the 28th U.S. president stands at 1705 Hampton St. in **Columbia.** The Victorian parsonage built for Wilson's father displays original family furnishings and period items. Wilson entered college from there in 1873. The house is operated by the Historic Columbia Foundation. (Open Wednesday–Saturday 10:00–4:00, Sunday 2:00–5:00; 803-252-7742; admission.)

(See GEORGIA, VIRGINIA in this chapter; also Chapter 1, NEW HAMPSHIRE; also Chapter 3, DISTRICT OF COLUMBIA, NEW JERSEY.)

TENNESSEE

The state's name is an ancient Cherokee word, but even the Cherokees had lost its derivation and meaning by the time of white settlement. Tennessee was obviously an appealing word, however, for it first named a native village, then a river, then a county—and finally the 16th state, when Andrew Jackson suggested its adoption in 1796. Walled villages and mounds characterized the first known human cultures. During the American Revolution, the territory officially existed as Washington County of North Carolina; but in 1784, residents of the northeastern settlements declared independence and formed the federally unrecognized "State of Franklin," named after Benjamin. Dr. Franklin, though flattered, would have none of it. A North Carolina faction won over most of the insurgents when the confusion and anarchy became absurd, and by 1788, the "State of Franklin" had expired. Two

years later, North Carolina ceded the territory to the federal government. Tennessee's official name just before its legitimate statehood was the Territory South of the River Ohio. Nashville became the permanent capital in 1843.

This border state initially preferred neutrality in the Civil War. Opinion was strongly pro-Union until Lincoln's call for troops, then tilted abruptly toward secession, which occurred in June of 1861. More than two-thirds of the state's approximately 150,000 soldiers fought on the Confederate side. With the gunfire at Shiloh, Chickamauga and Chattanooga, Tennessee became the second-bloodiest battleground (next to Virginia) of the war. Last to secede, Tennessee was the first to reenter the Union, in 1866. Though the state avoided carpetbag government, voting rights for blacks were withheld by every possible means. The birthplace of the nefarious Ku Klux Klan was Pulaski. Through crime, terror and the collusion of crooked officials, it largely succeeded for almost a century in its aim of negating the political power of blacks throughout the South. (The more recent organization of the Klan, a 1915 barbarity founded outside of Tennessee, continues to expose itself as a refuge of genuine American dregs.) Political differences from the Civil War survive vaguely in the fact that east Tennessee remains a Republican bastion, while the middle and west vote consistently Democrat.

The inverted-slipper shape of Tennessee stretches 432 miles from east to west. East Tennessee's mountain country extends from the Great Smokies to the middle basin 60 miles wide, centered by Murfreesboro. Westward, the state slopes to bluffs overlooking the Mississippi.

Manufacturing creates Tennessee's primary income, with chemicals ranking as the major product. Nashville, country music capital of North America, is also the foremost recording center for the entire music industry. Soybeans lead the farm crops, followed by cotton, tobacco and corn. Not the least of this state's contributions is its fine "sippin' whiskies." Its largest city—and the largest cotton market in the world—is Memphis. A crucial economic milestone was the construction of the huge Tennessee River system of federal dams and reservoirs slanting across the eastern state. Fiercely opposed by private power companies, the Tennessee Valley Authority (TVA), established in 1933, brought industry, recreation, flood control and commerce to seven states, providing a classic model of cooperation between federal and state governments.

Tennessee ranks high in its contribution of national political leaders, whose diversity reflected the great American controversies. Though none were natives, three presidents—Andrew Jackson, James Polk and Andrew Johnson (five if we include Confederate President Jefferson Davis and Texas President Sam Houston)—resided there, the first three for most of their lives. More recent native activists included Cordell Hull, Estes Kefauver and Sam Rayburn. Next to public servants in frequency, Tennessee has given us notable musicians of several genres—the blues of W. C. Handy and Bessie Smith, the country laments of Hank Williams and a pop-cultural explosion in the rhinestone person of Elvis Presley. Folk figures included Davy Crockett and Casey Jones. The lives of two enormously influential men—William Jennings Bryan and Martin Luther King, Jr.—ended there on varying levels of tragedy.

Tennessee has a fine record of memorializing the sites—and in many cases, the surviving structures—associated with these and other residents.

BRYAN, WILLIAM JENNINGS (1860–1925). His political career was long behind him when the popular orator and frequent presidential candidate went with his wife in July of 1925 to prosecute a young high-school teacher named John T. Scopes in **Dayton**. The celebrated "monkey trial" was a deliberate test of Tennessee's antievolution law. Theologically and scientifically naive, Bryan upheld the fundamentalist version of instant creation as opposed to the Darwinian evolution theory accepted by most scientists and taught by Scopes, who was defended by lawyer Clarence Darrow. Though Bryan won his case, those hot weeks in Dayton formed the ignoble end of the aged statesman's life and career, as Dayton's courthouse became a world spectacle and a butt of ridicule for aggressive ignorance. The law itself was later, of course, declared unconstitutional. Bryan's lodging throughout the trial and where he died five days afterward was the F. R. Rogers house at 711 South Market St., razed about 1935. The private dwelling that replaced it still occupies the site.

Exhibit: Rhea County Courthouse on North Market Street in **Dayton** preserves the courtroom where righteous Bryan thundered, sarcastic Darrow sliced, bewildered Scopes sat and astonished reporters like H. L. Mencken had a carnival. In 1978 county officials restored the chamber to its 1925 appearance; furnishings are almost entirely original. There is a small basement museum relating to the trial. (Open Monday–Tuesday, Thursday–Friday 8:00–4:00; Wednesday, Saturday 8:00–12:00; 615-775-1181; free.)

(See FLORIDA in this chapter; also Chapter 3, DISTRICT OF COLUMBIA; also Chapter 4, ILLINOIS, NEBRASKA.)

CROCKETT, DAVID "DAVY" (1786–1836). Tall tales about this colorful frontiersman, congressman and Alamo defender masked the real man even before his death; and he was not averse to helping along his legend. Though Crockett traveled far afield, he made his lifelong home in Tennessee. His birth site is now a five-acre park with a cabin replica, visitor center and picnic area. Visitors may see the flat limestone slab that was the doorstone of the original cabin. Davy Crockett Birthplace State Park, operated by the Tennessee Parks Department, is located on Crockett Highway off U.S. Highway 11E about two miles southwest of **Limestone**. (Open April–November, daily 7:00–10:00; 615-257-2061; free.)

At 2106 East Main St. in **Morristown** is the site of Crockett Tavern, operated by his parents and his boyhood home from 1794. The six-room tavern replica includes period furnishings and a basement museum of pioneer exhibits. Reconstructed a few yards from the original site during the 1950s, Crockett Tavern is operated by the Association for the Preservation of Tennessee Antiquities. (Open May 1–October 31, Monday–Saturday 12:00–5:00, other times by appointment; 615-586-6180; admission.)

Crockett built a log homestead northeast of **Lynchburg** in 1811 and hunted bears in this area until 1813. A marker on State Highway 55 identifies the site.

"Kentuck," Crockett's homestead from 1813 to 1817, stood about one mile south of **Maxwell;** a remnant well remains in a field on private land. West of Belvidere on U.S. Highway 64, a marker indicates the approximate location. Crockett left there to fight in the Creek War in 1813 and 1814; and his first wife, Polly Finlay Crockett, died there in 1815.

With Elizabeth Patton Crockett, his second wife,

Crockett moved to **Lawrenceburg** in 1817. There he became a militia colonel, local magistrate, state legislator and businessman. His house stood on the marked site at 218 North Military St.

Crockett's last home from 1823, stood on the Rutherford Fork of the Obion River about four miles east of **Rutherford**. Timbers of his original cabin were removed in 1932 and used in 1956 to reconstruct the dwelling on the grounds of Rutherford High School, U.S. Highway 45. Period furnishings include a rocking chair made by Crockett. This was his home during his rise to national prominence as humorist, hunter and congressman. Thoroughly rankled by his 1835 defeat for reelection, he left there for Texas, where he died at the Alamo less than a year later. The cabin is operated by the David Crockett Memorial Association of Gibson County. (Open May 15-September 30, Tuesday–Sunday 9:00–5:00, other times by appointment; 901-665-7166; admission.)

Exhibit: One mile west of **Lawrenceburg** on U.S. Highway 64 is David Crockett State Park, a preserve of 1,000 acres near the site of Crockett's grist mill, powder mill and distillery. A reconstructed grist mill like the one he operated on Shoal Creek from 1817 to 1822 is operated by the Tennessee Parks Department with a museum display of apparatus and tools. A swimming pool, tennis courts, picnic areas and nature trails are also provided. (Open daily.)

(See Chapter 6, TEXAS.)

DARROW, CLARENCE SEWARD (1857–1938).
Exhibit: See WILLIAM JENNINGS BRYAN.
(See Chapter 4, ILLINOIS, OHIO.)

DAVIS, JEFFERSON FINIS (1808–1889). The ex-president of the Confederacy never regained formal citizenship after the Civil War. Following his release from prison, he spent his last two decades traveling and trying to find an acceptable livelihood. He went first to **Memphis,** where he headed the Carolina Life Insurance Company until its 1873 failure; a tablet marks the site of his house at 129 Court Ave., where he lived from 1867 to 1875. Also marked is the site of his last Memphis residence (1875–78) at 216 Court Ave.

(See ALABAMA, GEORGIA, KENTUCKY, LOUISIANA, MISSISSIPPI, VIRGINIA in this chapter; also Chapter 3, DISTRICT OF COLUMBIA.)

DE SOTO, HERNANDO (1496?–1542).
Exhibit: The authenticity of the two sites associated with the Spanish explorer in **Memphis** is far from certain. De Soto Park at Delaware and California streets is reputedly the spot where he became the first European to lay eyes on the Mississippi River, on May 21, 1541. At Riverside Drive and Court Street, Jefferson Davis Park is supposedly the site of de Soto's shipyard, where his men built barges for crossing the river.

(See ARKANSAS, FLORIDA, MISSISSIPPI in the chapter.)

FARRAGUT, DAVID GLASGOW (1801–1870) The birthplace of the Union admiral was a log cabin on the north bank of the Tennessee River near the present village of **Concord**. The tract of 640 acres where he lived until 1807 lies mostly beneath the surface of Fort Loudoun Lake today. A marker in front of a more recent house on the private site indicates the cabin's location.

(See MISSISSIPPI in this chapter; also Chapter 2, MANHATTAN; also Chapter 3, NEW YORK.)

HANDY, WILLIAM CHRISTOPHER (1873–1958). The musician-composer, self-styled "Father of the Blues," lived at 659 Jennette Place in **Memphis** from 1912 to about 1918. Handy owned the three-room clapboard house and may well have written his famed "St. Louis Blues" (1914) there. "Hour after hour," he recalled of this place, "I sat at the piano pumping out new tunes." Today the somewhat enlarged, brick-sided house remains privately owned.

Exhibit: Beale Street Historic District National Historic Landmark is a restored commercial section of two blocks between Main and Fourth streets in **Memphis**. Far declined in appearance from its days at the turn of the century as a one and one-half-mile gaudy strip of night life, low life and irrepressible music, Beale Street was the "birthplace" of the blues; and Handy, it is said, wrote "Memphis Blues" (1912) on the cigar counter at Peewee's Saloon, which survives in restored condition. *Beale Street: Where the Blues Began* (1969 reprint) by George W. Lee gives an interesting history of the avenue, as does *Beale Black & Blue* (1981) by Margaret McKee and Fred Chisenhall.

(See ALABAMA in this chapter; also Chapter 2, MANHATTAN; also Chapter 3, NEW YORK.)

HOUSTON, SAMUEL "SAM" (1793–1863). The boyhood home of the soldier, Tennessee governor and president of the Republic of Texas stood near **Greenback** on Lambert Road, a two-story frame dwelling on 419 acres. The house lasted until the 1930s at a site located on private land. Houston lived there from 1807 to 1813.

Houston's **Nashville** residence during his governorship in 1828 and 1829 was the famed Nashville Inn, where he and his child bride occupied a second-floor suite during their marriage of three months. Houston resigned his position when Eliza Allen Houston deserted him there (see the entry on Andrew Johnson later in this section).

Exhibit: On Sam Houston Schoolhouse Road, five miles northeast of **Maryville** off U.S. Highway 411, stands the Sam Houston Schoolhouse, a rural log cabin where Houston taught one term in 1812. This 1794 structure, rebuilt with original materials in 1954 by the Sam Houston Memorial Association, is the only building closely identified with Houston that survives in the state. Though hardly schooled himself at age 19, he was a prolific reader and charged $8 tuition, which he collected in thirds of cash, corn and calico. A visitor center operated by the State of Tennessee displays memorabilia of the soldier and politician. (Open Monday–Saturday 9:00–6:00, Sunday 1:00–5:00; 615-983-1550; free.)

(See VIRGINIA in this chapter; also Chapter 6, TEXAS.)

HULL, CORDELL (1871–1955). Just west of **Byrdstown,** the restored log-cabin birthplace of the World War II secretary of state and "father of the United Nations" stands on State Highway 42. This was Hull's home until age four. The State of Tennessee operates the cabin and the adjacent museum, which displays numerous items of Hull memorabilia, including his Nobel Peace Prize medal, photographs, gifts from world statesmen and gavels he used. (Open Memorial Day-Labor Day, daily 10:00–6:00; 615-864-3247; free.)

(See Chapter 3, DISTRICT OF COLUMBIA.)

JACKSON, ANDREW (1767–1845). The seventh U.S. president made his permanent home in the Nashville area from 1788. Jackson bought a 425-acre tract in 1804, erected a two-story log house, and settled into his first "Hermitage" the following year. There the Indian fighter and hero of the Battle of New Orleans entertained Aaron Burr, Jefferson Finis Davis, President Monroe and other notable public figures (see the entry on Davis earlier in this section). In 1819, on a site selected on their estate by his wife Rachel Robards Jackson, Jackson built another two-story house, this time using bricks made on the estate. One-story wings were added in 1831, but an 1834 fire destroyed the entire interior except for the dining-room wing. Reconstruction immediately proceeded, based on the original plan; front and back porticos were added, and the front was painted white to cover smoke damage. Jackson retired there permanently in 1837 after eight years as president and died there 16 years after his beloved Rachel. Today the Ladies' Hermitage Association maintains 625 of the 1,050 acres owned by Jackson at the time of his death. Preserved in the mansion itself are the original furnishings and almost all of the Jackson's known personal effects; dining room, library, parlors and bedrooms appear just as they did when the fierce old ex-president retired there. Numerous outbuildings include the restored log house that was the first "Hermitage," a smokehouse, springhouse, various cabins, a museum, gift shop and offices. Visitors may also see "Rachel's garden," the "Tulip Grove" mansion of Jackson's nephew, the Old Hermitage Church completed in 1824, a barn and carriage house from Jackson's previous "Hunter's Hill" plantation and the Jackson tombs. The Hermitage National Historic Landmark stands on Rachel's Lane off U.S. Highway 70N, or via Old Hickory Boulevard off Interstate Highway 40, at **Hermitage,** about 12 miles east of Nashville. (Open daily 9:00–5:00; 615-889-2941; admission.)

(See NORTH CAROLINA, SOUTH CAROLINA in this chapter; also Chapter 3, DISTRICT OF COLUMBIA.)

JAMES, JESSE WOODSON (1847–1882). Laying low under the alias John Davis Howard, the outlaw bought a grain and livestock farm east of **New Johnsonville** on the Kentucky Lake bottomlands in 1879 and lived there until about 1881. Fire destroyed the house before 1955. Fieldstone markers in an overgrown meadow indicate the grave site of his twin infants born there. The privately owned property is currently known as "Link Farm," containing only a barn and outbuildings. It is located north of U.S. Highway 70.

(See Chapter 4, MISSOURI.)

JOHNSON, ANDREW (1808–1875). The 17th U.S. president, the only completely unschooled man to occupy that office, came to Tennessee in 1826 and made his permanent home in **Greeneville,** where he worked as a tailor until 1851. Johnson's first home in the town (1827–31) was a two-room board cabin, a combined shop and residence on Main Street, where his wife Eliza McCardle Johnson taught him to write and improve his reading. This structure has not survived. In 1831 Johnson bought the "Kerbaugh House," a two-story brick dwelling dating from the 1820s at College and Depot streets, and this remained his home for about two decades. There he began his political career. In 1851 he built the two-story, brick Johnson Homestead on West Main Street, his last permanent dwelling. The two latter residences now form Andrew Johnson National Historic Site, a tract of 17 acres at College and Depot streets that also includes the sheltered frame Tailor Shop containing the tools he used there. The earlier house is not presently open to the public, but the homestead displays the family's simple furnishings and possessions. Operated by the National Park Service, the tract's visitor center houses the shop plus exhibits on the life and career of this self-made courageous man, the worthy if ultimately frustrated successor of Abraham Lincoln (see the entry on Lincoln later in this section). (Open daily 9:00–5:00; 615-638-3551; admission.)

As Tennessee's Governor from 1854 to 1857, Johnson occupied **Nashville** quarters at the 1796 Nashville Inn, its site now marked on the north side of the Public Square. Johnson was living in the old inn when fire destroyed it in 1856.

(See NORTH CAROLINA, SOUTH CAROLINA in this chapter; also Chapter 3, DISTRICT OF COLUMBIA.)

JOHNSON, JAMES WELDON (1871–1938). From 1930 to his death, the author, civil rights reformer and diplomat taught literature at Fisk University. Johnson House National Historic Landmark is now the campus University Club at 911 18th Ave. North in **Nashville.**

(See FLORIDA in this chapter; also Chapter 1, MASSACHUSETTS; also Chapter 2, MANHATTAN.)

JONES, JOHN LUTHER "CASEY" (1864–1900). The railroad engineer and folk hero, who rode his locomotive into another train in Mississippi, lived in **Jackson.** Casey Jones Home and Railroad Museum at 211 West Chester St. in Casey Jones Village is the one-story frame dwelling he last occupied, probably from about 1890. Period items and Jones memorabilia plus miscellaneous railroad displays including early train equipment are displayed by the City of Jackson and operated by Brooks Shaw & Son Old Country Store. Of special interest is a steam locomotive in the yard, a duplicate of "Old 382" that Jones drove to his death. The house dates from 1880. (Open summer, Monday–Saturday 8:00–9:00, winter Monday–Saturday 9:00–5:00, Sunday 1:00–5:00; 901-668-1222; admission.)

(See MISSISSIPPI in this chapter.)

KEFAUVER, ESTES (1903–1963). Popular senator, investigator of organized crime and 1956 vice presidential candidate, Kefauver was born in **Madisonville,** where his first three homes remain privately owned and unmarked. His birthplace, built by his father about 1900, is a two-story frame house now veneered with brick on Cooke Street, his home until 1913. In 1912 his father built a new house at Main and College streets, now the Kefauver Hotel building, and the family lived there until about 1920. From 1920 to 1930 the family residence was an 1848 frame house on Main Street.

At **Lookout Mountain,** Kefauver lived atop the bluff at 619 Grandview Ave. (privately owned), a rented house with a cantilever balcony over the mountainside. He called the place "Mooneen" and resided there from 1935 to 1939 while practicing law in Chattanooga.

Kefauver's Tennessee home during his senatorial career was an isolated forest retreat loaned to the family by its owner. Called "Shangri-La," the lodge remains privately owned on Hickory Creek near **McMinnville.**

Exhibit: At **Knoxville,** Hoskins Library at 1401 West Cumberland Ave. on the University of Tennessee campus displays books, papers and political memorabilia in its Kefauver Collection. (Open Monday–Friday 9:00–5:30, Saturday except June–September 9:00–12:00; 615-974-4301; free.)

(See Chapter 3, DISTRICT OF COLUMBIA.)

KING, MARTIN LUTHER, JR. (1929–1968).

Exhibit: The two-story, cinder-block Lorraine Motel, where the civil rights activist was stalked and slain by sniper James Earl Ray, stands at 406 Mulberry St., **Memphis.** In Memphis to lead a nonviolent protest of sanitation workers, King occupied Room 306, where he slept one night and spent the day of April 4, 1968, in conferences. While standing on the outside balcony at 6:01 PM, he was shot from the window of a rooming house about 200 feet distant. Lorraine Bailey, wife of the motel owner in 1968, died of a stroke the day King was buried. The balcony, now glassed in, and King's room are set aside as a memorial to the slain leader. (Open 8:00–8:00; 901-525-6834; admission.)*

(See ALABAMA, GEORGIA in this chapter.)

LEWIS, MERIWETHER (1774–1809).

Exhibit: Near **Hohenwald,** the site of the soldier-explorer's death and burial is marked. A rustic log museum, operated by the National Park Service, depicts the life of this leader of the Lewis and Clark Expedition from 1804 to 1806. Meriwether Lewis Monument stands seven and one-half miles east of town on the Natchez Trace Parkway at the junction of State Highway 20. (Open daily 8:00–5:00; 615-796-2921; free.)

(See VIRGINIA in this chapter; also Chapter 3, DISTRICT OF COLUMBIA; also Chapter 4, MISSOURI, NORTH DAKOTA; also Chapter 6, OREGON, WASHINGTON.)

LINCOLN, ABRAHAM (1809–1865).

Exhibit: The most outstanding Lincoln collection in the South, and one of the best in the nation, is at Lincoln Memorial University in **Harrogate.** Lincoln Museum in Duke Hall on the campus displays personal memorabilia, papers, statuary and photographs of the 16th U.S. president. (Open January 1–November 30, Monday–Saturday 9:00–6:00, Sunday 1:00–6:00; 615-869-3611; admission.)

(See KENTUCKY in this chapter; also Chapter 3, DISTRICT OF COLUMBIA, PENNSYLVANIA; also Chapter 4, ILLINOIS, INDIANA, MICHIGAN, OHIO.)

---

*The motel was up for sale in late 1982, so visitors should inquire before stopping there.

POLK, JAMES KNOX (1795–1849). The 11th U.S. president was not a Tennessee native but resided there for most of his life. Only one house associated with him survives in the state, and it was not his own but his parents'. Polk House National Historic Landmark at 301 West Seventh St. in **Columbia,** a two-story brick dwelling built by Polk's father in 1816, was the young lawyer's frequent residence from 1820 to 1824, the beginning of his political career. The restored house, operated by the Polk Memorial Association, displays family furnishings plus fine woodwork and pieces used by the presidential couple in the White House. Polk's library and family lace, silver, and china are also exhibited. (Open April 1–October 31, Monday–Friday 9:00–5:00, Sunday 1:00–5:00; November 1–March 31, Monday–Friday 10:00–4:00, Sunday 1:00–5:00; 615-388-2354; admission.) Polk's own home in Columbia, from 1825 to his death, was a two-story frame house that he rented out during his frequent absences. It stood at 318 West Seventh St. until replaced by a funeral home parking lot in 1960.

Polk's boyhood home from 1806 to 1815 was a log cabin that stood on his father's 260-acre farm near **Kedron** in the Duck River valley. A marker on U.S. Highway 31 identifies the site.

In **Nashville,** Polk's last home, "Grundy Place," stood at the southwest corner of Seventh Avenue North and Union Street. Polk bought this 1815 mansion in 1847 and enjoyed a brief retirement before he died there. Sarah Childress Polk, his widow, resided there until her death in 1891, and the house was demolished in 1893. The Public Library of Nashville and Davidson County now occupies the site of the Polks' garden at Eighth Avenue North and Union Street.

(See NORTH CAROLINA in this chapter; also Chapter 3, DISTRICT OF COLUMBIA.)

PRESLEY, ELVIS ARON (1935–1977). Rock singer, film star and idol of a generation, Presley lived in **Memphis** from 1948. The first home he owned was a one-story ranch house he bought for his parents at 1034 Audubon Drive, his home in 1956 and 1957. Presley installed a swimming pool there and built a brick wall to separate his property from the street. The house remains privately owned. His last home, "Graceland," stands on a stone-walled estate of 13.7 acres at 3764 Elvis Presley Blvd. Presley bought his two-story, colonial-style limestone mansion and grounds in 1957, supported a constant entourage of about a dozen people and resided there almost constantly from 1970. His increasing drug addiction during the 1970s resulted in his death there from an apparent overdose. The 23-room mansion, which he redecorated almost annually, is still owned by the Presley estate and is operated by Jack Soden & Associates, which conducts tours. (Open daily 9:00–6:00; 800-238-2000; admission.)

Exhibit: In **Nashville,** the Country Music Hall of Fame and Museum, operated by the Country Music Foundation at 700 16th Ave. South (4 Music Square) displays Presley's custom-made gold Cadillac with the top cut away to show something of this performer's lavishly opulent life style. (Open June 1–August 31, daily 8:00–8:00; September 1–May 31, daily 9:00–5:00; 615-244-2522; admission.)

(See MISSISSIPPI in this chapter; also Chapter 6, CALIFORNIA.)

RANSOM, JOHN CROWE (1888–1974). The birthplace of the poet, critic and educator was "East Hill," his grandfather's house in **Pulaski** and Ransom's home for a year of his infancy. A private dwelling now occupies the site of the birthplace which was destroyed by fire at the southeast corner of East Jefferson Street and Sam Davis Avenue. There is no marker, but the Giles County Historical Society reports that it "may place one."

Ransom's Nashville residence in 1934 and 1935, now a private duplex, stands at 1610 17th Ave. South. The house dates from about 1930.

(See Chapter 4, OHIO.)

RAYBURN, SAMUEL TALIAFERRO "SAM" (1882–1961). Texas congressman for almost 50 years and speaker of the House for 17, "Mister Sam" was born in a log cabin on his parents' hardscrabble farm of 40 acres, located northeast of **Kingston** on Clinch Creek, his home until the family's 1887 move to Texas. This dwelling built by his father in 1868 stood until razed in 1958. A marker identifies the site in Roane County off Interstate Highway 40.

(See Chapter 3, DISTRICT OF COLUMBIA; also Chapter 6, TEXAS.)

RICE, GRANTLAND (1880–1954). The marked birth site of the sports writer and popular versifier is near the corner of North Spring and College

streets in **Murfreesboro,** his home to age four.

(See Chapter 2, MANHATTAN; also Chapter 3, NEW YORK.)

SMITH, BESSIE (1894–1937). "The greatest blues singer in the world" was born in what she described as "a little ramshackle cabin" in **Chattanooga.** The general vicinity of her birth site is marked in the 700 block of Martin Luther King, Jr., Boulevard (formerly East Ninth Street). The exact site remains unknown.

(See Chapter 3, PENNSYLVANIA.)

WILLIAMS, (HIRAM) HANK (1923–1953). Probably the nation's foremost country musician and composer, the uneducated but gifted Williams produced some of America's best-known popular songs before alcohol, in the best tradition of Grand Ole Opry pathos, destroyed him. He lived in **Nashville** from 1946 to 1953. "The house music built for me" in 1950 at 4916 Franklin Road became one of Nashville's show places. A feature of this low, rambling mansion, enlarged since his death, was a wrought-iron patio fence designed in the form of a musical score with the notes of his "Lovesick Blues" (1948) inscribed. Williams vacated the mansion in 1952, though his divorced wife continued to live there until her own death in 1975. It remains privately owned.

Exhibits: In **Nashville,** the Country Music Hall of Fame and Museum, 700 16th Ave. South (4 Music Square), displays Williams photos, songbooks and his guitar (see the entry on Elvis Aron Presley earlier in this section). At 116 Fifth Ave. North (Opry Place) stands Ryman Auditorium, the scene of Grand Old Opry performances from 1943 to 1974. Williams performed frequently there until he became more interested in the bottle than in audiences. Built in 1891, this two and one-half-story brick edifice was the Union Gospel Tabernacle until 1904. A small museum relating to Opry history is maintained by the Country Music Foundation. (Open daily 8:30–4:30; 615-749-1445; admission.)

(See ALABAMA in this chapter.)

VIRGINIA

As the first permanent English colony in America, Virginia is sometimes termed the "Old Dominion." Today's state is only a coastal fragment of the great British dominion of Virginia, which officially extended from Atlantic to Pacific between the latitudes of 34 and 45 degrees, thus including most of the present United States. A 1584 expedition sponsored by Sir Walter Raleigh had claimed the entire region between New-foundland and Florida for England. Elizabeth I, proud of her celibacy, named the colony after herself. More than a century later, the colony withdrew its western border claim to the Missis-sippi River. Augusta County, created in 1738, encompassed Kentucky, West Virginia and all of the Northwest Territory. After the Revolution, Virginia and several other seaboard states relin-quished their disputed western claims to the federal government.

Controversial as the product is today, tobacco provided the 1614 turning point for the strug-gling English colony established at Jamestown in 1607. John Rolfe, the husband of Pocahontas, exported the first crop. The first Indian conflicts began there when settlers established the soon-familiar strategy of mollifying native leaders with gifts and "treaties" while usurping lands. Such trickery didn't always work, even in Virginia—and had its frequent vicious cost in fire and massacre—but over the long haul, it worked supremely well. By the time the American natives united in common cause, it was far too late for them.

Virginia colony formed a representative assembly in 1619, and Middle Plantation (now Williamsburg), founded in 1633, remained the capital until Richmond took over in 1699. A plan-tation economy based mainly on tobacco brought prosperity, and Virginia's wealthy farmers considered themselves more as transplanted English country gentlemen than as frontier Americans. By 1765, however, this attitude was changing, expressed by some of the loudest hotheads and instigators that ever plagued old England. Patrick Henry, though not quite the political manipulator that his Massachusetts counterpart Sam Adams was, played roughly the same role in bringing Virginia's passion for inde-pendence to a boil. And Thomas Jefferson, no orator, framed the Revolution in written language that not only justified independence but related that quest to a definition of human aspirations that remains a beacon of world history. Subse-quent events, of course, amply proved that Jefferson's vaunted equality and rights—self-evident facts, he called them, not subject to

anyone's gift or grant—were often Sunday-reli-gious concepts that are still too advanced for many of us to handle. Not only did Virginia provide a national philosophy but also a solid, earnest beam of a man to activate it. Despite George Washing-ton's defects as a general, he did achieve what he set out to do, with the vital aid of British bungling and the abilities of a much better soldier, the later traitor Benedict Arnold. The Revolution-ary War ended at Yorktown following the 1781 British invasion, and Virginia became the tenth of the original 13 states to sign the Constitution.

Virginia's mills and seaports made it the lead-ing commercial state in the South before the Civil War. It was the eighth to secede, and Richmond became the capital of the Confederacy. The state's pro-Union northwestern portion, however, seceded from secession, creating thereby the state of West Virginia in 1863. As the main battle-ground of the Civil War, Virginia also hosted the final Confederate surrender at Appomattox. Statehood was restored in 1870.

Triangle-shaped Virginia shares the steplike topography of most other Atlantic states. The Allegheny and Blue Ridge Mountains descend to the Piedmont plateau, which covers about half the state. From Virginia's fall line, four large rivers—the Potomac, Rappahannock, York and James—empty into Chesapeake Bay and divide the coastal plain into three broad peninsulas. This "tidewater Virginia," where arose some of America's earliest white settlements, remains the nation's largest natural port: Hampton Roads, with its surrounding cities of Hampton, Ports-mouth, Norfolk and Newport News. Norfolk is Virginia's largest city, followed closely by Rich-mond and Virginia Beach. Tobacco, still an important crop, leads apple, grain and timber production. Today agriculture ranks third, however, behind manufacturing and tourism as a generator of income. Major industries, widely distributed over the state, include chemicals, tobacco products, textiles and food processing.

Virginia's list of national historic figures is one of the largest. Proximity to the District of Colum-bia accounts for many of its political and military residents, who mainly dwelled in the Arlington and Alexandria vicinities. Eight U.S. presidents, including four of the first five, were natives, more than any other state has contributed; and four others occupied homes there. Prominent mili-tary natives included, foremost, Robert E. Lee, but also George Rogers Clark, Sam Houston, Stonewall Jackson, Winfield Scott and Richard E. Byrd. Probably Virginia's best-known literary figure was Edgar Allan Poe. John Dos Passos, Sherwood Anderson and William Faulkner also lived and wrote there. Educator Booker T. Washington was born in the state, and William H. McGuffey died there. The supreme court's greatest chief justice, John Marshall, was a lifelong resident. Noted political figures included John Randolph and Richard Henry Lee. The state was inventor Cyrus H. McCormick's first home and rocket engineer Wernher von Braun's last.

History is "big" in Virginia; one would not expect otherwise. Extremely conscious of its crucial roles in national development, Virginia is not a state that begrudges the work of commemoration. Visitors are helped, in the policy of Southern hospitality, to find and appreciate the many surviving homes and relics of this state's impressive past. Sometimes guests are greeted like long-lost natives—which in some sense, most of us are.

ANDERSON, SHERWOOD BERTON (1876–1941). From 1927 the author's permanent home was Ripshin National Historic Landmark, the one and one-half-story house he built of logs and fieldstones in a U-shape near **Troutdale**. This house represents the royalties of his novel *Dark Laughter* (1925). Along with the house, two guest cottages and Anderson's log writing studio remain privately owned on State Highway 732.

(See LOUISIANA in this chapter; also Chapter 2, MANHATTAN; also Chapter 4, OHIO.)

ANDROS, SIR EDMUND (1637–1714). As British royal governor of Virginia from 1692 to 1698, Andros was the next to last governor to reside in **Jamestown** before the colonial capital's 1699 removal to Williamsburg. Jamestown National Historic Site has undergone extensive archaeological investigation since 1934, and excavation continues to identify foundations and ruins. The foundations of four succeeding statehouses, the last of which Andros occupied, have been unearthed and marked (see the entry on John Smith later in this section).

(See Chapter 2, MANHATTAN.)

BLACK, HUGO LAFAYETTE (1886–1971). The last home of the 34-year U.S. supreme court justice, from his 1937 appointment, stands at 619 South Lee St. in **Alexandria**. Black renovated this 1740 Georgian colonial mansion known as the "Snowden Home" and added a tennis court. His first wife died there in 1951, and he remarried in this house, which remains privately owned.

(See ALABAMA in this chapter.)

BRADLEY, OMAR NELSON (1893–1981). As the U.S. Army's chief of staff from 1949 to 1953, the World War II general occupied Quarters One National Historic Landmark at **Fort Myer** (see the entry on Douglas MacArthur later in this section).

(See GEORGIA in this chapter; also Chapter 3, PENNSYLVANIA; also Chapter 4, MISSOURI; also Chapter 6, CALIFORNIA, TEXAS.)

BRAUN, WERNHER VON (1912–1977). The last home from 1970 of the rocket engineer and nuclear scientist born in Germany was 816 Vicar Lane in **Alexandria**. It remains privately owned.

(See ALABAMA in this chapter.)

BYRD, RICHARD EVELYN (1888–1957). Admiral, pioneer aviator, and polar explorer, this direct descendant of William Byrd was born in **Winchester** at 326 Amherst St. (see the entry on William Byrd below). The unmarked site of the three-story house built in 1880 and torn down in 1968 is now a used car lot. Byrd lived there until about 1908 but returned at intervals to visit his mother, who died there the same year as her son. This was also the boyhood home of Senator Harry Flood Byrd, Sr., the admiral's brother.

(See CHAPTER 1, MAINE, MASSACHUSETTS; also Chapter 3, DISTRICT OF COLUMBIA.)

BYRD, WILLIAM (1674–1744). This colonial tobacco planter, official and scholar, known as "the American Pepys" and progenitor of the notable Byrd family in America, was a lifelong Virginia resident except for occasional stays in England. Byrd was born on his father's "Falls Plantation," 1,800 acres on the south bank of the James River in what is now **Richmond**. The Byrd property extended from about Hull Street encompassing the present James River Park area. The two-story stone house, long gone, stood behind Belle Isle. Byrd lived there until 1685. In that year his father built another house, "Belvidere," on Oregon Hill across the river, the present locale of Hollywood Cemetery (Cherry and Albemarle streets). Byrd laid out the first settlement of Richmond, originating in the present Church Hill National Historic District on East Broad Street, in 1737.

Westover National Historic Landmark, located on the James River seven miles west of **Charles City** off State Highway 5, is a two and one-half-story brick mansion that has been called "one of the finest Georgian houses in America." Byrd built his home in 1730 on the 1,200-acre estate purchased by his father in 1688. He lived in a 1690 wooden mansion built by the senior Byrd until the erection of the present house; the site of the first dwelling is probably just west of the 1730 structure at the end of the boxwood lane. Two fires extensively damaged the later house before 1745, and most of the interior woodwork probably dates from about 1750. Westover also has later historical associations: Both Benedict Arnold and Lord Charles Cornwallis, preparing to lead British raids on Richmond, were hosted by the Tory Byrds there in 1781. In 1938 friends offered by buy Westover for Adm. Richard Evelyn Byrd, thus restoring it to family possession, but the explorer's wife refused, fearing too much public exposure on the estate (see the entry on Richard Evelyn Byrd above). Today the old mansion remains privately occupied, but Westover's boxwood gardens and impressively landscaped grounds welcome visitors. (Open daily, 9:00–6:00; admission.)

CARTER, ALVIN PLEASANT DELANEY "A. P." (1891–1960). "Keep on the Sunny Side" and "Wabash Cannonball" were only two of the songs popularized by the Carter Family. Founder of the singing group, A. P. Carter was born at **Maces Spring,** where he resided for most of his life. "Carter Homeplace," the privately owned one and one-half-story dwelling of log and frame that was his birthplace and early home, stands near the junction of State Highways 614 and 691 about three miles east of Hiltons. Following his 1943 retirement, he lived in a nearby house with a daughter's family. The twin-gabled store he operated from 1943 at the crossroads no longer sells groceries but hosts occasional folk and country music performances.

CATHER, WILLA SIBERT (1873–1947). The birthplace of the novelist whose theme became midwestern pioneer life stands privately owned on U.S. Highway 50W near **Gore,** a two-story brick farmhouse dating from about 1800 that belonged to her grardmother. "Willowshade Farm" (no longer willow-shaded) was Cather's later home until age nine, when her family moved to Nebraska. She described this area in *Sapphira and the Slave Girl* (1940), her last novel. The house remains privately owned.

(See Chapter 1, NEW HAMPSHIRE; also Chapter 2, MANHATTAN; also Chapter 3, PENNSYLVANIA; also Chapter 4, NEBRASKA.)

CLARK, GEORGE ROGERS (1752–1818).
CLARK, WILLIAM (1770–1838).
The elder Clark brother, frontier soldier and "Conqueror of the Northwest," was born about two miles northeast of **Charlottesville** on his parents' 400-acre Rivanna River plantation. The Clarks were neighbors of Thomas Jefferson, whose boyhood home stood two and one-half miles southeast (see the entry on Jefferson later in this section). The Clark family lived there until about 1756.

Biographers have been unable to pinpoint the site of their next home, a Caroline County plantation on the Rappahannock River near the Spotsylvania County line—possibly near **Corbin** along U.S. Highway 17 or within the present A. P. Hill Military Reservation. This was soldier-explorer William Clark's birth site and the family home until 1784, though George Rogers Clark left in about 1772.

(See KENTUCKY in this chapter; also Chapter 4, INDIANA, MISSOURI, NORTH DAKOTA; also Chapter 6, OREGON, WASHINGTON.)

CLAY, HENRY (1777–1852). The site of "Slash Cottage," birthplace of the powerful pre-Civil War politician and frequent presidential candidate, is marked by a millstone monument on private land about four miles east of **Ashland** and about one mile north of Slash Church off State Highway 654. The one and one-half-story frame house with two large stone chimneys and slave quarters stood on 500 acres owned by his parents near Machump's Creek, a fairly prosperous estate for its time and place. This remained Clay's home until 1791. The town took its name from Clay's home "Ashland" in Lexington, Ky.

(See KENTUCKY in this chapter; also Chapter 3, DISTRICT OF COLUMBIA.)

DAVIS, JEFFERSON FINIS (1808–1889). The capital of the Confederacy from 1861 to 1865 was **Richmond,** and Davis resided there for the four turbulent years of his Civil War presidency. White House of the Confederacy National Historic Landmark, designed by architect Robert Mills and originally built as a two-story dwelling from 1816 to 1818, stands at 1201 East Clay St. A third story was added about 1852. In 1862 the building was offered as a gift to Davis. He refused it but agreed to use it as his official residence. Davis's young son Joseph died there when he fell off a back balcony in 1864. After Davis had fled, President Lincoln made a brief visit on April 5, 1865, a few days before his assassination. From 1893 until recently, this structure housed the Confederate Museum (see *Exhibit* below), but the mansion is currently closed for renovation. (Call 804-649-1861 for information.)

Following Davis's capture in 1865, he was imprisoned and quite harshly treated at Fort Monroe until 1867, when he was released on bail. Though indicted for treason, he was never brought to trial and never sought pardon or restoration of his citizenship. He spent his final years as an official anachronism and embarrassing nonperson, though a very famous and often worshipped one. Fort Monroe National Historic Landmark, built from 1819 to 1834 on the site of colonial military fortifications and still an active installation, stands on the Old Point Comfort peninsula jutting into Hampton Roads in **Hampton.** Davis was confined in a wall chamber, now called the Jefferson Davis Casemate, until his health suffered; he was then transferred to Carroll Hall in the fort until his parole. Fort Monroe Casemate Museum, operated by the U.S. Army, displays the restored original cell plus a Davis exhibit. (Open daily, 10:30–5:00; 804-727-3391; free.)

Exhibit: The new Museum of the Confederacy on the grounds of the Confederate White House at 12th and Clay streets in **Richmond** displays a large collection of Civil War relics including Davis furnishings from that mansion plus other possessions. (Open Monday–Saturday 10:00–5:00, Sunday 2:00–5:00; 804-649-1861; admission.)

(See ALABAMA, GEORGIA, KENTUCKY, LOUISIANA, TENNESSEE in this chapter; also Chapter 3, DISTRICT OF COLUMBIA.)

DIRKSEN, EVERETT McKINLEY (1896–1969). Mellifluous orator who believed that "the oilcan is mightier than the sword," the longtime senator from Illinois built a two-story house in 1959 after his wife's design near **Sterling.** A prominent feature of his three and one-half acres (as well as of his career) was his garden of marigolds, flowers whose symbolic patriotic virtues he likened to those of gallant men and the grand old flag. The privately owned property is known as "Broad Run Farms," located on Young Cliffs Road west of Sterling.

(See Chapter 3, DISTRICT OF COLUMBIA; also Chapter 4, ILLINOIS.)

DOS PASSOS, JOHN RODERIGO (1896–1970). His naturalistic, stream-of-consciousness novels portraying 20th-century beginnings reflected a radical outlook that grew increasingly conservative in his later works. One of the author's earliest homes—and also his last—occupied Sandy Point Neck near **Westmoreland.** His boyhood home was the "White House," a two-story colonial frame mansion on his father's scenic estate, 7,000 acres on the Potomac River. It had been owned by Col. George Eskridge, a friend of the Washington family and after whom, reputedly, George Washington was named (see the entry on Washington later in this section). Mary Ball, Washington's mother, lived there from 1721 until her 1730 marriage to Augustine Washington in Col. Eskridge's house. The author's father acquired this property in the 1880s, and it remained in the Dos Passos family until 1928. Twenty years later, the old house had disappeared, but John Dos Passos bought back 2,100 acres at Spence's Point, enlarged the two-story, brick mansion that is now Spence's Point National Historic Landmark, and made this his home base for the rest of his life. The 1806 house, located on State Highway 749, remains privately owned.

(See Chapter 1, MASSACHUSETTS; also Chapter 2, BROOKLYN, MANHATTAN.)

EISENHOWER, DWIGHT DAVID (1890–1969). During the early months of World War II just prior to his assignment as commander of U.S. forces in Europe, the eventual 34th U.S. President made his temporary home in 1941 and 1942 in **Falls Church** at the home of his brother Milton

Eisenhower. "Tallwood" at 708 East Broad St., a two-story house built during the 1870s, remains privately owned. Eisenhower's workdays were so lengthy that "I cannot remember ever seeing their house in daylight during all the months I served in Washington," he wrote.

From 1945 to 1948, as the U.S. Army's chief of staff, Eisenhower occupied Quarters One National Historic Landmark at **Fort Myer.** He wrote *Crusade in Europe* (1948) in his second-floor study there and also hosted British Prime Minister Winston Churchill (see the entry on Douglas MacArthur later in this section).

Exhibit: The U.S. Army Quartermaster Museum at A Avenue and 22nd Street at **Fort Lee** displays some of Eisenhower's army uniforms. (Open Monday–Friday 8:00–5:00, Saturday–Sunday 11:00–5:00; 804-734-4203; free.)

(See GEORGIA in this chapter; also Chapter 2, MANHATTAN; also Chapter 3, DISTRICT OF COLUMBIA, MARYLAND, PENNSYLVANIA; also Chapter 4, KANSAS, MICHIGAN; also Chapter 6, COLORADO, TEXAS.)

FAULKNER, WILLIAM CUTHBERT (1897–1962). In 1959 the Mississippi author bought a two-story brick house in **Charlottesville** at 917 Rugby Road; he had resided there at intervals from 1957 as writer-in-residence at the University of Virginia and continued to spend lengthy periods in the house until his death. Now owned by the university, the house serves as the White-Burkett Miller Center of Public Affairs.

(See LOUISIANA, MISSISSIPPI in this chapter.)

GRANT, ULYSSES SIMPSON (1822–1885). Commander of Union armies during the Civil War and 18th U.S. president, Grant brought the fighting to its conclusion in Virginia in 1865. His headquarters and home during the final 10 months of the war was a 25-x-27-foot log cabin built for him in 1864 at City Point in what is now **Hopewell.** President Lincoln visited Grant and Gen. William Tecumseh Sherman there just three weeks before the end of the war and Lincoln's assassination. This cabin, its vertical logs intact, was moved from City Point to Philadelphia in 1868 and exhibited for over a century in Fairmount Park there. In 1981, plagued by vandals and termites but mostly by neglect, the decrepit structure was returned; in 1982 it was reconstructed on its original site at the City Point Unit

of Petersburg National Battlefield. "Appomattox Manor," a one and one-half-story frame house also used by Union army headquarters on the same headland property, predates the Revolutionary War in its central portion. Operated by the National Park Service at the end of Cedar Lane, grounds only are currently accessible to visitors. (Open daily 9:00–5:00; 804-458-9504; free.)

Exhibit: Appomattox Court House National Historical Park, located three miles northeast of **Appomattox** on State Highway 24, preserves the site of the Confederate Army surrender on April 9, 1865. Gen. Robert Edward Lee met with Grant in the parlor of the 1848 Wilmer McLean House there and signed the surrender document (see the entry on Lee later in this section). The house was razed in 1893 with the intention of rebuilding it in Washington, D.C.; but the project came to nothing, and the original materials decayed and were scattered. The National Park Service has reconstructed this dwelling plus the entire village of Appomattox Court House (27 structures) to its 1865 appearance. Markers identify Grant and Lee headquarters sites. Some original furnishings have been returned to the McLean House, while others are displayed at the Smithsonian Institution and the Chicago Historical Society. The visitor center of the 1,318-acre park is located in the 1819 Clover Hill Tavern, which displays exhibits and distributes maps and literature. (Open daily 8:30–5:00; 804-352-8987; admission.)

(See Chapter 2, MANHATTAN; also Chapter 3, DISTRICT OF COLUMBIA, NEW JERSEY, NEW YORK; also Chapter 4, ILLINOIS, MICHIGAN, MISSOURI, OHIO; also Chapter 6, WASHINGTON.)

HALSEY, WILLIAM FREDERICK, JR. (1882–1959). The World War II Pacific naval commander bought a home in **Charlottesville** after the war and chaired the University of Virginia Development Fund. Halsey and his wife lived at "Four Acres," 1314 Rugby Road, from 1946 to 1950. When Mrs. Halsey required outside care for a declining mental condition, Halsey sold the house and spent his final years in New York City. The dwelling remains privately owned.

(See Chapter 2, MANHATTAN; also Chapter 3, NEW JERSEY.)

HARRISON, WILLIAM HENRY (1773–1841).

Frontier soldier and ninth U.S. president, Harrison was of aristocratic Virginia lineage. The ancestral Harrison home and his own birthplace, Berkeley National Historic Landmark, stands on the James River about six and one-half miles west of **Charles City** on State Highway 5. This two-story brick mansion, built by his grandfather on a 22,000-acre grant in 1726, was also the home of his father, a signer of the Declaration of Independence. Benedict Arnold's troops plundered the estate in 1781. Harrison never lived there after 1789 but returned for occasional visits and composed his 1841 inauguration address in the room where he was born. Berkeley was visited by every U.S. president from Washington to Buchanan. In 1862 the house became headquarters for Union Gen. George B. McClellan, and during this occupancy Gen. Daniel Butterfield composed the bugle call "Taps." This was also the site of the first thanksgiving service in America—on December 4, 1619, when English settlers arrived at the site. Privately owned, the restored house displays the interior alterations of 1790 and period furnishings plus a slide program. (Open daily 8:00–5:00; 804-795-2453; admission.)

(See Chapter 3, DISTRICT OF COLUMBIA; also Chapter 4, INDIANA, OHIO.)

HENRY, PATRICK (1736–1799). Colonial lawyer, political leader and Virginia's first governor, Henry was a lifelong Virginia resident. Several of his later homes have survived. A stone monument marks his birth site on County Road 605 at **Studley**. Foundations of the two-story, 30-x-40-foot brick house, itself destroyed by fire, were discovered there in 1936. This was Henry's home until age 14.

Hanover Tavern, built in 1723 and operated by Henry's Shelton in-laws, was his residence from 1757 to 1765, the period of his rise to eminence as a lawyer. British Gen. Charles Cornwallis stayed there briefly, during the summer of 1781. The restored, two-story frame structure on U.S. Highway 301 is now owned by the Barksdale Theatre in **Hanover**. (Open daytimes free, evenings for dinner and stage performances; 804-798-6547.)

Scotchtown National Historic Landmark, the 94-x-36-foot frame house occupied by Henry on a 960-acre plantation from 1771 to 1777 (and later by the family of Dolley Payne Todd Madison; see the entry on Dolley Madison later in this section)

stands on State Highway 685 about nine miles northwest of **Ashland** and east of **Beaverdam**. It was one of the largest houses in colonial Virginia when Henry lived there. Persistent tradition maintains that Sarah Shelton Henry, his wife, was confined in the basement there because of mental illness until her death in 1775. Having long vacated, Henry sold this property in 1784. Built about 1719, the restored house is operated by the Association for the Preservation of Virginia Antiquities and displays period furnishings. (Open April 1–October 31, Monday–Saturday 10:00–4:30, Sunday 1:30–4:30; 703-227-3500; admission.)

As Revolutionary governor, Henry occupied the Governor's Palace at **Williamsburg** from 1776 to 1779, immediately preceding the tenure of Thomas Jefferson there (see the entry on Jefferson later in this section). This building was the seat of Virginia's colonial governors from 1720 until Henry's wartime administration. Fire destroyed the original structure facing Palace Green in 1781 when it was serving as a hospital for American casualties from the Battle of Yorktown. The Governor's Palace, reconstructed on its original site, displays rare period furnishings, fine woodwork and formal gardens. It is part of Colonial Williamsburg National Historic Landmark, the 130-acre restoration begun in 1926 and financed by John D. Rockefeller, Jr. This project, the ultimate combined showpiece of historical scholarship, archaeology and restoration, has resulted in a faithful picture of Henry's seat of government. The entire complex, operated by the Colonial Williamsburg Foundation and a segment of Colonial National Historical Park, may be viewed individually or by guided tour. A visitor center northeast of the Governor's Palace on Colonial Parkway provides orientation and tickets. Automobiles, excluded from the historic area, may be parked at the center. (Open March 16–November 1, 8:30–10:00; November 2–January 1, daily 8:30–9:00; January 2–March 15, daily 9:00–6:00; 804-229-1000; admission.)

The site of Henry's two-room brick house on his 10,000-acre "Leatherwood Plantation," his home from 1779 to 1784, is marked near **Leatherwood** on State Highway 57.

Again Virginia's governor from 1784 to 1786, Henry lived in the new capital city of **Richmond**. The small wooden house on Shockoe Hill that served as the first Governor's Residence stood on the same site as the present Governor's

Mansion, which replaced it on the northeast corner of Capitol Square in 1813.

Henry disliked his cramped Richmond quarters and spent much of his two-year term at "Salisbury," a 1,263-acre plantation he rented southwest of the city. This is the present site of the Salisbury Country Club at **Midlothian**.

A reconstruction of Henry's last home, from 1796, is "Red Hill Shrine," located five miles east of **Brookneal** on County Road 677. The house was built on the right wing foundation of the original mansion, which fire destroyed in 1919. Henry family furnishings and personal possessions help flesh out the man from the elocutional image of his oratory; visitors may even see a lock of his red hair. Outbuildings include various cabins, a kitchen, stables, a smokehouse and Henry's small office, with his wing chair and filing cabinet. The latter structure is the original clapboard cabin on its original site. "Red Hill Shrine" on its scenic hilltop location—Henry called it "the Garden Spot of Virginia"—is operated by the Patrick Henry Memorial Foundation. Tours begin at the adjacent museum and visitor center. (Open April 1–October 31, daily 9:00–5:00; November 1–March 31, daily 9:00–4:00; 804-376-2044; admission.)

Exhibit: Henry is mainly remembered as the fiery Revolutionary orator who, on March 23, 1775, requested death in lieu of liberty. He flung this rhetorical challenge in the 1740 St. John's Episcopal Church at 2400 East Broad St. (at the corner of 24th Street) in **Richmond**. The Virginia Assembly was using the church in 1775 because it was the largest auditorium in Richmond at the time. The pew from which Henry spoke is marked. (Open March 11–November 30, Monday–Saturday 10:00–4:00; free.)

HOOVER, HERBERT CLARK (1874–1964). "All men are equal before fishes," declared the 31st U.S. president, an obsessed fly-rodder. In 1929 he wanted a vacation retreat that would fulfill three requirements: a trout stream within 100 miles of Washington, D.C., that was high enough to preclude mosquitoes. He soon purchased 12 cabins built by the Marine Corps near the headwaters of the Rapidan River in the Blue Ridge Mountains for his fishing camp. Camp Rapidan became the 164-acre Camp Hoover, where he vacationed and hosted numerous public figures until the end of his presidency in 1933. Hoover

spent most of that cataclysmic October weekend in 1929 on the telephone there as the stock market crash plunged the nation into the Great Depression. He donated the tract to Shenandoah National Park in 1933 as a retreat for future presidents, but his successor, Franklin D. Roosevelt, found the terrain too rough for his infirmity after an initial visit. While Camp Hoover served as a VIP hideaway for prominent cabinet and government officials (Secretary of the Navy Claude A. Swanson died there in 1939) as late as the Nixon and Carter administrations, the property remained mostly unused for several decades. The Boy Scouts of America leased Camp Hoover in 1948, to the ex-president's profound satisfaction, and burro trips there became a popular scouting activity. Hoover himself revisited the camp only once, in 1954. By 1958, however, the camp had become too costly to maintain, and the property again reverted to the National Park Service's control. All of the buildings except three were demolished by 1960; Hoover's own "Brown House" frame lodge, including his sun porch study, underwent restoration, and some of the original pine and wicker furnishings are still inside. Hoover's first priority for the camp—availability as a presidential retreat—remains in effect, but government use, even by cabinet members, is infrequent. Camp Hoover stands inaccessible to visitors by auto in a remote area of **Shenandoah National Park**. Hikers and horseback riders, however, may view the camp by a six-mile round-trip excursion from Byrd Visitor Center at Big Meadows (Milepost 51) on Skyline Drive. The camp is much more of a wilderness area today than when Hoover's entourage periodically invaded, and visitors will enjoy sights of wildlife that he rarely saw there. "Hoover Days," the park's annual weekend commemoration of the president's August 10 birthday, is the only time when buses conduct visitors directly to his lodge. Darwin Lambert's *Herbert Hoover's Hideaway* (1971) details the story of this historic camp where the famous fished. (Byrd Visitor Center open daily 9:00–5:00 except January–February; 703-999-2243; park admission.)

(See Chapter 2, MANHATTAN; also Chapter 3, DISTRICT OF COLUMBIA; also Chapter 4, IOWA; also Chapter 6, CALIFORNIA, OREGON.)

HOUSTON, SAMUEL "SAM" (1793–1863). Five miles south of **Fairfield**, a marker on U.S. Highway 11 indicates the birth site of the soldier, Tennessee governor and Texas president. "Timber Ridge Plantation," Houston's home until his father died in 1806, stood on a hilltop east of the highway.

(See TENNESSEE in this chapter; also Chapter 6, TEXAS.)

JACKSON, THOMAS JONATHAN "STONE-WALL" (1824–1863). Probably the best-known Confederate general after Robert Edward Lee (see the entry on Lee later in this section), Jackson owned only one home in his life. It stands at 8 East Washington St. in **Lexington**. Built in 1800, the modest brick house later served as a hospital until 1954. Jackson lived there from 1858 while teaching at Virginia Military Institute. The Historic Lexington Foundation displays Jackson memorabilia, original furnishings and a slide lecture in his restored home. (Open Monday–Saturday 9:00–4:30, Sunday 1:00–4:30; 703-463-2552; admission.)

Jackson resided during the winter of 1861–62 at what was then the new brick home of Col. L. T. Moore, now Stonewall Jackson's Headquarters National Historic Landmark at 415 North Braddock St., in **Winchester**. The Stonewall Jackson Foundation exhibits a large collection of Jackson relics and personal items. (Open daily 10:00–4:00; 703-667-3242; admission.)

Exhibits: At **Chancellorsville**, markers on State Highway 3 indicate the spot where, on May 2, 1863, Jackson was caught in the rifle fire of his own men and fell mortally wounded, and the site of the tent at Wilderness Tavern in which surgeons amputated his left arm in a vain attempt to save his life. At nearby **Guinea**, Stonewall Jackson Memorial Shrine National Historic Landmark is the 1828 restored plantation office building where Jackson was brought after surgery. Visitors may see the bed in which he died plus period furnishings. The house is operated by the National Park Service. (Open April 1–June 14, Labor Day–October 31, Friday–Tuesday 9:00–5:00; June 15–Labor Day, daily 9:00–5:00; November 1–March 31, Saturday–Monday 9:00–5:00; free.) The National Park Service Visitor Center of the 5,000-acre Fredericksburg and Spotsylvania National Military Park, in which these sites are located, stands at Lafayette Boulevard (U.S. Highway 1, at the corner of Sunken Road) and provides orientation to this historic battlefield. (Open June 15–Labor Day, daily 8:30–6:30; Labor Day–June 14, daily 9:00–5:00; 804-786-2880; free.)

New Market Battlefield Park commemorates the 1864 Civil War battle in which Virginia Military Institute cadets took to the field. Jackson was dead by the time of this battle, which continued his "valley campaign" strategy. Hall of Valor Visitor Center, operated by Virginia Military Institute on State Highway 305 north of **New Market**, shows a film on Jackson's campaign and an exhibit of personal items. (Open daily, 9:00–5:00; 703-740-3101; admission.)

Virginia Military Institute Museum in Jackson Memorial Hall on the **Lexington** campus also displays Jackson memorabilia. (Open Monday–Friday 9:00–4:30, Saturday 9:00–12:00, 2:00–5:00, Sunday 2:00–5:00; 703-463-9111; free.)

The Museum of the Confederacy in **Richmond** contains a Jackson sword and cap (see the entry on Jefferson Finis Davis earlier in this section).

(See Chapter 3, WEST VIRGINIA.)

JEFFERSON, THOMAS (1743–1826). Raw-boned and red-haired, the third U.S. president had an innovative mind and versatile skills not equaled by any president since. Except for official residences elsewhere, Virginia was his lifelong home. The 400-acre "Shadwell Plantation," Jefferson's birthplace, is located about three miles east of **Charlottesville** on U.S. Highway 250 within sight of his last home, Monticello. Jefferson lived at Shadwell until 1745, then returned in 1752 and lived there until the house burned in 1770. Foundation ruins of the 1737 house built by his father were discovered in 1955, and a conjectural reconstruction was erected in 1960 as a tourist attraction. This was removed, however, by the Thomas Jefferson Memorial Foundation, which now owns the site. A highway marker designates the spot, but visitors are not currently admitted to the home site itself.

Jefferson's boyhood home from 1745 to 1752 was "Tuckahoe Plantation," an H-shaped, two-story frame house built from 1712 to 1730. It stands privately owned on State Highway 650 about seven miles west of **Richmond**. Original outbuildings on the Randolph estate owned by his uncle include the small brick schoolhouse where Jefferson began his formal education.

Of all presidential homes, Monticello National Historic Landmark probably best represents its owner because Jefferson put so much of his creative energies into it. Almost everything there, from the layout of the gardens to the design, material and contents of his house, reflects the wide scope of an active mind that often regarded politics as an intrusion on his writing, inventing, architectural drawing and music. Jefferson inherited "Little Mountain" from his father in 1757, having picked the site himself. He began leveling the hilltop in 1768 and started building in 1770. The next year he moved into the first completed portion, the one-story brick cottage southeast of the main house, and brought his new wife, Martha Skelton Jefferson, in 1772; this structure is sometimes called "Honeymoon Cottage." Not until Martha Jefferson's death there in 1782 did Jefferson return to public life. In 1796 he began enlarging the house and by 1809 had completed the classical revival-style brick mansion with its familiar portico that visitors see today. After his presidency, Jefferson was financially hard-pressed to maintain his estate and its population of 14 permanent residents plus 25 household slaves and 75 field hands. Public contributions raised in 1825 relieved the immediate problem, and he died there the next year on July 4. The last of the Jefferson family vacated in 1829, and the estate declined through misuse and vandalism until 1836, when Commodore Uriah Phillips Levy of the U.S. Navy purchased it. His family maintained it extremely well—almost as a private trust, in lieu of national concern—for 89 years. The Jefferson Memorial Foundation bought Monticello in 1923, completed restoration in 1954 and now displays the 700-acre estate in the shape that Jefferson himself created. The 35 rooms contain his original furnishings plus a large variety of practical gadgets and inventions he designed for his own convenience—dumbwaiters, concealed mechanisms, adjustable desks and chairs, a polygraph, dozens of ingenious devices that predated the use of electricity and that work as well now as when he crafted them. Monticello is located three miles southeast of **Charlottesville** on State Highway 53. (Open March 1–October 31, daily 8:00–5:00; November 1–February 28, daily 9:00–4:30; 804-293-2158; admission.)

Near **Georges Tavern**, the site of Jefferson's "Elk Hill Plantation" is a high, grassy bluff near the end of County Road 608 off State Highway 6. Jefferson purchased the 307 acres in 1778 and added outbuildings to the one and one-half-story cottage built before 1766. Lord Charles Cornwal-

lis headquartered himself briefly there in June 1781, and Jefferson complained of the destruction and theft he discovered soon after the British left. No remnant of buildings remains on this privately owned site.

Another plantation that Jefferson maintained as a summer retreat from the constant stream of visitors at Monticello was "Poplar Forest," a 4,000-acre estate he acquired in 1781. It is said that Jefferson wrote his *Notes on the State of Virginia* (1785) there while recuperating after being thrown by a horse. The one-story, octagonal brick house that Jefferson designed and built over a high basement during his presidency in 1806 was severely damaged by an 1845 fire, but the exterior remains unchanged. It remains privately owned on State Highway 681 about seven miles southwest of **Lynchburg**.

Jefferson succeeded Patrick Henry as Virginia Revolutionary governor in 1779 (see the entry on Henry earlier in this section) and briefly occupied the Governor's Palace in **Williamsburg**.

(See Chapter 2, MANHATTAN; also Chapter 3, DISTRICT OF COLUMBIA, PENNSYLVANIA.)

JONES, JOHN PAUL (1747–1792). America's best-known naval hero was a felonious vagabond before he donned a Continental uniform. John Paul added his Jones surname as an alias after killing the ringleader of a mutiny in 1773. The sea captain born in Scotland began as a merchant shipper in the slave trade, commanded the *Bonhomme Richard* during the American Revolution and became one of the greatest sea warriors in naval history. He ended his mercenary admiral's career in the Russian navy. From about 1759 until he joined the Continental navy in 1775, he resided at intervals in **Fredericksburg** with his elder brother William Paul, a tailor. This half-brick, half-frame 18th-century house at the northeast corner of Lafayette Boulevard and Caroline Street, where Paul resided and operated his shop, remains privately owned.

(See Chapter 1, NEW HAMPSHIRE.)

KENNEDY, JOHN FITZGERALD (1917–1963).
KENNEDY, ROBERT FRANCIS (1925–1968).

As a senator, the eventual 35th U.S. president owned and occupied the estate called "Hickory Hill" near **McLean** from 1954 to 1957. The white

Georgian mansion on five and one-half rolling acres had served briefly as a headquarters for Gen. George B. McClellan during the Civil War. U.S. Supreme Court Justice Robert H. Jackson, who died in 1954, preceded Kennedy in ownership. When John and Jacqueline Kennedy moved back permanently to Washington, D.C., they sold this estate to his brother Robert Kennedy, the eventual attorney general, senator and presidential aspirant; and this remained Robert Kennedy's permanent family home from 1957. Privately owned, Hickory Hill stands at 1147 Chain Bridge Road.

(See FLORIDA in this chapter; also Chapter 1, MASSACHUSETTS, RHODE ISLAND; also Chapter 2, BRONX; also Chapter 3, DISTRICT OF COLUMBIA, MARYLAND, NEW YORK; also Chapter 4, MICHIGAN; also Chapter 6, CALIFORNIA, TEXAS.)

LEE, RICHARD HENRY (1732–1794). The patriot who first proposed the Declaration of Independence was a member of an old, distinguished Virginia family and granduncle of Gen. Robert Edward Lee (see the entry on Robert E. Lee below). Both of these Lees, as well as Revolutionary diplomat Arthur Lee, brother of Richard Henry, were born in Stratford Hall Plantation National Historic Landmark, the Lee ancestral home located at **Stratford** on State Highway 214. Richard Henry Lee's father, Thomas Lee, bought his 16,000-acre wilderness plantation in 1716 and built Stratford Hall from 1725 to 1730. This massive, H-shaped brick structure contains 18 rooms beautifully restored and maintained by the Robert E. Lee Memorial Foundation, which also operates the present 1,500 acres as a model colonial plantation. Stratford Hall sustained itself as a plantation for a century, remaining in the Lee family until 1828. Formal gardens, fields and recreated plantation industries vividly demonstrate the type of colonial prosperity familiar to Lee as well as to George Washington and other Virginia patriots (see the entry on Washington later in this section). Period furnishings in the house include some original Lee items. The foundation provides a reception center, museum, slide program and guided tours. (Open daily 9:00–4:30; 804-493-8038; admission.)

Near **Montross**, the site of "Chantilly," Richard Henry Lee's own plantation and last home from 1763, is marked about two miles northeast of the state highways 609 and 622 junction. Lee named his estate for a chateau he had seen while traveling as a youth near Paris. Lee died there, and fire destroyed the house, probably during the War of 1812.

LEE, ROBERT EDWARD (1807–1870). Virginia might still be Virginia if Thomas Jefferson or Jefferson Finis Davis hadn't lived there (see the entries on Jefferson and Davis earlier in this section). If Virginia's history was suddenly deprived of Robert E. Lee, however, the state would plunge into an immediate identity crisis. Except for his adversary Abraham Lincoln, probably no American hero has achieved brighter patriotic stardom, with a historical veneration approaching sainthood, than this soldier and Confederate commander who proved noblest in defeat. The United States was so far from being truly united during his lifetime that he always considered himself foremost a Virginian, though he personally opposed much of what the Confederacy stood for. Today Virginia's forest of Lee shrines stands as thick as the Lincoln markers in Illinois; any place remotely associated with the man is proudly called to public attention. Lee's birthplace stands in **Stratford**, where his parents occupied the ancestral Lee estate (see the entry on Richard Henry Lee above) from 1793 to 1810. His father, Revolutionary Gen. Henry "Light-Horse Harry" Lee had resided there with his first wife from 1782.

All of Lee's three boyhood homes in **Alexandria** survive, but only the last is open to the public. The family resided from 1810 to 1812 at 611 Cameron St. Lee's father died in the Barbados when the rest of the family were living (1816–18) in the rear portion of 407 North Washington St. (at the northeast corner of Cameron Street). From 1812 to 1816 and from 1821 until he entered West Point in 1825, Lee lived with his mother at 607 Oronoco St., a two-story Georgian mansion built about 1795. This house, containing period furnishings and Lee memorabilia, is operated by the Lee-Jackson Foundation. (Open Monday–Saturday 10:00–4:00, Sunday 12:00–4:00; closed December 15–February 1; 703-548-8454; admission.)

At **Arlington**, Custis-Lee National Historic Landmark (also called "Arlington House") was inherited by Lee's wife. Mary Randolph Custis, a great-granddaughter of Martha Dandridge

ROBERT E. LEE HOUSE. This was the Confederate general's home at the end of the Civil War as it looked then. It survives at 707 East Franklin St. in **Richmond**. The adjacent houses, however, have disappeared. (*Courtesy Virginia State Library*)

Custis Washington (see the entry on Martha Washington later in this section), married Lee in the parlor there in 1831. Mary Custis Lee's father built Arlington House from 1802 to 1817 on land owned by his father (who was Martha Washington's son by her first marriage). There the Lees spent most of their married life; six of their seven children were born in the mansion. Though Lee himself was often absent on various military assignments, he considered this place his permanent home and fully intended to retire there. His agonizing choice to ally with Virginia rather than the nation deprived the Lees of their home; one of the first acts of Union forces was to occupy the mansion, and it was officially confiscated by the federal government in 1864. Heart-

broken, the Lees never returned, having abandoned it in 1861. Lee's eldest son sued for the return of the property after the war and finally won his suit in 1882. By then, however, the estate had become a national cemetery, and George Washington Custis Lee sold his claim to the U.S. government for $150,000. Today the two-story, stucco-covered brick house with its Greek-columned portico remains one of the nation's most familiar landmarks, crowning Arlington National Cemetery and overlooking the Potomac River and Washington, D.C. The interior has been meticulously restored to its 1861 appearance by the National Park Service, displaying Custis and Lee family furnishings plus some personal effects of George Washington (see the entry on Washington later in this section). (Open April 1–September 30, daily 9:30–6:00; October 1–March 31, daily 9:30–4:30; 703-557-0613; free.)

Until 1864 Lee occupied numerous brief headquarters but no permanent home. In January of that year, his wife and daughter moved into a rented dwelling at 707 East Franklin St. in **Richmond**. Lee went there for occasional visits and resided there for two months after signing the 1865 surrender document at Appomattox. Civil War photographer Matthew Brady took his famed pictures of Lee there just a few days after the surrender. This three-story brick dwelling, variously called the "Norman Stewart House" or the "Robert E. Lee House," dates from 1844, the only surviving house in what was an elegant residential row in 1865. The Confederate Memorial Literary Society displays period furnishings plus such Lee relics as his camp bed and wash stand. (Open June 1–August 31, Tuesday–Saturday 10:00–4:00, Sunday 2:00–5:00; September 1–May 31, Monday–Friday 10:00–4:00; 804-644-7533; admission.)

On permanent parole from 1865, Lee resided for the rest of his life in **Lexington**, where he served as president of Washington College (now Washington and Lee University). Until 1869 he lived in the old President's House on campus, the "Lee-Jackson House" dating from 1842. Lee himself designed the new President's House on the campus, his last home from 1869 and still the private official residence of the university president. He died there after suffering a stroke.

Exhibits: The best, most comprehensive museum on Lee's military and academic careers is the Lee shrine at **Lexington**. The museum in Lee Chapel National Historic Landmark on the Washington and Lee University campus contains his study just as he left it plus numerous exhibits and family memorabilia. There is also preserved the skeleton of his horse "Traveler," with the horse's adjacent stable. (Open April–October, Monday–Saturday 9:00–5:00, Sunday 2:00–5:00; October–April, Monday–Saturday 9:00–4:00, Sunday 2:00–5:00; 703-463-9111; free.)

The Museum of the Confederacy in **Richmond** (see the entry on Jefferson Finis Davis earlier in this section) displays several Lee items including the sword and uniform he wore at Appomattox (see the entry on Ulysses Simpson Grant earlier in this section) and his death mask.

(See Chapter 3, NEW YORK.)

LEWIS, JOHN LLEWELLYN (1880–1969). Longtime powerful president of the United Mine Workers union, Lewis made his permanent home in **Alexandria** from 1934 in order to stay close to the national capital. He first rented the colonial dwelling at 209 Prince St. (privately owned), the former home of Dr. E. C. Dick, the private physician of George Washington (see the entry on Washington later in this section). Lewis occupied it until 1937, when he bought the Lee-Fendall House, another colonial residence built in 1785. Some 35 members of the notable Lee family had lived there from 1785 to 1903. This was Lewis's last permanent home, located at 429 North Washington St. Today, operated by the Virginia Trust for Historic Preservation, it functions as a memorial to Gen. Henry "Light-Horse Harry" Lee, father of Robert E. Lee (see the entry on Robert Edward Lee above). Period furnishings include many Lee family possessions. (Open Tuesday–Saturday 10:00–4:30, Sunday 12:00–4:30; 703-548-1789; admission.)

(See FLORIDA in this chapter; also Chapter 4, ILLINOIS, IOWA.)

LEWIS, MERIWETHER (1774–1809). Soldier and explorer of the Louisiana Purchase with William Clark (see the entry on Clark earlier in this section), the ultimately tragic Lewis was, like Clark, a Virginia native. The site of his birthplace, a plantation of 1,000 acres called "Locust Hill," is marked just north of **Ivy** off U.S. Highway 250. Lewis left with his family in 1784 but returned there in 1787 and remained until 1794, when he enlisted in the regular army.

(See TENNESSEE in this chapter; also Chapter 3, DISTRICT OF COLUMBIA; also Chapter 4, MISSOURI, NORTH DAKOTA; also Chapter 6, OREGON, WASHINGTON.)

MacARTHUR, DOUGLAS (1880–1964). The World War II Pacific commander with a god-like rectitude that both amused and antagonized those who had to work with him, MacArthur served as the U.S. Army's chief of staff from 1930 to 1935. During this period he resided with his mother in **Fort Myer** at Quarters One National Historic Landmark, built in 1899 and still the official private residence of the army's highest officer. Gen. Leonard Wood occupied this three-story, Victorian house of red brick on Grant Avenue from 1910 to 1914; and MacArthur's successors there included George Catlett Marshall, Dwight David Eisenhower and Omar Nelson Bradley (see the entries on Marshall, Eisenhower and Bradley in this section). The elevator installed in 1931 for MacArthur's mother remains in service. MacArthur emerged from Quarters One to conduct the 1932 "battle of Anacostia Flats," driving out the Bonus Army of 2,000 unemployed World War I veterans camped on lawns in the national capital. Fort Myer Historic District National Historic Landmark, with its elegant "Generals' Row" on Grant Avenue, is open daily for exterior viewing of buildings. (Call 703-545-6700 for information.)

Exhibit: An 1847 courthouse serves as the General Douglas MacArthur Memorial at MacArthur Square, 421 East City Hall Ave. in **Norfolk**. Surrounding MacArthur's tomb are numerous exhibits of his papers, medals, war souvenirs and mementoes. Included are his 1950 staff car, reconstructions of two of his offices with original furnishings and a continuously showing biographical film. (Open Monday–Saturday 10:00–5:00; 804-441-2382; free.)

(See ARKANSAS in this chapter; also Chapter 2, MANHATTAN; also Chapter 3, MARYLAND, NEW YORK; also Chapter 4, KANSAS; also Chapter 6, NEW MEXICO, TEXAS.)

McCORMICK, CYRUS HALL (1809–1884). The inventor of the mechanical reaper that revolutionized agricultural harvesting methods and vastly affected U.S. settlement patterns, McCormick was a Virginia native. Walnut Grove National Historic Landmark, his ancestral farm birthplace and where, with his father in 1831, he perfected and marketed the first grain reaper, stands on County Road 606 off U.S. Highway 11 northwest of **Steeles Tavern.** The 634 acres of the restored McCormick homestead, his home until 1848, include the large brick farmhouse where he was born, a gristmill and his blacksmith shop, where models and replicas of the implement are displayed. McCormick Memorial Museum is operated by the Virginia Polytechnic Institute. (Open Monday–Friday 9:00–5:00; 804-377-2255; free.)

(See Chapter 3, NEW YORK; also Chapter 4, ILLINOIS.)

McGUFFEY, WILLIAM HOLMES (1800–1873). The educator who authored the textbooks that taught most 19th-century American schoolchildren to read (besides imprinting many of the cultural values that, for better and worse, still influence our thinking) resided in **Charlottesville** from 1845. He taught moral philosophy at the University of Virginia, standing at a lectern in the east basement room of the campus Rotunda. McGuffey's home, still used for private faculty housing on the West Lawn of the campus, is known as "Pavilion IX," a square, two-story house with French windows and portico. (Information on University of Virginia Historic District National Historic Landmark tours are available at the Rotunda office, Monday–Friday 8:00–5:00; 804-924-0311; free.)

(See Chapter 3, PENNSYLVANIA; also Chapter 4, MICHIGAN, OHIO.)

MADISON, JAMES (1751–1836).
MADISON, DOLLEY PAYNE TODD (1768–1849).
The fourth U.S. president, a Virginia native, was born at the present site of "Belle Grove," built about 1770 and the largest colonial house in King George County. The original plantation, located on a Rappahannock River bluff above the village of **Port Conway** off U.S. Highway 301, was owned by Madison's grandparents. Madison probably spent considerable time there until his grandmother's death in 1760. The present house remains privately owned.

Madison's lifelong home from infancy was Montpelier National Historic Landmark, located four miles west of **Orange** on State Highway 20. The original 1730 homestead built by his grandfather stood, it is believed, on a knoll near the family graveyard about 300 yards south of the present two-story brick house, which was begun by his father about 1760. When Madison inherited the estate in 1801, it consisted of about 5,000 acres plus outlying lands. Madison himself enlarged the house and added the present wings. Dolley Madison shared Montpelier after their marriage, and Madison died there at age 85. Today Montpelier is one of the few major U.S. presidential homes that remain privately owned and closed to the public. Visitors may, however, enter the present 2,000-acre estate to view the Madison tombs.

While serving in the Virginia state legislature at **Williamsburg,** Madison lodged during 1778 and 1779 in the President's House, the official mansion of William and Mary College presidents since 1732. Rev. James Madison, second cousin of the eventual U.S. president, headed the college at that time. The President's House (privately occupied), a three-story brick mansion that was burned during the Revolution and later restored by the King of France, stands on the central campus at Richmond Road near North Boundary Street.

The childhood home of Dorothea Dandridge Payne, who took "the great little Madison" as her second husband in 1794 and became one of the nation's most brilliant first ladies, was Scotchtown National Historic Landmark near **Ashland.** Her family leased this estate from Patrick Henry (see the entry on Henry earlier in this section) in 1777 and resided there until 1783.

Exhibit: The James Madison Museum at 129 Caroline St. in **Orange** displays Madison possessions and memorabilia. "Sometimes I'd like to take out an ad in the *New York Times,*" said curator Stuart Downs in 1981, "and say, 'Somebody please adopt this president' "—a man whom John Fitzgerald Kennedy (see the entry on Kennedy earlier in this section) called one of the country's most underrated founding fathers. The James Madison Memorial Foundation, which operates this museum, hopes ultimately to acquire the Montpelier estate. (Open Monday–Friday 9:00–5:00, Saturday–Sunday 12:00–4:00; 703-672-1776; admission.)

(See NORTH CAROLINA in this chapter; also Chapter 2, MANHATTAN; also Chapter 3, DISTRICT OF COLUMBIA, PENNSYLVANIA.)

MARSHALL, GEORGE CATLETT (1880–1959). Army chief of staff during World War II and astute secretary of state after the war, Marshall occupied Quarters One National Historic Landmark at **Fort Myer** from 1939 to 1945. Katherine Brown Marshall wrote that the second-floor sun porch "proved to be where George and I practically lived . . . I think this room had much to do with my husband's good health in the difficult years ahead [from 1939], for it was flooded with sunlight." (See the entry on Douglas MacArthur earlier in this section.)

In 1940, the Marshalls bought their own permanent home, a brick Georgian house called "Dodona Manor," in **Leesburg.** It remains privately owned on Edwards Ferry Road.

Exhibit: The George C. Marshall Library and Museum, operated by Virginia Military Institute, houses and displays the general's papers and memorabilia plus interpretive exhibits on his life and career. It is located at the western end of the parade ground on the **Lexington** campus. (Open April 16–October 14, Monday–Saturday 10:00–5:00, Sunday 2:00–5:00; October 15–April 15, Monday–Saturday 10:00–4:00, Sunday 2:00–5:00; 703-463-7103; free.)

(See GEORGIA, NORTH CAROLINA in this chapter; also Chapter 3, DISTRICT OF COLUMBIA, PENNSYLVANIA; also Chapter 6, WASHINGTON.)

MARSHALL, JOHN (1755–1835). The nation's most notable chief justice, a man considerably less formal on the bench than his modern successors, was a lifelong Virginia resident. His birthplace and home to about 1765 was an ironworker's log cottage. A tall, conical stone marker identifies the site on County Road 649 near **Midland.**

Marshall's boyhood home from 1765 to 1773 stands "in a sad state of disrepair" east of **Markham** on State Highway 55. Col. Thomas Marshall, his father, built "The Hollow," a one and one-half-story frame house on 350 acres leased from the Lee family. The Friends of The Hollow, Inc., an organization formed in 1981, is currently working with Marshall descendants and architectural historians to restore and preserve this private dwelling.

In 1773 Marshall's father built "Oak Hill," a one and one-half-story frame house, and became one of the richest slave-owners in Fauquier County (he had 20). The son lived there until 1775, eventually inherited this homestead, and in 1819 built a larger, columned extension on the original house for his eldest son. Both homes are privately owned and are located about two miles southeast of **Delaplane** on U.S. Highway 17.

In **Richmond,** Marshall built his elegant, two-story permanent home in 1790, and Marshall House National Historic Landmark survives at 818 East Marshall St. as the city's only 18th-century brick dwelling. Marshall spent his remaining 45 years there, adding a small bedroom wing at the rear in 1810. The Association for the Preservation of Virginia Antiquities has restored this house with its original fine woodwork and furnishings plus papers and memorabilia of Marshall and his wife, whose 1783 wedding gown is also exhibited. (Open Tuesday–Saturday 11:00–

4:00, Sunday 1:00–4:00; 804-648-7998; admission.) (See Chapter 3, DISTRICT OF COLUMBIA.)

MONROE, JAMES (1758–1831). The fifth U.S president was born on his parents' small plantation, "Monrovia," near **Colonial Beach,** his home to 1769. The site is marked on State Highway 205.

At **Fredericksburg,** Monroe's first married home was built and owned by his uncle Joseph Jones, who offered the young lawyer and Elizabeth Kortright Monroe use of it in 1786. They lived there until 1791. Expanded before the Civil War into a three-story, stucco-covered townhouse, the Monroes knew it as a two-story brick dwelling. It remains privately owned at 301 Caroline St.

From 1791 to 1796 the Monroes occupied a two-story brick farmhouse in **Charlottesville.** This house stands west of the commons on the University of Virginia campus off Main Street and Fontaine Avenue (see the entry on William Holmes McGuffey earlier in this section). In 1796 Thomas Jefferson designed the rambling, hilltop "Ash Lawn" for his friend and neighbor Monroe on 800 acres that Monroe had purchased within sight of Jefferson's Monticello in 1789 (see the entry on Thomas Jefferson earlier in this section). This two-story, L-shaped frame house that Monroe called "Highlands," his home until 1820, stands on County Road 795 off State Highway 53 about five miles southeast of Charlottesville. The College of William and Mary operates it on 550 acres of Monroe's original plantation. Period furnishings include many Monroe possessions. (Open March 1–October 31, daily 9:00–6:00; November 1–February 28, daily 10:00–5:00; 804-293-9539; admission.)

From 1799 to 1802 and again in 1811, Monroe was Virginia's governor and resided in the first Governor's Mansion on the site of the present one in **Richmond** (see the entry on Patrick Henry earlier in this section).

In 1820, during his presidency, Monroe built Oak Hill National Historic Landmark, which stands privately owned about two miles north of **Gilberts Corner** on U.S. Highway 15. Monroe had inherited this property in 1808, and the small frame cottage he occupied before the 1823 completion of the mansion—where, it is said, he drafted parts of the Monroe Doctrine—also stands on the estate. White House architect James Hoban designed this two and one-half-story brick mansion, and a 1923 owner enlarged the original one and one-half-story wings to their present two stories. Elizabeth Monroe died there in 1830, and the ex-president left Oak Hill to make his last, brief home in New York City. Oak Hill furnishings include original Monroe items. (Open by appointment; 703-948-6246.)

Exhibit: In **Fredericksburg,** the James Monroe Museum and Memorial Library National Historic Landmark at 908 Charles St. occupies the restored 1758 brick building in which Monroe practiced law from 1786 to 1791. Numerous Monroe possessions displayed by the Commonwealth of Virginia include furniture he purchased in France and used in the White House; the desk on which he signed the Monroe Doctrine in 1824; court clothing worn by the Monroes in Europe; family jewelry, china and silver; plus Monroe letters and manuscripts. (Open daily 9:00–5:00; 703-373-8426; admission.)

(See Chapter 2, MANHATTAN; also Chapter 3, DISTRICT OF COLUMBIA.)

MOSES, ANNA MARY ROBERTSON "GRANDMA" (1860–1961). Long before she became known for her "American primitive" paintings of rural New York scenes, Anna and Thomas Moses, her husband, lived on five different farms in the Staunton area from 1887 to 1905. One of the earliest (1890s) stands on State Highway 780 northeast of **Verona,** a privately owned dwelling built in the early 1800s. Her painting "Apple Butter Making," done years later from memory, depicts the back yard scenery there. Nearby off U.S. Highway 11, a two-story brick house dating from the early 19th century has been identified as "Hilltop," a dwelling owned by the couple in 1901 and 1902. Anna Moses also called this house "Mount Airy" and "Mount Nebo," a name she gave all of her homes. Local residents who were children at the time recall that "Mrs. Moses often would serve all of the children bread, hot from the oven, spread with butter and brown sugar. Mrs. Moses made butter in a special way, and people from nearby farms preferred it over their own." The dwelling remains privately owned.

The last Virginia home of the Moses family (probably 1902–05) stood on the present site of King's Daughters' Hospital in **Staunton.** There the enterprising Anna Moses operated a potato chip business from her house.

(See Chapter 1, VERMONT; also Chapter 3, NEW YORK.)

PATTON, GEORGE SMITH, JR. (1885–1945). Long before he commanded in Europe, the wealthy World War II general occupied Quarters Number 5 (1923–25) in the "Generals' Row" of large brick residences at **Fort Myer.** Today this 1863 army post provides military personnel for ceremonial functions in and around the national capital (see the entry on Douglas MacArthur earlier in this section).

(See KENTUCKY in this chapter; also Chapter 1, MASSACHUSETTS; also Chapter 3, DISTRICT OF COLUMBIA; also Chapter 6, CALIFORNIA.)

POCAHONTAS (1595?–1617). Her personal name was Matoaka, "the playful one." This native Virginian, the apparent savior of Capt. John Smith in 1608 (see the entry on Smith later in this section), later became an important intercessor between Virginia Colonists and Indians and married Englishman John Rolfe. Her birth site remains unknown, but much of her childhood was spent at her father's village of Werowocomoco 10 miles southeast of today's **Gloucester** off U.S. Highway 17. This Purtan Bay site is marked by "Powhaten's Chimney," a reconstructed remnant of marl masonry that is supposedly part of a stone house built for the chief in 1609 by Smith. Whatever the history of this particular rockpile, the child Pocahontas (at least according to Smith) saved his life in this vicinity by placing her head on his own. There too, a few months later, the colonists "crowned" Powhaten a king, by order of a manipulative James I, with a tawdry copper headpiece made for the occasion. Philip L. Barbour in *Pocahontas and Her World* (1969) describes the hilarious attempts of the armored English to make the suspicious chief bow low enough to complete the ceremony.

Another of Powhaten's villages that Pocahontas would have known stood at the present location of Chimborazo Park, 3215 East Broad St. in **Richmond.** The Headquarters Visitor Center of Richmond National Battlefield Park, operated by the National Park Service, now occupies this site; exhibits relate to the Civil War Battle of Richmond. John Rolfe's experimental tobacco plantation, where the couple probably met in 1613 and lived after their marriage, was "Varina Farm." The present two-story brick house on the estate dates from 1857 and served as a Civil War headquarters for Union Gen. Benjamin F. Butler. Part of a much older brick house is attached as a wing;

this may have been a portion of Rolfe's original plantation house, which was also the later home of Rev. James Blair, founder of William and Mary College. Varina, still privately owned, stands on Varina Road about six and one-half miles south of Richmond off State Highway 5.

Pocahontas spent much time at **Jamestown** (see *Exhibit* below), where she was held hostage from 1613, and married John Rolfe there in 1614; they lived in the settlement at intervals until their 1616 departure for England.

The couple also lived on a plantation north of **Surry** that was apparently given to Rolfe as a dowry by Powhaten. This acreage, where their son Thomas Rolfe later settled, is today encompassed within Smith's Fort Plantation.

Exhibits: The Visitor Center of **Jamestown** Colonial National Historical Park on Colonial Parkway displays a set of earrings reputedly worn by Pocahontas that have descended through the Rolfe family—Thomas Rolfe's numerous progeny included John Randolph and Edith Bolling Galt Wilson, second wife of President Wilson (see the entries on Randolph and Woodrow Wilson later in this section). In Jamestown Festival Park is "Powhaten's Lodge," an Algonquin long house recreation based on a Smith drawing and the type of lodging in which Pocahontas would have spent her childhood.

POE, EDGAR ALLAN (1809–1849). "I am a Virginian; at least I call myself one," he wrote to a friend in 1841. Though born in Boston, the poet and author of macabre tales lived in **Richmond** for much of his life and considered it his native city. None of the homes he inhabited have survived. The John Allan house, the residence of his foster parents and Poe's home from 1811 to 1815, was a three-story, 12-room brick house that stood at 14th Street and the long-gone Tobacco Alley, just east of Capitol Square. From 1820 to 1825, following their return from Europe, the family lived in a two and one-half-story frame house that faced west on Fifth Street between Marshall and Clay streets; this house lasted until about 1900. "Moldavia," the two-story mansion bought by John Allan in 1825, was Poe's last parental home. He returned there at intervals until his final break with Allan in 1830. Demolished about 1890, this house stood at Main and Fifth streets. A two-story brick dwelling on the southeast corner of Bank and 11th streets was Mrs.

Yarrington's boardinghouse, where Poe, his 13-year-old wife and cousin Virginia Clemm, and Mrs. Clemm lived in 1835 and 1836. Poe married Virginia in a second "official" ceremony there in 1836—and there he began his serious literary career as the editor of a periodical. The house numbered among many city dwellings destroyed during the Civil War bombardment of 1865. Poe's last Richmond lodging, just before his death in Baltimore, was the Old Swan Tavern, a 1795 frame structure that stood until the early 1900s on the north side of Broad Street between Eighth and Ninth streets.

At **Charlottesville**, the room where Poe lived as a student during almost the entire year of 1826 has been restored on the University of Virginia campus. The only authentic Poe item among the few period antiques in Room 13 West Range is the bed he used at the Allan home in Richmond. Poe ran up gambling debts there but also read and wrote extensively, producing most of the verse in his first book *Tamerlane and Other Poems* (1827) in this room. The room is maintained by the campus Raven Society and may be seen on request (see the entry on William Holmes McGuffey earlier in this section).

Poe was stationed at Fort Monroe, **Hampton**, in 1828 and 1829 during part of his brief military career and there achieved the highest enlisted rank of sergeant major. He was discharged from the army at Fort Monroe in April of 1829. The Casemate Museum displays an exhibit relating to his months there (see the entry on Jefferson Finis Davis earlier in this section).

Exhibit: By far the best, most complete collection of Poe memorabilia is displayed in the complex of five **Richmond** buildings forming the Edgar Allan Poe Museum at 1914–16 East Main St., the locale of Poe's city neighborhood. The 1686 "Old Stone House," Richmond's oldest surviving structure, stands as part of this group. Named for his actress mother, the Elizabeth Arnold Poe building holds the few possessions Poe owned at his death, including his trunk, his wife's mirror and his walking stick. The desk and chair he used as editor of the *Southern Literary Messenger* from 1835 to 1837 are there, plus a transplanted staircase from "Moldavia" and furnishings from the demolished Allan homes where Poe grew up. The Edgar Allan Poe Foundation also exhibits photos, documents and art works relating to Poe. (Open Tuesday–Saturday 10:00–4:00, Sunday–Monday 1:30–4:00; 804-648-5523; admission.)

(See Chapter 1, MASSACHUSETTS; also Chapter 2, BRONX, MANHATTAN; also Chapter 3, MARYLAND, PENNSYLVANIA.)

RANDOLPH, JOHN (1773–1833). John Randolph of Roanoke was one of the most brilliant, erratic and ultimately tragic figures of our national political history. An aristocratic defender of states' rights in Congress, Randolph had few peers in his mastery of debate and parliamentary skills, but increasing mental instability and final insanity ruined his career. He was born at "Cawsons," his grandparents' plantation and his frequent childhood residence. The 30-room house, destroyed by fire sometime after Randolph's last visit in 1814, stood on a marked site at the end of North Fourth Street in **Hopewell**.

Randolph's parental home was "Matoax," which stood on a 1,300-acre plantation until burned in 1781 at the presently marked location in **Matoaca**.

Also marked at the northern edge of **Farmville** on State Highway 45 is the site of "Bizarre," another plantation of Randolph's grandparents. Randolph and his mother took refuge there in 1781 from Benedict Arnold's marauding troops, and this remained his home until 1810.

Randolph's last home, from 1810, was "Roanoke Plantation," located west of **Saxe** off State Highway 746. He inherited this estate from his father and erected two primitive log dwellings—one for summer, the other for winter. Despite their rude exteriors, Randolph's cabins housed fine furnishings and a large library. Only one cottage, a one and one-half-story frame structure, plus several outbuildings remain on this privately owned property.

REED, WALTER LAWRENCE (1851–1902). The army physician whose research in Cuba led to control of yellow fever was a Virginia native. His birthplace, a three-room frame house displaying period items, stands at **Belroi** four miles west of State Highway 614/616 junction. It is operated by the Association for the Preservation of Virginia Antiquities. (Open by appointment only; 804-693-3693; admission.)

(See ALABAMA in this chapter; also Chapter 4, NEBRASKA.)

SCOTT, WINFIELD (1786–1866). The foremost U.S. general between the Revolution and the Civil War, Scott devised the Union army "anaconda" strategy which, though widely ridiculed in 1861 when he retired, was the one ultimately adopted. He was born near **Dinwiddie** at the family plantation of "Laurel Branch," his home to 1803. The site is marked on U.S. Highway 1.

(See Chapter 2, MANHATTAN; also Chapter 3, NEW JERSEY.)

SHERIDAN, PHILIP HENRY (1831–1888). The Union army general and Indian fighter headquartered himself during the fall and winter of 1864–65 in a house that survives on the southwest corner of Braddock and Piccadilly streets in **Winchester**. From there, Sheridan—"twenty miles away," according to Thomas Buchanan Read's famous ballad *Sheridan's Ride* (1865)—set out on his famous "ride" to rally his men in the October 19, 1864 Battle of Cedar Creek. The two and one-half-story house, previously used as a headquarters by Union Gen. Nathaniel P. Banks, remains privately owned.

(See Chapter 1, MASSACHUSETTS; also Chapter 4, OHIO.)

SMITH, JOHN (1580?–1631). English adventurer, explorer, colonizer and founder of **Jamestown**, Smith resided there from 1607 to 1609. Without his leadership under the stern rule "He who would not work, would not eat," the colony probably could not have lasted more than a few weeks. There, in 1608, Smith wrote the first book in English on the American continent, his *True Relation*—also the first book about America actually written on the scene. Today this earliest colonial site, preserved as Jamestown Colonial National Historic Park, displays foundation remnants of colonial buildings and artifacts collected from ongoing archaeology. The locations of original excavated structures and streets have been well marked and diagrammed on the ground by the Jamestown Foundation. On Colonial Parkway, the Jamestown Visitor Center displays an audiovisual program plus archaeological exhibits, maps and brochures. (Open mid-June–Labor Day, daily 8:30–5:30; Labor Day–October 31, April 1–mid-June, daily 8:30–5:00; November 1–March 31, daily 8:30–4:30; admission.)

Smith's Fort Plantation near **Surry** is the preserved site of the frontier stockade erected by Smith in 1609. Traces of the mounded perimeter may still be seen. The present house on the site dates in its earliest portions from about 1652. Operated by the Association for the Preservation of Virginia Antiquities, Smith's Fort Plantation stands about two miles north of town on State Highway 31. (Open mid-April–September 30, Wednesday–Thursday 10:00–5:00, Friday–Saturday 10:00–1:00, Sunday 12:00–5:00; 804-229-3107; admission.)

Exhibit: **Jamestown** Festival Park, adjacent to Jamestown Island, displays replicas of the first fort constructed by Smith and his 104 "poor gentlemen, tradesmen, serving-men, libertines, and such like," as he described these forefathers. There too float replicas of the three small vessels in which they arrived. The Old World Pavilion exhibits a massive sea chest owned by Smith plus weapons and armor used by the colonists. (Open daily 9:00–5:00; 804-253-4838; admission.)

TAYLOR, ZACHARY (1784–1850). The first home of the rough-hewn frontier soldier and 12th U.S. president has long been a matter of dispute. But the general consensus is that his birthplace and brief residence as an infant is "Monte Bello," an 18th-century frame house that stands three miles west of **Gordonsville** on U.S. Highway 33. It remains privately owned.

(See ARKANSAS, KENTUCKY, LOUISIANA in this chapter; also Chapter 3, DISTRICT OF COLUMBIA.)

THURBER, JAMES GROVER (1894–1961). The humorist-cartoonist resided during the summers of 1901 and 1902 in **Falls Church**, in a two-story, 1895 frame house rented by his parents at 319 Maple Ave. In the large back orchard, Thurber suffered the arrow injury that cost him his left eye; he eventually went totally blind. This house fell in 1965 to make way for a townhouse development. The site is now numbered 201 James Thurber Court.

(See Chapter 1, CONNECTICUT; also Chapter 2, MANHATTAN; also Chapter 4, OHIO.)

TURNER, NAT (1800–1831). The leader of the South's largest and bloodiest slave rebellion in 1831, Turner was born a slave of farmer Benjamin Turner and spent his entire life in southwestern Southampton County as a piece of white man's property. Turner and his band of about 75 slaves cut a swath of death and destruction that sent shockwaves throughout the entire white South. State Highway 35 between **Courtland** and **Boykins** marks the eastern boundary of the uprising; country roads west of this highway traverse the backwoods area where blacks exploded into murderous rage, killing some 57 white men, women and children, and marching toward Courtland before state militia and armed townsmen intercepted them three miles northwest of town. About half of the victims lived (and died) on County Highway 658, locally known by its old name of Barrow Road. In 1969 one researcher found nine surviving houses that had figured in the massacre; only four were still being used as dwellings, however. The sites of Turner residences, including Samuel Turner's mill on Tarrara Creek (1822–30) and the house of Joseph Travis, his last master, where the massacre began, remain unmarked. Visitors interested in these sites are advised to study maps and learn something about the local area before penetrating this private farmland; local whites generally prefer not to review the event with strangers. Many blacks of the area are knowledgeable in traditional Turner lore, however. Excellent preparations for Nat Turner country include *The Southampton Slave Revolt of 1831* (1971), by Henry Irving Tragle; and *Fires of Jubilee* (1975) by Stephen B. Oates, particularly Oates's "Epilogue."

TYLER, JOHN (1790–1862). The tenth U.S. president, first to assume the office from the vice presidency, was a lifelong Virginia resident. His birthplace, "Greenway," a one and one-half-story frame house, was built in its earliest portions from 1650 to 1700 and centered the 1,200-acre family estate. Tyler lived there until his 1813 marriage, then purchased it in 1821 and resided until 1829. It stands privately owned about two miles west of **Charles City** on State Highway 5. "Mons-Sacer," a 500-acre section of the estate, was his first married home, from 1813 to 1815. On the same highway, about three miles east of Charles City, is Sherwood Forest National Historic Landmark, Tyler's home and 1,200-acre estate after 1842. He named his home after Robin Hood's domain in ironic recognition of his status as a political outlaw. Originally built about 1780, the two and one-half-story colonial structure was

remodeled and enlarged by Tyler in 1844. The 300-foot house is reputedly the longest frame house in the United States. Tyler used the present rear of the house as the front—a road ran between the mansion and the James River bank. A member of the Confederate congress in 1861, Tyler did not live to see the damage inflicted on his property by Union troops in 1864. His death went officially unnoticed by the federal government, and he remained in national limbo until 1911, when Congress finally memorialized him. Sherwood Forest, still a working plantation maintained by the Tyler family, consists of seven outbuildings plus the main house on 12 acres besides surrounding farmland. Original family furnishings and Tyler memorabilia are displayed. (Open daily 9:00–5:00; 804-829-5377; admission.)

Tyler's father was Virginia's governor from 1808 to 1811, and during this period the youth resided in the **Richmond** Governor's Mansion (see the entry on Patrick Henry earlier in this section).

(See Chapter 3, DISTRICT OF COLUMBIA, WEST VIRGINIA.)

WASHINGTON, BOOKER TALIAFERRO (1856–1915). Educator and dominant black leader of the early 20th century, Washington was born a slave at what is now Booker T. Washington National Monument, State Highway 122 at **Hardy**. The small Burroughs Plantation, the tobacco farm where Washington spent his first nine years, was more typical of the rural South than the huge plantations. Restored by the National Park Service, the farm with its log house and kitchen cabin again resembles the place that Washington remembered. The Visitor Center displays exhibits and a film on Washington's life (valued at $400 when he lived there); visitors may also picnic, wander along self-guided trails and watch farm demonstrations on this 224-acre preserve. (Open daily 8:30–5:00; 703-721-2094; free.)

(See ALABAMA in this chapter; also Chapter 1, MASSACHUSETTS; also Chapter 3, NEW YORK, WEST VIRGINIA.)

WASHINGTON, GEORGE (1732–1799). WASHINGTON, MARTHA DANDRIDGE CUSTIS (1731–1802).

The first U.S. president was also the first professional soldier among several to hold that office. While he summarily rejected the position

A VIEW OF MOUNT VERNON IN DECLINE. Taken from an 1858 glass plate negative, this view shows the derelict condition of Washington's mansion just before the Mount Vernon Ladies Association acquired and restored it. Identity of the photographer and persons in the picture remains unknown. *(Courtesy Rev. Guyron J. Philbert)*

and title of king, Washington was indeed one of our wealthiest presidents, and his administration displayed many more trappings of royalty than almost any since. Long before he died, he had become more icon than man to most citizens. And after generations of thoughtful quests, biographers still search for "the real Washington," so flag-draped and elusive a creature of the national psyche has he served for almost 200 years. Like Gilbert Stuart's portrait of him, Washington remains curiously "unfinished." Probably the best way to attempt a more realistic focus on the Olympian being is to visit his world, as represented by his homes and acres. This was no plebeian politician or log-cabin president—he would have found the notion offensive—but a rather standoffish Virginia aristocrat to whom good form, old family and broad estates were vital marks of personal distinction. Wealthy by inheritance, he became even more so after his expeditious marriage with rich widow Martha Custis. Meeting Washington on his own lush, placid turf—as a man whose deepest instincts owed much more to class-conscious England than to egalitarian American frontiers; as a quite mediocre soldier who looked good because many of his compatriots came off so incredibly bad and who preferred, after all, the life of country squire; and as a president much less gifted in actual leadership ability than some of his most banal successors in the job—we may begin to flesh out Stuart's unintentionally symbolic portrait on the dollar bill.

Washington Birthplace National Monument marks the ancestral home site of "Wakefield," also called "Pope's Creek." Washington's father, Augustine, built his plantation house in the 1720s, and a Christmas Day fire destroyed it in 1779. The present one and one-half-story brick mansion on the estate is not a replica but an "educated guess," built in 1931 as a typical plantation house of the period. Nobody knows what the original dwelling looked like, but the U-shaped foundation has been traced and is marked near the memorial house. Also on this property is the marked 1664 home site of John Washington, American progenitor of the family and George Washington's great-grandfather. Washington lived there until age three and perhaps at intervals from 1744 to 1746. Today the National Park Service operates this 538-acre portion of the Washington Plantation as a Colonial Living Farm, recreating 18th-century cultivation methods and types of livestock and produce raised by Augustine Washington. Located about five miles east of **Oak Grove** on State Highway 204, the house displays fine period furnishings. (Open daily 9:00–5:00; 804-224-0196; free.)

Washington spent most of his boyhood (1738–47) at "Ferry Farm," a site marked at 712 Kings Highway about one and one-half-miles east of **Fredericksburg**. If he ever did chop down a cherry tree or throw a Spanish dollar across the Potomac River—both highly dubious items of Washington apocrypha—this would have been the place. Washington's father, who died there in 1743, left Ferry Farm to George in his will. No original structure survives on this privately owned land.

Washington was 16 when he came to live permanently at Mount Vernon, the one and one-half-story house built in 1743 by his half-brother Lawrence on the foundations of an earlier house erected by his father and destroyed by fire. In this prior house, George Washington lived from ages three to six. After Lawrence died there in 1752, George first managed, then inherited the estate and began remodeling the house into the Georgian structure seen today. He added a second story in 1758, extended the ends in 1774 and 1776, built the river-view portico in the 1780s and added a pediment and cupola after that. He increased his father's original portion of the 1669 family grant from 2,500 acres to more than 8,000. By 1786 he was supporting five farms and almost 250 persons on the estate. His 500-acre "Mansion House Farm," intended as more of a country park for his pleasure than for serious agriculture, surrounded the main house and outbuildings. "No estate in United America is more pleasantly situated than this," he wrote. But Washington never made Mount Vernon pay its way commercially, despite diligent efforts to raise tobacco and other crops on his rather poor soil. The Washingtons resided at Mount Vernon continuously from 1759 to 1775, from 1783 to 1789, and from 1797 to his death. During his absences as colonial soldier, American military commander and president, overseers worked the plantation and made regular reports, which he studied carefully. Both George and Martha Washington died there. During the next 50 years, the estate declined in acreage and upkeep until by 1858, only 200 acres of the once vast holding remained in the Washington family, and the mansion itself sagged in decrepit shape. The formation of the Mount Vernon Ladies Association in 1858 to acquire the property began one of the first and most successful preservation-restoration efforts in national history.* Today the Association owns almost 500 acres of the original "Mansion House Farm," has retrieved most of Mount Vernon's widely dispersed contents, and provides a visual image

of the Washingtons' comfortable home life that offers a remarkable biography in itself. That home life was highly social—George and Martha declared themselves bored when they weren't entertaining guests—and especially notable is the parlor where they hosted some 2,000 notable visitors from 1768 to 1775. Other famous rooms include Washington's study and his bedroom, where his physicians bled away his life, in a medical barbarity typical of the times, to relieve a streptococcal throat infection. Rooms display the Washingtons' original furnishings plus many personal articles including clothing, gifts and the mundane sorts of items that make the first first couple a bit less remote as people who enjoyed living well. Outbuildings include stables, a kitchen, spinning house and greenhouse, reconstructed slave quarters and a museum. In 1979 the Mount Vernon Ladies Association began the first public fundraising campaign in its history, with a goal of $10 million for the improvements needed to accommodate more than a million visitors annually. "Get set for crowds," advises one experienced Mount Vernon visitor. "There is hardly a day in the year when you can commune privately with the spirit of George and Martha Washington. Avoid weekends, if possible, and try to get there early, before the crowds." Mount Vernon National Historic Landmark stands seven miles south of **Alexandria** on George Washington Memorial Parkway. (Open March 1–October 31, daily 9:00–5:00; November 1–February 28, daily 9:00–4:00; 703-780-2000; admission.)

Washington also occupied a town residence in Alexandria proper, and he considered this community his hometown; he helped survey and lay out its streets in 1749. His small, reconstructed brick townhouse at 508 Cameron St. is privately owned.

Martha Dandridge, wealthy from birth, was also a native Virginian (see the entry on Robert Edward Lee earlier in this section). None of her earliest homes in New Kent County have survived. She was born at "Chestnut Grove," the parental plantation home on the Pamunkey River. Its site is marked on County Road 623 off State Highway 33 near **New Kent**. The plantation house built by her father in 1722 burned down in 1927.

The site of the "White House," her home as the wife of Daniel Parke Custis in 1749, is marked on County Road 609 about six miles northeast of **Talleysville**. She married Washington there in

---

*A fine account of Mount Vernon's preservation history is Elswyth Thane's *Mount Vernon: The Legacy* (1967).

WOODROW WILSON BIRTHPLACE, STAUNTON. This handsome 1846 house has been recently restored to its appearance of 1856, the year when the 28th U.S. president was born in its main floor "chamber." The house fronts closely upon Coalter Street, but this rear garden-portico view gives some idea of the spaciousness of the yard. Wilson was too young to remember any of this when the family left, but he returned in later years to view the scene of his "rootage," *(Courtesy Woodrow Wilson Birthplace Foundation)*

1759. Fire destroyed the house in 1862.

Martha Custis also resided on a town plantation in **Williamsburg** during her first marriage. A remnant of the estate, a small brick cookhouse called the "Custis Kitchen," stands on the Eastern State Hospital grounds on Francis Street. Daniel Custis inherited the property; the surviving outbuilding dates from about 1714 and is not open to the public.

Exhibits: In **Winchester**, where Washington worked as a surveyor for Thomas Lord Fairfax in 1748, his small office of log and stone stands at Cork and Braddock streets. He also used the structure as his 1756 headquarters while building Fort Loudoun, the site of which is marked at Peyton and Loudoun streets. Washington's Office displays tools and items he used plus a scale model of Fort Loudoun. (Open May 1–October 31, Monday–Saturday 10:00–5:00, Sunday 1:00–5:00; admission.)

At **Fredericksburg**, the Mary Ball Washington House at 1200 Charles St. is the one and one-half-story dwelling that Washington bought for his mother in 1772. Washington visited there, though not as often as he should have, she

complained, and departed from there for his inauguration as the first U.S. president in 1789. Operated by the Association for the Preservation of Virginia Antiquities, the restored house displays some of Mary Washington's own furnishings plus period items. (Open April 1–October 31, daily 9:00–5:00; November 1–March 31, daily 9:00–4:00; 703-373-1569; admission.) The Masonic Bible on which Washington took his presidential oath on April 30, 1789, is exhibited at the 1815 Masonic Lodge, Princess Anne and Hanover streets. Portions of the first lodge on this site, where Washington was initiated a Mason in 1752, are preserved in the later structure. (Open Monday–Saturday 9:00–4:00, Sunday 1:00–4:00; 703-373-5885; admission.)

Another museum containing Washington Masonic relics is the George Washington Masonic National Memorial tower at the western end of King Street in **Alexandria**. Displayed here is the Mount Vernon clock stopped at his death by his doctor, furnishings of the Alexandria lodge he headed as Worshipful Master and the trowel he used when laying the cornerstone of the U.S. capitol in a 1793 Masonic ceremony. (Open daily,

9:00-5:00; 703-683-2007; free.)

(See Chapter 2, MANHATTAN; also Chapter 3, NEW JERSEY, NEW YORK, PENNSYLVANIA.)

WILSON, WOODROW (1856–1924). The first home of the 28th U.S. president was a Presbyterian parsonage at **Staunton**. "A man's rootage is more important than his leafage," Wilson believed (or said he did); and though he recalled nothing of the two-story, columned manse of white brick from his infancy, he returned to view the house just after his 1912 election. Wilson Birthplace National Historic Landmark, built in 1846, stands at 24 North Coalter St. According to Dr. Katharine L. Brown, Executive Director of the Woodrow Wilson Birthplace Foundation that operates the house as a Wilson museum, the restoration in 1978 and 1979 was painstaking: "It now looks more like it did when Wilson was born there than it did in 1912." Floors, mantels and many furnishings are original. Wilson's crib, parental possessions and memorabilia from his student and presidential days are among the items displayed. Especially noteworthy in the carriage house is the 1919 Pierce-Arrow sedan he bought from the White House motor fleet and used until his death. (Open March 1–November 30, daily 9:00–5:00; December 1–February 28, Monday–Saturday 9:00–5:00; 703-885-0897; admission.)

(See GEORGIA, SOUTH CAROLINA in this chapter; also Chapter 1, NEW HAMPSHIRE; also Chapter 3, DISTRICT OF COLUMBIA, NEW JERSEY.)

SIX

THE WEST

Fifteen states form the nation's largest, most populated and fastest growing region. From Texas and Oklahoma on the east, the Great Plains rise to the mountain and desert states of Arizona, Colorado, Idaho, Montana, Nevada, New Mexico, Utah and Wyoming. California, Oregon and Washington front the Pacific coast; and our most recent states, Alaska and Hawaii, lie far from contiguous American borders.* This vast region displays some immense contrasts. While California contains more people than any other state (about 24 million), the eight mountain states east of it encompass the nation's most thinly settled area (12 persons per square mile). Those same states are also the most arid in the country. Except for spots in Hawaii, however, coastal Oregon and Washington receive more rain than any other spot in America. The Great Plains begin their long roll eastward beneath the "rain shadow" of some of the most rugged crags and peaks on earth. In opposition to the desert extremes in Death Valley and Arizona's Sonora, few more fertile acres than California's Central Valley exist on the globe. Concurrent with the social progressivism of California and Oregon runs Arizona and Texas conservatism.

In the southern region, Spain and Mexico established the first colonies; and their influence

remains strong in the language, population ancestry and adobe styles of architecture. British traders contested the northern fur empire with an influx of American competitors until diplomacy instead of war settled this matter. Secretary of State James Buchanan relinquished the "Fifty-four Forty or Fight" slogan of President Polk's Democrats and, to avoid further friction, settled for the 49th parallel as the northern U.S. boundary line, signing the treaty in 1846. The 1848 Treaty of Guadalupe-Hidalgo, ending the Mexican War, ceded the territory now comprising most of Arizona, California, Colorado, Nevada, New Mexico and Utah. A separate American nation, the short-lived Republic of Texas, had achieved its own independence from Mexico in 1836 and gladly entered statehood in 1845; then, a few years later, it seceded as the only regional Confederate state. Hawaii, gradually taken over by 19th-century American business interests, owed its eventual, long-delayed statehood to its strategic location for national security.

"What do we want with this worthless area, this region of savages and wild beasts, of shifting sands and whirlwinds of dust, of cactus and prairie dogs?" In 1852 when Secretary of State Daniel Webster thus discouraged territorial acquisition of the mountain states, mapmakers had labeled this area the Great American Desert. For decades it was seen and experienced as only a hazardous barrier to California, to be traversed or circumvented as efficiently as possible. The 1854 Gadsden Purchase of lower Arizona and

---

*Because Alaska's most notable residents played no extensive roles in national history and the development of national culture, that state is not separately included in the following pages.

New Mexico was not for territory but a route. In a sense, America's true western frontier retreated east after the California gold rush; for not until then did settlers take a second look at opportunities left behind. The rancher replaced the prospector as the appeal of instant gratification focused into promises of slower success. Dispossession of the natives became the first priority, and official butchers like George A. Custer and people-herders like Kit Carson were excessively good at their jobs. Indians of numerous tribes, often more foreign to each other than to the whites, were literally "rounded up" when not massacred like bison, and squeezed into the nation's final Indian Territory of Oklahoma—where efforts proceeded to extinguish tribal identity in the ultimate spiritual as well as physical conquest. Fierce range wars between cattle and sheep ranchers replaced Indian conflicts; rustling became the region's typical felony; and the cowboy, a derisive term for plains "flunky," entered the national mythology as someone "free" and much larger than life. Though thousands of pioneers braved the Oregon and Santa Fe Trails, major settlement in this region did not begin until railroads spliced the continent in Utah.

To date, most of this region retains its pristine magnificence. But vast change is occurring almost too rapidly to measure. "The hard hat is edging out the Stetson," in James Kelly's words; for the largest reservoirs of America's fuel energy lie in and beneath these landscapes, and the region faces increasingly hard choices. The federal government holds disproportionate control over much of the West. It is Hawaii's biggest employer and the state of Washington's basic subsidizer. In the eight mountain states, it owns almost half the land and 80 percent of the mineral and energy resources. Westerners are torn by this immense attention and generosity. "As beneficiaries," recently admitted a former senator from Idaho, "we are reluctant to confront or confess the federal largesse because it cuts across the grain of our pioneer spirit." Economically, the region remains primarily agricultural—though by 1975 manufacturing, especially electronics firms, led both agriculture and mining in the mountain states, many of whose newest residents are ex-Californians. The following pages reveal that many more eminent persons made adulthood homes in this region than were born there—an indicator of the region's growth in population, industry and creative activity.

Today's West is obviously shaping up as a vastly different place than most prominent residents in this chapter knew or dreamed. Despite its wealth and busy prospects, the region seriously lags in the science of management and planning. One pattern hasn't changed much from the early days: Growth is still mainly hit-or-miss, based on the latest oil strike or new coal field, mimicking the early goldrush settlements and mining boomtowns. Almost automatically, wherever enough people gather is another Los Angeles in the making, as Phoenix smog demonstrates. The region also faces crucial water problems, with the bickering between agriculture and industry becoming as embittered as the old wars between open and fenced range. Today every Western river below Canada is used and overused. The 1,400-mile Colorado supplies seven states, ending as a trickle at the Gulf of California; and underground aquifers are seriously depleted. "There is not sufficient water to supply the land," flatly stated explorer John Wesley Powell in 1893—but again, and typically, the region defers any real strategy for the future. Can this region fulfill its enormous potential as America's prime energy resource and still retain its wilderness values for all Americans? Or will it come to represent colossal failure of a sort that lies beyond the capacities of drill rigs and power shovels to heal or prevent? Answers to those questions may well determine "who lives where" in the 21st century.

ARIZONA

The sixth largest state hosts one of the nation's largest native American populations, one person in twenty. Within more than two dozen tribal cultures in three linguistic families, acceptance of modern lifestyles varies widely. Some villages still reject electricity and grind corn by hand, but only traditional religious occasions draw back many who have otherwise embraced Little League, Sunday school and the work ethic. Nomadic peoples still travel, but with pickup trucks; and the agricultural Hopis and Pimas continue to farm as they have for centuries. Many of today's modern irrigation systems follow America's first known canals, established by the 14th-century Hohokams, whose descendants are notable artisans.

Water remains a controlling factor in the state's

economy. With an average annual rainfall of only 14 inches, Arizona has become a permanent field laboratory in water conservation and the science of irrigation. The Colorado, Arizona's only large river, forms most of the state's western border.

Arizona consists of mountain, desert and plateau. About 30 mountain ranges and high plains divide the southwestern Sonoran desert area from the canyons and mesas of the Colorado plateau country. One of the most awesome sights on the planet is the mile-deep gorge of the Grand Canyon. Other spectacular landforms and parks include the Painted Desert, Petrified Forest, Montezuma Castle cliff dwellings and Saguaro and Organ Pipe Cactus National Monuments.

Spanish missionaries and soldiers were Arizona's first known Caucasians. Coronado invaded the territory in 1540, and Jesuit father Eusebio Francisco Kino founded the first successful mission in 1692. Tucson, one of the oldest towns in the West, originated in 1776, but fierce Apache natives prevented much settlement until the mid-1800s. In 1848 the United States took the land north of the Gila River as a result of the Mexican War; and the 1854 Gadsden Purchase acquired southern Arizona to provide a route for California goldseekers. Arizona Territory, created in 1863, faced brutal years of Indian conflict and encompassed the growth of such turbulent "Wild West" mining towns as Tombstone. In 1912 Arizona became the 48th state.

Mining and cattle ranching were the main economic activities in the territorial days. Arizona's huge mineral wealth has made it the nation's main copper producer since 1910, and the state also ranks high in gold and silver production. Agriculture, especially commercial truck crops on reclaimed desert, replaced mining as the primary income producer in 1943; but since then, manufacturing and tourism have come to dominate the state's economy. Electronics, aircraft, missiles and copper refining are the major industries. Phoenix is the largest city and capital.

Early Arizona attracted footloose opportunists like Wyatt Earp and soldier-politicians like John C. Frémont, hardly settler types. Twentieth-century notable residents, by contrast, usually came to Arizona after active careers elsewhere to find semiretirement homes. Among these were Joseph Wood Krutch, Henry R. Luce, Westbrook Pegler and Margaret Sanger. Architect Frank Lloyd Wright made his final creative headquarters there, and author Zane Grey's tales are permeated by the Mogollon Rim country that he knew so well. Extant homes of Arizona notables, though not numerous, fairly well represent the span of this beautiful state's history and vitality.

EARP, WYATT (1848–1929). From 1879 to 1882, the frontier gambler lived in **Tombstone,** where his brother Virgil became marshal in the wild town "too tough to die." Wyatt Earp was first employed as a Wells Fargo messenger, then as a gambler and guard in the rowdy Oriental Saloon until deputized by Virgil in 1881—so tense a job, according to one story, that "his bowels refused to move properly for a year." With a third brother Morgan and John H. "Doc" Holliday, the Earps forced a showdown with the Clanton gang at the O.K. Corral on October 26, 1881, killing three of the five toughs, an act widely regarded at the time as simple murder. The Earp siblings quickly became unwelcome and soon drifted away. The Oriental Saloon (now the Oriental Steakhouse) remains at Allen and Fifth streets. Wyatt Earp's house stood at First and Fremont streets. In 1881, however, he lodged at the Cosmopolitan Hotel, which burned the next year.

Exhibits: **Tombstone** Historic District National Historic Landmark preserves portions of the old silvermining town that today lives mainly on its past. "Tombstone Historama," an audiovisual program about the town's history presented near the entrance to the O.K. Corral, is a good starting point. (Performance daily 9:00–4:00; 602-457-2227; admission.) The O.K. Corral, scene of the Earp-Clanton gun duel, stands at Allen and Fourth streets. Life-size mannequins of the participants—while positioned too far apart, according to some students of the episode—recreate the confrontation. And live reenactments are staged each Sunday. (Open daily, 8:30–5:00; 602-457-3456; admission.) The Wyatt Earp Museum at Toughnut and Fifth streets displays Earp family memorabilia. (Open daily 8:30–6:00; admission.) Wyatt Earp Days on the last weekend in May provide excuses for only one of the staged "shootfests" that draw tourists at various times throughout the year.

(See CALIFORNIA in this chapter; also Chapter 4, ILLINOIS, IOWA, KANSAS.)

FRÉMONT, JOHN CHARLES (1813–1890). A

sometimes reckless but enormously popular soldier, explorer and 1856 presidential candidate, Frémont served as Arizona's territorial governor from 1878 to 1883. His first residence, which he rented in 1878 and 1879 in the capital of **Prescott,** stands as part of the Sharlot Hall Museum Complex operated by Prescott Historical Society at 415 West Gurley St. The Frémont House dates from 1876. (Open Tuesday–Saturday 9:00–5:00, Sunday 1:00–5:00; 602-445-3122; donation.)

From 1879 to the end of his term, Frémont lived in **Tucson.** The 1858 Frémont House at 151 South Granada St., operated by the Arizona Historical Society, contains period items. (Open Wednesday–Saturday 10:00–4:00; 602-622-0956; free.)

(See CALIFORNIA in this chapter; also Chapter 3, NEW YORK.)

GREY, ZANE (1875–1939). In 1920 the prolific Western novelist built a small frame hunting lodge beneath the Mogollon (Tonto) Rim, came there frequently to hunt and roam the wilderness area, and used the setting for many of his novels (e.g., *Under the Tonto Rim,* 1920). Zane Grey's Cabin, renovated in 1963 to its 1920s appearance, stands in Tonto National Forest 17 miles east of **Payson** via State Highway 260 as indicated by signs. Displayed there are some of the original cabin furnishings, a Grey manuscript, first editions and movie posters. (Open March 2–November 14, daily 9:00–5:00; 602-478-4243; admission.)

(See CALIFORNIA in this chapter; also Chapter 2, MANHATTAN; also Chapter 3, PENNSYLVANIA; also Chapter 4, OHIO.)

KRUTCH, JOSEPH WOOD (1893–1970). From 1952 the literary critic turned naturalist made his permanent home in **Tucson,** where he built his dwelling at 5041 East Grant Road (privately owned). There Krutch wrote all of his later books, including *The Measure of Man* (1954).

(See Chapter 1, CONNECTICUT; also Chapter 2, MANHATTAN.)

LUCE, HENRY ROBINSON (1898–1967). The retirement home of the powerful publisher, whose *Time* and *Life* magazines widely circulated his own conservative political philosophy, was a rambling, pink stucco house near the 15th green of the Arizona Biltmore Hotel's golf course in **Phoenix.**

Luce bought this villa from international playboy Tommy Manville about 1957 and resided there until his death. The house at 43 Biltmore Estates remains privately occupied.

(See Chapter 1, CONNECTICUT; also Chapter 2, MANHATTAN, also Chapter 5, SOUTH CAROLINA.)

PEGLER, WESTBROOK (1894–1969). In **Tucson,** the newspaper columnist noted for his slashing, sometimes libelous attacks on public figures made his last home on West Magee Road near Oracle Road. "Casa Cholla," or "House of the Jumping Cactus," with its view of the Santa Catalina Mountains, was Pegler's adobe-style, stucco residence from 1941. He planted desert shrubs on his 40-acre estate, strangely serene environs for a man of such constant ire. The property remains private.

(See Chapter 2, MANHATTAN; also Chapter 3, NEW YORK; also Chapter 4, MINNESOTA.)

SANGER, MARGARET HIGGINS (1883–1966). From 1933 the birth-control activist, reformer and lecturer lived in **Tucson,** where she occupied several successive homes. During the 1940s (until 1949) she lived with her husband J. Noah Slee at 2133 East Elm St.; Slee died there in 1943. She designed her fan-shaped house with three gardens and a 40-foot glass frontage at 85 Sierra Vista Drive in 1949, her home until 1962. Both houses are privately owned. Sanger died in extreme senility at a private nursing home, her last residence from 1962, at 1107 East Adelaide Drive. Now known as The Haven, this 1950 structure is a private treatment center for alcoholic women.

(See Chapter 2, MANHATTAN; also Chapter 3, NEW YORK.)

WRIGHT, FRANK LLOYD (1867–1959). Near **Scottsdale,** the famed architect created "Taliesin West," his winter home and architectural school, in 1938. Wright designed his desert headquarters to blend and harmonize with this dry, brilliant landscape. Operated by the Frank Lloyd Wright Foundation, the complex and training center is located on 108th Street north of East Shea Boulevard. (Open June 1–September 30, daily tours 9:00–10:00; October 1–May 31, daily 10:00–4:00; 602-948-6670; admission.)

(See Chapter 4, ILLINOIS, WISCONSIN.)

CALIFORNIA

In 1982 one of every 11 Americans resided in California, keeping it the nation's most populous state. Los Angeles alone, the third largest American city, equals the combined population of Idaho, Montana, Nevada and Wyoming. The fastest growth occurred in the late 1960s and early 1970s, when a thousand new Californians arrived each day. That rate has since declined, but the state continues to host about 10 million tourists per year. Not so long ago, anybody who moved to California was never again seen east of the Sierras. Today newcomers do not invariably stay.

The attractions that drew so many people are as kaleidoscopic as the state itself. The first big influx was mercenary in the extreme, the 1849 gold rush. Many prospectors struck it rich; many more didn't, but fortune seekers sifted stream bottoms and washed away hillsides all over the state in quest of riches. California has, in a sense, been the heady national "dreamland" every since. The valley land, soil that would grow every commercial crop raised in the nation except tobacco, attracted another type of newcomer. But the foremost of California's magnets was its climate: an average yearly temperature variance of only 10 degrees, uncomplicated "wet" and "dry" seasons and sunshine some 350 days per year. Climate drew the motion picture industry, more dependent on good light than on talent or marvelous limbs and torsos. Broadcasting, aerospace and food industries also concentrated there. Mostly, however, the Mediterranean balm drew hordes of people tired of winter in their lives, seekers of good jobs, warm retirement and reliable weather reports. It was not, of course, true paradise on earth; California ground is not the steadiest rim of the globe—its periodic jolts somewhat balance the predictability scale, adding a disturbance factor. And heavy smog in the Los Angeles area frequently makes those 350 days of sunshine a moot point. Being poor in California is also more expensive than elsewhere; plain living can cost spectacular amounts, and housing is a seller's market.

It is often said that California represents the "wave of the future," the cutting edge of change and innovation in American society. Other observers see the "California phenomenon" as an intensified reflection of the national psyche, a mirror magnifying our awe of the smooth, new

and fast—and also our conflicts about that. Politically the state veers in bewildering shifts between progressive liberalism and jaw-clenching conservatism. Protectors of its matchless scenery vie with development schemes that often subvert the quality of the attraction. From California's spiritual growth centers have emerged new, humanistic options and aspirations for social living—at the same time that a new materialism treated brains as the highest market commodity for space-age industry. California is not unique in manifesting these kinds of paradox but simply exaggerates them more, as it has ever since 1849.

Long before the gold rush, California was the mission preserve of Spain, which established its claim in 1602. Colonization began much later, in 1768; by 1823, Franciscan fathers, notably Junípero Serra, had founded a chain of 22 coastal religious settlements along El Camino Real, the King's Highway (closely traced today by U.S. Highway 101). San Diego, founded in 1769 and today the state's second largest city, is considered the "birthplace" of California, though San Jose is the oldest incorporated city (1777). Russian colonizers built Fort Ross near Jenner in 1812 but withdrew in 1841. Mexican ownership, from 1822, ended with the Mexican War in 1847, and California became U.S. territory the next year. Two years later, it entered the Union as the 31st state, with Sacramento named capital in 1854. Railroads and agriculture brought waves of migrants; but the automobile dramatically influenced settlement patterns after 1920, giving rise to some of the country's largest, best-known suburbias.

The highest point in the nation outside Alaska is Mount Whitney, only 85 miles from the lowest and hottest point—Death Valley National Monument. Between California's mountainous Coast Range and the Sierra Nevadas stretches the Central Valley, 400 miles long and now the core of the state's agriculture. The state is the nation's third largest in area. California's varied landscapes include several separate "countries." The Mother Lode gold country, the Wine country, the Russian and Feather River country, the Desert, Big Sur and Eastern Sierra countries each provide a distinctive facet. North of Fresno, the state is largely forested, mountainous, cool and wet. Southern California is warm dry, urban and industrial.

California notables have spiced, enriched and occasionally disgraced our national history.

Natives included people of such diversity as William Randolph Hearst, Jack London, Marilyn Monroe, George Patton, John Steinbeck and Earl Warren. Two Californians during infancy only were poet Robert Frost and political leader Adlai Stevenson. But many more eminent people achieved fame in the state than were born there. Well-known Californians born elsewhere included scientists Luther Burbank, Lee De Forest, and J. Robert Oppenheimer; writers Zane Grey, Bret Harte, Eugene O'Neill, Upton Sinclair and Robert Louis Stevenson; industrialists Howard Hughes and Henry J. Kaiser; President Herbert Hoover; and the entire roster of America's best-known screen performers. Filmland residences, the nation's most lavish during Hollywood's "golden age," at first aped the palaces of Long Island gentry on America's opposite coast. Soon, however, they exploded into competitive styles of grandeur, ersatz adobe and Mediterranean villa crowning hilltops that resembled feudal domains. Though some of these structures survive, most are no more accessible to the public than they ever were. For years, a popular Hollywood tourist pastime has been "viewing the stars' homes," either by taking guided bus tours or by following often overpriced and inaccurate maps sold on street corners. The main attractions of this shirttail show business, however, are homes of today's "living legends," not those of their deceased predecessors—though many current performers do own or occupy dwellings of late Hollywood "greats." Two engaging accounts of residential Hollywood are Charles Lockwood's *Dream Palaces* (1981) and Richard Lamparski's *Lamparski's Hidden Hollywood* (1981). *Literary L.A.* (1981) by Lionel Rolfe provides interesting personal sidelights on California writers.

San Francisco produced and lodged many notable persons, but few homes predating the 1906 earthquake and fire survive today. City markers do identify some of their sites.

In proportion to the huge number of notables who lived in California, the quantity of homes displayed to the public is small when contrasted to most other states. Typically, the opulence of a few preservation efforts seems like an effort to outweigh the numerical deficiency, an exchange somehow characteristic of this immensely sensational state of paradoxes.

NOTE: The following communities mentioned in the text are located in the Los Angeles area:

Altadena	Monrovia
Avalon	Newhall
Bel Air	Newport Beach
Beverly Hills	North Hollywood
Brentwood Heights	Pacific Palisades
Canoga Park	Pasadena
Cheviot Hills	San Gabriel
Encino	San Juan Capistrano
Glendale	San Marino
Hawthorne	Santa Monica
Highland Park	Sylmar
Hollywood	Tarzana
Holmby Hills	Van Nuys
Long Beach	West Hollywood
Malibu	West Los Angeles
Mar Vista	Westwood
Mission Valley	Woodland Hills

BARA, THEDA (1890–1955). "Kiss me, my fool!" she commanded in her most famous subtitled line. According to Fox Studio, the sultry "vamp" of silent films was the illegitimate daughter of a French artist and an Arabian princess; her name meant "Arab Death." Actually she was Theodosia Goodman from Cincinnati. By 1918 audiences had started giggling, and her career was over. Her **Los Angeles** home from 1915 to 1919 was the Tudor mansion at 649 West Adams Blvd.—now a Roman Catholic rectory. Several notable Hollywood figures lived there after she sold the house, including comic actor Roscoe "Fatty" Arbuckle, director Raoul Walsh, executive Joseph M. Schenck and actresses Miriam Cooper and Norma Talmadge.

In later years, as the wife of British film director Charles Brabin, Theda Bara lived at 632 North Alpine Drive, **Beverly Hills,** still a private dwelling dating from 1927.

(See Chapter 2, MANHATTAN.)

BARRYMORE, ETHEL (1879–1959). From 1946 to 1950, the actress resided in **Palos Verdes Estates** at 1501 Chelsea Road (privately occupied).

Her last home, from 1958, was a duplex apartment at 135½ South Linden Drive, **Beverly Hills,** where she died. This dwelling also remains private.

(See Chapter 3, NEW YORK, PENNSYLVANIA.)

BARRYMORE, JOHN (1882–1942). The youngest and best-known of the Barrymore acting trio destroyed his career with alcohol and ended by doing pathetic film and radio caricatures of himself. His first **Los Angeles** address was the Ambassador Hotel, where he occupied a luxurious suite with his pet monkey Clementine in 1927 (see the entry on F. Scott Fitzgerald later in this section).

Barrymore owned one of the film colony's most lavish estates during his prime years. In 1927 he acquired a five-room, Spanish-style house formerly owned by director King Vidor on Tower Road, **Beverly Hills.** Barrymore soon enlarged his "Belle Vista" estate to seven acres and built another two-story, castlelike hacienda nearby. He joined this "Marriage House," with its tower hideaway, to "Liberty Hall," the former Vidor home, by a grape arbor. By 1937 Barrymore's estate numbered 16 buildings. He spared no expense on antique furnishings, art treasures, shrubs and rare trees, gardens, pools and a bowling green, skeet range, zoo and large aviary. His daughter Diana described Belle Vista as "a little village, a hacienda of buildings with red tiled roofs, iron grilled windows, and gardens." Fiercely jealous of his third wife, actress Dolores Costello, Barrymore had iron bars installed on the windows of "Marriage House" to prevent other men from "molesting" her. They divorced in 1935; and the estate, already declining from neglect, became an unkempt parody of former elegance. Barrymore began selling off his treasures for a fraction of their worth and finally declared bankruptcy in 1937. The estate he then called "that Chinese tenement" was put up for auction, but it never sold during his lifetime. Barrymore's home, as well as the aviary of his estate at 1400 Seabright Place, survive as private residences. He lived with his fourth wife, Elaine Barry, at 1020 Benedict Canyon Drive (privately owned) in 1936 and 1937.

One of their last homes (1937–40) was the secluded, two-story house they called "La Vida Nueva" at 11000 Bellagio Road, **Bel Air.** Barrymore bought this house in 1937 and lived there until 1940.

Between marriages, Barrymore was a frequent resident at the **West Hollywood** Garden of Allah (see the entry on the Garden of Allah later in this section), where he habitually fell into the pool.

(See Chapter 2, MANHATTAN; also Chapter 3, PENNSYLVANIA.)

BARRYMORE, LIONEL (1878–1954). The eldest, most versatile Barrymore sibling was not only a popular character actor but also a composer and writer. Crippled by arthritis in his later years, he played crusty, wheelchair-bound roles but was probably best known for his annual Christmas Eve radio portrayal of Scrooge in Dickens's *Christmas Carol.* His home from about 1924 to 1937 was 802 North Roxbury Drive, **Beverly Hills.** After his wife, Irene Fenwick Barrymore, long an invalid, died in 1936, Barrymore moved to the home of friends in Chatsworth but kept the Beverly Hills house as a shrine to her. "I did not want to live in it again," he wrote, "and I could not accept the idea of anyone else living in it." Ultimately, however, he sold it for tax purposes, and it remains privately owned.

(See Chapter 3, PENNSYLVANIA.)

BENCHLEY, ROBERT CHARLES (1889–1945). Critic, humorist and comic actor, Benchley's gentle satire found its largest audience in more than 40 film shorts on such subjects as *How to Sleep* (1935). From 1927 until his death, his frequent **West Hollywood** residence was the Garden of Allah, where he occupied various bungalows and became the enclave's most constant lodger (see the entry on the Garden of Allah later in this section).

(See Chapter 2, MANHATTAN; also Chapter 3, NEW YORK.)

BENÉT, STEPHEN VINCENT (1898–1943). The boyhood home of the author-poet was the Commandant's Quarters at **Benicia** Arsenal, which his father commanded from 1905 to 1911. Established as an infantry base in 1849, the post was deactivated in 1963. Twenty-one structures dating from 1854 to 1884 survive in what is now Benicia Industrial Park, a 252-acre remnant of the 2,200-acre barracks and arsenal complex at the foot of M Street, Army Point. Dating from 1860, the two-story, frame Commandant's House does not admit visitors. The fate of these buildings was uncertain in 1982.

(See Chapter 1, CONNECTICUT; also Chapter 2, MANHATTAN; also Chapter 3, NEW YORK, PENNSYLVANIA; also Chapter 5, GEORGIA.)

BENNY, JACK (1894–1974). The archetypal miser who remained 39 through decades of vaudeville, radio and television comedy was one of the century's most popular performers. In 1937 Benny built his home at 1002 North Roxbury Drive (privately owned) in **Beverly Hills,** a handsome, two-story brick mansion where he lived until 1966. "Gee, it sure is a long way from Waukegan," he often marveled when looking at the house.

From 1966 to 1969, Benny and his wife Mary Livingstone occupied a suite on the top floor of the Century Towers Apartments, 2220 Avenue of the Stars, **Los Angeles.**

Benny's last home, from 1969, was a private address in **Holmby Hills,** where he died.

(See Chapter 4, ILLINOIS.)

BEVERLY WILSHIRE HOTEL This 445-room structure at 9500 Wilshire Blvd. (at the corner of Rodeo Drive), **Beverly Hills,** was a favorite temporary lodging for Hollywood actors and actresses making films. By staying there, they did not have to commute from their outlying homes to meet rigorous early schedules at their studios. Among others who often bunked there were Clark Gable and Spencer Bonaventure Tracy (see the entries on Gable and Tracy later in this section). This 1926 structure has been called a "hybrid version of an Italian Renaissance villa."

BIERCE, AMBROSE GWINNETT (1842–1914?). The author occupied a number of California lodgings from 1867 to about 1912, but few survive. In **San Rafael,** the acerbic journalist roomed during 1870 and 1871 in a house of frame and shingle at 814 E St. while commuting to his San Francisco job on the *News Letter.* This house, built in 1868, recently burned down.

Bierce is also said to have used a studio apartment on the top floor of the private mansion at 737 Buena Vista West, **San Francisco,** probably about 1898 when it was new.

(See Chapter 4, INDIANA.)

BOGART, HUMPHREY DEFOREST (1899–1957). At intervals during and between marriages from 1935 to 1945, the tough-guy film star who became a cult hero after his death resided at the **West Hollywood** Garden of Allah (see the entry on the Garden of Allah later in this section), where his violent physical fights with third wife Mayo Methot and surreptitious courtship of actress Lauren Bacall achieved Hollywood notoriety.

Following his 1945 marriage to Bacall, the couple resided in **Beverly Hills** at 2707 Benedict Canyon

Drive until 1946.

Bogart's last home from 1946 was 232 South Mapleton Drive in **Holmby Hills.** "Bogey" died there after a long illness. Both homes remain privately owned.

(See Chapter 2, MANHATTAN.)

BOW, CLARA GORDON (1905–1965). Hollywood's famous "It Girl," she of the bee-stung lips, Clara Bow had a strong Brooklyn accent that virtually ended her film career by 1931, when sound came to the movies. Her home from about 1926 to 1931 was 512 North Bedford Drive (privately owned), **Beverly Hills,** a one-story, seven-room bungalow with pink stucco walls. She filled her house with Chinese furnishings, art objects and males, singly and in groups. "In her dark-red Chinese den," wrote Charles Lockwood, "she entertained dozens of men, among them Eddie Cantor, Gary Cooper, Bela Lugosi, and the eleven-man starting lineup of the University of Southern California football team, including tackle Marion Morrison, later named John Wayne."

At the **West Hollywood** Garden of Allah, during the early 1930s, she was courted by actor Roland Young, among others (see the entry on the Garden of Allah later in this section).

Her last home from the 1950s was a small stucco house at 12214 Aneta St. (privately owned), **West Los Angeles.**

(See NEVADA in this chapter; also Chapter 2, BROOKLYN.)

BRADLEY, OMAR NELSON (1893–1981). Gen. Bradley, World War II field commander, later chief of staff, and one of the few U.S. soldiers to wear the highest rank of general of the army, lived in **Beverly Hills** during his postwar business career with the Bulova Watch Co. from the 1950s to 1977. His home at 1720 Carla Ridge remains privately owned.

(See TEXAS in this chapter; also Chapter 3, PENNSYLVANIA; also Chapter 4, MISSOURI; also Chapter 5, GEORGIA, VIRGINIA.)

BRECHT, BERTOLT (1898–1956). The German Marxist playwright, director and drama theorist lived in **Santa Monica** through World War II. In 1941 and 1942 he lived at 817 25th St.; and from 1942 to 1947, at 1063 26th St. Both of these two-story frame dwellings remain privately owned.

BRUCE, LENNY (1926–1966). "His house was exactly like his nightclub act," wrote biographer Albert Goldman, "a record—in brick, stucco, wood, glass, and paint—of the endless flux of Lenny's fantasy life, becoming eventually a two-storied allegory of his soul." In 1960 the satirist and foremost practitioner of "black humor" bought his **Hollywood** "House on the Hill," shaped like a box and walled with glass, at 8825 Hollywood Blvd. (privately owned) for $65,000. He landscaped the acreage and continually renovated inside and out to convert his property to the image of his latest brainstorm. Ravaged by legal problems, drug addiction and powerful self-destructive urges, Bruce died there after a heroin overdose.

(See Chapter 3, NEW YORK.)

BURBANK, LUTHER (1849–1926). From 1875 the plant wizard made his permanent home in **Santa Rosa,** an area he carefully selected for its climate and soil properties, and there created hundreds of new fruit, vegetable and flower varieties through grafting and genetic experimentation. The small, two-story frame house he built from 1880 to 1884 stands on one and one-half acres in his four-acre gardens at 200 Santa Rosa Ave. (at the corner of Sonoma Avenue) along with the greenhouse he designed. Burbank's widow resided there until her death in 1977. The City of Santa Rosa operates Burbank House and Memorial Garden National Historic Landmark. Visitors may observe many growing examples of the species that Burbank cultivated there, along with family furnishings and memorabilia. (Gardens open daily 8:00–6:00, free; house open last weekend of April–mid-October, Tuesday–Sunday 12:00–3:30; 707-528-5195; admission.)

(See Chapter 1, MASSACHUSETTS; also Chapter 4, MICHIGAN.)

BURROUGHS, EDGAR RICE (1875–1950). The prolific pulp novelist and creator of "Tarzan" became a permanent California resident in 1919. That year, flush with writing success, he bought "Mil Flores," the 550-acre estate of Los Angeles publisher Harrison Gray Otis and named it "Tarzana Ranch." Otis had built his Spanish-style mansion on a 15-acre hilltop in 1911. Burroughs added a ballroom, garage and riding quarters and lived there until 1924, when he subdivided the land and sold 120 acres. The mansion leased from

Burroughs was adapted as a clubhouse in 1925 by the El Caballero Country Club; Burroughs occupied it again from 1930 to 1932, but it was later razed. His concrete-walled ballroom, however, survived and became the core of the present private mansion on the site at 18320 Tarzana Drive, **Tarzana.** The estate is now occupied by the commercial Cedar Hill Nursery, growing ornamental plants.

During the breakup of his marriage in 1935, Burroughs rented a house at 806 North Rodeo Drive, **Beverly Hills,** and stayed there until 1939; a previous occupant was singer-actor Maurice Chevalier. It remains privately owned.

The author's final home, from 1945, stood at 5465 Zelzah Ave. in **Encino.**

(See Chapter 4, ILLINOIS.)

CAPONE, ALPHONSE "AL" (1899–1947). From 1934 to 1939, the Chicago ganglord resided in California at federal expense, but he didn't enjoy his surroundings. Capone occupied a 9- × 5-foot cell at the end of the second tier ("B" Block) at **Alcatraz,** the island penitentiary for incorrigibles. Called "the Rock" for its stark isolation in San Francisco Bay, Alcatraz also hosted numerous other noted criminals including Alvin "Creepy" Karpis, Robert Stroud ("Birdman of Alcatraz"), George "Machine Gun" Kelly and Mickey Cohen. The U.S. Army, which established a fortification there in the 1850s, later used Alcatraz as a military prison and prisoner-of-war camp. Converted to a federal prison in 1934, it remained in service until 1964, when it became too costly to maintain. Only about 250 prisoners resided there at any one time; and over its 30 years of service, only 1,576 convicts lived there. During his confinement, the vicious Capone, convicted for income tax evasion, declined to premature senility, the result of neglected syphilis. By the time of his release, he was long past being a threat to anybody. In 1969 about 100 representatives of 78 native American tribes occupied the abandoned island and claimed it as their rightful territory. The last of the protesters were ejected in 1971, and in 1973 the crumbling fortress was opened to the public. Now part of Golden Gate National Recreation Area, Alcatraz is operated in unrestored condition by the National Park Service, which conducts two-hour tours. (Open daily 9:00–3:00, extended summer hours; reservations recommended one month in advance for May–

September, two weeks for October–April; 415-546-2805; admission.)

(See Chapter 2, BROOKLYN; also Chapter 4, ILLINOIS, WISCONSIN; also Chapter 5, FLORIDA.)

CARMICHAEL, HOAGLAND HOWARD "HOAGY" (1899–1981). The composer whose "Stardust" (1929) became one of the most popular songs of all time, Carmichael started out as a lawyer but soon turned to music. He lived in California from the 1940s, and all of his homes remain privately owned. His 1941 residence was 626 North Foothill Drive, **Hollywood.**

A home from later in the 1940s remains at 10281 Charing Cross Road, **Holmby Hills,** a one-story ranch house built about 1940 on two and one-half acres. "Compared to some over-ornate Hollywood houses," wrote Carmichael, "our place was Dogpatch."

During the 1950s and 1960s, he occupied a penthouse suite atop the office building at 9126 Sunset Blvd., **Beverly Hills.**

One of Carmichael's last homes, which he occupied from about 1950, was "Thunderbird Ranch," located on grounds of the Thunderbird Country Club at 40-267 Club View Drive, **Rancho Mirage.**

He spent his last years at 10250 Moorpark St. in **North Hollywood.**

(See Chapter 4, INDIANA.)

CARNAP, RUDOLF (1891–1970). The German-born philosopher made his final residence from about 1954 in the Los Angeles area, where he taught at the University of California until his retirement in 1962. His home at 11728 Dorothy St., **West Los Angeles,** remains privately owned.

(See Chapter 4, ILLINOIS.)

CHAPLIN, SIR CHARLES SPENCER "CHARLIE" (1889–1977). Gifted actor, director and producer, the British pantomimist became one of the biggest names in motion pictures, a comic genius and the first real "star" in the popular sense. His "Little Tramp" silents and such later masterpieces as *The Gold Rush* (1924), *Modern Times* (1936) and *Monsieur Verdoux* (1947) became film classics that still play to immense audiences. Harassment over his controversial political views and unconventional personal life finally drove him to 1952 exile in Switzerland, depriving the

nation of probably its greatest film artist. Old and harmless by 1972, he returned briefly to accept a ridiculously belated Academy Award.

Chaplin rented cheap rooms in Los Angeles when he arrived in 1915. In 1918 he and his 16-year-old bride, Mildred Harris, moved into the large mansion at 2010 De Mille Drive (privately owned) in **Hollywood.** When their child died soon after birth, "it became a sad house," wrote Chaplin, and the couple had separated by 1920. This house later held offices and guest rooms for Cecil Blount DeMille, who lived next door (see the entry on DeMille later in this section). Chaplin moved into 1416 North La Brea Ave., the studio-bungalow where he made all of his films from 1918 to 1940, now the headquarters of A&M Records. He also rented an East Indian-style "castle" at 6147 Temple Hill Drive (privately owned). Actresses May McAvoy and Mary Astor were later residents there.

In 1920 and later he also often lodged in an upstairs bedroom at "Pickfair," the lavish **Beverly Hills** estate of his friends and business partners Douglas Fairbanks and Mary Pickford (see the entries on Fairbanks and Pickford later in this section). In 1922 he finally built his own two-story, yellow stucco home, a 40-room Spanish-style mansion at "Cove Way," a six-acre plot at 1085 Summit Drive. The son of London slums was a notorious pinchpenny, however, especially during those years when many astute observers predicted that motion pictures were only a fad. Chaplin's false economies extended to the construction and contents of his house. His visitors tolerated decrepit furniture or none at all, mattresses on the floor and bare pipes in the shower stall. To save money, he had studio carpenters erect the house, and they built it like a studio set. It soon became known as "Breakaway House" for its tendency to shed doorknobs, lose fixtures and groan in its floorboards. Chaplin lived there through the tumultuous three years of his marriage to actress Lita Grey. Caring nothing about the Hollywood obsession for palatial homes to reinforce a screen image, he rarely entertained guests after his 1927 divorce. This remained Chaplin's home with succeeding wives Paulette Goddard and Oona O'Neill until his 1952 departure from the United States. For all of its apparently short life expectancy when built, Breakaway House has survived while many of the later homes built around it have not. It remains privately owned.

CLEMENS, SAMUEL LANGHORNE "MARK TWAIN" (1835–1910).

During his brief venture as a gold prospector in 1864 and 1865, the later author-humorist panned with a pal near **Tuttletown.** They got no gold, but Clemens expertly mined the experience for his book *Roughing It* (1872). The Mark Twain Cabin, a replica, stands on the site of their endeavors one mile west of town on State Highway 49. (Open daily; free.)

Exhibits: Two miles south of **Angels Camp** on State Highway 49, the Calaveras County fairground becomes "Frogtown" each year in late May, when the International Jumping Frog Jubilee commemorates the 1865 tale by which Clemens achieved his first national fame—"The Celebrated Jumping Frog of Calaveras County" (contact Calaveras County Chamber of Commerce, San Andreas, CA, 95249). Clemens reputedly heard the tale at the bar of the Angels Hotel, still at Main and Bird streets (see the entry on Bret Harte later in this section).

(See NEVADA in this chapter; also Chapter 1, CONNECTICUT; also Chapter 2, BRONX, MANHATTAN; also Chapter 3, NEW YORK; also Chapter 4, IOWA, MISSOURI.)

COBB, TYRUS RAYMOND "TY" (1886–1961).

A later residence of the "mean old man of baseball," one of the game's greatest hitters and base stealers (892), remains privately owned at 48 Spencer Lane in **Atherton,** his home from 1957. Cobb apparently divided his time between this two-story, Spanish-style house and homes in his native Georgia.

(See Chapter 3, NEW YORK; also Chapter 5, GEORGIA.)

COLE, NAT KING (1919–1965).

The musician and popular singer bought his 12-room Tudor mansion at 401 South Muirfield Road, **Los Angeles,** in 1948. When area residents pointedly expressed that they wanted no "undesirables" invading the neighborhood, the black showman said, "Neither do I. And if I see anybody undesirable coming in here, I'll be the first to complain." Civic harassment involving tax problems almost cost him the estate in 1951, but Cole weathered the bad times and remained there until his death. The house remains privately owned.

(See Chapter 5, ALABAMA.)

COOPER, GARY (1901–1961).

The lean, laconic film actor who made a cliche of understatement, Cooper lived with his parents in **Hollywood** at 7511 Franklin Ave. (privately owned), a Spanish-style house, from about 1926 to 1929, the first years of his acting career. He shared quarters from 1929 to 1931 in the Spanish house at 1826 Laurel Canyon Blvd. with actress Lupe Velez, the "Mexican spitfire." Cooper also rented the house at 1919 Argyle Ave. from 1930 to 1932.

Cooper's final home from 1954 remains privately owned in **Los Angeles,** built after his own design at 200 North Baroda Drive.

(See MONTANA in this chapter.)

CROSBY, HARRY LILLIS "BING" (1903–1977).

The popular crooner who recorded more than 1,600 songs was also an accomplished film actor, millionaire businessman and avid golfer. Crosby resided in the Los Angeles area from about 1930. His first home in the Toluca Lake area of **North Hollywood** dates from the early 1920s and remains privately owned at 4326 Forman Ave. There Crosby and his wife Dixie Lee began their large family and lived from 1930 to 1933. A feature of the house was a stained-glass front window displaying the lead notes of Crosby's theme song, "Where the Blue of the Night." The 20-room, two-story, colonial frame house that Crosby built on four acres at 10500 Camarillo St. was their home from 1933 to 1943. Fire razed this mansion when lights on the Christmas tree shorted in 1943, destroying many of Crosby's trophies and personal record collection.

Crosby lived at 594 South Mapleton Drive, **Holmby Hills,** from 1944 to 1964.

His two-story home in **Pebble Beach** overlooking the Pacific Ocean, stands near the 13th hole of the Pebble Beach Golf Club. In *Call Me Lucky* (1953), Crosby wrote that his sons liked to mingle outside with tourists, uttering such comments as "Wouldn't you think that Crosby would have a better house!" and "They say the guy who lives there is a terrible tightwad." He later sold the house.

Crosby's final home, from 1964, was a 25-room Tudor mansion, built in 1929, in **Hillsborough.** During the 1974 Patricia Hearst kidnapping, Crosby surrounded his estate with an eight-foot iron fence and electronic security systems; the Hearsts were Crosby's neighbors, and he feared "Symbionese liberation" of his own family. The estate remains privately owned at 1200 Jackling Drive.

(See IDAHO, NEVADA, WASHINGTON in this chapter.)

DEAN, JAMES BYRON (1931–1955). The young actor whose death in an auto crash propelled him to cult heroism in the 1950s, Dean roomed in several lodgings, all privately occupied. He lived in the Sigma Nu House at 601 Gayley Ave. in **Westwood** around 1950 as a graduate student at UCLA until expelled for punching a fraternity brother.

In **Hollywood,** he resided during the early 1950s at the Gower Plaza Hotel, 1607 North Gower St. While filming *East of Eden* in 1954, he roomed in the apartment building at 3908 Barham Blvd. directly across the street from Warner Brothers Studio, where the film was made.

(See Chapter 2, MANHATTAN; also Chapter 4, INDIANA.)

DE FOREST, LEE (1873–1961). Electronics genius whose inventions ushered in the modern age of telecommunications, De Forest lived and worked in **Palo Alto** from 1911 to 1913. The new cottage he bought in 1911 remains privately owned at 1301 Bryant St.

De Forest's permanent home from 1930 stands privately owned at 8190 Hollywood Blvd. in **Hollywood.**

Exhibit: A historical marker at 913 Emerson St. denotes the **Palo Alto** site of De Forest's Research Laboratory, where he devised the first vacuum tube amplifier and oscillator. The structure itself was razed in 1979.

The Space Science Center on the Foothill College campus at 12345 El Monte Road, **Los Altos Hills,** displays personal memorabilia of De Forest. (Open Thursday–Friday 9:00–4:30, Sunday 1:00–4:30; 415-948-8590; admission.)

(See Chapter 4, IOWA, NEBRASKA; also Chapter 5, ALABAMA.)

DeMILLE, CECIL BLOUNT (1881–1959). DeMille came to **Hollywood** in 1913, rented a barn studio at the southeast corner of Selma Avenue and Vine Street and there directed Hollywood's first feature film, *The Squaw Man* (1914), for the Jesse L. Lasky Feature Play Company. His first Hollywood home (1913–14) was a small, rented house at 6136 Lexington Ave., where he shared quarters with

the prairie wolf that appeared in scenes of the film. In 1916 DeMille joined two 1914 houses to create his final home at 2000 DeMille Drive. DeMille was one of the first of the Hollywood film colony to live in the grand manner befitting a large income, and his colleagues and stars soon emulated his lifestyle. Today, reports Charles Lockwood, DeMille's Spanish-style mansion, though somewhat declined, is maintained exactly as it was when its master reigned there from his comfortable wing chair. Though full of DeMille possessions and memorabilia, the house remains an essentially private memorial to the founder of the "Hollywood spectacular."

Northeast of San Fernando, DeMille bought the 600-acre ranch he called "Paradise," an estate surrounded by wooded hills, in 1916. He used the spread as a working retreat, usually came about twice a month and allowed no telephones or hunting on the property. Located in Angeles National Forest, DeMille Paradise Ranch remains privately owned off Little Tujunga Road near **Cottonwood Glen.**

(See Chapter 1, MASSACHUSETTS; also Chapter 3, NEW JERSEY.)

DISNEY, WALT (1901–1966). A gigantic Hollywood success who raked in a fortune from his development of animated cartoons and later built the giant Disneyland amusement park at Anaheim, the father of Mickey Mouse and Donald Duck resided in California from 1923. His earliest **Hollywood** lodging was his uncle's home at 4406 Kingswell Ave. (privately owned). In the small frame garage at the rear of this property, he began his first Hollywood work. At 4053 Woking Way, he built "Sleepy Hollow Hill," a large luxury mansion, in 1933 and resided there until 1950. Disney carved out his swimming pool there from the mountainside rock. The 1928 "birthplace" of Mickey Mouse was Disney's studio at 2719 Hyperion Ave., no longer standing.

In 1950 Disney built his final home at 355 Carolwood Drive (privately owned) in **Holmby Hills.** He also constructed an elaborate, narrow-gauge railway system over his extensive acreage, calling it the "Carolwood-Pacific Railroad," and enjoyed playing locomotive engineer for his guests.

(See Chapter 4, MISSOURI.)

DREISER, THEODORE (1871–1945). The pioneer

of literary naturalism in his fiction spent his last years in **Hollywood.** A house he occupied at 1426 North Hayworth Ave. in 1939 and 1940 remains privately owned. His final home from 1940 stood at 1015 North Kings Road, a six-room, Spanish-style stucco dwelling that he owned. Condominium apartments have occupied this site of Dreiser's death since about 1966.

(See Chapter 2, BROOKLYN, MANHATTAN; also Chapter 3, NEW YORK; also Chapter 4, ILLINOIS, INDIANA.)

EARP, WYATT (1848–1929). The frontier gambler and gunslinger was a lifelong itinerant but from 1885 resided mainly in California, where he long outlived the "Wild West" and faded away in rootless obscurity. He first came as a boy with his family to **Redlands,** where they settled on the Santa Ana River in the present vicinity of the San Bernardino County Museum, 2024 Orange Tree Lane. Earp hunted game for 20 people in this area from their 1864 arrival to 1868.

His brother Virgil settled in **Colton** in 1887, was elected marshal and built the one-story frame house at 528 West H St. (privately owned) the next year. Wyatt visited at intervals but never lived there himself.

Earp and his wife frequently occupied rented lodgings in Los Angeles and San Francisco during their decades of drifting. Between 1920 and 1929 alone, according to biographer Glenn G. Boyer, they resided at 13 separate addresses, mostly tourist cabins.

The only house they definitely owned was a desert cottage near the Arizona border at **Vidal** (U.S. Highway 95), where they spent winters near Earp's mining properties from 1906 to 1928. Vandals have long since destroyed the dwelling.

(See ARIZONA in this chapter; also Chapter 4, ILLINOIS, IOWA, KANSAS.)

EINSTEIN, ALBERT (1879–1955). From 1931 to 1933 the German-born physicist wintered in **Pasadena.** His first residence (1931–32) stands at 707 South Oakland Ave. Designed by architect Wallace Neff in 1924, this bungalow remains privately owned. Einstein resided during succeeding winters at the Athenaeum, the faculty club dating from 1930 on the California Institute of Technology campus, 551 South Hill Ave. J. Robert Oppenheimer also roomed there at intervals from 1933 to about 1940 (see the entry on

Oppenheimer later in this section).

(See Chapter 3, NEW JERSEY.)

FAIRBANKS, DOUGLAS (1883–1939). The dark, swashbuckling hero of numerous costume epics, Fairbanks was the kind of exhibitionist who liked to turn cartwheels or do pushups at odd times and places. The entire life of the athletic film star apparently consisted of chest-thumping performances of one sort or another. In 1919 he acquired the **Beverly Hills** estate later known as "Pickfair," a six-room hunting lodge built in 1911 on 14 acres—and, as Charles Lockwood wrote, "Beverly Hills was never to be the same again." He immediately set about renovating and enlarging the lodge to two wings and two stories, landscaped the dry grounds and installed a large swimming pool, canoe ponds and a stable. The mansion sat in splendid isolation atop its knoll. As one of the first homes in Beverly Hills, it was also the first filmland "dream palace," soon to be emulated by scores of actors, actresses, directors and producers. Fairbanks married actress Mary Pickford in 1920 (see the entry on Pickford later in this section), and their life there fell prey to the idyllic gaze and breathless prose of fan magazines, which mercilessly ogled every lavish party thrown by "Doug and Mary," at the same time portraying them as "just plain folks." The whole business was, of course, a careful orchestration of studio publicity. A dinner invitation to Pickfair represented the apex of Hollywood success; but Fairbanks also had a special liking for royalty, and a large proportion of European dukedom and crown princelings frequently stopped by, in addition to world celebrities of every stripe (but not hue). Fairbanks lived there until the couple's 1933 separation, so the whole lavish style that was Pickfair lasted little longer than a decade. Neither the largest nor gaudiest of filmland estates, it nevertheless ushered in the new generation of Hollywood status symbols that signified the "golden age" of stardom. Today Pickfair, still privately owned, survives on a 2.7-acre remnant of its original grounds at 1143 Summit Drive.

After 1935 until his death, Fairbanks and his new wife, Lady Sylvia Ashley, lived mostly in Europe but resided occasionally in the two-story stucco beach house he built during the 1920s at Pacific Terrace and Appian Way (privately owned) in **Santa Monica,** where Fairbanks died.

AMERICA'S SWEETHEARTS AT "PICKFAIR." This typical publicity photo of Douglas Fairbanks and Mary Pickford at their lavish **Beverly Hills** estate shows the hilltop house that remains essentially unchanged today. When this photo was posed, about 1922, "Pickfair" represented the apex of Hollywood glamour and success. The Fairbanks-Pickford marriage paralleled America's idolization of the glossy couple, but neither romance lasted much beyond a decade. *(Courtesy Security Pacific National Photo Collection/Los Angeles Public Library.)*

(See Chapter 2, MANHATTAN.)

FIELDS, W. C. (1880–1946). The misanthropic, beet-nosed film comedian "liked houses," wrote biographer Robert Lewis Taylor. "He was forever telling real estate men he was 'in the market for something good,' with the result that they rode him all over Southern California for years, showing him places. The comedian never bought a house, never had any intention of buying one, but he loved to look." The three homes he successively occupied from 1935 to 1946 remain privately owned.

In **Encino,** he rented an estate of five acres and

a Spanish-style dwelling at 4704 White Oak Ave. in 1935. This house, built about 1922, was later occupied by film people Martha Raye, Don Ameche and Roy Rogers. The property has since been subdivided.

Fields next rented the 1928 mansion at 655 Funchal Road in **Bel Air,** where he entertained more frequently from 1938 to 1940 than at any of his other homes. His landlord was not pleased when Fields, who had a phobia about kidnapping, installed heavy bars on the upstairs doors.

In 1940 Fields took a five-year lease on another Spanish-style house at 2015 De Mille Drive in **Hollywood.** He installed his pool table beneath a magnificent chandelier in the living room, regularly inspected his broad lawns and gardens for mythical "trespassers," and even bugged the house with hidden microphones during a period when he swore that the servants were plotting mischief. In severely declining health from years of martini breakfasts and further daily libations, Fields gave up the house in 1946. "I think it's back to the sanitarium for the nonce," he said.

He was referring to a cottage on the grounds of Las Encinas Sanitarium, his last residence at 2900 East Del Mar Blvd. in **Pasadena.** Once before, in 1937, he had undergone a months-long convalescence of several months there; on Christmas Day, 1946, he died.

(See Chapter 3, PENNSYLVANIA.)

FITZGERALD, F. SCOTT (1896–1940). The novelist first came to **Hollywood** in 1927 with his wife Zelda and stayed at the Ambassador Hotel, where they "raised holy hell," according to his later mistress Sheilah Graham. Zelda tried to burn the bed in their suite; then, after making themselves thoroughly obnoxious to the management, they piled all the furniture in the middle of the room and contemplated building a big bonfire. Instead, they left their unpaid bill on the stack and ducked out. The venerable, 500-room Ambassador still hosts less aggressive fun-seekers on its 23 acres at 3400 Wilshire Blvd.

A decade of hard living later, Fitzgerald was almost at the end of his physical and emotional resources. In desperation, he returned to California almost broke and minus Zelda, now hospitalized in a mental institution. Determined to make a literary comeback, he resided at the Garden of Allah, **West Hollywood,** in 1937 and 1938 (see the entry on the Garden of Allah later in this section).

Fitzgerald's last lodgings in 1940 were **Hollywood** apartments. He described the top floor rooms at 1403 North Laurel Ave. as being the least expensive he could find ($110 per month) without looking poor. After suffering a heart attack in November, he shared Sheilah Graham's suite on the ground floor at 1443 North Hayworth Ave. and died there while finishing *The Last Tycoon* (1941). Both buildings, dating from about 1930, still house private apartments.

(See Chapter 2, MANHATTAN; also Chapter 3, MARYLAND, NEW YORK; also Chapter 4, MINNESOTA; also Chapter 5, ALABAMA, NORTH CAROLINA.)

FLYNN, ERROL LESLIE (1909–1959). The Australian-born film actor who refused to take himself or anyone else very seriously appeared in dozens of grade-B swashbucklers that only enhanced his own legend as a world adventurer and voracious lothario. At the Garden of Allah, **West Hollywood,** Flynn resided at intervals from 1935 and between marriages through the 1950s (see the entry on the Garden of Allah later in this section). It was his first American lodging and, with French actress Lili Damita, his first married home. In 1955 and again in 1959, when the furniture was auctioned before the complex was razed, Flynn's beds were the most sought-after items.

During frequent periods of separation from his wife, Flynn and actor David Niven shared the rental of a house owned by actress Rosalind Russell at 601 North Linden Drive, **Beverly Hills.** Flynn lived there at intervals until the final breakup of his marriage in 1941. This privately owned house dates from 1926.

The two actors also rented a beach house at **Santa Monica** during these years, a bungalow that Carole Lombard labeled "Cirrhosis-by-the-Sea." It stood on the grounds of "Ocean House," the lavish estate owned by actress Marion Davies (see the entries on Lombard and William Randolph Hearst later in this section).

In 1942 Flynn built his one-story "Mulholland House" at 7740 Mulholland Drive overlooking the San Fernando Valley, and this remained the scene of his amorous escapades and turbulent marriages until 1955, when financial straits and a court order compelled him to forfeit "the place where girls dropped their panties as easily as others dropped writs through his mailbox," as biographer Michael Freedland wrote. Thereafter Flynn's bases were the Garden of Allah and his island home in Jamaica. Mulholland House remains privately owned and now faces Torreyson Drive, **Los Angeles.**

FRÉMONT, JOHN CHARLES (1813–1890). The soldier and later presidential candidate captured Los Angeles and secured California as national territory in 1847, also acquiring vast estates. Though the 1849 gold rush made him one of the region's wealthiest men, he eventually lost everything and died a near-pauper. His "Rancho Las Mariposas" ("Ranch of the Butterflies"), a land grant of almost 45,000 acres, encompassed today's Mariposa area. Until 1850 Frémont operated a quartz mill just south of Mount Bullion. His home, "The White House," stood in **Bear Valley,** where he lived from 1851 to 1863, the year he lost his ranch holdings. Only foundation stones of the mansion remain at the marked site. Both mill and home sites are located on State Highway 49.

(See ARIZONA in this chapter; also Chapter 3, NEW YORK.)

FROST, ROBERT LEE (1874–1963). So strongly associated with New England that few people think of the poet as a California native, Frost lived in **San Francisco** until age 11. None of his several family homes survive; at least two burned during the 1906 earthquake fire. His probable birthplace was a frame house on Washington Street between Larkin and Polk streets—though 1603 Sacramento St., his home as an infant until 1876, may have been the place. Frost's last California home (1883–85) stood at 1404 Leavenworth St.

(See Chapter 1, MASSACHUSETTS, NEW HAMPSHIRE, VERMONT; also Chapter 4, MICHIGAN; also Chapter 5, FLORIDA.)

GABLE, CLARK (1901–1960). Popular actor known as the "King of Hollywood," Gable lived with his first wife Josephine Dillon at 12746 Landale St., **North Hollywood,** in 1930 and 1931, the period of his first films. He awarded her title to this house in his will.

Gable and his second wife Rita Langham lived at 220 North Bristol St., **Brentwood Heights,** from 1931 to 1935.

From 1935 to 1939, his frequent residence, especially when making films, was the Beverly Wilshire Hotel in **Beverly Hills** (see the entry on the Beverly Wilshire Hotel earlier in this section).

Gable's last home, from 1936, was a 25-acre **Encino** ranch formerly owned by veteran director Raoul Walsh. The actor and his third wife, Carole Lombard, lived together there from their 1939 marriage until her death in a 1942 airplane crash (see the entry on Lombard later in this section). The nine-room house, built of white brick and frame about 1935 and modest by lavish filmland standards, stood in a citrus grove. It was, said Gable, "the first home I've had since I was a boy that I can really call my own." Nevertheless their alfalfa fields, barns and livestock became publicity sets for the studio-created "down home" image of the popular couple; milking cows and gathering eggs, rare occasions for the couple in everyday life, blew into media events. Gable continued to reside there during his last marriages and until his death. Located at 4525 Pettit St., the much enlarged house sold for about $200,000 in 1974, and its surrounding acreage was subdivided into building lots. Today Tara and Ashley Oaks streets—named for Gable's classic film *Gone With the Wind* (1939)—run through the actor's former property, now an expensive housing tract.

All of Gable's homes remain privately owned.
(See Chapter 4, OHIO.)

GARDEN OF ALLAH. This residential complex that stood on three and one-half tropical acres at 8150 Sunset Blvd. in **West Hollywood** achieved the kind of legendary status reserved for the film capital's most spectacular landmarks. Affectionate legend could not, unfortunately, save it, and today no remnant survives except in some well-preserved memories and endless anecdotes about the film stars, writers and musicians who lodged there. Almost all of the best-known actors and actresses of Hollywood's "golden age" called the Garden home at some time during their careers; a complete roster of its notable residents would fill several pages. The Garden of Allah consisted of a large, Spanish-style mansion, behind which stood 25 bungalows arranged around a swimming pool—Hollywood's biggest pool at the time, supposedly shaped like the Black Sea to remind its first owner of her Russian home. She was actress Alla Nazimova, who bought the house in 1918 during the height of her career in silent films.

There she lavishly entertained such stars as Rudolph Guglielmi Valentino, Russian singer Feodor Chaliapin and Italian actress Eleanora Duse, among many others (see the entry on Valentino later in this section). Almost a decade later, when Nazimova sought to provide for her own lifetime security, she converted the estate to a hotel. A company was formed which acquired the lease of the property, built the 25 bungalows and provided a lifetime apartment in the main house for Nazimova. She was forced to sell the property because of unpaid bills and taxes in 1928 but resided in the genteel poverty of her upstairs apartment until her 1945 death. On January 9, 1927, the Garden formally opened with an 18-hour party, most of Hollywood's biggest names in attendance. "In the thirty-two-year span of its life," wrote Sheilah Graham, "the Garden would witness robbery, murder, drunkenness, despair, divorce, marriage, orgies, pranks, fights, suicides, frustration and hope. Yet intellectuals and celebrities from all over the world were to find it a convenient haven and a fascinating home." Among the Garden's longtime or frequent dwellers were Robert Benchley, Humphrey Bogart, Errol Flynn, John Barrymore, Dorothy Parker, George Kaufman, F. Scott Fitzgerald, and many others (see the entries on each of these residents in this section). "The Garden of Allah," wrote Graham, "was the Algonquin Round Table [of New York City] gone west and childish." Though a deluxe hotel, its informal, strongly communal atmosphere of live-and-let-live attracted some of America's most notably individualistic temperaments. Producer Jed Harris said it "was always on the verge of being a glorified whorehouse, a place where a man could have a girl." After 1945 the Garden began its long, money-losing decline, undergoing patchwork renovation and three succeeding changes in ownership before a savings and loan company bought it for a building site in 1959. A "last blast" was held in August 1959, just before demolition, with many of the 1,000 guests impersonating the glamorous stars that had once cavorted there. "It had been a nonstop party from start to finish," wrote Graham. Her book *The Garden of Allah* (1970) fondly reminisced about this scene of so much Hollywood fun and games. A miniature encased reproduction of the Garden complex is displayed on the site.

Today the Garden's lavish, renovated barroom of 1956, its contents removed intact in 1959, survives in Ye Little Club, 455 North Canon Drive, **Beverly Hills.**

GARLAND, HAMLIN (1860–1940). From 1930 until his death, the author who long outlived the American "middle border" of his numerous books resided at 2045 De Mille Drive (privately owned), **Hollywood.** Garland enjoyed walking; in his later years, according to one observer, he became "a familiar sight pacing along De Mille Drive—a phenomenon in that land of motor transport."

(See Chapter 2, MANHATTAN; also Chapter 4, ILLINOIS, IOWA, SOUTH DAKOTA, WISCONSIN.)

GERSHWIN, GEORGE (1898–1937). The composer's last rented home, from 1936, stands privately owned at 1019 North Roxbury Drive, **Beverly Hills.**

(See Chapter 2, BROOKLYN, MANHATTAN.)

GETTY, JEAN PAUL (1892–1976). One of the world's richest men, the oil magnate and art collector considered his longtime **Los Angeles** family mansion his home base from 1907 to about 1941. The Tudor-style mansion stood at the present site of the 1974 St. Basil's Roman Catholic Church, 637 South Kingsley Drive (at the corner of Wilshire Boulevard).

Getty's **Santa Monica** beach house at 270 Ocean Front remains privately owned.

In 1945 Getty bought 65 acres along the beach at **Malibu** and built his Spanish-style "Ranch House" on the estate. After its 1948 completion, this became Getty's permanent U.S. home, though he lived mainly at his mansion in England. A major project of the billionaire's later years was the art museum he created on this estate to showcase the huge collection of his lifetime. A portion of Getty's house served as the first museum until 1974 when the present $16-million replica of a Roman villa opened (see *Exhibit* below). Getty never visited the new museum himself but supervised all acquisitions and endowed it with the bulk of his fortune, making it the largest-endowed art institution in the nation if not the world. His home on the estate is now closed to the public.

Exhibit: The J. Paul Getty Museum is located at 17985 Pacific Coast Highway, **Malibu.** (Open June 11–mid-September, Monday–Friday 10:00–5:00; mid-September–June 10, Tuesday–Saturday 10:00–

5:00; parking reservations one week ahead; 213-454-6541; free.)

(See OKLAHOMA in this chapter; also Chapter 2, MANHATTAN; also Chapter 4, MINNESOTA.)

GOLDWYN, SAMUEL (1882–1974). The Polish-born glove salesman, who became one of Hollywood's most powerful executives, made the first American feature film—*The Squaw Man* in partnership with Jesse L. Lasky and Cecil B. DeMille, in 1913—at the site of Lasky's Feature Play Company "barn," on the southeast corner of Selma and Vine streets, Hollywood. In 1932 Goldwyn bought two lots on the still-vacant slopes above Sunset Boulevard in **Beverly Hills** overlooking Coldwater Canyon. The design of the large, two-story colonial mansion that arose at 1200 Laurel Way (privately owned) was a source of contention between Goldwyn and his wife. She finally saw it through to completion after he declared himself too busy to argue about it.

GREY, ZANE (1875–1939). In 1920 the prolific "Western" novelist bought a two-story, Spanish-style house dating from 1906 on five acres at **Altadena.** He added a third floor and a two-story wing and resided there until his death, which also occurred there. Grey did virtually all of his writing after 1928 in his study on the third floor there. The house remains privately owned at 396 East Mariposa St.

His summer home, a massive hilltop castle called "Zane Grey Pueblo," stands at **Avalon,** Santa Catalina Island. Grey built this structure in 1924 after a Hopi Indian model. Now an expensive hotel, it hosts guests in pleasant accommodations at 199 Chimes Tower Road.

(See ARIZONA in this chapter; also Chapter 2, MANHATTAN; also Chapter 3, PENNSYLVANIA; also Chapter 4, OHIO.)

GRIFFITH, DAVID LEWELYN WARK (1875–1948). A pioneer motion picture director, the hawk-faced Griffith developed many aspects of film technique, creating a score of stars and laying the foundation for the entire industry. He was shunted aside after 1930—because of his "sentimental Victorian outlook," according to Leslie Halliwell—and never made another film. Griffith was mostly a "hotel vagabond" throughout his adult life and preferred it that way. From 1912, however,

he often resided at his San Fernando ranch, where he also made many of his films. Until the 1970s it stood on the marked site at the northeast corner of Vaughan Street and Foothill Boulevard in **Sylmar.**

In **Hollywood** during the early 1940s, Griffith occupied a suite at the Hotel Roosevelt Hollywood, 7000 Hollywood Blvd., a structure dating in its original portion from about 1931. His last home, from 1947, was the Hollywood Knickerbocker Hotel (now the Hollywood Knickerbocker Apartments) at 1714 North Ivar Ave.

(See Chapter 5, KENTUCKY.)

HARDING, WARREN GAMALIEL (1865–1923). The 29th U.S. president, returning from a trip to Alaska and apparently aware of scandals in his administration that would soon become public knowledge, spent his final days at the landmark Palace Hotel in **San Francisco.** Stricken with illness, Harding checked into the hotel with his entourage on July 29. The bedridden president died of an apparent heart attack on August 2 in Suite 8064—though rumors of poisoning and the lack of an autopsy fed sinister speculations for many years. Now the Sheraton Palace Hotel at 639 Market St., this 600-room structure is the second hotel on the site; the first Palace, opened in 1875, burned during the 1906 earthquake.

(See Chapter 3, DISTRICT OF COLUMBIA; also Chapter 4, OHIO.)

HARDY, OLIVER NORVELL (1892–1957). "Another fine mess!" was a frequent line of the fat, fuming member of the classic film comedy team of Laurel and Hardy. Unlike Stan Laurel (see the entry on Laurel later in this section), "Babe" Hardy considered himself primarily an actor who played comedy rather than a comedian as such. From about 1927 to 1929, he resided in the 1927 house at 621 North Alta Drive (private), **Beverly Hills,** with his second wife Myrtle Lee. Between marriages (1929 to 1940), Hardy occupied a rented suite in the Beverly Wilshire Hotel (see the entry on the Beverly Wilshire Hotel later in this section).

Hardy's ranch on two and one-half acres at 14227 Magnolia Blvd. in **Van Nuys** was his home from 1940 to 1956. There he raised poultry and hogs but made pets of them all, so the "ranch" was hardly an income operation. It remains privately owned.

He died at the home of his mother-in-law at 5421 Auckland Ave. **North Hollywood.**

(See Chapter 5, GEORGIA.)

HARLOW, JEAN (1911–1937). The "blonde bombshell" achieved renown for numerous tough-gal film roles, became a huge box-office attraction and was widely imitated for her platinum hair, wisecrack mannerisms and spectacular wardrobe. Her personal life, governed by unscrupulous parents and the conflict of her glamorous image with a basic disinterest in sex, became another Hollywood tragedy too real for fiction. At the beginning of her career, Harlow moved her family entourage into an expensive new home she rented in 1931 at 1535 Club View Drive (privately owned), **Westwood.**

The tragic outcome of her disastrous second marriage to film executive Paul Bern occurred in **Beverly Hills.** Bern's home, where the couple married and lived for two months in 1932 before his apparent suicide, remains privately owned at 9820 Easton Drive.

Late in 1932, Harlow built her two-story, white brick home on a hilltop lot at 214 South Beverly Glen, **Bel Air.** One observer called the house "an ice cream confection." Harlow let her mother do most of the decorating and resided there until her 1933 marriage to cinematographer Harold Rosson; and again after their 1934 separation until financial problems forced her to sell the mansion in 1935.

During the year of her marriage to Rosson (1933–34), the couple lived in an apartment on the third floor at the Chateau Marmont hotel complex, built about 1925 and still standing at 8221 West Sunset Blvd., **West Hollywood.**

In 1936 Harlow rented her last home, a two-story house at 512 North Palm Drive, **Beverly Hills.** There, afflicted with a kidney ailment apparently resulting from a savage beating by Bern, she declined into a coma, long kept from the medical treatment that would have saved her by "Mama Jean" Bello, her faith-healing mother. This house later became the first married home (1941–42) of singer-actress Judy Garland. It remains privately owned.

(See Chapter 4, MISSOURI.)

HART, MOSS (1904–1961). The last home of the playwright, stage director and screenwriter remains privately owned at 467 Via Lola in **Palm Springs.** Hart had moved there from New York City only two weeks before his sudden death.

(See Chapter 2, MANHATTAN; also Chapter 3, PENNSYLVANIA.)

HART, WILLIAM SURREY (1870–1946). A leading cowboy actor of silent films, Hart built his 1928 Spanish colonial ranch house in **Newhall** after his retirement, naming it "La Loma de Los Vientos." The original log ranch house dates from about 1910. Hart wrote his autobiography and several other books before he died there. "While I was making pictures," he said, "the people gave me their nickels, dimes, and quarters. When I am gone, I want them to have my home." Accordingly he willed his 253-acre "Horseshoe Ranch" and Western art collection to the public. Operated by the Los Angeles County Department of Parks and Recreation, William S. Hart County Park at 24151 North Newhall Ave. offers a picnic area plus tours of Hart's home with its original furnishings, art and historical artifacts. (Park open daily 10:00–8:00; home open Wednesday–Friday 10:00–3:00, Saturday–Sunday 10:00–5:00; 805-259-0855; free.)

Hart's home earlier in his film career, a two-story shingled dwelling at 1581 DeLongpre Ave. in **Hollywood,** is occupied by The Actors Studio.

HARTE, BRET (1836–1902). His tales of California mining camps brought this author to public attention. In 1857, after a period of working odd jobs and wandering, he settled at **Arcata,** where he wrote for a weekly newspaper. His editorial denunciation of an atrocity in which some 60 peaceful Indians were massacred by a band of white vigilantes forced his exodus from the town in 1860. Harte's frame house, enlarged in 1905, dates from the 1850s and stands privately owned at 927 J St. This is probably his only surviving residence in the state.

Earlier, from 1854 to 1857, he lived at intervals with his mother and stepfather in **Oakland.** The Bret Harte Boardwalk at 567-577 Fifth Street marks the vicinity of the parental home site.

Exhibits: **Angels Camp** and the "southern mine district" were the scenes of Harte's best-known stories. This area extends along State Highway 49 from Auburn south to Sonora. Angels Camp Museum on the highway displays memorabilia of the goldmining camps and tools used by pros-

TWO VIEWS OF HEARST'S "ENCHANTED HILL." "La Casa Grande," the main mansion built by William Randolph Hearst at **San Simeon,** surmounts his lavish hilltop estate like the temple to riches that it was and still is. The aerial view shows Hearst's giant "Neptune Pool" and guest houses in the foreground below the castle. These views date probably from the 1930's.
(Courtesy California Dept. of Parks & Recreation.)

pectors. (Open Thursday–Monday 11:00–5:00; 209-736-2963; admission.)

Calaveras County Museum at 30 North Main St. in **San Andreas** also exhibits historic items relating to the people and places that Harte described. (Open Memorial Day–Labor Day, Tuesday–Sunday 10:00–4:00; Labor Day-Memorial Day, hours irregular; 209-754-4203; admission.)

(See Chapter 2, MANHATTAN; also Chapter 3, NEW JERSEY.)

HEARST, WILLIAM RANDOLPH (1863–1951). A California native, the founding "Chief" of the Hearst publishing empire built enormous political muscle from his sensationalistic news treatment and circulation gimmicks. He is said to have almost singlehandedly aroused public support for the needless Spanish-American War through falsified reporting and slanted editorials. Few American industrialists have rivaled his personal power before or since—or so cynically and effectively manipulated public opinion. He also probably spent more for personal housing and decoration than any person in history. "At sixty," wrote biographer W. A. Swanberg, "Hearst was the

nearest approach to a Lancaster or a Burgundy in the democratic United States." A compulsively acquisitive art collector, Hearst had trouble finding space for the tons of statuary, furnishings and other pieces he obtained—many of which he never saw—in vast, random sprees of buying out entire shops and museums. In 1919 Hearst began construction of "La Cuesta Encantada" ("The Enchanted Hill"), his massive towered castle at **San Simeon,** as a palace for his treasures. His father had acquired some 48,000 acres of this area, an old Spanish grant called the "Piedra Blanca Ranch," in 1865. The elder Hearst built a large ranch house on the sea slope in 1878 and raised Hereford cattle; and the son employed architect Julia Morgan to follow his own design ideas for an "elegant, yet comfortable" castle on this site. Three palatial "guest houses" were completed first, and by 1923 Hearst began using parts of the finished complex for conferences. Begun in 1922, the twin-towered main castle, "La Casa Grande," built of concrete with limestone facing, stood in ornate splendor by 1930. With more than 100 rooms, an 83-foot assembly hall, 31 bathrooms and two libraries, the structure was never really completed; as Hearst acquired more warehouse-loads of art, he expanded and added chambers and wings for as long as he lived. In addition to the buildings, he enlarged his land holdings to about 240,000 acres; elaborate terracing and landscaping revised the former ranch-land hilltop into broad gardens, arboretums, a zoo and lawns. Hearst entertained hundreds there in his role of medieval potentate, and invitations to his lavish parties for political, business and entertainment figures were prized as royal edicts. Actress Marion Davies, his longtime mistress and protege, shared his baronial lifestyle there. In 1940 the U.S. War Department bought 164,000 acres of the barony for troop training grounds, leaving a mere 75,000. Hearst closed up "the Ranch," as he always called it, for two years in 1942 in order to save money and because it was feared that Japanese submarines might shell the estate from the bay. Old and ailing, he left it for the last time, weeping, in 1947. W. A. Swanberg estimated that the publisher had spent at least $30 million on San Simeon. "The Casa Grande offended classicists," wrote Swanberg, "because of its extravagant presumption, its hodge-podgery of art and architecture, its violence to tradition, its excesses in decoration. But it suited Hearst perfectly."

After Hearst's death, the huge castle complex presented a gigantic white elephant for his heirs. Too expensive for the Hearst Corporation or the University of California (to which he had willed it) to maintain, the State of California accepted it in 1957, with some misgivings, as a gift along with 123 surrounding acres. Tourist interest more than justified this decision, and the operation today (Hearst-San Simeon Historical Monument) is self-supporting. Today, visitors ushered in 90-minute tour groups of 40 by California Department of Parks and Recreation guides may view such Hearst treasures as a mosaic tile floor laid in 60 BC at Pompeii; the elaborate bed of Cardinal Richelieu; and roomfuls of furnishings and art objects from ancient temples, Spanish monasteries and English castles. Along with everything else, forests of statuary and two immense swimming pools plus herds of grazing animals will give some visitors pause to consider the newsstand transaction. Of Hearst himself, however, only a few forlorn items of dress are displayed in his own gothic suite. "La Casa del Sol," one of the guest houses, suffered heavy damage in a 1976 bomb blast apparently set off by a group involved in the kidnapping case of Patricia Hearst, the publisher's granddaughter. Visitors need more than a day there to digest all three tours offered. A feature of one tour is an interesting "home movie" showing Hearst as castle host. Hearst-San Simeon State Historical Monument is located off State Highway 1 about one mile east of San Simeon village. (Open June 1–August 31, daily 8:00–4:00; September 1–May 31, 8:30–3:30; reservations recommended, Ticketron, PO Box 26430, San Francisco, CA, 94126; 805-927-4621; admission.)

In order to have a residence closer to his increasing involvement with Hollywood film society, Hearst built a $7-million beach house compound at **Santa Monica** for Marion Davies in 1928. It became known as "the Versailles of Hollywood," consisting of five connected, colonial-style houses containing 110 rooms. The three-story central house was reserved for the couple, while other buildings held Davies relatives, guests and servants. Again, Hearst added and redecorated constantly. As at San Simeon, he imported entire antique rooms, including an Elizabethan pub for the mansion. A marble swimming pool of 110 feet lined one side, and 750 feet of Pacific beachfront spanned the other. Costume parties hosting 2,000 guests were not uncommon. "Guests were not selected for their prestige or wealth," wrote Swanberg, "but because they were likable or diverting, and the entertainments there were apt to be joyous and unconventional." Davies sold the estate for a paltry $600,000 in 1946, and the compound became the Ocean House Hotel, which failed after a few years. As another white elephant, all structures except a servants' wing were razed, despite protests, in 1956. Its site became a state-owned parking lot, but many of its period interiors and furnishings were acquired by film studios for sets. The surviving servants' wing is now part of the Sand and Sea Club at 415 Palisades Beach Road. Columns in front of the building at 9370 Santa Monica Blvd. in **Beverly Hills** were once part of "Ocean House."

Hearst's last home from 1947 was large and comfortable though considerably more modest than his castle. Marion Davies chose the three-story Spanish house of pink stucco at 1007 North Beverly Drive (privately owned) in **Beverly Hills** and moved some of Hearst's San Simeon statuary there to make him feel at home; eight acres, a high wall and armed guards surrounded the estate. The enfeebled Hearst gradually retired to his bedroom on the second floor, rallying occasionally to dictate instructions as in the old days to his editors, and died peacefully there at age 88. Marion Davies, immediately disavowed by the Hearst family, married Capt. Horace Brown and resided there until her own death in 1961. The later president John F. Kennedy and his bride, Jacquelyn Bouvier, spent part of their 1953 honeymoon there as guests of the actress.

In **Hollywood,** Hearst also rented a full floor at the Ambassador Hotel (see the entry on F. Scott Fitzgerald earlier in this section) from about 1926 for his frequent use.

(See Chapter 2, MANHATTAN; also Chapter 3, DISTRICT OF COLUMBIA.)

HITCHCOCK, SIR ALFRED JOSEPH (1899–1980). The pudgy English-born film director noted for his mastery of suspense and his mock-ghoulish manner, Hitchcock first rented, then bought a hillside dwelling in **Bel Air,** his home from 1939. The privately owned mansion at 609 St. Cloud Road (also given as 10957 Bellagio Road) was the former residence of Carole Lombard (see the entry on Lombard later in this section). Hitchcock died there.

HOOVER, HERBERT CLARK (1874–1964). The 31st U.S. president, a longtime California homeowner, built "San Juan Hill," his **Palo Alto** residence, in 1918. His wife Lou Henry Hoover had selected the site at 623 Mirada Ave., and she also helped design the two-story Mission Revival mansion. After assuming the presidency in 1929, Hoover was rarely there but made periodic visits until Lou Hoover's death in 1944, when Hoover gave the house to Stanford University for its President's Home. As such, it remains privately occupied.

Earlier, the Hoovers had intended to make their "geographical anchor" in **Monterey** with Lou Hoover's parents. But Hoover's peripatetic career prevented them from settling for any extensive stays during the period 1902 to 1907. This house remains privately owned at 600 Martin St.

Exhibit: The 280-foot Hoover Tower on the Stanford University campus at **Palo Alto** houses the Hoover Institution on War, Revolution and Peace. A collection of documents dedicated in 1941 by Hoover, the ex-president, pertain to the study of world conflict. There is also a display of Hoover memorabilia. (Open Monday–Saturday 10:00–12:00, 1:00–4:00, Sunday 1:00–4:00; 415-497-1754; admission.)

(See OREGON in this chapter; also Chapter 2, MANHATTAN; also Chapter 3, DISTRICT OF COLUMBIA; also Chapter 4, IOWA; also Chapter 5, VIRGINIA.)

HUGHES, HOWARD ROBARD (1905–1976). Where was Hughes? Usually in "San Limbo," a euphemism devised by his employees for "unknown." Even his chief lieutenants often didn't know the whereabouts of the industrialist, aviator and film producer they worked for. His reclusive tendencies gradually boxed him into an eremitic existence shared only by caretakers, drugs and nostalgic films. The billionaire lived at 211 Muirfield Road (privately owned), **Los Angeles,** during the 1930s, but he also kept additional city houses through his California years, mostly for 2:00 AM business conferences and secret dates with actresses. All of these dwellings, it is said, were arranged alike inside so that wherever he was, Hughes would know the locations of light switches, appliances and furnishings.

In **Beverly Hills,** he often occupied a bungalow for $100 per day in the 1911 Beverly Hills Hotel complex, 9641 Sunset Blvd., where he had a special chef assigned; this was probably his most frequent residence until his 1957 marriage to actress Jean Peters. The 1946 plane crash from which he never fully recovered occurred at 803–805 North Linden Drive.

In 1961 the couple occupied a hilltop French chateau, still privately owned and gated, at 1001 Bel Air Road, **Bel Air.**

Hughes rented a new mansion in 1958 at **Rancho Santa Fe** and occupied it at intervals for seven years. Built in "ancient fortress modern," according to one biographer, it remains on the private drive La Entrada.

Exhibit: The "Spruce Goose," Hughes' controversial wooden seaplane which he designed and piloted on its only flight in 1947, was intended as a prototype for use as a troop carrier in World War II, but the war ended before it was finished. Until his death, Hughes spent about $60 million to keep the plane in mint condition in case he might take a whim to fly it again. "If Mr. Hughes heard anyone call it the Spruce Goose," said longtime aide Phil Schmaeling, "he'd send them out to wash out their mouth with soap." The plane, actually constructed of laminated birch plywood covered with fabric and no spruce at all, measures 210 feet with a 320-foot wingspan and eight engines. After several years of litigation following Hughes' death, the massive aircraft went on public display in 1982 in **Long Beach** harbor. There, 35 years before, Hughes had coaxed it only 70 feet above the water. The exhibit, operated by the Wrather Corp., is housed in a domed hangar near the docked *Queen Mary,* approached via the Queen's Way Bridge off Ocean Boulevard or by the Long Beach Freeway (State Highway 7). (Call 213-435-4747, extension 1205, for admission information.)

(See NEVADA, TEXAS in this chapter.)

HUXLEY, ALDOUS LEONARD (1894–1963). The English novelist made his permanent home in California from 1939. Most of his California homes have been replaced by apartment dwellings or condominiums.

From 1945 to 1949 Huxley and his first wife occupied a small wooden dwelling built about 1920 as a forest ranger station at **Wrightwood.** The house, enlarged twice since then, stands privately owned at 1036 State Highway 2. Huxley wrote *Ape and Essence* (1948) there.

His last residence from 1961 stands privately owned at 6233 Mulholland Highway, **Los Angeles.** In this home of a friend, Huxley declined and died of cancer on the same day that President Kennedy was assassinated. Ever curious about mind-enhancing drugs, Huxley was given an LSD injection at his own request just hours before his death.

JARRELL, RANDALL (1914–1965). The influential poet and critic spent much of his boyhood (ca. 1920s) in **Long Beach.** His family home at 1819 East Fourth St., built about 1920, now houses private apartments.

(See TEXAS in this chapter; also Chapter 3, DISTRICT OF COLUMBIA; also Chapter 4, OHIO; also Chapter 5, NORTH CAROLINA.)

JEFFERS, ROBINSON (1887–1962). The somber poet who wrote of earth's endurance and humanity's "brief stain" on the globe, Jeffers occupied several California homes that survive, all privately owned. His boyhood home at 346 North Ave. 57 in **Highland Park** (1903–05), built

by his father, is currently a rental dwelling owned by Highland Park Guest Homes.

The poet's **Pasadena** home (1911–14) remains at 822 Garfield Ave.

In **Carmel,** Jeffers lived from 1914 to 1919 at Fourth and Monte Verde streets, still extant. The poet's last home in Carmel matched the cragginess of his face and poetic voice. He is one of the few persons in this book who built much of his dwelling with his own hands. "Tor House," most granite boulders of which he lifted from the Pacific beach, stands privately owned at 26304 Ocean View Ave. He began building the house in 1919, modeling it after an old Tudor barn he had seen in Surry, England. The redwood interior consisted of four downstairs rooms and one large workroom encircling the chimney on the second floor. He added the garage in 1920 and completed "Hawk Tower," the medieval turret incorporating gift stones from all over the world, in 1924. Later he also added a dining room, stone wall and courtyard. He refused to install electricity or a telephone; his stone fireplaces and a Franklin stove in his loft provided heat, and light came from kerosene lamps. "The elegant loneliness of Jeffers's cliffs," wrote Stephanie Kraft, "is now almost impossible to recreate even in the imagination, crowded as that part of Carmel is today by beautiful but densely set homes." Tor House remains in the Jeffers family and remains as it was when the poet died there. *The Stone Mason of Tor House* (1966), by Melba Berry Bennett, gives an interesting account. (Contact Tor House Foundation, Inc., PO Box 1887, Carmel, CA 93921, for information on occasional tours; 408-624-1813.)

Exhibit: Occidental College, Jeffers's alma mater at 1600 Campus Road, **Highland Park,** displays material on the poet in its Robinson Jeffers Room at Clapp Library (213-259-2640).

(See WASHINGTON in this chapter; also Chapter 3, PENNSYLVANIA.)

JOLSON, AL (1886–1950). In 1935, the entertainer born Asa Yoelson who made the first sound-film feature—*The Jazz Singer* in 1927—built his home with wife Ruby Keeler at 4875 Louise Ave. in **Encino.** Jolson remained there until 1945; actor Don Ameche later resided in the house, and Jolson bought it back before he died. It remains privately owned.

From 1945 to 1948, Jolson lived at 12101 Mulholland Drive (privately owned), **Los Angeles.**

Jolson's last home from 1948 stands at 570 Via Corta St. in **Palm Springs,** a one-story, private ranch house on spacious grounds.

KAISER, HENRY JOHN (1882–1967). The home of the portly entrepreneur who built an industrial empire was 664 Hadden Road (privately owned) in **Oakland.** Built in 1923, the house underwent almost constant renovation and enlargement during the dynamic Kaiser's long-time ownership.

(See HAWAII in this chapter; also Chapter 3, NEW YORK.)

KEATON, JOSEPH FRANK "BUSTER" (1895–1966). The deadpan film comedian, a master clown whose career sharply dived after sound movies arrived in 1930—but who enjoyed a minor comeback during the 1960s—Keaton occupied several rented Los Angeles mansions after his 1921 marriage to actress Natalie Talmadge.

In 1925 Keaton built a 20-room Italian-style villa on three acres on Hartford Way, **Beverly Hills,** just behind the Beverly Hills Hotel. "It took a lot of pratfalls," Keaton told his friends, "to build this dump." Keeping up appearances seemed vital to a star of Keaton's stature, though the financial strain was severe. He installed a large electric train set and a huge drape by which he swung from upstairs to the living room. Quail roamed the grounds, a trout stream flowed by switch and Keaton entertained crowds of guests at his notable Sunday barbecues. All of this ended with his declining career, increasing alcoholism and 1932 separation from his wife. Natalie Keaton sold the house in 1933. Later this mansion became the home of heiress Barbara Hutton. Today, privately owned, it survives at 1018 Pamela Drive off Hartford Way.

Keaton's home from 1933 to 1942, down-and-out years for him, was a much smaller place he owned at 3151 Queensbury Drive (privately owned) in **Cheviot Hills.**

From 1942 until about 1960, Keaton lived in the area west of **Mar Vista** at 1043 Victoria Ave. (privately owned), a one-story, nine-room house he had bought for his mother in the 1920s.

Keaton's last home, a one and one-half-acre "ranch," stands privately owned on Sylvan Way in **Woodland Hills.**

KENNEDY, ROBERT FRANCIS (1925–1968).

Exhibit: On June 5, 1968, the senator and 1968 presidential aspirant fell by an assassin's bullets just after he had spoken at the celebration of his primary election victory in the Embassy Room of the Ambassador Hotel, **Los Angeles.** Five people besides Kennedy were wounded in the shooting, which occurred in the serving kitchen on the ground floor behind the Embassy Room; but only Kennedy died, a day later. A small memorial plaque marks the spot (see the entry on F. Scott Fitzgerald earlier in this section).

(See Chapter 1, MASSACHUSETTS; also Chapter 2, BRONX; also Chapter 3, DISTRICT OF COLUMBIA, NEW YORK; also Chapter 5, FLORIDA, VIRGINIA.)

KERN, JEROME DAVID (1885–1945). The composer of numerous stage musicals and some of the best-known popular songs in the world, Kern lived in California from 1936. His last home stands privately owned at 917 Whittier Drive, **Beverly Hills.**

(See Chapter 2, MANHATTAN; also Chapter 3, NEW YORK.)

KEROUAC, JACK (1922–1969). Pop-Zen mystic and primary novelist of the "beat generation," Kerouac recorded the **San Francisco** North Beach scene of the 1950s in *The Dharma Bums* (1958). He lived at 29 Russell St. (privately owned) in 1951 and 1952 with Neal and Carolyn Cassady, writing in the attic. "It rained every day," he recalled, "and I had wine, marijuana, and once in awhile Neal's wife would sneak in." Vesuvio's Cafe at 255 Columbus Ave. was a popular beat hangout. There and elsewhere the beat guise of rebellion took the form, not of quiet meditation, but of a curiously logical extension of American mores—excessive motion and intoxication on several levels.

(See Chapter 1, MASSACHUSETTS; also Chapter 2, MANHATTAN, QUEENS; also Chapter 3, NEW YORK; also Chapter 5, FLORIDA.)

LAUREL, STAN (1890–1965). The partner of Oliver Norvell Hardy in film comedy (see the entry on Hardy earlier in this section), the English-born Laurel (whose real name was Arthur Stanley Jefferson) came to Hollywood in 1917. Despite his screen role as the halfwitted member of the team, Laurel was the brains behind most of their comic films, few of which were scripted. His first owned home (1927–32) stands at 718 North Bedford Drive, **Beverly Hills,** a brick colonial private dwelling. Close neighbors there included actress Marie Dressler and, at 722, actor Adolph Menjou.

The comedian designed and built "Fort Laurel" in **Canoga Park** as "his refuge from 'blondes' and 'ex-wives,' the terms in his case being synonymous," wrote biographer Fred Lawrence Guiles. A high brick wall and large garden there insured privacy with his fourth and fifth wives at 20213 Strathern St., now a private school, where he lived from 1938 to 1946.

"In his last years," according to biographer John McCabe, "Stan lived at the Oceana Hotel, 849 Ocean Ave., **Santa Monica.** He purposely had an apartment with only one bedroom simply to discourage relatives and friends from spending the night. He had had too much of such folk dropping in when he had a big house." Laurel resided at his last balconied address overlooking the Pacific from about 1958. The hotel still functions.

LEE, GYPSY ROSE (1914–1970). The strip-tease artist and author of detective novels, born Rose Louise Hovick, occupied her showplace **Beverly Hills** mansion from 1960. It remains privately owned at 1240 Cerrocrest Drive.

(See Chapter 2, MANHATTAN; also Chapter 3, NEW YORK.)

LLOYD, HAROLD CLAYTON (1894–1971). The bespectacled film comic who appeared in some 500 short comedies and features until his 1938 retirement, Lloyd was a California resident from 1907. He bought a shingled bungalow with his father in 1919 at 369 South Hoover St., **Los Angeles,** and convalesced there after being injured in a bomb accident while making a film. Lloyd lived there until 1923, when he married his leading lady Mildred Davis and occupied a new house at 502 South Irving Blvd. which remains privately owned.

In 1928 the Lloyds moved into "Greenacres," the 40-room Spanish-style mansion surrounding a courtyard on 22 acres at 1740 Green Acres Place off Benedict Canyon Drive in **Beverly Hills.** This estate, with its Olympic-size pool, 12 fountains, formal gardens, waterfall, canoe lake, golf course and staff of 32 was the film colony's largest and most expensive. Lloyd spent over $2 million on his estate. In 1928, when they moved in, they asked each other: "What are we—damn fools?" "By building the movie colony's finest architectural dream palace," wrote Charles Lockwood, "the Lloyds had become trapped by the formidable physical perfection of their enormous estate and by the 'a star has to live like a star' ideal." Nevertheless they stayed. Lloyd spent hours on his various hobbies and actively participated in the Shriners organization; but the estate and its contents slowly declined to genteel shabbiness, and the Lloyds didn't try to maintain or repair it. His Christmas tree, a 15-foot jungle of ornaments, became a year-round adornment when Lloyd found himself "too busy" one year to take it down. Lloyd willed his estate as a museum "for public viewing and scholarly research into the history of the motion picture." The Harold Lloyd Museum opened, but the Lloyd Foundation could not raise the funds necessary for the maintenance of what was then a 16-acre estate; also, residents of the exclusive neighborhood objected to the tourist invasion. The museum closed in 1974; grounds were subdivided into expensive building lots; and the mansion was sold to an Iranian businessman. In 1980 new owners bought and restored the house. Thus, despite its past declines, Greenacres, the biggest "dream palace" of all, survives under private ownership.

(See Chapter 4, NEBRASKA.)

LOMBARD, CAROLE (1908–1942). In 1930 and 1931 the Indiana-born film comedienne lived at 619 North Rexford Drive, **Beverly Hills,** with her mother; she married actor William Powell there.

The couple's **West Hollywood** home from 1931 to 1933 was 1416 North Havenhurst Drive, a Tudor mansion now called "Colonial House." Both dwellings remain privately owned.

Lombard's home from 1936 to 1939, just before she married Clark Gable, stands in **Bel Air** on St. Cloud Road, later the home of Sir Alfred Joseph Hitchcock (see the entry on Hitchcock earlier in this section).

Her last home, with Gable, was their **Encino** ranch (see the entry on Clark Gable earlier in this section).

(See Chapter 4, INDIANA.)

LONDON, JACK. (1876–1916). The prolific author best known for his Yukon tales, a Socialist with

JACK AND CHARMIAN LONDON AT THE "COTTAGE." The author's last home, from 1911, was a farmhouse on the old winery property that formed part of his "Beauty Ranch" near **Glen Ellen**. London died here on his sleeping porch, the one at left.
(Courtesy Russ Kingman).

oddly racist notions and distinctly baronial tastes, London was a California native and lifelong resident. His **San Francisco** birth site at Third and Brannan streets, where his unwed mother roomed in 1876, is marked by a California Historical Society tablet on the Wells Fargo Bank building now occupying the site. The actual site is about 60 feet south of the marker at the exit of the bank's parking lot. The two-story house burned down during the 1906 fire that destroyed the city.

London occupied 22 homes in **Oakland** from 1886 until his death (see Name Index and Gazetteer). Only four survive, all privately owned: at 1639 22nd Ave. when he attended high school in 1895 and 1896; 1645 25th Ave., the two-story home from which he left for the Klondike in 1896; 1914 Foothill Blvd., now an Oakland City Landmark, his home from 1898 to 1900 and the place where he wrote his first published stories; and 360 Palm Ave., the two-story frame house he bought for his mother in 1906, reserving the upper rooms as his frequently used Oakland town house. The last dwelling, now a four-unit apartment house, stood originally at 490 27th St. and was moved to its present location in 1955.

London wrote his best-known novel, *The Call of the Wild* (1903) at 575 Blair Ave. in **Piedmont.** The bungalow he rented in 1902 and 1903 is apparently the same structure which was moved and now houses physicians' offices at 2929 Summit St. in Oakland.

In **Glen Ellen,** Wake Robin Lodge at 4100 Wake Robin Drive (privately owned) was London's home from 1905 to 1911. It remains much as it was when he lived there. The 798-acre Jack london Ranch National Historic Landmark at London State Historic Park near Glen Ellen encompasses the original 130 acres of "Beauty Ranch," his last home. The author eventually owned some 1,400 acres on this scenic spot overlooking the Valley of the Moon. From 1905, when he bought the run-down farm, he spent thousands in restoring the land and trying to make the estate self-supporting through scientific agriculture. In this he never succeeded. He raised a variety of crops and livestock, including hogs and English Shire horses, and planted 150,000 eucalyptus trees. London moved there permanently in 1911, occupying the "Cottage," a small, frame, two-story farmhouse on the property. He enlarged the house, and the room he added on the west served as the study where he turned out most of his last novels and stories. In long-declining health and heavily dependent on drugs, he died on the glassed-in porch there after an apparent overdose of morphine taken for kidney pain. The most poignant sight at London's ranch is the stark, fire-blackened ruin of "Wolf House," the mansion of native stone and redwood begun in 1911 and completed in 1913. It "would last one thousand years," said London; but just 24 hours before he intended to move in, a fire of mysterious origin destroyed the mansion and his dream of years. Arson was strongly suspected but never proved. London vowed to rebuild, but the ruins remained untouched, as they do today. At some distance from both London houses, his widow, Charmian Kittredge London, built her stone "House of Happy Walls" in 1919 and resided there until her death in 1955. Willed as a museum for London memorabilia, it displays much of the custom-designed furniture intended for Wolf House plus

London's recreated study containing his desks and office equipment, his brass bed and miscellaneous items from South Pacific travels. Also displayed are some London manuscripts and a short "home movie" taken on the estate just before his death. The park has recently been expanded to include a walking trail that provides exterior views of London's Cottage, barns and five-acre lake. London Ranch, located one mile west of Glen Ellen at 2400 London Ranch Road, is operated by the California Department of Parks and Recreation. (Open daily, 10:00–5:00; 707-938-5216; admission.)

Exhibits: In **Glen Ellen,** London biographer Russ Kingman is associated with the Jack London Museum, owned by Martin Levy and Carolyn Boccuci at the London Lodge Motel, 13740 Arnold Drive. London's typewriter and other memorabilia collected by Kingman plus rare first editions are displayed. (Open daily; 707-938-8510; free.)

London exhibits in **Oakland** include the Jack London Room of the Oakland Public Library, 14th and Oak streets. In this building where London as a boy accomplished most of his self-education, visitors may see London books, pictures, memorabilia and a film. (Open daily; 415-273-3134; free.) Jack London Square, a commercial section on the waterfront bounded by Broadway, Webster and First streets, was a rowdy, red-light district during London's youthful days as an oyster pirate in these environs. Today the area, refined into shopping-mall dullness, bears little resemblance to the lively place that London knew. Only one building remains—the precariously leaning Heinold's First and Last Chance Saloon, where London was known to tip an elbow—at 90 Jack London Square. The dungeonlike little saloon, surrounded by concrete and subsided below pavement level, looks "forlorn at the party" though it's still open today. Items of musty London memorabilia decorate the walls; Robert Louis Stevenson also "watered" there (see the entry on Stevenson later in this section). (Open daily; 415-832-9933.) London's Yukon cabin is also planted amid the paving at the south end of Jack London Square. The 13-by-13-foot cabin was discovered on Henderson Creek, Yukon Territory, in 1967; London's name, carved on one of the logs, provided the basis for authentication. Half of the cabin went to Dawson City in the Yukon as a London memorial. The other half was restored in 1970 by the Port of Oakland and added to a reconstructed half supervised by the Alaskan Museum. London spent the winter of 1897–98 "holed up" with prospector cronies. They found little gold on Henderson Creek, but from the experience London took a lifetime of background for his Klondike tales. Since its original location was 15 miles from his winter camp, however, the cabin probably hosted him for a matter of days rather than weeks. It was probably not as sturdy then as it is now. Exhibits there include some of the paraphernalia described in his classic story "To Build A Fire" (1911). (Open daily; 415-444-3188; free.)

LOUIS, JOE (1914–1981). At 1171 Wellington Road, **Los Angeles,** the heavyweight boxer lived in retirement from 1957 through the mid-1970s. Louis boasted that his 10-room house, eventually sold when he moved to Nevada, contained nine television sets. It remains privately owned.

(See COLORADO, NEVADA in this chapter; also Chapter 2, MANHATTAN; also Chapter 4, ILLINOIS.)

McPHERSON, AIMEE SEMPLE (1890–1944). "Sister Aimee," the flamboyant, Canadian-born evangelist with a genius for spectacular self-promotion, "liked to remind people that she had arrived in **Los Angeles** with ten dollars and a tambourine," wrote biographer Lately Thomas, "and four years later opened Angelus Temple, built, equipped and paid for." In 1923 she erected a large parsonage adjacent to Angelus Temple in the Echo Park area. This building, her official home, has been converted to office use for the church's LIFE Bible College. It stands at 1800 Park Ave. (at the corner of Lemoyne Street). She usually resided, however, in the private estate located at 1982 Micheltorena St.—hardly the "small cottage" she described.

Sister Aimee also built a large, Moorish-style villa at **Lake Elsinore** in 1929 and used this for her lavish summer retreat from pastoral rigors. Some said it was an odd, heathen-looking thing for a gospel preacher to want, but McPherson seldom cared what folks said about her as long as they said something. She sold it about 1940. It was later operated as "a home for deficient children." In 1982 the stucco palace stood vacant, overlooking the lake on Graham Avenue.

Her last lodging was a suite on the tenth floor at the Leamington Hotel, the 230-room structure still at 19th and Franklin streets in **Oakland,** where she had come to conduct a revival. She overdosed on Seconal and died there; the death was kindly labeled accidental.

Exhibit: The 1923 Angelus Temple, flagship tabernacle of the International Church of the Foursquare Gospel, where the evangelist attracted huge crowds to her opulently choreographed sermons, stands at 1100 Glendale Blvd. in **Los Angeles.** According to Executive Secretary Charles Duarte, "we have not conducted any official tours for some time. However, we are always glad to take visitors through the building." (Office open Monday–Friday 9:00–12:00, 1:00–5:00; 213-484-1100; free or donation.)

MANN, THOMAS (1875–1955). The German novelist, a U.S. citizen from 1944, resided in California throughout World War II. In 1940 and 1941 he built his home at 1550 San Remo Drive in **Pacific Palisades.** There Mann wrote his epochal symbolic novel *Doktor Faustus* (1947) and resided until 1952, when he returned permanently to Europe. The privately owned dwelling remains in excellent condition, but it is hardly visible from the street.

(See Chapter 3, NEW JERSEY.)

MARX, ADOLPH ARTHUR "HARPO" (1893–1964). The Marx Brothers lived in the Los Angeles area from about 1930, when they began making films in Hollywood. Harpo, the mute, frizzy-wigged member of the vaudeville and film comedy team and an accomplished harpist, lived at the Garden of Allah, **West Hollywood,** from 1931 to 1933, his first years in California (see the entry on the Garden of Allah earlier in this section).

His home from 1936 to 1957 was 701 North Canon Drive (privately owned) in **Beverly Hills.** "At the end of the war we enlarged our house," he wrote in *Harpo Speaks!* (1961). "We threw out the butler . . . got rid of all the rest of the Beverly Hills nonsense and converted the dining room into a poolroom."

"El Rancho Harpo," the estate he built in 1957 and his last home, remains privately owned at 71-111 La Paz Road in **Cathedral City.** The house of timber and stucco with two wings at the end of a long lane stands adjacent to the 14th hole of Tamarisk Country Club, where he frequently golfed.

(See Chapter 2, MANHATTAN.)

MARX, JULIUS HENRY "GROUCHO" (1895–1977). The youngest, best-known brother of the frenetic comedy team, Groucho became a popular radio and television performer after the brothers' film career had ended and also authored several books. His caustic verbal ripostes, loping gait, leering eyebrows and ever-present cigar became widely caricatured trademarks of the man who was probably the nation's wittiest humorist. During the 1950s, at the height of his television career, he built his last home, a Spanish-style ranch house in the exclusive Trousdale Estates development at 1083 Hillcrest Road (privately owned), **Beverly Hills.**

(See Chapter 2, MANHATTAN; also Chapter 3, NEW YORK.)

MARX, LEONARD "CHICO" (1891–1961). The address trail of Chico, the eldest brother, pianist and fast-talking con man of the Marx trio, is devious. One of his homes was 123 North Elm Drive, **Beverly Hills.** His last was 409½ Spalding Drive. Both remain privately owned.

(See Chapter 2, MANHATTAN.)

MILLER, HENRY VALENTINE (1891–1980). From 1944 to 1964, the controversial author whose sexually explicit *Tropic of Cancer* (1934) and *Tropic of Capricorn* (1939) led to obscenity trials in the United States as late as the 1960s resided in **Big Sur,** where he wrote, painted and attracted a cult following as the nation's foremost underground writer. The address of his former house, built during World War II, is withheld by the current owner.

Miller's last home, from 1964, stands privately owned at 444 Ocampo St. in **Pacific Palisades.** The interior of the white, two-story Georgian house was described as "a visual feast" when the author lived there, with his array of posters, photos, paintings, tapestries and memorabilia surrounding him. In poor health for years, Miller finally declined to a bedridden existence but never lost his humor and sharp irreverence.

(See Chapter 2, BROOKLYN, MANHATTAN.)

MIX, THOMAS EDWIN "TOM" (1880–1940). An enormously popular cowboy actor of silent films, Mix developed the screen image of the wholesome, viceless hero, setting the stereotype for such later cowboy paragons as the Lone Ranger, Gene Autry and Roy Rogers, among numerous others. After his work day, however, Mix forgot all that and reverted to the earthier existence of the daredevil horse wrangler that he essentially was. The modest **Hollywood** bungalow where he lived from about 1917 to 1922 stands at 5841 Carlton Way. The site of the 60-acre William Fox Ranch, also called "Mixville," where Mix had his own permanent sets and made most of his "oaters," is 2450 Teviot St., now a Los Angeles housing tract.

In 1922 Mix built his dream palace, a two-story, stucco, Tudor mansion at 1018 Summit Drive in **Beverly Hills.** A cheerfully vulgar exhibitionist, Mix slapped his initials like cattle brands on everything he owned and on every part of his six-acre estate—including a neon TM on the roof. His parlor displayed his silver-embossed saddles, large gun collection and numerous trophies. In addition to creating the first movie saint of the range, Mix was probably the first "rhinestone cowboy." He loved jewelry, fancy clothes, expensive Stetsons and flashy cars. His parties there were legendary; on one occasion, roaring drunk, he galloped his horse up the main staircase, whooping and shooting holes in the ceiling. Recent private owners of Mix's last home have "de-Tudorized" the mansion, and all the gaudy TM's have long since disappeared.

(See OKLAHOMA in this chapter; also Chapter 3, PENNSYLVANIA.)

MONROE, MARILYN (1926–1962). The blonde film actress, whose robust physical endowments plus studio "love goddess" publicity gave her a public image she was emotionally unequipped to handle, was a native Californian. Born Norma Jean Mortenson, she lived until 1933 in a foster home at **Hawthorne** with the Bolender family. The house remains privately owned at 4211 West 134th St.

In 1935, after brief interludes in other foster homes, Norma Jean was sent to the Los Angeles Orphans' Home Society called "Hollygrove" when her mother, hospitalized for mental illness, refused to let the child be adopted. "I'm not an orphan!" she screamed, forcing staff members to drag her in. Hollygrove, the old brick complex still at 815 El Centro Ave. in **Hollywood,** established in 1880, was her home until 1937. "When she was finally liberated a few weeks after her eleventh birthday," wrote biographer Fred Lawrence Guiles, "the pattern of her life, a continuing quest for affection that seemed an end in itself, had been set."

In 1952 and 1953 she occupied an apartment at 882 North Doheny Drive (at the corner of Cynthia Street), **Beverly Hills.** She returned there briefly in 1961 and 1962 following her separation from third husband Arthur Miller. During 1960 she and Miller had resided in a large bungalow suite at the Beverly Hills Hotel, their last home together (see the entry on Howard Robard Hughes earlier in this section). Earlier, her home for five months in 1954 as the wife of Joe DiMaggio was the Tudor cottage at 508 North Palm Drive.

Long suicidal in behavior, the barbiturate addict finally met death in her last home, a one-story, Spanish-style "hacienda" dating from about 1930 on an acre lot at 12305 Fifth Helena Drive in **Brentwood Heights.** A 10-foot brick wall insured privacy at the end of the street. "I could never imagine buying a house alone," she said. "But I've always been alone, so why couldn't I imagine it?" She bought the house in early 1962, furnished it with Mexican pieces and resided there alone, except for a housekeeper, during her last months.

(See Chapter 1, CONNECTICUT; also Chapter 2, MANHATTAN.)

MONTEZ, LOLA (1818–1861). Marie Eliza Gilbert, the Irish-born exotic dancer and courtesan who concocted a Spanish ancestry, bewitched such world notables as Alexandre Dumas, Victor Hugo and Franz Liszt. As the Countess of Lansfeld, mistress of Ludwig I of Bavaria, according to one account, she infected him with syphilis, which eventually killed them both. She toured the United States in a stage show based on her legendary exploits, then retired from 1852 to 1854 in **Grass Valley.** Her elegant furnishings, collection of pets (including a bear) and parties for young miners made the town famous. Her modest cottage, restored by a public trust at Walsh and Mill streets, dates from the early 1850s. (Open daily 9:00–5:00; 916-272-6373; admission.)

NIMITZ, CHESTER WILLIAM (1885–1966). From 1948 to 1963, the retired Pacific naval commander of World War II resided in **North Berkeley** at the first home he ever owned. "Longview," his Spanish-style house at 728 Santa Barbara Road, remains privately owned.

The last home of Adm. Nimitz from 1963 was

Quarters One, the commanding officer's large residence made available for him on **Yerba Buena Island** in San Francisco Bay. The public is not admitted to this U.S. Navy Reservation property.

(See TEXAS in this chapter; also Chapter 3, DISTRICT OF COLUMBIA.)

NIN, ANAÏS (1903–1977). The author and diarist, whose lifelong journal of 35,000 handwritten pages chronicled her remarkable artistic growth and career, made her last home in **Los Angeles** at 2335 Hidalgo St. east of Silver Lake Reservoir. Built of natural materials in 1959 by architect Lloyd Wright, the one-level house remains privately owned.

(See Chapter 2, MANHATTAN).

O'NEILL, EUGENE GLADSTONE (1888–1953). Near **Danville,** Tao House National Historic Landmark is the two-story mountainside dwelling built with a tile roof by the playwright in 1937 with his 1936 Nobel Prize money. There O'Neill wrote *The Iceman Cometh* (1946) and *Long Day's Journey Into Night* (1956). "We stayed at Tao House for six whole years," said O'Neill's wife Carlotta Monterey, "longer than we lived anywhere else." O'Neill's deteriorating health forced them to vacate in 1944. The Eugene O'Neill Foundation has long planned to open the dwelling as a theater arts center. Recently the National Park Service presented a draft plan for developing the Eugene O'Neill National Historic Site, proposing three types of use: interpretive tours, creative and educational activities and theater performances. No date has been established for opening the home to the public. Located one and one-half miles west of town at the end of the private Kuss Road, the house remains presently inaccessible to visitors. (Contact Eugene O'Neill NHS, c/o John Muir NHS, 4202 Alhambra Ave., Martinez, CA, 94553; 415-228-8860.)

(See Chapter 1, CONNECTICUT, MASSACHUSETTS; also Chapter 2, MANHATTAN; also Chapter 5, GEORGIA.)

OPPENHEIMER, J. ROBERT (1904–1967). Physicist and "father of the atomic bomb," Oppenheimer later became a scapegoat victim of a postwar witch hunt because of his liberal sympathies. In 1963 President Johnson presented the scientist with the prestigious Fermi Award, certainly an odd honor for one whom the government still officially maintains was a "security risk." Oppenheimer taught for more than a decade at the California Institute of Technology and University of California before heading the Manhattan Project in 1942. At **Kensington,** adjoining Berkeley, he bought the house at 1 Eagle Hill (privately owned) in 1941 and lived there until 1943.

Oppenheimer also resided at intervals in **Pasadena** (see the entry on Albert Einstein earlier in this section).

(See NEW MEXICO in this chapter; also Chapter 2, MANHATTAN; also Chapter 3, NEW JERSEY.)

PARKER, DOROTHY ROTHSCHILD (1893–1967). The short story writer, poet and critic noted for her slashing wit and sometimes bizarre behavior, Parker and her husband Alan Campbell lived at what she called "Peyton Place West," where she worked on screenplays and collected unemployment from 1957 to 1963. The neighborhood of the house at 8983 Norma Place, **Los Angeles,** was the site of a studio owned by actress Norma Talmadge. Campbell died there in 1963.

Earlier (1933–34), Parker occupied a bungalow at the fabled Garden of Allah, **West Hollywood** (see the entry on the Garden of Allah earlier in this section).

(See Chapter 2, MANHATTAN; also Chapter 3, PENNSYLVANIA.)

PATTON, GEORGE SMITH, JR. (1885–1945). The birth site and boyhood home of the flamboyant World War II general is now a private housing tract called Lake Vineyard Patton Estates in **San Marino,** located at Kensington and Euston roads east of Lacey Park. The 13-acre estate where Patton's father also built a 21-room house in 1910 now holds 23 residential lots.

(See Chapter 1, MASSACHUSETTS; also Chapter 3, DISTRICT OF COLUMBIA; also Chapter 5, KENTUCKY, VIRGINIA.)

PERSHING, JOHN JOSEPH (1860–1948). Stationed at **San Francisco** Presidio National Historic Landmark in 1914 and 1915, the later leader of the World War I American Expeditionary Force suffered a tragic loss on August 27, 1915. The two-story frame house built in 1862 that he and his family occupied caught fire, and his wife and three daughters burned to death. Pershing himself was absent at the time. The site of the fire is marked by a 105½-foot flagpole, tallest in the San Francisco area, on Pershing Square south of the main parade ground. The 1,500-acre Presidio, established by the Spanish in 1776, is the headquarters of the U.S. Sixth Army. (Presidio grounds open daily: 415-561-3870; free.)

(See NEW MEXICO in this chapter; also Chapter 3, DISTRICT OF COLUMBIA; also Chapter 4, MISSOURI.)

PICKFORD, MARY (1893–1979). From 1918 to 1920, the actress whose little-girl roles made her immensely popular but also spelled the early end of her career lived with her mother at 56 Fremont Place, **Los Angeles.** The 1916 house remains privately owned.

From 1920 until her death, the actress lived at "Pickfair" in **Beverly Hills,** the estate built by her husband Douglas Fairbanks (see the entry on Fairbanks earlier in this section), becoming increasingly reclusive through remarriage and old age.

POLLOCK, JACKSON (1912–1956). In contrast to his later years in New York, the painter's early life was rootless, and he left few tracks. He had lived in six homes in three states by age 10, but even the precise location of his Cody, Wyo., birthplace remains unknown. One Pollock house has been definitely identified in **Riverside,** where the family resided from 1925 to 1928 and where Pollock attended high school. The one and one-half-story bungalow at 4196 Chestnut St. (a corner address also numbered 3985 12th St.) dates from about 1910. Pollock lived there in 1925; his next two homes in Riverside were demolished for the construction of the Riverside Freeway (State Highway 91). In 1982 the City of Riverside nominated the extant, privately owned house as a local "Structure of Merit."

(See Chapter 2, MANHATTAN; also Chapter 3, NEW YORK.)

PORTER, COLE ALBERT (1893–1964). The lyricist and composer rented the Spanish-style dwelling at 416 North Rockingham Ave. (privately owned), **Brentwood Heights,** from 1935 until his death, occupying it each year from June to October. With an outdoor swimming pool and tennis courts for his frequent guests, wrote biographer Richard G. Hubler, "it was a place of silence, of wide polished floors, glints of metal, and pleasant odors—with his omnipresent grand piano, his lifelong chaperon, dark-shining in a corner." The owner and former occupant of the mansion was actor Richard Barthelmess.

(See Chapter 2, MANHATTAN; also Chapter 4, INDIANA.)

PRESLEY, ELVIS ARON (1935–1977). Beginning his film career in 1956, the singer and actor moved to **Bel Air** in 1960 and, with his "Memphis mafia," successively rented three mansions until 1967. These, all privately owned, included 565 Perugia Way from 1960 to 1965; 1059 Bellagio Road briefly in 1964 ("too much like a mausoleum," he said); and 10550 Rocca Place from 1965 to 1967.

In 1967 he built a huge, multileveled house in the Trousdale Estates subdivision at 1174 Hillcrest Road (privately owned), **Beverly Hills,** but rarely lived there after 1970, spending most of his time at his home in Memphis, Tenn.

He bought another luxurious mansion in 1970 at **Palm Springs.** Though he still owned this estate at the time of his death, he seldom used it. It stands privately owned at 845 Chino Canyon Road.

(See Chapter 5, MISSISSIPPI, TENNESSEE.)

ROGERS, WILL (1879–1935). Humorist, satirist, vaudeville performer and film actor, Rogers lived in California from 1919. The next year he built the first home he ever owned at 925 North Beverly Drive, **Beverly Hills,** a rural area when Rogers settled there. He surrounded his several hilltop acres with an eight-foot brick wall and added stables, a pool and two log cabins. "Willie, you're just like an old fullblood," said his sister Maude, referring to his Cherokee ancestry. "You buy a big house, then build a little cabin at the foot of the hill and live in it." To attract residents to the new community, Rogers was named honorary mayor in 1926. By 1928, however, termites had infested his Spanish-style mansion; Rogers battled them for a while, then in disgust had the entire house razed, resigned as mayor and moved out.

His **Pacific Palisades** ranch was his last home. "Not really a ranch," he said, "but we call it that. It sounds big and don't really do any harm." Rogers bought acreage there in 1921 but occupied the original cabin only on weekends until 1928. In that year, he built the present sprawling, two-story house, incorporating the original one-

story structure as his living room in the left portion of the dwelling. He increased his holdings to 300 acres and installed a stable, corrals, riding arenas, horse trails and a polo field. Visitors may see his large collection of cowboy and Indian artifacts, trophies and curios, placed there by his widow. The California Department of Parks and Recreation operates the estate on 186 of the original acres at Will Rogers State Historic Park, 14253 Sunset Blvd. (Park open May 1–October 31, daily 8:00–6:00; November 1–April 30, 8:00–5:00; house open daily, 10:00–5:00; 213-454-8212; admission.)

(See OKLAHOMA in this chapter; also Chapter 3, NEW YORK.)

ROYCE, JOSIAH (1855–1916). The site of the philosopher's birth in **Grass Valley** is marked at the public library on Mill Street. The young Sierra town had been destroyed by fire just two months before he was born. "It is certainly a coincidence," wrote a local historian, "that a library should have been built at the actual birthplace of this man of high scholastic and literary attainments." Royce lived there until 1866.

(See Chapter 1, MASSACHUSETTS.)

RUSSELL, BERTRAND (1872–1970). While teaching at the University of California at **Los Angeles** in 1939 and 1940, the English philosopher and peace activist rented the two-story house at 212 Loring Ave. (privately owned) just east of the campus.

(See Chapter 3, PENNSYLVANIA.)

SCHOENBERG, ARNOLD (1874–1951). The Austrian expatriate composer lived and taught in California from 1934. His first residence (1934–36) was a rented dwelling at 5860 Canyon Cove (privately owned), **Hollywood.**

Schoenberg's last home, from 1936, was 116 North Rockingham Ave. in **Brentwood Heights.** Built about 1925, the Spanish-style dwelling also remains privately owned. One biographer records that when guides on tour buses pointed out actress Shirley Temple's house across the street (227) and not his, he became incensed at the supposed slight.

(See Chapter 1, MASSACHUSETTS.)

SERRA, JUNÍPERO (1713–1784). The Majorcan Franciscan missionary who established nine California missions between 1769 and 1782, Father

Serra resided for most of those years at Mission San Carlos Borroméo, founded at Monterey in 1770. The following year the mission was removed to **Carmel,** where it survives today as Carmel Mission National Historic Landmark, 3080 Rio Road. The present church was built from 1793 to 1797 and underwent extensive restoration in 1884. Mission relics and some of the priest's books and documents are displayed by the Franciscan fathers. (Open Monday–Saturday 9:30–4:30, Sunday 10:30–4:30; 408-624-9382; free.)

Exhibits: Mission sites established by Father Serra are well-marked along the coastal Mission Trail (U.S. Highway 101). They include the following:

The Serra Historical Museum, Library and Tower Gallery at 2727 Presidio Drive, Presidio Park, **San Diego**—the first site of San Diego de Alcalá, his first Upper California mission (1769). (Museum open Monday–Saturday 9:00–4:45, Sunday 12:00–4:45; 714-297-3258; donation.)

Mission San Diego de Alcalá, 10818 San Diego Mission road, **Mission Valley** (1774). (Visitor center open daily, 9:00–5:00; 714-283-7319; admission.)

Royal Presidio Chapel National Historic Landmark, Mission San Carlos de Borroméo, 550 Church St. (at the corner of Figueroa Street), **Monterey** (mission from 1770; present chapel from 1795). (Chapel open daily 8:00 AM–9:00 PM; 408-373-2628; donation.)

Mission San Antonio de Padua, northwest of **Jolon** off Highway G14 on the Hunter Liggett Military Reservation (1771). (Museum open Monday–Saturday 9:30–4:30; Sunday 11:00–5:00; 408-385-4478; donation.)

Mission San Gabriel Arcángel, Mission and Junipero Serra drives, **San Gabriel** (1798). (Mission open daily 9:30–4:30; 213-282-5191; admission.) The original 1771 site was located in Montebello.

Mission San Luis Obispo de Tolosa, Chorro and Monterey streets, **San Luis Obispo** (1772). (Museum open June 1–Labor Day, daily 9:00–5:00; Labor Day–May 31, daily 9:00–4:00; 805-543-6850; admission.)

Mission San Francisco de Asís (Mission Dolores), Dolores and 16th streets, **San Francisco** (1776). (Museum open May 1–October 31, daily 9:00–4:30; November 1–April 30, daily 9:00–4:00; 415-621-8203; donation.)

Mission San Juan Capistrano, Camino Capistrano and Ortega Highway, **San Juan Capistrano**

(1776). (Mission open daily 7:00–5:00; 714-493-1424; admission.)

Mission Santa Clara de Asís, University of Santa Clara campus, **Santa Clara** (1777). (Building open daily 6:30 AM–9:30 PM during the school year; 408-984-4023; free.)

Mission San Buenaventura, 225 East Main St., **Ventura** (1782). (Museum open Monday–Saturday 10:00–5:00, Sunday 10:00–4:00; 805-648-4496; admission.)

SHERMAN, WILLIAM TECUMSEH (1820–1891). A foremost Union general in the Civil War, Sherman earlier resided (1847–49) in **Monterey** as the chief military officer of California before its statehood. Sherman's Quarters, a small adobe structure on Main Street between Jefferson and Madison streets, is not open to the public.

(See OKLAHOMA in this chapter; also Chapter 2, MANHATTAN; also Chapter 3, DISTRICT OF COLUMBIA; also Chapter 4, MISSOURI, OHIO.)

SINCLAIR, UPTON BEALL (1878–1968). The prolific novelist and political reformer lived in California from 1916. His first **Pasadena** home (1916) survives at 1050 North Hudson St. Later houses at 1497 and 1513 Sunset Ave. were demolished for a freeway.

From 1927 to 1931, one of his most productive periods, Sinclair lived **in Long Beach,** at 10 58th Place, a modest house that remains privately owned.

Sinclair next lived in **Beverly Hills** at 614 North Arden Drive (1931–42), and used the home as the base for his unsuccessful EPIC ("End Poverty in California") gubernatorial campaign in 1934. His Republican opponent was the first candidate ever managed by advertising men, and the campaign became one of the most vicious smear jobs in political history; Sinclair was badly misrepresented, but still took 45 percent of the vote. The mansion remains privately owned.

Sinclair House National Historic Landmark, his home from 1942 to 1967, stands privately owned at 464 North Myrtle Ave. in **Monrovia.** The Spanish-style dwelling of concrete and stucco dates from 1923. He used the concrete double garage for his office and wrote several of his "Lanny Budd" novels there.

(See Chapter 3, DELAWARE, MARYLAND, NEW JERSEY.)

STEFFENS, LINCOLN (1866–1936). The prominent journalist and muckraking political reformer and lecturer spent his early years in **Sacramento.** His only remaining dwelling there is the Governor's Mansion (see the entry on Earl Warren later in this section), purchased by his father in 1888. Steffens himself, however, spent little time there.

Steffens also spent his final decade in the state. His last home, from 1927, became a devoted pilgrimage destination for his many admirers while he lived at **Carmel.** Located 100 yards from the beach, the frame house stands unnumbered but marked on San Antonio Street just southeast of Ocean Avenue and remains privately owned. A feature of the place was the writer's "wild, irregular" garden.

(See Chapter 1, CONNECTICUT; also Chapter 2, MANHATTAN.)

STEINBECK, JOHN ERNST (1902–1968). **Salinas** was first home of the novelist whose *The Grapes of Wrath* (1939) depicted a traumatic era of Southwestern history. The Victorian two-story, 15-room Steinbeck House, built in 1897 and Steinbeck's birthplace and home until about 1925, stands at 132 Central Ave. (at the corner of Church Street). Family memorabilia are displayed by the Valley Guild, which operates the house as a luncheon restaurant. Steinbeck was born in the first-floor front room on the left and eventually occupied the front upstairs bedroom. He wrote parts of *Tortilla Flat* (1935) and *The Red Pony* (1937) there during visits to his parents from 1932 to 1934. (Open Monday–Friday 11:00–3:00, lunch and tours by reservation; 408-424-2735.)

A longtime family cottage, where Steinbeck spent summers from boyhood and completed his first novels, stood at 147 11th St. in **Pacific Grove.** In 1941 he built a new house on Eardley Street; the present owners do not wish to publish the address. Steinbeck seldom went there after 1948.

From 1936 to 1938 the author and his first wife, Carol Henning Steinbeck, lived on a two-acre forested property about two miles west of **Los Gatos.** Steinbeck began work there on his best-known novel. The white, one-story ranch house remains privately owned on Greenwood Lane behind the high picket fence he built for privacy. Final lack of it ("This place is getting built up and we have to move . . . I can hear the neighbors' stomachs rumbling") drove them to a 50-acre ranch a few miles further west off State Highway 17. They lived in the old farmhouse on the property, subsequently a guest house, where Steinbeck finished *The Grapes of Wrath* while their new ranch house arose. By 1940 Steinbeck's marriage was on the rocks and he spent increasing periods away. "I sit upon this beautiful ranch in this comfortable chair with a perfect servant and a beautiful dog and I think I'm more homesick than ever," he wrote, "not for any home I ever had." He abandoned both ranch and marriage in 1941 and eventually sold the property, which remains privately owned in the Santa Cruz Mountains near Alma College.

In **Monterey,** Steinbeck owned and resided in the 1842 Casa Jesus Soto Adobe ("Soto House") at 460 Pierce St. (privately owned) during 1944 and 1945. He wrote *The Wayward Bus* (1947) in this dwelling that he called "a laughing house."

Exhibits: The Steinbeck Room in the John Steinbeck Library, 110 West San Luis St. in **Salinas,** displays a large collection of photos, first editions, manuscripts and memorabilia concerning the author. (Open daily; 408-758-7311; free.) "Steinbeck Country," the 85-mile Salinas Valley between Salinas and King City, formed the locale for many of his novels and stories. Information on self-guided tours identifying specific places may be obtained from the Salinas Chamber of Commerce, 119 East Alisal, Salinas, CA, 93901.

Steinbeck sites in **Monterey** include a marker at Cannery Row and Prescott streets, the once-thriving locale of *Cannery Row* (1945); and the Pacific Biological Laboratories at 800 Cannery Row ("Doc's Lab"), now a private social club.

(See Chapter 2, MANHATTAN; also Chapter 3, NEW YORK.)

STENGEL, CHARLES DILLON "CASEY" (1891–1975). "There comes a time in every man's life and I've had plenty of them," he said in typical Stengelese clarity when he retired. The seamed old wizard of baseball built his **Glendale** home in 1924. His two-story house, to which he permanently returned in 1965, stands privately owned at 1663 Grandview Ave.

(See Chapter 4, MISSOURI.)

STEVENSON, ADLAI EWING (1900–1965). The large, two-story frame house at 2639 Monmouth Ave. in **Los Angeles** was the birthplace and infant home of the diplomat and twice-defeated presidential candidate. Now a privately owned rooming house, it hosted a Stevenson visit during his 1952 national campaign when he addressed a crowd from the front porch.

(See Chapter 2, MANHATTAN; also Chapter 3, DISTRICT OF COLUMBIA; also Chapter 4, ILLINOIS.)

STEVENSON, ROBERT LOUIS (1850–1894). The Scottish author spent about a year in California, where he married Fanny Osbourne in 1880. While waiting for Fanny to obtain her divorce, he roomed and wrote in **Monterey** in the "French Hotel," the two-story adobe house at 530 Houston St., now included in the seven acres of Monterey State Historic Park. Stevenson, ailing and impoverished during the several months of his stay in 1879, enjoyed the town immensely despite his circumstances. The California Department of Parks and Recreation operates the restored dwelling, now called "Stevenson House," and displays period furnishings plus Stevenson exhibits. (Open Thursday–Tuesday 9:00–11:00, 1:00–4:00; 408-649-2836; admission.)

The site of Stevenson's long-gone boardinghouse in **San Francisco** (1879–80) is marked at 608 Bush St.

Seriously ill in the spring of 1880, the author recovered at his fiancee's home, which stood at 554 East 18th St. (on the northeast corner of 11th Avenue) in **Oakland.** The couple later married in San Francisco at 521 Post St., the site of a Presbyterian parsonage.

They honeymooned for two months in the old bunkhouse of an abandoned silver mine on Mount St. Helena (1880), where Stevenson began his book *The Silverado Squatters* (1883). A marker identifies the bunkhouse site in the 3,200-acre Robert Louis Stevenson State Park, eight miles northeast of **Calistoga** on State Highway 29. (Open daily; 707-942-4575; admission.)

Exhibit: One of the world's largest collections of Stevenson memorabilia, including manuscripts, letters, books, personal items and the desk from his last home in Samoa may be viewed at the Silverado Museum, operated by the Vailima Foundation at 1490 Library Lane in **St. Helena.** (Open Tuesday–Sunday 12:00–4:00; 707-963-3757; free.)

(See HAWAII in this chapter; also Chapter 3, NEW YORK.)

STILWELL, JOSEPH WARREN (1883–1946). Leader of U.S. forces in China, Burma and India during World War II, the bespectacled "Vinegar Joe" first viewed the **Carmel** area in 1912. He bought five lots on Carmel Point overlooking the Pacific in 1920 but did not build his permanent home until 1934. Gen. Stilwell spent little time there during the war but resided there from 1945. His widow occupied the estate until her death in 1972. The house remains privately owned but marked on Inspiration Avenue at San Antonio Street.

(See Chapter 1, MASSACHUSETTS.)

STRAVINSKY, IGOR FEDOROVICH (1882–1971). The longtime **Hollywood** home of the Russian-born composer was 1260 North Wetherly Drive, a small, one-story house with a large terrace. Stravinsky bought the house in 1941 and lived there until 1969. It remains privately owned.

(See Chapter 2, MANHATTAN.)

SUTTER, JOHN AUGUSTUS (1803–1880). The German-born California pioneer on whose lands began the Gold Rush of 1849, Sutter established an adobe fort on the 48,000-acre grant he called "New Helvetia" in 1839. By 1845 his ranch supported several thousand head of livestock, and he developed a thriving agriculture, fur trade and private 70-man army. His ranch became a main station for western immigrants and the nucleus of what became the capital city of **Sacramento.** For Sutter, however, the Gold Rush signaled personal disaster; his employees deserted, prospectors swarmed over his property and stole his cattle, and legal machinations swindled him of his land. In 1871 he fled to Pennsylvania, nearly a pauper. Sutter's Fort National Historic Landmark, the restored complex of ranch buildings and defensive structures where he lived until 1850, is operated by the California Department of Parks and Recreation at Sutter's Fort State Historic Park, 2701 L St. Only the two-story central building of oak and adobe is original. Exhibits of Sutter's life there and California pioneer existence are also displayed. (Open daily, 10:00–5:00; 916-445-4209; admission.)

On Garden Highway east of **Tudor** is the marked site of "Hock Farm" (corruption of the German *hohe,* "high"), Sutter's home from 1850 to 1868. His lands encompassed most of what is now southern Sutter County. When gold seekers overran his Sacramento property, Sutter drove all of his livestock to Hock Farm but could not salvage his rapidly depleting fortunes.

Exhibit: Marshall Gold Discovery State Historic Park off State Highway 49 southwest of **Coloma** marks the site where Sutter employee James W. Marshall discovered gold in 1848 at a sawmill on the American River. The preserve of 249 acres, which includes most of the town itself, is operated by the California Department of Parks and Recreation and contains a replica of Sutter's mill plus exhibits relating to Sutter and Marshall. (Open daily 10:00–5:00, longer Memorial Day-Labor Day; 916-622-3470; admission.)

(See Chapter 3, PENNSYLVANIA.)

TRACY, SPENCER BONAVENTURE (1900–1967). The highly respected film actor noted for his short temper but thorough professionalism, Tracy occupied several Los Angeles area homes from 1930. His **Beverly Hills** dwellings included 9191 St. Ives Drive (1950s–60s) and 1158 Tower Road (1960s). While making films, Tracy frequently took rooms at the Beverly Wilshire Hotel (see the entry on the Beverly Wilshire Hotel earlier in this section).

The actor retired to his final lodging ailing and exhausted after completing his last film, *Guess Who's Coming to Dinner* (1967). This rented cottage stands on the estate of his long-time friend, director George Cukor, located at 9166 Cordell Drive (privately owned), **West Hollywood.** Tracy died there.

(See Chapter 4, WISCONSIN.)

VALENTINO, RUDOLPH GUGLIELMI (1895–1926). The Italian-born matinee idol, one of the first film superstars, built an eight-room **Hollywood** house at 6776 Wedgewood Place in 1922 and lived there with his second wife, actress Natacha Rambova. Finding the property too modest for a star of his magnitude, the couple soon sought a larger estate; but Rambova left her husband before he vacated the place called by an auctioneer, after Valentino's death, their "temple of love." The foundation of this house, demolished in 1951 for the Hollywood Freeway (U.S. Highway 101), is visible from the Highland Avenue exit.

In 1925 with the help of his studio, the heartbroken Valentino bought for $175,000 his hilltop "Falcon Lair," named after *The Hooded Falcon*, a script that Rambova had written for him. He completely redecorated the red-tiled, Spanish-style house, built stables and kennels, walled in his eight and one-half acres and landscaped with exotic plantings. The interior with its rich furnishings and expensive antiques, collections of rare books, armor and jewelry, and a massive wardrobe resembled a Florentine nobleman's palace. Much of everything was taupe, his favorite color. Yet, as Charles Lockwood wrote, "by unwittingly turning Falcon Lair into almost a parody of a silent-star's showplace . . . Valentino had created a private compound where he could pursue his hobbies in peace and see his friends outside the public gaze." There the once-penniless immigrant "felt free to be himself, to wear dirty old clothes while he took car engines apart and put them back together again." But the estate virtually bankrupted him. After his death, Falcon Lair remained unsold until 1934, when it went for only $18,000. Today the estate at 1436 Bella Drive in **Bel Air** still survives under private ownership. Valentino's stables, now a private residence, stand nearby at 10051 Cielo Drive.

WARREN, EARL (1891–1974). A longtime governor, also a vice presidential candidate and one of the most influential chief justices in U.S. history, Warren was a California native, born at 457 Turner St. in **Los Angeles.**

His parental family resided at several addresses in **Bakersfield** during Warren's boyhood. The only house that survives is 707 Niles St. (privately owned), the family home from 1907 until Methias H. Warren, his father, was murdered there in 1938.

As district attorney for Alameda County and California's attorney general, Warren occupied two **Oakland** homes, both privately owned; at 958 Larkspur Road (1929–35), which he enlarged; and 88 Vernon St. (1935–43), presently known as Clausen House, a training home for retarded adults.

As governor from 1943 to 1953, Warren occupied the Governor's Mansion State Historical Monument at 1526 H St. (at the corner of 16th Street) in **Sacramento.** This three-story, Victorian gothic mansion, built for local merchant Albert Gallatin in 1877 and 1878, served as the official residence for 13 California governors between 1903 and 1967, including later Senator Hiram W. Johnson and Gov. Ronald Reagan, the last state executive to occupy it. Earlier, this house had been the family home of Lincoln Steffens (see the entry on Steffens earlier in this section). The building, declared unsafe during Warren's residence in 1941, several times verged on being destroyed until restoration was accomplished during the 1970s. Today the California Department of Parks and Recreation displays period furnishings, including many pieces donated by the former governors who occupied it. (Open daily 10:00–5:00; 916-445-4209; admission.)

(See Chapter 3, DISTRICT OF COLUMBIA.)

WAYNE, JOHN (1907–1979). The film actor born Marion Morrison who became a macho American prototype made his home in California from 1910. None of his boyhood homes in Palmdale or Glendale exist except the last of his seven **Glendale** addresses: a four-unit apartment dwelling at 207 West Windsor St. (privately owned). Wayne lived there in 1925 just before starting his film career.

Wayne's longtime estate in **Encino,** from the 1930s to 1966 stands at 14750 Louise Ave. (privately owned).

His last home, the seafront estate he occupied from 1966, remains privately owned at 2700 Bayshore Drive in **Newport Beach.**

(See Chapter 4, IOWA.)

WODEHOUSE, SIR PELHAM GRENVILLE (1881–1975). Humorist and sly satirist of British upper classes in his many novels, P. G. Wodehouse spent several short intervals in Hollywood as a well-paid screenwriter, but his talents remained largely unused. His residence in **Beverly Hills** (1936–37) remains privately owned at 1315 Angelo Drive. Built about 1932, this mansion was owned by food faddist Gaylord Hauser when Wodehouse rented it.

(See Chapter 2, MANHATTAN; also Chapter 3, NEW YORK.)

ZIEGFELD, FLORENZ (1869–1932). The last home of the stage producer, where he moved just before his death, was 2407 La Mesa Drive (privately owned) in **Santa Monica.**

(See Chapter 2, MANHATTAN; also Chapter 3, NEW YORK; also Chapter 4, ILLINOIS.)

COLORADO

The name originated from the Spanish word for "ruddy," the supposed color of the Little Colorado River. Amost a perfect rectangle, Colorado is one of two states delineated completely by lines of latitude and longitude. Great Plains, dominating the east, abut against the Rocky Mountains, which cover almost half the state.

James Michener's novel *Centennial* (1974), in many ways a fine history of Colorado, begins with the ancient geological forces that shaped this spectacular topography. The Rockies, a young range on the planetary scale, arose about 100 million years ago, making Colorado our highest state with a mean elevation of 6,800 feet. Minerals in these mountains, mainly gold and silver, drew the first rush of settlers to Colorado in 1859. Following U.S. acquisition of most of Colorado in the Louisiana Purchase, Col. Zebulon Pike led the first American party, discovering in 1806 the peak that bears his name. Mining towns like Central City, Cripple Creek, Golden and Georgetown boomed overnight. Colorado Territory, established in 1861, was admitted as the 38th state in 1876.

Minerals are still vital in Colorado's economy; the state produces more molybdenum than any other state plus large amounts of uranium, tin, zinc, coal and oil. The Rockies also supply quantities of high-grade stone. With irrigation, agriculture has become a major industry, concentrating on potatoes, sugar beets, wheat and livestock. Manufacturing, mainly of electronics and foundry products, is the primary source of income. Vail, Aspen and other noted resort areas draw thousands of skiers, boaters and climbers. Denver, the capital, is the largest city by far.

The oldest homes on display in Colorado date from the sixth to thirteenth centuries—those of the native cliff dwellers, probable ancestors of the modern Pueblo peoples. Caves and artifacts of their civilization may be viewed at one of the nation's major archaeological preserves, Mesa Verde National Park. Much later residents included political leaders Golda Meir and Dwight D. Eisenhower; journalists William Allen White, Lowell Thomas and Damon Runyon; and figures of such legendary renown as Molly Brown and Kit Carson. While most homes of eminent dwellers survive, very few admit visitors.

BROWN, MARGARET TOBIN "MOLLY" (1867–1932). In **Denver,** the flamboyant socialite, philanthropist and heroine of the 1912 *Titanic* disaster lived from 1894 at 1340 Pennsylvania St. The Molly Brown House, built in 1889, is a three-story, stone Victorian mansion. The rooms were restored during the 1970s and display both period and Brown family furnishings. She redecorated the interior many times, often having the rooms photographed as she completed them, and she entertained lavishly despite being ostracized by the soured cream of Denver society. The four carved lions she installed on front parapets still "guard" the dwelling. During her frequent travels, she often rented out the house, and it served as the state's Governor's Mansion in 1901. Historic Denver, Inc., operates this intriguing memorial to Margaret Brown, herself a monument of independence and unpretentious pleasure in good living. (Open Memorial Day–Labor Day, Monday–Saturday, 10:00–4:00, Sunday 12:00–4:00; March–Memorial Day, September, Tuesday–Saturday 10:00–4:00, Sunday 12:00–4:00; October 1–March, Tuesday–Saturday 10:00–3:00, Sunday 12:00–3:00; 303-832-4092; admission.)

(See Chapter 1, RHODE ISLAND; also Chapter 4, MISSOURI.)

BUFFALO BILL. See WILLIAM FREDERICK CODY.

CARSON, CHRISTOPHER HOUSTON "KIT" (1809–1868). The last command of the soldier and frontier scout was **Fort Garland** in 1866 and 1867. The restored adobe fort, now a State Historical Monument at the southern edge of town, originated in 1858 as an outpost of New Mexico Territory. Carson dealt sympathetically with the Ute natives there and thus averted attacks on white settlements of the area. Dioramas and frontier relics are displayed by the Colorado Historical Society. (Open June 1–September 30, daily 9:00–4:00; 303-379-3512; admission.)

Carson died at Fort Lyon No. 2 after a long period of declining health. The 1867 cabin he occupied has been converted to a chapel on the grounds of the 1934 Veterans Administration Hospital at **Fort Lyon,** County Road 183, the site of the old fort. Kit Carson Memorial Chapel, affiliated with the Veterans Administration Medical Center, displays Carson mementoes. (Open Monday–Friday 8:00–4:30; 303-456-1260; free.)

Exhibits: The Colorado Heritage Center at 1300 Broadway in **Denver** displays Carson possessions in the Colorado Historical Society Museum.

(Open Monday–Friday 9:00–5:00, Saturday–Sunday, 10:00–5:00; 303-839-3681; free.)

Kit Carson Museum, operated by the Pioneer Historical Society at 425 Carson St. in **Las Animas,** exhibits a Fort Lyon room with relics from the old fort where Carson last resided. (Open Memorial Day–Labor Day, daily 1:00–5:00; 303-456-0829; donation.)

(See NEW MEXICO in this chapter; also Chapter 4, MISSOURI; also Chapter 5, KENTUCKY.)

CODY, WILLIAM FREDERICK "BUFFALO BILL" (1846–1917).

Exhibit: At **Golden** atop Lookout Mountain Park, the Buffalo Bill Memorial Museum displays numerous relics of the showman's spectacular life and career. Located near Cody's grave five miles west of town on State Highway 5, the museum is operated by the City and County of Denver. (Open April 1–October 31, daily 9:00–5:00; November 1–March 31, Tuesday–Sunday 9:00–4:00; 303-526-0747; free.)

(See WYOMING in this chapter; also Chapter 4, IOWA, KANSAS, NEBRASKA.)

EISENHOWER, DWIGHT DAVID (1890–1969). Eisenhower's only permanent home address during his military career before and immediately after World War II was the **Denver** residence of his mother-in-law, Elivera C. Doud. Though their visits during the war were infrequent, the Eisenhowers resumed occasional stays there after he became the 34th U.S. president. The 1906 frame house at 750 Lafayette St. remains privately owned.

Exhibit: Eisenhower mementoes are displayed at the U.S. Air Force Academy Visitor Center, located 12 miles north of **Colorado Springs** on Interstate Highway 25. (Open spring and fall, Monday–Saturday 9:00–5:00, Sunday 1:00–5:00; summer, daily 9:00–5:00; 303-472-2555; free.)

(See TEXAS in this chapter; also Chapter 2, MANHATTAN; also Chapter 3, DISTRICT OF COLUMBIA, MARYLAND, PENNSYLVANIA; also Chapter 4, KANSAS, MICHIGAN; also Chapter 5, GEORGIA, VIRGINIA.)

LOUIS, JOE (1914–1981). "Home is a place you go when you want to rest," he always believed. During the mid-1960s, Louis clearly needed rest. The former heavyweight boxing champion experienced severe symptoms of mental illness, perhaps resulting from drug problems, and was eventually hospitalized for treatment. He lived in the brick ranch house, his summer residence, at 2675 Monaco Parkway (privately owned) in **Denver** during part of this troubled period.

(See CALIFORNIA, NEVADA in this chapter; also Chapter 2, MANHATTAN; also Chapter 4, ILLINOIS.)

MEIR, GOLDA MABOWEHZ (1898–1978). In 1912 the Ukranian-born future Israeli Prime Minister fled her parental home in Wisconsin to live with her sister Sheyna Korngold at 1606 Julian St. in **Denver** and attended high school during her year's residence there. The dilapidated structure, owned in 1981 by the Boys Club of Denver, was slated to be replaced by tennis courts until the Denver Landmark Preservation Commission declared the home "historical"; plans in 1982 involved moving the structure to Habitat Park on South Platte Greenway and restoring it as a nature center there. (Contact Platte River Greenway Foundation, 303-623-2252.) In 1913 and 1914 she occupied a small, solitary room at 1685 Cook St., still a private rooming house.

(See Chapter 4, WISCONSIN.)

MILLER, GLENN (1904–1944). The popular bandleader killed in World War II lived in **Fort Morgan** from 1918 to 1922, attending high school there. The peripatetic family occupied three successive homes. Two survive: at 318 Prospect St. and 202 Maple St. Miller also bought his mother the house at 825 Lake St. but never lived there himself. All remain privately owned.

(See Chapter 2, QUEENS; also Chapter 3, NEW JERSEY; also Chapter 4, IOWA, MISSOURI, NEBRASKA.)

RUNYON, DAMON (1880–1946). The sportswriter and Manhattan tale spinner began his journalistic career in **Denver,** where he occupied a series of rooms in 1905 and 1906. From 1906 to 1911 he resided at the Denver Athletic Club, still at 1325 Glenarm Place.

(See Chapter 2, MANHATTAN; also Chapter 4, KANSAS; also Chapter 5, FLORIDA.)

THOMAS, LOWELL JACKSON (1892–1981). Two boyhood homes of the pioneer broadcaster and world traveler survive (privately owned) in **Victor,** where he lived with his father from 1900 to 1912.

The three-room frame structure at 225 South Sixth St. dates from 1897. The second house, a two-story white dwelling, stands across from the town depot. Thomas last returned to Victor for a visit just days before his death. *Lowell Thomas' Victor* (1982), by Brian Levine, details his formative years there.

Exhibit: The Victor/Lowell Thomas Museum, operated by the Victor Improvement Association, displays furnishings from his homes and memorabilia relating to his life in **Victor** and his career. (Open summer, daily 10:00–4:00; admission.)

(See Chapter 3, NEW YORK; also Chapter 4, OHIO.)

WHITE, WILLIAM ALLEN (1868–1944). The longtime summer home of the influential Kansas journalist stands west of **Estes Park** at the Moraine Park Visitor Center, Rocky Mountain National Park, one mile south of the Beaver Meadows entrance. White's study was the main cabin of five board and log structures dating from the early 20th century. Owned by the National Park Service, the buildings are not open to the public. (Park open daily; 303-586-2371; admission; Moraine Park Visitor Center open May–October; free.)

(See Chapter 4, KANSAS.)

HAWAII

Located 2,315 miles southwest of San Francisco, Hawaii's chain of volcanic mountaintops protruding above the Pacific surface forms a 1,600-mile string of eight major islands ("High Islands") and some 125 "Leeward Islands." The tectonic plate below Hawaii carries the islands northwest about two inches per year, passing over a "hot spot" that forms one of the earth's many vents for the release of interior pressures.

The largest, easternmost island of Hawaii currently lies over this spot. Called "Big Island" to distinguish it from the state, Hawaii is the southernmost point in the United States and geologically the youngest of the islands, with volcanoes Mauna Loa and Kilauea remaining active. Oahu, the third largest island, holds more than three-fourths of the state's population; it is the seat of the capital, Honolulu, and the entrance point for about one million annual visitors.

Polynesians from the Marquesas and Tahiti arrived about 950 AD. Until British explorer James

Cook landed on Kauai in 1778, the peoples lived in Stone Age conditions under a semifuedal system of island chiefs. Cook named his discovery the Sandwich Islands after his sponsor, the Earl of Sandwich. Kamehameha I, using English weapons and ships, had conquered most of the islands by 1796 and ruled until 1819. Subsequent kings and queens dealt with increasing turmoil as Russia, England and the United States contended for influence and control. "American missionaries," it is said, "went to Hawaii to do good and their descendants did well." The Hawaiians themselves didn't do so well. Western diseases killed 15,000 in 1804 alone. Today less than one percent of the total population is pure Hawaiian; most of them live on the small, private island of Niihau, carefully preserving their culture and welcoming visitors only by invitation. American influence deposed Queen Liluokalani, the last monarch, in 1893, and the islands became a U.S. Territory in 1900. Pearl Harbor on Oahu bore the devastating bomb attack on December 7, 1941, the "day of infamy," plunging the nation into war. In 1959, Hawaii became the 50th state.

Sugar, pineapple, cattle ranching and tourism are important income producers, but federal maintenance of the numerous military installations on Oahu provides the state's major source of revenue.

Hawaii's unique blend of peoples—various mixes of Polynesian, Japanese, Filipino, Afro-American and Caucasian—make it one of the most physically mixed societies in the world. Racism there is a highly frustrating exercise; few bigots can handle this corner of America for long. Since few nationally prominent persons settled there, the roster of homes is unusually small.

KAISER, HENRY JOHN (1882–1967). In 1959 the industrialist, shipbuilder, and contractor built a lavish **Honolulu** estate, his last home, at 525 Portlock Road, Koko Head overlooking Maunalua Bay. Pink, Kaiser's favorite color, dominated his palace of concrete and marble with its lavish interior screens and glass partitions. Tropical gardens and numerous outbuildings surrounded the mansion on its seven acres. After Kaiser's death (occurring some 15 years before he expected), the estate fell into disrepair but was acquired in 1972 by wealthy private owners who have considerably modified and enlarged the buildings. According to a 1972 account by colum-

nist Lois Taylor, "The pure kitsch of most of the interior decorations left by the Kaisers included a plastic shell that opened to reveal a telephone, and enough plastic flowers to fill dozens of garbage cans." Interior designer Arthur Elrod said that "the Kaisers had a passion for purple and pink. They are dreadful colors to live with, constantly together." The house was twice used by President Johnson during 1968 meetings with South Vietnamese leaders; and also became a frequent setting for the "Hawaii Five-O" television series during the early 1970s.

(See CALIFORNIA in this chapter; also Chapter 3, NEW YORK.)

LINDBERGH, CHARLES AUGUSTUS (1902–1974). In the **Kipahulu** area south of Hana on the island of Maui, the aviator noted for his outspoken isolationism before World War II built a vacation retreat in the 1960s. Lindbergh permitted no modern amenities such as electricity or telephones on his four-acre property, where he spent a portion of each year until his death. The unaddressed house remains privately owned and inaccessible to the public off Pulaui Highway (State Highway 31).

(See Chapter 1, CONNECTICUT; also Chapter 3, DISTRICT OF COLUMBIA, NEW JERSEY, NEW YORK; also Chapter 4, MICHIGAN, MINNESOTA, MISSOURI.)

STEVENSON, ROBERT LOUIS (1850–1894). On the grounds of the Waioli Tea Room in **Honolulu,** the Salvation Army maintains Stevenson's "Grass House," the small structure where he lived for six months in 1889 as the guest of Princess Kaiulani. It stood originally on Waikiki beach. The grass roof is replaced every four years; period artifacts and Stevenson mementoes are displayed in this "little grass shack" at 3016 Oahu Ave. (Open Monday–Saturday 9:00–4:00; 808-988-2131; free.)

(See CALIFORNIA in this chapter; also Chapter 3, NEW YORK.)

IDAHO

After Lewis and Clark's traverse of Idaho in 1805, British fur trade dominated the area until 1846. The Oregon Trail brought thousands of immigrants through the region, but few except missionaries stopped to settle until the gold discovery at Pierce in 1860. Idaho Territory was organized in 1863, and Boise, founded the previous year, became its capital. Increasing numbers of miners and ranchers brought inevitable conflict with native residents, and the Nez Perce, Bannock and Sheepeater Wars from 1877 to 1879 culminated in the typical pattern of Indian withdrawal. The arrival of railroads in the 1880s inspired rapid growth, and Idaho became the 43rd state in 1890.

Dominated by the Rocky Mountains, this rugged boot of a state contains some of the wildest, most scenic topography on the continent. The large lakes Pend Oreille and Coeur d'Alene are prominent in the northern panhandle, and lava-enriched soil supports a highly varied agriculture in the south. Idaho is of course famed for potatoes, but wheat and livestock are also major products. A large Basque population in the southwest has developed a large sheep-raising industry. About 40 pecent of Idaho is timberland, a large income producer; and the state is heavily mined for lead, zinc, silver and phosphate, among other minerals. Industrial activity centers on food processing.

Notable Idaho residents included two literary giants. The state was Ezra Pound's first home and Ernest Hemingway's last. Mountain carver Gutzon Borglum was born there; and in national politics, William E. Borah achieved renown for his integrity and independence. None of their homes are currently open to the pubic.

BORAH, WILLIAM EDGAR (1865–1940). In 1895, the longtime Idaho Senator bought his 1891 frame house at 1101 Franklin St. in **Boise;** after 1908, however, he resided mainly in Washington, D.C. The house still exists west of **Garden City** on Chinden Street (U.S. Highway 20/26), where it was moved about 1959. Its original site is now the grounds of Boise High School. The home remains privately owned.

(See Chapter 3, DISTRICT OF COLUMBIA; also Chapter 4, ILLINOIS.)

BORGLUM, GUTZON (1867–1941). Near **St. Charles** on U.S. Highway 89, the private Wilhelmina Nelson House and Cabins mark remnants of the sculptor's birthplace and infant home on the Bear Lake plot cleared by his father. The present structures of log and sod and the two-story frame house were built from 1870 to the 1890s, possibly incorporating the original log hut where Borglum was born.

(See TEXAS in this chapter; also Chapter 1, CONNECTICUT; also Chapter 2, MANHATTAN; also Chapter 4, SOUTH DAKOTA.)

CROSBY, HARRY LILLIS "BING" (1903–1977). The popular singer and film actor built his summer vacation home near **Hayden Lake** in the early 1950s. It remains privately owned on English Point Road (U.S. Highway 2).

(See CALIFORNIA, NEVADA, WASHINGTON in this chapter.)

HEMINGWAY, ERNEST MILLER (1899–1961). The last home of the highly influential literary figure survives at **Ketchum.** Hemingway bought the two-story red structure in 1959. Still occupied at intervals by his widow, Mary Welsh Hemingway, it stands at the end of a rural road and a long drive in the Warm Springs area. Her autobiography, *How It Was* (1976), details Hemingway's final years of mental illness there and his ultimate suicide. Hemingway, familiar with the area for 20 years before he settled there, first came in 1939 and stayed in Suite 206 of the Sun Valley Lodge, still a popular resort complex, one mile north of Ketchum off U.S. Highway 75. There he wrote a part of *For Whom the Bell Tolls* (1940)—"the part with all the snow in it," he said.

(See Chapter 4, ILLINOIS, MICHIGAN; also Chapter 5, FLORIDA.)

POUND, EZRA LOOMIS (1885–1972). The birthplace of this poet, a major force of 20th-century literature, remains privately owned on Second Street South in **Hailey.** Built by his father, the two-story frame house was Pound's home until age one.

Exhibit: A small collection of Pound material, including books, photos and clippings may be seen at Blaine County Historical Museum on North Main Street in *Hailey.* (Open June 15–September 15, Wednesday–Monday 10:00–5:00; 208-788-4185; admission.)

(See Chapter 3, DISTRICT OF COLUMBIA, PENNSYLVANIA.)

MONTANA

A remote fringe of Louisiana Territory when Lewis and Clark ascended the Missouri River on their exploration journey to the Pacific, the Montana country soon attracted fur traders and missionaries. Jesuit Father Jean De Smet founded the first permanent settlement at Stevensville in 1841. During the 1860s gold mining camps exploded into towns at Bannack, Virginia City and Helena. Montana Territory, established in 1864, shifted its capital several times until placing it permanently at Helena in 1875. The next year brought the celebrated demolition of Custer's Seventh Cavalry; on a knoll above the Little Bighorn River, hard-pressed Sioux and Cheyenne defenders won a battle but knew they had lost the war. Territorial Montana exhibited much more of the stereotypical "Wild West" than most places that support a tourist industry by the claim. Cattle rustling, frontier gunslingers and vigilante justice were all part of an actual, though very brief, phase of its history. Following the arrival of the Northern Pacific Railroad in 1883, settlement proceeded rapidly, and Montana—the Spanish word for "mountain"—entered the Union as the 41st state in 1889. Its motto is refreshing among the usual pieties of the genre: "Gold and Silver."

Western Montana is mainly Rocky Mountains, and Glacier National Park in the north provides some of the nation's most enchanting wilderness. Eastern Montana undulates gradually to the mountain foothills. The foremost crops in this agricultural state are winter wheat and hay, though cattle and sheep ranching remains important. The Butte mining district produces a large percentage of the nation's copper and silver; and oil wells cluster in the Williston Basin. The fastest growing industry, however, is lumbering and the production of wood products.

The only native Montanan included here is laconic film star Gary Cooper, whose Helena birthplace survives. Calamity Jane roamed throughout the state and probably knew it better than most residents today—but she, like most of the early dwellers, left few tracks.

BURKE, MARTHA JANE CANARY "CALAMITY JANE" (1848?–1903). "She was real tall and built like a busted bale of hay," reported one observer who knew the wide-roaming, hell-raising frontier figure. Her movements and numerous brief lodgings in the gold camps, frontier forts and raw towns of several western states cannot be traced with any degree of accuracy.

The diary she wrote for her daughter is probably least accurate of all, and most scholars of western history downplay the significance that highly romanticized fiction and films have given her. No structure that she was known to occupy survives. Montana marks several sites associated with her, however, including that of her cabin at 213 Main St. in **Livingston.** The dates of her presence almost anywhere are uncertain.

Exhibit: The Western Heritage Center at 2822 Montana Ave. in **Billings** displays Calamity Jane memorabilia including personal knickknacks, pearl-handled knives and her battered diary. (Open Tuesday–Saturday 10:00–5:00, Sunday 1:00–5:00; 406-248-4901; donation.)

(See WYOMING in this chapter; also Chapter 4, MISSOURI, SOUTH DAKOTA.)

CALAMITY JANE. See MARTHA JANE CANARY BURKE.

COOPER, GARY (1901–1961). One of the few cowboy actors who ever actually ranched before facing a Hollywood camera, Cooper was a **Helena** native, born Frank James Cooper at 730 11th Ave., a large, two-story, brick house that remains privately owned. Subsequent family homes occupied successively until about 1926 remain privately owned at Fifth Avenue and Beatty Street, 15 Shiland St., and 712 Fifth St.

"Sunnyside," the 600-acre family cattle ranch acquired in 1906, was also known as the "Seven-Bar-Nine." After 1910 the boy resided there only during summers, working each year on the ranch until age 22—"the hardest work I ever did," he recalled. The "Seven-Bar-Nine" remains privately operated on the Missouri River off U.S. Highway 91 between the towns of **Craig** and **Cascade.**

(See CALIFORNIA in this chapter.)

CUSTER, GEORGE ARMSTRONG (1839–1876).
Exhibit: The site of the Little Bighorn massacre where Sioux warriors, led by Sitting Bull, Crazy Horse, Gall and others, wiped out Custer and his 225-man Seventh Cavalry regiment on June 25, 1876, is now a 1.2-square-mile memorial to this tragedy, which was also the last great Indian victory in North America. The Visitor Center at Custer Battlefield National Monument displays maps, photos and interpretive dioramas plus

lectures and battlefield tours.* Administered by the National Park Service, Custer Battlefield lies two miles southeast of **Crow Agency** on U.S. Highway 212, Crow Indian Reservation. (Monument open daily, 8:00–sunset; museum open June 1–Labor Day, daily 8:00–7:00; Labor Day–May 31, daily 8:00–4:30; 406-638-2622; free.)

(See Chapter 4, KANSAS, MICHIGAN, NORTH DAKOTA, OHIO; also Chapter 5, KENTUCKY.)

SITTING BULL (1831–1890).

Exhibit: See GEORGE ARMSTRONG CUSTER.

(See Chapter 4, MICHIGAN, SOUTH DAKOTA.)

NEVADA

Comstock Lode silver is seldom seen in Las Vegas gambling casinos, where the tender is paper money and silverless coins, but it brought wealth to many and helped the Union finance the Civil War. Until well into the 20th century, however, Nevada's main "function" lay in providing a trail to California's wealth. Today, of course, the state is one of the West's prime destinations for people with money to blow. The spectacular imported shows and dense "Vegas" crowds flourish in neon splendor and stark isolation, surrounded by desolate, uninhabited desert.

Nevada's first permanent town, Genoa, was settled in 1849 by family-oriented Mormons just 35 miles from later Reno, for many years America's divorce capital. Originally part of Utah Territory and admitted as the 36th state in 1864, Nevada experienced almost a century of economic ups and downs based on fluctuations in its gold and silver mines and the markets for these metals. It stabilized its economy by legalizing gambling in 1931, and the gambling industry now provides the state's chief revenue. Warehousing is also big business there, since Nevada assesses no income, inheritance or inventory taxes, and a very small sales tax. Mineral production remains important, and a large livestock industry thrives, though dependent on irrigation for feed crops.

Lake Tahoe and Lake Mead are major resort areas. The state's "boom-and-bust" history is amply reflected in large numbers of surviving 19th-century buildings, some of them elaborate. Few of them relate to nationally prominent persons, however. Nevada's most notable resident was probably Mark Twain, who began writing for a living in Virginia City; the flavor of his times is well preserved in this historic town.

BOW, CLARA GORDON (1905–1965). The retirement home of the film actress from 1931 to 1945 was the 300,000-acre cattle ranch owned by her husband, a former cowboy actor and Nevada Lieutenant Governor Rex Bell. She planned and built their Spanish-style ranch home in 1932. For publicity purposes, she once dyed some of the cattle red to match her hair color. Now known as the YKL Ranch, it remains a huge, privately owned cattle operation off U.S. Highway 95 in the state's extreme southern tip near **Searchlight.** (See CALIFORNIA in this chapter; also Chapter 2, BROOKLYN.)

CLEMENS, SAMUEL LANGHORNE "MARK TWAIN" (1835–1910). In 1863 and 1864 the eventual author-humorist frequently stayed with his brother Orion, Nevada's territorial secretary, at the latter's home in **Carson City.** This 1863 house veneered with stucco at 502 North Division St. (at the corner of Spear Street) remains privately owned. According to Clemens's somewhat jaundiced account, Orion's wife persuaded him to build this house. "Orion could be persuaded to do anything. He built and furnished the house at a cost of twelve thousand dollars and there was no other house in that capital that could approach this property for style and cost."

Exhibits: At **Virginia City,** "Queen of the Comstock Lode," Clemens began his professional writing career on a frontier newspaper, the *Territorial Enterprise,* and first used his nom de plume "Mark Twain." He lived there from 1862 to 1864. Much of the town has been restored to its 1860s appearance as Virginia City Historic District National Historic Landmark. A film at the Visitors' Bureau, on C Street between Taylor and Union streets, introduces the town's history and points of interest. (Open daily, 9:00–7:00; 702-847-0177; free.) The Mark Twain Museum, C and Taylor streets, displays Clemens's rolltop desk plus numerous historical items of the mining

---

*In 1976 the National Park Service was planning to recommend that the name be changed from Custer Battlefield National Monument to the Battle of the Little Bighorn National Monument. "It's not comfortable with a battleground named after the loser," according to reporter James Carrier. As of 1982, however, the loser had not yet lost this implied standing as some kind of "hero."

frontier. (Open May 1–September 30, daily 9:00–6:00; October 1–April 30, daily 10:00–5:00; 702-847-0454; free.) *Mark Twain in Virginia City* (1964), by Paul Fatout, details Clemens's rambunctious existence there.

(See CALIFORNIA in this chapter; also Chapter 1, CONNECTICUT; also Chapter 2, BRONX, MANHATTAN; also Chapter 3, NEW YORK; also Chapter 4, IOWA, MISSOURI.)

CROSBY, HARRY LILLIS "BING" (1903–1977). The singer and actor acquired his 3,000-acre cattle ranch—actually 11 pieces of property—between 1943 and 1952 near **Elko.** He herded his four sons there for several weeks every summer and worked them from dawn to sunset. Crosby owned about 3,600 head of cattle and sheep on what he called "a functioning cow-and-calf operation with nothing dudey about it." The privately owned ranch where the Crosby family resided is located on Mountain City Highway (State Highway 51) west of North Fork.

(See CALIFORNIA, IDAHO, WASHINGTON in this chapter.)

HUGHES, HOWARD ROBARD (1905–1976). The reclusive aviator, film producer and industrialist resided in **Las Vegas** during the 1960s, but nobody but his bodyguards ever saw him. He rented an entire wing of the Flamingo Hotel (now the Flamingo Hilton) at 3555 Las Vegas Blvd. South; then, from 1966 to 1970 he huddled in shade-drawn splendor on several top floors of the Desert Inn, which he owned along with most of the Las Vegas "strip" of hotels and gambling casinos. The Desert Inn stands at 3145 Las Vegas Blvd. South. Both hotels remain popular, expensive resorts.

(See CALIFORNIA, TEXAS in this chapter.)

LOUIS, JOE (1914–1981). During the 1970s, the former heavyweight boxing champion worked as an official "greeter" at the **Las Vegas** gambling casino of Caesars Palace, 3570 Las Vegas Blvd. South. Louis occupied a suite there. His last home, where he died at an infirm 66, remains privately owned at 3333 Seminole Circle.

(See CALIFORNIA, COLORADO in this chapter; also Chapter 2, MANHATTAN; also Chapter 4, ILLINOIS.)

TWAIN, MARK. See SAMUEL LANGHORNE CLEMENS.

NEW MEXICO

Remnants of the earliest known human in North America—Sandia Man, about 20,000 years old—were discovered just east of Albuquerque. Later nomadic hunters ate animals now extinct, as shown by bone evidence. Pueblo Indian culture, still thriving, began about AD 400; the high point of this remarkable democracy occurred between 1050 and 1300, when Europe writhed in medieval theocracy. Imposing remnants of this communal civilization are visible today in Chaco Culture National Historical Park and Gila Cliff Dwellings National Monument and in such "live" pueblos as Zuni.

New Mexico is not melting-pot America. Native and Spanish colonial cultures survive intact and continue to develop beneath Anglo-American overlay. Almost 40 percent of the state's population is of Spanish ethnic background. Geographers call New Mexico an "oasis civilization," with about one-third of all residents located in Albuquerque while vast reaches of landscape remain uninhabited. Almost half of the state is federal property, consisting mainly of national forests and military installations.

The state's topography is one of the most varied in the nation. In the east, the Great Plains abut against jumbles of mountain ranges that dominate the western two-thirds of the state. Six climatic life zones (from a U.S. total of seven) range from desert to Arctic-Alpine environments.

Pueblo natives peacefully farmed and irrigated corn, beans and squash hundreds of years before the Pilgrim landing in New England. Santa Fe, the nation's second oldest city, dates officially from 1610, but Indian pueblos stood there in 1200. Coronado explored the territory in 1540 and found Acoma (Sky City)—possibly the oldest continuously inhabited site in the country—well etablished. By 1628 Spain held firm control, and Franciscan missions were "enlightening" the major pueblos. United pueblo resistance in 1680, however, captured Santa Fe and held the province for 12 years, the only completely successful native revolt in American history. The Spanish returned, but by diplomacy and persuasion, not guns. Unlike the English colonial program of push, divide, conquer and remove, Spain exercised a policy of true coexistence with the native Pueblos, freely intermarrying and guaranteeing their lands by royal title. This cultural alliance resisted the aggressive Navaho, Apache and Comanche. Politically, however, this northern bulwark of New Spain suffered years of official neglect, not improved when Mexican authority replaced Spain's in 1821. The opening of the Santa Fe Trail from Independence, Mo., probably rescued the colony from oblivion. The Mexican War of 1846 resulted in 1850 cession of the province, including present Arizona, to the United States as New Mexico Territory. For the next 35 years, the main order of business was subjugating the Navaho and Apache, finally accomplished with Geronimo's surrender in 1886. Mining and cattle ranching became the dominant activities while successions of range wars contested land ownership and water rights. New Mexico entered the Union as the 47th state in 1912. In 1945 the testing of the first nuclear device near Alamogordo launched the world into the atomic age.

Mining remains the major industry, with New Mexico leading the nation in uranium production. Natural gas, oil, missile testing, tourism, electronics—and, still, cattle and sheep ranching—are important income producers.

The roster of these pages includes no native New Mexicans. Kit Carson resided in the state for much of his life, but most of the notables listed were atomic scientists, relatively brief dwellers. A more civilized creator was English novelist D. H. Lawrence. Perhaps New Mexico's greatest claim to world culture, however, must rely upon its pueblo-age natives for their early mastery of the skill of peace.

BILLY THE KID. See WILLIAM H. BONNEY.

BONNEY, WILLIAM H. "BILLY THE KID" (1859–1881). The merciless young killer had no permanent residence from about 1875, keeping constantly ahead of the law through New Mexico, Arizona and northern Mexico. Previously (1873–74) he had lived with his mother at **Silver City** in a long-gone house on Main Street.

Exhibits: One of the best preserved cowtowns of the old West is maintained in Lincoln Historic District National Historic Landmark, where Bonney led a faction in the Lincoln County cattle war. The restored Old Lincoln County Courthouse State Monument, which holds the jail cell from which he made a spectacular escape in 1881, stands on U.S. Highway 380, on the west edge of **Lincoln.** Dating from 1874, it served originally as a store. The State of New Mexico displays exhibits relating to the Lincoln County War and the violent life of Billy Bonney. (Open Memorial Day-Labor Day, daily 9:00–5:00; Labor Day-Memorial Day, Thursday–Monday 9:00–5:00, 505-653-4372; admission.)

At **Fort Sumner,** where Sheriff Pat Garrett caught up with the outlaw and shot him, little remains except the State Monument on the Pecos River marking the site of the vacated army post where Billy hid out and died at the Peter Maxwell house, razed in 1894. A visitor center about two miles east of town on U.S. Highway 60, operated by the state, shows exhibits on the fort's history. The outlaw's grave is nearby. (Monument open Thursday–Monday 9:00–5:00; free; museum open daily, 8:00–5:00; 505-355-2573; admission.) Also in Fort Sumner, Billy the Kid Museum, privately operated, displays Bonney memorabilia. (Open summer, daily 9:00–5:00; winter except January–February, Monday–Saturday 9:00–4:00; 505-355-2380; admission.)

(See Chapter 2, MANHATTAN.)

CARSON, CHRISTOPHER HOUSTON "KIT" (1809–1868). The frontiersman's longest continuous residence in his two New Mexico homes was between 1851 and 1861. Kit Carson House National Historic Landmark, his adobe house on Old Kit Carson Road off U.S. Highway 64 in **Taos,** dates from 1825. The frontier scout-soldier bought it in 1843 as his permanent home, where he and his wife Josefa Jaramillo raised their large family. The Kit Carson Memorial Foundation has restored the dwelling with its 30-inch-thick walls and displays Carson family furnishings and memorabilia plus Indian and Spanish artifacts. (Open April 1–October 31, daily 8:00–6:00; November 1–March 31, daily 8:00–5:00; 505-758-4741; admission.)

Five miles south of **Cimarron** on State Highway 21 lies Philmont Scout Ranch, the "Rayado Ranch" that Carson also owned and worked from 1851 to about 1860. This ground now forms a 137,500-acre national camping center for the Boy Scouts of America, hosting more than 15,000 Scouts each year. Seton Memorial Library there contains the artwork and books of naturalist Ernest Thompson Seton, while the Kit Carson Museum displays items relating to the controversial frontiersman and his ranch. (Library and museum open June 1–August 31, daily 8:00–5:00; September 1–May 31, Tuesday–Saturday 8:00–5:00; 505-376-2281; free.)

(See COLORADO in this chapter; also Chapter 4, MISSOURI; also Chapter 5, KENTUCKY.)

FERMI, ENRICO (1901–1954). After successfully achieving a sustained nuclear reaction at Chicago in 1942, the Italian-born physicist brought his secret Manhattan Project laboratory to **Los Alamos,** where the first atomic bomb was tested in 1945. Fermi's residence in 1944 and 1945 remains privately owned at 1964 Juniper St. on "Bathtub Row," a group of six structures built during the 1920s as part of the Los Alamos Ranch School for Boys. During the 1943 local population boom, where acres of cheap army housing arose, these dwellings were plush by comparison, containing the only bathtubs in town—hence the name.

(See Chapter 3, NEW JERSEY; also Chapter 4, ILLINOIS.)

GODDARD, ROBERT HUTCHINGS (1882–1945). The rocketry pioneer did much of his work from 1930 at a large testing range near **Roswell.** "Mescalero Ranch," the pueblo-style dwelling he occupied from 1930 to 1932 and from 1934 to 1942, stands a short distance east of town on Mescalero Road. It remains privately owned.

Exhibit: The Goddard wing of the **Roswell** Museum and Art Center, 100 West 11th St. (at the corner of Main Street) displays his laboratory equipment plus other exhibits on this brilliant engineer, widely regarded as something of a "mad scientist" during his lifetime. (Open Monday–Saturday 9:00–5:00, Sunday 1:00–5:00; 505-622-4700; free.)

(See Chapter 1, MASSACHUSETTS.)

LAWRENCE, DAVID HERBERT (1855–1930). E. M. Forster called this English author and poet "the greatest imaginative novelist of our generation." Lawrence and his wife Frieda visited briefly at Taos in 1922, then returned to what is now the Lawrence Ranch and Shrine on Lobo Mountain, located about five miles off State Highway 3 at **San Cristobal** as indicated by signs. Mabel Doge Luhan, their host in Taos, gave them the small ranch with its cabin residence, with which Lawrence was delighted. They stayed for about 10 months in 1924 and 1925, then returned to

Europe. Lawrence called it "Kiowa" after the natives who had once camped there. He carpentered, irrigated land and wrote during his stay, which was marred by serious illness. Frieda Lawrence returned as a widow in 1933 and built a nearby house, where she resided until her death in 1956. She also brought Lawrence's ashes from Europe, interred them in the 1934 chapel she built on the Lawrence Ranch and willed the entire property to the University of New Mexico, which uses the place for meetings and seminars. The ranch and shrine welcome visitors, but Lawrence's cabin remains closed to the public. His typewriter and clothing items are displayed in a small adobe museum. (Open daily, daylight hours: 505-776-2245; free.)

MacCARTHUR, DOUGLAS (1880–1964). The ruins of the World War II Pacific commander's boyhood home remain at Fort Selden State Monument—"a vivid and exciting place for me," he recalled—located on U.S. Highway 85 at **Radium Springs.** MacArthur's father commanded Fort Selden from 1884 to 1886. The site of the fort, an active frontier installation from 1865 to 1892, is operated by the Museum of New Mexico, which provides self-guided tours, a military museum and period demonstrations.

(See Chapter 2, MANHATTAN; also Chapter 3, MARYLAND, NEW YORK; also Chapter 4, KANSAS; also Chapter 5, ARKANSAS, VIRGINIA.)

OPPENHEIMER, J. ROBERT (1904–1967). Chief of the scientific staff that developed and tested the first atomic bomb during World War II, the physicist resided at **Los Alamos** during the crucial period from 1942 to 1945. He occupied the privately owned house at 1967 Peach St. in "Bathtub Row" (see the entry on Enrico Fermi earlier in this section).

From 1929 until 1950 Oppenheimer vacationed each year at his "Perro Caliente" ranch cabin in Santa Fe National Forest. The rustic lodge remains privately owned on the east side of Road 223 about one mile off State Highway 63 northeast of **Tererro.**

Exhibit: A one-day annual tour, usually in early October, is conducted from **Alamogordo** to Trinity Site in a remote section of the U.S. Army's White Sands Missile Range. There, in a fenced-off desolate area, a basalt cairn on "ground zero," where the bomb was set off, records that "The world's first nuclear device was exploded on July 17, 1945." The ruins of the McDonald Ranch, where Oppenheimer and his crew made final preparations for the blast that exploded the world into a new age, are also indicated. (Contact Alamogordo Chamber of Commerce, Alamogordo, NM 88310.)

(See CALIFORNIA in this chapter; also Chapter 2, MANHATTAN; also Chapter 3, NEW JERSEY.)

PERSHING, JOHN JOSEPH (1860–1948).

Exhibit: The Pancho Villa Museum at State Highway 11 and Lima Street in **Columbus** displays material relating to Gen. Pershing's 1916 punitive expedition into Mexico following Villa's bloody raid on Columbus. The museum is privately operated. (Open daily, 10:00–5:00; 505-531-2685; admission.)

(See CALIFORNIA in this chapter; also Chapter 3, DISTRICT OF COLUMBIA; also Chapter 4, MISSOURI.)

ROOSEVELT, THEODORE (1858–1919).

Exhibit: In 1898, three years before becoming the 26th U.S. president, Roosevelt achieved national recognition for a brazen act in a shoddy little war: leading his gang of "Rough Riders" up poorly defended Kettle Hill in Cuba during William Randolph Hearst's concocted Spanish-American War. A museum in **Las Vegas** commemorates this media event with material relating to the macho horsemen. Rough Riders Memorial and City Museum is located in the Municipal Building. (Open Monday–Saturday 9:00–4:00; 505-454-1401; free.)

(See Chapter 2, BRONX, MANHATTAN; also Chapter 3, DISTRICT OF COLUMBIA, NEW YORK; also Chapter 4, NORTH DAKOTA.)

OKLAHOMA

The prehistoric past of the 46th state includes the oldest mountain range in North America (the Wichitas), abundant dinosaurs and possibly runic stones. Mainly a prairie state, Oklahoma marks a western border of the Great Plains. A general rise in elevation occurs from southeast to northwest toward the Rocky Mountains.

Oklahoma became U.S. property with the Louisiana Purchase and was specified by Congress as Indian Territory. From 1817 to 1840 the government forcibly transferred the "Five Civilized Tribes"—Cherokee, Chickasaw, Choctaw, Creek and Seminole—to Oklahoma from the southeastern United States. About one-fourth of the Cherokee nation perished during this genocidal "Trail of Tears" from Georgia. The Indian Territory was chaotic from the beginning, with indigenous plains tribes pushed aside to make room for the newcomers. After the Civil War split the tribes into factions and devastated their property, the federal government forced the surrender of all the previously granted western Oklahoma. These lands soon attracted illegal white settlers, and strong political pressure mounted to open the area to homesteading. This was accomplished in the land rush of April 22, 1889, when thousands of land-hungry immigrants charged over the territorial borders to file claims— the "Sooners," from which the state took its nickname, were those who had sneaked across before the opening gun of April 22 and staked early claims. Oklahoma City arose almost overnight as a tent city of 10,000. Western Oklahoma became Oklahoma Territory in 1890, and the eastern half ostensibly continued as Indian Territory. But the Dawes Commission completed the extinction of tribal governments in 1899 by granting individual land allotments to those who could prove they were Indians. The Indian Territory was thus manipulated into unity with Oklahoma Territory despite considerable Indian opposition, and the combined halves entered statehood in 1907. As a result of this history, Oklahoma now boasts a larger Indian population, representing more tribes, than any other state. Most have been thoroughly integrated by generations of intermarriage, and the "reservation Indian" is virtually nonexistent.

Oklahoma's oil bonanza brought boom-town prosperity in the early 1900s. But disaster struck western Oklahoma during the 1930s as a result of ignorant farming techniques and prolonged drought. The "Dust Bowl," coincident with the Great Depression, was literally the surface of Oklahoma blowing away. John Steinbeck's novel *The Grapes of Wrath* and composer Woody Guthrie's *Dust Bowl Ballads* detail this experience more accurately than any purely factual account. Destitute thousands migrated west in search of new homes, and the derisive term "Okie" was applied by more fortunate Americans who still had something left to lose.

For a state with such a traumatic history, Oklahoma has more than recovered. Flood control, soil conservation and a proper emphasis on livestock production has mended the torn land, which remains primarily agricultural. Aerospace and aviation are major industries, and the state holds fourth place in national petroleum production.

Oklahoma's most notable sons were proud "Okie" Woody Guthrie, entertainer Will Rogers, part Cherokee, and athlete Jim Thorpe, a Sac and Fox. Prominent residents also included oilman Jean Paul Getty, cowboy actor Tom Mix and Apache warrior Geronimo, an unwilling Oklahoma guest. Rogers and Thorpe homes survive and admit visitors.

GERONIMO (1829?–1909).

Exhibit: The Apache war chief, kept under "house arrest" from 1894 at Fort Sill, prosperously farmed and sold handicrafts and photos of himself, resisted conversion by Dutch Reformed missionaries and hoped against all odds that the U.S. government would finally allow him to return to his Arizona homeland. The Old Guardhouse where he was briefly held on arrival houses exhibits relating to the frontier fort, its soldier and Indian inhabitants and the Oklahoma Indian Territory. Fort Sill Military Reservation National Historic Landmark, containing Fort Sill Museum, is now the headquarters of the U.S. Army Field Artillery. It is located five miles north of **Lawton** via U.S. Highway 277. (Open daily, 9:00–4:30; 405-351-5123; free.)

(See Chapter 5, ALABAMA.)

GETTY, JEAN PAUL (1892–1976). In **Tulsa,** the oil billionaire lived at two addresses during World War II. From 1942 to 1944, he resided at 2701 South Victor St., a house dating from 1939; and in 1945 and 1946 at 2929 South Utica St., built about 1937. Both remain privately owned.

(See CALIFORNIA in this chapter; also Chapter 2, MANHATTAN; also Chapter 4, MINNESOTA.)

GUTHRIE, WOODROW WILSON "WOODY" (1912–1967). The native town of the vagabond singer and prolific songwriter was **Okemah,** which needs another generation or so to feel quite comfortable about him. The yellow house built by his grandfather in 1909 burned down shortly after Guthrie's birth there. The "London House," where he lived from about 1912 to 1918, stood at Second and Birch streets until 1980. Despite pleas by the private owner and the Oklahoma Historical Society to save and restore the decrepit, white frame home of Okemah's noted son, the city council ordered it razed. According to a 1980 news release, "the city attorney called the house a gathering spot for high school students who crawl into the old structure to 'smoke marijuana and drink beer.'"

(See TEXAS in this chapter; also Chapter 2, BROOKLYN, MANHATTAN, QUEENS.)

MIX, THOMAS EDWIN "TOM" (1880–1940).

Exhibit: The prototype of the cowboy in the white hat, Mix led an adventurous life before becoming the screen idol of youngsters. For example, he served as marshal in **Dewey** from about 1909 to 1913. The Tom Mix Museum is operated by the Washington County Historical Society at the 1890 Dewey Hotel, 721 North Delaware St. (at the corner of Eighth Street). The museum displays personal effects including lots of his expensive cowboy gear and daily showings of several of his almost 400 silent films. (Open Tuesday–Friday 9:00–5:00, Saturday–Sunday 1:00–5:00; 918-534-1555; admission.)

(See CALIFORNIA in this chapter; also Chapter 3, PENNSYLVANIA.)

ROGERS, WILL. (1879–1935). Cowboy, vaudeville entertainer, slyly satiric humorist and film actor, William Penn Adair Rogers was born of Cherokee ancestry near **Oologah** in what was Indian Territory at the time. In 1875 his fairly prosperous parents built the house in which he was born, reputedly one of the largest and finest homes in the territory, and ranched 60,000 acres in the V of land between the Caney and Verdigris rivers. "It was a big two-story log house," Rogers said, "but on the back we had three rooms made of frame. Just before my birth, my mother . . . had them move her into the log part of the house. She wanted me to be born in a log house. She had just read the life of Lincoln. So I got the log house end of it O.K.; all I need now is the other qualifications." Will Rogers Birthplace National Historic Landmark, his home to about 1899, originally stood one mile east of its present location on a site flooded by the construction of Oologah

Dam and Reservoir. Moved in 1959, the house now overlooks the impounded Lake Oologah from a hilltop on U.S. Highway 169, two miles north of town; and the surrounding 993-acre Will Rogers State Park occupies part of the ancestral ranch. There are camping and picnic facilities, and the log house displays period furnishings. (Open daily 9:00–5:00; free.)

Exhibit: Will Rogers Memorial, operated by the Oklahoma State Park Department one mile west of **Claremore** on State Highway 88, is a ranch house museum dedicated to the entertainer on the 20 acres he bought in 1911 and where he intended to build his retirement home. This contains the largest collection of Rogers memorabilia, including his numerous saddles from all over the world, showbills, letters, ropes, photos and his typewriter. Dioramas of his life and recordings of his inimitable voice are also popular features there. Rogers is buried in the sunken garden terrace. (Open daily, 8:00–5:00; 918-341-0719; free.)

(See CALIFORNIA in this chapter; also Chapter 3, NEW YORK.)

SHERMAN, WILLIAM TECUMSEH (1820–1891). As commander of the U.S. Army in 1871, Gen. Sherman confronted Kiowa chiefs at Fort Sill, near **Lawton**, and narrowly escaped assassination at the post commandant's quarters where he lodged, a two-story stone dwelling now called the "Sherman House." The attacking Indian, called Stumbling Bear, apparently lived up to his name. The house is not open to visitors (see the entry on Geronimo earlier in this section).

(See CALIFORNIA in this chapter; also Chapter 2, MANHATTAN; also Chapter 3, DISTRICT OF COLUMBIA; also Chapter 4, MISSOURI, OHIO.)

THORPE, JAMES FRANCIS "JIM" (1888–1953). He was the world's greatest athlete, according to the International Olympic Committee of 1912. Thorpe set records and won gold medals that year in both the decathlon and pentathlon, but his awards were soon stripped from him when it was discovered that he had briefly played semi-professional baseball. The unjust decision was finally rectified posthumously by the Committee in 1982, when Thorpe's medals and records were restored. Of Sac and Fox ancestry, Thorpe was born south of **Prague** in a long-gone log cabin on the North Canadian river, where his father farmed 160 acres.

A transient for most of his life, the athlete made a last attempt to sink roots in 1917, when he bought a new hillside bungalow at 704 East Boston St. in **Yale**, his first permanent residence. He lived there until 1923. Containing period furnishings and Thorpe memorabilia, it is operated by the State Museum of Oklahoma. (Open Tuesday–Friday 9:00–5:00, Saturday–Sunday 2:00–5:00; 918-387-2815.)

(See Chapter 3, PENNSYLVANIA; also Chapter 4, OHIO.)

OREGON

Claimed by the United States in 1792, Oregon headquartered an early fur empire. The Lewis and Clark Expedition reached the Oregon coast in 1805, and John Jacob Astor soon established a post at Astoria; but until the 1840s, the "Oregon Country"—a vast tract with nebulous borders that included most of the northwestern United States plus parts of British Columbia—was mainly controlled by the British Hudson's Bay Company. Skilled diplomacy supported by increasing American settlement via the Oregon Trail, which ended at Oregon City, affirmed the U.S. claim; and Oregon Territory, including the present Washington, was established in 1848. Coincident with a gold rush that developed Portland into a major commercial center, Oregon entered the Union as the 33rd state in 1859. Railroads linked the state to the rest of the nation in 1883, and Oregon's population doubled in the next five years.

Oregon is divided by the Cascade Range which runs from north to south; its east is very different from its west, the big difference being precipitation. Green, rainy western Oregon, settled first, contains the state's largest population, mainly in the Willamette Valley between the Cascade and Coast ranges. Much of eastern Oregon, by contrast, is semi-arid desert and shortgrass ranchland. The leading timber state since 1900, Oregon also produces a huge variety of fruits, truck crops and livestock; and manufacturing is highly diversified. Oregon is justly noted for its leadership in environmental preservation and progressive social policies. The "common weal" receives considerably more than lip service there. All but a few miles of Oregon seacoast, for example, is public domain. No other state has matched its habitual concerns for women's equality, constructive law enforcement and insistence on clean air and water. Despite the fact that tourism is a major industry, Oregonians are not eager to welcome new residents; in a refreshing switch from the prevailing national sales syndrome, an Oregon journalistic "cult" only half-humorously conducts a campaign to discredit the state to outsiders.

Though Oregon's notable progeny are relatively few, Herbert Hoover's boyhood home welcomes visitors; and sites associated with early visitors Lewis and Clark are well-marked.

CLARK, WILLIAM. See MERIWETHER LEWIS and WILLIAM CLARK.

HOOVER, HERBERT CLARK (1874–1964). The 31st U.S. president, an orphan, resided in the **Newberg** home of Dr. Henry Minthorn, his uncle, from 1884 to 1889. The Minthorn House, an L-shaped, two-story frame structure dates from 1881 at 115 South River St. (at the corner of East Second Street). Hoover relics and memorabilia plus some original furnishings are displayed by the Herbert Hoover Foundation. (Open Wednesday–Sunday 1:00–4:00; 503-538-6629; admission.)

(See CALIFORNIA in this chapter; also Chapter 2, MANHATTAN; also Chapter 3, DISTRICT OF COLUMBIA; also Chapter 4, IOWA; also Chapter 5, VIRGINIA.)

LEWIS, MERIWETHER (1774–1809).
CLARK, WILLIAM (1770–1838).
The team assigned by President Jefferson to explore the Louisiana Territory reached its furthest point on the Oregon coast in 1805, 4,100 miles from its starting point in St. Louis, Mo. The expedition of 32 men and one woman built Fort Clatsop, two parallel, 50-foot buildings connected by picket walls at both ends, about three miles from the mouth of the Netul River (later renamed the Lewis and Clark River). They moved into their winter quarters on Christmas Day. Incessant rain, a "pore elk meat" diet, and frequent illness and injury marked their stay, which lasted until March 23, 1806. No remnant of the original fort survives; the present replica at Fort Clatsop National Memorial, dating from 1955, follows the plan sketched by Clark on the elk-hide cover of his

journal. There the captains spent three months updating their journals and drawing maps of the immense territory they had seen. The National Park Service visitor center displays exhibits and presents a living history program relating to the expedition. Fort Clatsop, named after a friendly local tribe, is located five miles southwest of **Astoria,** just south of U.S. Highway 101 (Business). (Open June 15–Labor Day, daily 8:00–8:00; Labor Day-June 14, daily 8:00–5:00; 503-861-2471; free.)

(See WASHINGTON in this chapter; also Chapter 3, DISTRICT OF COLUMBIA; also Chapter 4, INDIANA, MISSOURI, NORTH DAKOTA; also Chapter 5, KENTUCKY, TENNESSEE, VIRGINIA.)

REED, JOHN SILAS (1887–1920). A **Portland** native, the political journalist who became an official Soviet Hero of the Russian Revolution was born and spent his earliest years in "Cedar Hill," the luxurious French chateau of his grandparents. The long-gone mansion stood at 2368 Southwest Cedar St. Apartment towers now cover the site. A home Reed occupied later (ca. 1900–06), when attending Portland Academy, is a three-story private dwelling at the corner of Northwest 21st Avenue and Davis Street.

(See Chapter 2, MANHATTAN; also Chapter 3, NEW YORK.)

SUNDAY, WILLIAM ASHLEY "BILLY" (1862–1935). The flamboyant evangelist owned a small apple ranch at **Hood River** in his later years. It remains privately owned at 3024 Sunday Drive.

(See Chapter 4, ILLINOIS, INDIANA, IOWA.)

TEXAS

The third most populous and fastest growing state is also the second largest; Texas enormity is only vaguely expressed in numbers. Dawn takes about an hour to traverse the 773-mile width of the state. From the far northwest to the extreme south extend about 1,000 miles of peaks, plains, hills and canyons. Four major geographical zones—the Rocky Mountains, Great Plains, Central Lowlands and Coastal Plain—descend across the state, ending in the 624-mile Gulf shoreline.

When Spanish forces found La Salle's abandoned Fort St. Louis in 1690, they established

San Francisco de los Tejas on the Neches River near Beaumont, naming the settlement after a local Indian salutation that sounded like "teck-as." As a province of New Spain from 1691, the Spanish established San Antonio de Bexar as capital. The United States acquired Texas from France as part of the 1803 Louisiana Purchase but gave it up to Spain by the 1819 Florida Treaty. After Mexico took over in 1821, Stephen F. Austin founded the first American settlement under a Mexican grant. A period of political and military turmoil raged as American colonists poured in and Mexico tried to maintain control over its increasingly less Mexican province. The blood-thirsty Mexican dictator Antonio Lopez de Santa Anna brought matters to a head by capturing San Antonio, besieging the old, rundown mission called the Alamo and slaughtering its 187 defenders in 1836. Ironically, if Santa Anna had bypassed the Alamo to fight Sam Houston's meager army to the east, the Texas rebellion would undoubtedly have been crushed. As it was, Houston's army captured Santa Anna by surprise attack six weeks later at San Jacinto, and the Republic of Texas became an independent reality. Houston served as the president of Texas until its 1845 admission into the Union as the 28th state, an annexation that Mexico regarded as a declaration of war. Bumbling U.S. diplomacy at best or plain political opportunism at worst led to the needless Mexican War of 1846–48.

Sixteen years after gaining statehood, Texas became seventh of the 11 Confederate states to secede despite the strong opposition of Gover-nor Houston, who was promptly deposed and died shortly after. In many ways Texas still iden-tifies more deeply with the South than the Southwest, though this is changing. As one popular travel guide states, "for every school named after Sam Houston, there is one bearing the name of Robert E. Lee," but few Confederate battles occurred in Texas. Readmitted to the Union in 1870, Texas suffered economically under Reconstruction but soon became the nation's major producer of cotton. Longhorn herds ranged wild on arid plains in western Texas and also formed the basis of the Southwestern cattle industry. Between 1867 and 1887, some 10 million head were driven north over the Chisholm and other cattle trails to northern railheads. The tough, stringy longhorn, since replaced by heavier breeds, verged on extinction in 1927 and today

survives only as a zoo curiosity.

The state's economy remained agricultural until 1901, when the Spindletop strike near Beaumont brought oil to the forefront. Almost 200,000 active wells, scattered throughout plains, forests and Gulf waters, give Texas the national leadership in the production of petroleum and natural gas. Livestock and cotton are still major income producers, but agriculture has become highly diverse. In two generations the Texan population has shifted from 80 percent rural to 80 percent urban. Houston, the state's largest city and the nation's fastest growing major city, has ranked fourth largest in the United States since 1981; its inland seaport, third busiest in the country, makes it an international center with direct links to Middle Eastern and Chinese markets. The Dallas-Fort Worth area, a vast urban sprawl bearing the characteristic Texan label "Metroplex," encom-passes 11 counties and 3 million people. Austin, the capital since statehood, is the state's sixth largest city.

Prominent Texas natives included two U.S. presidents, Dwight Eisenhower and Lyndon Johnson. Adm. Chester W. Nimitz and Howard Hughes were born and raised there. Two native athletes, supreme in their times, were boxer Jack Johnson and Babe Didrikson Zaharias. Longtime residents born elsewhere included the two redoubtable political Sams, Houston and Rayburn. The most prominent resident writer was proba-bly O. Henry, who began his literary career in Austin. Visitors will find homes of the politicians and warriors generally open to the public; the homes of other notable Texans are in most cases privately owned and may be viewed only from the outside.

BEAN, ROY (1825?–1903). Self-declared "law west of the Pecos," the saloon keeper dispensed highly informal justice as a semi-official judge at the tent city of Vinegaroon from 1882. He renamed his settlement **Langtry** after developing a meno-pausal crush on beautiful English actress Lillie Langtry (though some claim that the town name originated more prosaically from another Lang-try, a civil engineer). The actress never answered Judge Bean's letters, but he named his saloon the "Jersey Lilly" (the signpainter misspelled her name) and continued to hold impromptu court sessions as needed before his bar. The Texas Department of Highways and Public Transportation maintains Bean's rustic saloon-courtroom on U.S. Highway 90. An adjacent visitor center exhibits dioramas about his colorful career. (Open daily, 8:00–5:00; 915-291-3340; free.)

Exhibits: In **San Antonio,** the Jersey Lilly Hospitality Center at the Pearl Brewery, 312 Pearl Parkway, is a replica of Bean's Langtry saloon. (Open June 1–August 31, Monday–Saturday 10:00–5:00; September 1–May 31, Monday–Friday 10:00–5:00; 512-226-0231; free.)

In **Del Rio,** the Whitehead Memorial Museum at 1308 South Main St. displays another replica of the "Jersey Lilly" plus Bean memorabilia. (Open Monday–Friday 8:00–4:30, Saturday 9:00–4:30; 512-774-3611; donation.)

BORGLUM, GUTZON (1867–1941). The sculptor of mountains maintained a three-room winter suite at the Menger Hotel on Alamo Plaza, **San Antonio,** from 1927 to about 1936. Operating since 1859, this hotel remains one of the city's most prestigious lodgings. Robert E. Lee guested there in 1861, and Theodore Roosevelt imbibed daily at the bar while recruiting his Rough Riders in 1898. During his residence there, Borglum used an old limestone building in Brackenridge Park, on U.S. Highway 281 in northeast San Antonio, for a studio.

(See IDAHO in this chapter; also Chapter 1, CONNECTICUT; also Chapter 2, MANHATTAN; also Chapter 4, SOUTH DAKOTA.)

BOWIE, JAMES "JIM" (1796–1836).
Exhibit: See DAVID "DAVY" CROCKETT.
(See Chapter 5, ARKANSAS, LOUISIANA.)

BRADLEY, OMAR NELSON (1893–1981). The last home of the General of the Army from 1977 was Quarters Number 1 in the Beaumont Army Medical Center complex at Fort Bliss. Dating from 1922, the house was occupied by Medical Center commanders before Bradley's occupancy; and current plans anticipate its continued use for this purpose. Fort Bliss military reservation and Beaumont Center are located on Fred Wilson Road in **El Paso.**

(See CALIFORNIA in this chapter; also Chapter 3, PENNSYLVANIA; also Chapter 4, MISSOURI; also Chapter 5, GEORGIA, VIRGINIA.)

CROCKETT, DAVID "DAVY" (1786–1836).
Exhibits: The Alamo National Historic Landmark at Alamo Plaza in **San Antonio**—known as the "Cradle of Texas Liberty"—is the 1744 chapel-fortress portion of the Mission San Antonio de Valero, established in 1718, which originally covered a much larger area on today's Alamo Plaza. With 5,000 troops, Mexican general Antonio Lopez de Santa Anna besieged the 187 rebel defenders, including Crockett and James Bowie, for 13 days. He finally stormed the chapel on March 6, 1836, and wiped out the entire garrison. Evidence gathered by Texas historian Dan Kilgore in *How Did Davy Die?* (1978) indicates that Crockett may have surrendered or been captured before being shot. The State of Texas displays the restored mission plus a museum of pioneer artifacts and dioramas. (Open Monday–Saturday 9:00–5:30, Sunday 10:00–5:30; 512-225-1391; free.) The Alamo Museum, operated near the Alamo by the Daughters of the Republic of Texas, exhibits relics of the 1836 battle. (Open Monday–Saturday 9:00–5:00; 512-225-3853; donation.) Remember The Alamo Theatre and Museum at 315 Alamo Plaza presents a multimedia program on the siege and battle. (Open daily, 9:00–5:30; 512-224-1836; admission.)

(See Chapter 5, TENNESSEE.)

DIDRIKSON, MILDRED ELLA "BABE." See MILDRED ELLA DIDRIKSON "BABE" ZAHARIAS.

EISENHOWER, DWIGHT DAVID (1890–1969). The 34th U.S. president's birthplace, a two-story frame house built about 1880, stands at 208 East Day St. (at the corner of Lamar Avenue) at Eisenhower Birthplace State Park in **Denison,** his home until 1891. As the popular World War II hero, Gen. Eisenhower reluctantly visited his birthplace in 1946. "Eisenhower's relationship with the place of his birth was almost traumatic," wrote Alfred Steinberg, "for it signified an unhappy period in his mother's life" when his father had temporarily deserted the family. Until his 1946 visit, Eisenhower invariably gave his birthplace as Tyler, Texas. The Eisenhower Birthplace Foundation has restored the home to its 1890 appearance with period furnishings and family memorabilia. The house is operated by the Texas Parks and Wildlife Department. (Open June 1–August 31, daily 8:00–5:00; September 1–May 31, daily

10:00–12:00, 1:00–5:00; 214-465-8908; admission.)

Exhibit: The Military Museum, Building 123 at Fort Sam Houston, displays a uniform and boots worn by Gen. Eisenhower during World War II. Fort Sam Houston is the headquarters of the Fifth U.S. Army and is located on North New Braunfels Avenue in **San Antonio.** (Open Wednesday–Sunday 10:00–4:00; 512-221-6117; free.)

(See COLORADO in this chapter; also Chapter 2, MANHATTAN; also Chapter 3, DISTRICT OF COLUMBIA, MARYLAND, PENNSYLVANIA; also Chapter 4, KANSAS, MICHIGAN; also Chapter 5, GEORGIA, VIRGINIA.)

GOULD, JAY (1836–1892).

Exhibit: The unscrupulous railroad tycoon lived in luxurious style while traveling, as manifested by his private railroad car, "Atalanta," an 88-foot "palace on wheels." Dating from 1890, its four staterooms, lounge and other rooms are richly paneled in mahogany and maple. It is owned by and stands opposite Excelsior House, the 1850 hotel still operating at 211 West Austin St. in **Jefferson.** Gould lodged there in a foul mood, displeased that town citizens had refused to permit railroads. "The end of Jefferson," he prophesied falsely in the hotel register now on display. ("Atalanta" open Monday–Saturday 9:00–5:00, Sunday 1:00–5:00; admission; Excelsior House tours daily, 1:00–4:00; 214-665-2513; admission.)

(See Chapter 2, MANHATTAN; also Chapter 3, NEW YORK.)

GUTHRIE, WOODROW WILSON "WOODY" (1912–1967). The balladeer and composer whose life and songs reflected a constant positive outlook despite crushing personal tragedies, Guthrie lived in **Pampa** at intervals from 1929 until about 1940, the period when he stopped painting signs and began his footloose performing career. His home with his first wife remains privately owned at 408 South Russell St.

(See OKLAHOMA in this chapter; also Chapter 2, BROOKLYN, MANHATTAN, QUEENS.)

HENRY, O. See WILLIAM SYDNEY PORTER.

HOLLY, BUDDY (1936–1959). Born Charles Hardin Holley at 1911 Sixth St. in **Lubbock,** the performer pioneered rock music with his group, the Crickets, during his short career. The small,

one-story frame house, built in the 1920s, fell during a 1970 tornado. Its site is now a vacant lot. He and his family also occupied subsequent dwellings in Lubbock. Some probably remain, but addresses remain uncertain.

HOUSTON, SAMUEL "SAM" (1793–1863). In Texas, Houston's pedestal ranks with Lee's in Virginia and Lincoln's in Illinois. The 15-acre Sam Houston Shrine, operated by the State of Texas at 1804 Ave. L, half a mile south of **Huntsville** on U.S. Highway 75 Business, displays several buildings associated with the soldier, president of Texas, governor and senator. The "Wigwam" or "Woodland" is the home he enlarged in 1847 from a one-room pioneer cabin and occupied until 1858. His 1847 law office, carriage house and a log kitchen are nearby. "Steamboat House," built in 1858 and Houston's last home from 1861, resembles a Mississippi riverboat in design. This house originally stood at Oakwood Cemetery three blocks north of the Huntsville courthouse. The Sam Houston Memorial Museum on the Shrine property at Sam Houston Avenue contains the major collection of his possessions, clothing and memorabilia. Houston Shrine is also affiliated with Sam Houston State University. (Open daily 9:00–5:00; 713-295-7824; free.)

In **Austin,** Governor's Mansion National Historic Landmark at 1010 Colorado St. (at the corner of 11th Street) was Houston's residence from 1859 to 1861. This stately, two-story house of white brick, still serving as State Executive Mansion, dates from 1855. One of the public rooms operated there by the State of Texas Board of Control displays Houston's massive four-poster bed. (Open Monday–Saturday 10:00–12:00, Sunday 2:00–4:00; 512-475-2121; free.)

Marked sites of other Houston homes include the southwest corner of the public square in **Nacogdoches** (1830s); White House of the Republic of Texas, southeast corner of Main Street and Preston Avenue in **Houston** (1836–38, 1841–44); and a location across from Old Baylor University campus on Farm Road 390 in **Independence** (1853–62). The last home of his widow, Margaret Lea Houston, stands privately owned two blocks east of the Farm Road 390/50 intersection (1863–67).

Exhibits: The Texas Baptist Historical Center Museum, operated on the site of Independence Baptist Church where Houston was baptized in 1854, displays Houston family artifacts and memorabilia. It stands at the Farm Road 390/50 junction in **Independence.** (Open Wednesday–Saturday 10:00–4:00, Sunday 1:00–5:00, other times by appointment; 713-836-5117; free.)

In **Galveston,** the Rosenberg Library, 2310 Sealy Ave., displays Houston letters and manuscripts. (Open Monday–Thursday 9:00–9:00, Friday–Saturday 9:00–6:00; 713-763-8854; free.)

(See Chapter 5, TENNESSEE, VIRGINIA.)

HUGHES, HOWARD ROBARD (1905–1976). Industrialist, aviator and film maker, the eccentric billionaire was a **Houston** native, born in a long-gone frame house at 1404 Crawford St., his home until 1918. In that year, his father built the two-story brick mansion at 3921 Yoakum Blvd. Though Hughes resided there only until his 1925 marriage to Ella Rice, he returned at intervals and continued to list it as his home address for years. His boyhood room was on the second floor north side. Today the structure houses the Modern Languages Department of Saint Thomas University.

(See CALIFORNIA, NEVADA in this chapter.)

JARRELL, RANDALL (1914–1965). Only one of the poet-critic's three Texas homes survive in **Austin,** where he taught at the University of Texas from 1939 to 1943. A private duplex residence he occupied in 1940 and 1941, it stands at 2501 Indian Trail.

(See CALIFORNIA in this chapter; also Chapter 3, DISTRICT OF COLUMBIA; also Chapter 4, OHIO, also Chapter 5, NORTH CAROLINA.)

JOHNSON, JACK ARTHUR (1878–1946). The boxer's probable birthplace was 808 Broadway in **Galveston,** a section hit hard by the 1900 hurricane. According to Rosenberg Library archivist Michael E. Wilson, "Today there is a small house on the site which does not seem to date back that far; but it well may, or have been moved from another site nearby." Thus evidence remains inconclusive as to whether this house was Johnson's actual birthplace. One biographer states that he spent most of his adolescence in the area of 11th Street and Avenue K.

(See Chapter 4, ILLINOIS.)

JOHNSON, LYNDON BAINES (1908–1973). The 36th U.S. president, a master politician with the features of a range foreman, was a fourth gener-

ation Texan. Three of his homes stand within the Lyndon B. Johnson National Historic Site, operated in two units by the National Park Service at Stonewall and Johnson City.

The LBJ Ranch Unit near **Stonewall** is reached only by free bus tour from Johnson State Historical Park (see *Exhibit* below). On the eastern edge of the Ranch Unit (Park Road 49) stands the reconstructed four-room farmhouse, dating originally from 1888, where he was born and lived until age five. Nearby on the same complex is the "Texas White House," the low, spacious ranch house of limestone and timber on the Pedernales River that became his permanent home. The original 1890 house, where Johnson lived from 1917 to 1923, had belonged to his aunt and uncle from 1912. Johnson acquired it from them in 1952 and enlarged the house to 13 rooms. Features that occasionally irritated visitors were an elaborate intercom system and Muzak playing constantly in every room. The LBJ Ranch encompassed some 438 acres at Johnson's death, only a small portion of his total property; during his vice presidency from 1961 to 1963, he bought 12,000 acres, including three entire ranches, in Blanco, Gillespie, Llano and Burnet Counties. In 1972 the ex-president and his wife donated more than 200 acres of the LBJ Ranch—his home, adjacent outbuildings and eight fields—to the public. Tours are limited to exterior views of the ranch buildings but also include visits to the one-room Junction School that Johnson first attended, his ranchland and the Johnson Family Cemetery where the former president lies. The ranch itself is still a working Hereford cattle operation. (Tours Memorial Day–Labor Day, daily 10:00–5:30; Labor Day–Memorial Day, daily 10:00–4:00; 512-868-7128; free.)

The **Johnson City** Unit, one block south of U.S. Highway 290, displays the small, white frame home, built in 1901, where Johnson lived as a boy from 1914 to 1917 and occasionally thereafter to 1924. During his presidency, he liked to take visitors there and expound about his poor boyhood, a tale true enough but often overstated to fetch a tear. Restored to its 1920s appearance, the house displays family furnishings and heirlooms. Visitors may also ride by wagon to the nearby Johnson Settlement Area, a restored complex of ranch buildings that includes the log house built by Johnson's grandfather. (Open daily, 9:00–5:00; 512-868-7128; free.)

Exhibits: The 269-acre Lyndon B. Johnson State Historical Park, located one mile east of **Stonewall** on U.S. Highway 290, contains the visitor center where LBJ Ranch tours begin and end. Displays, memorabilia and films relating to Johnson are shown there by the Texas Parks and Wildlife Department. (Open daily, 9:00–5:00; 512-644-2252; free.)

In **Austin,** the Johnson Library and Museum at 2313 Red River St., one block west of Interstate Highway 35, is the main repository for Johnson papers and memorabilia. The Museum occupies three floors of an eight-story structure on the University of Texas campus. Exhibits include items relating to his boyhood, political career and campaigns, life in the White House and controversies of the 1960s. Rooms display gifts from heads of state and the American people, a seven-eighths scale replica of the White House oval office during Johnson's tenure from 1963 to 1969 and a biographical film. The Library and Museum, operated by the National Archives, was dedicated by President Nixon in 1971. (Open daily, 9:00–5:00; 512-397-5279; free.)

The Alumni House of Southwest Texas State University, North Lyndon B. Johnson Drive in **San Marcos,** displays memorabilia of Johnson's student days there from 1927 to 1930.

(See Chapter 3, DISTRICT OF COLUMBIA, MARYLAND; also Chapter 4, MICHIGAN.)

KENNEDY, JOHN FITZGERALD (1917–1963).

Exhibits: "We're really in nut country now," remarked the 35th U.S. president to his wife as he viewed hostile headlines in their Hotel Texas room at Fort Worth on November 22, 1963. Later that day, in **Dallas,** an assassin's bullets killed him almost instantly as he rode in a motorcade past Dealey Plaza. A granite marker identifies the site of the shooting at Houston and Main streets on the grounds of a triple underpass. (This spot is very close to where Dallas pioneer John Neely Bryan built his cabin in 1843.) The Warren Commission contended that Lee Harvey Oswald (see the entry on Oswald later in this section) shot the president from the easternmost, sixth-floor window of the seven-story brick building which was then the Texas School Book Depository. This structure is still a brooding presence at 411 Elm St. (at the corner of Houston Street). It does not admit the public.

(See Chapter 1, MASSACHUSETTS, RHODE ISLAND; also Chapter 2, BRONX; also Chapter 3, DISTRICT OF COLUMBIA, MARYLAND, NEW YORK; also Chapter 5, FLORIDA, VIRGINIA.)

LAFITTE, JEAN (1780?–1825?). The privateer and smuggler moved his Louisiana colony to the eventual site of **Galveston** in 1817 and founded the settlement of Campeche, from whence he continued to molest Spanish shipping and steal slave cargoes. "Maison Rouge," his combination home, warehouse and fort with cannons at its corners, stood at 1417 Water Ave. Lafitte burned the town in 1821, before the U.S. Navy raided the colony, and sailed into the mists of history.

Exhibit: The Rosenberg Library at 2310 Sealy Ave. in **Galveston** displays Lafitte letters and papers. (Open Monday–Thursday 9:00–9:00, Friday–Saturday 9:00–6:00; 713-763-8854; free.)

(See Chapter 5, LOUISIANA.)

LA SALLE, ROBERT CAVELIER, SIEUR DE (1643–1687). "Somewhere in the course of developing scientific method," wrote James Gray, "we must have lost a technique of holding off death by sheer moral authority." Not once but many times was this "technique" evident in the superhuman but often self-destructive behavior of the French explorer. In 1685, three years after following the Mississippi to its mouth from Illinois, La Salle launched his last gamble in a life full of them—the attempt to establish, from the Gulf side, a French colony at the Mississippi mouth. His expedition somehow overshot the mark and landed on the shore of Matagorda Bay, probably near the old town of **Indianola** on State Highway 316, where his pink granite statue surveys the sand. Plagued by dissension, illness and loss of supplies, the 400 colonists erected Fort St. Louis on the west bank of Garcitas Creek about five miles above its mouth on Lavaca Bay. From there La Salle made several expeditions into the surrounding country in a futile attempt to locate the Mississippi. After his assassination, Karankawa Indians invaded the colony in 1689 and killed most of those who hadn't already succumbed to smallpox. The fort was discovered by Spanish soldiers later that year and burned. In 1722 Spaniards built Fort Nuestra Senora de Loreto on the site as a base of operations in the interior of Texas but abandoned it in 1726. Today this overgrown site lies on the private ranchland held by four generations of the Keeran family, located near **La Salle** off Farm Road 616.

Exhibit: A statue of La Salle on State Highway 90 in downtown **Navasota** marks the supposed vicinity where he was slain by mutinous followers. The actual site, according to Southwestern scholar Herbert E. Bolton, was just above the confluence of the Brazos and Navasota rivers, which would place the spot east of Navasota in the area of State Highway 105/Farm Road 159. A dissenting theory by E. W. Cole pinpoints the spot much further north: on the east bank of Larrison Creek, southeast of **Forest** in southern Cherokee County.

(See Chapter 4, ILLINOIS, MICHIGAN.)

MacARTHUR, DOUGLAS (1880–1964).

Exhibit: The Douglas MacArthur Academy of Freedom, affiliated with Howard Payne University on Austin Avenue and Coggin Street in **Brownwood,** displays some of the World War II general's personal souvenirs and memorabilia—gold-braided cap, sunglasses, medals, swords—plus a large electric map of his Pacific campaigns. (Tours daily, 1:30–3:30; also Monday–Friday 11:00, Saturday 10:00–11:00; closed during semester breaks; 915-646-2502; free.)

(See NEW MEXICO in this chapter; also Chapter 2, MANHATTAN; also Chapter 3, MARYLAND, NEW YORK; also Chapter 4, KANSAS; also Chapter 5, ARKANSAS, VIRGINIA.)

NATION, CARRY AMELIA MOORE (1846–1911).

Exhibit: The boardinghouse operated during the 1880s by the fierce temperance activist is long gone from Morton and Fourth streets in **Richmond;** but the Fort Bend County Museum at 500 Houston St. displays some Nation memorabilia. (Open Tuesday–Friday 10:00–4:00, Saturday–Sunday 1:00–5:00; 713-342-6478; free.)

(See Chapter 4, KANSAS, MISSOURI; also Chapter 5, ARKANSAS, KENTUCKY.)

NIMITZ, CHESTER WILLIAM (1885–1966). Admiral Nimitz State Historical Park at 340 East Main St. in **Fredericksburg** is a complex of buildings and gardens dedicated as a memorial to the World War II Pacific naval commander and the two million men and women he led. Nimitz was born in the back bedroom of the small limestone-adobe cottage built in 1866 at 247 East Main St. Before private owners acquired and restored this house to its original condition in 1981, it had stood vacant for almost 30 years. Renovation continues, but some of the rooms are currently open to public visitation at unspecified hours (inquire locally). The kitchen contains its original wood-burning stove. Steamboat Hotel, built in 1853 by Nimitz's grandfather and since restored, was Nimitz's home until 1891. Today it houses the Museum of the Pacific War, containing exhibits of the admiral's life and career. Operated by the Texas Parks and Wildlife Department, this complex is one of the nation's most impressive World War II memorials. (Open daily, 8:00–5:00; 512-997-4379; admission.)

Exhibit: Northeast of **Pasadena** on State Highway 134, San Jacinto Battlefield National Historic Landmark, a 325-acre site commemorating the final battle for Texan independence in 1836, also contains the moored *U.S.S. Texas.* A few exhibits on the famed World War II battleship relate to Adm. Nimitz. (Open daily 10:00–5:00; 713-479-2421; admission.)

(See CALIFORNIA in this chapter; also Chapter 3, DISTRICT OF COLUMBIA.)

OSWALD, LEE HARVEY (1939–1963). Apparent lone assassin of President Kennedy (see the entry on John Fitzgerald Kennedy earlier in this section), the rootless Oswald spent much of his short life in concocting and acting our bizarre ploys for attention. "Try a job. Fail. Do something dramatic," according to his brother Robert, was Oswald's typical pattern. In **Fort Worth,** the small family supported by his mother lived in a succession of houses from 1947 to 1952, including 1505 Eighth Ave. (1947); 3300 Willing St. (1947–48); and 7408 Ewing St. (1948–52), which his mother owned. Later he lived at 4936 Collingwood Ave., his 1956 apartment from which he enlisted in the U.S. Marines; and 2703 Mercedes St., a one-story duplex where Oswald and his Russian bride settled into a 1961 furnished apartment.

In **Dallas,** the scene of the "something dramatic" that capped all of Oswald's failures, the couple occupied a run-down, three-room apartment at 604 Elsbeth St. in the Oak Cliff section (1962–63), where their marriage grew rocky and they separated for a time. In March and April of 1963, Oswald lived alone in a balconied apartment on the second floor at 214 West Neely St. His final Dallas lodging before his arrest was a shabby room at 1026 North Beckley St., to which he returned immediately after the assassination and picked up the pistol with which he would kill police officer J. D. Tippett a few moments later.

The night before the assassination, Oswald stayed with his wife at her lodging—the Michael and Ruth Paine house, where he had also resided for about a month—at 2515 West Fifth St. in **Irving.** In the built-in garage of this four-room frame house, Oswald had previously stored the 6.5 mm Mannlicher-Carcano rifle he had obtained by mail order; and on the morning of November 22, 1963, carried it wrapped to his Dallas place of employment.

All extant Oswald lodgings (present local owners and authorities are exceedingly reluctant to confirm the presence of any house associated with him) remain private.

Exhibits: See the entry on John Fitzgerald Kennedy earlier in this section.

Though not officially marked, several **Dallas** sites were involved in the assassination. On April 10, 1963, Oswald attempted to kill retired Gen. Edwin A. Walker by firing into Walker's home at 4011 Turtle Creek Blvd. (privately owned); the shot narrowly missed. Oswald killed Officer Tippett near the intersection of 10th and Patton streets. He was finally disarmed and arrested about half an hour later in the Texas Theatre, 231 West Jefferson Blvd. On November 24 Oswald himself was shot in the basement garage of the Dallas Municipal Building, 2014 Main St. by Jack Ruby; and died a short time later in Parkland Memorial Hospital, 5201 Harry Hines Blvd.

(See Chapter 2, BRONX; also Chapter 5, LOUISIANA.)

PORTER, WILLIAM SYDNEY "O. HENRY" (1862–1910). Porter began his writing career in **Austin,** where he lived from 1884 to 1894 and returned at intervals until 1897. The home he occupied from 1893 to 1895 stood at 308 East Fourth St. Today this one-story frame cottage, built in 1886, stands at 409 East Fifth St. Moved there in 1956—despite the objections of at least one new neighbor who called the house "an old worn-out, worm-infested junkpile" and threatened a lawsuit—it has been restored by the Austin Heritage Society. The O. Henry Museum, now operated by the City of Austin Recreation Department, displays original and period furnishings plus Porter memorabilia. Visitors may see the mahogany desk on which he began his

serious literary efforts, doll furniture he made for his daughter, photos and facsimiles. (Open Tuesday–Saturday 11:00–4:30, Sunday 2:00–4:30; 512-472-1903; free.)

In **San Antonio,** Porter rented a two-story stone house on South Press Street in 1895 while publishing his humorous weekly magazine *The Rolling Stone,* an enterprise that soon folded. This house, built in 1855, was moved to the Buckhorn Hall of Horns Museum, operated by the Lone Star Brewery at 600 Lone Star Blvd. Displayed in the O. Henry House are first editions and photocopies of his weekly. (Open daily, 9:30–5:00; 512-226-8301; free.)

Exhibit: In **Austin,** the Old 1857 Land Office, where Porter worked from 1887 to 1891, is now the Daughters of the Confederacy and Daughters of the Republic of Texas Museum, 112 East 11th St. on the state capitol grounds. Pioneer and Confederate relics are displayed. (Open Monday–Friday 9:00–12:00, 1:00–5:00; 512-477-1822; donation.)

(See Chapter 2, MANHATTAN; also Chapter 5, NORTH CAROLINA.)

RAYBURN, SAMUEL TALIAFERRO "SAM" (1882–1961). Longtime Texas congressman and powerful speaker of the House for a total of 17 years, Rayburn migrated to the state with his parents in 1887. A fire in 1923 destroyed the first family home, which they occupied until 1912, south of Windom.

In 1916 Rayburn built a two-story, 12-room frame house near **Bonham** and occupied it as his "Home Place" until his death. Rayburn House National Historic Landmark, located two and one-fourth miles west of town on U.S. Highway 82, displays "Mister Sam's" original furnishings and possessions. Three vehicles owned by the speaker are also there. Rayburn expanded his original 120 acres to 250; his brother ran the farm, chiefly as a dairy operation, during his frequent absence. The Texas Historical Commission presents an audiovisual program relating to Rayburn's life and career and conducts tours through the house. (Open Tuesday–Friday 10:00–5:00, Saturday 1:00–5:00, Sunday 2:00–5:00; 214-583-5558; free.)

Exhibit: The Sam Rayburn Library, operated by a board of trustees on U.S. Highway 82 in **Bonham,** displays a wide variety of historical memorabilia relating to his political career. Papers, gavels, mementoes and a replica of his Washington speaker's office with original furnishings are shown along with exhibits tracing his life from Texas farm boy to congressional leader. (Open Monday–Friday 10:00–5:00, Saturday 1:00–5:00, Sunday 2:00–5:00; 214-583-2455; free.)

(See Chapter 3, DISTRICT OF COLUMBIA; also Chapter 5, TENNESSEE.)

RICKENBACKER, EDWARD VERNON "EDDIE" (1890–1973). During the 1950s the aviator and businessman owned a 2,700-acre ranch near **Hunt** that he eventually gave to the Boy Scouts of America. Now privately owned and known as "Patio Ranch," it is located on Farm Road 1340 west of town.

(See Chapter 2, MANHATTAN; also Chapter 3, NEW YORK; also Chapter 4, INDIANA, MICHIGAN, OHIO; also Chapter 5, FLORIDA.)

ZAHARIAS, MILDRED ELLA DIDRIKSON "BABE" (1911–1956). Probably the nation's foremost woman athlete, the versatile Babe Didrikson was a **Port Arthur** native. Her Seventh Street birthplace and home until 1915 was razed in 1962.

She resided longest at her family home in **Beaumont** (ca. 1916–36), which survives at 850 Doucette Ave. Her father continually added portions until, she wrote, "it became the biggest house on the block." In adulthood before her 1938 marriage, she resided in an apartment on the second floor there. She often revisited the house even after new owners occupied it. It remains privately owned.

Exhibit: The Babe Didrikson Zaharias Memorial Museum at 1750 East Interstate Highway 10 in **Beaumont** displays trophies, artifacts and memorabilia relating to her careers in several sports. (Open daily 9:00–5:00; 713-833-4622; free.)

UTAH

Deseret, meaning "land of honeybees" in the *Book of Mormon,* would have been this state's name if Mormon wishes had prevailed. The U.S. Congress rejected this name as too suggestive of "desert" and Mormon theology, imposing instead the name Utah after local tribes of native Utes. Separated from Upper California as Utah Territory in 1850, the area did not become the 45th state until 1896.

The first settlers were members of the Church of Jesus Christ of Latter-day Saints, an aggressive sect of visionary origins to whom persecution

and exile had become familiar traumas. Led by Brigham Young, their journey there was a literal pilgrimage across the plains to what they regarded as their "promised land." They entered Great Salt Lake valley in 1847, soon followed by other Mormon converts, built Salt Lake City and set about making the forbidding Utah desert flower. The industrious Mormons became the first white Americans to practice extensive irrigation. How well they succeeded is abundantly clear.

Today diverse manufacturing is the state's most important industry, followed by mining and agriculture. The renowned Mormon Tabernacle Choir is a brilliant national treasure, while Utah's spectacular landscape brings thousands of visitors annually.

SMITH, JOSEPH (1805–1844).

Exhibit: The founder of the Mormon church never arrived at Utah himself, but memorabilia—including a lock of his hair—may be viewed at the Temple Square visitor center, **Salt Lake City** (see the entry on Brigham Young below).

(See Chapter 1, VERMONT; also Chapter 3, NEW YORK, PENNSYLVANIA; also Chapter 4, ILLINOIS, MISSOURI, OHIO.)

YOUNG, BRIGHAM (1801–1877). Mormon leader and Territorial Governor of Utah, Young established and directed the religious colony from its 1847 beginning at **Salt Lake City.** Beehive House National Historic Landmark, his official residence from 1854 on East South Temple Street (at the corner of State Street), dates from that year and also served later presidents of the church. The cupola on this two-story house of buff adobe is in the shape of a beehive, symbol of Mormon industry. Twenty acres, including outbuildings and orchards, were enclosed by a 10-foot surrounding wall and guarded by armed sentry at the Eagle Gate entrance. Despite Young's roster of wives, he only "visited" them in their rooms, invariably returning to his own bedroom on the first floor to sleep alone. The Church of Jesus Christ of Latter-day Saints has restored the house to its original appearance. Some of the period furnishings belonged to Young. His adjacent office, built in 1852 and now a conference center, contains his pine desk. (Open Monday–Saturday 9:30–4:30, Sunday 10:00–2:30; 801-531-2672; free.) A simultaneous residence after 1856 and guarded by a stone "Lion of the Lord" over its portico, the adjacent 1856 "Lion House" with 10 gables held Young, seven of his wives, and numerous children. This structure of adobe and concrete where Young died is not open to the public. Eagle Gate, arched over State Street next to Beehive House, also survives.

Young Winter Home State Historical Site is a two-story, adobe house on a foundation of lava rock in **St. George;** the leader used it from 1873, when the north wing was added to the original 1869 structure. Also operated by the church and displaying period furnishings, the house stands at 89 West Second North St. (Open daily, 9:00–9:00; 801-673-2517; free.)

Exhibits: At Temple Square in **Salt Lake City,** the church visitor center at 50 West South Temple St. displays numerous items of personal memorabilia including Young's octagonal desk, a safe, articles of clothing and a lock of his hair. Tours of adjacent Mormon buildings and monuments begin there. (Open summer, daily 8:00 AM–8:30 PM; winter, daily 9:00–7:30; 801-531-2534; free.) The Museum of the Daughters of Utah Pioneers, 300 North Main St., exhibits other possessions: Young's carpetbag, a Panama hat he wore and the wagon in which he traveled over the plains. (Open April–October, Monday–Saturday 9:00–5:00, Sunday 1:00–5:00; November–March, Monday–Saturday 9:00–5:00; 801-533-5759; free.) Pioneer Trail State Park at 2601 Sunnyside Ave. marks the 1847 entrance to Emigration Canyon, where Young and his followers first viewed Salt Lake Valley and declared "This is the Place." Young's "Forest Farm Home," the cottage of adobe and pine centering the 100-acre farm that supplied Young's large households with dairy products, stood originally at 732 Ashton Ave. but is now in the park. A visitor center, operated by the Utah State Division of Parks and Recreation, displays exhibits on the Mormon arrival and settlement. (Open daily, 9:00–5:00; 801-582-2853; free.)

(See Chapter 1, VERMONT; also Chapter 3, NEW YORK; also Chapter 4, ILLINOIS.)

WASHINGTON

In 1980 national attention focused on the spectacular volcanic eruption of Mount St. Helens, which coated a large portion of the state in pulverized rock. Washington, larger than Pennsylvania, New Jersey, Delaware and Maryland combined, is nevertheless the smallest of the western continental states. As in Oregon, the Cascade Range divides the state into different climates and lifestyles. Coastal Washington in the mountain "rain shadow" receives some of the nation's heaviest annual rainfall—150 to 200 inches—and dripping, junglelike forests cover much of this rim. Eastern Washington is mainly a basaltic tableland dissected by the Columbia River. Sagebrush plains and rich farmland dominate this much drier half where wheat, orchard, truck and livestock agriculture thrive. Lumbering, formerly the state's primary producer of income, now ranks fourth. The state produces more aluminum than any other but nevertheless relies heavily for its economic well-being upon federal defense contracts for its aircraft industry. Puget Sound's harbor system and lowland area holds most of the state's population, including its largest city of Seattle plus Tacoma and the capital, Olympia.

Spanish, English and American sailors sought the fabled Northwest Passage along Washington's coast during the late 1700s. After Lewis and Clark's 1805 expedition, the fur trade brought competing English and American traders. Britain and the United States jointly occupied and disputed the area until an agreement in 1846 settled the border at the 49th parallel. Washington Territory, including the Idaho panhandle, separated from Oregon Territory in 1853. Missionaries, loggers and fishermen were early residents, but the real flood of settlers arrived only with the completion of the Northern Pacific Railroad in 1883. In 1889, thirty years after its southern neighbor Oregon achieved statehood, Washington entered the Union as the 42nd state. Seattle not only became the staging point of the Klondike Gold Rush of 1898 but also the commercial center and main port of the Pacific Northwest, a position it maintains.

Prominent Washington natives included two popular musical showmen, Bing Crosby and Jimi Hendrix. Justice William O. Douglas, two generals—Ulysses S. Grant and George C. Marshall—and two poets, Vachel Lindsay and Theodore Roethke—also resided in the state for varying periods. Most of their homes exist, but visitors will find few of them open to the public.

CLARK, WILLIAM. See MERIWETHER LEWIS and WILLIAM CLARK.

CROSBY, HARRY LILLIS "BING" (1903–1977).
The popular singer and actor was born in **Tacoma**
in the 1903 home built by his parents at 1112
North Jay St., a white frame, two-story house
that remains privately owned. Crosby's father sold
the house in 1906. The Bing Crosby Historical
Society is in process of acquiring this house and
intends to display Crosby memorabilia there.
(Contact Bing Crosby Historical Society, PO Box
8013, Tacoma, WA 98408; 206-627-2947.)

In **Spokane,** the family rented a yellow, two-
story house on Sinto Avenue. There, about 1910,
Crosby acquired his nickname from a boyhood
chum's fondness for a newspaper humor column
called "the Bingville Bugle." The family lived there
from 1906 to 1913. They next built a two-story
house at 508 East Sharp St., the birthplace of
Bing's musician brother George Robert "Bob"
Crosby in 1913. Bing Crosby lived there until 1925
and returned frequently until his 1930 marriage
to actress Dixie Lee. This dwelling now serves as
an alumni house for Gonzaga University.

Exhibit: The Crosby Library at Gonzaga
University, the crooner's alma mater, displays a
collection of Crosby records and memorabilia at
East 502 Boone Ave. in **Spokane.** (Open Monday–
Saturday 8:00–5:00; Sunday 1:00–5:00; 509-328-
4220; free.)

(See CALIFORNIA, IDAHO, NEVADA in this
chapter.)

DOUGLAS, WILLIAM ORVILLE (1898–1980).
"Absolutely nothing happened on this spot,
September 6, 1859." That was the sign erected
by the puckish jurist outdoorsman, as his own
comment on historical markers, in front of his
Cascade Mountain lodge near **Goose Prairie.**
Douglas built "Prairie House," his isolated home
in 1964 and resided there at every opportunity,
sometimes for weeks, hiking wilderness trails and
entertaining guests. "Goose Prairie is my place
in a sense that Washington, D.C. never could
be," he said. A rail fence surrounds the house
and two acres of pastureland and forest. Still
privately owned, Douglas's home stands south
of State Highway 410 just east of Mount Rainier
National Park.

(See Chapter 1, CONNECTICUT; also Chapter
3, DISTRICT OF COLUMBIA; also Chapter 4,
MINNESOTA.)

GRANT, ULYSSES SIMPSON (1822–1885). Grant

House Museum at 1106 East Evergreen Blvd. in
Vancouver was the brevet captain's office and
living quarters when he served as quartermaster
at Fort Vancouver in 1852 and 1853. The museum
displays furnishings and books owned by the
eventual Union army commander and 18th U.S.
president. Built in 1849, the two-story log building, now sided, with its broad, columned porches,
remains the oldest in the Vancouver Barracks and
forms part of "Officers' Row." A portion of clapboard has been removed on the house to show
its original construction. It is operated by the
Soroptimist Club of Vancouver. (Open Monday–
Wednesday, Friday 1:00–4:00; Saturday–Sunday
1:00–5:00; 206-693-9743; admission.) Vancouver
Barracks, established in 1849, was inactivated in
1946, retaining only 64 of its original 640 acres
for army reserve training.

(See Chapter 2, MANHATTAN; also Chapter
3, DISTRICT OF COLUMBIA, NEW JERSEY,
NEW YORK; also Chapter 4, ILLINOIS, MICHI-
GAN, MISSOURI, OHIO; also Chapter 5, VIR-
GINIA.)

HENDRIX, JIMI (1943–1970). Born Johnny Allen
Hendrix in **Seattle,** the virtuoso rock guitarist was
renamed James Marshall Hendrix, then took the
name Jimi when he began performing. He lived
mainly with his father during infancy and youth
at numerous untraceable addresses in Seattle's
"underside." "Jimmy and his father were like two
roomers," wrote biographer David Henderson,
"two old men who moved often from place to
place, always at the mercy of one authority or
the other: a new landlord, the unemployment
officer, the schoolteacher, the welfare office, the
foster home, the police." In 1946 the two occupied Room 580 at 124 10th Ave., still a private
hotel.

(See Chapter 2, MANHATTAN.)

JEFFERS, ROBINSON (1887–1962). In 1910 and
1911, just before moving permanently to California, the poet occupied a suite in the Forty-two
Fifteen Brooklyn Avenue NE Apartments, **Seattle,** still private lodgings.

(See CALIFORNIA in this chapter; also Chapter 3, PENNSYLVANIA.)

LEWIS, MERIWETHER (1774–1809).
CLARK, WILLIAM (1770–1838).

Exhibits: The Lewis and Clark Interpretive Center at Fort Canby State Park marks the site of the explorers' first view of the Pacific Ocean in 1805. Exhibits and multimedia programs portray numerous aspects of their two-year, 8,000-mile expedition. This is probably the best, most comprehensive Lewis and Clark exhibit in the nation. Operated by the Washington State Parks and Recreation Commission, it is located on Cape Disappointment four miles southwest of **Ilwaco** off U.S. Highway 101. (Open Memorial Day–October 1, daily 9:00–6:00; October 2–Memorial Day, Wednesday–Sunday 9:00–5:00; 206-642-3078; free.)

Sacajawea State Park Museum and Interpretive Center, also operated by the State Parks and Recreation Commission, occupies an 1805 camp site of the expedition on Road 40 East, three miles southeast of **Pasco.** Named for the Shoshone guide who accompanied the explorers to the Pacific, museum and center detail expedition activities at this spot and display many native artifacts. (Open April 16–October 7, Wednesday–Sunday 10:00–6:00; other times by appointment; 509-545-2361; free.)

Expedition artifacts are also displayed at Fort Lewis Military Museum, operated by the U.S. Army at **Fort Lewis.** (Open Wednesday–Sunday 12:00–4:00; 206-967-7206; free.)

(See OREGON in this chapter; also Chapter 3, DISTRICT OF COLUMBIA; also Chapter 4, INDIANA, MISSOURI, NORTH DAKOTA; also Chapter 5, KENTUCKY, TENNESSEE, VIRGINIA.)

LINDSAY, VACHEL (1879–1931). The wandering poet-minstrel lived in **Spokane** from 1924 to 1928. His first residence (1924–25) was Room 1129 of the Hotel Davenport, still at 807 West Sprague Ave. From 1925 to 1928, he lived at 2318 West Pacific Ave. (privately owned).

(See Chapter 4, ILLINOIS.)

MARSHALL, GEORGE CATLETT (1880–1959). In **Vancouver,** the soldier-statesman commanded the Fifth Infantry Brigade at Vancouver Barracks from 1936 to 1938. He resided during this period in the frame Victorian mansion at 1310 East Evergreen Blvd. in "Officers' Row." This 1886 structure, later occupied by the American Red Cross, was restored and opened in 1981 as the Marshall House Restaurant (see the entry on Ulysses Simpson Grant earlier in this section).

(See Chapter 3, DISTRICT OF COLUMBIA, PENNSYLVANIA; also Chapter 5, GEORGIA, NORTH CAROLINA, VIRGINIA.)

MURROW, EDWARD ROSCOE (1908–1965). From 1913 to 1925, the eventual journalist and news broadcaster lived with his family in **Blanchard.** Their first home (1913–18) survives at 387 Chuckanut Drive. The two-story frame structure, built in 1883 and moved there from a nearby location in 1922, has been sided and remains privately owned by a Murrow relative.

(See Chapter 2, MANHATTAN; also Chapter 3, DISTRICT OF COLUMBIA, NEW YORK; also Chapter 5, NORTH CAROLINA.)

ROETHKE, THEODORE (1908–1963). The poet lived in **Seattle,** where he taught English at the University of Washington from 1947. Until 1950 he lived in the Malloy Apartments, still at 4337 15th St. NE. He rented several other dwellings for brief periods until 1957, when he purchased the only house he ever owned at 3802 East John St. near Lake Washington. Roethke and his wife, financially pressed because of his frequent hospitalization for a manic-depressive condition, began furnishing the large, 10-room dwelling with Salvation Army and Goodwill items but gradually made it into a showpiece of fine decoration. This privately owned home was Roethke's last.

(See Chapter 1, VERMONT; also Chapter 3, PENNSYLVANIA; also Chapter 4, MICHIGAN.)

WYOMING

Its rugged landscape capping vast reserves of oil and coal—with all the financial opportunity and ecological problems this involves—Wyoming has become one of the nation's main energy resources. Oil drilling centers in the boom-town of Evanston, formerly a sleepy railroad village, and oil rigs sprout like forests across the center of the state. And almost 20 million acres of bituminous reserves make Wyoming the nation's leading coal state. Along with its surge in population and prosperity, however, have come big-city problems in communities ill prepared to deal with them.

Where Wyoming isn't mountain, mine or oil well, it is pasture, supporting one of the nation's foremost cattle and sheep industries. Grassland covers about 15 percent of this elevated state on plains rimmed by mountains. The climate is dry and cool in summer, extremely cold in winter. The first national park, Yellowstone, was established in northwestern Wyoming in 1872.

The first whites to view Wyoming were probably the French Vérendrye brothers in 1743. A century later trappers had decimated the "beaver gold," and Wyoming channeled thousands of overland travelers through its South Pass, a corridor of the Oregon Trail. Two small but important settlements—Fort Laramie and Fort Bridger—provided supplies and rest stops for this westward traffic and became the best-known stations in the Rockies. Fierce native resistance could not prevent the penetration of stage lines, or later of the Union Pacific Railroad, which gave rise to a line of cities in the late 1860s. One of the first acts of Wyoming Territory, created from a part of Dakota Territory in 1868, was to give equal suffrage to women. In 1890 the territory became the 44th state.

Wyoming today, as all the mountain states, confronts hard, challenging choices. As giant shovels chew into the scenery for coal and oil rigs become ubiquitous, its residents must weigh their values—between vast development potential and the matchless environment—as never before. There are mighty temptations toward short-sightedness. Today Buffalo Bill and mountain man Jim Bridger would still recognize much of the spectacular landscape they knew so well. Whether that will be true in the year 2004, Bridger's 200th birthday, is far from certain.

BRIDGER, JAMES "JIM" (1804–1881). The frontiersman and fur trader established **Fort Bridger** on the Oregon Trail in 1842 and made it the base of his trading and scouting operations for a decade. It also became a convenient supply point for pioneers headed west. The Mormons took charge in 1853, and five years later it became an official military post. Abandoned by the army in 1890, fort buildings centered a large cattle ranch until the 1920s, when the state acquired the property. The 15 oldest buildings at Fort Bridger State Historic Site National Historic Landmark date from the army's earliest occupation in 1858; Bridger's original fort was a mud-and-pole construction, relocated several times before 1842. Operated by the Wyoming State Archives and

Historical Department, the park and Fort Bridger Museum display artifacts of the fort's history plus living history demonstrations on the military and pioneer past as experienced there. An excellent account is *Fort Bridger: Island in the Wilderness* (1975), by Fred R. Gowans and Eugene E. Campbell. Fort Bridger stands on U.S. Highway 30 South. (Museum open June 1–Labor Day, daily 8:00–6:00; April 1–May 31, Labor Day–October 15, daily 9:00–5:00; grounds open daily; 307-777-7510; free.)

(See Chapter 4, MISSOURI.)

BUFFALO BILL. See WILLIAM FREDERICK CODY.

BURKE, MARTHA JANE CANARY "CALAMITY JANE" (1848?–1903). Legends concerning this free-roaming alcoholic wrangler, scout and prostitute are considerably larger than her rather dismal life. Hardly the nubile lass that Hollywood made of her, Calamity Jane could outcuss and outshoot most of "the boys" in a lifetime that bordered on macho parody. She ranged throughout Wyoming and Montana for more than 30 years, seldom "holing up" for long; accounts vary widely concerning her presence at any given time. She was, however, a frequent lodger and transient at all of the frontier forts at one time or another. These include **Fort Bridger** (see the entry on James "Jim" Bridger above) and Fort Laramie, where a marker states that Calamity Jane and a woman friend once borrowed cavalry uniforms and "roamed the fort saluting puzzled officers." Fort Laramie National Historic Site, established in 1836, became one of the major trading centers and army posts of the old West. Now operated by the National Park Service, 23 of its original buildings survive on 860 acres located three miles southwest of the town of **Fort Laramie** on State Highway 160. A visitor center provides exhibits and historical programs. (Open June 1–Labor Day, daily 8:00–8:00; Labor Day–May 31, 8:00–4:30; 307-837-2221; free.)

(See MONTANA in this chapter; also Chapter 4, MISSOURI, SOUTH DAKOTA.)

CALAMITY JANE. See MARTHA JANE CANARY BURKE.

CODY, WILLIAM FREDERICK "BUFFALO BILL" (1846–1917). "Being a hero," wrote Dixon Wecter, "grew to be the prime vocation of his life; he professionalized the role more than any other American in history." The Iowa birthplace of the frontier scout and showman was moved to Wyoming in 1934 and is now a featured display at Buffalo Bill Historical Center, operated by private trustees at 720 Sheridan Ave. in **Cody,** a town he helped establish in 1895. The two-story frame house, built by Cody's father, dates from 1840, and his family occupied it until 1851; some of its original furnishings are displayed (see *Exhibit* below). In 1902 Cody built the two-story, sandstone Irma Hotel in the center of town (U.S. Highway 14/20), naming it after his daughter. He filled the structure with fine furniture and paintings, including the 36-foot mirror over the cherrywood bar imported from France, and welcomed streams of noted guests. The hotel remains active. Cody's last home, from 1895, was the "TE Ranch," named after his cattle brand, where he hosted cowboys, celebrities, native Americans, preachers, journalists and painters, including Frederic Remington (see the entry on Remington below). Cody established his ranch retreat at the extreme southern end of the South Fork valley of the Shoshone River. TE Ranch survives about 30 miles southwest of Cody on South Fork Road (State Highway 291) as a privately owned cattle operation.

At **Sheridan,** Cody operated Sheridan Inn National Historic Landmark, the large, three-story, frame hotel built in 1893 at Broadway and Fifth Street. There he glad-handed his sportsman cronies from 1894 to 1896. Restored to its original appearance, the structure remains privately operated as a bar and restaurant.

Exhibit: Buffalo Bill Museum, part of the Buffalo Bill Historical Center complex at **Cody,** exhibits the largest collection of Cody memorabilia, including numerous gifts, firearms, saddles and Wild West Show paraphernalia. The museum is housed in a replica of Cody's house at the TE Ranch. (Open March 1–April 30, October 1–November 30, Tuesday–Sunday 1:00–5:00; May 1–31, September 1–30, daily 8:00–5:00; June 1–August 31, daily 7:00–10:00; 307-587-4771; admission.)

(See COLORADO in this chapter; also Chapter 4, IOWA, KANSAS, NEBRASKA.)

REMINGTON, FREDERIC (1861–1909).

Exhibit: The studio from the painter's long-gone home in New Rochelle, N.Y. (see Name Index and Gazetteer), has been recreated in the Whitney Gallery of Western Art at Buffalo Bill Historical Center, **Cody.** Remington created many of his best-known scenes in the vicinity of Cody the person and Cody the place (see the entry on William Frederick Cody above). Numerous Remington artifacts plus paintings and sculptures are displayed in the replica of his studio.

(See Chapter 1, CONNECTICUT; also Chapter 3, NEW YORK.)

NAME INDEX AND GAZETTEER

Listed here in chronological order are all the known homes and residence sites for each noted person included in this book. A gap in dates, where no home or site is listed, usually means that the person (a) resided outside the United States during that period, (b) resided at a number of brief, transient addresses, or (c) resided at addresses that remain unknown to biographers. Uncertain whereabouts at given times, even for some of our country's best-known historic persons, continue to frustrate and intrigue researchers. For lesser-known lives, this problem becomes common. Some listings are therefore more complete than others.

KEY TO SYMBOLS AND ABBREVIATIONS

* Open to public visitation.
□ Extant dwelling but privately owned or occupied; not open to public visitation.
△ Site of dwelling, now vacant land or reoccupied by later structure.
X Site unknown to biographers or local authorities.
Et seq. between two dates indicates that the house or site was occupied at irregular intervals between those dates; after one date only, it indicates occupation at irregular intervals for a lengthy but undetermined period from that date.
NHL National Historic Landmark
NHP National Historical Park
NHS National Historic Site
Exhibits are separately indexed only for pertinent locations in states not listed as residences.
Italicized page numbers indicate illustrations.

Philadelphia, Pa. Slate Roof House, Second and Sansom streets, 1774 △, 212

Quincy, Mass. Adams Mansion NHS, 135 Adams St., 1788 et seq. 1826 *, 23

New York, N.Y. Richmond Hill, Charlton Street, 1788–90 △, 79

Philadelphia, Pa. Bush Hill, 18th and Buttonwood streets, 1790–93 △, 212

———— Morris Mansion, 526–30 Market St., 1797–1800 △, 212

District of Columbia. Union Hotel, M and 30th streets NW, 1800 △

———— White House, 1600 Pennsylvania Ave. NW, 1800–01 *, 135

ADAMS, JOHN QUINCY (1767–1848).

Quincy, Mass. John Quincy Adams Birthplace NHS, 141 Franklin St., 1767 et seq. 1784 *, 23

1768–1788: See JOHN ADAMS.

Quincy, Mass. Adams Mansion NHS, 135 Adams St., 1788 et seq. 1848 *, 23

Boston, Mass. 39 Hanover St., 1801–05 △

———— Tremont and Boylston streets, 1807–09 △

District of Columbia. 1333 F St. NW, 1817–25, 1834–48 △, 135

———— White House, 1600 Pennsylvania Ave. NW, 1825–29 *, 135

———— Meridian Hill, Meridian Hill Park, 16th Street NW, 1829–34 △, 136

ADAMS, SAMUEL (1722–1803).

Boston, Mass. Adams Birthplace, Purchase Street, 1722–75 △, 24

Lexington, Mass. Hancock-Clarke House NHL, 36 Hancock St., 1775 *, 24

Boston, Mass. 24 Winter St., 1776–1803 △, 24

ADDAMS, JANE (1860–1935).

Cedarville, Ill. Addams Birthplace, Mill Street, 1860–81 □, 238

Chicago, Ill. Hull House NHL, 800 South Halsted St., 1889–1935 *, 238

AGASSIZ, LOUIS (1807–1873).

Cambridge, Mass. 12 Oxford St., 1847–54 △

Cambridge, Mass. 36 Quincy St., 1854–73 △, 24

ALCOTT, AMOS BRONSON (1799–1888).

Wolcott, Conn. Alcott Birthplace, Spindle Hill Road, 1799–1815 □, 4

Boston, Mass. 12 Franklin St., 1828–30 △

Philadelphia, Pa. 91 South Third St., 1831 △

1832 to 1855: See LOUISA MAY ALCOTT.

New York, N.Y. 81 St. Marks Place, 1857 △

Concord, Mass. Orchard House NHL, 399 Lexington Road, 1858–77 *, 25

———— Thoreau-Alcott House, 255 Main St., 1877–85 □, 25

Boston, Mass. 10 Louisburg Square, 1885–88 □, 25

ALCOTT, LOUISA MAY (1832–1888).

Philadelphia, Pa. Alcott Birthplace, 5425 Germantown Ave., 1832–33 △, 213

Boston, Mass. 21 Bedford St., 1834 △

———— 3 Somerset Court, 1835 △

———— 6 Beach St., 1836–40 △

Harvard, Mass. Fruitlands Museums NHL, Prospect Hill Road, 1843–44 *, 24

Concord, Mass. Wayside House NHL, Lexington Road, 1845–48 *, 24, 25

Boston, Mass. 50 High St., 1850 △

———— 20 Pinckney St., 1851 △

———— 34 Chauncy St., 1855 △

Concord, Mass. Orchard House NHL, 399 Lexington Road, 1858–77 *, 25

Boston, Mass. Bellevue Hotel-Apartments, 21 Beacon St., 1864 et seq. 1885 □, 25

———— 6 Hayward Place, 1867–68 △

———— 43 Pinckney St., 1869 △

Concord, Mass. Thoreau-Alcott House, 255 Main St., 1877 et seq. 1885 □, 25

Boston, Mass. 81 Pinckney St., 1880 △

———— 31 Chestnut St., 1884 △

———— 10 Louisburg Square, 1885–88 □, 25

———— 10 Dunreath St., Roxbury, 1886–88 △

ALDEN, JOHN (1599?–1687).

Plymouth, Mass. Town Square at School Street, 1620–27 △

Duxbury, Mass. Alden House, 105 Alden St., 1627–87 △ *, 25

ALGER, HORATIO, JR. (1832–1899).

Revere, Mass. Alger Birthplace, 88 Beach St., 1832–44 □, 25

Marlborough, Mass. 9 Broad St., 1844–48 □, 25

Natick, Mass. The Parsonage NHL, 16 Pleasant St., 1852–60 □, 25

———— 29 Florence St., 1860 et seq. 1899 □, 26

Brewster, Mass. 1944 Old King's Highway, 1864–65 △, 25

New York, N.Y. Newsboys' Lodging House, William and New Chambers streets, ca. 1860s et seq. 1890s △, 79

———— 26 West 34th St., 1872–76 △, 79

———— 133 East 46th St., 1877–79 △

———— 107 West 44th St., ca. 1880 △

———— 52 West 26th St., 1886–87 △

———— 36 West 33rd St., ca. 1888 △

Brooklyn, N.Y. 196 20th St., 1890–96 △

New York, N.Y. 223 West 34th St., 1891–94 △

———— 227 West 34th St., 1895 △

———— 44 East 10th St., ca. 1896 △

ALLEN, ETHAN (1738–1789).

Litchfield, Conn. Allen Birthplace, Old South Road and High Street, 1738–40 □, 5

North Cornwall, Conn. Southwest corner of Town Street and Cogswell Road, 1740–63 △

Lakeville, Conn. Allen Forge, State Highway 41 and U.S. Highway 44, 1763–65 △

Sunderland, Vt. Ethan Allen Inn, U.S. Highway 7, 1770s □, 63

Arlington, Vt. Studio Tavern, (see text), 1780s △, 63

Burlington, Vt. Ethan Allen Park, State Highway 127, 1787–89 △, 63

ANDERSON, SHERWOOD BERTON (1876–1941).

Camden, Ohio. Anderson Birthplace, 142 South Lafayette St., 1876–77 □, 296

Clyde, Ohio. 120 Spring Ave., 1884–96 □, 297

Chicago, Ill. 5654 Rosalie Court, 1904–06 △

Elyria, Ohio. Gray Apartments, West and Second streets, 1907–08 □, 297

———— 229 Seventh St., 1908–12 □, 297

Chicago, Ill. 735 Cass St. (later Wabash Ave.), 1912–15 △

New York, N.Y. 427 West 22nd St., 1918–19 □, 80

———— 12 St. Luke's Place, 1922 □, 80

Chicago, Ill. 12 East Division St., ca. 1922–24△

New Orleans, La. Upper Pontalba Building, 540B St. Peter St., 1924–25 □, 348

———— Casa Correjolles, 715 Governor Nicholls St., 1925 □, 348

Troutdale, Va. Ripshin NHL, State Highway 732, 1927 et seq. 1941 □, 373

New York, N.Y. 54 Washington Mews, 1930s □, 80

ANDRÉ, JOHN (1751–1780).

Lancaster, Pa. Cope House, Lane and Grant streets, 1775–76 △, 213

Carlisle, Pa. Carlisle Tavern, South Hanover Street, 1776 △

Philadelphia, Pa. Franklin Court, Orianna Street, 1777–78 △, 213

New York, N.Y. Kennedy House, 1 Broadway, 1779 △, 80

———— Beekman House, 455 East 51st St., 1779–80 △, 80

Tappan, N.Y. Mabie Tavern ('76 House), Main Street, 1780 *, 179

ANDROS, SIR EDMUND (1637–1714).

New York, N.Y. White Hall, Whitehall and State streets, 1675–81 △, 81

Boston, Mass. Fort Hill, Fort Hill Square, 1686–88 △

Jamestown, Va., Virginia Statehouse, Jamestown NHS, 1692–98 △, 373

ANTHONY, SUSAN BROWNELL (1820–1906).

Adams, Mass. Anthony Birthplace, East Road at East Street, 1820– 26 □, 26

Battenville, N.Y. Anthony House, State Highway 29, 1833–39 □, 180

Center Falls, N.Y. Anthony House, Battenkill River, 1839–45 △

Rochester, N.Y. Anthony Farm, Brooks Avenue (State Highway 204) and Genesee Park Blvd., 1845–66 △

—— Anthony Home NHL, 17 Madison St., 1866–1906 *, 180

New York, N.Y. 44 Bond St., 1868–69 △

—— 116 East 23rd St., 1869–70 △

ARENDT, HANNAH (1906–1975).

New York, N.Y. 317 West 95th St., 1941–51 □, 81

—— 130 Morningside Drive, 1951–60s □, 81

Chicago, Ill. Quadrangle Club, 1155 East 57th St., 1960s □, 239

—— 1126 East 59th St., 1960s et seq. 1967 □, 239

New York, N.Y. 370 Riverside Drive, 1960s–75 □, 81

ARMSTRONG, LOUIS DANIEL (1900–1971).

New Orleans, La. Armstrong Birthplace, 2723 Jane Alley, 1900– ? △, 348

—— Vicinity of Liberty and Perdido streets, ca. 1905–10 △, 348

Chicago, Ill. Armstrong House, 44th Street, early 1920s X

—— Cottage Grove and 33rd Street, ca. 1926–29 △

—— 3529 Martin Luther King Jr. Drive, 1934–37 △

Queens, N.Y. Armstrong House NHL, 34–56 107th St., 1942–71 □, 126

ARNOLD, BENEDICT (1741–1801).

Norwich, Conn. Arnold Birthplace, Washington Street and Arnold Place, 1741–61 △, 5

New Haven, Conn. 87 George St., 1764–71 △

—— 155 Water St., 1771–78 △, 5

Philadelphia, Pa. Slate Roof House, Second and Sansom streets, 1778–79 △, 213

—— Morris House, 526–30 Market St., 1779–80 △, 213

Garrison, N.Y. Robinson House, State Highway 9D, 1780 △, 180

New York, N.Y. Watts House, 3 Broadway, 1780–81 △, 81

ARTHUR, CHESTER ALAN (1829–1886).

East Fairfield, Vt. Arthur Birthplace, off State Highway 36, 1829 △ *, 64

Perry, N.Y. 7 Elm St., 1835–37 □, 180

Greenwich, N.Y. Arthur House, Woodlawn Avenue, 1838–43 □, 180

New York, N.Y. 34 West 21st St., 1859–61 △

—— Arthur House NHL, 123 Lexington Ave., 1867–86 □, 81

District of Columbia. Butler House, Independence and New Jersey avenues SE, 1881 △

—— Northwest corner of G and 14th streets NW, 1881 △

—— White House, 1600 Pennsylvania Ave. NW, 1881–85 *, 136

—— Anderson Cottage, U.S. Soldiers' and Airmen's Home NHL, Rock Creek Church Road and Upshur Street NW, 1882 et seq. 1884 □

ASTOR, CAROLINE SCHERMERHORN (1831–1908).

Rhinebeck, N.Y. Ferncliff, River Road, 1870–1908 △, 180

New York, N.Y. 350 Fifth Ave., 1880s–94 △, 81

Newport, R.I. Beechwood, Bellevue Avenue, 1880s–1908 *, 60

New York, N.Y. 1 East 65th St., 1894–1908 △, 81

ASTOR, JOHN JACOB (1763–1848).

New York, N.Y. 362 Pearl St., 1785–90 △, 82

—— 40 Little Dock St., 1790–94 △

—— 149 Broadway, 1794–1802 △, 82

—— 223 Broadway, 1803–20s △, 82

—— 585 Broadway, 1820s–48 △, 82

Hoboken, N.J. Astor Villa, 132–34 Washington St., 1828 et seq. △, 169

New York, N.Y. Astoria, East 87th Street, 1834–47 △, 82

AUDEN, WYSTAN HUGH (1907–1973).

New York, N.Y. 237 East 81st St., 1938–39 □, 82

Brooklyn, N.Y. 1 Montague Terrace, 1939–40 □, 73

—— 7 Middagh St., 1940–41 △, 73

Ann Arbor, Mich. 1223 Pontiac St., 1942 □

Swarthmore, Pa. 16 Oberlin Ave. 1943–45 □

New York, N.Y. 7 Cornelia St., 1945–53 □, 82

—— 77 St. Marks Place, 1953–72 □, 82

AUDUBON, JOHN JAMES (1785–1851).

Audubon, Pa. Mill Grove, Pawling and Audubon roads, 1804– 06 *, 213

New York, N.Y. 175 Pearl St., 1806–07 △

Audubon, Pa. Bakewell Estate, Pawling Road, 1808 □, 213

Louisville, Ky. Gwathmey's Indian Queen Hotel, North Third Street waterfront, 1808–10 △, 340

Henderson, Ky. Audubon Cabin and Store, Main and Second streets, 1813–19 △, 340

Cincinnati, Ohio. 414 East Third St., 1820 △

New Orleans, La. 706 Barracks St., 1821 □, 349

St. Francisville, La. Audubon State Commemorative Area (Oakley Plantation), State Highway 965, 1821 *, 349

New Orleans, La. 505 Dauphine St., 1821–22 □, 349

Wakefield, La. Weyanoke Plantation, off State Highway 124, 1822, 1824–25 △, 349

New York, N.Y. 86 White St., 1839–41 △

—— Minnie's Land, 765 Riverside Drive, 1841–51 △, 82

Exhibit: 326

BANCROFT, GEORGE (1800–1891).

Worcester, Mass. Bancroft Birthplace, Salisbury Street, 1800–11 △

Northampton, Mass. Round Hill School, 49 Round Hill Road, 1823–30 △, 26

Springfield, Mass. Dwight House, 49 Chestnut St., 1835–38 △

Boston, Mass. 1 Winthrop Square, 1838–45 △

District of Columbia. Blair House NHL, 1651 Pennsylvania Ave. NW, 1845–46 □

Newport, R.I. Roseclyfe, Bellevue Avenue, 1850–91 △, 60

New York, N.Y. 32 West 21st St., 1849–50 △

—— 17 West 21st St., 1850–67 △

District of Columbia. 1623 H St. NW, 1874–91 △, 136

BARA, THEDA (1890–1955).

Cincinnati, Ohio. Theodosia Goodman Birthplace, 1890–? X

Los Angeles, Calif. 649 West Adams Blvd. 1915–19 □, 400

New York, N.Y. 132 East 19th St., 1916–19 □, 83

—— 500 West End Ave., 1920 □, 83

Beverly Hills, Calif. 632 North Alpine Drive, 1940s–55 □, 400

BARNUM, PHINEAS TAYLOR (1810–1891).

Bethel, Conn. Barnum Birthplace, 55 Greenwood Ave., 1810–30s □, 5

New York, N.Y. Barnum Boardinghouse, 52 Frankfort St., 1835– 40 △, 83

Bridgeport, Conn. Iranistan, Park and Fairfield avenues, 1846– 57 △, 5

—— Lindencroft, Fairfield and Clinton avenues, 1860–69 △

New York, N.Y. 438 Fifth Ave., 1868–70s △, 83

Bridgeport, Conn. Waldemere, Waldemere Park, 1869–90 △, 5

Stratford, Conn. Portion of Waldemere, 1 Pauline St. □, 5

Bridgeport, Conn. Court Marina, Waldemere Park, 1890–91 □, 5

BARRYMORE, ETHEL (1879–1959).

Philadelphia, Pa. Barrymore Birthplace, 119 North Ninth St., 1879–ca. 1881 △

—— 2008 West Columbia Ave., ca. 1881–83 △, 214

—— 140 North 12th St., ca. 1883–85 △, 214

District of Columbia. Sheraton Park Hotel, 2660 Woodley Road NW, ca. 1926–30 □

——— Wesley Heights NW, ca. 1930–37 X

Alexandria, Va. 619 South Lee St., 1937–71 □, 373

BLACKWELL, ELIZABETH (1821–1910).

Cincinnati, Ohio. Blackwell Houses, Third, Fourth, Eighth Streets, 1838–44 X

Geneva, N.Y. 1847–49 X

New York, N.Y. 44 University Place, 1851–53 △

——— 79 East 15th St., 1853–60 △

——— 126 Second Ave., 1860–69 △, 85

BLAINE, JAMES GILLESPIE (1830–1893).

West Brownsville, Pa. Indian Hill Farm (Blaine Birthplace), State Highway 88, 1830–40s △

Augusta, Maine. Stanwood Homestead, 22–24 Green St., 1851–62 □, 16

Augusta, Maine. Blaine House NHL, Capitol and State streets, 1862–93 *, 16

District of Columbia. 821 15th St. NW, 1868–81 △

——— Blaine House, 2000 Massachusetts Ave. NW, 1881–83 □, 137

——— Marcy House, 736 Jackson Place NW, 1883–84 △

——— Windom–Munn Mansion, 1601 Massachusetts Ave. NW, 1885–89 △

Bar Harbor, Maine. Stanwood, Norman Road, 1886–93 △

District of Columbia. Rodgers House, 17 Madison Place NW, 1889–93 △, 137

BLOOMER, AMELIA JENKS (1818–1894).

Homer, N.Y. Jenks Birthplace, 43 North Main St.? 1818–24 △, 183

Waterloo, N.Y. Two residences, 1824–40 X

Seneca Falls, N.Y. 53 East Bayard St., 1840–49 *, 183

——— Bloomer Home, Cayuga and Fall streets, 1849–53 △

Mount Vernon, Ohio. 1853–54 X

Council Bluffs, Iowa. 123 Fourth St., 1855–94 △, 260

BOGART, HUMPHREY DEFOREST (1899–1957).

New York, N.Y. 245 West 103rd St., 1899–1917 □, 85

West Hollywood, Calif. Garden of Allah, 8150 Sunset Blvd. 1930s et seq. 1945 △, 402

Beverly Hills, Calif. 2707 Benedict Canyon Drive, 1945–46, 402

Holmby Hills, Calif. 232 South Mapleton Drive, 1946–57, 402

BONNEY, WILLIAM H. "BILLY THE KID" (1859–1881).

New York, N.Y. Bonney Birthplace, Rivington Street, 1859–60 X, 85

——— 386 East 10th St., 1860–62 △, 85

——— 271 East 12th St., 1862–?, △, 85

Indianapolis, Ind. 58 Cherry St., ca. 1867 △

Wichita, Kan. Market Street, 1870–71 X

Silver City, N.M. Main Street, 1873–74 X, 439

BOONE, DANIEL (1734–1820).

Baumstown, Pa. Boone Homestead (Boone Birthplace), Boone Road, 1734–50 △ *, 214

Lexington, N.C. Boone Memorial State Park, off State Highway 703, 1751–52 △ *, 356

Mocksville, N.C. Boone Farm, U.S. Highway 64, 1754–56 △, 356

Farmington, N.C. Boone Farm, Rainbow Road, 1756–66 △, 356.

Boone, N.C. Boone Cabin, Faculty and Newland streets, 1766–75 △, 356

Boonesboro, Ky. Fort Boonesborough State Park, State Highway 388, 1775–78 △ *, 340–41

Maysville, Ky. 1786–88 △

Charleston, W. Va. Fort Lee, 1202 East Kanawha Blvd. 1788–95 △, 232

Point Pleasant, W. Va. City Park, U.S. Highway 35, 1790–91 △, 232

Carlisle, Ky. Boone Cabin, U.S. Highway 68, 1795–97 *, 341

Matson, Mo. Boone Farm, State Highway 94, 1799–1804 △, 282

Defiance, Mo. Boone Home NHL, County Road F, 1810–20 *, 282

BOOTH, EDWIN THOMAS (1833–1893).

Bel Air, Md. Tudor Hall, Tudor Lane, 1833 et seq. 1840s □, 161

Baltimore, Md. East side of High Street, north of Gay Street, ca. 1842 △

——— 72 North Front St., ca. 1845 △

——— 152 North Exeter St., 1846–52 △, 162

New York, N.Y. 28 East 19th St., 1862–65 △

Boston, Mass. Tompkins House, 12 Franklin Square (11 St. George St.), 1865 △

Boston, Mass. 29A Chestnut St., 1883–87 □, 27

Middletown, R.I. Boothden, Indian Avenue, 1883–87 □, 60

New York, N.Y. Players Club NHL, 16 Gramercy Park South, 1888–93 □, 85

BOOTH, JOHN WILKES (1838–1865).

1838–1852: See EDWIN THOMAS BOOTH.

District of Columbia. National Hotel, Pennsylvania Avenue and Sixth Street NW, 1864–65 △, 137

——— Surratt Boardinghouse, 604 H St. NW, 1865 □, 137

Exhibit: 214

BORAH, WILLIAM EDGAR (1865–1940).

Fairfield, Ill. Borah Birthplace, Jasper Township, 1865–83 △, 239

Boise, Idaho. 1101 Franklin St., 1895–1908 △; moved to Garden City, Idaho. Chinden Street □, 435

District of Columbia. Windsor Lodge NHL, 2139 Wyoming Ave. NW, 1913–29 □, 137

——— 2101 Connecticut Ave. NW, 1929–40 □, 137

BORDEN, LIZZIE ANDREW (1860–1927).

Fall River, Mass. 234 Second St., 1860s–92 □, 27

——— Maplecroft, 306 French St., 1893–1927 □, 27

BORGLUM, GUTZON (1867–1941).

St. Charles, Idaho. Borglum Birthplace, U.S. Highway 89, 1867 △, 435

Ogden, Utah 1867–74 X

Fremont, Neb. Fifth Street between Union and D streets, 1875–ca. 1880 △

——— Park Avenue, ca. 1880 X

Los Angeles, Calif. Temple Street, 1884–86 X

——— Fort Street, 1886–89 X

——— Second Street, 1889–90 X

Sierra Madre, Calif. El Rosario, 205 West Orange Grove, 1893–96 △

New York, N.Y. 166 East 38th St., 1902–1912 △, 85

Stamford, Conn. Borgland, Wire Mill Road, 1910–27 △, 6

San Antonio, Texas. Menger Hotel, Alamo Plaza, 1927–36 □, 446

Hermosa, S.D. Borglum Ranch and Studio, State Highway 36, 1929 et seq. 1940 *, 310

Montecito, Calif. 6 Ayala Lane, ca. 1937 △

BOW, CLARA GORDON (1905–1965).

Brooklyn, N.Y. Bow Birthplace, Bergen Street, 1905 X, 73

——— 857 73rd St., ca. 1915–20s □, 73

Beverly Hills, Calif. 512 North Bedford Drive, 1926–31 □, 402

West Hollywood, Calif. Garden of Allah, 8150 Sunset Blvd., 1930s △, 402

Searchlight, Nev. YKL Ranch, off U.S. Highway 95, 1931–45 □, 437

West Los Angeles, Calif. 12214 Aneta St., 1950s–65 □, 402

BOWIE, JAMES "JIM" (1796–1836).

Russellville, Ky. Bowie Birthplace (reputed), Logan County, 1796–ca. 1800 X

Gallatin, Tenn. Bowie Birthplace (reputed), Elliot's Branch, 1796–99 X

New Madrid, Mo. Bowie Farm, Mississippi River, 1799–1802 X

Catahoula Parish, La. Bowie Homestead, Section 40, 1802–12 △, 349

Opelousas, La. 1790 South Union St., 1812–20 △, 349

Lecompte, La. Bowie Sawmill, Bayou Boeuf, 1824–27 X
San Felipe, Texas. Bowie Ranch, 1830s–36 X
Exhibits: 324, 446
BRADFORD, WILLIAM (1590–1657).
Plymouth, Mass. Bradford House, Main Street and Town Square, 1620–57 △, 27
BRADLEY, OMAR NELSON (1893–1981).
Higbee, Mo. Bradley Birthplace, 2 1/2 miles west of town, 1893–? △, 282
Clark, Mo. Railroad and Cross streets, ca. 1895 ☐, 282
Higbee, Mo. East Grand Street, ca. 1900–ca. 1911 ☐, 282
Fort Benning, Ga. 126 Rainbow Ave., Fort Benning Infantry School, 1930–34 ☐, 332.
West Point, N.Y. U.S. Military Academy, 1934–38 X
Fort Bennings, Ga. Riverside (Quarters One), Fort Benning Infantry School, 100 Vibbert Ave., 1941–42 ☐, 332
Fort Myer, Va. Quarters One NHL, Grant Avenue, 1949–53 ☐, 373
Beverly Hills, Calif. 1720 Carla Ridge, 1950s–77 ☐, 402
El Paso, Texas. Quarters No. 1, Beaumont Army Medical Center, Fort Bliss, 1977–81 ☐, 446
Exhibit: 214
BRADSTREET, ANNE DUDLEY (1612?–1672).
Boston, Mass. 1630–31 X, 27
Cambridge, Mass. 2 Boylston St., (1374 Massachusetts Ave.), 1631–35 △, 27
Ipswich, Mass. South Main Street, 1635–45 X
North Andover, Mass. Osgood Street, 1645–72 △, 27
BRADY, JAMES BUCHANAN "DIAMOND JIM" (1856–1917).
New York, N.Y. Brady Birthplace, Cedar and West streets, 1856–67 △, 85
——— 7 West 86th St., 1900–17 △, 85
South Branch, N.J. Ellesdale Manor Farm, Raritan River, 1901 et seq. 1915 X, 169
Atlantic City, N.J. Shelburne Hotel, Boardwalk and Michigan Avenue, 1917 ☐, 169
BRADY, MATTHEW B. (1823–1896).
Warren County, N.Y. Brady birthplace, 1820s X
New York, N.Y. Brady Studio, Broadway and Fulton Street, 1844–53 △, 86
——— Brady Studio, 359 Broadway, 1853–60 △, 86
——— Brady Studio, Broadway and East 10th Street, 1860s △
District of Columbia. National Hotel, Pennsylvania Avenue and Sixth Street NW, 1858–80, 1881–87 △, 137
——— Brady National Photographic Gallery, 627 Pennsylvania Ave. NW, 1880–81 △, 137
——— 494 Maryland Ave. SW, 1887–95 △, 137
New York, N.Y. 127 East 10th St., 1896 △, 86
BRANDEIS, LOUIS DEMBITZ (1856–1941).
Louisville, Ky. Brandeis Birthplace, 500 block of Armory Place, 1856–75 △, 341
Boston, Mass. 114 Mount Vernon St., 1900s ☐, 27
——— 6 Otis Place, 1900s ☐, 27
Dedham, Mass. 194 Village Ave., 1900s ☐, 27
District of Columbia. Stoneleigh Court Apartments, Connecticut Avenue and L Street NW, 1916–26 △, 137
Chatham, Mass. Brandeis House NHL, Neck Lane off Cedar Street, 1922 et seq. 1941 ☐, 27
District of Columbia. 2205 California St. NW, 1926–41 ☐, 137
BRAUN, WERNHER VON (1912–1977).
El Paso, Texas. Beaumont Army Hospital annex barracks, east of Fort Bliss National Cemetery, Fort Bliss, 1945–50 △
Huntsville, Ala. 907 McClung St., 1950–57 ☐, 320
——— 1516 Big Cove Road, 1957–70 ☐, 320
Alexandria, Va. 816 Vicar Lane, 1970–77 ☐, 373
BRECHT, BERTOLT (1898–1956).
Santa Monica, Calif. 817 25th St., 1941–42 ☐, 402

——— 1063 26th St., 1942–47 ☐, 402
BRIDGER, JAMES "JIM" (1804–1881)
Richmond, Va. Bridger birthplace, 1804–12 X
Dupo, Ill. Bridger Farm, 1812–18 X
Fort Bridger, Wyo. Fort Bridger State Historic Site NHL, U.S. Highway 30 South, 1842–53 △ *, 456
Kansas City, Mo. Bridger Farm, 10600 block of Wornall Road, 1853–57, 1868–81 △, 282
Fort Laramie, Wyo. Fort Laramie NHS, State Highway 160, 1854 et seq. 1868 *
Story, Wyo. Fort Phil Kearney NHL, off U.S. Highway 87, 1866–67 *
BROWN, CHARLES BROCKDEN (1771–1810).
Philadelphia, Pa. Brown Birthplace, 117 South Second St., 1771–97 △, 215
New York, N.Y. 45 Pine St., 1798 △
Philadelphia, Pa. 124 South 11th St., 1805–10 △, 215
BROWN, JOHN (1800–1859).
Goshen, Conn. Brown Birthplace, John Brown Road, 1800–05 △, 6
Hudson, Ohio. 1842 Hines Hill Road, 1818–25 ☐, 297
New Richmond, Pa. Brown Homestead and Tannery, Local Road 20118, 1825–35 △, 215
Akron, Ohio. John Brown Home Museum, 514 Diagonal Road, 1842–46 *, 297
Lake Placid, N.Y. Brown Farm, John Brown Road, 1855–59*, 183
Oswatomie, Kan. John Brown Memorial Park, 10th and West Main streets, 1855–56 *, 264
Tabor, Iowa. Todd House, Park Street, 1856 *, 260
Chambersburg, Pa. 225 East King St., 1859 *, 215
Samples Manor, Md. John Brown Headquarters NHL, Chestnut Grove Road, 1859 ☐, 162
Charles Town, W. Va. Old Jail, South George and Washington streets, 1859 △, 233
BROWN, MARGARET TOBIN "MOLLY" (1867–1932).
Hannibal, Mo. Tobin Birthplace, Denkler Alley and Butler Street, 1867–84 *, 283
Leadville, Colo. East Fifth Street, 1886–92 X
——— East Seventh Street, 1892–94 X
Denver, Colo. Molly Brown House, 1340 Pennsylvania St., 1894 et seq. 1932 *, 431
Newport, R.I. Mon Etuí, 44 Bellevue Ave., 1913–22 △, 61
BRUCE, LENNY (1926–1966).
Bellmore, N.Y. Myron Schneider Shoe Store, 1926–37 X
Lawrence, N.Y. 710 Hughes St., 1937–42 ☐, 183
Hollywood, Calif. 8825 Hollywood Blvd., 1960–66 ☐, 403
San Francisco, Calif. Swiss American Hotel, 534 Broadway, 1965 ☐
BRYAN, WILLIAM JENNINGS (1860–1925).
Salem, Ill. Bryan Birthplace, 408 South Broadway, 1860–62 *, 239
——— Bryan House, Bryan Lane, 1862–75 △
Jacksonville, Ill. Jones House 505 West College Ave., 1875–81 △
——— 1225 West College Ave., 1884–87 △, 240
Lincoln, Neb. 1425 D St., 1888–1902 ☐, 292
District of Columbia. 131 B St. (Independence Ave. SE), 1892–94 △
Lincoln, Neb. Fairview NHL, 4900 Summer St., 1902–21 *, 292
District of Columbia. 2101 R St. NW, ca. 1900s ☐, 138
Mission, Texas. Bryan House, Bryan Road and 2 Mile Road, ca. 1910 ☐
District of Columbia. Calumet Place, Clifton and 13th streets NW, 1913–15 △, 138
Asheville, N.C. 107 Evelyn Place, ca 1920 ☐
Miami, Fla. Villa Serena, 3115 Brickell Ave., 1921–25 ☐, 326
Dayton, Tenn. Rogers House, 711 South Market St., 1925 △, 366

BRYANT, WILLIAM CULLEN (1794–1878).

Cummington, Mass. Bryant Birthplace, Potash Hill Road, 1794–99 △

—— Bryant Homestead NHL, State Highways 9 and 112, 1799–1816, 1865–78 *, 28

West Bridgewater, Mass. Baylies House, 58 South St., 1814 ☐

Brockton, Mass. 815 Belmont St., ca 1817 ☐

Great Barrington, Mass. 362 Main St., 1821–22 ☐, 28

New York, N.Y. 92 Hudson St., 1825–26 △

—— Meigs Boardinghouse, 88 Canal St., 1826–ca. 30 △

—— Broome Street, ca. 1830–31 X

—— Fourth Street and Broadway, 1831–? △

Roslyn, N.Y. Cedarmere, Bryant Avenue, 1843–78 ☐, 183

New York, N.Y. 24 West 16th St., 1867–78 ☐, 86

BUCHANAN, JAMES (1791–1868).

Mercersburg, Pa. Buchanan Birthplace State Historic Park (Cove Gap), State Highway 16, 1791–94 △; moved to Mercersburg Academy *, 215

—— James Buchanan Hotel, 17 North Main St., 1796–1807 ☐, 215

Lancaster, Pa. 42 East King St., 1813–48 △

District of Columbia. 1331 F St. NW, 1845–48 △

Lancaster, Pa. Wheatland NHL, 1120 Marietta Ave., 1848–68 *, 215

District of Columbia. White House, 1600 Pennsylvania Ave. NW, 1857–61 *, 138

——Woodley, 3000 Cathedral Ave. NW, 1857 et seq. 1860 ☐

—— Anderson Cottage, U.S. Soldiers' and Airmen's Home NHL, Rock Creek Church Road and Upshur Street NW, 1857 et seq. 1860 ☐, 138

BUCK, PEARL SYDENSTRICKER (1892–1973).

Hillsboro, W. Va. Buck Birthplace NHL, U.S. Highway 219, 1892, 1901–09 *, 233

Dublin, Pa. Green Hills Farm NHL, 520 Dublin Road, 1934–73 *, 215, 216

New York, N.Y. 35 East 85th St., 1940s–50s ☐

Danby, Vt. Danby House, Boro Hill, 1950s ☐, 64

Winhall, Vt. Mountain Haunt, off State Highway 30, 1950s ☐, 64

Philadelphia, Pa. 2019 Delancey Place, 1960s–73 ☐, 217

BUFFALO BILL. See WILLIAM FREDERICK CODY.

BULFINCH, CHARLES (1763–1844).

Boston, Mass. Bulfinch Birthplace, north side of Bowdoin Square, 1763–94, 1837–44 △, 28

—— 8 Bulfinch Place, 1794–96 △, 28

—— Bowdoin Street, 1796–97, 1799–1800 X

—— Howard Street, 1797–99 X

—— Clap-Bulfinch House, Bulfinch and Howard streets, 1799–1815 △, 28

—— 5 Tremont St., 1816–17 △

District of Columbia. Sixth Street NW, 1817–30 X

Boston, Mass. 3 Bumstead Place, 1833–37 △, 28

BUNKER, CHANG and ENG (1811–1874).

Traphill, N.C. Bunker Farm, Little Sandy Creek, 1839–45 △

Mount Airy, N.C. Chang Bunker House, U.S. Highway 601, 1845–74 ☐, 357

White Plains, N.C. Eng Bunker House, U.S. Highway 601, 1845–74 △, 357

Exhibit: 217

BURBANK, LUTHER (1849–1926).

Lancaster, Mass. Burbank Birthplace, Harvard Road, 1849–70 △; moved to Dearborn, Mich., 28

Dearborn, Mich. Burbank Birthplace, Greenfield Village, 20900 Oakwood Blvd. *, 269

Lunenburg, Mass. 42 Main St., 1872–75 ☐, 28

Santa Rosa, Calif. Burbank House and Memorial Garden NHL, 200 Santa Rosa Ave., 1880–1926 *, 403

BURGESS, THORNTON WALDO (1874–1965).

Sandwich, Mass. Burgess Birthplace, 6 School St., 1874–? ☐, 28

Springfield, Mass. 61 Washington Road, 1906–57 ☐, 29

Hampden, Mass. Laughing Brook Education Center, 789 Main St., 1928–65 *, 28

BURKE, MARTHA JANE CANARY "CALAMITY JANE" (1848?–1903).

Princeton, Mo. Canary Birthplace, U.S. Highway 136, 1848?–ca. 1865 △, 283

Livingston, Mont. 213 Main St., ca. 1870s △, 436

Fort Bridger, Wyo. Fort Bridger State Historic Site NHL, U.S. Highway 30 South, ca. 1880s et seq. △ *, 456

Fort Laramie, Wyo. Fort Laramie NHS, State Highway 160, ca. 1880s et seq. *, 456

Rock Springs, Wyo. M Street, ca. 1888 X

Terry, S.D. 1903 X, 310

BURR, AARON (1756–1836).

Newark, N.J. Burr Birthplace, Broad and William streets, 1756 △, 169

Princeton, N.J. President's House NHL, Nassau Street, 1756–58 ☐, 169

Philadelphia, Pa. Shippen-Wistar House, 240 South Fourth St., 1758–60 ☐, 217

Litchfield, Conn. Reeve House and Law School NHL, South Street, 1774–75 *, 6

Albany, N.Y. 110 Washington Ave., 1782–83 △, 183

New York, N.Y. 10 Cedar St., 1780s △

—— 3 Wall St., 1783–84 △, 86

—— 10 Maiden Lane, 1784–90 △, 86

—— 4 Broadway, 1790–94 △, 86

—— Mortier House (Richmond Hill), Charlton Street, 1794–1804 △, 86

Philadelphia, Pa. Todd Boardinghouse, 96 North Third St., 1790s △

District of Columbia. 1336–38 F St. NW, ca. 1800–04 △

Jersey City, N.J. White House, northwest corner of Sussex and Hudson streets, ca. 1830 △

New York, N.Y. Morris-Jumel Mansion NHL, Edgecomb Avenue and West 160th Street, 1833–34 *, 86

Staten Island, N.Y. Port Richmond Hotel, 2040 Richmond Terrace, Port Richmond, 1836 △, 129

BURROUGHS, EDGAR RICE (1875–1950).

Chicago, Ill. Burroughs birthplace, Washington Boulevard between Lincoln and Damen streets, 1875–91 X, 240

—— 2005 Park Ave., 1900, 1904–08 △

—— 35 South Damen St., 1902—03 △

—— 2008 Park Ave., 1909 et seq. 1910 △

Oak Park, Ill. 821 Scoville Ave., 1910–11 △

Tarzana, Calif. Tarzana Ranch, 18320 Tarzana Drive, 1911 et seq. 1932 △, 403

Oak Park, Ill. 325 North Oak Park Ave., ca. 1914 △

—— 700 Linden St., ca. 1915 △

—— 414 Augusta Blvd., 1917–19 ☐, 240

Tarzana, Calif. 5046 North Mecca Ave., 1926–32 △

Malibu, Calif. 90 Malibu La Costa Beach, 1932–34 △

Beverly Hills, Calif. 806 North Rodeo Drive, 1935–39 ☐, 403

—— 716 North Rexford Drive, 1939–40 ☐

Encino, Calif. 5465 Zelzah Ave., 1945–50 △, 403

BYRD, RICHARD EVELYN (1888–1957).

Winchester, Va. Byrd Birthplace, 326 Amherst St., 1888–1908 △, 373

Boston, Mass. 9 Brimmer St., 1934–57 ☐, 29

East Sullivan, Maine. Wickyup NHL, State Highway 183, 1937 et seq. 1957 ☐, 16

Exhibits: 138

BYRD, WILLIAM (1674–1744).

Richmond, Va. Falls Plantation, James River Park, 1674–85 △, 373

—— Belvidere, Cherry and Albemarle streets, 1685–90 △, 373

Charles City, Va. Westover NHL, State Highway 5, 1690–1744 *, 374

BYRNES, JAMES FRANCIS (1879–1972).

Charleston, S.C. Byrnes birthplace, 1879–ca. 1900 X, 363

Aiken, S.C. Magnolia Cottage, 1900–25 △

District of Columbia. Shoreham Hotel, 2500 Calvert St. NW, 1930–47 ☐, 138

Spartanburg, S.C. 1925–41 X

Columbia, S.C. Governor's Mansion, Richland and Lincoln streets, 1951–55 ☐, 363

—— 12 Heathwood Circle, 1955–72 ☐, 363

CALAMITY JANE. See MARTHA JANE CANARY BURKE.

CALDER, ALEXANDER (1898–1976).

Philadelphia, Pa. Calder Birthplace, 1903 North Park Ave., 1898–1906 △, 217

Pasadena, Calif. 534 South Euclid Ave., 1906–08 △

—— 555 Linda Vista Ave., 1908 △

Croton-on-Hudson, N.Y. Old Gate House, 1184 Old Post Road, 1911–12 ☐, 183

San Francisco, Calif. 1654 Taylor St., 1914–15 △

New York, N.Y. 111 East 10th St., 1923–24 ☐

—— 11 East 14th St., ca. 1924 ☐

—— 7 Bleecker St., 1925 ☐

—— 249 West 14th St., 1925 ☐, 86

Roxbury, Conn. Old Painter Hill Road, 1933–76 ☐, 6

CALHOUN, JOHN CALDWELL (1782–1850).

Abbeville, S.C. Calhoun Birthplace, State Highway 823, 1782–1800 △, 363

Litchfield, Conn. Reeve House and Law School NHL, South Street, 1805–06 *

Willington, S.C. Bath Plantation, between Savannah and Little rivers, 1811–25 △

District of Columbia. Rodgers House, 17 Madison Place NW, 1817–20s △

—— 618 E St. NW, 1820s et seq. 1829 △

——Dumbarton Oaks, 1703 32nd St. NW, 1823–26 *, 138

Clemson, S.C. Fort Hill NHL, Clemson University campus, 1825–50 *, 363

District of Columbia. Hills' Boardinghouse, First and A streets NE, 1849–50 △, 138

CALVERT, LEONARD (1606–1647).

St. Marys City, Md. Church Point, State Highway 584, 1634–44, 1646–47 △, 162

CAMP, WALTER CHAUNCEY (1859–1925).

New Britain, Conn. Camp birthplace, 1859–? X

New Haven, Conn. 34 Hillhouse Ave., 1909–22 △, 6

—— 460 Humphrey St., 1925 △

CAPONE, ALPHONSE "AL" (1899–1947).

Brooklyn, N.Y. Capone birthplace, Navy Street, 1899–1907 X, 74

—— 38 Garfield Place, 1907–15 ☐, 74

Chicago, Ill. 7244 South Prairie Ave., 1922–33 ☐, 240

Cicero, Ill. Hawthorne Inn, 4833 West 22nd St., 1923–29 △, 240

Couderay, Wis. The Hideout, County Highway CC, 1925–30s *, 313

Miami Beach, Fla. 93 Palm Ave., Palm Island, 1928–33, 1939–47 ☐, 327

Alcatraz Island, Calif. Alcatraz Penitentiary, 1934–39 *, 403

CARMICHAEL, HOAGLAND HOWARD "HOAGY" (1899–1981).

Bloomington, Ind. Carmichael birthplace, South Grant Street, 1899–1903 X, 253

Indianapolis, Ind. Carmichael Apartment, East and Lockerbie streets, 1903–05 △

Bloomington, Ind. South Fess Avenue, 1905–09 X

—— 907 East Atwater St., ca. 1915–16 △

—— 214 North Dunn Ave., ca. 1900s ☐

Indianapolis, Ind. 27 North Warman Ave., ca. 1916 ☐, 253

New York, N.Y. 121 East 52nd St., ca. 1934–36 △

Hollywood, Calif. 626 North Foothill Drive, 1941 ☐, 404

Holmby Hills, Calif. 10281 Charing Cross Road, 1940s ☐, 404

Rancho Mirage, Calif. Thunderbird Ranch, 40-267 Club View Drive, ca. 1950–81 ☐, 404

Beverly Hills, Calif. 9126 Sunset Blvd., 1950s–60s ☐, 404

North Hollyood, Calif. 10250 Moorpark St., 1970s–81 ☐, 404

CARNAP, RUDOLF (1891–1970).

Chicago, Ill. 5110 South Kenwood Ave., 1936–37 ☐

—— 5438 South University Ave., 1937–41 ☐, 240

—— 5724 South Kenwood Ave., 1941–44 ☐, 240

—— 5642 South Drexel Ave., 1944–52 ☐, 240

West Los Angeles, Calif. 11728 Dorothy St., ca. 1954–70 ☐, 404

CARNEGIE, ANDREW (1835–1919).

Pittsburgh, Pa. Rebecca Street, 1848–52 X, 217

—— Hancock Street, 1852–? X

Homewood, Pa. 1860–67 X, 217

Cresson, Pa. Braemar Cottage, U.S. Highway 22 and State Highway 53, 1879 et seq. 1886 ☐, 217

New York, N.Y. Windsor Hotel, 571 Fifth Ave., 1880s △

—— 5 West 51st St., 1887–1901 △, 87

—— Carnegie Mansion NHL, 2 East 91st St., 1901–19 *, 87

Lenox, Mass. Shadowbrook, West Street, 1916 et seq. 1919 △, 29

CARNEGIE, DALE (1888–1955).

Ravenwood, Mo. Carnegie Birthplace, Harmony Church vicinity, 1888–98 △, 283

—— Carnegie House, Section 32, off State Highway 46, 1898–1906 △

—— Ira Moore Farm, Harmony Church vicinity, 1906–08 X

Belton, Mo. Carnagey Street, ca. 1910 ☐, 283

Queens, N.Y. 27 Wendover Road, 1930–55 ☐, 127

CARSON, CHRISTOPHER HOUSTON "KIT" (1809–1868).

Richmond, Ky. Carson Birthplace, Tates Creek Road, 1809–11 △, 341

Boonville, Mo. Boone's Lick State Historic Site, County Road MM, 1811–24 △ *, 283

—— Old Franklin, State Highway 87, 1824–26 △, 283

Taos, N.M. Kit Carson House NHL, Old Kit Carson Road, 1843–61 *, 439

Cimarron, N.M. Rayado Ranch, State Highway 21, 1851–60 △ *, 439

Window Rock, Ariz. Fort Defiance, State Highway 264, 1863–64 △

Fort Garland, Colo. Fort Garland State Historical Monument, 1866–67 *, 432

Fort Lyon, Colo. Kit Carson Memorial Chapel, County Road 183, 1868 *, 432

CARSON, RACHEL LOUISE (1907–1964).

Springdale, Pa. Carson Birthplace, 613 Marion Ave., 1907–29 *, 217

Silver Spring, Md. 204 Williamsburg Drive, 1949–57 ☐, 162

West Southport, Maine. Summer home, Dogfish Head Road, 1953 et seq. 1963 ☐, 16

Silver Spring, Md. 11701 Berwick Road, 1957–64 ☐, 162

CARTER, ALVIN PLEASANT DELANEY "A. P." (1891–1960).

Maces Spring, Va. Carter Birthplace, near junction State Highways 614/691, 1891 et seq. ☐, 374

Hiltons, Va. 1943–60 ☐

CARUSO, ENRICO (1873–1921).

New York, N.Y. Hotel Knickerbocker, Broadway and West 42nd Street, 1908–20 ☐, 87

—— Vanderbilt Hotel, Park Avenue and East 34th Street, 1920–21 △, 87

CARVER, GEORGE WASHINGTON (1864?–1943).

Diamond, Mo. Carver National Monument, County Road V, 1864?–80s *, 283

Beeler, Kan. Carver Homestead, State Highway 96, 1886–88 △, 264

Tuskegee, Ala. Rockefeller Hall, Tuskegee Institute NHS, U.S. Highway 80, 1903–43 □, 320–21

CASSATT, MARY (1844–1926).

Pittsburgh, Pa. Cassatt birthplace, Reedsdale Street, 1844–48 X, 217

Lancaster, Pa. Hardwick, 1848–51 X

Philadelphia, Pa. 496 West Chestnut St., 1849–51 △

———— 1436 South Penn Square, 1858–65 □

———— 1418 Spruce St., 1908–09 △

CATHER, WILLA SIBERT (1873–1947).

Gore, Va. Cather Birthplace, U.S. Highway 50W, 1873 □, 374

———— Willowshade Farm, U.S. Highway 50W, 1873–82 □, 374

Red Cloud, Neb. Cather Grandparents' Homestead, Bladen Road, 1883–84 △, 293

———— Cather Childhood Home NHL, Third and Cedar streets, 1884–90 *, 292

Pittsburgh, Pa. McClung House, 1180 Murray Hill Ave., 1896–1906, 1912–13 □, 218

New York, N.Y. 82 Washington Place, 1908–13 □, 87

———— 5 Bank St., 1913–27 △, 87

Jaffrey, N.H. Shattuck Inn, Dublin Road, 1917 et seq. 1938 □, 55

New York, N.Y. Grosvenor Hotel, 35 Fifth Ave., 1927–32 □, 87

———— 570 Park Ave., 1932–47 □, 87

CERF, BENNETT ALFRED (1898–1971).

New York, N.Y. Douglas Apartments, 201 W. 121st St., ca. 1900–11 △

———— Riviera Apartments, 790 Riverside Drive, 1911–? □, 87

———— Navarro Apartments, 112 Central Park South, 1940s □, 87

Mount Kisco, N.Y. The Columns, Orchard Road, 1940s–71 □, 184

New York, N.Y. 132 East 62nd St., 1950s–71 □, 87

CHAMPLAIN, SAMUEL DE (1567?–1635).

St. Croix Island, Maine. St. Croix Island National Monument, 1604–05 △, 17

CHAPLIN, SIR CHARLES SPENCER "CHARLIE" (1889–1977).

Hollywood, Calif. 2010 De Mille Drive, 1918–20 □, 404

———— 1416 North La Brea Ave., 1920s □, 404

———— 6147 Temple Hill Drive, 1920s □, 404

Beverly Hills, Calif. 1085 Summit Drive, 1922–52 □, 404

CHURCHILL, JENNIE JEROME (1854–1921).

Brooklyn, N.Y. Jerome Birthplace, 197 Amity St., 1854–58 □, 74

New York, N.Y. Jerome Mansion, Madison Avenue and 26th Street, 1860–67 △, 88

CLARK, GEORGE ROGERS (1752–1818).

Charlottesville, Va. Clark Birthplace, Rivanna River, 1752–56 △, 374

Corbin, Va. Clark plantation, 1756–72 X, 374

Louisville, Ky. Corn Island, Ohio River, 1778 △, 342

———— Clark Fort, 12th Street, 1778–82 △

———— Fort Nelson, West Main and Seventh streets, 1782–85 △, 342

———— Mulberry Hill, George Rogers Clark Park, Poplar Level Drive, 1785–1803 △, 342

Clarksville, Ind. Clark Mill, Harrison Avenue, 1803–09 △, 254

Louisville, Ky. Locust Grove NHL, 561 Blankenbaker Lane, 1809–18 *

CLARK, WILLIAM (1770–1838).

Corbin, Va. Clark birthplace, 1770–84 X, 374

Louisville, Ky. Mulberry Hill, George Rogers Clark Park, Poplar Drive, 1785–89, 1796–1803 △

1803–06. See MERIWETHER LEWIS.

St. Louis, Mo. 103 North Main St. (Jefferson National Expansion Memorial Riverfront Park vicinity), ca. 1806–36 △

———— 418 Olive St., 1836–38 △

CLAY, HENRY (1777–1852).

Ashland, Va. Slash Cottage (Clay Birthplace), off State Highway 654, 1777–91 △, 374

Lexington, Ky. Ashland NHL, 1400 Richmond Road, 1811–52 △ *, 342–43

District of Columbia. F and 15th streets NW, 1823–25 △

———— Rodgers House, 17 Madison Place NW, 1825–27 △, 139

———— Decatur House NHL, 748 Jackson Place NW, 1827–29 *, 139

———— National Hotel, Pennsylvania and 6th Street NW, 1840s–52 △, 139

CLEMENS, SAMUEL LANGHORNE "MARK TWAIN" (1835–1910).

Florida, Mo. Clemens Birthplace, State Highway 107, 1835 △; moved to Mark Twain Birthplace Memorial Shrine NHL, State Highway 107 *, 284

Hannibal, Mo. Mark Twain Boyhood NHL, 206 Hill St., 1839–46, 1847–53 *; 284, 285

———— Pilaster House, Hill and Main streets, 1846–47 *, 285

Muscatine, Iowa. 109 Walnut St., 1853–54 △

Keokuk, Iowa. Ivins House, Second and Main streets, 1854–56 △, 260

Carson City, Nev. 502 North Division St., 1863–64 □, 437

Tuttletown, Calif. Mark Twain Cabin, State Highway 49, 1864–65 △ *, 405

Buffalo, N.Y. 472 Delaware Ave., 1869–71 △, 184

Hartford, Conn. John Hooker House, Forest and Hawthorn streets, 1871–74 □

———— Mark Twain House NHL, 351 Farmington Ave., 1874–91 *, 7, **8**

Elmira, N.Y. Quarry Farm, Crane Road, 1874–1903 □, 184

New York, N.Y. 14 West 10th St., 1900–01 □, 88

Bronx, N.Y. Wave Hill, 675 West 252nd St., 1901–03 *, 70

New York, N.Y. 21 Fifth Ave., 1904–08 △, 88

Redding, Conn. Stormfield, Redding Road (State Highway 53), 1908–10 △, 7

CLEVELAND, GROVER (1837–1908).

Caldwell, N.J. Cleveland Birthplace, 207 Bloomfield Ave., 1837–41 *, 170

Fayetteville, N.Y. 109 Academy St., 1841–50 □, 184

Buffalo, N.Y. Porter House, 1145 Niagara St., 1860s △

———— 284 Main St., 1873–83 △

Albany, N.Y. State Executive Mansion, 138 Eagle St., 1883–85 □, 184

District of Columbia. White House, 1600 Pennsylvania Ave. NW, 1885–89, 1893–97 *, 139

Deer Park, Md. Cleveland Cottage, Deer Park Hotel Road, 1886 □, 162

District of Columbia. Red Top, 3536 Newark St. NW, 1886–88 △, 139

Bourne, Mass. Gray Gables, President's Road, Monument Point, 1891–1904 △, 29

New York, N.Y. 816 Madison Ave., 1891–92 △

———— 12 West 51st St., 1892–93 △

District of Columbia. Woodley, 3000 Cathedral Ave. NW, 1893–97 □

Princeton, N.J. Westland NHL, 58 Bayard Lane, 1897–1908 □, 170

Tamworth, N.H. Cleveland House, Cleveland Hill Road, 1906–08 □, 55

CLINTON, DE WITT (1769–1828).

Little Britain, N.Y. Clinton Birthplace, Bull Road, 1769–85 △, 184

New Windsor, N.Y. Clinton House (reputed), River Road, 1769–73 □, 184

Queens, N.Y. Clinton Farm, 56th Terrace, 1796–1828 △, 127

New York, N.Y. Mortier House, Charlton Street, 1811–15 △, 88

———— 3 or 9 Cherry St. (see text), ca. 1817 △, 88

Albany, N.Y. Yates Mansion, Broad and Westerlo streets, 1817–22 △

———— Clinton House, North Pearl and Steuben streets, 1825–28 △

CLINTON, GEORGE (1739–1812).

Little Britain, N.Y. Clinton Birthplace, Bull Road, 1739–70 △, 184

New Windsor, N.Y. Clinton Farm, Maple Street, 1770–77 □, 184

Poughkeepsie, N.Y. Crannell House, 448 Main St., 1777–84 △, 184

New York, N.Y. 80 Pine St., 1784–91 △, 88

———— Government House, State Street and Bowling Green, 1791–94 △, 88

———— Clinton Farm, 1230 York Ave., 1794–1800 △, 88

Albany, N.Y. Caldwell House, 60 State St., ca. 1801 △

Poughkeepsie, N.Y. Clinton Home, Sheafe Road, 1806–12 △, 184–85

District of Columbia. O'Neale's Hotel, 21st and I streets NW, 1811–12 △, 139

COBB, TYRUS RAYMOND "TY" (1886–1961).

Narrows, Ga. Cobb birthplace, 1886–? X

Royston, Ga. South Cobb Street, 1890s–1904 △, 333

Glenbrook, Nev. 1940s X

Atherton, Calif. 48 Spencer Lane, 1957–61 □, 405

Royston, Ga. Grier Street, 1957–61 □

Cornelia, Ga. Chenocetah Mountain, 1958–61 □, 333

Exhibit: 185

CODY, WILLIAM FREDERICK. "BUFFALO BILL" (1846–1917).

LeClaire, Iowa. Cody Birthplace, 1034 North Cody Road, 1846–51 △; moved to Cody, Wyo., 260

Cody, Wyo. Cody Birthplace, Buffalo Bill Historical Center, 720 Sheridan Ave. *, 457

McCausland, Iowa. Cody Homestead, off U.S. Highway 61, 1851–53 *, 260

Leavenworth, Kan. Cody Homestead, U.S. Highway 73, 1853–61 △, 265

Hays, Kan. Fort Hays Frontier Historical Park, U.S. Highway 183A, 1867–68 *, 265

———— Scouts Rest Ranch State Park, Buffalo Bill Avenue, 1886–1917 *, 293

———— Welcome Wigwam, 1877–92 X, 293

———— Welcome Wigwam, 1200 block of West Fourth St., 1892–1908 △, 293

Sheridan, Wyo. Sheridan Inn NHL, Broadway and Fifth street, 1894–96 □, 457

Cody, Wyo. TE Ranch, State Highway 291, 1895–1917 □, 457

Denver, Colo. Decker House, 2932 Lafayette St., 1917 △

COHAN, GEORGE MICHAEL (1878–1942).

Providence, R.I. Cohan Birthplace, 536 Wickenden St., 1878 △, 61

North Brookfield, Mass. 34 Bell St., 1880s–90s □, 29

Highland Mills, N.Y. Cohan Farm, Bakertown Road, 1909 et seq. 1942 □, 185

Atlantic City, N.J. Shelburne Hotel, Boardwalk and Michigan Avenue, 1909 et seq. 1924 □, 170

Kings Point, N.Y. 100 Kings Point Road, 1914–27 □, 185

New York, N.Y. Hotel Knickerbocker, Broadway and West 42nd Street, ca. 1910 et seq. □, 89

———— 993 Fifth Ave., ?–1942 □, 88

COLE, NAT KING (1914–1965).

Montgomery, Ala. Cole Birthplace, 1524 St. John St., 1919–23 □, 321

Chicago, Ill. 1923–? X

Los Angeles, Calif. 401 South Muirfield Rd., 1948–65 □, 405

COLE, THOMAS (1801–1848).

Steubenville, Ohio. 105 North Fourth St., 1820–21 △

Catskill, N.Y. Cole House NHL, 218 Spring St., 1820 et seq. 1848 □, 185

New York, N.Y. Cole Studio, Greenwich Street, 1825–26 X

COLTRANE, JOHN WILLIAM (1926–1967).

Hamlet, N.C. Coltrane Birthplace, 318 Bridges St., 1926–29 □, 357

High Point, N.C. 1929–43 X

Philadelphia, Pa. North 12th Street, 1943–51 X

———— 1511 North 33rd St., 1951–56 □, 218

New York, N.Y. 203 West 103rd St., 1957–59 □, 89

Queens, N.Y. 116-60 Mexico St., 1959–63 □, 127

Huntington, N.Y. Candlewood Path, 1966–67 □, 185

COMSTOCK, ANTHONY (1844–1915).

New Canaan, Conn. Comstock Birthplace, Country Club Road vicinity, 1844–63 △, 9

Brooklyn, N.Y. 354 Grand Ave., 1871–83 △, 74

Summit, N.J. 59 New England Ave., 1883–97 △

———— Breeze Crest, 35 Beekman Road, 1897–1915 □, 170

COOLIDGE, CALVIN (1872–1933).

Plymouth Notch, Vt. Coolidge Homestead NHL, State Highway 100A, 1872–90s *, 64

Northampton, Mass. 21 Massasoit St., 1906–23, 1929–30 □, 29, 30

District of Columbia. Willard Hotel, Pennsylvania Avenue and 14th Street NW, 1921–23 □, 139

———— White House, 1600 Pennsylvania Ave. NW, 1923–29 *, 139

———— 15 Dupont Circle NW, 1927 □, 139

Game Lodge, S.D. State Game Lodge, U.S. Highway 16A, 1927 *, 310

Northampton, Mass. The Beeches, Hampton Terrace off Monroe Street, 1930–33 □, 29

COOPER, GARY (1901–1961).

Helena, Mont. Cooper Birthplace, 730 11th Ave., 1901–06 □, 436

———— Cooper Houses, Fifth Avenue and Beatty Street, 15 Shiland St., 712 Fifth St., ca. 1906–26 □, 436

Craig, Mont. Seven-Bar-Nine Ranch, off U.S. Highway 91, 1906 et seq. 1926 □, 436

Hollywood, Calif. 7511 Franklin Ave., 1926–29 □, 405

———— 1826 Laurel Canyon Blvd., 1929–31 □

———— 1919 Argyle Ave., 1930–32 □, 405

Encino, Calif. Cooper Ranch, Ventura Freeway (U.S. Highway 101), 1933–35 △

Brentwood Heights, Calif. ca. 1935–54 X

Holmby Hills, Calif. 200 North Baroda Drive, 1954–61 □, 405

COOPER, JAMES FENIMORE (1789–1851).

Burlington, N.J. Cooper Birthplace, 457 High St., 1789–90 *, 170

Cooperstown, N.Y. The Manor, Main Street, 1790–98 △, 185

———— Otsego Hall, Main Street opposite Fair Street, 1798–1811, 1814–17, 1833–51 △, 185

Mamaroneck, N.Y. DeLancey House, 404 West Post Road, 1811–14 □, 185

Scarsdale, N.Y. Angevine Farm, Mamaroneck Road, 1818–22 △, 185

New York, N.Y. Broadway and Prince Street, 1821–23 △, 89

———— 3 Beach St., 1823–25 △, 89

———— 345 Greenwich St., 1825–26 △, 89

———— 145 Bleecker St., 1833–36 □, 89

———— 6 St. Marks Place, 1834–? □, 89

COPLEY, JOHN SINGLETON (1738–1815).

Boston, Mass. Copley Birthplace, Long Wharf, vicinity of 148 State St., 1738–48 △, 30

———— Lindall's Row, Exchange Place and Congress Street, 1750s △

———— Orange Tree Tavern vicinity, Hanover and Court streets, 1760s △

———— Mount Pleasant, 42–43 Beacon St., 1772–74 △, 30

CORNELL, KATHARINE (1893–1974).

Buffalo, N.Y. 484 Delaware Ave., 1894–ca. 1920 □, 186

New York, N.Y. 23 Beekman Place, 1921–52 ☐, 89

Vineyard Haven, Mass. Chip Chop, 1937–74 ☐, 30

Palisades, N.Y. Peter Rock, Woods Road, 1951–61 ☐, 186

New York, N.Y. East 51st Street, 1961–74 X, 89

COWARD, SIR NOEL PIERCE (1899–1973).

New York, N.Y. 1 Beekman Place, 1933 ☐, 89

———— 450 East 52nd St., 1936–40 ☐, 89

———— Hotel des Artistes, 1 West 67th St., 1950s ☐, 89

———— 404 East 55th St., 1960s ☐, 89

CRANE, HART (1899–1932).

Garrettsville, Ohio. Crane Birthplace, 10688 Freedom St., 1899–1903 ☐, 297

Warren, Ohio. 340–350 High St., 1903–08 ☐, 297

Cleveland, Ohio. 1709 East 115th St., 1908–20 ☐, 297–98

New York, N.Y. 54 West 10th St., 1917 ☐, 89

———— 25 East 11th St., 1917–19 ☐, 89

———— 24 West 16th St., 1919 ☐, 89

Cleveland, Ohio. 11431 Euclid Ave., 1920 et seq. 1925 △, 298

New York, N.Y. 45 Grove St., 1923–24, 1930 ☐, 89

———— Charles St., 1924 ☐, 89

Brooklyn, N.Y. 110 Columbia Heights, 1924 et seq. 1929 ☐, 74

———— 77 Willow St., 1928 ☐, 74

———— 130 Columbia Heights, 1929 △, 74

Chagrin Falls, Ohio. Canary Cottage, 87 West St., 1929 et seq. 1932 ☐, 298

CRANE, STEPHEN (1871–1900).

Newark, N.J. Crane Birthplace, 14 Mulberry Place, 1871–74 △, 170

Paterson, N.J. Hamilton Street, 1876–78 X

Port Jervis, N.Y. 49–51 Sussex St., 1878–80 △

New York, N.Y. 136 West 15th St., 1893 △

———— Art Students League, 143 East 23rd St., 1893–94 △, 90

———— 33 East 22nd St., 1894, 1896 △

———— 111 West 33rd St., 1894 △

———— 281 Sixth Ave., 1894 et seq. 1896 △

———— 165 West 23rd St., 1895–96 ☐, 90

CROCKETT, DAVID "DAVY" (1786–1836).

Limestone, Tenn. Crockett Birthplace State Park, Crocket Highway, 1786–94 △ *, 366

Morristown, Tenn. Crockett Tavern, 2106 East Main St., 1794–1800s △ *, 366

Lynchburg, Tenn. Crockett Homestead, State Highway 55, 1811–13 △, 366

Maxwell, Tenn. Kentuck, U.S. Highway 64, 1813–17 △, 366

Lawrenceburg, Tenn. 218 North Military St., 1817–23 △, 367

Rutherford, Tenn. Crockett Cabin, Obion River, 1823–35 △; moved to U.S. Highway 45 *, 367

Exhibit: 446

CROSBY, HARRY LILLIS "BING" (1903–1977).

Tacoma, Wash. Crosby Birthplace, 1122 North Jay St., 1903–06 ☐, 454

Spokane, Wash. Sinto Avenue, 1906–13 X, 454

———— 508 East Sharp St., 1913–25 ☐, 454

North Hollywood, Calif. 4326 Forman Ave., 1930–33 ☐, 405

———— 10500 Carmarillo St., 1933–43 △

Pebble Beach, Calif. Crosby House, Pebble Beach Golf Club, 1940s–60s ☐, 405

Elko, Nev. Crosby Ranch, State Highway 51, 1943–70s ☐, 438

Holmby Hills, Calif. 594 South Mapleton Drive, 1944–64 ☐, 405

Hayden Lake, Idaho. Crosby Summer Home, U.S. Highway 2, 1950s–70s ☐, 435

Hillsborough, Calif. 1200 Jackling Drive, 1964–77 ☐, 405

CUMMINGS, EDWARD ESTLIN (1894–1962).

Cambridge, Mass. Cummings Birthplace, 104 Irving St., 1894–1918 ☐, 31

Silver Lake, N.H. Joy Farm NHL, Salter Hill Road, 1899 et seq. 1962 ☐, 55

Lynn, Mass. 135 Nahant St., 1901–03 ☐, 31

New York, N.Y. 4 Patchin Place, 1923–62 ☐, 90

Cambridge, Mass. 6 Wyman Road, 1952–53 ☐

CUSTER, GEORGE ARMSTRONG (1839–1876).

New Rumley, Ohio. Custer Memorial State Park (Custer Birthplace), State Highway 646, 1839–52 △ *, 298

Monroe, Mich. Custer Home, Monroe and Second streets, 1852 et seq. 1876 △; moved to 703 Cass St. ☐, 269

Manhattan, Kan. Fort Riley Military Reservation, State Highway 18, 1866–67 ☐, 265

Elizabethtown, Ky. Custer House, North Main Street, 1871–73 △, 343

Mandan, N.D. Fort Abraham Lincoln State Park, 1873–76 △ *, 295

Exhibits: 310, 436

DALEY, RICHARD JOSEPH (1902–1976).

Chicago, Ill. Daley Birthplace, 3502 South Lowe Ave., 1902–39 ☐, 240

———— 3536 South Lowe Ave., 1939–76 ☐, 240

DARROW, CLARENCE SEWARD (1857–1938).

Farmdale, Ohio. Darrow Birthplace, 1857–64 X

Kinsman, Ohio. Darrow Octagon House, State Highways 5 and 7, 1864–78 ☐, 298

Andover, Ohio. 1880–84 X

Ashtabula, Ohio. 4744 Park Ave., 1884–87 △, 298

Chicago, Ill. 4219 Vincennes Ave., 1892–97 ☐, 240

———— 1397 Sheridan Road, 1903–07 △

———— 1537 East 60th St., 1907–38 △, 240

Exhibit: 367

DAVIS, JEFFERSON FINIS (1808–1889).

Fairview, Ky. Davis Monument State Park (Davis Birthplace), U.S. Highway 68, 1808–10 △ *, 343

Woodville, Miss. Rosemont Plantation, State Highway 24, 1810–25 *, 353

Lexington, Ky. Ficklin House, 102 West High St., 1821–24 △, 343

Davis Island, Miss. Hurricane Plantation, 1835–38 △, 353

———— Brierfield Plantation, 1838–61 △, 353

District of Columbia. Everett House, G Street NW between 17th and 18th streets, 1853–57 △

———— 1736 I St. NW, 1857–60 △, 140

Montgomery, Ala. First White House of the Confederacy, Bibb and Lee streets, 1861 △; moved to 626 Washington St.*, 321

Richmond, Va. White House of the Confederacy NHL, 1201 East Clay St., 1861–65 *, 375

Hampton, Va. Fort Monroe NHL, Old Point Comfort, 1865–67 *, 375

Memphis, Tenn. 129 Court Ave., 1867–75 △, 367

———— 216 Court Ave., 1875–78 △, 367

Biloxi, Miss. Beauvoir NHL, U.S. Highway 90, 1877–89 *, 353

New Orleans, La. Forsyth House, 1134 First St., 1889 ☐, 350

Exhibit: 333

DEAN, JAMES BYRON (1931–1955).

Marion, Ind. Dean Birthplace, South McClure and East Fourth streets, 1931–36 △, 254

Jonesboro, Ind. Winslow Farm, 7184 South 150th Road East, 1940–49 ☐, 254

Westwood, Calif. Sigma Nu House, 601 Gayley Ave., 1950 ☐, 406

Hollywood, Calif. Gower Plaza Hotel, 1607 North Gower St., 1950s ☐, 406

New York, N.Y. 19 West 68th St., 1954 ☐, 90

Hollywood, Calif. 3908 Barham Blvd., 1954 ☐, 406

DEBS, EUGENE VICTOR (1855–1926).

Terre Haute, Ind. Debs Birthplace, 457 North Fourth St., 1855–59 △, 254

———— Debs Grocery, northeast corner Wabash Avenue and 11th Street, 1859–85 △

—— Debs Home NHL, 451 North Eighth St., 1890–1926 *, 254

Atlanta, Ga. Federal Penitentiary, McDonough Road and South Boulevard, 1919–21 ☐

DECATUR, STEPHEN (1779–1820).

Berlin, Md. Decatur Birthplace, Decatur Street, 1779 △, 162

Philadelphia, Pa. 611 South Front St., 1780s–96 △, 218

—— Mount Airy, 10000 Decatur Road, 1779–1802 △, 218

Norfolk, Va. 517 Warren St., ca. 1807–08 △

District of Columbia. Decatur House NHL, 748 Jackson Place NW, 1819–20 *, 140

DEERE, JOHN (1805–1886).

Rutland, Vt. Deere Birthplace, 1805–30s X

Grand Detour, Ill. Deere House NHL, State Highway 2, 1837–47 *, 240

Moline, Ill. Deere House, 11th Avenue and 12th Street, 1880s–86 ☐, 241

DE FOREST, LEE (1873–1961).

Council Bluffs, Iowa. De Forest Birthplace, 523 Fourth St. (see text), 1873–76 X, 260

Waterloo, Iowa. 1876–78 X

Muscatine, Iowa. 1878–79 X

Talladega, Ala. 702 West Battle St., 1882–91 ☐, 321

New York, N.Y. Yale Eyrie, West 97th Street and Riverside Drive, ca. 1902–09 △

Palo Alto, Calif. 1301 Bryant St., 1911–13 ☐, 406

Bronx, N.Y. Riverlure, 1391 Sedgwick Ave., 1913–25 △

Hollywood, Calif. 8190 Hollywood Blvd., 1930–61 ☐, 406

Exhibit: 293

DeMILLE, CECIL BLOUNT (1881–1959).

Ashfield, Mass. DeMille Birthplace, Main Street, 1881 ☐, 31

Wayne, N.J. Pamlico, 266 Terhune Drive, 1892–96 △, 170–71

Hollywood, Calif. 6136 Lexington Ave., 1913–14 ☐, 406

—— Cahuenga Boulevard (Hollywood Freeway, U.S. Highway 101), 1914–15 △

—— Hollywood Boulevard, 1915–16 X

—— 2000 DeMille Drive, 1916–59 ☐, 406

Cottonwood Glen, Calif. Paradise, Little Tujunga Road, 1916–59 ☐, 406

DE SOTO, HERNANDO (1496?–1542).

Tallahassee, Fla. Anhayea, 1539–40 X, 327

Tupelo, Miss. De Soto winter camp, 1540–41 X

Camden or Calion, Ark. Utiangue, 1541–42 X, 325

Exhibits: 354, 367

DEWEY, GEORGE (1837–1917).

Montpelier, Vt. Dewey Birthplace, State Street, 1837–51 △, 64

District of Columbia. Northeast corner of Connecticut Avenue and K Street NW, 1900s △

—— 1601 K St. NW, 1908–17 △, 140

Exhibit: 218

DEWEY, JOHN (1859–1952).

Burlington, Vt. Dewey Birthplace, 186 South Willard St., 1859–63 ☐, 64

—— 14 George St., 1867–76 △

—— 178 South Prospect St., 1876–79 ☐, 64

Ann Arbor, Mich. 601 South Forest Ave., 1889–94 △

Chicago, Ill. 1895–1913: Del Prado Hotel, 1414 East 59th St., △; 213 East 61st St., △; 5813 South Kenwood Ave., △; 5238 South Woodlawn Ave., △; 6036 Harper Ave., △; 6016 Stony Island Ave., △, 241

Huntington, N.Y. Dewey Home, Greenlawn Road, 1910–23 △, 186

New York, N.Y. 2880 Broadway, 1913–27 △, 90

—— 125 East 62nd St., 1927–38 ☐, 90

—— 1 West 89th St., 1939–45 ☐, 90

—— 1158 Fifth Ave., 1945–52 ☐, 90

DEWEY, THOMAS EDMUND (1902–1971).

Owosso, Mich. Dewey Birthplace, 323 West Main St., 1902–? ☐, 270

—— 421 West Oliver St., 1915–19 ☐, 270

New York, N.Y. West 122nd St., 1923–25 X

—— East 73rd St., 1929–34 X

—— 1148 Fifth Avenue, 1934–40s ☐, 90

Tuxedo Park, N.Y. 1934–? X

Pawling, N.Y. Dapplemere, Reservoir Road, 1938–71 ☐, 186

Albany, N.Y. State Executive Mansion, 138 Eagle St., 1942–55 ☐, 186

New York, N.Y. 141 East 72nd St., 1955–71 ☐, 90

DICKINSON, EMILY ELIZABETH (1830–1886).

Amherst, Mass. Dickinson Home NHL, 280 Main St., 1830–40, 1855–86 *, 31

—— 161 Pleasant St., 1840–55 △

DICKINSON, JOHN (1732–1808).

Trappe, Md. Crosiadore (Dickinson Birthplace), Grubin Neck Road, 1732–40 △, 162

Dover, Del. Dickinson Mansion NHL, Kitts Hummock Road, 1740–50 *, 133

Philadelphia, Pa. Fair Hill, Germantown Avenue, 1770–77 △, 218

—— Dickinson Town House, Chestnut Street between Fifth and Sixth streets, 1774–77 △

Wilmington, Del. Dickinson Home, northwest corner of Eighth and Market streets, 1785–1808 △

DIDRIKSON, MILDRED ELLA "BABE." See MILDRED ELLA DIDRIKSON "BABE" ZAHARIAS.

DILLINGER, JOHN HERBERT (1903–1934).

Indianapolis, Ind. Dillinger Birthplace, 2079 Cooper (now Caroline) St., 1903–20 △

Mooresville, Ind. Dillinger Farm, 535 State Highway 267, 1920–24 ☐, 254

Manitowish Waters, Wis. Little Bohemia, U.S. Highway 51, 1934 *, 313

Chicago, Ill. 2509 North Crawford Ave., 1934 ☐

Exhibits: 140, 241

DIRKSEN, EVERETT McKINLEY (1896–1969).

Pekin, Ill. Dirksen Birthplace, 802 Catharine St., 1896–1900s ☐, 241

—— 1201 Hamilton St., 1900s–27 ☐, 241

—— 335 Buena Vista, 1927–69 ☐, 241

District of Columbia. Mayflower Hotel, 1127 Connecticut Ave. NW, 1939–48 ☐, 140

—— Berkshire Apartments, 4201 Massachusetts Ave. NW, 1950–59 ☐, 140

Sterling, Va. Broad Run Farms, Young Cliffs Road, 1959–69 ☐, 375

DISNEY, WALT (1901–1966).

Chicago, Ill. Disney Birthplace, 1249 Tripp Ave., 1901–06 △

Marceline, Mo. State Highway 5 and West Broadway, 1906–09 ☐, 285

Kansas City, Mo. 508 North Kansas Ave., 1910–11 △

—— 2706 East 31st St., 1911–14 △

—— Disney Home NHL, 3028 Bellefontaine Ave., 1914–17, 1919–21 ☐, 285

Hollywood, Calif. 4406 Kingswell Ave., 1923–? ☐, 406

——Sleepy Hollow Hill, 4053 Woking Way, 1933–50 ☐, 406

Holmby Hills, Calif. 355 Carolwood Drive, 1950–66 ☐, 406

DIX, DOROTHEA LYNDE (1802–1887).

Hampden, Maine. Dix Memorial Park (Dix Birthplace), U.S. Highway 1A, 1802–14 △, 17

Boston, Mass. 499 Washington St., 1814–36 △, 31

Trenton, N.J. Trenton State Hospital, Sullivan Way, 1881–87 △, 171

DOOLITTLE, HILDA "H.D." (1886–1961).

Bethlehem, Pa. Doolittle Birthplace, 10 East Church St., 1886–95 △, 218

Upper Darby, Pa. Flower Observatory vicinity, 9 West Chester Pike (St. Lawrence Road), 1895–1910 △, 218

Richmond Hill, Ga. Ford Estate, State Highway 144, 1936–47 □, 333

FOSTER, STEPHEN COLLINS (1826–1864).

Pittsburgh, Pa. Foster Birthplace, 3600 Penn Ave., 1826–30 △, 219

────── William Foster homes, East Common vicinity, 1830s et seq. 857 △, 219

Cincinnati, Ohio. Griffin Boardinghouse, 421 East Fourth St., 1846–50 △, 298

Hoboken, N.J. 601 Bloomfield St., 1854 □, 172

New York, N.Y. 97 Greene St., 1860–61 △, 92

────── 6 Greenwich St., 1860s △, 92

────── New England Hotel, 15 Bowery, 1864 △, 92

Exhibits: 327, 343

FRANKFURTER, FELIX (1882–1965).

District of Columbia. 1727 19th St. NW, 1912–14 □, 142

Cambridge, Mass. 192 Brattle St., 1919–39 □, 35

District of Columbia. 1511 30th St. NW, 1930s–40s □, 142

────── 3018 Dumbarton Ave. NW, 1947–62 □, 142

────── Massachusetts Avenue NW, 1962–65 □

FRANKLIN, BENJAMIN (1706–1790).

Boston, Mass. Franklin Birthplace, 17 Milk St., 1706–12 △, 35

────── Blue Ball, Union and Hanover streets, 1712–18 △, 36

────── James Franklin shop, 17 Court St., 1718–23 △, 36

Philadelphia, Pa. Read House, 314–16 Market St., 1723 △

────── 139 Market St., 1728–39 △, 220

────── 131 Market St., 1739–48 △, 221

────── Franklin Home, Second and Race streets, 1748–50 △

────── 325 Market St., 1750–57 △, 221

────── 326 Market St., 1762–64 △

Franklin Court, Orianna Street, 1775–76, 1785–90 △ *, 221

FRÉMONT, JOHN CHARLES (1813–1890).

Savannah, Ga. Frémont Birthplace, 563–565 West Bay St., 1813 △

Charleston, S.C. 1820s X

Bear Valley, Calif. The White House, State Highway 49, 1851 et seq. 1863 △, 410

New York, N.Y. 56 Ninth St., 1855–56 △

San Francisco, Calif. Commanding Officer's Quarters, Fort Mason, Bay and Van Ness streets, 1859–61 △

North Tarryton, N.Y. Pokahoe, 7 Pokahoe Drive, 1860–73 □, 188

New York, N.Y. 21 West 19th St., 1860s–70s △

Prescott, Ariz. Frémont House, 415 West Gurley St., 1878–79 *, 398

Tucson, Ariz. Frémont House, 151 South Granada St., 1879–83 *, 398

FRENCH, DANIEL CHESTER (1850–1931).

Exeter, N.H. French Birthplace, 34 Court St., 1850 □, 56

────── 43 Pine St., 1850s △; moved to 5 Nelson Dr. □, 56

Concord, Mass. 342 Sudbury Road, 1858–88 □, 38

Amherst, Mass. Stockbridge House, Stockbridge Road, University of Massachusetts campus, 1867 □

New York, N.Y. 125 West 11th St., 1888–1931 □, 93

Stockbridge, Mass. Chesterwood NHL, two miles west of town off State Highway 183, 1896–1931 *, *38*

FROST, ROBERT LEE (1874–1963).

San Francisco, Calif. Frost Birthplace, Washington Street, 1874 X, 410

San Francisco, Calif. 1603 Sacramento St., 1874–76 △, 410

────── Abbotsford House Hotel, Broadway and Larkin Street, 1877, 1881–82 △

────── 1404 Leavenworth St., 1883–85 △, 410

Lawrence, Mass. 370 Haverhill St., 1885 △, 38

Salem, N.H. Loren Baily Homestead, 8 Sullivan Court, 1886–90 □, 56

Derry, N.H. Frost Farm NHL, State Highway 28, 1901–09 *, 56

Franconia, N.H. Frost Place NHL, Ridge Road, 1915–20 *, 56

South Shaftsbury, Vt. Frost Summer Home, Buck Hill Road, 1920–28 □

Ann Arbor, Mich. 1523 Washtenaw Ave., 1921–22 △, 271

Amherst, Mass. 10 Dana St., 1923–24 □

Ann Arbor, Mich. Ann Arbor House, 1223 Pontiac Road, 1924–26 △; moved to Dearborn, Mich. 271

Dearborn, Mich. Ann Arbor House, Greenfield Village, 20900 Oakwood Blvd. *, 272

North Bennington, Vt. Shingle Cottage, Harlan Road, 1927 □, 67

South Shaftsbury, Vt. Frost Farm NHL, Buck Hill Road, 1929–38 □, 65

Amherst, Mass. 43 Sunset Ave., 1932–38 □, 38

Boston, Mass. 88 Mount Vernon St., 1938–41 □, 38

Ripton, Vt. Frost Farm NHL, off State Highway 125, 1940–62 *, 65

Cambridge, Mass. 35 Brewster St., 1941–63 □, 38

South Miami, Fla. Pencil Pines, 5340 Southwest 80th St., 1941–62 □, 328

FULLER, MARGARET (1810–1850).

Cambridge, Mass. Fuller House NHL, 71 Cherry St., 1810–26 □, 38

────── Dana Mansion, 5 Dana St., 1826–32 △

────── Brattle House, 42 Brattle St., 1832 □, 38

Groton, Mass. Wharton House, head of Farmers Row, 1832–38 □, 38

Jamaica Plain, Mass. Willow Brook, 1838–42 X

West Roxbury, Mass. Brook Farm Site NHL, 670 Baker St., 1841–42 △, 38

New York, N.Y. Greeley Farm, East 48th and 49th streets, 1844–46 △, 93, 94

FULTON, ROBERT (1765–1815).

Goshen, Pa. Fulton Birthplace NHL, U.S. Highway 222, 1765–71 △ *, 221

Philadelphia, Pa. Fulton Studio, Second and Walnut streets, 1779–ca. 85 △

District of Columbia. Kalorama (Joel Barlow Estate), vicinity of S Street and 22nd Street NW, ca. 1807 △

Linlithgo, N.Y. Teviotdale, 1805–15 □, 188

New York, N.Y. 1 State St., ca. 1810–15 △, 93

GABLE, CLARK (1901–1960).

Cadiz, Ohio. Gable Birthplace, 138 Charleston St., 1901–02 □, 298

Hopedale, Ohio. Gable Home, Mill Street, 1905–17 □, 298

Akron, Ohio. 1163 Getz St., 1917–18 □, 299

North Hollywood, Calif. 12746 Langdale St., 1930–31 □, 410

Brentwood Heights, Calif. 220 North Bristol St., 1931–35 □, 410

Beverly Hills, Calif. Beverly Wilshire Hotel, 9500 Wilshire Blvd., 1935–39 □, 410

Encino, Calif. 4525 Pettit St., 1936–60 □, 410

GARFIELD, JAMES ABRAM (1831–1881).

Moreland Hills, Ohio. Abram Garfield Farm Site Park (Garfield Birthplace), S.O.M. Center and Jackson roads, 1831–50 △, 299

Hiram, Ohio. 6825 Hinsdale St., 1863–72 □, 299

District of Columbia. Garfield House, 13th and I Streets NW, 1869–81 △, 142

Mentor, Ohio. Lawnfield NHL, 8095 Mentor Ave., 1876–81 *, *299*

District of Columbia. White House 1600 Pennsylvania Ave. NW, 1881 *, 142

Long Branch, N.J. Franklyn Cottage, 6 Garfield Terrace, 1881 △, 172

GARIBALDI, GIUSEPPE (1807–1882).

Staten Island, N.Y. Cross Street, Clifton, 1851–53 △; moved to 420 Tompkins Ave., Rosebank (Garibaldi and Meucci Memorial Museum) *, 129

GARLAND, HAMLIN (1860–1940).

West Salem, Wis. Garland Birthplace, Garland Street, 1860–68 △

Osage, Iowa. Boyhood home, Burr Oak Township, 1869–76 □, 261

Ordway, S.D. Garland Homestead, State Highway 10, 1881–84 △, 310

West Salem, Wis. Garland Homestead NHL, 357 West Garland St., 1893–1915 *, 314

Chicago, Ill. Elm Street, ca. 1890s–1901 X

New York, N.Y. 23 Gramercy Park South, 1897 □, 93

Oregon, Ill. Eagle's Nest, Lowden State Park, State Highway 64, 1898 et seq. 1920s □, 242

Chicago. Ill. 6427 South Greenwood Ave., 1907–15 □, 242

New York, N.Y. 71 East 92nd St., 1916–29 △, 93

Lake Onteora, N.Y. Garland Summer Home, 1920s–30s □

Hollywood Calif. 2045 De Mille Drive, 1930–40 □, 411

GARRISON, WILLIAM LLOYD (1805–1879).
Newburyport, Mass. Garrison Birthplace, 5 School St., 1805–12 □, 38

Boston, Mass. 14 Dix Place, 1850s–64 △

——— Garrison House NHL, 125 Highland St., Roxbury, 1864–79 □, 38

New York, N.Y. Westmoreland Apartments, Broadway and 17th Street, 1879 △

GEHRIG, HENRY LOUIS "LOU" (1903–1941).
New York, N.Y. Gehrig Birthplace, 1994 Second Ave., 1903–ca. 1905 △, 93

New Rochelle, N.Y. 9 Meadow Lane, 1928–32 □, 188

——— 5 Circuit Road, 1932–37 □, 188–89

Bronx, N.Y. 5204 Delafield Ave., 1937–41 □, 70

GERONIMO (1829?–1909).
Clifton, Ariz. Geronimo Birthplace, upper Gila River X

Pensacola, Fla. Fort Pickens State Park, State Highway 399, 1886–88 *

Mount Vernon, Ala. Fort Stoddert, County Road 96, 1888–94 △, 321

Lawton, Okla. Fort Sill Military Reservation NHL, 1894–1909 △, 442

GERRY, ELBRIDGE (1744–1814).
Marblehead, Mass. 44 Washington St., 1744–86 □, 38

Cambridge, Mass. Elmwood NHL, Elmwood Avenue and Mount Auburn Street, 1786–1814 □, 38–39

District of Columbia. 1901 Pennsylvania Ave. NW, 1814 △

GERSHWIN, GEORGE (1898–1937).
Brooklyn, N.Y. Gershwin Birthplace, 242 Snediker Ave., 1898–99 □, 75

New York, N.Y. 520 West 144th St., 1919 □, 93

——— Amsterdam Avenue and 110th Street, 1919–25 △

——— 316 West 103rd St., 1925–28 □, 93

——— 33 Riverside Drive, 1928–33 □, 93

Beverly Hills, Calif. Chevy Chase Drive, 1930–31 X

New York, N.Y. 132 East 72nd St., 1933–36 □, 93

Bevely Hills, Calif. 1019 North Roxbury Drive, 1936–37 △, 411

GETTY, JEAN PAUL (1892–1976).
Minneapolis, Minn. Getty Birthplace, 900–912 Fourth Ave. South, 1892–1906 □, 279

Los Angeles, Calif. 637 South Kingsley Drive, 1907 et seq. 1941 △, 411

New York, N.Y. 1 Sutton Place South, 1936–42 □, 93

Tulsa, Okla. 2701 South Victor St., 1942–44 □, 442

——— 2929 South Utica St., 1945–46 □, 442

Malibu, Calif. 17900 block of Pacific Coast Highway, 1948–76 □, 411

Santa Monica, Calif. 270 Ocean Front, 1950s □, 411

GIBBS, JOSIAH WILLARD (1839–1903).
New Haven, Conn. Gibbs Birthplace, 86 Crown St., 1839–46 △, 9

——— 125 High St., 1846–1903 △, 9

GODDARD, ROBERT HUTCHINGS (1882–1945).
Worcester, Mass. Goddard Birthplace, 1 Tallawanda Drive, 1882–83, 1899–1914, 1924–34 □, 39

Boston, Mass. 63 Forest St., Roxbury, 1883–99 □, 39

Worcester, Mass. 5 Bishop Ave., 1914–24 □

Roswell, N.M. Mescalero Ranch, Mescalero Road, 1930–32, 1934–42 □, 440

Tydings-on-the-Bay, Md. 1942–45 X

GOLDMAN, EMMA (1869–1940).
New York, N.Y. 42nd Street 1889–91 X

New Haven, Conn. 27 Silver St. (present vicinity of Prince and Hill streets), 1890–91 △

New York, N.Y. 210 East 13th St., 1903–13 □, 94

Ossining, N.Y. 1906 et seq. 1912 X

New York, N.Y. 74 East 119th St., 1913–14 △

——— 125th Street, 1914–17 X

Jefferson City, Mo. Missouri State Prison, Lafayette and State streets, 1918–19 □

GOLDWYN, SAMUEL (1882–1974).
Gloversville, N.Y. Kingsborough Hotel, ca. 1900s □

Hollywood, Calif. Hollywood Bloulevard, ca. 1913–34 X

Beverly Hills, Calif. 1200 Laurel Way, 1933 –74 □, 412

GOMPERS, SAMUEL (1850–1924).
New York, N.Y. Houston and Attorney streets, 1863–64 △, 94

——— East 91st Street, ca. 1888–90s X, 94

——— Hotel Washington-Jefferson, 318 West 51st St., 1895 et seq. 1924 □, 94

District of Columbia. 2122 First St. NW, 1902–19 □, 142

——— 3501 Ordway St., NW, 1919–24 □, 142

GOODYEAR, CHARLES (1800–1860).
New Haven, Conn. Goodyear birthplace, South Howard Avenue vicinity, 1800–? △, 9

Naugatuck, Conn. North Main and Bridge streets, 1810s–20s △, 9

Philadelphia, Pa. 200 block of Church Street, 1826–34 △, 221

Woburn, Mass. 280 Montvale Ave., 1838–40 △, 39

Hamden, Conn. 151 Watie St., 1840s □

New Haven, Conn. 2 St. John Place, 1845–47 △

——— 191 Church St., 1850s □

——— 541 Chapel St., 1859–60 □

District of Columbia. 1728 I St. NW, 1859–60 △

Exhibit: 300

GOULD, JAY (1836–1892).
Roxbury, N.Y. Gould Birthplace, West Settlement Road, 1836–52 □, 189

New York, N.Y. 33 East 17th St., 1870s–80s △

Tarrytown, N.Y. Lyndhurst NHL, 635 South Broadway, 1878–92 *, 189

New York, N.Y. 579 Fifth Ave., 1882–92 △, 94

Exhibit: 447

GRANT, ULYSSES SIMPSON (1822–1885).
Point Pleasant, Ohio. Grant Birthplace State Memorial, State Highway 232, 1822–23 *, 300

Georgetown, Ohio. Grant Boyhood Home, 219 East Grant Ave., 1823–39 *, 300

Detroit, Mich. 1369 East Fort St., 1849–50 △; moved to Michigan State Fairgrounds, State Fair and Woodward avenues *, 272

Vancouver, Wash. Grant House, 1106 East Evergreen Blvd., 1852–53 *, 454

St. Louis, Mo. Hardscrabble, 10501 Gravois Road, 1854–60*, 285

——— Grant Cabin, Rock Hill Road, 1854–60 △, 285

Galena, Ill. 121 High St., 1860–61 □, 243

Hopewell, Va. Grant Cabin, Cedar Lane, City Point Unit, Petersburg National Battlefield, 1864–65 *, 376

District of Columbia. Grant Mansion, 550 17th St. NW, ca. 1865–67 △

————509 West 121st St., 1917 ☐, 97

Great Neck, N.Y. 40 Shore Drive, 1926–40 ☐, 190

New York, N.Y. 1067 Fifth Ave., 1930–31 ☐, 97

Doylestown, Pa. Highland Farm, 70 East Road, 1940–60 ☐, 222

HANCOCK, JOHN (1737–1793).

Quincy, Mass. Hancock Birthplace, 8 Adams St., 1737–44 △

Lexington, Mass. Hancock-Clarke House NHL, 36 Hancock St., 1744–45, 1775 *, 39

Boston, Mass. 25 Beacon St., 1745–93 △, 39

Philadelphia, Pa. Arch and Fourth streets, 1776 △

HANDY, WILLIAM CHRISTOPHER (1873–1958).

Florence, Ala. Handy Birthplace, 620 West College St., 1873–? *, 321–22

Memphis, Tenn. 246 Ayres St., ca. 1911–12 △

————659 Jennette St., ca. 1913 ☐, 367

New York, N.Y. 400 Convent Ave., 1920s–30s ☐, 97

Tuckahoe (Yonkers), N.Y. W. C. Handy Place (19 Chester Drive). Colonial Heights, 1930s–58 ☐, 190–91

HANNA, MARCUS ALONZO "MARK" (1837–1904).

Lisbon, Ohio. Hanna Birthplace, Park Avenue and Market Street, 1837–52 ☐, 300

Cleveland, Ohio. Hanna House, Prospect Street between Granger and Cheshire streets, 1852–64 △

————2905 Franklin Ave., 1866 et seq. 1890 ☐, 300

Lakewood, Ohio. Lake Avenue, 1890–1904 ×, 301

Thomasville, Ga. 830 North Dawson St., 1895 et seq. 1900 ☐, 334

District of Columbia. Tayloe-Cameron House, 23 Madison Place NW, 1897–1901 ☐, 143

————Arlington Hotel, southwest corner of Vermont Avenue and I Street NW, 1901–04 △

HARDING, WARREN GAMALIEL (1865–1923).

Blooming Grove, Ohio. Harding Birthplace, State Highway 97, 1865–? △, 301

————Harding Home, State Highway 97, ca. 1870–73 ☐, 301

Caledonia, Ohio. Harding Home, South and Main streets, 1873–80 ☐, 301

Marion, Ohio. 500 East Center St., 1882–91 △, 301

————Harding House NHL, 380 Mount Vernon Ave., 1890–1921 *, 301

District of Columbia. 2314 Wyoming Ave. NW, 1915–21 ☐, 143

————White House, 1600 Pennsylvania Ave. NW, 1921–23 *, 143

San Francisco, Calif. Sheraton Palace Hotel, 639 Market St., 1923 ☐, 412

HARDY, OLIVER NORVELL (1892–1957).

Harlem, Ga. Hardy Birthplace, behind City Hall, 1892–? △, 334

Milledgeville, Ga. 1890s ×

Madison, Ga. Hardy Boardinghouse, 1890s–1910 △

Beverly Hills, Calif. 621 North Alta Drive, 1927–29 ☐, 412

————Beverly Wilshire Hotel, 9500 Wilshire Blvd., 1929–40 ☐, 412

Van Nuys, Calif. 14227 Magnolia Blvd., 1940–56 ☐, 412

North Hollywood, Calif. 5421 Auckland Ave., 1956–57 ☐, 413

HARLOW, JEAN (1911–1937).

Kansas City, Mo. Harlean Carpenter Birthplace, 3344 Olive St., 1911–27 ☐, 286

Westwood, Calif. 1535 Club View Drive, 1931–32 ☐, 413

Beverly Hills, Calif. 9820 Easton Drive, 1932 △, 413

Bel Air, Calif. 214 South Beverly Glen, 1932–33, 1934–35 ☐, 413

West Hollywood, Calif. Chateau Marmont Hotel, 8221 West Sunset Blvd., 1933–34 ☐, 413

Beverly Hills, Calif. 512 North Palm Drive, 1936–37 ☐, 413

HARRIS, JOEL CHANDLER (1848–1908).

Eatonton, Ga. Harris Birthplace, 1848–60s ×

————Turnwold Plantation, Phoenix Road, 1862–66 △, 334

Atlanta, Ga. 201 Whitehall St., 1876–81 △, 334

————Wren's Nest NHL, 1050 Gordon St., SW, 1881–1908 *, 334

HARRISON, BENJAMIN (1833–1901).

North Bend, Ohio. Harrison Birthplace, Symmes and Washington avenues, 1833 △, 301

————Point Farm, Harrison State Memorial, Loop Avenue, 1833–53 △

Indianapolis, Ind. East Vermont Street, 1850s–60s ×

————North New Jersey Street, 1860s ×

————North Alabama and Washington streets, 1870s–76 △

————Harrison Home NHL, 1230 North Delaware St., 1874–1901 *, 255

District of Columbia. White House, 1600 Pennsylvania Ave. NW, 1889–93 *, 143

HARRISON, WILLIAM HENRY (1773–1841).

Charles City, Va. Berkeley NHL (Harrison Birthplace), State Highway 5, 1773–89 *, 377

Cincinnati, Ohio. Fort Washington, Fort Washington Way, 1795–96 △, 301

North Bend, Ohio. Harrison Home, Symmes and Washington avenues, 1796 et seq. 1841 △, 301

Vincennes, Ind. Grouseland NHL, 3 West Scott St., 1804–12 *, 255

Columbus, Ohio. Oberdier House, 570 West Broad St., 1813–14 ☐

District of Columbia. White House, 1600 Pennsylvania Ave. NW, 1841 *, 143

HART, MOSS (1904–1961).

New York, N.Y. Hart Birthplace, East 103rd Street, 1904–? ×

Brooklyn, N.Y. 1930s ×

New York, N.Y. 1185 Park Ave., 1930s–61 ☐, 97

Aquetong, Pa. Hart House, Aquetong Road, 1940s ☐, 222

New York, N.Y. Waldorf Towers, 100 East 50th St., 1940s ☐

Palm Springs, Calif. 467 Via Lola, 1961 ☐, 413

HART, WILLIAM SURREY (1870–1946)

Newburgh, N.Y. Hart Birthplace, 165 Front St. (reputed), 1870–80s △

New York, N.Y. 205 West 56th St., 1888–93 △

Hollywood, Calif. 1581 DeLongpre Ave., ?–1928 ☐, 413

Newhall, Calif. Horseshoe Ranch, 24151 North Newhall Ave., 1928–46 *, 413

HARTE, BRET (1836–1902).

Albany, N.Y. Harte Birthplace, 15 Columbia St., 1836–? △

New York, N.Y. 487 Hudson St., ca. 1849 ☐, 97

Oakland, Calif. 567-577 Fifth St., 1854–57 △, 413

Arcata, Calif. 927 J St., 1857–60 ☐, 413

San Francisco, Calif. 524 Sutter St., 1862–? △

New York, N.Y. 16 Fifth Ave., 1870–73 ☐, 97

Morristown, N.J. The Willows, Mendham Avenue, 1874–75 ☐, 173

New York, N.Y. 713 Broadway, 1875 △

HAWTHORNE, NATHANIEL (1804–1864).

Salem, Mass. Hawthorne Birthplace, 27 Union St., 1804–08 △; moved to 54 Turner St. *, 40

————10½-12 Herbert St., 1808–28 ☐, 40

Raymond, Maine. Hawthorne Home, Hawthorne and Raymond Cape roads, 1818–19*, 17

Salem, Mass. 16 Dearborn St., 1828–32 ☐, 40

West Roxbury, Mass. Brook Farm Site NHL, 670 Baker St., 1841 △, 40

Concord, Mass. Old Manse NHL, Monument Street, 1842–46 *, 40

Salem, Mass. 18 Chestnut St., 1846–47 ☐

————14 Mall St., 1847–49 ☐, 40

Lenox, Mass. Red Cottage, West Hawthorne Street, 1850–51 △, 40

Concord, Mass. Wayside House NHL, Lexington Road, 1852–53, 1860–64*, 40

HAYES, RUTHERFORD BIRCHARD (1822–1893).

Delaware, Ohio. Hayes Birthplace, East William and Winter streets, 1822–36 △, 302

Cincinnati, Ohio. 383 Sixth St., 1853–67 △

Fremont, Ohio. Spiegel Grove NHL, 1337 Hayes Ave., 1874–93 *, 302

District of Columbia. White House, 1600 Pennsylvania Ave. NW, 1877–81 *, 143

————Anderson Cottage, U.S. Soldiers' and Airmen's Home NHL, Rock Creek Church Road and Upshur Street NW, 1877 et seq. 1880 □

HEARN, LAFCADIO (1850–1904).

Cincinnati, Ohio. 215 Plum St., 1872–74 △

————114 Longworth St., 1874–77 △

New Orleans, La. Bustillos Boardinghouse, 813 Baronne St., 1877 □, 350

————516 Bourbon St., 1880 □, 350

————Higgins Boardinghouse, 1565 Cleveland St., 1881–87 □, 350

New York, N.Y. 438 West 57th St., 1887–88 △

————149 West 10th St., 1889–90 □, 97

HEARST, WILLIAM RANDOLPH (1863–1951).

San Francisco, Calif. Stevenson House (Hearst Birthplace), California and Montgomery streets, 1863 △

————Rincon Hill, 1863–65 ×

————Chestnut Street, 1865–73 ×

————Van Ness Avenue, 1875–ca. 1880 ×

————Nob Hill, ca. 1880s ×

Sausalito, Calif. 1887–94 ×

San Francisco, Calif. Palace Hotel, 639 Market St., 1894–95 △

New York, N.Y. Madison Square, 1895–98 ×

————Worth House, Broadway and West 25th Street, 1898–1900 △

————Arthur House NHL, 123 Lexington Ave., 1900–07 □, 98

District of Columbia. 722 Jackson Place NW, 1903–07 △, 144

New York, N.Y. Clarendon Apartments, 137 Riverside Drive, 1907–26 □, 98

San Simeon, Calif. Hearst-San Simeon State Historical Monument, State Highway 1, 1923–47 *, 414

Hollywood, Calif. Ambassador Hotel, 3400 Wilshire Blvd., 1926–40s □, 416

New York, N.Y. Ritz Tower Hotel, Park Avenue and East 57th Street, 1928 et seq. 1938 □, 98

Santa Monica, Calif. Ocean House, 415 Palisades Beach Road, 1928–46 △, 415

McCloud, Calif. Wyntoon, McCloud River, 1942–44 △

Beverly Hills, Calif. 1007 North Beverly Drive, 1947–51 □, 415

HECHT, BEN (1894–1964).

Racine, Wis. Castello Boardinghouse, 838 Lake Ave., 1890s–1910 △, 314

Chicago, Ill. 5210 South Kenwood Ave., ca. 1920s–24 □, 243

Upper Nyack, N.Y. Hecht Home, Perry Lane, 1929–64 □, 191

New York, N.Y. 39 West 67th St., 1950s et seq. 1964 □, 98

HEMINGWAY, ERNEST MILLER (1899–1961).

Oak Park, Ill. Hemingway Birthplace, 339 North Oak Park Ave., 1899–1905 □, 243

Petoskey, Mich. Windemere NHL, Walloon Lake, 1900–20 □, 273

Oak Park, Ill. 600 North Kenilworth Ave., 1906–17 □, 243

Petoskey, Mich. 602 State St., 1919 □, 273

Chicago, Ill. The Belleville, 1239 North Dearborn St., 1921 □, 243

Key West, Fla. Hemingway Home and Museum NHL, 907 Whitehead St., 1931–39 *, *328*

Ketchum, Idaho. Hemingway House, Warm Springs area, 1959–61 □, 435

HENDRIX, JIMI (1934–1970).

Seattle, Wash. 124 10th Ave., ca. 1946 □, 454

New York, N.Y. Theresa Hotel, 2090 Seventh Ave., 1963–64 □, 98

————210 West 118th St., 1964 □

————Howard Johnson Motor Lodge, Eighth Avenue and West 51st Street, 1960s □, 98

————Electric Lady Studio, 55 West Eighth St., ca. 1968–70 □, 98

————Drake Hotel, 440 Park Ave., 1968–70 □, 98

HENRY, JOSEPH (1797–1878).

Albany, N.Y. Henry birthplace, 78 South Pearl St., 1797–? △

————105 Columbia St., 1820s–30s △

Princeton, N.J. Henry House, Princeton University, 1836–48 □, 173

District of Columbia. Smithsonian Institution, 1000 Jefferson Drive SW, 1847–78*, 144

HENRY, O. See WILLIAM SYDNEY PORTER.

HENRY, PATRICK (1736–1799).

Studley, Va. Henry Birthplace, County Road 605, 1736–50 △, 377

————Mount Brilliant Plantation, southeast Hanover County, 1750–53 ×

Hanover, Va. Pine Slash Farm, south off State Highway 2, 1754–57 △

————Hanover Tavern, U.S. Highway 301, 1757–65 *, 377

Louisa, Va. Henry Farm, Roundabout Plantation, State Highway 208, 1765–71 △

Ashland, Va. Scotchtown NHL, State Highway 685, 1771–77 *, 377

Williamsburg, Va. Governor's Palace, Palace Green, Colonial Williamsburg NHL, 1776–79 △ *, 377

Leatherwood, Va. Leatherwood Plantation, State Highway 57, 1779–84 △, 377

Richmond, Va. Governor's Residence, Capitol Square, 1784–86 △, 377

Midlothian, Va. Salisbury Plantation, 1784–86 △, 378

Farmville, Va. Henry Farm, Appomattox River, 1786–92 △

Gladys, Va. Henry Estate, Long Island, Staunton River, 1792–96 △

Brookneal, Va. Red Hill Shrine, County Road 677, 1796–99 △ *, 378

HERBERT, VICTOR (1859–1924).

Pittsburgh, Pa. 503–519 Aiken Ave., 1898–1904 △, 222

Lake Placid, N.Y. Camp Joyland, 69 Victor Herbert Drive, 1903–24 □, 191

New York, N.Y. 300–321 West 108th St., 1904–24 □, 98

HICKOK, JAMES BUTLER "WILD BILL" (1837–1876).

Troy Grove, Ill. Hickok Birthplace, Main Street, 1837–? △, 243

————Hickok Farm, 1830s–56 ×, 243

Leavenworth, Kan. Fort Leavenworth NHL, U.S. Highway 73 and Seventh Street, ca. 1856 *

Manhattan, Kan. Fort Riley Military Reservation, State Highway 18, 1866 ×

Hays, Kan. Fort Hays Frontier Historical Park, U.S. Highway 183A, 1869 *

Abilene, Kan. 1871 ×

Deadwood, S.D. Hickok Camp, Sherman Street, 1876 △, 311

HILL, JAMES JEROME (1838–1916).

St. Paul, Minn. 34 Canada St., 1869–71 △

————11 Canada St., 1873–75 △

————Hill House, Ninth and Canada streets, 1877–78 △

259 East Ninth St., 1878–91 △

North Oaks, Minn. North Oaks Farm, State Highway 96, 1883–1916 △, 279

Jekyll Island, Ga. Jekyll Island Club House, Millionaires Village NHL, 1888–1916 *, 334

Albany, N.Y. 50 North Pearl St., 1845–47 △

New York, N.Y. 57 West 14th St., 1840s–50s △, 100

Newport, R.I. 13 Kay St., 1860–62 □, 61

———— 465 Spring St., 1860s □, 61

Boston, Mass. 13 Ashburton Place, 1864–66 △

Cambridge, Mass. 20 Quincy St., 1866 et seq. 1882 △, 42

New York, N.Y. 111 East 25th St., 1875 △, 100

Boston, Mass. 102 Mount Vernon St., 1882 □, 42

———— 131 Mount Vernon St., 1882–83 □, 42

New York, N.Y. 21 East 11th St., 1904 □, 100

Cambridge, Mass. 95 Irving St., 1910 □

JAMES, JESSE WOODSON (1847–1882).

Kearney, Mo. James Homestead, Jesse James Farm Drive, 1847 et seq. 1882 *, 286

New Johnsonville, Tenn. James Farm, off U.S. Highway 70, 1879–81 △, 368

Kansas City, Mo. Woodlawn Avenue, 1881 X

St. Joseph, Mo. James House, 12th and Penn streets, 1882 *, 286

JAMES, WILLIAM (1842–1910).

New York, N.Y. James Birthplace, Astor House Hotel, 125 Broadway, 1842 △, 100

1843–1878: See HENRY JAMES.

Cambridge, Mass. 387 Harvard St., 1878–80 △

———— 14 Garden St., 1880–94 △

———— 95 Irving St., 1889–1910 □, 42

Chocorua, N.H. James Summer Home, State Highway 16, 1887–1910 □, 57

JARRELL, RANDALL (1914–1965).

Nashville, Tenn. Jarrell Birthplace, 1914–20s X

Long Beach, Calif. 1819 East Fourth St., 1920s □, 417

Gambier, Ohio. Walton House, 103 College Drive, 1937–39 □, 302

Austin, Texas. 707 West 25th St., 1939–40 △

———— 2501 Indian Trail, 1940–41 □, 448

———— 2202 Leon St., 1941–43 △

Greensboro, N.C. 1924 Spring Garden St., 1947–51 △

———— 1200 West Market St., 1954–56 □, 357

District of Columbia. 3916 Jenifer St., NW, 1956–58 □, 145

Greensboro, N.C. 123 Tate St., 1958–60 □, 357

———— 5706 South Lake Drive, 1960–65 □, 357

JAY, JOHN (1745–1829).

New York, N.Y. Jay Birthplace, 1745–? X

East Fishkill, N.Y. Van Wyck-Jay House, State Highway 52, 1776–81 □, 191

New York, N.Y. 133 Broadway, 1788 △, 100

———— Government House, State Street and Bowling Green, 1795–1801 △, 100–101

Katonah, N.Y. Jay Homestead, Jay Street, 1801–29 *, 191

JEFFERS, ROBINSON (1887–1962).

Pittsburgh, Pa. Jeffers Birthplace, 723 Ridge Ave., 1887–88 △, 222

Sewickley, Pa. 44 Thorn St., 1888–93 □, 222

Edgeworth, Pa. Twin Hollows, Beaver Road, 1893–ca. 1900 △

Highland Park, Calif. 346 North Ave. 57, 1903–05 □, 417

Manhattan Beach, Calif. Third Street, 1905 △

———— Jeffers Ranch, Sepulveda and Manhattan Beach boulevards, 1905–06 △

Los Angeles, Calif. 1623 Shatto St., ca. 1907 □

Seattle, Wash. 4215 Brooklyn Ave. NE, 1910–11 □, 454

Pasadena, Calif. 822 Garfield Ave., ca. 1911–14 □, 417

Carmel, Calif. Jeffers House, Fourth and Monte Verde streets, 1914–19 □, 417

———— Tor House, 26304 Ocean View Ave., 1919–62 □, 417

JEFFERSON, THOMAS (1743–1826).

Charlottesville, Va. Shadwell Plantation (Jefferson Birthplace), U.S. Highway 250, 1743–45, 1752–70 △, 379

Richmond, Va. Tuckahoe Plantation, State Highway 650, 145–52 □, 379

Charlottesville, Va. Monticello NHL, State Highway 53, 1771–1826 *, 379–80

Philadelphia, Pa. Graff House NHL, Seventh and Market streets, 1776 △ *, 222

Georges Tavern, Va. Elk Hill Plantation, County Road 608, 1778–et seq. △, 380

Williamsburg, Va. Governor's Palace, Palace Green, Colonial Williamsburg NHL, 1779 *, 380

Lynchburg, Va. Poplar Forest Plantation, State Highway 681, 1781 et seq. 1826 □, 380

New York, N.Y. 57 Maiden Lane, 1790 △, 101

Philadelphia, Pa. Leiper House, 274 Market St., 1790–93 △, 223

District of Columbia. Conrad and McMunn Boardinghouse, New Jersey Avenue and C Street SE, 1800–01 △, 146

District of Columbia. White House, 1600 Pennsylvania Ave. NW, 1801–09 *, 145

JEWETT, SARAH ORNE (1849–1909).

South Berwick, Maine. Haggens House (Jewett Birthplace), Portland Street, 1849–60s *, 17

———— Jewett Memorial, 101 Portland St., 1860s–1909 *, 17

JOHNSON, ANDREW (1808–1875).

Raleigh, N.C. Johnson Birthplace, 123 Fayetteville St., 1808–24 △; moved to 1 Mimosa St. *, 357

Laurens, S.C. Johnson Cabin, Town Square, 1824–25 △, 364

Greeneville, Tenn. Johnson Cabin, Main Street, 1827–31 △, 369

———— Kerbaugh House, Andrew Johnson NHS, College and Depot streets, 1831–51 □, 369

———— Johnson Homestead, Andrew Johnson NHS, College and Depot streets, 1851–75 *, 369

Nashville, Tenn. Nashville Inn, Public Square, 1854–56 △, 369

District of Columbia. Kirkwood Hotel, Pennsylvania Avenue and 12th Street NW, 1865 △

———— Blair-Lee House NHL, 1651–53 Pennsylvania Ave. NW, 1865 □

———— White House, 1600 Pennsylvania Ave. NW, 1865–69 *, 146

Elizabethton, Tenn. Stover Farm, one mile southwest of town, 1875 △

JOHNSON, JACK ARTHUR (1878–1946).

Galveston, Texas. Johnson Birthplace, 808 Broadway (reputed), 1878–90s △?, 448

Chicago, Ill. 3344 South Wabash Ave., ca. 1909–11 △, 244

———— Cafe de Champion, 42 West 31st St., 1911–12 △, 244

JOHNSON, JAMES WELDON (1871–1938).

Jacksonville, Fla. Johnson Birthplace, 138 Lee St., 1871–1901 △, 329

New York, N.Y. Marshall Club, 260 West 53rd St., 1901–? △, 101

———— 2311 Seventh Ave., 1920s □, 101

———— 187 West 135th St., 1925–38 □, 101

Great Barrington, Mass. Five Acres, Seekonk Road, 1925 et seq. 1938 □, 42

Nashville, Tenn. Johnson House NHL, 911 18th Ave. North, 1930–38 □, 369

JOHNSON, LYNDON BAINES (1908–1973).

Stonewall, Texas. Johnson Birthplace, Park Road 49, Johnson NHS, 1908–13 *, 448

Johnson City, Texas. Johnson Boyhood Home, Johnson NHS, 1914–17 et seq. 1924 *, 448

Stonewall, Texas. LBJ Ranch, Johnson NHS, 1917–23, 1952 et seq. 1973 *, 448

District of Columbia. Dodge House, North Capitol and E streets, NW, 1932–34 △

Austin, Texas. 2808 San Pedro, 1935–36 □

———— 4 Happy Hollow Lane, 1937, 1939, 1941 □

———— 3119 Tom Green St., 1938–39 □

District of Columbia. Chatham Courts, 1938 X

———— Woodley Park Towers, 2737 Devonshire Place NW, 1941–42 □

Las Vegas, Nev. Caesars Palace, 3570 Las Vegas Blvd. South, 1970s □, 438

—— 3333 Seminole Circle, 1970–81 □, 438

LOVECRAFT, HOWARD PHILLIPS (1890–1937).

Providence, R.I. Lovecraft Birthplace, 454 Angell St., 1890–1904 △, 62

—— 598 Angell St., 1904–24 □, 62

Brooklyn, N.Y. 259 Parkside Ave., 1924 □, 75

—— 169 Clinton St., 1924–26 □, 75

Providence, R.I. 10 Barnes St., 1926–33 □, 62

—— 66 College St., 1933–37 △; moved to 65 Prospect St. □, 62

LOWELL, JAMES RUSSELL (1819–1891).

Cambridge, Mass. Elmwood NHL (Lowell Birthplace), Elmwood Avenue and Mount Auburn Street, 1819–56, 1889–91 □, 44

—— Dr. Estes Howe House, 13 Kirkland St. (corner of Oxford Street), 1856–61 △

Southborough, Mass. Burnett House, 1885–89 X

LOWELL, ROBERT TRAILL SPENCE, JR. (1917–1977).

Boston, Mass. Lowell Birthplace, 1917–? X

—— 91 Revere St., 1924–27 □, 44

—— 170 Marlborough St., 1927–50 □, 44

Gambier, Ohio. Walton House, 103 College Drive, 1937–40 □, 302

New York, N.Y. 12 Gansevoort St., 1943–? △

Boston, Mass. 239 Marlborough St., 1954–60 □, 44

Castine, Maine. Summer home, Castine Commons, 1957 et seq. 1968 □, 18

New York, N.Y. 154 Riverside Drive, ca. 1959 □

—— 15 West 67th St., 1960–70 □, 104

LUCE, HENRY ROBINSON (1898–1967).

New York, N.Y. 514 West 122nd St., 1920s □, 104

—— 234 East 49th St., 1927–33 □, 104

—— River House, 435 East 52nd St., 1936–65 □, 104

Moncks Corner, S.C. Mepkin Plantation, River Road, 1936–49 *, 364

New York, N.Y. Waldorf Towers, 100 East 50th St., 1938–50 □, 104

Greenwich, Conn. The House, 1275 King St., 1938–46 □, 10

Ridgefield, Conn. Sugar Hill, Limestone Road, 1946–60s □, 10

Phoenix, Ariz. 43 Biltmore Estates, 1957 et seq. 1967 □, 398

New York, N.Y. 950 Fifth Ave., 1960–65 □, 104

MacARTHUR, DOUGLAS (1880–1964).

Little Rock, Ark. MacArthur Birthplace, MacArthur Park, East Ninth Street, 1880–81 *, 325

Radium Springs, N.M. Fort Selden State Monument, U.S. Highway 85, 1884–86 △, 440

Milwaukee, Wis. 575 North Marshall St., 1907–08 △

Leavenworth, Kan. 12–14 Sumner Place, Fort Leavenworth, 1908–11 □, 266

West Point, N.Y. Superintendent's Quarters, Jefferson and Washington roads, U.S. Military Academy, 1919–22 □, 194

Owings Mills, Md. Rainbow Hill, Park Heights Avenue, 1925–28 □, 164

Fort Myer, Va. Quarters One NHL, Grant Avenue, 1930–35 □, 383

New York, N.Y. Waldorf Towers, 100 East 50th St., 1952–64 □, 104

Exhibit: 450

McCARTHY, JOSEPH RAYMOND (1908–1957).

Center, Wis. McCarthy Birthplace, 5711 West Broadway Drive (North McCarthy Road), 1908–23 □, 315

Shawano, Wis. 404 South Main St., 1936–40 □, 315

Appleton, Wis. 1508 Lorain Court, 1940–41 □

—— 514 South Story St., 1942 et seq. 1957 □, 315

—— Hotel Appleton, 127 North Appleton St., 1945–? △

District of Columbia. 3335 C St. SE, ca. 1950 □, 149

—— 20 Third St. NE, 1953–57 □, 149

McCLELLAN, GEORGE BRINTON (1826–1885).

Philadelphia, Pa. McClellan Birthplace, 700 Walnut St., 1826–42 △, 223

District of Columbia. H and 15th streets NW, 1861–62 △, 149

New York, N.Y. 22 West 31st St., 1863–65 △, 104

West Orange, N.J. Maywood, St. Cloud, 1870–85 X, 174

District of Columbia. 1730 Massachusetts Ave. NW, 1882–83 △

McCORMICK, CYRUS HALL (1809–1884).

Steeles Tavern, Va. Walnut Grove NHL (McCormick Birthplace), County Road 606, 1809–48 *, 384

Chicago, Ill. 230 North Dearborn St., 1859–64 △

—— 128 Michigan Ave., 1864–66 △

New York, N.Y. 40 Fifth Ave., 1866–72 △

Chicago, Ill. 62 North Sheldon St., 1872–75 △

—— 363 Superior St., 1875–79 △

—— 675 North Rush St., 1879–84 △, 248

Richfield Springs, N.Y. Clayton Lodge, Sunset Hill, 1882–84 △, 194

McCULLERS, CARSON SMITH (1917–1967).

Columbus, Ga. Smith Birthplace, Fifth Avenue and 13th Street, 1917–27 △, 335

—— 1519 Starke Ave., 1927–34 □, 335

—— 2417 Wynnton Road, 1925–27 □

Saratoga Springs, N.Y. Yaddo, Union Avenue, 1930s et seq. 1950s □

Charlotte, N.C. 311 East Blvd., 1937 □, 358

—— 806 Central Ave., 1938 △

Fayetteville, N.C. 1104 Clark St., 1938–40 △, 358

New York, N.Y. 321 West 11th St., 1940 □, 104

Brooklyn, N.Y. 7 Middagh St., 1940–41, 1943 △, 75

Nyack, N.Y. Graycourt Manor, 127 South Broadway, 1944–45 △

—— 131 South Broadway, 1945–67 □, 194

MacDOWELL, EDWARD ALEXANDER (1861–1908).

New York, N.Y. MacDowell Birthplace, 220 Clinton St., 1861–76 △, 104

Boston, Mass. 1888–97 X

Peterborough, N.H. MacDowell Colony NHL, MacDowell Road, 1896 et seq. 1908 *, 57

New York, N.Y. Central Park West and West 96th Street, 1898–1902 X, 104

—— Westminster Hotel, Irving Place, 1904, 1908 △

McGUFFEY, WILLIAM HOLMES (1800–1873).

Washington, Pa. McGuffey Birthplace, West Finley Township, 1800–02 △; moved to Dearborn, Mich., 223–24

Dearborn, Mich. Greenfield Village, 20900 Oakwood Boulevard *, 275

Coitsville Center, Ohio. McGuffey Boyhood Home Site NHL, McGuffey Road, 1802–15 △, 302

Oxford, Ohio. McGuffey House NHL, 401 East Spring St., 1833–36 *, 302

Athens, Ohio. McGuffey House, East Union Street, 1839–43 △, 303

Charlottesville, Va. Pavilion IX, West Lawn, University of Virginia campus, 1845–73 □, 384

McKINLEY, WILLIAM (1843–1901).

Niles, Ohio. McKinley Birthplace, Main Street, 1843–52 △, 303

Poland, Ohio. 210 Main St., 1852–66 △

Canton, Ohio. McKinley Home, North Market Avenue and Eighth Street, 1871–77, 1899–1901 △, 303

District of Columbia. Ebbitt House, F and 14th streets NW, 1876 et seq. 1897 △, 149

Columbus, Ohio. Neil House Hotel, South High Street, 1891–96 △, 303

District of Columbia. White House, 1600 Pennsylvania Ave. NW, 1897–1901 *, 149

Buffalo, N.Y. Milburn House, 1168 Delaware Ave., 1901 △, 194

Tenafly, N.J. 1 Byrne Lane, 1939–42, 174

Duarte, Calif. Miller House, adjacent to Satellite Park, 1941–42 △

MILLER, HENRY VALENTINE (1891–1980).

New York, N.Y. Miller Birthplace, 450 East 85th St., 1891–92 □, 106

Brooklyn, N.Y. 662 Driggs Ave., 1892–1900 □, 75

——— 1063 Decatur St., 1900–12 △, 75

New York, N.Y. 244 Sixth Ave., 1916

Brooklyn, N.Y. 91 Remsen St., 1924 □, 75

Big Sur, Calif. Miller House, 1944–64 □, 423

Pacific Palisades, Calif. 444 Ocampo St., 1964–80 □, 423

MITCHELL, MARGARET MUNNERLEIN (1900–1949).

Atlanta, Ga. Munnerlein Birthplace, 296 Cain St., 1900–03 △, 335

——— 1401 Peachtree St. NE, 1912–24 △, 335

——— 979 Crescent Ave. NE, 1925–32 □, 335

——— 4 East 17th St., 1932–39 □, 335

——— 1268 Piedmont Ave. NE, 1939–49 □, 335

MIX, THOMAS EDWIN "TOM" (1880–1940).

Mix Run, Pa. Mix Birthplace, Bennett's Branch Road, 1880–84 △, 225

Driftwood, Pa. Front Street, 1884–88 △ X, 225

DuBois, Pa. 1888–98 X

Dewey, Okla. 1909–13 X, 442

Hollywood, Calif. 5841 Carlton Way, 1917–22 □, 423

Beverly Hills, Calif. 1018 Summit Dr., 1922–40 □, 423

MONK, THELONIOUS SPHERE (1920–1982).

Rocky Mount or Palmyra, N.C. Monk birthplace, 1920–24 X

New York, N.Y. 243 West 63rd St., 1924–82 □, 106

Weehawken, N.J. 1970s–80s X

MONROE, JAMES (1758–1831).

Colonial Beach, Va. Monrovia (Monroe Birthplace), State Highway 205, 1758–69 △, 386

Fredericksburg, Va. Jones House, 301 Caroline St., 1786–91 □, 386

Charlottesville, Va. Monroe House, University of Virginia campus, 1791–96 □, 386

——— Ash Lawn, County Road, 795, 1796–1820 *, 386

Richmond, Va. Governor's Mansion, Capitol Square, 1799–1802, 1811 △, 386

District of Columbia. Caldwell-Monroe House NHL, 2017 I St. NW, 1811–17 *, 150

——— White House, 1600 Pennsylvania Ave. NW, 1817–25 *, 151, 158

Gilberts Corner, Va. Oak Hill NHL, U.S. Highway 15, 1820–30 *, 386

New York, N.Y. Gouverneur House, Lafayette and Prince streets, 1830–31 △, 106

MONROE, MARILYN (1926–1962).

Hawthorne, Calif. Bolender House, 4211 West 134th St., 1926–33 □, 423

Hollywood, Calif. Baker House, now Hollywood Bowl parking area, Highland Avenue, 1933–35 △

——— Hollygrove, 815 El Centro Ave., 1935–37 □, 423

Van Nuys, Calif. 4524 Vista Del Monte, 1942 □

Hollywood, Calif. YWCA Studio Club, 1215 Lodi Place, 1948 □

Beverly Hills, Calif. 882 North Doheny Drive, 1952–53, 1961–62 □, 424

——— Beverly Hills Hotel, 9641 Sunset Blvd. 1954, 1960 □, 424

——— 508 North Palm Drive, 1954 □, 424

New York, N.Y. Waldorf Towers, 100 East 50th St., 1955–56 □, 106

——— 444 East 57th St., 1957–59 □, 106

Roxbury, Conn. Arthur Miller Farm, Tophet Road, 1957–60 □, 11

Brentwood Heights, Calif. 12305 Fifth Helena Drive, 1962 □, 424

MONTEZ, LOLA (1818–1861).

Grass Valley, Calif. Lola Montez House, Walsh and Mill streets, 1852–54 *, 424

Brooklyn, N.Y. Old Clover Road, 1860 X

Queens, N.Y. Astoria, 1860–61 X

New York, N.Y. 194 West Seventh St., 1861 △

MOORE, CLEMENT CLARKE (1779–1863).

New York, N.Y. Moore Birthplace, West 22nd Street, 1779-ca. 1850 △, 106

——— Moore House, Ninth Avenue and West 23rd Street, 1850s–63 △, 106

Newport, R.I. Tudor Hall, 26 Greenough Place, 1850–63 □, 62

MOORE, MARIANNE CRAIG (1887–1972).

Kirkwood, Mo. 325 North Taylor St., 1887–94 △, 287

Carlisle, Pa. 343 North Hanover St., 1894–1905, 1911–16, 225

Chatham, N.J. Ogden Memorial Church Manse, Elmwood and Main streets, 1916–18 △

New York, N.Y. 14 St. Luke's Place, 1918–29 □, 106

Brooklyn, N.Y. Cumberland Apartments, 260 Cumberland St., 1931–66 □, 75–76

New York, N.Y. 35 West Ninth St., 1966–72 □, 106

MORGAN, JOHN PIERPONT (1837–1913).

Hartford, Conn. Morgan Birthplace, 153 Asylum Ave., 1837–40 △, 11

——— 108 Farmington Ave., 1840–51 △, 11

Boston, Mass. 15 Pemberton Square, 1852–54 △

New York, N.Y. 227 Madison Ave., 1865–70s △

Highland Falls, N.Y. Cragston, 1871 et seq. 1913 X

New York, N.Y. 243 Madison Ave., 1870s △

——— 6 East 40th St., 1870s–82 △

——— 219 Madison Ave., 1882–1913 △, 107

District of Columbia. Arlington Hotel, southwest corner of Vermont Avenue and I Street NW, 1890s–1912 △

Jekyll Island, Ga. Sans Souci Apartments, Millionaires Village NHL, 1899–1913 *, 336

MORGENTHAU, HENRY, JR. (1891–1967).

New York, N.Y. Morgenthau Birthplace, Beresford Apartments, 211 Central Park West, 1891–? □, 107

Hopewell Junction, N.Y. Morgenthau Farm, East Hook Road, 1913–67 □, 195

MORSE, SAMUEL FINLEY BREESE (1791–1872).

Boston, Mass. Morse Birthplace, 199–205 Main St., Charlestown, 1791–1817 △, 47

Charleston, S.C. Munro Boardinghouse, 81 Church St., ca. 1819 △

New Haven, Conn. Kingsley-Apthorp House, 31 Hillhouse Ave., 1819–21 △

——— 320 Temple St., 1821–26 □, 11

New York, N.Y. New York University, Washington Square North and University Place, 1835–40s △, 107

Poughkeepsie, N.Y. Locust Grove NHL, 370 South St., 1847–72 *, 195

New York, N.Y. 5 West 22nd St., 1850s–72 △, 107

MOSES, ANNA MARY ROBERTSON "GRANDMA" (1860–1961).

Greenwich, N.Y. Robertson Birthplace, 1860–70 X

Verona, Va. Moses Farm, State Highway 780, 1890s □, 386

——— Hilltop, off U.S. Highway 11, 1901–02 □, 386

Staunton, Va. King's Daughters' Hospital site, 1902–05 △, 386

Eagle Bridge, N.Y. Moses Farm, Grandma Moses Road, 1905–51 □, 195

——— Moses Home, Grandma Moses Road, 1951–61 □, 195

MOTT, LUCRETIA COFFIN (1793–1880).

Nantucket, Mass. Coffin Birthplace, Fair Street, 1793 △, 47

——— 15 Fair St., 1793–1804 □, 47

Philadelphia, Pa. South Second Street near Walnut Street, ca. 1809–10 X

Staten Island, N.Y. Tosomock Farm, 4515 Hylan Blvd., Eltingville, 1848–54 ☐, 129

Brookline, Mass. Olmsted House NHS, 99 Warren St., 1883–98 *, 47

Sunset, Maine. Summer home, State Highway 15, 1893 et seq. 1898 ☐, 18

Belmont, Mass. Hope Cottage, McLean Asylum, 115 Mill St., 1898–1903 ☐, 47

O'NEILL, EUGENE GLADSTONE (1888–1953).
New York, N.Y. O'Neill Birthplace, Barrett House Hotel, Broadway and West 43rd St., 1888 △, 108

New London, Conn. Monte Cristo Cottage NHL, 325 Pequod Ave., 1890–1914 ☐, 11

New York, N.Y. Jimmy the Priest's Saloon, 252 Fulton St., 1911 △, 108

———— 38 Washington Square South, 1915 △, 109

———— 42 Washington Square South, 1916 △, 109

Provinceton, Mass. 577 Commercial St., ca. 1919 ☐, 47

———— Peaked Hill Bar, 1919–30 △, 47

Ridgefield, Conn. Brook Farm, 845 North Salem Road, 1922–25 ☐, 11

Sea Island, Ga. Casa Genotta, Agramont Street, 1932–36 ☐, 337

Danville, Calif. Tao House NHL, Kuss Road, 1937–44 ☐, 424

New York, N.Y. 35 East 84th St., 1946–48 ☐, 109

Marblehead, Mass. Point O'Rocks Lane, 1948–51 ☐, 47

Boston, Mass. Shelton Hotel, 91 Bay State Rd., 1951–53 ☐, 47

OPPENHEIMER, J. ROBERT (1904–1967).
New York, N.Y. Oppenheimer Birthplace, West 94th Street, 1904–? X

———— 155 Riverside Drive, 1912–22 ☐, 109

Tererro, N.M. Perro Caliente, Road 223, 1929 et seq. 1950 ☐, 440

Pasadena, Calif. 160 South Los Robles, 1932 △

———— Athenaeum, 551 South Hill Ave., 1933 et seq. 1940 ☐, 425

Altadena, Calif. 205 East Las Flores, ca. 1935 △

Berkeley, Calif. 10 Kenilworth Court, 1941 ☐

Kensington, Calif. 1 Eagle Hill, 1941–43 ☐, 425

Los Alamos, N.M. 1967 Peach St., 1942–45 ☐, 440

Princeton, N.J. Olden Manor, Olden Lane, 1947–67 ☐, 175

OSWALD, LEE HARVEY (1939–1963).
New Orleans, La. 1010 Bartholomew St., ca. 1941 ☐, 351

———— 831 Pauline St., 1941–43 ☐, 351

———— Bethlehem Children's Center, 4430 Bundy Road, 1943–44 ☐, 351

Fort Worth, Tex. 1505 Eighth Ave., 1947 ☐, 450

———— 3300 Willing St., 1947–48 ☐, 450

———— 7408 Ewing St., 1948–52 ☐, 450

Bronx, N.Y. 1455 Sheridan Ave., 1952 ☐, 71

———— 825 East 179th St., 1952–54 ☐, 71

Fort Worth, Tex. 4936 Collingwood Ave., 1956 ☐, 450

———— 2703 Mercedes St., 1961 ☐, 450

Dallas, Tex. 604 Elsbeth St., 1962–63 ☐, 450

———— 214 West Neely St., 1963 ☐, 450

———— 1026 North Beckley St., 1963 ☐, 450

Irving, Tex. 2515 West Fifth St., 1963 ☐, 451

PAINE, THOMAS (1737–1809).
York, Pa. Cookes House, 438–40 Cordorus St., 1777–78 ☐, 225

Bordentown, N.J. 2 West Church St., 1783–1803 ☐, 175

New Rochelle, N.Y. Paine Cottage NHL, North and Paine avenues, 1803–06 *, 196

Brooklyn, N.Y. Sands and Fulton streets (see text) △, 76

New York, N.Y. 16 Gold St. 1804 △, 109

———— 36 Cedar St., 1804–06 △, 109

———— 85 Church St., 1806–07 △, 109

———— West Fulton Street, 1807–08 △, 109

———— 309 Bleecker St., 1808–09 △, 109

———— 59 Grove St., 1809 △, 109

PARKER, CHARLES CHRISTOPHER "CHARLIE" (1920–1955).
Kansas City, Kan. Parker Birthplace, 852 Freeman St., 1920–? △, 267

Kansas City, Mo. 1535 Olive St., 1942–? △

New York, N.Y. 411 Manhattan Ave., 1940s ☐, 109

PARKER, DOROTHY ROTHSCHILD (1893–1967).
West End, N.J. Rothschild birthplace, 1893 X

New York, N.Y. 57 West 68th St., 1890s ☐

———— Broadway and 103rd Street, 1916–17 △

———— 57 West 57th St., ca. 1920 ☐, 110

West Hollywood, Calif. Garden of Allah, 8150 Sunset Blvd., 1933–34 △, 425

Tinicum, Pa. Fox Hollow Farm, Mt. Airy Road, 1934–45 ☐, 225

Beverly Hills, Calif. 602 North Bedford Drive, 1937 ☐

New York, N.Y. Volney Hotel, 23 East 74th St., 1953–57, 1963–67 ☐, 110

Los Angeles, Calif. 8983 Norma Place, 1957–63 ☐, 425

PARRISH, MAXFIELD FREDERICK (1870–1966).
Philadelphia, Pa. Parrish Birthplace, west side of the 700 block of North 10th Street, 1870–90s △

Plainfield, N.H. The Oaks, State Highway 12A, 1898–1966 ☐, 57

PATTON, GEORGE SMITH, JR. (1885–1945).
San Marino, Calif. Patton Birthplace, Lake Vineyard Patton Estates, Kensington and Euston roads, 1885–ca. 1905 △, 425

District of Columbia. Woodley, 3000 Cathedral Ave. NW 1920–23 ☐, 151

Fort Myer, Va. Quarters 5, Generals' Row, 1923–25 ☐, 387

District of Columbia. 3117 Woodland Drive NW, 1928–31 ☐, 151

South Hamilton, Mass. Green Meadows, 650 Asbury St., 1928 et seq. 1941 ☐, 47

Columbus, Ga. 601 Baltzell Ave., Fort Benning, 1941 ☐

———— Second Armored Division Road, Fort Benning, 1941–42 △

Exhibit: 346

PEALE, CHARLES WILLSON (1741–1827).
Centreville, Md. Peale Birthplace, vicinity of State Highway 18 and Tilghman Neck Road, 1741–42 △, 165

Chestertown, Md. Kent County School, 1742–49 △

Annapolis, Md. Peale home, North Street, 1769–75 X, 165

Philadelphia, Pa. 238–240 Lombard St., 1780–94 △

———— Philosophical Hall, 104 South Fifth St., 1794–1810 ☐, 226

———— Belfield NHL, 2100 Clarkson Ave., 1810–21 ☐, 226

———— 617 Walnut St., 1821–27 △, 226

PEARSON, DREW (1897–1969).
Evanston, Ill. Pearson Birthplace, 1104 Foster St., 1897 ☐, 249

———— 1100, 1117, 1103, 1121 Garnett St., 1898–1901 ☐, 249

Swarthmore, Pa. Benjamin West Birthplace NHL, Swarthmore College, 1903–13 ☐, 226

———— 516 Walnut Lane, 1913–19 ☐, 226

District of Columbia. 2820 Dumbarton Ave. NW, 1926–69 ☐, 151

Potomac, Md. 13130 River Rd., 1937–69 ☐, 165

PEARY, ROBERT EDWIN (1856–1920).
Cresson Pa. Peary Birthplace, State Highway 176 and U.S. Highway 22, 1856–59 △ *, 226

Portland, Maine. Oxford Street, 1870–73 X

Brunswick, Maine. 12 Page St., 1873–77 ☐, 19

Fryeburg, Maine. 9 Elm St., 1877–79 ☐, 19

District of Columbia. 405 East Capitol St., 1879–80s △

Philadelphia, Pa. 43 South 19th St., ca. 1890 ☐

———— 4118 Elm Ave., 1890–91 △

Eagle Island, Maine. Sawungun, 1904 et seq. 1920 *, *19*

District of Columbia. 1831 Wyoming Ave. NW, ca. 1910–20 △, 152

PEGLER, WESTBROOK (1894–1969).
Minneapolis, Minn. Pegler Birthplace, 2838 Eighth Ave. South, 1894–1904 ☐, 280

Chicago, Ill. 1529 South Kenmore Ave., 1904–? △

Bronx, N.Y. Walton Avenue, 1922–24 X

Larchmont, N.Y. 10 Harmony Drive, 1926–29 ☐, 197

Pound Ridge, N.Y. Eastwoods Road, 1929–41 ☐, 197

New York, N.Y. Park Lane Hotel, 299 Park Ave., 1930s–40s ☐, 110

Tucson, Ariz. Casa Cholla, West Magee Road, 1941–69 ☐, 398

PEIRCE, CHARLES SANDERS (1839–1914).

Cambridge, Mass. Peirce Birthplace, 11 Mason St., 1839–50s ☐, 48

Baltimore, Md. 1020 North Calvert St., 1883–? ☐, 165

Milford, Pa. Arisbe, U.S. Highway 6, 1888–1914 ☐, 226

PENN, WILLIAM (1644–1718).

Philadelphia, Pa. Letitia Court, 1683–84 △, 226

——— Slate Roof House, Second and Sansom streets, 1694–1701 △, 226

Tullytown, Pa. Pennsbury Manor NHL, off U.S. Highway 3, 1700–01 *, 226–27

PERELMAN, SIDNEY JOSEPH (1904–1979).

Providence, R.I. 8 Bernon St., ca. 1905–? ☐, 62

Erwinna, Pa. Perelman Farm, Geiger Hill Road, 1932–70 ☐, 227

West Hollywood, Calif. Garden of Allah, 8150 Sunset Blvd., 1930s △

New York, N.Y. Gramercy Park Hotel, 52 Gramercy Park North, 1972–79 ☐, 110

PERRY, MATTHEW CALBRAITH (1794–1858).

Newport, R.I. Perry Birthplace, 31 Walnut St., 1794–1810 ☐, 62

Wakefield, R.I. Perry Homestead, 184 Post Road (U.S. Highway 1), 1794 et seq. ☐, 62

Boston, Mass. Commandant's Quarters, Boston Navy Yard, Charleston, 1827–30 ☐

North Tarrytown, N.Y. The Moorings, U.S. Highway 9 near State Highway 17, 1839–52 △

Brooklyn, N.Y. Perry House NHL, New York Naval Shipyard, Hudson Avenue and Evans Street, 1841–43 ☐, 76

New York, N.Y. 38 West 32nd St., 1855–58 △, 110

PERRY, OLIVER HAZARD (1785–1819).

Wakefield, R.I. Perry Birthplace, 184 Post Road (U.S. Highway 1), 1785–99 ☐, 62

Newport, R.I. 31 Walnut St., 1790s ☐, 62

Westerly, R.I. 172 Main St., 1808 △

Exhibit: 227

PERSHING, JOHN JOSEPH (1860–1948).

Laclede, Mo. Pershing State Park (Pershing Birthplace), U.S. Highway 36, 1860–66 △, 287

——— Pershing Boyhood Home NHL, State and Worlow streets, 1866–82 *, 287

Cheyenne, Wyo. Officers Quarters, Fort D. A. Russell, Francis E. Warren AFB, Randall Avenue, 1912 ☐

San Francisco, Calif. Pershing Square, San Francisco Presidio NHL, 1914–15 △, 425

District of Columbia. Carlton-Sheraton Hotel, 16th and K streets NW, ca. 1925–? ☐

——— Metropolitan Club, 17th and H streets NW, 1920s–30s ☐

——— Walter Reed Center, 6825 16th St. NW, 1941–48 ☐, 152

Exhibit: 441

PHILLIPS, WENDELL (1811–1884).

Boston, Mass. Phillips Birthplace, Beacon and Walnut streets, 1811–27 ☐, 48

——— 26 Esssex St., 1841–82 △, 48

——— 37 Common St., 1882–84 △

PICKFORD, MARY (1893–1979).

New York, N.Y. Pickford apartment, Broadway above Central Park, 1915–16 X

Santa Monica, Calif. 49 Mayberry Road, 1916–17 ☐

Hollywood, Calif. 1403 Western Ave., 1917–18 △

Los Angeles, Calif. 56 Fremont Place, 1918–20 ☐, 425

Beverly Hills, Calif. Pickfair, 1143 Summit Drive, 1920–79 ☐, 425

PIERCE, FRANKLIN (1804–1869).

Hillsboro, N.H. Pierce Homestead NHL, State Highway 31, 1804–34 *, 57

Concord, N.H. Pierce Manse, 14 Penacook St., 1842–46 *, 57

District of Columbia. 219 Third St. NW, 1840s–53 △

——— White House, 1600 Pennsylvania Ave. NW, 1853–57 *, 152

Concord, N.H. 52 South Main St., 1857–69 ☐, 57

PLATH, SYLVIA (1932–1963).

Jamaica Plain, Mass. 1932–36 X

Winthrop, Mass. 92 Johnson Ave., 1936–42 ☐, 48

Wellesley, Mass. 26 Elmwood Road, 1942–55 ☐, 48

POCAHONTAS (1595?–1617).

Gloucester, Va. Werowocomoco, off U.S. Highway 17, 1590s–1600s △, 387

Richmond, Va. Chimborazo Park, 3215 East Broad St., 1590s–1600s △, 387

——— Village of Orapaks, Cold Harbor Battlefield vicinity (reputed), State Highway 156, 1609 △

Jamestown, Va. Jamestown Colonial NHP, ·Colonial Parkway, 1613–16 △, 387

Richmond, Va. Varina Farm, Varina Road, 1614–16 △, 387

Surry, Va. Rolfe Plantation, Smith's Fort Plantation, State Highway 31, 1614–16 △, 387

POE, EDGAR ALLAN (1809–1849).

Boston, Mass. Poe Birthplace, 62 Carver St., 1809–10 △, 48

Richmond, Va. John Allan House, 14th Street and Tobacco Alley, 1811–15 △, 387

——— Allan House, Fifth and Clay streets, 1820–25 △, 387

——— Moldavia, Main and Fifth streets, 1825 et seq. 1830 △, 387

Charlottesville, Va. Room 13 West Range, University of Virginia campus, 1826 *, 388

Hampton, Va. Fort Monroe NHL, Old Point Comfort, 1828–29 *, 388

Baltimore, Md. 408–410 Eastern Ave., 1831–32 △

——— Poe House NHL, 203 North Amity St., 1832–35 *, 165, 166

Richmond, Va. Yarrington Boardinghouse, Bank and 11th streets, 1835–36 △, 387

New York, N.Y. Sixth Avenue and Waverly Place, 1837 △

——— 113½ Carmine St., 1838 △

Philadelphia, Pa. Fourth and Arch streets, 1838–? △

——— 16th Street near Locust Street, 1840–41 △

——— Fairmount Avenue, near 25th Street, 1841–42 △

——— Poe House NHS, 530–32 North Seventh St., 1842–44 *, 227

New York, N.Y. 130 Greenwich St., 1844 △

——— 18 West Third St., 1844 △

——— 85 West Third St., 1845 ☐, 110

——— 195 East Broadway, 1845 △

——— Broadway and West 84th Street, 1846 △, 110

Bronx, N.Y. Poe Cottage, 2640 Grand Concourse, 1846–49 *, 71

Richmond, Va. Old Swan Tavern, Broad Street, 1849 △, 388

POLK, JAMES KNOX (1795–1849).

Pineville, N.C. Polk Memorial State Historic Site (Polk Birthplace), U.S. Highway 521, 1795–1806 △ *, 359

Kedron, Tenn. Polk Boyhood Home, U.S. Highway 31, 1806–15 △, 370

Columbia, Tenn. Polk House NHL, 301 West Seventh St., 1820–24 *, 370

——— Polk House, 318 West Seventh St., 1825–49 △, 370

District of Columbia. Rodgers House, 17 Madison Place NW, 1845 △

——— White House, 1600 Pennsylvania Ave. NW, 1845–49 *, 152

Nashville, Tenn. Grundy Place, Seventh Avenue North and Union Street 1847–49 △, 370

—— Elkhorn Ranch (see text), 1884–86 △, 295

Oyster Bay, N.Y. Sagamore Hill NHS, Cove Neck Road, 1885–1919 *, *202, 203*

District of Columbia. 1215 19th St. NW, 1889–95 ☐, 154

New York, N.Y. 689 Madison Ave., 1895–97 △

District of Columbia. 1910 N. St. NW, 1897–98 ☐

Albany, N.Y. State Executive Mansion, 138 Eagle St., 1899–1901 ☐, 203

District of Columbia. White House, 1600 Pennsylvania Ave. NW, 1901–09 *, 153

—— Marcy House, 736 Jackson Place NW, 1902 △, 153

Exhibit: 441

ROOT, ELIHU (1845–1937).

Clinton, N.Y. Root Birthplace, Buttrick Hall, Hamilton College campus, 1845 ☐, 204

New York, N.Y. 20 Irving Place, 1871–78 △, 115

District of Columbia. 1775 N St. NW, 1899–1904 △

—— 722 Jackson Place NW, 1903–05 △, 154

New York, N.Y. 733 Park Ave., 1903–12 ☐, 115

District of Columbia. 1333 16th St. NW, 1905–07 △

Clinton, N.Y. Root House NHL, 101 College Hill Road, ca. 1906 et seq. 1937 ☐

District of Columbia. Bell-Morton House, 1500 Rhode Island Ave. NW, 1907–09 ☐, 154

—— 1155 16th St. NW, 1909–15 △, 154

New York, N.Y. 998 Fifth Ave., 1912–37 ☐, 115

ROSS, BETSY (1752–1836).

Philadelphia, Pa. 233 Arch St., ca. 1776 △, 228

—— 241 Arch St., 1800s △, 228

ROTHKO, MARK (1903–1970).

Portland, Ore. 2000 SW Second St., 1913–21 △

New York, N.Y. 19 West 102nd St., 1924–29 △

—— 231 East 25th St., 1929–32 △

—— 313 East Sixth St., 1936–40 ☐, 116

—— 29 East 28th St., ca. 1941 ☐,

New York, N.Y. 165 East 31st St., ca. 1943 ☐

—— 22 West 52nd St., ca. 1946 ☐

—— 1288 Sixth Ave., 1946–54 ☐

—— 102 West 54th St., 1954–60 ☐

—— 118 East 95th St., 1960–64 ☐, 116

—— 157 East 69th St., 1964–70 ☐, 116

ROYCE, JOSIAH (1855–1916).

Grass Valley, Calif. Royce Birthplace, Mill Street, 1855–66 △, 426

San Francisco, Calif. 1032 Folsom St., 1866–70 △

East Oakland, Calif. ca. 1870–80 X

Berkeley, Calif. Head House, Addison and Oxford streets, 1880–82 △

Cambridge, Mass. 14 Sumner Road, 1882–85 ☐, 50

—— 20 Lowell St., 1885–89 ☐, 50

—— 103 Irving St., 1889–1916 ☐, 50

RUNYON, DAMON (1880–1946).

Manhattan, Kan. Runyon Birthplace, 400 Osage St., 1880–82 ☐, 267

Wellington, Kan. ca. 1885–87 X

Pueblo, Colo. Mount Pleasant Boardinghouse, 522 Albany St., 1890s-ca. 1905 △

Denver, Colo. 1439 California St., 1905 △

—— 1420 Logan St., 1905△

—— 1458 Court Place, 1906 △

—— Denver Athletic Club, 1325 Glenarm Place, 1906–11 ☐, 433

New York, N.Y. 111th Street and Broadway, 1913–? X

—— 251 West 95th St., ca. 1917 ☐, 116

—— 320 West 102nd St., 1920–28 ☐, 116

—— 224 West 49th St., 1928–32 ☐, 116

Miami, Fla. Las Melaleuccas, 271 Hibiscus Island, 1933–40 ☐, 331

Beverly Hills, Calif. 1940–43 X

Holmby Hills, Calif. Gertrude Neisen House, 1943–44 X

New York, N.Y. 350 West 57th St., 1940s ☐, 116

—— Hotel Buckingham, 101 West 57th St., 1945–46 ☐, 116

RUSSELL, BERTRAND (1872–1970).

Los Angeles, Calif. 212 Loring Ave., 1939–40 ☐, 426

Malvern, Pa. Little Datchet Farm, Street Road, 1941–43 ☐, 229

RUSSELL, LILLIAN (1861–1922).

Clinton, Iowa. Helen Leonard Birthplace, (see text), 1861 △, 262

—— 408 Seventh Ave., 1861–63 △, 262

Chicago, Ill. 1865–70s X

New York, N.Y. 57 East 54th St., 1880s ☐, 116

—— 58 East Ninth St., ca. 1885–93 △

—— West 77th Street, 1893–? X

—— 161 West 57th St., ca. 1901–07 ☐

—— Wilbraham Apartments, 284 Fifth Ave., 1900s ☐, 116

Pittsburgh, Pa. 328 Penn Ave., 1912–22 △, 229

RUTH, GEORGE HERMAN "BABE" (1895–1948).

Baltimore, Md. Ruth Birthplace, 216 Emory St., 1895–96*, 167

—— Boyhood homes, Frederick Avenue, Woodyear Street, 1890s X

—— 426 West Camden St., ca. 1900 △

——— St. Mary's Industrial School for Boys, Wilkens and Caton avenues, 1903–14 △, 167

Sudbury, Mass. Home Plate, 558 Dutton Rd., 1916–26 ☐, 50

New York, N.Y. 110 Riverside Drive, 1935–48 ☐, 116

Exhibit: 204

SAARINEN, EERO (1910–1961).

Bloomfield Hills, Mich. Saarinen House, Cranbrook Academy, 1929–30s ☐, 276

—— 1045 Vaughan Rd., 1930s–61 ☐, 276

SAARINEN, ELIEL (1873–1950).

Bloomfield Hills, Mich. Saarinen House, Cranbrook Academy, 1929–50 ☐, 276

SAINT-GAUDENS, AUGUSTUS (1848–1907).

New York, N.Y. Saint-Gaudens lodgings, Duane, Forsyth, Broome streets, 1848–50s X

—— 41 Lispenard St., 1850s–60 △

—— 21st Street between Second and Third avenues, 1860–67 △

—— Sixth Avenue and 57th Street, 1880–84 △

—— 148 West 36th St., 1884–? △

—— 22 Washington Place, 1880s–90 △, 116

Plainfield, N.H. Saint-Gaudens NHS, off State Highway 12A, 1885 et seq 1907 *, 58

New York, N.Y. 51 West 45th St., 1890–97 △, 116

SANDBURG, CARL (1878–1967).

Galesburg, Ill. Sandburg Birthplace, 331 East Third St., 1878–81 *, 249

—— 641 East South St., 1881–82 ☐, 249–50

—— 808–810 East Berrien St., 1882–99 ☐, 250

—— 809 East Berrien St., 1899–1905 ☐, 250

Milwaukee, Wis. 907 18th St., ca. 1911 △

Chicago, Ill. 4646 North Hermitage Ave., 1911–14 ☐, 250

Milwaukee, Wis. 3325 Cambridge Ave., ca. 1912 ☐, 315

Maywood, Ill. 616 South Eighth Ave., 1914–19 ☐, 250

Elmhurst, Ill. 331 South York St., 1919–28 △, 250

Harbert, Mich. Chikaming Goat Farm, Birchwood Court, 1928–45 ☐, 276

Flat Rock, N.C. Sandburg Home NHS, Little River Road, 1945–67 *, 359, *360*

SANGER, MARGARET HIGGINS (1883–1966).

Corning, N.Y. 238 West Second St., 1890s ☐, 204

Hastings-on-Hudson, N.Y. 155 Edgar's Lane, 1908–11 ☐, 204

New York, N.Y. 4 Perry St., 1914 ☐, 116

—— 236 West 14th St., 1917–? △, 117

Fishkill, N.Y. Willowlake, Van Wyck Lake Rd., 1924–43 ☐, 204

TIFFANY, LOUIS COMFORT (1848–1933).
New York, N.Y. Tiffany Birthplace, 57 Warren St., 1848–53 △, 120
——— 255 Madison Ave., 1860–? △
Irvington, N.Y. Tiffany Park, ca. 1860–ca. 1904 △, 207
Oyster Bay, N.Y. Laurelton Hall, 1904–33 △, 207
New York, N.Y. 19 East 72nd St., ?–1933 △, 120
Exhibit: 331

TILDEN, SAMUEL JONES (1814–1886).
New Lebanon, N.Y. Tilden Birthplace, 1814–35 △, 208
New York, N.Y. 11 Fifth Ave., 1850s △, 120
——— 15 Gramercy Park South, 1864–86 □, 120
Albany, N.Y. State Execution Mansion, 138 Eagle St., 1875–76 □, 207
Yonkers, N.Y. Graystone, 919 North Broadway, 1879–86 △, 207

TILLICH, PAUL JOHANNES (1886–1965).
East Hampton, N.Y. 84 Woods Lane, 1943–65 □, 208
Cambridge, Mass. 16 Chauncy St., 1955–62 □, 52
Chicago, Ill. Windermere Hotel, 1642 East 56th St., 1962–65 □, 251

TOSCANINI, ARTURO (1867–1957).
Bronx, N.Y. Villa Pauline, Independence Avenue, 1939–42; 1940s–57 □, 72
——— Wave Hill House, 675 West 252nd St., 1942–? *, 72
Exhibit: 176

TRACY, SPENCER BONAVENTURE (1900–1967).
Milwaukee, Wis. Tracy Birthplace, Prospect Avenue, 1900–? X
——— Prospect Avenue, ca. 1900s–17 X
——— Marietta Street, ca. 1917–20 △
——— 2970 South Kinnickinnic Ave., 1900s □, 315
——— 2447 South Graham St., 1900s □, 315
——— 3004 West St. Paul Ave., 1900s △
——— 335 Howell Ave., ca. 1929 △
——— 2935 South Moffett St., ca. 1933 △
Encino, Calif. Tracy Ranch, Ventura Freeway (U.S. Highway 101), 1936–40s △
Beverly Hills, Calif. Beverly Wilshire Hotel, 9500 Wilshire Blvd. 1940s et seq. 1950s □, 430
——— 9191 St. Ives Drive, 1950s–60s □, 430
——— 1158 Tower Road, 1960s □, 430
West Hollywood, Calif. Cukor Estate, 9166 Cordell Drive, 1967 □, 430

TROTSKY, LEON (1879–1940).
Bronx, N.Y. 1522 Vyse Ave., 1917 □

TRUMAN, HARRY S. (1884–1972).
Lamar, Mo. Truman Birthplace NHL, 1009 Truman Ave., 1884–85 *, 288
Belton, Mo. Frank Farm, 4.5 miles southeast of town, 1885–87 □, 288–89
Grandview, Mo. Truman Farm, 12300 South 71st Highway, 1887–90, 1906–17 □, 289
Independence, Mo. 619 South Crysler St., 1890–96 □, 290
——— 909 West Waldo St., 1896–1902 □, 290
——— 902 North Liberty St., 1902 □
Kansas City, Mo. 2108 Park Ave., 1902–05 □, 290
——— 2650 East 29th St., ca. 1905 □
——— 1314 Troost Ave., 1905–06 □
Independence, Mo. Truman House NHL, 219 North Delaware St., 1919–72 □, *289*, 290
District of Columbia. 3016 Tilden Garden, 3000 Tilden NW, 1935–36, 1939–40 □
——— Sedgwick Gardens, 3726 Connecticut Ave. NW, 1936–37 □
——— Carroll Arms, 301 First St. NE, 1937–38 □
——— Warwick Apartments, 3051 Idaho Ave. NW, 1938–39 □
——— 3930 Connecticut Ave. NW, 1940–41 □
——— 4701 Connecticut Ave. NW, 1941–45 □, 155
——— White House, 1600 Pennsylvania Ave., NW, 1945–48, 1952–53 *, 156
Key West, Fla. Little White House, Front and Caroline streets, 1946 et seq. 1953 □, 331
District of Columbia. Blair-Lee House NHL, 1651 Pennsylvania Ave. NW, 1948–52 □, 156
Exhibit: 276

TRUMBULL, JOHN (1756–1843).
Lebanon, Conn. Trumbull House NHL, State Highway 87, Lebanon Common, 1756–70s *, 14
New York, N.Y. 128 Broadway, 1804–08 △, 121
——— 27 Park Place, 1818–25 △, 121
——— 256 Broadway, 1825–37, 1841–43 △, 121
New Haven, Conn. Silliman House, Hillhouse Avenue, 1837–41 △; moved to 87 Trumbull Street □, 14

TRUTH, SOJOURNER (1797?–1883).
Hurley, N.Y. Isabella Van Wagener Birthplace, Hardenbergh House, School House Lane, 1797?–1800s □, 208
Bloomington, N.Y. Van Wagener House, Main Street, 1800s □, 208
West Park, N.Y. Dumont Farm, U.S. Highway 9W, ca. 1810 △
New York, N.Y. 73 Nassau St., 1829–30 △
——— 177 Duane St., 1830–31 △
——— Fourth Street, Franklin Street, Third Street, 1830s X
Florence, Mass. 45 Park St., 1850–57 □, 52
Battle Creek, Mich. 38 College St., 1867–83 △, 277

TUBMAN, HARRIET (1820–1913).
Bucktown, Md. Tubman Birthplace, Greenbriar Swamp Road, 1820–50s △, 168
Auburn, N.Y. Tubman House NHL, 180 South St., 1857–1913 *, 208

TURNER, NAT (1800–1831).
Courtland, Va. Benjamin Turner Farm, 1808–09 X
——— Samuel Turner Mill, Tarrara Creek, Southampton County, 1819–21 △, 390
——— Thomas Moore Farm, 1821–30 X
——— Joseph Travis House, Southampton County, 1830–31 △, 390

TWAIN, MARK. see SAMUEL LANGHORNE CLEMENS.

TWEED, WILLIAM MARCY (1823–1878).
New York, N.Y. Tweed Birthplace, 1 Cherry St., 1823–44 △, 121
——— 193 Madison St., 1844–46 △, 121
——— 35 Vandewater St., 1846–50s △
——— 197 Henry St., 1860s △
Greenwich, Conn. Tweed Mansion, East Putnam Avenue, 1865–78 △, 14
New York, N.Y. 41 West 36th St., 1866–70 △, 121
——— 511 Fifth Ave., 1870–76 △, 121
——— Ludlow Street Jail, 350 Grand St., 1876–78 △, 121

TYLER, JOHN (1790–1862).
Charles City, Va. Greenway (Tyler Birthplace), State Highway 5, 1790–1813, 1821–29 □, 390
Richmond, Va. Governor's Residence, Capitol Square, 1808–11 △, 390
Charles City, Va. Mons-Sacer, Greenway Estate, State Highway 5, 1813–15 △, 390
Williamsburg, Va. Tyler House, Dunmore Street, 1837–41 △
District of Columbia. Tyler House, Madison Drive NW between Fourth and Sixth streets, 1841 △
——— Brown's Indian Queen Hotel, northwest corner Pennsylvania Ave. and Sixth Streets NW, 1841 △
District of Columbia. White House, 1600 Pennsylvania Ave. NW, 1841–45 *, 156
——— Woodley, 3000 Cathedral Ave. NW, 1841 et seq. 1845 □

Alexandria, Va. Mount Vernon NHL, George Washington Memorial Parkway, 1799–1802 *

WAYNE, ANTHONY (1745–1796).

Paoli, Pa. Waynesborough NHL, 2049 Waynesborough Road, 1745–96 ☐, 231

Valley Forge NHP, Pa. Wayne's Quarters, Many Springs Farm, Walker Road, 1777–78 ☐

WAYNE, JOHN (1907–1979).

Winterset, Iowa. Marion Morrison Birthplace, 224 South Second St., 1907–10 *, 263

Palmdale, Calif. Morrison Farm, State Highway 14, 1913–15 △

Glendale, Calif. 121 South Isabel St., 1915–16 △

———— 115 North Geneva St., 1917–18 △

———— 443 West Colorado St., 1919–20 △

———— 815 South Central Ave., 1921–22 △

———— 129 South Kenwood St., 1922–23 △

———— 245 South Orange St., 1924 △

———— 207 West Windsor St., ca. 1925 ☐, 431

Encino, Calif. 14750 Louise Ave., 1930s–66 ☐, 431

Newport Beach, Calif. 2700 Bayshore Drive, 1966–79 ☐, 431

WEBSTER, DANIEL (1782–1852).

Franklin N.H. Webster Birthplace, off State Highway 127, 1782–84 *, 58

———— Elms Farm, off U.S. Highway 3, 1784–1806, 1830 et seq. 1852 ☐, 58

Hanover, N.H. Webster Cottage, North Main St., 1800–04 ☐, 58

Portsmouth, N.H. 139 Vaughan St., 1808–09 △

———— Northwest corner of Court and Pleasant streets, 1809–13 △

———— 58 High St., 1813–16 △; moved to Strawberry Banke, Hancock and Marcy streets ☐, 58

Boston, Mass. 57 Mount Vernon St., 1816–19 ☐, 52

———— 37 Somerset St. (1 Center Plaza), 1819–22 △

———— High and Summer streets, 1824–32 △, 52

Marshfield, Mass. Green Harbor, Webster Law Office and Library NHL, Webster and Careswell streets, 1832–52 △ *, 52

District of Columbia. Corcoran House, 1611 H St. NW, 1841–43 △, 157

———— Vine Cottage, D St. NW, 1845–52 X, 157

WEBSTER, NOAH (1758–1843).

West Hartford, Conn. Webster Birthplace NHL, 227 South Main St., 1758–74 *, 14

Sharon, Conn. Smith Mansion, State Highway 41, 1781–82 ☐, 14

Goshen, N.Y. 1782–83 X

Hartford, Conn. Wadsworth House, 600 Main St., 1789–93 △, 14

New Haven, Conn. 155 Water St., 1798–1812 △, 15

Amherst, Mass. 46 Main St., 1812–22 △, 53

New Haven, Conn. Temple and Grove streets, 1823–43 △; moved to Dearborn, Mich., 15

Dearborn, Mich. Webster New Haven House, Greenfield Village, 20900 Oakwood Blvd. *, 277

WEILL, KURT (1900–1950).

New City, N.Y. Brook House, 116 South Mountain Road, 1941–50 ☐, 209

WESLEY, CHARLES (1707–1788).

St. Simons Island, Ga. Fort Frederica National Monument, Frederica Road, 1736–37 △ *, 338

WESLEY, JOHN (1703–1791).

Savannah, Ga. Wesley Parsonage, Reynolds Square, 1736–37 △, 338

Exhibit: 361

WEST, BENJAMIN (1738–1820).

Swarthmore, Pa. West Birthplace NHL, Swarthmore College, 1737–43 ☐, 231

Clifton Heights, Pa. Darby-Springfield Tavern, Springfield Road, 1743–44 X

Springfield, Pa. Newtown Square, 1744–56 X

Lancaster, Pa. William Henry House, East King Street, 1756 X

Philadelphia, Pa. 1756–58 X

WESTINGHOUSE, GEORGE (1846–1914).

Central Bridge, N.Y. Westinghouse Birthplace, off State Highway 7, 1846–56 ☐, 209

Schenectady, N.Y. 1416 State St., 1865–68 △, 209

Pittsburgh, Pa. Solitude, North Murtland and McPherson streets, 1871–1914 △, 231

Lenox, Mass. Erskine Park, Stockbridge Road (State Highway 7), 1890–1914 △, 53

District of Columbia. Blaine House, 2000 Massachusetts Ave. NW, 1898–1914 ☐, 157

WHARTON, EDITH (1862–1937).

New York, N.Y. Edith Jones Birthplace, 14 West 23rd St., 1862–82 ☐, 123

Newport, R.I. Pencraig, Harrison Avenue, 1872 et seq. 1890 △

New York, N.Y. 7 Washington Square North, 1882 ☐, 123

———— 28 West 25th St., 1882–85 △, 123

———— Madison Avenue, 1889–91 X

———— 884 Park Ave., 1891–93 △, 123

Newport, R.I. Land's End, Ledge Road, 1893–1902 ☐, 62

Lenox, Mass. The Mount NHL, U.S. Highway 7, 1901–12 ☐, 53

WHISTLER, JAMES ABBOTT McNEILL (1834–1903).

Lowell, Mass. Whistler Birthplace, 243 Worthen St., 1834–37 *, 53

Stonington, Conn. Amos Palmer House, Main and Wall streets, 1837–43 ☐, 15

WHITE, STANFORD (1853–1906).

New York, N.Y. White Birthplace, 110 East 10th St., 1853–58 ☐, 123

St. James, N.Y. Box Hill, Moriches Road, 1884–92 ☐, 209

New York, N.Y. Madison Square Garden, Madison Avenue and East 26th Street, 1890–1906 ☐, 123

———— 122 East 22nd St. 1890s–1906 △, 123

———— 22 West 24th St., 1890s–1906 ☐, 123

St. James, N.Y. Harbor Road, 1892–1906 ☐, 209

New York, N.Y. Lexington Avenue and Gramercy Park North, 1901–06 △, 123

WHITE, WILLIAM ALLEN (1868–1944).

El Dorado, Kan. South Main Street, 1870–74 △

———— White House, U.S. Post Office lot, 1874–91 △

Kansas City, Kan. 1892–95 X

Emporia, Kan. White House NHL, 927 Exchange St., 1899–1944 ☐, 267

Estes Park, Colo. White Summer Home, Moraine Park Visitor Center, Rocky Mountain National Park, ca. 1920s–44 ☐, 433

WHITMAN, WALT (1819–1892).

Huntington Station, N.Y. Whitman Birthplace, 246 Walt Whitman Road, 1819–23 *, 209, *210*

Brooklyn, N.Y. Front Street near Fulton Ferry, 1823–24 X

———— Cranberry Street opposite Plymouth Church NHL, 1824 X

———— Johnson Street north of Adams Street, 1825 X

———— 251 Adams St., 1826–27 △

———— 41 Tillary St., 1827–32 △, 77

———— 120 Front St., 1833–44 △, 77

Huntington, N.Y. 313 Main St., 1838–39 ☐

New York, N.Y. 12 Centre St., 1842 △, 124

Brooklyn, N.Y. Adams Street near Myrtle Avenue, 1846–48 X

———— 106 Myrtle Ave., 1849–52 △, 77

———— Cumberland Street north of Atlantic Avenue, 1852–54 X

———— 142 Skillman St., 1854–55△, 77

———— Ryerson Street north of Myrtle Avenue, 1855–56 X

Columbia, S.C. Wilson Boyhood Home, 1705 Hampton St., 1872–75 *, 365

Princeton, N.J. 72 Library Place, 1890–96 □, 178

——— 82 Library Place, 1896–1902 □, 178

——— Prospect, Princeton University, 1902–10 □, 178

——— 25 Cleveland Lane, 1910–13 □, 178

Sea Girt, N.J. Governor's Mansion, Stockton Lake, 1910 et seq. 1912 △

District of Columbia. White House, 1600 Pennsylvania Ave. NW, 1913–21 *, 159

Cornish, N.H. Harlakenden, State Highway 12A, 1913 et seq. 1915 △, 59

West Long Branch, N.J. Shadow Lawn, Shadow Lawn campus, Monmouth College, 1916 △, 178

District of Columbia. Wilson House NHL, 2340 S St. NW, 1921–24 *, 159

WINCHELL, WALTER (1897–1972).

New York, N.Y. Winchell Birthplace, 117th Street and Madison Avenue, 1897–? X, 124

——— 124 West 116th St., ca. 1907–10 △

——— Whitby Apartments, 325 West 45th St., 1930s □

——— St. Moritz Hotel, 50 Central Park South, 1930s–40s □, 124

——— Park Central Hotel, Seventh Avenue and 56th Street, 1940s □

Scottsdale, Ariz. Paradise Valley, 1968–70 □

Hollywood, Calif. Ambassador Hotel, 3400 Wilshire Blvd., 1970 et seq. 1972 □

WINTHROP, JOHN (1588–1649).

Boston, Mass. Harvard Mall, Charlestown, 1630 △, 54

——— 53 State St., 1630–43 △, 54

Somerville, Mass. Ten Hills Farm, Governor Winthrop Road and Shore Drive, 1631 et seq. 1649 △, 54

Boston, Mass. 310 Washington St., 1644–49 △, 54

WODEHOUSE, SIR PELHAM GRENVILLE (1881–1975).

New York, N.Y. 375 Central Park West, 1914–15 □, 124

Great Neck, N.Y. 121 Arrandale Ave., 1918–21 □, 210

Hollywood, Calif. 1930–31 X

Beverly Hills, Calif. 1315 Angelo Drive, 1936–37 □, 431

New York, N.Y. Hotel Adams, 2 East 86th St., 1947–48 □, 124

——— 1000 Park Ave., 1948–52 □, 124

Remsenburg, N.Y. Blandings Castle, Basket Neck Lane, 1952–75 □, 210

WOLFE, THOMAS CLAYTON (1900–1938).

Asheville, N.C. Wolfe Birthplace, 92 Woodfin St., 1900–06 △, 361

——— Thomas Wolfe Memorial NHL, 48 Spruce St., 1906–23 *, 361

New York, N.Y. Albert Hotel, University Place and East 11th Street, 1923–27 △, 125

——— 13 East Eighth St., 1927 △, 125

——— 263 West 11th St., 1927–28 □, 125

——— 27 West 15th St., 1928–29 □, 125

Brooklyn, N.Y. 40 Verandah Place, 1931 □, 77

——— 111 Columbia Heights, 1931–32 □, 77

——— 101 Columbia Heights, 1932–33 △

——— 5 Montague Terrace, 1933–35 □, 77

New York, N.Y. 865 First Ave., 1935–37 □, 125

——— Chelsea Hotel, 222 West 23rd St., 1937–38 □, 125

WOOD, GRANT (1892–1942).

Anamosa, Iowa. Wood Birthplace, Rural Route 3, 1892–1901 △

Cedar Rapids, Iowa. 318 14th St. NE, 1903–14 □, 263

——— 1532 B Ave. NE, 1914–16 □, 263

——— 3178 Grove Court, 1918–25 □, 263

——— 800 Second Ave. SE, 1925–35 □, 263

Iowa City, Iowa. 1142 East Court St., 1935–42 □, 263

WOODHULL, VICTORIA CLAFLIN (1838–1927).

Homer, Ohio. Claflin birthplace, 1838–48 X, 307

Mount Gilead, Ohio. 1840s–53 X

Cincinnati, Ohio. 422 West Fifth St., 1864–66 △, 307

New York, N.Y. 15 East 38th St., 1868–71 △, 125

——— 118 East 23rd St., 1871–72 △, 125

——— 44 Broad St., ca. 1872 △

——— 237 Fourth Ave., ca. 1872 △

——— 6 East 34th St., ca. 1873 △

——— 75 East 10th St., ca. 1876 △

——— 17 Great Jones St., 1870s X

WRIGHT, FRANK LLOYD (1867–1959).

Richland Center, Wis. Wright Birthplace, 300 South Church St., 1867–69 □, 316

McGregor, Iowa. 1869–71 X

Pawtucket, R.I. 1871–74 X

Weymouth, Mass. 95 Broad St., 1874–77 △

Madison, Wis. 804 East Gorham St., 1880–87 △

Oak Park, Ill. Wright House and Studio, 951 Chicago Ave., 1889–1909 *, 251–52

Spring Green, Wis. Taliesin East NHL, State Highway 23, 1911–38 *, 316

Chicago, Ill. 19 Cedar St., 1915 □

Scottsdale, Ariz. Taliesin West, 108th Street, 1938–59 *, 398

WRIGHT, ORVILLE (1871–1948).

Dayton, Ohio. Wright Birthplace, 7 Hawthorne St., 1871–78, 1885–1912 △; moved to Dearborn, Mich., 308

Dearborn, Mich. Wright Dayton Home, Greenfield Village, 20900 Oakwood Blvd. *, 277

1878–1912: See WILBUR WRIGHT.

Dayton, Ohio. Hawthorne Hill, Harmon and Park avenues, 1914–18 □

Exhibits: 159, 231

WRIGHT, RICHARD (1908–1960).

Natchez, Miss. 20 Woodlawn Ave. (reputed), 1911–14 □, 355

Elaine, Ark. 1916–20 X

Jackson, Miss. 1107 Lynch St., ca. 1920s △

Memphis, Tenn. 570 Beale St., 1925–26 △

——— 875 Griffith Place, 1926–27 △

——— 370 Washington St., ca. 1927 △

Chicago, Ill. 4804 South St. Lawrence Ave., 1931 △

New York, N.Y. 235 West 26th St., 1937 □, 125

Brooklyn, N.Y. 175 Carlton Ave., 1938–40 □, 77

——— 343 Grand Ave., 1940 □

——— 7 Middagh St., 1942 △

——— 87 Lefferts Place, 1939–40 □, 77

——— 11 Revere Place, 1941–42 □, 77

——— 89 Lefferts Place, 1943–45 □, 77

New York, N.Y. 82 Washington Place, 1945 □, 125

——— 13 Charles St., 1946–47 △, 125

WRIGHT, WILBUR (1867–1912).

Millville, Ind. Wilbur Wright State Memorial, County Road 750 East, 1867–68 △*, 258

Dayton, Ohio. Orville Wright Birthplace, 7 Hawthorne St., 1871–78, 1885–1912 △; moved to Dearborn, Mich., 308

Dearborn, Mich. Wright Dayton Home, Greenfield Village, 20900 Oakwood Blvd. *, 277

Cedar Rapids, Iowa. 184 Iowa Ave. (now on the 600–700 block of First Ave.), 1878–81 △

Richmond, Ind. 211 North 14th St., 1881–82 □, 258

——— 309 North 12th St., ca. 1882–83 □, 258

——— 38 South 13th St., ca. 1883–84 □, 258

Kill Devil Hills, N.C. Wright Brothers National Memorial, 1900 et seq. 1903 *, 361–62

Exhibits: 159, 231

YOUNG, BRIGHAM (1801–1877).

Whitingham, Vt. Young Birthplace, State Highway 100, 1801–03 △ *, 67

Smyrna, N.Y. Cole Road, 1803–13 △, 211

Tyrone, N.Y. ca. 1820s X

Port Byron, N.Y. Main Street, 1820s □

Mendon, N.Y. Southeast corner of Boughton Hill and Pittsford-Ionia roads, 1829–32 △, 211

Kirtland, Ohio. Chillicothe Road (State Highway 306), 1833–38 △

Nauvoo, Ill. Kimball and Main streets, 1841–46 *, 252

Omaha, Neb. Winter Quarters, Florence Park, North 30th Street, 1846–47 △

Salt Lake City, Utah. Beehive House NHL, East South Temple Street, 1854–77 *, 452

———— Lion House, East South Temple Street, 1856–77 □, 452–53

St. George, Utah. Young Winter Home, 89 West Second North St., 1873–77 *, 453

YOUNGER, COLE (1844–1916).

Lees Summit, Mo. Younger birthplace, 1844–50s X

Harrisonville, Mo. ca. 1858–63 X

St. Paul, Minn. 551 State St., ca. 1903 △

Lees Summit, Mo. Younger House, Market Street, 1903–16 △

ZAHARIAS, MILDRED ELLA DIDRIKSON "BABE" (1911–1956).

Port Arthur, Tex. Didrikson Birthplace, Seventh Street, 1911–15 △, 452

Beaumont, Tex. 850 Doucette Ave., 1916–36 □, 452

Tampa, Fla. 1955–56 X

ZENGER, JOHN PETER (1697–1746).

New York, N.Y. 81 Pearl St., 1711–19 △, 126

———— William Street, near Maiden Lane, 1726–34 X, 126

———— City Hall, Wall and Nassau streets, 1734–35 △, 126

———— Broad Street, 1735–46 X, 126

ZIEGFELD, FLORENZ (1869–1932).

Chicago, Ill. Ziegfeld Birthplace, 298 East Chicago St., 1869 △

———— 44 Loomis St., 1870s–82 △

———— 1448 West Adams St., 1882 et seq. 1930s △, 252

New York, N.Y. Netherland Hotel, 781 Fifth Ave., 1890s △, 126

———— Ansonia Hotel, 2109–2119 Broadway, 1900–32 □, 126

Hastings-on-Hudson, N.Y. Burkeley Crest, 360 Broadway, 1916–31 △, 211

Santa Monica, Calif. 2407 La Mesa Drive, 1932 □, 431

GEOGRAPHICAL INDEX

GEOGRAPHICAL INDEX

This index refers only to places appearing in the narrative section of the book and excludes additional listings in the Name Index and Gazetteer.